DICKENS

By the same author

DICKENS

PETER ACKROYD

HarperPerennial
A Division of HarperCollins*Publishers*

This book was originally published in Great Britain in 1990 by Sinclair-Stevenson Limited. It is here reprinted by arrangement with Sinclair-Stevenson Limited. The first U.S. edition of this book was published in 1991 by HarperCollins Publishers.

HarperCollins books may be purchased for educational, business, or sales promotional use. For information, please call or write: Special Markets Department, HarperCollins Publishers, Inc., 10 East 53rd Street, New York, NY 10022. Telephone: (212) 207-7528; Fax (212) 207-7222.

First HarperPerennial edition published 1992.

LIBRARY OF CONGRESS CATALOG CARD NUMBER 90-55522

ISBN 0-06-092265-6 (pbk.)

92 93 94 95 96 RRD 10 9 8 7 6 5 4 3 2 1

Contents

Acknowledgments

I believe that I have read all of Dickens's extant correspondence, published and unpublished, and I would like to thank the institutions and libraries which made their holdings available to me. The most significant collections of Dickens's letters are to be found at the Houghton Library, Harvard; the Pierpont Morgan Library; the Berg Collection of New York Public Library; the Beinecke Rare Book and Manuscript Library, Yale; the Dickens House; the Manuscript Department of the British Library; the Humanities Research Centre of the University of Texas at Austin; the Huntington Library; the Rare Book Collection of the Free Library of Philadelphia; the Robert H. Taylor collection of Princeton University Library; the Brotherton Library, Leeds; the John Rylands Library, Manchester; the Newberry Library, Chicago; Duke University Library, North Carolina; Mugar Memorial Library, Boston; the University of Keele Library; Brown University Library; Trinity College Library, Cambridge; Department of Rare Books at Cornell University Library; University of Virginia Library; Stanford University Library; Rosenbach Museum and Library, Philadelphia. Other invaluable material is to be found in the Forster Collection of the National Art Library, Victoria and Albert Museum.

I would like to thank the editors of the Pilgrim Edition of the *Letters of Charles Dickens*, published by Oxford University Press, for allowing me to quote from Volumes One to Six of that gigantic enterprise. In accordance with the wishes of those editors, I am happy to quote only occasional and brief phrases from Dickens's unpublished correspondence. I would also like to thank Christopher Dickens, the holder of the copyright in the unpublished writings of Charles Dickens.

My debt to Dickens scholars is extensive and profound, but in particular I would like to thank Graham Storey, Michael Slater, Philip

Acknowledgements

Collins, David Parker, Kathleen Tillotson, Thelma Grove, George Curry and Janine Watrin for their assistance and encouragement. I would particularly like to thank Katharine M. Longley, who allowed me to read her unpublished study of Ellen Ternan and the Ternan family, from which I have derived inestimable benefit.

In the span of this biography I have tried to incorporate all known material on the life of Charles Dickens, and as a result I have often redeployed the arguments or speculations of other Dickens critics and scholars, both past and present; to that vast multitude, my thanks. I would also like to thank Michael Slater, Catharine Reynolds, and Douglas Matthews for their comments upon my completed work. My research assistant, Brian Kuhn, has provided invaluable help over the past five years. But, most especially, I would like to thank Christopher Sinclair-Stevenson, my editor and publisher, without whose assistance this book could not have been written in the first place.

Illustration Acknowledgements

The pages from the first edition and corrected proofs of *Bleak House* and the picture of Dickens, Catherine and Mary Hogarth are reproduced courtesy of the Board of Trustees of the Victoria and Albert Museum; the portrait of Wilkie Collins and the picture of Dickens reading *The Chimes* are from the Mary Evans Picture Library; the drawing of Dickens by Samuel Laurence is reproduced by permission of the National Portrait Gallery, London; the illustration by Phiz from the first edition of *Domby and Son* is reproduced by permission of Michael Brown. Apart from the illustration of the cover of Nicholas Nickleby, all the remaining pictures are reproduced by kind permission of the Dickens House Museum.

Prologue

"... deeper than all, if one has the eye to see deep enough, dark, fateful, silent elements, tragical to look upon, and hiding amid dazzling radiances as of the sun, the elements of death itself."

Thomas Carlyle on Charles Dickens.

"Remember that what you are told is really threefold: shaped by the teller, reshaped by the listener, concealed from both by the dead man of the tale."

The Real Life of Sebastian Knight. Vladimir Nabokov.

"Ippolit Kirillovitch had chosen the historical form of narration, preferred by all anxious orators, who find in its constraints a check on their own exuberant rhetoric."

The Brothers Karamazov. Fyodor Dostoevsky.

CHARLES DICKENS was dead. He lay on a narrow green sofa – but there was room enough for him, so spare had he become – in the dining room of Gad's Hill Place. He had died in the house which he had first seen as a small boy and which his father had pointed out to him as a suitable object of his ambitions; so great was his father's hold upon his life that, forty years later, he had bought it. Now he had gone. It was customary to close the blinds and curtains, thus enshrouding the corpse in darkness before its last journey to the tomb; but in the dining room of Gad's Hill the curtains were pulled apart and on this June day the bright sunshine streamed in, glittering on the large mirrors around the room. The family beside him knew how he enjoyed the light, how he needed the light; and they understood, too, that none of the conventional sombreness of the late Victorian period – the year was 1870 – had ever touched him.

All the lines and wrinkles which marked the passage of his life were now erased in the stillness of death. He was not old – he died in his fifty-eighth year – but there had been signs of premature ageing on a visage so marked and worn; he had acquired, it was said, a "sarcastic look". But now all that was gone and his daughter, Katey, who watched him as he lay dead, noticed how there once more emerged upon his face "beauty and pathos". It was that "long-forgotten" look which he describes again and again in his fiction. He sees it in *Oliver Twist*, in the dead face which returns to the ". . . long forgotten expression of sleeping infancy", and in that same novel he connects "the rigid face of the corpse and the calm sleep of the child". In Master Humphrey's death, too, there was something "so strangely and indefinably allied to youth". It was the look he recorded in William Dorrit's face in death; it was the look which he saw in the faces of the corpses on view in the Paris Morgue. This connection between death and infancy is one that had haunted him: sleep, repose, death, infancy, innocence, oblivion are the words that formed a circle for him, bringing him back to the place from which he had begun. Here, in Gad's Hill, close to the town in which he had lived as a small child, here in the house which his father had once shown him; here the circle was complete.

A death mask was made. He had always hated masks. He had been frightened by one as a child and throughout his writing there is this refrain – "What a very alarming thing it would be to find somebody with a mask on . . . hiding bolt upright in a corner and pretending not to be alive!" The mask was an emblem of Charles Dickens's particular fear; that the dead are only pretending to be dead, and that they will suddenly spring up into violent life. He had a fear of the dead, and of all inanimate things, rising up around him to claim him; it is the fear of the pre-eminently solitary child and solitary man. But was there not also here some anticipation of the final quietus? The mask was made, and he was laid in his oak coffin. This wooden resting place was then covered with scarlet geraniums; they were Charles Dickens's favourite flowers and in the final picture of the corpse covered with blossom we can see a true representation of Dickens's own words echoing across the years – "Brighten it, brighten it, brighten it!" He always wanted colour about him, and he was notorious for his own vivid costumes. Especially in youth: and, on the wall above the coffin, his family placed a portrait of him as a young man. It was no doubt that painted by Daniel Maclise, and it shows the Dickens of 1839 looking up from his desk, his eyes ablaze as if in anticipation of the glory that was to come. Georgina Hogarth, his sister-in-law, cut a lock of hair from his head. On his prior instructions, his horse was shot. And so Charles Dickens lay.

The news of his death, in that age of swift communication, soon travelled around the world. In America Longfellow wrote that "I never knew an author's death to cause such general mourning. It is no exaggeration to say that this whole country is stricken with grief." But this perhaps is no surprise in a country which had greeted the arrival of the latest sheets of *The Old Curiosity Shop* with cries of "Is Little Nell dead?" Carlyle wrote, "It is an event world-wide, a *unique* of talents suddenly extinct . . ." And at once a certain aspect of his significance was seen clearly; as the *Daily News* wrote on 10 June, the day after his death, "He was emphatically the novelist of his age. In his pictures of contemporary life posterity will read, more clearly than in contemporary records, the character of nineteenth century life."

And yet, if he was the chronicler of his age, he also stood apart from it; he was always in some sense the solitary observer, one who looked upon the customs of his time as an anthropologist might look upon the habits of a particularly savage tribe. And there is no more direct evidence for this than in his own will, read now as he lay in his coffin. ". . . I emphatically direct that I be buried in an inexpensive, unostentatious and strictly private manner . . . that those who attend my funeral wear no scarf, cloak, black bow, long hat-band, or other such revolting absurdity . . . I conjure my friends on no account to make me the subject of any monument, memorial or testimonial whatever. I rest my claims to the remembrance of my country upon my published works . . ." It was presumed that this meant that he wished to be buried quietly in the vicinity of Gad's Hill and his childhood haunts, and at once a grave was prepared for him in the crypt of Rochester Cathedral.

But a compromise was reached between Dickens's family and what might be called the interests of the nation; he was to be buried in Westminster Abbey, after all, but with a completely private service. He had once said, ". . . the more truly great the man, the more truly little the ceremony . . .", thus emphasising that simplicity which was an essential part of the man. And so it was on Tuesday morning, 14 June, that his body was taken from Gad's Hill to Higham Station, and from there conveyed in a special train to Charing Cross. A small procession of three coaches made its way down Whitehall, and the great bell of the Abbey began to toll as they drove under the archway into Dean's Yard; then the small group of family and friends entered Westminster Abbey, where Charles Dickens was to be laid in Poets' Corner. Around him were the busts of Shakespeare and Milton, and at the end of the short ceremony the organ sounded the Dead March. In Rochester, the city in which he had as it were begun life and in which his last novel was set, the bell of the cathedral tolled as he was interred. His grave at Westminster Abbey was left open for two days. At the end of the first day, there were still one thousand people outside waiting to pay their respects. So for those two days the crowds of people passed by in procession, many of them dropping flowers onto his coffin – "among which," his son said, "were afterwards found several small rough bouquets of flowers tied up with pieces of rag."

There, in the ragged bundles of flowers, no doubt picked from the hedgerows and fields, we see the source and emblem of Charles Dickens's authority. Even to the labouring men and women there was in his death a grievous sense of loss; they felt that he had in large measure understood them and that, in his death, they had also lost something of themselves. It is often said that the great Russian novelists of the nineteenth century capture the soul of the Russian people with their fervour, their piety, and their wonderful tenderness; but can we not say that Dickens captured the soul of the English people, as much in its brooding melancholy as in its broad humour, in its poetry as well as in its fearlessness, in its capacity for outrage and pity as much as in its tendency towards irony and diffidence? And can we not see something of the national outline, too, in Charles Dickens's brisk, anxious stride across the face of the world – a man of so much assurance and of so much doubt, of so much energy and so much turmoil? It might be said, in fact, that it was his peculiar genius to represent, to bring together, more aspects of the national character than any other writer of his century. As a man he was sharp, exuberant, prone to melancholy and a prey to anxiety; as a writer he was filled with the same contrasts, so concerned with the material world and yet at the same time so haunted by visions of transcendence. The evidence for that divide is to be gathered throughout his work. In the nineteenth-century Russian novelists, the material and the spiritual are in a certain sense interfused; and in the French novelists of the nineteenth century it is the very genius of the material world to have no transcendental echoes: it remains splendidly itself. But, in the work of Charles Dickens, the real and the unreal, the material and the spiritual, the specific and the imagined, the mundane and the transcendental, exist in uneasy relation and are to be contained only within the power of the created word. The power of Charles Dickens.

To all Victorians, then, the death of Dickens came as the evidence of a giant transition; in these last decades of the nineteenth century, the English people were witnesses to the fatal disruptions of an old order and the unsteady beginnings of a new. There are times, when looking at Dickens, or when looking at the people who mourned him, the years between his time and our own vanish. And we are looking at ourselves. Just as these who came to mourn in the Abbey were looking at themselves. When they buried him, and surrounded his grave with roses and other flowers, they were registering in symbolic sense the end of an age of which he was the single most visible representative; more so than Palmerston, now dead, more so than Gladstone, who stood in an uneasy relation to the period yet to come, and more so than the Queen herself who had not, like Dickens, seen all the transitions of the century. He had more than seen them; he had felt them, had experienced them, had declared them in his fictions. From a distance, then, he embodied the period from which he sprang; and in the course of the succeeding pages we will see how it was his particular genius to turn his life itself into an emblem of that period – instinctively, almost blindly, to dramatise it. But when we come closer to him still, when we observe his life and his work in continuous motion and combination, will these biographical certainties remain or will they dissolve?

For there is a sorrowfulness, a self-contained sorrowfulness, almost a coldness, about aspects of Dickens's life on earth – just as the same sorrowfulness and coldness can be glimpsed within the heart of his narratives. We might use here the imagery of the seascape which fascinated him always: on the surface there is the light and the turbulent water, the currents and the cross-currents, the whole vast edifice of the natural world seen as a wall of glass, or as foam, or as wave, or as rainbow. There are often great scenes of tempest on the face of this water – and how Dickens seemed to live in the storm – but even at quieter times there is still the track of the sailing vessel, the current of the steam-ship; always activity; always busyness. But if we go further beneath the water, beneath the active and busy world of light, what then? If we dive down deeper, dive into the unfathomable depths, what then do we see of him? Lost objects which have drifted down, now flattened beyond recognition. Darkness and silence.

Strange phosphorescent images. Is this what Carlyle meant – a man whose radiance contained the presence of death itself?

But this is to move ahead of our history, and surely it is from Dickens, of all writers, that we learn that it is in details that the spirit fully lives. And if it is true, as David Copperfield says, that ". . . trifles make the sum of life", will we see in the "trifles" of Dickens's life all the constituents of his great works – see in them, too, the true shape of the world in which he lived? For this is the challenge, to make biography an agent of real knowledge. To find in a day, a moment, a passing image or gesture, the very spring and source of his creativity; and to see in these details, too, the figure of the moving age.

Chapter 1

CHARLES DICKENS was born on the seventh of February 1812, the year of victory and the year of hardship. He came crying into the world in a small first-floor bedroom in an area known as New Town or Mile End, just on the outskirts of Portsmouth where his father, John Dickens, worked in the Naval Pay Office. His mother, Elizabeth, is reported to have claimed that she went to a ball on the night before his birth; but no ball is mentioned in the area for that particular evening and it is likely that this is one of the many apocryphal stories which sprung up around the birth and development of the great writer. He was born on a Friday, on the same day as his young hero David Copperfield, and for ever afterwards Friday became for him a day of omen. Whether like his young hero he was born just before midnight, when the tide was in, is not recorded; but this strange association between himself and his fictional characters is one that he carried with him always. He said once, during a speech in memory of Shakespeare's birthday, that: "We meet on this day to celebrate the birthday of a vast army of living men and women who will live for ever with an actuality greater than that of the men and women whose external forms we see around us . . .". He was thinking here of Hamlet and Lear, of Macbeth and Prospero, but is it not also true that in this small front bedroom in Portsmouth, in the presence of a surgeon and a monthly nurse, there was born on this February day Pecksniff and Scrooge, Oliver Twist and Sairey Gamp, Samuel Pickwick and Nicholas Nickleby, Pip and David Copperfield, Miss Havisham and Little Nell, the Artful Dodger and Wackford Squeers, Thomas Gradgrind and Little Dorrit, Sydney Carton and Paul Dombey, Fagin and Edwin Drood, Uriah Heep and Wilkins Micawber, Quilp and Sam Weller, Barnaby Rudge and Bill Sikes, Tiny Tim and Tommy Traddles, all of them tumbling out into the light? It is impossible to say precisely how many characters Charles Dickens has created – almost two thousand of them, born with Dickens but not dying with him, living on for ever. Whether Dickens himself shall turn out to be the hero of his own life, therefore, or whether that station will be held by others, these pages must show.

There was already one man who had set his mark upon him, and in the local newspaper there was inserted an advertisement: "On Friday, at Mile-end Terrace, the Lady of John Dickens Esq., a son." Three weeks later John Dickens and his Lady, whom their son was later savagely to satirise, walked through the lanes and fields to the church of St Mary's Kingston. Here the infant was christened with the names of Charles John Huffam Dickens – Christopher Huffam, who will later play no inconsiderable part in this story, being a friend of John Dickens and godfather to the child. Then they walked back to their small house – not exactly genteel, despite the flourish of John Dickens's announcement in the newspaper, but certainly respectable, in a semi-rural neighbourhood away from the clamour of Portsmouth, a home for someone of modest means but one who could lay definite claims to being a part of the middle classes. It may seem strange that Charles Dickens, who in his work was excessively nostalgic about the years of his childhood, never showed any signs of sentimental interest in the house of his birth: "I can't say I usually care much about it," he once wrote and indeed on the one occasion he seems to have revisited the area he could not find the exact dwelling. One house might serve as his birthplace, he said, because "it looks so like my father"; and another because it looked like the cradle of a weak and puny child. But then he and his companion passed on, until in a square nearby he was happy to lie down on one of the doorsteps in imitation of a lovesick clown until he was chased away by the irate householder. Not a sentimental man in life, therefore; a humorous man, an energetic man, but not a sentimental one. All he remembered of this first house was the fact that it possessed a small garden in the front; and so it does still. A basement kitchen and washroom, a parlour and dining room on the ground floor, two bedrooms on the first floor – in one of them, in the room that he was born, two windows look down onto the front garden – and two garrets above those. A modest house, with a small garden also at the back. A house furnished in the sparse, light pre-Victorian style, the wooden floors echoing the tread of feet, the plain rooms fitfully illuminated either by oil or by candle, the house itself looking out over fields of hay and vegetables, the sight of some windmills along the shore, and the familiar presence of Portsmouth Harbour beyond.

Charles Dickens was not the first child – eighteen months before John and Elizabeth Dickens had had a daughter, Frances Elizabeth, called Fanny all her life. A servant lived with them, too, so this was by no means a large house for them all. The infant memories of Dickens, if such they be, would have been of people moving around in small rooms; mainly female voices, female tears, echoing through the small house. And is there not in his constant description of parts of the body – the face, the hand, the leg, seen in distinction to other limbs – some mark of the first stages of infant perception? No other memories can be traced from a period almost as remote to him as it is to us, unless it be the fact that the first object remembered by David Copperfield is of ". . . my mother with her pretty hair and youthful shape". In later life Dickens was heard to deny the belief that a child had any "divine instinct" of love for its mother, but his own helpless and instinctive affections do not always consort easily with his ordinarily articulated opinions. It is also in *David Copperfield*, after all, that David identifies himself with a baby at the breast, just as at the opening of *Master Humphrey's Clock* the narrator was "happy to nestle in her breast – happy to weep when she did – happy in not knowing why". This is the young mother whose image Dickens was later to pursue both in his own amatory life and in the gentle young women of his fiction: young, beautiful, and good. It is the memory that belongs to all living things but, like all the matters that touched him, Dickens was able to ridicule it even as he celebrated it. "An excellent woman that mother of yours, Christopher," Dick Swiveller says in *The Old Curiosity Shop* – ". . . who ran to catch me when I fell, and kissed the place to make it well? My mother. A charming woman." Dickens here is recalling the famous nursery rhyme of the period, now forgotten.

> Who fed me from her gentle breast,
> And hush'd me in her arms to rest,
> And on my cheek sweet kisses prest?
> My Mother.

And what of the rest of the Dickens family at this time? Charles Dickens never seemed to know much about his grandparents, and even less about those who had come before them, and yet there is no doubt that they always stood silently around him. The actual origins of his family remain quite unknown. There was a Dickens family of

Babbington, Staffordshire, who were lords of the manor of Churchill from 1437 until 1656, and a contemporary biographer records that ". . . it is said that from this family Mr Dickens, the author, is descended", "it is said", always, in this context, being a synonym for unreliable gossip or conjecture. There was also a long line of John and William Dickens (the names of his father and grandfather respectively) who had first lived in Derbyshire but who were memorialised frequently in London records of the seventeenth and eighteenth centuries: and, if there is to be an origin for Dickens, it is perhaps more appropriate to look for it here in generations of Londoners. Surely the image of the city which Dickens creates comes from sources as deep as himself, as deep as his own inheritance?

More is known of those immediately preceding him. His mother's maiden name was Barrow, and the Barrows came from Bristol. There appear to have been clerics in this family but, more importantly, they were the makers of musical instruments. Both his maternal grandparents were connected with this business, and his grandfather also practised as a music-master – although his later and less worthy activities were to leave a different kind of mark upon his grandson. And yet the figures who influenced him most are to be found on the father's side of his family. There is no doubt that, in the lives of writers, the shadows of a grandfather or grandmother (most potent even when they are not clearly discerned) can be seen lying across the paths they follow. It is as if the peculiar chemistry of genius sometimes skips a generation, as if it is the nature of the grandparents which really accounts for the temperament and even behaviour of the one who comes after them. Dickens's grandparents were both servants, a fact which was not revealed until after his death. He generally disliked the more superior kind of servant (with the exception of housekeepers, as we shall see), preeminently because they were of a fluid class, part of the aristocracy but not belonging to it, part of the lower-middle class and yet not attached to it. They shifted between the classes, often exhibiting the vanity of one and the hardness of the other. In his fiction Dickens's characters are always being – they believed – observed by butlers and it is worthy of notice that Dickens's grandfather, William, was a butler. He was dead long before his grandson was born, and yet one sees in him all the virtues which Dickens himself cultivated and which were so signally absent in the writer's parents. William Dickens was butler or steward for the Crewe family, who possessed houses in both London and the country; all the available evidence suggests that he was a thrifty and conscientious man, one who could not have risen to that level of service without considerable administrative abilities and with a reputation for financial probity. These were all qualities which his grandson possessed, even to abundance.

But there were also characteristics which Dickens inherited from his grandmother, the only grandparent whom he ever really knew. She died when he was twelve and, although there are no records of their meeting (how could there be records of the activities of so relatively undistinguished a family?) there can be little doubt that he knew her and that he liked her. She was a housekeeper for the Crewe family, and in his fiction he shows an especial fondness for such conscientious old ladies. She had married her husband early in life; before her marriage she was a servant to a certain Lady Blandford in Grosvenor Square, and there are unconfirmed reports that she came from a small village named Claverley, near Tong, and that she had been housekeeper at Tong Castle. The only interest to be found in these shadowy reports lies in the fact that it is often claimed that Little Nell meets her quietus in the church at Tong; if so, a strange pilgrimage for one of Dickens's small and sickly heroines – towards death in a place marked by the presence of his grandmother! After her marriage in 1781, however, she joined the Crewe family and was eventually promoted to the post of housekeeper, a post she retained until she was seventy-five. She, too, was trusted and competent. But, more importantly, she was known as a fluent story-teller; one of the Crewe children later recalled that ". . . not since that time had she met anyone who possessed so surprising a gift for extemporising fiction for the amusement of others". Another report has it that "Mrs Dickens was an inimitable story-teller, and she loved to have the children around her, and to beguile them, not only with fairy tales, but with reminiscences of her own, and stories from the pages of history". Towards the end of her life she gave her grandson a fat old silver watch which had belonged to her husband, but it is also possible that he inherited much more interesting gifts from her.

His grandfather dead before his birth; his grandmother dead when he was twelve; and his father's brother died childless: he had really only a small circle of relations, therefore, not at all like the extended Victorian family which he was later both to celebrate and to curse. And yet the image of the family haunts him. Practically all of his novels are concerned with the life within families, after all, specifically in the degradation and unsatisfactoriness of familial relationships. This is the fount from which all forms of social evil are seen by him to spring, but the conclusions of his novels tend nevertheless to reinstate some idealised family group which can withstand change and the world. In Dickens's fiction that idealised family becomes an image both of social and religious life; so, by that strange alchemy of his genius, he turns private longings for a more ordered and stable life into a positive social force. Does it also come as a surprise, then, that he all but destroyed his own family, and that he was perpetually beset by the failures and weaknesses of his own relatives? We must look for the origins of these compulsive, contradictory feelings in those closest to him – and no one ever came as close to him as his parents, John and Elizabeth Dickens. In them we see half of his strength and half of his weakness, and in his baffled troubling relations with his parents we observe also the root source of that art through which he was later to encompass them.

Elizabeth Dickens, his mother, was twenty-three at the time of his birth – a young woman, then, and it would be most unwise to transpose all of the stories about her in later life to this much earlier period. Still more unwise, therefore, to take the stock portrait of Mrs Nickleby, assumed to be Charles Dickens's portrait of her, and use this as a stick with which to beat her. His relationship to his mother was central to his life, but it was necessarily a complex one established upon guilt and rejection but combined with a kind of hopeless love. All the maternal figures in his novels are in fact ways of reinstating someone else in her place. He did not want to see her too clearly. He did not want to get too close to her. And yet there are occasions when the reports of others, and Charles Dickens's own casual asides, help us to see the mother of the genius more clearly. "It is an undoubted fact that all remarkable men have had remarkable mothers, and have respected them in after life as their best friends" – these words are put into the mouth of the put-upon and somewhat foolish Mr Tetterby. But they contain a particle of truth; as Charles Dickens himself casually observed in one of his journalistic papers, "Excuse my curiosity, which I inherit from my mother . . ." There is another reference, too, in the mouth of Dick Swiveller, generally called "Dick" which was itself one of Dickens's own nicknames: ". . . My mother must have been a very inquisitive woman; I have no doubt I'm marked with a note of interrogation somewhere. My feelings I smother, but thou hast been the cause of this anguish, my – upon my word." And so he breaks off, the word missing from his lips of course being that of "mother". It is the word often missing from Dickens in his adult life – his references to Elizabeth Dickens are in fact very rare – but, even if he did not necessarily recognise the inheritance, others were more observant. An early biographer records that "her famous son, it is said, resembled her greatly in his later years. She was a cheerful soul, fond of joining in the amusements of young people, and especially in dancing . . ." Another contemporary account talks of her "entering into youthful amusements with much enjoyment" as well as having "a good stock of common sense". The inheritance is there, even if its attributes were so much a part of Dickens, so knit into his brain and flesh, that he could not always be expected to see them clearly. He was fond of dancing, too, but he did not like to see his mother dance; he is said ". . . to have regarded her performances with disfavour". And here also we trace the strange alchemy of the mother–son relationship, the son despising in his mother what is implicit in himself, just as in his fiction he sees her as a stranger without realising that he is also looking upon his own face.

He was close to her in other ways, too. A report of her in middle-age deserves to be quoted in full: she "was a little woman who had been very nice-looking in her youth. She had very bright hazel eyes –" Dickens's eyes were hazel also – "and was as thoroughly good-natured, easy-going, companionable a body as one would wish to meet." We must remember the "easy-going", since it will be of considerable importance later. "She possessed an extraordinary sense of the ludicrous, and her power of imitation was something quite astonishing. On entering a room she almost unconsciously took an inventory of its contents and if anything happened to strike her as out of place or ridiculous, she would afterwards describe it in the quaintest possible manner." This gift of rapid and keen observation was one which Dickens possessed to the highest possible degree, and from where else might it have come? "In like manner she noticed the personal peculiarities of her friends and acquaintances. She had also a fine vein of pathos, and could bring tears to the eyes of her listeners when narrating some sad event . . . Mrs Dickens has often sent my sisters and myself into uncontrollable fits of laughter by her funny sayings and inimitable mimicry." So the mimicry, the pathos and the comedy exist in the mother as well as in the son. Of course in the son it was controlled and magnified to an unimaginable extent but the mystery of inheritance remains. And it *is* a mystery, how such gifts and qualities can be transmitted from generation to generation, until there comes a time when in one particular person they blaze out and, in a sense, devour all those around.

There is a drawing of Elizabeth Dickens in her middle years, and even in the features, which had not grown old, one can see the lineaments of the young woman: something sardonic about her but also amused and alert, her wide eyes showing an enthusiasm or impetuosity barely kept in check. There was one occasion when Dickens himself alluded to her as the origin of Mrs Nickleby but we must look here for the evocation of something more rarefied and more important than external character or temperament: in the ceaseless tumbling speech of Mrs Nickleby we catch an echo of the infant child hearing the sound of his mother's voice. The comforting ebb and swell of words, the easy chatter, the full flow concealing something close to anxiety, the flood of language upon which the infant could float. And in this he seems to have returned again to his memories of the mother as the young woman, upon whose breast he could rest; this is the mother as girl, perpetually memorialised among the heroines of Charles Dickens, the real maternal figure, young, beautiful and good. "The mother who lay in the grave, was the mother of my infancy; the little creature in her arms was myself, as I had once been, hushed for ever on her bosom."

So how are we to see Elizabeth Dickens during her son's earliest years? Cheerful, good-tempered, enjoying social pleasures (hence the report about the ball before his birth); but also by all accounts sensible, practical and, as was to be demonstrated in later years, with a fair stock of courage in enduring the misfortunes inflicted on her by her husband. There were earlier family misfortunes as well: two years before the birth of her son, her father, Charles Barrow, had been found guilty of embezzling money from the Navy Pay Office (in which department he had a much superior position to that of her husband), and on the revelation of his theft he absconded to the Isle of Man. There was, in other words, in Charles Dickens's immediate family a grandfather who was both an embezzler and a fugitive from justice. The problems of class had surfaced with his paternal grandparents, the servants, and now criminality – specifically criminality tied to the misuse of money – also marked those around him. Is it not appropriate, then, that the major themes within his novels lie in the making and spending of money, and the effect that this pursuit can have on families? Certain themes, it seems, run in the blood.

Elizabeth Dickens called her husband D. We know that. As for John

Dickens himself, there is also a great deal known, some of it verifiable and some of it apocryphal. He had been brought up by his mother in the various Crewe households, his father having died a few months before his birth; it is often claimed that Dickens draws his fictional orphans from his own blighted experience as a boy, but can we not also see in his father's own partial orphanhood a ready source of fantasies and stories? He had a brother, William, who was three years older and who seems to have inherited his parents' sense of responsibility and fiscal caution which John notably lacked. William died as the keeper of a coffee house in Oxford Street, not a particularly exalted occupation, and one which the Dickens family never seems to have mentioned. But on the available evidence he appears to have been his mother's favourite son; John, on the other hand, was called by her "that lazy fellow . . . who used to come hanging about the house" and one "against whose idleness and general incapacity she was never tired of inveighing". Certainly she left him nothing specific in her will, stating that instead he had obtained diverse sums from her on different occasions; in other words, the pattern of his life was set early and in succeeding years he would dun his son much more heavily than ever he dunned his mother.

So here was a feckless youth, brought up in the purlieus of a rich and respectable family – the son of a servant but nonetheless it is clear from everything recorded about him that he suffered from no visible sense of inferiority as a result. Quite the contrary; whether out of insecurity or resentment or plain imitation, he carried himself as a gentleman, dressed fashionably as a gentleman and always insisted upon being treated as a gentleman. His accent must have been trained early in life – there was no sense in which he was what was called low – and he grew up in an environment which paid no little respect to all the special proprieties and in particular to book-learning. (The fact that, by the time his son had discovered literature, John Dickens had really only a "standard set" of English classics suggests that he himself was not an adventurous or omnivorous reader.) A different atmosphere, then, from any which a normal boy of the lower middle classes would have enjoyed, and it is possible that it was the presence of wealth and its apparent ready availability which made him so remiss in his own financial matters. Growing up without a father, he found a father in the world. He believed, all his life, that he would be sheltered; and, indeed, as it turned out, he was not so wrong in that belief even if it was his son who had to shelter him.

John Dickens stayed with his mother in the Crewe household until he was about twenty or twenty-one, and there is no doubt that by then his character was almost completely formed. Perhaps with the influence of Lord Crewe, he went to Somerset House in 1807 as an extra clerk in the office of the Treasurer of His Majesty's Navy; here he met another new recruit, Thomas Barrow, the brother of Elizabeth. Two years later he was given a more permanent position of assistant clerk in the Pay Office, and in succeeding years he steadily moved forward through the ranks of promotion, but even before this welcome security of employment he began his serious pursuit of his colleague's sister. By 1808 he had been transferred to a more responsible position in Portsmouth, which must have entailed a certain amount of commuting in his courtship of Elizabeth Barrow who still lived in London. On 13 June 1809 they married at the Church of St Mary-le-Strand, and then travelled back to Portsmouth and to their new house in Mile End Terrace. Frances was born in the following year, and Charles two years later.

And what of the father in these early years? He was a clerk, but the work was not of that ordinarily bureaucratic kind which the word now suggests. He was with others responsible for paying both the naval workmen in port and the crews upon ship, which meant physically handing over the money; sometimes, with a crowd around them, it might lead to disagreements, and sometimes even to fights. Portsmouth itself was then a relatively violent place, and many of the men whom John Dickens encountered had been actively engaged in the naval battles which marked the Napoleonic Wars; one must imagine the smell, the bravado, the drunkenness, the sheer physical stamina which marked those involved in warfare. By no standard was early nineteenth-century England safe or particularly salubrious, and a naval town such as Portsmouth would have been almost as bad a spot as you could find; it would not have had the sheer overcrowded slums of the capital or of the Northern cities, but nevertheless the streets would not have been safe at night, the houses and highways not secure against robbery. The danger, in outlining the characters of those who make up this history, is that in some sense we place them within the context of our own period. In fact everything has changed to such an extent that the social and economic relations between individuals are not easily to be recaptured. Nor is the atmosphere and quality of the world in which they moved – we must think of it as a less secure, a more invidious, a more *angular*, world. If a late twentieth-century person were suddenly to find himself in a tavern or house of the period, he would be literally sick – sick with the smells, sick with the food, sick with the atmosphere around him. It is an unimaginable journey we must take, therefore, a journey back through time.

So what of John Dickens the naval clerk? He was always well-dressed, always polite, always affable. He was good-looking – better looking than his children, it was generally thought – and well-built, although inclining to stoutness in later years. According to one contemporary in the Navy Pay Office he was ". . . a fellow of infinite humour, chatty, lively and agreeable". This seems to be the general report. "A chatty pleasant companion"; "most genial and courtly . . . of kindly disposition"; ". . . possessing a varied fund of anecdote and a genuine vein of humour"; "very courteous, imposingly so"; ". . . the jolliest of men". He described himself as an optimist and once compared himself to "a cork which, when submerged, bobs up to the surface again none the worse for the dip". Strangely enough his son, in one of his earliest pieces of journalism, describes just such a man as "one of the careless, good-for-nothing, happy fellows, who float, cork-like, on the surface, for the world to play at hockey with . . . always reappearing and bounding with the stream buoyantly and merrily along". (There is no doubt that he has his father in mind here, and from his earliest sketches Dickens seems to be describing him, reinventing him, readdressing him.) Most of his colleagues' remarks were of course made with the beneficence of hindsight, and many of them without the knowledge that John Dickens had all but ruined his family through his own negligence and incompetence. Yet even his wife said of him, after his death, "Certainly there never was a Man more unselfish, and ever a Friend to those whom he could serve and a most affectionate kind Husband and father." "Ever a Friend to those whom he could serve" no doubt but, like many amicable and companionable people, he did not in his turn scruple to be served by his friends when the occasion required it.

Yet there is more to him than that, or how else could it be that his character so bewildered and exasperated his son? Certainly he was more complicated than these first reports suggest; his mother thought of him as lazy, but it is also true that he could on occasions work with great energy and alacrity. He perspired a lot as he grew older. He suffered from asthma, about which complaint one might quote his own words: "One must have something wrong, I suppose, and I like to know what it is." He may have been jolly, but he had a fearful temper; on one occasion, according to a story, he had been asked to allow no one behind the scenes during the course of one of his son's theatrical ventures and, on entering the green room, flew at his own reflection in the glass and bruised his knuckles. Dickens called these his "passion bursts" and admitted that he suffered from them himself – the subject of Dickens's anger is a large one and will be addressed elsewhere. There was also about John Dickens "more than a shade of gentility" and he was ". . . a little pompous". Asthmatic, fits of anger, self-invented gentility; all of these suggest someone who was far more nervously insecure than his general amiability would suggest. We must imagine a man who was agreeable, courteous, but also with a certain impenetrability; there is a sense in which he never seems properly connected with the world, his own elaborate diction confirming that sense of dislocation, and as a result there is a sense of unreality about him. He was always short of money, always spending money, always borrowing money. This improvidence and recklessness, when seen in combination with his courteous and amiable personality, also suggest that there was a callowness or even a coldness at his centre. There is a sort of emptiness, an infantilism, a refusal to confront himself. This is no more than in a million other men: it comes to our notice only because it was noticed and recorded by his son. "How long he is," Dickens once complained, "growing up to be a man." And we recall in Dickens's fiction how universal it is that the child looks after the adult, and how the adult remains so dependent upon the child that he becomes something worse than merely child-like.

In fact Charles Dickens's relations to his father were of the most complicated sort; not the "half-admiring and half-ashamed" response of Little Dorrit to her imprisoned father, but something at once more violent and less easy to understand. There were times in later life when John Dickens became for him a creature of nightmare, forever weighing upon his life, but long before that time it is clear that the image of his father haunted him in some generalised and unspecified way. He is even mentioned in his first published story. It seems that John Dickens liked to tell an anecdote about the time he escorted Sheridan's wife in a coach to London, and how once he kissed Sheridan's hand – Sheridan being the Paymaster to the Forces between 1807 and 1812 – and there, in Dickens's first published piece, we find a grandiloquent and "little smirking man" who has been "endeavouring to obtain a listener to some stories about Sheridan". It has been said that his father then reappears everywhere after this; in William Dorrit, in Wilkins Micawber, in Joey Bagstock (originally christened "John" by Dickens) and in that succession of false fathers and social parasites who sometimes bear the name "John" but who can be recognised in any case as images of that father who haunted him. He liked to parody his father in his letters, also, and the authentic sound of John Dickens's voice and phraseology is to be glimpsed in the echoes which his son gives of him; in phrases such as "she has sown and must reap", "your promised communication", "manifest to any person of ordinary intelligence" and in a longer passage which, to judge from John Dickens's extant correspondence, is a fair summary both of its appeal and of its emptiness: ". . . to be deprived, to a certain extent, of the concomitant advantages, whatever they may be, resulting from his medical skill, such as it is, and his professional attendance, in so far as it may be so considered." Here is the grandiloquence and the theatricality which Dickens on occasion could himself assume, but it is clear that once again in the various versions of his father which he is said to have created he does not so much parody the character of his father as parody the sound of his words – the circumlocutions, the elongated constructions, the sudden turnings and cul-de-sacs. In short, his speech.

But his attitude to his father was not one that could be resolved by parody or imitation; there were other feelings at work. If he admired him he despised him, too, but he also recognised the presence of his father within himself so that, at times of great distress, his own self-pity spilled over into pity for the man who had begotten him. He was forever accusing him during his life of rapacity and ingratitude but, after his death, his constant refrain was "my poor father". His mother was never so sympathetically described, and we will see how it was that Dickens believed her to have rejected him in ways that his father had not. And yet it was his father who was to ruin his family, just as in turn Charles Dickens was to ruin his. Thus the strange burden of inheritance, something deeper and darker than those mannerisms which Dickens may have employed as material in his novels. It may be that we inherit precisely those qualities which we cannot recognise or understand, that it is our fate to resemble our parents in ways that can never be clear until, perhaps, the moment of death itself. But inherit them we do. Even on the most superficial level it is clear enough that Dickens owed something of his observation and inquisitiveness to his mother, something of his rhetoric and grandiloquence to his father. One might notice here how the feminine characters in

Dickens tend to talk on and on without the benefit of grammar or syntax; and how the male characters use language very deliberately constructed and shaped. Dickens had heard both. And he contained both of these possibilities within himself. And if there was a certain unreality about the father's presence in the world, it is an unreality which can be supposed to have affected all the rest of the family including Charles Dickens; there is always something about them which is out of key, out of touch, like a family of travelling actors who have no secure place in the world. And what also of the impetuosity and self-destructiveness which, as we shall see, seem to have been a feature of his parents' life in these earliest years? What about the insouciance, almost the coldness, which is also present? Do they in their turn find a place within Charles Dickens himself? And how is it in any case that all of these characteristics and qualities so combined with each other that they formed the greatest novelist ever to have written in the English language? What power made that?

"Speaking of memory one day he said the memory of children was prodigious; it was a mistake to fancy children ever forgot anything." This was Charles Dickens's constant refrain, but of course some things are forgotten. Some things must be forgotten. In any case no one can know what early childhood is, really, like, because it can only be re-experienced in the act of remembering; in the act, therefore, of interpretation and explanation. The exceptional visions are those of stray objects and scenes, which seem to loom up without context and which are invested with a mysterious stillness. These are the true memories of infancy, and the rest is folded forever within natural and instinctive oblivion. The point about origins is that they cannot be recalled; that is why they remain so powerfully influential in the course of any life. The real springs of childhood exist before language and even before proper consciousness itself; and so, when discussing Dickens's childhood, we must conceive of purposiveness without purpose, aptness without intent, a glowing expectancy. Of course no one more willingly defined and described himself in language than Charles Dickens – there is a sense in which his identity actually depended upon his deployment of language – and there are many passages in his journalism or fiction where he unveils incidents and passages of his childhood with a clarity which seems extraordinary. It is a point to which he draws attention, all the time emphasising the nature and the powers of his observation. "I was a child of close observation," he says; "I looked at nothing that I know of, but saw everything . . . ," he says, again; and he makes the same point in part of the autobiographical fragment he once wrote of his childhood, "Their different peculiarities of dress, of face, of gait, of manner, were written indelibly upon my memory." This is a constant refrain – this idea of seeing everything without having to focus closely upon anything – and there is no need to doubt Dickens's word on the subject. Indeed throughout his life it is clear that he retained a very strong visual memory so that he could, as it were, effortlessly recall the visual details and elaborations of a scene without necessarily understanding its context or purpose. It is a rare and strange gift, currently believed by psychologists to be related to obsession (it is sometimes found, for example, in children who are mentally un- stable), and one which Dickens was able to harness for the purposes of his creativity so that there are occasions when a perfectly visualised scene rises out of the context of his writing and takes on a haunting, irremediable quality of its own. In his childhood memories, however, these scenes are to be distinguished from those passages in which he links specific incidents with the spectacle of his own abandonment and unhappiness; this is memory as nostalgia, and no writer was more adept at using it than Dickens, though it does mean that such passages have to be examined rather more closely.

But Dickens did more than emphasise the intensity of his own childhood observation. Again and again he makes the larger point that children in general can be said to have such powers. "He considered," one contemporary wrote, "that an intelligent child's observation was accurate and intense to a degree" and he himself said in a later essay that "it would be difficult to overstate the intensity and accuracy of an intelligent child's observation. At that impressible time of life, it must sometimes produce a fixed impression. If the fixed impression be of an object terrible to the child it will be (for want of reasoning upon) inseparable from great fear." There do indeed seem to have been moments of great fear in Dickens's own childhood, but the significant point to notice is that here and elsewhere Dickens is suggesting that the child is in an important sense father of the man. As he says in *Nicholas Nickleby*, ". . . perhaps a word, a laugh, a look, some slight distress, a passing thought or fear – and yet more strongly and distinctly marked, and better far remembered, than the hardest trials or severest sorrows of but a year ago". This passage has an Augustan sententiousness which is not absent from Dickens's earlier novels, but the point is one that he often returned to; in a sense he was proclaiming here the

springs of his art, but just as importantly he is reiterating the importance of childhood memory in the understanding and appreciation of
the world. Memory for him is inseparable from fancy, from creativity
and from social beneficence. Implicitly he believed to it to be a
humanising force, just as he believed that his novels, springing in part
from childhood memories, were themselves agents of social and
private benevolence. The art of fiction was for him the art of memory,
and now in our turn we must try, as it were, to remember Charles
Dickens's childhood. Just as we must "remember" the age from
which he came.

The Dickens family did not stay long in the little house in Mile-End
Terrace, and five months after his birth they removed to Hawk Street,
the first of many moves which were to mark Dickens's childhood and
which even at this very early age must in some sense have affected
him. (It is curious, in fact, how many other writers were similarly
unsettled in early life; fiction may in that sense be a way of controlling
and dominating an otherwise fluctuating reality.) This particular street
was beside the port itself – for John Dickens it was no more than three
minutes' walk to the small naval pay office just within the gates. The
street has now gone (although its name and the pay office itself
remain), but at the time it was considered a perfectly respectable
thoroughfare where many officers were placed in lodging houses. In
Dombey and Son Dickens recounts in vivid detail a certain Mrs Pipchin,
boarding-house keeper, and in particular he dwells upon her clothes
like "the . . . black bombazeen garments of the worthy old lady
[which] darkened the audience chamber". After he had composed
this his older sister, Fanny, is reported by him to have exclaimed,
"Good heavens! What does this mean? You have painted our lodging-
house keeper and you were but two years old at the time." Whether it
was indeed a portrait of the lady, or whether it was simply based upon
fugitive infant impressions, is one of those conundrums which regularly occur in trying to assess the processes of Dickens's extraordinary
imagination. Perhaps best to suggest that it was rather like little
Florence Dombey's memory of another ancient crone, ". . . her
childish recollection of that terrible old woman was as grotesque and
exaggerated a presentment of the truth, perhaps, as the shadow on the
wall". And then eighteen months later the family were on the move
again, this time to the new extension of Portsmouth which was
known as Southsea, at 39 Wish Street. The rent here was twice that of
their previous house, which confirms what the records themselves

demonstrate, that John Dickens was steadily climbing through the preordained ranks of preferment. (He had also subscribed to Campbell's *Lives of the Admirals* which suggests, if nothing else, a certain attachment and even affection for his profession.) They were joined here by Elizabeth Dickens's sister, Mary Allen, known as Aunt Fanny, who no doubt contributed her own portion of the larger rent. They had moved in by Christmas 1813, and for the first time we see signs of Dickens's powers of recall. His friend, John Forster, was to write in his life of Dickens: "He has often told me that he remembered the small front garden to the house . . . from which he was taken away when he was two years old, and where, watched by a nurse through a low kitchen-window, almost level with the gravel walk, he trotted about with something to eat, and his little elder sister with him."

They spent New Year's Day in that house, a New Year's Day apparently remembered by Dickens forty-six years later in an article for his journal, *Household Words*. "So far back do my recollections of childhood extend," he wrote, "that I have a vivid remembrance of the sensation of being carried down-stairs in a woman's arms, and holding tight to her, in the terror of seeing the steep perspective below." This has the ring of truthful memory, a recollected experience of anxiety, and so does the picture which greeted him when he peeped into the celebrations in the ground floor room – ". . . a very long row of ladies and gentlemen sitting against a wall, all drinking at once out of little glass cups with handles, like custard-cups . . . There was no speech-making, no quick movement and change of action, no demonstration of any kind. They were all sitting in a long row against the wall – very like my first idea of the good people in Heaven, as I derived it from a wretched picture in a Prayer-book – and they had all got their heads a little thrown back, and were all drinking at once." This is an extra-ordinary picture; it was one that he said always haunted him when anyone talked of a New Year's Day party. But in this vision of a row of strangely silent people, leaning against a wall with their heads thrown back, there also is revived the picture of a lost age, a vanished age – lost to Charles Dickens himself when he looks back, but also how much lost to us.

Three months later there was a birth in Wish Street; a male child, on 28 March, who was christened Alfred Allen Dickens. Those who profess to understand the nature of infant consciousness might suggest that the emergence of another male child when Dickens himself was just a little over two years old would have inspired anxiety and resentment in the sibling's breast – that he would have felt, as Dickens put it in another context, "an alien from my mother's heart". Would he have been denied the pampering which he might have desired, and would he then have felt rejected by his mother? It is difficult to be sure; certainly the idea of maternal rejection is a very strong thread both in his fiction and in his own reminiscences. And then six months later Alfred Allen died, of "water on the brain", and for reasons which remain unclear was buried in the churchyard of the obscure village of Widley. If the infant Charles had harboured resentful or even murderous longings against the supplanter, how effectively they had come home to roost! And how strong the guilt might have been. *Might have been* – that is necessarily the phrase. And yet when the adulthood of Dickens is considered, with all its evidence that Dickens did indeed suffer from an insidious pressure of irrational guilt, and when all the images of dead infants are picked out of his fiction, it is hard to believe that this six-month episode in the infancy of the novelist did not have some permanent effect upon him.

Then in January of the following year the family were on the move again; the Portsmouth administration was being curtailed after the ending of hostilities, and John Dickens had been recalled to Somerset House. And so for the first time Charles Dickens entered London, a journey about which he remembered nothing except the fact that they left Portsea covered with snow. But already the capital must have been associated with privation, if not exactly hardship – John Dickens had a reduced income in the city, largely because he was not paid an Outport Allowance. They went into lodgings at 10 Norfolk Street, now 22 Cleveland Street, on the corner of Tottenham Street. The house is still there; now the ground floor contains a sandwich shop, but then it was a grocer's. The grocer was also the landlord, a certain John Dodd who was later to become one of John Dickens's many creditors, and it seems possible that it was during this London period that Dickens's father first ran into debt. They stayed here two years – Aunt Fanny and perhaps a servant with them – and although nothing else is specifically recorded of their life in that period there can be no doubt that it affected Dickens. It was not only that another child was born in this period, Laetitia Mary Dickens in April 1816, but, rather, that it was in his third and fourth years that the infant Dickens gradually awakened to further consciousness of the world. A world that was now not one of fields, but of streets. Of course there were areas close to Tottenham Court

Road which were still rural – the fields of Camden Town were relatively close – but the sense of urban reality was quite a new one. Even in the somewhat restricted surroundings of Hawk Street the sea had been only a few hundred yards away; but here they were beside the thoroughfares of Oxford Street and Tottenham Street, that somewhat blighted area where a few years before the forsaken boy, Thomas De Quincey, had met the friendless girl and together they had trudged weary and fainting. De Quincey had memoralised this episode in his *Confessions of an English Opium Eater* published in 1822: "when I walk at this time in Oxford-street by dreamy lamplight, and hear those airs played on a barrel organ which years ago solaced me and my dear companion (as I must always call her) I shed tears . . ." Dickens was later to shed tears when he paced some other London streets and, although it would be too much to say that the small child was aware of the miseries which existed close to him, it would be a foolish person indeed who did not believe that the strange mysteries and sorrows of London did not in some way pierce or move his infant breast. And what is that cry repeated more than once in Dickens's fiction, the words of the dying child who cries out, "Mother! . . . bury me in the open fields – anywhere but in these dreadful streets . . . they have killed me"?

It was in January 1817 that they returned to those "open fields"; to Sheerness, which was John Dickens's next posting, a somewhat isolated port and about which little is known in connection with the migratory Dickens family. It seems that they rented a small house next door to the Sheerness Theatre, and one mid-nineteenth-century chronicler said of John Dickens that "of an evening he used to sit in this room, and could hear what was passing on the stage, and join in the chorus of 'God Save the King' and 'Britannia Rules the Waves'". Songs and theatres are to feature large in Dickens's childhood, and here is perhaps the first intimation of that long-forgotten world – in the vision of John Dickens singing patriotic songs in his sitting room, listening eagerly to the sounds coming from a small wooden theatre. A world in which nautical or comic songs and theatrical farces were the most popular form of entertainment. This is the world beside which Charles Dickens grew up.

Four months later, at the beginning of April 1817, they moved from Sheerness along the coast to the much more populous port of Chatham. It is here, in what was sometimes called "the wickedest place in the world", twinned, as it were, with the cathedral town of

Rochester, from which it is impossible geographically to separate it, that we first begin to see Charles Dickens *in situ*; that we first begin to see Dickens's childhood clearly, and can trace from it the lines which connect his infancy with his maturity, his childish imagination with his later fiction. It is the area with which he felt himself to be most closely associated, and it is the one to which he returned in later life. Rochester provides a setting for his first novel and for his last; Chatham itself, once described by him as a "mere dream of chalk, and drawbridges, and mastless ships, in a muddy river", was also to become one of the primary landscapes of his imagination.

Chapter 2

THEY moved to Ordnance Terrace, on the brow of a hill – "the most airy and pleasant part" of the parish, Dickens was to say later. It was a comfortable although by no means a spacious house; John Dickens always seemed to prefer *new* buildings, and the houses in this terrace had only recently been constructed. And it was a typical building of its period: the narrow hallway, the dining room on the first floor, and the parlour above it. There was a bedroom on this floor, too, for the parents and then up a further staircase to two attic rooms, one for the servants and one for the children. Charles Dickens seems to have spent half his childhood in such small rooms; and in his fiction also we find attic rooms, musty rooms, parlours, tiny kitchens, sets of chambers, all of them suggesting that Dickens's fictional imagination could best work within the ambience of the small spaces he had known as a child. In Ordnance Terrace there were now three children, two nurses, Aunt Fanny and the Dickenses themselves – a complement of eight in what was effectively a six-room house. And do we not hear also in this somewhat overcrowded house the echoes of all those people moving through small rooms, arguing, fighting, grieving, which play so large a part in his later novels? And yet in his later sketches, part fiction and part autobiography, there is a characteristic image of a child or children looking from the windows of such small rooms up at the stars. They would have seemed much brighter then than they ever are now.

Chatham was of course a naval town, and from the window of his attic bedroom the young Dickens would also have looked out across the hayfields to the prospect of the harbour and dock beyond; he would have seen the tall masts of the sailing ships and the chimneys of the dockyards outlined against the hillsides and orchards beyond them. And beyond them, too, were the Chatham Lines, that system of hollows, pits, drawbridges, subterranean passages and bomb-proof rooms where the soldiers garrisoned in Chatham would engage in manoeuvres or what today would be defined as "war-games". It was here that in a later essay he remembers having fought an inconclusive duel over the hand of a very young lady, but Dickens's more elaborate childhood memories – at least those under the guise of a narrator such as the "Uncommercial Traveller" – are not to be mistaken for the real thing, and this pretty episode may be nothing more than an echo of a more famous inconclusive duel close to the same spot in *The Pickwick Papers*. These Lines, Dickens wrote later, were "grassy and innocent enough on the surface, at present, but tough subjects at the core". There were to be found here mysterious "dark vaults" with gratings and with a "smell so chill and earthy". That grave-like odour is one of the most significant of his childhood – it will occur in other contexts, both in Rochester and in Chatham – and it is as if he smelled it for the rest of his life. Ordnance Terrace itself was on the brow of a hill which led to Fort Pitt, one of the many fortifications around the Medway, and beyond the small front garden of the Dickens residence the ground ran down to the old town and to the river beyond. There was a field just in front of the house where the young Dickens used to play with his sister and with his nurse; when he returned many years later, that field had been removed in order to make way for the railway which linked London to Chatham, and here as in so many aspects we may discern how the childhood of Dickens was spent in an older country which was already receding into the far distance when he reached maturity. This was, then, a genteel neighbourhood, and on certain occasions Dickens mentions the neighbours to whom the family became greatly attached; later he was to represent them in his fiction as "the old lady" and the "Half-pay captain" and, although it is always dangerous to assume that he was in any sense realistically portraying the people whom he knew, there is no doubt that there *was* an old lady, who was later to leave money to the family, that there was a retired seaman and that there *was* even a young girl, a certain Lucy Stroughill, who was the playmate of the young Dickens and whom he later remembered as "golden-haired Lucy".

The Dickens family lived here for four years. One of the earliest accounts of this period talks of him as "a lively boy of a good, genial, open disposition, and not quarrelsome as most children are at times"; certainly these were some of the happiest years of his childhood, and in later evocations of the area he was to describe "the sheaved corn . . . in the golden fields . . . Peace and abundance". And yet Chatham itself hardly deserved so golden a description. It was a rough and dirty place, the haunt of the sailors and soldiers who were stationed there at a time when the Napoleonic Wars had just come to an end, leaving the inheritance of wasted lives, maimed bodies, popular discontent and a repressive domestic government. A place known for being "as lawless as it is squalid" and one in which the numerous frowsy drinking places were matched only by the number of equally frowsy brothels. We can be sure that the young Dickens noticed all of this; how much he understood is another matter. But, at a time before the moral restraint of what we have come to call the "Victorian period", the less salubrious sights and odours were simply taken for granted; certainly John Dickens must have done so (even if he did not necessarily enjoy them), and there is nothing of the prude or puritan about the later Charles Dickens which would suggest that he was in any way horrified or repelled by what he saw as a boy. Quite the contrary; there is evidence to suggest that "low life" in a certain way always exhilarated him, and the tone of Mr Pickwick's remarks about the Medway towns (no doubt Chatham in particular) has all the hallmarks of Dickens's own ebullient spirits: "The streets present a lively and animated appearance, occasioned chiefly by the conviviality of the military. It is truly delightful to a philanthropic mind, to see these gallant men, staggering along under the influence of an overflow, both of animal, and ardent spirits; more especially when we remember that the following them about, and jesting with them, affords a cheap and innocent amusement for the boy population." In this same litany of merit Mr Pickwick chooses to mention the marine-stores and the stalls which sold apples, flat-fish and oysters. But this was also a town in which the merchants of old clothes thrived; as well as marine-store shops, there were "salesmen, outfitters, tailors, old clothesmen, army and navy accoutrement makers", so it comes as no particular surprise that, on his pilgrimage away from London, the young David Copperfield should pass through Chatham and there sell his jacket to a mad dwarf. Of course old clothes were also an important part of the Victorian social economy; not only were most of the lower classes too poor to buy new clothes of their own but these old coats and shirts represented the emblems of a higher class which over a period of years were slowly passed down through the ranks of society. An interesting symbol, this, for the changes which were taking place within the culture itself. In any case Dickens himself always had a fascination for old clothes, and in one of his earliest exercises in journalism he speculates about the bodies which once inhabited them – finding, in a panoply of old garments, a crowd of forgotten human beings dispersed through the community. It would not be surprising, therefore, if the old shops of Chatham had first provided him with the materials of that obsession. And if we are looking for other seeds of his genius in this early period (as search we must, since every good story must have a beginning as well as an end) it is not inappropriate to notice that in the registers of a Chatham church are to be found the names of Weller, Tapley, Wren and Jasper. Perhaps one might note here also that one of John Dickens's colleagues in the Navy Pay Office had been an extra clerk by the name of S. Tupman. One can never overestimate the power of names spoken in the presence of the young boy, names that find some lodging in his consciousness and, without any prior effort on his part, re-emerge in his work as faultlessly as if they had been coined just the day before.

Chatham itself imperceptibly merges with the cathedral town of Rochester, which was of course considerably more "respectable" than Chatham itself; it was an ancient market-town with its own castle, cathedral, and guildhall. Almost as soon as he arrived in the neighbourhood, John Dickens subscribed to *The History of Rochester* which, like his earlier subscription to the *Lives of the Admirals*, suggests his urgent need to become a part of whatever environment in which he found himself, to fit in and as it were to aggrandise himself by attaching himself to the grander elements of the reality around him. The experience of Rochester for his son was quite a different one; it has a narrow high street and on market days it must have been especially crowded and noisy. And yet in Dickens's later descriptions it becomes "the silent High-street" which, with its gables, its ancient clocks, its fantastically carved wooden faces, and its "grave" red-brick buildings, is an emblem of past time. Of course, in the early chapters of *The Pickwick Papers*, Rochester and its environs become the scenes of farce but even during this sport of excitement and of activity, fuelled more than anything else by Dickens's own youthful high spirits, the atmosphere of the cathedral and of the ruined castle cast their own shadow; "frowning walls," says Alfred Jingle, "– tottering arches – dark nooks – crumbling staircases – Old cathedral too – earthy smell – pilgrims' feet worn away the old steps . . .". Thus in his first book; and thus also in his last when, in *The Mystery of Edwin Drood*, Dickens describes the ancient city in just such terms, "A monotonous, silent city, deriving an earthy flavor throughout"; and when a certain Grewgious peers through the great western doors into the cathedral he mutters, "Dear me . . . it's like looking down the throat of Old Time." In his beginning is his end but, in the years between, Dickens constantly sees Rochester in similar terms as reflecting "universal gravity, mystery, decay, and silence" and as thus reflecting upon his own precarious existence: ". . . what a brief little practical joke I seemed to be, in comparison with its solidity, stature, strength, and length of life." Age; dust; mortality; time. These are the images of Rochester drawn from him again and again, and is it too much of a hyperbole to leap from the adult Dickens to the child once more and to suggest that this low, mournful note was one that sounded for him throughout his childhood?

Yet of course there were other notes. Other sounds swirling around him. And none more evocative for him than "the splash and flop of the tide". Dickens grew up beside water – beside the sea, beside the tidal waters, beside the river – and there is no doubt that it runs through his imagination no less strongly than the Mississippi ran through that of T. S. Eliot. Of course he is the novelist of the city, the novelist of the huddling tenements and of the crowded streets; nevertheless, it is hard to think of one of Dickens's novels that does not take place within earshot of the river or of the tides. Just as Dickens himself preferred to spend long periods in the coastal regions of England or of France, so many of the settings in his novels are by the sea's edge and there are few of them which are not haunted by the presence of the river. From a very early age he was acquainted with the sea and the things of the sea. There were occasions, for example, when with his sister Fanny he used to accompany his father on expeditions on the Navy Pay yacht, a very old boat known as the *Chatham*, and upon this he travelled up the Medway to Sheerness. The river itself was then filled with ships and schooners and barges and yachts: here he would have seen the two prison ships, the *Euryalis* and the *Canada*, and the hospital ship, the *Hercules*. In the dockyard itself he glimpsed those vast wooden walls which loom up and which only by an act of imagination can be seen as the sides of ships; and in the dockyard, too, he would have heard the pile-driving and the sluice-driving, the blacksmiths and the carpenters, the mills and the mast-houses, the oar-making and the rope-making; and, everywhere, "the smell of clean timber shavings and turpentine". It was in the Chatham dockyard that he felt the ". . . gravity upon its red brick offices and houses, a staid pretence of having nothing worth mentioning to do, an avoidance of display, which I never saw out of England". And yet even in this aspect of his childhood there was a sense of change all around him; the end of the sailing ship was approaching, and already steamers plied between Dover and Calais.

As a child, too, he first nourished that love for the naval service which is everywhere apparent in his fiction, no less in the wrinkled countenance of Captain Cuttle than in the heroic adventures of shipwrecked mariners. Hence the many nautical expressions which he uses or on some occasions misuses and hence, too, the connection which Dickens generally makes between sailors and neatness or cleanliness; as if life on board ship was for him the epitome of the safe, private and carefully arranged world to which he was always drawn. In his last novels, also, those things which are most cherished by his imagination are those things which are connected with water; with the running tide, the drifting river, the enormous sea, even the reflection of the moon upon water which as a very young child he believed "was a path to Heaven, trodden by the spirits of good people on their way to God . . ." And then there were the ships themselves "filled with their far visions of the sea". On more than one occasion in his published writings he quotes from Campbell's "Ye Mariners of England":

> As I sweep
> Through the deep
> Where the stormy winds do blow . . .

And all through his life he loved to read accounts of maritime travels. Of course it would be wrong to point to Dickens's childhood and say: This is where it all began. Here are the origins of his genius. But the child hears and sees without needing to understand the meaning of its perceptions; the atmosphere of earliest childhood can seep into later writings without the writer himself being aware of any such source. So it was with the age and silence of Rochester; so, too, was it with the ebbing tides of the Medway, the gulls and crows and herons among the marshes which surround that region; and beyond them all the sea, the sea. The sea that Paul Dombey stared into; the sea that killed James Steerforth; the sea at which David Copperfield looked as a child and from which source he derived some of his finest impressions: ". . . the sun, away at sea, just breaking through the heavy mist, and showing us the ships, like their own shadows." And then again: ". . . I have never beheld such sky, such water, such glorified ships sailing away into golden air."

That Dickens was an observant child, we know; that he was also a very clever one is no less open to proof. His mother was his first teacher; she taught him every day and, to the best of his own recollection, she taught him well. (The fact that she later instructed him in Latin tells us two things – that she was a much better educated woman than has been suggested and that, despite her son's later animadversions against her, there was no sense in which she neglected him.) "I faintly remember," he once told his friend John Forster, "her teaching me the alphabet; and when I look upon the fat black letters in the primer, the puzzling novelty of their shapes, the easy good nature of O and S always seem to present themselves before me as they used to do." We might say, then, that it was to his mother that Dickens owed the first awakening of his childish imagination, the first entry into that world of words which so enthralled him; and even here, in his first steps forward, it is clear how the words themselves satisfy him, how he finds peace in the letters. Was it some such concatenation of reasons that led him once to claim that "I dreamed my first dreams of authorship when I was six years old or so . . .", a sufficiently startling claim, but one which he subsequently modified to the age of eight.

Then in 1818, with his sister Fanny, he was sent to a dame-school in Rome Lane. These archaic institutions – which lasted well into the nineteenth century but had their roots back in the fifteenth – were based on nothing more than the belief that an old lady who could write or read, and who had a few chapbooks at her command, might profitably be employed as the educator of infant minds. That there were some good dame-schools it is impossible to doubt but Charles Dickens was implacable in his hostility to them, and it is likely that his attitude was acquired from his own experience. In later life he said that his particular dame school was "over a dyer's shop", but in a speech he once gave he seems to come closer to the actual feelings of that time when he was ". . . under the early dominion of an old lady, who to my mind ruled the world with the birch"; and under her auspices, too, one senses the power which the young Dickens found and felt in words. "I never now see a row of large, black, fat staring Roman capitals, but this reminiscence rises up before me." What rises up before him, especially, are the *clothes* which his fellow pupils wore – a brown beaver bonnet, a black dress, a pinafore. The dyer's shop, too, suggests nothing so much as odours. And, yes, these are the perceptions which a child would have, perceptions which he is quite likely to recall.

In this period he was educated with his slightly older sister, Fanny, and those who seek reasons for the ubiquity of that name in his fiction might start their search here (the name itself might have been given added resonance by the presence of Aunt Fanny living in the house with them). On that criterion alone his response to the name is, to say the least, somewhat ambiguous; there is Fanny Dombey, the doomed mother of little Paul who dies in childbirth, but then of course there is also Fanny Squeers, the grotesque and ugly daughter of the famous Yorkshire schoolmaster. And then – in between, as it were – there is Fanny Dorrit, the imperious and petulant elder sister of Little Dorrit. There are also eight other characters who bear the same name. Now there is no doubt that Dickens did use Christian names which for some reason were emblematic for him – that is why the names of his father and sister crop up so often – and there is no doubt, too, that this was on occasions a deliberate device. But the range of Fannies in his fiction is so great that it suggests at the very least a most complicated relationship with his sibling. But we know also that, for Dickens himself, the relationship between brother and sister became the paradigm for human relationships in general; that loving sexless union of siblings is commemorated again and again in his novels, whether it is in an idealised bond such as that between Ruth Pinch and Tom Pinch in *Martin Chuzzlewit*, or whether it is as an element in those childish relationships which Dickens loved to describe. There are times when he becomes almost maudlin on the subject, and throughout his prose one hears as if in echo the words of one brother left behind on earth after his young sister has died: "'Oh, sister, I am here! Take me!'" It would not be going too far to say, then, that this image of the platonic bond between brother and sister – truly platonic, in the sense that for Dickens it seems to mirror some heavenly unity and harmony – is the dominant image of beneficence in his account of the relations between the sexes. And we will come to see its presence, too, in the relationships which he himself formed in his adult years.

What we know of Fanny herself is that she was both quick and gifted (her career as a musician will provide ample evidence of that). In later life she was described as possessing "decision of character" as well as a "natural buoyancy of spirits and fondness for society"; she was also said to be self-reliant "in no ordinary degree – together with almost restless activity and practical energy". In some respects she resembled her younger brother, therefore; together, they seem actively to have differentiated themselves from their parents in a way that their younger siblings were not to do. There is a difference, however; it was said that "there was nothing of the romantic in her composition".

So it was that in these infant years he went to school with his sister, was taught by his mother, and began to read. His first companions were 'picture books', as he said later, ". . . picture books: all about scimitars and slippers and turbans and dwarfs and giants and genii and fairies, and Blue-beards and bean-stalks and riches and caverns and forests and Valentines and Orsons: and all new and all true." As so often happens when the mature Dickens starts to indulge in lists, or elaborate upon his childhood, specific memories are mixed up with more general perceptions, the chronology is thrown in doubt, and a sort of hybrid mixture emerges of Dickens as he was and Dickens as he would like to be. We are often on much better ground when he makes only oblique or passing reference to specific details culled from his childhood, brief moments of vision that really do seem to have glanced upward from the otherwise inchoate mass of his earliest years. So on two occasions he refers to the colour and texture of his first books, with their "bright, smooth, cover" and their "deliciously smooth covers of bright red or green", offering a sudden access into the consciousness of another time. He could recall certain of the picture books at which he gazed; *Jack the Giant-Killer* was one and *Little Red Riding Hood* was another, "my first love," he said of the latter. No doubt she has been the first love of other small children, too, and in the rhymes and stories of the nursery we can trace a real human continuity in the life of this country over the last two or three centuries. It has been said that the childhood of most men and women is, through the generations, much the same. This may or may not be true – the conditions of the early nineteenth century are in some ways now irrecoverable, so the statement can be neither proved nor disproved – but it is the case that much of its imaginative climate remains the same. No doubt that is why the work of Dickens still retains such a powerful hold; it springs from the roots that we all in some part share.

There are other sudden illuminations of this shared past from Dickens, and characteristically he remembers a particular scene or image which for some reason has never left him – a coloured engraving of Mrs Skipton "in a florid style of art", the picture of a bull pulling a bell rope in the *Cock Robin* saga, a shaft of light illuminating Cain as he murders his brother, a Russian serf amid the snows; all these images returned to him. But not all these memories were to do with death or deprivation, and in a later essay he was able to recall the verses printed in a picture book entitled *The Dandies' Ball, or High Life in the City*; he quotes these verses from memory, from a book which he read when he was seven years old, and the astonishing fact is that, with one or two minor mistakes, he actually gets them right. There is no doubt that he had a remarkable memory, both verbal and visual. In 1850 he was able to remember the initials of his next-door neighbour in Ordnance Terrace – a certain W. H. Drage – and he was in the late stages of his life able to remember the details of his schoolfellows' lives as if he had seen them yesterday. Memory in itself is perhaps not proof of anything but, in Dickens's case, it is only one example of what was a remarkable mental organisation. For it is not just a question of memory; Dickens's visual imagination was formed early and, together with the work of William Hogarth, these early prints from the picture-books were to affect his own fiction – fiction which itself was, of course, largely illustrated.

But he was not only a reader; like all good children, there were times when he was an avid listener. Children's stories. Nursery stories. Bedtime stories. Whether these were told by a nurse or by his mother is now no longer clear. There were two young female servants with the family at Ordnance Terrace – a Mary Weller and a Jane Bonny – but in later essays he also describes one called Mercy and another called Sally Flanders. One of these figures was apparently "a sallow woman with a fishy eye, an aquiline nose, and a green gown, whose specialty was a dismal narrative" of a landlord who turned his guests into meat pies. And Dickens goes on to say that this narrator "had a Ghoulish pleasure, I have long been persuaded, in terrifying me to the utmost confines of my reason" as well as making disparaging comments about his friends and relatives. Then there was the nurse who told him stories about a certain Captain Murderer, about the curse of a talking rat with its cry "Oh Keep the rats out of the convicts' burying ground!". That last phrase has a convincing resonance with the more Gothic elements in Dickens's fiction; but for that reason alone we would be wise to be cautious about its plain matter-of-fact truth. He describes these imaginative nurses in one of his Christmas stories as well as in a series of journalistic essays, and although most biographers have taken them to be true transcripts from memory, considerably enlivening Dickens's childhood as a result, it is more than likely that he was simply making up little narratives for the delectation of his audience. We are on firmer ground only on one aspect of these early narratives; he declared, and his real nurse herself confirmed, that there was a time when he was lulled to sleep by the words of the "Evening Hymn" as he cried upon his pillow. In a later story one of his characters ascribes the recitation of these pretty verses to a mother but, mother or nurse, there is no doubt that it was one of the first poems he would have heard.

> Glory to Thee, my God, this night
> For all the blessings of the light;
> Keep me, O keep me, King of kings,
> Beneath Thy own Almighty wings.

And so these early years passed, with little to report except for the slow increase of the Dickens family and the somewhat insecure ability of John Dickens's finances to support them: in August 1819, just three weeks before the birth of another daughter, he borrowed the large sum of two hundred pounds from a certain James Milbourne, at an annual repayment of twenty-six pounds for life. In March of the following year Dickens's salary was raised according to precedent but nevertheless he never managed to keep up with the necessary repayments and eventually his brother-in-law, Thomas Barrow, whom he persuaded to countersign the debt, was forced to repay it for him; this in part accounts for something of the later coolness of Elizabeth's family towards her husband, and the document itself, known as "the Deed", was later to figure largely in Dickens's childhood. Then in August 1820 another child emerged – this time a son, Frederick, who was in succeeding years to be a source of great annoyance to his famous brother. So already there are signs here of all the calamities which Dickens was later to visit upon his fictional families: the burgeoning household, the debts, the threats of legal action all suggesting an atmosphere of strain, if not exactly of anxiety, which the young Dickens himself knew well.

But John Dickens was not without resources, and the pursuit of esteem under difficulties is clearly a mark of his character: thus it was that in March 1820 he reported for *The Times* on a fire at Chatham. Even if this did not earn him immortal fame, it at least ensured him a place on the vestry committee which was organising help for those affected by the disaster. It would be too much to claim that his son's subsequent interests, both in journalism *and* in fires, owe anything to John Dickens's activities; but there is one mark of paternal influence of which there can be no doubt. A young companion of Charles Dickens in these Chatham years – a certain J. H. Stoqueler who in a late reminiscence called his friend "Charley Wag", no doubt on the principle that a childhood companionship earns at least the right to be jocular – describes how he and the young Dickens used to idle their time together on Rochester Bridge or walk up the road which leads to a house known as Gad's Hill Place. It was, it seems, a favourite journey of Dickens and there is no doubt that his goal was of a private character. For it was this house which his father had once pointed out to him; Dickens used to tell the story to his friends whenever he later passed it, and he recorded it at least twice in print. So, for once, we can be sure of its authenticity: ". . . upon first seeing it as he came from Chatham with his father," Forster once wrote, "and looking up at it with much admiration, he had been promised that he might himself live in it or in some such house when he came to be a man, if he would only work hard enough." Dickens himself was to say, "I used to look at it as a wonderful Mansion (which God knows it is not) when I was a very odd little child with the first faint shadows of all my books in my head – I suppose." And then again: "And ever since I can recollect, my father, seeing me so fond of it, has often said to me, 'If you were to be persevering and were to work hard, you might some day come to live in it . . .'" And so, thirty-six years later, he bought it. Anyone who doubts the influence of Charles Dickens's childhood upon his later predilections and obsessions may take their scepticism no further, for without doubt only a man heavily influenced by his father's praise would spend the next thirty years of his life trying to earn it. Gad's Hill Place might have been a house that his father picked at random, a convenient emblem of prestige and property; and yet it continued to haunt his son. It is intriguing, too, that as a boy he did so often walk to this house outside Rochester: he wanted to see it again and again as an image of his possible future, he wanted a fine house even then. Even at that time he seems to have wanted to escape the narrow and over-populated domesticity of his real home.

There are other less striking memories to be drawn up from the depths of his childhood and, once again, it is better to rely upon Dickens's stray asides that upon his more elaborate attempts either at autobiography or at fictional reconstruction. Thus it is we can believe him when he was passing through Chatham and pointed to a particular wall, exclaiming, "I remember . . . my poor Mother, God forgive her, put me on the edge of that wall so that I might wave my hat and cheer George IV – then Prince Regent – who was driving by." One can believe the brief memory of ". . . the kite that once plucked at my own hand like an airy friend". One can believe that he really did have his ears boxed "for informing a lady visitor . . . that a certain ornamental object on the table, which was covered with marbled-paper, 'wasn't marble'", for it fits in with the evident fact that, as we shall see, the young Dickens had a great belief in literal meaning. Certainly we can believe a strange episode that his sister seems to have confirmed, when, for reasons that he could not remember, and in a period about which he is vague, ". . . we stealthily conducted the man with the wooden leg – whom we knew intimately – into the coal cellar, and that, in getting him over the coals to hide him behind some partition there was beyond, his wooden leg bored itself in among the small coals . . ." There were a lot of gentlemen with wooden legs in this naval port (it was, you might say, an occupational hazard) and this anecdote has all the hallmarks of some small intrigue between the servants "below stairs". In fact Dickens seems to have had something of an obsession with wooden legs – they pop up time and again in his fiction – and the recollection of this man with his stump thrust among the small coals was to be revived in *Our Mutual Friend* as the spectacle of Silas Wegg with ". . . his self-willed leg sticking into the ashes about half-way down". So are childhood scenes revived in fiction, the lost images restored.

There are other apparent childhood memories of Dickens which are not necessarily to be taken literally. It suits his genius to grow lyrical over the spectacle of infant romance, and so his account of his relationship with Lucy Stroughill, the girl in a neighbouring house, is perhaps to be seen as an idealised reconstruction of what a romance might be; as they sit beneath a table imbibing "saccharine substances and liquids" which later necessitate the taking of a stomach powder, or as they slumber together peacefully during a demonstration of an "Orrery", that elegant instrument for the delineation of the heavens. They are pretty stories, like that of the young Dickens first putting on a pair of trousers "stiff, angular, hard, wooden". Or like his memories of Christmas at home. For in his idealised memory Christmas was always associated with a family group which "bound together all our home enjoyments, affections and hopes" and it might seem that in the glowing accounts of these seasonal festivities in his fiction he is trying to revive the benevolence of his lost childhood. "Heaven's fallen sister – Home . . ." he once wrote, and there is no doubt that at times of domestic celebration he seems able to suffuse the concept of "Home" with an almost spiritual belief in its potency. And yet the home, and the domestic hearth, are always defined by what lies outside them; beyond the glow of the protective fire lie misery, poverty and death. (In view of the fact that Dickens can be said to have almost single-handedly created the modern idea of Christmas, it is interesting to note that in fact during the first eight years of his life there was a white Christmas every year; so sometimes does reality actually exist before the idealised image.) We are always conscious of the difficult world banished from the domestic hearth, and there is a sense in which Dickens's generalised accounts of "Home" owe as much to fear and nostalgia as they do to any observable reality from Dickens's own childhood. There is no reason to doubt, however, that the Dickens family took Christmas more seriously than many of their contemporaries. For the first nineteen years of his life, John Dickens would have experienced that festival in the opulent setting of Crewe Hall, and there is every reason to suppose that he would try to recreate such an atmosphere in his own home with conjurings, dances, recitations, charades, forfeits, blind-man's-buffs, and card games like Pope Joan or Speculation.

But when Dickens actually and deliberately sets out to recreate the specific details of his childhood Christmases, there is no mention of family or of celebration. Instead, characteristically, he concentrates upon objects – upon presents – and the accuracy of the detail suggests the workings of something which is very close to involuntary memory. A wooden tumbler, its hands in its pockets, always rolling upon the floor; a figure "in a black gown, with an obnoxious head of hair, and a red cloth mouth, wide open" who sprang out of a snuff box; a toy donkey with skin made of real hide; a Jacob's Ladder "made of little squares of red wood, that went flapping and clattering over one another, each developing a different picture"; a Noah's Ark complete with little animals, including "the goose, whose feet were so small, and whose balance was so indifferent, that he usually tumbled forward . . ."; a dolls'-house, with its own "soft fire-irons", its own wooden plates with little wooden hams and turkeys glued to them, its own set of blue crockery. All these things are striking childhood memories, the memories of someone staring at small objects very closely and not forgetting their peculiarities of taste, texture and movement; forgotten toys, forgotten times, redolent of a world more distant from us than even it was from Dickens himself. These lost objects speak to us of the past in ways that generalisations cannot do; we are in the early nineteenth century when children were happy with wooden acrobats and wooden animals. It is a time irrecoverable to us, but one that Dickens himself did his best to recover. There are toy-makers and doll-makers dotted throughout his fiction, always affectionate but always somewhat sorrowful, always somehow having lost their way in the world as if in making toys they had become accustomed to the usual process of decay and forgetfulness which marks such childhood pleasures. But in his fiction, too, there are times when Dickens sees his own characters as toys, his houses as dolls'-houses, and there is a hint that on occasions he took the same kind of fascination in creating his characters as he had once done in observing, and playing with, the wooden creatures of his childhood.

But, if we are to talk of his infancy in these terms, then there is one aspect of early nineteenth-century England which, perhaps more than anything else beside his own solitary reading, marks him out for his eventual fate: it is his childhood love for the theatre, for pantomime. There were occasions when he was taken by relatives to London, and there can be little doubt that this was primarily to visit the theatres; he specifically remembers, on one occasion, being taken to see Grimaldi, "in whose honor I am informed I clapped my hands with great precocity". And John Forster adds this in his biography: "By Lamert, I have often heard him say, he was first taken to the theatre at the very tenderest age." Lamert was a friend of the family – his stepfather eventually married 'Aunt Fanny' – and the theatre was the Theatre Royal in Rochester, on the New Road which leads out of Chatham and connects it with the cathedral town. The building survives still, a small, narrow place, in which it is hard to see the crucible of young Dickens's imagination. And yet so it proved. "The sweet, dingy, shabby little country theatre" Charles Dickens was to call it, with the odour of sawdust, orange-peel and lamp-oil which he savoured all his life. And it was here that he saw *Richard III* and *Macbeth*, Lillo's *The London Merchant or the History of George Barnwell* and Rowe's *Jane Shore*; the world here was transformed into farce and melodrama, and in all his accounts of his childhood expeditions to the theatre there can be sensed the unmistakeable hunger and intensity of Dickens's gaze. He missed nothing; the funny man "in a red scratch wig" who sings a comic song about a leg of mutton while imprisoned in the deepest dungeon, the hole in the green curtain, Richard III pretending to sleep on a sofa that is too small for him, the reappearance of the Witches and

King Duncan in various walk-on parts, the words of the irate rustic ("Dom thee, squire, coom on with thy fistes then!"); and he believed everything. One of his standing jokes, reappearing throughout his published work, rests upon the mannerisms of acting and of actors – the props, the standard phrases, the stage embraces "which, as everybody knows, are performed by the embracer's laying his or her chin on the shoulder of the object of affection, and looking over it", and the "stage walk, which consists of a stride and a stop alternately"; he appreciated, too, "the captain who courts the young lady, whose guardian unaccountably persists in dressing himself a hundred years behind the time . . . the lady's young brother, in white kid gloves and trousers, whose position in the family would appear to be to listen to all the female members of it when they sing, and to shake hands with them between all the verses . . . the peasant . . . who may usually be observed to turn his glass upside-down immediately before drinking the Baron's health". He loved the bad acting and the stage costumes, the absurdity of the actors and the banality of the plays, almost as if they were simulacra of life itself, and in all these accounts he conjures up the rapt vision of the child sitting in that "Dear, narrow, uncomfortable, faded-cushioned, flea-haunted, single tier of boxes" in the Theatre Royal. It was a vision which never left him, even though it might fade each time he left the bright theatre in order to return to the dreary, dull and settled world beyond it. But, if actors and acting, theatres and theatrical props, become a dominant motif in Dickens's life and work, it is nevertheless hard now to recover that lost sense of reality which the nineteenth-century theatre represented. It is hard to hear the noises once again, the stamping on the floor, the clapping, the groaning, the cheering, the open weeping. It is hard to evoke the sight of the theatregoers waving their hats or handkerchiefs to signal their acclaim for a scene or for a play. And it is hard, too, to hear once again the bells which were rung to stop or to start the music from the orchestra (a play without music was not to be thought of), or the sound of whistles coming from the wings to announce a change of scenery; to envisage the sheer length of performances, which might go on for six or seven hours; to evoke the smell, the odour of the unwashed which mingled with the tang of the oranges and oil lamps. Yet it was amid such scenes as these that the imagination of the young Dickens struggled to be born.

If there was one theatrical art which truly inspired him, it was that of pantomime, "that jocund world," he called it, ". . . where there is no affliction or calamity that leaves the least impression . . . where everyone, in short, is so superior to all the accidents of life, though encountering them at every turn". A bright, safe, world in which comedy mingled with tragedy, scenes of farce with scenes of pathos, love and death, Pantaloon and Columbine, dark scenes and trans-formation scenes, processions and patriotic songs, comic dances and rhymed couplets, everything to be sung and not spoken. "No words can express," one contemporary wrote, "the animation, the gaiety, the boldness, the madness, the incoherence, the coarseness, the splen-dour, the whimsical poetry, the brutality of these Christmas panto-mimes." The young Dickens was taken to London to see them, on the day after Christmas, but he also watched them when they were performed by the travelling fairs in Rochester itself. He would have seen the "opening" in which a mythological fable or love story was presented with a kind of lyrical seriousness – an old man trying to wed his daughter to a wealthy suitor although her heart is promised to another, until the doomed love of the two young people is resolved by the intervention of a benevolent spirit (and does this plot not appear time and again in Dickens's own fiction?). And then after this the harlequinade, with its comic songs and farce ballets and mime and slapstick. "What mattered it that the stage was three yards wide and four deep? *We* never saw it. We had no eyes, ears, or corporeal senses but for the pantomime", for the spangled Harlequin "covered all over with scales of pure gold", the white-faced Clown, the Pantaloon crying "Now, I sawed you do it!". In *Great Expectations* there comes a point when Pip remembers how he had laid down his head after a Fair because it had been "too much for my young senses". And we must picture the young Dickens in a similar way – over-wrought, over-eager, screaming with delight, watching everything and forgetting nothing. In later life he enjoyed nothing so much as imitating the postures and the manner of the clown; on one occasion, he "began playing the clown in pantomime on the edge of a bath" and then by accident tumbled into the warm water, and, on another, he demon-strated on a train journey how the clown "flops and folds himself up like a jack-knife"; he was also adept at improvising the "patter" between clown and pantaloon. We see that same spirit in the older Dickens who, even in the years close to his death, would still stoop down in order to read the bills advertising the London pantomimes.

It is in this spirit, too, that we must see him constructing and working a toy theatre in his more wretched childhood years after

Chatham; he had it in Camden Town, London, complete with the sheets of characters (penny plain and twopence coloured) to be cut out, pasted onto cardboard and glued to wires or sticks. These then would be pushed onto the small stage, with its backdrops, props and scenes; in full costume, and in suitable postures, the tiny cardboard creatures would then act out the play. Here it was that Dickens performed *The Miller and His Men* and *Elizabeth, or The Exile of Siberia*; his brothers moved the little players, which sometimes had an unfortunate habit of creasing up or becoming unglued, while Charles himself read and acted out the scenes. He was even writing now, and he said later that his first piece was composed when he was nine or ten years old – *Misnar*, a tragedy based on *Tales of the Genii* and concerning a gracious and wise young prince (no doubt Dickens himself) who has a habit of uttering wise thoughts when surrounded by demons or monsters. Dickens once declared that "I was . . . an actor and a speaker from a baby" and in this vision of the young boy, book in hand, taking on the roles in this miniature theatre we see, in miniature too, an emblem of Dickens's own relation to the world. His daughter once observed that, when he was writing his fiction, he would literally act out the words in front of a mirror before placing them down on paper, and of course eventually he came to read out the words of his novels to the audiences of England and America. He never abandoned his inheritance; when many years later he was living at Gad's Hill Place, a toy theatre was given to his son and at once Dickens became fascinated by it – he set to work to produce the first piece, called *The Elephant of Siam*, and, his son recalled, he "pegged away at the landscapes and architecture of Siam with an amount of energy which in any other man would have been something prodigious, but which I soon learned to look upon as quite natural in him". So, in his later life, in his constant attendance at the theatre, and in his own skills as a performer, we understand how much the garish light of the stage represented for him both the memory and the intensification of childhood experience.

One component of that experience was something which Dickens himself called "conviviality". The idea of entertainment, of an audience sharing in a certain pleasure, the idea of friendship, the idea of the family, all things which he tried helplessly to resurrect throughout his life precisely because they derive from the memory of his early childhood. Mary Weller, his young nurse at Ordnance Terrace, has a distinct recollection of him in that light. "Sometimes Charles would come downstairs and say to me, 'Now, Mary, clear the kitchen, we are going to have such a game.'" There is no doubt that this is a true memory, and here for the first time we have a clear echo of Charles Dickens's voice; it is one repeated in his own writing, with "I've got sitch a game for you, Sammy" in *The Pickwick Papers* and "There's *such* a goose, Martha" in his public reading of *A Christmas Carol*. So does the voice of the child re-emerge in the man. George Stroughill, a friend from Ordnance Terrace, would sometimes bring in his Magic Lantern but also "they would sing, recite, and perform parts of plays". Charles himself had a "favourite piece for recitation" which was "The Voice of the Sluggard" by Dr Watts; "the little boy," according to Mary Weller, "used to give it with great effect, and with *such* action and *such* attitudes" (one sees here also the older Dickens, head thrown back, hand in the air, reciting from his novels):

> 'Tis the voice of the sluggard; I heard him complain,
> You have wak'd me too soon, I must slumber again.

He would have recited passages from the classics, too, and no doubt much of his acquaintance with Shakespeare came from such a source. And then he liked to sing. He had a "clear treble voice" and at this time, Mary Weller remembers, "sea-songs were . . . his especial favourites". There are many sea-songs quoted or mentioned in his fiction, too, and no doubt little Dickens delivered the song which Mr Micawber is also supposed to sing –

> Sweet is the ship that under sail
> Spreads her white bosom to the gale;
>   Sweet, Oh! sweet's the flowing can;
> Sweet to poise the labouring oar,
> That tugs us to our native shore,
>   When the boatswain pipes the barge to man;
> Sweet sailing with a fav'ring breeze;
> But, oh! much sweeter than all these,
>   Is Jack's delight – his lovely Nan.

There were other songs of his childhood; there was a vogue for sentimental ditties, fuelled largely by the success of Thomas Moore's *Irish Melodies*, but there were also songs which satirised such sentiment. There were comic songs, love songs, pathetic songs such as "Begone, Dull Care", "And She Shall Walk in Silk Attire", "Over the Water to Charlie", "I'll tell thee how the maiden wept", "The Soldier's Tear", and "The Peasant Boy" with its sad melodies:

> Thrown on the wide world, doom'd to wander and roam,
> Bereft of my parents, bereft of my home,
> A stranger to pleasure and to comfort and joy,
> Behold little Edmund, the poor Peasant boy.

The young Dickens would have sung them while accompanying the words with the appropriate postures and gestures, the clear small voice echoing into a later time when many of these songs are mentioned in his last completed novel, *Our Mutual Friend*; how touching and yet how typical of Dickens that in the last years of his life he should still recall the songs of infancy.

He sang at birthday parties and at Twelfth Night parties. He was also writing his own songs; he composed and sang a comic number entitled "Sweet Betsy Ogle", and this delight in comic performance is to be seen also in his rendition of a "monopolylogue" in the manner of the great comedian Charles Mathews; these performances consisted, as the name suggests, in one person playing all the parts of a short play and in doing so by means of stock phrases, comic mannerisms and the mimicry of dialect. All these features would later reappear in his mature fiction, of course, and it will soon also become clear what a gifted mimic Dickens was; but it is here, in these infantile performances, that we see the beginning of the use of such gifts. It is one of the most important images of Dickens's childhood – the young boy, beaming, eyes shining, singing, striking attitudes, giving a perfect performance, being cheered and applauded. He was not always unaccompanied, however; Fanny sometimes used to sing with him, or accompany him on the piano and there were times, too, when they performed for more general audiences than that of the immediate family. On occasions they clambered onto the dining table of the Mitre Inn in Rochester (the proprietor was a friend of John Dickens) and sang a duet:

Charles – Long time I've courted you, Miss,
      And now I've come from sea
      We'll make no more ado, Miss
      But quickly married be.
Fanny – I ne'er will wed a tar, Sir
      Deceitful as yourself;
      'Tis very plain you are, Sir
      A good for nothing elf.

The last line of each of these verses comprised what was then the rage for "bow wow wow" choruses, a typical example of which (and one which Dickens himself no doubt sung) goes:

> Fol lol de iddy row dow row
> Sing toodledy, teedledy, bow wow wow.

Once again this refrain reappears in *Our Mutual Friend*, confirming how much the songs of his childhood echo through his writing; and perhaps nowhere more clearly do we hear the voices of the period itself, touching now in their gaiety and insouciance, their ready patter and their open sentiment, their clear melody and their strong expression. And it is possible, too, to see the young boy standing on the table of the inn and singing them to invited guests – perhaps, like his own David Copperfield, with "a simple, earnest manner of narrating". The young Dickens was already with an audience, already sensing the power of words and enjoying the praise which his performances elicited. He was in a sense being "shown off" by his father, and can we not see in these early performances a hint of that theatricality which seemed always to surround him in his later life? And, if we have cause to thank Mary Weller for these first authentic reminiscences of him, it is perhaps interesting to note that, when he came back as a rich and famous man to read at the Mechanics' Institute in Chatham, she was too shy to be reintroduced to him. There are always such people in the lives of great men; those who nourished them, supported them, loved them, but who then fade away. Who dare not come too close.

At some point during the early months of 1821 Dickens left the dame-school in Rome Lane and moved to a larger and more promising school in Clover Lane – a school run by a young man of twenty-three, William Giles, the son of a Baptist minister and himself a Dissenter. Giles had a reputation in the Chatham neighbourhood "as a cultivated reader and elocutionist". He seems to have spent some time at Oxford, teaching at a school there, but although he was debarred from residence at the university because of his nonconformist faith it is possible that he was given permission to attend certain courses. Certainly he was a well-educated young man and some indication of the nature of his Chatham establishment can be glimpsed in an advertisement for another of his schools which he placed some years later – "The English Department is distinguished by an approved analytical method of tuition, by due attention to Letter-writing,

Translating and the composition of Theses and Essays. In the Commercial department, great care is observed in securing to the Pupils a good hand-writing . . ." This is close to the syllabus in which the young Dickens himself would have been instructed, with the addition, too, of lessons culled from Lindley Murray's grammar, a book to which the schoolmaster Wackford Squeers alludes in *Nicholas Nickleby*. "It's me, and me's the first person singular . . ." Dickens himself was equally punctilious about such matters of grammar and, although there are occasions when the momentum and expansiveness of his style lead him to neglect the niceties of syntax, he was always able to spot and pounce upon the mistakes of others.

Dickens remembered many details of his time at this Chatham school; he remembered its playing fields where, according to his daughter, Mamie, "he and his friends went through – in play – all sorts of wonderful and heroic achievements"; he remembered the time of his first school examination when he recited some verses from the *Humourist's Miscellany* and received, according to his own memory of the occasion, a double encore from all those present. In a letter to his schoolmaster many years later Dickens observed that ". . . you magnify, in my bewildered sight, into something awful, though not at all severe". We may acquit Giles, then, of being the prototype for any of the grotesque schoolmasters in Dickens's fiction; and in this same letter, too, there are brief but evocative recollections of his early education. He remembers the phrase, "If you please, sir, may I leave off?" And he remembers also how often he made a bow to his teacher. (There is another small echo, too, perhaps in the importance which in his fiction Dickens imparts to someone helping a small boy with his homework – Paul Dombey is helped by his older sister, and Agnes helps the young David Copperfield. Can we see in these two consonant pictures an image of Dickens's older sister, Fanny, helping him?) This is not much, perhaps, but it conjures up a vivid impression of the formality and discipline which prevailed in such places; and we can in turn conjure up the young Dickens, with his tall white beaver hat, his blue jacket, his broad white collar and what he later remembered to be a ". . . a dreadful, high-shouldered sleeved strait-waistcoat . . . over which their dreadful little trousers were buttoned tight". During the course of his two years at this school he came to be on close terms with the Giles family itself; two of William's younger brothers were also enrolled here, and William's sister remembered him as ". . . a very handsome boy, with long curly hair of a light colour".

The Giles family seem to have played some part in the next move of the Dickens family for, soon after Dickens entered the school, the family migrated to a house at 18 St Mary's Place (known as "the Brook") which was next to the Baptist meeting house where William's father was the minister. It was a "plain-looking whitewashed plaster-front" sort of house, complete with the regulation small garden before and behind, a semi-detached six-room affair. It could not have been much smaller than the house in Ordnance Terrace, but there is a definite possibility that it was in social terms a step down for John Dickens from the airy and pleasant purlieus of the Terrace to an area which was essentially for humble dockyard officials. It was of course conveniently closer to the dockyard itself, and other contemporaries have described it as an area "of singular architectural beauty and charm" – even if that charm might have been of a somewhat poignant kind, since from the upper windows of the house the young Dickens could see the church and churchyard which he later memorialised in "A Child's Dream of a Star". It is not clear, then, whether the Dickens family had begun that slow descent which was eventually to lead to a debtors' prison, but certainly there seems to have been some change of atmosphere here; and Mary Weller has recalled that "there were no such juvenile entertainments at this house as I had seen at the Terrace". Of course they now had different neighbours, and instead of the little old lady, the half-pay captain and golden-haired Lucy there was now only a somewhat unprepossessing Baptist chapel.

Yet what better place could be found to speculate about Dickens's own religious leanings during his childhood years? He does not seem to have leaned very far in any particular direction, his most striking religious memory being of the fireplace in St Mary's Place, of which the tiles were illustrated with scenes from the Scriptures (he gave it to Scrooge, perhaps in revenge, in *A Christmas Carol*). There is one more lengthy memory of his childhood experience of religion, but again it is not designed to make converts; the little Dickens, according to Dickens himself, was on occasions "dragged by the hair of my head" to listen to a preacher, or, as he puts it, ". . . to be steamed like a potato in the unventilated breath of the powerful Boanerges Boiler and his congregation". This may be a reminiscence of a time when he was taken to the Baptist chapel next door – perhaps under the combined influence of the Giles family weighing down upon the Dickenses – but, since this narrative is part of his writing as the "Uncommercial Traveller", it is also possible that Dickens is only imagining the scene.

That he did undergo some form of religious education does seem likely, however; in one letter he specifically mentions ". . . the immense absurdities that were suggested to my own childhood by the like injudicious catechising" about such matters as "the Lamb of God". (The idea of the infant Dickens already recognising "absurdities" is an interesting one.) More important evidence of his religious torture is perhaps to be found in his fiction; he never ceases to ridicule and parody Dissenting preachers of whatever persuasion, and the roots for such a violent dislike are generally to be found somewhere within his own experience. He tended to take such things very personally, and half of his attacks can be seen to spring from some resentment or fear first provoked in him as a child. Yet if there was such religious instruction it must have been of a quite desultory kind. We have his own sister's word for it; when in her maturer years she herself became a Dissenter she wrote to her minister that "I was brought up in the Established Church but, I regret to say, without any serious ideas of religion. I attended Divine worship as a duty, not as a high privilege . . ." When her father and mother once came to stay with her in these later years, she told her husband, "Don't omit family prayer, morning and evening, during their stay with us. They have never been used to it, but that should not prevent us from continuing usual habits . . ." During their visit John and Elizabeth Dickens "appeared to be much interested in the new character and new associations of their daughter". Interested, no doubt, but perhaps somewhat astonished.

In any case, even if Charles Dickens was not properly introduced to the beauties and mysteries of Christianity, he found beauties and mysteries elsewhere. For it was in this little house, in St Mary's Place, that he himself locates his first awareness of books and his first entry into literature. In the room next to his own, his father kept what seems to have been a standard set of volumes: "From that blessed little room, *Roderick Random*, *Peregrine Pickle*, *Humphrey Clinker*, *Tom Jones*, *The Vicar of Wakefield*, *Don Quixote*, *Gil Blas* and *Robinson Crusoe* came out, a glorious host, to keep me company. They kept alive my fancy, and my hope of something beyond that place and time – they, and *The Arabian Nights*, and the *Tales of the Genii* – and did me no harm . . ." *My hope of something beyond that place and time* – here are the irremediable longings, the aspirations, of the small boy in the somewhat nondescript little house.

"Little Charles was a terrible boy to read," Mary Weller once recalled, "and his custom was to sit with his book in his left hand, holding his wrist with his right hand, and constantly moving it up and down, and at the same time sucking his tongue." To her own son Mary Weller told much the same story. "She used to speak of the future author as always fond of reading, and said he was wont to retire to the top room of the house on the Brook, and spend what should have been his play hours in poring over his books or in acting to the furniture of the room the creatures that he had read about . . ." And again we notice here the acting, the need fully to enter the world of fancy which he had imbibed, the need to lose his identity and, as it were, to enter the books themselves. "I recollect everything I read then," he once wrote, "as perfectly as I forget everything I read now . . ." – the truth of this is to be found in his own fictions as clearly as anywhere else, and there does seem to have been a sense in which his childhood reading became for him a living presence, almost a magical presence, which he could summon, like Tom Pinch in *Martin Chuzzlewit*, by rubbing "that wonderful lamp within him".

That wonderful lamp, of course, is to be found in *The Arabian Nights* which is arguably the most important of all literary influences upon Charles Dickens. That saga, together with *Tales of the Genii*, which he read in a small pocket edition, is constantly recalled both in his fiction and in his journalism; recalled, too, in his life on those occasions when his own anxious musings send him plummeting back to that magic world first opened to him in his childhood. And how could it not be so? Coleridge perhaps expressed it best in a letter which he wrote about his own childhood: ". . . from my early reading of fairy tales and genii etc. etc. my mind had been habituated *to the Vast* and I never regarded *my senses* in any way as the criteria of my belief. I regulated all my creeds by my conceptions, not by my *sight*, even at that age. Should children be permitted to read romances, and relations of giants and magicians and genii? I know all that has been said against it; but I have formed my faith in the affirmative. I know no other way of giving the mind a love of the Great and the Whole." Given some changes of emphasis and vocabulary, this is precisely Charles Dickens's own belief, and he pointed to the childhood reading of these fantastic tales as the way to nourish both the Fancy which leads to gentleness and the Imagination which encourages sympathy or mercy – the tales' "simplicity, and purity, and innocent extravagance" eliciting in turn "Forebearance, courtesy, consideration for the poor and aged, kind treatment of animals, the love of nature, abhorrence of tyranny and brute force . . ." It lies at the very centre of his belief, and its source is to be found here, in the small room at Chatham. He read *Tales of the Genii* in the Cooke's Pocket Library series; it was in very small print (perhaps accounting for Dickens's later short-sightedness), and its engravings were sometimes of a risqué nature. But we are not in the Victorian period, not yet, and these tales imbibed during the Regency had not been placed within the terrible straitjacket of adult disapproval. In fact we may take this book as the symbol of many such, filled as it is with repetition and with extravagance. It is easy to imagine the ten-year-old boy (the date at which significantly he places the onset of his reading days) lost in a world of chariots of pearl, of · thousands of archers, thousands of camels, cars of beaten gold, hundreds of musicians, wandering in a country where "appeared the most glorious palaces that eye could conceive, glittering with silver, gold and precious stones . . . he found the ground he trod on to be gold dust, and the stones pearls: these were covered with flowers which seemed formed of vegetable crystal, emeralds, and amethysts." These are the words from one of the tales, "The History of the Merchant Abudah"; these are the words which he read in his small room.

His own appetite for such marvels seems to have been endless. "In all these golden fables," he once wrote, "there was never gold enough for me. I always wanted more. I saw no reason why there should not be mountains and rivers of gold, instead of paltry little caverns and olive pots . . . For, when imagination does begin to deal with what is so hard of attainment in reality, it might at least get out of bounds for once in a way, and let us have enough." And this vision stayed with him. When in later life he discusses gold and money, he almost always alludes to *The Arabian Nights* as if his own appetite for such things were boundless; when in his journalism he discusses the most modern industrial or commercial processes, he similarly invokes the spirit of these tales, in part no doubt to romanticise that which seems alien and ugly, but also in part to create a sense of fabulous communion with his readers, using childhood and the values of childhood as the arena common to all people and one which can naturalise the most forbidding contemporary phenomena. The attempt is rarely successful, however, and the introduction of this magical landscape only serves to emphasise its difference from the real landscapes of nineteenth-century Britain. In his reading of *The Arabian Nights*, in fact, there is something so eager, so overwhelming, so obsessive that it really suggests images of childhood anxiety and deprivation – so it is that, in his use of *The Arabian Nights* in his later writing, there is often latent within his references an overwhelming mood of incongruence and sadness. Childhood has gone for ever, his own and that of his age.

There were other books, too, and to the list which Charles Dickens draws up one might add *Gulliver's Travels*, *The Pilgrim's Progress*, and the works of Addison, Steele and Johnson. There was also George Colman's *Broad Grins*, a sequence of verses which for the young boy conjured up magical visions of London; Mrs Inchbald's collection of farces, not entirely free of sexual innuendo which may or may not have gone over little Dickens's head (the general tone of these plays is in fact very weak, not unlike the kind of drama Dickens himself was to write in his early career); and there was Thomas Day's *History of Sandford and Merton*, an author whom Dickens actually detested "because he was so very *instructive* and hinting doubts with regard to the veracity of Sinbad the Sailor". These are representative items of the eighteenth century, both classic and staple, and Dickens remained true to them; there were copies of all of these books in his library at the time of his death. Even George Gissing considered Smollett and Fielding "strong food" for a young boy but, as Dickens himself said, there was no harm for him to be found in them. Only that smooth, dry, agreeable eighteenth-century prose, the formality of diction combined with the farce of adventure, the rhetoric creating an ordered and harmonious world. (And did he not hear in the syntax of these novels an echo of his father's own orotund voice?) It is possible that children read in order to make sense of their world, and when Dickens read these novels from the century before his own he would have at once been confronted by their strange mixture of elegance and impropriety, of formal diction and violent behaviour. And, since the characteristically picaresque plots are combined with theatricality of action and character, this reading could have done nothing other than to complement the sense of life which he had already derived from the theatre of his own period. This was the world of the early nineteenth century, therefore, in its artistic forms – optimistic, casually violent, high-spirited, grotesque. And now it was Charles Dickens's world.

Reading ". . . was my only and my constant comfort. When I think of it, the picture always rises in my mind, of a summer evening, the boys at play in the churchyard, and I sitting on my bed, reading as if for life." These lines come from *David Copperfield*, but they are a literal transcription from his own autobiographical fragment. Books were, he says, his consolation and it is curious to note how, in his fiction and in his own memories, accounts of childhood reading are always placed close to accounts of childhood agonies; they are inseparable in his mind, and was it then so early in life that he gained the faculty of transference, always able to turn his suffering into characters and stories, his pain into fables and fantasies? Perhaps that is why, in *Oliver Twist*, the young boy's reading and writing are seen as part of an idyllic pastoral, as the singular and proper relief for a wounded spirit. And so it was, too, that the young Charles Dickens comforted himself "by impersonating my favourite characters" and avenged himself on his enemies by putting them "into all the bad ones". These fictional characters literally came alive to him; he could *see* them. "Every barn in the neighbourhood, every stone in the church, and every foot of the churchyard, had some association of its own, in my mind, connected with these books, and stood for some locality made famous in them. I have seen Tom Pipes go climbing up the church steeple; I have watched Strap, with the knapsack on his back, stopping to rest himself upon the wicket-gate; and I *know* that Commodore Trunnion held that club with Mr Pickle, in the parlour of our little village alehouse." This is the other significant image of Dickens's childhood, to be placed beside that of the young boy singing and acting upon a tavern table – it is the image of the solitary child, lost in his book, preoccupied with his own fancies, creating his own world. Creating his own world so vividly that it supplanted the one around him. There is a reflection of this when, in *A Christmas Carol*, Ebenezer Scrooge is led helplessly back to his childhood and sees "his younger self, intent upon his reading. Suddenly a man, in foreign garments: wonderfully real and distinct to look at: stood outside the window, with an axe stuck in his belt, leading an ass laden with wood by the bridle. 'Why it's Ali Baba!' Scrooge exclaimed in ecstasy . . . One Christmas time, when yonder solitary child was left here all alone, he *did* come, for the first time, just like that. Poor boy!'" And Scrooge sees, too, Valentine and Orson and the Sultan's Groom and Robinson Crusoe's parrot, all of them parading in dumb-show in front of him as they had done once before. And once again he whispers of his old self, "Poor boy!" Here in Dickens's fantastic interweaving of reality and fiction, of sorrow and fantasy, pain and play, we see something of the sources of his own later fiction; the boy "reading as if for life" became the man who wrote as if for life, taking the world and recreating it in more consoling form.

Of course such a picture of the young Dickens is quite different from the memories of him in the same period. One contemporary at

William Giles's school recalled his "marked geniality" and "his proficiency in all boyish sports such as cricket etc.". William Giles's sister also remembers that ". . . he was of a very amiable, agreeable disposition . . . Charles was quite at home at all sorts of parties, junketings and birthday celebrations" and she especially remembers "that he took great delight in Fifth of November festivities around the bonfire". Again the description complements that of Mary Weller: high-spirited, active, convivial. There will be many such descriptions of Dickens's maturity, too, but in a very real sense they are deceptive; there was that within him which avoided the notice of other people, a stiller and more attentive person, a darker and deeper temperament which he literally kept to himself. It is not surprising, therefore, that in his later semi-autobiographical accounts of childhood another self steps out of the gaiety and the good humour; there emerges a child who is guilty and anxious, sensitive and quick to anger, filled with apprehensions but never expressing them to anyone.

That is why, in later life, he always looked back upon his childhood with something very close to self-pity. He was, he said, "a very queer small boy", "not a very robust child", "once a lonely boy". A friend later recalled how ". . . he used to say he *always was* a puny, weak youngster", and never used to participate in games ". . . with the same zest that other boys seemed to have. He never was remarkable, according to his own account, during his younger days, for anything but violent spasmodic attacks, which used to utterly prostrate him, and for indomitable energy in reading – cricket, 'chevy', top, marbles, 'peg in the ring', 'tor', 'three holes', or any of the thousand and one boys' games, had no charm for him, save such as lay in watching others play . . ." His daughter, Mamie, described how ". . . his knowledge of games was gained merely from long hours of watching others while lying upon the grass". This idea of "watching" others was clearly very important to him, and it suggests both passivity and anxiety, the security of being bound up in one's self and a concomitant separation from the "real" world. The nature of his "spasmodic attacks" has often been discussed, not least because they occurred throughout his life. They seemed particularly to attack his left side and Dickens believed them to stem from an inflamed left kidney, calling it in later life "the torment of my childhood". No doubt he was right to think so, the symptoms suggesting some form of renal colic, perhaps provoked by a stone in the kidney passage itself. His was not a long-lived family (lung diseases of various kinds carried off a brother, a sister and two of his own children), and it is perhaps interesting – as another aspect of the inheritance from father to son – to note that John Dickens died of a stone in the bladder. One biographer who has studied Dickens's medical history in some detail suggests that Dickens was "foredoomed from his youth", the kidney stone eventually leading to a deterioration of the smaller arteries and an eventual paralysing stroke. But in a sense we are all foredoomed from youth, dying perhaps from the same network of disease which kills our parents and their parents before them; more importantly, in Dickens's case, these youthful spasms or fits of agony seem frequently to have occurred at times of crisis or anxiety. Yet even this is to be expected, since the body is only part of our general consciousness of the world, and there does seem to be a sense in which Dickens withdrew at such moments, enacted a kind of death, writhing in agony under the weight of the world – the pale doomed children of his fiction, Paul Dombey, Little Nell, Smike, being images of his own self.

So what kind of imagination was being formed by this boy who appeared cheerful and gregarious, but who believed himself to be weak and lonely? It is hard to forget those images of death which the mature novelist seems particularly to associate with childhood, in part deriving from self-pity, but perhaps also an echo of his two siblings who died in infancy. More significantly, however, it is clear that for Dickens childhood is often associated with the experience of sudden terror and of inexplicable fear, just as Scrooge's blood was ". . . conscious of a terrible sensation to which it had been a stranger from infancy". So it is that on other occasions Dickens refers to ". . . the enduring sharpness of a fearful impression made at that early period of life" and to the fact that ". . . few people know what secrecy there is in the young, under terror". And what of his dreams? These too seem to have taken on the shape of his own fears. ". . . I can see back to very early days indeed, when my bad dreams – they were frightful, though my more mature understanding has never made out why – were of an interminable sort of ropemaking, with long minute filaments for strands, which, when they were spun home together close to my eyes, occasioned screaming." This is close to another childhood nightmare of ". . . an immense area of shapeless things . . . slowly coming close to my eyes, and receding to an immeasurable distance". Shapeless-ness, strands being melted together: and close enough to Esther Summerson's fevered hallucinations in *Bleak House* (". . . there was a flaming necklace or ring, or starry circle of some kind, of which *I* was one of the beads . . . it was such inexplicable agony and misery to be a part of the dreadful thing . . .") to suggest that these dream images of objects or perhaps lives being tightly bound together, somehow incurring loss of identity, are of deep and continuing significance to him. Could it be that as a child he did, in some deep sense, fear and loathe the idea of connection with other people – perhaps in revulsion from his enforced intimacy with his family? But there is a limit to any such analysis, beyond which no one can go. There is something in Dickens's infancy, something which cannot now be recovered or understood, some primal fear which left him casting about for images with which to express it and which gave him as a novelist that sensitivity to the adult world which is most often to be found in the eyes of a frightened child.

There were specific images that he could recall, those shadows that make "the wondering child, half-scared and half-amused, a stranger to itself"; one such was the image in *Tales of the Genii* of "the terrible old woman hobbling out of the box". He evokes this childhood image on three separate occasions, thus confirming the fascination it continued to exert over him; it is easy to image a child morbidly sensitive to horror, unable to stop listening, unable to stop reading, unable to forget. Other images return. In adult life he could remember the gaol he had seen in Rochester in those early days, and he recalled how he had watched a line of convicts bound together with manacles upon an iron chain, that whole dark world of fear and imprisonment which is brought back to life in the opening chapters of *Great Expectations* where Dickens alludes to the convict ships and the gibbets which he had known as a child by the Medway. He could also remember some crumbling houses outside Chatham which were being mined by soldiers to make way for a prison; the place was known locally as "Tom-all-Alones", and in *Bleak House* he transferred this area of decay and dissolution to a dark district of London. There was one other memory too, and perhaps the worst because it seems so trivial an occasion for terror. "It is a figure that I once saw, just after dark, chalked upon a door in a little back lane near a country church – my first church . . . it horrified me so intensely – in connection with the churchyard, I suppose, for it smokes a pipe, and has a big hat with each of its ears sticking out in a horizontal line under the brim, and is not in itself more oppressive than a mouth from ear to ear, a pair of goggle eyes, and hands like two bunches of carrots, five in each, can make it – that it is still vaguely alarming to me to recall (as I have often done before, lying awake) the running home, the looking behind, the horror, of its following me . . ." The hands like carrots in fact resemble those of a Chatham "Idiot" whom Dickens was also to recall – ". . .a dreadful pair of hands that wanted to ramble over everything – our own face included". But in the figure chalked upon the wall there are other connotations too – the churchyard, the idea of the dead coming alive, the horror of being pursued. For we recall that the convict ship and the Medway gibbet at the beginning of *Great Expectations* lead Pip to another overwhelming fear of ". . . the hands of the dead people, stretching up cautiously out of their graves". All the evidence suggests that these were truly the fears of his childhood, and indeed they eddy through Dickens's fiction like a tidal flow beneath the surface, bringing up stray images and associations, pulling his narrative in one direction rather than another, controlling the movement of his consciousness.

And sometimes foundering? ". . . near *foundering* (what a terrific sound that word had for me when I was a boy!)", and it must not be forgotten that, for the child lost in his books, words were the only proper token of reality. The rest was a game, a spectacle, a phantasmagoria, a nightmare. The first evidence for this lies in the extent to which in childhood he believed himself to "see through" the adult world; in many of the short reminiscences of his early life, there is a sense in which he is eager to point out the hypocrisy and theatricality of other people's behaviour. Just as he saw through the stock conventions of the theatre, so also he believed himself to be above the ritual pieties of adult life. As he said of the recently bereaved widow at a funeral he attended as a small boy, "She formed a sort of Coat of Arms, grouped with a smelling-bottle, a handkerchief, an orange, a bottle of vinegar, Flanders's sister, her own sister, Flanders's brother's wife, and two neighbouring gossips – all in mourning, and all ready to hold her whenever she fainted. At sight of poor little me she became much agitated (agitating me much more) and having exclaimed, 'Oh here's dear Master Uncommercial!' became hysterial, and swooned as if I had been the death of her . . . I was not sure but that it might be manners in *me* to faint next, and I resolved to keep my eye on Flanders's uncle, and if I saw any signs of his going in that direction, to go too, politely." There is a nephew here, also, eating plum cake, ". . . but he felt it to be decent mourning that he should now and then stop in the midst of a lump of cake, and appear to forget that his mouth was full, in the contemplation of his uncle's memory".

This again may all be the fiction of Dickens in his "Uncommercial" guise, but it does provide at least an impressionistic glimpse of his own childhood – the life of a child who watched and saw the adults, in his own phrase, "making game". He was a boy who saw literal meanings in things; we have already noticed how he explained to a guest that the marbled-paper ornament in the parlour "wasn't marble" and we have seen him marvelling at the literal absurdities conjured up in his mind by the phrase "Lamb of God". The same aptitude for taking things literally occurs also in another story which his mother used to relate to her friends: "Once, when Charles was a tiny boy, and the family were staying down in Chatham, the nurse had a great deal of trouble in inducing him to follow her when out for his daily walk. When they returned home, Mrs Dickens said to her 'Well, how have the children behaved?' 'Very nicely indeed, ma'am – all but Master Charley.' 'What has he done?' 'Why Ma'am he will persist in always going the same road every day.' 'Charley, Charley, how is this?' 'Why mamma,' answered the urchin, 'does not the Bible say we must walk in the same path all the days of our life?'" Apocryphal, perhaps, but Dickens used the episode in order to describe Pip's character in *Great Expectations* and he employed the phrase again almost forty years later when he was attacking the bureaucracy of mid-nineteenth-century England and declaring that ". . . with God's leave I shall walk in the same all the days of my life . . ." A later glimpse of Dickens in the same mood is to be found when, in his fifties, he heard a friend talking "of somone having been 'bashed' by someone else. Boz caught the then rather unusual word, and began to ask for a literal explanation." The idea of the great fabulist and romancer so preoccupied with the literal meaning of words or phrases may seem disconcertingly odd, but it is not really so. It has to do with Dickens's fascination, and reverence, for words in themselves. ". . . near *foundering*" – always he was moved by words, by their sound and by their connotations. Yet there is something of a paradox here; the boy who delighted in theatre condemning the theatrical behaviour of those around him, the boy revolted by the hypocrisy of adults who became the novelist revelling in the hypocrisy of the characters he created, the man fascinated by literal meaning who was also the author who effortlessly transcended such meanings. But it has to be remembered that the good writer will be at pains to withstand the pressures within his own writing, just as the sensitive child notices most clearly those weaknesses to which he himself is most susceptible.

That he was a sensitive child is not now in any doubt, of course, and his last years at Chatham would for him have been marked, if not by the slow decline of his family at least by the gradual increase in its problems. Although his father was progressing through the ranks of the bureaucracy in pre-ordained fashion – he became a third clerk in Chatham in 1821, and in the December of that year was transferred from the Pay Office to the branch which inspected seamen's wills and powers of attorney – his own financial position was less secure. In May, as a result of his inability to pay the interest owed on the money he had borrowed from James Milbourne, his brother-in-law was forced to cancel the Deed by paying John Dickens's creditor a total of two hundred and thirteen pounds; from this date, relations between the Barrows and the Dickens were little short of frosty. Then the family itself began to change, an experience which is uniquely un-settling to a small child. His aunt, Mary Allen, married Thomas Lamert in December 1821 and the newly wedded couple moved to Ireland, together with one of the servants, Jane Bonny. The next year, however, was one which remained more prominently in Dickens's memory – in March 1822 a child was born, and christened Alfred Lamert Dickens in memory of the infant who had died eight years before. But this birth was followed by the calamity of another death; Dickens's infant sister, Harriet, died from the smallpox (the disease which disfigures Esther Summerson in *Bleak House*). Again the death of the sibling may have provoked in him feelings of fear and of guilt: this cannot be known, although it is curious how often in the lives of writers there is to be found the early death of a younger brother or sister. Whether Harriet died in Chatham or in London is not clear, because it was in June of this year that John Dickens was formally recalled to work at Somerset House. The house in St Mary's Place was relinquished, and there was a sale of some of the Dickenses' household effects; a local shipwright, who was about to marry Mary Weller, bought the best set of chairs. Mary Weller herself left, and an orphan from Chatham Workhouse was taken on as the new servant. The remaining furniture was sent ahead by water and the Dickens family made their way to London in a carriage; they travelled to Camden Town and settled in a new house in Bayham Street.

For reason or reasons unknown, Charles Dickens did not travel with them. He remained behind in Chatham, staying in the house of his schoolmaster, William Giles, for about three months. Perhaps he asked to stay in order to complete some phase of his education – even as a ten-year-old boy he was no doubt determined and ambitious – or perhaps his parents, knowing his sensitive disposition, wished him to remain there until they were properly settled in the capital. Perhaps he had been ill. It does not matter. It meant only that his departure from Chatham was delayed, but depart he must. On the night before he went away ". . . my good master came flitting in among the packing-cases to give me Goldsmith's *Bee* as a keep-sake. Which I kept for his sake, and its own, a long time afterwards." The next morning he went to Simpson's coach office in Chatham and, while he waited there for the coach which was to take him to London, he had time to notice an oval transparency in the window of the office representing one of the coaches ". . . in the act of passing a milestone on the London road with great velocity, completely full inside and out, and all the passengers dressed in the first style of fashion, and enjoying themselves tremendously". Once he saw something, with that quick glance of his, it was never forgotten. And then he was placed inside the coach, the "Commodore", a "light coach" with four horses which left each morning at nine-thirty; and the young boy was driven out of Chatham. Driven out of the place which had been the harbour of his infant imagination, where he had first gone to school. Driven away from the scenes which he had populated with the characters out of the novels he had read. "It was the birthplace of his fancy," his friend John Forster wrote, "and he hardly knew what store he had set by its busy varieties of change and scene, until he saw the falling cloud that was to hide its pictures from him for ever." He was the only passenger inside the coach. "Through all the years that have since passed have I ever lost the smell of the damp straw in which I was packed – like game – and forwarded, carriage paid, to the Cross Keys, Wood Street, Cheapside, London?" And so he had left his infancy behind. He was on the road to London. ". . . and I consumed my sandwiches in solitude and dreariness, and it rained hard all the way, and I thought life sloppier than I had expected to find it." There is no knowing what other thoughts afflicted him on this journey away from home – anxiety, nostalgia, a longing for the past and fear of the future – but what else do we see in his fiction but that great divide between the country and the city, between the place of innocence and the place of poverty or hardship? And was it even now that the great myth of London which he was able to create – with its close-packed streets, its darkness, its mystery – first began to stir within him, as the open fields of his infancy rushed past and the city loomed before him?

Chapter 3

LONDON. The Great Oven. The Fever Patch. Babylon. The Great Wen. In the early autumn of 1822 the ten-year-old Charles Dickens entered his kingdom. He was met at the end of his journey from Chatham, and rejoined his family in their new house in Camden Town – 16 Bayham Street, a recently erected house (no more than ten years old) in what was then an area only just being developed. Houses were always important to Dickens; in his fiction they become almost animate objects, taking on the features of their owners or, like abandoned children, betraying all the symptoms of neglect and vacancy. Their expressions can be blank or stern or forbidding; their façades can be cheerful or sullen, according to the mood of occupants, neighbours or the locality itself. He always remained acutely sensitive to their appearance and to their condition, as if the sight of certain houses sent an actual shock through his nervous system; and always, for him, there were certain buildings which resurrected the feelings of his childhood, feelings of being stifled, of being betrayed, of being abandoned. So what did Dickens see on first looking up at his new home? A two-storey building of characteristic London yellow brick, one in a small terrace of houses. He was given a tiny garret room at the top of the house, which looked out over a small garden surrounded by a wall. There were two rooms on the first and ground floors, as well as a basement, and within this somewhat confined space there were now the Dickens parents, their five children, the servant whom they had brought from Chatham Workhouse and James Lamert, the stepson of the man whom Aunt Fanny had married. He was a lodger, whose payments must materially have helped the family but whose effect upon the life of Charles Dickens was to be little short of catastrophic.

Camden Town itself was a quiet and respectable semi-rural area, almost "genteel" despite the problem of robberies which always beset those whose houses abutted upon lanes and open fields. There was grass growing up in the newly paved road, and water was to be taken from a pump almost opposite Dickens's new house. To the south was Somers Town, but there were fields between; to the north the wooded heights of Highgate and Hampstead; to the east and west there were fields and market gardens, notable amongst them the tea-gardens of the famous Mother Red Cap, a place of resort, and if not quite a sylvan retreat at least something very different from the gin shops of the metropolis. Where Euston Station now stands there were fields of sheep and cows. The road between Camden Town and the hamlet of Kentish Town led through open fields, unlit, solitary and the haunt of footpads. Bayham Street was in fact one of the few roads already put down upon this area, of which the chief occupations were still haymaking and cricket, and to one contemporary at least it was nothing less than the countryside itself: "To my childish apprehension it was a country village. It seemed a green and pleasant spot." And another resident has described how in those early years of the nineteenth century ". . . gas was unknown. We had little twinkling oil-lamps. As soon as it became dark, the watchman went his rounds, starting from his box at the north end of Bayham Street, against the tea gardens of the Mother Red Cap." So an area agreeable enough, and the houses already built in Bayham Street were inhabited by what would have been considered a "respectable class" of persons – among them an engraver, a retired linen-draper, an artist, a retired hairdresser, a retired diamond merchant and a jeweller. John Dickens, in other words, had chosen a house and a street which fully fitted with his own notions of gentility and at a not exorbitant rent of £22 per annum. It was of London but not exactly in London, and the likelihood is that John Dickens would have walked to work; omnibuses were not introduced for another six years, and the stage would have been too expensive to use on a daily basis. So we must imagine, then, a few straggling streets among the fields, like an outcrop of London stone in the countryside. For those brought up in the town it would have had all the hallmarks of a "country village" but for those who came from the country it must already have seemed to have an indefinable urban atmosphere, the first intimations of the city that would soon engulf the whole area. But placid and genteel nonetheless.

Dickens's recollections were somewhat different. Some thirty-two years later he was to describe it as touching "the outskirts of the fields" but "at that period it was as shabby, dingy, damp and mean a

neighbourhood as one would desire not to see . . . quiet and dismal
. . . crazily built houses – the largest eight-roomed – were rarely
shaken by any conveyance heavier than the spring van that came to
carry off the goods of a 'sold up' tenant . . . we used to run to the doors
and windows to look at a cab, it was such a rare sight". And he
remembers, too, the band playing in the Mother Red Cap tea-gardens.
". . . They used to open with 'Begone Dull Care' and to end with a
tune which the neighbourhood recognised as 'I'd rather have a Guinea
than a One-pound-note'." To John Forster, he described his house
itself as "a mean small tenement, with a wretched little back-garden
abutting on a squalid court". In fact neither the house nor the area was
as mean or as dismal as the locale of Dickens's imagination: it is as if the
young child, distracted by his own unhappiness from seeing the actual
nature of the place, had already fastened his misery upon his surroundings. Forster himself makes the same point in another sense, claiming
for Camden Town the merit of being the place which fuelled the
young boy's imagination; thus ". . . he took, from the very beginning
of this Bayham Street life, his first impression of that struggling
poverty which is nowhere more vividly shown than in the commoner
streets of the ordinary London suburb, and which enriched his earliest
writings with a freshness of original humour and quite unstudied
pathos . . . 'I certainly understood it,' he has often said to me, 'quite as
well then as I do now.'" And it is a curious if perhaps accidental fact
that for the rest of his life Dickens lived near this area of London; just
like the characters in his own fiction who seem rooted to one part of
the metropolis as if they had been created by it, as if the darkness of
London had compressed itself into their tiny wandering forms. So, as
the strains of the music from the band in the tea-gardens floated across
to his garret in Bayham Street, the little Charles Dickens had a vision
of the street no force of reality or changing circumstance would ever
diminish.

For the fact was that the young boy remembered Camden Town as
the place where he first fell into neglect. Of his father he wrote in an
autobiographical fragment, ". . . in the ease of his temper, and the
straitness of his means, he appeared to have utterly lost at this time the
idea of educating me at all, and to have utterly put from him the
notion that I had any claim upon him, in that regard, whatever. So I
degenerated into cleaning his boots of a morning, and my own; and
making myself useful in the work of the little house . . . and going on
such poor errands as arose out of our poor way of living." He seems to

have referred to this episode to John Forster on many occasions, and his first biographer recalls his words: "As I thought, in the little back garret in Bayham Street, of all I had lost in losing Chatham, what would I have given, if I had had anything to give, to have been sent back to any other school, to have been taught something anywhere!" It is to be noted that Dickens here re-emphasises the loss of schooling; in the unlikelihood of any more education all the agony of the little boy seems to be encompassed. The future was snatched away, the dreams and visions of his youth thrown off, all the hope he had of becoming a famous man and all the knowledge of the talent within his own breast (for even children have that knowledge) were of no account. For a talented and ambitious child there is no hell worse than this; all the dirt, all the dreariness, all the poverty which he summons up in his account of Bayham Street spring from it. James Lamert built him a toy theatre, and he seems to have written small sketches (one of a deaf and elderly lady who waited on them at table); but these could only have been stray and brief entertainments, all the more sorrowful because they reminded him of the life he had left behind and the skills which seemed to him now about to waste away for ever; as if, when his consciousness of himself were soiled, then his whole small world became soiled also.

He makes his little hero, David Copperfield, ten years old when he begins work at Murdstone and Grinby's – "a little labouring hind" – which is precisely the age when he came to London, and there are countless passages in his fiction where he places all the poverty and horror of the world in London, all of its peace and seclusion in the neighbouring countryside of Kent. Yet sometimes the reality seemed to him worse than anything he could profitably put in his fiction; in the published version of *David Copperfield*, the sentence which describes the onset of this period in his life reads, "And now I fell into a state of neglect, which I cannot look back upon without compassion". But an examination of the emendations in his manuscript revives the lost sentence which he originally wrote: "And now I fell into a state of dire neglect, which I have never been able to look back upon without a kind of agony." And in his fiction, too, the house of Bayham Street is recalled; it is the house where the poor Cratchits celebrate their Christmas feast in *A Christmas Carol*, and it is the house of Mr Micawber in *David Copperfield* which displays an air of "faded gentility" in a "rank and sloppy street"; his own garret room appears in the same novel as ". . . a close chamber; stencilled all over with an ornament which my young imagination represented as a blue muffin; and very scantily furnished".

It was here, then, that he sank into what he once described as "a solitary condition apart from all other boys of his own age". Alone, friendless, bereft of any possible future or any alternative life, he would sometimes walk down the little paved road of Bayham Street and look south towards the city itself just as he had once looked out to sea in Chatham; from here the great city, smoky in the grey light, might have seemed to him like "a giant phantom in the air". To stand on this spot, according to Forster, "and look from it over the dust heaps and dock-leaves and fields . . . at the cupola of St Paul's looming through the smoke, was a treat that served him for hours of vague reflection afterwards". The roofs, the chimneys, the churches, the light upon the river and there, towering above them, the great cross on the summit of St Paul's. This is what the crossing-sweep, Jo, sees in *Bleak House*, and "from the boy's face one might suppose that sacred emblem to be, in his eyes, the crowning confusion of the great, confused city . . ."; it is the dome which Little Nell could have seen "looming through the smoke, its cross peeping above the cloud", clear of "the Babel out of which it grew"; it is "the great black dome" which Pip sees on his first visit to London in *Great Expectations*; it is the cross which the young Dickens cannot take his eyes from even as he wanders lost through the streets of the metropolis, as recorded in his essay, "Gone Astray". It is the very symbol of London, of its grimy and labyrinthine ways in which we all might lose our path. It was his first view of the city. The lonely boy looking down at the city, the city which bewildered him, which seemed a symbol of his own loss of hope and peace, the city which he would eventually master.

There was death at home, as well; it is possible that his young sister, Harriet, died here and not in Chatham; certainly his Aunt Fanny died, in Ireland, in the autumn of this year. There were other relatives, however, whom the young boy seems to have been encouraged to visit. No doubt one of them was his grandmother, who had now retired from service and was living with her other son, William, above his coffee shop in Oxford Street. Curiously enough there is no record of such visits left by Dickens, except for the fact that she presented him with a silver watch which had once belonged to her husband, but since she died in April 1824 it is possible that they met infrequently or that she left no lasting impression upon his memory. Certainly his visits to another relative are better documented – his uncle, Thomas Barrow, lodged at the house of a bookseller in Gerrard Street, Soho. "Lodged" is not really the word, since in fact he was laid up there; he had broken his thigh, was unable to move, and Charles Dickens became, as the novelist himself put it later in a gracious letter, "your little companion and nurse, through a weary illness". This might have been in fact after his leg was amputated, thus suggesting one other reason for Dickens's later obsession with wooden legs as both ridiculous and somehow menacing. (Of course the operation would have been performed without anaesthetic and it is recorded that, when Thomas Barrow recovered from his swoon of pain, he asked "Where's my leg?" and was told that it was "Under the table".) Generally the influences on the young Dickens were of a more literary nature, however, and it was during these visits to his maternal uncle that the widow of the bookseller in whose house Barrow lodged lent him such books as Holbein's *Dance of Death* and George Colman's *Broad Grins*, the latter being a rather ghastly collection of verse stories, published in 1802. There were certain lines in one of those narratives, however, which seem to have affected Dickens very much. In a story of "The Elder Brother" George Colman utters this encomium to Covent Garden:

> Centrick, in London noise, and London follies,
> Proud Covent Garden blooms, in smoky glory;
> For chairmen, coffee-rooms, piazzas, dollies,
> Cabbages, and comedians, famed in story.

Dickens was so taken with these lines that, according to Forster, "he stole down to the market by himself to compare it with the book . . . snuffing up the flavour of the faded cabbage leaves as if it were the very breath of comic fiction". He was already now writing himself; by his own account he composed a little sketch of a barber who lived in Gerrard Street and who has since been tentatively identified as William Turner, the father of the painter, one of those coincidences in the culture of the time which will reoccur in the pages of this book. But, more importantly, London was also the arena for those eighteenth-century novels which he read, and continued to read, so avidly; it was the place where Peregrine Pickle sets out for the Haymarket in the habit of Pantaloon, where Matthew Bramble is "pent up in frowzy lodgings" and watches a "barrow-bunter" in Covent Garden clean her dusty fruit with her own spittle, where Tom Jones and Roderick

Random hurry on their endless quests. ". . . I should have been perfectly miserable," his hero wrote in *David Copperfield*, "I have no doubt, but for the old books. They were my only comfort; and I was as true to them as they were to me, and read them over and over I don't know how many times more." And no doubt the young Dickens *saw* these figures in London just as he had seen them in Chatham.

That the city was in part for him an enchanted place is not in doubt. In an essay already mentioned, "Gone Astray", he records how in this period he was taken by an unnamed "Somebody" to see St Giles, and how he somehow managed to become separated from his adult companion. So he wanders through the streets of London quite alone, all the time noticing how "grand and mysterious" everything seemed; he meets a dog, eats a sausage, sees the giants of Guildhall and thinks of every City merchant as a creature of fable. Even in his forlorn lost condition he was "inspired by a mighty faith in the marvellousness of everything". How precise a recollection this is may be a matter of dispute; he himself says, however, that it was "literally and exactly how I went astray. They used to say I was an odd child, and I suppose I was." Indeed the image of the little boy, filled with both wonder and apprehension, seems genuine enough. And there is one other incident in the story which carries a certain conviction; he decides to visit the theatre and: "Whenever I saw that my appearance attracted attention, either outside the doors or afterwards within the theatre, I pretended to look out for somebody who was taking care of me, and from whom I was separated, and to exchange nods and smiles with that creature of my imagination." Here is a timely reminder of the potential horror awaiting some children in the streets of London but here, more especially, is an image of the ten-year-old boy who is already something of an actor.

For the skills of his Chatham youth had not completely been abandoned. John Dickens still retained the friendship of Christopher Huffam, Charles Dickens's godfather, and there were many occasions when the young boy was taken to Huffam's house and shop in Limehouse. Christopher Huffam, together with his brother, was a sail-maker and ship's chandler who lived in Church Row, just behind the great Limehouse church of Nicholas Hawksmoor, and their business was in Garford Street almost opposite Limehouse Hole. It was in the house of this prosperous merchant that John Dickens placed his young son upon the dining room table and prevailed upon him to sing. "The Cat's Meat Man" was one of his favourites:

> Down in the street cries the cat's meat man,
> Fango, dango, with his barrow and can.

And on one occasion, according to Charles Dickens himself, he was declared by one of the audience of neighbours to be nothing less than a "prodigy". But there were other reasons for the young boy to remember this place with affection. In his novels marine-stores like that of Solomon Gills in *Dombey and Son* are treated with great affection, as Dickens always did with the sea and with the things of the sea, and it seems likely that the atmosphere of Limehouse reminded the young boy of the ambience of Chatham which he had known just a few months before. On his journeys to see Christopher Huffam he would have passed forges, ropeyards, mast-makers, oar-makers, boat-builders. All the familiar smells and sights of his recent childhood would then have returned; and beside the Huffams' brick-walled workshop, where they made sails, stored rope and piles of chain, the Thames still flowed. So did he here discover the comfort of childhood associations? Yet was it also in the prosperity of the Huffam household that he began to feel the disparity between this life and the life of Bayham Street? Pip's words may be relevant here: "It is a most miserable thing to feel ashamed of home. There may be black in-gratitude in the thing, and the punishment may be retributive and well-deserved; but that it is a miserable thing I can testify . . ."

And to be made more miserable still; there is a wonderful scene in *Dombey and Son* when Walter Gay, learning of the bankruptcy of his uncle, runs in desperation to Limehouse to seek the aid of Captain Cuttle. Is it fanciful to see in this flight – past "slopsellers' shops . . . anchor and chain-cable forges . . . rows of houses, with little vane-surmounted masts uprearing themselves from among the scarlet beans. Then, ditches. Then, pollard willows. Then, more ditches . . . Then, the air was perfumed with chips; and all other trades were swallowed up in mast, oar, and block making, and boat building" – is it possible to see here the panorama of the young Dickens's own flight to seek the help of Christopher Huffam at the time of his father's bankruptcy? Certainly John Dickens was, all the time, coming closer to that fate. The poor-rate due to be paid in April of 1823 was only met by him after a summons, and in the following year he seems not to have made any attempt to pay the local rates for paving and lighting. By moving to London he had also lost various "outport allowances" and it has been calculated that his salary dropped by some ninety pounds a year. This would not have been a welcome development but nonetheless, on a salary of approximately £350 per year, he ought to have been able to meet all the expenses of his household. Instead there seems to have been a steady drain on his resources, the reasons for which remain unclear. It has been suggested that he drank, evidently on a stray remark of Charles Dickens many years later that a man might procure bread and meat on credit but that – gesturing at a bottle – ". . . has no right to do this sort of thing in the same way". It is hard to believe that he was a drunkard, however, and there is no evidence to support that fact. It has also been suggested that he was a secret gambler, and this on the evidence of Little Nell's grandfather in *The Old Curiosity Shop*, whose addiction to gambling Dickens describes with such success. But these speculations are perhaps not necessary; the fact is that John Dickens was simply and recklessly improvident, one of those people to whom no thought of responsibilities can avert the need to assuage the pleasure of the moment.

The effects are clear enough, too. "One dirty-faced man, I think he was a bootmaker, used to edge himself into the passage as early as seven o'clock in the morning, and call up the stairs to Mr Micawber – 'Come! You ain't out yet, you know. Pay us, will you? Don't hide, you know; that's mean. I wouldn't be mean if I was you.'" This of course is fiction or dramatised reconstruction, but anyone who knows the impact on the sensitive child of his parents' misfortune – let alone the impact made by creditors invading the home and making threats – will understand how it was that the adult Dickens still felt the horror and could thus evoke it with such shuddering authenticity.

Not all of John Dickens's expenditure was of a reckless kind, however, and in April 1823 Fanny Dickens was enrolled as a pupil and boarder at the Royal Academy of Music (fee: 38 guineas per annum), where she studied piano – or "entered for piano" as it says in the records of that institution – on the nomination of a certain Thomas Tomkisson, a pianoforte-maker in Dean Street. While here she also studied grammar, moral and religious education, arithmetic and Italian; she had a good soprano voice and was already a talented pianist, and no doubt the parents decided to make this investment in their eldest daughter's education as a prospective source of earnings in the future. The effect on her brother could not have been anything other than severe, however; here was a boy whose education had been begun only to be abruptly curtailed, whose hopes and ambitions had been destroyed almost without thought, and whose sister was now taken out of the home to be properly educated. To be granted a future which he could not possess. ". . . he has told me," Forster wrote, "what a stab to his heart it was, thinking of his own disregarded condition, to see her go away to begin her education, amid the tearful good wishes of everybody in the house." That it was a "stab" cannot be in doubt, if only for the fact that he remembered and wished to discuss it with a friend so many years later. He must have suffered not only a sense of hurt and of exclusion, but also a sense of betrayal; his sister had been his companion at their first school, and now she, too, was in a sense abandoning him. Theories of maternal abandonment with their subsequent rage and guilt abound in explanations of Dickens's adult conduct and attitude towards women, but surely the departure of his sister can be seen to be of equal significance – his anger and hostility framing themselves in the thousand different portrayals of treacherous women and empty-headed girls? It was yet another betrayal; and there were others to come.

At some point in this period he fell into a "fever", some prostration of the spirit and the body, from which he emerged to find his parents ever deeper in debt. It was now, it seems, that his mother decided that she "must do something". She decided to start a school for young ladies, no doubt with the encouragement of Christopher Huffam who helped to draw up the prospectus and whose connection with the East Indies, from which quarter the children of English residents were sent home for the required learning expected of young ladies in the period, might be of some advantage. Just after Christmas in 1823 they moved into a house in Gower Street North – their most expensive yet, more than double the rent of the Bayham Street residence, and the tenancy of which was in Mrs Dickens's name. It was a new house, comfortable, almost elegant, with two tall windows on the first floor reaching from ground to ceiling; and outside, in the street now totally claimed by University College Hospital, a brass plate was affixed to the door bearing the legend "Mrs Dickens's Establishment". Perhaps the young Charles Dickens hoped that he might receive some form of education here, too, but his role at this time was simply to push handbills through the letter-boxes of prospective clients. And nothing came of the scheme: ". . . nobody ever came to school, nor do I recollect that anybody ever proposed to come, or that the least preparation was made to receive anybody." Slowly their affairs grew worse, and it was during this period that the young Dickens became acquainted with the interiors of the myriad of pawnbrokers' shops then existing in the metropolis. The pawnbroker was generally called in the euphemism of slang "My Uncle", and in a later essay Dickens has described "the timorous, irresolute glance at the three golden balls; the transparent hypocrisy of looking at the silver forks . . . the furtive, skulking slide round the corner, to the door in the court where the golden balls are emblazoned again . . . the mental perplexity as to which of the little cell doors looks the most benevolent . . ." The "cells" were the private boxes or cubicles where the embarrassed customer might bolt himself within and conduct his affairs in reasonable privacy. As it might be for a frock and silk handkerchief:

"What do you want upon these?"

"Eighteen pence."

"Lend you ninepence."

"Oh, make it a shillin'; there's a dear – do now."

"Not another farden."

"Well, I suppose I must take it."

Dickens was no stranger to these places, nor was he a stranger to a little drunken bookseller in the Hampstead Road where by degrees he pawned his father's small library of books. But he never did pawn Goldsmith's *Bee*, his schoolmaster's final gift to him, and in the retention of that little volume one senses the last remaining hope of the boy himself; to have given up that book would have been to have given up all his past and the hopes that were part of it. This bookseller liked to hear Dickens conjugate his Latin verbs, and one must picture the little boy, amidst all the hopelessness and degradation of his position, lifting up his head and chanting the precious lessons he had learned in an easier and better time. Later in life he once again purchased all of the books of his childhood reading, but the melancholy experience of the pawnshop is one that stayed with him always; again and again it emerges in his fiction, and the fact that when in his adult years he always needed to know, on his trips from home, where every article of furniture *was* and *must remain* seems like the echo of a childhood where familiar household objects might suddenly disappear. The need for security, for safety, is something that always drove him onwards. But there is another reason for that need, which is to be found in the most dolorous passage of Dickens's childhood.

When Dickens first came to Bayham Street, the "nightlife" of London fascinated him; particularly he was struck by the world of Seven Dials – ". . . what wild visions of prodigies of wickedness, want, and beggary, arose in my mind out of that place!" But now there came a time when that life would come all too close to him. It began with James Lamert. He was no longer living with the Dickens family – no doubt the want of space and the noise of small children had something to do with his decision – but he had been approached by his cousin, George Lamert, to become the chief manager of a business he had just purchased. This was Warren's Blacking of 30 Hungerford Stairs, a manufacturer of boot blacking, and it was James Lamert's suggestion that Charles, now entering his twelfth year, should also be employed there at a salary of six or seven shillings a week. Dickens himself put the matter baldly: ". . . the offer was accepted very willingly by my father and mother, and on a Monday morning I went down to the blacking warehouse to begin my business life." The date generally fixed for this inauspicious occasion is Monday, 9 February, 1824, just two days after his twelfth birthday. It might have seemed to him ". . . some dark conspiracy to thrust him forth upon the world", to use the words in *Oliver Twist*, but to his parents it must have been a welcome opportunity for their son to be gainfully employed and to help with their own straitened finances. In a business run by their kind relative, after all, what rungs might their son not climb on the journey towards gentility?

And so on that fateful Monday he walked the three miles from Camden Town to the Strand, down Hampstead Road and Tottenham Court Road, crossing the High Street which leads into Broad St Giles's and then down St Martin's Lane. Then across the Strand into an area of squalid corners and alleys, and descending Hungerford Stairs to the river itself. His destination was the last house on the left, beside the Thames itself, ". . . a crazy, tumbledown old house, abutting of course on the river, and literally overrun with rats. Its wainscotted rooms and its rotten floors and staircase, and the old grey rats swarming down in the cellars, and the sound of their squeaking and scuffling coming up the stairs at all times, and the dirt and decay of the place, rise up visibly before me, as if I were there again." In fact this ancient house did haunt him; there is the mouldering house in *Nicholas Nickleby* with a Thames wharf behind it; there is the house in *Oliver Twist* with the "dark and broken stairs" where Fagin dwells and the manufactory in the same novel where "the rat, the worm, and the action of the damp, had weakened and rotted the piles on which it stood; and a considerable portion of the building had already sunk down into the water beneath . . ."; and there, too, in *The Old Curiosity Shop* is the summer-house overlooking the Thames which is ". . . a crazy building, sapped and undermined by the rats, and only upheld by the great bars of wood which were reared against its walls . . ." This is the haunted place of Dickens's imagination. Dampness. Ruin. Rottenness. Rats, familiar to him from the books he read and stories he heard. Woodworm. The smell of decay. And beside it the river, the Thames which flows through his fiction just as it flowed through the city itself, ". . . lapping at piles and posts and iron rings, hiding strange things in its mud, running away with suicides and accidentally drowned bodies faster than midnight funeral should . . . this river looks so broad and vast, so murky and silent, seems such an image of death in the midst of the great city's life . . ."

This was the place to which the twelve-year-old Dickens came, then. James Lamert greeted him, and took him to the counting house on the first floor; there was an alcove there, looking down at the Thames, which was to be his place of work. A boy who worked downstairs, Bob Fagin, was called up to show Dickens of what that work would consist: he was to take the bottles of blacking and prepare them for sale. Not bottles exactly, but receptacles rather like small flower pots made of earthenware and with a rim around them for string. Dickens's job was ". . . to cover the pots of paste-blacking: first with a piece of oil-paper, and then with a piece of blue paper; to tie them round with a string; and then to clip the paper close and neat all round." When he had finished a few gross of these, "I was to paste on each a printed label". He worked for ten hours a day, with a meal break at twelve and a tea-break in the late afternoon. The boy himself, ". . . of singular abilities: quick, eager, delicate, and soon hurt, bodily or mentally", now sitting at a work-table with scissors and string and paste, looking out at the dreary river just beneath him, bearing away his hopes. It is not too much to say that his childhood came suddenly to an end, together with that world of reading and of imagination in which the years of his childhood had been passed. But it was not gone; it had ended so quickly that it did not gradually fade and disappear as most childhoods do. Instead it was suspended entire in the amber of Dickens's rich memory. "My whole nature was so penetrated with the grief and humiliation of such considerations, that even now, famous and caressed and happy, I often forget in my dreams that I have a dear wife and children; even that I am a man; and wander desolately back to that time of my life."

It was not the only catastrophe of that time since, no more than a few days after the boy's introduction to Warren's, John Dickens was arrested for debt. It was at the instigation of a certain James Karr, a baker who lived round the corner of Bayham Street in Camden Street, and the contested amount was a large one, forty pounds. It was not the only debt of John Dickens – there were still claims outstanding even from Rochester as well as London – and after his arrest he was taken to a "sponging house" or "half-way house" where debtors about to be imprisoned tried to obtain relief before the prison doors closed upon them. Now "with swollen eyes and through shining tears" his young son ran errands and carried messages for John Dickens, no doubt some to his father's mother and brother. But it seems that John Dickens had either claimed too much in the past or on this occasion had gone too far; no aid was forthcoming. On 20 February, he was incarcerated in the Marshalsea Prison as an insolvent debtor. It was a common offence in this period and for some years after – it has been estimated, for example, that in 1837 there were between thirty thousand and forty thousand arrests for debt – but nevertheless the insolvent debtor was classed as a quasi-criminal and kept in prison until he could pay or could claim release under the Insolvent Debtors' Act. It often happened that such a prisoner remained indefinitely within the prison and John Dickens himself, immediately before being taken away, announced that "the sun was set upon him for ever". "I really believed at the time," Charles Dickens told Forster, that these last words "had broken my heart". They are of course repeated in a similar situation by Mr Micawber who a few hours later is found playing skittles with perfect equanimity, and Charles Dickens's later ambiguous reaction to his father's plight is evident in the way in which he places them in the mouth of the notorious Wackford Squeers when he, too, finds himself behind bars – " 'The coat of arms of the Squeerses is tore, and their sun is gone down into the ocean wave!' "

But that it seemed to be a catastrophe at the time there can be no doubt; for one thing, it brought back into prominence all those fears about low social class and indeed criminality which remained submerged within the family. It was not so many years before that Dickens's maternal grandfather had absconded as an embezzler, and there were theories in this period concerning some inherited propensity towards crime as well as towards madness. It might have seemed to the young Dickens that this was indeed his true inheritance, which is perhaps why some critics have believed that Dickens's great contribution to the description of childhood lies in his depiction of infantile guilt. But the calamity had more immediate consequences, also, which resonate no less profoundly through his novels. The family was in a literal sense being broken apart; whatever joy and conviviality it possessed, so amply demonstrated in the young boy's ". . . we are going to have such a game", had gone. There is a further interpretation to be granted to this event, however, for when the destruction of the family is placed beside the young Dickens's own descent into manual labour, we can see how the fate of the Dickens household might be seen as an emblem of the transition through which the entire country was going. Just as debt and labour began to destroy this once middle-class family, so the country itself was now in the process of losing its eighteenth-century character and moving toward a period in which the exigencies of industrial production became the single most important factor in disrupting family life and in emphasising the social power of money. This may seem a fanciful comparison but somewhere within it lies the nature of Dickens's génius; his private situation, nourished and transformed by his imagination, became a symbol of the public world. When he speaks of the need for labourers and manufacturers to come together, when he speaks of the need for one family within the nation, when he describes Christmas as the spirit of benevolence and family harmony, we need look no further than the events of this one month in 1824 to find a pressing source for his visions, a pressing pain which he needed continually to explain and to assuage.

When David Copperfield first enters the debtors' prison to visit Mr Micawber, his somewhat disinterested status in the novel, merely as lodger and no relation, is dissolved in what seems to be the flood of Dickens's own filial memory: ". . . and when at last I did see a turnkey (poor little fellow that I was!), and thought how, when Roderick Random was in a debtors' prison, there was a man there with nothing on him but an old rug, the turnkey swam before my dimmed eyes and my beating heart." Certainly this bears all the marks of Dickens's private memory. For once again the characters of his reading return to his bewildered sight, and the real world wavers in the air like an hallucination; not for the first or the last time in his life the boundary between fiction and reality, what is real and what is imagined, seems to disappear. On his first visit to the Marshalsea the young Dickens arrived at the main gate and was directed to the turnkey's house. "My father was waiting for me in the lodge, and we went up to his room (on the top storey but one), and cried very much. And he told me, I remember, to take warning by the Marshalsea, and to observe that if a man had twenty pounds a year, and spent nineteen pounds nineteen shillings and sixpence, he would be happy; but that a shilling spent the other way would make him wretched." Which salutary piece of advice has since attained immortality in *David Copperfield* through the words of Mr Micawber, showing that Dickens imports reality into fiction just as surely he allows fiction to change or distort reality itself.

First for the reality. The prison which he entered was just off Borough High Street, the main entrance and turnkey's lodge at the end of a narrow court now known as Angel Place. Pass the lodge and you enter a small yard in front of the prison itself, with its strongly barred windows. Within this prison there were rooms, on an average some eight feet by twelve feet, and eight and a half feet in height; each room had a fireplace, a cupboard and small window from which the sky but not the street could be seen. There was an "airing yard" beyond the prison building and, in addition, a "tap" and common room where the prisoners might resort. And around this whole area was of course the high wall, with the spikes upon it. It was not a large place, and it would have been crowded, noisy, squalid and malodorous; a dank and desperate reality, indeed, the despair seeping into its bricks, its stone staircases and unswept floors. A bell was rung at ten in the evening, warning visitors that the gates were about to be locked for the night. (Greetings and partings are very important in Charles Dickens's fiction – it is as if at this point his characters become most real, caught in that charmed temporary light in which we can see their true feelings.) After the bell had been rung those like the young Dickens who did not have to reside in this place would walk out into the night, into the grimy streets of the Borough fitfully illuminated by oil lamps.

This was the place and the area which haunted Dickens throughout his life, this place he had come to as a child. In his autobiographical fragment he could recall scenes and details as clearly as if they had happened just the day before yesterday; how his father had drawn up a petition and, when it was being read out loud by another prisoner, how he had listened "with a little of an author's vanity, and contemplating (not severely) the spikes on the opposite wall"; how as a visitor he watched and noted everything which happened within his view as a prisoner might study with wide eyes the cracks and surfaces of his cell; how he ruminated on all the peculiarities of the prison and the prisoners as he sat over the blacking bottles in Warren's; how "in that slow agony of my youth" he made up histories for the shabby and wretched people whom he saw here. Most of the prison episodes find their way, practically unchanged, into the pages of *David Copperfield*; but there is one small difference. In the novel it is the young boy who runs back to tell Mrs Micawber stories of prison life; in his autobiographical fragment, he remarks that ". . . I was always delighted to hear from my mother what she knew about the histories of the different debtors in the prison". No doubt the truth lies equally in both accounts, and we can imagine the mother and eldest son taking almost a grim delight in recounting stories to each other; it is an image of closeness, of course, and one that must be placed beside Dickens's later declarations of maternal ineptitude and betrayal.

The Marshalsea does not appear only in *David Copperfield*, however, and it is a mark of the hold which the prison had over Dickens that its presence continually re-emerges in his fiction – in just the same way that Little Dorrit, the "child" of that gaol, expects the Marshalsea to be waiting for her even when she travels in Switzerland and Italy, the sad building and its inmates being "lasting realities that had never changed". He came to know the neighbourhood of the Borough well and in *The Pickwick Papers* we learn how "all the busy sounds of traffic, resound in it from morn to midnight, but the streets around, are mean and close; poverty and debauchery lie festering in the crowded alleys, want and misfortune are pent up in the narrow prison; an air of gloom and dreariness seems, in my eyes at least, to hang about the scene, and to impart to it, a squalid and sickly hue". And so it seemed to him, then, both as a child and in his recollections as a man. No less powerful is his account in *Little Dorrit* of morning in the Marshalsea: "A blurred circle of yellow haze had risen up in the sky in lieu of the sun, and he had watched the patch it put upon his wall, like a bit of the prison's raggedness. He had heard the gates open; and the badly shod feet that waited outside shuffle in; and the sweeping, and pumping, and moving about, begin; which commenced the prison morning". But, perhaps more than anything else in these accounts of the Marshalsea, the one which seems most to echo the young Dickens's own experience is the sight of the children playing within the prison walls. In *Little Dorrit* there are ". . . the games of the prison children as they whooped and ran, and played at hide-and-seek, and made the bars of the inner gateway 'Home'"; and in *David Copperfield* it is Micawber's memory of ". . . the shadow of that ironwork on the summit of the brick structure . . . reflected on the gravel of the Parade, I have seen my children thread the mazes of the intricate pattern, avoiding the dark marks." These accounts of prison life are some of the most evocative in all of Dickens's writing, and it is hard in particular to forget the early chapters of *Little Dorrit* in which the heroine, so strange an image of the young Charles Dickens himself, is seen to live and work within the prison. For here, in these scenes, is the most extraordinary invocation of London and its dispossessed – the stuffy close rooms, the clouds rolling across the sky, the wind, the mud, the streets, the mad, the afflicted. Those people who wait patiently outside the prison at daybreak – "Such threadbare coats and trousers, such fusty gowns and shawls, such squashed hats and bonnets, such boots and shoes, such umbrellas and walking-sticks . . .' – might seem in fact to comprise the entire populace which swarms through Dickens's novels, existing on the margins, just beyond the open arena in which the major characters play their parts, but visible and audible nonetheless, the great faint crowd which give his novels their fullness and their life.

Dickens's parents never mentioned this episode in their lives to their son in later years, and their silence might suggest that they were as traumatised by it as he; but we can never be certain. The younger children would not have been affected to anything like the same degree; it may even be the pictures of their playing which Dickens recalled in his fiction. His older sister, Fanny, must clearly have been humiliated and bewildered by her father's incarceration; but at least she was still enrolled at the Royal Academy of Music, even if she could not have been certain how long she might remain there. But of Charles's reaction there can be little doubt. Certainly of all the family he seems to have been the one most affected by its downfall. We have seen him watching and musing and dreaming through all this "slow agony", but there must also have been the agony of uncertainty – it was not clear to anyone at the time but that John Dickens might remain incarcerated until his death. And then, too, there must have been the boy's fear that he would for some reason be imprisoned himself; Bramah locks and keys were a great innovation of Dickens's childhood, and they occur frequently in his published writings as if the image of them was fixed in his mind at some early age. There was a feeling of terror, then, and one of revulsion. But more than anything else he must have begun to understand the nature of failure, and at the same time to wish to banish it from his own life. As he says of Little Dorrit, "What that pitiful look saw, at that early time, in her father, in her sister, in her brother, in the jail; how much or how little of the wretched truth it pleased God to make visible to her, lies hidden with many mysteries. It is enough that she was inspired to be something which was not what the rest were, and to be that something, different and laborious, for the sake of the rest." Thus the image of the Marshalsea never left him. The high wall with the spikes on top of it, the shadows cast by the prison buildings, the lounging shabby people – all of these images return again and again in his narratives. But the gaol is even more central than that; there are times when within his fiction the whole world itself is described as a type of prison and all of its inhabitants prisoners; the houses of his characters are often described as prisons, also, and the shadows of confinement and punishment and guilt stretch over his pages. In his own life he never ceased to be affected and intrigued by prisons; he visited them often, almost as a matter of routine, and on his visits to other countries never failed to pay attention to their penal institutions. Imprisonment was with him everywhere; how much a symbol of infantile guilt, how much a recollection of childish privation, and how much emanating from the very being of the man, cannot be known. But it is there. The Marshalsea is always there.

The uncertainty of these months continued, and no more distressingly so for the child than in continual changes of address. For a few weeks after the incarceration of John Dickens, Elizabeth and her children remained at Gower Street North; most of their possessions had now been sold and they were encamped in two or three rooms, the meagre remains of their furniture and their other belongings around them. It seems that she was, in someone's immortal words, waiting for something or someone to "turn up" to solve her husband's financial problems – probably a member of his family or of her own – but, at the beginning of April, despairing of any immediate aid, she and the youngest children moved into the Marshalsea alongside John Dickens. Fanny remained at the Royal Academy, and Charles was taken to lodge with a friend of the family, a Mrs Roylance who lived only a short walk away from Gower Street North in Little College Street. She had formerly lived in Brighton, and in fact had given refuge there to Elizabeth's absconding father, but this familial tie does not seem to have endeared her to her young charge. According to his own account she sat for certain characteristics in the depressing and sometimes rather terrifying Mrs Pipchin in *Dombey and Son*, and in *The Pickwick Papers* he describes Little College Street itself as ". . . a desolate place enough, surrounded by little else than fields and ditches". Once again, however, it is likely that his own feelings of hurt and loneliness charged the reality around him with its own shapes of oppression; hence no doubt Mrs Roylance's reappearance as an "Ogress" in *Dombey and Son* and Dickens's own faint response to the area itself. Of his time with this lady he gave an equally dismal account in his autobiographical fragment; it seems that he shared a bedroom with another child who lodged here but "My own exclusive breakfast, of a penny cottage loaf and a pennyworth of milk, I provided for myself. I kept another small loaf, and a quarter of a pound of cheese, on a particular shelf of a particular cupboard: to make my supper on when I came back at night . . . No advice, no counsel, no encouragement, no consolation, no support, from anyone that I can call to mind, so help me God." This pitiable and self-pitying account is perhaps too carefully crafted to be altogether true, but it is certainly the case that for the first time he was separated entirely from his family (with the exception of his stay with his schoolmaster) and left to fend for himself. He also might have felt aggrieved at being compelled to continue earning his own living; the Dickens family were much more comfortable, and actually rather better off, within the safety of the prison walls and he might have expected them to bring him with them. In addition there was a school in Blackman Street for the children of prisoners in the King's Bench or the Marshalsea, but no effort seems to have been made to place the young Dickens there; all the evidence suggests that the Dickens family needed the money he was now able to earn.

John Dickens was still drawing his salary from the Pay Office but, a month after entering the prison, he applied for retirement with pension; no doubt he feared that his bankruptcy might lead to his dismissal, and wanted to preclude that possibility. But he lodged his appeal on the grounds of his ill health; he was, according to the medical report he sent with his application, suffering from "a chronic infection of the urinary organs" which in his covering letter he described more grandiloquently as an "unfortunate calamity". There is no doubt that he was suffering from just such a painful complaint – indeed he died of it – but his application seems to have lapsed as events in his life took a different turn. On 26 April his mother died at her son's house in Oxford Street at the age of seventy-nine and, although John Dickens was not named as an executor in her will, without a doubt this was something that had indeed "turned up".

There were no immediate consequences, however. John Dickens

remained in the prison, and his eldest son remained in Little College Street; every Sunday he picked up his sister from her college near Hanover Square, and together they spent the day in the Marshalsea. On Sunday evenings he returned her to the school while he took his own solitary way back to Camden Town; all that can safely be said about these days is that Charles Dickens's feelings on the matter were as usual kept within his own secret, struggling, anguished self. There was one outburst, however: after three weeks or so he complained to his father about his isolation "so pathetically, and with so many tears . . . It was the first remonstrance I had ever made about my lot, and perhaps it opened up a little more than I intended." Here one notices again the extraordinary reserve and secrecy of the boy, just like the child Pip in *Great Expectations* who feels everything and says nothing, but the effect of this single disclosure was beneficial. He was removed from Little College Street, and a new lodging was found for him in Lant Street, a small narrow street, dull, restful enough to the senses to provoke "a gentle melancholy upon the soul", and within two minutes' walk of the Marshalsea itself. Here Dickens was placed in a house owned by a certain Archibald Russell, an agent for the Insolvent Court and therefore used to transactions of such a kind; the landlord and his wife, according to Dickens's own account, were later immortalised as the Garlands in *The Old Curiosity Shop*. His was a garret room once again, and its "little window had a pleasant prospect of a timber yard" but in comparison to what had gone before it seemed to him to be "a Paradise". Yet paradise had really been lost, and it was in this attic room that one night the young boy once more fell into a spasm which lasted until the morning.

For this was the shape his life had taken; in the morning he would lounge around the old London Bridge until the gates of the prison were opened – this was the bridge which was completely roofed over with houses and buildings and where, as he loitered, he would entertain the Chatham workhouse servant with his own vivid fictions of the life around him – and then he would breakfast with his family before setting off for the blacking factory. When his day's work was completed, he would return to the Marshalsea, generally crossing Blackfriars Bridge, turning into Great Surrey Street until he took a side-turning into Great Suffolk Street. He would have supper with his family, and then at nine go back to his lodgings in Lant Street. In later life he placed Jo, the crossing-sweeper, upon Blackfriars Bridge, like some emblem of his own lost self, and, many years after these events had passed, "my old way home by the Borough made me cry, after my eldest child could speak". How terrible these memories must have been to him, then, to weep over the stones where his childish feet had trod – and then in even later years to keep on coming back, to look at the old image of "a golden dog licking a golden pot over a shop door" which he had seen many times as a child, to peer into a shop where he used to purchase boot-laces, to smell once again the odour of hat-making in the manufactories which had been there when he had known them as a child. What terrible memories, but ones which he endlessly relived. And on the site of that dolorous way there are now streets named after the characters of his imagination – Little Dorrit Court, Pickwick Street, Quilp Street – and in Lant Street, his old lodgings long since demolished, there now stands the Charles Dickens Primary School for children under eleven. If this could have been prophesied to him as a small and lonely child, what wonder and disbelief would have been his? I, who cry here, on this same spot will I one day be remembered for ever?

And each day he walked through these streets to Warren's blacking warehouse, back to the rats and the rotting wood and the black paste. The original plan had been for him to stay on the first floor, within sight of James Lamert, and for Lamert to give him lessons during the dinner hour of twelve to one. But the exigencies of commercial life over-rode such schemes; he was not taught by Lamert, and eventually he migrated to the ground floor where the other boys worked. Here his companions were Bob Fagin, an orphan, and Paul Green, whose father was a fireman. "No words," Dickens wrote in his autobiographical fragment, "can express the secret agony of my soul as I sunk into this companionship;" both in his fictional and autobiographical accounts, again and again he emphasises the "degradation" involved in his companionship with these working-class boys. They were "common men and boys", "common companions", to be associated with whom was "shame" and "humiliation" – even though he insists that "my conduct and manners" were different and that he was characteristically called "the young gentleman". Here one senses some imitation of his father's own projection of a genteel persona (it is clear enough how John Dickens's fear, stemming from the fact that he was so perilously hovering between classes, was transmitted to the son). It also tells us much about his instinctive reaction to the labouring poor, although it is one that would have been widely shared in his lifetime; the "working classes" were in a very real sense a race apart, a substratum of society which bred in those above them a fear of disease, a horror of uncleanliness and of course the dread of some kind of social revolution if ever these individual Fagins and Greens became a "mob". For Dickens, the boy who had hopes "of growing up to be a learned and distinguished man", such close contact and the resultant fear of contamination must have been appalling; it is often forgotten how precarious early nineteenth-century society could be, how easy it was for a person to slip downwards through the social classes – through drink, or improvidence, or misfortune – and in a sense to disappear. There was no "safety net" and without all the accoutrements of a "welfare state" ordinary existence was a much tougher and more forbidding business; it was, to use a phrase of the period, truly "the battle of life". So although it seems that even by Dickens's own account Bob Fagin was gentle and considerate to him, his very presence evoked a horror greater than any gratitude Dickens might have felt – the horror of being a part of the poor. That is why the child's name is used for the terrible figure of Fagin in *Oliver Twist*; just as Bob Fagin "in a ragged apron and a paper cap" trained Charles Dickens in the skills of tying string around the blacking bottles, so Fagin instructs Oliver Twist in the art of stealing. Both are introductions to that soiled amorphous world of privation, of beggary and want, which the young Dickens wanted so desperately to avoid; even little Bob Fagin's kindness seemed to the young Dickens no more than another way in which the darkness might stick to him, another possibility of degradation drawing him further downwards on a level with the "common men and boys". That is why he had fears of growing up to be "a shabby moody man" (as David Copperfield expresses it), unable to wipe off the stain steadily encroaching upon him; his fear was one of becoming permanently "low", even of becoming "a little robber or a little vagabond". This is of course the fate that seems to engulf Oliver Twist, and that novel might be said to mark Dickens's first memorial to his life as a child. But there are echoes of Dickens's childhood also in *Great Expectations*, when Pip feels himself degraded even by working with the kindly Joe in his forge. ". . . I used to stand about the churchyard on Sunday evenings, when night was falling, comparing my own perspective with the windy marsh view, and making out some likeness between them by thinking how flat and low both were, and how on both there came an unknown way and a dark mist and then the sea."

Of course he was not utterly thrown away. His mother often came to visit him at the blacking warehouse, which suggests that she was not as heartless as her son later cared to believe; and sometimes, no doubt in those moments of hilarity or exhilaration which visited the young boy, he would play with his companions on the Thames coal-barges. He was also earning six or seven shillings a week, which was not at all a bad salary for a boy of his age, and as he told Forster later it ". . . was a grand thing to walk home with six shillings in his pocket" on a Saturday night. And even amidst all the grief and loneliness certain salient characteristics of Dickens do emerge. There is for one thing his decision to do his work as well as possible – "I soon became at least as expeditious and as skilful with my hands as either of the other boys" – and there is also the small child's determination to exercise as firm a control over his life as he possibly could by proper organisation. He attempted, for example, to make his money last all week "by putting it away in a drawer I had in the counting-house, wrapped into six little parcels, each parcel containing the same amount, and labelled with a different day". He would be equally methodical when he grew up to be a famous man; indeed both loneliness and self-reliance mark his adult character, and it would seem that the hardest lessons are those which we learn first.

But one notices the emphasis on "little" in his description of "little parcels" here; that adjective is constantly employed in his memories, and the dominant image which Dickens gives of himself in his passages of autobiography is of a small, wretched, frail child wandering alone through a city in which adults seem to loom above him like the giants in a fairy story. There is the waiter, for example, watching this "strange little apparition" eat his dinner in the best dining room in a beef-house off Drury Lane. Dickens tips him a halfpence which he could ill afford but, in his sturdy determination to sit down and order such food, in what must have seemed to him so wonderful a place, one sees both the ambition and the helplessness of the child, both the desire to be something better than a "labouring hind" and the anxiety which accompanied it. There is also his story of entering a public-house in Parliament Street and ordering ". . . your very best – the VERY *best* – ale . . ." He hears his childish self saying, ". . . Just draw me a glass of that, if you please, with a good head to it." The words echo down the years, down to Dickens himself as an adult, and then down to us, the echo of a childish voice as the landlord and the landlady came to watch him drink. "They asked me a good many questions, as what my name was, how old I was, where I lived, how I was employed, etc. To all of which, that I might commit nobody, I invented appropriate answers . . . and the landlord's wife, opening the little half-door and bending down, gave me a kiss that was half-admiring and half-compassionate . . ." But there was little other compassion for him, and the dominant image of these memories lies in his taking his solitary way through the streets of London; looking in at the pudding shops and at the stale tarts in dusty tins, eating raisin pudding, buying a saveloy and a penny loaf for his dinner or going to a coffee-shop and ordering half a pint of coffee with a slice of bread and butter. The intensity of these experiences cannot be in doubt. When he ate alone in the coffee room, for example, he could read its inscription backwards on the interior glass, "MOOR EEFFOC", and whenever as a man he happened to catch sight of the same reverse image "a shock goes through my blood". The shock of being abandoned, as he thought, of being thrust into the world with only his own quick wits for protection, was one that never left him; many years after these events, he still "could not endure to go near" Hungerford Stairs and the site of his degradation.

It is possible even at the time that he contemplated the idea of escape; escape back to William Giles's house, perhaps, and to the scenes of his happier years. Back to the hope of being "learned and distinguished" once more. Or at least of "going away somewhere, like the hero in a story, to seek my fortune . . ." Certainly this is the dream he gives to David Copperfield, who leaves the warehouse in which he works and makes his own pilgrimage to Chatham, where Dickens had once lived, and to his kind aunt there. Yet if he had such dreams they soon faded; ". . . transient visions," as he records in *David Copperfield* again, "day dreams I sat looking at sometimes, as if they were faintly painted or written on the wall of my room, and which, as they melted away, left the wall blank again." So he suffered, but he suffered in secret; never once did he complain to his working companions, or even to his parents. "I never said, to man or boy, how it was that I came to be there, or gave the least indication of being sorry that I was there . . . I kept my own counsel, and did my work." This repression of his feelings, this silence, will be seen to be characteristic of the mature Dickens – never wanting to show himself as he truly was, to express how he truly felt, is a remarkable characteristic of the man who in his fiction seems so open to all the sentiments of the world. But it is true nonetheless; his children knew it, and his closest friends knew it. He was always a reticent, almost a repressed, man.

But he did in Warren's what he did later on a more elaborate scale. He told stories, to beguile his companions and to retain some image in his heart of the reading to which he had been so attached. In some instances he told stories merely to protect himself against ridicule or spite; when his father was incarcerated in the Marshalsea, and Bob Fagin wanted to walk home with him, the young Dickens stopped at a house across the river and pretended to live there. "As a finishing piece of reality in case of his looking back, I knocked at the door, I recollect, and asked, when the woman opened it, if that was Mr Robert Fagin's house." Remember also how he had invented answers to the questions of the landlord of the public house where he had purchased the "very best" ale. How he told the orphan servant from the Chatham Work-house "quite astonishing fictions" as he lounged on London Bridge. He was in other words a good liar – it is impossible to know how many stories he told at the blacking warehouse in order to assert his position as "the young gentleman", but the wish to believe in such things was so strong that he no doubt did indeed convince himself of their truth even as he invented them. The longings of young children are sometimes so powerful that fantasies come to seem the merest truths. And in the child, so in the man.

But the stories were also those familiar tales from the books he had read. In *Oliver Twist*, that first expression in fable of the currents which run through Dickens's childhood, the reading of books is itself seen as an alternative to a life of crime; reading is part of the gentle, respectable world to which Oliver so fervently aspires. And so it was for Dickens; the old stories were a reminder of his past life, and in *David Copperfield* his pain is anatomised thus: "All this time I was so conscious of the waste of any promise I had given, and of my being utterly neglected, that I should have been perfectly miserable, I have no doubt, but for the old books." "Reading as if for life" – that was a phrase used of him before, finding in books the only refuge against the world and the only harbour for his own self so grievously threatened. But there is more to it than that; this entry into his old books seems in turn to have prompted the young boy to extend their spell and their protection by recreating the world in their image. This was, he says in *David Copperfield*, ". . . the manner in which I fitted my old books to my altered life, and made stories for myself, out of the streets, and out of men and women . . ." And here in embryo is part of the urge which led him towards the writing of fiction, this need to rewrite the world, to make it a more vivid and yet more secure place, to dominate and to control a reality which might otherwise bear him away into a life of degradation; to turn even the details of this childhood into the fictional narratives of *Great Expectations* and *David Copperfield* so that the child himself can be remade and thus redeemed. That is why, even as we may quote from these novels, citing evidence for the account of his early years, we must always do so with circumspection; any reality behind Dickens's well-chosen words would have been dirtier, scruffier, more ambiguous, more amorphous, and apparently endless.

He could not escape the stain of this reality, however hard he tried. There was at least one occasion when he had a recurrence of the old spasms to his side, the agony of "my old disorder". The attack lasted all afternoon and Dickens tells how Bob Fagin in particular was kind to him, and how he was laid in some straw while empty blacking bottles were filled with hot water and applied to his side. In his novels there are two characters who fall into fits – both of them marked men who go pale, sweat dreadfully and then swoon or descend into paroxysm. In both cases an analogy is made with "a wild beast" in its torment, and in later years Dickens would sometimes compare himself to an animal prowling behind bars. Can we see something of his own memory in these accounts? But do we not also see in the agony which Dickens suffered some image of himself as the innocent victim? But there is also punishment and self-imposed pain here – guilt, perhaps, at taking the role of breadwinner away from the father. Anxiety. Solitude. Defilement. Despair. Blacking. All these things come together, and we are left with the image of the young boy writhing in agony on the rat-infested floor.

Chapter 4

IT was impossible to say for how long John Dickens might be incarcerated; so, in other words, it was impossible for his son to know the length of his service in the blacking factory. But that John Dickens, unlike William Dorrit, did not intend to settle in the gaol is obvious from the fact that, very soon after his arrival in the Marshalsea, he was preparing for his freedom under the Insolvent Debtors Act. This meant that he could be released after being declared insolvent, if he could demonstrate that his debts were incurred unintentionally, that all property of his own was surrendered, and that all goods over a combined value of twenty pounds would be used to pay off his debtors. He had been left four hundred and fifty pounds in his mother's will but, since the will was proved only after his release, it was not of much immediate material benefit. But it is noteworthy that his brother, William, swiftly paid off the original debt to James Karr which had begun the process of imprisonment in the first place. (It is interesting to remember, in this connection, how important a part wills and legacies play in Charles Dickens's fiction; they represent a staple plot in use from *Oliver Twist* to *Our Mutual Friend*, and although they were also a characteristic of nineteenth-century fiction, a way of handling the twin themes of money and intrigue, they seem also deeply implicated in the processes of Dickens's imagination. A legacy, in his world, can often free you from unmerited suffering.) The legal process of the Insolvent Debtors Act now had to go on until its end: in order properly to evaluate the worth of John Dickens's belongings, his son had to appear before an official appraiser in order to have his own clothes valued. So he arrived in his white hat, small jacket and corduroy trousers and, on being told by a gentleman smelling of beer that "that would do" and "it was all right", he gave a bow and left the room. The habit of bowing was far more customary then than now;

and we must imagine the young Dickens bowing in acknowledge-
ment of an adult, bowing to his schoolmaster, bowing on receiving a
favour of some kind. In such a simple act it is possible to glimpse far
more clearly than in any number of statistics the pressure of a highly
defined and stratified society, literally forcing the young boy down
into a position of deference.

John Dickens's case was brought before the Insolvent Court,
described later by Dickens in *The Pickwick Papers* as a badly lit and
badly ventilated room which was ". . . always full. The steams of beer
and spirits perpetually ascend to the ceiling, and, being condensed by
the heat, roll down the walls like rain: there are more old suits of
clothes in it at one time, than will be offered for sale in all Houndsditch
in a twelve-month; and more unwashed skins and grizzly beards . . ."
and so forth, all the stench and noise of the place being recaptured in
what reads like an act of memory on his part. Here his father was
placed in an enclosure to the left of a panel of judges, his case reviewed,
debts both in Rochester and in London detailed, and an appointee
assigned to handle the payment of these (in fact John Dickens had to
find a considerable sum in the November of the next year, and a
further sum in the following November). Case over.

And so, on 28 May, having spent fourteen weeks in the Marshalsea,
John Dickens was released into the world. If he was not taken in
procession to the prison gates, as happens both to Samuel Pickwick
and to William Dorrit, the relief and celebration must nevertheless
have been much the same. At first the whole Dickens family, with the
exception of Fanny, who was still at the Royal Academy of Music, went
to stay with Mrs Roylance in Little College Street; the orphan servant
seems to have been discharged at the same time, one further example
of the severity of behaviour in a period when people had to struggle for
mere survival. They came "not as lodgers", Mrs Roylance's grand-
daughter later explained, "but as welcome guests". It is not clear how
long they stayed here – and who indeed would have bothered to record
the wanderings of a poor family? – but at some point they moved
further north, to Hampstead, remaining there until late in December.
Then at the end of this year the Dickens family moved to 29 Johnson
Street, in Somers Town, only a few minutes' walk from their original
house in Bayham Street; in an area which soon declined into squalor
but was then what might be called "shabby genteel", the home of
shopkeepers and clerks. The street was some thirty years old, and
overlooked the fields which still bordered Camden Town; it was

narrow and had a sort of intimacy – a "family circle" was the way in which it has been described – but it could not have been entirely unaffected by the closeness of the city. For one thing no gas light had as yet reached it and, since most of the inhabitants would have been too poor to afford an inexhaustible supply of oil-lighting, the street would have been plunged into profound darkness at the end of the day.

The house itself was relatively small – "a charming little villa" was one description of it before it was demolished in 1934 – with a red brick façade, a small door with an arched fanlight, a narrow passage running the whole length of the house, and two floors with two rooms on each floor. There was a small garden at the back, with an 'outhouse' used for multifarious purposes, and there was a high garden wall broken in places to allow for the passage of air. Dickens's own room seems to have been once again an attic or garret just beneath the sloping roof of the house; he had at this, or a slightly later, stage his own library of books, and there was a small "basket grate" to keep him warm. From his window the young boy would have looked across the green fields to Camden Town, and to the Hampstead Road along which the old stage coaches still travelled. It was the road which carried Tom Jones and Partridge from St Albans, it was the road upon which Defoe's Captain Jack had made his way: no doubt these literary associations were still very strong for him, and it is poignant to note that many years later, in the first years of the twentieth century when the area had degenerated into a slum, it was in this house that a certain John Langstaff established the David Copperfield Library for the poor children of the neighbourhood. So the dreams of each generation can be transmitted through books – from the time when the young Dickens read *Tom Jones*, and looked out upon the area where some of its events had taken place, to the time when another young boy might read *Great Expectations* a few yards from the house where its author had spent a portion of his own disordered childhood.

During the course of these various moves John Dickens continued his work as a clerk in Somerset House, his first application for retirement having lapsed; and, with the knowledge that most if not all of his colleagues had heard about his imprisonment for debt, this could not have been the easiest of periods for him. Certainly he was soon reapplying for retirement, which suggests that he was no longer happy with the work upon which he had been engaged for some nineteen years. Yet he went to the office every day still, walking from Hampstead and then Somers Town to the Strand (the distance from

Hampstead being something like five miles). On these journeys he would have been accompanied by his son, himself working in that same neighbourhood, and it is tempting to speculate upon their relationship to each other in this period – the father continuing with a job he was finding more and more disagreeable (and of course still troubled by that infection of the urinary organs which seems to have flared up at times of crisis), and the son going daily to a place he hated and feared in equal measure. It is not evident why John and Elizabeth Dickens wanted their son to continue working in the blacking warehouse after the release from the Marshalsea; but no doubt they still needed the money which he brought home each Saturday night, and in any case he clearly never uttered a word about his own feelings of being unloved and abandoned. It may be, in addition, that it was necessary for Charles Dickens to keep on working in order to prove that his father was truly an "insolvent" person. And, as they walked together, around them sprang the morning life of the metropolis; the clerks and office boys already streaming in to the city from the outlying areas, the apprentices sweeping their shops and watering the pavements outside, the children and servants already crowding the bakers' shops, the fast coaches going on their appointed rounds. But, for the young Dickens, above all the sun rising over another blank day, over the dreariness and the subdued low pain of loss.

A loss made all the greater, from his own account, by the spectacle of seeing his older sister win a prize – or, rather, two prizes. On 29 June of this fatal and memorable year she was awarded the Academy's silver medal for good conduct as well as a second prize for the piano. There were to be problems later when John Dickens could no longer afford to pay the tuition fees of his daughter but on this occasion her prospects seemed bright indeed; bright compared with those of her brother who was one of the family assembled to see Princess Augusta congratulate Fanny on her achievement: "I could not bear to think of myself – beyond the reach of all such honourable emulation and success. The tears ran down my face. I felt as if my heart were rent. I prayed, when I went to bed that night, to be lifted out of the humiliation and neglect in which I was. I never had suffered so much before." And then he adds, "There was no envy in this." In part this last remark is simply a reflection of Dickens's usual inability to admit that he possessed any faults – on all such occasions he adopts a passive role as sufferer or victim – but in a sense the experience he had was too deep to be that merely of "envy". His whole life seemed to have been thrown away, and on an occasion such as this the full truth of his situation must have impinged very deeply upon him. When in the company of Bob Fagin and Paul Green, no doubt his hurt was assuaged by routine duties and by companionship; but to see his sister in a world above his own, with companions far cleverer and cleaner than his own, to see her petted and praised by his parents, all this was a deep humiliation which nothing in his life afterwards ever seems to have eradicated.

And so he went on, the small boy walking through the streets of London to his place of work and then walking back again. Walking, and wandering, seem to comprise a large part of Dickens's early years in London; but that was quite usual in the period, and most people would not think it surprising to make a round trip of ten miles as John and Charles Dickens had done each day on their journey from Hampstead to the Strand. Such efforts were taken for granted. But by his own account Dickens's wanderings were of a more shiftless and dreamy nature. Particularly he came to know the area around the warehouse itself – the Strand, Covent Garden, Blackfriars Bridge and old London Bridge. The major thoroughfares were already lit by the new gas, but this was not the bright and even glare of the late Victorian period: the light flared and diminished, casting a flickering light across the streets and lending to the houses and pedestrians a faintly unreal or even theatrical quality. He had already shown his interest in the noting and creating of "characters" – he had, after all, completed his sketch on the barber of Gerrard Street and the deaf old lady who had waited on the Dickens family in Bayham Street – and it is hard to avoid the conclusion that the young Dickens, walking through these fitfully illuminated streets, watching the passers-by, did not create his own stories out of his head just as he had done in the Marshalsea. Creating stories out of his own misery. Out of his own sense of loss and of wonder.

Of course there were many streets without gas, with perhaps only the occasional oil-lamp to light the way, and Dickens would have known these also. The darker side of London was pre-eminently to be found in those streets congregating around Southwark and the Borough but, if he had strayed from the main route back to his house in Somers Town, he would have passed through narrow unlit streets like his own in Johnson Street. "To pace the echoing stones from hour to hour," he was later to write in *Barnaby Rudge*, "counting the dull chimes of the clocks; to watch the lights twinkling in chamber windows, to think what happy forgetfulness each house shuts in . . . to feel, by the wretched contrast with everything on every hand, more utterly alone and cast away than in a trackless desert; – this is a kind of suffering, on which the rivers of great cities close full many a time . . ." He may have experienced this mood as a child, and certainly he understood it; it is his vision of the threatening city which is exemplified by Little Dorrit's cry, "And London looks so large, so barren and so wild." She utters this while at Covent Garden, so close to the scene of Dickens's own youthful agony at Warren's, and in fact Dickens's characters tend to track the same streets as he did as a child: the Strand, the Borough, Covent Garden, Waterloo Bridge, Camden Town, all these sites of his youthful anguish emerge again and again in his fiction. If there is such a thing as the landscape of the imagination, then it lies for Dickens within these few square miles of early nineteenth-century London.

In particular he describes certain areas which seem in his account to be imbued with sullen mystery or strange enchantment. There were the Adelphi arches, described by one near-contemporary as "malodorous caverns where a fish tail gas-jet, fluttering blue in the gusty half-light . . . showed ragged forms huddled against the curving bulkheads of the blackened slimy brick walls". There was Newgate Prison, which Dickens often passed, and which in the period of his childhood still exhibited for public edification the bodies of those recently hanged. Dickens does not mention these – although all his life he had an "attraction of repulsion" and in particular for the sight of dead bodies – but the blankness and horror of the Newgate walls is never far from his descriptions of London. There was also the patch of waste ground behind Montague House, not far from Somers Town, overrun with nettles and dock-weeds which "looked rather like a barbarous place of execution". And there was the strange sight, outside a public house by the river near Scotland Yard, of "some coal heavers dancing; to look at whom, I sat down upon a bench". Again a vision of lost time, of a life gone forever – so far from us now, this vision of "coal heavers dancing" and yet within it can be recognised something of the spirit of early nineteenth-century England, the privation and also the gaiety, the occupations adopted like a talisman, and nevertheless within this firmly stratified society the high spirits and the measured dance.

In later years Dickens evoked several memories of his early life in London and, although there was a sense in which he was creating yet another fiction in the process (he could not help himself, the making of fiction is an inseparable part of his being), there are details within his narratives which have all the suddenness and unpredictability of recovered memory: a bowl filled with a tape worm, with "ears like a mouse", taken from someone's stomach; a mad woman dressed in black, deranged by the death of her brother; the White Woman, also mad, with "mincing step and fishy eye"; a tea-tray shop in Covent Garden, one of its items being a tray showing two brothers going off to school; and somehow, always, the shadow of Newgate prison, "the same blank of remorse and misery". When this is placed alongside his memories in "Gone Astray" we have the picture of a London crowded with the mad, the oppressed and the miserable but in which stray objects or sights offer the vision of an imaginary world beyond.

Of course there are things which Dickens never mentions, although he must have been quite aware of them. In *The Pickwick Papers* Sam Weller's father says of his son: "I took a good deal o' pains with his eddication, Sir; let him run in the streets when he was wery young, and shift for his-self. It's the only way to make a boy sharp, Sir." To be sharp means to be knowing and to be observant; and no child with these faculties can have failed to notice that the streets were a breeding ground not only for disease but also for all forms of sexual licence; that Dickens's wanderings in London coincided with the onset of his own sexuality and puberty suggests that he must have been profoundly affected by the far from decorous world he saw around him. Alleys and bushes were used as lavatories; sexual intercourse in the streets with prostitutes was not uncommon and one only has to read some of the more direct reporting from the public houses and "low" quarters of the period to realise that, of all the entertainments open to the indigent, just sex was free and was, as one historian put it, "the only pleasure of the poor". In addition Dickens's entrance into the working life of Warren's, at his particular age, must have meant that he received from his boyish companions something close to a complete sexual education. Child molestation was not infrequent in the period and theft from children was something of an industry (known as a "kinching lay"); of course that fate was not visited upon Dickens, but the fact does at least indicate the peril which a small child ran in these dark and squalid streets.

But on all such matters he remains silent, except for an oblique reference in *David Copperfield* to ". . . how knowing I was (and was ashamed to be) . . ." – in that phrase alone can we decipher what it was that Dickens had seen and had understood. Information about his early knowledge of, or attitude towards, sexuality can therefore only be discovered indirectly. In his adult life he was clearly not promiscuous. His was a passionate nature kept severely under control, and there was a sense in which he was always too *hard* and too *driven* a man to be also a sensuous one. In his novels sexuality remains unconscious but everywhere apparent; when directly expressed, it tends to be thwarted or blocked off. In his novels, too, childhood relations are merely "affections of the heart" and at least seem to have no connection with sexuality of any kind. It is as if he did not want to focus upon the matter, as if he did not want to bring it to the surface. Of course this has a great deal to do with the narrative conventions of the period, but there seem also to be vivid private associations which make his reticence more than just another example of Victorian decorousness: sex in Dickens is almost entirely linked with the idea of confusing class boundaries, for example, of bringing *down* its "victims", of consigning them to the same dirt and squalor and disease which his vision of London visits upon the poor. It is also associated with the idea of death – Lady Dedlock, Arthur Gride, Oliver Twist's mother, all die as a result of their sexual "sin" and the females in particular are those who have broken the taboos of the class structure. One cannot help but think that the youthful wanderings of Dickens through the streets of London – and indeed his youthful experience of the Marshalsea, where promiscuity must have been rife – provide at least some of the reasons why he should characteristically link the sexual appetite with poverty and with degradation. Why he should associate it with failure, too, and with the idea of dirt. Of blacking. Of course this vision of the city, as one of dirt and dankness and disease, is very close itself to literary myth, but, if it is a myth which Dickens himself did so much to foster and to expand, it is only because it was established upon a reality he had experienced at first hand.

Yet not all his experiences in this period of his life, not all his experiences of London, were of a disagreeable sort. It is not clear – since he never mentions the fact – whether he saw any of his relations, whether he continued his visits to the Huffams in Limehouse, whether he made any friends outside the blacking warehouse (there is one mention of a young boy of eleven with whom he explored London, but no further reference to him is to be found). What is clear, however, is that somehow he managed to keep his youthful imagination alive. The world of theatres and "penny gaffs" was just around the corner, almost literally so, but he makes particular mention of one aspect of his reading during this period – it was a twopenny weekly, *The Portfolio*, which professed in conventional style to combine instruction with amusement but which was essentially a compendium of horror stories, fables, executions, disasters ("All Of Us In Danger of Being Buried Alive"), murders, and sketches of London life. Dickens always loved reading of such things and, at this particular stage of his life, it is not premature to view the formation of his genius within the context of a very popular culture. Indeed within the culture of London itself. This was a time, for example, when according to one contemporary ". . . people did their best, or their worst, to show their love of music, and express their gaiety, or possibly their vacancy of mind, by shouting in the streets the songs of the day". There was always a popular song being whistled in the streets, sung in tap-rooms, ground out by barrel organs. In this period Dickens would have loitered among singers of all forms of street ballads – political, religious, criminal, romantic – many of them giving to topical events the haunting romance of the stories which he read in *The Portfolio*. And there were songs like "Unfortunate Miss Bailey" or "The Ballad of George Barnwell":

> As soon as he had shut the shop up,
>   He went to the naughty dicky-bird,
> And vhen he vent home next morning,
>   Blow me if he could speak a vord!

"Dicky-bird" was slang for a young lady and here, in these now ancient songs, it is possible to hear something of the spirit and the diction of the period – in songs that Dickens remembered all his life, and which echo through his novels. The culture of London had other manifestations as well, none more colourful or more pervasive than that of the popular print. Sometimes these prints (or indeed illustrations torn out of books) were sold in the streets, characteristically being placed inside upturned umbrellas. And in the windows of the booksellers the crowds would gather to look at the latest offerings, whether pictures of prize fights or caricatures of the famous, engravings of murders or the finer work of Cruikshank, Gillray and Hogarth. These prints, like the animated descriptions of *The Portfolio*, turned the city into a place of mystery and of intrigue. The city which Dickens in turn inherited. And so here is a further picture: the boy, really still only a child, surrounded by music, diverted by illustrations, entertained by songs, haunted by cheap fiction, the whole panoply of London entertainment rolling over him, so impressionable and sensitive as he was. The Adelphi arches. The coal heavers. The Strand. The flaring gas. All to be born again within his imagination.

And, as he walked through these streets, there was another life – the running patterers or "flying stationers" as they were called, the coster girls, the oyster stalls, the baked potato men, the groundsel men, the piemen, the sellers of nutmeg-graters and dog-collars and boot-laces and lucifer matches and combs and rhubarb and crockery ware; men and women who, according to Mayhew writing even some years later, were "allowed to remain in nearly the same primitive and brutish state as the savage". There were the street conjurors, the acrobats, the negro serenaders, the glee-singers; and there were the cries of London, "Chesnuts all ott!", "Half a quire of paper for a penny!", "An aypenny a lot!"; amid the shouts of the people themselves. So, when we wonder at the elaboration and quirkiness that spring from the mouths of Dickens's characters, we ought also to remember that this was a period in which the colour and the originality of London speech would have been taken for granted. One can recall the words of a street patterer interviewed by Mayhew: "Two murderers together is never no good to nobody . . . in course the public looks to us for the last words of all monsters in human form and, as for Mrs Manning, they were not worth the printing . . . Ratcliffe highway – that's a splendid quarter for working – there's plenty of feelings – but, bless you, some places you go to you can't move no how they've hearts like paving stones . . ." When the nature of Dickensian caricature and dialogue is considered, it is wise to remember the rich tumult of voices from which it sprang and which encircled him as he walked through crowded thoroughfares.

He knew them well. He knew the red brick of the City squares, he knew the weavers' houses of Spitalfields and the carriage-makers of Long Acre, the watch-makers of Clerkenwell and the old clothes stalls of Rosemary Lane. It was a much smaller city than that in which he was soon to find his fame; the great building projects were of the Thirties and Sixties, and in the year of his entry into London Trafalgar Square did not exist – it marked only the site of an old inn and some horse stables. The Haymarket was still what its name suggests, the resort of farmers bringing their produce to sell. There was not as much traffic as even twenty years later; there were no omnibuses yet and instead the streets of London resounded to the noises of carts, waggons, hackney coaches, cabs and the old four-horse staging coaches. There was still the danger from footpads, or street robbers, and at night linkboys still bore lights to take the wary pedestrians homewards. And of course all the roads out of the capital were in this period guarded by turnpike gates. That is why, when old men in the 1880s looked back to the London of their childhood, they remembered a city which still retained its eighteenth-century identity; characteristically they recalled the dog fights, the cock fights, the numerous public hangings, the pleasure gardens of Cremorne and Vauxhall, the pillory, the theatres with their playbills put up in the local tobacco shop or pastry cook's, and what one historian has called ". . . the passionate craving for excitement and display". This is the city in which the young Dickens worked and lived. There were no restaurants then, but taverns and chop-houses. There were eating houses with fourpenny plates and sixpenny plates, penny bread and penny potatoes. There were no railways and urban sanitation did not exist. Water was expensive to buy, as were clothes and newspapers; there were no "holidays" for working people but the city had not yet become a prey to that wild and violent energy which now seems so characteristic of the Victorian period. It was a slower-paced city, a city of small shops and houses, a compact city, a city in which the public savagery of the hangman and the pillory was matched by private entertainments in the tavern clubs and song societies. It was a city with its heart still in the eighteenth century, and it is important to realise that this was the city in which Dickens's imagination was formed. It would be true to say, in fact, that the London of his novels always remains the London of his youth; even at the end of his life, in *Our Mutual Friend*, he pays no attention to the great urban developments of the period but goes back to his first vision of the terrible river, the wretched buildings around it, the fetid alleys and the bright, bewildering life of the streets. "And now he approached the great city, which lay outstretched before him like a dark shadow on the ground, reddening the sluggish air with a deep dull light, that told of labyrinths of public ways and shops, and swarms of busy people . . . Long lines of poorly lighted streets might be faintly traced, with here and there a lighter spot . . . Then sounds arose – the striking of church clocks, the distant bark of dogs, the hum of traffic in the streets; then outlines might be traced – tall steeples looming in the air, and piles of unequal roofs oppressed by chimneys . . ." This is the London of 1775 as Dickens imagined it, in *Barnaby Rudge*, but it is the London in which he grew up and it is the

London in which his imagination continued to live. And with it, too, we can put the other constituents of his vision. Uncertainty. Poverty. Dirt. Squalor. Interconnectedness, the rich living beside the poor. Fog. Mist. Fever. Madness. A place of crime and of punishment. Prisons. Executions. Monsters created out of the mud, and crawling out of the mud. This is the London he saw as a child.

Yet at last his stay in the blacking factory was coming to an end. At the close of 1824 John Dickens had once again requested permission to retire from the Navy Pay Office on a fixed pension – the circumstances, according to his superior who backed the application, being of a "mixed nature" but including his urinary infection and his release under the Insolvent Debtors' Act. The petition was accepted on this second occasion, and John Dickens retired from his naval work on 9 March, 1825 after service of some twenty years. He had a pension of one hundred and forty-five pounds a year but he was in the process of paying off his debts, and was still poor; still what his son might later have called "shabby genteel". Some months before his final departure his son's place of work had changed, when Warren's left the mouldering warehouse by the Thames and moved to Chandos Street just off Covent Garden. This was a larger establishment, but, more importantly, it seems that Dickens had now attained as much dexterity in his tasks of pasting and tying as Bob Fagin. The two boys sat in front of a window, to gain the light for their tasks, ". . . and we were so brisk at it, that the people used to stop and look in. Sometimes there would be quite a little crowd there. I saw my father coming in at the door one day when we were very busy, and I wondered how he could bear it." There is a passage in *Great Expectations*, where Pip is fearful of being seen at work with Joe Gargery; in fact this fear of being seen is again and again emphasised in his fiction, and the scenario is only partly transformed in *Oliver Twist* when Fagin is suddenly to be found at a window peering in at little Oliver among his books. Here everything is reversed; the father looking at the harmless Bob Fagin and Charles Dickens becomes the evil Fagin looking at Oliver Twist. All the elements are here working together; if it is not "the primal scene", as some commentators have suggested, Charles Dickens's memory of his father watching him tie pots in the company of Bob Fagin evokes sensations of pleasure and degradation, the adult father turning into a monstrous figure of nightmare, the child always in peril of being permanently consigned to the "low" world from which he wishes to escape.

". . . I wondered how he could bear it." And it seems that John Dickens, for reason or reasons unknown, finally could not bear it. His son was the object of a fierce quarrel between himself and James Lamert, letters were exchanged, and Charles Dickens left the establishment in Chandos Street with a ". . . relief so strange that it was like oppression". The cause of the quarrel is not known; Dickens himself suggested that it was the sight of his son working in the window which prompted his father to act, but this seems unlikely. It may have been to do with money; it may have been to do with pride. Or perhaps that combination of the two which would have been so important to a person in John Dickens's position; he, like his son, was always susceptible to slights and it is not hard to understand why eventually he did choose to quarrel with the employer of his labouring child. So the boy went home – relieved, as he said, and no doubt also oppressed because his sudden departure meant that he had to begin a new kind of life altogether. Then his mother stepped between Lamert and her husband; in a move for which Dickens never forgave her, she resolved the quarrel between them and came back from Chandos Street with "a request for me to return the next morning". But John Dickens, in a moment which perhaps more than anything else saved Dickens for posterity, refused. He wanted his son to be sent to school, to retrieve all those hopes and ambitions which father and son seemed to share. "Home, for good and all. Home, for ever and ever." This is the infant Scrooge's cry in *A Christmas Carol* – Home, from this time forward so much the centre of Dickens's faith, so obvious a yearning in the period of the blacking factory. But Dickens ". . . never afterwards forgot, I never shall forget, I never can forget, that my mother was warm for my being sent back".

The time which he spent at Warren's is unclear, and he himself did not seem to be sure. "I have no idea how long it lasted; whether for a year, or much more, or less." Recent commentators have varied their estimates between a matter of six months to a year, but the real point is that the young boy did not know how long he was likely to remain in that employment. He might, as far as he could see, be thrown away for ever. It is interesting to speculate what he would have become, what kind of man this genius would have turned into, if he had remained at Warren's for the formative years of his development. There are occasions in his fiction when Dickens himself seems to be speculating, seems to be *imagining*, what it would have been like to have been left at the factory – particularly in his evocations of those children or young people whom nobody notices, who slink through the streets, who live without a kind word addressed to them. In little Dick who dies in the workhouse from which Oliver Twist is removed, in Jo from *Bleak House*, in Smike from *Nicholas Nickleby*, and in a host of others, it is almost as if Dickens were populating his fiction with images of his own potentially lost self. He himself believed that he might have turned into a thief, or vagabond, or one of those "shabby moody" men whom he saw frittering away their lives. And how easy it might have been for a child of such sensitivity, such susceptibility to hurt, such great gifts, to have turned against the world which had so baffled and defeated him; there is always that tendency in Dickens's fiction, even when he is upholding the principles of social cohesion, to be at one with rioters, to enter the gates of the prison and to tear it down, to throw flame alongside those with brands in their hands. It is a kind of anger – an anger against the institutions of the world – which his childhood experience nourished within him and which might, under other circumstances, have had quite a different outcome. As it is, however, he transformed his fears. And, if in the account of Warren's he has poured all the horror and distress of the passage to adolescence, there is remarkably little anger in the autobiographical fragments themselves. He removes from his childhood awakening any sexual element and any aggression towards his father, for example, and instead paints that always traumatic period with the more vivid hues taken from the blacking bottle. In his novels the good tend to be the helpless, the self-effacing, the gentle; and this, too, is how he chooses to present himself in these terrible times when a form of self-knowledge and an early maturity were thrust upon him. But he emerged triumphant.

The episode itself was never discussed in his later life. His parents never referred to it, and, although his relatives must have known all about it, there is only one example on record of its ever being mentioned. This was when Dickens was applying for employment as a journalist and his uncle, John Barrow, wrote to say only that "at one time he had assisted Warren the blacking man in the conduct of his extensive business, among other things had written puff verse for him . . ." This is most unlikely, but the expedient lie might well have been told to Barrow by Dickens himself. Whatever the motive, the fact remains that his juvenile employment would not have been considered a recommendation. So it remained his secret. He told Forster, who was to become his biographer, but it was still a matter of dispute whether he ever told his wife. Certainly he never told his children. Just as secrecy and guilt are some of the characteristic themes of Dickens's fiction, so reticence was the key to his own life. ". . . the secret was such an old one now," Pip says in another context, "had so grown into me and become a part of myself, that I could not tear it away." The secrecy was a part of Dickens's being, too.

And yet of course it haunted him; the image of boot blacking appears in *The Pickwick Papers* and carries through his novels to the last, *The Mystery of Edwin Drood*. Blacking bottles, blacking brushes, boot black advertisements, even a blacking warehouse itself, make their appearances in Dickens's novels like some secret transaction between his fiction and his private self; as if in the repetition of this episode he was signalling one of the sources of his strength. That it *was* a source of strength is not really in doubt. Of course the episode, as Forster says, "haunted him and made him miserable, even to that hour". And yet it is often a calamity of such a kind which elicits strengths of which the sufferer may have little idea. Dickens at least seems to have realised the fact that "all these things have worked together to make me what I am", and in a pseudo-biographical passage of *David Copperfield* he makes the point more dramatically: "As the endurance of my childish days had done its part to make me what I was, so greater calamities would nerve me on, to be yet better than I was . . ." Always this idea of striving forward, of purposefulness, of rising above circumstances – and always, in his own life, the same almost primitive urge to conquer.

So in a sense his adult imagination and character were formed by the experience of Marshalsea and of Warren's. "When I tread the old ground," his narrator says in *David Copperfield*, "I do not wonder that I seem to see and pity, going on before me, an innocent romantic boy, making his imaginative world out of such strange experiences and sordid things!" And a world it is, a world conjured out of all the agony of that year. And what of his old, secure, familiar world? When he entered the ruined warehouse at a stroke it disappeared, as if he had lost his connection with it, and it had become a kind of shadow play. In its place were the stories he told and the fictions which he invented, fictions which seem so close to the lies he also told in order to protect himself. As Pip explains it in *Great Expectations*, ". . . I knew I was common, and that I wished I was not common, and that the lies had come of it somehow . . ." One cannot help but think that, when Dickens was abandoned in the blacking factory, he fantasised about kind strangers looking desperately for him and seeking to relieve him, just as he saw adults who he thought were beating him down and using him with no regard for his welfare. In moments of crisis or uncertainty, the adult Dickens often returns to that childhood and to that childhood apprehension of reality. These were the figures he carried in his head, and the figures which he transposed to his fiction. Why else is it that adult reality is always, and at every turn, threatening? – how different a sense of life from his Augustan forebears who described death and disaster but never accompanied them with that calamitous low note which sounds so loudly throughout Dickens that there are times when the reader says, "I can't bear it if this happiness is destroyed, or this outing ruined, or this little boy's money stolen, or this child kidnapped!" And yet these are precisely the things which come to pass.

It could further be said that everything in his mature life became a kind of flight from his childhood. Of course there is no doubt that he was a very ambitious infant, wanting to be "learned" and to live in a great house, but his time in the blacking factory immeasurably deepened and hardened him. He once told John Forster that "he used to find, at extreme points in his life, the explanation of himself in those early trials". Certainly, from the other side of the experience at Warren's, he emerges almost self-created – fluent with words, self-sufficient, funny. In addition he always retained throughout his life a morbid susceptibility to any form of slight – his "shrinking sensitiveness", as he called it – and we see in his huge appetite for success, his huge will for what he himself called "power", the need to remove the taint of poverty and social disgrace. This latent fear of social degradation and his memory of the past clearly led him to overwork as well (how easy, after all, it was to "go under"!), just as it was his childhood association with the soiled life of the blacking factory which made him as a man so extraordinarily neat and so particularly clean. (How hard it must have been to remove the blacking from his nails and hands!) Even his penchant for bright clothes suggests the self-created man fashioning his own image of himself quite different from any past he might or might not possess. Dogmatism. Satire. Determination. Hardness. Energy. Persistence. Thoroughness. Inflexibility. That *driven* quality which others noticed in him – all of these qualities, although latent in the child, seem to have been released into active life by his time among "common men and boys". So it was, too, with his extraordinary concentration on food and drink in his fiction. "I . . .

had to win my food," he once wrote of his childhood, and that equation of food with protection and sustenance is one that never left him. To be fed and to be loved. Are these not the twin claims of the young boy moving through London, looking in the window of the pastry cook and remembering the affection, however slight, of the adults who pitied him? And in his later life, in his enormous appetite for applause, his boundless need for admiration, his continual desire for money, do we not see echoes of his childhood state, echoes of that need to be recompensed for the absence of love? John Forster noticed all these things; he describes Dickens's "too great confidence in himself . . . the tone of fierceness . . . his resolves insuperable", but he goes on to make a more general point about the strange amalgam of passivity and aggression, victim and conqueror, that establishes Dickens's relations with the world. An amalgam which he describes as "a stern and even cold isolation of self-reliance side by side with a susceptivity almost feminine and the most eager craving for sympathy . . ." And everything leads on, as it must, to his novels; in novels where he conquers his isolation and his fears by creating a community of love; where he can create his own world as a blessed alternative to the one which so threatened him. Here are some lines from *Nicholas Nickleby*:

> "There were hyacinths there this last spring, blossoming in – but you'll laugh at that, of course."
> "At what?"
> "At their blossoming in old blacking bottles."

And yet throughout the novels we are left not only with this celebration of Dickens's imaginative authority but also with the image of the child who still dwells somewhere within it. Insecure. Maltreated. Starved. Frail. Sickly. Oppressed. Guilty. Small. Orphaned. Of course there are healthy children to be found in his pages but, like the schoolchildren in *The Old Curiosity Shop*, they are merely players. *His* children are somehow separated from the world, forced to keep their distance. "'Has my dream come true?' exclaimed the child again, in a voice so fervent that it might have thrilled to the heart of any listener. 'But no, that can never be. How could it be – Oh! How could it!'"

I

BUT WHAT IF it were possible, after all, for Charles Dickens to enter one of his own novels? To bow his head and cross the threshold, into the world which he had created? And then to meet Little Dorrit with her companion, the simpleton Maggie, as they walked slowly away from London Bridge in the darkest reaches of the night. Dickens was coming upon them when he heard the cry of the disturbed woman to Little Dorrit, "I never should have touched you, but I thought that you were a child." Then the woman hurried away, brushing against the sleeve of Dickens's coat; she gave him an agonised, fearful glance as once more she hid within the dark margins of the novel.

He did not look back at her, because he knew where she was going. He walked on towards Little Dorrit and, as he approached her, she looked up at him in alarm. "Pray do not be frightened," he whispered. "At all costs do not be frightened. I mean you no possible harm."

The quietness of his voice comforted her. "It is so dark, sir. And London is so barren and so wild."

"Those are my own sentiments, I assure you . . ." He was about to add something else, some further reassurance, but he checked himself. "Shall we walk on a little?" He offered Maggie his arm which she took with great aplomb (he still felt constrained with Little Dorrit) and, with the child of the Marshalsea beside them, they retraced their steps towards London Bridge. They stopped for a moment and looked down at the dark water flowing beneath them. "You know," he said, "I have often stood here as a boy. Telling stories to the small maid who once lived with us. Stories of the past. Stories of the future."

"And did they all come true, sir?" Maggie asked. "Stories are meant to come true."

"Yes. They all came true." He looked at her curiously for a moment. "And I am telling stories still."

Little Dorrit was, for some reason she could not understand, particularly interested in this slender, middle-aged man in his tightly buttoned overcoat and shining stove-pipe hat. "Why did you come here, sir? Why did you come here as a child?"

"My father –". He stopped, almost out of habit. Then he smiled. "But I can tell you, if I can tell anyone in the world. My father was incarcerated in the prison close by here. In the Marshalsea."

The young woman clasped her hands together. "Can that really be true? For that is my story, too!"

"Yes," he said. "I know."

"How do you know?" Her enthusiasm faltered for a moment. "How do you know of us?"

He smiled and said nothing. "I will tell you something else, Little Dorrit. My father was released, and all was well." He hesitated, not sure whether he should go on. "Shall we walk down the High Street?" And as they passed down the narrow thoroughfare towards the Borough, he added, "Just as your father will be set free in good time. I am sure of it."

Little Dorrit drew Maggie nearer to her, as if she needed protection from the exhilaration of this unanticipated and welcome news. "Set free at last, sir? And you are so sure?"

"Quite certain. All will be revealed in good time."

Little Dorrit kept hold of Maggie, and it seemed as if it were the simpleton who was guiding her forward; for in truth she was now so lost in her inner vision of her father's freedom that she had no eyes for the reality around her. Then she looked up at Dickens, who was striding thoughtfully beside them. "Will you come and tell him this yourself, sir? He would be so glad. So glad."

"I am not . . . It is not the time."

"Please come."

Reluctantly he accompanied the two young women down Borough High Street towards the Marshalsea Prison. But this was not the street he knew in the outer world; this was a darker and narrower thoroughfare, the shadows deeper, the noises much clearer, the colours of the doors and shop-fronts under the round moon fuller and more distinct than anything in reality. The street seemed to go on forever, and Dickens had the curious sensation that there was nothing beyond it. The houses were smaller than anything he remembered, also, and from the open windows of one he recognised an odour of soap and beer and unwashed clothes that he had not sensed since infancy. And, as he walked past that window, he saw the silhouettes of various people crossing, recrossing, crossing again in front of a flaring oil-lamp.

In this last stretch of the night there were still men and women to be found loitering in doorways, too, whistling to one another, slinking down the many alleys which lead away from the High Street. There was an old man with a wooden leg, screaming "Where am I?" at a dwarf who followed a few paces behind him; there was a thick-set man with the inexpressibly weary but determined face of a transported convict; there was a young vagabond, wearing a cloth top-coat a size too large for him; and, most curiously of all, there was an old woman dressed entirely in white. Some of these men and women passed Dickens and, as they passed, smiled at him in recognition; he seemed to recollect them, also, but at this point he could not remember how or when he had first met them.

He was aroused from his reverie by Little Dorrit, who gently touched his arm.

"Here we are, sir. The house of my father. And of your

father." They were at the corner of Angel Place, an alley which branched left off the main thoroughfare, and the three strange companions walked down towards the very gate of the prison. "This is all as it was," Dickens murmured to himself as they approached the turnkey's lodging, "but, oh, how strangely altered. How much larger than I recall. How much darker and more permanent." He followed Little Dorrit's quick steps into the main courtyard, and was astonished to see her turning into the second entrance on the right. "This is the very staircase where my father's room was! It is the very same."

He followed her up the stairs, although he knew the worn stone so well that he might have been walking in some dream of the past. He turned around to wait for Maggie but, unaccountably, she had disappeared. "This is the gentleman," he heard Little Dorrit saying from behind a half-open door. "This is the gentleman who says you will be rescued, father."

He did not want to enter. Not yet. "I am greatly indebted to the gentleman, whoever he may be." He could hear the familiar voice of William Dorrit. "I am indebted in every sense, of course. But to be offered hope – this, to one who is so hopelessly immured . . ." He had been speaking in a loud voice, obviously addressing Charles Dickens who still remained outside the small room. There was no help for it: Dickens entered. William Dorrit bowed, and Dickens bowed in return. "My daughter, sir, has been conveying your sentiments on, shall we say, a delicate matter?"

Dickens did not know how to reply. You are very like my own father, he thought. Very like.

William Dorrit noticed the strange expression on Dickens's face, and reddened.

"Of course she may have misconstrued your meaning, sir. She is only a young woman. But you were talking of release?"

"I feel certain that your relief is at hand, sir. That is all

I meant. I have no special knowledge of your circumstances."

William Dorrit breathed heavily and turned to the small window which looked down onto the prison yard. But he was used to such disappointments and after a few moments he turned to face him. "As for my circumstances, sir, you can see them now." Instantly, almost unconsciously, he looked down at Dickens's pockets. "As for relief, sir, I am accustomed to small tokens. Small tokens of faith. Small signs, may I say it, of charity?" Dickens knew what he meant and delved into his overcoat for a guinea-piece. It was now Little Dorrit's turn to move to the window in order to hide her face, and for the rest of the interview that is where she remained. "This is most kind, sir." William Dorrit took the coin at once, and slipped it into the pocket of his threadbare waistcoat. "But you have probably gathered that I am not a materialist. No, by no means. One needs philosophy to endure here, sir. After all, we are the sport of fate. Of forces that we do not understand."

Dickens bowed. "That is true, sir."

At this moment some footsteps could be heard on the stone stairs, and Dickens assumed that Maggie was now at last making her way to them. But it was not her at all; into the small chamber rushed a young man, elegantly dressed and carrying a pair of lilac gloves in his left hand. "Sir," he said to William Dorrit. "I have come to congratulate you on your great expectations. My name is –".

"No!" Dickens shouted, as the room seemed to darken. "No! This place is not for you!"

The young man turned towards him. "I know you," he said. "I know you very well."

Dickens put out his hand to stop him from saying any more. "There is no room for you here. I must take you away from this place before it is too late."

He took the young man's arm and, much to William Dorrit's displeasure, seemed intent on leading him away. "There is no need to fear the taint of prison, sir. You are free to come and go as you wish." Clearly he had been hoping for some further "token" from the elegant young man. "The bell for visitors will not be rung for another hour at least."

"No," Dickens replied. "I must go at once. I must go before I am imprisoned in another sense." But the room was now completely dark, and he could see no one in front of him. He looked down, and he could not even see the outline of his own body. It was as if he were floating, floating in a dark place, waiting once more to be born.

Chapter 5

A ND so Charles Dickens left the blacking factory and, with it, the formative years of his childhood. Almost at once he was enrolled by his father at Wellington House Academy, a school only a short walk from their house in Johnson Street and one which had a good reputation in the neighbourhood. He was to remain for two years, and what is surprising about the record of his stay there is the extent to which he had changed from the passive, suffering "labouring hind" of only a few months before; all his contemporaries concur that he was lively, agreeable, high-spirited, healthy, and very clearly the "son of a gentleman". Dickens had, as it were, "come through" the experiences which had so secretly scarred him; he was in that sense self-created and already in the thirteen- and fourteen-year-old schoolboy we can discern the lineaments of the mature Dickens. The fact that he made the transition so successfully suggests how supple and yet how sturdy a temperament he possessed; he was not one to be bowed down by misfortune, but to use and to conquer each calamity as it arose. His own early impressions were no doubt more uncertain than this suggests – we have already described how the young David Copperfield sees his new schoolboy companions and wonders, "How would it affect them, who were so innocent of London life and London streets, to discover how knowing I was (and was ashamed to be) in some of the meanest phases of both?" The fear of David Copperfield is that some of his new companions might have once seen him in his earlier degraded working life but, only a few pages later, he recounts how he shook off his uneasiness at the same time as he increased his prowess both in his studies and in his games; how, in a very short while, his old embittered existence "became so strange to me that I hardly believed in it". This sounds like a true account but it is likely, also, that once Dickens had escaped from the anxiety inherent in his past – and his fear of the knowledge of it which others might possess – this childhood experience of the darker aspects of London was one that actually lent him a certain sense of power and of authority. He *knew* more than his companions, and this sense of having had a larger and deeper experience may well have been one that spurred him forward.

The school itself stood in the Hampstead Road, facing the fields of a large dairy farm (on his way from Johnson Street, Dickens's quickest route would have been a road alongside the fields), and was of a conventional kind. One large schoolroom, made of timber and holding something like two hundred boys with their "rough notched" forms arranged in rows; there was a modestly sized playground outside, with the house of the owner and headmaster just beside it. We must imagine the schoolroom divided by learning abilities rather than age, the boys conning their lessons by rote (an older boy often being deputed to teach the younger ones) amid the noise of voices, slate pencils, and quill pens being sharpened. Charles Dickens's own memories of this school are far from complimentary, and in a speech much later in life he declared that "the respected proprietor of which was by far the most ignorant man I have ever had the pleasure to know, who was one of the worst-tempered men perhaps that ever lived, whose business it was to make as much out of us and to put as little into us as possible . . ." In more fictionalised accounts, particularly in an essay entitled "Our School", Dickens adds more flesh to these bones of memory with a description of a headmaster who had a strange fondness for the cane, a timid usher (a sort of junior teacher) who was supposed "to know everything" and was "a bony, gentle-faced, clerical-looking young man in rusty black", a wan Latin master, a "fat little dancing master who used to come in a gig", and a morose serving man called Phil. The young narrator, in this account, distinguishes himself, and wins prizes. Of course it has to be remembered that Dickens characteristically attacked schools of all kinds, and there are times when it seems that he always bore a grudge against anyone who was ever set in authority over him, but his contemporaries have supported the general accuracy of his account. They confirm, for example, that the owner of the school was indeed a man of irascible temper, a Welshman named Jones, who was addicted to the caning of boys in tight trousers – "Ah! ah! had you there: you can't rub that off: you can't rub it off" has all the melancholy of a pupil's sober but vivid memory. There was a boy called Horne "known as Kiddy or Dandy because he appeared in a long-tailed coat", a boy called Jordan "who had the pluck to call out 'Shame! Shame!' when some act of brutality was committed", and Morgan, the natural son of a soap-boiler who spoke of a bench being 3 feet 16 inches long. There were also two boarders here, mulattoes whose parents lived in the East Indies; are these two raised up again in Dickens's memory as Neville and Helena Landless in *The Mystery of Edwin Drood*? Certainly, in the recollections of these quondam schoolfellows, an old generation emerges once more, in ducks, in coat-tails, in tall beaver hats, a generation long gone, in a culture long forgotten.

His contemporaries' recollections of Dickens himself are in some ways striking – "a healthy-looking boy, small but well built, with a more than usual flow of spirits . . . He usually held his head more erect than lads ordinarily do, and there was a general air of smartness about him." This erectness of posture and smartness of dress ring true because they were also the salient characteristics of Dickens in later life. Another description suggests that there was ". . . nothing heavy or dreamy about him . . . I never should have thought that he had been employed at humble work. He appeared always like a gentleman's son, rather aristocratic than otherwise." One gets some indication here of the direction the boy had taken, and the need he felt to distance himself from his "soiled" past. Another contemporary account has a similar air of authenticity: ". . . rather short, stout, jolly-looking youth, very fresh coloured, and full of fun, and given to laugh immoderately without any apparent sufficient reason." This apparently "immoderate" laughter is true to character, too – true to the character of this short but well-built boy who is prone to sudden acts of hysterical excitement. What is immediately noticeable is that there is no trace of the ill health which dogged him while he was at Warren's; in fact he emerges here as a very robust child indeed, a transformation which suggests that he had attained some kind of fulfilment or tranquillity in his new state of schoolboy. The general impression, as we shall discover, is of a child industrious, affectionate, ambitious to please, self-willed but, when being watched or judged, sometimes surprisingly awkward and anxious.

His training at the school does not seem to have been of any remarkable kind. "Depend on it," one contemporary wrote, "he was quite a self-made man." Which echoes John Dickens's remark that his son "may be said to have educated himself!" (a phrase which Dickens later liked to imitate in his father's own manner). And yet at Wellington House Academy Dickens was taught Latin, and seems to have distinguished himself enough to carry off the Latin prize one year; in return he gave his tutor a copy of Horace's verses. Other people have disputed Dickens's claim that he was taught the language, but on the evidence of his novels themselves there seems little doubt of it – indeed, at a much later date, he is to be found consulting the works of Virgil. He was also apparently taught the violin, according to an early biographer, "which study Dickens could by no means make progress in, and had to relinquish". Even if his knowledge of the English language was acquired, as one colleague remarked, "by long and patient study after leaving" it still seems that he already possessed more than the rudiments of his tongue; he astonished his school-fellows by being the only one able to spell theatre, a feat which suggests not only his own early attachment to that place of entertain-ment but also the woeful ignorance of his classmates. Certainly his own reading was of a varied if not always educational sort. From references in his later work it is clear that he was well acquainted with the intricacies of English grammar – Lindley Murray has already been noticed – as well as the knottiness of the Latin one. In addition he had a working knowledge of various school textbooks, among them Harris's *Scenes* of England, Europe, Asia, Africa and America, the flavour of which can be gathered in the full title of Harris's *Scenes of British Wealth in Produce and Manufacture for the Amusement and Instruction of the little Tarry-at-home Travellers*. But his favourite reading seems to have been a sixteen-page weekly, with close print and amateur wood-cuts, known as the *Terrific Register*. In later life he extolled its virtues for ". . . making myself unspeakably miserable, and frightening my very wits out of my head, for the small charge of a penny weekly; which, considering that there was an illustration to every number, in which there was always a pool of blood, and at least one body, was cheap." This fascinating compendium included accounts of plague and of cannibalism but the major emphasis was on the various details of such cruel and unusual punishments as immolation or disembowelling. The "headlines" tell the same story: "Horrible Murder of a Child", "Miserable Fate of a Female Slave", "A Most Extraordinary and Diabolical Murder". It might be noted that in one number of 1825 – precisely the time when Dickens was poring over it – there was a detailed account of an incident of spontaneous combustion. This was an effect Dickens was himself to employ with the death of Krook in *Bleak House*, and we may take what may be no more than a coinci-dence to evoke the popular context through which the young boy came to fiction and to melodrama. But, even if all the concerns of that period's more melodramatic fiction were in one way or another to be refracted through Dickens's own novels, it would be wrong to suggest that Dickens "inherited" the tradition of popular fiction or that his own works reflect it in some simple manner. This is clearly not the case. It should only be noted that Dickens could take the pre-occupations of the lowest form of periodical journalism and turn them into something much richer and stranger, but no less appealing to those who were educated upon the staple fare of the cheap popular prints.

Most of the memories of his time at school, however, concern not his academic or literary prowess but his "animation and animal spirits". He is remembered for having sung "The Cat's Meat Man" and entering "into all the vulgarity of the composition"; how touching, this, that the young boy still sang the songs he learnt at the time of his privation. Similarly he was remembered for improvising upon the "lingo" or the "gibberish" of the schoolboys, and for posing as a poor boy in order to beg from old ladies before whom he "would explode with laughter and take to his heels" – how strange that already he should begin mimicking the fate which only a few months before had in fact been his, although it is true that his ability to translate the events of his life into theatre was a natural and permanent gift. One of his first jokes is also remembered – one friend remarked that his trousers seemed well worn and that they needed a rest.

Dickens: "Ah yes! You are right, it *is* a long time since they had a *nap*."

These general high spirits seem to have been kept up everywhere; one day at church, according to a contemporary, "I am sorry to say Master Dickens did not attend in the slightest degree to the service, but incited me to laughter by declaring his dinner as ready and the potatoes would be spoiled, and in fact behaved in such a manner that it was lucky for us we were not ejected from the chapel". The school, perhaps, was not as severe as Dickens paints it, therefore; and indeed it had at least in one respect a pleasantly literary aspect. According to one of Dickens's first biographers, "Tales and plays were written, recited and performed, and the current works of fiction eagerly sought after and studied by 'a sort of club' consisting of some of the older boys". Dickens, with a friend named Bowden who sat beside him in the schoolroom, "used to write short stories on scraps of paper, pin them together, so as to form a book with a few leaves, and lend them to the other boys to read for the small charge of a piece of slate pencil". In addition he and the same friend began an occasional periodical entitled *Our Newspaper*, "lending it to read on payments of marbles and pieces of slate pencil". Bowden himself recollected that one of the "bits of fun" included:

"*Lost*. By a boy with a long red nose, and grey eyes, a very bad temper. Whoever has found the same may keep it, as the owner is better without it."

Dickens is also remembered for having made puns on "Peregrine" in the name of his friend, Owen Peregrine Thomas. These might conceivably be the later inventions of nostalgic adults, anxious to share some glory in their own memories of the great genius who grew up amongst them. But their veracity is a little more firmly established by the fact that, almost without exception, they state that at no time did the young Charles Dickens give any sign of the talent or genius which he was later to reveal. He was just another high-spirited and mischievous boy, the recorded jokes of whom seem authentic when they are compared with Dickens's first extant letter. This is to a schoolfellow, the same Owen Peregrine Thomas, and it rings the changes on the idea of a "Leg" or lexicon – "I am quite ashamed I have not returned your Leg but you shall have it by Harry to morrow. If you would like to purchase my Clavis you shall have it at a very *reduced price*. Cheaper in comparison than a Leg." This is followed by Dickens's signature, already with a slight hint of the "flourish" under his name which was to become his trademark. And there follows a postscript, on one of his favourite subjects – "I suppose all this time you have had a *wooden* leg. I have weighed yours every saturday Night."

The young Dickens was also remembered for his interest in the theatre and in amateur theatricals. It is recorded how with two schoolfriends he "used to act little plays in the kitchen" of a friend's house. One contemporary observed that ". . . he was very fond of theatricals. I have some recollection of his getting up a play at Dan Tobin's house, in the back kitchen . . . we made a plot, and each had his part; but the speeches every one was to make for himself". He was still adept with the toy theatre constructed for him by James Lamert at Bayham Street, and for that small but fiery stage he condensed such plays as *Cherry and Four Star* and *Elizabeth, or The Exiles of Siberia* – the latter being a book which Fanny had won as a prize at her musical academy, a *roman sentimental* describing the plaintive adventures of a young girl who journeys to Moscow to meet the Czar. It is not known what role Dickens himself played in this little romance but the nature of his interest is clear; these innocent plots with their heightened dialogue and strident effects, these "cut-outs" moved to and fro upon small rods, these small but perfectly detailed sets, are at the centre of Dickens's imaginative response to the world. It is not a theatre which encourages anything like psychological exploration or social realism, but these were not matters that ever moved Dickens; he was entranced by the bright surfaces and the powerful stories, the vivid unnatural colours and the shuffling movement of the cardboard creations.

Particularly he enjoyed watching *The Miller and His Men*, in which robbers pose as millers and where there is a climactic scene at the end when the mill is blown up (in his own small theatre, this effect was achieved by the judicious use of crackers among the stage machinery). In later life he knew the scenario by heart, and in his published work often alluded to the most famous phrases from it. This dialogue with Percy Fitzgerald, much later in life, suggests how much he appreciated it:

Dickens (seeing Percy Fitzgerald carrying a parcel): What! More sacks to the mill!

Fitzgerald: Oh yes, and you know when the wind blows, then the mill goes.

Dickens: Oh Lord bless me! Do you know *The Miller and His Men*?

This vignette is narrated by Fitzgerald himself but Dickens's exclamation – "Oh Lord bless me" – was certainly typical of him. The whole anecdote itself suggests a truth about Dickens which Fitzgerald himself understood: "He delighted in calling back all his youthful pictures, which seemed to him more dramatic and suggestive than the more brilliant business of actual life." In fact he and Fitzgerald attended a revival of *The Miller and His Men* but, alas, actual life even took its toll upon childhood memories; the play was not a success and Dickens, announcing that he "could stand it no longer", left during the second act. He soon cheered up, however, and later that same night was to be heard with Fitzgerald singing old songs. And there, in the still jovial and somehow innocent man, we see the jovial schoolboy – taking the parts of a play in a friend's back kitchen, laughing immoderately, mimicking the gait and actions of poor children as he went home by the fields of Somers Town.

He stayed at Wellington House Academy for only two years, once again his father's wastrel habits confounding his son's ambitions. The point was that, despite his pension from the Pay Office and the strong possibility that he was already working as a journalist, John Dickens's means did not encompass his ends. Some debts were still being taken directly from his pension, and sums had to be disgorged to his debtors in both 1825 and 1826; as a result he was in arrears with the payment of his daughter's fees to the Royal Academy of Music. In October 1825 there was an outstanding debt almost equal to the amount of the next quarter's fees and he wrote a letter to the administrators explaining that "a circumstance of great moment to me will be decided in the ensuing term which I confidently hope will place me in comparative affluence . . .", these rolling words being precisely the sound which his son so carefully adopted and parodied. Then seven months later, "comparative affluence" having eluded him once again, he asked to pay off his debt in monthly instalments. Then yet again he failed even to maintain this modest hope, so in June 1827 Fanny was compelled to leave the Royal Academy – and this after some notable successes, not least being asked to perform at a benefit for J. P. Harley, an eminent musician who was later to play an important role in her brother's life. But John Dickens's chronic indebtedness must have affected other members of his family as well; the fact that one of Dickens's school-friends described Elizabeth Dickens as "a delicate-looking woman" may signify some of the strain under which she laboured.

But it cannot be said that John Dickens was a lazy man, even though he was an improvident one. At some point in this period – and the likelihood is that it was very soon after his retirement from Somerset House – he began what was for him a new career as a journalist. He was employed by *The British Press*, both as a parliamentary reporter and also as a contributor of articles on the subject of marine insurance. He was now entering his forties, and it is a sign of his undaunted spirit that he should so quickly embark upon a quite new career; if, as seems probable, he also undertook to learn the difficult art of shorthand then his application and industry have to be admired. J. P. Collier, who was working for *The British Press* at this time, suggested that John Dickens was "a gentleman of no great intellectual capacity", but Charles Dickens himself said that he was "a first-rate shorthand writer on Gurney's system, and a capital reporter . . ." In the latter role he had already had a certain amount of practice – he had described the fire at Chatham for *The Times* – but evidence of his journalistic skills is no longer at hand. The only articles of his which can be identified with any certainty are those on the subject of marine insurance when, in a prose as fulsome as it is precise, he extols the claims of Lloyds over competing agencies. There is a statement from Collier that Charles Dickens himself was a contributor to the paper – "Now and then there came to the office a smart, intelligent, active lad who brought what was then called 'penny-a-line' stuff: that is to say, notices of accidents, fires, police reports, such as escaped the more regular reporters, for which a penny a printed line was paid". Penny-a-line journalism was an accepted staple of the public prints (". . . a good murder is a great godsend . . ."), and it is not inconceivable that the fourteen-year-old schoolboy, who had already written scraps for *Our Newspaper* and various character sketches of his own, might not find such casual work great fun. And of course it does at once suggest that attachment to journalism which Dickens was to maintain for the rest of his life; it should never be forgotten that, although he used topical events in his fiction with the same symbolic power as Shakespeare adopted North's translations, his actual and prosaic links with popular journalism were strong and continuous.

The particular link with *The British Press* could not have lasted long, however, since the newspaper collapsed in October 1826. John Dickens then took the not unusual step of applying for money from the firm, Lloyds, which he had championed in print; they responded by giving him ten guineas. But such small sums were not enough to avoid a further visitation of financial chaos; a few months later the family were evicted from their house in Johnson Street, and took lodgings just around the corner at The Polygon in Clarendon Square, so named because it consisted of five blocks facing inwards with their courts and gardens running into a central point. This was in fact a more "respectable" area than Johnson Street, and it is unlikely that temporary lodgers of the Dickens sort were entirely welcome. Nine or ten months later the family had returned to Johnson Street, however, whether in a midnight sortie, through a composition with the rating authorities, or by a technique which later became known in this same area as "Home Rule" (possession being nine tenths, etc.), is not clear. In fact these have been called Charles Dickens's "silent years" and certainly one of the aspects of Dickens's adolescent life which can never now be recovered consists of those slights or indignities to which he must necessarily have been subject, and which in a young man of his sensitive disposition must have rankled.

In the short term, John Dickens's financial failure meant that his son had to be removed from Wellington House Academy; he was now fifteen and had, as he said in a letter some years later, "to begin the world". His two years of schooling were over but, curiously enough, there is no sign or sense that he resented this abrupt removal from a standard middle-class education. Perhaps he really did wish to "begin the world" and held the belief which David Copperfield possessed at a similar juncture ". . . that life was more like a great fairy story, which I was just about to begin to read, than anything else". Certainly he seems never to have regretted not attending a university and, if further proof were needed, perhaps it lies in the fact that he showed no great inclination for his own children to do so – he seems to have preferred that they left school young and went into "business" or some allied worldly pursuit.

The "business" in which Charles Dickens now made his way was the law. His parents, and once again particularly his mother, made the first move. Elizabeth Dickens was the niece of a certain Mrs Charlton, who kept a boarding house in Berners Street. One of her lodgers here was a young lawyer, Edward Blackmore, to whom Mrs Dickens was introduced. Blackmore explained what happened: "His mother expressed a great wish to get him employment in my office, and the boy's manners were so prepossessing that I agreed to take him as a clerk . . ." He was also, Blackmore says, ". . . extremely good-looking and clever". And so in May 1827 Charles Dickens began the world as a junior clerk in the office of Ellis and Blackmore, "a poor old set of chambers of three rooms" in Holborn Court, at a starting salary of 10/6 a week eventually rising to fifteen shillings. The firm moved at the end of the year to Raymond Buildings, a short walk away; it was on the second floor, and it seems that the young Dickens used to amuse himself here by dropping cherry stones on the hats of passers-by, confronting any complainant "with so much gravity and with such an air of innocence, that they went away . . ."

It was not necessarily very hard work, therefore, but it was clearly very dull. It was by no means an exalted position; John Dickens did not have the means to enrol his son as an articled clerk and instead Dickens was a "writing clerk", which was really only the glorified equivalent of an office boy with very few prospects of promotion beyond the level of a salaried clerk. His duties would have included the copying of documents, administering the registration of wills and visiting on errands the various lawyers' offices and courts of law; in Dickens's fiction the law is always a place of barren mystery and labyrinthine ways, and there is no doubt that something of its intricacy and its sterility were impressed upon him as he trudged to and fro between such public offices as the Alienation Office, the Sixpenny Receivers Office, the Prothonotaries Office, the Clerk of the Escheats, the Dispensation Office, the Affidavit Office, the Filazer's, Exigenter's and Clerk of the Outlawry's Office, the Hanaper Office and the Six-Clerk's Office. But he never undertook anything without wishing to surpass in it: there are notations of his in the petty cash book, and they show how carefully he tried to attain a proper standard of legal penmanship with a neat and legible hand.

His first day at work was not altogether a success, however. He had turned up in what was undoubtedly a brand new uniform – a blue jacket and a "military-looking cap which had a strap under the chin". He was, as his schoolfriends had noticed, small but of a nervously erect bearing and, in addition, he carried this cap "rather jauntily on one side of his head". Just the young man to attract attention, therefore. He had been sent upon an errand down Chancery Lane, only a minute or so from the office, but when he returned he was bearing a black eye. Dickens explained to a fellow clerk that "a big blackguard fellow knocked my cap off as I was crossing over Chancery Lane . . . He said 'Halloa, sojer' which I could not stand, so I at once struck him and he then hit me in the eye." There is no reason to doubt this story, emanating from two separate contemporaries, and at once it does illustrate what became in Dickens's later life his enormous suscepti-bility to slights, whether real or imagined. Once again we see the man in the boy, just as we will, later, see the boy in the man.

The blue jacket and military cap were a concession to the fashion of the period, and there is no doubt that the young Dickens wished to "keep up appearances" just as he had done at Wellington House Academy; all traces of the poor boy at Warren's had been removed and one legal companion explains how "he looked very clean and well fed and cared for . . ." He also possessed that "dapper smartness, strug-gling through very limited means" which, in a pamphlet, he once characterised as the birthright of a junior clerk. A fellow clerk, George Lear, describes him thus: "His appearance was altogether prepossess-ing. He was a rather short but stout-built boy, and carried himself very upright – and the idea he gave me was that he must have been drilled by a military instructor." The only instructor who ever drilled him was his own sense of himself, however, and he held himself erect in order to make himself look taller or more dignified; his height was about five feet nine inches, small enough to surprise some of his admirers when they first met him. And in that military bearing one hears an echo of Henry James when he saw the great Charles Dickens towards the end of his life and noticed "a straight inscrutability, a merciless *military* eye, I might have pronounced it, an automatic hardness . . ." Here is someone, it seems, who always understood the "battle of life".

But to return to the young law recruit: "He wore a frock-coat buttoned up, of dark blue cloth, trousers to match, and . . . buttoned with leather straps over the boots; black neckerchief, but no shirt collar showing. His complexion was of a healthy pink – almost glowing – rather a round face, fine forehead, beautiful expressive eyes full of animation, a firmly-set mouth, a good-sized rather straight nose . . . His hair was a beautiful brown, and worn long, as was then the fashion . . . His appearance was altogether decidedly military." And once again is noticed that "military" air in a good-looking youth with expressive eyes and long brown hair – the latter part of the description suggesting an almost feminine aspect to him upon which other contemporaries remarked over the years, but which was firmly kept in check by his "hardness" and by his highly disciplined demeanour. Perhaps it is also worth mentioning here that this same observer, George Lear, believed Charles Dickens "much resembled his father".

He was, it seems, a "universal favourite" at Ellis and Blackmore. For one thing he was that great comic relief in any office, a good "mimic". There was an old laundress in Holborn Court – a particular type of dirty, snuff-taking servant at which Dickens was later to excel in his fiction – and Dickens "took great interest in her and would mimic her manner of speech, her ways, her excuses etc to the very life". He had seen her, understood her, had perhaps even been drawn to her by what he later called the "attraction of repulsion", and reproduced her in his own person – only clever people become good mimics, because the primary act is one of understanding and empathy, a kind of helpless abnegation of one's own character in favour of that which has supplanted it. So it was that in this period "Dickens could imitate, in a manner that I have never heard equalled, the low population of the streets of London in all their varieties, whether mere loafers or sellers of fruit, vegetables, or anything else". As the "labouring hind" wandering through the streets behind Warren's or beside the Marshalsea, he had seen everything and missed nothing; with that quick, bright, humorous glance which was so characteristic of him. In the process, of course, he had come to know London very well. "His knowledge of London was wonderful," his employer reported, "for he could describe the position of every shop in any of the West End streets." Again evidence of that remarkable visual memory which was to be of such importance in the unfolding of his genius. "Having been in London for two years," George Lear recollected, "I thought I knew something of town, but after a little talk with Dickens I found that I knew nothing. He knew it all from Bow to Brentford." And this is of central importance to any understanding of Dickens: there were plenty of mimics in early nineteenth-century London, plenty of office-boys with an intimate acquaintance with London, but somehow stirring within the imagination of Dickens was a vision which would encompass all of his gifts. His was a much more intimate, almost obsessive, knowledge, one born in secrecy and in "low" company but enlarged by his own good humour and extended by his own energetic curiosity about the city which had at first so overwhelmed him. Everything was working towards one end – the time, not so many years ahead, when Dickens even as a young man would emerge as the chronicler *non pareil* of that peculiar urban civilisation which was only then growing up. In his signature in the cashbooks of the office of Ellis and Blackmore, one sees the characteristic flourish under his name which already suggests the inscription of someone who believes himself to be set apart. Even as he worked in the dingy chambers he was still watching, and learning. Observing, for example, how at the beginning of each day, as he was to put it in *The Pickwick Papers*, "Clerk after clerk hastened into the square by one or other of the entrances, and looking up at the Hall clock, accelerated or decreased his rate of walking according to the time at which his office hours nominally commenced; the half past nine o'clock people suddenly becoming very brisk, and the ten o'clock gentlemen falling into a pace of most aristocratic slowness."

Of course the law itself appears in many of his novels, even if its entry is sometimes by humble means. In the petty cash book of Ellis and Blackmore there are such names as Weller, Mrs Bardell, Corney, Rudge and Newman Knott – all names which he would use, one way or another, in his later work. Newman Knott, according to a colleague, was a man "whose eccentricities and personal history were a source of great amusement to the clerks", and he was popularly supposed to be the real antecedent of Newman Noggs in *Nicholas Nickleby*; apparently there was also in this period a Little Old Lady of the Court of Chancery upon whom Miss Flite was later based. But such derivations have to be taken very cautiously – there is no doubt that on many occasions Dickens used certain salient characteristics of the people whom he met or knew, but there are very few instances when he simply transcribed what he had seen and heard onto the page. The novelist's art is not of that kind: Dickens perceived a striking characteristic, or mood, or piece of behaviour, and then in his imagination proceeded to elaborate upon it until the "character" bears only a passing resemblance to the real person. In his fiction Dickens entered a world of words which has its own procedures and connections, so that the original "being" of any individual is subsumed into something much larger and generally much more conclusive.

In fact the only passages where comparisons or associations can be drawn with even the remotest conviction are to be found in Dickens's own journalistic "memories" of the period; when, for example, in an early sketch entitled "Making A Night Of It", he creates a certain clerk known as Robert Smithers who bears some resemblance to Dickens's idea of himself at that period. "There was a spice of romance in Mr Smithers's disposition, a ray of poetry, a gleam of misery, a sort of consciousness of he didn't exactly know what, coming across him he didn't know precisely why . . ." His friend in the sketch is Thomas Potter, and there was indeed a Potter in the office of Ellis and Blackmore – it is this Potter who in real life is supposed to have uttered the immortal line about his hangover, *"It was the salmon"*, which Dickens later placed in the mouth of another in *The Pickwick Papers*. That first novel, too, bears traces of Dickens's own association with Ellis and Blackmore, for in his descriptions of the law clerks there are intimations of his life and attitudes at this time – at least in "the office lads in their first surtouts, who feel a befitting contempt for boys at day schools, club as they go home at night, for saveloys and porter, and think there's nothing like 'life'". Toiling amongst these sprigs is the salaried clerk who is dressed in "dirty caricature of the fashion, which expired six months ago" and the middle-aged copying-clerk "who is always shabby, and often drunk". It is worth considering, however, that, in this middle-aged copying-clerk, the young Dickens would have seen the very image of the fate awaiting him if he remained in the law. These are relatively sympathetic portraits, but there is no doubt that Dickens carried hatred enough for all forms of the law itself – specifically for those who are in charge of the law's arrangements, who live by it and who die by it. There is only one good judge in the whole of Dickens's work, few good solicitors, and really nothing but loud-mouthed barristers. It is possible that Dickens actually was savage about these people largely because he had once been employed by them: both as a young man and an eminent author, he always managed to disparage anyone who held, or had once held, any kind of moral or financial authority over him. He could not bear to be anything other than at "the top" and was generally hostile towards anyone who impeded his progress or who once tried to browbeat or humiliate him; preachers, teachers, lawyers are all pilloried in his writings with a vindictiveness which often far outstrips any possible cause.

There were compensations, however, in a life which ahead of him promised nothing but unrelieved drudgery. There was the theatre. He was, as his employer noted, "very fond of theatricals" and some years later Dickens recalled that "I went to some theatre every night, with a very few exceptions, for at least three years: really studying the bills first, and going to see where there was the best acting . . . I practised immensely (even such things as walking in and out, and sitting down in a chair) . . ." He is talking about a period just a little later than his days at Ellis and Blackmore, although even in these early years he was a keen and frequent attender at all forms of dramatic entertainment. Certainly his time outside the office was largely taken up by theatrical outings; Blackmore again remembers that Dickens and Lear "took every opportunity, then unknown to me, of going together to a minor theatre . . ." On Lear's own account they sometimes went to a small theatre in Catherine Street to see their colleague, Potter, in one part or another (this was a period in which aspiring players paid to take on roles in the smaller theatres), but the extent and variety of Dickens's acquaintance with the stage are emphasised in another recollection of his companion: "He could also excel in mimicking the popular singers of that day, whether comic or patriotic; as to his acting he could give us Shakespeare by the ten minutes, and imitate all the leading actors of that time." In later life, as we shall see, he went to some trouble to become acquainted with the leading actors of the period, and himself carved out something of a career as an amateur player, but the roots of these activities are to be seen in his adolescent enthusiasm.

Such enthusiasm was by no means uncommon, of course, since the theatre was the main staple of popular entertainment and popular performance. The kind of plays Dickens watched were not necessarily of the first rank, therefore – Gothic · melodrama, corrupted

Shakespeare, sentimental comedy, domestic farce, romantic drama, burletta, extravaganza, the whole gamut of early nineteenth-century drama in which sentimentality was matched only by grotesquerie, pathos by sensationalism. The theatres themselves were not attractive; gas-lighting was very unusual still, and most of the establishments which Dickens and his friends attended were lit only by candles or oil-lamps (the candles stayed alight during the performance). They would have entered the pit, which was filled with wooden backless benches, and become part of an audience which was often willing to spend many hours in the theatre, remaining intent on the performance or talking cheerfully to each other at moments of low tension. Blackmore's own hint of slight disapproval at these outings of his employees ("then unknown to me") would have been quite in keeping with his sense of himself and his dignified profession, since most of the smaller theatres were known to be resorts of prostitutes – the audiences themselves possessing, according to a famous German observer, "unheard of roughness and coarseness . . . the noise and mischief so incessant that it is difficult to understand how such distinguished artists can perform at all with so brutal, indifferent and ignorant an audience". Here, as in so many other areas of the early nineteenth-century, we feel the presence of the more strident and more "vulgar" life of the previous century. Of the small theatres known as "penny gaffs" we learn this, for example, from Henry Mayhew: ". . . shops which had been turned into a kind of temporary theatre (one penny admission) where dancing and singing take place every night. Rude pictures of the performances arranged outside . . . children often attending scenes of debauchery and immorality . . . women, girls and boys bringing an overpowering stench with them . . ." Mayhew is here writing of the late 1840s but the fact that such scenes should stretch well into the century suggests how much more vivid and brutal and "obscene" London life could be – at least when it is compared to the stereotypical images of Victorian "decorum" and "propriety" which twentieth-century writers like Lytton Strachey did as much to manufacture as to pillory. And yet, although Dickens often attacks the brutish audiences of the period, it is clear that the theatrical experience was for him one whose power overrode any other considerations. Thus, when David Copperfield sees a pantomime at the age of seventeen, ". . . it was, in a manner, like a shining transparency, through which I saw my earlier life moving along" and the young Copperfield is most effectively swayed by ". . . the poetry, the lights, the music, the company, the smooth stupendous changes of glittering and brilliant scenery".

It is a moot point whether the young Dickens himself acted in any of the minor theatres, although most of the evidence suggests that at some point in this period as a clerk he may well have put at least a tentative foot upon the boards. Many years later he told John Forster that he had once played the character of Flexible in a now forgotten drama entitled *Love, Law and Physic*, and George Lear records that "he told me he had often taken part in amateur theatricals before he came to us". He may have been referring here to private family gatherings, but a school-friend does state that "at about the age of fourteen Dickens took parts at the small playhouse in Catherine Street". This was the Minor Theatre where Lear and Dickens went to see Potter attempt his own parts but, since the charge for playing such roles as Othello was then approximately fifteen shillings, it is unlikely that the schoolboy Dickens could afford such sums even if he had the ambition to take the largest parts: he may have been one of those who attend a scene or two, and in later years was quite happy to forget the fact. Hence the paucity of references.

It does not make it any the less surprising, however, that in one of his early journalistic sketches, "Private Theatres", he should attack these small-time actors and their audiences for "lamentable ignorance and boobyism" as well as for their "imbecility" – the principal patrons of such places being, as far as Dickens was concerned, "dirty boys" and "low copying-clerks in attorneys' offices". Yet the fact that he had been just such a clerk, attending just such theatres, may in some way account for the asperity of his remarks; Dickens was often at his best when he attacked those vices or failings of which he himself was guilty, and there is in these comments a strange amalgam of forgetfulness about his own past and a fierce assault upon it which will come to be characteristic of his adult manner. He wrote such things when he had left the narrow boundaries of his adolescent self behind and in some spirit of strange revenge wished to attack those boundaries, even though it also means that he was indirectly attacking his own adolescence. As he was himself to say later, people's ". . . snarling at the little pleasures they were once glad to enjoy, because they would rather forget the times when they were of lower station, renders them objects of contempt and ridicule". It is not clear here, or on other occasions, whether Dickens's self-knowledge or self-forgetfulness is most in evidence. What is clear, however, is that while he remained as the copying clerk in an attorney's office, the stage – and a possible career on the stage – offered him both the best hope of release from drudgery and the only palliative to it.

In fact he stayed with Ellis and Blackmore for approximately eighteen months, during which time, it seems, "he grew so very much"; this from George Lear, who goes on to say, "I remember his having a new suit of clothes, brown all alike, coat cut like a dress coat, and with a high hat: he seemed to grow into a young man at once." After he left Ellis and Blackmore in November 1838 he spent a brief period in similar employment at the office of Charles Molloy – it seems that he moved here on the recommendation of another clerk, a certain Thomas Mitton, who knew Dickens well. The origins of their friendship remain unclear, the general presumption being that Mitton attended Wellington House Academy; certainly on one occasion Dickens described him as an old school-friend. Mitton's sister, Mary Ann Cooper, later recalled in vivid detail the relationship between the two young men – how Dickens had a habit of giving a nickname to all of his acquaintances (one might see this as another way of drawing them into a fictional world of his own devising), how he took her to various city haunts, how he told Thomas Mitton, "I can't stand this law work, Tom." None of this sounds entirely convincing – the memories of old ladies are notoriously inaccurate, especially when it comes to chronicling their relationship with the illustrious dead – but it is true enough that Dickens and Mitton did strike up a friendship which, with various lapses, was to last until Dickens's death. Mitton was eventually to practise as a solicitor, and in his early years Dickens often consulted him at times of trouble or on matters of business. In middle age they saw less of each other, and Dickens's affairs were handled by another solicitor; it is certain, too, that some of Dickens's friends did not care very much for Mitton, and Georgina Hogarth, the novelist's sister-in-law, went so far as to call him "odious". But the salient fact is that Dickens remained close to one of his first friends for over thirty years, and this during a period when he became the most famous novelist on earth while Mitton remained a provincial solicitor. If it says nothing else, it testifies at least to Dickens's passion for maintaining friendship, part of that general appetite within him for conviviality, for the warmth of the small circle around the hearth.

He did not stay long in the office of Charles Molloy, however, even with Mitton for company. His previous employer, Blackmore, assumed that Dickens did not continue with his legal life because of its "drudgery" and Dickens later told Wilkie Collins that he "didn't much like it". This seems fair enough, but it is not simply a case of weariness or boredom. Dickens was and remained a most ambitious person – how could he, who had already suffered so much and proved to himself that he could rise above such suffering, how could he endure the life of a "writing clerk"? In fact, even while he was with Ellis and Blackmore he was planning a new career. He was learning shorthand, and this specifically to become a reporter in the press gallery of the House of Commons. This may not appear to be a particularly exalted position but, in that period, it was a well-established commencement for many great careers and, in addition, it was the best-paid work then available for a stenographer. And so he set to work to master a system which, on average, took a person of moderate capacity some three years to learn. Dickens seems to have managed it in almost as many months. He taught himself the Gurney method (no doubt persuaded to do so by his father or even by his uncle, who had both gone through the same tuition) and while teaching himself what he called "a very difficult art" he was "walking miles every day to practise it all day long in the Courts of Law". The best general description of the process comes again from *David Copperfield*. The arduousness and length of the task ahead of him only serve to fuel Copperfield's determination – he went, "axe in hand", to work his way forward. The metaphor changes a few pages later: "It was one of the irons I began to heat immediately, and one of the irons I kept hot, and hammered at, with a perseverance I may honestly admire." Perseverance was certainly necessary since the acquisition of shorthand skills is a painful and frustrating business at the best of times, what with its dots and lines and circles and squiggles and "marks like flies' legs".

In *David Copperfield*, his surrogate parents dictate parliamentary speeches to the young hero in order that he might acquire the skill not only to write, but also to re-read what he had written, and there may here be an echo of occasions when Mr and Mrs Dickens took part in mock debates in order to help their son. Eventually, and swiftly, Dickens mastered it – to such an extent that a few years later he was generally credited with being the best shorthand reporter in Parliament. Whatever he did, he did extremely well; this in itself, as much as anything else, is a mark of his especial genius. But this is to move ahead a little; all that needs to be said at this juncture is what David Copperfield says of himself: "I will only add, to what I have already written of my perseverance at this time of my life, and of a patient and continuous energy which then began to be matured within me, and which I know to be the strong part of my character, if it have any strength at all, that there, on looking back, I find the source of my success." David Copperfield then proceeds to extol the virtues of "punctuality, order, and diligence" which Dickens himself emphasised throughout his life as the first and most solid foundation for any kind of enterprise. "My meaning simply is, that whatever I have tried to do in life, I have tried with all my heart to do well; that whatever I have devoted myself to, I have devoted myself to completely; that, in great aims and in small, I have always been thoroughly in earnest." This statement from *David Copperfield* contains Dickens's own creed, and there is no doubt that his belief in the virtues of perseverance, endurance and hard work stem from these formative years when he was beginning to make his way in the world. They were maxims which he applied to all of his activities – even his writing of fiction seems to come from the same potent combination of determination and hard work, enormous ability and almost phenomenal energy, as if his very novels were a task which had to be conquered in the same way as he had once conquered shorthand. And there is also another aspect to this settled determination to master such skills: Dickens always liked to achieve that which other people considered to be impossible.

There were other advantages which accrued to the study of shorthand, even if they were ones which he might not then have fully valued. His use of phonetic spelling, and the graphic embodiment of speech which is a part of shorthand, led him to listen very carefully to the sounds of words; and, once he had distinguished them, to put them down very quickly and with absolute accuracy upon paper. It is often said that his transcripts of Cockney or American speech are to a certain extent exaggerated, but in almost all instances one finds Dickens noting down very exactly the phonetic variants of local demotic. Shorthand also taught him literal "short" cuts in the transition from speech to writing, so that something of the freedom and spontaneity of speech is retained within his own prose. That is also why his novels are never harmed by being read aloud – Dickens himself was eventually to make another career out of doing so – since the elements of sound and speech are as intrinsic to them as the more literary virtues which critics have uncovered. It was a skill which Dickens never lost: when he dictated letters to a secretary he would often make the same movements as if he were himself taking it down in shorthand, and an old colleague, George Dolby, noticed that when Dickens was interested in a speech being delivered he would "follow the speaker's words by an almost imperceptible action, as if taking down the speech in shorthand".

It was with these skills that Dickens now wanted to start a new career, working for himself as a freelance transcriber, and there is a passage in *Martin Chuzzlewit* which may plausibly be taken as a commentary upon his state of mind: "He had his moments of depression and anxiety, and they were, with good reason, pretty numerous; but still, it was wonderfully pleasant to reflect that he was his own master, and could plan and scheme for himself. It was startling, thrilling, vast, difficult to understand; it was a stupendous truth, teeming with responsibility and self-distrust . . ." And so it was. Dickens had wanted to enter the parliamentary press gallery, like his father and uncle before him, but either there were no vacancies or his lack of experience momentarily told against him. So he resolved to gain experience elsewhere, and at some time in the spring of 1829 – in his eighteenth year – he enrolled at Doctors' Commons.

It was not a place which in itself encouraged ambition, just two quadrangles with their main entrance in Knightrider Street south of St Paul's Cathedral, with the paved stone and red-brick buildings which in the secluded recesses of the City harboured nothing but somnolence, stunted trees and dusty sparrows (there are some such places left still, although Doctors' Commons itself is long gone). Here were a series of courts which were convened in the same Hall and which, for a variety of reasons, took for their jurisdiction both ecclesiastical and naval matters. A Consistory Court, a Court of Arches, the Prerogative Court, the Delegates Court and the Admiralty Court; in his later fiction Dickens used the tangled legal system to mirror the confusions of the world, and there is no doubt that his experience as a young man, caught up in a system of which the absurdity was palpable, helped to strengthen this sense of life as convoluted, indeterminate, capable of infinite complexity and procrastination. ". . . always a very pleasant profitable little affair of private theatricals", as Steerforth says in *David Copperfield*, "presented to an uncommonly select audience".

For the first few months, it seems, Charles Dickens was hired by one particular firm of proctors – "very self-important-looking personages" Dickens called them in a later sketch – to take notes on evidence and on judgments (there is the legend of the stool he sat upon, one of the material props which always seem to haunt the reputations of the great). But it was not long before he established himself as an independent shorthand reporter; he rented a reporter's box in the Court itself, and also shared the costs of a probate office or transcribing room in Bell Yard nearby. He even had a business card engraved to give definite announcement of his independent status: "Mr Charles Dickens / Short Hand Writer / 10 Norfolk Street, Fitzroy Square". This latter address was the first in a series to which the Dickens family would move over the next few years, each one in turn seeming to be a way to escape the attentions of creditors. This, beside other matters, suggests that it may not have been a particularly happy time for Dickens: in particular, his work itself involved what was for him the tedious task of keeping records of the court proceedings in shorthand and then transcribing them in longhand. One such transcript, in Dickens's rather elaborate writing, has been preserved; it concerns two judgments "relative to a disturbance in the vestry room of St Bartholomew the Great", and is memoralised as Jarman *v* Bagster, the case being heard on 18 November, 1830. It is a long transcript, and would have required some four or five hours to complete; an expert who examined it many years later declared that the manuscripts "by reason of their slipshod production, convince me that they are the original work of a young shorthand writer, with no long experience behind him . . ." In a later and rather virulent sketch of Doctors' Commons, Dickens uses this squabble in the vestry as the crowning absurdity of an absurd system but he does, indirectly, provide some extenuation for his own apparent difficulties as a transcriber. Where the shorthand expert proclaims Dickens sometimes "uncertain here and there", it is also the case that the judge in Dickens's sketch "spoke very fast"; and, when the shorthand expert suggests that "here and there, he might have misheard", Dickens tells us that the judge also spoke "rather thick". In this sketch the more racy sentences of the accused – "You be blowed" – are placed against the more orotund prolixity of the bewigged gentlemen, thus suggesting once more how closely Dickens had familiarised himself with the speech patterns and the vocabulary of both "high" and "low". They were to be an important element within his novels, too.

It was arduous and monotonous work. "It wasn't a very good living (though not a *very* bad one)," he wrote later, "and was wearily uncertain . . .". It is the precariousness of it which lingers in his memory, then, and indeed the post of a freelance shorthand writer, so dependent upon the patronage of proctors or upon sudden commissions, would not necessarily have appealed to anyone as sensitive and anxious as the young Dickens seems to have been. We must imagine a young man, already aware of the powers latent within him but still living with his family in difficult circumstances, walking each day through the City to his tedious work. ". . . I could settle down into a state of equable low spirits," his hero David Copperfield says, "and resign myself to coffee; which I seem, on looking back, to have taken by the gallon . . ." The general impression of Dickens in these "silent years", the period of incubation (you might say) between his eventful childhood and his no less eventful maturity, is of someone both ambitious and purposeful but as yet uncertain in which direction his ambitions were to be driven.

That he had some stake in some undefined future is clear enough from the energy with which he pursued multifarious activities; it seems likely that while he was at Doctors' Commons he did part-time shorthand work in the parliamentary gallery, and there is no doubt that he still harboured theatrical ambitions. This was the period, after all, in which he assiduously practised his exits and his entrances, finding out from approved models such as the comic Charles Mathews how to do such apparently simple theatrical tricks as sitting upon a chair. But even as he was preparing for a possible career upon the stage he was also engaged in more literary pursuits – in February 1830 he obtained a reader's card to the British Museum, and in the library there he began a course of voracious reading. Among the books he ordered, and for which the call slips are preserved, were the works of Addison and Goldsmith as well as *The Dance of Death* painted by Holbein and engraved by Hollar. He had already known this particular volume in his childhood, and the fact that he ordered it especially here testifies to his perhaps somewhat obsessive interest in the subject. (It ought always to be remembered that, in all the later accounts of Dickens's high spirits and vivacity, there was a lurking morbidity, a fascination with death and disaster, which he barely managed to keep in check.) It seems that, in addition to his reading in the British Museum, he joined a circulating library at 24 Fetter Lane which was kept by a printer and curio-dealer, a certain Mr Haines. A peculiar place, this, filled with ancient silver, foxed engravings, cracked paintings, old china and a supply of books to be borrowed at a small price. It is not hard to see the young Dickens mooning around such an establishment, seeing in those books the promise of immortality but observing in the old broken curios the wreckage of human hopes. It is not hard to see him as Haines remembers him, with his "pleasant face" and his habit "whenever he laughed of throwing up his upper lip"; a little harder, though, to credit Haines's statement that he had a "passion for sensational novels which he took away by the pile". This sounds like an exercise in hindsight unless, by "sensational", Haines means the novels of Harrison Ainsworth, Bulwer-Lytton and Mrs Radcliffe. There is no doubt that narratives of that more advanced kind – in many ways the staple of the age – influenced him, although it is not at all clear that Dickens himself at this stage had any ambitions to join their illustrious company. If these "silent years" are to be remembered for anything, in fact, it is not primarily for the slow and uncertain progress of Dickens's youthful career as for a more immediate revelation: it was now he experienced what he described as "real first love", during an episode which, he claimed later, marked him for life.

Chapter 6

FIRST love. This was not the infantile love for his little neighbour in Chatham, nor was it the love for his mother and sister. This was infatuation. Her name was Maria Beadnell; she was fifteen months older than Charles Dickens. She was quite short – apparently her nickname at one time was "the pocket Venus" – dark-haired, dark-eyed with that kind of slightly plump beauty which can so easily dissolve in later life; and, from all the available evidence, she was something of a flirt if not quite a coquette. Her "Album" contained verses and drawings from more than one admirer, but it has the honour of being the volume to contain Charles Dickens's first extant writing, an acrostic on the name of Maria Beadnell which opens:

"My life may chequered be with scenes of misery and pain,
And it may be my fate to struggle with adversity in vain . . ."

How Dickens met her is not known, although a friend, a young bank clerk by the name of Henry Kolle, is thought to have been one possible intermediary. Her father was a banker and they lived next door to the "shop", as it were, in Lombard Street. They met in the spring of 1830, as Dickens commemorated in a set of verses he wrote for the Beadnell family in the following year:

"And Charles Dickens, who in our Feast plays a part
Is a young Summer Cabbage, without any heart;
Not that he's *heartless*, but because, as folks say,
He lost his a twelve month ago, from last May."

The name "Charles Dickens" then meaning nothing – just another admirer, a friend of the family, an amateur versifier.

The course of their relationship is difficult to chronicle, but that it was one of passionate admiration on Dickens's part is clear from his subsequent distress when matters deteriorated. There is also his account of David Copperfield's early infatuation with Dora Spenlow: "She was more than human to me. She was a Fairy, a Sylph, I don't know what she was – anything that no one ever saw, and everything that everybody ever wanted. I was swallowed up in an abyss of love in an instant . . ." The first extant and recorded letter from Dickens to Maria Beadnell dates from the latter part of 1831 and it is clear that their "romance" was hardly a settled or determined matter. He wishes to present her with an Annual – "Surely, surely you will not refuse so trivial a present: a mere commonplace trifle; a common present even among the merest 'friends'." Already it is possible to see Dickens's assured handling of tone and style in such a letter and, if this sounds an unnecessarily dispassionate observation, it ought to be remembered that in Dickens's novels the characters are only seen to be deeply moved when they make speeches; there is a clear correlation for Dickens between emotion and words. "Do not misunderstand me: I am not desirous by making presents or by doing any other act to influence your thoughts, wishes or feelings in the slightest degree. – I do not think I do: I cannot hope I ever shall . . ." It was the first of a number of passionate attachments to young women – all of them, with perhaps one exception, being of a "platonic" nature – and we can see here in the fervour of his young nature what was a central characteristic of his temperament. One senses the words of someone intensely in love but still holding himself back, frightened of some shock running through his blood and terrified of a rebuff. Tense. Anxious. All the precarious side of Dickens's character comes forward, implicated as it always is in the need to fight, to battle forward, but expressed also in the wish to "hope and trust" – he employs the phrase twice in this letter – and in his vast appetite for the experience of love. That his was a genuine passion cannot be in doubt. He told Forster that his love "excluded every other idea from my mind for four years . . . I have positively stood amazed at myself ever since! . . . the maddest romances that ever got into any boy's head and stayed there". And yet somehow this passion is connected with his ambition and the exercise of his will; it was his love for Maria Beadnell, he says, which inspired him "with a determination to overcome all the difficulties, which fairly lifted me up into that newspaper life . . ." – which, in other words, helped him to climb upward from the life of Doctors' Commons to that of parliamentary reporting.

In his memory of these events many years later, at a time of great distress in his own life when a sudden letter from Maria opened the floodgates of the past, he characteristically recalls small objects and scenes – a pair of blue gloves, a "sort of raspberry coloured dress", "a tendency in your eyebrows to join together"; such disparate memories can in turn be compared with David Copperfield's recollection of Dora, with "a little black dog being held up, in two slender arms, against a bank of blossoms and bright leaves". This is not any Proustian exercise of memory, because it is neither elaborately perceived nor fully *felt*: Dickens sees things vividly and instantaneously, describes them, and then moves on. But if his memories of Maria Beadnell are of her clothes or of parts of her face – *disjecta membra* indeed – his real nostalgia about this aspect of his past is reserved for himself and for his own feelings. ". . . there never was such a faithful and devoted poor fellow as I . . ." he told her later and, in another letter, he wonders if it is not ". . . ungrateful to consider whether any reputation the world can bestow is repayment to a man for the loss of such a vision of his youth as mine". Dickens was a man of infinite nostalgia about himself; what is real, and what remained real for him, is the ambitious boy moving through adolescence to maturity. That is why this period of struggle, which really "made" him long before he achieved success, was the one which he could never forget. The one which he continued to interpret in his fiction. The one around which he was most willing to cast a roseate light.

But struggle he did. He fought to make headway – with Maria Beadnell, with the world, with his own career. Even while he was working as a shorthand reporter in Doctors' Commons, at some point early in 1831 he joined the parliamentary staff of the *Mirror of Parliament*. His uncle, John Henry Barrow, was both editor and proprietor of this periodical; and, since his father was already working in the same capacity in the press gallery, it hardly comes as a surprise that the young man should join the ranks of its reporters. The journal had been founded three years before, specifically to provide a weekly account of the proceedings in the House of Commons and the House of Lords; in this it had already succeeded, and had acquired a reputation higher than that of its rival, *Hansard*. After a while Charles Dickens played some role in the management and editing of the newspaper, but his primary duty consisted in attending Parliament and keeping an accurate shorthand record of what transpired there. It was well-paid but exhausting work. In the days of the old Parliament –

the building was destroyed by fire in 1834 – reporters were consigned to the back bench of the Strangers' Gallery, where it was hard to hear what was taking place on the floor of the chamber below them. In addition, as one parliamentary reporter recalled, "It was dark: always so insufficiently lit that on the back benches no one could read a paper and so ill-ventilated that few constitutions could long bear the unwholesome atmosphere . . .", a reminder that, in those days, the washing of bodies and the cleaning of clothes were not considered to be absolute priorities.

It was in this dark and unwholesome place that the young Dickens would have to push his way, find a seat and sit there for his own "shift" – of between three quarters of an hour to an hour – transcribing everything that was said by speakers and interrupters alike. He worked on with numbed wrist and aching back, listening to the words of Palmerston and O'Connell, Peel and Russell, ". . . Members," as he wrote in "A Parliamentary Sketch", "some with their legs on the back of the opposite seat; some with theirs stretched out to their utmost length on the floor; some going out, others coming in; all of them talking, laughing, lounging, coughing, o-ing, questioning, or groaning; presenting a conglomeration of noise and confusion, to be met with in no other place in existence . . ." "Night after night," David Copperfield says of that same period in his fictitious past, "I record predictions that never come to pass, professions that are never fulfilled, explanations that are only meant to mystify. I wallow in words." Dickens never had a high opinion of the House of Commons, and even from his earliest days he treats it either as a pantomime – "My lords and gentlemen, here we are!" – or as a savage farce. He became very well acquainted with it – its city members, its country members, its pompous officials, even the waitress in its refreshment-room with her "pastoral friskings and rompings" – and never ceased to mock or insult it. Not that it was a wholly irrelevant or redundant assembly. Dickens himself transcribed, after all, the debates on factory conditions, on penal reform, on educational provision, and on the workings of the Poor Law. Significantly, too, he was a spectator of the great crises and interventions which preceded the Reform Bill of 1832 – a contest which Croker described as no longer "between two political parties for the ministry but between the mob and the government . . . the conservative and subversive principles". Yet in all of Dickens's accounts Parliament remains an unreal place; unreal, perhaps, because of his consuming love for Maria Beadnell in this period (there is nothing like love for placing every other human experience in attenuated perspective) but unreal, too, because these eminent representatives of the people were talking about such matters as child employment and urban poverty which he had experienced at first hand. And, as always, that unreality is expressed by Dickens through the nature of the words people use: ". . . our honourable friend knows, and did from the first know, both what he meant then, and what he means now; and when he said he didn't mean it then, he did in fact say, that he means it now. And if you mean to say that you did not then, and do not now, know what he did mean then, or does mean now, our honourable friend will be glad to receive an explicit declaration from you whether you are prepared to destroy the sacred bulwarks of our nationality."

It is possible that he engaged in more than parliamentary reporting as a young man and in the Dexter collection of Dickens material, housed in the British Library, there is a report of the trial of a certain Williams, Bishop and May for the murder of "the Italian boy". It took place on 12 February, 1831, and on the frontispiece it is stated that the court proceedings were "taken in shorthand". There is no direct evidence to link it with Dickens, but in the descriptions of the murderers there is something which seems very close to the kind of prose Dickens was writing only a few years later: "Bishop advanced to the bar with a heavy step, and with rather a slight bend of the body; his arms hung closely down, and it seemed a kind of relief to him, when he took his place, to rest his hand on the board before him. His appearance, when he got in front, was that of a man for some time labouring under the most intense mental agony, which had brought on a kind of lethargic stupor . . ." And of a co-defendant the unknown shorthand reporter writes, ". . . his look was that of a man who thought that all chance of life was lost . . . there appeared that in his despondency which gave an air of – we could not call it daring, or even confidence – we should rather say, a physical power of endurance . . ."

Perhaps the work of Dickens; perhaps not. All that we can say with certainty of this period is that his skill as a shorthand reporter was growing, and that as a result of his work on the *Mirror of Parliament* he was becoming more widely known among the London journalists. Certainly he was asked to do occasional work for another journal, the *True Sun*, on its inception in March 1832; the nature of the work is unclear and now impossible to verify, but the salient fact is that

Dickens was becoming deeply involved in the reporting of political affairs at precisely the time when the life of the nation was undergoing a profound change. As one contemporary novelist put it, "London was in a strange situation at that period. It was in a manner half-besieged and half its population was discontented. The grievances of the subjects were enormous, and yet with all these corroding abominations the face of things was gay." It was a period both of discontent and of vitality, when the middle-classes emulated aristocratic and upper-middle-class life even as they resented its power; a period of exuberance in which social and religious reformers alike saw the possibility of working on material flexible enough now to take on a different stamp. Throughout the post-Waterloo era in England the habits and techniques of political suppression, provoked by the conditions of war and maintained by the habitual fear of social revolution (the events of 1789 were still of the very recent past), had been only gradually removed; there were sporadic food riots and scenes of mob violence which were put down within the terms of the barbaric criminal code of that period, but by the Twenties it was clear that a change was taking place within the country which the exercise of ordinary social or political authority could not avert. In fact, in 1820, Peel had wondered whether the social tone of England was not "more liberal – to use an odious but intelligible phrase – than the policy of the government". The need for change could not at this juncture be long delayed, therefore, and in the late Twenties the Tory government of Lord Liverpool did attempt to dismantle some of the more oppressive legislation inherited from the eighteenth century – various Emancipation Acts were passed, and the brutal Criminal Law was modified. There would still be public hangings – they survived until 1868 – but the sight of the bodies of the dead left along the walls of Newgate was one of the more nefarious practices which were abolished. During Dickens's childhood and adolescence, therefore, there was an awareness of change and of the need for change – some denied it, some tried to ride it out, some tried to direct it, and some tried to analyse it. And although the eventually Reformed Parliament of 1832 was "reformed" only in a very limited sense – to suggest that it marked the political supremacy of the middle-class householder would be quite wrong – it was at least a visible sign of the transformation of the country; a transformation of which Dickens himself was, in a sense, one of the major beneficiaries.

Yet, in his novels and journalism, Dickens rarely mentions this period of his life in such terms; in his own accounts of his distraught and thwarted existence, political conditions go unregarded. But he did not disregard them at the time and in a speech he gave five years before his death he makes it clear how much he knew and understood about the world around him: ". . . the newsman brought to us daily accounts of a regularly accepted and received system of loading the unfortunate insane with chains, littering them down on straw, starving them on bread and water, denying them their clothes, soothing them under their tremendous affliction with the whip, and making periodical exhibitions of them at small charge, rendering our public asylums a kind of demoniacal Zoological Gardens. He brought us constant accounts of the destruction of machinery . . . In the same times he brought us accounts of riots for bread, which were constantly occurring and undermining the State, of the most terrible animosity of class against class, and of the habitual employment of spies for the discovery, if not for the organisation of plots, in which the animosity on both sides found in those days some relief. In the same times the same newsmen were apprising us of the state of society all around us in which the grossest sensuality and intemperance were the rule . . . This state of society has discontinued in England for ever." These are Dickens's clearest memories of the period in which he was brought up and went to school; how far away he must have seemed from them when he made this speech in the spring of 1865 and yet, as we shall see, they remained an inalienable part of his imaginative life.

But can Dickens himself be said in this period to possess the "radical" or "subversive" instincts which so many of his more articulate contemporaries shared? It is interesting to note that the newspaper to which he was attached, the *True Sun*, was a London evening journal with professed Radical and Benthamite sympathies – the Benthamites or philosophic radicals being, of all the groups within the state, those most committed to the need for, and acceleration of, social change. Its editor, W. J. Fox, was a Benthamite utilitarian whose faith in the necessity for social progress was matched only by his belief in the need for "general intellectual emancipation". The Benthamites criticised in particular the established Church, condemned aristocratic rule, believed both in universal suffrage and in complete freedom of speech. That is why the *True Sun* was called by one contemporary an "ultra-liberal" paper, and when Dickens joined it he was to establish a link with radical journalism which he never really severed. Whether it could be said that he entirely approved of the Benthamite or utilitarian polity is quite another matter, however; it is likely that his own observant and ironic nature, combined with his experience of what politics was really like in the House of Commons, would quickly have mitigated any excessive zeal for such matters as universal suffrage. In addition it ought to be remembered that he became one of the fiercest critics of such Benthamite measures as the New Poor Law. No doubt he enjoyed the company of his new colleagues, agreed with some of what they said and remained silent about the rest. He *was* a radical, but one in quite a different tradition.

Walter Bagehot later called him a "sentimental radical", which was less an insult than an attempt to place Dickens in the exuberant and in some ways grandiose days of the early Thirties. It is a true description only in the sense that Dickens was a radical by instinct rather than by ideology; he was one of the growing number of middle-class people who both envied and despised the mores of the upper-middle-class, and who revolted against the social constraints which were designed specifically to hold them down, to control their ambition and their power. But these reformers also possessed a new earnestness, what one contemporary called an "unusual ardour", in their desire to mitigate more general social burdens, and their mood (if it is possible to anatomise something so abstract and now so remote) seems to have been one of quite extraordinary purpose and animation, with all the manifest confidence and eagerness of a new class emerging into the light. Dickens certainly shared that eagerness but, unlike many others of his generation, he was not an *intellectual* radical. He was not someone who believed that governments might work on the basis of a few enlightened principles; he was a radical by reason of his own position in society, and his own determination to transcend it. But it was not simply a question of individual ambition – in his novels, by that act of general identification which makes him so much the most powerful writer of his period, he infuses the whole of the struggling middle-class with his own life and animation, so that instinctively he embodies their concerns and expresses the changes which were even then altering the country beyond recognition. That is why in his novels the lower-middle-class and the middling-middle-class become, almost for the first time, objects of sympathetic attention – no longer a mob, no longer a statistic (the curse of this period in one sense was the vast growth of statistical enquiry), but English men and women whose distinctive sensibility was at the very centre of Dickens's imaginative vision. This might be classified as a "political" or "radical" manoeuvre but it was Dickens's skills as a mimic, as a reporter and as a fabulist which were needed to engineer so large a transition. There was mixed up in this pity, self-pity, humour, pathos; and all of these qualities served to bring before the English public a vision of life that they had been waiting to see and to understand. To say, therefore, that Dickens was a "radical" in any party sense or in any ideological sense would be to mistake the unique nature of his perceptions.

Perhaps Dickens's special and somewhat ambiguous position is best expressed by Oscar Wilde, that figure at the end of a century whose fin-de-siècle perceptions do sometimes have some relevance to its beginning: "Art is the only serious thing in the world. And the artist is the only person who is never serious." The mature Dickens would indignantly have denied his own lack of seriousness – he like other Victorian writers made much of his moral and didactic powers – but whether the young Dickens would have so readily dissented is another matter. He *was* serious, but in ways his journalistic colleagues and Benthamite contemporaries would probably not have understood. One could put the point differently by noting that, even at the time when he was recording the parliamentary debates on Reform, and working as a more general reporter on the radical *True Sun*, he was seriously considering the idea of a career in the theatre. His own account of the episode to Forster provides the key – at this point in his life, he explained, he was not sure if he might not make a better business out of the stage than out of shorthand reporting. Part of his interest in a career in the theatre was for prudent financial reasons, then, but no doubt there was also some over-riding interest which impelled him in this direction. He still attended the theatre all the time, just as he had in his days as a law clerk, and he had gone to the trouble of perfecting a system to learn the words of various parts (a technique which would be very useful to him in later years). There is even a suggestion that, while he was reporting the proceedings of Parliament, he was also appearing nearby at a minor theatre called The Westminster in Tothill Street. But this is probably false. What is without doubt however is that in March or April of 1832 – still only twenty – he wrote to the stage manager of Covent Garden, a Mr Bartley, ". . . and told him how young I was, and exactly what I thought I could do; and that I believed I had a strong perception of character and oddity, and a natural power of reproducing in my own person what I observed in others".

The significant point here is that he was deliberately modelling his routine upon that of Charles Mathews, a comic actor whose smartness and quickness had already made him the idol of the hour – "the beau ideal of elegance," one contemporary wrote. "We studied his costumes with ardent devotion." Dickens himself was always greatly interested in the possibilities of sartorial display, but there were other reasons which drew him towards Mathews. It is worth recalling, for example, that this actor's real skill lay in the swiftness and dexterity with which he could change both voice and dress so that he could represent "seven or eight different, and very varied, characters in an evening". The ability of one man to assume a variety of characters and voices was of extreme significance to Dickens, suggesting as it does both a mastery of the world and an evasion of the personality. In years to come such versatile acting would indeed become for him a way of lifting the burden of selfhood – an American observer in those later years noted of Dickens that "his rapid change of voice and manner in the impersonation of character was almost like what we read of the elder Mathews". A newspaper subsequently declared that Dickens was very much like Mathews in his walk and manner and voice – although it was quick to point out that the author possessed an "earnestness" which the comic actor lacked. It is worth recalling, too, that the characters whom Mathews most often imitated were those of the garrulous female, the urchin, the foreigner with his broken English – these had always been stock types, but they are also precisely the types which Dickens introduces into his fiction. Dickens would also have known the staccato monologue which Mathews had perfected in a now forgotten piece by Thomas Holcroft called *The Road to Ruin*, since it is one the novelist later immortalised in Alfred Jingle, the first truly comic character he ever created. It would be wrong to press these resemblances too hard, but no great artist works in a vacuum and there seems little doubt that it was under the direct inspiration of Charles Mathews that Dickens first explored the comic possibilities latent within him.

But a career on the stage was not to be his, after all. Mr Bartley, the stage manager to whom Dickens had addressed his letter, wrote back quickly enough. "There must have been something in my letter that struck the authorities . . ." Dickens told Forster later. "Punctual to the time another letter came, with an appointment to do anything of Mathews's I pleased, before him and Charles Kemble, on a certain day at the theatre." Fanny was to go with him in order to accompany him on the piano, here re-enacting their childhood roles when the young Dickens sang for his father's companions. Yet on the appointed day Dickens was "laid up", as he put it, "with a terrible bad cold and an inflammation of the face". Never can there have been a more fortunate illness. He would not have been a great stage actor; he was too small for romantic leads, and there was a certain spareness and lightness about him which would have made him suitable really only for servants, dandies and assorted comic roles. The stage was not his destiny, and so he became ill on the day which that particular future opened for him. Somehow he knew – or at least his body knew – that this was not the life for which he was intended. There is in great artists a secret momentum that always draws them forward so that they can ride over obstacles and avoid side-tracks without even realising that they are doing so – so it was with Dickens. Whether it be called a power of will or of ambition, whether it is a form of self-awareness or even of self-ignorance, there was something which ineluctably led him forward to his proper destination. He told Bartley that he would renew his application the following season, but he never did so.

It has just been suggested that Dickens lost something of his own troubled identity in theatrical performance, and this may even be true of these youthful years when the way ahead of him seemed so un-certain, his own life so perplexing. For even though he had implicitly rejected a career on the stage, he was always almost obsessively involved with amateur theatricals. Most of these quintessentially early nineteenth-century domestic pastimes have been lost to us, but there is still documentary record of a trio of plays which Dickens, with family and friends, worked up in their lodgings in Bentinck Street just a year after Dickens missed his encounter with the managers of Covent Garden. The performance was given in honour of Shakespeare's birthday on Saturday, 27 April, 1833 ("at seven o'clock precisely," the poster intimates – that "precisely" sounding very much like the addition of Dickens) and, with his sister, Fanny, his father, his friend Mitton, and others, Dickens presented an opera-drama entitled *Clari*, an interlude entitled *The Married Butler*, and a farce called *Amateurs and Actors*. *Clari* itself would have been the major production, since it was a play which already enjoyed great esteem and was principally favoured because of the rendering of its central song, "Home Sweet Home" (a tune that Dickens was in later life to play on the accordion). Fanny played the title role, the daughter of a farmer who falls in love with a passing duke and is persuaded to elope with him; the various crises and entanglements are better imagined than described, although it is worth pointing out for the sake of the historical record that Dickens, in the role of aggrieved father and Italian farmer, wore a long coat or smock, a large white collar and slouch hat. The dialogue itself is to be adduced from one example – "Help! Curse her not! She is not lost! She is innocent!" It might be easy to sneer at such innocent manifestations of the theatrical spirit, but of course its action and dialogue do not materially differ from those currently available in television "soap opera". The appetite for fictions which are both easily understandable and provoke readily identifiable emotions is a permanent and capacious one – what is different about the domestic entertainments of the last century is the care with which the illusion was constructed and maintained by the individuals themselves. Enormous trouble was taken over the creation of a proper stage, for example, and over the provision of costumes or theatrical props; *Clari* would have been a real *production*, and nothing is more remarkable about this era than the length to which middle-class families and friends would go to amuse each other. It was a culture which, like the social and economic life of the time, depended crucially upon a form of "self-help", of familial cohesion and small group activities.

It was the kind of communal and convivial activity which Dickens maintained all his life and on this occasion, as on almost all others, he himself took on the role of stage-manager as well as actor. He once said of amateur theatricals that it was like "creating a book in company" and in this twin emphasis on invention and administration, organisation and imagination, we see the poles of Dickens's own character. The role of stage-manager was one uniquely suited to him, in fact, and even in this first attempt he manifested all the self-discipline and authority which were later to become his hallmarks in other theatricals; for *Clari* he drew up a list of regulations, and explained in a circular letter that ". . . it should be distinctly understood by his friends that it is his wish to have a series of weekly Rehearsals for some time . . ." He insisted upon punctual attendance at these rehearsals, repeated practice of roles and an early but entire knowledge of parts. He was, in fact, something of a martinet although he drove himself just as hard – if not harder – than any of the others. He did everything, from finding the proper costumes to helping the "stage carpenter", and in this insatiable attitude towards even domestic entertainment we see once again the determination and assiduity of a young man whose energy seemed at this stage to be illimitable.

And, as was only to be expected, he was also writing for the stage at this point. He composed a humorous piece, *O'Thello* – "for private performance" according to his father, who eventually sold manuscript pages of this early Dickens work when he found himself once more in financial difficulties. The pages he bartered were those relating to his own part – the "Great Unpaid", he was called – and the extracts reveal an occasionally flat but often funny range of songs and rhyming couplets. There is a parody of "Begone dull care" entitled "Begone dull Mike" and a specimen of the verse runs as follows:

> "Bung the porter in the Pewter
> And be sure they draw it mild."
> "If he suspects his wife he'll shoot her,
> And I am for vengeance wild."

If Dickens knew Shakespeare well enough to be heavily influenced by him (and all the signs of his fiction demonstrate this), he also understood him well enough to want to parody him. The things closest to Dickens's heart are those he most readily turns to laughter.

The spring performance of *Clari* in 1833 was notable also for something else: it marked the final stage of his separation from Maria Beadnell. "Separation" is perhaps not quite the right word, since they seem not to have been in any tangible sense together. It is a familiar story, but its familiarity does not render it any the less painful for the young men and women who experience it for the first time – passion on one side and reserve on the other, the love of love on the one hand and the love of intrigue on the other. What seems to have happened is this: for some three years Dickens had been paying court to Maria Beadnell. His advances were at first favoured and then neglected and finally rebuffed; there was a slow but steady falling off between them, and in the period towards the end of their acquaintance Dickens would, in the early hours of the morning, walk after work from the House of Commons to Lombard Street just to see the place in which she slept. There were clandestine letters, conducted through mutual friends like Henry Kolle. But by March 1833, almost three years after he had first met her, he began to lament the futility of his pursuit. The attitudes of the parents of both parties are not recorded, although it is clear that there must have been something like coldness or indifference on the part of the Beadnells. Maria's mother called him "Mr Dickin" and it is possible that the Beadnells did not approve of the young Dickens, although surely his ambition and his post in the press gallery would have weighed against the fact that his father was a convicted debtor and had at the end of 1831 once again been taken to the Insolvent Court: nevertheless there are suggestions in Dickens's extant correspondence that his family during this period felt in a sense "unwanted" and were more than usually susceptible to real or imagined slights. But the real problems seem to have been with the young couple – clearly Dickens's ardent temperament and nervous manner were not of the kind that fully appealed to Maria Beadnell, and the unpleasant scene at *Clari* involved the attitude of Maria's best friend and confidante, Mary Anne Leigh, who for reasons best known to herself seemed to be pretending that Dickens was also paying court to her. Somehow his sister, Fanny, was involved in the confusion and in his distraction he vowed that he would never forgive her. A month later he was best man at the wedding of Maria's sister, Ann, to his friend Kolle; the night before the ceremony he dispatched a letter to Maria but nothing, it seems, could shake her indifference to him.

The letters which Dickens sent to her during these difficult months still make "good" reading in the sense that Dickens himself seems in a way to have enjoyed writing them – "I had never had the remotest intention of sending any of those letters," he wrote later in a journalistic essay, "but to write them, and after a few days tear them up, had been a sublime occupation." This is an account of a fictional lover, of course, but the boundaries between fact and fiction in Dickens's remembrance are often difficult to draw and there is no doubt that, in the letters which survive, there is a genuinely theatrical display of feeling. Here the thwarted lover emerges as sensitive, anxious, impatient for immediate results, unhappy, always alive with self-pity and generally preoccupied with the need to defend and to justify himself.

On 18 March, 1833, to Maria Beadnell: "*My* feelings upon any subject . . . must be to you a matter of very little moment still I *have* feelings in common with other people . . ."

On 15 April, 1833, to Henry Kolle: ". . . you are, or at all events will be what I never can – happy and contented . . ."

On 14 May, 1833, to Maria Beadnell: ". . . the miserable reckless wretch I am . . ." And in the same letter: ". . . I have been so long used to inward wretchedness, and real, real, misery that it matters little very little to me what others may think of or what becomes of me."

On 16 May to Maria Beadnell: "Destitute as I am of hope or comfort I have borne much and I dare say can bear more."

On 17 May to Mary Anne Leigh: "I am perfectly aware of my own unimportance . . ."

He sent one further last plea for some kind of reconciliation in late May – ". . . all that any one can do to raise himself by his own exertions and unceasing assiduity I have done, and will do." But it was not successful.

That he was thwarted and stalled and frustrated and wounded there is no doubt; he was always afraid of being rebuffed and now, for the first time, he had been rejected. Three years marks a long period in the life of a young man, and now three years of courtship had come to nothing. Wasted. His heart laid bare, and also wasted. In later life he seemed to regard it as a traumatic event – one which he had "locked up" in his own breast and which, he said, had led directly to a "habit of suppression" which meant that he could never display his true feelings to anyone, not even to his children. This is true enough of his mature character – no author can have been at more pains to conceal his emotions than Dickens, despite the "emotion" of his fiction – but it is by no means the whole story. His rejection by Maria Beadnell was the one which he could most plainly lament and most clearly feel, but the fact that it provoked such deep emotion within him suggests that it was in a sense an echo or reprise of earlier abandonments; those by his mother and by his sister were prominent in his own memories of his childhood, and there is every reason to suppose that the experience of female rejection determined much of his emotional life. He had an appetite – indeed a demand – for total love, which no human being could really satisfy; in addition he seems to have sought a total identification with the object of his love, and in so desperate a situation any sign of resistance or retreat would be treated by him as a severe calamity. The humiliation and despair then revive echoes of earlier betrayals, stretching back like the milestones in Dickens's amatory pilgrimage, and a pattern begins to emerge. ". . . A vague unhappy loss or want of something", was one of Dickens's favourite phrases and it registers that perpetual and inescapable emptiness which he experienced even at moments of triumph in later life – surely it has its roots here in his hopeless need for total love. There was a yearning, an aching, towards some idealised woman – mother, sister, child, girl – which no real woman could satisfy. The want of something; the ache; the loneliness; the closeness to tears. Dickens suffered from this at periods throughout his life and it became related to feelings of being trapped, of life ebbing away, the loss of romance equivalent to the loss of youth. It is an inexhaustible feeling, and one whose origins lay beyond Maria Beadnell even though they were revived by her. She was not the first, nor the last woman, to leave him, to betray him, as he thought, and to hurt him: he saw the pattern, too, and there is some reason to believe that he deliberately set out on occasions to revive it so that he might once again relive the agony of his childhood.

The abortive romance with Maria Beadnell sets the pattern for these years in Dickens's life in another sense, also, marked as they are by apparent uncertainty and confusion even as the real direction of his life was implicitly being set. There were of course still the problems of his family to waylay and beset him. John Dickens had again been declared insolvent in November 1831, and his name had appeared in the *London Gazette* as being sued in the Insolvent Debtors' Court, but he carried on with his new career; he was working for the *Mirror of Parliament* (one of his duties being to send MPs proofs of their speeches for correction) and had joined the parliamentary reporting staff of the *Morning Herald*. He had, like his son, also become a reader in the library of the British Museum – which suggests, if nothing else, that despite the difficulties of these years he had not entirely abandoned certain literary aspirations. There was another child in this already overstretched family, little Augustus, known as "Moses" or "Boz" after the son of Doctor Primrose in *The Vicar of Wakefield*. Dickens's two other brothers, Alfred and Frederick, were now being sent to a school in Hampstead; they only attended the school for two years, however, since once again John Dickens's improvidence meant that he could no longer afford to keep them there. (It seems to have been one of Dickens's duties to collect his brothers from school at the end of the day and, in a real sense, he would have to look after these siblings for the rest of their lives.) His elder sister, Fanny, had, as we have seen, also been compelled to leave the Royal Academy of Music because her father did not keep up the payments; but she had returned there as a sub-professor and throughout this period was giving instruction in harmony for seven shillings a week. All in all, it seems to have been a more ragged and desultory family life than the amateur theatricals might suggest – the uncertainty of which was compounded by the number of moves which they undertook, moves which characteristically took place during periods of John Dickens's "pecuniary embarrassment" when he needed to vanish from the gaze of his more importunate creditors. Norfolk Street; North End, Hampstead; Belle Vue, Hampstead; Margaret Street, Cavendish Square; Fitzroy Street;

North Road; Bentinck Street. Dickens generally stayed with his family, although on at least two occasions he took lodgings of his own – in Buckingham Street and later in Cecil Street, no doubt because of the fact that these addresses were more convenient for his work in the House of Commons as much as for the absence of space in whatever temporary encampment the Dickens family had established.

Uncertainty, then, in his domestic life; uncertainty in his romantic aspirations; and great uncertainty, too, concerning his eventual destiny. He had already approached the purlieus of three occupations – the stage, the legal profession, and journalism – but it seems that at some time during this period he also took very seriously the possibility of emigrating to the West Indies. A relative, a certain Mrs Margaret Hadfield, had just returned from there and "on the occasion of that visit," a cousin later recalled, "and whilst he was still brooding over the choice of a career, Dickens questioned her very closely as to the prospects for pushing his fortune in the West Indies, wanting but a little encouragement to try his luck there."

Any writing of his own was of an appropriately desultory kind, and the most complete examples of his compositions are in fact the occasional verses which he composed for Maria Beadnell's album. They are not without merit, however – "The Devil's Walk", "The Bill of Fare", "The Churchyard", and "Lodgings to Let" show great skill in versification and demonstrate his ability to evoke a mood of sentimental pathos as well as one of comic parody. These are the familiar characteristics of the poetry of young writers, and would not be remarkable, perhaps, except for the name which was being appended to them –

> Still I'm most proud, amongst these pickings,
> To rank the humblest name.
>
> *Charles Dickens*

There were other writings; his parody of *Othello* has already been mentioned, and it is likely that, if he had any literary ambitions at all in this period, they were at least partly directed towards writing for the stage. Certainly, besides *O'Thello*, he composed what was described by him as a "Venetian comedietta" entitled *The Stratagems of Rowena* – those portions which survive are in his mother's handwriting, and it was no doubt acted in the back-parlour on another familial occasion. But he was also doing some drawing – there are three pen-and-ink drawings extant, two of which are in the style of the early nineteenth-century cartoon. One concerns two Indian gentlemen and includes a joke about the reincarnation of their parents as ducks and drakes, while another shows a man out riding and continues what was then the popular joke about the Cockney sportsman. "Vell I declare Nankeen breeches are famous for riding in."

Not much here to divert the attention, or to detain the reader, except as a symptom of Dickens's general restlessness. His main work was simply to earn his living in a family which he must also have helped to support. In December 1832 he found work as a polling clerk (the Member for whom he was working, Charles Tennyson, was the poet's uncle but perhaps more significantly a Reformer), and in the parliamentary recess of 1833 he was trying to obtain extra employment as a shorthand writer: he asked a friend to recommend him as such if "the opportunity arises". A little later in the same year, he went to dinner with a certain John Payne Collier who was on the staff of the *Morning Chronicle*. His uncle, John Barrow, wanted to obtain a position for his "clever nephew", as Collier put it, on that paper and had brought the two men together. Collier retold the story many years later: ". . . [Barrow's] nephew wished of all things to become one of the parliamentary reporters of the *Morning Chronicle*. I asked how old he was, and how he had been employed before he had connected himself with the *True Sun*. The answer was rather ambiguous; the uncle only knew that his father's family distresses had driven Charles Dickens to exert himself in any way that would earn a living . . . at Barrow's instance, I agreed to meet Dickens at dinner, his uncle also informing me that he was cheerful company and a good singer of a comic song." And so it proved, although it seems that Dickens "would not make the attempt until late in the evening and after a good deal of pressing". Eventually he sang "The Dandy Dog's-Meat Man" and his own composition, "Sweet Betsy Ogle"; both songs of his youth. But the dinner was wasted in all other respects – Collier either could not or would not help Dickens in his journalistic progress, and it was not until late in the following year that he fulfilled his ambition and joined the *Morning Chronicle*.

His main occupation, then, was simply in pursuit of a decent living; but even now, even in the period when his skills were to a certain extent quiescent, he was working at a rate and with a consistency which underline how hard he drove himself (and would continue to do so). He had a surplus of energy, to be sure, more energy than most human beings possess, but he was employing it all the time. He seemed, through unhappiness or uncertainty (both of which qualities, to judge from his letters, he possessed extensively), to wish to *tire* himself, to occupy himself so much that he did not have time to think or contemplate the course of his life; there was almost a need to punish himself. As his fictional hero, David Copperfield, puts it at a similar point in his own life: "I made it a rule to take as much out of myself as I possibly could, in my way of doing everything to which I applied my energies. I made a perfect victim of myself." And then again, in the same narrative, "I fatigued myself as much as I possibly could . . ." Dickens, too, could not bear to relax. He had to keep going, keep moving forward, using time as a precious commodity that could not be wasted, thinking of himself as a *working* being for whom the meaning of life came through labour and the financial rewards of labour. For perhaps behind all this endless, wearying effort there was always that latent fear of failure which pursued him – the fear which had approached him and almost destroyed him when he worked in the blacking factory. Failure, the effects of which he had seen with terrible clarity in the yard of the Marshalsea prison. Only a few years after this, in conversation with an American journalist, he is reported to have said, "In the haunts of squalid poverty I have found many a broken heart too good for this world. Many such persons, now in the most abject condition, have seen better days." That was the fate he had once feared for himself – that "abject condition". Now it is true that in the first decades of the nineteenth century the tangible benefits of success were available to the hard-working members of the middle- or even lower-middle-class (Samuel Smiles's *Self-help*, a wonderful document, is filled with such examples) but there was no smooth or easy path to such rewards. It would require all the determination and ambition which Dickens possessed. In *David Copperfield*, the young hero finds one of his chief occupations in haunting "the old spots" of his childhood. And is this what Dickens did also, returning to the scenes of poverty and distress, and like Copperfield having "reflections at these times [that] were always associated with the figure I was to make in life, and the distinguished things I was to do. My echoing footsteps went to no other tune . . ."? "But the fame –" David begins to say to his old friend Steerforth who disqualifies himself from a conventional "career". This was what Dickens wanted, "the fame", and in *Barnaby Rudge* he presents the thoughts of one of his "villains" in words which might have been applicable to himself at this period (it is typical of Dickens to infuse some of the less attractive aspects of his own temperament into his less attractive characters). "But to drag out a ignoble existence unbeknown to mankind in general – patience! I will be famous yet. A voice within me keeps on whispering Greatness. I shall burst out one of these days, and when I do, what power can keep me down?"

So we may now step back and see him in his twenty-first year, perhaps even on the eve of his twenty-first birthday party – an evening party, beginning at eight o'clock, with "Quadrilles" although "Heaven knows I had nothing to 'come into' save the bare birthday, and yet I esteemed it as a great possession". A young man, a little less than middle height, slight, with light brown hair worn fashionably long, of a somewhat dark or muddy "London" complexion but with expressive eyes and an apparently "feminine" cast to his features. He spoke quickly and nervously, with a slight lisp or thickness in his speech; always animated, seeming always to laugh. He was a young man of some spirit and indeed honour – always punctual, always quick to pay his debts. Ironic sometimes, sometimes facetious. He was an impatient person, quick to take offence, but a tendency towards self-pity and even petulance was curbed by his natural high spirits. He had many "gloomy" thoughts – he admitted as much – but his vivacity and alertness seem generally to have kept them at bay when he was in the company of others. Manifest, too, was the "desperate intensity of my nature . . ." But there were things within him which had not yet been made manifest. This slight, eager, impatient, comic young man was truly a child of his time. One contemporary wrote, much later, that ". . . he was the man of his epoch and had the spirit-time throbbing within him . . ." We must wait to see how true this description may be.

Chapter 7

DICKENS began seriously to write at some time in the summer or autumn of 1833, perhaps spurred on by Maria Beadnell's rejection of him, perhaps wishing to make good use of his time during the parliamentary recess, or perhaps just rising into his own gifts at the appropriate moment. It was a short story entitled "A Dinner at Poplar Walk". There were revisions for later editions (and indeed its title was eventually changed to "Mr Minns and His Cousin") and in its final version it opens, "Mr Augustus Minns was a bachelor, of about forty as he said – of about eight-and-forty, as his friends said." Mr Minns was "a clerk in Somerset-house", just as John Dickens had been, and the story is a light sketch concerning the misadventures which happen when families pursue putative legacies with too much earnestness. One senses here the pressure of the young Dickens's own concerns with money and familial pride, and there can be no doubt that in his early writing he grabbed almost blindly at any material close to hand. Yet the general mood of the piece is theatrical and almost farcical; it reads largely like a piece for the stage which has been transmitted onto paper. But funny, nonetheless.

Later he said that, in his first stories written for publication, he had used "plain penmanship and a sheet of paper large enough to hold the lines"; and, for that first publication, he had chosen the *Monthly Magazine*, a periodical of no great reputation or circulation (it had just been taken over by a certain Captain Holland). It was published in Johnson Court, off Fleet Street, and Dickens had brought his piece which he "dropped stealthily one evening at twilight, with fear and trembling, into a dark letter-box, in a dark office . . ." But the darkness did not last for long. When he went back to the same address to buy the next issue of the magazine, he found printed there "A Dinner at Poplar Walk". "I walked down to Westminster Hall, and turned into it for half an hour, because my eyes were so dimmed with joy and pride that they could not bear the street, and were not fit to be seen there." All the excitement and barely suppressed emotion here say more about the pleasures of authorship than any later and more experienced reports: to see his work in print for the first time was, for Dickens, something like a revelation of himself and yet, more importantly, a revelation of what he might become. His eyes could not bear the streets because his interior sight had beheld a larger and more capacious vision than anything which his present reality could encompass; it was a vision of his own fame. Quickly he wrote a letter to Henry Kolle, who seemed to have surpassed him in affairs of the heart, in order proudly to announce the publication – "I am so dreadfully nervous," he wrote, "that my hand shakes . . ."

Over the next few months he wrote another eight stories for the *Monthly Magazine* (for none of which, incidentally, was he paid). In January 1834 he wrote a story about some amateur theatricals which go awry (the play was *Othello*, which of course he had already parodied elsewhere), and in the following month a story about a draper's assistant whose manner belies his "low" status. There are flashes of acid if high-spirited wit in all these sketches (in some respects like Jane Austen's juvenilia), but both plot and humour are generally farcical and almost vulgar – like that of the kind of London "spark" Dickens was later to satirise. These stories are about loss of face or respectability, of the perils involved in trying too hard to impress, of theatrical mannerisms which go wrong; all themes, of course, likely to be of some consequence to a young man who was himself intent upon rising in the world. And it is clear, in fact, that this particular young man already had larger ambitions than could be easily satisfied by a small magazine; he was planning a series of sketches or stories to be entitled "The Parish" and by the end of 1833 he had already been talking about a "proposed Novel". It has been suggested that this plan concerned *Oliver Twist* and, since it is undoubtedly true that most proposed first novels contain more than their fair share of autobiographical material, it is likely that Dickens would have hit upon some such theme – the poor boy rescued from oblivion and misery – which would so closely touch upon the events and fantasies of his own childhood.

And already the characteristic style of Charles Dickens was beginning faintly to emerge – in a story published in April 1834, "The Bloomsbury Christening", there is a foretaste of Scrooge in a misanthropic old party, Nicodemus Dumps, and in the Kitterbells an anticipation of those happy, helpless, feckless families which later became something of a Dickens speciality. In another story two months later there is a preview of another type of Dickensian humour: in a love letter within that story we find an anticipation of Jingle in "Ere this reaches you, far distant – appeal to feelings – love to distraction – bees'-wax – slavery". And finally, in August of 1834, another very funny story (the important thing to remember about these early stories is just how comic the young Dickens could be) is succeeded by the pseudonym, "Boz". At one stroke he created an identity which could unite these scattered pieces, while at the same time fabricating a minor mystery about the author himself. That he had good reason to be proud of his authorship is not in doubt; there were already appearing favourable if short reviews of his stories, and he had also received the further if unwelcome compliment of being reprinted – or pirated, rather – both in England and in the United States. What he had always wanted, "the fame . . ." It was beginning to happen. One of the recurring words in his correspondence now is "flare", a term which he uses variously to describe an appearance in print, a party, an argument, and any kind of concerted or violent activity. But the real meaning is clear enough: to brighten, to erupt, to come alive at last.

It is not that these early stories are altogether extraordinary or unique. The prevailing taste of the reading public may have been for sensational or sentimental fiction, but there had always been a tradition of comic urban *facetiae* which was even then being continued by Hook, Hood and Pierce Egan. But it is a vain exercise to explain Dickens in the context of this tradition, or that of his eighteenth-century predecessors, or that of the comic print which his more static narratives sometimes copy. It was rather that Dickens had fastened upon middle-class London as his realm (in these early stories, like Daniel Defoe before him, he is always very particular about street names, which is the real sign of a Londoner writing about London) and that he had found his proper subject in the agonising if self-inflicted ordeals which the middle-class and respectable lower-middle-class suffered when they addressed themselves to matters of fashion and social manners. There are times when he is supercilious and even callow, but the sharpness and exuberance of his humour are still evident because they spring from an almost overpowering natural energy. Often the stories are theatrical in tone, and concern themselves with people who conduct themselves in a theatrical or hypo-critical manner; how could that not be so when the chief medium of popular entertainment and popular understanding was in fact the theatre itself? But what is astonishing about these early stories, coming from a young man still in his twenty-first year, is the extent of Dickens's certainty about the real nature of the world which is matched only by his certainty about his ability to describe it. That assurance is nowhere more evident than in his willingness to linger over the trivial or mundane aspects of middle-class life – the green window-frames, the marigolds in the tiny flower beds of suburban gardens, the stale-smelling passages "denominated by courtesy 'Hall'", the signs of "Beware of the Dog", the attempt at genteel speech – which lesser writers would have scurried over in alarm. One of the characteristics of nineteenth-century fiction may be said to lie in this solid belief in the external world and the possibility of real knowledge about it, and Charles Dickens possessed this gift *in excelsis*. On the tacit assumption that most human beings like to have their world, and their place in it, properly described, perhaps we have already stumbled across at least one reason why Dickens became so popular.

But he was not a *successful* author. Not yet. He still had to earn his living in the employment of others. In the autumn of 1833 he was helping his uncle, John Barrow, with business on the *Mirror of Parliament* but he soon found a larger sphere in which to move. It so happened that in the earlier part of the following year a Liberal politician, Sir John Easthope, became the new proprietor of the *Morning Chronicle*, a serious London daily newspaper that under its previous owner had somehow lost its way. Easthope's purchase of it, primarily as a mouthpiece for the Whig and reformist cause, heralded a re-organisation of its journalists. A certain Thomas Beard had joined its parliamentary staff, and suggested that Charles Dickens should also become its representative in the press gallery – Beard had met Dickens when he had worked with John Dickens on the *Morning Herald*, and it seems that almost at once they had become good friends. Certainly Dickens knew him well by 1832, and indeed it became a friendship that was only eventually severed by death. But it is not a friendship easy to chronicle – it is clear that Dickens relied upon Beard's advice and in turn advised him, and it is also clear that there were several occasions when Dickens was able to help his old friend. Yet the character of Beard himself remains somewhat obscured. This is in large part no doubt how Beard wanted it; all the evidence shows that he was one of those quiet and unassuming men who become the friend of genius without ever advertising the fact. He was a shy man, a retiring man, who warmed to Dickens's company and yet in a sense always seems to have felt slightly unworthy of him; Beard clearly held back from him in the years of Dickens's great fame, and this is largely because he thought himself too staid, too mediocre, too *grey* to be a fitting companion for the great author. And yet Dickens seemed to need people like this around him, people who were willing to fade into the background but upon whose friendship and good sense he could rely. Certainly, at this stage in his life, Beard materially assisted him: his recommendation was taken up, but not before a period of uncertainty. In later life Dickens remembered when "I, wanting employment in my path of life, had to call a dozen times upon a busy man, and yet bore it with a Christian fortitude – though conscious of my own deserts, as most men are". Easthope was not an easy man, in any case – his employees called him "Blast-hope" – but eventually Dickens was enrolled upon the staff.

The *Morning Chronicle*, in its new incarnation, became a paper of some stature; John Stuart Mill described it as "the organ of opinions much in advance of any which had ever before found regular advocacy in the newspaper press", by which he meant that it was the first serious daily newspaper to introduce Benthamite theory "into newspaper discussion". In other words, the *Morning Chronicle* was on the more intellectual and fervent end of the Liberal spectrum. In fact it increased its popularity as a result – its circulation rose within a few years from one thousand to six thousand. Its editor, John Black, seems to have shared generally in Benthamite principles, and John Stuart Mill said of him that he was "the first journalist who carried criticism and the spirit of reform into the details of English institutions". Of course Dickens was at this stage a radical but not, as we have seen, necessarily of the same Benthamite stamp as Black and Easthope – indeed he was later to engage in arguments with Black about the results of that Benthamite measure, the New Poor Law, which in the cause of political theory had organised a system of poor relief both barbaric and simplistic. The important thing about Black, however, was that, like any good editor, he knew talent when he saw it and it was not long before he became, in Dickens's own words, "my first hearty out-and-out appreciator". That this is not simply Dickens's own opinion is clear from the evidence of other contemporaries, one of whom recalls that "I have often heard Black speak of him, and predict his future fame". And another erstwhile colleague recalled how Black tried to rescue Dickens as much as possible from the conventional hack-work of the office, "having the highest opinion of his original genius". Others were not so sure – according to John Dickens, ". . . my brother-in-law Barrow . . . and other relations anticipated a failure".

Yet proof of that genius was to come very shortly, even though Dickens was certainly not spared the ordinarily rigorous and arduous life of a general reporter. At a salary of five guineas a week he was employed as one of twelve parliamentary reporters of the paper but over the next two years his duties included theatre reviews and, during the parliamentary recesses, he travelled widely to report on election campaigns, dinners, public meetings and the like. For once his internal energy and restlessness had found a suitable outlet, and Dickens has left his own record of how "I have often transcribed for the printer from my shorthand reports, important public speeches in which the strictest accuracy was required . . . writing on the palm of my hand, by the light of a dark lantern, in a post chaise and four, galloping through a wild country, all through the dead of night . . ." He recollected the time when two colleagues, on a rainy day, held a handkerchief over his head when he was taking down an election speech by Lord John Russell; the times when he wore down his knees, resting his papers on them, while huddled in the press gallery. But his abiding memories were of travelling and the excitement which it seems always to have provoked in him; rushing back in the middle of the night, giving his copy to messengers on horses at convenient stops, travelling on the express and the post-chaise. "I have had to charge for half-a-dozen break-downs in half a dozen times as many miles. I have had to charge for the damage of a great-coat from the drippings of a blazing wax-candle, in writing through the smallest hours of the night in a swift-flying carriage and pair . . . I have charged for broken hats, broken luggage, broken chaises, broken harness . . ." The important thing here was the rivalry between newspapers (principally between the *Morning Chronicle* and the more conservative *Times*) to provide, the next morning, as full and accurate a transcription of speeches from the previous evening in locations far removed from the capital. So the journalists raced each other back to the city, dispatching their "copy" as they finished it to messengers waiting for them. Dickens loved it all, and no other occupation – beside writing and acting – could have given him so keen a pleasure.

Working against time. The need for accuracy. And, above all, the desperate need for *speed*. These were all the qualities he loved to display, and even at the end of his life he would describe in vivid detail the stories of his travels as a young reporter. "Often and often this work would make him deadly sick," he told an American woman just two years before his death, "and he would have to plunge his head out of the window to relieve himself; still the writing went steadily forward on very little slips of paper which he held before him, just resting his body on the edge of the seat and his paper on the front of the window underneath the lamp." Here in the detail we hear an echo of Dickens's own vivid descriptions. On these long and desperate rides the mud often dashed up through the open windows of the post chaise and "they would be obliged to fling it off from their faces and even from the papers on which they wrote". The American woman goes on to say, "As Dickens told us he flung the imaginary evil from him as he did the real in the days long gone, and we could see him with the old disgust returned." Disgust at being soiled once more. Mud. Blacking.

But the travelling – that, despite the mud, was the thing which entranced him. These were the days before railways, the old "coaching days", the days when the chaises often lost their wheels in the mud, the days of fast coaches, too – of drivers calling out, just when the horses were about to move off, "All right!", of the inn-yards smelling of tobacco, of the stables, of the famous *Book of Roads*, of exhausted horses and drunken post-boys. Of course as he travelled over the country Dickens, for the first time in his life, saw the industrial cities of the Midlands and the North; saw, for the first time, exactly what was happening in a country still expanding its industrial base. But for him, essentially, it was the rush and the speed which entranced him, the rush of the wind and whirling roads which he was now experiencing for the first time and which constantly he evoked in later fiction like *Martin Chuzzlewit* – "Yoho, past streams, in which the cattle cool their feet, and where the rushes grow; past paddock-fences, farms and brickyards; past last year's stacks, cut, slice by slice . . . Yoho, past market-gardens, rows of houses, villas, crescents, terraces, and squares; past waggons, coaches, carts; past early work-men, late stragglers, drunken men and sober carriers of loads . . ." This, too, from *The Old Curiosity Shop*: "There was a freedom and freshness in the wind, as it came howling by, which, let it cut never so sharp, was welcome. As it swept on with its cloud of frost, bearing down the dry twigs and boughs and withered leaves, and carrying them away pell-mell, it seemed as though some general sympathy had got abroad, and everything was in a hurry like themselves."

His work was rewarding, too, for the praise which he began to receive. Within a few months Dickens was "universally reputed to be the rapidest and most accurate shorthand-writer in the gallery" and another colleague wrote that "a more talented reporter never occupied a seat in the Gallery of either House of Parliament". Yet the curious aspect of this repute among his colleagues was the fact that he was in no sense a necessarily popular or expansive young man; in fact, according to one contemporary, he was "exceedingly reserved in his manners, although interchanging the usual courtesies of life with all whom he came in contact in the discharge of his professional duties". This "reserve" will often be noticed in Dickens – surprising, perhaps, in a man whose work testifies to the virtues of cheerfulness and sociability, but there is no doubt that on many occasions he was quiet to the point of taciturnity, agreeable enough when met or spoken to but fundamentally a man who kept his opinions to himself. A man who, in a certain sense, always stood apart. He could be difficult company, and one of the images we must carry with us through this narrative is of a man who never liked to reveal his true feelings and who sometimes relapsed into a glum silence in the company of others. It is possible, too, that his reserve in these youthful days was also the reserve which springs from pride; he did not want to be properly known until he had proved himself, until he had become the kind of person he knew himself to be. He did not want to be met *on the wrong terms*. It should not be forgotten, either, that even if he made a "great splash" in the sphere of journalism, as he said, he nevertheless came to think of it as essentially a "little world".

And so, as it were, his merit shone through despite himself. It was not long, either, before he was being seen as a "man of mark" for whom a great future was predicted. It was not the first time he had triumphed over difficulties and conquered arduous tasks, but it was the first time that he had been able to make an impression among his peers. He said later of this period of his life that ". . . he could not forget that his first entry into life, his first success in life, his first view of the bearings of life around him, were in connexion with a London daily newspaper . . ." And, of course, he became more than ever convinced of the benefits and virtues of hard work and sustained effort. "To the wholesome training of severe newspaper work, when I was a very young man, I constantly refer my first successes . . ." he came to say. That training was of help in more ways than one; he learnt how to produce "copy" to a deadline with a punctiliousness that would prove invaluable for his novels in later life but, more importantly, it is significant that the greatest novelist of the English language should have been trained first as a journalist and reporter. He was at once made aware of an audience which he had to address, and whose tastes he would need to satisfy, if he were to be taken seriously at all.

Not that the common newspaper style of the period was of any great use to him, characterised as it was by a ponderous Latinate verbosity and filled with periphrasis and cliché. (Those who are interested in the effect of economics upon prose might note that this particularly ponderous style was popular in part because it filled up more lines for those working on a "penny-a-line" basis.) Dickens himself was of course quite aware of its faults and was inclined to parody this putative "high" style wherever he found it; it is possible, also, that he detected within it something of his father's tone, and was inclined to suspect it for that reason alone. His own early contributions to the *Morning Chronicle* are in fact remarkably free from it, and the first piece he ever wrote seems to emerge fully armed, as it were, from the soil of Dickens's sharp observations. He had gone up with Thomas Beard by boat to Leith, en route to Edinburgh where a public dinner was to be given for Earl Grey; in Beard's recollection, that journey was enlivened by a commercial traveller laughing out loud at something Dickens had written in the *Monthly Magazine*, a circumstance which endeared him to the young author at once, and by Dickens's suddenly being "prostrated" by sea-sickness. The dinner itself was rich material for Dickens's first reportorial assignment: it seems that the guests started eating before the principal visitors had arrived and, as Dickens stated, ". . . this is, perhaps, one of the few instances on record of a dinner having been virtually concluded before it began". But there was also at once in his writing a vein of pathos; on an earlier occasion that day in Edinburgh, at a "Promenade" for a Blind Asylum and the Deaf and Dumb Institution, the young reporter noticed how cowed and unsettled the blind people were who ". . . appeared very glad to be filed off from a scene in which they could take little interest, and with which their pensive careworn faces painfully contrasted". Here in embryo is Dickens the observer: ready to see the farce and absurdity inherent in human behaviour but always alert to the darker music beneath it. It is so instinctive to him that it comes out in this first piece quite naturally, and the force of Dickens's perceptions and language are such that he is quite able to avoid the stereotypical phrases of conventional journalism. Of one politician muddling his speech Dickens wrote, for example, "Lord Lincoln broke down, and sat down." Not surprisingly his skills were appreciated by Black, and Dickens's contributions to the *Morning Chronicle* were soon of a varied kind. On the dismissal of the Melbourne ministry by William IV he wrote a political satire in the manner of a fairy tale "translated from the German by Boz", and almost as soon as he had joined the paper he began writing individual "sketches" which were quite different from the "stories" he was still placing in the *Monthly Magazine*: the first of them, "Omnibuses", immediately establishes the London tone and setting with its sharp dialogue and swift observations of urban life. Five appeared in the *Morning Chronicle* by the end of the year and, as we shall see, became the first engine of Dickens's fame.

There is a small possibility, however, that even at this stage Dickens did not envision a literary career for himself since he wrote to the Steward of New Inn stating that he intended ". . . entering at the bar, as soon as circumstances will enable me to do so". In fact Dickens seems on other occasions to have considered the possibility of a legal career – there would even come a time when he would apply to become a magistrate, like Henry Fielding before him – but in this period it seems most likely that Dickens simply wanted to find chambers for himself. He wanted his independence, in other words, and he wanted to put some distance between himself and his family; a fact about which his father seemed a little bitter, since he referred to "Charles's determination to leave home, on the first occasion of his having an annual engagement . . ." with the *Morning Chronicle*. The wisdom of Dickens's decision was soon evident, however, for only a week after he wrote to New Inn his father was once more arrested for debt – this time on the initiative of wine merchants to whom he owed money. Once again, just as the young man was beginning to find the world and to make his mark upon it, his old childhood humiliations and miseries threatened to descend upon him. And this time matters were worse than usual; Dickens had apparently backed some of his father's bills and would therefore also be liable for arrest. "I have not yet been taken," he wrote to Thomas Mitton when asking for his help, "but no doubt that will be the next act in this 'domestic tragedy.'" His father was escorted to Sloman's detention house for debtors at 4 Cursitor Street; Dickens was too busy with his newspaper work that morning to deal with the problem, and asked Mitton to visit him instead. Dickens then went to Cursitor Street at six, just two hours before starting work on the night's session in the parliamentary gallery, and managed to give his father enough money to escape the immediate consequences of his debts (some of this money came from Dickens's "French employer", about whom nothing is known – an indication, at any rate, of the extent to which he was forced to take many and varied employments in these first years). What is most interesting about this episode, however, is not the helplessness with which the father relied upon the son, nor the precariousness of Dickens's family life, but rather the fact that no more than two months later he used the experience in a story which he wrote for the *Monthly Magazine*. "A Passage in the Life of Mr Watkins Tottle" has a long section in which the aforesaid Mr Tottle is taken to a "lock-up house in the vicinity of Chancery Lane", this establishment and its guests being described in great detail and with an obvious air of authenticity. "The room – which was a small, confined den – was partitioned off into boxes, like the common-room of some inferior eating-house. The dirty floor had evidently been as long a stranger to the scrubbing-brush as to carpet or floor-cloth; and the ceiling was completely blackened by the flare of the oil-lamp by which the room was lighted at night." Dickens was using his private family experiences even though they have no direct relation to the plot of the story which he was composing – either he was being a good reporter and wanted to make use of the material which he had observed so woefully at first hand, or he simply had to put down the episode in fictional form in order to deal with it properly and so come to terms with his own feelings. That is why there are times in Dickens's sketches and stories of the period when a somewhat penny-drama plot is redeemed by intense observation, by exactly that "intensity of . . . nature" which he had diagnosed in himself.

His father was released, but only at the expense of his son's borrowing from his friends on the security of his own salary. But this did not deter John Dickens himself from almost immediately writing to those same friends in turn asking for money; he informed Thomas Beard, for example, that the household was about to break up, with various members of the family going into lodgings but "your humble servant 'to the winds'". His son, Alfred, he told Beard in a subsequent letter, "is walking to and from Hampstead daily in dancing Pumps". Colourful letters – certainly more colourful than apologetic – and it is hard not to be entertained by that air of self-dramatisation which the father brings to the most dismal situations. Which was a gift, of course, he transmitted to his famous son.

The son, meanwhile, had, as it were, fled; in December 1834 he moved with his younger brother, Frederick, into chambers at Furnival's Inn. He rented what was then known as a "three pair back" at what was then the not inconsiderable rent of £35 a year – three modest rooms, a cellar and a lumber room in a not very prepossessing congeries of buildings which had been expressly built as chambers. It was a "good" address but somewhat gloomy, according to all reports, and in his later writings Dickens always referred to the loneliness and dilapidation of such places – describing them once as "that stronghold of Melancholy" and dilating on the unpleasant habits of the "laundresses" who were supposed to clean them and look after their tenants. One can be sure, then, that the "gloomy thoughts", of which Dickens admitted he was a prey, would still have visited him even at this time when his whole career seemed to stretch before him in bright prospect. Yet, as he noted during this period, "We have much more cause for cheerfulness than despondency after all; and as I for one am determined to see everything in as bright a light as possible . . ." This is always to be remembered about Dickens: cheerfulness keeps on breaking through.

Events, in any case, conspired to make him very busy in this period. The dissolution of the Melbourne ministry precipitated a general election (the proximate cause had been the King's aversion to Melbourne's Irish church policy, one of those disputes which seem infinitely remote to us until we realise that all the political controversies of the period – the Irish Question, the need for municipal reform, the protection of certain kinds of employee – have their counterparts in our own time), and the election in turn meant that Dickens was at once sent on a number of reporting assignments to meetings, dinners and all the paraphernalia of what was slowly and uncertainly becoming a "democratic" process, his duties taking him to Colchester, Braintree, Chelmsford, Sudbury, Bury St Edmunds and elsewhere. This election has been called "the most violent electioneering struggle ever witnessed in England" (it resulted in the return to power of a Conservative government under Robert Peel) and such violence must be remembered, together with the intelligence which the young reporter gathered about corruption and bribery, when we come to consider *The Pickwick Papers*. But in the same period he was also visiting the London theatres in order to write notices. "This gentleman's vocal powers we have yet to discover," he said, for example, of a certain Mr Anderson appearing in *The Farmer's Son* at the Queen's Theatre in Tottenham Street. In other words, Dickens was part of the general movement of his age – participating in it, reporting on it, buoyed up by the energy and momentum of it.

And, at the same time, he was writing his sketches which, fortuitously, found a slightly wider audience. For it was at some point in the autumn or winter of 1834 that he made the acquaintance of George Hogarth, who was about to become the editor of the *Evening Chronicle* – a tri-weekly offshoot of the *Morning Chronicle* which was delivered mainly to the rural areas around London. Hogarth "begged" the young man to write sketches for his new venture, to which Dickens graciously assented – although adding, in a not unfriendly manner, that he would expect "*some* additional remuneration" above his *Morning Chronicle* salary. Upon that everybody seems to have agreed, and for an extra two guineas a week Dickens embarked on a series which was to become known as "Sketches of London".

George Hogarth, however, was to play an even more important role in his life. Hogarth was a music critic and journalist. He had known Walter Scott – his sister married Scott's printer, James Ballantyne – and had had a relatively distinguished if peripatetic career as editor of local newspapers in Exeter and Halifax. He had moved to London in the early autumn of 1834 in order to take up a position as musical and dramatic editor of the *Morning Chronicle* but, as we have seen, he was soon appointed as editor of the *Evening Chronicle*. He had taken 18 York Place, one in a terrace of houses the gardens of which bordered the south side of the Fulham Road (the area of Fulham was in those days known for its nurseries and tulip gardens, but perhaps as a result was also a byword for dullness). He had a large family, was slightly "Bohemian" in his tastes but was apparently a genial and gentle man. Forster described him as "a kindly and accomplished man" and there is no reason to doubt that judgement. Certainly he soon established a friendship with Charles Dickens, the young man whose occasional journalism he so obviously admired, and it was not long before Dickens was making social calls to Fulham. One of Hogarth's daughters, Georgina, remembered "some delightful musical evenings" in which Dickens joined and during which her father performed upon the violoncello. Another episode in their acquaintance was more lively; one day, it seems, while the Hogarths were sitting in the drawing room, a "young man dressed as a sailor jumped in at the window, danced a hornpipe, whistling the tune jumped out again, and a few minutes later Charles Dickens walked gravely in at the door, as if nothing had happened, shook hands all round, and then, at the sight of their puzzled faces, burst into a roar of laughter". The incident has the ring of truth – it comes from Dickens's daughter who had heard it from Mrs Hogarth. And it expresses too in characteristic form something of Dickens's own powerful and mercurial temperament – the sudden dance, the "grave" demeanour as if nothing whatever has happened, and then the burst of laughter. It is true, too, that Dickens was adept at performing the sailor's hornpipe (it may have been something his father had taught him at Chatham) and many years later, towards the end of his life, he did the same dance for two companions while travelling in a railway compartment. He could be very merry, and these sudden effusions of high spirits, expressing themselves in dance, are typical even of Dickens's more mature years.

So Dickens became a welcome guest at the Hogarths, and he in turn welcomed them. Hogarth's eldest daughter, Catherine, told her cousin in a letter of February 1835 that she had attended a birthday party for him at his chambers in Furnival's Inn: ". . . it was a delightful party I enjoyed it very much – Mr Dickens improves very much on acquaintance he is very gentlemanly and pleasant . . ." And so was heralded one of the most famous marriages of the nineteenth century. Three months later, Charles Dickens and Catherine Hogarth were engaged. She was the oldest of the Hogarth children – nineteen when she met Dickens, whereas her sister Mary Hogarth was fourteen and Georgina seven – but all three girls were to exercise a permanent influence upon Dickens's life, in one capacity or another. Mary, for example, was not yet of an age to marry but there is no doubt that the affection between her and the young Dickens was strong; she gave him presents, a fruit knife and silver inkwell, very soon after he had come to know the Hogarths and it is clear from all later reports that her gentle and selfless nature deeply impressed the young man. But little else is known about her – only a "spiritual" quality which she seemed to possess and, since she died at an early age, it can only be said that her proper character remained as it were in the womb of time, leaving behind only the faint intimations of a personality from which Dickens in later life was to create his own beloved "Mary".

Catherine, by contrast, is a much more tangible and definite figure.

There are many descriptions of her, but the most comprehensive and accurate comes only a few years after her meeting with Charles Dickens: ". . . a pretty little woman, plump and fresh-coloured, with the large, heavy-lidded blue eyes so much admired by men. The nose was slightly retroussé, the forehead good, mouth small, round and red-lipped with a genial smiling expression of countenance, notwith-standing the sleepy look of the slow-moving eyes." In other words she was the same physical "type" as Maria Beadnell, Dickens's last romantic attachment, and this similarity may give added weight to Dickens's childhood wish "to marry a Columbine". But Catherine seems to have been quite without Maria's flightiness or flirtatiousness – clearly Dickens, now so busy with his journalism, could do without the strain of these. Yet certain qualities seem significant enough to have impressed everyone, first among them Catherine's general amiability and cheerfulness; "sweet-natured", "sweet" and "kind" are some of the adjectives used about her and, according to Mrs Stowe some time later, "a friend whispered to me that she was as observing and fond of humour as her husband". She had other qualities, too – "placid", "easy-going", "peace-loving", "a certain womanly repose" (this last from Hans Christian Andersen) and these suggest the other side of her nature. She was characterised by a native slowness, or what she herself called "procrastination", which would have been much more visible beside Dickens's own extraordinary enthusiasm and vivacity. Her daughter, after her death, said that there were times when she could be "negative" and this suggests that there was about her a certain resistance to the energetic flights of Charles Dickens, a certain inability or unwillingness to respond in the same quick, excitable manner as he. There is no doubt that she was highly affectionate but there were moments, in the early months of her relationship, when she also tended to be insecure. In later life she suffered from migraines (it is possible she also suffered from them when she was a girl), and this suggests a certain latent anxiety about herself and about the world. She lacked confidence in herself, it seems, and there are times when such lack of confidence can make for awkwardness and even for petulance. There were occasions, then, when she could be uneasy and distrustful; but whatever "scenes" occurred were quickly settled – she was difficult on occasions, but she did not resist being managed. In addition, since she was the oldest daughter, and since her mother seems to have been a trifle hysterical, it is likely that many of the responsibilities of household management fell upon her – certainly she was a most capable "wife" in the conventional nineteenth-century sense of that term. And the important thing is that she was clearly also capable of deep affection; her devotion to her husband, despite events which would have alienated almost anyone else, continued until her death.

The young Dickens would have seen all this at a glance, of course, and there can be no doubt that the characteristics she possessed as a middle-aged woman could at least be glimpsed in the young girl. All the evidence is that, at nineteen, she was what she would always be; so here, in miniature, is the girl to whom Dickens quickly became engaged. It was not so long after his rejection by Maria Beadnell, of course, but if in their extant correspondence there is plenty of love and affection there is none of that thwarted passion or hysteria which are present in his letters to Maria. Everything is much calmer, more open, more equable and, on those occasions when Catherine upset or annoyed him, he seems deftly to have asserted his "rights" and used his occupation as an excuse for not being quite so much in her company. If this sounds like a relationship of convenience, there is at least one sense in which that was exactly what it was – Dickens needed the security and stability of a home almost as soon as he had gone into chambers. And clearly, too, that perpetual "want of something" would have sent him spinning towards a girl who was as pretty as she was accomplished, and whose more equable temper would have been a welcome change after the mercurial behaviour of Maria Beadnell. The course of their engagement was an easy one, as we shall see, and it is remarkable only for the fact that by the end of it Charles Dickens was set to become the most famous and most successful novelist of his day.

He was already getting into his stride with his "Sketches of London" for the *Evening Chronicle*, and his development as a writer is to be observed even as he worked upon these occasional pieces of journalism. For one thing he was extending his range. In his first months he had rigidly separated his "stories" from his "sketches" but it would always be part of his genius to reconcile the opposing tendencies of his mind, and now in a new series he began for the *Evening Chronicle* – it was entitled "Our Parish" and was certainly related to the novel he still wanted to write – he began to combine fiction and observation in new ways. The stories had always tended to be more supercilious, more farcical, owing a greater debt to the theatre. The sketches are more benign, more purposeful, more concerned with elucidating the world. It is as if the creative side of Dickens was still being held back by his early allegiance to the stage, while his hitherto untried powers of observation were growing ever stronger. What was interesting now, too, was the intermittent expression of his social indignation; he was no longer the ironic or supercilious farceur and in his first pieces for the *Evening Chronicle* his social concerns began to emerge very clearly. In a short piece entitled "Gin Shops", for example, he made the connection between intemperance and poverty which he maintained for the rest of his life. And all the time Dickens knew the direction in which he was going; he was in the position of someone who is "fighting to get on", as he said of another colleague later, and he was quite aware how in that position the exposure of a name "before the public", as he put it, was very important. In later life he tended to disavow these sketches as the product of a juvenile sensibility, but at the time he was very concerned to get them right; there is no doubt, either, that it was their publication, rather than that of *The Pickwick Papers*, which first gave Dickens a measure of fame.

The fact is that, even if they were not wholly original, they were distinctive. There was a tradition of urban sketches stretching right back into the seventeenth century – they were a significant feature of the eighteenth-century periodicals he had read as a boy – and there is no doubt that Dickens can be placed in that long tradition of English humour which owes as much to journalism as it does to the novel. But if there were times when Dickens drops into the occasional stateliness of the eighteenth-century essayist, he is a million miles away from that urbane or weary tone, that use of language as a moralistic or sarcastic device to hedge the reader against the oppressive indignities and hardships of what was often then a savage world. Dickens removes this protective veneer, and his own pieces are much funnier, much more vivid and reportorial. It is true that he was still as much of the stage as of the world, but as a result he is able to bring the light and exaggeration and animation of the theatre to the streets of London. "I wished again and again that the people would only blow me up, or pitch into me – that I wouldn't have minded, it's all in my way . . ." You might say that this extract from the conversation of a broker's man in one sketch is just another aspect of Dickens's theatrical techniques – that he can, as it were, jump up on stage and do all the voices. Which accounts for this extraordinary mixture of display and directness, exterior irony and internal identification. But what his contemporaries heard *were* the voices, and the prevailing admiration for Dickens's early work came from what was described as the "vivid" and "graphic" way in which he had described the speech of London. "The vernacular idiom is given in all its truth and richness," was one newspaper comment and it is this "truth" which causes the most comment – this "startling fidelity" to the language of "the middling and lower orders". The fact that this was also a comment applied to Dickens's earlier novels emphasises what an important aspect it became of his art. "Niver mind . . . niver mind; *you* go home, and, ven you're quite sober, mend your stockings." This, again, is from one of the sketches, but the speech is not really an invention of Charles Dickens. Here is a transcript from an actual trial of 1833, taken from *The Times*: "I'se quite hinnocent, your vorship. I was a valking along, and I see these here trousers a hanging, vich I vishes I'd a never seed at all . . ." It is the same vernacular, the same idiom, the same cadence. Dickens heard it, and employed it: it is the gift of any great writer to lend permanent expression to the demotic of his period – to give it *form* by making it part of the larger world which he has created. And this is what the young Dickens, instinctively, eagerly, hastily, was doing now.

Astonishing, too, was the detail as well as the directness. For the readers of the sketches it was as if they were seeing in front of their eyes, for the first time, almost as if they were daguerreotypes, all the things that no one had ever noticed before – down to the way in which London cab-drivers will greet one another by "the solemn lifting of the little finger of the right hand". And equally astonishing, now, is the high degree of stylistic control which Dickens was able to exercise. At first he never seems quite sure what tone he ought to adopt, and so he veers from the distant irony of the superior observer to the anger of the denouncer of social evils; it is as if he is not sure of his own position, or perhaps that of his audience. But then slowly the alchemy of his genius begins its work upon the world around him and his own passionate, comic, direct, plangent, farcical, lachrymose prose takes shape. Prose as a principle of animation. Thus he takes a walk from Oxford Street towards Drury Lane, which means going through a congeries of alleys known as the "Rookery" (these streets have now disappeared and only the edifice of St Giles and the narrow streets around Seven Dials testify to the ancient area), passing the "wretched houses with broken windows patched with rags and paper", past "the fruit and 'sweet-stuff' manufacturers in the cellars", past the "clothes drying and slops emptying from the windows", past the "girls of fourteen or fifteen, with matted hair, walking about barefooted, and in white great-coats, almost their only covering". And on another evening he walks down Oxford Street, Holborn, Cheapside, Coleman Street, and Finsbury Square and visits a public house where he overhears animated conversation –

"Not at all extraordinary – not at all . . . Why should it be extraordinary? – why is it extraordinary? Prove it to be extraordinary!"

"Oh, if you come to that –"

"Come to that! . . . But we must come to that . . ."

As he walks he broods, and his broodings become impressions. He meditates on misery living side-by-side with wanton excess. He wanders. He becomes the people he observes. He cannot describe a scene without also becoming a part of it, and living within it. His genius lay in an imaginative sympathy so strong that the world overpowers him; in a linguistic mastery so great that in turn he can recreate both himself and the world.

So what are the subjects that animate him, that pluck at his coat, that disarm him, that wring his heart? Condemned men; drunkards; vagrants; and the poor – ". . . the miserably poor man (no matter whether he owes his distresses to his own conduct, or that of others) who feels his poverty and vainly strives to conceal it, is one of the most pitiable objects in human nature". His own childhood experience had left him prey to fears of poverty, sudden degradation and even villainy – only a little while before he had been in danger of arrest for his father's debts – so it is often to the "low" quarters of the city and its inhabitants that, fascinated, he returns. Seven Dials. Monmouth Street. Newgate. The Old Bailey. This is the particularly alert young man who in his tour of Newgate notices every detail of the condemned pew which "will haunt us, waking and sleeping, for months afterwards"; who observes all the "broken-spirited and humbled" men with a painfully rapt and alert sympathy as if he had only to see them to take their place.

But these were not his only themes. "Somehow," he said, "we never can resist joining a crowd . . ." There are also passages when he is as animated and excited as any passer-by watching an incident in the street so that, when he writes of the pleasure gardens at Vauxhall, the circus performances at Astley's or the fairs at Greenwich, he perfectly reflects the vigour and disorder of the city. And of its inhabitants: what impressed his contemporaries as much as the vivacity of his style was the way in which he was able to chronicle the lives of "the people" even at the time they were first struggling to find social and economic expression. This was how he found his great subject, in crowd scenes, in streets, in the lives of people who are uniquely tied together, for better or worse, and who are part of the city which rises like an hallucination through these early sketches. It was sometimes said during this period that, in the years of Reform agitation, interest in literature had perforce given way to the political controversies but that now, after the Reform legislation had been passed, the interest in literature had resumed. This is true as far as it goes, and it goes as far as Charles Dickens: the interest in literature came back precisely because of the kind of work upon which he was now engaged. This young man who was rushing back to his lodgings in order to dramatise his wanderings or his observations, to write them down while the fit of inspiration was still upon him, scribbling always against a deadline while trying to keep his own perceptions in order.

And, at the same time, he was working in the press gallery of the House of Commons. He was becoming increasingly weary, in other words, often working until dawn and then sleeping until ten or eleven in the morning. And then getting up to write at once to Catherine: "I wrote till 3 oClock this morning (I had not done for the paper till 8) and passed the whole night, if night it can be called after that hour, in a state of exquisite torture from the spasm in my side far exceeding anything I ever felt." So on occasions of more than usual stress the pain in his side, the legacy of his childhood, still returned. (It was generally allayed, however, by potions from Thomas Beard's brother, Francis, who was then a medical student and who later became Dickens's family doctor.) Already he was doing too much: in June 1835 he stopped writing his "Sketches" for the journal of his putative father-in-law, but began writing them for a magazine called *Bell's Life in London*. This was partly because they offered him more money, and partly because to appear on the front page of that metropolitan journal was better than being tucked away inside a newspaper primarily designed for the rural areas. In addition he had a great admiration for its editor, Vincent Dowling. It was to Dowling that he sent his famous "business card", written on the spur of the moment in an inn opposite Dowling's offices: "CHARLES DICKENS, Resurrectionist, In Search of a Subject". The "resurrectionist", or grave-robber who took corpses and sold them to medical faculties for dissection, had been lately in the news; and Dickens, with his own subdued infant fear of the dead coming alive, was still fascinated enough by the profession in later days to place one of its exponents in *A Tale of Two Cities*. But in this instance he seems to be no more than poking macabre fun at his own life as reporter and observer rather than active participant.

Of course it is easy to miss, in describing his work and attitudes so generally, the actual moments and occasions when a theme would germinate, a subject be found, a new skill established. It is intriguing to notice, for example, that in November of 1835 the theme of prisons and executions suddenly becomes much more prominent in his work. It began with a visit to Newgate Prison. He wanted material for an essay with which to crown the publication of the first volume of his sketches, and he realised that there he was most likely to find it; he knew what he was looking for and, together with the real sympathy with which he invested the hapless scene, there was also an alert sense of how best to mould that sympathy for the benefit of his audience – "You cannot throw the interest over a year's imprisonment," he told his publisher, ". . . that you can cast around the punishment of death." So out of this excursion came the extraordinary "A Visit to Newgate". But he also had an unwearying sense of comedy even in the darkest situations; on his visit to Newgate with this same publisher, for example, he had seen a Quakeress in the prison office and had turned to his friend saying "Mrs Fry". Elizabeth Fry was a prominent prison-visitor, of course, and here Dickens is turning the whole thing into a joke – it is the kind of humour which might be described as theatrical, sharp, almost (to use an old-fashioned term) "camp". And when we come to read of Dickens's jollity, his good spirits, it ought to be remembered that characteristic of his humour is the quick remark, the sudden lance of wit, the sharp observation. A few days after the visit to Newgate he published "The Prisoners' Van", another sketch detailing the pathos and misery of those who had fallen in this savage city. Then almost at once the idea of a story, "The Black Veil" – the saga of a hanged man and his mother – occurred to him, and he set to work on what is really his first proper story; it is no longer a sketch or a scene or a farcical interlude but a finished narrative. Thus we see, in miniature, the formation of the artist, reacting to the events of the life around him, using them and being used in turn.

All the while he was trying to balance the needs of his career against his duties to Catherine who, on occasions, seems to have been disturbed by his attention to his work at the expense of herself. It was not unreasonable for her to be so: it must have looked as if this was the shape their marriage was about to take, and indeed in that she was not much mistaken. Nevertheless, in order to be closer to her he had moved to lodgings in Selwood Terrace, a row of houses just north of the Fulham Road and only a short walk from the Hogarths' own house. He took the place in May, at the time of his engagement, and remained here for six months – thus assuming the obligation of rents both here and at Furnival's Inn. Despite minor and temporary disagreements, in fact, the course of their engagement was a relatively smooth one; at no stage was she anything other than what he described as "My dearest life" or "My dearest love", "dearest Pig" or simply "Mouse", and there is evidence, too, that their affection for each grew during the course of their engagement. Although he was often ill and dispirited (often hard-up, as well, and forced to borrow money from Beard or from Mitton), his unfailing resource seems to have been Catherine. Sometimes she even came around to Selwood Terrace in the morning, after he had risen from his bed after a late night; and of course there were evenings with the Hogarths themselves. The relationship between the two families is not recorded, although there is no reason to doubt that it was a friendly one: George Hogarth probably forgave Dickens for his desertion of the *Evening Chronicle* in favour of *Bell's Life in London* on the grounds that anything which helped his future son-in-law's career was to be welcomed. In addition Dickens agreed to correct the proofs of a book by Catherine's uncle, *Two Journeys Through Italy and Switzerland*, while George Hogarth wrote an enthusiastic notice of Fanny Dickens's *soirée musicale* at the Royal Academy in May. When Catherine became ill with scarlet fever in October 1835, Dickens reported himself to be "in great distress of mind" because of it; she recovered, but not before experiencing the full force of Dickens's extraordinary will. "Should you not be so well," he wrote, "I *must* see you, and *will not be prevented*." He was to use italics like this all his life. At some point he gave her, as a present, a copy of Johnson's life of Richard Savage – since this short life is notable for its exposure of the bad treatment meted out to Savage by his mother and for its account of the hazards of a writer's life, it might have been intended by Dickens either as an explanation or as a warning.

There was now a great deal for him to do, and it seems that there came a time when Catherine acquiesced in the fact that he would always be "busy", always overwork himself. But she was still capable of becoming upset, or "coss" as he puts it on occasions, at his frequent absences in the evenings, even while he himself never ceased complaining about the solitude and misery of life in lodgings. "I am writing by candle-light shivering with cold, and choked with smoke," he told one colleague. But he always saw the comedy even in his own distress – "My Laundress who is asthmatic, has dived into a closet . . . and is emitting from behind the door, an uninterrupted succession of the most unearthly, and hollow noises I ever heard." And all the time what is driving him, what is shaping his life, is the pre-eminent demand of his writing. "You know," he wrote to Catherine in extenuation for yet another absence or missed engagement, "I have frequently told you that my composition is peculiar; I never can write with effect – especially in the serious way – until I have got my steam up, or in other words until I have become so excited with my subject that I cannot leave off . . . ." This is the first description of the ardour of his creative process, and throughout these months there are constant intimations of his weariness and anxiety as a result – intimations, too, of that quick temper which he had inherited from his father. At some point he committed an "assault" upon a butcher's boy, according to the boy himself, but the nature and outcome of the episode are not known. No doubt it had something to do with a slight or affront which the young Dickens believed to have been perpetrated upon him – such matters generally aroused his anger.

Still the work piled up. In January 1836 he began once more writing sketches for the *Morning Chronicle* and during these months, also, he wrote frequent theatre reviews, carried on working in the press gallery of the House of Commons (according to one report he was so overpowered by a speech by Daniel O'Connell on the hardships of the Irish peasantry that he burst into tears and could not continue), he reported on a dinner for Lord John Russell in Bristol, reported on a fire at Hatfield House, and attended a by-election which he summed up as ". . . bells ringing, candidates speaking, drums sounding . . . men fighting, swearing drinking, and squabbling . . .", during the course of which Dickens holed up in a hotel room with other representatives of the press and played bagatelle. He also attended a stone-laying ceremony (which ceremony he later used, to great effect, in *Martin Chuzzlewit*). His life as a journalist, then, was a wearying if various one. But he was indisputably a success, and the favourable wind of his career seems, as often happens, to have given him self-confidence and even stridency in his dress: ". . . a fresh, handsome, genial young man," one of his parliamentary colleagues described him now, "with a profusion of brown hair, a bright eye . . . rather inclined to what was once called 'dandyism' in his attire, and to a rather exuberant display of jewellery on his vest and on his fingers." Another colleague has a similar story: ". . . he had bought a new hat, and a very handsome blue cloak, with black velvet facings, the corner of which he threw over his shoulder *à l'Espagnol.*" The same colleague recalls an incident which epitomises the merry side of Dickens: they were walking together through Hungerford Market "where we followed a coal-heaver, who carried his little rosy but grimy child looking over his shoulder; and CD bought a halfpenny worth of cherries and, as we went along, he gave them one by one to the little fellow without the knowledge of the father. CD seemed quite as much pleased as the child." And as he walked through the market Dickens, in that expressive but comic manner of his, alluded to the difficulties which he himself had experienced as a child – "He informed me, as we walked through it, that he knew *Hunger*ford Market well, laying unusual stress on the two first syllables." Yet within a matter of months Dickens's life was to change in ways that he could not, even in the days of his childhood fantasies, possibly have imagined.

Chapter 8

IN the autumn of 1835 a young publisher, John Macrone, approached Dickens with the idea of reprinting his stories and sketches in volume form, offering £100 for the copyright. Dickens seems to have leapt at the chance, not least because it would provide a welcome additional income just before his marriage, and almost at once he began to plan and arrange the proposed collection. The title was one difficulty; "Bubbles from the Bwain of Boz and the Graver of Cruikshank" was the first suggestion, by Macrone himself, but Dickens considered the idea of bubbles emanating from a steel engraver to be a little far-fetched. He in turn suggested the less facetious but more accurate title of "Sketches by Boz and Cuts by Cruikshank" – the important name in both titles, however, really being the second. It was something of a coup for Macrone to enlist the services of this illustrator, George Cruikshank, in the cause of a young author of only modest fame. To have his name on the title page was, if not a guarantee of success, at least a provident hedge against failure. He was called the "Illustrious George", and was already very well known as a caricaturist and illustrator of books – he was in some ways a difficult man, with powerful perceptions but equally powerful opinions. He could be truculent and assertive, even though this self-assertive manner often gave way, in his famous drinking bouts, to one of drunken clowning and gaiety. He was dark-haired, swarthy, with prominent eyes and nose; he looked as if he might have walked out of one of his own caricatures, and indeed he most resembled his own later illustration of Fagin in his condemned cell, of which G. K. Chesterton, perhaps Dickens's best critic, said that ". . . it does not merely look like a picture of Fagin; it looks like a picture by Fagin". Cruikshank called Dickens "Charley", and although at first their working relationship seemed perfectly amicable (with Cruikshank quite aware of his preeminent position) it soon became clear that the young author was in no sense about to defer to the older and more famous man. Quite the opposite, in fact; with a self-assurance and even self-assertiveness which are entirely characteristic of Dickens even when young, he began to badger Cruikshank for the illustrations to his first book – an event which Cruikshank, in a letter to Macrone, described as an "unpleasant turn". Matters were, as they generally are, resolved but the episode does suggest how Dickens already had a sure enough sense of his own worth to put himself on equal terms with the much more eminent artist; the episode reveals, too, something of the tension which existed between author and illustrator in a period when most of the popular forms of publishing depended upon the use of cartoons and illustrations. In fact it was often the illustrator who created the theme and organised the plot of serial works, with the author providing merely the written extensions of the artist's work – this was a "visual culture" just as much as our own, even if that visual dimension were established upon a quite different set of moral and theatrical stereotypes. But clearly it was important for Dickens to assert control over his own project – in the first edition of *Sketches by Boz* he paid fulsome tribute to Cruikshank, but all subsequent editions removed references to him in anything but a nominal sense. His relationship with the artist was in later years to be a most uneasy one (Cruikshank said in the 1860s, "When I and Mr Dickens meet on the same side of the way, either Dickens crosses over or I do") and this small preliminary skirmish did in fact delay the publication of the first edition for some two months. Eventually it appeared in February 1836.

It was a great success. Dickens had not organised his stories or journalistic pieces to any discernible plan, and in fact seems to have been at pains to suggest the range and heterogeneity of his talent (in a preliminary puff for the book in his own newspaper, he added the word "versatile" in proof to describe himself). But he had gone to some trouble to prepare the material for this more permanent form of publication – as we have already seen, he had written his essay on Newgate, perhaps the most powerful of his short pieces, solely for publication in the volume. In fact he would always have an intuitive and astute notion of public taste and public response, and on this first occasion he deliberately revised the sketches to make them more suitable for the readership of a book rather than that of a newspaper; he cut opening and closing paragraphs which were no longer relevant or suitable, he softened some of his social criticism, erased political or topical allusions and, as far as possible, removed any harshness or clumsiness which had inevitably crept in during the course of their rapid composition. In other words he was trying to make himself look less like a reporter and more of an author, an ambition emphasised in the preface he wrote for this rather small-sized two-volume edition: "Unlike the generality of pilot balloons which carry no car, in this one it is very possible for a man to embark, not only himself, but all his hopes of future fame, and all his chances of future success." It meant as much to him as that. In fact he tried to guarantee that success in advance, and showed a natural talent for expediting the business of "puffs" from fellow journalists and writers. He hardly needed to have done so, however, since the reviews were on the whole excellent – one newspaper summarising the general reaction with its compliment on "a perfect picture of the morals, manners and habits of a great portion of English Society". Later in life he was to dismiss this first work as "juvenile and hasty" but in fact it is not so; of course *Sketches by Boz* has suffered from public inattention in comparison with Dickens's novels, but it is nevertheless still a remarkable production which not only offers invaluable evidence for the growth of Dickens's genius but also acts as a tableau of English life at a time when the country itself was in the process of inevitable transition.

But a more important proposal, and more significant enterprise, was just about to come. *Sketches by Boz* appeared on 8 February, and just two days later a certain William Hall called upon Dickens at his lodgings in Furnival's Inn. At once Dickens, with his power of visual recognition, remembered him to be the man who had sold him, more than two years ago, over the counter in Johnson Court, the issue of the *Monthly Magazine* which had contained Dickens's first story. And what kind of young man did Hall now see? John Forster was to say of Dickens in this period that he had "eyes wonderfully beaming with intellect and running over with humour and cheerfulness" – a somewhat lax description, perhaps, to have eyes "running over" in quite that fashion. But it contained a grain of truth, as did his description of the young writer's energy "that seemed to tell so little of a student or writer of books, and so much of a man of action and business in the world". Dickens, by any standard, was certainly a man of "business" as well as busy-ness. Which is precisely what they discussed: William Hall was now one of the partners in the publishing firm of Chapman and Hall, a relatively new venture for which Hall supplied the financial acumen while Thomas Chapman provided the "literary" dimension (not an uncommon divide among publishers, and it may have been one that contributed to Dickens's later portrait of "Spenlow and Jorkins").

The previous year Chapman and Hall had engineered a success with a publication called the *Squib Annual of Poetry, Politics, and Personalities*, which was more or less a vehicle for the cartoons of Robert Seymour; now they wanted to repeat that success and Seymour had come up with the idea of publishing in shilling monthly parts a record of the exploits of something known as the "Nimrod Club"; this would concern the misadventures of a group of Cockney sportsmen (a familiar comic subject at the time, suggesting as it does that growing awareness of the uniqueness of urban experience). Seymour's drawings would be the important thing, however; the provider of the words, or "letterpress", definitely the subsidiary. The job of appending those words had been offered to Charles Whitehead, a writer who had just taken up the post of editing the *Library of Fiction* for Chapman and Hall, but he demurred; and it seemed that it was he who suggested the newly fashionable Boz for the task. No doubt Seymour was consulted before any decision was made but, when it came, it was entirely in Boz's favour. So Hall had arrived at Furnival's Inn in order to offer the job to Charles Dickens, for a payment of nine guineas per sheet and at a rate of one and a half sheets per month (a sheet being a publishing term for sixteen pages of the finished product). He accepted almost at once, and that evening Dickens wrote to Catherine saying that "the work will be no joke, but the emolument is too tempting to resist". Especially since now they were making active preparations for their marriage and, a week after receiving the offer from Hall, Dickens moved to larger quarters in Furnival's Inn at an additional cost of fifteen pounds a year. He was buying furniture, too, for this new home – rosewood for the drawing room, mahogany for the dining room. It would be here that he began the novel which would bring him world-wide fame.

But there were other matters to settle in advance: once again Dickens's self-command and determination prompted him to change the nature of the task he was about to perform. He may not yet have known the nature of his especial genius but, with the instinct of a "professional" writer, he knew what to avoid; the idea of a sporting club had been worked to death in recent years, as had the notion of "Cockney sportsmen", and from the beginning Dickens decided to turn the project on its head in order to give him room for the full use of his particular powers. He told Hall that ". . . it would be infinitely better for the plates to arise naturally out of the text; and that I should like to take my own way with a freer range of English scenes and people, and was afraid I should ultimately do so in any case." In other words, he had no intention of being a mere accompanist for Robert Seymour's illustrations. As in all the projects he ever undertook, he insisted that he should take the pre-eminent role. He was being all the more assertive because, at this time, Seymour was, as one contemporary noted, "the most varied and the most prolific" caricaturist of his day. Chapman and Hall, with the grudging acquiescence of Seymour, concurred.

It was almost time to begin. He needed a title, and a hero. In deference to Seymour's original notion he imported the idea of a club or society of urban "types", although they would have very little to do with the "sportsmen" whom the artist had envisaged. More significantly, he needed a name. Names would always be very important to him. In later years he could not begin a book until he had hit upon the right title, and in a notebook he made lists of fanciful or odd surnames to assist with his inspiration. It is simply that, without the name, the essence could not and did not exist; he was a man who trusted in the power of words and the name seemed to call forth the character whom then he could begin to portray. So it was with this new project: he remembered the name of a coach proprietor from Bath, a man whose coaches he would have seen or used during his peregrinations as a journalist on the *Morning Chronicle*. This man was Moses Pickwick. And so Mr Pickwick was born. And, with him, *The Pickwick Papers*.

Charles Dickens had now moved into his new chambers. The House of Commons was not sitting, so he had his mornings and evenings for his own writing. He needed all the time he could get. He had agreed to provide the first number by early in March, and the second at the end of the same month – each number would be longer than anything he had ever written before, some twelve thousand words, but the length did not daunt him. He sat down, on 18 February, 1836, and began. He began with a metaphor of the rising sun. He began, in another sense, with the rising of his own hopes and ambitions, powerfully brought forth in the first words of the book which was to win him immortality: "The first ray of light which illumines the gloom, and converts into a dazzling brilliancy that obscurity in which the earlier history of the public career of the immortal Pickwick would appear to be involved . . ." The first sentences of a novel are very important to the novelist, and here Dickens is at once setting his imprint upon a venture that began in high spirits even as it marked the onset of a journey of which he did not know the end. "Pickwick is at length begun in all his might and glory," Dickens told his publishers that evening. "The first chapter, will be ready tomorrow." He was working quickly and with great energy – trying to plan out each chapter in advance as he went along but all the time being caught up in the processes of his own invention, finding in this new work a bright glass in which other aspects of his genius began to manifest themselves. He could not have worked so quickly if it had not been for his journalistic experience, however, and indeed there was a sense in which he saw *The Pickwick Papers* as a continuation in a higher key of his skills as a story-teller and sketch-writer; that is why he could begin it without trepidation, and with the assurance which allowed him to invent rapidly and easily. He had finished the first chapter the next day, and three days later he had got Mr Pickwick and his faithful followers on the coach to Rochester and to the scenes of his happy childhood. Already he had thought of Jingle, so firmly modelled on his comic favourites, but nevertheless a recognisable Dickensian creation – he had that "jaunty impudence and perfect self-possession" which he had already noticed in the cab-drivers of London and which seems so close to his own image of himself in these youthful years. As soon as he thought of him, he *saw* him just as he had seen the heroes of his childhood reading. There he was, "a rather tall thin young man, in a green coat" who talks in breathless and disjointed phrases. And as soon as he talks Dickens hears him; he is, as it were, simply listening to the character and transcribing what he says: ". . . other day-five children-mother-tall lady, eating sandwiches-forgot the arch-crash-knock-children look round-mother's head off-sandwich in her hand-no mouth to put it in . . ." As he writes Dickens rarely pauses to correct; his handwriting is large and firm, springing from him with extraordinary ease. He has found his great subject, and it is not long before he has taken Mr Pickwick to a ball, installed him in the Bull Inn, Rochester, and begun to digress upon the characteristics and adventures of his companions. There is great humour and even joy in all this; it is the joy of the young Dickens able for the first time to write and invent upon a large scale. Of course he still retains some of the supercilious and ironic manner-isms of his journalistic work, and of course he almost at once incorporates the topical and trivial events of the day; but the important thing is that he is now beginning to enlarge himself, to expand everything he had previously done, to find himself as a writer at just the appropriate time.

In what sense appropriate? It would take a few months to make its mark, but the fact was that the form and manner of *The Pickwick Papers* heralded a revolution in the circulation and appeal of narrative fiction. Of course the idea of shilling monthly parts for this enterprise had originally been that of Robert Seymour, and the form itself was not a particularly new one; there had been similar excursions in the same field of light humour and *facetiae* with heroes such as Mr Jorrocks and Dr Syntax. Serialisation of fiction in magazines was equally common (much of the work of Marryat and Galt was first published in this way) and there were even examples of fiction being published in monthly parts – the difference being that such serialisation was really only employed for old and familiar tales like *The Pilgrim's Progress*. What was unfamiliar about Dickens's venture was the idea of a *new* story being marketed in this way, and within a matter of months it became clear exactly what it was that Dickens had initiated.

He was working quickly now. He introduced the character of Mr Winkle in order to satisfy the "sporting" humour of Seymour's first illustrations, although the artist himself was also forced to change his work in compliance with the narrative Dickens was producing. Originally he had drawn Mr Pickwick as a thin man but agreed to revert to an earlier conception and turn him into that plump figure who became part of Victorian popular mythology (Chapman, the literary "half" of the publishing firm, later said that this persona was based upon a real Richmond *beau*). In fact the inspiration was coming from all around Dickens as he wrote – already he had gone back to his childhood haunts, had employed many of the comic tags and characters which he had seen upon the stage, but he was also drawing material from the very life of the city and the nation during this period. He had even managed to write too much – so prodigal was his invention that within a few days he had introduced Pickwick, Jingle, Winkle, Tupman, Snodgrass, a ball, a duel, and consequently had overwritten by two pages. For the first and last time in his writing career (for he learnt quickly) one monthly number ended with only part of a chapter. By the end of March he had already finished the second number, and it was on the thirty-first of that month that the actual first instalment was published of *The Posthumous Papers of the Pickwick Club, containing a faithful record of the Perambulations, Perils,*

Travels, Adventures and Sporting Transactions of the Corresponding Members. It was "Edited by 'Boz'", came in green wrappers, with 32 pages of print and 4 engravings by Seymour, and was priced at one shilling. The exact number printed is in doubt, but it can be assumed that approximately 400 were distributed by Chapman and Hall. It had been hard work, but it was finished. He wrote his own advertisement for the *Library of Fiction* in which facetiously he heralds the appearance of a work to be placed alongside that of Gibbon's *The History of the Decline and Fall of the Roman Empire*.

Buoyed up by his exhilaration at a labour completed he now went on to the next event of his life, his marriage – "went on" being the appropriate phrase here, since there was a sense in which these extraordinary months in the life of the young writer were like a series of hurdles, over each of which he leapt as he went along. Certainly it was the success of *Sketches by Boz*, and the prospect of extra financial reward from *The Pickwick Papers*, that persuaded him to marry sooner than he had originally intended. He and Catherine Hogarth had been engaged for less than a year and, since she was still a minor, Dickens had to return to the scene of his old employment, Doctors' Commons, in order to obtain a special marriage licence. The ceremony itself took place on 2 April in the Hogarths' parish church, the newly built St Luke's in Chelsea. The only people present were the Dickens and Hogarth families, John Macrone, Henry Burnett – a young singer soon to be married to Fanny – and Thomas Beard who acted as best man. "It was altogether a very quiet piece of business," Beard said many years later in a characteristic piece of under-statement. Burnett in turn remembers Dickens "helping his young wife out of the carriage after the wedding, and taking her up the steps of the house of quiet, intellectual, unobtrusive Mr Hogarth". The wedding breakfast here was a quiet affair, too: "A few common, pleasant things were said, healths drunk with a very few words said by either party – yet all things passed off very pleasantly, and all seemed happy, not the least so Dickens and his young girlish wife." As a wedding present Dickens gave his wife a sandalwood work-box inlaid with ivory, and after the breakfast at York Place he took his bride down for their honeymoon to a small cottage (a two-storey wooden building, whitewashed) in the Kentish village of Chalk; this was only a few miles from Rochester, and it seems that the letting of the cottage was arranged by the Dickenses' old neighbour, Mrs Newnham, from Ordnance Terrace days. The decision to take his honeymoon in an area he had known as a child is not perhaps as sentimental as it seems: it is quite likely that Dickens, at a time when he was deluged with work, decided to take the easiest option and rely upon the help of old family friends to secure him a place to rest. And, since he was in the process of writing a narrative set in the same area, no doubt the thought of returning to it for an additional examination was a welcome one.

The newly-married pair stayed in Chalk for less than two weeks, and then returned to the new lodgings at Furnival's Inn; the three rooms here were larger than those which Dickens had originally possessed but nevertheless they must have seemed somewhat small to Catherine after her life in the capacious Hogarth household. But at once Dickens went back to work. On the eighteenth of the month he had his first meeting with Robert Seymour; he had invited him to Furnival's Inn together with Chapman and Hall, to "take a glass of grog" (his younger brother, Frederick, to whom Dickens was especially attached, was also a member of the little party), but in the same letter Dickens asserted his proprietorial rights over their venture by suggesting that Seymour alter one of his illustrations – a task which Seymour, no doubt against his wishes, carried out. Nothing is known of the ensuing party, and it is noteworthy now only because, two days later, Seymour went into the summer-house of his garden in Islington, set up his gun with a string on its trigger, and shot himself through the head. He was, like many illustrators, a melancholy and in some ways thwarted man. It has been suggested that Dickens's request to change the illustration was one of the causes of his suicide, but this is most unlikely. Seymour was used to the imperatives of professional life, and it seems that it was essentially anxiety and overwork which eventually killed him. He was in any case of disturbed mind at the time – in later life Dickens, who always professed great regard for him, told the story that some days before his death Seymour had asked his wife to try on a widow's cap. In any event he left a short note for his wife "blaming himself, and making some reference to the Creator" and at the subsequent inquest a verdict of "temporary insanity" was reached.

The suicide of Seymour was of course a most unwelcome surprise both to Dickens and his publishers since the whole project, originally established on the popularity of the artist, might quickly founder without him. More immediately, the second number was about to be printed and at once a search was made of the artist's working-room; three engravings were found, and these were duly published as Seymour's last contribution to *The Pickwick Papers*. But the essential problem remained: since his return from his honeymoon Dickens had already written half of the succeeding number, and some decision about the future shape of the serieswithout Seymour had to be made. At once the search began for a suitable artist. A young man who had already illustrated one of Dickens's stories, R. W. Buss, was first chosen: although he had had no real experience of steel engraving (a difficult and then novel process which involved etching upon a steel plate with a needle and then "biting in" the image with acid), he agreed to begin work upon the third number. Later he said that he practised this new craft for a fortnight "almost day and night" though in the end he had to give his designs to a professional etcher; even then, they were not satisfactory. It seems that Dickens now stepped in. He was unhappy with the results and arranged for Buss to be taken off the job. Or, perhaps, merely acquiesced in his publishers' decision to remove him. It was at this point that he, or Chapman and Hall, came up with the idea that saved the project and helped to increase its success: it was suggested that he should write an extra half a sheet (or eight pages) each month and that the quantity of illustrations should be halved to two plates. In other words, he was able to take command of the project and to proceed with it in a manner unhampered by the demands for too many illustrations or by the requests of a too-powerful illustrator: it is clear also that at this point he had every confidence in his ability, and a good idea of the kind of work *The Pickwick Papers* could become. At such moments of decision, it is possible to see both those intuitive and managerial qualities which hastened the progress of Dickens's career. The effect on Buss was severe, however, and it is reported that "he locked up his engraving tools" and destroyed much of his work relating to *The Pickwick Papers*. "For the rest of his life," it was said, "he could not bear to have the matter mentioned in his presence." And yet it is touching that, after the author's death, it was Buss who painted the famous portrait of Dickens dreaming, all the characters of his imagination surrounding him as he slept.

Now came the moment, after the removal of Buss, that Dickens chose the illustrator who more than anyone else came to be associated with his work – Hablot Knight Browne. He was a little younger than Dickens and, although he had had no academic training, had been apprenticed to an engraver; he had left his apprenticeship a short while before, and was still making up his mind whether he wanted to be a painter or an illustrator when he encountered the novelist. He had already been working with him on a small pamphlet and, although he had had scarcely more experience than Buss in etching, he was chosen to continue work on *The Pickwick Papers*. This may have been for personal reasons as much as anything else: Dickens had already met him and no doubt saw in him those qualities of steadiness, perseverance and, above all, pliability which he knew that he needed. Browne was a quiet, unassuming, unobtrusive and almost painfully shy man; he hated going out "in company" and to the end of his life remained something of a "loner", a man who was content with his lot in life and performed it satisfactorily. In some ways he resembled Thomas Beard, in fact, and it seems that Dickens was attracted to just this type of character – not necessarily because it complemented his own more vivacious and gregarious temperament, but rather because these qualities of self-effacement and shyness were precisely the ones he admired and precisely the ones which he felt most lacking in himself. Thus, paradoxical though it may sound, his friendship with the artist in a way helped to recompense him for his own strengths. So Browne was chosen and, as we shall see, no better illustrator could have been found – not only did he at once fall into compliance with Dickens's ways and requests (even adopting the name of "Phiz" to complement "Boz") but he learned from the novelist's own art and, in a sense, grew with it. Of course his relationship with Dickens changed the direction of his life, and the ensuing success of *The Pickwick Papers* made his reputation in a way that a hundred smaller successes over a number of years could never have achieved. In fact he was not a particularly good draughtsman, and there are weaknesses in many of his compositions, but he became a wonderful caricaturist – his ability to match the mood and the atmosphere of Dickens's work compensating for the occasional failure of his technical skills.

Dickens himself was, despite the setbacks of this new endeavour, taking on work and commitments almost blindly – as if he felt that no task or range of tasks was impossible to him. Even while he had been preparing *Sketches by Boz* for the press, John Hullah – a composer who met him through his sister, Fanny, while they were both at the Royal Academy – was proposing a collaboration with him on a musical venture. He wanted a libretto for a Venetian subject (Italian opera was then very popular in London) but once again Dickens demurred at something which he could not undertake with equanimity, and instead suggested to Hullah that it would be best if he worked on something closer to home and closer to his own interests. This is precisely what happened: Dickens began writing a "burletta", adapted from one of his own stories, the first version of which he finished by the end of January and which was entitled *The Village Coquettes*. But he was revising it even while working on *The Pickwick Papers*, albeit with the help of his more musical father-in-law, and had finished it by July. Then almost at once he took on the task of turning another of his stories, "The Great Winglebury Duel", into a farce for the stage. In later life he admitted that ". . . I don't feel the writing of a farce to be quite suited to me. I am continually trying to get a meaning into it, of which a farce is not susceptible", but, at this stage in his career, anything seemed possible. Certainly he had not lost his wish to write for the theatre – an aspiration which would, in fact, intermittently return to him throughout his life. He was also finishing *Sunday Under Three Heads*, a pamphlet directed against the Sunday Observance Bill, an Evangelical measure which would have severely curtailed the Sunday amusements of the labouring and middle classes. It is a polemical pamphlet but one conducted not so much through argument or discussion as through imaginative accounts of various characters. What is noticeable in Dickens's approach, in particular, is his barely concealed disdain for the rich and the fashionable – this is partly his own natural defensiveness, but there is also within it the pride of the self-made man convinced that such people are somehow less substantial than he is.

By early May he had also signed an agreement with John Macrone to write a novel entitled *Gabriel Vardon, The Locksmith of London*. This may have been the novel he had been proposing to himself ever since he began writing the sketches and, if so, since it only eventually emerged in completed form as *Barnaby Rudge*, it has the claim to being the novel most delayed by Dickens. He received two hundred pounds for this, and then three months later accepted a further one hundred pounds when he agreed to write for Thomas Tegg a children's book to be called *Solomon Bell the Raree Showman*. Then in the same month he made an agreement with yet another publisher, Richard Bentley, for two novels, each to be of the conventional three-volume length. He had also agreed to write sketches for a new weekly paper, *The Carlton Chronicle* – and all this at the time he was writing *The Pickwick Papers*, continuing with his parliamentary duties for the *Morning Chronicle*, and preparing another volume of *Sketches* to be published by John Macrone. In other words, he had committed himself to the eventual publication of some five books while still heavily engaged upon his first novel. ". . . more irons in the fire:" he had told Catherine earlier, "more grist to the Mill . . .", in conscious or unconscious adaptation of the line in *The Miller and His Men* which had so powerfully affected him when he was young; was it the image in that play of unceasing work ("More sacks to the mill") which had so entranced him?

The reasons for placing such an extraordinary burden of work upon his shoulders are various, however, the first being that he needed the money. No doubt he was already planning to leave the *Morning Chronicle* (a step he eventually took in November) and no doubt he was even now trying to measure his funds for the months and years ahead, estimating the loss of the *Morning Chronicle* income against the payments for the proposed works of fiction. Throughout his life Dickens had an obsessive need for the security which money could bring – it ought to be remembered that he would soon be casting the childhood of the miser, Ebenezer Scrooge, at least partly in the image of his own. It is clear enough that he knew as well as anyone, at least as well as any of his biographers, from what troubled origins this demand for money came. It was not that he himself was a miser or loved money for itself. He was on all occasions a most generous and open-handed man. It was just that his early experiences in the Marshalsea and blacking factory provoked an anxiety which only the assurance of financial well-being could assuage. Money was a defence for him. But there were other reasons for his over-activity in this period – it is clear that he wanted to write "serious" fiction. His friends had told him, when he embarked upon *The Pickwick Papers*, that ". . . it was a low, cheap form of publication, by which I should ruin all my rising hopes" and, although this was clearly not the case, he must have worried about the possibility that he had sold himself short and must still have wanted to attempt something which was of a much more conventionally literary kind; hence the agreement to write three-volume novels on the familiar pattern which, he told Richard Bentley, would be ". . . a work on which I might build my fame . . ." And beyond all this, too, is the boundless self-assurance of a young man who clearly believes that he can achieve so much without wearing away his unnatural energy, who realises that in starting *The Pickwick Papers* he had come across an inexhaustible well of creativity within himself. And also he simply wanted to *work*, to exhaust himself, to place burdens on his own shoulders like those of the miller and his men to whose unwearying progress he had once been so mightily attracted.

All the while he was still living with Catherine in Furnival's Inn: it was not so small a lodging for a young couple, perhaps, although his brother, Frederick, was often in attendance and Catherine's young sister, Mary Hogarth, was a frequent visitor. In fact there were times when she must have seemed almost a permanent one. She stayed for a month with them just after they had returned from their honeymoon, but there is no doubt that Dickens appreciated her company just as much as her own sister did. Mary herself reciprocated their feelings, and on her return after the month in Furnival's Inn told her cousin that Catherine "makes a most capital housekeeper and is as happy as the day is long – I think they are more devoted than ever since their Marriage if that be possible – I am sure you would be delighted with him if you knew him he is such a nice creature and so clever he is courted and made up to by all literary Gentlemen, and has more to do in that way than he can well manage." Somehow he *did* manage, yet no doubt it was partly the pressure of such constant hard work, just as much as the early Victorian belief in a "change of air", that persuaded Catherine and her husband to take a cottage in the country during the late summer – in August and September they absconded to Petersham, from which rural retreat Dickens made occasional sallies into London until they returned on 24 September. It was here, during this interval, that he placed Pickwick drunk in a wheelbarrow and that he introduced to his readers the legal partnership of Dodson and Fogg.

He came back to London particularly in order to superintend the rehearsals of his first farce, *The Strange Gentleman*. In fact he had originally started work on *The Village Coquettes*, but problems with his collaborator and with the text meant that *The Strange Gentleman* was the one to be staged first. He composed it quickly enough in that clear, round hand which is characteristic of Dickens in this period; and it may be worth noting, too, simply to prove that John Dickens was gainfully employed in this period of his son's first success, that his father made a fair copy to be given to the censor of plays, the Lord Chamberlain. Dickens had written it for John Braham, a fine singer who had the year before built the St James's Theatre of which he was also the manager: Braham would not only put on the play but take the leading singing role within it. His stage manager, John Pritt Harley, was also the leading comedian of his company and would perform as well, their dual roles suggesting how closely acting and management were combined in this period. Writing and acting could be, too, and there were persistent reports over the years that Dickens himself played a role in his first drama.

The Strange Gentleman opened on 29 September. It is essentially a farce on the theme of mistaken identity, in which the prospect of a duel so frightens a young man that he sends a letter to the mayor in order to prevent it. Most of the action takes place in the room of an inn; doors open and close; various personages make their exits and entrances; the finale suggests the importance of those twin deities, marriage and money: altogether a rather conventional exercise in stage comedy and Dickens admitted as much later: "I just put down for everybody what everybody at the St James's Theatre wanted to say and do, and that they could say and do best, and I have been most severely repentant ever since." The point is that Dickens, possessed as he was by the theatre and influenced so heavily by the stage, could not in fact write plays at all. He failed, in one sense, because he was too much in awe of the theatre; he had been affected by it too much to be able to break away from the origin of those effects. But essentially his was a literary rather than a dramatic genius; his gift lay in symbolic narrative rather than in dialogue, in creating characters who dwell in language rather than ones who dwell upon the boards. This in itself should give pause to those people who in our own time suggest that Dickens, because he was such a "popular" author of serial fiction, would necessarily in the late twentieth century have written for television. Nothing could be further from the truth. The closest equivalent to television in the previous century was the theatre, and certainly he could not write in *that* medium.

The Strange Gentleman was at the time a modest success, however, and continued its run until Dickens's second theatrical effort, *The Village Coquettes*, was ready for presentation on 6 December. This too was of a conventional turn, a story of forbidden love between those of different "stations" in life which is set in an English village of the previous century. Conversations, comic and sentimental in turn, are interrupted by song; the general atmosphere of the piece (as well as of Charles Dickens's dramatic writing) can be glimpsed in a short episode:

Main character sees fallen leaves as he wanders disconsolate and remarks: "What a contrast they present now, and how true an emblem of my own lost happiness."

Then he proceeds to sing:

> "Autumn leaves, autumn leaves, lie strewn around me here;
> Autumn leaves, autumn leaves, how sad, how cold, how drear!
> How like the hopes of childhood's day,
> Thick clustering on the bough!"

A sentimental drama, in other words, with exits and asides and soliloquies and moral generalisations – "Be the high-souled woman: not the light and thoughtless trifle that disgraces the name." But it is not without humour, as you would expect from an author who was embarked upon *The Pickwick Papers*, some of it not a million miles removed from Alfred Jingle – ". . . give us your hand, hearty squeeze, good shake . . ." In his own preface to the published version of the work, Dickens was rather defensive about his effort, and indeed despite the playbill written after the first night's performance – ". . .one of the most triumphant receptions ever known" – it only ran for nineteen performances. The critics too were almost uniformly unimpressed by the libretto of "Boz", and remarked chiefly upon the unprecedented appearance of the author before his audience on the first night. It was not usual even for the actors to take applause afterwards in that manner, and the arrival on stage of Dickens was considered somewhat disgraceful; the author had his own reasons, however, and one of them was his need to give "Boz" flesh and publicity at a time when there were rumours about the identity or even identities behind the pseudonym. And of course since he loved performing, being applauded, being seen, what better role could he choose than that of himself? In later life he rejected the burletta just as he had the farce – when asked if he still possessed a copy of *The Village Coquettes* he replied that ". . . if I knew it was in my house and if I could not get rid of it in any other way, I would burn the wing of the house where it was". Enough said.

Of course his defensive preface suggests that even at the time he knew that his major work lay in quite a different direction. For a while he had wanted to be known both as a dramatic writer and as a writer of fiction, but the failure of one and the relative success of the other made it clear to him in what department he ought to expend his energies. In October his publishers, Chapman and Hall, were already discussing a possible sequel to *The Pickwick Papers*, for throughout this period that narrative was moving slowly ahead, growing in power as it proceeded. He was writing quickly but such is the sureness of his invention that the manuscript in his strong and confident hand is remarkably free of corrections. He numbers each page at the top as he goes along with his flowing quill pen – there are two or three small deletions on each page which look as if they were made at the actual time of writing, and there are others which were clearly made when he looked over the manuscript after he had completed it. He was often writing early in the morning or late at night, and often when exhausted from his reportorial duties. The narrative, as a result, contains a few repetitions and obvious occasions when the seed for a later scene has been sown in Dickens's mind as he went along. There is a vignette in the Fleet Prison where a poor man's mind is slowly breaking down as he "was riding, in imagination, some desperate steeplechase . . .", for example, and this image is worked up into a whole story a few numbers later. Dickens's imagination caught fire as he went along, then, the energy and speed making it burn all the brighter. It is this sense of moving life which runs through it almost from the beginning, and within a few weeks he had started to tie the month of the fictional narrative to the very month in which that number would appear. By October he had already planned the probable course of the next three numbers and, in the December issue, he is looking forward to the events of the next spring. By the conclusion of his labour he had so harnessed the time of his narrative to the real time of chronology, and had been so successful at relating the impact of brief stories and events to the larger movement of each episode, that in *The Pickwick Papers* he came close to incorporating the rhythm of life itself.

That again marks something of the novelty of his enterprise: unsure as to exactly what type of work he was beginning, he did not feel constrained by literary etiquette and was able to include anything which occurred to him at the time. He was putting in short stories, for example, most of them invented on the spot. Each number had as a result something of the heterogeneity and variety of a magazine, with comic narrative, sentimental vignette and Gothic "horror" jostling alongside each other as they did in journals like the *Penny Magazine*. He was beginning to imitate, incorporate and to change all the aspects of popular and literary culture around him and that, in turn, accounts for the appeal of *The Pickwick Papers* as it unfolded: in a sense it became a work of journalism as well as of fiction, and the audience increased immeasurably when it was realised that such a work did not have the conventional inhibitions of ordinary fiction. He had been working towards something of the same kind in his sketches, where fictional material was being introduced into a realistic setting, but now in *The Pickwick Papers* he was able, and indeed forced, to work on a much larger scale. He was writing about debtors' prisons, for example, with a range of feeling and observation that he had not been able to introduce into his previous prison sketches, and the whole landscape of his imagination – scenes of poverty and death in London counterpointed by scenes of peace and seclusion in the countryside – was now lent much more imaginative and thematic coherence. It works in smaller ways, too: the scene of Pickwick falling asleep drunk in a wheelbarrow is a reprise of a scene concerning a pickpocket which Dickens had already employed in an earlier sketch, "The Hospital Patient". There was no need to waste a good "picture", to use one of his favourite terms. But the relation between the sketches and the novel is even closer than that, since there are times when it is clear that the same group of concerns in any one month inter-animates both. He is writing *Sunday Under Three Heads* and emphasising the right of the urban "masses" to entertainment, for example, in the latter part of June at exactly the same time he is writing the scene of the cricket match in *The Pickwick Papers* which is followed by the happy drunkenness of the Pickwickians. The idea of the need for recreation, and for harmless pleasure, infuses both the pamphlet and this episode in the book. Then again in a sketch of the same period, "A Little Talk about Spring and the Sweeps", he emphasises the need for happiness and recreation in the lives of children, all of a piece with the magical landscape of childhood which he is conjuring up at the same time in *The Pickwick Papers*. And, when he talks in that sketch about how these "merry sports" are being swept away leaving "degradation and discontent" in their place, we see how in all three works – pamphlet, sketch and novel – he is describing the need for enjoyment and for recreation, linking it both to politics and to childhood, introducing into it the spectre of authorities who might try to crush it, infusing it with memories of his own ruined infancy and then resurrecting it in the idyllic scenes of *The Pickwick Papers*.

The closeness of Dickens's imaginative concerns worked also in another sense: only a few days after he has reflected upon the importance of clothes in one of his finest sketches, "Meditations in Monmouth Street", and had expatiated upon "Hackney Cabs and their Drivers" in the *Carlton Chronicle*, he brings both sets of observations together in *The Pickwick Papers* with his wonderful portrayal of Sam Weller's father, Tony Weller. In the sketch on hackney cabs, the driver is philosophical about accidents he inflicts upon those he transports – "On'y the fare, Sir," he says of the injured party, ". . . bump they cums agin the post, and out flies the fare like bricks." In Monmouth Street the narrator had stood meditating upon the old clothes hanging in this street of stallholders – "these extensive groves of the illustrious dead," he calls them – and as he speculates about the former wearers of these skeleton suits, overcoats, coarse frocks, and ancient trousers he notes a pair of "jolly, good-tempered, hearty-looking" boots and invents an owner equal to them in placidity and cheerfulness of temper. Both of these moods come together in the number he was writing at the same time, where he describes Mr Weller – stage coachman and wearer of boots – in just such a manner. So the progress of inspiration ran from one medium to the next, his thoughts revolving on the work to hand and irradiating everything else which he wrote.

He wrote so quickly, so freely, with so little sense of formality that he picked up material wherever he could find it. The scenes in the Fleet prison are in part derived from his own childhood observations of the Marshalsea but it is also quite evident that he took details from a book published the year before, *Scenes and Stories by a Clergyman in Debt*; it also seems likely that he introduced this sobering element into Mr Pickwick's progress precisely because, in this period, there were many pamphlets and much journalistic discussion on the need for debtors' reform. The impact of topical and journalistic events on *The Pickwick Papers* has never been properly studied (perhaps with good reason, since it would take a lifetime to pick out all the obliquities and passing references) but there is no doubt that this monthly series was very much "up to the minute" in its details and references, as for example in the impact of the Melbourne-Norton trial for adultery on Dickens's own dramatisation of Bardell *v* Pickwick. There is one point during this very trial scene when Sam Weller tells the prosecuting counsel that if his eyes "wos a pair o' patent double million magnifyin' gas microscopes of hextra power" he might be able to see through a door but, given that they weren't, he couldn't. This sounds like another example of Dickens's humorous invention, but in fact there was at this time a "double million magnifying gas microscope" being exhibited and discussed. So he took in everything he saw, he incorporated what might have seemed the most recalcitrant or alien material and brought it to life. That was the extraordinary and startling achievement of *The Pickwick Papers* – for the first time it made sense of the world around Dickens's contemporaries by finding a common place where the most recondite and the most familiar, the most disagreeable and the most comic, elements of early nineteenth-century England could be organised and controlled.

Of course the novel did not spring up from nowhere. We have seen how indebted Dickens was to his earlier training as a journalist but, equally significantly, *The Pickwick Papers* came out of his early reading; it is a refraction, as it were, from his own childhood. Much critical and scholarly ink has been spent on finding the literary predecessors of Pickwick (it is one of the sins of scholarship to assume, however unconsciously, that there is nothing original in the world), and indeed there are many sources or resemblances to be located. The election scenes at Eatanswill may owe something to Fielding, something to Maria Edgeworth, something to Peacock, something to Galt, and something to Surtees; the duel in the novel is related to duels in Smollett; some of the comic scenes might have been taken from the farces by Mrs Inchbald which Dickens had read as a boy; the whole idea of Pickwick's adventures might have come from Pierce Egan. In fact the novel does begin in the manner of Egan, but then Dickens's own vision gets the better of him as he proceeds. And that is the point. *The Pickwick Papers* had begun as an extension of his sketches, and also bears traces of its origin in the eighteenth-century novel and its offshoots. But the differences become obvious almost from the start: if we look at Pierce Egan's series on Tom and Jerry, whose adventures were always said most to resemble those of Mr Pickwick, there is an absolute contrast between them. Egan has the characteristic eighteenth-century belief in rationalisation and generalisation, together with a certain eighteenth-century syntactical politesse most obvious in his sometimes arch circumlocutions. Despite the apparent raciness of the theme, the material is always somehow set at a distance from the reader, a characteristic nowhere more in evidence than in the fact that Egan always prints colloquialisms in italics as if they were part of some alien language. Dickens is never that kind of writer. He abolishes the distance, he incorporates the slang of his period as if it were instinctive to him, he infuses his prose with an energy and a vivacity that preclude the kind of reserve Egan always maintained. Of course there are geniality, farce and high spirits within eighteenth-century fiction; Dickens incorporates these, too, but he also removes from them the harshness and the violence so endemic in earlier fiction and instead irradiates his narrative with geniality and with sentiment.

The writing of *The Pickwick Papers* is in that sense also the education of Charles Dickens; education in public response, education in his powers of human observation, education in his talent for comic narrative. Just as he finds new meaning and new life in the figure of Mr Pickwick as he proceeds – Mr Pickwick soon ceases to be merely a humorous figure and becomes instead the embodiment of natural benevolence – so Dickens discovers new power and capacity within himself. And it is a young man's book, too, because it has no sense of an ending. All of his life up to that point is somewhere within these pages, and in that spirit *The Pickwick Papers* becomes an exercise in self-definition as well as in the telling of a story. That accounts for its charm, that instinctive, compulsive, exhilarating sense of discovery. The scenes in Rochester, no less than the scenes in prison, testify to the sense of enlargement and liberation which Dickens was now feeling; the real Rochester, the real Bull Inn, the real debtors' prison, were not as large and as echoic as they become in these pages where they are labyrinthine, incalculable, chaotic. There were times when Dickens was overworked and ill – violent headaches, and something he described as "rheumatism in the face", afflicted him in the winter of 1836. Such apparently minor ills were not insignificant in a period when even a common ailment such as a cold might prove fatal and where the techniques of medicine and surgery were quite rudimentary. But even during such periods of stress Dickens managed to work on, his invention and humour undiminished.

Of course he was now also working closely with Hablot Browne, his illustrator, but the speed with which he himself was forced to work sometimes made matters difficult for his new colleague. Generally, however, it was possible for Dickens to send portions of the manuscript to Browne who would then within twenty-four hours be able to produce an appropriate drawing; this he would in turn despatch to Dickens, who would comment upon it. He often suggested changes and, although these were of a minor kind, his interventions do emphasise how closely Dickens felt himself to be involved in all aspects of the novel's appearance – "Winkle should be holding the Candlestick above his head I think," he wrote above one of Browne's sketches involving Mr Winkle's misadventures in Bath. "It looks more comical, the light having gone out." And these suggestions underline, also, how closely Dickens understood the conventions of caricature. But there were occasions when there was no time to give "Phiz" any manuscript material, and he would rush over to Browne's house, outline the story he had in mind and allow him to work "blind". In fact Browne rarely failed to rise to the appropriate occasion. His first work in *The Pickwick Papers* is not very distinguished, and at times somewhat clumsy, but he rapidly and steadily improved so that by the sixth number he had evolved a much cleaner and more detailed style. And he was able to work quickly, too – he could design, etch a plate and have it "bitten in" (for this he had a partner, Robert Young, who coincidentally also had rooms in Furnival's Inn) within twenty-four hours. It is important, in considering the composition of *The Pickwick Papers*, to realise that this was the speed and the pace at which both author and illustrator were working.

Nevertheless Dickens understood very well the importance of visual aids both in the understanding and in the reception of his monthly parts. The etchings were the first things to be seen in each number, just as it was the etchings which were characteristically displayed in the windows of booksellers. There was still in the early nineteenth century, as we have discovered, a popular visual culture which had been nourished on the tradition of Hogarth, Gillray and Cruikshank: it was a tradition that bolstered the "progress" of a Hogarth character or the precise moral lesson to be adduced from one of Cruikshank's cartoons. It was the tradition of graphic satire which Dickens himself had known as a boy, and the illustrations of "Phiz" helped to enlist it in the service of Dickens's own imagination; his characters could be fixed in the public mind by visual means, thus allowing the narrative to acquire continuity and identity, and the book itself was given the added weight and resonance which derived from a precise tradition in which clothes, gesture and facial appearance could signal the intentions of the author even before his actual words were read. It was a kind of static theatre. That Browne's illustrations were important for the author, too, is not in doubt. Dickens will often arrange his climaxes so that they can be epitomised by an illustration, and he will often write "up to" whatever illustration he requires. Of course it was also important for him to be able to visualise a character as he went along, and so the illustrations of Pickwick or Winkle or Sam Weller acted for him as a form of visual aide-mémoire, and one of enormous help in the processes of composition because he was able to see them in front of him without any additional creative effort. Thus Dickens's world is created, a world first revealed in his sketches but now for the first time being given depth and life – a world of shrewish women and good-hearted men, of amorous widows and jovial Cockneys, of poor abandoned children and virginal young women, of self-important hypocrites and ridiculous judges. At times of stress, this was also the world which Dickens himself believed that he lived in; but, at this stage, it was the dream of his youthful creativity billowing in clouds around him.

The success of *The Pickwick Papers* was not long in coming.

Chapman and Hall had printed approximately four hundred copies of the first monthly number. By the end, they were selling some forty thousand. It began to happen at the time of the fourth number, or instalment, when Sam Weller is introduced and when Hablot Browne's illustrations appear for the first time. In July, also, Boz's identity was first revealed, and in that same month William Jerdan printed extracts from the novel in his influential *Literary Gazette*. And, since *The Pickwick Papers* appeared monthly, it reaped the benefit of being mentioned or reviewed each month in the other public prints – although there seems to have been some difficulty in categorising the material from which they were quoting. Some journals placed it not under fiction but under journalism or "miscellanies". But there is no doubt that its comic appeal – its human appeal – was steadily being seen and its audience steadily growing. That is also why in the fourth number there first appeared the "Pickwick Advertiser", a section of advertisements placed in front of the main text like advertisements in a newspaper. In this first edition of the "Advertiser" the only goods to be sold are books, among them *A Popular Treatise on Diet and Regimen*, *Les dames de Byron* and *The Angler's Souvenir*, but the success of Pickwick was such that by the ninth number there were more pages of advertisement (some thirty-nine) than pages of text (thirty-one). The range of the advertisements had also widened from the merely literary, and now included Rotterdam Corn and Bunion Solvent, Simpson's new Antibilious Pill, a gentleman's water-proof cloak "in all respects superior to the shabby-looking India Rubber" and – a firm favourite, this – Rowlands's Macassar Oil.

The extent of the advertising was an indication of one significant fact: *The Pickwick Papers* had become an extraordinary success. ". . . no sooner was a new number published," one contemporary wrote, "than needy admirers flattened their noses against the booksellers' windows eager to secure a good look at the etchings and to peruse every line of the letterpress that might be exposed to view, frequently reading it aloud to applauding bystanders . . . so great was the craze, Pickwick Papers secured far more attention than was given to the ordinary politics of the day". Lord Denman used to read it on the bench while jurors were deliberating their decisions and the fashionable doctor, Sir Benjamin Brodie, read it in his carriage as he travelled between patients. One gentleman on a "grand tour" in 1840 found "Pickwick" inscribed on one of the pyramids, and there is the famous story of the dying man who seemed to find no comfort in his spiritual minister but who was heard to say, "Well, thank God, Pickwick will be out in ten days, anyway." A contemporary wrote to her friend in the year of the novel's success, "All the boys and girls talk his fun – the boys in the streets," and so great was the "craze" for these monthly narratives that there emerged for sale the Pickwick cigar, the Pickwick hat (with narrow brims curved up at the side, like that of Mr Pickwick himself), and the Pickwick coat (with brass or horn buttons and cloth of dark green or dark plum). But perhaps the most important evidence for the success of Dickens's work is to be found in the report of one of his first biographers who, at the time of the novel's appearance, had visited a locksmith in Liverpool: "I found him reading Pickwick . . . to an audience of twenty persons, literally, men, women and children." It was hired by them all for twopence a day from the circulating library, because they could not afford a shilling for the monthly number, and the observer never forgot how these humble people, who themselves could not read, laughed with Sam Weller and cried with "ready tears" at the death of the poor debtor in the Fleet prison. This was the audience which Charles Dickens had found – not only the judges and the doctors, but the labouring poor. By some miracle of genius he had found a voice which penetrated the hearts of the high as well as of the low. Truly he had created a national audience.

The appeal of *The Pickwick Papers* to its first readers, then, was of an especial kind. It has been said of the businessman of the period that he "thought of work as supreme" but "dreamed of retiring from work"; this was true of others, too, and there is in the peregrinations of Pickwick that dream of idleness, that dream of ease and freedom, which accounts for its idyllic aspects. No God here. No sex. Just a timeless world in which good feelings win through and in which Pickwick enters Eden, as it were, after ploughing through the world of discord. And, more importantly, this is a world in which father and son are reconciled, in which the classes of society come together, in which master and servant are happily united. This is, in other words, a world of union and brotherhood; and it is precisely here that one will find the true source of Pickwick's appeal and Pickwick's greatness. There are very good reasons why the young Dickens, buoyed up by his good fortune and by his marriage, should have created this world of benign comedy, of brotherhood, of love and blessed unity – but the real miracle was that his mood, and the world which he created from it, corresponded with the deepest dreams and desires of his readers.

For there is a theory that it was only in the late eighteenth and early nineteenth centuries that a real sense of nationhood developed; that nationalism, and a sense of national identity (in contrast to simple patriotism), became a potent force. Typically this was a middle-class phenomenon, rooted in part in instinctive dislike of the Europeanised upper-class and what might now be called its "internationalism" of dress and culture. But nationalism took its strength, too, from the increase of literacy among the middle-class, from the growth of industrialism and from the belief in the need for the moral regeneration of the nation. It may also be significant that this new sense of nationalism sprang from people who had previously been at a social disadvantage, and who had keenly felt the slights against their national identity and national inheritance. It was, in other words, the creed of the middle-class as they even now began to emerge from under the shadow of the aristocracy in order to become the pre-eminent economic power of the land. It was precisely this class which took to its heart *The Pickwick Papers*, for it was precisely *The Pickwick Papers* which first crystallised in comic form a real sense of national cohesion and national identity – Sam Pickwick and Samuel Weller, master and servant, being in this guise the new union of the nation.

Of course the formulations of hindsight tend to be couched in too abstract and definitive a mode, the cohesion and the union described here being no more than a glow, an intimation, an extra resonance emerging from the narrative. And there is no doubt that Dickens was working purely and instinctively out of his own energetic creativity. But yet cannot it also be said that he too had embraced the notions of brotherhood and conviviality precisely because he had in his youth undergone slights and humiliations of no small kind? Had he not felt oppressed by those in authority even as he knew his own strength? And was he, too, not looking for social and cultural values by which he could guide himself and through which he could claim his truthful identity? All these things mirror in human form the situation of the country which in his work he was addressing, and the miracle of *The Pickwick Papers* – for miracle it was, catapulting the young author to international fame with his first book – may in part have something to do with the manner in which it reflected and described and strengthened the real needs or desires of the readers who waited impatiently for each monthly part. In finding his own art, Dickens also came to idealise the English "people" in that rich procession of characters – Bob Sawyer, Sergeant Buzfuz, Jingle, the Fat Boy, and of course the inimitable Sam Weller – whom he saw in front of him as he wrote.

What his contemporaries enjoyed most of all was the new sense of their own selves.

There are of course other reasons for the success of *The Pickwick Papers*, not least among them the fact that this book was in fact *reaching* the people whom it idealised, the locksmith in Liverpool no less than the doctor in London. This was in large part due to the novelty and the success of issuing it in shilling monthly parts. There is the obvious point that such serialisation encourages suspense and maintains the continuity of interest which more conventional publication *in toto* would have precluded, and there is no doubt also that serial publication encouraged precisely the kind of breathless, and almost topical, excitement which the newspapers also satisfied. But the success of the novel also derives from the fact that it appealed to a national audience at precisely the time when it could effectively and cheaply reach such a national audience; in these first decades of the nineteenth century new ways of manufacturing paper, the accelerated speed of printing, improvements in transport and in the network of distribution meant that the demands of a middle-class public could more easily be met. The spread of literacy, too, encouraged precisely the growth in demand which these new technical arrangements were able to satisfy. It was in 1832 that the first of the penny weeklies, like Charles Knight's *Penny Magazine* and Chambers's *Edinburgh Journal*, had been inaugurated, thus beginning an era of cheap but not necessarily "low" literature. And so everything came together in *The Pickwick Papers* – Dickens's comic imagination, his dream of brotherhood and companionship, his reflection of the national mood, his exploitation of new forms of publication and his creative use of the old traditions of graphic satire. Everything entered into the wonderful flow of Dickens's own creativity at this first and most crucial period of his life.

And how did he seem now to his contemporaries? "A slim, trimly built figure; an oval face eminently handsome; long silken hair, and slight down whiskers; a swallow-tail coat with a very high velvet collar; a voluminous satin stock with a double breast-pin; a crimson velvet waistcoat over which meandered a lengthy gold chain . . ." Everyone noticed his dress, which was colourful to the point of vulgarity: here was someone who was intent upon proclaiming himself in the society of men. But there was something else about him, too. John Forster noticed it when he first met him; there was of course his "look of youthfulness" and the very definite air of sprightliness and firmness with which he carried himself but there was also "the quickness, keenness, and practical power, the eager, restless, energetic outlook on each several feature . . . Light and motion flashed from every part of it." Mrs Carlyle said that it was as if his face "was made of steel" and Leigh Hunt observed that "it has the life and soul in it of fifty human beings". And he observed everything. He noticed everything. "Nothing seemed to escape him," another contemporary wrote, and a newspaper account of his presence remarked that "he seemed to be scanning you, not obtrusively but unobservedly, from head to foot." This was another characteristic which almost everyone noticed – this *scanning* of the person whom he was with. And had the success of *The Pickwick Papers*, in the cant phrase, "gone to his head"? There is a revealing passage in *David Copperfield*, at a time when the hero of that novel has attained his first eminence as an author – "I was not so stunned by the praise which sounded in my ears, notwithstanding that I was keenly alive to it . . . a man who has any good reason to believe in himself never flourishes himself before the faces of other people . . . I retained my modesty in very self-respect." And this is not the invention of the author in hindsight, because at the time it is precisely this quietness, this modesty, this self-possession which most charac-terised him. But it was also something of an act. As he said in a letter at the time, "Since I have been a successful author, I have seen how much ill-will and jealousy there is afloat, and have acquired an excellent character as a quiet, modest fellow." It was not that he was modest at all; far from it. He had a proper sense of his own importance, and a proper sense of his own role in life. That is why he dressed as he did. He said in a speech many years later that "when I first took Literature as my profession in England, I calmly resolved within myself that whether I succeeded or whether I failed, Literature should be my sole profession . . . I made a compact with myself that in my person Literature should stand, and by itself, of itself, and for itself." This is the true measure of the man, young or old: the strength of his will, the apparent coolness and reserve, the composure with which he was able to hide his feelings of triumph or pleasure, the determination, and the self-control. All the more remarkable, as we shall see, are those times when that control broke down; but this image of the steady young author is the one which we must have most firmly before us as we trace his progress through the world.

Chapter 9

NOW at last he could make his own way. He could make his own terms. He could shake off his old employers, and work fully for himself. So it was that at the beginning of November 1836 he signed an agreement with Richard Bentley, the publisher, to edit a new magazine which was originally to be called the *Wits' Miscellany* but which was later changed to *Bentley's Miscellany* – "Would not that be going to the other extreme?" one real wit asked at the time. He had already agreed to supply Bentley with two three-volume novels, as we have seen, and this agreement to edit Bentley's new enterprise tied them even closer together. There would come a time when disagreements between them became so heated that he denounced Bentley as "the Burlington Street Brigand" but at this point it seemed a winning combination. Bentley himself has been described by Percy Fitzgerald as "a short, pink-faced man, with great white whiskers and bristly, wiry hair; smart of speech . . . with a cordiality and bonhomie that some may have considered was affected". Fitzgerald was adept at brief caricatures of his contemporaries and in this short portrait of a brisk, pink-faced, cordial but perhaps too smooth man the lineaments of a quintessential publisher rise up. But Bentley knew what he was doing: he wanted to turn his *Miscellany* into the foremost monthly of the period, and clearly decided to spare very little expense in making sure that it became so. He had already hired Cruikshank to do the illustrations and in employing Boz – who also agreed to contribute each month an original article of some sixteen pages – he had in a sense captured the tide of early nineteenth-century taste. Certainly Dickens himself, in a prospectus he drafted in Furnival's Inn, said that the new journal would include "all the best known and most successful writers of the present time" (as well as talented beginners, an undertaking that editors always include but rarely fulfil), with its management "entrusted to 'Boz' – a gentleman with whom the public are on pretty familiar terms".

He had agreed to edit the journal for one year, and set to work upon it with no misgivings. It was his first experience of editing, although he had been involved in the more technical administration of the *Mirror of Parliament*, and had spent enough time on the *Morning Chronicle* not to be overawed by the responsibility; almost at once he began to write to various authors whom he hoped would contribute, perhaps the most famous of them being Douglas Jerrold. Jerrold himself, a radical journalist who had literally worked his way upwards like Dickens from humble origins, was indeed the type of writer and man with whom Dickens seemed most at ease and most in sympathy; he always preferred the company of writers of working-class or lower-middle-class origins and suitably robust views. Dickens was part of a radical generation growing to maturity in the 1830s, and it is important to see his fiction, as well as his journalism, in the sometimes fierce and polemical light which his colleagues or contemporaries cast.

Of course the *Morning Chronicle* was itself a radical journal, but it also had the disadvantage of being Dickens's employer; no doubt he had been considering the possibility of leaving it ever since the success of *Sketches by Boz* and *The Pickwick Papers*, and in fact he was so little overawed by his employers that on one occasion he led a short but successful reporters' dispute against Easthope. But he picked his moment to resign carefully. No doubt he continued to draw his usual salary during the summer recess of Parliament, thus leaving him more time for his other commitments, but the day after he signed his agreement with Richard Bentley he formally left the newspaper's staff. He had been reporting on parliamentary debates for the last five years, a long and weary time, and there is a passage in the life of *David Copperfield* which covers precisely the same transition: ". . . when my new success was achieved, I considered myself reasonably entitled to escape from the dreary debates. One joyful night, therefore, I noted down the music of the parliamentary bagpipes for the last time, and I have never heard it since . . ." That this was no fictional embellishment is proved by a conversation which Dickens had in 1867, when he declared that since the time of his reportorial duties he had never once entered the House of Commons again because of "his hatred of the falseness of talk, of bombastic eloquence . . ." It was to be a hatred always renewed and deepened, as Dickens observed the behaviour of parliament at times of war and economic difficulty. His detestation of "bombastic eloquence" might in part represent some suppressed hatred of his father, but there is no doubt that it also sprang directly out of his parliamentary duties and must in turn have been fuelled by his sense of the subsidiary and even undignified role he was forced to play as an amanuensis to the hypocrite and the liar. Of course he was proud enough of his own achievements as a journalist, and it was characteristic of him that he felt at the time of his resignation that he was slighted by the proprietor, John Easthope, and that his gifts were not fully appreciated. ". . . I *did* expect," he wrote to him, ". . . to receive some slight written acknowledgment from the Proprietors of the Morning Chronicle of the sense they entertained of the services I had performed . . . I have again and again . . . done what was always before considered impossible, and what in all probability will never be accomplished again." This stress on his own uniqueness, well founded if more than slightly imperious, is again typical of Dickens, especially at times when he believes his own worth is being slighted or his reputation assaulted. Nevertheless, he had been well enough liked by his colleagues on the *Morning Chronicle*; at the time of his departure from their company they presented him with a silver goblet. Now he was truly on his own.

It seems that John Macrone, the publisher of *Sketches by Boz* for whom Dickens had agreed some time before to write a novel, *Gabriel Vardon*, only now heard about Dickens's agreements to publish two novels with Richard Bentley – and this only when Dickens sent him a letter asking if he might withdraw from his previous contract. It was a difficult situation, especially since Macrone was just about to publish the second series of the *Sketches*, and Macrone was not sure how to proceed. Certain colleagues advised him to keep Dickens to his earlier contract, although the publisher himself must already have at least guessed the self-willed and stubborn determination of Dickens in matters of this kind. He was in fact becoming much better able to deal with publishers and publishing demands; he made sure, for example, that the songs from *The Village Coquettes* were not published by Macrone (as Macrone had suggested) but by John Hullah and himself in a private edition sold within the theatre itself. Even as Dickens and Macrone argued over the withdrawal from his agreement, the second series of *Sketches by Boz* was issued. On this occasion it appeared in one volume only, partly because of Dickens's usual niggling disputes with Cruikshank, but largely because Dickens himself, overworked and sometimes ill, was not able to provide enough material for two volumes. He gave Macrone much of the material which he had left out of the first series, but also some more recent prose – this collection, it has to be said, is rather less carefully edited than the previous series but is nonetheless an important clue to Dickens's development during this period. The problem with Macrone remained, however, and it was only after some complicated negotiating – settling largely on the question of whether a quid pro quo could be worked out by assigning Macrone the copyright to the *Sketches* – that the matter was finally resolved. Dickens would now only be writing novels for Richard Bentley.

He had handled these negotiations himself, but there now entered his life a man who was in future years to take many of these business burdens from him. It was in late 1836 that Dickens encountered John Forster. They met at the house of Harrison Ainsworth. How Dickens had fist come across Ainsworth is not clear, although it seems likely that their joint publisher, Macrone, at some point introduced them. And they, too, had become friends. It could be said that they were well matched. Ainsworth was seven years older than Dickens, and only two years before he had won enormous acclaim as a novelist for his *Rookwood.* Certainly he was as well known as Dickens himself, and the later publication of *Jack Sheppard* even seemed at one point to be eclipsing Dickens's own *Oliver Twist.* In many ways they were alike. Ainsworth was a very handsome, forceful and somewhat mercurial man. He was also rather short, like other of Dickens's friends (Forster and Maclise among them), and it seems that Dickens did not like to be at a disadvantage in any sense. Ainsworth shared Dickens's passion for the theatre (he too had once mounted a juvenile production of *The Miller and His Men*) and was full of the same kind of confidence and enthusiasm as his contemporary. They both worked hard, like to walk immense distances, liked to ride. They were both also extraordinarily convivial; they celebrated their various successes with large dinners, and in these years Ainsworth was giving parties at Kensal Lodge, on the Harrow Road near Willesden, which he shared with his cousin's widow – a sprightly, somewhat sarcastic, party, known as Mrs Touchet. He and Dickens were, in all these ways, very much part of the same generation, part of that eminently social, gregarious, energetic, vivacious group which we have come to call "Early Victorians". It was through Ainsworth that Dickens met those men who became his closest friends – among them Count d'Orsay,

Bulwer-Lytton, Daniel Maclise, T. N. Talfourd and, of course, pre-eminently, John Forster.

If anyone is connected with Dickens's name, it is Forster; and indeed he was the most likely person to walk down through posterity as the friend and companion of genius. He was the same age as Dickens and, when they met, they would have already known or at least soon discovered how much they had in common. Forster, too, had come from lowly origins; he was the son of a Newcastle butcher (in later life he was infuriated by enemies who taunted him behind his back as a "butcher's boy"), and it was said that his mother was the "daughter of a cow-keeper". But he was one of those young men who, at this period in English history, seemed ready and able literally to push their way forward through the world – a feat only a little more easily achieved at this time of social transition and political confusion. Like Dickens, he had first gravitated within the sphere of the law; after attending University College, London, he was enrolled as a law student at the Inner Temple but, again like Dickens, he soon found out that law suited him less well than journalism and literature. Thus he had worked for the *True Sun* at about the same time as Dickens. The two young men never met then, however. But Forster had lately moved on to become literary and dramatic editor of *The Examiner*, in which position he found himself when he was first introduced to Dickens. In fact it had been Forster who had written a bad notice of *The Village Coquettes*, although it was a review witty enough to make Dickens laugh and, for that, he could forgive almost anything. Dickens was no doubt in any case impressed by this exact contemporary of his, not less because Forster had already become acquainted with Charles Lamb and Leigh Hunt, Bulwer-Lytton and William Macready, all men of an earlier generation and all of whom Dickens admired. It was clear that Forster was already in the process of carving out for himself a literary "career" in other words, and, like Dickens himself, he was always ready to emphasise the dignity of literature. So the two young men impressed each other. They were alike, too, in other ways. They were both very precise and very punctual but, perhaps most importantly, Forster shared Dickens's own high spirits. He was well known for his loud laugh, and his equally boisterous energy (there is a famous story of his throwing a water jug during the course of an argument) and, like Dickens, he liked to perform impromptu comic dances. He loved the theatre, clubs, excursions, dinners and was in these days a Radical – a "rational Unitarian" is how he has been described, which, if nothing else, suggests the moral rigour and direction of the politics of these young men. And in such characteristics as these do we not once again see the quintessential virtues of the men of the new century?

Forster was a kind and generous friend, as this narrative will show. But the fact remains that there were some people who never could understand how it was that Dickens became so attached to him. Forster could, after all, be very difficult indeed. He seems to have felt keenly his low origins, and there were often occasions when he became uneasy or defensive. He was inclined to bluster as a result, had an almost comical sense of his own dignity, and frequently assumed an air of overpowering infallibility: there is the notorious occasion when he corrected Macready, one of the greatest nineteenth-century actors, for his delivery of Shakespeare. In fact he often gave the impression, typically to those who did not know him well or had not become accustomed to his foibles, of being rude, pompous or just ordinarily bad-tempered. Above all he could be overbearing, and there are some wonderful recollections of his conversation that capture the tone if not necessarily the essence of the man. "It was in*tol*-er-able. *In*-*tol*-erable!" He had some favourite interjections – "Monstrous!" "Incredible!" "Don't tell me!" He was also something of a snob, and some of his favourite phrases almost assumed the status of catchphrases among his friends. "As Lord X said to me in this room . . ." Or "Lord X has been saying, with much force . . .", etcetera. But the most famous stories about Forster concern both his generosity as a host and the quickness of his temper with his hapless servants. "Biscuits," muttered in a low growl. Then "BIScuits!" And finally roared out, so that all the table could hear, "*BIS*cuits!" Then there was the occasion when Count d'Orsay came to dinner, prompting an exchange between Forster and his servant which was remembered by Percy Fitzgerald. "Sauce to the Count," he murmured. And then louder: "*Sauce* to the Count." And then finally, in a very loud voice, "*Sauce for the flounders of the Count!*" There was another occasion, which Fitzgerald also remembered, when in a Dublin hotel a servant told Forster that he could not smoke in one of the public rooms. "Leave the room, you scoundrel!" Forster is said to have replied, all his dignity roused. "How dare you, sir, interfere with me! Get out, sir!"

So one can imagine the manner of this loud, burly man, with his ponderous jokes, his loud laugh, his delivery of his judgments. Put beside him the young Dickens – much lighter in company, more pleasantly humorous, quicker, more composed, sharper, more perceptive. But no doubt Dickens saw in Forster other qualities, too, which less perceptive acquaintances might not have understood; he would have seen at once Forster's generosity of spirit, his genuine love of literature and, perhaps above all, his social unease and his loneliness. It was often said that in manner Forster resembled Macready on stage, but it is possible, too, that Dickens saw in this sometimes pompous and orotund young man something of the mystery of his own father. Certainly this would in part explain their complicated and ambivalent relationship for, even as he loved and respected Forster, Dickens could not help but make fun of him. He used to call him "the Mogul" or "the Lincolnian mammoth". He loved to imitate him, just as he loved to imitate his father, and there were times when he literally rolled on the floor in agony of laughter at some absurd story about him. One friend said that he "revelled" in Forsterian anecdotes. Once he had to leave the room when Forster attempted to dance in leather shoes too big for him – Dickens could *not* control himself on these occasions – and Forster was the frequent butt of jokes which he would tell even to passing acquaintances. When it was heard that Forster was purchasing a bath, Dickens said that "he would squeeze every *drop* of water out of it", and he loved to mimic his more ponderous pronouncements. Once he remarked sarcastically that Forster was going through one of his "nice face" periods – at a time when Forster was saying of practically everyone that he or she had a "nice face". And he remembered with delight a dismissive comment by Forster about "a very offensive and improper young person, and I wish to hear no more about her". This, no doubt, with a wave of his hand. Dickens revelled, too, in his friend's very loud "whisper" which, said Dickens, "seems to go in at your ear and come out at the sole of your boot". There are times when there was less good humour in his remarks, however, and he once said in a letter to a mutual friend: "I have always a vicious desire to electrify Mr Forster (when he is acting) violently, in some sensitive part of his anatomy . . ." Of course there are accounts of them together, as Forster "was ever bustling around his friend, interpreting and explaining him". Another contemporary records how "I have known Forster pay some compliments to 'the Inimitable' in his patronising way . . ." – how Forster often called him "My dear Dickens" or "My dear boy", ". . . which the other would acknowledge in his drollest manner".

Forster was everybody's friend – no one in the nineteenth century had such a wide acquaintance among social, political and literary figures – but pre-eminently he remained Dickens's friend and companion. Within a few weeks of their first meeting Forster was aiding and advising him in various tangled matters of publishing business, and it is not going too far to say that he became Dickens's literary agent, editor, proof-reader and critic. Dickens himself seems to have realised quite soon just how astute Forster was, and in literary matters tended to use him as a representative audience; that is why there were many times when he also gave him literal *carte blanche* to alter or amend his manuscripts. Forster had a hatred of sensation and melodrama for their own sakes, and it is quite probable that Dickens curbed his natural tendencies in these directions in implicit recognition of his friend's disapproval. Of course there were many differences between them; no men of such unequal temperaments could hope to avoid them. There were periods of coolness, there were sometimes terrible arguments and, towards the end of Dickens's life, when Forster became a fully paid-up member of Society at precisely the time when Dickens had become totally disenchanted with it, there was a definite lessening in the warmth if not in the attachment between the two men. Yet he was always Dickens's best friend and staunchest ally; in a sense it might be said that he devoted much of his life to Dickens, perhaps seeing in him all the genius which he knew that he himself did not possess. And it was Forster who said, after Dickens's death, that ". . . the duties of life remain while life remains, but for me the joy of it is gone for ever more". Thus does our knowledge of later events reflect our understanding of those which precede them, and in the beginning we see something of the end.

A beginning of such ambition and energy, though, this time in the mid-1830s when Forster, Dickens and Ainsworth were close companions. Often from Kensal Lodge they would mount their horses and ride over the surrounding countryside – Brent, Perivale, Greenford and Ruislip or, in the other direction, over Old Oak Common towards Acton and Shepherd's Bush (Dickens was never altogether easy on a horse, and in general the sarcastic Mrs Touchet described the trio as "Cockney riders"). Dinners. Festivities. The shared enthusiasm of young men – Ainsworth and Dickens both prominent and highly successful novelists, Forster their friend and confidant making a career for himself as a literary "figure". Of course it all dissolved in the end. Ainsworth drifted apart from the other two, and in fact his fame vanished almost as quickly as it had first come to him. He moved to Brighton in the early Fifties, and very little is heard of him from that time forwards. Perhaps the saddest postscript of all to this record of friendship and ambition lies in the Sixties when, at a dinner party, Robert Browning remarked that "a sad, forlorn-looking figure stopped me today, and reminded me of old times. He presently resolved himself into whom do you think? – Harrison Ainsworth!" Forster replied, in one of those hasty but nevertheless resonant remarks, "Good heavens! Is he still alive?" And so the world goes. By the Sixties men such as Forster were looking over their shoulders at their own past, coming to the end of their own lives in a Victorian era to which it cannot be said that they truly belonged by instinct or temperament. They were now part of a solid, middle-class, and somehow more enclosed world than that of their youth – one which if it could boast greater achievements had also less vigour, which if it was more secure also had less sense of the need for progress and discovery. All the old youthfulness gone. "Is he still alive?"

This was not the world of the 1830s. Their world then was full of venture and change, of optimism and reform – the "circle" of Dickens and Forster was soon to be filled with other young men who had the same confidence and enthusiasm as they. Perhaps with a hint of that period's coarseness or vulgarity, too, because this was still a time when men and women were hanged in public and when it was common for a deformed or crippled person to be openly mocked in the streets. These new friends were, in another sense, all of a type. They were "outsiders" in one way or another, most of them having found their way to eminence after severe hardships and struggle and self-denial. One of Dickens's closest friends was Daniel Maclise, for example, an Irishman just a year older than he, who had left school at fourteen in order to concentrate upon a career as an artist. In that he was highly successful – he came to London at the age of sixteen, and two years later won a gold medal at the Royal Academy for the best historical painting; in his period he was best known for his idealised "story-book" canvases, sometimes executed on a large scale, although it is one of the ironies and perhaps injustices of history that he is now best remembered for his portrait of Charles Dickens. By the time he met the young novelist, however, he was an artist of great reputation. But he was a paradoxical man, with a complexity of temperament that appealed to Dickens. On the surface he seemed to have an air of ease and almost of indifference, even in the most difficult circumstances. But he was also something of a solitary, and there is some evidence that his moods varied wildly from enthusiasm to depression. Certainly in later life he became a sick and moody recluse, from which isolation not even Dickens's fondest promptings could move him. But we must see him in this early period, when he was one of Dickens's closest friends and, responding to Dickens's own gaiety and energy, a young artist with as great a future before him as the novelist.

Another close friend was an older man, William Charles Macready. By the time he met Dickens he was already the most famous Shakespearean actor of his day, and someone for whom Dickens would have felt immediate respect and sympathy. He was in some ways acutely theatrical, with an expressive face, a powerful voice, and sonorous manner, but in addition he would have appealed to Dickens's own sense of professionalism by being an absolute professional himself. As a colleague wrote, "He was a thorough artist, very conscientious, very much in earnest." His dramatic style would also have attracted Dickens for, although Macready took on the great roles, he seems to have been better at those expressing passion rather than nobility; he was a master of pathos, remorse, the more bravura aspects of melodrama, and nothing moved Dickens more than these. Macready was very intelligent, if inclined to be short-tempered; he was also a "gentleman" who suffered terribly from the suspicion that his was not a gentlemanly profession – "over-sensitive to the imaginary disrespect in which his profession is held," one contemporary wrote of him, "and throughout his career hating the stage, while devoting himself to the art." In other words a complicated and sometimes difficult man, but he was always devoted to Dickens; in some ways, in fact, he seems to have been another "father" to the novelist, or at least he willingly took on the role of the older man to whom Dickens could go for advice and assistance. And it is likely, too, that Dickens saw beneath the surface of this sensitive and often despondent man the true genuineness of his nature. He was a fine actor, indeed, and as Dickens said in another context, ". . . the more real the man the more genuine the actor . . ."

In this period, then, the inner circle of Dickens's friendships comprised Forster, Ainsworth, Maclise and Macready (this is not of course to forget his earliest friends, Beard and Mitton, who remained close to him). But there was also an outer circle which reflects if nothing else the kind of people, and the kind of world, in which Dickens felt most comfortable and which most clearly embodies his own interests and predilections. This world was, essentially, of a socially radical nature.

There was Albany Fonblanque, editor of *The Examiner*, to whom Dickens was introduced by Forster: he was never close to Dickens, being for one thing a much older man, but he was a leading "philosophic radical", had been a close friend of Bentham, and was most associated with the cause of law reform. Dickens's friendship with Bulwer-Lytton was established for similar reasons; although he was by no means the "self-made" man so common in Dickens's acquaintance, he would first have met Dickens when he had a reputation for radicalism. In his novel, *Paul Clifford*, published at the beginning of the decade, there was an apostrophe close to Dickens's own feelings: "I come into the world friendless and poor – I find a body of laws hostile to the friendless and the poor! To these laws hostile to me, then, I acknowledge hostility in my turn. Between us are the conditions of war." Dickens's real friendship with Bulwer-Lytton was yet to flourish, however, and at this time he established a more important relationship with Douglas Jerrold who, like many men of this era, managed to combine two or three different careers and roles at once. He had been the son of an itinerant actor and had himself played on the stage when he was young; he then became a midshipman and, after leaving service at sea (which disgusted him), he set himself up as a writer of plays and farces. His first great dramatic success had been *Black-Eyed Susan* in 1829, but by the time he met Dickens he was also well known for his satirical and radical journalism. He was a small man with a massive head and sharp features: he was noticeable also for his intense nervous energy, tossing his long hair "like a lion does with its mane" at moments of excitement, and afflicted by a "peculiar restlessness of eye, speech and demeanour". He could also be very funny. When asked with whom his wife was dancing he replied, "Some member of the Humane Society;" and when asked why one particular playwright had such dirty hands he said, "From his habit of constantly putting them up to his face."

Then there was T. N. Talfourd, another example of early nineteenth-century catholicity of talent; by the time he came to know Dickens, he was a Serjeant at the Bar (a peculiar position, like that of barrister, but one only allowed to practise in certain courts), a Liberal MP for Reading, and a successful playwright. He was seventeen years older than Dickens, and bore the traces of the eighteenth century perhaps more obviously than his young friend: "I remember how he kept the tradition of the then past generation," one contemporary noted, "and came into the drawing room with a thick speech and unsteady legs." He had been a friend of Lamb and Coleridge (we must remember how the Romantic movement, as it has become known, spilled over into the nineteenth century to such an extent that Dickens might even be seen as its true heir), which would have impressed, if not necessarily endeared him to, Dickens. But he was sometimes vain and self-centred, albeit innocently so; he also had an unfortunate inability to pronounce his "r"'s, a habit which Dickens used to imitate and mock. It is worth noticing, in passing, that, with Talfourd as with Jerrold, there is the same connection between the theatre and journalism or politics; clearly drama can be seen as one of the dominant activities and images of the period, and when we come to describe certain "theatrical" qualities both in Dickens's manner and appearance (as well, of course, as in his fiction) it must be with due recognition of the society in which he was formed. More immediately, however, it is also worth noting that Dickens's friends came almost exclusively from the journalistic or theatrical professions. This would be the case for the rest of his life (his younger friends in a later period were known as "Bohemians" because of this slightly raffish characteristic), and many contemporaries remarked how little he mixed with other serious writers or with what one might call "intellectuals". He preferred the company of those who in all important respects were inferior to himself but who shared his own interests, and it could fairly be said that he would not have been so much at ease in a society which he could not in a certain sense dominate. He was not one of nature's "followers" or "partners"; it was he, the Inimitable, as he liked to call himself, who had to lead while others followed.

This was also true of his domestic life and, although his novels are filled with the images of the gentle or weak husband being dominated by a vicious or vigorous female, this is one of the many instances when Dickens's life had absolutely no relation to his fiction. He and Catherine were still living in Furnival's Inn but his brief reminiscences of this period have characteristically much more to do with Catherine's sister, Mary Hogarth, than with Catherine herself. He does seem to have grown very close to her; on the New Year's Day of 1837 he bought her a desk, and in a later diary he notes the day of his first son's birth with a further account of Mary:

"*Saturday, January 6, 1838*: This day last year, Mary and I wandered up and down Holborn and the streets about, for hours, looking after a little table for Kate's bedroom which we bought at last at the very first Broker's we had looked into, and which we had passed half a dozen times because *I didn't like* to ask the price. I took her out to Brompton at night as we had no place for her to sleep in; (the two mothers being with us). She came back again next day to keep house for me, and stopped nearly the rest of the month. I shall never be so happy again as in those Chambers three Stories high – never if I roll in wealth and fame. I would hire them to keep empty, if I could afford it." Later events were to be partly responsible for this tone of melancholy, but the essential facts of Dickens's domestic life in this period can be glimpsed easily here: Mary a welcome and often long-staying guest with the young couple, and a general air of happiness which was not in later life to be recovered. That Dickens was not alone in his admiration for his sister-in-law is clear from a letter written by a contemporary to Macrone in the same month: "Our acquaintance, Boz, seems not to be sleeping. His name appears to irradiate at least three publishers' lists. How does his pretty little sister-in-law get on? She is a sweet interesting creature."

Catherine herself was not in quite so interesting a condition. The first son was born on 6 January, and it seems that she suffered from some post-natal disorder, the first signs of that nervous condition which was frequently in later years to recur. Mary Hogarth wrote to her cousin about her sister's condition: ". . . my dearest Kate . . . I am sorry indeed to say has not got on so well as her first week made us hope she would. After we thought she was getting quite well and strong it was discovered she was not able to nurse her Baby so she was obliged with great reluctance as you may suppose to give him up to a stranger. Poor Kate! it has been a dreadful trial for her . . . It is really dreadful to see her suffer. I am quite sure I never suffered so much sorrow for any one or any thing before . . . Every time she sees her Baby she has a fit of crying and keeps constantly saying she is sure he will not care for her now she is not able to nurse him." Catherine was suffering from severe depression, therefore, which sounds like the exacerbation of some general nervous anxiety. Perhaps she never was completely well. As for her brother-in-law, Mary Hogarth goes on, ". . . his literary career gets more and more prosperous every day and he is courted and flattered on every side . . ." In the same period, however, Dickens himself was ill with a variety of symptoms which ranged from cold to violent headache, but in the absence of Mary (there was now no room for her in Furnival's Inn, with Mrs Dickens and Mrs Hogarth in attendance after the birth), he too must have helped minister to his wife. It has been suggested that he was unsympathetic

to his wife's condition, both because he was unsettled by her pregnancy which evoked echoes of his mother's own confinements
and because he was too busy and preoccupied to deal with her nervous
depression, but there is no evidence for this. Quite the reverse: as
Mary Hogarth said in the letter to her cousin, Dickens "is kindness
itself to her, and is constantly studying her comfort in everything . . ." He was a conscientious and practical husband, and since
Catherine's health did not seem to be improving he decided that, at
some inconvenience to himself at such a busy time, they should move
to the healthier air of Kent. With Mary back in attendance, they
returned to Chalk; and with them, of course, came the baby soon to
be christened Charles Culliford Boz Dickens, the "Boz" apparently
an error, resulting from John Dickens's shouting out the name beside
the font. (Dickens's father, by the way, was not always so benign a
presence: even now, so early in his son's career, he was trying to
"borrow" money from the publishers, Chapman and Hall, "recollecting how much your interests are bound up with those of my son".)

Dickens could not himself rest at Chalk, and during the two months
they stayed there he was constantly engaged in all the work to which
he had committed himself. He was now of course an editor, and he
estimated that he was reading some sixty or eighty manuscripts a
month for possible publication in *Bentley's Miscellany*. But that was
only one aspect of his editorial work, which also included proof-
reading as well as the revising and cutting of articles. He arranged the
payments for each contributor, and worked upon his own article each
month. It ought to be remembered, too, that he was collaborating
closely with George Cruikshank who, as the official illustrator of the
magazine, had a position of some significance; they worked together
amicably enough, however, despite their recent arguments over the
Sketches, the general plan being that Dickens suggested which articles
ought to be illustrated and then left it to Cruikshank to decide upon a
particular passage or scene. There is no doubt that he enjoyed his
work. On one occasion he compares being an editor to that of being a
stage manager, and it is clear that he brought the same skills to this
editorial venture which he had brought to bear upon his management
of amateur theatricals. In both areas, after all, he liked to be an
impresario of all the talents even while reserving the central position
for himself. Certainly he became fond of the direct connection with his
audience of readers in the "Proclamations", "Addresses" and
"Announcements" which appear in this magazine as well as in all the

others which he edited in future years. He seems to have needed that link with his audience, established as it was upon his assumption of personal intimacy and approaching something like a relationship with an extended substitute family. In one such address, in the second issue of *Bentley's Miscellany*, Dickens also emphasises in jocose fashion the real attitudes which he wished to adopt toward this readership: "It has been the constant aim of my policy to preserve peace in your minds, and provoke merriment in your hearts: to set before you the scenes and characters of real life, in all their endless diversity; occasionally (I hope) to instruct, always to amuse, and never to offend." Although this is written in the style of a royal speech to parliament, the sentiments are to be taken as representative of his own; in particular, in his wish "never to offend" and in that decorous acquiescence in the new proprieties of the century, it is clear that his own genius is to be seen working within restraints which at this period in his life he entirely accepted. Both as an editor and as a novelist, he always knew precisely the demands and expectations of the public and at no stage in his career did he deliberately or knowingly thwart them. It was only towards the end of the century, when the "public" became synonymous with "public opinion", that artists felt the need expressly to defy it; Charles Dickens came from a period in which the popular arts were also the most important and the most energetic, and at a time when it was nothing if not exhilarating to appeal to and to capture a new and rapidly growing audience. No doubt Bentley considered the magazine to be an extension of his own skills as a publisher, but it is clear that in turn Dickens thought of it primarily as a vehicle for his own growing fame.

It ought to be remembered, too, that he was still writing a whole number of *The Pickwick Papers* each month, and the pressures of work and ambition were now so intense that he was composing right against the deadline, sometimes not finishing a particular instalment of the novel until a few days before its actual publication. The reason for such haste was, largely, because Dickens found himself embarked almost at once upon another series. The first number of the new magazine, in January 1837, had opened with a sketch by him entitled "The Public Life of Mr Tulrumble" and then the next month another sketch, a continuation of the first, appeared under the title "Oliver Twist". The first had been set in "Mudfog", a pseudonym for Chatham, and was a pleasant enough satire on the idiocies of provincial authorities with the moral that "puffed-up conceit is not dignity". The second, with

"Oliver Twist" as its title, begins in a workhouse in the same town of Mudfog. In other words, at this point, harassed by family difficulties, exhausted by overwork, and suffering from a variety of ailments, Dickens himself did not at first seem to realise that he was embarking upon the novel which in later years would perhaps more than any other be identified with his name. He had the idea only of a series of articles in mind ("The Chronicles of Mudfog" perhaps), but then almost as soon as he began he found that he had "hit on a capital notion". For he had created the figure of Oliver, the child born and brought up in a workhouse, the child who dared to ask for more, and at once he saw the possibilities which could be extracted from it. The idea of a series of sketches was abandoned.

There is some dispute about the origin of *Oliver Twist*, largely engineered by George Cruikshank who many years later (and after the novelist's death) insisted that he had been the principal begetter of young Oliver and of his sad history. On the face of it this is unlikely – Dickens was not the kind of writer or person who acquiesced in the ideas of others – but it is at least possible that Cruikshank suggested the notion of writing something like an Hogarthian poor boy's "progress" through poverty and misery. In any case Cruikshank and Dickens shared many of the same preoccupations; they were both fascinated by London, particularly in its more squalid and darker aspects, and by images of prison or punishment. There is no doubt, for example, that Cruikshank had sketched the "condemned cell" of Newgate long before he made Fagin its occupant. This proves nothing about *Oliver Twist* itself, only the fact that author and illustrator were eminently well suited to work together upon this saga of London "low life".

What *is* clear is that as soon as Dickens had hit upon his "capital notion" of the deprived and abused child, the whole conception caught fire in his imagination. It is even possible that this was in essence the "proposed Novel" which he had been contemplating ever since he began seriously to write, and it has been said, rightly, that *Oliver Twist* is the first novel in the English language which takes a child as its central character or hero; a revolution, perhaps, although not one which was widely noticed at the time. This is largely because factual "orphan tales" were actually quite common in the period, and Dickens himself had often read autobiographies which emphasise the miseries and privations of childhood: even Johnson's life of Richard Savage has a long passage on the horrors of his infancy. There was also an ancient but still healthy tradition of "rogue literature", which in part chronicled the dramas of lost or abandoned children. So the theme of *Oliver Twist* was not in that respect new. Nevertheless it was one that directly appealed to Dickens's own sense of himself and his past, and was therefore one in which all the resources of his imagination could be poured. In the original sketch Oliver was born in Mudfog or Chatham, the site of Dickens's own infancy, and the figure of the parish boy's "progress" was one that at once attracted a cluster of childhood feelings and associations. Oliver Twist's forced association with Fagin, which seems like a savage reprise of the young Dickens's companionship with Bob Fagin in the blacking factory; Oliver's flight towards respectability; his journey from dirt to cleanliness and gentility. Thus does Dickens seem able to work through his own childhood in disguised form, both in its troubled reality and in its disturbed fantasies of escape. The life of Warren's, the foul streets of London, the sheer helplessness of the lost child resound through a narrative which becomes the echo chamber of Dickens's own childhood. In the March number of *The Pickwick Papers* Tony Weller had mentioned "Warrens's blackin'" and in the following month's episode of *Oliver Twist* a "blackin' bottle" is mentioned by the notorious beadle. The associations come flooding back as Dickens writes.

But his childhood does not pass untrammelled into his fiction; that is one reason why he was an artist and not a memoirist. And that is also why it is important to realise that he was working on *The Pickwick Papers* and *Oliver Twist* at the same time – in fact he was writing the opening chapters of the poor boy's progress, filled as they are with suffering and abandonment, at precisely the time he was also writing some of the most comic passages in *The Pickwick Papers* concerning as they do the misadventures of Bob Sawyer and the skating party at Dingley Dell. In fact Dickens soon adopted the characteristic rhythm of writing *Oliver* first, and *Pickwick* after, and it could plausibly be maintained that as a result *The Pickwick Papers* assumes a more buoyant form, as if much of the pathos which he had once introduced into the comic narrative has now been transferred to the monthly serial in *Bentley's Miscellany*. But the relationship between the novels cannot be taken too far since they have quite different forms. For one thing *Oliver Twist* is much shorter, with some nine thousand words in each episode compared to *Pickwick's* eighteen or nineteen thousand; in addition, the publication of a narrative in monthly parts was quite a different undertaking, with quite different rules, from that of publishing a monthly serial in a magazine. *Oliver Twist* was surrounded by other fiction (although it was always placed *first* in *Bentley's Miscellany*) and those who came to read it would approach it with habitual assumptions about the kind of "adventure" it was likely to provide: monthly magazine serials were commonly of the adventure or mystery sort, and relied to a large extent upon formal devices of suspense and plot to maintain that mood. In that sense, it could not be said that *Oliver Twist* disappointed them. It conformed to type even as it transcended that type, and in the brilliant exploitation of familiar material part of Dickens's genius is to be found.

There were other differences between Dickens's first two novels. It is quite clear, for example, that from the beginning he had decided to give a polemical air to *Oliver Twist* which had not been present in *The Pickwick Papers*. Presumably this is because *Oliver Twist*'s appearance in a magazine format gave him both the context and the licence to introduce more overtly propagandistic elements within it, but it is equally likely that Dickens was already aware that his range was being artificially restricted while he remained a "comic" novelist. Indeed the imperatives of his own childhood suffering must have led him ineluctably forward to the more sharply "up to date" tone of the first chapters of *Oliver Twist*. The point is that these early chapters were aimed at the workings of the New Poor Law – not so much a Law as a series of measures introduced three years before, which were only now attracting public attention because of the abuses which were arising from their provisions. In the early months of 1837 a Select Committee of Parliament had been examining the working of the Law, and it was also in this period that its principles were first introduced into the metropolis. That *Oliver Twist* was part of the contumely directed against the New Poor Law is not in doubt – *The Times*, which attacked the "BENTHAMITE cant" involved in these rationalised administrative measures, printed sections of the novel as it appeared, and Dickens himself believed that he was directing a blow against it. It meant that he was also ranging himself against some of his more radical friends, who would have approved of the measures precisely because they were "Benthamite" in character; the idea, after all, was to cut down on the cost of the poor by precluding the able-bodied pauper from relief and by making the life of the workhouse distinctly unpalatable. But Dickens's distaste for these measures was instinctive and immediate. What, after all, was the New Poor Law doing? It was tearing families apart, by consigning sexes to different quarters within the same workhouse and, with the abolition of the "search for the father" clause (which meant it was no longer required that the fathers of illegitimate children should be traced), it constituted a total disregard of the need for family life among the poor and needy. Together with the new dietary provisions, which were satirised by Dickens precisely in Oliver's asking for ". . . some more", it is possible to see why the New Poor Law provoked in Dickens angry memories of his own deprivation, of his own separation from his family, and his own obsessive comparison of the need for food with the need for love. So when he began work upon the novel his own childhood experiences merged ineluctably with the national experience; Dickens was detailing the miseries of the poor and of those being crushed by "the system", as the new workhouse regulations were already being called, even as he recalled the phantoms of his own childhood.

Everything was close to him again. In fact, as he wrote the scenes within Fagin's lair in Field Lane, and as he described the squalid alleys and ditches around it, we do well to remember that he was himself living almost beside them; Field Lane itself was no more than a minute or two from Furnival's Inn or from Doughty Street (where he was soon to move). Given the fact that the twin preoccupations of the urban middle-class were the fear of disease and the fear of theft, and that both of these were thought literally to spread in a miasma from the rookeries and courts of the poor, it is important to note that Dickens was living alongside one of the most squalid areas in the whole metropolis. A short stroll would have taken him to Saffron Hill, and the neighbourhood of Field Lane where "excrement was thrown into a little back yard where it was allowed to accumulate for months together"; and there, beside it, Fleet Ditch, which was no more than an open sewer of fetid water. He knew of what he wrote, and it is a tribute to the power of his imagination that even those desperate elements of urban life, physically so close to him, are transposed by the power of his imagination into a larger theme. Never before had a novelist so closely aligned his narrative with topical and familiar events. Never before had the roles of novelist and journalist been so cunningly combined. So for his audience there was a double fascination – as the *Spectator* said in a review which criticised Dickens's use in fiction of the "popular clamour against the New Poor Law", the author nevertheless possessed "remarkable skill in making use of peculiarities of expression, even to the current phrase of the day". It was a kind of genius, the instantaneous transformation of the speech and events and locales of the moment, and it is one which his contemporaries were quick to recognise.

And Dickens was doing it quite instinctively, making it up literally as he went along. Apparently the name of Oliver had come from an omnibus conductor's conversation which Dickens overheard; he had seen a pauper's funeral at Cooling Church (how often that church upon the marshes is connected in Dickens's mind with death) and transposed it to the novel; he knew of a magistrate, Mr Laing of Hatton Garden, whom he went to see before turning him into Mr Fang of *Oliver Twist*; an enquiry was being conducted into the deaths of workhouse children who had been "farmed out" (that is, adults were paid to take care of them in private houses), and he used *that* too. At first he had difficulties with the length – the first instalment was too short – but within a matter of weeks he was getting into his stride. There had been nothing quite like it before – *The Pickwick Papers* and *Oliver Twist* running together, two serials of quite different types appearing simultaneously. What was admired then, and what one admires still, is the sheer fluency and easy flow of these narratives; the humour itself lies almost as much in Dickens's unflagging invention as in the scenes themselves, since it is the laughter and gaiety of human creativity. For Dickens is enjoying it, too; never can a writer so young have had such easy access to all the resources of the language, effortlessly wielding what was for him an instrument of power, the only instrument of power he had ever possessed.

Nothing could stop him now: even as he was writing the two fictions, he was superintending rehearsals for yet another farce, *Is She His Wife? or, Something Singular!* at the St James's Theatre. It is a pleasant concoction, but is perhaps worthy of remark now only for the fact that its allusions to bigamy, seduction and adultery place it in the eighteenth-century tradition of broad humour; it is more earthy than anything which appeared later in the nineteenth century, and suggests just how firmly part of Dickens's taste was rooted in the past. Yet perhaps *Is She His Wife?* is also notable for the fact that on the same bill the principal comedian of the theatre, Harley, appeared on stage as Mr Pickwick and recited a song written by Dickens on the theme of a whitebait dinner. This was only the prelude to a number of Pickwick "dramatisations" (in fact the prelude to innumerable dramatisations of all Dickens's novels over the years), the point being that his plots and characters could be used without any payment or reference to the author himself. Edward Stirling adapted *The Pickwick Papers* in April, but there was another version in May and then another two months later; and so it went on, perhaps the most important aspect of these stage versions being the fact they were billed as something quite unusual – as being realistic dramas dealing with "ordinary life". They read now like ordinary hack-work but the initial reception does explain something about the kind of impact Dickens's novels were making.

Of course he had to return frequently to London from Chalk in order to attend the rehearsals of *Is She His Wife?* – he was commuting between his family and the city in any case on editorial business – but one of his major preoccupations in this period was also to find a larger house. The birth of their son meant that he and Catherine would have to move out of the chambers in Furnival's Inn, and Dickens's own growing fame would also seem to have demanded it. He offered for one house, but did not get it, and then rented temporary lodgings at 30 Upper Norton Street when the family returned to Furnival's Inn; it is possible that he needed somewhere quiet in which to work. He was so busy, in fact, that he employed house agents on his behalf, although he also found time to travel around London with Mary Hogarth in order to inspect available premises. And at last he came across the right one – on 18 March, 1837 he made an offer for 48 Doughty Street and, after agreeing to a rent of eighty pounds per annum, he moved in two weeks later. It was a pleasant house of the last century, situated in a private road with a gateway and porter at each end. He had borrowed money from Richard Bentley in order to pay for such things as moving expenses and, at the time, it struck him as a ". . . frightfully first-class Family Mansion, involving awful responsibilities". It was indeed larger than anything in which Dickens had ever lived before – a twelve-roomed house on four floors, for which relatively large edifice Dickens also employed a cook, a housemaid, a nurse and, eventually, a manservant called Henry. So far had the young author already come. His study was on the first floor, at the back of the house and overlooking the garden. On the floor above were two bedrooms, in one of which Mary Hogarth seems often to have slept, and on the ground floor there was the dining room and back parlour. The drawing room, where the family would often sit, was next door to Dickens's study. It is difficult now to evoke the actual living presence of the house, although it is clear that at once it was given several Dickensian touches – the woodwork was painted pink, a veined marble hearth was brought in, a complete set of "standard novels" was

purchased to furnish his study, and bright flowered carpets introduced. (Since he seems to have had a nervous terror of fire, one of his
first moves was to insure everything with the Sun Fire Office.) The
furniture would have been of the Regency and William IV style, and it
was one which for the rest of his life Dickens preferred over more
gloomy and more sober mid-Victorian interiors. He loved elegance
but just as importantly he loved brightness; that is why he installed
mirrors in whichever house he occupied. An era in which candles and
oil lamps provided interior lighting was surely one in which the use of
mirrors to reflect light was of paramount importance, although some
unkind critics have suggested that Dickens's love of mirrors was based
on vanity as much as anything else. Certainly one cannot overrule this
possibility entirely. Dickens *was* a rather vain man in dress and
appearance – although there are times when vanity seems to have
become something closer to obsession. He had, for example, a
preoccupation with combing his hair. He would pull out a comb even
at dinner parties and, at any time he thought his hair was at all ruffled,
he would dive at once into his pocket, take out a comb, and straighten
it. A colleague in later life recalled that "he would go through the
performance a hundred times a day and in fact seemed never to tire of
it".

Of course, in Doughty Street, Dickens would have arranged and
rearranged all of the furniture as well; one of the most remarkable of
his characteristics was his ability to visualise exactly where every piece
of furniture was in any room in which he had stayed. Order was of
extreme importance to him, and he had a nervous habit of placing
chairs and tables in *precisely* the right position before he could get
down to a day's work. He could not bear anything to be out of place
and, when he stayed in hotels or rented houses, one of his first tasks
was to rearrange the furniture according to his own interior plan. Even
in this trivial way he stamped his personality upon everything around
him, since he could not breathe in an atmosphere which was not
permeated by him. He always had a superstitious habit, by the way, of
turning his bed in a north–south direction – a lifelong habit since,
according to one friend, "he maintained that he could not sleep with it
in any other position; and he backed up his objections by arguments
about earth currents and positive and negative electricity. It may have
been a mere fantasy but it was real enough to him . . . Nervous and
arbitrary, he was of the kind to whom whims are laws, and self-
control in contrary circumstances was simply an impossibility". Thus

in small things do we see the shadow of permanent realities (he had other superstitions, like touching certain objects three times for luck). He was in addition extremely neat and methodical – he frequently "tidied up" after friends, and became vexed to the point of anger by sloppiness or untidiness. His children soon discovered this, and it is no doubt a lesson which Catherine and Mary had learnt early on. Certainly Dickens liked to take charge of such household arrangements – the cash book of Doughty Street is in his hand, and not that of his wife.

Here in Doughty Street he gave dinners and entertained his friends (as well, no doubt, as his parents); on so grand a scale, in fact, it seems that some people believed that he was spending money too lavishly even for so young and successful an author. There are a few reminiscences from friends about this period, all of them suggesting a perfectly happy domesticity of the kind which Dickens had not enjoyed since the first years of his childhood – he had one son already, and with the constant attendance of his brother, Frederick, and with his sister-in-law, he already had the makings of a suitably large family. His publisher, Bentley, recalled one evening: "It was a right merry entertainment; Dickens was in force, and on joining the ladies in [the] drawing room, Dickens sang two or three songs, one the patter song 'The Dog's Meat Man' and gave several successful imitations of the most distinguished actors of the day. Towards midnight, it was Saturday, I rose to leave but D. stopped [me] and pressed me to take another glass of Brandy and water. This I wd. gladly have avoided, but he begged Miss Hogarth to give it me." Here the memory of Dickens singing the "patter" song, and of imitating various actors, evokes very much the same Dickens who had entertained his parents and his parents' friends when he was a child; we get a measure of the kind of entertainment he continued to enjoy all his life. His brother-in-law, Henry Burnett, had his own recollections: "One night in Doughty Street, Mrs Charles Dickens, my wife [Fanny] and myself were sitting round the fire, cosily enjoying a chat, when Dickens, for some purpose, came suddenly from his study into the room. 'What, you here!' he exclaimed; 'I'll bring down my work.' It was his monthly portion of *Oliver Twist* for *Bentley's*. In a few minutes he returned, manuscript in hand." They carried on talking, as he instructed them to do, ". . . he, every now and then (the feather of his pen still moving rapidly from side to side), put in a cheerful interlude. It was interesting to watch, upon the sly, the mind and the muscles working (or, if you please, *playing*) in company, as new thoughts were being dropped upon the paper. And to note the working brow, the set mouth, with the tongue slightly pressed against the closed lips, as was his habit." Dickens was at this time, in other words, convivial even as he worked; but there were also odd lacunae when, as Burnett said, he "withdrew within himself" (these episodes were often remarked upon in his later life), and such was his presence that he managed to reduce the whole party to silence in the process, until on one occasion he broke from his reverie after a few minutes and said gently, "Will – somebody – just sniff?" Then they all began talking again. That it was a happy family there is no doubt, even though in much later life Dickens would insist that almost from the beginning he had felt estranged from his wife. At the time Catherine herself had no such doubts – "Oh dear Mary," she wrote to her cousin, "what pleasure it would give me to see you in my own house, and how proud I shall be to make you acquainted with Charles. The fame of his talents are now known all over the world, but his kind affectionate heart is dearer to me than all." It might have seemed that this domestic idyll was set indefinitely to continue, as Dickens slowly made his way forward in the world. He was already now "accepted"; he had been elected to the Garrick Club; and on 3 May he had delivered his first public speech. It was at the anniversary festival of the Literary Fund, and when a toast was made to "the health of Mr Dickens and the rising Authors of the Age" it was received with "long-continued cheering". But then, four days later, an entirely unanticipated event changed everything.

Chapter 10

ON 7 May, 1837, Mary Hogarth died at the age of seventeen. She had been the previous night with Dickens and Catherine to see a performance of his farce *Is She His Wife?* at the St James's Theatre. They had returned home to Doughty Street at about one in the morning; Mary went to her room but, before she could undress, gave a cry and collapsed (the doctors were to diagnose her condition as one of heart failure). Mary's mother, Mrs Hogarth, was called, and in her grief became insensible; Catherine and Dickens stayed with Mary as she lay in her bed in the little back room, but she never recovered. At three o'clock the following afternoon she died in Dickens's arms. Or, rather, it seems that she was dead for some time before he fully appreciated the fact. An undertaker was summoned – in an essay many years later he recalled "the one appalling, never-to-be-forgotten undertaker's knock" on the door – and she was placed in a coffin which remained in the bedroom overlooking the garden of 48 Doughty Street. She was buried six days later. Mrs Hogarth became hysterical after her collapse and had to be kept from the bedroom by force, while Catherine on the other hand showed surprising and what seemed to Dickens almost excessive calmness and strength. But, in this situation, clearly it was she who had to remain strong.

For the effect upon her husband was of the most extraordinary kind. His grief was so intense, in fact, that it represented the most powerful sense of loss and pain he was ever to experience. The deaths of his own parents and children were not to affect him half so much and in his mood of obsessive pain, amounting almost to hysteria, one senses the essential strangeness of the man. He cut off a lock of Mary Hogarth's hair and kept it in a special case; he took a ring off her finger, and put it on his own. These are all very natural reactions but, more eccentri-cally, he kept all of her clothes and two years later was still on occasions taking them out to look at them – "They will moulder away in their secret places," he said. He also continually expressed a wish to be buried with her in the same grave. To keep the clothes of a seventeen-year-old girl, and to desire to be buried with her, are, even in the context of early nineteenth-century enthusiasm, unusual sentiments.

It has been surmised that all along Dickens had felt a passionate attachment for her and that her death seemed to him some form of retribution for his unannounced sexual desire – that he had, in a sense, killed her. The fact that she died immediately after seeing his farce upon the problems of married life has added fuel to these speculations. But all this is unproven and unprovable. Far more likely, in fact, that he kept her clothes, and that he expressed the wish to be buried with her, because in a sense he identified himself with her – "Thank God she died in my arms," he said just after her death, "and the very last words she whispered were of me." That sounds like the most unfortunate kind of self-obsession, but it is not so; it is an indication of the fact that he imagined some form of union between them. For the next nine months he dreamed of her every night – he called these nocturnal phantoms "visions" of Mary – and in addition he used to say that her image haunted him by day. So what precisely *was* the significance of Mary to him, apart from being his companion during the first happy months of his marriage? In his public remarks he describes himself as having a "father's pride" in her, and his descriptions of her suggest something like paternal closeness: "From the day of our marriage," he wrote, "the dear girl had been the grace and life of our home, our constant companion, and the sharer of all our little pleasures." In an announcement to the readers of *Oliver Twist* he went even further, in words that could not have been entirely acceptable to Catherine since he describes Mary as one ". . . whose society had been for a long time the chief solace of his labours". But the death of even such a close companion cannot explain the depth of Dickens's grief, and it seems likely that there were other forces at work which compounded his misery. Particularly after Catherine became pregnant, it is to be expected that he would draw close to his seventeen-year-old sister-in-law: he had a deep desire to retain certain elements of his childhood (as in his singing of the old songs) and it is more than likely that, whereas Catherine now represented the adult world of responsibility and work, Mary for him was still a child with whom he could recapture the world of his own happy childhood. She became another sister, like

the sister he had known at Chatham. So it is not surprising that all the
qualities he wished to retain from childhood – principal among them
that passivity and gentleness which he had already celebrated elsewhere – were precisely the ones which he believed her to have
possessed, and which he mourned in her passing. It ought to be
remembered that, in the melodrama of the period, the good were
passive and the bad essentially thrusting and aggressive; all the experiences of Dickens's own life would lead him to trust that sense of life,
and in his novels the good characters would follow the same pattern of
helpless passivity and gentleness. In that sense he identified his own
best self with Mary Hogarth, the gentle and innocent girl. But there is
also an important chronological point. Her death led once more to the
destruction of his childhood at precisely the time when, in the early
episodes of *Oliver Twist*, he was also exploring the death of innocence
in the life of the parish boy. Everything came together, and the death
of Mary merely intensified the autobiographical anguish which he was
transposing to his fiction. That is why all his early sorrow and
loneliness come back in his distraught letters after her death, and why
once again he experiences the savage pain in his side which had
disabled him in the blacking factory. Dickens's mood was ostensibly
one of adult grief and even prostration, but there would also have been
moments of desolation, moments when in this new separation from a
loved one he felt again all the anguish and fear of his infancy. For his
evident happiness during the time at Furnival's Inn – the only time in
his life when it can be said that he was truly happy – was due as much to
the presence of Mary Hogarth as to that of his wife. Both the
passionate and sexual aspects of his nature were then being assuaged
(or perhaps we can say both his infantile and adult aspirations). After
Mary Hogarth's death there came once more that emptiness, that
ache, that yearning perpetually renewed, always fresh and yet always
the same, which by his own account became one of the guiding aspects
of his life.

As a result she became for him the idealised image of the female.
"Young, beautiful, and good" were the words he had inscribed upon
her gravestone, and he uses the same words in his later descriptions of
Rose Maylie, Little Nell and Florence Dombey. He had said in one of
his mourning letters that "the love and affection which subsisted
between her and her sister, no one can imagine the extent of . . .", and
again in his fiction there is a constant tendency to idealise the relationship between sisters as if in their happy companionship there

dwells some holy bond. And of course the image of the virtuous and innocent girl – "she had not a single fault," he said – is one that emerges throughout his fiction and acquires a mystical, semi-religious, significance; it would not be going too far to state, in fact, that Dickens's own religious sensibility began to develop as a result of Mary's death. It is known that he started regularly to attend the chapel of the Foundling Hospital in Great Coram Street nearby, and since he mentions a visit to church in the immediate aftermath of her death it seems likely that it was at this time in particular that he began to feel the need for religious hope or consolation. He was consoled "above all" by "the thought of one day joining her again where sorrow and separation are unknown"; when we come to consider Dickens's Christianity it is as well to remember from what private roots of suffering and relief it sprang. And hence, too, the religious significance which he attached to the concept of memory; as soon as she was dead he was reminiscing about their lives together. "I can recall everything we said and did in those happy days," he said, and for him the memory became a blessed faculty aligned with fancy and the imagination, linking the living with the dead and thus earth with heaven; it became a way of infusing reality with spiritual grace, and there can be no doubt that it was the death of Mary Hogarth which awakened those elements in his nature which had up to this time been overshadowed by his appetite for fame. Dickens had learned another hard lesson early – he was still only twenty-five – but in a sense it was his good fortune that the profound experiences which shape a writer's imagination happened to him sooner rather than later.

But he could not write just yet – for the first and last time in his life he missed his deadlines, and the episodes of *The Pickwick Papers* and *Oliver Twist* which were supposed to be written during that month were postponed. Instead he went with Catherine to a rural retreat, Collins's Farm in Hampstead, which, curiously enough, is in much the same location as the one to which Dickens was soon to consign Bill Sikes after his murder of Nancy. They remained here for a fortnight, although in the last week Dickens was travelling back daily to Doughty Street. Quiet and rest were certainly needed since, although Catherine had seemed so calm at the time of Mary's death, she had in fact suffered a miscarriage – although it is possible that this was as much in reaction to her husband's hysteria as to her own grief. But clearly the thought of death was now very much on her mind; she wanted to have her infant son, Charles, christened as soon as possible and wrote to ask her cousin to take the place of Mary as godmother. "We have learned from sad experience," she wrote, "the uncertainty of life."

By the beginning of June they were back in Doughty Street and Dickens at once began work on the postponed chapters of *Oliver Twist*. Much critical acumen has been expended in trying to locate the time when Dickens first decided that this series should take on the definite shape of a novel and not be simply a parish boy's "progress" in the conventional sense – when in other words he provided a circular rather than simple linear shape to the narrative, and began to tie up all the loose ends which previously he had been happy to leave trailing on the ground. But there is another change which has been less widely noticed since it is in the episode after the death of Mary Hogarth, and in those that follow, that Dickens begins to lose interest in the topical and polemical intent of the first chapters. The suppressed poetry of the narrative begins more clearly to emerge as a result, and what had been in part a series of sharp satirical sketches turns into a narrative at once more romantic and more mysterious. It may be unwise to suggest a firm connection between this transition and the death of Mary, but her presence does also become visible in certain direct ways. So it is that he now creates Rose Maylie, a young girl of seventeen ". . . so mild and gentle; so pure and beautiful; that earth seemed not her element . . ."; and so it is that she passes through a perilous illness, comes close to death, but then miraculously recovers. He raises Mary Hogarth in his words, and the theme of loss and return is one that becomes central to the story as Dickens now begins to develop it.

The experience of the death of Mary Hogarth enters the novel in other ways, also. It occurs in the words of Mr Brownlow, the kind gentleman who has rescued Oliver from a life of degradation – "The persons on whom I have bestowed my dearest love, lie deep in their graves . . ." – no less than in the account of Oliver watching over the bedside of the languishing Rose Maylie. "The suspense, the fearful, acute suspense, of standing idly by while the life of one we dearly love, is trembling in the balance; the racking thoughts that crowd upon the mind, and make the heart beat violently, and the breath come thick . . . the desperate anxiety *to be doing something* to relieve the pain . . . what tortures can equal these . . ." And there in the italicised words one captures something of Dickens's own agony as he watched by the bedside of the dying girl. Since Mary's death also aroused in Dickens his old, one might even say primal, fears of abandonment, it is perhaps not surprising that after her death the portrait of London in *Oliver Twist* should once more take the shape of that dark, threatening and contaminated city which he had experienced as a child, a city in which it seems that Oliver is "languishing in a wretched prison". It may be significant, too, that the chapters of *The Pickwick Papers* which Dickens wrote immediately after Mary's death concern Mr Pickwick's own entry into the Fleet prison. The image of prison rises up before him once again; in his desolation of spirit it is always the one which returns.

This is not to suggest that such chapters or passages are uniquely determined by Dickens's experience of Mary Hogarth's death – the pull of the narrative comes from sources deeper and darker than even the most appalling of recent events – but rather that certain aspects of Dickens's creative imagination were thereby strengthened or aroused. That is why there now develops in *Oliver Twist* a constant sense of the need for sleep, for forgetfulness, for that blessed slumber "which ease from recent suffering alone imparts"; and there are episodes in the book now where Oliver hovers between sleep and wakefulness, in which suspended state he experiences what Dickens calls "visions" – visions in which "reality and imagination become so strangely blended that it is afterwards almost a matter of impossibility to separate the two". Was it in that state that he had his own "visions" of Mary? Yet it is also appropriate to the nature of the novel itself. It is on one level a realistic tale in which the Artful Dodger is arraigned for pick-pocketing and calls out ". . . this ain't the shop for justice", in which Fagin, about to be condemned to death, gazes idly over the spectators at his trial and notices that "some of the people were eating, and some fanning themselves with handkerchiefs; for the crowded place was very hot. There was one young man sketching his face in a little note-book. He wondered whether it was like, and looked on when the artist broke his pencil-point, and made another with his knife, as any idle spectator might have done." These scenes could have come straight from Dickens's own days as a reporter but then, beside them, are the other elements in this tale – the resurrection of Rose Maylie, the magical restoration of Oliver himself to gentility, the terrible flight of Bill Sikes from the phantoms of his own making. These scenes belong to another order of reality, and suggest how it is that dream and actuality, fantasy and observation, mingle within the narrative quite freely. Dickens's imagination burns, and the reality wavers above it as it does above a fire – for was not Dickens himself at the time in that state of sleeping wakefulness, of respite stolen from suffering, where reality and imagination are in his words "so strangely blended"?

All that strangeness coming also from Dickens's own state now, as the early fame and success and ambition are so cruelly undermined by the death of his sister-in-law. But in that fall from youthful insouciance and brilliance Dickens himself is broken open and the style that emerges after these events is one which will pervade the rest of his writing. For what are the essential themes brought to life in *Oliver Twist* as he now continued it? Home. Death. Childhood. All of them so curiously blended in the wish to revert to some primal place, some Eden of remembrance, some innocent state, ". . . some pleasant dream of a love and affection he had never known; as a strain of gentle music, or the rippling of water in a silent place, or the odour of a flower, or even the mention of a familiar word, will sometimes call up sudden dim remembrances of scenes that never were, in this life; which vanish like a breath; and which some brief memory of a happier existence, long gone by, would seem to have awakened . . ." And here we glimpse all the memories of Dickens himself – his memory of early infancy when nothing could separate him from his mother, his memory of the life before the blacking factory, his memory of the life he thought that he had led with the blessed companionship of Mary Hogarth – all these things utterly torn from him but returning now, returning in his memory, returning in his fiction as the parish boy himself wakes to find himself saved. Once again Charles Dickens is propelled towards some quite exceptional achievement in *Oliver Twist*, as if it were his fate that all the blessings and miseries of his life were to be transformed into words.

There is a poetry in this novel which is quite unlike anything which is to be seen in previous fiction, a poetry of barely whispered notes that sets up a deep refrain within the text, for it was Dickens's great achievement to bring the language of the "Romantic" period into the area of prose narrative. He was the first novelist really to possess the "sympathetic imagination" of his great poetic predecessors, through which he was able to grasp and integrate an entire world. So, when we come to consider the inconsistencies and difficulties of his view of the world, perhaps we ought to remember Sir Henry Taylor's contemporaneous remarks on the Romantic poets themselves: "A feeling came more easily to them than a reflection, and an image was always at hand when a thought was not forthcoming." These remarks might well be applied to the novelist, too, but it is not enough to say that he inherited the imaginative dispensation of the Romantic poets. Even in *Oliver Twist* itself we see another poetry, the poetry which appears in certain Gothic novels and which in Dickens's writing becomes the poetry of London, the poetry of darkness and isolation, the poetry which Bulwer-Lytton described only a few years later as "the vast and dark Poetry around us – the Poetry of Modern Civilisation and Daily Existence . . . He who would arrive at the Fairy Land must face the Phantoms". The poetry of Civilisation. The poetry of Daily Existence. The poetry of urban suffering. This is the new poetry of the novel. That is why there are times when the world becomes for Dickens one vast orphanage or one echoing blacking factory.

But then one cannot forget in *Oliver Twist* the hysterical humour, the vamping, the mimicry, the farce, the broad comedy. The words of the Artful Dodger defending himself in court: "Oh! You know me, do you? . . . Wery good. That's a case of deformation of character, any way." The remarks of Mr Bumble in sententious mood, "If you had kept the boy on gruel, ma'am, this would never have happened."

"'Dear dear!' ejaculated Mrs Sowerberry, piously raising her eyes to the kitchen ceiling, 'this comes of being liberal!'"

Humour; poetry; declamation; melodrama. All of these elements are here, as they will be in every one of Dickens's novels. But in that variegated mixture do we not also glimpse something of the mercurial character of the author himself as it will slowly be revealed to us – the sudden gaiety and the equally sudden withdrawal within himself, the seriousness and the mimicry, the high spirits and the anger? There is a deep resemblance always between a writer and his work, but it has nothing to do with his expressed opinions or sentiments; it is rather that the form of his work embodies the form of his personality. But it is important to note, also, that if we can in some sense describe the books as general representations of Charles Dickens – his presence in language as related to his presence in the world – it is also true that the books in turn managed to change and even to "rewrite" him. It can be argued that the books helped to create Dickens's mature personality, strengthening and deepening its possibilities as he came to recognise what each time he had achieved.

Of course it is not to be imagined that each mood or feeling of Charles Dickens can be formulated and expounded in an analytical way; what one observes are various appetencies and reactions, instincts and memories, each jostling against or working with one other, a bundle of striving impulses for a few of which at any time we give appropriate names. Clearly the Charles Dickens who emerges through the pages of *Oliver Twist* would not be easily or immediately recognisable to those who knew him; indeed, after his brief sojourn at Collins's Farm, he returned to London and to his working life for, to those who mixed with him, it might have seemed that nothing in particular had happened. He had already inserted advertisements in *Bentley's Miscellany* explaining the omission of the usual *Oliver Twist* episode and, in the next number of *The Pickwick Papers*, he explained why the June number had not been published as the result of "a severe domestic affliction of no ordinary kind". This last announcement is more interesting, however, for its denunciation of "various idle speculations" about the reasons for the non-appearance of the number: "By one set of intimate acquaintants, expressly well impressed, he has been killed outright; by another driven mad; by a third imprisoned for debt; by a fourth sent per steamer to the United States; by a fifth rendered incapable of any mental exertion for evermore . . ." Such reports were in fact to become a perpetual irritant to Dickens – he was always the subject of rumour and gossip, with madness and imprisonment for debt tending to be the two favourite scandals attached to his increasingly eminent name. But now he went back to work at once. Back to his old activities. He went to the prison at Coldbath Fields (at Clerkenwell, and so within walking distance of his house in Doughty Street) with Macready, and they had dinner with the comedian, Harley, afterwards – "Our evening was very cheerful," Macready wrote in his diary; on another evening he had dinner at the house of Talfourd with Macready and Forster; he attended the wedding of his sister, Laetitia, to Henry Austin (an architect and engineer who, with Dickens's assistance, became an active proponent of sanitary reform); he attended a dinner at Greenwich for the Literary Fund; he was even planning a comedy, and discussed the project with Macready. And, for a week in July, he travelled to France and Belgium together with his wife and Hablot Browne. Very little is known about this excursion, since neither Browne nor Mrs Dickens was in later years particularly communicative about their respective relationships with the great novelist, and it is perhaps notable only for the fact that this is the first foreign journey which Dickens ever made. In later years he was to become a regular traveller, indeed almost a resident, in France and Italy; but what soon became a matter of necessity with him here has the nature of an agreeable "jaunt". At this stage in his life he did not seem particularly interested in other countries at all; he was, in one sense or another, devoting all of his energies to understanding and conquering his own. It was only when his position in England became more assured that he felt the need to get away.

In fact even while he was travelling he was thinking of his London "career", and he sent a letter to Forster thanking him for a review in *The Examiner* as well as one to Bentley asking for the renegotiation of his contracts. For it was only now that Dickens began to do something about the proliferation of agreements he had undertaken in the first flush of his youthful ambition; the point was that he had not only over-extended himself (there were at least three novels contracted to two different publishers) but had also begun to realise that the publishers were making more money out of his work than he was. This was the kind of situation which Dickens found unbearable, and now for the first time he had an ally who could fight his battles for him: his friendship with John Forster, confirmed by their frequent riding and dining expeditions together, had become very important to him for just such a reason. He knew that in the past Forster had acted on behalf of Ainsworth, so now he enrolled him for his own negotiations with various publishers. It was from this time, also, that he showed everything he wrote to Forster – either in manuscript or in proof – and his friend became his critic as well as his unofficial "agent". The first difficulties had arisen with Macrone: when Dickens learned that the publisher was about to issue *Sketches by Boz* in monthly parts he became fearful that the presence of three different productions under his name might seriously damage the interests of all. *Pickwick?* And *Oliver?* And the *Sketches* as well? So Forster was despatched to reason with Macrone, but without any noticeable effect. Of course Macrone was justified in anything he chose to do with the volume or volumes; in return for having cancelled Dickens's agreement to write a novel for him, he had been assigned the entire copyright in the *Sketches*. Clearly he wanted to capitalise upon his ownership at a time when Dickens was growing ever more famous, but Dickens was adamantly opposed to any such scheme. It was his fixed belief and intention that the *Sketches* should not be republished by Macrone and eventually he called in the aid of Chapman and Hall, the publishers of *Pickwick*; it was finally decided that they should buy the copyright from Macrone for the then enormous sum of two thousand pounds.

But this altercation with Macrone was only a prelude to his arguments with Richard Bentley, the pink-faced publisher whom at various times in the course of the next few months and years Dickens was to describe as the Burlington Street Brigand, Fagin and the old Jew. His first cause for disagreement was over Bentley's apparent meddling in *Miscellany* business; if there was one thing Dickens could not endure it was interference in projects which he considered to be his own, and on this occasion, as on others, he threatened to resign if his conditions were not instantly met. Matters were resolved, however, only to be overshadowed by Dickens's next demands. He had decided that the series which he had begun in the magazine, *Oliver Twist*, ought to be counted as one of the novels for which he had been contracted by Bentley – even though the *Miscellany* was quite a separate matter. The fact that he had absolutely no right to do so does not seem to have entered his mind on this occasion; he had decided what was right and proper, and no force on earth could stand in his way. He suspected that he was being ill-used financially, but he now believed that his increasing fame and earning power meant that he had the absolute right to cancel agreements which were no longer satisfactory to him. It is in fact the natural instinct of any author who feels himself compromised by agreements negotiated in less fortunate days, and the fact that Dickens had no legal justification for his attitude did not lead him in any way to mitigate his somewhat importunate conduct. There were arguments, meetings between third parties, offers and counter-offers, legal threats and, for one month, Dickens literally downed tools, or quill pen, and refused to write that month's episode of *Oliver Twist*. Bentley even visited Doughty Street in order to talk matters over with him – "I approached him," he wrote later, "in the usual friendly manner, but was met on his side with an air of coldness and restraint . . . he exhibited considerable irritability, threatening amongst other intemperate expressions that he would not write the novel at all." Throughout the crisis Forster acted as Dickens's representative on earth – there could not have been a more stubborn or determined one – and in the end, of course, as he always would, Dickens won. Bentley renegotiated the contract, making *Oliver Twist* one of the two novels for which he had paid an advance. But this was not the end of the matter. There would be more disagreements, more demands by Dickens, and more victories as his supreme position in English letters meant that he was literally able to force publishers to do his bidding. And of course he had to win. That erect posture, that almost military bearing, suggest what his forceful will and determination have already intimated – if life was a "battle", then he would never settle for anything other than complete victory.

These ancient disputes are in fact of not much interest now, except in so far as they do provide evidence about the nature of Dickens's character. Throughout all of these crises, for example, the salient point was that he expected instant responses to his demands, and much of the anxiety and anger which he experienced during the course of the negotiations lay in the fact they could not be settled at once. ". . . negotiation and delay are worse to me than drawn daggers," he wrote later in life; any kind of suspense destroyed "rest, sleep, appetite, and work" until matters were "definitely arranged". When he had made up his mind to do something, he once said, he resembled a hot air balloon which when not encumbered simply has to go up. He was in fact a most impatient human being – when he agreed to building alterations with various contractors, the work had to be finished "at once". There are numerous vignettes of his "hurrying" Catherine, whether in finishing a letter or simply in walking down the street. Whether for coach or (later) train, he always arrived a quarter of an hour before departure. He was in everything utterly punctual, and he detested unpunctuality in others.

So the episodes with Bentley, which seemed for a while unresolvable, acted upon him like some prolonged torture, although it is clear from Bentley's own reminiscences that Dickens's impatience was matched only by his imperiousness and irritability. It has already been noted how he had inherited a short and sometimes violent temper from his father – as a contemporary said, ". . . he could be angry, as those with whom he had been angry did not very readily forget" – but he knew as much himself. Throughout his letters there are constant and sometimes almost self-congratulatory references to a temperament which could be "indomitable, savage, unalterable". He described on many occasions how in moments of rage he could turn "Demoniacal", how he had a "spice of the Devil" within him. To seize by the throat is one of his favourite expressions; another is to lay violent hands upon. On one occasion he notes, "(I am of rather a fierce turn, at times) . . . a vague desire to take somebody by the throat and shake him – which was rather feverish." Here the presence of violence, fierceness and fever are united in one short outburst, and it is interesting, too, how often Dickens works himself up into what he describes as a "fever of excitement". Thus the man. And so the novelist? Certainly in his fiction he is interested in murder, in the bodies of the dead, in the speculations of the man condemned to death. He also wrote sanguinary notes to himself about the need to "kill" one character and to "slaughter" another. "Jo?" he writes of the poor sweeping boy of *Bleak House*. "Yes. Kill him –." And can we not see in the spectacle of Dickens himself irate, irritable, savagely angry, the human behaviour of the writer whose work seems permeated by the shapes of a sometimes violent and macabre imagination – who can hardly see a child without condemning him or her to death, who revels in the incendiary rages of the mob in *A Tale of Two Cities* and *Barnaby Rudge*, who relishes Krook's extraordinary death by spontaneous combustion, who takes an almost lascivious pleasure in detailing the senile simperings and gentilities of various elderly parties? Yet nothing exists without its opposite and there is that other aspect of his character, too, in the need to be self-possessed, in the desire to exercise self-restraint. Characteristically, in the face of emotions from others, Dickens tends to congratulate himself on remaining calm and utterly composed. When greeted with cheers and roars of applause he stayed "as cool as a cucumber", he once wrote; when people mentioned his name in speeches or even in theatres where he was present, he would pretend that he did not know of whom they were talking and would look unconcernedly at the ceiling. This is the other side of the anger – this need to restrain himself, to conceal his true feelings – and in that constant struggle between his self-discipline and impatience we sense something of the conflicting art which comprises his narratives.

In the midst of his troubles with Bentley, he had gone down with the family to Broadstairs at the end of August, taking with them Mrs Hogarth, Mary's mother, who had still not recovered from her daughter's sudden death four months before. It is not known why he chose Broadstairs but, even today, it has an air of enclosure, of being *cut off*, which may have appealed to him after the arduous engagements and negotiations in London. They took a small, two-storey wooden house with its parlour overlooking the High Street which, as it does still, sloped steeply downwards to the sea which was no more than three minutes' away. This place had been fashionable in the late eighteenth century but was now once more a quiet fishing village, built upon the steep chalk cliffs which overlook a semi-circular bay with its pleasant sands and short wooden pier. Clearly Dickens liked it here. He fell ill but recovered quickly, and became acquainted with the landlord of Ballard's Hotel which overlooked the sea. He walked the few miles along the sands to Ramsgate, and joined the local subscription library. The main point, however, was that Broadstairs was secluded and that it was quiet – conditions in which Dickens could rest and also work. He liked it so much, in fact, that he and his family returned there in the summer or autumn months for almost fourteen years. It may even have been Dickens's presence there that made it more popular – some years later *Punch* described it as "a shrine to which certain fashionable people make a yearly pilgrimage, in order to take penance". Particularly it was favoured by "theatrical" people (of course, a group very close to Dickens's heart) but at no point did it become a "resort" in the twentieth-century sense. There was no such phenomenon then – travellers either did the grand tour of Europe or they migrated to various health "spas" (Bath, for example, was still immensely popular). In Broadstairs Dickens would have seen only a place of refuge after the cares of the metropolis, and, in particular, a place where he could resume his contemplation of the sea.

So it was here at the beginning of September that he recommenced work on *The Pickwick Papers* (having refused to write a number of *Oliver Twist* for *Bentley's Miscellany*) but now, in this penultimate instalment of a narrative that had taken him so far, there are certain signs, if not of weariness, at least of his creative interests being diverted elsewhere. He was in a sense tired of Mr Pickwick, and he was already thinking of new novels he wished to write – the much-postponed *Gabriel Vardon*, or *Barnaby Rudge*, was clearly on his mind, and he was to begin work on *Nicholas Nickleby* within three or four months. So he reverts to his earlier borrowings from the contemporary theatre, and tries to round off *The Pickwick Papers* as if it were a play; he reintroduces characters like Bob Sawyer, Mr Pott of the *Eatanswill Gazette*, the red-nosed preacher Mr Stiggins, the notorious Fat Boy, and engineers the final appearance of other characters such as Jingle and Job Trotter, Mr Dodson and Mr Fogg. But the book ends as it began, with the "immortal Pickwick" whom Dickens had created when he was a struggling reporter in his lodgings in Furnival's Inn. It ends with Dickens, the most famous author of his day, writing these words in his study in Doughty Street: ". . . he is invariably attended by the faithful Sam, between whom and his master there exists a steady and reciprocal attachment, which nothing but death will sever." But of course death has not intervened, for Mr Pickwick is indeed "immortal" – his narrative will never die because it is imbued with the irresistible energy and the unfeigned humour of creativity which Dickens enjoyed throughout the period in which he wrote it.

The Pickwick Papers could now at last be published in one volume, complete with illustrations and preface (in the course of which Dickens changed the description of himself from novelist to writer, and then changed it back again, suggesting some confusion or at least hesitation on his part). In order to celebrate the event a Pickwick banquet was held at the Prince of Wales Hotel off Leicester Square; present on that occasion were Talfourd, Macready, Browne, Forster, Ainsworth, Chapman, Hall, John Dickens and others. Talfourd proposed Dickens's health, "and Dickens replied – under strong emotion – most admirably". Thus Macready recorded the event in his diary. In later years Dickens seems not to have been quite as emotional. He once confided to a friend that ". . . he did not much care for *Pickwick*" and one of his colleagues reported that "he never spoke of it himself, nor did he much care to hear it spoken of". But that is the natural reaction of any author to an early success, especially when it is one that might threaten to engulf any reputation he may acquire for subsequent books. He knew later, just as he knew at the time of the Pickwick dinner, that he had in fact produced something quite unprecedented in the history of English literature. It has not been a popular book in recent years, primarily because those who discuss such matters professionally have tended to look for "ambiguity", "complexity", "darkness", or "irony" in the fictions they recommend. *The Pickwick Papers* has all of these things, but they are at the service of a comic energy which has a momentum of its own. It is that rare thing in literature – a pure shout of creation that rings out like the laughter of a child on a frosty day, for it is the laughter of the child that Dickens once was when he burst into the room and exclaimed, ". . . we are going to have such a game."

Yet there was always his imperiousness even in the midst of his highest spirits and, as one friend commented after his death, he "had a strain of hardness in his nature which was like a rod of iron in his soul". It was with this rod that he was still in the process of beating back Richard Bentley, who in this period eventually acquiesced in all the new demands which Dickens had made. And, now that *Oliver Twist* was formally agreed by Bentley to be the first novel under contract, it seems that Dickens himself started considering the possibilities of turning the magazine serial into a work approaching the shape of conventional literary fiction – in other words, a narrative in which the beginning, middle and end are more than temporally aligned. This may also have had something to do with his dissatisfaction with the somewhat rambling way he was even then concluding Mr Pickwick's adventures. So, in October, not long after his new agreement with his publisher and just as he was finishing *The Pickwick Papers*, he asked for a complete volume of the first issues of *Bentley's Miscellany* so that he could reacquaint himself with Oliver's history; this is a sure sign, if nothing else, that he wanted to ensure that the later episodes were properly connected to the earliest. Three weeks later he seemed to have found a character upon whom some of the complexity of the newly evolved novel might fall – "I hope," he told Forster, "to do great things with Nancy. If I can only work out the idea I have formed of her, and of the female who is to contrast with her . . ." The contrasting female was of course Rose Maylie, the alter ego of Mary Hogarth who *does not* die. Certainly something seems to have boosted his enthusiasm and energy – the end of *Pickwick*, the resolution of his dispute with Bentley, the month "off" *Oliver Twist* as a result of that dispute, all are possibilities. Whatever the cause, he was writing the next episode of *Oliver Twist* very quickly indeed and managed to finish one chapter in the space of one day. It was coming easily to him at this point, and it is perhaps worth noting that it is in this quickly written chapter that Dickens makes his famous observations about the alternation of "the tragic and the comic scenes" like layers in "streaky well-cured bacon"; this passage was written as quickly as it was conceived but, for that very reason, it is a clear expression of Dickens's instinctive methods. He went down to Brighton for a week, ostensibly to rest, but while there he bought and started to read Daniel Defoe's *Political History of the Devil* – a strange choice for Dickens, perhaps, except that at this point he knew that he was about to switch the interest in his story away from topical matters and to explore what must have seemed to him the instinctively religious dimensions of his recent experience of Mary Hogarth's death. He wanted to learn more about the devil, too, in order effectively to portray Fagin – he said later that, at this time in his life, "Fagin the Jew would never let him rest".

Yet, in any case, he would never let himself rest – since the completion of *The Pickwick Papers* he found that he had time on his hands, and at once he began to employ what might have seemed to him to be the merely wasted days of not working. Of course he still had the same two proposed novels in mind – *Nicholas Nickleby* to be published by Chapman and Hall in monthly numbers from April 1838, and *Barnaby Rudge* to be published by Bentley at some time in the autumn of that same year. But neither of these projects was as yet ready to begin; for one thing, Chapman and Hall had started publishing *Sketches by Boz* in monthly form, and he did not want to clog the market with too much material. So instead, after some prompting, he agreed to fill the empty days by editing the memoirs of the famous clown, Joe Grimaldi, and by writing a short pamphlet entitled *Sketches of Young Gentlemen*. The latter need not detain us long; it is a volume of sharp and well sustained comic sketches in which Dickens characteristically turns human beings into various "types" in the approved early nineteenth-century manner. *Memoirs of Joseph Grimaldi* is another matter. Dickens began it unwillingly, since the task of bringing order and purpose to Grimaldi's papers (already once revised) was a cumbersome business, and he only eventually agreed when the payment for his editorial services was increased by Bentley. It was to be published in time for the pantomime season, and Dickens's method was to cut an already abridged account and then dictate the results to his father who came to Doughty Street for the purpose. In fact he seems to have warmed to his task in the process, not least because of his fascination with pantomime in general and with clowns in particular – all his life he admired this world in which no harm came to anyone, and in which the conflicts and assaults of human existence were resolved in laughter. It is not surprising, either, that he became interested in Grimaldi himself, since that clown's character and temperament bear in many ways striking resemblances to Dickens's own. Grimaldi, too, was a spirited, quick-witted and inventive artist, whose life as Dickens dictated it to his father might have been seen as a cautionary tale for the novelist himself. "This immense fatigue, undergone six days out of every seven," he wrote, "left Grimaldi at the conclusion of the week completely worn out and thoroughly exhausted, and, beyond all doubt, by taking his bodily energies far beyond their natural powers, sowed the first seeds of that extreme debility and utter prostration of strength from which in the latter years of his life, he suffered so much." Exactly the same things would be said of the novelist, too. In fact Dickens's account of Grimaldi's miserable childhood, his extreme punctuality, his inability to stop working ("Idleness wearied him more than labour . . ."), his horror of letting any audience down, sound very much like a projection of Dickens himself. But Dickens was not a contemplative or self-aware man in the conventional sense, and it is likely that he composed those words without considering his own fate, and certainly without realising that, when he began to describe Grimaldi's "premature old age and early decay", he would be granted an acute premonition of his own last years.

That was to be in another time altogether, and now the year 1837 came to an end with a New Year's party at which Dickens entertained a few friends and relatives in Doughty Street. "It was near the hour of twelve," his brother-in-law, Henry Burnett recalled, "when up went the windows, and each person became mute, excepting an excusable whisper now and then from two or three ladies. The constrained silence was at an end as soon as the first stroke of a distant clock came upon the ear. Then a muffled counting was heard from one or two, and then the clear voice of our Host called out 'Best Wishes and a kiss for each lady, and a Happy New Year to us all!'" It was the year which had seen the culmination of *The Pickwick Papers* as well as the beginning of *Oliver Twist*, the year in which he had moved into his first house and the year in which his first child was born. Perhaps in response to his own sense of all the things which were happening to him with such bewildering speed, he resolved from this time forward to keep a diary; but the first entry he makes does not concern his triumphs but the fate of Mary Hogarth. Lamenting her death and expressing his wish that he may one day join her – thus beneath the convivial and successful surface of Dickens's life there emerges this other persistent note of grief and loneliness.

At first he tried hard to keep up his entries in this new memorial of his life. That for the second of January, 1838, for example, reads: "With Ainsworth all day, at Macrone's place on business. Afterwards to the ruins of the fire in the Borough, thence to the top of Saint Saviour's Church; back to his Club to dinner, and afterwards to Covent Garden where we met Browning. Ainsworth has a fine heart." We might gloss this by noting that Dickens had agreed with Ainsworth to "illustrate ancient and modern London in a Pickwick form". The book was never written (no doubt because of the sudden death of its putative publisher, Macrone, later that year), but this may in part explain their perambulations around the city. In any case Dickens would probably have gone to see the site of the recent fire in the Borough, since he had a fascination for such spectacles – whether it was the fire itself, or the smoking ruins which marked its progress, he loved the violence of it, the sense of desolation and destruction which it provoked. (Often he applied a similar image to himself, as he sat "blazing away" over his work.) In this same diary he mentions his attempt a week later to insure his life with Sun Insurance – on the application form he said that he had once had "cowpox" but falsely denied that he had "any fit or Fits"; a few days later the company denied his application, no doubt on the grounds of general worries about his excessive working habits. The following day he attended a quadrille party at which his sister, Fanny, sang. Another guest recorded of this occasion, "Met Boz – looks quite a boy. His sister was there; she sang beautifully . . ." But Dickens only says in his diary, "City people and rather dull." There are a few other entries relating to his work and amusements, but on Monday, 15 January, 1838, he simply writes: "Here ends this brief attempt at a Diary. I grow sad over this checking off of days, and can't do it. CD." Strange sentiments, perhaps, for a young man enjoying enormous success but it is clear enough that he had by no means recovered from the shock of his sister-in-law's death: the emptiness he felt in this "checking off of days" is evident enough, as is the sadness which seems to have been a companion more faithful even than his companions at the Pickwick banquet. But it is not just Mary's death which provokes or sustains this mood. It is a permanent one, to be glimpsed intermittently throughout his life and noticed by his more percipient contemporaries. The sadness was always with him.

The diary did not in fact end at this point, and he takes it up again for his various travels and expenses; it seems that he kept a diary each year of his life, but he noted in it only the sparest details and made a habit of burning it at the conclusion of each year: there were things within it which he did not "paint", to use his word for the processes of ordinary literary composition, and which he did not want anyone to see. (This particular diary for 1838 survived accidentally, as did a later one.) But, if he had kept on with his regular "checking off of days", what else might he have recorded?

There were, first of all, his frequent visits to demonstrations of hypnotism, or "mesmerism" as it was then described. On at least four occasions in this year he attended mesmeric sessions, principally those conducted by John Elliotson (a professor of clinical medicine) at University College Hospital in London. "I am a believer," he said some time later, ". . . I became so against all my preconceived opinions and impressions." Elliotson's skills lay in placing his subjects in a deep trance and, although he was most concerned with the curative powers of mesmerism, his demonstrations also emphasised the more "sensational" aspects of its effects in inducing apparently prophetic or intuitive states as well as provoking various kinds of extraordinary behaviour; the famous Okey sisters, epileptics, were seen to sing, to dance and to possess second sight. In addition Dickens was much impressed by the exploits of the French "magnetic boy" who seemed able to read cards and watches while his eyes were thickly bandaged. It was as a result of these experiences that Dickens himself became acquainted with Elliotson, the manner and work of this doctor so impressing the novelist that he referred to him as "one of my most intimate and valued friends". He supported him when he resigned from his position as lecturer at University College later this year, primarily because of the obloquy he received from the authorities as a result of his mesmeric demonstrations. Indeed he was to become the doctor for the Dickens family although, typically, it was Dickens who in turn tried to help Elliotson when in later life he became despondent and suicidal.

So what was it in mesmerism that so attracted the attention of Charles Dickens? The theory itself was intimately related to the belief in "animal magnetism"; the belief, in other words, that the powers of the human body could be conducted and controlled by an invisible fluid, and that by the careful management of this mesmeric fluid the sick human subject could be cured or revived. Mesmerism was in that sense an aspect of the guiding principles of the age; it became a subject of debate and controversy in the late Thirties and Forties, which was precisely the period when Faraday was investigating the association of electricity and magnetism – in particular the production of an electric current from a magnetic field – so that we can see both in the scientist's own experiments and in the idea of mesmerism a strongly developed interest in the same forces of nature. In fact the various manifestations of any age should be viewed together; and, in this period, in theories of heat, of light, of velocity, of electricity, scientific research was typically concerned with the dynamic nature of energy. It was thus intimately associated with the other leading ideas of the period – notably the belief in work, in progress, in the force of industry, in the dynamism of society itself. The local connection with mesmerism is clear enough, certainly, since in Elliotson's theory they were energies and powers within the human body (as well as within the world) which could be harnessed by the human will and employed efficaciously. Of course all this was connected, too, with nineteenth-century ideas of power and dominance – particularly the male over the female, the stronger over the weaker, the more energetic over the less energetic. Everything, in every age, is of a piece.

Dickens was fascinated by such developments and, as he said himself, became a professed believer in mesmeric powers. In fact Elliotson taught him how to make use of them himself – the movements around the head with the hands in order to induce a magnetic sleep, the brushing of the eyebrows with the thumbs, and the quiet breathing onto the face in order to wake the sleeper. All these things he learned, and indeed he proved himself to be an extraordinarily powerful magnetiser. His son often saw him send people into a "strange sleep". He experimented successfully with his own family (on one occasion even sending Catherine into a trance without either of them intending so to do) and, as we shall see, healed certain of his friends. What kind of healing it was we cannot of course know; whether it meant simply the relief from hysterical symptoms, or the ability to promote rest, or whether some other occluded element was involved, is impossible now to determine. It can only be said, with some degree of certainty, that the ills of any one period often find their most appropriate balm in the remedies invented by that period. And all we can say of Dickens's powers is that they are congruent with everything else we know of his personality, his behaviour and his will. In mesmeric demonstrations great importance was attached to the eyes of the mesmeriser, for example, and Dickens himself always emphasised the force and power of his own "Visual Ray". "(Keep your eye on me) . . ." he once commanded Forster in a letter, as he narrated a story to him, and in later life when he gave his public readings he always insisted that the audience should be able to see his face. When they did not respond he sometimes complained that they were not "magnetic", which suggests that Dickens deliberately (and generally successfully) managed to induce in his audiences a highly suggestible state which was in some ways close to that of the mesmeric trance. The curious thing is that he would never allow himself to be mesmerised, not on any account, and this in turn emphasises other aspects of these powers: in Dickens it was part of his need to control, to dominate, to manipulate. He even did this in his fiction by impressing his images upon his audience and, while writing one of his Christmas tales, he informed Forster that ". . . my eyes have grown immensely large". This abiding fascination for mesmerism is naturally to be linked with his belief in phrenology, his half-humorous interest in the occult, his liking for magical tricks and his own successful appearances as a conjuror at children's parties. But of course it is also to be seen in more intimate connection with the whole nature of his life, particularly with that ability effortlessly to dominate those around him which makes up so large a part of his social behaviour. So once more we see how the forces of his own personality blend with the guiding forces of his period, lending him almost an emblematic strength of character in his dealings with the world and with other people.

And what else might one have read in his diary, if he had bothered to keep it up? He would soon be entering what might be called "Society", although one hostess of the period, Lady Holland, first had the prudence or impudence to ask "if Boz was presentable" before inviting him to one of her evenings at Holland House. She was one of the last great Whig hostesses, and she pronounced afterwards that "he is a young man of 26, very unobtrusive, yet not shy, intelligent in countenance . . ." In fact, in later life, Dickens was to come to despise "Society" of the conventional kind; even in his early days, it is clear that he maintained his reserve and composure with people who were merely "well-known" or "fashionable". And why should he not do so? He had a perfectly good notion of his own worth, and he was shrewd enough to know that these people – in particular the Whig grandees who were "liberal" enough to admit him into their circle – were on the whole remarkable for nothing except their presumption. They would be utterly forgotten, whereas he . . .

And in his diary, too, he might have mentioned the numerous clubs which he either joined or initiated. Ainsworth, Forster and he established the Trio Club or Cerberus Club, with only themselves as members, and at a later date he organised Beard, Forster and Burnett into something known as the Balloon Club. Its principal business was to provide balloons for the children while on holiday, but this small aim did not prevent Dickens from writing long facetious letters and sending them to the other members. Of course there were ostensibly more serious associations; in this year he joined the Athenaeum, for example, a club he is said to have disliked. Certainly he was not a very "clubbable" man in the first place and, as one fellow member put it, "he seldom spoke to anyone unless previously addressed". Another member presents a similar picture with rather more detail: "He used to eat his sandwich standing at the centre table, or striding about". Such clubs were never really to his taste, and in 1838 he resigned from the Garrick, one of a number of occasions on which he did so. But there were other less pompous associations – the Parthenon Club (a small dining club), the Literary Fund Club, the Antiquaries Club, and the Shakespeare Club which met every Saturday evening in the Piazza

Coffee House in Covent Garden in order to discuss such subjects as, "is the present system of periodical publication calculated to raise the character of Literature?" The location of this last-named club in fact suggests something of the reason why clubs of all sorts were popular in the first decades of the nineteenth century; they were essentially a continuation of an eighteenth-century social tradition, itself based upon the prevalence of coffee houses where men could read the newspapers and exchange the latest gossip. Once again we see how the mores of the previous century could stretch into the "Victorian era". But this tradition also had another, and more personal, significance for Dickens. The very idea of a club is one that deeply attracted him, and indeed it was one to which he attempted to give a permanent expression in later periodicals; the idea of a little association of men (and women) impressed him almost as deeply as the idea of home and household for, in each case, there lurks the image of a small, cosy, tight-knit group which by reason of its intimacy and closeness manages to shut out all the threatening life beyond. It is a buttress against a world which, in this period, is characteristically seen as a place of harsh usage and violent struggle. Where there are clubs, of course, there are also dinners; and, if Dickens had kept up his diary, it would have amply demonstrated what his existing entries already suggest – that the most important and indeed frequent aspect of early nineteenth-century social life revolved around food and drink. Dinners of all sorts; dinners to celebrate the publication of a novel, or to venerate a dead author, or to support a favourite charity or "fund", or simply for the express purposes of conviviality. All through Dickens's life these affairs crop up with almost monotonous regularity, and in this period alone there are vignettes of Dickens being escorted through the fog by two men with torches in order to attend one of Ainsworth's dinners at Kensal Lodge; of Dickens, Catherine and Forster going out to the Star and Garter Hotel in Richmond in order to celebrate the joint anniversary of the Dickenses' wedding and Forster's birthday (a tradition which was kept up for the next twenty years); of Dickens attending an Artists' Benevolent Fund dinner where his name was greeted "with such a burst of enthusiasm, again and again renewed, as we have never heard equalled in a meeting of this sort".

Of course there were also the dinners which Dickens celebrated in his fiction. In his later novels there is less of a festive spirit, when intimations of poison and cannibalism creep in, but in the early novels dinners indeed become what Dickens in *American Notes* describes as "social sacraments". It has been estimated that in *The Pickwick Papers* there are some 35 breakfasts, 32 dinners, 10 luncheons, drink itself being mentioned on 249 separate occasions. There is a variety of reasons why Dickens should be so entranced by food and the processes of eating; it will be remembered that he lays much stress upon it in his records of his days at the blacking factory, as if food and drink provided him with the only kind of security and sense of well-being which in that unhappy period he could claim. (It is to be noted, too, that most of the meals he describes in these early books contain the kind of food he would have liked as a child.) But, if food can be a register in his fiction for something very close to the need for love, so also it can be a proper measurement of human pride and social respectability. The fact is that in the end it might be said to stand for anything or everything, and it is perhaps best to notice that its prominence in Dickens's early fiction captures if nothing else the primacy which Dickens afforded to the need for oral satisfaction of every kind. Eating. Drinking. Speaking. Yet here is the paradox: the man who expatiates so imaginatively upon the delights of food was himself a very abstemious person. He drank and ate very little; when he was a host in later life, one of his guests noted that he "seemed to participate in other people's enjoyment of what was laid before them rather than to have any pleasure in the good things himself". And an American friend, at the end of Dickens's life, confirmed that "I have rarely seen a man eat and drink less. He liked to dilate in imagination over the brewing of a bowl of punch, but I always noticed that when the punch was ready, he drank less of it than any one who might be present. It was the sentiment of the thing and not the thing itself that engaged his attention." His office boy provided more immediate corroboration: "He wasn't," he said, "but a light eater himself." These reports are from the latter part of his life, when in any case his appetite might have been diminished by age and weariness, but there is no evidence to suggest that he was anything other than abstemious even in his younger days; there are no accounts of his being drunk, no accounts of his eating to excess. We must be very careful, therefore, before drawing easy parallels between his life and his work. He enjoyed the *sentiment* rather than the *thing*, and the human being who releases all his wonderful words into the public sphere may have only the most ambiguous or intangible relationship with them. The man who dilated upon huge meals himself ate very little. Will not this perhaps give us a clue to the complicated tangle of his social relationships, as well as to the somewhat ambiguous nature of his political opinions?

Is there anything else he might have mentioned in his diary? Perhaps the fact that, as soon as *The Pickwick Papers* was completed, he opened a bank account with Coutts and Company by depositing five hundred pounds. That balance, as might be expected, grew over the years; so great was his concern for money matters, in fact, that he always took great pains to make sure that he remained in credit and was horrified if he found himself even a few pounds overdrawn. This concern might in part have sprung from the close relationship which grew up between him and the heiress to that particular banking fortune, Miss Angela Burdett-Coutts, a tall and thin, somewhat plain, young woman, whose generosity and philanthropic ventures led to her close association with the equally philanthropic if poorer Dickens. He might have noted in his diary, too, that he was sitting to the painter Samuel Laurence in this same period; it was the first of the many portraits which he endured rather than enjoyed. And he might have noted, also, that he was a witness in a prosecution brought against a man for mistreating his horse, during which trial he spoke out warmly against the offender. The headline in *The Times* for this minor matter was: "Charles Dickens in the Witness Box", one more indication of how famous this author in his mid-twenties had now become. He might also have mentioned a fight in which he and his friends were involved when one night they paid a visit to one of the slums, or rookeries, of London. There were many occasions when Dickens made such visits to the poorest quarters of the city, often with no aim in mind other than engaging in something very close to a spectator sport; but he missed nothing and, as one of his first biographers noted, at the time of *Oliver Twist* "it began to be whispered . . . that Dickens was well acquainted with low life".

He wished to be acquainted with much else besides and in the first weeks of 1838, just at the time he was revolving in his mind the possibilities for his next novel (the first episode of which was promised to Chapman and Hall in the spring), he decided to travel with Hablot Browne to Yorkshire. But this was no "jaunt" – he had a definite aim in mind, and planned his trip accordingly. As a child he had heard vaguely about the notorious Yorkshire schools, and in particular he remembered the story of a "suppurated abscess that some boy had come home with in consequence of his Yorkshire guide, philosopher and friend" – in other words, the schoolmaster – ". . . having ripped it open with an inky pen-knife". He remained "curious" about these schools, which were in many instances nothing but convenient dust-bins for unwanted children, bastards or orphans; the advertisements for them often included the chilling words, "No Vacations", which meant that the children were retained there indefinitely. And the conditions, to judge by contemporary reports, were often as harsh as it is possible to conceive. Clearly Dickens had been encouraged by the success of his topical allusions in *Oliver Twist*, and determined that he could direct his polemic against new targets; the idea of poor children being almost literally imprisoned in squalid conditions, and of being tyrannised by brutal adults, was one that in any case struck to the centre of his imagination. So once again his childhood reading, and the memories or fantasies of his own childhood, helped to fashion his ideas for a new novel; the inter-animating process had begun. He became "bent upon destroying" the Yorkshire schools, and, with that aim in mind, he concocted a scheme in which he would pose as the friend of a widowed mother who wished to place her child in just such an establishment. The trip was intended to be a "mighty secret" but a legal colleague of Thomas Mitton knew a lawyer who practised in that Northern neighbourhood, and he gave Dickens a letter of introduction. For the occasion Dickens took the name of Hablot Browne – it is clear that he did not want his own identity, as the author of *Oliver Twist*, and the attacker of workhouses, to be revealed to his new intended subjects or victims – and at the end of January he and the real Browne travelled up to Yorkshire in order to investigate the conditions under which these poor schoolchildren existed. (He took his illustrator with him so that he might have the benefit of seeing the landscape and its figures for himself.) They stayed in Yorkshire for only two days, but during that time Dickens, with an ability to organise his impressions as successfully as he organised everything else (he variously compared his brain to a number of pigeon-holes and to a photographic plate sensitive to the slightest impression), absorbed everything of significance for his own design.

They travelled up on Tuesday morning by a slow coach, paradoxi-cally called the "Express", which left the Saracen's Head at Snow Hill at eight o'clock in the morning; they stayed at Grantham overnight and then took the Royal Glasgow Mail to Greta Bridge – these coach trips themselves, uncomfortable and wearying though they were, providing Dickens with scenes and characters that would be trans-mogrified in his fiction. A mistress of a Yorkshire school who was carrying a letter to one of her recalcitrant pupils from his loving father, demanding to know why he refused to eat "boiled meat", was turned into young Mobb's mother-in-law who "took to her bed on hearing that he would not eat fat". The Yorkshire schoolmistress in question, Dickens went on to note in a letter to Catherine, "was very communicative, drank a great deal of brandy and water, and towards evening became insensible . . ."; which was just the sort of behaviour which appealed to his comic sense. Then there was the lady's maid continually expecting a carriage to greet her; she also reappears in *Nicholas Nickleby*. As does the inn at Greta Bridge where Dickens and Browne stayed; as does the snow which impeded them as they travelled further north. In other words Dickens, alert to every impression, was absorbing as much local detail as he could, knowing all the time that such specific truths would buttress the larger designs which he already had in mind. From Greta Bridge they travelled on Thursday morning to Barnard Castle by post chaise; here, according to local report, Dickens "questioned every likely person he encountered, in order to elicit information regarding incidents of local school life"; and it was here, too, that he met the local solicitor to whom he had been given a letter of introduction. Yet this man proved curiously unwilling to discuss the schools of the area – Dickens gives a fair impression of his Yorkshire speech in one of his eventual prefaces to the novel – and so on the following day he and Browne travelled the short distance to Bowes, a small village on the moors near the River Greta, in order to see for themselves.

It was here that Dickens encountered Mr William Shaw and his academy. He wrote later in his diary, "Shaw the schoolmaster we saw to-day, is the man in whose school several boys went blind sometime since, from gross neglect . . . Look this out in the Newspapers." It is clear that Dickens did not go up specifically to find Shaw, and the information about his neglectful conduct probably came from a disgruntled usher (or teacher) whom according to local report Dickens met at the time. Shaw himself was obviously less communicative; it seems that Dickens's real identity was discovered, and that Shaw's attitude towards the novelist's investigations into his establishment was not particularly friendly. But Dickens had seen all he needed of the school and its owner; it is probable that all along he knew approximately how he would deal with the subject, and was looking merely for those details which might give his imaginative design a local habitation and a name. It was while at Bowes, too, that he wandered into the local churchyard and found there many tombs of dead schoolchildren; in twenty-four years, some thirty-four young "scholars", from the cheap schools of the district, had died at ages varying from ten to eighteen. In particular Dickens was struck by one gravestone which read: "Here lie the remains of GEORGE ASHTON TAYLOR Son of John Taylor of Trowbridge, Wiltshire, who died suddenly at Mr William Shaw's Academy of this place, April 13th, 1822 aged 19 years. Young reader, thou must die, but after this the judgement." It was a dismal winter's afternoon, with the snow laying thickly about, as Dickens read the epitaph. "I think his ghost put Smike into my head, upon the spot," he told a friend later in the year. (Perhaps it ought to be remarked, in passing, that the year of the boy's death, 1822, was the year in which the young Dickens was taken to London.) And so, as Dickens's mind wandered around the themes of his new novel on that dreary day, the elements of its conception began to emerge and to blend together; the coach-ride, the school, the area, the churchyard, all of them slowly being populated by the phantoms of Dickens's imagination. And perhaps it was the ghost of Smike, the poor ruined boy, which helped to expel another spirit: Dickens had written to his wife from Greta Bridge and mentioned for the first time that Mary Hogarth had appeared every night in his dreams. But after this the "visions" suddenly stopped; Dickens always explained this by reference to his letter to Catherine, as if his telling of the dreams had exorcised them. But it is at least as likely that the imaginative energies now circling around this new book, and the ghosts of the poor sick children he was about to raise, displaced the memory of Mary Hogarth and his distraught identification with her. Pausing only to write a letter of complaint concerning a biographical article which had appeared about him in the *Durham Advertiser* (he complained chiefly about the amount of money he was described as earning), he and Browne travelled on to York and then back to London. They had been away for little over a week.

Almost at once Dickens tried to begin work on the novel itself, combining the new enterprise with his labours over *Oliver Twist* and *Bentley's Miscellany*, but he could not settle down to the task until he had clared his mind of the anxiety he felt over yet another novel; this was *Barnaby Rudge*, which he had promised to Richard Bentley by October. Of course none of it was written, or was likely to be under present circumstances, and so he wrote to Bentley suggesting that it should appear in monthly instalments in the *Miscellany* after *Oliver*

Twist had completed its run there – thus buying time, and clearing the ground for *Nicholas Nickleby*. Or, to give the novel its full title, *The Life and Adventures of Nicholas Nickleby, Containing a Faithful Account of the Fortunes, Misfortunes, Uprisings, Downfallings and Complete Career of the Nickleby Family. Edited by "Boz"*. Bentley acceded to this new request and Dickens, able to forget about *Barnaby Rudge* for the time being, set to work, fitfully at first, on his Yorkshire novel. It is worth noting, too, as he begins to write, that there is in this period a change in his handwriting; he has finally lost the old school-formed style and has evolved his own distinctive, clear but nervous hand. In fact to see a chronological selection of his signatures is to see a pattern of contraction and expansion – the earliest letters signed in approved schoolbook fashion and then slowly drawing inward, becoming bunched up with a certain kind of intensity which reaches its peak in 1837 before beginning to broaden and expand into the more elaborate signature of his later years. In addition, in 1836 he stops placing the "flourish" of his signature under *Charles* and puts it instead under *Dickens*; and, approximately from the end of January 1837, he begins to write out in full the dates of his letters at the top of his notepaper, as if signifying a new self-consciousness about the chronology of his life. Certainly the change in his handwriting at the time he was writing *Nicholas Nickleby* suggests that, at last, he was beginning to see himself as a major novelist.

All the evidence suggests, too, that Dickens, after he had surmounted his fitful start, was working quickly and easily on the new novel; the surviving manuscript pages of *Nicholas Nickleby* show that it was written very clearly and smoothly, with very few deletions and additions. Since it opens with an account of the Nickleby family quickly followed by scenes at the inauguration of the United Metropolitan Improved Hot Muffin and Crumpet Baking and Punctual Delivery Company, there is almost certainly an intention on Dickens's part to recapture that inventive, free-wheeling and almost picaresque spirit which had been so much the inspiration of *The Pickwick Papers*. And yet, if the narrative were to be improvised in this way, how was it that Dickens had taken such trouble to enquire into the conditions of the Yorkshire schools with clear reference to their use in the same novel? The reason lies with Dickens's own ambitions at this point in his career; he wanted to do something larger than either of his first two novels, and this mainly by combining their best elements. He knew that the pathos of *Oliver Twist* had been just as much a success as the comedy of *The Pickwick Papers*; and he realised, too, that at a time when, he said later, "the stability of my success was not certain" he did not want to lose either his reputation as a topical and polemical novelist or his fame as a comic one. So in *Nicholas Nickleby*, he devised a plot capacious enough to include both aspects of his genius; and so congenial a task was it that, after some initial hesitation over the first pages, he was, as we have seen, working with very little difficulty upon it. He began seriously in the last week of February and had finished the preliminary number on the ninth of the following month; many of the main characters had thus been introduced, among them Ralph Nickleby, Mrs Nickleby and the rest of that unhappy family, Newman Noggs and the ineffable Mr Squeers. Clearly he knows in which direction he is travelling – a metaphor much employed by Dickens himself when discussing the process of his fiction – but he is in no hurry to get there and, in the interim, he is quite happy to employ all the effects he has already used and which he knows to work. He had a broad overall conception of the general story, but he is playing it by ear as he goes along. So it is that in the final chapter of the first instalment he takes young Nickleby to Snow Hill, where he and Browne had set out for the North and where Fagin had been only a few weeks before in *Oliver Twist*: the landscape of Dickens's wonderful imagination was, in a physical sense, small indeed. As soon as the first number had been finished, in his elation and relief he summoned Forster for a ride (these riding jaunts by the two of them were now very common until the time came when, for reasons of health, Dickens gave up riding for walking). But he started working on the next episode of *Oliver Twist* almost immediately afterwards, until eventually he was able to settle down into a more congenial routine whereby he wrote *Oliver Twist* before embarking upon that month's number of *Nicholas Nickleby*, generally finishing the latter task only two or three days ahead of publication.

At the end of his labours on *Nicholas Nickleby* Dickens told his friends that it "had been to him a diary of the last two years: the various papers preserving to him the recollection of events and feelings connected with their production". This may be Dickens's own understanding of the fact that his novel reminded him of the circumambient world in which it was written – his moods and difficulties over certain sections, the locales where he composed them, and so forth. But it raises, too the question which bedevils *Nicholas Nickleby* perhaps more than any other of his novels. To what extent, and for what purposes, did Dickens base his characters upon "real" people? There is the obvious case of Squeers and Dotheboys Hall, since the description of both provoked many threats of libel writs from various real Yorkshire schoolmasters; notably, it seems, from William Shaw himself who eventually came to realise the folly of suing the famous "Boz". Many scholarly articles have been devoted to exploring the precise degree of truth and fiction in Dickens's account of that Yorkshire school, with the perhaps predictable conclusion that in some cases he exaggerated, in some cases he under-emphasised, and in some cases faithfully recorded, the reality. Of his exaggerations there can be little doubt, since the physiognomies of Mr Squeers and his spouse are clearly based upon the grotesques of the Hogarthian tradition; it also seems possible that he exaggerated the moral villainy of the schoolmaster since, after the publication of *Nicholas Nickleby*, various voices were raised in William Shaw's defence – all to the effect that he was, in the context of his period and of his profession, by no means the worst of a motley collection. Yet there are also parts of the narrative which are very firmly modelled on the actual conditions of the period, not least in the absurd advertisements which the Yorkshire schoolmasters (in fact Shaw himself was a Londoner) placed in the public prints. Shaw's own advertisment includes the fact that "YOUTH are carefully instructed in the English, Latin and Greek languages . . . Common and Decimal Arithmetic; Book-keeping, Mensuration, Surveying, Geometry, Geography and Navigation . . . No extra charges whatever, Doctor's bills excepted. No vacations, except by the Parents' desire." It is clear from examination of the surviving exercise-books from Bowes Academy that his pupils were in fact proficient only in handwriting and in the mere copying by rote from various textbooks, but no doubt it was the absurdity of including "Navigation" in the list of special subjects that prompted Dickens's own version of the advertisement in which the subjects include "fortification, and every other branch of classical literature". The somewhat ominous last sentence of Shaw's real advertisement must in turn have prompted Dickens's "No extras, no vacations, and diet unparalleled". There is a clear connection here, then, between Dickens's observations and his subsequent composition, just as the episodes on his trip to the North were re-employed in the novel itself.

But there is also a great deal of evidence to suggest that Dickens actually underplayed the horror of life in the Yorkshire schools; that, for reasons of decorum or credibility, he purposely ignored the worst excesses of which men like William Shaw were capable. When he looked up the old prosecution against Shaw in 1832, for example, he would have read a real account of the conditions at Bowes Academy by a pupil who had been afflicted by blindness while there: ". . . their supper consisted of warm milk and water and bread, which was called tea . . . five boys generally slept in a bed . . . On Sunday they had pot skimmings for tea, in which there was vermin . . . there were eighteen boys there beside himself, of whom two were totally blind. In November, he was quite blind and was then sent to a private room where there were nine other boys blind . . . Dr Benning used to come to the school when the boys had nearly lost their sight. He merely looked at the boys' eyes and turned them off; he gave them no physic or eye-water, or anything else. There was no difference in his fare during his illness, or his health." Accounts from other schools were equally bad, malnutrition and subsequent disease being the most serious problems (if you except the violence against the pupils, which seems to have been perpetrated almost as a matter of form). But such gruesome physical incidents do not really play any part in Dickens's own narrative, which is conceived only in terms of sentimental pathos or grotesque comedy; even in the spectacle of the "pale and haggard faces, lank and bony figures, children with the countenances of old men, deformities with irons upon their limbs . . ." there is, according to Dickens, something "grotesque . . . which . . . might have pro-voked a smile". The real filth and suffering have been transformed, and typically Dickens attacks not the government, or the lack of educational provision, which allow such things, but only the charac-ters of the Squeers family – as if the reality were the reality of a play in which only the actors on the stage can really be seen or condemned. If there is horror here, it is the horror he imagines he would have felt in the situation and there is nothing like that "objective" description of social or educational ills which was once claimed as Dickens's pre-eminent contribution to the English novel. It ought always to be remembered that Dickens is rarely if ever a "realistic" writer in any accepted sense; all of his polemic and observation are at the service of the larger themes or moods with which he animated his narrative. What he saw, and remembered, was determined by what he felt; his temperament, grave or gay, filled the world with its own shapes.

One must be wary, therefore, of any identifications which have been made between the fictional and the real – his mother and Mrs Nickleby is perhaps the most famous, although parallels have also been drawn in the past between the Infant Phenomenon and a certain youthful Jean Davenport (the playbills for whom he might have seen when he visited Portsmouth during the composition of the novel), between Nicholas Nickleby and Dickens's brother-in-law Henry Burnett (there is some evidence, however, that Hablot Browne used Burnett's figure and appearance for his depiction of the young hero), between the Cheeryble brothers and the Grant brothers whom Dickens may have met in Manchester. Of course Dickens said as much in his preface to *Nicholas Nickleby* when he assured his readers that "the Brothers Cheeryble live" and were modelled upon real people, although such assurances were largely the result of his wish to seem "accurate" and "truthful", not a run-of-the-mill fabulist. As a result he received "hundreds upon hundreds" of begging letters addressed to these worthy gentlemen and, even six years later, a clergyman inserted an advertisement in *The Times*: "To the brothers Cheeryble, or any who have hearts like theirs." But sometimes this confusion between fact and fiction – even, or perhaps especially, when it was exacerbated by the novelist himself – had more significant consequences. Certainly Dickens's description of Dotheboys Hall provoked a severe public reaction against those Yorkshire schools of which it was taken to be representative. Pupils were withdrawn; establishments closed and, within a year of the publication of *Nicholas Nickleby*, the *Quarterly Review* stated that ". . . the exposure has already put down many infant bastilles" – the reference to "bastilles" linking them to the London workhouses which had the same nickname. An American observer five years later remarked that the original of Dotheboys Hall was "deserted utterly". Shaw's advertisement appeared for the last time in *The Times* in 1840, and only one such school was still advertising in 1848. A school commissioner in 1864 (the first period when such officials were actually appointed) reported that "I have wholly failed to discover an example of the typical Yorkshire school with which Dickens has made us familiar". There seems indisputable evidence, then, that the lurid descriptions in *Nicholas Nickleby* did in fact have a permanent effect upon the real world; single-handedly Dickens had been able, by exaggeration and grotesquerie, to extirpate a national abuse.

". . . what a thing it is to have Power," he once told Catherine; and indeed it was with this novel and its effect upon the schools that, for the first time, Dickens realised the full force he had at his command. From this time forward he could make a person or place famous just by describing it. There was a certain inmate of a Philadelphia prison, for example, who, after Dickens's account of him in *American Notes*, became a penal celebrity – to such an extent that he wanted to stay in prison when the time came for his release because "he pined for the curious attention bestowed on him by visitors". It seems that he was happy only in prison, like Amy Dorrit, and is the only case on record of a man turning into a Dickensian character after the novelist's own intervention in his life. Of course Dickens's writing could have equally unfortunate consequences of another kind. All of his ridicule in *Nicholas Nickleby* had been directed upon the family of the Squeerses and, although at least three Yorkshire schoolmasters felt themselves to be personally injured by the portrait, it became clear that the real originals were indeed William Shaw and his family. Their own livelihoods were destroyed, naturally, and it is said that he and his wife died prematurely as a result of Dickens's satiric assault; even their daughter, Miss Shaw, "the sweetest and kindest of women" according to one of her contemporaries, was mocked as the original of the appalling Fanny Squeers. It is likely that Dickens never calculated the human cost of his portrayals (even much later in life he was notably cavalier about his allusions to real people in his fictional portraits), which in turn provides some evidence of Dickens's blindness to reality in the act of composition itself. In ordinary life he saw everything – no man was more observant – but when he wrote he saw only the reality of his own devising.

But the public confusion of fact and fiction is not simply a matter of his characters' reality being impressed upon the readers by Dickens's own unparalleled imagination, a process exemplified by one young woman, who saw an illustration in a bookseller's window and rushed into her house screaming, "What DO you think? Nicholas has thrashed Squeers!" It is easy to laugh at the credulity of such readers, perhaps, but it is no different from the reaction of audiences to most television soap operas, where the activities of imagined people become as real as those of anyone actually living in the world. The most significant effect was of a slightly different kind, however, since it was the *difference* between what was real and what was imagined which became wholly confused by a reading of Dickens's novels. This could of course have beneficial results, for it was said at the time that Dickens's accounts of the poor and the neglected actually increased the amount of concern for, and knowledge of, those real people who lived in the vicinity of Saffron Hill and Field Lane, Yet, in hindsight, this seems doubtful; the movements for social reforms and for social analysis were part of that same early Victorian ardour which Dickens's own novels exemplify but did not necessarily create. We must see Dickens's own writings and the social movements of the period as complementary, animated by the same energy and faith, but as distinct. Much more likely, however, is the contemporaneous belief that Dickens's loving accounts of the middle-class and lower-middle-class actually brought those classes more vividly present *to themselves* and as a result rendered them more confident, more aware, more completely alive. It was his ability, as one contemporary account puts it in somewhat elaborate fashion, "to describe impressions respecting peculiarities in persons or objects around them which, without such ready hints, they would never perhaps have been susceptible of". Dickens opened up the world for those who were already living in it. It comes as no surprise, for example, that a police commissioner reported that young thieves spent their time playing games like pitch-halfpenny and reading books like *Oliver Twist*. Characters like Mr Micawber, Mrs Gamp and Smike became wholly real to those who read of them; their verbal expressions were copied and terms like "Pecksniff" or "Gamp" were used to describe certain types of people. The identification was, in that sense, complete. There were also Pickwick clubs, in which each member took on the name of a Pickwick character. The verger at Rochester Cathedral seemed to enjoy being known as "Mr Tope", the name of the chief verger in *The Mystery of Edwin Drood*, and when Dickens was instrumental in sending one boy to Ragged School, he became known to his companions as "Smike".

In addition there were certain streets or areas which seemed to have been imaginatively colonised by Dickens – people would look for "Fagin's walks", George Gissing walked in a dream down Bevis Marks, and Henry James talked of Craven Street which "absolutely reeked to my fond fancy with associations of the particular ancient piety embodied in one's private altar to Dickens . . . the inscrutable riverward street packed to blackness with accumulations of suffered experience". In that last phrase resides something of the mystery of Dickens and of the London he created in his fiction – he had seen in London what few of his contemporaries or predecessors had seen. He had seen the horror and the filth of London as somehow integral to its being, the shadow which it must necessarily cast, and he had populated that darkness with figures which seemed to emerge and return to it naturally. His own childhood experiences had been a fall into the centre of the city, and that fall had broken him open – leaving him always vulnerable, always aware, of that "suffered experience" which created London just as surely as its stones and bricks had done. But now a further process was taking place; Dickens's own vision of London came to be added to the reality itself, so that a further note of darkness was added to the city. His own suffered experience became part of its fabric as well: when we see London now, it is in part his own city still. During his lifetime, too, certain spots were of course consecrated by association with him and admirers would visit the inns and localities which he mentioned in his novels. Thus in particular there came to exist that "Dickens land", particularly of Kent, which is half-real and half-fictional, and yet wholly familiar, wholly reassuring because it has the permanence of imagined things. It ought to be added, however, that Dickens himself was normally quite impervious to these literary associations; when on one of his journeys he stayed at the old Bull Inn in Rochester, he was quite unaffected by the fact of its previous appearance in *The Pickwick Papers*. For he knew what his admirers did not; the real places marked only the arena in which his imagination had come to life, and were not to be confused with it.

But such confusion seemed perpetually to follow him. It is an odd but noticeable fact that mad people were very much attracted to him; they would write letters, they would seek interviews, and even mistook themselves for the characters in his books (the theme of madness in fact seems to hover around Dickens, notably in the occasional newspaper reports that he himself had gone mad, indicating if nothing else the intuitive awareness of the strangeness of his imagination). But such confusions were not restricted to those whose wits had fled. Often his friends would quote his own words back to him, and members of the public would write to him with ideas he might care to use. When the son of a certain Basil Hill lay dying, Hill exclaimed, "Oh, here's a point for Dickens." So strong was Dickens's imaginative hold upon his readers, in fact, that it is also entirely probable that people began to behave in a "Dickensian" fashion when they were in his presence; in other words they unconsciously exaggerated their own mannerisms and behaviour in order to conform to the types which he had already created. "We had a Pickwickian luncheon," one of his American admirers said when he visited the great novelist, and there are often reports of how a certain garrulous party behaved exactly like Mrs Nickleby when addressing him, and so forth. There were even occasions when Dickens himself deliberately decided to behave in a Dickensian manner. When showing American friends around Rochester and Chatham, for example, he ordered an old coach in the style of Pickwick. But, more importantly, the reality of his characters was impressed as much upon him as upon any of his readers. In certain amateur theatricals, for example, he sometimes dressed up and acted the parts of Samuel Weller or Mrs Gamp (of course the entire course of his public readings was one long assumption of various Dickensian roles), and in his correspondence he will frequently sign off or even compose letters in the guise of Wilkins Micawber or Edward Cuttle or Toots. In a short letter to his office manager he once wrote, "Scrooge is delighted to find that Bob Cratchit is enjoying his holiday . . ." And, when he was manager of his amateur theatricals, he was often addressed by his cast as "Mr Crummles". In other words Dickens relished the idiosyncrasies and mannerisms of his characters; once they had been created they continued to live within him as so many imaginary companions whom he delighted to introduce to others on appropriate occasions. What is more significant, perhaps, is the fact that he "saw" his characters in the same way that he had seen the characters of his childhood reading. He said that, while writing *A Christmas Carol*, Tiny Tim and Bob Cratchit were "ever tugging at his coat sleeve, as if impatient for him to get back to his desk and continue the story of their lives". More curiously, perhaps, as one friend remembered, "he said, also, that when the children of his brain had once been launched, free and clear of him, into the world, they would sometimes turn up in the most unexpected manner to look their father in the face. Sometimes he would pull my arm while we were walking together and whisper, 'Let us avoid Mr Pumblechook, who is crossing the street to meet us'; or, 'Mr Micawber is coming; let us turn down this alley to get out of his way.' He always seemed to enjoy the fun of his comic people, and had unceasing mirth over Mr Pickwick's misadventures."

The adjective to stress here is "comic"; he saw comedy everywhere and with a novel such as *Nicholas Nickleby*, so often diagnosed and analysed, it is at least appropriate to suggest that it is primarily and overwhelmingly a comic narrative; that Dickens himself, the novelist of a thousand moods, is also primarily and overwhelmingly the greatest comic writer in the English language. That is why, as he was toiling over the more solemn adventures of poor Oliver Twist, all the humour of the recently completed *Pickwick* is reaffirmed in *Nicholas*

Nickleby which has some title to being the funniest novel Dickens ever wrote; it is perhaps the funniest novel in the English language.

There is of course the grotesque humour of the Squeers family – ". . . here's richness!" Squeers exclaims as he pours out thin milk and water for the abandoned children and, in his later encomium on his lovely wife, he declares, "One of our boys – gorging his-self with vittles, and then turning ill; that's their way – got a abscess on him last week. To see how she operated upon him with a pen-knife! Oh Lor! . . . what a member of society that woman is!" And as Dickens continues to write the humour overflows, as if it came from a source within him which was inexhaustible, even when his own life was dogged by misfortune or depression. There are the Crummles, the itinerant theatrical troupe – one of their stars is a certain Miss Petowker whose virtues are extolled by Mr Crummles: "'The Blood Drinker' will die with that girl; and she's the only sylph *I* ever saw who could stand upon one leg, and play the tambourine on her other knee, *like* a sylph." And on his devoted wife's own noted performance of "The Blood Drinker": "Nobody could stand it. It was too tremendous. You don't quite know what Mrs Crummles is, yet." Within a few pages Miss Petowker is married to a man some years older than herself, one of the bridesmaids on that occasion being the younger Crummles, more popularly known as the "Infant Phenomenon" and so covered with artificial flowers that "she was rendered almost invisible by the portable arbour in which she was enshrined". As they proceeded up the aisle her noble mother advanced with the famous "stage walk, which consists of a stride and a stop alternately". And then there is Mrs Wititterly, the lady of advanced sensitivities who spends most of her day reclining on a sofa in Cadogan Place. Of course her husband adores her: "'. . . The society in which you move – necessarily move, from your station, connexion, and endowments – is one vortex and whirlpool of the most frightful excitement. Bless my heart and body, can I ever forget the night you danced with the baronet's nephew, at the election ball, at Exeter! It was tremendous.'

'I always suffer for these triumphs afterwards,' said Mrs Wititterly."

She suffers, too, in the cause of art and drama: "'I'm always ill after Shakespeare,' said Mrs Wititterly. 'I scarcely exist the next day; I find the re-action so very great after a tragedy, my Lord, and Shakespeare is such a delicious creature.'"

And of course the Mantalinis emerge from Dickens's imagination complete and inimitable, Mr Mantalini forever trying to hold off the wrath of his rich wife by the most agreeable endearments. "'Ashamed – of *me*, my joy? It knows it is talking demd charming sweetness, but naughty fibs,' returned Mr Mantalini. 'It knows it is not ashamed of its own popolorum tibby.'" And then again, "'. . . my essential juice of pine-apple!'" And, when this fails, "'Will she call me Sir!' cried Mantalini. 'Me who doat upon her with the demdest ardour. She, who coils her fascinations round me like a pure and angelic rattle-snake! It will be all up with my feelings; she will throw me into a demd state.'"

But perhaps there is nothing to equal the famous letter from Fanny Squeers, written to complain of Nicholas Nickleby's behaviour after he has "thrashed" her father in front of the boys of Dotheboys Hall. It has with some justice been described as the funniest letter in English literature, with the possible exception of Oscar Wilde's "De Profundis":

"Sir. My pa requests me to write to you. The doctors considering it doubtful whether he will ever recuvver the use of his legs which prevents his holding a pen.

"We are in a state of mind beyond anything, and my pa is one mask of brooses both blue and green likewise two forms are steepled in his Goar. We were kimpelled to have him carried down into the kitchen where he now lays. You will judge from this that he has been brought very low.

"When your nevew that you recommended for a teacher had done this to my pa and jumped upon his body with his feet and also langwedge which I will not pollewt my pen with describing, he assaulted my ma with dreadful violence, dashed her to the earth, and drove her back comb several inches into her head. A very little more and it must have entered her skull. We have a medical certifiket that if it had, the tortershell would have affected the brain.

"Me and my brother were then the victims of his feury since which we have suffered very much which leads us to the arrowing belief that we have received some injury in our insides, especially as no marks of violence are visible externally. I am screaming out loud all the time I write . . ."

But if one character emerged from this novel as the comic favourite, it was Mrs Nickleby, the garrulous old party who always experiences difficulty in remembering what she is talking about. "'Hackney coaches, my lord, are such nasty things, that it's almost better to walk at any time, for although I believe a hackney coachman can be transported for life, if he has a broken window, still they are so reckless, that they nearly all have broken windows. I once had a swelled face for six weeks, my lord, from riding in a hackney coach – I think it was a hackney coach,' said Mrs Nickleby reflecting, 'though I'm not quite certain, whether it wasn't a chariot; at all events I know it was a dark green, with a very long number, beginning with a nought and ending with a nine – no, beginning with a nine, and ending with a nought, that was it, and of course the stamp office people would know at once whether it was a coach or a chariot if any inquiries were made there – however that was, there it was with a broken window, and there was I for six weeks with a swelled face . . .'" And so she goes on, the first and perhaps the finest example of those women in Charles Dickens who simply cannot stop talking. The females in his novels are characteristically very loose with their words; they rattle on regardless, their free flow quite different from the more ornate and measured speech of the men. But there is a further distinction here. The men are rhetorical and sententious but they are at the same time often false; the women may be breathless and apparently random, but they are at the same time real. Dickens combines both qualities in his writing, just as he seems to combine the story-telling gift of his mother with the rhetorical richness of his father; perhaps that is why his novels, which seem so artless and natural, are also so carefully constructed.

This renders it all the more difficult, however, to locate the sources of Dickens's humour, if they ever *can* be located. The search for origins may in any case be a profitless one, and it might be better to revert to the conventions of the period which we are describing; a period, after all, in which gesture, appearance and dress were of far greater importance than any internal psyche from which they might or might not have sprung. Analysis was then less important than observation, which is one of the reasons why the photographs of the nineteenth century give so false an impression of the era; it was in many ways brighter, or at least more colourful, than our own because it was one in which external representation was the most important aspect of reality. It is this sense which Dickens evokes so well in his novels; particularly in *Nicholas Nickleby* itself, where his prodigal humour is so implicated in theatrical conventions, where false seeming and misrepresentation hit the grace-notes of his comedy. Even as he was writing the novel with so many of its scenes concerned with acting, good or bad, he was also noticing with some pleasure the theatrical antics of those around him. Talfourd's wife had apparently been over-complimentary to William Macready, and the great actor was annoyed when Dickens told him that "I saw her after, and she told me she was quite *fatigued* with over-*acting*". A few months later he was noticing in a play sent for his approval all the elements he was parodying in *Nicholas Nickleby* at the time – "The father is such a dolt and the villain *such* a villain, the girl so especially credulous and the means used to deceive them so very slight and transparent, that the reader *cannot* sympathise with their distresses." But he was not above a little theatrical behaviour himself; under the pen-name of "Louisa" he wrote a touching love letter to John Forster: "I have seen you – met you – read your works – heard you speak – listened, in a breathless state, to your eloquent and manly expressions of the sentiments which do you honor; and still by no word or sign have I discovered that you recognised in me the giver of the simple worthless riding whip which I have often seen in your hand and once . . . nearly touched."

His high spirits and his theatrical comedy existed as much in his own life as they did in his fiction, therefore, and if there is one constant memory of him among his friends and contemporaries it was precisely this quality of humour; "he had an inimitably funny way," one remarked, and there are memories of the time he "roared" with a friend during a dinner party, of the occasions when he literally cried with laughter, of his quickness and animation, of his enthusiasm in telling a funny story, of "his strangely grotesque glances" when he was dramatising a comic scene, of the way in which the sides of his mouth quivered when he was trying hard not to laugh. There were times when his humour inclined to the facetious; he was well-known for his "gagging" on stage during amateur theatricals, for example, as on the occasion when one player forgot his lines and Dickens came in with "he must be in an awful state of mind, his memory is going now". Sometimes he even inclined to the farcical; he loved to act out the gestures and tricks of the clown, and on more than one occasion improvised a whole dialogue between clown and pantaloon in approved pantomimic style. On occasions, in this facetious vein, he could also be sarcastic; when a friend of his emerged in some strange fashionable article of dress Dickens was heard to say: "Stock? Oh I'm so glad to know it is meant for a stock. It was so painful to think you might have intended it for a waistcoat."

His own son noted that, of all the men he knew, Charles Dickens was the quickest to see the ludicrous aspect of any situation.

Misplaced gravity especially amused him, and there was one occasion when he had to leave a church service which was taking place on a steamer during a heavy sea. He simply could *not* help bursting out in laughter. One remembers here the immoderate and sometimes hysterical laughter of the boy attending Mr Jones's school in Hampstead, the boy who laughed during the service in chapel and complained that his potatoes would be spoiled. There is that same hint of suppressed hysterics in an incident when he and Cruikshank attended a funeral. Funerals often provoked hilarity in Dickens, and he himself recounted how he "cried" with laughter at some of Cruikshank's philosophical asides during the ceremony; and, when Cruikshank was decked out in a black coat and a very long black hat band by an undertaker, "I thought I should have been obliged to go away". There were times like this when Dickens could only just manage to control himself, his laughter often relieving stress or panic but also acting as some destructive or purging force and overpowering all the conventions of the world. The high spirits of his childhood seemed to return, too, in another incident – Dickens was at a dinner party when suddenly one of the women turned to her husband and called him "Darling". This was not a common form of endearment at the time and Dickens slid out of his chair, lay on his back and raised one foot in the air. "Did she call him darling?" he asked no one in particular, and then got back up, sat in his chair and resumed the conversation. It is in this spirit, also, that he liked to introduce private jokes within his novels – the dissolute brother of Little Nell is called Fred, for example, which was the name of Dickens's own brother. Here the joke would be shared by only a very few people, but that was often the kind Dickens most enjoyed. He would sometimes refer to Mrs Gaskell as "Mary Barton" and called George Eliot "Adam Bede", but one glimpses sometimes in his comic remarks or asides a certain hardness, like the hardness of temperament which others had noticed. Once in the company of Chauncy Hare Townshend he was touring an asylum for the deaf-and-dumb and, when a poor afflicted boy seemed to Townshend to be trying to repeat his name, Dickens laughed out loud at the man's well-meaning presumption. He laughed at another friend's "ridiculous confusion" when he lost his luggage, and he said of George Eliot and George Henry Lewes, "They really are the ugliest couple in London." When that same Lewes contributed a series of articles on the theme of "Success in Literature", Dickens was heard to say, "Success in literature? What on earth does George Lewes know about success in literature?" So Dickens had sarcasm as well as wit. One can see him even now, this relatively small man, his hands deep in his trouser pockets, his erect posture, with the head thrown slightly back as he laughed or talked – and, as he laughed, what his daughter and many others have called "the wonderful and quickly changing expression of his face", his bright eyes moving from one interlocutor to the next; and, as he talked, that slight "burr" in his speech, something like a lisp which gave a slightly metallic sound to his "s".

There were other notable aspects to his humour as a man. He liked to repeat phrases for certain of his friends. One of his closest was the painter, Augustus Egg, and it was a habit of Dickens when they were together suddenly to call out "Augustus!" – and, when that gentleman looked up, to add gravely, "God bless you, Augustus!" There were times when he seemed to have the most oddly comic perceptions of the world; of particularly colourful cushions he observed that "they looked as if they have been sat upon by a damp Harlequin"; and of a one-sided couch against a window he said that "whenever I see that couch, I think the window is squinting". Sometimes he was genuinely witty. When he was told by a guest at dinner that a certain clergyman was taking up astronomy "to see further into Heaven –", Dickens interrupted with "– than his professional studies have enabled him to penetrate." He was once asked by a French priest if the English had "strong" ships. "Well," he replied, "your trade is spiritual, my father: ask the ghost of Nelson." This was part of his quickness, too, the quickness with which he "took in" somebody's character, the quickness with which he sensed an atmosphere or understood a mood, the quickness of his eyes, the quickness of his repartee. At one solemn dinner a barrister began, "Speaking for the ladies . . ." and then went on mistakenly to say, ". . . and for myself as one of them." "I just caught a gleam from his wonderful eyes," a companion said of Dickens at this moment; then the novelist got up to reply with the opening words. "The learned lady who has just sat down . . ."

But his greatest social talent, apart from the telling of stories, droll or macabre according to the occasion, was his enormous skill as a mimic. Sometimes it was a physical mimicry; once he told some friends how he had seen a man, as a cure for sea-sickness on a boat, begin to cut up slices of brown paper in order to plaster them on his breast and in a wonderful manner Dickens mimicked this man's "sympathetic motions of the jaw" as he used his scissors on the paper. He liked, too, to imitate the movements of animals – of, for example, a lion in a cage (a situation in which he sometimes found himself) – and once he "gave a capital imitation of the way a robin redbreast cocks his head on one side preliminary to a dash forward in the direction of a wriggling victim". But above all he liked to imitate his closest friends; "he delighted to recall," one of those friends remembered after Dickens's death, "the peculiarities, eccentricities and otherwise, of dead and gone as well as living friends." He imitated Forster and Hood and Sydney Smith; he mimicked the slow drawl of Samuel Rogers and the sometimes absurd longueurs of Macready. This gift extended to his writing also and, on one occasion when Wilkie Collins seemed to be too ill to complete a series, Dickens offered to write it for him "so like you as that none should find out the difference". In some ways, perhaps, a rather insulting offer.

Dickens was in fact something of a ventriloquist, and his talent in later life for doing "all the voices" of his characters in his public readings was anticipated by his ability, as a sort of party act, to mimic many voices immediately after one another. On one occasion, at a meeting of a particular society, he and a young man were the only members who had actually turned up; and so Dickens made all the resolutions and speeches of the various members in a voice appropriate to each and with "the appropriate gravity never departed from". It was an extraordinary gift, and one can very clearly see, or, rather, hear, how it works within his fiction. It is often said of mimics that they can only successfully imitate characters whom they admire or in some way care for; and it is true of Dickens, too, that he literally *became* the characters and the friends whom he mimicked. That is why, even in his greatest villains, there is more than a trace of fellow feeling and sympathy.

Of course he could also imitate himself; he liked to tell stories against himself, and on more than one occasion seemed to parody the excesses of his own style. He said of a peculiarly affecting episode in *David Copperfield*, when David's mother dies: "Get a clean pocket-handkerchief ready for the close of 'Copperfield' No 3; 'simple and quiet, but very natural and touching' – *Evening Bore*." This was part of the comedy he found in quoting advertisements out of context – "No family should be without it," he would say of one object or another. We have here intimations of a man who found it difficult, if not impossible, to take anything absolutely seriously for very long; often in the middle of scenes of distress and poverty in the worst rookeries of London, for example, something would strike him as "irresistibly comic". Nothing was excluded from the range of his humour, whether it took a farcical or satirical turn, and although it is proper that the work of Dickens as a social reformer and even propagandist ought to be made plain (he would have been horrified if these activities were to be ignored, since he invested so much energy in them) one should never lose sight of the fact that his anarchic, liberating and sometimes harsh laughter was his immediate and even instinctive response to the world. And one can see him, also, withdrawing into himself once more after he has amused everyone; going back to his own communings, where the steady low note of his melancholy is not to be separated from that constant spring of humour that was with him always. We will leave him as he left the company of others in just such a mood: "Just as we were in a tempest of laughter over some witticism of his, he jumped up, seized me by the hand, and said goodnight."

Chapter 11

S O the daily life of Charles Dickens continued as, in the first years of his fame, he worked on *Oliver Twist* and *Nicholas Nickleby*: his writing in the mornings, his riding in the afternoons, alone or with Forster, his supper at five and then more work, or a trip to the theatre, or perhaps an evening at home. He was a man of relatively fixed habits, even when young, since a regimen of work and rest was the only one that could have supported such continuous and energetic production; that and the knowledge of his success, emphasised all the more when the first number of *Nicholas Nickleby* sold fifty thousand copies (it did not significantly fall off from that number for the whole of its run). There were problems, however. Catherine had given birth to her second child on 6 March, 1838 – this was Mary, generally called Mamie – and once again she was plunged into that condition of physical debility and post-natal depression which had afflicted her after the first child. Dickens took her to Richmond for a few days to help her to recuperate, and then in June they moved for the summer to 4 Ailsa Park Villas in Twickenham, a peaceful and rural retreat, perfect for those long rides which he enjoyed but also for the multifarious sports of summer – bagatelle, battledore, quoits, bowling, bar-leaping. There were, as always, frequent open invitations to his friends to come and stay with them (Dickens always liked to create around him a family more extended than his immediate one); there were boating trips up the Thames; there were expeditions to Hampton Court. Of course he was still busy here with both novels and, with the sometimes unwelcome assistance of Bentley, he conducted all his usual work on the *Miscellany*. Quite regularly he commuted to Doughty Street, however, and not just for business reasons: this was the time of the new Queen's coronation (and thus the proper beginning of the Victorian era, to be dated some years after Dickens's rise to eminence), and he attended the festivities in Hyde Park about which he wrote an article for *The Examiner*. For Doughty Street itself he had bought a carriage and horses (the latter, however, may have been hired), and he was already well-known to his neighbours. John Coleman, who lived directly opposite, remembered him very well: "He used to turn out pretty punctually between one and two, either with a pony and trap or on horseback . . . There was an abounding vitality about him. His eyes were bright, his hair was long and wavy, his whiskers luxuriant. His costume was peculiar and pronounced . . ." Yet another reference to the loud bright colours which Dickens always delighted to wear, as if he were constantly treading upon the stage. Coleman always raised his hat to the young novelist, but his civilities were not necessarily returned and on one occasion, when Macready was leaving the house, the actor saw Coleman and whispered something to Dickens. "They both laughed as they drove off, little dreaming the pain their laughter left behind . . ."

There were other trips in this period of his fame; at one point he fell ill just when he should have been finishing his fictional instalments and later told a friend that he took a steamer for Boulogne, hired a room in an inn and there "secure from interruption" was able to get on with his postponed work and "to return just in season for the monthly issues with his work completed". He was also speculating about a journey to America, and it is possible that even now he was chafing against the strains of domesticity, with two infants around him and a wife who found it difficult by herself to cope. There is often a sense in his life of his wishing to break away from bonds even as he was tying them for himself. His most important task, however, was to finish *Oliver Twist*. In March he was ". . . sitting patiently at home waiting for Oliver Twist who has not yet arrived", and only days later "fallen upon him tooth and nail". We will see later how great was his sympathetic identification with his characters, often miming their features in the mirror before he wrote, and in this period we can imagine him doubling over in pain as Oliver Twist is shot and then, moments later, miming the comedy of Brittles ". . . with his mouth wide open, and his face expressive of the most unmitigated horror". He worked rapidly on the story from August to October; he wrote no episode specifically for the September issue of the *Miscellany* in order to give himself a clear run to the end of the book, but also in order to forestall any more dramatisations of the novel (instead he wrote very quickly a facetious and ironic "Mudfog" paper in the same vein as the one with which *Oliver Twist* had opened twenty-one months before). This was the period in which he unravelled the mystery of Oliver's parentage, a complicated exercise which he seems to have had to make up as he went along. In intervals carefully mapped out in advance he also wrote his instalments of *Nicholas Nickleby* and even managed to write an article for *The Examiner* attacking the publishers of Sir Walter Scott. It was the first of three, in fact, a cathartic exercise at a time when, as usual, he was trying to renegotiate his own contracts with Richard Bentley. Indeed his virulence against Scott's publishers suggests the real state of his feelings: ". . . the extravagance, thoughtlessness, recklessness and wrong have been upon the part of these pigmies, and the truest magnanimity and forbearance on the side of the giant who upheld them and under the shadow of whose protection they gradually came to lose sight of their own stature, and to imagine themselves as great as he." There are times when Dickens, in oblique or unguarded moments, does reveal something of his true opinion of himself, an opinion he would never in the ordinary course of events vouchsafe to anyone.

He went to the Isle of Wight in September in order to work undisturbed – staying at Alum Bay and then at Ventnor – and such was his fluency that he managed to write eight chapters in the twelve weeks from July to the end of this month. As soon as he came back, he applied himself to *Nicholas Nickleby*, but then once more turned his attention to the last chapters of *Oliver Twist*. He pretended to many people to be "out of town", managed to see hardly anyone, and composed few letters; in this period he also frequently wrote after dinner into the late hours, a practice which in later life he regarded with abhorrence. But it was of this closing sequence that he told Bentley ". . . I am doing it with greater care, and I think with greater power than I have been able to bring to bear on anything yet . . ." These were indeed the most powerful scenes. He killed Nancy – "I shewed what I have done to Kate last night who was in an unspeakable '*state*'" – and then went on to hammer out the flight of Sikes, the pursuit of him by the mob, his death, the trial and punishment of Fagin. While of course leaving Oliver, the parish boy, at the end rich and happy. He managed to write the final six chapters in three weeks but, as always, he hated to leave his creations once he had brought them so vividly to life; he became as much a part of their world as they were part of his, and at the end of his narrative he wrote, "I would fain linger yet with a few of those among whom I have so long moved . . ." But he could not. The book was complete. It would appear in *Bentley's Miscellany* for a few months yet, but the three-volume printed edition was about to be published. He had finished it at last, "this marvellous tale" as he called it.

It had become a superstition with him that he should be out of London on the day of publication, so almost as soon as he had completed *Oliver Twist* he was off. On this occasion, however, the superstition was combined with the opportunity to "work up" some more scenes for his remaining novel, *Nicholas Nickleby*: he left on a tour of the Midlands and North Wales with Hablot Browne. Their main destination was Manchester, for it seems that Dickens had arranged to visit some of the cotton mills with the express purpose of somehow fitting them into the plot and once more reasserting his claim to be the single most important topical and polemical novelist in England. He had already been impressed by Lord Ashley's attempts to alleviate the plight of child labourers in England, and at this stage he was clearly in accord with what was known as the Ten Hours Movement, which campaigned to limit the amount of time children could be employed; now he decided that he wanted to see for himself the conditions of the operatives in the factories and "to strike the heaviest blow in my power for these unfortunate creatures". And so, a week after he had completed *Oliver Twist*, and entrusting the reading of the final proofs to Forster, he set out.

He and Brown travelled first to Leamington, then on to Stratford, Birmingham, Shrewsbury, Llangollen, Bangor, Chester and on to Manchester; he kept a record of his journey in his diary together with all of the expenses he incurred, noted down neatly to the last jot and tittle, including such items as one shilling for a mountain guide. Perhaps as a result of exhaustion after his most recent efforts he once more suffered those painful seizures in his side which always seemed to hit him at times of mental or physical debility; but he took henbane and was so pleased with the effectiveness of this drug that he mentioned it in the early chapters of *Barnaby Rudge*. They reached Manchester on 5 November, at which point Forster joined them; Ainsworth, a native of the town, had given them a letter of introduction to one of the local worthies and over three days Dickens and his companions saw all that they needed or wanted to see; in particular they met the Grant brothers, the benevolent factory-owners who were to be immortalised as the Cheeryble Brothers in an impending number of *Nicholas Nickleby*. Dickens did not however include in that novel any scenes from the cotton mills which he visited, a sure sign that he was even at this early stage more interested in eccentric characters than in social conditions; in later life, he was in fact to change his opinion about the nature of industrialism, and to come, in some senses, to applaud it. The Mancunians also remembered Dickens; Ainsworth's cousin recalled "a smart looking young man of rather effeminate appearance" and particularly remembered his highly polished boots. Another citizen remembered Dickens at dinner with the Grant brothers, one of whom at once generously entered the spirit of the occasion by inviting him to breakfast the next morning: "Dickens appeared to be much tickled with the 'character' and his frank invitation at such a short notice, that he did not utter one word, but soon after retired to a corner of the room, pondered for a few moments, turned his head to the wall, put his hands before his face, and burst out into an uncontrollable fit of laughter." Apocryphal?

Three days in Manchester seem to have been enough, and at this point Dickens cut short what was to be a more protracted visit. His abrupt departure was in part because he was desperate to see *Oliver Twist* in its new volume form; it was the novel over which he had taken the most care and in which he had invested so much of his energy, and he could no longer deny himself the luxury of seeing it printed and bound. It is also possible that Forster alerted Dickens to some of the illustrations which Cruikshank was preparing. So he travelled back rapidly by train, the first such journey he is ever recorded as taking and quite likely the first he ever made – the trunk route from Birmingham to London was the first established, and had been opened only this year. No record survives, however, of Dickens's reaction to this novel mode of travelling. That it might have been somewhat alarming is attested by those who did leave accounts of their first trips but for Dickens, who loved speed and movement for their own sake, the alarm might well have been displaced by sheer exhilaration. Certainly the passage of the railway was to figure largely both in his life and in his fiction, although his attitude towards it remained somewhat ambiguous – resembling, as it did, his later attitude towards the industrial age itself, compounded both of admiration and distrust, realisation of the need for progress and nostalgia for the recent past, a worship of speed and a hatred of the destruction which it wrought. In his ordinary life he tended to admire the development of the railway as a sure index of human progress; in his fiction his attitude is darker and more ambivalent. All one can say, at this stage in his life, is that the pages of *Nicholas Nickleby* are suffused with the idea of movement and of energy, a momentum forward which is undoubtely related to Dickens's own sense of himself at this period but one which can only have been corroborated by the rapid movements on the metalled rails which were beginning to cover the country.

He returned in time to see the final proofs of the book edition of *Oliver Twist*, and at once took exception to some of Cruikshank's final illustrations; he seems to have been disappointed with the whole series but had the good sense to curb his temper with the "Illustrious George" and ask him to remove only one, a painfully sentimental print of Rose Maylie and Oliver by the fireside. Cruikshank at first prevaricated, limiting himself to making minor changes in the existing plate, but finally he agreed to substitute another for the next printing. Dickens had already made his own changes for the volume edition of the text, by not only altering such minor details as the Artful Dodger's height (originally three foot six inches but altered to a more credible four foot six inches), but also excising those passages from the original instalments which had emphasised the serial elements and origins of the tale. Thus did Dickens attempt to transform it into a much more coherent and consistent piece of work. He also suddenly decided to use his real name; the first printing had its author as "Boz" but all subsequent ones amended this to "Charles Dickens". In fact his care for the book was quite unusual. Of all his novels it was the one most revised in future editions, and, three years after its first appearance, he wrote a preface in which he attempted to prove that all along his task had been to demonstrate ". . . the principle of Good surviving through every adverse circumstance and triumphing at last". In reality he did not want to be grouped with the often very popular "sensation novelists" or "Newgate novelists", for even now he had a proper sense of his own worth and his own seriousness. He did not even want to be associated in the public mind with the work of his friend Harrison Ainsworth, whose own series, *Jack Sheppard*, was to command as much attention as *Oliver Twist* itself. He had in fact once praised Ainsworth's *Rookwood* in a footnote to one of his sketches but, in the 1839 edition of *Sketches by Boz*, he removed the reference – not the only change in a volume which, reissued now at a time of Dickens's fame and popularity, underwent something like a surgical operation. No doubt with Forster's help, he removed slang and toned down any passage or reference which might smack of indelicacy. He was now, after all, a celebrated and important novelist. He had to create the appropriate conditions for his own developing reputation.

That is perhaps one reason why Dickens treated his second novel with much more seriousness than his first: even as he was writing *Oliver Twist* he had decided that he wanted to dramatise it for himself, perhaps hoping in this way to knock out of the field any inferior imitations. Nothing came of this idea but there was a dramatisation at the St James's Theatre on 27 March; since this was the theatre with which Dickens had been heavily involved, and since Harley and Braham were still in charge there, it has been suggested that Dickens himself did in fact write this first adaptation. Certainly he may have had some involvement with it – no doubt attending rehearsals, if nothing else – but the more likely candidate for authorship is Gilbert à Becket, a man of Dickens's age but one who epitomises the fate of moderately successful nineteenth-century "hacks" who wrote a plethora of cheap plays and edited a variety of unsuccessful cheap journals. The play was not a success, however, and the reaction was such that it closed after two or three nights. But this did not stop others attempting the same trick. In some ways, in fact, *Oliver Twist* was ready made for the stage adapters, who merely excised the social criticism and cut down the plot until it encompassed only the main scenes and characters – although, even in this truncated form, the dramas of *Oliver Twist* (and indeed of most of Dickens's novels) were generally taken to be extremely "realistic" and not "melodramatic". What might seem to us now stale, faded, sentimental and grotesque then hit audiences with a fresh blast of life and truth. For of course every new "realism" eventually seems pale and thin, as "reality" itself changes its form.

There were six versions of *Oliver Twist* in 1838, representing at least in a literal sense the most dramatic aspect of what was called "Bozmania" or "Boz-i-ana" and although at one such version Dickens, embarrassed by what was being perpetrated upon his book, lay down in his box from the middle of the first act until the end of the play, the sentiments of such adaptations are some indication at least of the taste of the audience; a taste that Dickens himself found that he needed to satisfy. The particular version just mentioned ended thus, as Dickens remained lying on the floor of his box, refusing to watch it:

Mr Brownlow. The next request I will make for you, dear Oliver, myself, and will make it here – to you (*to audience*). Our hero is but young; but if his simple progress has beguiled you of a smile, or his sorrows of a tear, forgive the errors of the orphan boy, Oliver Twist.

Tableau. And *Curtain.*

It is not that Dickens objected in principle to the dramatisations of his novels, just that he disliked the poorer ones. He did in fact admire or at least enjoy some aspects of an adaptation of *Nicholas Nickleby*, for example, which was running simultaneously with the dramas made out of *Oliver Twist*: in particular he appreciated the portrayal of Smike by Mrs Keeley, although he took exception to her uttering sentiments about "the pretty harmless robins". Mrs Keeley reported a scene at the dress rehearsal which the novelist attended: "I shall never forget Dickens's face when he heard me repeating these lines. Turning to the prompter he said. 'Damn the robins: cut them out.'" Damn the robins: there we hear the true creative voice of the man who was later dubbed by Trollope "Mr Popular Sentiment". In any event he was not so disheartened by all these dramatic versions that he did not go on to suggest to Macready that he himself should adapt *Oliver Twist* for Macready's company at Covent Garden. The actor turned down the suggestion, probably wisely, but this did not deter Dickens from suggesting to him a month later that he should put on a farce, *The Lamplighter*, which he had written. At the beginning of December he visited Macready and read this short play to him – "The dialogue is very good, full of point . . ." Macready wrote in his diary, "but I am not sure about the meagreness of the plot. He reads as well as an experienced actor would – he is a surprising man." But once again Macready, with the willing or unwilling consent of all parties concerned, dropped the idea. Clearly Dickens was not to succeed as a dramatist, and it is at this point that we can see the end of his ambitions in that particular direction. The success of his novels no doubt made the breach all the easier to bear, for the time had come for him to concentrate upon his purely literary career. Already he was being publicly honoured for it. On his last visit to Manchester he had made a "rash promise" that he would return in order to attend a public dinner in his honour; or rather it seems that the dinner was originally to be in honour of Harrison Ainsworth, the native Mancunian, but as soon as Dickens agreed to accompany his friend it became clear that Dickens himself would be the paramount guest. An uncomfortable situation for Ainsworth, perhaps, but one that he seems to have surmounted with at least the appearance of courtesy and tact. They travelled up to Manchester, together with Forster, at the beginning of January 1839 –

Dickens staying five days which, in view of the work he was supposed to do, no doubt seemed a long and weary time.

Work he was supposed to do, as well as work he was contracted to do. Almost as soon as he returned to London, in fact, he turned his attention to the serial novel which he had promised to bring out in *Bentley's Miscellany*, in May, immediately after the final chapters of *Oliver Twist*. By this stage he seems to have had no more than a rough idea of the nature of the story he was going to write; it was to be called *Barnaby Rudge*, and was in part to be concerned with the Gordon Riots of 1780; but the thought of having to complete the first episode by May, even as he continued his work on *Nicholas Nickleby*, seems to have exacerbated his belief that he was being exploited by Richard Bentley. That there was no ground for such a belief is not the point; he saw his work being applauded and dramatised, but he also saw Richard Bentley taking a large share of the proceeds from the serialisation of *Oliver Twist* which he believed ought to be his. So he stopped working on *Barnaby Rudge*. Then he seemed about to break off the agreement to write the novel altogether but, at Forster's urging, he decided merely to postpone its appearance for six months. Bentley, perhaps somewhat rashly, agreed to this proposal on condition that Dickens himself should extend his contract to edit the *Miscellany* for a further six months; and on condition, too, that he should engage in no other writing except *Nicholas Nickleby* until *Barnaby Rudge* was ready. At this Dickens lost whatever self-control he possessed: ". . . if you presume to address me again in the style of offensive impertinence which marks your last communication, I will from that moment abandon at once and for ever all conditions and agreements that may exist between us . . ." Here, when aroused, is the clear sense of his own dignity and worth. And then, two days later, he resigned from the editorship of *Bentley's Miscellany*. Pages from his diary for these days have been torn out – perhaps coincidentally, or perhaps because he revealed something of himself which he or his executors did not want to disclose. He continued his negotiations with Bentley's solicitors over the matter of the outstanding novel but, in the meantime, persuaded Harrison Ainsworth to take over the editorship of the magazine; apart from anything else, it is possible that he wanted the *Miscellany* in relatively safe hands at least until the serialisation of *Oliver Twist* had come to an end. Ainsworth seemed at first reluctant to take on what must have looked like Dickens's abandoned project but, after a series of urgent missives and protracted meetings, finally he agreed. Bentley demurred in the arrival of Ainsworth (although later saying that he was "forced upon me") and Dickens wrote a sentimental farewell to *Bentley's Miscellany*, addressed as "My Child", in the February issue; it is notable, perhaps, only for the reference to the new railway as the symbol of necessary change and progress. His publicly stated affection for Ainsworth, however, did not prevent Dickens from sending him a few weeks later a stern and very cold letter in which he all but accused Ainsworth of spreading scandals about Forster's role in the editorial transition – ". . . I must speak strongly because I feel strongly." Matters were resolved, but there is no doubt that from this time there arose a distinct cooling in the relations between the two men – Dickens, on this occasion as on so many others, being guided principally by his impetuosity in private dealings as well as by his readiness to take offence. Notable, too, in this instance, and again in so many others, is his refusal to believe that he is ever mistaken or ever in the wrong; throughout his life he always needed to be *right*, and any attempt to suggest that he was not wholly without blemish was met at once with irritable aggression.

Thus over a period of years we can trace certain permanent traits of his temperament even though, in the local and immediate perspective, we may see only a number of events. If we turn to the diary for this period which he was still fitfully keeping, for example, there are recorded only minor incidents and somewhat abbreviated comments – "Forster preposterous" on something, and the son of Wordsworth "decidedly *lumpish*". On his birthday he thanks God for a "most prosperous and happy year", and then continues with the diurnal round.

> "*Saturday February 9th*:
> At Smithson's by appointment, with Ainsworth and Forster, going over the drafts of new agreements prepared by Bentley's Solicitors. Objected to by mine, and the matter stands over.
> To the Zoological Gardens afterwards – home to dinner. Alone all the evening, reading the Curse of Kehama and thinking about Nickleby.
> Kate at the Promenade Concert."

Thus it went on. The reference to the Zoological Gardens is the first but not the last since Dickens had an extraordinary interest in this institution. One friend recalled, "What a treat it was to go with him to the London Zoological Gardens, a place he greatly delighted in at all times! He knew the zoological address of every animal, bird and fish of any distinction; and he could, without the slightest hesitation, on entering the grounds, proceed straightway to the celebrities of claw or foot or fin. The delight he took in the hippopotamus family was most exhilarating. He entered familiarly into conversation with the huge, unwieldy creatures, and they seemed to understand him. Indeed he spoke to all the unphilological inhabitants with a directness and tact which went home to them at once. He chaffed with the monkeys, coaxed the tigers and bamboozled the snakes, with a dexterity un-approachable." It is worth quoting this passage at length to emphasise the innocence and simplicity of Dickens's character, even at the time he was engaged in this curious internecine warfare with friends and publishers: he liked what might seem to be the crudest of entertain-ments, and it ought to be remembered that when he talks about the need for entertainment among the populace he was divining his own need for it also. And, when he returned to Doughty Street, he was still ". . . thinking about Nickleby".

Nicholas Nickleby paramount, then, in this period when he had no other book upon which he was engaged; it was the first time since the early days of *The Pickwick Papers* that he had only one novel to write. But there were always domestic preoccupations to mitigate his literary ones. He had to dismiss his manservant, Henry, for some unspecified but obviously glaring "impertinence to his 'Missis'", Catherine; then he hired a small man with very bright red hair, William Topping, to take his place (as always, he preferred to deal with smaller men). More serious were his problems with his parents, and particularly with his father whose importuning and indebtedness were becoming a per-petual trial to his son. John Dickens seems to have made a habit, for example, of begging – the word is scarcely too strong – from Chapman and Hall, Dickens's publishers. Many letters between son and father were destroyed, both by Dickens himself and by his executors after his death. What these letters contained is obviously not known but Georgina Hogarth, who was responsible for destroying many of them, said that ". . . there were letters to CD from his father, from his mother, brothers and other relations, almost all of them in the same tone, money difficulties, applications for money . . . *And most especially from his father* . . . not only debt and difficulties, but most discreditable and dishonest dealing on the part of his father towards his son . . ." More evidence for this "discreditable" behaviour will emerge later, but it was in this period that matters once more reached a crisis. John Dickens's debts had come to such a point that bankruptcy proceedings must again have been threatening; and Dickens took an immediate decision. In the February 1839 number of *Nicholas Nickleby* he had despatched Kate and Mrs Nickleby to a country cottage and now, at the beginning of March, he decided to find a similar place for his parents; just as in his fiction he had a tendency to dispose of characters who were no longer necessary for the narrative, there is a sense now in which he wanted to remove his parents from the scene of action. And by what better means than those he had already found in his novel?

He travelled quickly down to Devon and, with his usual impatience and impetuosity, found a new house for them the same day; it was called Mile End Cottage, Alphington, just a mile outside Exeter, and, to judge from Dickens's descriptions in his ecstatic letters back to his wife and Forster, you would think that it was indeed a cottage constructed in his fiction. It was a "jewel of a place . . . in the most beautiful, cheerful, delicious rural neighbourhood I was ever in . . . excellent parlour . . . a capital closet . . . a beautiful little drawing-room . . . noble garden". He found it by accident, simply by walking along the road, and at once decided that this was the place. Not only did he arrange for it to be rented by his parents, looked over and signed the necessary documents, but he also furnished it and purchased such things as the crockery, the glass, and the stair-carpet. No detail was too small for his attention – just like the details of his fiction – and of course by the time he had finished ". . . the neatness and cleanliness of the place is beyond description". It is possible to get a good measure of the man, too, in his dealings with the various rustic parties; how with the old people who owned it he was "facetious and at the same time virtuous and domestic"; how he summed up the landlady at a glance "or I have no eye for the real and no idea of finding it out"; how he practised various "virtuous endearments" upon the upholsterer's daughter to keep the bill down; how he stayed in the same hotel as the actor, Charles Kean, and wandered into the lavatory where "a man's voice (of tragic quality) cried out – 'There is somebody here!'" He turned everything into a story, a narrative, a little piece of truth which is "stranger than fiction", even as he stored up impressions for his own later use. All this done, down to the stair-carpet and the crockery, and he was back within seven days.

The fact that Dickens wanted his mother to come down to Alphington to help with the arrangements, just as he was to ask her to attend during Catherine's next pregnancy, suggests that she was a more willing and practical person than is to be presumed from the descriptions of those who take her to be the living original of Mrs Nickleby. Clearly, too, it was John Dickens who was most at fault on this as on other occasions. They had been living in King Street, Holborn, and Dickens wanted to get them off to Devon without alerting his father's creditors; in addition he gave his father an allowance of seven pounds and ten shillings a quarter, no doubt on condition that he did not return to London. The parents acquiesced in the move, although they really had no choice in the matter and in any case could hardly withstand the force of their famous son's will. Indeed it seems that their relationship to him had altered somewhat since the days of his newspaper reporting. One friend saw Dickens with his family in this period and noted that "they appeared to be less at ease with Charles than with anyone else, and seemed in fear of offending him. There was a subdued manner, a kind of restraint in his presence . . . because his moods were very variable." In other words Charles Dickens had become the master of the family, and was already playing the role of "father", both supporter and disciplinarian; the parents had become children again, just as Mrs Nickleby becomes a child to be guided by her son.

And all the time he was ". . . thinking about Nickleby", working hard on it, or "powdering away", to use one of his favourite expressions. There were "very late hours at my Desk", and there were times when he seemed about to "'bust' the boiler" of his imagination. He turned the Grants into the Cheerybles almost as soon as he returned from his second trip to Manchester, which suggests how eager he was to employ new material while it was still fresh. And it is an odd though permanent fact in his life that, at times of most crisis and anxiety, he is actually at his funniest – some of the best scenes with the Mantalinis and Squeerses appear at the time when he was most heavily involved in his arguments with Bentley. Yet, despite his immediate ways of working, he had a clear idea of the shape which the finished novel was to take. This was why he found it necessary to "spoil a number" with a great deal of plot machination "for the sake of the book". He was also aware of the difficulties involved precisely in plot construction, and pointedly allows one of his characters to remark, "Why, I don't believe now . . . that there's such a place in all the world for coincidences as London is." London is in fact as great a presence in *Nicholas Nickleby* as it had been in *Oliver Twist* and, although it has become customary to separate the two novels as two quite different achievements, it is perhaps better to see the continuity of Dickens's concerns in this period of his life. Pre-eminently, of course, both Nicholas Nickleby and Oliver Twist are "gentlemen", even though circumstances might suggest the contrary, and both novels set out to prove that fact. That in a sense is the dominant theme of both novels – this need to be a gentleman in the face of a world which denies or threatens such a claim, even if people like Fagin must die in the process. There is a good deal of self-assertion and even aggression involved in this, just as there must also have been in Dickens's own progress through the world. For, if there are resemblances between the two novels, how could there not be when his own life was, as it were, the nourishment for both? Nevertheless he was generally writing with such fluency and speed on *Nicholas Nickleby* that it seems much freer than *Oliver Twist*; it is a book of hurry, of rapidity, of characters emerging then fading and, in those strange pulses of energy, clause following clause with the barest comma to mark their territorial bounds, we see something of the nature of Charles Dickens himself.

Its story itself is the familiar one of a young man's journey through life, with the cry "The world is before me, after all", and his subsequent encounters with villains and misers and virgins; but Dickens has added to it suffering children, insufferable or crazy women, comic or broken-down wretches, and a family life which is seen characteristically as a place of torment. He is trying to introduce everything within the confines of the prose narrative – romance, melodrama, tragedy, comedy – but if there is one large distinction between this novel and its predecessor it is that in *Oliver Twist* Dickens used a romantic vocabulary whereas in *Nicholas Nickleby* he uses a theatrical one. Perhaps in mute recognition of the fact that he was introducing so many different styles in the novel, they remain precisely that – *styles* – and the characters always seem to be enacting a role which has been given to them. The book itself was eventually dedicated to Macready, and everything about it has the feel of the theatre; it is as if Dickens saw human life conducted among the bright lights of the stage, making it somehow larger and brighter than the reality. If he had any image of the world in his head as he wrote, it was that narrow and highly magnified one which he observed from the stalls or from the pit. One could put it differently by noting that *Nicholas Nickleby* is written by someone whose understanding of appearance, of gesture, of speech and of character has been very strongly influenced by his experience of acting; the effect is heightened by Hablot Browne's illustrations which characteristically portray everything as if it were indeed taking place upon the stage. But if the novel is close to the theatrical conventions of the period (which were also the conventions employed by most popular literature) this is not to suggest that it lacks power or effectiveness as a result. Quite the contrary. The most obviously theatrical scenes in the book – the rescue of Madeline Bray from the clutches of the hideous miser Arthur Gride, the discovery that Smike is really Ralph Nickleby's son – are moments of great power which still have an enormous ability to intrigue and to move the reader. One of the lessons in reading Dickens comes from understanding how little our responses to this form of action have changed, and how close we still are to our ancestors who wept and laughed in the small theatres of London. And yet at the same time Dickens, with that extraordinary double-awareness he possessed, satirises the theatre even as he displays his love and admiration for it; much of the novel is concerned with parodying bad acting, for example, a subject which always fascinated him. On the other hand, some of the serious scenes and events in the novel are themselves parodied with the same élan. Many learned disquisitions have been devoted to the parallels between the comic and serious elements of the action, but surely they can be seen as another aspect of Dickens's high-spirited inventiveness in which he plays with ideas and events as lightly and as gaily as he invents a comic scene or describes a character, the very epitome of what is described here as ". . . those strange contradictions of feeling which are common to us all".

Yet even if theatrical effects suffuse *Nicholas Nickleby*, they are not confined to that one novel and it can be said with some assurance that there is not one work of Dickens which is unaffected by the vision of the stage which he had had as a child and as a young man. He said as much himself, in a speech which he once gave at a dinner and in which he claimed that ". . . every writer of fiction, though he may not adapt the dramatic form, writes in effect for the stage". That is why there are always in Dickens's novels elements of burlesque, of melodrama, of farce, of sentimental comedy. In the days of his maturity, the presence of large and unruly audiences in the theatres necessitated the use of extravagant colours, large props, and highly exaggerated gestures or expressions; Dickens saw all these things, often mocked them, but noticed their potential in his own bright fiction. Of course this interest was by no means unreciprocated; the number of adaptations of his novels suggests how much he influenced the theatre in turn and, in general, it can be said that eighteenth- and nineteenth-century drama was as much affected by contemporaneous fiction as the fiction was influenced by drama. That is why Dickens was always attracted by the more theatrical writers of the previous century; he talks often of Smollett but hardly mentions Jane Austen, a novelist with whom he was deeply out of sympathy. Since he himself was always concerned with his audience and with the effect he was having upon that audience, his preference was for writing which offered a direct and immediate appeal. Not only was he attracted to the more theatrical novelists but also he expressed a preference for what might be called middle-class drama; he liked to quote from Robert Browning's *A Blot on the 'Scutcheon* and Bulwer-Lytton's *Not So Bad As We Seem*, and he had a fondness for such plays as Douglas Jerrold's *Time Works Wonders*. It is easy and conventional to dismiss melodrama, and thus to dismiss much of Dickens as well as the dramatists whom he admired, but it ought not to be forgotten that melodrama, subsisting as it does on highly patterned language, is in fact an art of great discipline and often of verbal dexterity. It ought to be remembered, too, that this style, which at times appears sentimental or forced to a modern audience, would seem quite natural to one of the nineteenth century: that is why Dickens, in the same speech where he suggested that novelists were essentially writing for the stage, declared that the two most permanent attributes of that stage were "truth" and "passion".

Yet so much of this theatrical momentum within Dickens's novels depends upon his own personality. There is, first of all, that constant delight which he took in mimicry. His ferocious humour. His ability to parody himself. His delight in acting. But he also performed in his novels the roles which he adopted in his amateur theatricals; in his fiction, too, he is both stage manager and central performer. In *Nicholas Nickleby* and elsewhere, there tends to be the same troupe of players surrounding him, to each of whom he gives instructions about pitch or tempo or rhythm, and who come on or go off like actors at the appointed time. The endings of novels are extremely important clues to a writer's real intentions, because it is often at that concluding point (when the novelist has, as it were, come to an end of the self-imposed tasks and the necessary difficulties) that real meanings emerge in the most relaxed and unhindered way. That is why it is so significant that most of Dickens's novels end with the same kind of tableau and curtain that marked the dramas of the period. The actors all return, their past and futures mapped out; they link hands and bow; then suddenly the curtain comes down and they are gone.

But if there are many occasions when the theatre and the novel resemble each other, it is really only because they shared a specific kind of nineteenth-century reality; of course it is to be found in caricature, too, but it is also present in the glee clubs, the singing clubs, the taverns, the dress, and the art. It is a spirit congruent with the gin-palaces and taverns of the period as well, with their garish bar fittings, brightly painted barrels inscribed "Old Tom" or "Cream of the Valley", their glittering bottles and – what seemed most important of all to contemporaries – their "immense blaze of gas light". It is a sense of life which goes with the stock phrases of the mid-Thirties, those inconsiderable scraps of speech which pass from person to person and become the repertoire of the streets, and the words of the labouring poor – "There he goes with his eye out!", "How are you off for soap?", "Flare up and join the union!", "Does yer mother know yer out?" This is part of the background to Dickens's own fictions, and what makes everything cohere in his own art is the momentum, the inventiveness of Dickens himself writing late at his desk, transferring his energy to the page, his own life exemplified in the prospect of London which he introduces in the book – "Streams of people apparently without end poured on and on, jostling each other in the crowd and hurrying forward . . ." And in this jostling London Dickens elbows his way forward, identifying within it all his own contrasts and contradictions: "Life and death went hand in hand; wealth and poverty stood side by side; repletion and starvation laid them down together."

But he wanted to get away from the city, and at the end of April he and Catherine took a place in Petersham, Elm Cottage, where they remained until the end of August. Of course, Dickens's hospitality and appetite for company were in no way abated; there were constant invitations to friends to spend the weekend there. On one occasion he visited the Hampton races close by, and used the material he gathered in the next number of *Nicholas Nickleby*. Of course the novel was his main task even while he was resting in the countryside of Surrey; there were times when he was "shut up" in the cottage in order to write, and he would frequently send his copy direct to the printers, Bradbury and Evans, in London. In fact he generally stayed at Petersham from Saturday until Monday, and then during the week made various commuting excursions to London. These were not always of a business nature: he came up for the Macready banquet, for example, held in honour of the actor after he had given up his management of Covent Garden. One of the ladies at that feast, who according to the practices of the time sat in the gallery and did not join the men at the table, noted Dickens's "remarkably observant faculty, with perpetually discursive glances at those around him, taking note as it were of every slightest peculiarity in look, or manner, or speech, or tone that characterised the individual". And, when he came to speak in honour of Macready, his speech "was like himself, genial, full of good spirit and good spirits, feeling and cheerful vivacity". Later he went to Elstree for three days in order to attend the christening of Macready's baby, and in the same month he attended the wedding of George Cattermole in London; Mrs Cattermole remembered in later years how Dickens had been "foremost in making hearty and graceful congratulations, and as we drove away, he energetically pelted the carriage, its occupants, postilion and horses with handfuls of rice". Cattermole himself was an artist and illustrator whom Dickens had met through Forster; he was already well known for his "quaint" or picturesque style, had executed illustrations for the novels of Scott and Bulwer-Lytton, and was in fact to illustrate elements of Dickens's fiction. But, since the author had met the painter socially before he ever employed him, their relationship remained cordial and unsullied by Dickens's sometimes peremptory demands on Hablot Browne; although Cattermole himself, curiously like other illustrators of the period, became much more nervous and retiring as he grew older.

There were others whose friendship Dickens cultivated – or, more likely, who cultivated *his* friendship – during the same period. He came up to London from Petersham on at least one occasion to dine with Miss Burdett-Coutts, for example, the young heiress whose philanthropic nature and steady spirit were to impress Dickens to such an extent that, of all the women with whom he had to deal, she was the one whom he always held in most respect; Miss Burdett-Coutts's first impression of him was of "restlessness, vivacity, impetuosity, generous impulses, earnestness and frank sincerity"; it is notable, perhaps, that restlessness was the very first characteristic she mentions and her pen portrait might even act as a commentary upon the painting of the author which his friend, Daniel Maclise, finished at this time. A "face of me," Dickens said, "which all people say is astonishing." Two years before Samuel Laurence had drawn Dickens – it was, according to his brother-in-law, "a *facsimile*" of the man who had just married

Catherine and was then writing *The Pickwick Papers*. Yet how much the artists' perceptions have changed in those two years. The Laurence drawing is of a more fleshy and sensual Dickens, even though the large eyes and penetrating glance are also prominent. The Maclise portrait of 1839 shows a much more poised and self-assured young man; his glance still has that bright animation but there is something about the stance and expression which suggest a writer who knew exactly where he was – "at the top of the tree". This was an expression used by Thackeray, and it was he who said of the portrait, ". . . a looking glass could not render a better facsimile. Here we have the real identical man Dickens . . ."

The young man, with oval face and long brown hair, is looking out of a window and his face reflects the light which is in turn absorbed by his acute and penetrating gaze; the eyes themselves seeming to emanate light. He is sitting upon a chair but he is not relaxed, far from it. His legs are nervously crossed, his left hand touches the pages of an open book, and his right hand is poised in the air in front of him; the hands, too, are caught in the rays of light and it is as if he were directing those rays down onto the book itself, as if that were the proper place for them. The figure is carefully dressed, and yet the furnishings depicted in the painting have a fullness and opulence which contrast strangely with the eager, nervous gaze of the sitter. It is the picture of a man who has made his own way in the world, and knows it. And he was still only twenty-seven years old.

On the desk in front of him there are three eighteenth-century volumes lying on top of each other, and in that echo of a previous age – and of previous writers – Maclise has caught something of the spirit of Dickens at this precise point in his life. For already, even as he was working on *Nicholas Nickleby*, he was contemplating a quite different project. He wanted to establish a periodical which would bear a very close resemblance to those eighteenth-century journals he had read as a child, to Addison's *Spectator* and to Goldsmith's *Bee*. Clearly his own unhappy experiences on *Bentley's Miscellany* had not diminished his appetite for editorship, but now at least he had learnt enough to insist upon total control of any new venture. This was, more or less, the proposal he put to Forster in a letter from Petersham, and it was one which he wished him to conduct to Chapman and Hall – the publishers who, in any case, had never done anything but accede to his wishes from the beginning. His plan was first to complete *Barnaby Rudge*, that much delayed and much argued-over novel which, in the final set of negotiations, Dickens had agreed to deliver to Richard Bentley by January of next year. And then, as soon as he was clear of all previous publishing commitments, he would begin to edit a publication "consisting entirely of original matter"; it would be established around the idea of an informal club of characters who would tell different stories but would also include essays and sketches, letters "from imaginary correspondents" and running series on such themes as "Chambers" and "ancient London". He wanted, in other words, something quite different from the very knowing and up-to-date *Miscellany*. In Elm Cottage he had copies of Goldsmith and other English essayists, no doubt specifically brought to assist him with his plans, and he seems to have been reading *Gulliver's Travels* for a similar purpose, one of his aims being to satirise the topical events of the day in oblique form. It is remarkable too that he planned to reintroduce such old fictional characters as Samuel Pickwick and Tony Weller, which suggests that he believed these characters to have an independent existence beyond the confines of the novel in which they first appeared. Which in turn suggests that Dickens still had ambitions which had very little to do with the writing of novels.

In fact the idea of the new venture had taken such a hold upon him that it led him to neglect his work on *Nicholas Nickleby*, and induced "great worrying and fidgeting of myself"; again one sees how even the most tentative plan, once it is conceived by him, is seized as if it were already a burning reality which had to be put into practice immediately. He could not sit still. The idea of a weekly periodical for which he would receive a regular income without having to extend his energies once more on a long novel clearly appealed to him, together with the fact that a periodical under his sole guidance and authority would confirm that link with his audience for which he was always searching and which might have been in danger if he had simply embarked upon another monthly series. He had a good idea of his audience and he knew that, to keep it, surprise and novelty were potent instruments. Of course this new idea had the great merit of binding Chapman and Hall even closer to him, but in a partnership as beneficial to himself as it was to them – he proposed the idea of *Master Humphrey's Clock*, as the new weekly periodical was to be called, at the same time as he suggested that in the matter of *Nicholas Nickleby* they "behave with liberality to me". In fact they paid him an extra £1,500, and it seems partly the fact that he had outlined a new agreement for future co-operation which persuaded them to be so generous; the pattern emerges here which was to become constant in Dickens's later career, of dangling both the carrot of a future work and the stick of his well-known wrath to keep his publishers in line. The agreement with Chapman and Hall which he eventually signed for *Master Humphrey's Clock* was almost ideal from Dickens's point of view; he was paid a weekly salary while Chapman and Hall covered the expenses, and he shared equally in all profits. Henceforward in his career, having suffered from fixed payments in the past, he insisted that he would always participate in the profits and thus increase his own income as his sales increased. He was perhaps the first professional author to *act* as a professional, and to put what would have been notable skills as a Victorian businessman to good use. And, as he became more and more enthusiastic about his ideas for the new periodical and his own future, *Nicholas Nickleby* itself began to suffer from slight inattention; those episodes written at Petersham show no evidence of flagging invention, but they do show some sign of his loss of interest in construction.

Dickens still did not want to return to London, however, and this largely because he was no longer happy with Doughty Street. He had given notice that he did not intend to resume the tenancy agreement which was just about to expire, and no doubt the presence of two children, with his wife pregnant yet again, made the somewhat cramped rooms of the house seem even more constricted. So as soon as they left Petersham they went down to Ramsgate to search for lodgings. There were none to be obtained there, and instead they went back to the nearby town of Broadstairs; they no longer stayed in the small house in the High Street, but instead took a commodious house on the sea-front. It was here, at 40 Albion Street, that he set to work on the final number of *Nicholas Nickleby*. And here, too, he experienced one of those episodes concerning servants which might have been pathetic but which always seemed to Dickens to be irresistibly comic: his cook "got drunk – remarkably drunk – on Tuesday night, was removed by constables, lay down in front of the house and addressed the multitude for some hours . . ." Not that he did not miss London; and, in one of those strangely self-revealing letters which on the surface seem merely animated and cordial, Dickens suggests that because of his absence any number of dreadful events might have taken place in the capital. "I almost blame myself for the death of that poor girl who leaped off the Monument . . . neither would the two men have found the skeleton in the sewers", and he goes on to describe an imaginary portrait by Cruikshank of someone stuffing a dead child down the little hole of the privy. Another aspect of a vision which was sometimes truly grotesque.

Fred was with the family at Broadstairs. Of all Dickens's brothers he was undoubtedly the favourite, and Dickens took a constant interest in his welfare; together they climbed down to the beach one night during a ferocious storm, and crept within the shelter of a boat beside the little pier in order to observe the breaking sea. But for most of the time here his diary mentions just one word – "Work". Writing at his study looking out at the turbulent sea, composing the final chapters of *Nicholas Nickleby* in which Squeers is undone, Ralph Nickleby's treacheries unmasked, the terrible story of his son, Smike, is told, Dotheboys Hall breaks up at last and everything ends cheerfully for the hero and his bride, for the hero's sister and her betrothed. Nicholas Nickleby becomes "rich and prosperous" just like his creator but the novel ends with a vision of the grave of poor Smike, a character so much like a simulacrum of the author as he might have been if he had remained a ". . . labouring hind". But now dead and buried for evermore. Then, on Friday, 20 September, 1839 Dickens wrote in his diary: "Finished Nickleby this day at 2 o'clock, and went over to Ramsgate with Fred and Kate, to send the last little chapter to Bradbury and Evans in a parcel. Thank God that I have lived to get through it happily." He had already written his preface to the newly completed novel, in which for the first time he adopts that fond and agreeable tone towards his audience which he wished to continue in his projected journal, *Master Humphrey's Clock* – his aim being, he said, that of ". . . one who wished their happiness, and contributed to their amusement". Here is Dickens as the man of feeling, uniting all his readership in a concord of affection and brotherhood.

The morning after he had completed his task of some nineteen months he went by steamer to London in order to correct the last proofs with Forster. Then he returned to Broadstairs and for the next few days broke off all work and all thought of work in order to rest after his labours. This could hardly be called "relaxation", however, because he put himself through a regimen of walking, riding and swimming that on its own terms seems as exhausting as any of his literary labours; "out from breakfast time until dinner" was the routine for most of the days after completing *Nicholas Nickleby*, and particularly it ought to be noted how important his walks became for him. These "daily constitutionals", as he sometimes called them, in fact turned into something of an obsession and it came to be his settled opinion that it was important for him to spend as many hours walking as he did working. It became what he described as a "moral obligation". His steady pace was some four and a half miles per hour, and it was quite common for him to walk twenty or even thirty miles at a stretch. The covering of such distances was not an uncommon feat in those early nineteenth-century years; before the onset of cheap public transport, walking long distances was a positive necessity. But what was different about Dickens was the speed and the determination of his perambulation. In later life it was to be a means of warding off melancholy or a way of fighting off the worries which beset him but, in these early years, it can be most fruitfully seen as the blowing off of superfluous energy. As his brother-in-law put it, after seeing him return from one of his excursions, ". . . he looked the personification of energy, which seemed to ooze from every pore as from some hidden reservoir; and as we got towards home a watcher looking at him might have said. 'He is seeing written in the air, Excelsior, at every turn on the way.'" But we might remember Nicholas Nickleby's own determined or desperate walks, and speculate that Dickens himself was aware of the nervous fury which also sent him marching forwards – ". . . I must move rapidly, or I could not draw my breath . . ." And earlier in the same novel: ". . . he felt so nervous and excited that he could not sit still. He seemed to be losing time unless he was moving."

The completion of *Nicholas Nickleby* was celebrated by a dinner which Macready described as "*too* splendid". It was held at the Albion in Aldersgate Street, and Maclise's painting of Dickens was given pride of place on the occasion – a painting, incidentally, of which the engraved copies became so popular that the plate from which the impressions were taken deteriorated beyond repair. Apparently it was not a particularly inspiring occasion. In a speech in honour of Dickens Macready compared him to Wordsworth, which seems to have prompted Dickens to tell a fellow guest that he enjoyed Wordsworth's pretty but somewhat morbid poem, "We Are Seven", one of the few indications that Dickens admired the first generation of Romantic poets. The party broke up "very late".

Very late, and then back to Doughty Street, where Catherine was now in the last stages of her fourth pregnancy; in fact she had been pregnant for most of the time since her marriage, despite what must have now become the evident fact that she suffered post-natal depression and anxiety of a particularly severe kind. Her health was slowly being drained away. Despite, or perhaps because of, Dickens's energy and success, it could not always have been an easy household. Dickens had brought up his mother to assist Catherine in her confinement, and it may have been of this period that a friend remarked, "I never saw him at all very serious but once, and that was when he said 'his house in Doughty Street was nothing but a hospital ward'." The sentiment could, however, have applied to any of the three other occasions when Catherine suffered depression and listlessness. It is hard to take adequate stock of their marriage at this point. It is clear that the expressions of love and affection in his letters are quite genuine, but it is true also that he did not take his wife into "society" very often (although in any case she may have been reluctant to go). It is an odd relationship, hard to fathom, hard to describe. Even during their courtship Dickens had found cause to lecture Catherine about her "dismal forebodings" and her uneasiness, and clearly this was an aspect of her character for which he had little time. Certainly there are occasions when he speaks of her with considerably less than sympathy; when she was convalescing after the birth of this most recent child, she requested books to read and Dickens told Forster, ". . . If you have any literary rubbish on hand, please to shoot it here;" and, remarking on a mistake Catherine made, he refers sarcastically to "Kate's accustomed cleverness". More serious, perhaps, is the incident reported some time later by a friend: Catherine had pressed Dickens to read out loud an extract from a Scottish book, but ". . . he turned abruptly and made off muttering, 'I hate Scotch stories and everything else Scotch' which was not any more complimentary to his wife than to me, as she was also Scotch. She flushed, laughed nervously and said, 'Don't mind him, he doesn't mean it.'" So there were at least occasional strains, and it is unlikely that Dickens, hard pressed as he was with work and with anxiety over contracts, always curbed what he himself knew to be a short and sometimes violent temper. It is possible, too, that the spirit of Mary Hogarth seemed less beneficent to her sister than to her brother-in-law; it was even said at the time that, because of the death of Mary, "those who know him say that he has not yet thoroughly recovered his former spirits". This is likely (his references to Mary are as fulsome as ever) and there may have been some resentment on Catherine's part at the spectacle of a husband who was clearly in love with the dead girl. Sorrow, too, perhaps that she was somehow displaced as the principal object of his love. All these tensions were of course exacerbated by the considerable distress she suffered after giving birth. One must imagine a quiet and often passive or uncomplaining woman who yet suffered perceptibly from tremulous anxiety and intermittent depression.

And what of Dickens himself? High-spirited, energetic, apparently unaffected by arduous labour and by equally arduous leisure; and yet a man who was, as his children will later testify, much less affectionate and easy with his immediate family than he was with his friends. He was often taciturn, often something of a martinet in household matters, and notably irritable and impatient with his wife's "slow-ness". But how did he see himself? It is significant how in these early books, written in the full flood of his success, he so often projects himself into images of privation and imprisonment. "Dick", the name by which he was known to Cruikshank, Maclise and others, is also the name he gives to a blind blackbird in *Nicholas Nickleby*, and to the frail orphan boy destined to die in *Oliver Twist*. He seems to have felt himself to be in some profound manner ill-used, and again in *Nicholas Nickleby* there is an image of a child which might come from Dickens's own childhood – "It is a sad thing . . . to see a little deformed child sitting apart from other children, who are active and merry, watching the games he is denied the power to share in." With the exception of the deformity, this is very much the image of his own infancy which Dickens remembered, and such references manifest an overwhelming and almost helpless self-pity. There is a sense in which Dickens always imagines himself to be neglected, and no doubt this permanent vague dissatisfaction with the world must on occasions have been directed at his immediate family. The birth on 29 October of Kate Macready Dickens, the child who in many respects was to be the one most like her father, could only have served to increase that sense of imprison-ment which was one of the disadvantages of his domesticity.

And one of the reasons, too, why he wanted to move – as soon as he had returned to London from Broadstairs, he began to search in earnest for a new house. Dickens suggested that he should leave Doughty Street by the Christmas of 1839 on condition that the landlord bought from him all the fixtures he had installed, yet another example of his practical canniness in financial matters, and at the beginning of December the Dickens family and servants moved into a much larger house. One Devonshire Terrace was on the Marylebone Road, almost opposite the York Gate into Regent's Park; in some ways it was a grander address than Doughty Street and certainly a grander house. It was the last in a terrace of three and stood on the corner of Marylebone Road and Marylebone High Street, its square garden protected by a high wall. It was on two floors, contained some thirteen rooms, and was soon to be well furnished with candelabra, rosewood chairs covered with silk, silk damask curtains, large mirrors, sofas, sofa tables and – the only homely touch – a cottage piano which Dickens had originally bought for his lodgings in Furnival's Inn. He also had the front door and exterior railings painted bright green, one of his favourite colours, although this did not prevent it from being seen by some observers as a rather conventional and even dreary mansion. One French journalist said that its front resembled "a badly washed sepulchre" and some years later George Gissing, that epicure of London's uglier aspects, considered it to be "as plain and dull-looking a house as can be found in London". But it was solid, it was genteel, it was respectable, and thus precisely the kind of house which Dickens wanted; this was the period, after all, in which he joined the Middle Temple with definite ideas of being one day called to the Bar. He could not yet be absolutely certain that his popularity would last, and no doubt his own histrionic and analytic skills would have earned him more than a modest income if he had ever become a barrister. But for the time being, at least, he was the writer of the day and his new house, according to his brother-in-law, became "a general meeting place for men of mark, especially literary men and artists". One such literary man, George Henry Lewes, had not been particularly impressed by Dickens in Doughty Street. He had been appalled to find in the young writer's library just a standard set of books and presentation copies, and came away with a genuine appreciation of Dickens's energy but not with any real "sense of distinction". But when he visited him in his first year at Devonshire Terrace he found the author changed. "His conversation turned on graver subjects than theatres and actors, periodicals and London life. His interest in public affairs, especially in social questions, was keener. He still remained completely outside philosophy, science, and the higher literature . . . But the vivacity and sagacity which gave a charm to intercourse with him had become weighted with a seriousness which from that time forward became more and more prominent in his conversation and his writings." Lewes was being absurdly sententious about "higher literature" but there was no doubt that Dickens's personality had indeed developed; in fact this was largely the result of his appreciation of his own growing importance, particularly in the effect which he had already exerted upon public opinion in such matters as the Yorkshire schools and the New Poor Laws. Certainly his relation with his readers was beginning to change, and one contemporary dated from this period "that curiously reverent attitude . . . paid to him by the public". It was in this period that he was interviewed by an American writer and is reported to have said that, "I am trying to enjoy my fame while it lasts, for I believe I am not so foolish as to suppose that my books will be read by any but the men of my own times;" when the reporter replied that it would be hard to convince the world of this, Dickens added with a smile that "I shall probably not make any very serious efforts to do so". And yet even now doubts persisted about his "seriousness" – as the American writer, Dana, put it, "He is the *cleverest* man I ever met. I mean he impresses you more with the alertness of his various powers. His forces are all light infantry and light cavalry, and always in marching order. There are not many heavy pieces, but few *sappers* and *miners*, the scientific corps is deficient, and I fear there is no chaplain in the garrison." And there was also Dickens's inherent strangeness, his susceptibility, his uniqueness – like the time in January of the new year when he was so overcome by being a member of a jury at the inquest into the death of a young child that he had "a most violent attack of sickness and indigestion" which would allow him neither sleep nor rest; as a result he and Catherine sat up all night. (It ought to be recorded of this incident that it was as a result of his own intervention on behalf of the mother that the child was declared stillborn rather than murdered.) And there is also the strangeness, too, of his sudden obsession with the young Queen who was about to celebrate her marriage – "The presence of my wife aggravates me. I loathe my parents. I detest my house." Of course this was part of the "fun and raillery" of which he so often speaks, but one notices here the way in which his fantasies chafe at the banks of reality, and how quickly he slides into a dream of discontent.

The move to Devonshire Terrace had taken up a great deal of time, and he had to make up for the loss by cancelling most other engagements in order to work on *Barnaby Rudge*, which he had begun again in October only to break off. But he contracted a bad cold in his chest and, in addition, had agreed to write another selection of essays, *Sketches of Young Couples*. This is in many respects a particularly bad-tempered selection of portraits of the marital state but it does contain one notable article of faith which Dickens was to maintain for the rest of his life: ". . . all men and women, in couples or otherwise, who fall into exclusive habits of self-indulgence, and forget their natural sympathy and close connection with everybody and everything in the world around them, not only neglect the first duty of life, but, by a happy retributive justice, deprive themselves of its truest and best enjoyment." This is a fine statement – the fine statement of an *idea* – yet it ought to be remembered that, as even these slight sketches demonstrate, Dickens's imagination most closely and naturally twined itself about the actual conduct of human beings. But these *Sketches of Young Couples* were light work. He had more important tasks ahead of him. There was *Barnaby Rudge* . . . and then, even as he was working on his much postponed novel, he saw an advertisement which had been placed by Bentley in the *Morning Herald* and which announced *Barnaby Rudge* as "preparing for publication". At once he wrote to his solicitors, Smithson and Mitton, charging them to tell Bentley that the book would not be ready on time; and that, in fact, he refused altogether to produce it. He gave as his principal reason the fact that Bentley had for some time past been associating Dickens's work with that of his other authors (such as Harrison Ainsworth) and "hawking them about in a manner calculated to do me serious prejudice". Now it is certainly true that Dickens had a dislike, amounting almost to a phobia, of having his own novels associated with those of other writers, but in truth he was desperate to get out of his contract to supply *Barnaby Rudge* to Bentley. It was not even close to being finished, he was about to begin work with Chapman and Hall on the new periodical he had proposed, and he had in any case no high regard for Bentley himself; so he seized upon the advertisement as an excuse to cancel his contract. Of course Bentley himself was astonished by Dickens's sudden and peremptory declaration – "one of the most extraordinary effusions that even Mr D ever sent forth," his solicitor commented, and Bentley's son later added, "It is a brick in the building of Dickens's character. He wished to break his agreement, and so he made up the account herein. Dickens was a very clever, but he was not an honest man."

This was not the only occasion on which Dickens was charged with dishonesty, and his enemies sometimes accused him of being an outright liar. Of course he was very fond of superlative expressions, and he had an innate taste for excessiveness: never has he been so willing to do something, never has he had so large an audience, never has he sold so many copies, and so forth (although it is often odd to see these superlatives, in his correspondence, couched in his characteristically neat and tidy hand). It is also undeniably true that he would make up or at least embellish incidents when it suited his purpose to do so, even though this native tendency towards exaggeration also had its more beneficent side; as one contemporary noted, he was often guilty of "the amiable magnifying of the merits of persons . . ." But the point is more complicated than that, and certain comments which Dickens made at different times of his life all point in the same direction: ". . . any impression of mine is, I need not say, much better than a fact . . . I promised to tell you the truth, and this is the truth, as I feel it . . . I have created a legend in my own mind – and consequently I believe it with the utmost pertinacity . . ." And so forth. This comes close to the truth of the matter: Dickens believed what he saw, or what possessed him, at that moment. If he felt something, it became at once true for him; in the same way that he *saw* his characters, immediately he seized upon an opinion or a belief it possessed absolute truth and reality in his own mind. Everything in the world, therefore, took on the shape of his own principles or obsessions; this has nothing to do with lying unless creation itself is a lie. And, although it may be poor comfort for those who suffered from his misrepresentations (his wife principal among them, in the end), there is no doubt that Dickens would have felt able to put his hand upon his heart and swear that he was always telling the truth.

Which was precisely why his animus against Richard Bentley was inspired by a real sense of outrage, even though it was Dickens himself who was principally in the wrong. From that time forward it was, as he put it, "war to the knife . . . with the Burlington Street Brigand". He was no doubt counting on Bentley's unwillingness to take him to court – it is rare for a publisher to sue an author – and in that belief it turned out he was not very much mistaken. And in the meantime, having abandoned work on *Barnaby Rudge*, he turned his attention eagerly to his proposed periodical, *Master Humphrey's Clock*. He proceeded very much as he had planned; he conceived the idea of a club, and began writing a series of tales which were linked to the members of that club. This idea of the "framed tale" was one that satisfied some aspect of his imagination; stories had appeared within the narratives of *The Pickwick Papers* and *Nicholas Nickleby*, too, and it is probable that this notion of linked but separate tales was closely connected with his memory of his childhood reading; not only his reading of periodicals like the *Bee* and *The Spectator*, but also, and most importantly, of *The Arabian Nights*, the fantasies of which had so deeply stirred him. What is unusual about the first number he was now writing of *Master Humphrey's Clock*, however, is the narrator, for here Dickens casts himself in the role of an old man whose essential memory is of his childhood as a "poor crippled boy". Just as Somerset Maugham gave the hero of his *Of Human Bondage* a club-foot, as some physical symptom of the inadequacies Maugham believed himself to possess, so in the figure of Master Humphrey we see once again that projection of injury and vulnerability which Dickens had already explored in earlier characters and which he would use once again in such creations as Tiny Tim. As Master Humphrey says of himself, ". . . my heart aches for that child as if I had never been he, when I think how often he awoke from some fairy change to his own old form, and sobbed himself to sleep again". He is now an old man, taking "all mankind" as "my kindred, and I am on ill terms with no one member of my great family". Much like Dickens's image of himself, of course, and Master Humphrey also wanders through the city streets, as Dickens did, "for ever lingering upon past emotions and bygone times", losing his "sense of my own loneliness" while imagining the scenes in the various houses which he passes or seeing an interesting face within a crowd. Clearly Dickens here is setting up the context for the kind of human stories which he will place in *Master Humphrey's Clock* – it is likely that the little tale which burgeoned into *The Old Curiosity Shop* was intended to follow one such imaginary journey – but clearly also it refers to Dickens's own pensive habits of imagination.

And there is London, too, the London which he celebrated in *Nicholas Nickleby* and which once more is defined in his new periodical as a place which contains "within its space everything, with its opposite extreme and contradiction", holds together a "thousand worlds"; a city where the narrator has "some thought for the meanest wretch that passes". Here Dickens is establishing the framework in which he will tell his stories, but once again he is firmly drawing the boundaries of his own imagination. The first stories he wrote were certainly of a London kind. He opens with an episode concerning the twin urban deities of Gog and Magog, no doubt partly inspired by his original plan to write a book about old London with Harrison Ainsworth but also clearly linked with his own imaginative interests at that time. The first chapters of *Barnaby Rudge*, which he had already written, were concerned with eighteenth-century London, and it is significant that all the ensuing short tales in *Master Humphrey's Clock* were set in the sixteenth or seventeenth centuries. His whole thinking was revolving around the past, therefore, and in the month he began writing *Master Humphrey's Clock* he visited an antiquarian bookseller, a Mr Upcott, who called himself "bibliophile and publisher", and wrote in the visitors' book – ". . . this most extraordinary antiquarian mansion, whereto I mean to return at the earliest possible opportunity to refresh myself with a few dusty draughts from its exhaustless wells." Old London. The crippled childhood of the narrator. Old books. So in *Master Humphrey's Clock* the idea of the past, the specific past of London and his own lost childhood are once more intertwined. As if in exploring the history of the city he was in some way exploring and animating his own past. Combining ". . . past emotions and bygone times". Which adds substance, perhaps, to G. K. Chesterton's comment that in these periodical tales lay "the stuff of which his dreams were made".

He was still meditating on the next episode of *Master Humphrey's Clock* when he went down to Bath with Forster in order to visit Walter Savage Landor. They had met through Forster (it was Forster, more than anyone, who introduced Dickens to the representatives of that age of literature before his own) and Landor seems to have appealed to Dickens at once; he was almost forty years older than Dickens and the younger man treated him with that mixture of admiration, deference and light comic teasing which seems always to have comprised his attitude to older authors. He was in fact something of a "character", an apparently ferocious and belligerent party whose determined manner actually camouflaged a highly tender and even sentimental person. He was very much a representative of the previous age, an eighteenth-century or at least Regency figure who had survived into the age we may now begin to call "Victorian". They stayed in Bath for only three days – Mrs Lynn Linton, a friend of Landor, had dinner with them all one evening and described Forster as "snubbing and satirical" whereas Dickens was "most kind and gay with me". (In later life she was to compare Dickens less favourably with Thackeray, and said that he was "infinitely less plastic, less self-giving, less personally sympathetic".) It was at Bath, apparently, that Dickens found the original of his ferocious dwarf, Quilp; there was here "a frightful little dwarf named Prior, who let donkeys on hire" and who beat his wife and animals equally. Such "originals" have to be admitted with extreme caution, as we have seen, but there is no doubt that the visit to Bath did affect Dickens's fiction in one significant way. For it was at Landor's house that he conceived of the character of Little Nell, and at once fell to plotting a short tale for her in *Master Humphrey's Clock*. Of course Little Nell came not only to dominate a whole novel but also to master the entire nation, and Landor said later that he wished he had burned down his house so that ". . . no meaner association should ever desecrate the birthplace of Little Nell". A typical piece of exaggeration, this, from Landor and one that no doubt contributed to the portrait of him as Boythorn in *Bleak House* – this is one occasion when the character really does resemble the original, to such an extent that most readers who knew Landor saw the likeness at once. Landor himself was not amused. When he was asked if he had read *Bleak House*, he replied "No! And never shall!", and Mrs Lynn Linton reports that afterwards he spoke of Dickens "with a certain acerbity of tone". Dickens was not always the wonderful and devoted friend whom most of his contemporaries seem to remember; there were times when those closest to him also became disenchanted with his behaviour, and Landor is one notable example.

But another friendship made in this period was to be of far more importance to Dickens. At the house of Edward Stanley, a Whig politician who had "taken up" the famous novelist as so many others in the fashionable world had done or were at least attempting to do, he met Thomas Carlyle. In later life Dickens told one of his sons that Carlyle was the man "who had influenced him most" and Dickens's sister-in-law said to Carlyle himself that "there was *no one* for whom he had a higher reverence and admiration". There is the famous photograph of Dickens on the lawn at Gad's Hill Place, reading Carlyle's *History of the French Revolution*. In his admiration for him, of course, Dickens was by no means alone and there is a strong case to be made for Carlyle being the single most important writer in England during the 1840s; Dickens, although he was by no means intimately acquainted with his writings when they met, would have known of him by repute in the radical circles in which they both moved and was certainly aware of some of his work. For already, at the beginning of the year, Dickens had initiated a correspondence with a certain John Overs, a working man who wished to earn his living as a writer; theirs was in some ways a complicated and difficult relationship, in which Dickens's real sympathy for Overs's plight (there is a sense in which he seems to treat him as the kind of person he himself might have become if he had not been successful) was tinged with a certain peremptory and even domineering manner towards this working-class man. Yet he had lent Overs a copy of Carlyle's *Chartism*, a pamphlet in which he addresses what had become known as "the condition of England question". This was largely a debate about the rights of the working classes and in his pamphlet Carlyle stresses the need for both proper education and efficient emigration, together with the urgent necessity for the repeal of the Corn Laws – with all of which panaceas Dickens himself agreed. Carlyle was some seventeen years older than Dickens, and had already ensconced himself with his wife in their house in Cheyne Row. That there was some sympathy between them is at once made clear by Carlyle's own description of Dickens at this first meeting as ". . . a fine little fellow . . . a face of most extreme *mobility*, which he shuttles about – eyebrows, eyes, mouth and all – in a very singular manner while speaking". Carlyle goes on to comment, like so many others, on Dickens's colourful and dandified dress but adds that he is ". . . a quiet, shrewd-looking, little fellow, who seems to guess pretty well what he is and what others are".

Dickens's own first impressions are not recorded, although he would no doubt have considered Carlyle to be in the same "camp" as himself; not just because of his radical sympathies but also because, earlier in this year, he had given a course of lectures which were later published as *Heroes, Hero-Worship and the Heroic in History*. Dickens was always to have reservations about Carlyle's worship of power, and the men of power, but he could not have helped but be stirred by Carlyle's encomia on "The Hero as Man of Letters" in which he declared that ". . . since it is the spiritual always that determines the material, this same Man-of-Letters Hero must be regarded as our most important modern person. He, such as he may be, is the soul of all. What he teaches, the whole world, will do and make . . . Men of Letters are a perpetual Priesthood, from age to age, teaching all men that a God is still present in their life . . . I say, of all Priesthoods, Aristocracies, Governing Classes at present extant in the world, there is no class comparable for importance to the Priesthood of the Writers of Books . . ." This of course, shorn of its Idealistic elements, is precisely the position which Dickens was moving towards; and precisely the role which he seems to have wanted to assume.

And yet it cannot be said that Carlyle had any very high opinion of Dickens's merits as a writer – this primarily because Dickens was a novelist and thus consigned to the world of Appearances rather than that of the Real. Of course he was entertained by Dickens's writing, and sometimes moved by it, but there is no doubt that his most permanent attitude was one of slight disparagement aptly expressed in his idea of Dickens as a "little fellow". He said as much later when in *Past and Present* he obliquely described Dickens's progress through America: ". . . if all Yankee-land follow a small good 'Schnuspel the distinguished Novelist' with blazing torches, dinner invitations, universal hep-hep-hurrah, feeling that he, though small, *is* something . . . Possible to worship a Something, even a small one . . ." And when describing the idea of Genius he again disparages the very kind of work on which Dickens was engaged – "What! The star-fire of the Empyrean shall eclipse itself, and illuminate magic-lanterns to amuse grown children? He, the god-inspired, is to twang harps for thee, and blow through scrannel-pipes; soothe thy sated souls with visions of new, still wider Eldorados, Houri Paradises, richer Lands of Cockaigne?" Yet at the same time as he hated the sin he liked the sinner. "I truly love Dickens," he once said, "and discern in the inner man of him a tone of real Music, which struggles to express itself as it may . . ."

Again not an overwhelming compliment and Dickens, astute as he was, must have known from the start what a relatively low opinion Carlyle held of fiction and fiction-writers who, faced with the light of the Absolute, were happy to settle for the coloured shades of a magic lantern. Carlyle's father had believed fiction to be "*false* and criminal" and to a certain extent his son adopted that attitude. But it has to be said that there was always within Carlyle a brighter and more cheerful aspect; this was the person who responded to Dickens. That there was a certain wariness, or strain, in their relationship cannot be doubted – but there was also amity, a genuine warmth and a genuine sympathy. These were two men who thought, in their own different ways, that they were trying to find and to express the "Time-Spirit". Indeed there were enough real resemblances between them to ensure that they maintained friendly relations, even in such specific things as their common distaste for the more overt forms of philanthropy (especially to other races), for model prisons, and indeed for most conventionally "liberal" activities and ideals. Both of them were from a much rougher, and tougher, school. Yet there were also sympathies of a deeper kind between them, sympathies which put them in close contact with the driving spirit of the age. It was Thomas Carlyle who said, after all, that "Man is created to fight; he is perhaps best of all definable as a born soldier; his life 'a battle and a march' under the right General". Dickens shared precisely the same sentiments, just as he shared Carlyle's distaste for the aristocracy in *Past and Present* – "the impotent, insolent Donothingism in Practice, and Saynothingism in Speech". It might almost be the epigraph to *Little Dorrit*. There were temperamental affinities, too, expressed perhaps best in Carlyle's account of ". . . that nameless unrest, the blind struggle of a soul in bondage, that high, sad, longing Discontent"; he was here describing Goethe, but had he not also seen the same "unrest" in Dickens? Was it not that which eventually led him to talk of the "dark, fateful silent elements" within the great novelist?

Of course Dickens's beliefs were on the whole instinctive, passionately held but not necessarily carefully considered, and in Carlyle's writings he would have found a strenuous idealism, a high purpose and an essential seriousness which would help to bind his own notions into a coherent whole. Certainly Carlyle's speculative idealism and his distrust of philosophic radicalism would have helped to set Dickens's own more scattered ideas into some sort of order. Both men agreed, for example, or would come to agree, on the parlous state of England at this time, a time which seems to us so strident and so fruitful but which seemed to them to be barren of meaning and empty of faith. In *Past and Present*, published three years after their first meeting, Carlyle spoke of the condition of the country in terms that Dickens would have understood and admired: "All England stands wringing its hands, asking itself, nigh desperate, What farther? Reform Bill proves to be a failure; Benthamee Radicalism, the gospel of 'Enlightened Selfishness' dies out, or dwindles into Five-point Chartism, amid the tears and hootings of men: what next are we to hope or try?" These were times when the men of the early Forties were ". . . mumbling to ourselves some vague janglement of Laissez-faire, Supply-and-demand, Cash-payment the one nexus of man to man: Free-trade, Competition, and Devil take the hindmost, our latest Gospel yet preached!" These were some of the assaults that Dickens himself was to direct against his contemporaries, and, like Carlyle, over all social and political matters Dickens erected a vast shadowy symbolic structure so that the London of *Bleak House*, for example, might be said to act as an echo-chamber for Carlyle's words on "Sooty Manchester, – it too is built on the infinite Abysses; overspanned by the skyey Firmaments; and there is birth in it, and death in it; – and it is every whit as wonderful, as fearful, unimaginable, as the oldest Salem or Prophetic City. Go or stand, in what time, in what place we will, are there not Immensities, Eternities, over us, around us, in us . . ."

This is the vision of Carlyle, but it is also the vision of Charles Dickens. It is the true vision of the first half of the nineteenth century.

To say that Carlyle was the single most important philosophical writer of his period, then, is to throw a different light upon an age which has often seemed in retrospect to represent no more than the beginning of a staid Victorian dispensation. It was nothing of the kind. It had its own unique energies and patterns; we see how in Carlyle and in Dickens they spread and eddy, reaching from the innermost imagination to the large circle of readers who picked up each episode of *Oliver Twist* or the latest of Carlyle's pamphlets. Indeed from this greater distance we can see distinct resemblances between them. Both writers marrying philosophical or social analysis with the vivid scene or detail, both of them moving away from that strict separation of genres which had marked eighteenth-century writing, both of them uniting the most unlikely opposites – a private self-communing speech with public rage and denunciation, an almost apocalyptic vision with a strict determination to tell the "truth", a Gothic stance with the need also to be "real" and to be "immediate". All of these elements are contained as much within Carlyle's prose as that of Dickens; in both men we may discern the true lineaments of the 1830s and the 1840s, that period of passion and responsibility, of faith and scepticism. But Carlyle was the older man, and it was Dickens who really came to maturity in an age of transition.

II

CHARLES DICKENS at the time of Pickwick, and of Oliver Twist, and of Nicholas Nickleby; the young man hurrying along, turning suddenly, looking up at the rolling clouds of a London sky, laughing at something in the street ahead of him. "Look at that! I have never been so surprised in all my life!"

"Tell me. Do please stay, and tell me where you are going."

"Where am I going? Where am I going? Why –" Dickens did stop for an instant, and scratched his head. "Why, that is a nice question. Oh Lord, yes. A very nice one." He saw a face moving past him, staring out of the window of an old-fashioned stage-coach, and he continued to watch it as the coach moved slowly down the street. Then he turned back, his span of attention as capacious and as impersonal as that of a cat. "I'll tell you where. I am going forward. I have been going forward ever since I began."

"Began?"

Two elderly women, fidgeting nervously as they talked to each other in loud voices, meandered past; Dickens watched them eagerly, restraining his urge to laugh out loud by compressing his lips together. Then, as soon as they had gone by, he imitated their worried, puckered faces and their slightly nasal Cockney: "Vy, that one wos the commonest dirt, yes she wos." And then he carried on as if nothing whatever had happened. "Ever since I began the world." He stared fully at his questioner – straight at him, for a second or two, as if he were taking the measure of his entire life.

Before he turned around again, alerted by a voice raised suddenly in the pawnbroker's outside of which we were standing. A young woman came running out from the dilapidated shop (its wooden boards were damp and crumbling); Dickens stepped aside and let her pass, but looked at her so sharply that she felt the brightness of his glance upon her. She looked up at him as she ran off. "Did you see that face? I have never seen anything like it before! Truly, never!" But his questioner had seen only the startled appearance of a young woman caught by Dickens, as it were, while in pursuit of her own life. "What a fate she will have!" He murmured this with some satisfaction.

"Good day to you," he said abruptly. "I must be on my way." He started walking briskly down this main thoroughfare, Kingsland Road, towards the great church of Shoreditch. Several inhabitants turned to watch him as he continued on his way and indeed, in his green and scarlet top-coat with its facings *à l'Espagnole*, he was an unusual person to be found in this desolate neighbourhood. Eventually I was able to catch up with him and to walk beside him; he merely nodded to acknowledge my presence, and carried on with his quick, jaunty step. We walked beside several decaying houses, straggling along this unlit and unpaved road, and as he passed each one Dickens peered inside; his lingering gaze had an air of absorbed melancholy striated with something very like recognition, and it was as if in these coarse dwellings of ragged yellow brick he saw a part of his own self.

"I knew this place as a boy," he said. "There was a pie-shop, Berry's it was called, where there is now this lodging house for travellers. And here stood the estab-lishment of a carriage-maker, by the name of Jasper. He had in his window two engravings of his work – the Berkshire Fly, all in green and red with heraldic arms of yellow, and the famous London Immaculate. No doubt they are both still on the road. Both on the road." He had a slightly thick accent, very much like a lisp, and in his effort to conceal it he pronounced his words almost too distinctly.

"You remember so much."

"I remember *everything*." He inhaled deeply. "Even the smells are the same. It is always the smell which brings back the truest memory." For a moment I might have believed that tears had started up in his eyes but, instead, he burst out laughing. "I was just thinking," he went on, "of what that child said when he saw you."

"I recall no child."

"He came up behind you when you first stopped to talk to me. I noticed him at once." All the time I had been talking to Dickens during those first moments I had observed nothing, and he himself had given no sign. "He said, when he stood behind you, 'What a shocking bad hat!'" Then he laughed again. "Nothing like a street child to see the comedy of life. Even here." And you, I thought, you too were once a street child. And now you might be king of this little island of misery around us. "Yes, a child," he went on. "No home should be without one. Excellent in novels, too." And I could have sworn that, when he turned towards me, he actually winked – a brief, funny wink – although it might have been a trick of the waning light. We walked together a little more but gradually his footsteps grew faster, leaving me further and further behind. The last I saw of him was when his slight, slender figure was swallowed up in the dusk.

Chapter 12

AT the beginning of April 1840 Charles Dickens travelled to Birmingham with Catherine and Forster; he had already written "the little child-story" about Nell for his new periodical, the story which had occurred to him while visiting Landor in Bath and which was eventually to become the first chapter of *The Old Curiosity Shop*. No doubt he visited this manufacturing city for some more general purpose connected with his new venture, but in any case it was his practice to be out of London when anything of his began publication; and, on the day after they left for the Midlands, the first number of *Master Humphrey's Clock* duly appeared. It cost threepence a week (monthly parts sold at a shilling) and in appearance it was very distinctive. It was larger than the regular monthly parts of *Nicholas Nickleby*, on creamy white paper, and with twelve pages of text; the engravings were not placed at the beginning of each issue, as they had been with the monthly numbers, but were "dropped" into the text. All this demonstrates Dickens's fine eye for detail, and the care he lavished upon the project was matched only by his hopes for its success. The prospects were, he said, "beyond calculation". It was a "very difficult game" but "with very high stakes before me" and, when he heard that the first number had sold some seventy thousand copies, he was elated. At this rate, he told Macready in the first flush of his optimism, he could make ten thousand pounds a year. And already he was devising ways of improving the effectiveness of the magazine; he was going to insert the story of the child into the third number but then changed his mind and decided to put it in the fourth, his primary aim at this stage being to lend coherence to what was an assemblage of different materials. He wanted to give his journal "a less discursive appearance". And his instincts were right: the page proofs of numbers five and six were already prepared when it became clear that the public appeal of this heterogeneous collection of essays was not as great as Dickens and his partners had anticipated. Within two weeks sales had dropped almost thirty per cent to around fifty thousand copies, and it was at this juncture that Dickens decided to cut his losses. He realised that the public had been expecting another story from him, and, like the professional journalist he was and always remained, he set out to provide them with just that; it is likely that he had already seen possibilities in the "child-story", this story of the little girl whom Master Humphrey finds wandering in the streets of London, and perhaps intended to return to this charming theme from time to time. But now he decided to elaborate upon it and to transform it into a story of weekly instalments. There is no doubt that it exercised a strong fascination for him in any case; at this juncture, as he later told a friend, Little Nell "followed him about everywhere", as did so many of his creations once he had imagined them. As with *Oliver Twist* what had once been simply a short story about a child had grown almost at once into an entire narrative. It is as if the plight of a solitary child provoked Dickens into full-scale conceiving and scheming and designing, as if it would not let him rest until he had (in Little Nell's case, literally) laid it to rest.

And so the fourth number of *Master Humphrey's Clock* opened with the new story. He had other material which he wanted to use up, of course, and so we find the tale of Little Nell preceded by a short story about the murder of a child and followed by a piece of romantic parody – "'Can you?' said he with peculiar meaning. I felt the gentle pressure of his foot on mine; our corns throbbed in unison . . ." – displaying, if nothing else, the essential amorphousness of Dickens's talent at this stage. He was ready to try his hand at anything. But so it was, out of occasional pieces and stray inspirations, that the great story of Little Nell and her grandfather emerged. By the time the novel had finished its run sales of *Master Humphrey's Clock*, which had now become its vehicle, had reached one hundred thousand. John Forster, who took on for Dickens the task of reading the final proofs of the novel, said that thus *The Old Curiosity Shop* emerged "with less direct consciousness of design on his own part than I can remember in any other instance throughout his career". Yet it was this particular narrative which more than any of his other works made "the bond between himself and his readers one of personal attachment". By the beginning of May he was writing the third, fourth and fifth chapters and already the characters were emerging in abundance; Little Nell herself, Quilp the rebarbative dwarf, Kit Nubbles the golden-hearted "grateful fellow" and Dick Swiveller.

It was clear by now that he was again embarked upon a long story, and it was with the intention of concentrating all his energies upon it that he decided quite suddenly to go down to Broadstairs; but the evident fact that he wished to work undisturbed did not prevent him from sending letters to such friends as Beard, Mitton, Maclise and Forster asking them to join him and his family by the sea. They were back in Albion Street, along the sea-front, and it was here that he really embarked upon *The Old Curiosity Shop*. The first thing he did, however, was to rearrange and tidy his rooms; "the writing table is set forth with a neatness peculiar to your estimable friend," he wrote to Beard, "and the furniture in all the rooms has been entirely rearranged by the same extraordinary character." Here, in the half-whimsical references to himself, one detects at least a brief note of genuine pride. And at once he began his routine. He rose at seven, started work at about 8.30 and generally finished before two – an arduous enough schedule, but he found the difficulties of working within the limits of weekly numbers (as he had done with *Oliver Twist*) no less exhausting. Since *The Old Curiosity Shop* was also to be published in monthly instalments it was necessary for him to plan both on the smaller and the larger scales, fashioning the narrative so that it might continue unimpeded through its various divisions; it seems clear, too, that he began to keep written memoranda to assist him in this. Small notes on three of the numbers survive, and there is no reason to assume that he did not make such jottings for other parts as well. In fact the keeping of memoranda would become an indispensable part of his procedure in the later novels, where the complexities both of story and of character demanded something in the nature of an aide-mémoire. But, even now, he had difficulties; as he sat at his desk in Broadstairs, he began to write down the wanderings of Little Nell and her grandfather but there were occasions when, as he told Forster, the cramped space of each instalment meant that "I hadn't room to turn". He was writing sixteen or seventeen pages each week, characteristically as one long chapter followed by a shorter one. The point about his capacious imagination is that it was also a disciplined and habitual one: once he had hit upon the form which seemed most truly to reflect the exigencies of the story and the demands of his own time, he kept to it throughout the entire book. And not just a book; all his life, for example, he maintained the pattern of monthly numbers which had so fortuitously begun with *The Pickwick Papers*.

At the beginning of the story he was only working two weeks ahead of the printer, which, in a venture so much depending upon regular appearance, was cutting it somewhat fine. The nervous strain upon him, the constant need for unwearying effort in order to meet his commitments to what he now considered to be his "public", were severe: perhaps this is the best explanation for his sudden decision to escape, to travel, to go on a "jaunt". For, after about four weeks in Broadstairs, he visited Chatham and Rochester with Forster and Maclise. He always found a kind of sustenance in his returns to his childhood haunts, and it is almost as if they reminded him of how far he had already come; of how far he might yet travel. Yet even the longest journey had the same necessary end; it was on the occasion of this visit that he is reported to have said of the little burial ground just beneath Rochester Cathedral, "There, my boy, I mean to go into dust and ashes." Then he was back in London, back in his study at Devonshire Terrace, where he complained that "I am more bound down by this Humphrey than I have ever been yet" and where he continued the narrative of Little Nell's wanderings, of the meeting with Mrs Jarley and her waxworks, of the machinations of Quilp. "Bound down" in one sense, but at least he had now freed himself from Richard Bentley; he paid him £2,250 (which he had borrowed from his publishers, Chapman and Hall) and with that money was able to purchase back his copyright in *Oliver Twist* and also to release himself from the contract to write *Barnaby Rudge*. For the first time in his writing career he had cancelled all hasty or irksome contractual obligations, and a few days later he celebrated at the house of his publisher, Hall, where he drank bad wine and had to stay in bed the next morning.

It says something about the contrasts of life in this century that, two days before the party at Hall's, Dickens had attended a public hanging – to witness the execution of François Benjamin Courvoisier, a valet who had cut the throat of his employer. He had not planned to become a part of this gruesome occasion. He had been dining with Maclise and his brother-in-law, Henry Burnett, when he suddenly remembered that Courvoisier was to be hanged the next morning; no sooner had he conceived the idea of witnessing the scene than he was impetuously set upon it, and with his two friends he went down to Newgate prison. They walked about, noting the preparations for the execution, all the time struggling against the crowds who were already gathering for the spectacle. Nearly all the windows which overlooked the prison had already been booked, as was the custom, but Dickens was determined that he, too, should see the ceremony: "Just once," he said, "I should like to watch a scene like this, and see the end of the Drama." So he went into a nearby house and found one upper room still to let, from the window of which they watched the crowd beneath and the building of the scaffold. Dickens had of course been about to embark upon a history of the Gordon Riots in *Barnaby Rudge*, so he was particularly interested in the gathering crowds and often directed the attention of his friends to the noise and confusion beneath them. And when Henry Burnett muttered something about the state of mind of Courvoisier about to be hanged, Dickens replied, "No, the man sleeps soundly. They always do!" All the time he was scanning the crowd, observing the people, and at one point cried out "Why, there stands Thackeray!" (In fact, Thackeray had come expressly to write a piece about the occasion.) The time drew on to eight, the bell of Saint Sepulchre's was sounded, the crowd roared, the cry given of "Hat's off in front!" and then, four minutes late, Courvoisier stepped out. He lifted up his fettered hands and seemed to pray. Then he was hanged and cut down, his body carried on a wooden bier back within the walls of the prison. Among the mob who witnessed this scene Dickens said later that there was ". . . nothing but ribaldry, debauchery, levity, drunkenness and flaunting vice in fifty other shapes. I should have deemed it impossible that I could have felt any large assemblage of my fellow creatures to be so odious." It is like a scene out of Doré; the mob of the poor and the outcast, the ragged clothes, the swearing and the debauchery, the loud cries, the smell, and Dickens himself looking down from the upper room at the spectacle of these, his countrymen, the surging mob living in the shadows cast by his civilisation and inseparable from them. The experience stayed with him – his account of it was written some six years later – but, in any case, it can truly be said that his interest in punishment was equalled only by his interest in the crimes which provoked it. In particular he was always fascinated by murders and by murder trials, but it ought to be noted that his observation of the Courvoisier hanging seems for some time to have turned him against the notion of capital punishment altogether. Of course as he grew older he became more conservative and even more authoritarian, and by the Fifties he was extolling the necessity of hanging while at the same time wishing it to take place within the privacy of prison walls and without the unwelcome attendance of the

London public. And we can see, too, in his reaction to the crowd who surrounded Courvoisier in his last moments something of the instinctive dislike and even fear of "the mob" which was also part of his political and social attitudes. It was part of that "hardness" which others noticed and, if he was sometimes a martinet in domestic life, he was also sometimes a strict disciplinarian in social matters. It is not so odd, then, that in this same year he should write to Lord Normanby, the Home Secretary, with an offer to write a description of the horrors of life in an Australian penal colony as some kind of popular cautionary tale.

So he was still restless as he worked on *The Old Curiosity Shop*, the story he found it so difficult to "turn". He went down with Catherine to see his parents at the cottage in Alphington which he had found for them. "They *seem* perfectly contented and happy," he told Forster. "That's the only intelligence I shall convey to you except by word of mouth." In that last sentence, of course, lies all the difficulty of biography, for how is it possible now to guess at what was passed by mouth, by the sudden expression or by the unintentional phrase? The whole meaning of a life may be evoked in such moments which cannot now be reclaimed – like the life itself disappeared utterly, leaving behind just written documents from which we can only attempt carefully to reconstruct it. But the biographer does know some things which may not even have been clear to Dickens himself as eagerly he moved forward through the world, each day a new confirmation and extension of his being; we know that the parents were *not* happy, for example, and that John Dickens would soon be forging bills with his son's signature.

After the short visit to Alphington Dickens went again to Broadstairs and rented a larger place, Lawn House, for the rest of the summer. Once more he was close to the sea, and once more he invited friends and relatives to join him. It was an unusual holiday only in one respect, inasmuch as a certain Eleanor Christian, a friend of the family, left a detailed account of her stay with the Dickens entourage and gave in particular a sharp portrait of Dickens himself. He does not emerge particularly well largely because, in Eleanor Christian's account, he is marked by facetiousness, a propensity for a certain kind of savage fun, and a wilful unpredictability in his moods. The small details are right; how his clothes were too "*loud*" ("Young as I was, I was aware of the vagaries of dress indulged in by authors and artists; but this was something unusual . . ."); how, like his brothers and father, he had a slightly thick speech and tended to talk in low and hurried tones; how when he was concentrating he would suck his tongue and pull upon his hair; all these things are confirmed by other contemporaries. And in his behaviour, too, Eleanor Christian remembers what others also saw; how his humorous remarks "were generally delivered in an exaggerated, stilted style", and how misleading was the "rapt, pre-occupied, far-off look" which he sometimes adopted when in the company of others. In fact he was "taking in" everything and would eventually indulge in "most amusing but merciless criticisms" of everything that had been said. But above all else she remembered the variability of his moods. There were times when he was boisterous and amicable, even though some of the effects of his high spirits, like dragging Eleanor Christian into the sea while she was wearing her new and only silk dress, were not altogether pleasing. He would sing snatches of popular songs as they travelled in carriages on various excursions, he would attend the local dances (even though he stayed in the shadows so that he would not be recognised), he played charades and party games with all the excitement and gusto of his nature – at one time, during charades, putting on a lady's broad-brimmed hat with bedraggled feather. But there were also times when he was moody, silent and unsociable. There were even occasions when his eyes were like "danger lamps" and it was then that "I confess I was horribly afraid of him".

There is one refrain here. A little while after Broadstairs Eleanor Christian was about to go, uninvited, to a charade party at Dickens's house. But the friend who was to take her demurred: "If it was anybody else but Charles Dickens I should not hesitate an instant," she told Eleanor Christian. "But he is so odd!" His brother, Frederick, also said that he was "*odd* sometimes" and this is a description repeated by others. Odd. Mercurial. Unpredictable. Talking in low and rapid tones. This was the man who was then engaged upon a novel where tearfulness and grotesquerie, farce and tragedy, lie side by side. A novel which reads like a cross between *The Pilgrim's Progress* and *Tales of the Genii*, where the little heroine mixes with dwarves and giants, where the child-like are parodied by the childish, where there are dead children and waxworks, where the impulse towards Gothic historicity is continually displaced by the distorted figures of contemporary nightmare, where sexuality is everywhere apparent but nowhere stated. A novel, too, where there are constant references to wildness and to the wild. "I was wild myself once," Quilp says to his poor berated wife and mother-in-law, Quilp the dwarfish figure who has been seen as a simulacrum of Dickens in his savage state – even down to the detail, which the author later removed in manuscript, of the dwarf taking a shower bath in true Dickensian fashion. There are references here also to the "wild boy" and to "wild boys". Wildness. With Dickens's own eyes like "danger lamps". And it was in this period, too, that Dickens argued with Forster so ferociously that, according to Macready, he ". . . flew into so violent a passion as quite to forget himself and give Forster to understand that he was in his house, which he should be glad if he would leave". Catherine, meanwhile, had gone out of the room in tears; from this anecdote and others she comes to life once more, always trying to turn away his wrath from others, always excusing him, her quieter and gentler nature acting as the counterbalance to his nervous and sometimes difficult manner.

There were other reports of his "wildness", too, which seemed to have been passed around very quickly; that he had "fallen under the power of the demon Drink" and, most persistently, that he was mad and was undergoing treatment in an asylum. It is said that these reports of his madness originated from a joke about the raven which Dickens kept at Devonshire Terrace, a creature called Grip in whose attitudes and behaviour he took a keen interest. And, so the report goes, Landseer had said that Dickens was "raven mad". But this seems unlikely. It is more probable that the feverish pace which he maintained, as well as the usual rumours which surround someone already so celebrated as he, had crystallised into some easy formulation about insanity. That it was a serious report is not in doubt, since Dickens himself went to the unusual step of denying it in the preface which he was soon to write for *The Old Curiosity Shop*. There is even the strange testimony of a contemporary who talked to Dickens without realising who he was. It was one evening at an inn where he fell into conversation with this unknown companion, and had brought up the subject of the famous novelist: "'. . . I heard a worse affliction than that had befallen him,' I rejoined half-laughing, 'it has been said and currently reported that Boz has, what is generally called, gone out of his mind.' I have already observed we had been for some time in the twilight, and whilst I was speaking I could scarcely discover the features of my companion, so rapidly had it deepened; the lights were at this moment brought in, and as the waiter placed them on the table I continued – 'Yes not only has he been reported imbecile but downright mad'.

Whilst I uttered this my look met the gaze of my companion, and the expression of his eyes at this moment, was of a character I find impossible to describe; I observed a slight colouring steal over his features – it was of a momentary duration, leaving his countenance pale as before. 'I believe that he was aware of that report,' replied my companion after a little hesitation, 'and in noticing it publicly, observed that it had afforded him and his friends not a little amusement.'" So may Dickens have talked of himself, quietly, in an inn at twilight.

At Broadstairs he kept up the momentum of *The Old Curiosity Shop*, and one night as he walked along the cliffs he had a sudden vision of the stars reflected in the water and of "dead mankind a million fathoms deep" after the Flood. It was a vision which he placed within his story when Little Nell sees the same stars reflected in the river and then ". . . found new stars burst upon her view, and more beyond, and more beyond again, until the whole great expanse sparkled with shining spheres . . ." And all the time new images were crowding in upon him – images "in my mental Museum", he called them – images of the sea, of dreaming faces, of the road between Birmingham and Wolverhampton which he had travelled with Catherine and Forster at the beginning of the year, images of the mob, images of the pilgrimage of Little Nell and grandfather towards her death, wonderful images of the fire-watcher who sits before the furnace of a factory. "It's my memory, that fire, and shows me all my life."

Images of sublimity, then, even as his own diurnal life continued. He was not feeling well; he was suffering from severe pain in his face, which he ascribed either to rheumatism or *tic douloureux*. Then, as soon as he returned from Broadstairs to London at the beginning of October, he discovered that the profits he had expected to accrue from *Master Humphrey's Clock* were not, after all, there; the expenses of producing what was a very handsome periodical were proving heavy. And he managed to contract a bad London cold – "I have been crying all day," he said. But of course tears could not stop him working. He was helping to supervise Frederick Yates's adaptation of *The Old Curiosity Shop* at the Adelphi, although he could not eventually bring himself to attend any of its performances. He was already planning to begin *Barnaby Rudge* in *Master Humphrey's Clock* immediately after the conclusion of the present novel. And he was "revolving" the general idea of *The Old Curiosity Shop*, bringing Little Nell to live by the old church, and foreshadowing her death. All the themes came together in these winter months of 1840: the interest in death, the pre-pubescent girl, the ruins of the old church all speaking of some time of innocence so unlike the industrial landscape of the Midlands through which his heroine had passed. Yet there can be no permanent innocence. The buildings must fall into ruins. The girl must die. All through the late autumn and early winter he was working on this, sometimes taking long walks at night through the streets of London to restore his spirits. "All night I have been pursued by the child," he wrote, "and this morning I am unrefreshed and miserable." It was at this juncture that he began once more to contemplate Mary Hogarth's death a few years before, in the little room in Doughty Street overlooking the garden. And so through December and January he worked towards a fresh death. "I am breaking my heart over this story," he told George Cattermole, "and cannot bear to finish it." Later, to Macready: "I am slowly murdering that poor child, and grow wretched over it. It wrings my heart. Yet it must be." Then again, as he approached even nearer to the death-bed, "It casts the most horrible shadow upon me, and it is as much as I can do to keep moving at all." By the sixth of January he was murdering the child, and then by the thirteenth he had performed the task. He had killed her at last. "I am, for the time being, nearly dead with work – and grief for the loss of my child." He had a bad cold again, and his face became swollen as if with grief. He read the chapters containing the death of Little Nell to Forster, who was mightily affected by them, and then finally finished the novel at four o'clock on the morning of the seventeenth. Finis. Dead.

And yet there was an aspect of his character which exulted in this death – "I think it will come famously," he said in the same letter in which he described his grief. In fact there is no doubt that he deliberately worked himself up into a state of pity and holy terror in order to write of this death with the proper sympathy – that is why he had begun thinking once more of the death of Mary Hogarth, almost as if he were relishing the experience of the pain of loss. And then a strange reversal takes place, a reversal which is of considerable importance in understanding Dickens's own sense of his fiction. Clearly he needed to remember the pain of loss in order properly to describe the death of Little Nell – this is a familiar importation of life into art – but then, strangely, the art begins to affect the life. The very state which Dickens provokes in himself in order to write is transferred to the world so that, for a while, his heart actually becomes as open to real people as it does to his own creations. It was while he was killing Little

Nell, for example, that he tried to resolve a quarrel between Forster and Ainsworth and gave his experience of writing *The Old Curiosity Shop* as the crucial reason why he was "sorry in my heart that men who really liked each other should waste life at arm's length". His involvement in his art materially affected his attitude towards life, so that it can be said with some justice that his fiction recreated the world for him even as he was composing it. And yet of course it would be wrong to think of Dickens in this period as some lachrymose bundle of unhappy instincts; quite the contrary. For much of the time he was very merry, even boisterous and signally unsentimental. He mocked Forster's grief at the death of one of Macready's daughters, for example, even as he was "killing" his own child. On Saturday, 2 January, he told an acquaintance that "all next week I shall be laid up with a broken heart" while finishing *The Old Curiosity Shop*, but on the following Monday he is up till five-thirty in the morning dancing and playing charades. There were other parties, too (one of them in honour of his son's birthday), and on New Year's Eve he invited his friends – Cruikshank, Ainsworth and Cattermole among them – to celebrate the turn of the year at Devonshire Terrace. So these states of pity or sorrow are discontinuous but easily recoverable, like the state of creativity itself which he was able to marshal at the appropriate time each morning. His habitual external response to the world is one of quickness and vivacity, his habitual interior temperament one of loss and anxiety; it is in the revolution of these two spheres around each other that we begin to understand why he seemed so odd and so mercurial, even to those who knew him best.

Of course his own grief at the death of Little Nell was matched by the public response. It is always said that the crowds gathered on the harbour front of New York and asked the incoming passengers from across the Atlantic, "Is Little Nell dead?" Given Dickens's popularity in the United States, and Bret Harte's famous poem about the cowboys listening to Little Nell's story in the Wild West, this is not at all unlikely. The response at home was also very encouraging to Dickens; Little Nell was even compared to Cordelia, perhaps the first but certainly not the last occasion when the names of Dickens and Shakespeare were placed together. Lord Jeffrey was found in tears after reading the death scene, and Daniel O'Connell threw the book out of a railway window exclaiming, "He should not have killed her!", a complaint echoed by many others who sent letters to Dickens imploring him to avert that unhappy fate. And perhaps it was a little impolitic of Dickens to send a copy of the closing chapters to Macready, since the actor had lost his own daughter only three months before (an instance of Dickens's curious insensitivity about the effects of his own work upon others). "I dread to read it," Macready wrote in his diary, "but I must get it over." And later: "I never have read printed words that gave me so much pain. I could not weep for some time." Those who have some image of the Victorian male as conventionally and almost gruffly "masculine" may be surprised to discover how easily all these men cried over the fate of a fictional heroine. But it is not so strange. Open displays of feeling were not uncommon; men walked arm-in-arm with each other if they so wished, and the theatres were filled with people who wept without embarrassment. In this period all the evidence suggests, in fact, that open and even violent feeling was seen as an aspect of moral judgment; whether in the popular drama of the period, or even in the style of newspaper reports, there is no doubt that emotion was seen as a testimony to sincerity and not as a vehicle for any kind of self-indulgent sentimentality.

But what was it about the death of Little Nell which provoked such a response – such a significant reaction, in fact, that one later critic described it as "a movement in the history of modern sensibility"? Of course this is an exaggeration, and even at the time not everyone found the death-bed of Little Nell as moving as the author intended. There were many readers who disliked the "sentimentality" of the scene just as much as anyone in the latter part of the nineteenth century. But that it did have a marked effect upon others is not in doubt, and it is as if in the death of the virginal child there were many readers who lamented the death of their own innocence. Some of the feeling aroused might be seen, therefore, as a form of vicarious self-pity, which is surely the most potent form of emotionalism, then and now. But there is more to it than that. Dickens was lamenting the death of a child when the deaths of children in ordinary life were quite familiar; in 1839, for example, almost half of the funerals in London were conducted for children under the age of ten, carried off by sickness or malnutrition. There was of course also the contemporary trade of child prostitution. When we first see Little Nell, this "pretty little girl" is wandering lost through the streets of London, and as Master Humphrey watches over the house in which she lives he is filled with thoughts "of all possible harm that might happen to the child" – no one in 1841 would have had the least doubt that one of her possible fates was that of being forced "upon the streets". So there is a sense in which these Victorians were lamenting the state of the society which they themselves had created. In the death of Little Nell lay the memory of other deaths, and worse fates, and the tears shed over her lifeless body were the luxurious tears of pity at a situation which was of their own making. Yet people also pity the things which cannot harm them and, in the death of Little Nell, there was a threnody for the gentler and more innocent part of themselves which in actual existence had to be discarded in the "struggle" or the "battle of life". The Victorians wept over the very things they were destroying, and perhaps there is a latent cruelty here which is very much like Dickens's own hardness. Innocence *has* to be destroyed in order that civilisation may grow and prosper. In the same way, Dickens *had* to kill Little Nell. If she had lived on she would either have been corrupted or remained a stunted figure like the dwarves she meets upon her journey, even like the malevolent little figure of Quilp himself. She had to die. That is why the religion of work and effort tends always to be accompanied by the religion of death, the cultivation of pain and the worship of sorrow. All these elements are present in *The Old Curiosity Shop*.

Yet illuminated throughout always by Dickens's wild humour, making light of the things that most closely touched him, parodying the very passions he could barely withstand. Above all, too, the sheer joy of invention and of creativity. Many years later – in fact only two years before his death – a friend found him reading the novel once more and "laughing immoderately" because the story of the sad pilgrimage reminded him of the circumstances in which the book was written. He had not forgotten the sorrow he felt when coming close to the death of Little Nell, but that sorrow is subsumed in a larger and more powerful burst of laughter. And at this point, perhaps, it is appropriate to consider the question of Dickens's own sentimentality, since it has often been assumed that the ready emotionalism in his fiction somehow spilled over into his own life. It has been reported that in *The Old Curiosity Shop* someone weeps about every tenth page, and in *Dombey and Son* Florence Dombey is calculated to have broken down in tears on eighty-eight separate occasions. (By the Fifties, however, the fashion for fictional tears somewhat abated and Dickens's characters remain much more firmly dry-eyed in his later books.) But Dickens himself was not inclined to weep, and it may be significant that he tended to shed tears only when reading books or watching action upon the stage. "I invariably begin to cry whenever anybody on the stage forgives an enemy or gives away a pocket book . . ." he once said, suggesting how much theatrical generosity moved him. How much it recalled, perhaps, childhood aspirations and wishes. He was sometimes seen to cry when listening to popular romantic songs, and over the incidents in certain novels. But that is all. One of his colleagues in later life, Edmund Yates, said that "he was in no sense an emotional man", and even though he wept at events on the stage he was not particularly moved by real places or real people. It is significant, for example, that he showed no particular nostalgia for the place of his birth, and we have already seen that when he visited inns he had made famous in *The Pickwick Papers* or elsewhere – inns such as the Angel at Bury St Edmunds or the Great White Horse in Ipswich – those with him remembered that "he seems to have been quite unaffected by any Pickwickian associations". Of course that might just have been because he was heartily sick of Pickwick and all his works, but it is at least another aspect of a temperament which really does seem almost entirely devoid of conventional sentimentality. And why should it not be so? It is his ability to recognise and refine human feeling which makes him so great a novelist.

After he had completed *The Old Curiosity Shop*, at four o'clock on a January morning, there were only a few extra editorial tasks he had to perform on the complete story in order to prepare it for the volume edition; he had to remove certain extraneous material concerning Master Humphrey himself, for example, and in the extra space provided he added a few paragraphs. It is interesting that at this point he adds a remark about the presence of "wild grotesque companions" around Little Nell and obliquely alludes to *The Pilgrim's Progress*; it is clear that both these elements of his art had occurred to him only as he was writing the story. In addition one perceptive reviewer had noticed a few months before the allegorical tendency of the story, and Dickens himself took up the hint by now saying of Little Nell that ". . . she seemed to exist in a kind of allegory". Thus it is that novelists come to understand what they have actually been doing. But once more, at the end of his labours, he found it difficult to break away from the characters he had invented, and can we not see his own reaction to this work completed in his recent description of Sir Christopher Wren regarding St Paul's: "I imagined him far more melancholy than proud, and looking with regret upon his labour done."?

Little time for regret in Dickens's case, however, since at once he turned his attention to that much-delayed story, *Barnaby Rudge*, which he had decided to serialise in *Master Humphrey's Clock* as soon as *The Old Curiosity Shop* had finished its run; it was the best way of maintaining the circulation of the periodical and, of course, the attention of his public. He had already written two chapters at the time of the abortive negotiations with Richard Bentley, and to give himself more room for manoeuvre he now added a few passages which turned the two chapters into three – enough material for two numbers of the magazine. But there were problems and distractions. Catherine was now expecting another child and, once again, she began to suffer from the illness or illnesses which had left her prostrate in the past. Dickens felt compelled to remain at her side, and for forty-eight hours got no sleep at all. There was also the difficulty of turning his mind to *Barnaby Rudge* when he had been so recently exhausted by Little Nell; but a few days later, as he told Forster, "I imaged forth a good deal of *Barnaby* by keeping my mind steadily upon him". He began writing on the twenty-ninth of January, just eight days after finally completing *The Old Curiosity Shop*, and managed to finish a third number of the new story. But he was restless. Even though Catherine was still in acute distress, he had to get out. He had to walk around. He went to see Forster at about ten in the evening, and rapped on his window with his stick; but his friend was out, and instead Dickens went on alone to the Parthenon Club where he met someone else and sat drinking gin and water till three in the morning. A few days later, on 8 February, his second son, Walter, was born; in the census return for this year Dickens described himself in the usual Victorian manner as "Gentleman", and declared that his household at Devonshire Terrace now consisted of one wife, four children, four maid-servants and one man-servant. He had come a long way from the Marshalsea.

At the end of the month the family went down to Brighton, largely in order to enable Dickens to work undisturbed on the new novel, and remained there for a week. On his return to London he suffered a small private loss. His pet raven, Grip, had died. He had always been fascinated by the bird, and followed its antics closely – comparing its clumsy run to that of a "playful cow", for example, in one of his touches of exact observation. The death provoked a series of facetious letters to his friends, wherein Dickens expatiates upon the life and death of the bird: "On the clock striking twelve he appeared slightly agitated, but he soon recovered, walked twice or thrice along the coach-house, stopped to bark, staggered, exclaimed 'Halloa old girl' (his favourite expression) and died. He behaved throughout with a decent fortitude, equanimity, and self-possession, which cannot be too much admired." And so on and so forth; facetiousness was Dickens's one besetting vice. But there were also domestic affairs of a more troublesome kind. His family were still a burden upon him and would remain so for the rest of his life; he had just written a letter of recommendation for his brother, Alfred, who wished to begin a career in New Zealand as an engineer (he was in fact the only Dickens brother who made any kind of name for himself). But the real problem was with his father, since it was only now that Dickens realised that John Dickens had not only been continuing his wastrel ways in Devon but had also been forging his son's name, or using his son's name as a guarantor for certain debts. It is not difficult to imagine Dickens's reaction to this news; he had sent him down to Alphington precisely in order to avert this kind of fecklessness, but the terrible shadow of his parents – first glimpsed when they consigned him to the blacking factory so many years before – now once more threatened him. He took swift action, and placed an advertisement in all the leading London newspapers that "certain persons bearing, or purporting to bear, the surname of our said client" had been obtaining credit, and that Charles Dickens would not be responsible for any debts so incurred. It was the most public manner he could possibly contrive to distance himself from his father. He refused to speak to him personally, and demanded through his solicitors that John Dickens should leave England altogether and reside on a fixed stipend on the continent. In fact John Dickens, for reasons unknown, continued to live in Alphington with his wife but the whole episode only served further to deepen the antagonism between father and son.

So it is not very surprising that the early episodes of *Barnaby Rudge*, upon which he now set to work again, should themselves be animated by conflicts between fathers and sons, and that the theme of filial rebellion is central to the development of the entire novel. Significant, too, that the men who do most to ignore or abuse or distrust their sons – Chester and Willet – both have the Christian name of John. And there is anger in the sons, an anger that seems at least consonant with Dickens's own injured feelings – just as there is a connection, too, between the reports of madness which so infuriated Dickens and his creation here of the mad Barnaby whose imaginings are so much more interesting than the stolid or civilised orthodoxies of the people by whom he is surrounded. It is curious, perhaps, how Dickens suggests that Barnaby carries a curse which he has inherited from his father; did he believe, in turn, that John Dickens had bequeathed some fatality to his own children, even if it was only the fatality of financial reckless-ness? Of course this is not to say that the incidents of Dickens's emotional life have a direct bearing upon the novel he was even then creating, but rather that they are the atmosphere in which his writing develops. They are the clouds that bring rain. So when a notably unnatural father, John Chester, remarks that "the relationship be-tween father and son, you know, is positively quite a holy kind of bond . . ." it is important to realise that Dickens was expressing such ironic sentiments at a time when he was alienated from the behaviour of his own father. Dickens is not attempting directly to use his own experience, or even necessarily directly remembering it; the point is that he takes what in other hands might be a wholly private theme and makes it much larger, transforms it into the emblem of a much more general dislocation of authority.

Of course the novel had been with him now for five years, ever since he had first contracted to write it, and there is no doubt that its major public theme – the civil riots of 1780 – was one which continued to fascinate him. Much of the research had already been done; he had read the main historical narratives, and had even ranged further afield in the quest for accuracy and detail. His copy of Waterton's *Essays on Natural History* has pencil marks beside the chapter on ravens. But although *Barnaby Rudge* is an "historical novel" it is one, which, like all good historical novels, is actually concerned with its own time. His interest in the London mob which had rampaged through the streets of London and set fire to Newgate Prison, for example, must have been considerably increased by the fact that now in his own period Chartism and the Chartists seemed about to provoke civil rebellion of a similar kind. It must be remembered that the passage of the Reform Act in 1832 had not appreciably affected the vast body of wage-earners, who remained underpaid and unrepresented. 1837 had been a year of severe depression, not really alleviated until the end of the decade, and it was in such a climate that the disillusionment over the political reforms of 1832 emerged in the demands of "the Charter" – demands which included universal male suffrage, the secret ballot, the payment of Members of Parliament, the abolition of the property qualification for Members of Parliament, equal constituencies and annual elections. But these demands were in turn fuelled by popular hatred of the New Poor Laws, and by increasing public clamour for factory reform. Dickens clearly sympathised with the thrust of working-class grievances in regard to those last two elements, if not to the parliamentary demands, and it is equally clear that in his fiction he was attempting to put the case of those who felt themselves to have been actively neglected by "the system" in these recent difficult years. That is no doubt why extracts from *Nicholas Nickleby* had been reprinted in a Chartist magazine for working men, the *Penny Gazette of Variety and Amusement*. But that was as far as it went. The portrait of the mob and of poor apprentices in *Barnaby Rudge* was by no means a flattering one; the point was that, although Dickens understood the grievances of those at the rough end of this new industrial age, he never sympathised with those who tried to create a revolutionary movement in England. He disliked the "physical force" Chartists and despised those who tried to exploit the genuine grievances of the working-class for their own ends – typically in *Nicholas Nickleby* he had pitied the individual children at Dotheboys Hall but found them repulsive when they engineered an uprising *en masse*. He describes them in revolt as ". . . the malicious crowd, whose faces were clustered together in every variety of lank and half-starved ugliness . . ." Dickens can pity individuals and individual suffering, just as he can sympathise with criminals when they become quintessential victims of society; but he changes his attitude when such individuals are grouped together in a crowd, or "mob", because it is precisely at that point they cease to be an image of himself. In that sense Bagehot's description of him as a "sentimental radical" was a correct one, and there is no indication that in this period of Chartist insurrection – the Convention in London was followed by the battles of Birmingham in May 1839 and the Newport uprising in November – Dickens played anything but the part of a concerned spectator who did not feel himself to be actively engaged in any of the popular credos of the moment. Nevertheless, in dealing with the Gordon Riots of 1780, Dickens was able to introduce quite contemporary anxieties about the possibilities of Chartist insurrection and mob rule. The political conditions of this period were such that the ultra-Tories were aligned with the "physical force" Chartists in their dislike of the Whig government, and it was these Tories themselves who used the cry of "No popery" in particular in order to lend credence to their attacks upon the government. There had even been a Protestant Association formed in 1839 in direct imitation of Lord George Gordon's own association. Not for the first time did Dickens find a range of contemporary references which would give his story the immediacy which it needed in its weekly format.

And yet, even though he attacked those who would tear down lawful authority, he takes delight in the anarchy of the scenes he portrays; he is there with the eighteenth-century mob, running amok, burning, destroying, exulting in the savage festivals of chaos which he describes. The sources of that fascination come essentially from his own double nature. His experience of the "mob" at the Courvoisier hanging had shown him directly what he already knew from his own life in London – that the populace, left unchecked, could be a fearsome thing. Yet he started working once more on *Barnaby Rudge* at a time when his non-revolutionary but "radical" instincts were stronger than ever. In the summer of this year the Tories were returned to power under the leadership of Peel, and throughout this period Dickens attacked them as "people whom, politically, I despise and abhor". He gave further expression to these sentiments in a number of small items which were published anonymously by Forster in the *Examiner* – the most notable being a verse parody, "The Fine Old English Gentleman", in which Dickens attacks the prevailing worship of authority and the "good old days" before Reform. In fact, just before he began to work upon *Barnaby Rudge* in earnest, he imagined himself in the position of "a poor labouring man" who sees in the windows of booksellers certain aristocratic pufferies such as *Portraits of the Nobility* – ". . . I should think of my own children and the no-regard they had for anybody, and be a greater Radical than ever". So there is a part of him that swayed with the revolutionary mob; he even made it clear that if Wat Tyler and his followers had been able to burn down London "I should still entertain some respect for their memory". Yet even now at the height of his disgust with the political situation, when he half-humorously suggested emigration as the only possible answer to a Tory government, he declared, "I wonder, if I went to a new colony with my head, hands, legs, and health, I should force myself to the top of the social milk-pot and live upon the cream! . . . Upon my word I believe I should." Sentiments which suggest that it would be unwise to think of Dickens's radicalism as in any sense egalitarian. He feared lawlessness but understood the motives of those who rose up against authority, and this Janus-like attitude towards society enters *Barnaby Rudge* in a direct way, just as his own troubled relationship with his father lends further depth to his presentation of a world in which most forms of lawful authority are corrupt or corrupting. In which the great secret desire is the breaking of all locks, all chains, all forms of social or domestic servitude. His imaginative sympathy is with the rioters and with the poor mad boy, Barnaby Rudge, so like Dickens himself in his eagerness and restlessness, but it also ought not to be forgotten that the real hero of the novel – and the one after whom it was once to be called – is Gabriel Varden, the locksmith, the man who constructs the great locks which enclose the prisoners.

As the story gradually took possession of him, he began his wanderings through London "searching for some pictures I wanted to build upon". He had always been interested in the historical essence of London, that deeply imbued spirit of dirt and misery with which he could bind his own past to that of the city itself, and in these first weeks of composing *Barnaby Rudge* he visited "the most wretched and distressful streets" to find images which could move him. He also went to see in prison a certain William Jones who had been charged with unlawfully entering Buckingham Palace and who was generally considered to be of "unsound mind"; on Dickens's visit, no doubt, he was unwittingly posing for Barnaby. In fact he entered gaols on at least two occasions in one week – another visit was to see a tailor, whose wits were considered to be "ricketty" and who once again might stand in for Barnaby as Dickens closely watched him. Watching as his own imagined character comes alive in front of him. (It ought to be pointed out, however, that Dickens was never merely the spectator extracting vicarious interest from the sufferings of others; part of his ethic was one of active helpfulness in the world and, after seeing the imprisoned tailor, he sent him money and clothes.) But to all these scenes and characters he imparts a dream-like quality, London itself becoming "a mere dark mist – a giant phantom in the air". The narrative itself is marked by references to ghosts, dreams, phantoms, as if Dickens's own private material was so deeply implicated in the unfolding of the story that he wished to keep it somewhat remote, occluded, apart from himself. Private dreams and public hallucinations come together, therefore, as Dickens continued to compose the story which had been with him so long; a proper *novel* this time, far more carefully planned than any of its predecessors, a novel that with its historical sweep might rival comparison with the works of Scott and which in its depiction of the revolutionary mob would be an attempt to create a quite new effect in English fiction.

After he had completed the first three numbers he stopped for a week – he felt "lazy", he said – but then once more he began work upon it in earnest. There could never be any real repose for him. In any case the life of London never pressed so heavily upon him as when he was trying to write; there were constant dinners or gatherings and constant attempts to enlist him in the service of one cause or another. It was now, for example, that he was offered the candidature of MP for Reading, an offer he declined principally on the grounds that he could not afford the expense of running for parliament. In the meantime he busied himself with a project for establishing a Sanatorium for the middle-classes, on a subscription basis. Such duties occupied too much of his time, however, and there is no doubt that he was both depressed (he admitted as much) and desperate to get away. So once more his thoughts turned to Broadstairs, and he opened negotiations for the rental of another house there for the summer; in the meantime he took up an invitation which had been proffered to him during the spring, a proposal that he should visit Edinburgh in order to be publicly welcomed and entertained there. He wrote back to a Scottish friend, ". . . I would not for the world reject any compliments they, or any of them, sought to offer me. Therefore I say, stop *nothing* . . ." in the way of dinners or ceremonies. He was also thinking of Catherine, whose native home was Scotland, and plans were quickly made for a visit of some three or four weeks. Once he had made the arrangements he was, as usual, very anxious to put them into effect as quickly as possible. ". . . I am on the highest crag of expectation," he wrote – while all the time composing as much as he could of *Barnaby Rudge* before he went away. And indeed he was working very fast upon it; at the beginning of June he finished four chapters within six days, on average about 2,300 words a day.

On 19 June he and Catherine left for Scotland, a journey both by the new railway and by road which took some three days. The first engagement of this tour was a public dinner to be given in his honour in Edinburgh which, as he said many years later, was "the first public recognition and encouragement I ever received . . ." It was in fact a striking occasion, one spectator noticing this "little, slender pale-faced, boyish-looking individual" arriving in the Waterloo Rooms to an extraordinary reception: "I felt as if the tremendous cheering which accompanied his entrance would overwhelm him." Another guest noticed his "cheeks shaven like those of a comedian, black stock surmounted by no collar, in accordance with the fashion of the day, elaborate shirt front and general showy get-up". He dined at the top table, raised upon a platform, and himself noticed how odd it was that so young a man should be surrounded by so many elderly worthies who had come to honour him; "I felt it was very remarkable to see such a number of grey-headed men gathered about my brown flowing locks." Here was the man who had written *The Pickwick Papers*, *Nicholas Nickleby*, *Oliver Twist*, *The Old Curiosity Shop*; and he was not yet thirty years old. After the dinner was completed, Catherine Dickens and the other ladies arrived in the gallery to hear the speeches. Professor John Wilson, a remarkable writer under the name of Christopher North, rose to propose Dickens's health by saying that they had come "to honour one that has outstripped them all in the race", a sentiment which led to "great cheering", according to the newspaper reports; Wilson went on to talk of Dickens's "genius" and of his being "perhaps the most popular writer now alive". Again, how remarkable in a young man not yet thirty. When Dickens rose to reply "there was", according to a spectator, "silence deep as in the tomb". He began: "If I felt your warm and generous welcome less, I should be better able to thank you . . ." and the same spectator noted that "from the commencement to the end [Dickens] never hesitated a moment or misplaced a word". This was the extraordinary thing, this self-possession, as if all the cheering and acclamation which greeted him were perfectly natural. It was as if he had been preparing for this success all his life, as if it were his birthright, and it was noticed that he remained "calm as if speaking to an amanuensis". Dickens recognised this trait in himself with approval – "notwithstanding the enthoosemoosy, which was very startling," he wrote to Forster the next day, he remained "as cool as a cucumber". This was always his way: to pretend not to be moved by the praise of others even though everything about him – his manner, his "general showy get-up" – proclaimed a young man who knew exactly how far he had come and how prominent he was. He had once said that he played his modest role simply in order to avoid envy, and indeed even in his speech to the citizens of Edinburgh he adopted the tones of a young man not spoiled by success and humbly grateful for the chance of adding a little to the "stock of harmless cheerfulness". That he did feel something of this is not in doubt, but there was also an inward tone of exultation which he displayed only in letters to his friends – "It was the most brilliant affair you can conceive . . ."

In fact there was a sense in which he was now becoming public property. He was given the Freedom of the City of Edinburgh and when he made a chance entry into one of the theatres there "the whole audience rose spontaneously in recognition of him, the musicians in the orchestra, with a courtly felicity, striking up the cavalier air of 'Charley Is My Darling'". And yet, even as he wrote of his success, he wanted to return to the familiar ways of home and his friends. "For God's sake be in waiting," he told Forster when he mentioned the longed-for date of his return to Devonshire Terrace, yet another indication of the way in which Dickens craved for the comfort of what was essentially his extended family. One senses here in "For God's sake" his terrible appetite for affection even at this time of triumph. A time when he attended dinners and various receptions or parties in Edinburgh. A time for playing the part of the famous author. But no time for some things: it is odd that he did not bother to accompany Catherine when she visited the Edinburgh house in which she was born.

On 4 July they left the city for a ten-day journey through the Highlands, their guide and companion on this trip being Angus Fletcher, a Scottish sculptor who had completed a bust of Dickens two years before and whose somewhat eccentric manner had endeared him to the novelist. He had even stayed with them at Broadstairs where his peculiarities – on one occasion advancing naked into the sea in front of the horrified populace – were sometimes embarrassing but had always provided Dickens with what he called a "store" of anecdotes. He was precipitate, loud, ungainly and even uncouth but with a curiously innocent unawareness of his own eccentricity which appealed to the novelist who specialised in characters who lacked self-knowledge. In the Highlands, however, Fletcher's peculiarities were something of an advantage since it was he who seems to have dealt with the crofters, and the keepers of inns, on what was on occasions an exhausting and even dangerous journey. The route took them from Edinburgh to Melrose via Stirling, Glencoe, Ballachulish, Inveraray and Glasgow, an ellipsoid track that passed through ravines and mountain passes, across rocks and torrents – the whole panoply of nature assuming in Dickens's descriptions the fervent and tempestuous shape of his own imagination as he looked in wonder at the kind of landscape he had never before seen. In particular he enjoyed the horrors of Glencoe – ". . . perfectly *terrible*. The pass is an awful place. It is shut in on each side by enormous rocks from which great torrents come rushing down in all directions . . . such haunts as you might imagine yourself wandering in, in the very height and madness of a fever. They will live in my dreams for years . . ." In fact he exulted in the awfulness of the place, and was glad to be able to revisit it on the following day when they were forced to retrace their steps. Dickens always loved the wilder qualities of landscape – the mountains, the volcanoes, the ravines and the deserts – as if it were only in them that he could find any real confirmation of his own imaginings. Certainly he was now contemplating the riots which were just about to begin in *Barnaby Rudge*, and there is some consonance of inner and outer moods when he describes how in Glencoe ". . . torrents were boiling and foaming, and sending up in every direction spray like the smoke of great fires. They were rushing down every hill and mountain side, and tearing like devils across the path, and down into the depths of the rocks." Fire. Devils. Rushing. He might have been describing the rioters in the streets of eighteenth-century London. "As to the Riot," he had written a few days before he left for Scotland, "I am going to try if I can't make a better one than he [Gordon] did." And so he sees the scenes of his imagination everywhere, the shape of old London glowing through the mists of Glencoe as he travels onward. Onwards but also backwards. Backwards through time. As soon as he returned from the Highlands to Edinburgh he spent the whole day at the house of Sir Walter Scott, Abbotsford, and while there pondered over the dead novelist's "old white hat, which seemed to be tumbled and bent and broken by the uneasy, purposeless wandering hither and thither of his heavy head". And in that sad relic Dickens saw an emblem of "broken powers and mental weakness". Scott, who was in part the inspiration of *Barnaby Rudge*, also became for Dickens an example of what can happen to a novelist who writes too much, who never rests. It was a warning which, as we shall see, was never far from his mind in the months to come.

But, as soon as he returned to London in the middle of July, he at once began work on those scenes of riot he might have seen in the very rocks of Glencoe; he was writing very quickly, and managed to finish six chapters in twelve days before setting off for Broadstairs with the family. Once again his friends were invited to come and stay with them and, in a curious letter to Maclise, Dickens intimates that the painter might like to favour the prostitutes of Margate – "I know where they live". He himself confined his attentions to *Barnaby Rudge*. "I am in great heart and spirits with the story," he said, although this may have been just his own way of cheering himself up: he knew by now that the sales of *Master Humphrey's Clock* with the new novel had fallen markedly since the end of *The Old Curiosity Shop*, and were now running at something like 30,000 a week. In addition the magazine itself was so expensive to produce that there were still no real profits at all. That is no doubt why Chapman and Hall, publishers who had been signally generous to Dickens, were keen to discuss with him the possibility of a new novel, to be published in monthly parts and to begin in the spring of the following year; they knew that large sales, at least, could be expected from the old and tested formula. Dickens came up to London to discuss the matter with Forster; he was early as usual and, walking around Lincoln's Inn Fields, where Forster lived, he was suddenly seized by something which seems part inspiration and part fear. He recalled the image of a feeble and broken Scott, rendered so vivid to him a few weeks before, and realised that it was a fate which might conceivably be visited upon him: he seems always, in fact, to have had an irrational fear of incapacity, of going "dry". He had now been continually before the public for five years. He may even have considered the possibility that the low sale of *Barnaby Rudge* owed something to his own fatigue or over-familiarity. Whatever the cause, he decided there and then that it was time "to *stop* – to write no more, not one word, for a whole year – and then to come out with a complete story in three volumes . . . and put the town in a blaze again". Of course the three-volume novel would be for him, at least, quite a new form: and almost at once the prospect invigorated Dickens. He explained his proposals to Forster who, acting as Dickens's intermediary even when Dickens was present, explained the plan to Chapman and Hall over dinner. The publishers were astonished, not least because Dickens wanted his year "off" to be financed in advance by them, even though he already owed them three thousand pounds over the purchase of his copyrights and contracts from Richard Bentley; but Dickens's will was not one that was easily brooked, and eventually, after some discussion, they agreed to the new proposals. They would pay Dickens another eighteen hundred pounds, in order to finance his year of idleness, and he would reward them with a story the following spring (in fact he realised soon after that it would be easier for him to revert to the old monthly numbers, written as the months went by, rather than compose a three-volume novel which would necessarily have to be completed during the preceding year). In other words, he had purchased a temporary freedom from his responsibilities but only at the cost of leaving himself heavily in debt to Chapman and Hall. But he was elated by that prospect of freedom, and went back to Broadstairs in something like a "holiday" mood even though he was still in the middle of writing *Barnaby Rudge*. "I have just burnt into Newgate," he told Forster – of that point in the narrative when the rioters storm the great prison – and then, a week later, "I have let all the prisoners out of Newgate . . . I feel quite smoky when I am at work." And no doubt his smokiness was increased by this sudden burst of vicarious radical anger. At times like these he *becomes* the rioters, and the scenes of burning London in the novel are some of the most extraordinary in all of his fiction. One can sense behind them the eagerness of Dickens's research as if in his pursuit of the past he were also pursuing the secrets of his own mysterious self, just as one can sense in his furious prose the alacrity of his own long walks along the London thoroughfares which in his imagination were bathed in blood red. Already he had the close of the story in mind, and was sending off instructions to George Cattermole for the illustrations which he was preparing. And yet, and yet . . . the prospect of a year's idleness was beginning to affect him; he was, he said, becoming "hideously lazy" and was only just finishing each instalment of *Barnaby Rudge* in time for the printer.

He was becoming preoccupied, too, with other matters since, for some time past, he had been revolving in his mind the idea of visiting America. Originally he had the idea of writing a series of essays for *Master Humphrey's Clock*, or perhaps a little book, on the subject of travels there; there were in these years no end of studies of American life by various English worthies, but no doubt Dickens thought that he might supply something of a novelty for that particular market. The idea had remained with him, and a fulsome letter of tribute from the American writer, Washington Irving, seems to have been the deciding factor – Irving told him that ". . . if I went, it would be such a triumph from one end of the States to the other, as was never known in any Nation". And it is possible that his present fierce "Radicalism" while writing *Barnaby Rudge* also played a part in his decision. Would he not be visiting a country which remained untainted by all the Tory tricks and unhampered by any aristocratic burdens? He would, in a sense, be visiting a country which was very much like himself; which had risen unimpeded from all the trials of circumstance. Once he had conceived the plan, characteristically nothing would shake him from it. He was, he told Forster, "haunted by visions of America . . ."; but there were problems, chief among them being Catherine who did not want to go, and who certainly did not want to leave the children behind. Walter, after all, was a still only a baby of nine months. She "cries dismally" every time Dickens mentioned the subject. But he was not a man to let family considerations stand in his way and by the nineteenth of September, only six days after he had broached the plan with Forster, he had finally decided to go. At once he fell into the "stir and bustle of anticipation" which always preceded the enactment of any plans he made; "he was in his usual fever," Forster wrote, "until its difficulties were disposed of." The major difficulty, at this juncture, still being Catherine. She still remained to be convinced, and he asked Macready, who had travelled to America on just such a tour as he was planning, to write to her and to reassure her. Dickens was still not sure if he should take the children, and all these preliminary problems "to a gentleman of my temperament, destroy rest, sleep, appetite, and work, unless definitely arranged". Somehow or other, Catherine was brought round to agreement; no doubt Dickens's own fevered impatience and impetuosity carried her in the direction she did not really want to travel. For in his own mind the trip had become "a matter of imperative necessity" and not even the tears of his wife could affect it. It was agreed that the children should remain in London, under the care of his brother, Fred, and that Anne Brown, Catherine's maid, should accompany her across the Atlantic. In fact Catherine was eventually able to face the prospect with more equanimity, although even now Dickens did not tell her precisely how long they would be away. Perhaps this was because there were times when she was still uneasy – "I have seen her *looking* (very hard) at the Sea, but she has *said* nothing." It should be noted at this point that it was he who persuaded her to leave behind the children, despite the insinuations he would make against his wife in later and more troubled years. But, even as he was impatiently making his plans for America, he was in his imagination anticipating his return from that country to the delights of home and the arms of his friends. He told Forster at the end of September, three months even before he sailed, "I am already counting the days between this and coming home again." How *odd*, as his friends would no doubt have said.

Just before finally returning to London from Broadstairs, he set off for a short visit to Rochester with Forster and Catherine but, while there, began to feel the agonising pains which heralded the onset of a fistula – a gap in the rectal wall through which tissue had been forced. He had suffered from rectal pains just recently, ascribing them to the fact that he spent much of his day sitting at his desk, and seems to be recollecting them in a short passage of *Barnaby Rudge* which he wrote in Broadstairs, where the sleeper's consciousness of pain is described as "a phantom without shape, or form, or visible presence; pervading everything . . ." The pain had now grown worse; he went back to London with Catherine, and three or four days later endured an operation at the hands of Frederick Salmon, a surgeon famous for his work in that area of the human body: thirteen years before he had published *A Practical Essay on Stricture of the Rectum*. The fact that he was in capable and experienced hands did not of course minimise the pain of the operation. The rectum would have been opened up, and then held apart by some kind of surgical appliance, while the tissue was cut away and the sides of the rectal wall then sewn together. And this difficult operation was performed without any anaesthetic at all. It sounds almost unbearable and, when Dickens described it to Macready, Macready wrote that "I suffered *agonies* as they related all to me, and did violence to myself in keeping myself to my seat. I could scarcely bear it." And yet, having consciously suffered the cutting of his flesh by the knife, Dickens seemed remarkably cheerful and even active. It was true that he could not walk about, and was compelled to lie upon the sofa to write the always pressing instalments of *Barnaby Rudge*, but the fact that he could write at all only days after such torture is proof of his extraordinary energy and powers of revival. "Never *say* die," he wrote to the working man, John Overs, whom he had befriended, and that philosophy of cheerfulness and activity is one that served him well. He was writing the last chapters of the novel in great pain of course, and yet it is precisely in these chapters that all the comedy breaks through again – in particular the comedy of Miss Miggs, the appalling maid of acid visage, whose hypocritical holiness was always one of Dickens's favourite subjects. And something else happened, too, as he wrote. "I don't invent it – really do not – *but see it*, and write it down . . ." and it is in this act of seeing that his pain abates, to return only when he has finished his writing.

It was nevertheless hard to keep his mind fully upon the task. He had to dictate letters to Catherine, not being well enough to answer them for himself, and then in the midst of this physical trouble, with all the stir and anticipation of America upon him, Catherine's brother died and, according to his wishes, was to be buried in Mary Hogarth's grave. This was the place which Dickens had always wanted to reserve for himself, and the death of George Hogarth seems to have revived those earlier experiences of loss and weariness. "It seems," he wrote, "like losing her a second time." So it is not perhaps surprising that he now finished *Barnaby Rudge*, the novel conceived so many years before, on a slightly weary and mechanical note. As soon as he had completed it, he went to Windsor with Catherine in order properly to recuperate; here he suffered from various small pains and "an odd sort of nervousness", but they soon passed. He dictated the preface for the novel to Catherine; *Master Humphrey's Clock*, the vehicle for *The Old Curiosity Shop* and *Barnaby Rudge*, was wound up at last.

In fact he seems to have finished the latter with less emotion than any of his other novels, and there is a sense in which at the end it became almost a distraction from the pursuit of his American adventure. Certainly all his most pressing activities were directed to that end. In preparation for his journey he insured his life with the Eagle Insurance Company for five thousand pounds, and by what appears to be curious chance let his house in Devonshire Terrace to a director of that company for the duration of his absence. He took lodgings for Fred and the children in Osnaburgh Street, which had the advantage of being close to the Macreadys who had promised to superintend his brother's care of them. It was at this time, too, that Catherine's younger sister, Georgina, was brought in to help with the children as well; Georgina was then fifteen years old, bright, attentive, and what might be described as a "quick study". In fact the move from the familial atmosphere of the Hogarths to the more bright and bracing climate of the Dickens ménage appealed to her, and it was not long before she became an integral part of that household.

Dickens, meanwhile, was assiduously studying for his trip. He had something like twenty-seven different American guide books and, when he was interviewed by an American journalist some weeks before his departure, the reporter noticed that "his study was piled with Marryat's, Trollope's, Fidler's, Hall's, and other travels and descriptions of America, and blazed with highly-coloured maps of the United States . . ." Of these bright maps the novelist made a typically Dickensian remark: "I could," he said, "light my cigar against the red-hot State of Ohio." Nevertheless the last month of 1841, the month before the departure of Dickens and his wife, was a very quiet one. He had finished the novel, of course, and now dined out with friends and relatives. The last week in particular he wished to spend with his children, who would not see their parents for another six months, but he also paid farewell calls upon Macready and Miss Burdett-Coutts. These must have been difficult interviews for him because he had a rooted distaste for saying "Goodbye" to anyone, even those closest to him; this may have been part of his own emotional reserve on the most deeply felt occasions but it suggests, also, that fear of estrangement and separation which he had experienced so deeply in his younger days.

Then on the second day of the new year, 1842, in company with Forster, together with Dickens's siblings Alfred and Fanny, Charles and Catherine Dickens left London for Liverpool. According to Dickens, Catherine was now "in glorious spirits", despite the fact that she was suffering from intermittent toothache, and Forster corroborates her good humour; he told Maclise that he "never saw anything better" than her cheerfulness. They were to sail on the *Britannia*, a steamship of some 1,154 tons and capable of carrying 115 passengers. The great advantage of the steamship was, for Dickens, of course its *speed* but the first ship powered by that means had crossed the Atlantic only four years before and this modern form of transportation had its dangers. To cross the Atlantic in stormy January, too, posed something of a risk – as Dickens was soon to discover – but as usual he wanted to leave as early, and travel as quickly, as possible. In fact he was not at first impressed by the ship; its size in particular seems to have discomfited him and he described his cabin as too small to take in even their portmanteaux. "The pillows are no thicker than crumpets" and his bed was like "a muffin, beaten flat". Forster himself described Dickens's "indescribably comic shadow of momentary bafflement and discomfiture" when he saw this tiny room where he was to spend the next two weeks, but noticed how quickly his animal powers of humour revived at the absurdity of it. Dickens laughed so much, as Dickens himself said, that "you might have heard me all over the ship" – suggesting, perhaps, the idea of Dickens filling and dominating any space in which he found himself. He went on shore a little while before departure, leaving Catherine and Anne Brown upon the ship. He returned on the last packet-boat, apparently, according to a fellow passenger, "slightly drunk"; he disembarked and, as Forster and his family rowed away and cheered, "the now passive object of this fugitive homage but faintly responded by now and then raising his right hand out of his overcoat pocket in a somewhat abstract manner, clearly indicating that his interest in the proceedings was measurably diminished". In *American Notes*, however, the book about his travels which even now he was contemplating, Dickens conjures up a more animated scene. "Three cheers more: and as the first one rings upon our ears, the vessel throbs like a strong giant that has just received the breath of life; the two great wheels turn fiercely round for the first time; and the noble ship, with wind and tide astern, breaks proudly through the lashed and foaming water." Charles Dickens was on his way to America.

Chapter 13

IT was not an easy journey. A fellow traveller made a sketch of
Dickens on the deck of the *Britannia*; he seems to be wearing some
kind of cap and his hands are plunged deep into the pocket of his
overcoat; he looks somewhat woebegone. And well he might. He
always suffered greatly from sea-sickness, until in later life he
literally willed himself to withstand its effects, and for the first two
days he stayed in his cabin. The sea remained rough and then, five days
out, the little steamship was caught up in a mighty storm – "Picture
the sky both dark and wild, and the clouds, in fearful sympathy with
the waves, making another ocean in the air." This is from Dickens's
own account in *American Notes*, and he went on to say of the *Britannia*,
". . . she stops, and staggers, and shivers, as though stunned, and
then, with a violent throbbing at her heart, darts onwards like a
monster goaded into madness, to be beaten down, and battered, and
crushed, and leaped on by the angry sea . . ." Perhaps these passages
owe something to his own childhood reading of travellers' adventures
but, even though other passengers' recollections of the same journey
are not so fearsome, there is no doubt that there was a terrible storm
which might, just might, have killed them. Catherine "was nearly
distracted with terror", as she herself wrote, "and don't know what I
should have done had it not been for the great kindness and composure
of my dear Charles". It is odd here for a wife to mention the "great
kindness" of her husband as if in some sense they remained strangers,
but the rest is true enough; on other occasions, as this history will
show, he generally found the strength to remain composed at times of
crisis. This is not to suggest that he was inwardly collected, however;
all his life he had a nervous dread of fire, and in particular he now
feared a conflagration upon the ship if by any chance its chimney
should crumble in the heavy seas. Such were his fears, in fact, that

he decided to travel by sail rather than steam on the homeward trip.

Yet everything in his account in *American Notes* suggests that he was the epitome of sociability, the soul of conviviality, on this Atlantic crossing. Another passenger, who wrote his own memoir of the journey, suggests quite the opposite, however, and remarks that Dickens was noted by all the passengers for his "reserve"; he spoke to three or four chosen companions, and that was all. As so often in his life the sentiment of the thing, rather than the thing itself, captures his imagination: he feels he ought to have been jolly, almost Pickwickian, on his travels, and this is what he remembers; while in fact other people noticed only his oddness or taciturnity. While on the *Britannia* he spent much of his time reading (he had taken with him a collection of stories known as "The Child's Fairy Library") and he liked to patrol the deck at night as others slept. He generally wore a pea-coat of some coarse-haired dark brown material, a pair of steel-grey trousers striped, as was then the fashion, with black along the outer seams, and cork-soled boots for the slippery deck. "Imagine this traveller," his fellow voyager, Pierre Morand, wrote, "quietly standing or strolling about with both hands in his pea-coat pockets, and the slight stoop peculiar to most men of thought." Catherine was the more sociable of the two, it seems, holding informal levées, trying "to make herself as agreeable as possible while he sought fresh air in another direction". In fact there seem to have been many occasions when she was the pleasant and cheerful party, her famous husband going off on his own account and not bothering particularly to entertain or impress his fellow passengers. But Morand also noted that, despite Dickens's reserve, "nothing escaped his unobtrusive, yet watchful eye". In fact Morand was saved from "card sharks" by Dickens. The incident is worth recalling for the light it throws upon Dickens's manner in the world – he stopped Morand playing cards "with a soft but significant touch upon my right shoulder . . . a pair of large and wonderfully eloquent eyes beckoning me to come away. Comprehending the situation, I quietly rose under some pretext and took a walk on deck, where Mr Dickens made his appearance an hour later, apparently unconscious of my presence. Seeing me approach he waived the formality of my expression of gratitude with a sweeping gesture, merely inquiring whether I meant to play again in that company." Then he gave "a brief injunction of secrecy regarding his intervention" and "gently bowed himself away". And there we see the man in front of us: watchful, reserved, somewhat isolated, even as his own accounts of the journey are filled with animation and a propensity for vivacious exaggeration.

On the nineteenth of January the *Britannia*, approaching land at last, suddenly ran aground upon a mud bank; it was clear that the winds or the pilot had steered them in a false direction but Captain Hewitt, whose nautical common sense seems to have impressed Dickens mightily (with sailors, as with detectives or prison governors, he admired any kind of technical proficiency and expertise), knew where they had struck and after a night of great confusion safely steered the vessel into the harbour at Halifax. Now came Dickens's first taste of his fame on the other side of ocean. A man came aboard ship, calling out Dickens's name, and as soon as he found the novelist he announced himself to be the Speaker of the local assembly and dragged Dickens off to attend a meeting of that sovereign body. "I wish you could have seen the crowds cheering the inimitable in the streets," Dickens wrote to Forster – for the first time using that self-description, "the inimitable", as if his reception in Canada and America now somehow justified it. "I wish you could have seen judges, law-officers, bishops, and law-makers welcoming the inimitable." Then from Halifax they sailed further south, along the coastline of the north-eastern States, a New World indeed to Dickens, and in *American Notes* he remembered the ". . . indescribable interest with which I strained my eyes, as the first patches of American soil peeped like molehills from the green sea . . ." Then, on the twenty-second of January, the steamship sailed into Boston Harbour.

As soon as the *Britannia* had reached its berth a group of Boston editors and journalists rushed on board in order to see and to interview Dickens; he was still dressed in his pea-coat and, when Catherine gently remonstrated with him about changing clothes, he replied that such formalities did not matter now that they had reached "the other side". At once he was grabbed, his hand shaken, his comments taken down, his appearance scrutinised, until he could be rescued by Francis Alexander, an artist for whom Dickens had agreed to sit, and taken to the Tremont House Hotel. One of the many people waiting to see and to greet him noticed how he "flew up the steps of the hotel, and sprang into the hall. He seemed all on fire with curiosity, and alive as I never saw mortal before." Then, when he entered the lobby, he greeted the curious bystanders with the old pantomime phrase: "Here we are!" He dined that evening in the hotel with the Earl of Mulgrave, who had also been a passenger on the *Britannia*, and then at about midnight on a bright cold night he went out with him into the streets of Boston. A boy, who was later to become a great friend of Dickens, James Fields, was one among a number of people who watched and followed Dickens in his first visit to the town; he records how he was "muffled up in a shaggy fur coat" and "ran over the shining frozen snow . . . Dickens kept up one continual shout of uproarious laughter as he went rapidly forward, reading the signs on the shops, and observing the 'architecture' of the new country into which he had dropped as if from the clouds." And indeed he might have come from some other world, so familiar and yet so strange was this new country to him: it is a curious fact, confirmed by other English visitors, that America at first seemed too bright, too vivid, and almost artificial in its size. Dickens could do nothing but run around the streets and laugh. He said later that ". . . every thoroughfare in the city looked exactly like a scene in a pantomime", and when we remember how he had uttered the famous words of the clown, "Here we are!", as soon as he had arrived at his hotel, one can see exactly how the scene would have appeared to Dickens, and exactly the role which he was, in these first hours of his discovery of America, playing. It was all unreal to him, and as a result he too becomes slightly unreal; an actor, a performer, a comedian in his fur coat. The young man following him in this first uproarious progress remembers how Dickens pulled the bell-handles of the doors as he passed them – "Dickens seemed quite unable to keep his fingers off the inviting knobs that protruded from the doors as he went past, and he pulled them with such vigour that one actually came off in his hand." In his *American Notes* he described these very knobs "so marvellously bright and twinkling"; he could *not* resist touching them because they seemed to him too bright, unreal, mere props in a wonderful scenic illusion, the colours and shapes of this new world uncannily echoing the exaggerated and colourful backdrops in the London theatres. And then, when he came to the old South Church of Boston, "Dickens screamed". One would give almost anything to have heard that scream – that scream of undiluted pleasure and freedom, of sudden astonishment at the fact that he was actually living and breathing in a world so much like that of the stage on which he always longed to be. He was in a play, and it was also real; nothing could have suited Dickens's needs more than that. It was like inhabiting one of his own fictions.

But, to paraphrase his own words, we are all either going to the play or just leaving it; leave it he must, in the end, since that first sensation of unreality in America was soon succeeded by other impressions of a graver and more permanent kind. But first he had to settle in. On the following day he attended to his baggage and already such was the press of people waiting to meet him, and the number of journalists wanting to interview him, that he came to an arrangement with the British consul in Boston; Dickens agreed that he should hold daily receptions in his hotel at which the consul would introduce him to the various guests who flocked to see him. "Flocked" is, for once, the appropriate word. When he sat to Francis Alexander, the staircase and hall of that artist's studio were filled with people waiting to catch a glimpse of him and one lady is reported to have said, "Mr Dickens, will you be kind enough to walk entirely round the room, so that we can all have a look at you?" He doodled as he sat for Alexander, and such was his fame that even these doodles have been preserved. Curiously enough he transcribed from memory extracts from *The Pickwick Papers* and *The Old Curiosity Shop* (how close to him his own inventions must always have seemed); he wrote down "Little Nell", then "Charles", and then the phrase "Poor Dick was dead". And the poor boy Dickens was indeed dead now, in his place emerging the young and famous author who was followed by crowds wherever he went, who was waited for on corners, who was entertained to breakfast and to lunch and to dinner, who was the recipient of literally hundreds of letters. The press of business was in fact so great that Dickens felt the need for a secretary and just five days after his arrival he hired a young man, George Putnam (in fact only a little younger than Dickens himself), who was a pupil of Alexander's and whose "flamboyant" but "serious-minded" manner (to quote two of the descriptions given of him) recommended him to Dickens. Putnam was employed at once, and was thus in an uniquely good position to record Dickens's characteristics; he described his "quick, earnest, always cheerful, but keen and nervous temperament" and contrasted it with Catherine's own gentler and somehow more dignified behaviour. But this was not to say that he disapproved of his temporary employer; he describes with pleasure how when Dickens was writing letters home his "face would be convulsed with laughter at his own fun", he talks about *the lighting up of the face* at a humorous remark or incident, as others did, and, like others too, he notices how his large and expressive eyes seemed to be "searching every face, and reading character with wonderful quickness". Everyone saw that, how Dickens seemed literally to be able to penetrate each person when he looked at them. Indeed it was a gift which Dickens himself knew he possessed; only a few months before he had described his custom of trying "to understand what people *think* when they are talking to me . . ." He also noticed the more absurd mannerisms of other people with an alert and watchful eye. Because of Putnam's somewhat flamboyant manner, for example, he nicknamed him "Hamlet" or "the Prince" and noticed as well that he tended to lie about his past. But he was a good secretary, in addition to being a useful foil for Dickens's humour, and he remained with the English visitors for the whole of their stay.

The first important public event for Dickens in America was the dinner given to him by the "Young Men of Boston" on the first evening of February. Not the first public dinner in his honour (Edinburgh, as we have seen, had had that privilege) and certainly not the last, but in some ways typical of a nineteenth-century social entertainment which had become something of an institution. For this was a lengthy affair; it began at about five in the evening and continued till one in the morning and, beside the meal itself, there were long speeches punctuated by songs, comic or otherwise, so that the whole occasion had something of the gaiety of a stage performance. The president of the occasion rose at one point to greet their guest and remarked how "a young man has crossed the ocean with no hereditary title, no military laurels, no princely fortune, and yet his approach is hailed with pleasure by every age and condition . . ." This emphasis upon Dickens's unaristocratic if not exactly lowly origin marked precisely the bond which he hoped to form with the United States, and in his speech in turn Dickens emphasised what might be called the democratic or egalitarian aspects of his particular genius. "I believe," he said, "that Virtue shows quite as well in rags and patches as she does in purple and fine linen." In other words, he was setting himself up as an unofficial laureate of the nation and its beliefs; there is no doubt that at this stage, fêted on all sides, he felt some *consonance* with this new country. Yet it was not to last, and there were warning signals already when in this first major speech he touched upon the question of international copyright, by politely alluding to the fact that his work and that of other British authors was being generally pirated by American publishers and American magazines without any recompense being paid. He did not mention the subject before his visit, but the fact that he raised it so soon suggests that it had been very much on his mind; later he was indignantly to deny that it was the primary reason for his visit to America, but the very fact that he did not mention the subject in advance to anyone might only suggest that the prospect of earning more money from his American sales was one that he was wary of mentioning for fear of seeming mercenary. Certainly it was not the message which the Americans wished to hear from the great young novelist.

Yet he was still buoyant and excited. "How can I tell you what has happened since that first day?" he wrote to Forster. "How can I give you the faintest notion of my reception here; of the crowds that pour in and out the whole day; of the people that line the streets when I go out; of the cheering when I went to the theatre; of the copies of verses, letters of congratulation, welcomes of all kinds, balls, dinners, assemblies without end?" He was not exaggerating and, at a time in America when there were no stirring domestic crises, Dickens was indeed the sensation of the moment. But already he and Catherine were becoming very tired, "on duty" as they were from morning until night, and he was beginning to regret his decision to be quite so open to the advances of the American public. "He says in future that he will pursue a totally different course," one Bostonian wrote, "– shut himself up on particular days and see no one;" he was tired, it seems, of "giving himself up as a spectacle". The welcome was "all heart", one of his American acquaintances, Dr Channing, had written to tell him – a happy phrase, perhaps, but one which Dickens was suspicious enough to satirise. A few years later he placed it in the mouth of that most unnatural of creatures, Mrs Skewton. And clearly there was already something within him which rebelled against the "spectacle" of himself and even against the fulsome praise he was receiving on every side. For now, at the very height of his reception, he found himself thinking of the dead Mary Hogarth, "that spirit which directs my life", as if only so could he "keep his head" amidst the turmoil that every day surrounded him. Similarly, in his account of Boston in *American Notes*, he does not remark upon his own reception but instead dwells upon the case of Laura Bridgman, a deaf, dumb and blind girl whom he had encountered at a Boston institute for the blind; how strange, perhaps, that at this time of his greatest triumph (for nothing in England had ever equalled the treatment he was receiving in the United States) he should revert to the plight of a young girl struggling towards communication from the depths of her entombed spirit. In his speeches, also, he referred frequently to the sorrows of Little Nell. It is almost as if in this royal progress he felt it necessary to keep a quiet heart by sympathising or identifying with the plight of a suffering child. A child, he liked to think, as he had been.

In fact *American Notes*, and much of his own travels through the United States, are largely concerned with what might be called the mournful institutions of American life; the asylums, the workhouses, the prisons, the orphanages, the blind institutes. Of course this was not uncommon in other travellers' accounts of America; in this new age when the role of the state and social provision was being endlessly debated, public institutions of all kinds were at the centre of contemporary argument. Indeed, in a period of social transition, such places were almost the touchstone of national progress. In England eighteenth-century attitudes towards various forms of governmental control, in prisons and asylums in particular, were only gradually being displaced by the sometimes more "stream-lined" and sometimes more humane methods of the radicals and utilitarians. But in America the experiment had as it were started from the beginning and, in the accounts which Dickens wrote of the Boston institutions in particular, it is clear that he believed himself to be witnessing a much more effective and modern form of public care. He had seen the future here, and it worked. His only quarrel with the Boston prison system, in fact, was that it was not harsh enough; as far as he was concerned, a jail should be "a place of ignominious punishment and endurance" and he was surprised to see American prisoners engaged in the ordinary forms of manual labour rather than picking oakum or walking the treadmill. For him ". . . the subject of Prison Discipline is one of the highest importance to any community", and we see in his attitudes something which might be described as liberal authoritarianism. When he visited the industrial town of Lowell he was deeply impressed by the factories and the factory workers there, for example, and this primarily because the places and the people were clean, neat, and organised upon paternalistic lines: ". . . I like to see the humbler class of society careful of their dress and appearance, and even, if they please, decorated with such little trinkets as come within the compass of their means." He was in many respects, therefore, an enlightened disciplinarian, but can we not see in his visits to prisons and to asylums, in his constant interest in the imprisoned and the mad, something more than the philanthropic instinct of a nineteenth-century public man – is there not also something darker, and deeper, something to do with his own feelings of anxiety and guilt expressed in what Putnam called his "nervous" manner?

On the day after his visit to Lowell, he attended a breakfast with Henry Wadsworth Longfellow, the American writer who after Washington Irving seems to have meant most to him. Apparently it was a sufficiently literary occasion, although Longfellow himself stopped a friend from reading out his verses to the honoured guest. Longfellow's younger brother, also present on the occasion, was a little disappointed by the Englishman, however, and noticed the "slightest possible tincture of rowdyism in his appearance". He noticed what others had seen also: "His features are in constant play while he talks, particularly his eyebrows . . . He speaks fast and rather indistinctly." In fact in most of the published accounts of Dickens in America there does seem to be an indication that people were, if only at first, disappointed by his manner and appearance. He was later to claim that America was not "the Republic of my imagination" but it is also true that the young Englishman was not always the novelist of the Americans' imagination. "The very first sight of him may not wholly please you," Dana wrote to William Cullen Bryant, and the President's daughter observed after meeting him that he was "rather thick set, and wears entirely too much jewellery, very English in his appearance and not the best English . . ." Someone else noted his "unkempt hair", and Dickens seems to have caused some offence among the Bostonians by ostentatiously combing it while at dinner. They noticed his shortness, his quick and expressive eyes, the lines around his mouth, the large ears, and the odd fact that when he spoke his facial muscles slightly drew up the left side of his upper lip (that is what was meant by the slight "sneer" which sometimes seemed to cross his countenance), as well as the long flowing hair falling on either side of his face. He was "very fidgety", another observed, a diagnosis confirmed by Dickens's own statement many years later that "I was less patient and more irritable then . . ." There are other descriptions, also, making a composite portrait of Dickens at this point in his life – ". . . a dissipated looking mouth with a vulgar draw to it, a muddy olive complexion, *stubby* fingers . . . a hearty, off-hand manner, far from well-bred, and a rapid, dashing way of talking." One of these hearty remarks caused something of a scandal, in fact; when at the house of a learned judge Dickens entered an argument about the relative beauty of two ladies he said, "Well, I don't know, Mrs Norton perhaps is the most beautiful; but the duchess, to my mind, is the more kissable person." This was not the kind of language these descendants of the Puritans were used to hearing, and there is in fact a sullen, slightly suspicious, New England narrowness which marks many of the descriptions of Dickens. There was particular comment upon his vivid waistcoats, his jewellery and generally bright "get-up". "His whole appearance is foppish," one newspaper reported, "and partakes of the flash order." In other words he was not at all American; he was a Londoner *in excelsis*, and one of the causes for his subsequent disappointment must necessarily be traced to his failure to forge that bond between himself and the new country which at first he tried to claim. It ought to be added, however, that once Americans had got over their surprise at his appearance he was generally reckoned to be cordial, lively, agreeable and perfectly natural. He did not like to play the part of "the Lion", and there is no doubt that his gay manner and lively high spirits found a welcome where the jewellery and the coloured waistcoats might, by themselves, not. Much was written about Catherine Dickens, too – "the Queen and Albert" as Dickens on occasions referred to their appearances together. And it is not perhaps surprising that, on the whole, she was seen as altogether more kindly and satisfactory than her husband. "She is natural in her manners," Dana wrote, and "seems not at all elated by her new position". Longfellow described her as "good-natured – mild . . . not beautiful but amiable". Another observer described "Mrs Dickens's mild, unexacting character and manners". So the accounts have the same burden: "plain and courteous in her manner, but rather taciturn, leaving the burden of conversation to fall upon her gifted husband . . . Her position as the lion's mate seemed embarrassing to her . . . she evidently found satisfaction in quiet conversation with me concerning the best shops in Oxford Street . . . amiable and sensible . . . modest and diffident . . . kind and patient." This was how she was then and how she would be always; the quiet presence beside Dickens, proud of his fame but not in any sense exploiting it, gentle and somewhat shy but courteous and natural in her conversation. And always having to withstand the nervous and quick moods of the person she called "my impatient husband". In the end his impatience was to become the juggernaut which almost destroyed her, but in these early years of their marriage they seemed to all who met them to be fundamentally compatible. The genius and his quiet wife, each one somehow needing the support of the other.

They had been in Boston for two weeks, and on Saturday, 5 February they took the three o'clock train for Worcester; it is reported by several witnesses how crowds waited along the line to get a glimpse of "Boz"; even as the train was moving in or out of the station heads would be thrust through the window with the enquiry "Is Mr Dickens here?", and at each station the crowds surged towards the train in order to catch a glimpse of the famous novelist. They spent Saturday and Sunday in Worcester, their time now filled by the characteristic dinner parties and levées. It was here that the Governor of the state, when discussing the Bostonians with Dickens, enquired, "Did they sound *hash* to you?" By which he meant, did their accent sound disagreeable? Dickens replied, "I beg your pardon. What did you say?" It took time for a translation to be given to him, but in that question – "What did you say?" – one can hear an echo of Dickens's fascination with American speech which was at once so familiar and so alien to him. He noted how "Possible?" was used as a mere habit of reply; how "Yes?" was also used as a simple interrogative; how "Where do you hail from?" meant "Where were you born?" Dickens had a wonderful ear for the quirkiness of speech – phonetic analysis of Cockney speech in the 1830s suggests how accurate and natural the conversations of Sam Weller would have read to a native Londoner – and he stored up all of these Americanisms for use at a later date. But even at the time he could not resist imitating it, and in one letter to Forster managed to include a number of words and phrases which were quintessentially "Yankee" – ". . . it does use you up com-plete, and that's a fact . . ."

From Worcester they travelled a little further south to Hartford where once more in a speech at a banquet in his honour he emphasised the democratic spirit of his writings, as if uniting himself with his audience, and then launched into a plea for international copyright, using the spectre of a broken and exhausted Walter Scott as an example of a writer who was unjustly deprived of his rightful income. The fate of Scott, then, had stayed in his mind – it was the sad end of that novelist which had first warned Dickens of the perils of over-production and thus led indirectly to the American trip itself. And now he employed him once more. "My blood so boiled as I thought of the monstrous injustice that I felt as if I were twelve feet high when I thrust it down their throats." His American friends had tried gently to dissuade him from pursuing the theme of copyright while in the United States, and already there were paragraphs of adverse criticism appearing in reference to Dickens's apparent determination to bite the hands that were applauding him. The point was that magazines and publishers alike "pirated" any available material from England, and thought themselves justified in doing so; their argument was that the spread of Dickens's writings through the land of the free and the brave was more important than any monetary reward to which, in some theoretical sense, he might be entitled. They might also have pointed to the current economic depression as a hindrance to the export of American funds. But we have already seen how important money, and monetary fair play, were to him – and how easily he felt himself to be cheated and misused; what he was doing in America was to address the whole publishing industry as if it were Richard Bentley writ large. But he had not yet lost his sense of humour; when he and Catherine were being serenaded in their hotel room in Hartford, Dickens suddenly remembered that he had left his boots outside the door for cleaning. The absurdity of the situation, for it was almost as if these Americans were serenading his *boots*, was such that he had to muffle his laughter under the bed-clothes as they kept on singing.

Then on to New Haven, where the hotel in which they stayed was besieged by well-wishers; then on by boat to New York where, at the landing, a "press of people" was waiting for him. At once he was taken to the Carlton House Hotel, on Broadway, where the usual panoply of distinguished public figures, literary men, unannounced visitors, press representatives and members of the public began their ritual greetings. Nevertheless there were some people he really did want to see – Washington Irving, the American writer closest in spirit to Dickens and with whom he had corresponded, arrived at the hotel and they spent the evening together. Later, after the publication of *American Notes*, Irving was to turn against Dickens and to describe him as "outrageously vulgar – in dress, manners and mind" but there is no doubt of the friendship which grew between them during this period, and Putnam described them as being "greatly delighted with each other". Irving was to discover in good time that Dickens the friendly companion could be very different from Dickens the writer.

He was fascinated by New York; from his hotel-room on Broadway he could see a scene almost like any in London but somehow with more vivacity, more animation, more colour than in his own city. Here were omnibuses, hackney cabs, coaches, phaetons, but among them all the pigs which wandered through the city. Pineapples and water-melons on display. Bowling saloons. Ten-pin alleys. Oyster bars in basements. The ladies with their brightly coloured dresses. The hum. The stench. The sheer momentum of the city. It was an energy and display which he was soon to experience at first-hand, in fact, since the great coming event here was the "Boz Ball" to be held in the Park Theatre. The theatre itself had been turned into a ball-room with chandeliers and drapes and candelabra; the walls had been covered in white muslin and punctuated by large medallions representing each one of Dickens's novels; and in the centre was a portrait of Dickens with a laurel crown hovering over his head in the grip of an eagle. The stage had been extended, turned into a Gothic set and, in front of some three thousand people and between dances, there were tableaux vivants representing scenes from his fiction. It could only have happened in New York, and indicates how that city's extraordinary energy and enthusiasm were of very early date. Which in turn suggests how, through the decades and even through the centuries, cities retain their proper characteristics; how their unique identity endures and indeed fashions the progress of the generations who inhabit them. So it is that New York in particular, and America in general, had an effect upon Dickens which we can still understand in our time. Everything seemed too large, too bright, and yet somehow *temporary*. Every-thing, to his eyes, became *excessive* so that in the end he could not recognise himself in the descriptions and reactions which he elicited from his hosts. Perhaps even on this night, the night of the "Boz Ball". He was led through the Park Theatre by David Colden, a New York "figure", and General George Morris took Catherine's arm; "Boz", according to the local press, "looked pale and thunderstruck – his charming wife was completely overpowered". In fact Dickens seemed to have thoroughly enjoyed this extraordinary tribute, dancing until he and his wife were so tired that they slipped out and went quietly back to their hotel. Now, at last, he had really seen the *éclat* of his fame.

But he became sick; he retired to bed with a sore throat, and stayed within his hotel for the next three days. How much this was genuine illness, and how much the need simply to rest, is not clear. But this three-day relief from activity gave Dickens time to consider what had happened in the last extraordinary three weeks, and try to understand why it was that, despite the compliments and the festivities, he was beginning to feel so angry and ill-used. A week later he was complain-ing that "I am sick to death of the life I have been leading here – worn out in mind and body – and quite weary and distressed". What in particular distressed him? The fact was that he was also experiencing the reverse side of fame, both in the open way in which the newspapers discussed his life or his behaviour and in the aggressive manner with which they attacked his opinions on international copyright. "You must drop that, Charlie," the Boston *Morning Post* said, "or you will be dished; it smells of the shop-rank." Dickens, for all his apparent composure in the face of "enthoosymoosy" or indeed its reverse, was in fact acutely and painfully sensitive to anything written about him; he always professed not to read the reviews of his books, for example, but his reluctance was largely due to the fact that he could not bear to be criticised. Now, for the first time in his life, after years of praise and fame and success, he was actually being lampooned in public. Certain newspapers, for example, began to speculate that his motives for coming to America were simply mercenary, that he was only interested in obtaining royalties from his works, that he was not a gentleman but merely the "son of a Haberdasher". Some writers would have been able to laugh off such attacks, as merely the customary barbs of the infamous against the famous, but Dickens was not of their sturdy breed. He winced under every attack. "I vow to Heaven," he wrote to one of his American friends, "that the scorn and indignation I have felt under this unmanly and ungenerous treatment has been to me an amount of agony such as I never experienced since my birth." Curiously, however, he seems to have expressed his feelings to no one else – and, he said, he had not even told his wife. Such was the astonishing reserve of the man. He had not spoken to anyone about the blacking house where he worked as a child, either. And now he was being humiliated and rejected all over again. It is easy to forget that, in this record of achievement and of fame, he was still a young man – he was only thirty years old – with all the susceptibility of a young man. He had confidently expected that in America he would be hailed as the emblem of radical social change and liberal democracy; he expected to be as greatly loved here as he was in England. And, up to a point, of course he was. But he did not expect, and he could not endure, the public attacks. His anger and his strange reserve about that anger might arguably have had another dimension also: in the attacks upon his mercenary motives in appealing for international copyright, and in the suspicion of hypocrisy which was cast over his behaviour, did he perhaps recognise some truth? A truth which he preferred to conceal even from himself?

But there is another aspect to his bewilderment in the United States; despite his conviviality and his need for friendship and love, he was in many respects an utterly private and enclosed man. He needed time alone; time for writing, of course, but also time for the kind of self-communing through which, as he said, he was able "to understand my own feelings the better". The isolated child was also the isolated man and he needed that isolation, however temporary it was; he hugged it to him as if in its enclosure he might remain true to himself. But here he had obtained no rest and no privacy; "everything public, and nothing private," he exclaimed. He hated, it was reported, "giving himself up as a spectacle". One of his great fears, as we shall see in later accounts of his dreams and imaginings, was of becoming an *object* in the world, one bead among thousands of beads on the great chain, one strand among many strands, one thing among many things. But this was what was happening to him now. When he arrived at any railway station the crowds peered in the window at him "with as much coolness as if I were a Marble image". There were other indignities. "If I turn into the street, I am followed by a multitude. If I stay at home, the house becomes, with callers, like a fair . . . I go to a party in the evening, and am so inclosed and hemmed about by people, stand where I will, that I am exhausted for want of air. I dine out, and have to talk about everything, to everybody . . . I can't get out at a station, and can't drink a glass of water, without having a hundred people looking down my throat when I open my mouth to swallow." He was featured in advertisements; copies of his bust were on sale at Tiffany's; it is even reported that the barber who cut his hair then sold strands of it to Dickens's admirers. He was becoming an object, and all this perpetual wearying attention meant that ". . . I never knew less of myself in all my life, or had less time for those confidential Interviews with myself, whereby I earn my bread . . ." In other words his secret self – the self in collaboration with which he created his fiction – had to all intents and purposes disappeared. He no longer exercised that mastery over his environment which had been his for the last seven years of writing and creating.

It took America to teach him that fame and success were not enough, that humanitarian ideals were not enough, since his own sense of personal injury now affected everything. Even his radicalism. ". . . I tremble for a radical coming here," he wrote, "unless he is a radical on principle, by reason and reflection . . . I fear that if he were anything else, he would return home a tory . . ." He had expected in America to find the conflicts of English life resolved, but in fact the "free press" and the representatives of the people were as dishonest and as hypocritical as anything he had found in his own country. Perhaps even more so: "I have a yearning after our English customs and english manners" he wrote, for the first time explicitly affirming his national identity rather than that free-spirited, liberal, radical one which he had hoped to have confirmed in the United States. It may or may not be significant that he was also constantly reading from a pocket Shakespeare which Forster had given him at Liverpool just before the Atlantic crossing. He believed, too, that in the United States he would not have been a successful author at all and "I should have lived and died, poor, unnoticed, and a 'black sheep' . . ." As if the humiliation and rage he now felt were so close to his experiences in the blacking factory that for him America became one vast Warren's from which he would never have escaped. And now he began to notice how much Americans *spat*, almost as if he believed that they were spitting at him. On a train, "the flashes of saliva flew so perpetually and incessantly out of the windows all the way, that it looked as though they were ripping open feather-beds inside, and letting the wind dispose of the feathers". This is a wonderful image, of course, to be put beside this other account of the same American habit: "And in every bar-room and hotel passage the stone floor looks as if it were paved with open oysters . . ." It is prose like this which suggests one of the reasons why Dickens was writing so many and such long letters to England; it was his one way of controlling the reality he was faced with, the only creative outlet at his disposal and one which allowed him at least in part those "confidential Interviews with myself" which sustained his fiction but which were now creating an alternative America based upon his own impressions. He could not speak about his disgust and humiliation, but he could write it down.

Of course no one could have had such a reception from other writers and indeed from the American public without being in some way moved by it. "They are friendly," he said of the people, "earnest, hospitable, kind, frank, very often accomplished, far less prejudiced than you would suppose, warm-hearted, fervent, and enthusiastic . . . when they conceive a perfect affection for a man (as I may venture to say of myself), entirely devoted to him . . . The State is a parent to its people; has a parental care and watch over all poor children, women labouring of child, sick persons, and captives." And he made friends on this visit who would remain attached to him for the rest of his life – Washington Irving was one of the exceptions – and with whom he had the closest relations. There was Charles Sumner, one of the leaders of the anti-slavery faction; David Cadwallader Colden, a philanthropist; Jonathan Chapman, the Whig Mayor of Boston. In particular he struck up a close friendship with Cornelius

Felton, who was Professor of Greek at Harvard University. This was not the kind of friend he made in England but Felton was quite different from his English counterparts; he was the son of poor parents who, like Dickens himself, had made his way in the world through effort and industry. These were the kinds of Americans he most liked – Bostonian (except for Colden, who was a New Yorker), "self-made" men, liberal, courteous, magnanimous.

But they were a world away from the "Boz Balls" (there was in fact a second one, a commercial undertaking which Dickens did not attend) and the press comments and the crowds. And it was while Dickens was sick in his New York hotel room, beset on all sides, that he determined he would travel for the rest of his stay in America as a private citizen, accepting no public engagements and attending no public dinners or levées. It was in that capacity, with as little noise as possible, that, a few days later, he visited an asylum for the insane off Long Island, the City penitentiary and the County workhouse; all of these places offered invaluable material for the *American Notes* he had already decided to write although, as always, one senses in these long visits to the imprisoned and the mad the reach of his own preoccupations or obsessions. He also had time to visit the notorious "Tombs", the New York House of Detention, as well as the City watch-house where men and women were taken "below the surface of the earth; profoundly dark; so full of noisome vapours that when you enter it with a candle you see a ring about the light, like that which surrounds the moon in wet and cloudy weather; and so offensive and disgusting in its filthy odours, that you *cannot bear* its stench." Yet he stayed, and watched, and remembered everything. That he had time to visit all these subterranean places was largely because he and Catherine had decided to remain in New York until they received the letters which had been sent to them from England; Catherine, in particular, wished to have news of the children. But the mail was delayed, and there were reports that the ship carrying the letters had been sunk in a storm. Catherine also became unwell; like her husband she developed a violently sore throat, which malady he put down largely to the American love for central heating in hotels and public buildings. Still no letters had arrived, after three weeks – Dickens, characteristically, imagined them as living things which were now drowning beneath the Atlantic – and on 5 March they travelled from New York to Philadelphia. He had sent Putnam ahead, in order to prepare their way and explain the delay in their arrival, and almost at once Dickens's determination to make no more public engagements was forestalled by the always eager and determined attitudes of his putative hosts. A local politician had visited them after their arrival, and asked if he could introduce the famous author to a few friends; Dickens assented, no doubt somewhat wearily, and in the next day's newspapers there was an announcement that he would "receive the public" at a specified time. In his own account Putnam, describes how "at the time specified the street in front was crowded with people, and the offices and halls of the hotel filled". Dickens was indignant but, informed that a refusal on his part would now provoke a riot, agreed to meet everyone; he stationed himself in the hotel parlour and for the next two hours shook the hands of a steady stream of Philadelphians. One journalist noticed that he simply "shook the proffered hand feebly, and let it fall", although Putnam himself remembers how "the humorous smiles played over his face . . . the thing had its *comic* side". The scene appears in more colourful guise in *Martin Chuzzlewit*, as the hero of that tale is forced to "receive" a multitude of Americans:

"'Mr Chuzzlewit, I believe?' said the gentleman.

'That is my name.'

'Sir,' said the gentleman, 'I am pressed for time.'

'Thank God!' thought Martin.

'I go back Toe my home, Sir,' pursued the gentleman, 'by the return train, which starts immediate. Start is not a word you use in your country, Sir.'

'Oh yes, it is,' said Martin.

'You air mistaken, Sir,' returned the gentleman, with great decision: 'but we will not pursue the subject, lest it should awaken your preju-dice. Sir, Mrs Hominy.'"

It is not clear whether at any point on this American journey Dickens considered the possibility of creating such fiction out of his experiences in the United States, but the inadvertent comedy with which he was daily confronted was very suggestive – "Oh!" he wrote to Forster, "the sublimated essence of comicality that I *could* distil, from the materials I have!" And thus to take charge of the reality, to control it, to master it with laughter.

That same afternoon of the unwanted reception in the Philadelphia hotel, he visited the Eastern Penitentiary, plunging at once from the excessive and unwelcome sociability of the levée to the profoundest depths of gloom and silence. For this was one of the new American prisons, much admired by certain penal reformers in England, which had introduced the Separate System: "Every prisoner who comes into the jail, comes at night; is put into a bath, and dressed in the prison garb; and then a black hood is drawn over his face and head, and he is led to the cell from which he never stirs again until the whole period of his confinement has expired. I looked at some of them with the same awe as I should have looked at men who had been buried alive, and dug up again." Dickens, as we have seen, was not at all liberal in terms of penal policy – in fact he was more "reactionary" than many prison governors – but as soon as a prisoner became a victim, or, rather, as soon as Dickens could imagine himself in the prisoner's place, his tone changes to one of terror and pity. "A horrible thought occurred to me when I was recalling all I had seen, that night," he told Forster later, of a similar prison. "*What if ghosts be one of the terrors of these jails?* . . . The more I think of it, the more certain I feel that not a few of these men . . . are nightly visited by spectres." What an extraordinary conclusion to reach; as if his imagination had reverted to the days of his childhood reading of *The Terrific Register*, to the days of the Marshalsea prison itself. Clearly his visit to the prison – he went from cell to cell and spent some seven hours in the place – affected him deeply, so strangely did his mind attach itself to these visions of the night. What seems to have happened is this: the theme of "buried alive" is often associated in his fiction with the idea of the dead coming back or signalling their presence, and so his horror at the living burial of these prisoners prompted him in turn to think of ghosts. It is all the more unusual an association since, in normal circumstances, he dismissed reports of such phenomena as the product of mere trickery or credulity.

In fact his attitude towards "the occult", like many of his other attitudes, was various and contradictory. There is no doubt that he was personally superstitious; Friday was his "lucky" day, he felt the need to touch certain objects three times, he always left London on publication day, and so forth. Clearly he was fascinated, too, by the powers of mesmerism and its twin phenomenon of clairvoyance; there are many occasions when he personally believed that a certain "magnetised" subject had been gifted with second sight. He is known to have attended at least one seance and, with family or friends, even to have practised the occult art of table-spinning. He was also fascinated by ghosts – "I have always," he wrote, "had a strong interest in the subject, and never knowingly lose an opportunity of pursuing it." It was that dark and melodramatic aspect of his personality which also made him a wonderful teller of ghost stories. His closest friend, Forster, noticed as much and commented that "such was his interest generally in things supernatural, that, but for the strong restraining power of his common sense, he might have fallen into the follies of spiritualism". Sometimes this interest in the supernatural went no further than a kind of morbid jokiness; there was one reported occasion when he placed two skeletons in a cupboard, locked it, and then asked a local carpenter to force open the door, with predictable results. But there were also times when he seems genuinely to have felt the presence of the uncanny; on two occasions he passed in the shadow of the Burlington Hotel, and on both occasions, so he said, he was invaded by a feeling of numbness and of cold.

Yet these responses are perhaps only to be expected in a novelist who delighted in creating mysteries within his fiction, who used all the panoply of Gothic effects when he considered them to be appropriate and who, in a much more general sense, is filled with the morbid poetry of fantasy and death. Alexander Blok, the Russian poet, said that ". . . in reading Dickens I have felt horror, the equal of which Poe himself does not inspire", and there is no doubt that there was within Dickens's consciousness a private world built upon nightmares and fantasies and anxieties which he chose not to reveal to anyone; except, of course, to the readers of his fiction. He was fascinated, too, by his own dreams and by the visions which appeared in them – visions of Mary Hogarth, once, but also visions which entailed some form of pre-cognition. On one occasion he dreamed of a lady in a red shawl who turned to him and said, "I am Miss Napier;" the next evening, he met the same lady, wearing the same shawl and bearing the same name. There were other dreams, too, and in a long letter he once sent to a writer on the subject Dickens suggests that the strongest dreams are those which create a kind of allegory of the world; that dreams are, in that sense, at the root of all fiction. A strange genesis, one might think, for novels as elaborate as *Bleak House* or *Oliver Twist* but there are many occasions when Dickens points to "the land of shadows" as the origin of his fiction and when he even describes his serial fiction as "my month's dream". There are also times when that dream casts a veil over the actual world, when he could say of his fiction – ". . . to believe it the only reality in life, and to mistake all the realities for short-lived shadows". Thus the real world sometimes becomes for him a place of memory and shadow only; "I think what a dream we live in, until it seems for the moment the saddest dream that ever was dreamed." And in remarks such as this, where it is clear that the world of his fiction has become utterly confused with the world of his waking life, we see how it was that the sadness of his own novels is turned into the nature of the world itself; and how Dickens himself is sometimes to be found wandering desolately inside one of his own fictions. It is worth noticing also his remark that, in his own dreams, he always returned to the time of his early manhood when, as a young reporter, he was just beginning the world. And when we recall also how he remembered all the details of that period in his life – "I forget nothing of those times," he once wrote – we may be able to see how it was that Dickens was haunted by his own past, how its bright images burned in his imagination and obscured all the fame and success which the adult had come to know. But now it is time to awake and return with him to that waking landscape of renown and honour.

From Philadelphia he and Catherine travelled on to Washington. From this time forward, his resolution to travel merely as a private citizen was to a certain extent maintained; press reports about him became scarcer after this date, also, although that may simply be due to the evident fact that his "novelty value" had by now all but vanished. But of course there were many who had not yet met the distinguished stranger; he was taken to visit President Tyler, for example, who on seeing Dickens remarked, "I am astonished to see so young a man, Sir." He also attended the President's levée where, once again, he became the main object of attention; when he moved among the guests, according to one report, it had the same effect as corn thrown before chicken. It was while he attended a private dinner in the capital that news came of the arrival of the long-awaited letters from England: he left the dinner as soon as he decently could, and rushed back to the hotel. Catherine was waiting for his arrival before she opened the letters, which demonstrates how submissive or self-sacrificing she could be, and together they read them until two in the morning.

It was now that their real travels in America began. From Washington they travelled to Richmond; in particular Dickens wanted to visit the tobacco plantations there, and to see a "slave state" in action. It was here that he was told that he must not let success turn his head. He replied that he would do his best to keep his head in its natural position. A son of an American friend visited him in his hotel: "Entering the room with somewhat of a tremor . . . I was seized by the hand and almost *slung* across the room, and a dozen remarks and questions were addressed to me in a breath." Dickens was still very eager, very active, very observant. It was in Richmond, for example, that he noticed the air "of decay and gloom" which for him seemed to be an expression of slavery itself. From Richmond back to Washington. From Washington to Baltimore. Here he wrote a number of long letters home to Macready, Maclise, Mitton, Lord Brougham, Lady Holland, his brother Frederick, Samuel Rogers, T. N. Talfourd and Forster – in themselves enough to make up a short book, and indeed many passages in this correspondence were later used in *American Notes*. By now, in fact, he seems to have decided that he knew all there was to know about America. Like Mr Pickwick in the Fleet prison he had seen enough, and now in the evening he was accustomed to play "Home Sweet Home" on an accordion which he had bought in New York. Yet if he had known what was happening in one part of "Home" he might have been less sanguine about its charms; taking advantage of his absence, his father had written begging letters to Miss Burdett-Coutts and Coutts bank itself. One such letter exists still, in beautiful handwriting and fine lines, the writer apparently calm and dignified: "Contemporaneous events of this nature place me in a difficulty from which, without some anticipatory pecuniary effort, I cannot extricate myself . . ." He wanted an advance of twenty-five pounds to help him on his removal from Alphington to London, but it is not known whether Miss Burdett-Coutts gave him the money. Certainly it was not enough, if she did, for in succeeding months he sold off at least two pages of his son's manuscript version of *O'Thello*, written so many years before. On each occasion John Dickens authenticated the work as that of "Charles Dickens".

From Baltimore the Dickenses travelled on the mail coach to Harrisburg – what he thought to be a parcel on the roof of the coach turned out to be a small boy who, observing the heavy rain that was falling as they made their way, remarked to Dickens, "Well now, stranger, I guess you find this, a'most like an English a'ternoon,-hey?" Dickens liked small boys, although he often pretended not to, and adds in his letter on the incident, "I thirsted for his blood." And then across a wooden bridge, roofed over, for more than a mile, with all its echoes and its rumblings, so that it seemed to Dickens to be like a journey in a dream. From Harrisburg onto the canal boat which was to take them to Pittsburgh – in frowsy and dirty shared sleeping quarters where all the men spat and where no one washed except, of course, Dickens and his party. "I make no complaints, and shew no disgust. I am looked upon as highly facetious at night, for I crack jokes with everybody near me until we fall asleep." It is easy to see him, the young man, already almost too famous but with no hint of superiority about him, making jokes. Also "I am considered very hardy in the morning, for I run up, bare-necked, and plunge my head into the half-frozen water, by half past five o'clock". One recognises the energy and the hardiness of the man; and notices, too, the scrupulous desire for cleanliness even in conditions such as these. "I am respected for my activity, inasmuch as I jump from the boat to the towing-path, and walk five or six miles before breakfast . . ." Of course these American travellers had their own eccentricities, of which he would make good use in *Martin Chuzzlewit*. "I remained as grave as a judge," he wrote later. "I catch them looking at me sometimes, and feel that they think I don't take any notice." They were wrong. This is a perfect picture of Dickens, keeping a grave demeanour even when he finds the situation extremely funny. And afterwards, when he sat upon the deck with Catherine, they saw the landscape slowly being colonised by the new settlers; log cabins with their windows stuffed with old hats or old clothes to withstand the wind, areas of forest which had been burned and cleared, swamps, morasses, broken trunks of dead or rotten trees. All of these things lingered in his mind as the elements of a landscape of despair, and it is one which he revives in *Martin Chuzzlewit*.

Then Pittsburgh, where once more he was surrounded and hemmed in and bothered and bewildered by callers both expected and unforeseen. Anne Brown and George Putnam were stationed at the door of his hotel room, to take cards and to announce each visitor in turn. He held one conversation in the course of which an American apologised for his seeing the country under such unfavourable circumstances with "commerce and manufacture destroyed, credit paralysed and spirits of people depressed in a corresponding degree". This was something which interested him for two days later, in a letter to Macready, he made much the same point – "Look at the exhausted Treasury; the paralyzed government; the unworthy representatives of a free people . . ." It was in Pittsburgh, too, that he encountered an Englishman he had known many years ago in London; he had failed in business and was now a portrait painter, and such was the hospitality of Dickens that he dined with them for each of the three days they remained in the city.

Then onwards again. Dickens having arranged this tour so that they were almost continually moving, they went now by steamboat down the Ohio River to Cincinnati. This river journey was more pleasant than that on the canal boat: they had a little cabin to themselves and generally sat together in a gallery at the stern of the boat away from the other passengers, Dickens wanting to avoid the number of "bores" who pestered him for his opinions continually. He and his wife walked for exercise upon the hurricane deck, sometimes for hours. He wrote letters to Forster and to Macready, balancing the paper on his knee in order to write and his handwriting is as a result rather shaky. Dickens admired Cincinnati, ". . . a beautiful city; cheerful, thriving, and animated". He wrote another letter to Forster from there and, just as he turned the page, he went over to the window of his hotel room in order to describe what he saw in the street below. And all at once the America of one hundred and fifty years ago comes to life. A large bread bakery, a book-binding establishment, a dry goods store, and a small shed which calls itself a Carriage Repository. "On the pavement under our window, a black man is chopping wood; and another black man is talking (confidentially) to a pig." Dinner has just been eaten and "the diners are collected on the pavement, on both sides of the way, picking their teeth, and talking". It is a warm evening, and many people are sitting on chairs in the street. "The loungers, underneath our window, are talking of a great Temperance convention which comes off here tomorrow. Others, about me. Others, about England." And so the conversation on this warm evening floats up to Charles Dickens as he peers out of the window, and in the echo of these scattered voices we are returned through time to an April evening in 1842 – Dickens, thousands of miles from home, listening to the diners talking about him and about England.

From Cincinnati they travelled by boat to Louisville, and then on to the farthest extension of their journey, down the turbid Mississippi to St Louis. It was in some ways an unpleasant trip on that river since every five minutes a bell rang to warn the captain of floating logs; the company on the boat was dreary and monotonous, too, with the usual conversations about money, the usual rush for food which was eaten rapidly and in silence. And then the arrival at St Louis, which in its French quarters, with its narrow crooked thoroughfares and wooden houses, seemed more like a European than an American city. Here there was the usual levée and the usual ball, but for once Dickens managed to break out of the routine which others set for him: he wished to see the famous wide and flat prairies of the region, and with a party of fourteen rode out to the Looking Glass Prairie. One of his hosts on this occasion was the local Unitarian minister, William Greenleaf Eliot, a young man who is chiefly remembered now as the grandfather of T. S. Eliot – so by chance do the generations of writers touch each other. Dickens was not much impressed by the prairie, however, which seemed to him like an inferior version of Salisbury Plain. (He *did* like the Reverend Eliot.) Then back by steamboat to Cincinnati; then on from that city to Columbus in a stage-coach, Dickens taking his favourite seat on the box with the driver. At Columbus yet another levée, and by this stage of his exhaustion and familiarity Dickens was describing his experiences in a wholly comic way: "They shake hands exactly after the manner of the guests at a ball at the Adelphi or the Haymarket" (in other words, exactly as if they were all on stage, all playing out their roles) and they "receive any facetiousness on my part, as if there were a stage direction 'all laugh', and have rather more difficulty in 'getting off' . . ." By now in fact Dickens himself has become facetious or merry; he had seen all that he really needed to see (although there were to be two or three small outings later), had more than enough material for the travel-book he intended to write, and was now relaxing into a broadly comic mood brought on by the imminent end of their American journey and the prospect of their return home. Already he had arranged to travel back across the Atlantic by sail rather than by steam, and their passages were booked on the *George Washington*.

From Columbus they hired their own stage-coach to a place called Tiffin; they took a hamper with them, and dined on the way, but the roads were now very bad. For a long stretch they were travelling across something known as a "corduroy road", a name merely for logs which had been laid across marsh land, and the coach bumped and heaved as it passed across each log. En route they stayed at an "inn" which was no more than a number of bare rooms without locks on the doors or proper facilities, and then on to Tiffin itself where another landlord – hearing that they needed to be taken to the railroad station – put them all in an open wagon and paraded them around the main streets of the small town before they arrived at their destination. Then on by rail to Sandusky; American railway trains were too hot and too stifling for someone of Dickens's energetic and breezy nature, but he managed. From Sandusky on to Cleveland by steamboat but, when they landed there, ". . . the people poured on board . . . and stared in at the door and windows *while I was washing, and Kate lay in bed*". At

Sandusky he had already read an editorial in the *Cleveland Plain Dealer* which had urged war with England – "Despised and feared by all, she sits like a surly mastiff in her island kennel, thirsting for blood, yet afraid to leave her litter" – and as a result he indignantly refused to meet the mayor of the town who had come on board to greet him. He was no longer declaring himself to be almost an honorary American, as he had done in his first speeches, but was now almost a conventional Englishman, displaying wounded pride at any attack upon his country as if it were an attack upon himself. If there was one thing which Dickens discovered in America, it was his essential Englishness, then, and he had to come thousands of miles in order properly to recognise and to understand it. On from Cleveland across Lake Erie to Buffalo. From here they had to travel only a very short distance by railroad into Canada and the "English side" of Niagara Falls. He was free at last. He had left America behind, albeit for a month before their journey home from New York, and he had left behind all the boredom and inconvenience of being an honoured foreign guest.

As they approached Niagara in the train from Buffalo, Dickens eagerly awaited the sound or the sight of the Falls; just as before, in the vale at Glencoe, it was Nature in its more gigantic forms which appealed to his imagination. Then, as they arrived at the station, he saw "two great white clouds rising up from the depths of the earth". All at once he was frantic to see it, and immediately he ran off to the ferry which took travellers to the very Falls themselves. "I dragged Kate down a deep and slippery path leading to the ferry boat; bullied Anne for not coming fast enough; perspired at every pore . . .", as if he himself were like the waterfall, the sweat pouring from him. Once on the boat he saw what it was: blinded by spray, deafened by the roar, he was close enough to see more than that "vague immensity" which at first he had glimpsed. Then he rushed to the inn where they were to stay for the next few days, changed his clothes and hurried out again to see the phenomenon; this time he went down into the basin and looked up at the cascading waters. "There was a bright rainbow at my feet; and from that I looked up to – great Heaven! to *what* a fall of bright green water . . ." Here he felt at peace again, that peace of wonder and self-communing which had been snatched from him in America. No more crowds. No more levées. No more curious spectators watching him, noting him, writing about him. Here was "Beauty, unmixed with any sense of Terror" and "Peaceful Eternity" and as he gazed upon it, as he continued to gaze upon it over the ten days they remained here, he began to recover that sense of his inner life which had been denied him on his travels. And here, once more, he thought of the dead girl, Mary Hogarth. Her image was presented to him in this other image of the eternal, and there can be very little doubt that he did truly believe her to be a "spirit" looking down upon him from some place of eternal repose. All these images and associations sanctified Niagara Falls for him, and so his anger was compounded when he read in the visitors' books various facetious or indelicate expressions from those who had visited the spot before. "If I were a despot," he wrote, "I would force these Hogs to live for the rest of their lives on all Fours, and to wallow in filth expressly provided for them by Scavengers, . . . every morning they should each receive as many stripes [whippings] as there are letters in their detestable obscenities." Which, if nothing else, is an apt indication of the kind of anger to which Dickens could on occasions be roused.

Otherwise, for the days they spent here at the inn, their rooms overlooking the Falls, Dickens relaxed. Catherine, too, was in need of relaxation. She had been the almost silent partner of her husband on the last arduous stages of their American journey, mentioned by him only in passing except in one letter where he laughs at her propensity for accidents – "She falls into, or out of, every coach or boat we enter . . ." But this was less than fair, as he must have realised as soon as he had written it down, for he goes on to say that she now "made a *most admirable* traveller in every respect . . ." and was "perfectly game". There had also been one rather curious episode back in Pittsburgh: Dickens had been extolling the virtues of "magnetism" at dinner, although he had never tried his own mesmeric powers upon her. Catherine had laughed at the idea, and at once Dickens decided to try and hypnotise her. It worked. "I magnetised her into hysterics, and then into the magnetic sleep." He tried again the following night with equal success, and in later years Dickens was to find that he could mesmerise her with extraordinary ease; which suggests, if nothing else, how obedient Catherine was to her husband's will. Yet of course the spectacle of her, no doubt desperately weary and anxious to return home to her children, accompanying him on these arduous and sometimes unpleasant journeys across America, is ample evidence of that. More will be supplied in later years.

More letters were written home, and on the first day of May he woke up in his bed and shouted "Next month!" to Catherine – only five weeks before they embarked on the ship to take them back to

England. They had arranged a short tour of Canada to help fill the days between; they went to Toronto for a few days and then travelled on to Montreal where a British garrison was stationed. One of the officers here, the Earl of Mulgrave, had become acquainted with Dickens and his wife on the journey across the Atlantic. It must have been at his instigation, or certainly on his urging, that they stayed until the end of the month. "As the time draws nearer," Dickens wrote, "we get FEVERED with anxiety for home . . ." Home was now the word he was using as a litany; spelling it out, mentioning it to Catherine, thinking of the children, picturing all the rooms in Devonshire Terrace as neat and as orderly as he had left them. Yet once again he whipped himself up into a further state of intense excitement by participating in the theatricals of the Garrison Amateurs in Montreal although, as usual, he did not so much participate as manage and control. Clearly Mulgrave had found out his propensity for theatricals on the long voyage out, but it would have taken no very hard persuasion to elicit help from Dickens. Three plays were planned for one evening, and at once he began to drill his cast, arrange for props and scenery, direct the plays and of course act in all of them himself. "The furor has come strong upon me again; and I begin to be once more of opinion that nature intended me for the Lessee of a National Theatre . . ." – Although there are some who might think that the author of *The Pickwick Papers* and *Nicholas Nickleby* had already created a kind of national theatre within the pages of his own novels. The plays to be performed were *A Roland for an Oliver*, *Past Two o'Clock in the Morning* and *Deaf as a Post*; the first two were light comedies of a conventional kind, the last a farce. It was the first time Dickens had acted since the days – now seeming so long ago, so far away – when he had put on family theatricals in Bentinck Street. But he found himself to be as adept as ever, both in stage management and of course in his acting: "I really do believe that I was very funny . . ." Certainly the audiences seemed to share in Dickens's delight at his own perform- ance; the three plays were a great success, and one newspaper account said of Dickens's acting that it was "a sort of mixture of the late Charles Mathews and Mr Buckstone's". This was in fact high praise since Mathews had been the comic actor non pareil and Buckstone had a very high reputation. Catherine acted as well, although there is no real account of her own performance; since she rarely acted again, despite the fact that her husband arranged a number of theatrical events in later years, it seems likely that she did not take so easily to the stage. They performed for two nights (between engagements they went on a short visit to Quebec with Lord Mulgrave), and then at the end of the month travelled back south again by steamboat, rail and stage-coach to New York.

They were within a week of their departure and, to pass the time now already filled with so much anticipation, they made an excursion up the Hudson River for one last look at another part of the country. They visited a "Shaker" community, part of a religious sect for which Dickens apparently had nothing but contempt; he was never a devotee of the more extreme forms of religious worship, and the Shakers impressed him as nothing so much as irresponsible or depressing bores. "I so abhor," he wrote later in *American Notes*, "and from my soul detest that bad spirit, no matter by what class or sect it may be entertained, which would strip life of its healthful graces, rob youth of its innocent pleasures, pluck from maturity and age their pleasant ornaments . . ." And what he seems to have noticed among them, too, was their hypocrisy and their cant – in that respect his reaction against them was part of his general reaction against America itself. Certainly it is no coincidence that his next novel would be primarily concerned with that theme, since there was no other aspect of human behaviour which struck him more forcibly in all these months of travelling. Cant everywhere. Cant in the newspapers. Cant from the self-styled leaders of public opinion. Cant from the businessmen. And did he now, having at first identified himself with this new world, sense a certain amount of hypocrisy also within himself?

But at last the day had come. On 7 June, 1842, he had breakfast with some of his more steadfast American friends; then he and Catherine embarked upon the *George Washington* in order to begin their voyage home. They had taken various mementoes with them – amongst them two American rocking chairs, of which Dickens became especially fond, and a small white spaniel whom he christened "Timber Doodle" just as if he had trotted from the pages of one of his own novels. Dickens had chosen to come back by sail rather than steam because he feared drowning by water much less than he feared death by fire; as a result, the journey home had few of the terrors which had afflicted them on board the *Britannia*. By Dickens's account it was a pleasant and uneventful crossing; he organised a facetious little club, called the United Vagabonds, and entertained himself with various games of whist, chess, cribbage, backgammon and shovel-board. But he noticed, too, the poor passengers who kept "below decks" in their

John Dickens

Elizabeth Dickens

From an unsigned miniature, said to be the
earliest portrait

Dickens at eighteen

Dickens at nineteen

Dickens at twenty-four from a
painting by Samuel Laurence.

Dickens at twenty-three

Georgina Hogarth, painted by Frank Stone

Catherine Dickens, 1842

Catherine Dickens in later life

Charles Dickens, painted by Daniel Maclise, 1839

Tavistock House

Mile End Terrace,
Portsea, Dickens's
birthplace

No 1 Devonshire
Terrace

48 Doughty Street

16 Bayham Street,
Camden Town

Maria Beadnell

Mary Hogarth

(*Left*), Dickens, Catherine and Mary Hogarth,
c. 1835

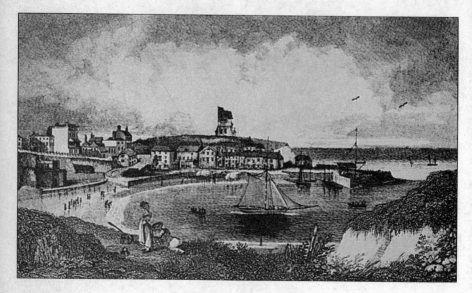

Broadstairs, Kent

(*Right*) Charles Dickens, painted by William Powell Frith in 1859

The Dickens children, 1841.
Charley, Mamey, Katey and
Walter with the raven

Henry Fielding and Francis Jeffrey
Dickens, c. 1862

Mary Dickens

Walter Landor Dickens

Katey Macready Dickens

Charles Dickens, Jr.

Edward Bulwer Lytton Dickens,
1868

Alfred D'Orsay Tennyson Dickens

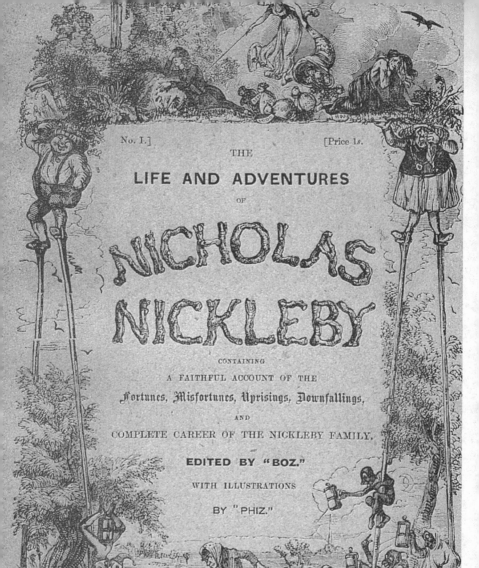

No. I.]   [Price 1s.

THE

LIFE AND ADVENTURES

OF

NICHOLAS NICKLEBY

CONTAINING

A FAITHFUL ACCOUNT OF THE

Fortunes, Misfortunes, Uprisings, Downfallings,

AND

COMPLETE CAREER OF THE NICKLEBY FAMILY.

EDITED BY "BOZ."

WITH ILLUSTRATIONS

BY "PHIZ."

LONDON: CHAPMAN AND HALL, 186, STRAND.

1838.

$\frac{1}{102}$

Reading *The Chimes*, December 1844

Dickens as Captain Bobadil in *Every Man in His Humour*

Above: An illustration by Hablot K. Browne (Phiz) reproduced from the first edition of *Dombey and Son*.
Left: Henry Burnett, said to be the original Paul Dombey

own "little world of poverty", and he took pains to find out from some of them their histories as they sailed on to England. Home. Dickens was leaving behind a country which, despite the friends he had made there and the progressive state institutions he had visited, he seems to have viewed with little emotion other than contempt. In fact his dislike intensified even as he returned to England; no doubt reflecting, all the while, upon the way he was treated both by those idle crowds who had watched him and by those newspapers which had attacked him. What had he found in that country? Everywhere business and money, money and business, coarseness of manner and a dismal concern with commerce. More enlightened penal and social policies, certainly, but no humour. No laughter. And newspaper politics; it was the newspapers which had attacked him, and it was with the newspapers that he was primarily indignant. In that sense he suffered a sea-change on the journey back from America and, even though it is unlikely that he reflected upon his own identity in any general sense, it is quite clear that he returned to England a very different person, a very different writer, from the one who had so eagerly embarked at Liverpool six months before. He had taken everything for granted before – England, his own success, his political radicalism – but his experience of the United States opened his eyes to the particular nature of all those things which characterised him and which gave him life.

Yet not every impression of American life had been negative. Of his radicalism, for example, it can be said that he retained it but with significant alterations. Before his visit to America he had been much closer to the anti-industrialist or at least anti-manufactory bias of men like Lord Shaftesbury; on his return, having seen the way in which a well-run factory system such as the one at Lowell was conducted, and understanding how closely that enlightened factory system was re-lated to the public institutions of the state, he changed direction. No longer did he attack industrialism or industrialists, but instead came to believe that the twin evils of protectionism and aristocratic govern-ment were the real enemies of progress. Flunkies, corn laws, nepot-ism, red-tapeism of all descriptions became his principal targets both in his journalism and in his fiction. This did not happen overnight, of course, but his American journey marks an important stage in his understanding of social matters. He was a man of his time, after all, and became as convinced of the merits of industrial development as he had previously been persuaded of the need for the progress of the railway. But all of these interests were related to that one central experience of the factories of Boston: it was important that workers and industrialists came together, as part of a well-organised paternal system of government, and the only real obstacle to such enlightened progress in England lay in those relics of the past which still hampered the free development of the country.

His attitude towards England changed in private no less than in public matters, however, and in his six months' absence from the country (which, before, he had left only for a week or two during his travels through France and Belgium), he discovered his essential Englishness; indeed, his need for English life. In America he had found the loss of privacy to be deeply unsettling: he had told Macready that he could never live in America, but probably this is because he realised that he could never *write* in it. He needed England, and his sojourn on alien shores made him realise just how English in fact he was. He needed his own patch of ground, his territory, more than he needed anything else. Yet he must also have returned home with a heightened sense of his own fame and what he was later to call "Power"; he had been greeted by President and Senators, dined with ex-Presidents, been followed by crowds, mobbed in the streets, welcomed by thousands at balls and dinners, praised in speeches. Such glory had never come to him in England where, as always, literary fame was taken rather less seriously and where native diffidence prevented the kind of triumphal scenes which had accompanied his progress in America. But now, having seen the response of New York and Boston and St Louis, he knew how great a success he had become. Of course he also came back chastened and, in the hostile newspaper comments which had so angered and depressed him, for the first time he had come to see the reverse aspect of fame. To be pilloried as mercenary, to be described as common, to be satirised – this had never happened to him before and in the attacks upon him, as well as in his own horrified reactions to them, he became much more self-aware. Previously he had risen almost instinctively to fame and applause but his experiences in America, as we shall see, fostered in him a new kind of maturity. But is there not some other more secret experience to be divulged here? He had arrived in America with the determination to attach himself to what he saw as the liberal and progressive aspects of this new world, but it was not long before he saw how mistaken he was; how a new tyranny, that of "public opinion" fostered by a rancid press, had simply usurped older forms of authoritarianism. But there was something more than that. In the very qualities which he saw in Americans – their self-righteousness, their "smartness", their insecurity and constant appetite for praise – did he not also recognise certain qualities within his own self? Had there not also been the suspicion of a mercenary motive, just a trace of hypocrisy, in his own handling of the controversy over international copyright? Perhaps he averted his gaze from any such resemblance even in the savage way which, in *Martin Chuzzlewit*, he satirised American characteristics. Perhaps, as so often in his fiction, his laughter at these externalised aspects of his own self was his particular way of acknowledging them without necessarily understanding, or having to deal with, them. Perhaps. All that can be said with certainty is that, after his stay in America, his own understanding of character is deepened and that a troubled mist of self-awareness lingers around such figures as Martin Chuzzlewit, Mr Dombey and of course David Copperfield. Dickens's American journey had also been a journey towards himself.

Chapter 14

IN the early morning of Wednesday, 29 June, 1842, the *George Washington* docked at Liverpool. Charles and Catherine Dickens had come home. They returned to London by train and then in the evening arrived at Osnaburgh Street, where Fred and the children were staying. Mamie Dickens, who was then four years old, remembers a hackney coach coming up to the door and "before it could stop, a figure jumped out, someone lifted me up in their arms, and I was kissing my father through the bars of the gate". The shock of their sudden arrival – they had not been expected until the next day – sent Charlie into convulsions; Dr Elliotson was called at once, and the boy quickly recovered. He was "too glad", he said and some time before had told the washerwoman (his "confidential friend", as Dickens described her) that he would "shake very much" when his parents returned. But there was also Dickens's extended family to visit. He went straight to Macready's house, hurried in and before Macready could see who it was found "dear Dickens holding me in his arms in a transport of joy". Then Dickens rushed off to see Forster at his house in Lincoln's Inn Fields – but he had gone out to dinner. Dickens found out where he was dining and sent a message by servant to tell him "that a gentleman wanted to speak to him". But Forster realised who it was, came out of the house, jumped into the carriage and began to cry. So much for the sternness and masculine reticence of the "Victorians".

And, since this was a period of communal sentiment as well as of high feeling, a dinner was arranged almost at once to celebrate Dickens's return. It was held in Greenwich – among the guests was Thomas Hood who remembered how the novelist spoke of "the embarrassing attentions of the Transatlantickers, who made his private house and private cabin particularly public". Clearly this aspect of his journey was still on his mind. "Then," Hood goes on, "we had more songs. Barham chanted a Robin Hood ballad, and Cruikshank sang a burlesque ballad of Lord Bateman" – in fact this was a ballad which Dickens himself had written some years before – "– and somebody, unknown to me, gave a capital imitation of a French showman. Then we toasted Mrs Boz and the Chairman, and the Vice, and the Traditional Priest [a certain Father Prout, writer of articles and critic] sang the 'Deep, deep sea' in his deep, deep voice." And, after this, there were more toasts and speeches and songs. Of course there were other quieter dinners with friends like Samuel Rogers, Captain Marryat and Lady Holland. And, in addition, Dickens had to catch up with a great deal of correspondence. They moved back to Devonshire Terrace the day after their arrival, with all the domestic upheaval which this entailed, and it seems that from this time forward Catherine's younger sister, Georgina, came to live with her sister and brother-in-law in order to help with the children. She became a sort of unofficial governess, known after a time as "Aunt Georgie". She was eager, punctilious, and helpful; indeed, what young woman would not have tried to impress a famous brother-in-law, leading a life so much more glamorous than any she had known before? More importantly, perhaps, she came to the Dickens household at the age of fourteen and thus was only a little younger than Mary Hogarth when Dickens first knew her; it seems, in fact, that at once he noticed a resemblance between the two girls: ". . . so much of her spirit shines out in this sister," he wrote of Mary, "that the old time comes back again at some seasons, and I can hardly separate it from the present." Was this one of the reasons why Dickens invited Georgina to join his family? If so, there is no cause to suppose that Catherine, at this stage, disapproved of such a decision.

Such was the energy of Dickens himself that immediately after his return he launched into several projects at once; he composed a long circular on the absence of copyright in America and sent it to various writers, and at the same time wrote a letter to the *Examiner* in which he publicly declared that he would never sign a publishing contract with an American firm (a promise which he did not in fact keep). He also became marginally involved in a scheme for a Union or Guild of writers, a project which at this time came to nothing but which he would revive with more success at a later date. Then a few weeks later he wrote a long letter to the *Examiner*, supporting the provisions of Lord Ashley's Mines and Collieries Bill, which was about to prohibit the employment of women and children in the mines. It is indicative of his real politics, however, that he attacks the aristocratic owners of the mines (in particular the vacuous Lord Londonderry) rather than the industrial civilisation which depended upon them. He signed it merely "B", for "Boz", but all those who knew him recognised who the writer was. Clearly he was troubled by the idea of children being involved in such a dangerous and dirty trade (did he remember his own time in the blacking factory as he wrote this eloquent condemnation of the aristocratic mill-owners who were trying to defeat the Bill?) but clearly, also, he had come back from America with a greater awareness of his own fame and a greater sense of his power as a public figure. That is no doubt why he also seems to have welcomed the opportunity of becoming a newspaper editor – the occasion was the disappearance of the liberal newspaper, the *Courier*, and Dickens believed that there was what we would call a "gap in the market" for a radical journal under his own direction. He wrote at once to Lady Holland, broaching the idea and asking her to contact the leaders of the Whig party to see if they would finance the venture. It came to nothing (a later project would be more successful, at least temporarily) but the fact that Dickens made such a sudden decision to take on such an arduous job suggests that he was eager to place himself in a new and more authoritative relationship with his public. It is of course difficult to see how he could have edited an evening newspaper and maintained the writing of his fiction, except that he always possessed a grandiose but not necessarily misplaced confidence in his own powers and perseverance. It is also possible that, still so much in debt to Chapman and Hall, he wanted to secure a regular source of income beyond the exigencies of the monthly numbers of his novels. Yet clearly now, after his American journey, he saw himself as an eminent man, an important man – not simply an entertainer who, to use his phrase of only a few months before, was adding to the stock of harmless cheerfulness. Or, rather, he believed himself to be capable of doing both things at once. He wanted to be a leader of opinion as well as an entertainer. He wanted to be everything. And he was also very impetuous: once an idea like this had "struck" him, he would work himself up into a fever of excitement and impatience, even if it was one which abated almost as quickly as it had arisen. That is why there are many times in his life when he takes up a cause with huge zeal only to weary of it; certainly his interest in international copyright, so important a part of his life at this time, was not one that endured. A few years later, he had for all practical purposes lost interest in the subject.

Thus his energy and enthusiasm redoubled on his return from the United States and, within two weeks, he had also begun work on an account of his travels which he finally entitled *American Notes for General Circulation*. He had gone there with the idea of writing such a book, and there was no reason to believe that it would not achieve a high sale; and, if there was one thing he needed now, it was money. Money to help pay back the debt to Chapman and Hall. Money to support his ever-enlarging family. Money to support his spendthrift father and younger brothers who seemed incapable of making their own way. And so, with the images of the New World fresh in his mind, he began. His opening chapter was a salvo directed against what he anticipated to be a hostile American reception; he read this to Macready almost as soon as he had written it, but the actor was not impressed by Dickens's excessively defiant and almost hostile tone. "*I do not like it*," Macready wrote in his diary and in fact, at Forster's instigation, Dickens later and reluctantly dropped the offending chapter from the published book. Of course accounts of American travels by English notables were not at all rare phenomena: in *The Pickwick Papers*, the elder Weller is heard to say of Mr Pickwick: ". . . let him come back and write a book about the 'Merrikins as'll pay all his expenses and more, if he blows 'em up enough." If Dickens did not exactly blow them up, he certainly rocked them a little. The task was congenial enough to come easily to him, and Mary Shelley wrote to a friend that "Charles Dickens has just come home in a state of violent dislike of the Americans – and means to devour them in his next work – he says they are so frightfully dishonest". He borrowed as many of his letters to friends as he could, especially those to Forster which he had been writing at the time as a record to be consulted at a later date. He also used material from various pamphlets and newspapers which he had collected in the course of his journeys; and there was, of course, his wonderfully adept memory. It has often been asserted that his account is less than accurate, that he sometimes, as the *Edinburgh Review* put it, "mistakes pictures in his mind for facts in nature". There are occasions when he transposes a detail from one scene to another, and there are also two or three passages where he does seem to falsify his description for imaginative reasons. But to a large extent his is an accurate account, even if he has a habit of interpreting events in the most unflattering or unfavourable light. For, although Dickens employed the material from his letters, *American Notes* is a much more elaborate and self-conscious narrative than his general correspondence, and the sometimes bare detail of his private reports is here lent more careful and even artful shape. He also decided not to introduce his own experiences to an inordinate degree; all those paragraphs in his letters about his enthusiastic and sometimes bizarre reception in the United States are excised, and Dickens is at pains to compose a serious, objective account of his experiences. Yet of course the personality of Dickens cannot help but invest these pages with an extra resonance, and he emerges here indirectly as punctilious, watchful, high-spirited, extremely susceptible to atmosphere. Whenever he does appear, in fact, the narrative takes on a more fiery and pantomimic quality – "Here we are!" had been his cry when he entered the Boston hotel, as we have heard already, and that same joyous and almost reckless spirit is on occasions visible in the pages of a sometimes sombre book. It was a qualified success in England; the quarterly reviews were not impressed by Dickens's sprightly manner, but the daily newspapers found little to which they wanted to object. Of course *American Notes* was almost at once pirated in the United States, although Dickens had cleverly arranged for its publication (in two volumes) on 19 October so that it could not be taken aboard the *Caledonia* which was bound for Boston on that very day. As a result the pirates were delayed by three weeks. Nevertheless, in its various editions, it had a sale in America as enormous as the criticism which it provoked. The *New York Herald* described Dickens's mind as the "most coarse, vulgar, impudent and superficial" and as a direct result of these two slim volumes Dickens's reputation in the United States plummeted except among those intimate friends who continued to support him. Dickens was quite aware of the controversy he had aroused, and even years later was to say of the representative American, "Sometimes he seems disposed to consider me a sort of Monster, at first, but he soon gets over it."

In fact *American Notes* was in many ways a serious discourse on the nature of American society and American institutions in particular, and by far the most controversial and topical aspects of the book concerned the regime of prisons in America. The country was considered by many to be a leader in penal reform, as we have already described, and in particular English penal experts were interested in that "Separate System" which Dickens had seen in Philadelphia and which was about to be introduced at the new "model prison" of Pentonville. The alternative penal method was known as the "Silent

System" which was more purely punitive in character; prisoners worked on the treadmill, or picked oakum, while rigid silence was maintained. Dickens infinitely preferred the latter system. He believed the "model prisons" to be too lenient to their inmates and extolled instead the virtues of hard and unrewarding labour. Certainly he preferred a regime which relied more upon punishment than upon moral improvement; ". . . it is a satisfaction to me," he wrote some years later, "to see that determined thief, swindler or vagrant, sweating profusely at the treadmill or the crank." Nor did he approve of those prison chaplains or enlightened reformers who put their trust in the confessions or conversions of prisoners; as Scrooge might have said for him, he considered it the merest humbug, and the remarks of "pet prisoners" were treated by him with incredulity. "If a notion arose," he wrote in the *Examiner*, "that the wearing of brass buttons led to crime, and they were questioned to elucidate that point, we should have such answers as 'I was happy till I wore brass buttons', 'Brass buttons did it', 'Buttons is the cause of my being here . . .'" This is the authoritarian Dickens, the man who was on intimate terms with police inspectors and prison governors; one particular friend was G. L. Chesterton, the governor of Coldbath Fields, which had a reputation as one of the most severe of the London penitentiaries. But, as always in Dickens's personality, one attitude or belief is expressed only to call forth its opposite, for is it not also true that in Dickens's fiction the prisoner or convict is often a figure treated with the greatest sympathy? If there are times when the world is constructed in his fictions as if it were itself a kind of prison, so the most forceful and the most imaginative of his own creations are prisoners either in fact, like Magwitch, or in spirit, like Miss Havisham. For there is a sense in which Dickens, toò, seems imaginatively to share their fate. In one of his letters to Chesterton he in fact adopts the tone and style of a prisoner, and there is no doubt that he begins to pity and to sympathise with prisoners as soon as they are turned into victims of "the system". He may have wanted to see them punished in the treadmill but, when he comes to identify himself with them, all the powers of his imagination are lavished upon them; so he becomes both gaoler and jailed, condemning others and in turn condemned. It is this crucial act of personal identification which led him specifically to denounce the treatment of juvenile prisoners in England. The sight of a child in a cell was enough to set off all the alarm bells within his nature and, as a contemporary noticed, ". . . the subject was one which at all times raised him to passionate indignation; at all seasons, at his own table, in private conversation as well as public occasions, he denounced the treatment of unfortunate juveniles as inhuman and unnatural, a monstrous evil calling for immediate reform". Such paradoxes make it difficult to describe Dickens's attitudes in any schematic way. There are times when he is more reactionary than any of his contemporaries (with the possible exception of Carlyle), but there are also occasions when he condemns the evils of the nineteenth century in tones that recall the most liberal reformers of that time. The fact that his journalism tends to be harsher or more "prejudiced" than his fiction suggests what is really only to be expected: the artist is more capacious and less obsessive than the man.

Almost as soon as they had returned to England, he and Catherine were planning to make what had now become an annual visit to Broadstairs, and on the first day of August they set off with the children to that resort which in a fake legal deposition Dickens described now as a "seaside dipping, bathing, or watering-place". They were back in a house on Albion Street, along the front and facing the sea, and it was here that Dickens began the fifth chapter of *American Notes*. Throughout the whole of this summer he kept up a steady pace of a chapter a week, his own antagonism towards America, and to the American press in particular, being refreshed by the publication of a faked letter purporting to come from him and in which he attacked friends and enemies alike. It was a clumsy forgery, but the interest in the scandalous Boz was enough to place it on several American front pages. Dickens sent off a series of angry letters to his American friends denouncing this fake, but there was little action he could take except, perhaps, to direct his anger into his writing. It is notable that in the chapter he began to write after he had been informed of the forged letter he dwells once more with some disgust upon the American habit of spitting in all places and on all occasions. And yet even as he was writing *American Notes* he was turning over in his mind the possibilities for a new novel. According to his contract with Chapman and Hall it was to begin in November, but at this stage he seems to have had no clear idea of the direction in which he wanted to move. His ideas simmered, as it were, as he continued with the travel book and engaged in all pastimes of the seaside; he was taking his usual long walks along the coast or along the beach, he was bathing in the sea, he was visiting the theatres in Margate and Ramsgate (there was none in Broadstairs), he was reading Tennyson, he was welcoming friends who came to stay for brief periods. Nothing unusual in any of this, and it might seem representative of "holidays" at any time, but there are sometimes scenes which establish people and events in a time so different from our own that all the familiarity of resemblance fades away. It was during this holiday, for example, that Charles Dickens found a deaf and dumb boy who had been abandoned and was lying "half dead" upon the beach at Broadstairs. "A most deplorable case," Dickens adds, in a phrase which suggest how familiar such "cases" were, but he stirred himself into action; Dickens had the boy taken to the infirmary of a local workhouse, and he is never mentioned again. One of the thousands of homeless children, many of them in some way disabled from ordinary life, who seem to drift across the landscape of the nineteenth century, discarded and forgotten.

Dickens had almost finished *American Notes* by the time the family returned to London at the beginning of October; he had only two chapters to write and, for the first of them, he simply reprinted a number of newspaper cuttings to give his readers some idea of the horrors of slavery in the Southern states. The last chapter, an odd mixture of exhortation and comic observation, was also written hurriedly, and this principally because Dickens's time was taken up by an unexpected visitor in the shape of Henry Wadsworth Longfellow. There had been other interruptions. William Hone, a radical author and compiler of miscellanies, was dying and asked for him on his death-bed. Dickens knew him as a friend and collaborator of George Cruikshank, but it seems that Hone had recently been reading nothing but Dickens's novels and wanted to shake hands with the author before he died; a touching last request and one which Dickens could hardly refuse. So great was his power that even those leaving the world wanted to see and to thank him. So he visited the dying man in the company of Cruikshank. And then, that same night, Longfellow arrived unexpectedly at Devonshire Terrace. Dickens had liked the man in the United States and, in his usual impetuous and convivial manner, had invited him to stay with him on his next journey to London; and now he was here. "I write this from Dickens's study," he told a compatriot. "The raven croaks in the garden; and the ceaseless roar of London fills my ears." Longfellow was just five years older than Dickens and at this time not particularly well known in England as a poet. No doubt that is why Dickens referred to him as "the American Professor" – he had been Professor of Modern Languages and Belles Lettres at Harvard since 1836 – but he also called him "the best of the American Poets" and admired the three volumes of poetry which Longfellow had published. So for the next two weeks he became his guide, host and social secretary; there were trips to the theatre, breakfasts and dinners with a variety of friends, visits to the available literary grandees, excursions to the country (Rochester, of course, and Bath, to visit Landor). He also took Longfellow on a tour of the "rookeries" or slums of London, to see how the vagrant and indigent population of the city managed to survive in the narrow alleys, courts and passages of the poorer quarters. There are times, in fact, when Dickens's nocturnal expeditions seem indistinguishable from his trips to the London Zoological Gardens or to Astley's, where other forms of entertainment were also guaranteed. Forster and Maclise went with them on this particular expedition to a lodging house in an area of the Borough known as The Mint: the usual stench emanated from the place and Maclise "was struck with such a sickness on entering" that he had to remain outside with the policemen who were guarding them in this area of theft and vice.

Of course Dickens was more accustomed to the odours of the poor, since part of his knowledge of London came from his journeys into its interior where thousands of people lived in close-packed rookeries or jerry-built tenements without ventilation or sanitation. But familiarity did not breed neglect. He was never anything other than appalled by what he saw, as all were who ventured into what for most respectable nineteenth-century citizens was unknown and forbidden territory. And he knew, too, how dangerous in every sense such places were. Westminster, Southwark, Bermondsey, Whitechapel, Rotherhithe, St Giles, a world within a world. But one that affected the larger world. Just two weeks before this visit with Longfellow to the Borough, Dickens had been reading Edwin Chadwick's *Report on the Sanitary Condition of the Labouring Population*; it is not a document for the squeamish, Chadwick himself being a social reformer of the direct, Benthamite breed who never allowed propriety to interfere with his good intentions. Dickens had received this report from his brother-in-law, Henry Austin (who had married Laetitia five years before), an architect and civil engineer. Austin had worked with Robert Stephenson on the construction of the Blackwall Railway and in the course of that work had been appalled by the slums through which the railway line was supposed to pass, for one of the major benefits of the new mania for laying down railways was precisely the extent to which it opened up a world of dirt and indigence which had previously been obscured from view. Its effect on Austin was such that he became actively involved in founding the Association for Promoting the Improvement of the Dwellings of the Labouring Class; thus did the railways materially assist the cause of social reform. Austin went on to become secretary of the 1847 Sanitary Commission and eventually Chief Inspector for the Board of Health, but even at this stage he was known to be Chadwick's "favourite engineer" and one whose personal contact with Dickens was invaluable for the movement of sanitary reform. As Chadwick told him, "Mr Dickens will have possession of the ear not only of America but of Europe . . ." And indeed it was after reading Chadwick's report that he emphasised the importance of sanitary reform in the last and hurriedly written chapter of *American Notes*. We shall see at a later date how a number of important themes rise up from this sanitary activity and find their place in Dickens's novels but it is important to note here that, from the beginning, he was deeply concerned with the most important reform activity of the day – the reform of public health.

For London was growing too fast. The "Great Oven", as Dickens sometimes called it, was spreading through Bloomsbury, Islington, and St John's Wood in the North and, in the West and South, through Paddington, Bayswater, South Kensington, Lambeth, Clerkenwell and Peckham. The population of London at the beginning of the nineteenth century was something like one million but, by the end, it had reached four and a half million; in the 1840s alone it has been estimated that there was a net migration into the city of some quarter of a million people. They came in from outlying areas looking for work; they came from Ireland; they came from all the counties of England into the Great Wen, the Fever Patch, London. Most of them were so poor that they found their way ineluctably into the already-overcrowded slums, and there were areas of London in which the population took up every inch of available space. One survey of the Forties found that, in the area of St Giles, the rookery close to the Seven Dials and immortalised by Hogarth in 'Gin Lane', 2,850 people were crowded into just 95 small and decrepit houses. It was not unusual for families of seven or eight people to inhabit one room. And we must not see London as the city so familiar today; much of *that* was a later development of the Victorians themselves who, by the closing years of the century, had transformed whole areas of the metropolis.

In fact the London of the 1840s was very much the London of the eighteenth century; a city of small shops and small trades, a city of dirty red brick, a city which was covered by a patina of fog and decay, a city which simply had no resources for those who poured into its dens and courtyards. Poured into the narrow streets; poured into the jerry-built houses constructed back to back without drainage; poured into the cellars; poured into the frowsy lanes which had a channel of sewage running along them; poured into the once-grand buildings which had become a jangling honeycomb of tenements; poured into the cheap lodging houses where men, women and children mingled promiscuously together. In some of these places, according to an Inspector in 1847, "the filth [by which he meant excrement] was lying scattered about the rooms, vaults, cellars, areas and yards, so thick, and so deep, that it was hardly possible to move for it". In 1856 when a death occurred in one of the tenements of Clerkenwell, "the living and the dead must be together in the same room, the living must eat, drink and sleep beside a decomposing corpse, overheated by a fire required for cooking, and already filled with the foul emanations from the bodies of the living and their impure clothes". The housing conditions for what might be called the labouring poor are best summarised in this short official report on the death of one woman who lived with her husband and son in a small room, without furniture, in Bermondsey: "She lay dead beside her son upon a heap of feathers which were scattered over her almost naked body, there being neither sheet nor coverlet. The feathers stuck so fast over the whole body that the physician could not examine the corpse until it was cleansed, and then found it starved and scarred from the bites of vermin. Part of the floor of the room was torn up, and the hole used by the family as a privy." Dead, and dying around them every day. Dr Simon, the great worker for public health reform, saw these poor people as a race apart: ". . . swarms of men and women who have yet to learn that human beings should dwell differently from cattle – swarms to whom personal cleanliness is utterly unknown; swarms by whom delicacy and decency in their social relations are quite unconceived." These were the men and women whose lives and habitations Dickens would periodically visit; in those passages of *Bleak House* or *Oliver Twist* when he describes such things, and has often been unjustly accused of fantasy or melodrama, he was speaking less than the barest truth. But of course they were not a race apart. They lived in the next street or in an adjacent district, unseen and unknown by respectable men and women but there nonetheless, packed in houses very close to those of

Regent Street or Hanover Square, the unseen host whose presence meant danger. They did not provoke a fear of social revolution, although the presence of this underclass often induced strange fears among those who walked within the pale of "civilisation", but rather the fear of disease. "All smell is disease," Edwin Chadwick had once proclaimed, and it was commonly believed that the pestiferous winds and gases from the rookeries were literally the bearers of fatality.

The essential problems were obvious enough to the health reformers, therefore, even if the various authorities were strangely unwilling to act upon their recommendations. One of the main problems was that of drainage or, rather, the lack of it. What sewers existed were already falling apart, and many of them simply emptied into areas known as "cess lakes". Gutters in the middle of the street were used as avenues for excrement and urine to run until they were stopped up in a court or alley; a certain backyard would be chosen to contain the heaped-up piles of the neighbours' dirt; privies were often emptied into the open sewers and ditches which ran across the metropolis and in most places the detritus oozed through the foundations and cellars of the buildings and collected into the myriad of cesspools; that is why the soil of London was literally sodden with filth of all descriptions. The Fleet Ditch which ran beside Holborn Hill was no more than an open sewer which emptied out into the Thames; as did two hundred other sewers, so that during the hot summer of 1858, for example, the stench of the great river became insupportable and it was recorded at the time that ". . . the sewerage of nearly three million people had been brought to seethe and ferment under a burning sun, in a vast open cloaca lying in their midst". And yet the very same Thames water was pumped into the domestic cisterns of London householders or into standing pipes, without any attempt at filtration. It is recorded that the water had a strange taste and was brownish in colour, and it needs not the wildest flight of imagination to realise what was actually in the water when it was used for washing or cooking. Of course many thousands of poor people had no access to water at all. If they were fortunate they might be able to make use of a standing pump which was turned on for a short period each week or, if they could afford to do so, they might buy water from the travelling water carts.

It was said by foreigners or countrymen arriving in London that the city smelt characteristically of horse dung, largely because of the number of horses on the thoroughfares; but there were other smells, too, and the public health reformers did not turn their attention only to the poor state of sanitation and drainage. There was another and equally insidious threat to the health of the citizens – it came from the burial grounds within the city which were now overflowing and in which the bodies were piled high upon each other, sometimes breaking through the soil and emitting noxious gases which poisoned or even killed those in the vicinity. One report noted that in Clement's Lane there were no less than four graveyards where "the living breathe on all sides an atmosphere impregnated with the odour of the dead". The soil was "saturated, absolutely saturated, with human putrescence". It was common for those who worked among the tombs literally to pick up pieces of the overflowing dead and burn them. One graveyard worker reported that "I have been up to my knees in human flesh by jumping on the bodies so as to cram them into the least possible space at the bottom of the graves in which fresh bodies were afterwards placed".

And so disease spread like a stain. There were four epidemics of cholera within Dickens's own lifetime and, beside these mortal visitations, there were periodic and regular outbreaks of typhus, typhoid fever, epidemic diarrhoea, dysentery, smallpox and a variety of ailments which were classified only as "fevers". Between November and December of 1847 500,000 people were infected with typhus fever out of a total population of 2,100,100, and it seemed to many that London was indeed becoming what *The Lancet* described as a "doomed city". The average age of mortality in the capital was 27, while that for the working classes was 22, and in 1839 almost half the funerals in London were of children under the age of ten. Dickens is often criticised for the number of child-deaths which occur in his fiction but, again, he was reflecting no more than the simplest truth. Dead, and dying around him every day. That is the forgotten aspect of Victorian London. No Londoner was ever completely well, and when in nineteenth-century fiction urban life is described as "feverish" it was a statement of medical fact and not a metaphor. In the opening pages of *The Old Curiosity Shop* Dickens describes the capital as "the stream of life that will not stop, pouring on, on, on . . .", and here we see the image of feverish sweating superimposed upon a city that was filled with the dank cold perspiration of its inhabitants.

It was not in fact until the end of Dickens's life that the sanitary conditions of London were improved. For most of his period the sundry and various official bodies in the metropolis – vestries, parishes, water authorities, gas authorities, improvement commis-sioners, poor law guardians – took specific responsibility for only a small number of activities and refused to work together in any meaningful sense. Not until the inauguration of the Metropolitan Board of Works in 1855, and the creation of the new London sewers by the mid-Sixties, was there any proper attempt to create a healthy or decent environment in what was then the greatest city in the world. And so for most of his life Dickens lived in a city in which the odour of the dead emanated from metropolitan graveyards, where adults and children died of malnutrition or disease, where open sewers and cesspools spread their miasma into the foggy air, where it took only the shortest period to turn off one of the grand thoroughfares or respectable streets of the city and enter a landscape of filth and destitution, death and misery. We have here glimpses of an urban life which is so alien to us as to seem almost incredible; but which for Dickens and his contemporaries was both common and familiar.

On 21 October Dickens and Forster travelled from London to Bristol in order to "see off" Longfellow on his voyage back to the United States and on the following day, now that all his duties in London had been dispatched, he began to make plans for another journey – this time to Cornwall with Forster, Maclise and Stanfield. He was supposed to deliver the first instalment of his new novel within a month to Chapman and Hall, but it was already clear that publication would have to be deferred, at least for a short while. Of course the new book was very much on his mind, and in fact his decision to go to Cornwall seems to have been determined by it; he wanted to visit the "very dreariest and most desolate portion of the sea-coast" and, in addition, he wanted to go down one of the tin mines there. Only a few weeks before he had written in support of Lord Ashley's Mines and Collieries Bill, as we have seen, and clearly he was aiming to strike at the mines and mine-owners as once he had struck at Yorkshire schools in *Nicholas Nickleby* and the New Poor Law in *Oliver Twist*. After the historical fiction of *Barnaby Rudge*, and no doubt fired imaginatively by his recent experiences in America, he wanted to write another fiction of the present day. So he set off in search of material.

On his way to the South-West, he stopped at Alphington to see his parents – not perhaps a happy visit, after John Dickens's attempts to raise money in his son's absence, and in light of the fact that they were about to move away from the cottage which their son had found for them. From there the party went on to Plymouth and started on a week's trip which would take them through Liskeard, Bodmin, Truro and Land's End. Apparently it was a successful holiday. "I never laughed in my life as I did on this journey," Dickens wrote to one of his American friends. "It would have done you good to hear me." The others were no doubt, as always, infected with Dickens's high spirits, although even at this stage Daniel Maclise was becoming much more difficult and reclusive. "I suppose I shall be expected to make myself agreeable," he said of a different occasion. And no doubt there was also the unstated rivalry between Maclise and Forster for the closest friendship with Dickens; unstated but not unnoticed, since Count d'Orsay at a slightly later date mocked what he told Maclise was "your little dam ridicule coquetterie avec that good Forster and Dickens". But Forster was too useful and important, Maclise too wayward and uncertain, for there to be any real doubt about the outcome of such a contest. Meanwhile, they visited such famous sites as the Logan Rock, stayed at variously colourful local inns, descended into at least one mine, rode, and drew (even Dickens made some sketches). But what gained Dickens's attention did not necessarily engage his imagination, and nothing of that trip finds any place in the novel he was just about to begin; unless it be the fact that *Martin Chuzzlewit* has initially a rural rather than an urban setting. The tin mines were to appear elsewhere, however, when Dickens came to write *A Christmas Carol* in the following year: nothing he saw was ever really lost, but the right conditions were necessary for it to emerge transformed.

And what were the conditions surrounding *Martin Chuzzlewit* itself? Dickens was back in London by 4 November and almost at once began to plot his new work. Clearly he was in a heightened and excitable state. A week later he had to attend the funeral of William Hone, and in an account of this event for Cornelius Felton he constructed a scene which might have come from the pages of Balzac or, indeed, of Dickens, since it is concerned with the "comicality" which can arise at the most solemn moments as Dickens finds himself almost sobbing with laughter at the funereal absurdities of George Cruikshank and others. When his letter was published many years later, after Dickens's death, it became clear from the outraged comments of other participants at the funeral that he had not been entirely truthful. Cruikshank himself said that Dickens's account was the merest "fiction", and one of the relatives of the long-dead Hone commented that Dickens seemed ready "to sacrifice everything that stands in the way of his making a point" – that he lied, in other words.

And this in a letter in which he had written "I give you my word" about one of the incidents later called into question by less imaginative observers. Not a particularly interesting incident, perhaps, except to the extent which it displays Dickens's propensity and indeed his need to create fictions just as he was beginning his new work.

For all this time he was "plotting and contriving" *Martin Chuzzlewit*, a process which meant that he shut himself away, doodled, looked out of the window, walked up and down, became ferociously impatient with his family, despaired, and then wrote. In many respects *Martin Chuzzlewit* was to be a novel quite different from any of its predecessors, a fact which might be put down to Dickens's "development" as long as we attempt to understand of what that development might have consisted. It is of course difficult to chart the course of anyone's inner life, especially of one so prone to self-dramatisation as Dickens, and there are times when the biographer must behave like an archaeologist and go field walking over the life of his subject, looking for those faint traces and furrows which indicate the presence of a time long gone. So it is that, in Dickens's life in the period he began to write *Martin Chuzzlewit*, we begin to mark several faint strands of meaning, several episodes which in·themselves may suggest nothing but which may have a cumulative significance. He had, for example, started regularly to attend Unitarian services at a chapel in Little Portland Street. He had also just written a plea for a sanatorium for the impoverished middle-classes, in which he spoke of those "trodden down amidst the busy concourse struggling for existence". Charles Dickens's Christianity was of an eminently practical kind, as we shall see later, and his attachment to Unitarianism at this time indicates the extent to which he was concerned less with theology and more with the social and moral obligations of faith; good works and public service were the key phrases of Unitarianism, in both the American and English versions of what has been called its predominantly "ethical culture". And, if traces of a more elaborate moral consciousness are to be detected in *Martin Chuzzlewit*, it is from evidence of this kind that we can confirm the direction in which Dickens was travelling. But there are other influences around him. He had been reading Tennyson in Broadstairs and had been particularly struck by the threnodies to death and beauty in his *Poems* published that year. And he had been overwhelmed by Robert Browning's *A Blot on the 'Scutcheon*, a play lent to him by Forster in which a fourteen-year-old girl becomes the secret and innocent lover of a doomed young hero. In particular he admired the lines: "I had/No mother – God forgot me – and I fell." Clearly here his immediate and powerful reactions – "Browning's play has thrown me into a perfect passion of sorrow" – are to be attributed to his memories of Mary Hogarth, sorrow for whom always instilled in Dickens confused images of death and beauty; but such unsettling images and influences are also to be found in *Martin Chuzzlewit*.

What other events in Dickens's life, inconsequential in themselves, lead towards the great act of divining energy and passion with which he always informed his work? He had also been much struck by another play – John Marston's *The Patrician's Daughter*, again a drama about love and death – and had even agreed to write a preface for it when Macready produced it at Drury Lane. Its great strength came from its contemporary setting, a "realism" which Macready emphasised in his production; and this was precisely what Dickens noticed, too. He described it in a letter to Longfellow as a "tragedy of the present day" and in his prologue introduced an invocation to "the Present!":

> "Not light its import, and not poor its mien;
> Yourselves the actors, and your homes the scene."

Dickens wished to use that last line as an epigraph for *Martin Chuzzlewit*, but was persuaded otherwise by Forster. Nevertheless the connections are clear. Even as Dickens was stirred by tales of lost love and fatality, he was equally intrigued by the idea of setting such tragedies within the sphere of the present day (an interest confirmed when a stage version of *Martin Chuzzlewit* itself was eventually performed with a prologue which stressed its "powerful romance of common life"). The fact that Dickens makes his central comic character, Pecksniff, an architect is another example of his deliberate topicality at this point, since architecture and its practitioners were very much "in the air" during the period when he was beginning the novel. The rebuilding of the House of Commons after the fire seven years before, the construction of the great new railway stations, and the expansion of London itself, had combined to turn the architect into one of the central and most controversial figures of the period. Only two years before, in fact, Dickens's brother-in-law, Henry Austin, had written a pamphlet entitled *Thoughts on the Abuses of the Present System of Competition in Architecture*. Nothing escaped Dickens's attention and so, when he needed a figure to represent the commercialism and vainglory of his own age, he found an architect.

Everything comes together, so that even in the smallest incidents the origin of great works may be found: in these months, for example, Dickens was commissioning work from several artists in order to decorate the walls of Devonshire Terrace. George Cattermole gave him two watercolour drawings based upon scenes from *The Old Curiosity Shop* and, through an anonymous "buyer", Dickens had managed to obtain from Daniel Maclise a painting of a Cornish waterfall they had seen together on their recent excursion. Recently, too, he had met W. P. Frith and had commissioned him to paint two of his characters, Dolly Varden and Kate Nickleby; one sees in these commissions, by the way, how Dickens granted reality to the creatures of his imagination. He asked Frith who had been the model for Dolly and, in doing so, had pronounced the word with its then accustomed French intonation, modèle. Frith had replied and used the now standard pronunciation – model (moddle). Dickens then interjected, with what Frith considered a certain "sarcasm", "Oh, Mr Frith, you call it 'moddle', do you?" So it is that in *Martin Chuzzlewit* a Mr Augustus Moddle makes his appearance. Thus, in the months and weeks and days before Dickens set to work, his growing moral concerns, his attachment to the themes of love and death, his interest in a modern and realistic setting, even the occasions of his sarcasm, are moulded together.

He still needed a name to begin. On a sheet of paper he transcribed all the titles of his previous novels, and then wrote Martin chuzzlewig, then Martin chubblewig, then chuzzletoe and chuzzlebog. Then on another sheet he wrote down a whole range of surnames; Martin was clearly right, but now he put after it chuzzlewig, Sweezleden, chuzzletoe, Sweezlebach, Sweezlewag. Then he decides on Chuzzlewig, writes out a longer title, only to change his mind and on another sheet put Martin Chuzzlewit. He had found it. For names were very important to Dickens. When he started a new periodical he told Forster that "I shall never be able to do anything for the work until it has a fixed name", and it is the same with his characters also. They did not exist for him until he had given them a name and it is that which, like a spell, brings forth their appearance and behaviour in the world. Whenever he saw or heard an odd name he would remember it and then later note it down. He kept lists of them – one such was in fact compiled from a Privy Council Education List – and he had a copy of *Bowditch's Surnames*. Perhaps that is why there are such odd and perhaps not coincidental clusters of names in areas which he knew;

Fanny Dorritt is on a gravestone beside Rochester Cathedral, and at the small church at Chalk are Guppy, Twist, and Flight on three adjacent tombstones. In the church register at Chatham are Jasper, Sowerby and Weller while in the register of St Andrew's, Holborn, are to be found Chadband, Twist, Krook, Boffin, Guppy, Dorrit, Marley and Varden. He devoted so much care and attention to the name because within it, when eventually it emerged, he saw the lineaments of the character who possessed it; when he brooded over his lists he was selecting and defining all the qualities he needed. The name, then, works as an almost objective pressure on the novelist's imagination. The fact that he gave his friends and his own family various nicknames – the Ocean Spectre, the Lincolnian Mammoth, the Prince – suggests also how readily he converted the people of the real world into characters of his own devising, all of them inhabiting that private imaginative world which he had constructed for them. And can we not also trace at least part of his constant preoccupation with names to the fact that his own name, Dickens, now so hallowed because of its association with the great novelist, was at the time considered funny and even vulgar? In *The Merry Wives of Windsor* he would have read, "I cannot tell what the Dickens his name is"; he would also have known the phrases of the time, "how the Dickens" and "I'll play the Dickings with you", where variants of his name were used as a euphemism for the devil. He even plays with his own name in all the Dicks of his fiction, as well as in such surnames as Pickwick and Wickfield.

And even Chuzzlewit. Now that he had the name he could set to work upon the complete title and he eventually emerged in the fifth draft with: "The Life and Adventures of Martin Chuzzlewit, His relatives, friends, and enemies. Comprising all His Wills and his Ways, With an Historical Record of what he did, And what he didn't. Shewing Moreover who Inherited the Family Plate; who came in for the Silver Spoons, And who for the wooden ladles. The whole forming a complete Key To The House of Chuzzlewit. Edited by 'Boz'. With illustrations by 'Phiz'." So this is to be the story of a family or a dynasty, its concerns money and inheritance. He began with a parody of genealogical research, then went on to chronicle the progress of an autumn wind in evening as it blows its way towards Mr Pecksniff and his two lovely daughters, Charity and Mercy ("Not unholy names, I hope?" as he is later to ask). The youngest Miss Pecksniff is all simplicity and innocence, all girlishness and playfulness, a tender gushing thing. The elder Miss Pecksniff, in lovely contrast, is all gravity and demureness. Mr Pecksniff himself is a very pattern of the moral man, an architect, a pillar of the little community, who warms his hands before the fire "as benevolently as if they were somebody else's, not his . . ." These opening chapters were written quickly – he had finished them by the middle of December, only six weeks after his return from Cornwall – but they are composed with extreme carefulness, almost self-consciousness, on Dickens's part. Two number plans of the novel survive in which he plots the course of particular chapters, sometimes foreshadowing events which will transpire much later in the narrative, and from this evidence alone it is clear that he was now beginning to take care over the construction and elaboration of his fictions where before he had been happy to proceed on an almost spontaneous or improvisatory basis, most of his plots having been of a picaresque nature which allowed him to introduce characters and arrange incidents as he went along with his characters in the discovery of their world.

But not with *Martin Chuzzlewit*. He had a theme – according to Forster, it was to display "the number and variety of humours and vices that have their root in selfishness" – and in the preface he wrote at the conclusion of the tale he declares that he had endeavoured ". . . to keep a steadier eye upon the general purpose and design". It was a novel about "Selfishness", as he himself said five years later, and so we have the family of Chuzzlewit in desperate eagerness for an inheritance vying with the self-interest of the hypocrite Pecksniff. How much of this springs from his experiences in America and his own understanding of himself, how much from his disgust at his father's behaviour, how much sheer unacknowledged chance and coincidence, it is impossible to say. If the book is arranged around the theme of selfishness it could also plausibly be said to concern money; wrong investments, anticipated inheritances, borrowing and lending, all create the fabric of a highly commercialised world but nevertheless one which also accurately reflects Dickens's own preoccupations at a period when he was in debt to his publishers and when his family were making their own financial demands upon him. The novel is close to Dickens's experience in another sense, also, since the narrative itself is preoccupied with the role of brother and sister, or sister and sister; Tom Pinch's loving relationship with his own sister, and the hapless Mr Moddle's uncertainty about which of two sisters he should love, has at least its analogue in the Dickens household where two sisters now lived with the novelist in apparent perfect amity.

And yet in *Martin Chuzzlewit* there is a great change in Dickens's conception of moral characteristics. In the earlier novels the heroes and villains were of a dramatic and indeed theatrical order; there are such characters in this novel, too, but, in his portrait of the young Martin Chuzzlewit and of the saintly if credulous Tom Pinch, Dickens incorporates the idea of a changing moral world, of characters who develop under the infliction of circumstances, who become ethically responsible in ways that Dickens's earlier creations did not. And this, too, may have been the indirect consequence of his American journey, in the course of which he had felt himself to be changed. For the first time Dickens begins to explore the contradictions and difficulties of the contemporary human world; these are no longer figures defined by a single characteristic or animated by the wilful principle of a "humour", but ones who are seen to change with the changing world, to live and grow. In fact Dickens was so pleased with the opening chapters – so pleased, in other words, that his grand conception was coming to life in front of him – that he rushed around to Forster's rooms and, as his friend lay ill, read to him the descriptions of Pecksniff and Tom Pinch. As soon as he had finished it seemed to him, as always, the best thing he had done. The manuscript was delivered to the printers by 18 December and, on the last day of that month, the first number of *Martin Chuzzlewit* was published. From now on he set himself a routine of writing the next episode in the first half of the month, and correcting proofs in the second half. He was on his way again.

So, in the first days of January 1843, he began the second number. Until there came Twelfth Night. 6 January. And also the sixth birthday of his first son, Charles or "Charlie", for which occasion, as on many subsequent Twelfth Nights, Dickens gave a party for children and adults alike. The Twelfth Night cake to be ceremoniously cut. Dances, in particular Sir Roger de Coverley which Dickens loved. Crackers. Sweets. A magic lantern entertainment. And, most important of all, Dickens's appearance as conjuror and magician. He had bought the stock-in-trade of a conjuror at Hamley's of High Holborn, and spent days within his own room preparing his feats of magic: coins flying through the air, a box of bran miraculously transformed into a guinea pig, a plum pudding emerging from an empty saucepan. It was said that ". . . when dressed as a magician he would make the children scream with laughter . . .", and at a later date he called himself "The Unparalleled Necromancer Rhia Rhama Rhoos" amongst whose tricks were The Travelling Doll Wonder, The Pudding Wonder, and The Conflagration Wonder. Experts in such matters, on examining all the available evidence, incline to the belief that Dickens was no more than a competent magician, relying upon simple mechanical tricks of illusion, but that he was an unparalleled "patterer" as he talked his way through the various sleights of hand. This we can readily believe, and it is not the first occasion we have seen the writer as performer, the writer as illusionist, the writer as a child among other children.

But all parties come to an end, and through the next cold days he applied himself to *Martin Chuzzlewit*, took long walks in the snow, even rushed down to Devon with Catherine in order to attend to his father's usual tangled affairs. Soon there came more alarming news; the monthly sale of *Martin Chuzzlewit* was of only twenty thousand copies, far fewer than that of his other serials, and within a relatively short time advertising revenue from the inserts in each monthly number also declined. Dickens was in fact extremely pleased with what he had achieved in the new novel, and believed himself to be in some ways at the height of his powers, and so he was not ready to blame himself for this decline in his popularity. In fact posterity may largely support his own judgment: *Martin Chuzzlewit* is among his greatest novels, primarily because of its rich comic mood, and there was a general book trade depression in the period which was making it difficult for writers and booksellers of every kind. But Dickens was severely disappointed, not to say alarmed, about the course of his finances, now that he was earning much less than he had anticipated. As soon as he had seen the Chapman and Hall accounts in March, he gave up the idea he had envisaged of buying a house or cottage out of town.

Instead he took rooms at Cobley's Farm in the rural retreat of Finchley, and here he contemplated the relative failure of *Martin Chuzzlewit*. The eventual shape of the novel was still at this stage fluid enough for him, if he wished, to change its course and catch more public attention. One possibility was to align the novel even more closely with the most important issues of the period; after all, he had originally considered including the abuses of the Cornish mine-owners. It might have been fortuitous, then, that Dr Southwood Smith, one of the members of the Children's Employment Commission, should now have sent him a copy of its second report. South-wood Smith is one of those social reformers who in large part illuminate the active forces of the era; once a Unitarian minister, he had been private secretary to Bentham and all his life had interested himself both in the problems of sanitation and in the working conditions of the poor. He was also a staunch member of committees; he had been part of the Society for the Diffusion of Useful Knowledge, the Health of Towns Association, and the Metropolitan Association for the Improvement of the Dwellings of the Industrial Classes (where he had become closely acquainted with Henry Austin). He was almost twenty-five years older than Dickens but, like Edwin Chadwick, he realised the importance of the young novelist in diffusing the ideas and ideals of social reform; in any case the nexus of Unitarianism, Benthamite utilitarianism and social reform was one in which Dickens himself still largely moved. But his relationship with such reformers was not always easy. Only a few weeks before, for example, he had turned down Southwood Smith's request to help in the campaign to limit the number of working hours: Dickens's characteristically sensible belief was that, as long as working men remained poor, no attempt should be made artificially to curtail their earnings. But the report which exposed the harsh and sometimes unbearable conditions in which children, some as young as five or six, were forced to work was quite another matter. Here all the Dickens's instinctive sympathies came into play and, even as he was writing *Martin Chuzzlewit*, he dashed off a letter to Southwood Smith in which he declared that he would write a pamphlet on the question. A few weeks later he had changed his mind, however, and decided to forget about any pamphlet in order to exert a "Sledge hammer" blow at a later date. It is indeed possible that Dickens had decided to include in *Martin Chuzzlewit* an exposure of child employment. In theory it might have been a good idea and a welcome addition to the range of the novel; in practice it was to emerge in quite a different form.

But there still remained the problem of the novel itself, a novel which Dickens knew to be good but which had failed to capture or to hold the public imagination. And it seems likely that it was at this time, while he was trying to get ahead with the narrative in his retreat at Finchley, that he conceived the idea of sending his "hero", Martin Chuzzlewit, to the United States – a decision which, if it did owe something to his desire to provoke public attention, was also in large part determined by the venomous and abusive tirades which had been reaching him from across the Atlantic. He always said that he made a point of never reading such material in the American newspapers but this sounds like the defence of tremulous and wounded pride; it seems probable that he had learnt the gist of their attacks and, after the relative restraint of *American Notes*, decided to unleash all the fury of his comedy upon them. (It should never be forgotten that, for Dickens, comedy was often a weapon to use against those who threatened or attacked him, which is no doubt why he made such fun of women.) In fact the introduction of American episodes only marginally helped to improve sales – they went up from 20,000 to 23,000, whereas the sale for *Nicholas Nickleby* had been approximately 50,000 for most of its run – and Dickens was hugely offended when one of the partners in the publishing firm, William Hall, mentioned a clause in their contract which stipulated that they could subtract from Dickens's income the sum of fifty pounds each month if sales did not seem to be adequately repaying the advance. In Dickens's tender and vulnerable state, any legalistic attempt to take money from him (money which he now presumed to be *his*) roused him to fury and at once he began considering the idea of abandoning Chapman and Hall altogether, and, curiously enough, making an agreement instead with Bradbury and Evans, the actual printers of his novels with whom he was on very friendly terms (they sent him a turkey each Christmas).

In fact this was a period in which he seems to be uneasy and unsettled at every point. Catherine was expecting another child and, although this condition can scarcely be blamed solely upon her, his references to her during this period are notably bad-tempered; he had already called her "a Donkey" at one point. He was also more than angry with his father, seeming positively to disown him and refusing to have any communications with him. "He, and all of them, look upon me as a something to be plucked and torn to pieces for their advantage," he said later in the year. ". . . My soul sickens at the thought of them . . . Nothing makes me so wretched, or so unfit for what I have to do, as these things . . ." John Dickens, who had removed with his wife from Alphington to lodgings in Lewisham, was again cadging money off almost anyone who had dealings with his famous son. He even wrote to Chapman and Hall, asking them to procure for him a free ticket on the Thames river-boat so that he could visit the library of the British Museum; "If not why then I must doze away the future . . . in my armchair in re-reading the works of Boz." But Dickens's impatience and anger were not directed solely at his family. In this period he had conceived a violent dislike for the Established Church and in particular for those apparently ignorant and bigoted clergymen who quarrelled over the "forms" of the service and of their faith. He also hated going into "society". And he was tired of the endless speeches and meetings with which his fame had encumbered him. This in itself is not surprising, for within a matter of three months he made speeches at the Printers' Pension Society, the Hospital for Consumption and Diseases of the Chest, the Charitable Society for the Deaf and Dumb, the Literary Fund, and the Sanatorium; in the same period he had also agreed to organise the testimonial dinner for Macready, who was about to leave the Drury Lane Theatre, to chair a meeting of authors wishing to form a Guild, to chair a meeting about copyright, and in addition to become chairman of a committee established to provide for the children of Edward Elton, an actor who had drowned. It was not that he was dilatory or incompetent in such duties – as one member of the Elton committee recalled, Dickens managed the meetings with ". . . remarkable tact and dominating power without any undue assumption". It was just that there were now far too many of them. And then there were also balls which, despite his hatred of "society", he sometimes felt obliged to attend. At one of them Thackeray was also present and wrote, somewhat caustically and even snobbishly, "How splendid Mrs Dickens was in pink satin and Mr Dickens in geranium and ringlets." And then, too, there were the various public dinners at which Dickens was the honoured guest. The curious nature of his bad temper in this period is to be seen, perhaps, in his complaints about the dress of his old friend, Thomas Mitton – ". . . he came out in a waistcoat that turned my whole mass of blood – a flowery waistcoat, with buttons like black eyes . . ."; it is as if he did not have the self-knowledge to realise that he was more guilty of dandyism than perhaps any other contemporary. His anger emerges again when at a dinner for the Charterhouse Square Infirmary he describes the other guests as "sleek, slobbering, bow-paunched, overfed, apoplectic, snorting cattle . . ." Dickens's rage could be terrible, turning its scorching light upon everything and everyone. He also suffered intermittent pains in his face, which he put down to "rheumatism" although they sound suspiciously like nervous spasms. There were too many dismal engagements, too many dinners, too many problems with his family and, when this is placed alongside the evident fact that Dickens was still deeply in debt with no present means of releasing himself from it, it is no wonder that he should begin contemplating the idea of living abroad for a while. He was angry because he felt himself to be trapped. The final decision was not made until later in the year, but the restlessness and uneasiness which are so prevalent during these months mark the beginnings of his determination to get away. To escape.

And yet this was also the period when he was writing some of the funniest passages in *Martin Chuzzlewit* – not only the American episodes but also the events at Todgers's, the boarding house in darkest London where Pecksniff and his lovely daughters temporarily reside. As so often in the past, Dickens's private unhappiness, restlessness and anxiety seem only to fuel still further the extravagances of his comedy. A French journalist met him during this period, and remarked upon his "long, brown, rather untidy hair" which falls "over the forehead of an unhealthy pallor. The bright, restless eyes testify to an unusual sagacity and quick intelligence"; yet this is the pale, restless author who ". . . nearly killed myself with laughing at what I have done of the American No . . ." as he told Mitton. And then: "I seem to hear the people talking again." Among the voices he hears is that of the American, Mr Putnam Smif, who sends a letter to Martin in which he declares, "I am young, and ardent. For there is a poetry in wildness, and every alligator basking in the slime is in himself an Epic, self-contained. I aspirate for fame. It is my yearning and my thirst." There is no indication that Dickens knew anything about the poetry of Walt Whitman, and so it is doubly remarkable here how he is able to parody what might be called a quintessential American tone, a tone he captures also in Mrs Hominy who in letters to the newspapers signs herself "The Mother of the Modern Gracchi", and of course also in the American literary lady who speaks thus: "'Mind and matter,' said the lady in the wig, 'glide swift into the vortex of immensity. Howls the sublime, and softly sleeps the calm Ideal, in the whispering chambers of Imagination. To hear it, sweet it is. But then, outlaughs the stern philosopher, and saith to the Grotesque, What ho! arrest for me that Agency. Go, bring it here! And so the vision fadeth.'" As always one can do nothing but admire Dickens's facility at evoking hypocrisy or self-delusion, theatricality and false feeling; they represent indeed the bedrock of his comic talent, upon which he builds everything else, and this essentially linguistic humour is always couched in elaborate form so that he seems instinctively to be reaching for the orotund language of his own father when he wishes to portray baseness or folly. And if

Martin Chuzzlewit is indeed a novel about "Selfishness", as Dickens claimed, then surely one can interpret this in the light of a remark he made a little later to the effect that ". . . the greater part of my observation of Parents and children, has shewn selfishness in the first, almost invariably". Does the shadow of John Dickens, at this period an appalling burden and nightmare for Dickens, hang over this comic novel more than has previously been thought? Is it not the case that all these forms of comic, obfuscatory, prolonged speech are all designed to hide pure selfishness, so that for Dickens elaboration of speech, like that of his father, is actually a way of hiding reality – in just the same way as the Americans in this novel profess virtues without ever possessing them? But why is it, then, that Dickens takes such delight in creating that obfuscatory language? For the same reason that he loves the monsters of his own devising like Pecksniff and Scrooge. In monsters like these he was caricaturing certain aspects of his temperament; that is why there is always that particle of affection which springs from self-love, and it is precisely that affection which makes these characters so vividly alive.

There is another monster besides for, while he was composing his novel on retreat at Cobley's Farm, walking as was his custom along the green lanes and across the fields, and at the very time when he was so irate with William Hall that he comes close to absolute disgust with his publishers, even now he creates the character of Mrs Gamp. The midwife and night nurse, the decrepit party who announces herself, mysteriously but unforgettably, "Gamp is my name, and Gamp my nater," the female whose rallying cry in company is, "Drink fair, wotever you do!", is perhaps the most famous and certainly the funniest of all Dickens's creations. There was a real Mrs Gamp, or, rather, there was an original upon whom the monster was established. The secretary and companion of Miss Burdett-Coutts, a certain Miss Meredith, had recently been taken ill but not so ill as to be unaware of her nurse's strange habits; one of which was "to rub her nose along the top of the tall fender", and another to sup vinegar with the flat of her knife while eating cucumbers. This was all Dickens needed. Mrs Gamp emerged as he wrote or walked at Cobley's Farm; he once said that on waking the head is generally full of "words" and it is likely that in the creation of such a character her words came first. He seemed to hear her talking, taking down the words as they issued from her capacious mouth; and, as she talks, he sees what she is wearing and understands what she will do within the plot. In Dickens's novels there are always certain characters who emerge only to be dropped altogether (except sometimes at the end when the *dramatis personae* reappear for a final curtain call), but there are other characters who spring out from the ground fully armed with their own quirkiness and in whom Dickens at once glimpses immense possibilities; that is why even secondary characters, like Mrs Gamp, can almost steal the whole show. An instinctive process, perhaps, but one which is nevertheless consciously and carefully controlled.

For we must never forget the minutiae of his verbal art. It is sometimes assumed that Dickens wrote so much because he wrote quickly and even carelessly. Nothing could be further from the truth of the matter. To use Oscar Wilde's phrase, he was a lord of language, albeit a generally unacknowledged one, who possessed a poet's ear for cadence and euphony, as well as a painter's eye for fine visual effect. In the first manuscript version of one passage in *Martin Chuzzlewit*, for example, he wrote of Pecksniff that "Of his doings in the architectural way no other record existed than a framed plan which was suspended over the chimney piece in the back parlour and lettered . . ." Dickens then turned the page and began again – "Of his architectural doings, nothing was clearly known, except that he had never designed or built anything; but it was generally understood that his knowledge of the science was almost awful in its profundity." One sees in changes such as these the pulses of Dickens's creative imagination, the onrush of humour, the quick revision, and the final effect. There are other changes in the novel which may be a matter of artful choice or instinct. It is revealing, for example, that as soon as Mercy Pecksniff begins to suffer at the hands of her brutish husband she ceases to be the object of light scorn from Dickens and instead becomes the recipient of his pity. In *Martin Chuzzlewit* he is always sharp, parodic, unsympathetic to those who do not suffer or who do not understand the sufferings of others; pain becomes his touchstone, and in Dickens's fiction it ennobles anyone who must endure it.

And so from effects such as these Dickens creates what is the richest gallery of fictional characters ever to have issued from the imagination of one man. They spring up all around him and there are times when he seems even effortlessly to anticipate some of his later characters, as if the seed were planted early in a name or a phrase; in *Martin Chuzzlewit* itself, a certain Pip appears briefly and we hear that "Pip's our mutual friend". In addition characters seem to shuffle into one another so that the same spirit is reincarnated, as it were, in a variety of human beings – Murdstone in *David Copperfield* becomes Merdle in *Little Dorrit* becomes Headstone in *Our Mutual Friend* becomes Durdles in *The Mystery of Edwin Drood*, all distinct but all related. Even closer resemblances abound – Mrs Nickleby in *Nicholas Nickleby* becomes Flora Finching in *Little Dorrit*, Nadgett in *Martin Chuzzlewit* becomes Bucket in *Bleak House*, Moddle in *Martin Chuzzlewit* becomes Toots in *Dombey and Son*. It is generally a case of these characters sounding like one another; one of Dickens's favourite and repeated habits of speech, for example, lies in what might be called the false emphasis. *You* won't get into trouble, *you* won't. Not *you*. You're too smart. That's what *you* are. Indeed it is so much a mannerism of Dickens's writing that it is hard to believe that it was not one of his own conversational tricks. But there are also times when Dickens's comprehension of character is entirely gestural: "'That's all at present,' said Nadgett, putting up his great pocket-book, which from mere habit he had produced when he began his revelation, and had kept in his hand all the time . . ." These are things which Dickens invariably notices; the small nervous habits, the professional gestures, the unconscious movements.

But there is much else that is mysterious and instinctive in Dickens's creation, and he always recognised that fact. He was once with friends, discussing these matters, when he took up a wine glass. "Suppose," he said, "I choose to call this a *character*, fancy it a man, endue it with certain qualities; and soon the fine filmy webs of thought, almost impalpable, coming from every direction, we know not whence, spin and weave about it, until it assumes form and beauty, and becomes instinct with life." He called this process of individuation an "unfathomable mystery". Even as he was composing *Martin Chuzzlewit* he wrote to Forster on Pecksniff and Tom Pinch, "As to the way in which these characters have opened out, that is, to me, one of the most surprising processes of the mind in this sort of invention. Given what one knows, what one does not know springs up; and I am as absolutely certain of its being true, as I am of the law of gravitation – if such a thing be possible, more so." So there is a mystery in the origins of his characters, whom he seems to summon up when they are already half-formed in the ante-chambers of his imagination, but then a further and deeper mystery is involved in their assumption of life itself. "I have often and often heard him complain," his son, Charles, was to record later, "that he could *not* get the people of his imagination to do what he wanted, and that they would insist on working out their histories in *their* way and not *his*. I can very well remember his describing their flocking round the table in the quiet hours of a summer morning . . . each one of them claiming and demanding instant personal attention." It was the same son who also said that ". . . the children of his brain were much more real to him at times than we were". "I can as distinctly see with my own eyes," Dickens once told Charles Collins, "any scene which I am describing as I see you now; and indeed on one occasion when I had shadowed a certain course for one of my characters to pursue, *the character took possession of me* and made me do exactly the contrary to what I had originally intended." So he becomes the observer – he *"heard"* every word of what they said and took it down as if in dictation.

His daughter, Mamie, said that her father in fact lived in his books, and there is indeed a sense in which his characters were so real, and so independent, that he himself merely dwelt among them; "I often say to Mr Gradgrind . . ." he wrote to one correspondent. In the public readings of his later years he actually took on all the characteristics of his creations and played them to the life; they ". . . *took possession of me* . . .", as he had said. But there is another form of possession, too. Many of Dickens's characters have in the past been described as copies of real originals, with Harold Skimpole as Leigh Hunt, Lawrence Boythorn as Walter Savage Landor, and so forth. There is a truth to this, but it is only a partial one. Dickens might begin with the appearance or behaviour of a certain individual but, as he writes, the character takes on the novelist's own feeling and expression far more than it copies the eccentricities of any presumed original. The novelist, not the external model, infuses himself into the creation; Harold Skimpole has more to do with Charles Dickens than with Leigh Hunt, and all the thousands of characters in Dickens's world may be seen as emanations from the amorphous personality of the novelist himself.

Part of him always realised that they were unreal, however, that they were phantoms of his own imagining; he revealed to one friend that in fact he never dreamed of his characters precisely because he *knew* that they were not real. There is a mystery here – the mystery which to Dickens is "unfathomable" because it is also the mystery of his genius and his own self. The mystery of his imagination which created an alternative world sometimes more real than the world in which he lived and moved. The mystery of a man who even sometimes approaches that living world as if it obeyed the laws of his imagination. There are many portraits of Dickens, sitting deep in thought and surrounded by the various characters of his books; in such presentations he almost seems to be one of the characters, too, as if he had somehow managed to write himself. Which, in a sense, is precisely what he did all his life. But there is one sketch, "Dickens Receiving His Characters", in which they seem to be imploring him to bring them to life, to let them grow and change; there is something rather sinister about them here, as they creep from behind a curtain into Dickens's darkened study. There are other portraits, too, in which his characters swarm around him as he sleeps, like small creatures intent on stealing his breath, on taking the life out of him. In fact it has often been said that they eventually did kill him, that his public readings, when he assumed many of his finest creations, destroyed him just as surely as if Bill Sikes had plunged a knife in his back.

So by the end of June he was "quite weary and worn out" with *Martin Chuzzlewit* and at the beginning of July he travelled with Catherine and Georgina to stay in Yorkshire with the Smithsons at Easthorpe Park, a late eighteenth-century house which Dickens called ". . . the most remarkable place of its size in England and immeasurably the most beautiful . . ." Here he rested, organised picnics and games, embarked on nocturnal expeditions to the local ruins, and took long rides into the surrounding countryside. While here he read the newspapers, too, and in *The Times* he saw reports of American support for Daniel O'Connell and his campaign for Home Rule in Ireland, support which was hastily withdrawn in some quarters when O'Connell attacked slavery in one of his more fiery speeches. Dickens kept the material, and on his return to London from Yorkshire included it in one of the novel's American chapters which he was now writing. He was starting work at about eight in the morning, in order to make up for the time spent idling in Yorkshire, and once again his humour was in full flood; that "distilled essence of comicality" which he had noted at the time of his American travels was now suffusing his own pages. It would be a weary task to compare, page for page, *American Notes* with *Martin Chuzzlewit*; it need only be said that the random experiences portrayed in the book of travels are here thoroughly condensed and lent what might be described as a thematic purpose. The river journeys into the interior had in *American Notes* contained some "pure delights", for example, whereas in *Martin Chuzzlewit* the journey is one which offers only "the weary day and melancholy night", a journey that reminds Dickens of the progress of time and a passage to the "grim domains of Giant Despair". There had been an incident which Dickens retold in *American Notes* – how a young woman had taken the riverboat to St Louis in order to be reunited with her husband and how she found him waiting eagerly for her, "a fine, good-looking, sturdy young fellow!" The incident is recast in *Martin Chuzzlewit* as concerning a young woman who crosses the Atlantic in order to be reunited with her husband; in the novel she finds him, too, but he is now only a "feeble old shadow". The difference is one of symbolic intent, Dickens's imagination recasting the duller shades of reality to suit his native chiaroscuro.

He had started the September number of the novel after his return to London from Easthorpe Park in July but now, restless as ever, he and the family decamped to Broadstairs for their annual visit. On this occasion Georgina was with them; she had bought her brother-in-law a pair of binoculars and through these he would watch the children disporting on the sand or riding the donkeys with Georgina herself, now the young "Aunt Georgie", being deputed to look after them. But Broadstairs was becoming very noisy or, more likely, in his own restless and irritable state he became disturbed by the familiar noises of the place. Yet amid these distractions Dickens set to work on *Martin Chuzzlewit*, continuing with the American chapters even as they seemed increasingly to create problems for him. There is a sense, in fact, in which the very form of the novel was becoming irksome to him; it was proceeding along the lines of its internal development which accounts for its organic firmness and consistency, but clearly there were now many things that he wanted to say, and could not say, in such a book. He had abandoned the idea of introducing the hard-pressed mine-workers, and his promise to Southwood Smith that he would bring a "Sledge hammer" down upon the question of children's employment was one that he had not fulfilled. There are even episodes within the book itself which suggest something of this dissatisfaction; when Tom Pinch is contemplating the ruins of all his amatory hopes he comforts himself and his sister with the following conclusion: "You think of me . . . and it is very natural that you should, as if I were a character in a book; and you make it a sort of poetical justice that I should, by some impossible means or other, come, at last, to marry the person I love. But there is a much higher justice than poetical justice . . ." Here Dickens seems to be suggesting the limitations of precisely the kind of novel he had been inclined to write, and the "higher justice" of which Tom Pinch speaks is part of his perception of inequality and injustice in the living world – injustice which by some means or other he was determined to discuss and to expose. But the monthly serial novel in general, and *Martin Chuzzlewit* in particular, was not the right medium for such work. It seems possible – more than possible, probable – that Dickens himself now wished to write something quite different, something that would allow him to use all of the dismay and angry public concern which had been accumulating within him since his return from America, boiling up in him together with his own private irritations. But it was only when Dickens travelled up from Broadstairs to London, in order to visit a ragged school, that his new imaginative journey began.

He was visiting the ragged school on behalf of Miss Burdett-Coutts who, by now, had become a close friend. They were a strange pair. She, plain and somewhat self-conscious but also calm and very determined, with her immense wealth as a bulwark against the world; and Dickens, eager, nervous, impetuous, with his fame matching her wealth. Yet they both observed in each other something which they recognised in themselves, a genuine concern and compassion for the poor which went beyond the political or social mores of the time. That is why Dickens began to act as her unpaid agent, revealing to her some of the more remediable evils in nineteenth-century London and collaborating with her in the effort to alleviate them. The understanding between them had already rendered them almost intimate; earlier in the year he had asked her to help his brother, Alfred, to find work as an engineer, "knowing the kind interest you take in any application or design of mine". So it was with her interests, as well as his own, that he visited the Field Lane ragged school in Saffron Hill. An advertisement had appeared in *The Times*, seeking charity for this particular establishment, and it seems to have been this which originally attracted his attention. Saffron Hill was of course not unknown to him. He had lived very close to it for some years, and had set parts of *Oliver Twist* in its vicinity. When he visited the school, in fact, he described it as being on exactly the same spot where Fagin had once worked, that coincidence emphasising how certain parts of the old city were haunted, haunting, filled with the blackened relics of the real and the imagined past. The establishment itself was sufficiently real and has some claim to being the first of the self-styled ragged schools, although charitable schools were not in themselves a new thing. There had always been a concern in England for the general reclamation of the very poor (education or training of any specific kind was really out of the question) and the Ragged School Movement, under the guidance of a certain Mr Starey, was established to make use of that tradition and properly to direct it.

The Field Lane school which Dickens visited was wretched enough, three rooms on the first floor of a dilapidated house among the swarming courts and alleys of Saffron Hill and its environs. The area itself was considered by many to be the worst in London, a place of filth and disease and every kind of vice, the inhabitants of which were separated from their fellow-citizens by a gulf wider than any city thoroughfare, a separate race who found the shortest route to prison or the gallows, and who were in a very real sense steeped in what Dickens called "profound ignorance and perfect barbarism". It was their children who were enticed to come to the ragged school, set up by Evangelicals primarily to reclaim the souls of the errant young but at the same time trying to inculcate in them the rudiments of learning. Many of these young boys and girls already earned their miserable "living" by thievery or prostitution, and all of them were filthy, reckless and of course illiterate; when Dickens visited them, he found ". . . a sickening atmosphere, in the midst of taint and dirt and pestilence: with all the deadly sins let loose, howling and shrieking at the doors". He was wearing a pair of white trousers and bright boots and, as soon as he entered the room, they began to laugh at him; his companion, Clarkson Stanfield, found the smell too much and quickly left. But Dickens stayed, and by dint of perseverance got them to answer some of his questions. But he was appalled by the ragged figures he had observed here. "I have very seldom seen," he told Miss Burdett-Coutts, "in all the strange and dreadful things I have seen in London and elsewhere, anything so shocking as the dire neglect of soul and body exhibited in these children."

He had, in truth, many reservations about the kind of teachers and the kind of teaching involved in the ragged school movement, but, from this first visit, his interest in it was intense and prolonged. Of course he recommended the charity as a fit object for Miss Burdett-Coutts's capacious purse, and, characteristically, he was severely practical about what should or should not be done to assist the scheme. The first task, as far as he was concerned, was to find somewhere for the children to be washed; sanitation came before any other attempt to alleviate their benighted condition. Miss Burdett-Coutts provided funds for this, and also for the renting of better-ventilated and better-kept schoolrooms. But Dickens did not stop there. His anger at the conditions of the poor children was such that immediately he suggested to the *Edinburgh Review* that he should write an article on the conditions in Saffron Hill; it seems that he also approached the government and asked them to consider making a grant from the Education Committee which had been established ten years before to assist the efforts of charitable and voluntary schools. No such grant was forthcoming.

The situation was, and remained, desperate. Until the very end of Dickens's life only one child out of three attended school of even a rudimentary kind, and it has been estimated that in the London of the Forties there were more than one hundred thousand children of the poor who had never attended even a ragged school. It was a vast sea of ignorance into which, Dickens feared, the whole country might sink. Of course such was the direction of his temperament that he was always most interested in those institutions which catered for the poor or deprived. So, although he often refers to the ragged schools, there are few extant commentaries by him on the network of British or National Schools, and his comments on charity schools and Sunday schools are at best weakly dismissive. That is one reason why it is difficult to elucidate from Dickens's scattered documents any general theory of education – certainly, in his fiction, he never seemed to like any existing school very much. He sent his own sons to typical if good private schools, before they were pitched upon the world to earn their living, and his daughters were taught at home by governesses in the standard manner. Taken as a whole, his more overt comments suggest that the state should provide education for the very poor or the unwanted child, and that this education should be of a practical and "industrial" kind. Although he was to attack the state training of teachers he does seem to have come round to the belief that, at some stage and in some way, the state should also be able to provide the outline of "certain moral and religious truths". In particular he wanted the children to be trained away from crime, and in this area his interest was not altogether theoretical; on at least two occasions he paid for a child to be trained in various crafts, and gave the money for one boy to emigrate to the colonies after his training. Education and emigration – these were the two radical or Benthamite solutions to the problems of crime and poverty, but they were also the most practical response to a social disease which grew with the children it fed upon. The fact that Dickens was always immensely pragmatic in social matters is further emphasised by his efforts, with another educational reformer, James

Kay-Shuttleworth, to set up his own ragged school and to establish it along model lines; but the attempt came to nothing. In any case even the ragged schools themselves were criticised by him; desperate as he knew the situation to be, and sympathetic as he was to many of the courageous men who taught in them, he was clearly dismayed by the excessive attention to religious dogma and by the general evangelical spirit which seemed at work in these establishments. He disliked creeds, religious forms, and sectarianism of every kind; this is why he so often attacked the ragged schools as inadequate to the task set for them. In fact, confronted with the general and universal ignorance of the poor, he came eventually to believe that they were the merest palliative and that more general action of a concerted kind was necessary.

It never happened in his lifetime, and he saw before him always the twin phantoms of Ignorance and Want. He saw what others also saw. He saw what Lord Ashley saw: "Many of them retire for the night, if they retire at all, under the dry arches of bridges and viaducts; under porticoes; sheds and carts; to outhouses; in sawpits; on staircases . . ." Dickens saw the legions of what he called "doomed childhood" and believed that, unless they were properly instructed and their wants alleviated, they would rise up one day and tear down the very edifice of nineteenth-century civilisation. As he was to put it in the *Examiner* some time later, "Side by side with Crime, Disease, and Misery in England, Ignorance is always brooding, and is always certain to be found". It was out of this vision of the world that Dickens now found his new subject; his imagination was seized by the conditions of the ragged school in Saffron Hill and within a few weeks he had created *A Christmas Carol*, the wonderful story of redemption in which appear the two children, Ignorance and Want, infants who are "wretched, abject, frightful, hideous, miserable". This was the book he had been wanting to write all along; and so this powerful Christmas tale, which has achieved a kind of immortality, was born out of the very conditions of the time.

Dickens actually thought of it on a short trip to Manchester which he made three weeks later, specifically to help another educational enterprise. The Manchester Athenaeum, founded to provide a place of education and recreation for the labouring men and women of that city, was desperately short of funds and he had agreed to make a speech in order to raise money. He had been persuaded to do so by Fanny, his sister, who had moved to Manchester with her husband

Henry Burnett; both of them by now had become pious Evangelicals, and there is a great deal of evidence to suggest that Dickens did not much care for his brother-in-law. But his sister had been close to him always – close to him as an infant in Chatham, close to him as a child in London before the terrible separation – and on his arrival in Manchester at the beginning of October he went to stay with them in the suburb of Higher Ardwick. Thomas Mitton had travelled with him and stayed at a Manchester hotel but Dickens, "not caring to be under hourly observation" by the public, according to his brother-in-law, elected to stay with Fanny and Henry. It was here that he was reunited with his old schoolmaster, William Giles, who had established a private school in the area; nothing is known of their conversation. What we have, instead, are the recollections of Edward Watkin, the director of the Athenaeum; he particularly remembered the way in which Dickens raised his eyebrows and nodded his head whenever a point was put to him, and he noticed "a quick, funny glance" which was provoked by a reference to *The Pickwick Papers*. He also noted that Dickens had a habit of murmuring "Oh, lord" or "Oh, law, no", a true cockneyism, which may have been one of the reasons that some thought him slightly "vulgar" (or, as the Americans had put it, "rowdy"); and, like many others, Watkin mentions the strange impediment or thickness in the novelist's speech. Of course their conversation centred on the best way to appeal for funds and Dickens said, "Get the tea all over – I must confess to a sort of horror of tea things, or tea on a grand scale – and I think the best way to excite and keep up the interest would be to appear immediately after tea *and go to work at once.*" This has the true Dickensian ring and indeed, as planned, he made his speech. He was sharing a platform that day with Cobden and with Disraeli, two powerful political figures whose presence beside Dickens emphasises just how important he himself had become. And, in his speech itself, he once again underlined the need for education and the fact that ignorance was "the most prolific parent of misery and crime". He went on to extol the virtues of the self-made and self-educated man (in which company no doubt Dickens implicitly included himself) and ended with a peroration on the need for workers and employers to come harmoniously together since they shared "a mutual duty and responsibility".

Here in abbreviated form, then, were Dickens's central social concerns. The ragged schools. His experience of industrialism in America. The "Sledge hammer" blow he had promised for the labouring children. The working men of Manchester. His own past. All these things came together, and flowed towards the little book which now emerged blinking, as it were, into the light of Dickens's imagination. So it was that, in Manchester, *A Christmas Carol* was born. Of course it was not entirely unmotivated by other factors. He needed to earn more money, both for himself and for the alleviation of his outstanding debts to Chapman and Hall, and he had been casting around for some extra method of earning income. This in itself explains the *idea* of a small festive book, a specifically Christmas book, but it does not account for its power. Within a week of his return to London he started to work upon it, his "little scheme", as he called it. Of course it shares the same family of concerns as *Martin Chuzzlewit* which he was writing almost literally alongside it (he took a break from *A Christmas Carol* to finish the next number of the novel). Ebenezer Scrooge is a more fantastic image of the unreformed elderly Chuzzlewit, Bob Cratchit only a slightly more careworn Tom Pinch – and Chuzzlewit's apparent conversion to beneficence, which excited Dickens so much that he carried on writing it until three in the morning, takes place only a few days after that of Scrooge. *A Christmas Carol* becomes almost a dream reworking of *Martin Chuzzlewit* in which the themes of "Selfishness", money, greed, and the commercialised society which results from them, are conveyed in condensed and fantastic form. There were other derivations, too, and curiously enough some of its earliest words, "Old Marley was as dead as a door-nail", are taken from a dream which Dickens remembered from that summer in Broadstairs – a dream in which "a private gentleman and a particular friend" is pronounced to be "as dead Sir . . . as a door-nail". This was a dream, also, in which his apparent frustration at the fact that Catherine was about to have another child, thus adding to his already large family's demands, is expressed in the image of a baby being skewered on a toasting fork. The dream stayed with him, and by using it in *A Christmas Carol* his own feelings of helplessness and indebtedness are strangely allied with his reaction to the children of the ragged school and the labouring men of the Manchester Athenaeum. So it is that public concerns and private fantasies come together in a complete statement.

He worked on it quickly, the plot itself deriving from a memory, conscious or unconscious, of the story of Gabriel Grub in *The Pickwick Papers* – an interpolated tale in which a surly old man is visited by various goblins who show him past and future. He had a bad cold, tried not to attend too many social engagements, but as he worked the story grew under his hand. Clearly the narrative of Scrooge and his conversion had been simmering within him for some time, emerging now and again in the history of Martin Chuzzlewit, but it took all the accidental circumstances here related to release it. That is why it emerges almost ready-made. Forster recounts with what "a strange mastery it seized him", how he wept over it, laughed, and then wept again; in the course of its composition he took long night walks through London, sometimes covering ten or fifteen miles, and during these lonely nocturnal excursions he no doubt recalled that sense of life – and that vision of the world – which he had experienced in these same streets as a child. For in *A Christmas Carol* he returns to his childhood and relives it. Not just in the sense that this Christmas story itself is strangely reminiscent of the tales and chapbooks which he had read as a child ("No one was more intensely fond than Dickens of old nursery tales," Forster wrote, "and he had a secret delight in feeling that he was here only giving them a higher form") but also in the more important sense that, for the first time in his published writings, the whole nature of Dickens's childhood informs the little narrative.

In Scrooge's infancy, after all, the familiar elements of Dickens's own past are dispersed. The blacking factory and Gad's Hill Place are wonderfully knit together in an image of a decaying building which is made of red brick and has a weathercock on the top of it: it is here that Scrooge sees, literally *sees*, the heroes of his boyhood reading just as Dickens had once done; and it is from this place, where the plaster falls and the windows are cracked, that his sister, "little Fan", rescues him. How much a reworking of Dickens's own fantasies is this, as the young sister, whom he had thought had abandoned him, returns and leads him "Home, for good and all . . ." But the resemblances to Dickens's own childhood do not end here. The Cratchit family live in a small terraced house which is clearly an evocation of that house in Bayham Street where the Dickens family had moved after their arrival in London, and their crippled infant had first been christened not Tiny Tim but "Tiny Fred" – the name of his own brother who was two years old at the time of their journey to the capital. Some of his earliest memories are here fused together, creating such an entirely new shape that it is perhaps pointless to look for the various scattered "sources" of which *A Christmas Carol* is made up. It is enough to say that much of its power derives from the buried recollections which animate it.

And is not Dickens waiting for us here in other guises, too? It should not be forgotten that he created the character of Scrooge exactly at the time when he was desperate for money and when he was trying to fend off the demands of his own relatives, or those "blood petitioners", as he called them. All through Dickens's life, in fact, we will see the power which money held over him. It is one of the constant themes of his correspondence, and the desire to earn as much money as possible is noticeable both in his business dealings with publishers and in the exultation with which he greeted the *amounts* he was able to earn, for example, at public readings. Of course he was as ambivalent about money as he was about any matter which touched him deeply. He said quite genuinely to his brother that ". . . there is not a successful man in the world who attaches less importance to the possession of money . . ." And yet in the following month he was saying, of one of his plans to republish his works, ". . . I hope to get a great deal of money out of the idea . . ." Of course there is no necessary contradiction here; the man who values money simply as a defence against the world does not necessarily value it in itself. Like many men who have made their own way in the world and have come from poverty to relative wealth, as Scrooge had done in *A Christmas Carol*, Dickens was instinctively cautious in matters of finance: he made sure that Catherine was careful about the domestic budget (there were often occasions when at the beginning or end of the week he would go through the household accounts with her), and he avoided unnecessary expenditure wherever it was possible to do so. Of course, as Scrooge's nephew tells the miser, "You're rich enough". And yet Dickens did not think of himself as a rich man; "I am never rich," he once wrote, "and never was, and never shall be." Of course by the standards of his time he was not particularly wealthy – Miss Burdett-Coutts and the industrial princes of the era had a great deal more – but it was also important to Dickens that he should never think of himself as rich, that there should always be that fear of "ruin" or poverty beneath the surface of his apparently affluent life. It was, in a true sense, a spur to his energy and even to his creativity.

So it is perhaps only in fiction such as *A Christmas Carol* that his real preoccupation with money can come to the fore. Miserliness as vice. Generosity as virtue. How people obtain money. How people exert power over others because of money. How money can be an aspect of cruelty. How money can destroy a family. How the want of money is oppressive. How the greed for it is a form of unworthiness, a form of human alienation. And, central to *A Christmas Carol*, how the experiences of childhood can lead ineluctably to miserliness itself. For, if Scrooge is in one sense an exaggerated aspect of Dickens himself, it is clear that the author knew where the springs of at least his fictional character were buried – not only in the doomed childhood of the miser but also in the anxiety which can emerge from it. "You fear the world too much," a woman tells Scrooge, ". . . All your other hopes have merged into the hope of being beyond the chance of its sordid reproach." In that sentence one sees the clearest analysis of Dickens's own need to earn money as a defence against the world. And yet he was also a generous and philanthropic man. He was on the list of begging-letter writers as a regular giver of alms, and throughout his life there are many examples of his charity and kindness to those who needed it: children whose education he paid for; men and women whose fate so touched him that he sent them money in secret; prisoners whose plight led him to send money to the prison officials on their behalf. There is no evidence at all that he was ever mean in his personal dealings, either, and do we not see in Scrooge's reformation yet another exaggerated aspect of Dickens's own character – so that Scrooge as both a mean and generous man is a fantastic, dream-like image of Dickens himself? In *A Christmas Carol* Dickens imagines what he once was and what he might have become. As Forster said, he wanted to recreate the atmosphere of the fairy stories which he had read as a child; but one in which he was the real hero.

He finished it at the beginning of December so that, in total, it had taken him a little over six weeks to compose. He had already come to an agreement with Chapman and Hall that they would publish the book solely on the basis of a commission and, since it was to be very much *his* Christmas book, he went to great pains to procure for it the best possible appearance. It was bound in red cloth, with a gilt design on the cover and the edges of the pages themselves were gilt; John Leech provided four full-colour etchings, and there were also four black-and-white woodcuts within the text of the book. Altogether a handsome volume and, at the relatively low price of five shillings, it became the most successful Christmas book of the season; some six thousand copies were purchased by Christmas Eve, and it kept on selling well into the new year and beyond. Indeed the response of the public was so enthusiastic that it seems quite to have blotted out both the relative failure of *Martin Chuzzlewit* and any fears Dickens might have had about his waning popularity as a writer. As *Fraser's Magazine* put it, the little book was "so spread over England by this time, that no sceptic . . . could review it down . . . who can listen to objection regarding such a book as this?" In fact it quickly became what one critic called a "national institution" or what Thackeray described as a "national benefit". There is the story of the American factory-owner who on reading the book gave his employees another day's holiday, and the story of Carlyle ordering a turkey after he had finished it. Of course, in its attack upon those who spurn the poor and the unemployed, *A Christmas Carol* takes its place among other pieces of radical literature in the same period, particularly Thomas Hood's "The Song of the Shirt" and Elizabeth Barrett Browning's "Cry of the Children". But clearly, too, there are many religious motifs which give the book its particular seasonal spirit; not only the Christmas of parties and dancing but also the Christmas of mercy and love which binds a community to itself. But it combined all these things within a narrative which has all the fancy of a fairy tale and all the vigour of a Dickensian narrative. There was instruction for those who wished to find it at the time of this religious festival, but there was also enough entertainment to render it perfect "holiday reading"; it is rather as if Dickens had rewritten a religious tract and filled it both with his own memories and with all the concerns of the period. He had, in other words, created a modern fairy story. And so it has remained.

He knew instinctively what he had done, and in subsequent years his Christmas Books and Christmas Stories make up as important a part of his writing as they constitute a significant extension of his relation to his audience. He did not invent Christmas, however, as the more sentimental of his chroniclers have suggested. Robert Seymour, the suicidal first illustrator of *The Pickwick Papers*, had in 1835 been responsible for *The Book of Christmas* which has many of the genial ingredients of Dickens's own commemorations of the period. But Dickens could be said to have emphasised its cosy conviviality at a time when both Georgian licence and Evangelical dourness were being questioned. It was not yet the "festive season" which Dickens desired to make of it; it did not possess what he described as the "Christmas spirit, which is the spirit of active usefulness, perseverance, cheerful discharge of duty, kindness and forebearance!" Christmas cards were not introduced until 1846, and Christmas crackers until the 1850s. Typically it was still a one-day holiday when presents were given to children, but there was no general orgy of benevolence and generosity. It was a time of quiet rest. Acting. Reading aloud.

Music. Games. What Dickens did was to transform the holiday by suffusing it with his own particular mixture of aspirations, memories and fears. He invested it with fantasy and with a curious blend of religious mysticism and popular superstition so that, in certain respects, the Christmas of Dickens resembles the more ancient festival which had been celebrated in rural areas and in the north of England. In addition he made it cosy, he made it comfortable, and he achieved this by exaggerating the darkness beyond the small circle of light. It might be said, in fact, that his real contribution to the depiction of Christmas lay in his talent for chiaroscuro. Beyond the hearth were the poor, the ignorant, the diseased, the wretched; and do we not enjoy the flames of the Christmas fire more because of the very shadows which it casts? Dickens had an acute sense of, and need for, "Home" – it sprang from his own experience of being banished from that blessed place – which is why in *A Christmas Carol*, and the stories that succeed it, there is a constant contrast between warmth and cold, between the domestic interior and the noisome streets, between the rich and the poor, between the well and the ill, between the need for comfort and the anxiety about homelessness. And in that ambivalence he touched upon one of the real spirits of the age. In many Victorian homes the exterior world seems literally to be kept at bay by a whole artillery of protective forces – screened by thick curtains and by lace inner curtains, muffled by patterned wallpaper and patterned carpets, held off by settees and ottomans and what-nots, mocked by wax fruit and wax candles, its metaphorical and literal darkness banished by lamps and chandeliers and candles. The central idea is one of ferocious privacy, of shelter and segregation, and it was in *A Christmas Carol* that Dickens divined it and brought it forth to the surface. Once again his own obsessions take on the very shape and pressure of the age.

That is why the effect of *A Christmas Carol* on Dickens himself should not be underestimated. Most importantly, he had for the first time been able to complete an entire fiction without being compelled to write in serial portions. He had had the opportunity to design the book in every sense, and carefully to calculate the plot in advance. He had done it all in one bound, as it were, and as soon as he had written "The End" he added three double underlinings. Then, he said, he ". . . broke out like a Madman". On 26 December he attended a party given by Mrs Macready (her husband being away in America). Jane Welsh Carlyle was also there and told a friend, "Only think of that excellent Dickens playing the *conjuror* for one whole hour – the *best* conjuror I ever saw . . ." And then came the dancing: "Dickens did all but go down on his knees to make *me* – waltz with him!" as the party grew madder and madder still. Madder and madder as Charles Dickens whirled through the last days of 1843.

Yet all the pressures of his life were still there, and the only alternative still seemed to him to be escape. Even as he was writing *Martin Chuzzlewit* and *A Christmas Carol*, he was planning to get away. He wanted to make a clean break. To travel in Switzerland, France and Italy. He wanted a rest after his labours on the novel and, always now aware of the perils of over-production, to disappear from public view for at least a year. He had made the decision as *Martin Chuzzlewit* continued with its relatively small sales, but he was defiant about that. "You know, as well as I," he told Forster, "that I think *Chuzzlewit* in a hundred points immeasurably the best of my stories." But the low sale of the novel made it also a matter of pressing economy that the Dickens family should decamp, let their house in Devonshire Terrace, and live more cheaply on the Continent. So everything propelled him in this direction, and not even the fact that Catherine was still expecting the baby could deter him – "We have spoken of the baby, and of leaving it here with Catherine's mother. Moving the children into France could not, in any ordinary course of things, do them anything but good." Clearly no one except himself wished to travel abroad; certainly not Catherine, now in the last stages of her pregnancy. But Dickens's will was not something to be questioned in such matters. If it was good for him, it must be good for them; "And the question is, what it would do to that by which they live: not what it would do to them." In fact as soon as Catherine had given birth to their new son, Francis, Dickens began to write about her with more than a trace of irritation and annoyance. Once more she was suffering from post-natal depression, of which Dickens reports ". . .her health is perfectly good, and I am sure she might rally, if she would". Later he was complaining about how slow she was, and seems to have had no very strong affection for the new baby who would place a further drain upon his dwindling resources. "I decline (on principle) to look at the latter object," he wrote in what may or may not be a mock facetious tone. And this the man who had only a short time before been extolling the familial virtues of Christmas with his final words, "God Bless Us, Every One!" In fact neither the sentiments nor the success of *A Christmas Carol* materially affected his resolve to leave England, and his decision to do so was if anything now being strengthened by the behaviour of his always importunate father; although Dickens's finances were far from healthy, John Dickens seems to have made further and further demands upon him. Dickens wrote to Thomas Mitton, from whom he had already borrowed money, and who acted as his agent in all transactions with his father, "I really think I shall begin to give in, one of these days. For anything like the damnable Shadow which this father of mine casts upon my face, there never was – except in a nightmare." God Bless Us, Every One!

Other problems beset him. Within two weeks of the publication of *A Christmas Carol*, Parley's Illuminated Library brought out a "condensed" but essentially pirated edition of that work. Two days later Dickens had filed an injunction to stop publication; his wrath against American "pirates" might do him no good, but he could at least win some kind of victory in the English courts. And indeed he did: he hired Talfourd to represent him, and the injunction was granted while Dickens sued the printers and publishers for breach of copyright. "The pirates are beaten flat," he said in his triumph but, unfortunately, his was something of a Pyrrhic victory. The defendants declared themselves bankrupt and as a result Dickens had to pay his own costs, which amounted to the not inconsiderable sum of seven hundred pounds. It is often said that it was Dickens's experiences as a shorthand writer in Doctors' Commons which turned him against the legal system and which found such memorable expression in the nightmare Chancery of *Bleak House*, but it is possible, too, that the sources of his anger and disgust are to be found in the way this particular case turned against him even at the time of his legal success. Nothing seemed right in England any more and then, when no worse could be expected, the accounts of *A Christmas Carol* arrived. He had expected to earn something like one thousand pounds from the sale of the book, but the costs of producing it had cut heavily into the profits. He wrote to Forster, "The first six thousand copies show a profit of £230!" – in fact the profit was closer to £130, and Forster seems to have misread Dickens's hand when he transcribed the letter into his biography. In any case the sum was very small, far smaller than anything Dickens had anticipated, and he fell at once into an anxiety which came close to hysteria. "Such a night as I have passed! I really believed that I should never get up again, until I had passed through all the horrors of a fever . . . I shall be ruined past all mortal hope of redemption." And indeed this was his panic fear: the fear of ruin, of being thrust down again into poverty, to go the way of his father into a debtors' prison, all the success and fame he has achieved to be stripped from him as he is cast back into the state of childhood. There must have been times when it seemed to him that all his achievement was a dream, and that he would wake up once again in Bayham Street or the little attic room of Lant Street. There was still so much fear behind the bright appearance of the eminent novelist.

Yet his financial panic seems to have been connected with anxieties about the future as well as those induced by the past, since it is linked to what was becoming a general uncertainty about the course his life was about to take. From this time, for example, one can trace a certain loss of affection for, or connection with, Catherine; as if in some way she was hemming him in, narrowing his possibilities, consigning him to a domestic fate. In fact his disaffection with his wife was signalled in a very curious manner. It happened in Liverpool. He had agreed to travel there, and to Birmingham, once more in the cause of adult educational reform – to speak at a *soirée* of the Mechanics Institution in Liverpool and at a *conversazione* for the Polytechnic Institution in Birmingham. Two worthy causes, and the huge national success of *A Christmas Carol* rendered Dickens all the more popular a spokesman for the worthy poor and the working men of the country. Of course it should not be assumed that Dickens's attitude towards working men was in any sense an idealised one. In his own dealings with John Overs, for example, the poor cabinet-maker who had literary ambitions, we have already seen how his assistance and sympathy are precisely measured out. Dickens is always aware of his own position in the world, and sometimes wrote to Overs in what can only be described as seigneurial tones; his own pity and sympathy for the man are not in doubt, nor are his many practical attempts to help him, but Dickens always remained the gentleman who was stooping towards someone more unfortunate than himself. In a preface which he wrote in June of this year for a collection of Overs's pieces, in fact, he described the ". . . unobtrusive independence of his character, the instinctive propriety of his manner, and *the perfect neatness of his appearance* . . ." (my italics); and it was thus that Overs "has risen superior to the mere prejudices of the class with which he is associated". There is an ambivalence here which one can detect flowing just beneath the surface of Dickens's somewhat patronising recommendation; imaginatively he understood the anxieties and privations of Overs's life, and in imagination he may even have shared them with him, but as a man of the world, as a famous writer, he was at some pains to put a distance between himself and the object of his patronage. It is almost as if he still needed to put a distance between himself and his own similarly wretched childhood. So Dickens often exhibits an odd mixture of the most sensitive sympathy and the sternest authoritarianism. In May of this year, for example, he had received a begging letter from a certain John Walker. He was accustomed to such letters and in fact was usually generous in his response, on this occasion sending his brother, Fred, to make enquiries about the man before sending him money on two separate occasions. But then Dickens discovered that Walker had been lying about his circumstances, and as a result had him hauled up before the magistrates of the Marylebone Police Court. In fact the man was in real distress, despite his misrepresentations, and Dickens was genuinely relieved when the case was dismissed on a technicality. This is not unlike Dickens, to be giving sums of money to the indigent while at the same time not scrupling to bring the force of the law against any poor people who tried to cheat him. Of course this mixture of philanthropy and authoritarianism was not unusual in the period (they might even be said to fit together perfectly) but Dickens's own haunted nature reacted much more positively and much more powerfully than most of his contemporaries'. For was there not always a sense in which he thought – there, but for the grace of God . . . ?

He had been nervous about making a speech at the Liverpool Mechanics Institution – "rayther shakey", he told Catherine on the day he was to speak. But once more only his popularity was evident. When he arrived on the platform the organ played "See The Conquering Hero Comes" and his speech, in which once more he emphasised the "just right" of every man to education and extolled the virtues of self-help as well as the need for "mutual forebearance among various classes", was often interrupted by what the shorthand reporters called "Laughter and applause". But the occasion remained in Dickens's memory for quite another reason: at a suitable moment in the proceedings, a native of Liverpool, Miss Christiana Weller, then eighteen years of age, was called upon to give a piano recital. Her name, with its echo of a more famous Weller in *The Pickwick Papers*, seemed to amuse Dickens and a local newspaper said that as she played the famous novelist "kept his eyes firmly fixed on her every movement". Then he was introduced to her and also to her father, "at the same time making some observation which created much laughter among those immediately around". Then, in his concluding remarks, Dickens went on to say that "the last remnant of my heart went into that piano". (He actually finished by quoting Tiny Tim, "God Bless Us, Every One!", a sure sign that he knew on what basis his current and immediate popularity rested.) Clearly he was in some way attracted to Christiana Weller since he invited himself to lunch with her, at her brother-in-law's house, the very next afternoon, and on that occasion inscribed some verse in her album, part of which read:

"I love her dear name which has won me some fame
But Great Heaven how gladly I'd change it!"

In other words, how glad he would be to marry her. If he could. If he were free of Catherine.

In fact this first attraction came somewhere close to infatuation, an infatuation all the more significant in light of the fact that Miss Weller was thought to resemble Mary Hogarth – at least this is what other members of the Hogarth family came to notice about her. On his eventual return to London Dickens told T. J. Thompson, the friend with whom he had stayed in Liverpool, that "I cannot joke about Miss Weller; for she is too good; and interest in her (spiritual young creature that she is, and destined to an early death, I fear) has become a sentiment with me. Good God what a madman I should seem, if the incredible feeling I have conceived for the girl could be made plain to anyone!" Clearly all the thwarted yearning of Dickens's nature became attached to this young woman, that endless appetite for love and affection once more aroused by the sight of a girl who looked so much like Mary Hogarth; and yet how odd, too, that his feelings for her should also be associated with the idea that she would die young. One might interpret it as meaning that, as a result of his love for her, she *must* die young; thus in a way pre-empting her sexual maturity or sexual identity while at the same time implicitly disavowing any sexual interest in her. He calls her "spiritual" for precisely this reason, even though in the same letter he declares that "I shall never be a wise man" and contrasts his own excited state of feeling with that of "ice". When only a few weeks later Thompson astonished him by explaining in a letter that he wanted to marry Christiana, Dickens "felt the blood go from my face . . . and my very lips turn white". But such was the passionate discipline of his nature that he could not confess to anything like sexual jealousy; quite the reverse. He encouraged and abetted Thompson in his efforts to marry Christiana, but he had a strange request of his own in anticipation of that happy union. "Ask her to save the dress – the dress with the fur upon it." This was the dress in which he had first seen her. "Let it be laid up in Lavender. Let it never grow old, fade . . ." Dickens had also preserved Mary Hogarth's dress after her death, and in this strange concatenation of infatuation, obsession and disavowal of sexuality we move a step closer towards his own most instinctive feelings. But what emerges here, more strongly than anything else, is the curious innocence of Dickens – the innocence of such a direct expression of his own feelings, even if it is an innocence that may well be accompanied by a lack of self-knowledge. This will prove to be of some importance when we examine his later relationships; enough to say that, even at this point in his life, at the age of thirty-two, his sexual responses and energies were sublimated by, or channelled towards, that strange pattern of passivity, innocence, spirituality and death which emerges so often in his fiction and in his extant correspondence. Why else did he treat Christiana Weller as if she were one of the heroines of his novels, doomed to an early death as soon as the possibility of sexual attraction becomes evident?

It is interesting to note, however, that she was not the only young woman to resemble Mary Hogarth. Certainly Georgina Hogarth recalled Mary to his mind, and she was now living with the rest of the Dickens family in Devonshire Terrace. And, if he had to control or to deny certain feelings which he had for his young sister-in-law, is that yet another reason why they broke out again so ferociously in the company of Miss Weller? And is it not also possible that the lament of Tom Pinch, cruelly deprived of the love of Mary Graham in the chapters of *Martin Chuzzlewit* which Dickens was just about to write, is in part established upon his own yearning and his own sense of loss? "Ah, Tom! The blood retreated from his cheeks" – just as that of Dickens had done when he learnt of Thompson's love for Christiana Weller – "and came rushing back, so violently, that it was pain to feel it; ease though, ease, to the aching of his wounded heart." Christiana Weller did eventually marry T. J. Thompson, and at first Dickens did all he could to help her career as a concert pianist, for a while acting like an unofficial impresario. Eventually he tired of her and even turned against her, not before, however, entangling the families of the Wellers and the Dickens, as we shall see, in a series of unfortunate episodes. But the over-riding impression of this incident must surely be the extent to which he was dissatisfied with his wife at a time when she was continually bearing his children. How else can one explain almost the hysteria or at least the desperation of Dickens's attachment to a young girl of eighteen, if it did not spring from real emotional unhappiness which his wife had been able neither to divert nor to assuage?

From Liverpool and Miss Weller he went on to Birmingham where, in the town hall crowded with people, the words "Welcome Boz" had been fashioned out of artificial flowers and constructed some six feet high. "Dick," he said later of himself in that slightly disturbing third person he regularly used, ". . . made decidedly the best speech I ever heard him achieve. Sir, he was jocular, pathetic, eloquent, conversational, illustrative and wise – always wise." It was a speech in which once more he extolled the importance of education and went on to declare to his large audience, "As long as I can make you laugh or cry, I will . . ." The next day he returned to London "dead, worn-out, and Spiritless". He knew already that fame and applause could not in themselves assuage that aching, empty yearning, that perpetual "want of something" which the sight of Christiana Weller had provoked once more within him.

The "want of something" which made him restless. Eager to move on. He still wanted to get away, even if, as Forster maintained, he was being driven away principally by what were "imaginary fears" about his own work. He had also now decided definitely to leave Chapman and Hall and to make new agreements with his printers, Bradbury and Evans, all this merely because of the chance remark by William Hall about the terms of his contract. How much Dickens resented slights, and how impetuously but implacably he reacted to them, is evident from this alone. In the agreement which he eventually signed with Bradbury and Evans, he promised only to provide another little Christmas book on the lines of the albeit very successful *A Christmas Carol* and, in addition, to explore with them the possibility of starting a new periodical. (It was a period when printers often transcended their technical skills, and became publishers as well.) But he had a travel book in mind and was also eager, after he had finished *Martin Chuzzlewit*, to start work on a novel which would have a continental setting; this was another reason why he wanted to move to Europe. But he did not wish to write the projected novel in monthly numbers. His experience with *A Christmas Carol* had led him to believe that it would be better for any new novel to come out in complete and coherent form. The fact was, also, that he was happy to consider these various schemes because he needed money badly. That is perhaps why he approached the publisher, Thomas Longman, in the period after his break with Chapman and Hall; and why he opened negotiations with the *Morning Chronicle* for a series of regular articles. Neither of these two ideas came to anything, but they are indicative of his generally unsettled state of mind just at the point when he was about to leave England.

There were various duties to perform before that departure: the sudden death of Charles Smithson meant that he had to travel up to Yorkshire for the funeral, and of course he was still heavily in demand as a giver of speeches for a variety of worthy causes. In April of this year, for example, he addressed the Governesses' Benevolent Institution; it might be thought an odd charity for Dickens to support, if it were not for the fact that his sister had for a while been employed as a governess and the humiliations of that still lowly profession had been described by him in some of the earlier chapters of *Martin Chuzzlewit*. In fact the man who made the speech that evening and the man who wrote the novel expressed precisely the same opinions on the subject, one of the few instances when Dickens's social attitudes moved unscathed from art to life. He also delivered a speech on behalf of the Artists' Benevolent Society, and one for Southwood Smith's projected sanatorium; the latter occasion was notable for the fact that, apparently for the first time, the females were not banished to the gallery and sat on equal terms with the males at the dinner table. Dickens mentioned this in his speech, during which he praised women as "our dearest companions and our constant and unchanging friends", a sentiment which may have had as much to do with his still-passionate feelings for Christiana Weller as the more familiar presence of his own wife.

One observer at the Artists' Benevolent Society complained to his wife that Dickens's speech had "a very cut and dried air", although in fact he had now gained a reputation for his merits as a public speaker. There were some people who believed him to be the greatest speaker of his day, and this at a time when Disraeli and Cobden were possible contenders for that honour. Certainly he impressed and charmed most of the people who heard him: one contemporary remembers his "opening wide his mouth to give full effect to the charm of oral delivery" and it seems likely that he trained himself to speak clearly and precisely, to lose that faint thick or metallic burr that others had noticed in his speech as a young man. But his was not just a triumph of elocution over natural disadvantages – many years later he spoke quite extemporaneously to a group of boys and ". . . with a few words so magnetised them that they wore their hearts in their eyes as if they meant to keep the words forever". The astonishing thing was that Dickens never made or kept notes but seemed to speak spontaneously and effortlessly, all the more extraordinary since the speeches themselves are as graceful and as fluent as anything he ever wrote. The truth was that, as his early life as a reporter may have suggested, he had an extraordinary verbal memory. He did not make notes because he memorised everything he wished to say, and this for speeches that lasted some twenty or thirty minutes. Even after he had finished, he could still repeat what he had said verbatim to reporters anxious for "clean" copy: another astonishing gift in a man who never ceases to astonish.

How did he achieve this? The morning before he was due to speak, he would take a long walk and in the course of that journey he would decide what topics he was going to raise. He would put these in order, and in his imagination construct a cart wheel of which he was the hub and the various subjects the spokes emanating from him to the circumference; "during the progress of the speech," he said, "he would deal with each spoke separately, elaborating them as he went round the wheel; and when all the spokes dropped out one by one, and nothing but the tire and space remained, he would know that he had accomplished his task, and that his speech was at an end." He said it was easy, but nothing about this method would render it easy for most people. Only someone with the concentration, determination and orderliness of Dickens himself could perform such a feat. Interesting, too, that one of his closest friends noticed that at public dinners he did indeed "dismiss the spoke from his mind by a quick action of the finger as if he were knocking it away . . ."

There is a portrait of him at precisely this period in his life. He is sitting, or rather lounging, in a chair; his face has a slightly quizzical expression, the hair still long, the features still fresh, everything about the picture emphasising how young Charles Dickens still was. At the age of thirty-two he had written novels which would have secured the reputation of a writer twice his age. Yet he was restless, dissatisfied, wanting to move on. One of his favourite phrases in this period is "Sledge hammer blow", as we have seen, but in his correspondence he employs it to describe a variety of different activities – to write, to appear in print, to attack. But in the phrase there is also that constant sense of having to force his way forward. Mill said of him in this period that "he reminds me of Carlyle's picture of Camille Desmoulins, and his 'face of dingy blackguardism irradiated with genius'". That he did possess "genius" was now not really in doubt. There had been many people who had considered *Martin Chuzzlewit* to be a failure but the huge impact of *A Christmas Carol*, together with the range of novels which Dickens had written before he was even thirty, were indication enough of the extraordinary author which England possessed. Indeed it was in this year that R. H. Horne wrote a book, *A New Spirit of the Age*, in which he gave Dickens pride of place. It was not uncritical of him, and in particular Horne noticed Dickens's inability to construct a coherent or organised plot: "Dickens evidently works upon no plan; he has a leading idea, but no design at all." But then Horne went on to say that "Mr Dickens is manifestly the product of his age. He is a genuine emanation from its aggregate and entire spirit . . . Popularity and success, which injure so many men in head and heart, have improved him in all respects. His influence upon the age is extensive – pleasurable, instructive, healthy, reformatory." Dickens read this account of himself, and was dissatisfied with it; it is hard to see why, except insofar as Horne criticised his inability to construct or manage an entire plot. It is more than probable, in fact, that it was partly in response to the criticisms (and there were others similar in the newspapers) that Dickens himself made a major effort to do precisely the things he was accused of neglecting: from this time forward, all of his novels would build upon the achievement of *Martin Chuzzlewit* and would aspire to some larger architectonic unity quite different from those previous narratives which Horne had described as "a series of short stories".

By spring his plans for his European journey were very well advanced: after much hesitation and consulting of better-travelled contemporaries (like Lady Holland) he had decided upon Genoa as his headquarters, a city which was inexpensive, picturesque and, as he thought, healthy. So he asked Angus Fletcher, the sculptor whose eccentricities had amused him both in Broadstairs and in Scotland but who was now living in that city, to find an appropriate house for the family. Dickens had also been looking for suitable transport. It would have been difficult and no doubt expensive to hire coaches or carriages at every stage of their journey, and he went to the Pantechnicon near Belgrave Square where he found what seems to have been an old stage coach – large enough, in any case, to hold a party of twelve people and equipped, according to Dickens, "with night-lamps and day-lamps and pockets and imperials and leathern cellars, and the most extra-ordinary contrivances". It was a shabby giant of a coach, priced at sixty pounds, but he bargained it down to forty-five. Unlike many English travellers he and Catherine had also decided to take Italian lessons. These were conducted twice a week by a certain Luigi Mariotti, whom they had first met on the *Britannia* en route to the United States; Dickens was a quick study in such matters and, although he continued to have some difficulty with the spoken language, his written Italian (in letters) is perfectly competent. Mariotti remembered Dickens as "a bright-eyed, ready-witted, somewhat gushing, happy man, cheered by the world's applause, equally idolised by his wife, by his children, by every member of his family". It is as well that his wife and family did idolise him, since it seems unlikely that Catherine in particular would otherwise have relished the prospect of a year in a strange city without the comforts of home. Dickens had also hired a "courier", Louis Roche, whose job it was to guide the family across the continent with the minimum of fuss and delay. In addition, in preparation for his sojourn in Italy, he grew a moustache; whether this was in obeisance to the romantic character of the journey he was about to make, or whether it was another way of affirming a different kind of identity he wanted to assume after his "escape" from England, is not clear.

They had managed to let Devonshire Terrace and, since the new tenants wished to move in without delay, a detailed inventory was made of the contents of the house, in the course of which it was stated that the library contained more than two thousand volumes. Then the whole family decamped to the house in Osnaburgh Street where the children had stayed during the American tour; the dog, Timber Doodle, was to go with them on their journey but Dickens left with Edwin Landseer a pet raven and pet eagle. Even as the complicated preparations were going ahead, Dickens was still trying to finish *Martin Chuzzlewit*. Never had the composition of any of his books been so beset by the general accidents of life, and yet he still pushed forward; during the last stages of Catherine's difficult pregnancy, during the Chancery suit against the pirates of a *A Christmas Carol*, during his infatuation with Christiana Weller, he had been able to write rapidly, sometimes improvising as he went along, sometimes making minor mistakes as a consequence. Even when fearful of "ruin" after his disappointment at the receipts for *A Christmas Carol*, he was able to write some of the funniest passages in the narrative – as Mrs Gamp watches a young lady being taken on board a packet boat to Antwerp which she calls "The Ankworks package" and which she wishes "in Jonadge's belly, I do". For some reason this auspicious occasion prompts memories of her own children: "'My own,' I says 'has fallen out of three-pair backs, and had damp doorsteps settled on their lungs, and one was turned up smilin' in a bedstead, unbeknown . . .'" And of her dead departed husband, too: "'. . . there's a wooden leg gone likeways home to its account, which in its constancy of walkin' into wine vaults, and never comin' out again 'till fetched by force, was quite as weak as flesh, if not weaker.'" In April he was working on two consecutive numbers; and one passage here, which details the last movements of a man about to be murdered, is written so clearly and with such little hesitation that it might almost be a fair copy from some unknown original. Even still, he was writing against time; it was not in fact until June, and after their removal to Osnaburgh Street, that Dickens finally completed *Martin Chuzzlewit*. Finished at last, perhaps the most comic of his books, the novel in which he immortalised Mr Pecksniff and Mrs Gamp, but written during one of the most difficult periods of his life. There was no time for him to "break out like a Madman" after this novel; he barely had time to make all his farewells before departure, although of course he ensured that his affairs were left in secure hands. Those of Thomas Mitton, for finance; those of John Forster, for publishing. The final number of *Martin Chuzzlewit* was published on the last day of June. Two days later he and his family left for Italy, an event which Forster described as "the turning-point of his career".

III

A TRUE conversation between imagined selves.

Chatterton. Indeed not. The truest poetry is not the most feigning. It is that which is most often borrowed, passed down from poet to poet.

Eliot. I originally entitled *The Waste Land* "He Do The Police In Different Voices". I took that line from *Our Mutual Friend.*

Wilde. You did not take it. You rescued it.

Dickens. I was perpetually being accused of stealing work from other novelists, but I did so without realising it at the time.

Wilde. That is the definition of inspiration.

Chatterton. It is of no consequence in the sum of things. For what do any of us do but return helplessly to the past? It is the part of us that creates our music.

Eliot. Or rather, shall we say, it is the informing presence of which we become a part? It is the tradition.

Wilde. You make literature sound like a philanthropic society. Really, one might as well join the Salvation Army as appear in print. In any case there is absolutely no necessity to look backwards, since one need not look at all. If art has one merit, it is that of inventing reality.

Eliot. What *precisely* do you mean by invention? And by reality? And by art? It seems to me –

Wilde. I mean *precisely* what I do not say.

Dickens. Nevertheless you are perfectly right. Perfectly. Art – but I do not like the word. Can we say literature? Literature discloses reality as it truly is –

Wilde. That is not what I meant at all –

Dickens. It shows its inner spirit and its proper harmonies. It displays its meaning and its direction. Its progress.

Chatterton. There is no such thing. All around is anarchy, and artifice, and –

Wilde. Alliteration?

Eliot. I am afraid that I must tend to agree. We live in a fallen world.

Dickens. No, not fallen at all. But rising. Rising all the time. Rising to the beat of time.

Wilde. (Obviously bored by this theme.) That must be the explanation for your use of blank verse. I do not know if I should say this – but, now that we are beyond the reach of time, what harm can come from literary criticism? Reading the more purple aspects of your prose was like reading Shakespeare by the light of a penny sparkler.

Dickens. (Laughing.) Better than not reading me at all. (Yet somewhat uneasily changing the subject.) And who can say what oblivion eventually lies in wait for all of us?

Eliot. I would appreciate that. Oblivion.

Chatterton. But you did not suffer from it in your own lifetime, as I did.

Wilde. And I suffered from my fame. Curious, is it not? Presumably it was my own definition of the artist as a unique personality that contributed to my destiny. There is nothing like self-revelation to seal one's fate.

Chatterton. But I saw poets like craftsmen, like the builders of the great cathedrals. Like the stone masons who worked on the church beside which I was born. How I longed to have my own signature imprinted upon stone rather than upon vellum.

Eliot. And then to achieve a glorious anonymity. Is that not so? To become invisible . . .

Wilde. I cannot think of a more unattractive posture. One might as well be a model in the window of Whiteley's.

Eliot. But if I were to say impersonality instead of invisibility?

Wilde. I would be forced to issue a pamphlet in my own defence.

Dickens. But stop a minute. Do stop a minute. There is something greater than either impersonality or invisibility, although it might be said to include them. Have you considered the artist as the proclaimer of truths? Of truth? Let us take the *Four Quartets* –

Chatterton. If that is a title, it contains a tautology.

Wilde. He may not know what you mean. Grammar is the respect which the low-spirited pay to the high-minded.

Dickens. (Ignoring the interruption.) Literature can reveal the true shape of the world, and thus of its Maker.

Wilde. But how can you say that? You of all people, who made the world laugh with Mrs Gamp and Quilp? In my lifetime you were remembered for your grotesquerie and not for your sanity, for your caricatures and not for your truth. It was the reason I admired you, even as I pretended not to do so.

Dickens. I do not understand you.

Wilde. That is another reason why I admire you.

Dickens. There was no – what was your word? – grotesqueness. No caricature. It was an entire world, as real as the one in which I moved. I saw it all. I copied faithfully the reality. It was my vision.

Wilde. Ah, at last, a paradox.

Chatterton. Now that you talk of visions, what truer vision is there than of one's own self. I have been unjustly criticised –

Wilde, Eliot and *Dickens* (together). So have I!

Chatterton. – criticised for my vision of the past. But

really it was a vision of my own dead father. A vision of the possibilities latent within me.

Wilde. He is the only Romantic among us.

Chatterton. What is a Romantic?

Wilde. It happened after your lifetime. Amusing, is it not, to find that the originator of a movement has not the least idea what it is? That is true inventiveness.

Dickens. When you speak of visions, why, I agree. All writing is a form of revelation, by which we can move into the shadowy world and borrow from there all the emblems and images which comprehend our own state. If William Blake were here –

Chatterton. He will be joining us shortly.

Eliot. It seems to me that all this is mere hyperbole. There is nothing more damaging than literature seen as a form of religion. It is a heresy. An abomination.

Wilde. But highly suggestive, don't you think? Can we not say in turn that all religion is a form of literature, at least of the more sensational kind.

Eliot. The religion of your century, perhaps.

Wilde. I came at its end. I cannot be responsible for its beginning. Does the butterfly look back at the grub?

Eliot. Yes, you were of the fin-de-siècle. If I understood anything at all about my own career – my own art, I mean to say – it was that I came at the beginning of a period in every sense.

Chatterton. So is that why I suffered? Coming in the middle of the century, as I did? Neither before nor after –

Eliot. I have heard that before somewhere.

Chatterton. (Turning to Dickens.) And what of you?

Dickens. I lived through most of my own century, so I saw myself as an integral part of it. Part of the great machine. There was neither beginning nor end, just the steady march, the steady movement forward.

Wilde. When I looked forward, I saw only an age of which I could not be a part.

Eliot. When I looked forward, I saw only darkness and barbarism.

Chatterton. When I looked forward, I saw . . . why should I lie to you now? I never looked forward. I was too young.

Wilde. Another paradox.

Dickens. And really I never looked forward.

Wilde. You were always too young.

Dickens. I had no need to look forward. It was reality that impressed itself upon me. The living, moving world.

Wilde. The only thing that has ever impressed me is my own command of style.

Chatterton. I was impressed by the glorious past.

Eliot. I was impressed by posterity.

Dickens. But none of you looked at the world as it is?

Wilde. There is no such thing.

Dickens. None of you listened to the voices around you?

Eliot. Delusion. Impotence. Vacancy.

Chatterton. Visions only. Hallucinations. Trances.

Wilde. Artifice. Fantasies.

Dickens. But there was truly a world beyond us.

Wilde. Not in my period.

Eliot. Nor in mine.

Chatterton. I never stopped to see it. I was too eager to earn my bread.

Dickens. But are we all then mere individuals, lost in some dream of the world?

Wilde. That would be true contentment.

Eliot. No. Individuality is the thing we must lose in order to save ourselves.

Dickens. So there is no great world. No thriving concourse of reality. Is that what you all firmly believe?

Chatterton. How do we know what we believe? Is the truest poetry the most feigning, after all?

Eliot. The truest poetry is that which is closest to prayer.

Wilde. There is no truth.

Dickens. I do not understand you. I do not understand any of you.

Wilde, *Eliot* and *Chatterton*. (Together.) Of course you do. You are part of us. Of me.

Chapter 15

THEY left on the Channel boat from Dover on 2 July – Charles Dickens, Catherine Dickens, Georgina Hogarth, Charley Dickens, Mamie Dickens, Kate Dickens, Walter Dickens, Francis Dickens, Louis Roche (the courier), Anne Brown (Catherine's maid who had accompanied her mistress on the American tour) and two domestic servants who will become much less anonymous in Italy than they ever were in London. A party of twelve in all, plus dog, travelling together inside the ancient coach across the countryside of France and Italy. At Boulogne Dickens entered a French bank to change some money and made a long request in his inexpert French. "How would you like to take it, sir?" – the clerk replied to him, in English. And from Boulogne to Paris. A city he had never seen, and at once he was enthralled by it. "My eyes ached and my head grew giddy, as novelty, novelty, novelty; nothing but strange and striking things; came swarming before me." It was all new to him, and he told Forster that it was as if he had grown another head beside his old one. On later occasions he would describe Paris as variously light, brilliant, sparkling, glittering; he was affected by its glare rather than its gloire and, since it is well known how Dickens always loved to have mirrors around him in his own homes, it is clear that the French city fulfilled his own needs for light and brilliancy.

Cities do not change over the centuries. They represent the aspirations of particular men and women to lead a common life; as a result their atmosphere, their tone, remain the same. Those people whose relations are founded principally upon commerce and upon the ferocious claims of domestic privacy will construct a city as dark and as ugly as London was. And is. Those people who wish to lead agreeable lives, and in constant intercourse with one another, will build a city as beautiful and as elegant as Paris. This is precisely what Dickens saw on his first journey there: "I cannot conceive any place so perfectly and wonderfully expressive of its own character; its secret character no less than that which is on its surface . . ." This is a wonderfully apt description of the city (and one which should give the lie to those who believe that Dickens was always a Cockney tourist); one might think of the contemporary Pompidou Centre, which is a miracle of lucidity in exactly the sense Dickens conveys. It is a true affirmation of the Parisian spirit: everything exists in a clear and even light. The pavement cafés in the nineteenth no less than in the twentieth century were places where people went to sit and watch, and be watched in turn, as if the Parisians had invented glass, that medium which imparts brightness but not heat. The clearness, the unambiguity, the lucidity were everywhere: the relentless clarity of French realism, the lucid structures of French philosophical thought, the inordinate attention paid to appearances so that waiters really looked like waiters, tramps really looked like tramps. This sense of life was very close to Dickens's own, which is why the city made an "immense impression" upon him and why he returned to it so often in later years. Its closeness to Dickens's own vision of the world is undoubtedly the reason that, while he walked excitedly through the streets, ". . . almost every house, and every person I passed, seemed to be another leaf in the enormous book that stands wide open there . . . There never was such a place for a description." In Paris, the world is turned into a spectacle. And, when Dickens likens it to a book, it is one of his own that he means. His party spent two days in the capital before moving on through the countryside. On to Lyons where, to the dismay of the sacristan, he mistook a model of the Angel Gabriel in the clock of the cathedral for a representation of the Evil One. On to Avignon where a "she-devil" who showed him gleefully around the torture chambers of the Inquisition was unwittingly to sit for some of his less flattering portrayals of French women. On to Marseilles, which he detested, and by boat across the Mediterranean to Genoa.

He had arrived in Italy. What had he expected in advance? What was the Italy of his imagination? Of course its towers and churches and villas had been familiar to him from earliest childhood as the backdrop to various burlettas and comic operas; he knew it from the theatre, too, as the place for stabbings, poisons and other secret villainy, a vision of darkness tempered only by Shakespeare's more graceful visions and sweeter airs. Clearly it was a place associated by him with the theatre in all its forms – is that one reason why he had grown a moustache, like a stage villain? – and it is not surprising that almost at once he was describing Genoa in grotesque or pantomimic terms.

Angus Fletcher had hired for them a large house, the Villa Bagnerello, in Albaro, which was then a district just outside the city. It was on the slope of a hill and was reached by a narrow lane which wound its way from the sea-coast to the via Albaro above: a large but not a grand house, surrounded by high walls but overlooking vineyards and the Bay of Genoa; the courtyard opened onto a small front hall, where a marble staircase led upwards to commodious and well proportioned rooms. And yet it did not seem altogether to please Dickens or his family. His name for it was the "pink jail", despite the magnificent views over the Bay, and, in addition, it was swarming with fleas. Genoa itself seems at first to have disappointed Dickens as well. It was a very frowsy and dirty city, not at all that place of Mediterranean brightness which he must at least have half-anticipated. It was crowded. It was noisy. It was slow. And yet he came to love it for, if America had been a journey into an unworkable future, this was a journey into the dismal and ruined past which he had already recreated in his novels. It is not hard to see how he came to appreciate it, even at its worst – with the alleys and high buildings of its ancient town; the palaces and the fine public buildings which crowd against each other on streets no more than twelve feet across; the cavernous dim churches filled with the prayers or sighs of worshippers and fitfully illuminated by the splendour of gilt and marble. But there was another reason why he came to love this place. The frescoes on the walls of the public buildings, the gestures of the people, the very life of the streets, must have given him an unmistakable impression of some theatrical reality, the frescoes themselves looking uncannily like backdrops for the voluble and excited life of the inhabitants. It may well be that the stinking alleys reminded him of London, but this was London seen as a form of theatre. He was at home.

And yet if it was theatre, it was the theatre of decay. He had written "Notes" from America, suggesting a journalistic record of contemporary life, but his book concerning these travels was to be more appropriately entitled "Pictures" from Italy. Pictures of ruin. Neglect. Darkness. The past haunted and lost. Catholicism. Lamps. Flowers. Monks. High houses. The sudden sight of dark interiors. The sedan chairs carrying people through the narrow ways. The smells. The odours of desolation and death. The crumbling churches packed among the tenements of the old city. The plaster cracked and peeling.

The strange words scrawled upon walls. The statues of the Virgin in the dirtiest corners of the city. The stray dogs. Mould. The end of time. "It seemed," he wrote, "as if one had reached the end of all things." And he went to look at the Italian puppet theatres – a strange phenomenon to be found among "the end of all things", perhaps, but one that Dickens had anticipated in *The Old Curiosity Shop* where the dying Nell is surrounded by Punches and Judies and waxworks.

Yet of course there was more to Genoa, and to Italy, than the mere confluence of decay. There was the countryside and the sea, with the Alps beyond. Blue. Scarlet. Lilac-green. The blue Mediterranean which, Dickens said in a memorable phrase, would "make a great blue blank of your intellect". Heat. Brightness. Perhaps over-brightness. The rotten fruit dropping off the trees in that heat. "Everything is in extremes," he wrote. And yet, after the secrecy and mournfulness of London, how wonderful a change to have "all manner of show and display". All these things were quite new to him and, as soon as he arrived in Albaro, he started sending long accounts of his observations to his friends in England. Of course this was partly in anticipation of a book of travels to be elicited from these letters; but he *needed* to write. He needed to share his feelings and perceptions with others before they became properly real to him; in addition, he needed to use words, to master with language the unfamiliar reality in front of him, to control this "bewildering phantasmagoria, with all the inconsistency of a dream, and all the pain and all the pleasure of an extravagant reality!" Once more it is as if he is describing one of his own novels but on this occasion, at least, he is not turning Genoa into a fiction; this is simply the way his imagination curves around all things, bending them slightly out of shape but in the process making them brighter, more visible, more real.

So the outline of his new travel book may already have been clear to him but nevertheless, in this ancient place, he had to turn his mind to the Christmas Book which he had promised to Bradbury and Evans and which he wished to finish by mid-October, only three months away. The atmosphere, however, was not yet conducive to work. His daughter, Kate, was very ill for a time but then recovered, and the servants were at first horrified by Italian food and Italian manners; their usual method of communication with the natives was to speak English very loudly and very slowly, as if they were deaf rather than Italian, and Dickens later employed this mannerism in *Little Dorrit* when the inhabitants of Bleeding Heart Yard try to converse with

John Baptist Cavalletto: "E pleased," Mrs Plornish interprets for him in what she believes to be very good Italian, "E glad get money." Dickens's cook was the first to master enough of the language to buy whatever food was wanted, and very shortly after the servants began, as it were, to settle in. They remain the permanent but alas unacknowledged backdrop to Dickens's life. We hear little from him about his valet, Topping, for example, no more than that he had violent red hair and a habit of becoming confidential when not entirely sober. In turn Topping, who of all the men of the period was probably the one who knew Dickens best, left no memoir and no reminiscences of his employer. Perhaps he never read his novels. It is not even clear whether he was in Italy with the family – since Louis Roche acted as guide, interpreter and man-servant on most occasions, it is likely that he was left behind in some supernumerary capacity in Devonshire Terrace.

Meanwhile, as the family began to start its new European life, Dickens lazed in the Villa Bagnerello. He continued to learn Italian and, although on most occasions he left Catherine to deal with unexpected guests, he attended a few parties and visited the theatres of the town. But most of all he loved to walk, through the city and through the countryside, getting lost in the narrow streets, coming upon "the strangest contrasts; things that are picturesque, ugly, mean, magnificent, delightful, and offensive, break upon the view at every turn." In this period he also managed to complete a task which he did not even think worth mentioning in his correspondence: he completely revised *Oliver Twist* in readiness for its publication by Bradbury and Evans for the first time in a single volume. (Since he was once more suffering from agonising pains in his side, is it possible that the return to Oliver's infancy had reawakened once more something of his own anguished childhood?) This exercise in revision would in itself only be of interest to textual scholars were it not for the fact that, in the process, he imposed a quite new system of punctuation upon his narrative. He seems to have gone through it thoroughly, making many small excisions and changes, but most importantly he gave his words a punctuation which suggests a more rhetorical or declamatory style; it is almost as if he had revised it so that it could be more easily read aloud. It has been suggested that this is an anticipation of his later public readings, but this seems improbable; he had recently been delivering many speeches, in England and just previously in America, and it is more likely that, for the first time, he was now beginning to realise both the power of his voice and the sense of an audience listening to him. It was a new conception of himself, gathered largely in America, his own presence as somehow central to his authorial personality; which is no doubt why he wished to rush back to London later this year precisely in order to read his second Christmas Book out loud to his friends.

But this is to anticipate his movements; at this stage, in the first months of his travels, he went only so far as Marseilles in order to meet his brother, Frederick, who was to join the family in Genoa. He was gone only for a few days, during the course of which he and his brother were forced to remain on the boat outside Nice in official quarantine for several hours – an incident which he later embellished and used at the opening of *Little Dorrit*. On his return with Frederick, he began to make plans to move out of the Villa Bagnerello into a more habitable place. Not only did he find the Villa somewhat grim, but he realised also that it would be very difficult to keep warm during the Italian winter. So, with the help of an expatriate Englishman, he managed to rent a palace in Genoa itself; it was a real palace, known as the Palazzo Peschiere, on account of two large and ornamental ponds at the front of the house which were filled with goldfish. It had been built in the late sixteenth century, and was conceived on a very grand scale; the sala on the ground floor was some fifty feet in height, covered with frescoes, and most of the rooms Dickens and his family used led off from this large hall. The walls and ceilings of the rooms were also painted with frescoes, and Dickens later recalled how he wandered from room to room, from bed chamber to bed chamber, as if he were in a vision. From its large windows Dickens could look down at the old city of Genoa; although the Palazzo Peschiere was in fact within the walls of the city it was upon the side of Monte Bartolomeo and therefore slightly above the main congeries of streets and buildings; and from here, too, he could hear the bells of the churches below him. The gardens were filled with "statues, vases, fountains, marble basins, terraces, walks of orange-trees and lemon trees . . ." Dickens described it as "like an enchanted place in an Eastern story" in its splendour – and to think that they had left their modest house in Devonshire Terrace because they could not afford to live there. Odd too, perhaps, that it was in these very grand surroundings that Dickens wrote what was to become his most outspoken defence of the poor and the working men of England.

The Palazzo Peschiere was also reputed, according to Dickens, to be "very badly haunted indeed" but in the months the Dickens family stayed there they saw nothing. Dickens himself did in fact experience *something* but he would not have described it as a haunting: he explained it variously as a dream, or a vision within a dream. For, almost as soon as he moved into their new quarters, he saw Mary Hogarth once again. It was the first time she had appeared to him since she had vanished in the wilds of Yorkshire, after he had told his dreams to Catherine, but here in Italy she came again. It happened like this. He had been suffering his old childhood pains, in his back and side, and had found it difficult to sleep. But when eventually he managed to slumber he dreamed of a Spirit wrapped in blue drapery, like a Madonna by Raphael. His memory of Mary Hogarth was now rather generalised – he was not even sure of her voice – but somehow he knew that this was "poor Mary's spirit". He stretched out his arms and called her "Dear". And then, "Forgive me! We poor living creatures are only able to express ourselves by looks and words. I have used the word most natural to *our* affections; and you know my heart." The Spirit said nothing and Dickens began to sob. "Oh! give me some token that you have really visited me!"

> *The Spirit*: "Form a wish."
> *Dickens*: "Mrs Hogarth is surrounded with great distresses. Will you extricate her?"
> *The Spirit*: "Yes."
> *Dickens*: "And her extrication is to be a certainty to me, that this has really happened?"
> *The Spirit*: "Yes."
> *Dickens*: "But answer me one other question! What is the True religion? You think, as I do, that the Form of religion does not so greatly matter, if we try to do good? Or perhaps the Roman Catholic is the best? Perhaps it makes one think of God oftener, and believe in him more steadily?"
> *The Spirit*: "For *you*, it is the best."

Then Dickens awoke, roused Catherine from her sleep, and repeated the words of this strange visitation over and over again so that he could the more easily remember them.

By any standards a curious incident, but one not without its echoes and parallels deep within Dickens's own consciousness. His previous Christmas Book, which had at the time so powerfully affected him, did of course introduce Spirits to a sleeping Ebenezer Scrooge in much the same manner. So the imaginative conditions were appropriate, perhaps, for a further nocturnal visitation. Curiously enough there is a picture of the Virgin in Cattermole's drawing of the death of Little Nell; it is just above her bed, too, so that in a sense the sleeping Dickens is taking the place of his little heroine. Part Little Nell, therefore, and part Scrooge? But there were also more immediate references. He had been sleeping in a room where a great altar was placed; in the terraces which led to the Palazzo Peschiere there were many ancient sculpted figures, also, and that very night he had heard the interminable convent bells around him. So was his a vision of Mary Hogarth, or of the Virgin Mary? Perhaps the consonance of names suggests the truth; that here was the idealised virgin figure which played as large a part in Dickens's own imagination as it did in the rituals of the Roman Catholic Church. Genoa itself seems almost to have been devoted to the Virgin Mary, with altars raised in reverence to her in all of the churches, pictures of her on public buildings, and in the slums of the old town an astonishing number and variety of statues placed in crumbling niches and festooned with flowers. This was the city of the Virgin, therefore, and it is not hard to see how in his mind the Virgin Mary might come to resemble the Virgin Mary Hogarth. And yet this is a Church which extols Mary as the Virgin Mother. Dickens mentions Mrs Hogarth in his dream, Mary's mother, but is it not possible that his real yearning is towards his own mother, a yearning he so frequently and often denied? Is this what is exemplified in the Spirit's suggestion that the Catholic church, the church of Mariolatry or mother-worship, was for Dickens the best? Was he in this dream expressing all the real pining of his nature for the young mother who had once nursed and nourished him, and whose later apparent abandonment of him led to so much bitterness and even coarseness in his relationship to her? Was he returning to his origins in such a dream? It cannot be known. All we can say is that the dream was not easily forgotten by Dickens: the hooded figure of a woman reappears in his later fiction and his next Christmas Book, *The Chimes*, was also to deal with ghosts and spirits and visitations.

Of *The Chimes* itself he was soon to say, ". . . it has a grip upon the very throat of the time". This was the Christmas Book he had agreed to write for Bradbury and Evans but, in Genoa, he found it difficult to begin. It was the first time he had attempted to write a book outside England, and "plucked . . . out of my proper soil" he felt ill at ease; a cavernous Italian palace was perhaps not the best place to paint the careful miniatures of benevolence and good will which he needed for the Christmas season. He could not work, and he was vexed by the clangour of Genoa's bells borne upon the wind. These were the noises which eventually saved him, however, and at the beginning of October he sent a one-sentence letter – or, rather, quotation – to Forster: "We have heard THE CHIMES at midnight, Master Shallow!" This short missive has often been quoted as an example of Dickens's boisterous good spirits, but it seems more remarkable for its entire but perfectly unconscious preoccupation with himself and with his own problems.

It was in another letter to Forster that he explained his story's "grip" upon "the time" and indeed all of his recent remarks on public matters culminate here in the story of a poor man, Trotty Veck, who comes to believe that he has no right to exist in the world at all – just as Thomas Malthus had once said, in a controversial paragraph of *An Essay on the Principle of Population*, the impoverished man "has no business to be where he is. At nature's mighty feast there is no vacant cover for him. She tells him to be gone . . ." This is extreme social Darwinism at a time before Darwinism existed, and in these brief but telling remarks is contained everything that Dickens detested and despised. He detected the same attitude, the same disdain for the poor in the battle for life, in other and apparently more emollient statements. Part of the inspiration for *The Chimes* came from a dismissive review of *A Christmas Carol* in the *Westminster Review*, for example, where it was said that the question of "Who went without turkey and punch in order that Bob Cratchit might get them . . . is a disagreeable reflection kept wholly out of sight" by Dickens. But Dickens had come across much more terrible reports in the newspapers. He had been reading in *The Times* the accounts of the trial of a young woman who, in her terror of the workhouse, had thrown herself with her baby into the Thames; the child had slipped from its mother's arms, had drowned, and the rescued mother was found guilty of murder and condemned to death. Thus did the New Poor Law wreak havoc upon the lives of the destitute. And Dickens had read, too, of the activities of a certain Sir Peter Laurie, magistrate, who had made it his business to "put down" the crime of suicide by sentencing to the treadmill any wretches who tried but failed to kill themselves. (It should be added that some putative suicides were in fact acts designed to elicit charity, but how desperate must such men and women have been to go to such extreme lengths to find relief?) Dickens had read, as well, this year, about the arson and insurrection of the Dorset labourers who were already close to destitution. He knew of such matters at first hand, since his efforts to help John Overs had shown him the difficulties and resentments which could embitter and destroy those who wished to rise out of their "station". All these specific matters found their way into the text of *The Chimes*, as Dickens considered the horrors in store for those who tried unsuccessfully to find release from lives of want and toil; but he also attacked those who relied upon statistics, or the myth of "the good old days", to avert their eyes from present circumstances.

So he set to work. The bells of Genoa had reminded him of Time, and Time had reminded him of the Sea. Of Motion. Of necessary Progress. Everything came together in a story in which the poor man has a vision of death and sorrow, only alleviated at the end by one of those acts of mercy and charity which Dickens always tried to celebrate in his Christmas fiction. He had started by the second week of October and images of his violence, anger, excitement, are to be found in his description of the writing: "I am in regular, ferocious excitement with the *Chimes*; get up at seven; have a cold bath before breakfast; and blaze away, wrathful and red hot . . ." There could not be a better description of Dickens when "taken by the throat" by a conception. He could not rest until he had got it down on paper. "It has great possession of me every moment in the day; and drags me where it will . . ." He was being dragged forward all the time, forward through all the sorrow and horror of the London poor which he was imagining here in a Genoese palace. Forward to the beat of Time which "cries to man, Advance!" – how much of the real meaning and self-confidence of the age in this phrase from the story, and how appropriate for Dickens's fiction which matches the spirit of its time with its own relentless momentum. Forward through the insults given to the labouring poor, through the despair of those who have no place to sleep, forward through the shame of women forced upon prostitution to support their children. All these things were true – all these things were happening around the readers of *The Chimes* – and all these things invaded Dickens as he wrote. "My cheeks, which were beginning to fill out, have sunk again," he told Forster; "my eyes have grown immensely large; my hair is very lank; and the head inside the hair is hot and giddy." Dickens was making an overtly political and social statement; he knew Carlyle, and from him he seems to have borrowed a worried apocalyptic manner; he knew the work of Douglas Jerrold, too, and for once he used his topical, satirical, sarcastic tone. He blazed away through the whole of October, having to take violent exercise to still his beating mind. One day he walked twelve miles in mountain rain; another day he walked six miles under the hottest sun of the day; another day he walked fifteen miles. He sent each section of the tale to Forster, who then took it to Bradbury and Evans; Dickens meanwhile, faithful to his old profession, kept a shorthand copy of each instalment. He worked on, and when he finished at the beginning of November "had what women call a 'real good cry!'"

He had already decided that he wanted to come to London when it was printed; and not just because he wanted to see the volume itself, which he believed would knock *A Christmas Carol* "out of the field". More importantly, he wanted to read the story out loud. He was so pleased by it, so excited by its novelty, that he wanted to see its effect upon a group of chosen friends; particularly those like Carlyle and Jerrold who would understand what a leap Dickens had made from his other fiction. In fact the book did cause something of a sensation and, because of its overtly radical tones, was more vigorously attacked and more stoutly defended than any of Dickens's previous works. Here he brands himself as a true radical, even revolutionary: in this Christmas Book, so hard a present for those who defended the status quo, it is quite clear that Dickens really did despise the political system of his country as much as he loathed its social mores. Of course there were more personal objections to the book too. Sir Peter Laurie, whose campaign against suicides had been satirised here under the name of Alderman Cute, called it "most disgraceful". In fact Laurie had once taken Catherine Dickens to a Lord Mayor's dinner and thought he was on good terms with the famous author. "He is a dangerous man to meet," he said. *The Morning Post* went further and accused Dickens of romanticising "the ruffian and the wanton, the rickburner and the felon". But all this was to come – now that he had finished *The Chimes*, Dickens first had to make his way across the continent to London.

He was accompanied by his courier, Louis Roche, but even so it began as a lonely and dispiriting journey. He travelled over-night in a very slow coach without refreshment of any kind until at daybreak he came to Alessandria; according to Murray's Handbook there were at least two good hotels in this little town but, according to Dickens, all he could find was "the damndest Inn in the world". And then on through mud and rain for Stradella, sleeping in a large bare room which opened onto a courtyard where the waggons and horses were kept. He saw streets which in their filthiness reminded him of a London scene, but he was in low spirits and without real company he felt isolated. As a result he held onto whatever certainty he could: "Keep things in their places," he told his wife. "I can't bear to picture them otherwise." One sees in this remark the boy within the man, the boy with such wide fears of desolation and abandonment still within the man who travels across this alien landscape, "houseless Dick" as he called himself in a letter to Forster. And then on to Piacenza, a "brown, decayed, old town . . .", thus adding yet another tincture to the desuetude and weariness that Dickens found all around him. The point is that he rarely changed his first impressions of a place, but merely elaborated upon them; on his first arrival in Italy he had pronounced it to be in decay, and thus he saw decay everywhere he looked. It was the same with every place he visited. "As soon as I have fixed a place in my mind," he told Forster, "I bolt . . ." And bolt he did, always travelling onward, never resting for very long, seeing everything in a flash and then again going forward – and as he rides through the towns and the villages, along the muddy roads and the beaten paths, he comes almost to be persuaded that ". . . there is no more human progress, motion, effort or advancement . . ." And yet there is always his own advancement and his own unwearying effort. "My only comfort is, in Motion." The noun is capitalised with good reason because he literally equates Motion with the idea of human progress. The Italians, he said, should thank heaven "that they live in a time when Iron makes Roads instead of Prison Bars . . ." And he describes how the railway to Leghorn has brought "punctuality, order, plain dealing, and improvement". It is worth repeating that Dickens was in no real sense opposed to industrialism or the Victorian industrial temper. In some ways he even embodies it, for in his own constant motion he becomes almost a human image of the railway and of advancement, truly a representative of his country at this time.

In Parma he visited a circus troupe and a desolate theatre; he had already conjured up both images within his fiction of previous years, and in that sense he had a store of pictures ready for any available reality. Or, rather, the reality is always conceived by him within certain terms. *Pictures from Italy* is very much like one of his novels, in fact, but without what he once called "the great idea". And from Parma to Modena, from Modena to Bologna, from Bologna to Ferrara. Seeing churches and galleries and streets and gardens and monks and amphitheatres. Rushing around with the same energy and almost hysterical determination which he applied to everything: ". . . insisting on having everything shewn to me whether or no, and against all precedents and orders of proceeding, I get on wonderfully," he said in a letter and, in *Pictures from Italy*, he also explained how it was "such a delight to me to leave new scenes behind, and still go on, encountering newer scenes . . ." Maclise analysed the phenomenon: Dickens "has a clutching eye – gets his impressions at once – is given to activity, and would not care to linger for contemplation". But that is not quite true. He did sometimes linger, and there are even occasions when he slows down, stops, and remains silent; just such a time came when he was walking at sunset towards Ferrara. "In the blood-red light, there was a mournful sheet of water, just stirred by the evening wind; upon its margin a few trees. In the foreground was a group of silent peasant girls leaning over the parapet of a little bridge, and looking, now up at the sky, now down into the water; in the distance, a deep bell; the shadow of approaching night on everything." This scene was responsible for an ". . . emphatic chilling of the blood", but for reasons that he did not understand. Yet one sees here what one also sees in his fiction: the sudden quietness amidst activity, a momentary picture but one that leaves a permanent imprint. Dickens actually associated this scene with murder, and indeed it is like a vision just glimpsed before death. The world is quiet, and these small figures beside calm water have a significance at once both close and remote, as if the visible world had been touched by the invisible and thus redeemed.

In Venice he recovered his composure and, indeed, one purpose of his long journey was to restore himself after the fever involved in the composition of *The Chimes*. So for him Venice became a place of dreams, of withdrawal from the pressures of ordinary reality, and in *Pictures from Italy* it is represented as such. It is a place of water, too, and the presence of water seems always to instil in Dickens memories of his childhood by the sea; perhaps it is that infantile reminiscence in itself which persuaded him to treat the city as if it were part of a fairy tale he may once have read. "Then, coming down some marble staircase where the water lapped and oozed against the lower steps, I passed into my boat again, and went on in my dream." Yet even in this magical place there are intimations of horror and darkness, just as his own beneficent childhood had been plunged downwards into dirt and blacking; for beneath the silver lamps and silent galleries, beneath the lofty houses and glittering arcades, are "dismal, awful, horrible stone cells" where men were once tortured and destroyed.

Then he moved onward again. From Venice to Verona. To Mantua. To Cremona. To Milan. Then from that foggy city he crossed into the Alps and climbed the Simplon, sledged across the top in snow and descended the other side of this "wild, and bleak, and lonely . . ." country. Then to Strasbourg. And then by coach he travelled fifty hours until he reached Paris. He was so filthy after this eternity in a rusty coach that he was almost unrecognisable to himself. He imagined someone in the Hôtel Bristol, where he expected to stay, asking, "Are you Charles Dickens?"

"No. I never heard of him."

Eager to get home, he stayed only one night in Paris before taking off again for Boulogne and England. The journey was over.

As soon as he had arrived in London he took rooms at the Piazza Coffee House in Covent Garden (his house in Devonshire Terrace of course still being let) and then went at once to see Forster in Lincoln's Inn Fields. Forster remembered many years later ". . . the eager face and figure, as they flashed upon me so suddenly this wintry Saturday night that almost before I could be conscious of his presence I felt the grasp of his hand." But of course he had really come back for *The Chimes*, and the next night he read the whole Christmas story to Macready. "If you had seen Macready last night – undisguisedly sobbing, and crying on the sofa, as I read – you would have felt (as I did) what a thing it is to have Power." This was how he described that reading to Catherine. "Power." Power over others. Power to move and to sway. The Power of his writing. The Power of his voice.

And it was that same Power which he demonstrated the following evening when he read his story to a selected group of friends. Forster had called them together in his rooms – Carlyle, Daniel Maclise, Clarkson Stanfield, W. J. Fox, Laman Blanchard, Douglas Jerrold and of course Forster himself, all of them keenly in sympathy with the political and social emphases of *The Chimes*. "It is a tea-party," Forster told one of them in advance, "D. objecting to anything more jovial, and we assemble *punctually at half past six* . . .", that last emphatic command sounding suspiciously like something from Dickens's own lips. Such an early start was necessary because, on an approximate reckoning, *The Chimes* would have taken over three hours to read; which is longer even than Tennyson took to read *Maud* out loud to his friends (although the poet did on occasions read it more than once if he believed that it was not being properly understood). But there was no mistaking Dickens's intention or his effect. Maclise drew the scene with the novelist sitting before a desk, the book opened in front of him (he must in fact have used a proof copy which he had received from Bradbury and Evans), his companions around him in a semi-circle – Forster his hand upon his knee in robust attitude, Carlyle leaning upon his left hand, two others crying and the rest looking on and wondering. Maclise himself provided the best commentary to his own picture when he wrote to Catherine in the following week (he, of all Dickens's friends, appeared to have most respect and understanding for Catherine; he had a similarly quiet temperament, and must have realised how difficult it was for her to deal with her quixotic husband): "I send you a sketch of a scene," he said, "that took place last Tuesday . . . of Charles reading to a few of his friends, in the Rooms of Forster, his new book of *The Chimes*, when (as the saying is) there was not a dry eye in the house . . . We should borrow the high language of the minor theatre and even then not do the effect justice – shrieks of laughter – there were indeed – and floods of tears as a relief to them – I do not think that there ever was such a triumphant hour for Charles . . ." Laughter and tears. These were precisely the effects at which Dickens aimed, and nothing in his reception that night needed to change his opinion that he had indeed delivered a "Sledge hammer" blow for the poor. For it is the poor in whom he is really interested, just as it is the tears which he most readily provokes; he once told a close friend that "he preferred the power of making the world cry rather than laugh" and in a comment on *The Chimes* itself he told Lady Blessington that "I am in great hopes that I shall make you cry, bitterly". He told his sister, Fanny, that even the printers had "laughed and cried over it strangely" and added, ". . . when you come towards the end of the 3rd part you had better send upstairs for a clean pocket handkerchief". ". . . *very* dramatic," he said of his story in later years, "but very melancholy on the whole." He gave a second reading two evenings later, at which the principal guest was Albany Fonblanque, and it might fairly be said that the success of these occasions gave Dickens the first hint, the first intimation, that he might be just as successful with other readings of his works – readings, perhaps, to a larger audience than that comprised of his friends. Certainly it was on one of these evenings, as Forster relates, that Dickens and others conceived the idea of enacting plays in private with a sort of radical amateur theatricals. In fact the stage was never far from Dickens's mind and even now, on this brief and hectic visit to London, he gave permission to Gilbert A'Beckett and Mark Lemon to dramatise *The Chimes* at the Adelphi. From this time forward, Dickens never wrote a Christmas Book which did not at least have the potential for dramatic adaptation; when this is taken in conjunction with the rhetorical punctuation which he was perfecting (he had been recasting *Oliver Twist* in precisely that style) one can see how Dickens's art was changing even as his own sense of his role was being transformed.

Of course Dickens attempted to do more during that week in London than most people manage in a month; apart from dealing with *The Chimes*, for example, he took care to mend the fortunes of John Overs's family. Overs had died a few months before, never really having had the opportunity to harvest the gifts which he sensed within himself. A melancholy story; but Dickens was not one to allow melancholy to triumph over practicality, and within two days he had organised a fund for Mrs Overs and her six children, arranged for one of the children to enter an Orphans' Working School, and had written to Miss Burdett-Coutts on behalf of one of the daughters. As soon as he had completed this task, he moved on again. Macready was about to perform in Paris, and Dickens travelled over to join him there for two days. Together they visited the various theatres of that city, good and bad alike; Macready no doubt took a sterner view of such matters than Dickens, who still seems positively to have exulted in any kind of poor acting. And then on again. To Marseilles where he was to board the ship bound for Genoa. It was on this voyage that an American recognised him strolling on deck: "I am blarmed," he said, "if it ain't DICKENS!" Such recognition was becoming increasingly common and would, in later years, become more frequent still until there came a time when he could not walk down an English street without people turning back to look at him, or shake his hand, or smile. It was his custom studiously to ignore such manifestations wherever possible, and to go about his business perfectly serenely, but in these earlier years he was less blasé. In any event he struck up a travelling friendship with these Americans, while observing their absurdities and eccentricities with his usual keen eye. He was back in Genoa by 20 December and, pausing only long enough to resolve some difficulty with his passport, he rushed back to the Palazzo Peschiere and to Catherine, whom Forster has described as "disconsolate" at his earlier departure. She was about to be more troubled, however, by her husband's behaviour on his return. For within three days he had started mesmerically to "treat" a certain Augusta de la Rue, the English wife of a Swiss banker residing in Genoa. Thus opens a curious episode in his life, not least because it represents the first notable occasion when his wife opposed his will.

Madame de la Rue suffered from a pronounced and disagreeable nervous "tic" or spasm on her face but this was only the physical symptom of a debilitating anxiety. It is said that she resembled Dickens's sister, Fanny, and this may in part account for his interest in her: in any event, he told her husband that he had particular powers of animal magnetism and that he was "ready and happy" to assist her. So began a course of treatment which was to last some months, Dickens seemingly able effortlessly to induce a trance in Madame de la Rue; in that hypnotised sleep he was able not only to assuage the nervous spasms but also, by the technique of verbal free association, to help to elicit the fears which had induced this nervous disorder. It became for him an intense, consuming, interest. He had no book to write, not yet, and all his energies focused upon the sad state of a helpless woman who was lost in her dreams and who sometimes so recoiled in fright that she became almost unmanageable. At first he tried only to cure her physical disorder but very quickly he became drawn in to the very depths and caverns of her consciousness. He sat in the de la Rues' drawing room, with the woman in the trance he had imposed, and questioned her –

"Well! Where are you today? On the Hillside as usual?"

"Yes."

"Quite alone?"

"No."

"Are there many people there?"

"Yes. A good many."

And so it went on, Dickens taking notes in pencil as the hypnotic trance continued and then showing them to her husband. (The editors of the indispensable Pilgrim edition of his letters note that he signs off these memoranda with the kind of flourish he used to mark the end of a chapter in one of his novels; so, for him, this was also a kind of creation.) Clearly Dickens was an effective hypnotist, and his course of therapy began to show results; Madame de la Rue began to sleep at night, a feat which seems previously to have eluded her, and her appearance improved. But gradually Dickens learnt of problems more serious than nervous spasms. She believed that she was being pursued by an indistinct figure, a phantom who appeared in her dreams and would not let her rest. At this point Dickens seems to have become very interested indeed; he began to magnetise her each day and to question her about the phantom, for was it not an entity rather like those he had been invoking in his Christmas Books? He and the rest of the family were about to tour Italy, but even while he was away he remained in constant contact with his "patient"; he asked her husband to keep a journal of her progress and send it to him, and he wrote both husband and wife long, reassuring letters about the alleviation of her condition. Certainly he believed that there was some psychic or magnetic connection between himself and Madame de la Rue; he would concentrate upon her and attempt to hypnotise her from a distance, while on his travels, and there were times when he was afflicted by "uncommon anxiety" which he believed to be emanating from her. One night in Rome he woke up at two o'clock in the morning "in a state of indescribable horror and emotion" which he believed to be connected with the woman's condition. There is another curious circumstance also. One morning he decided to try to "magnetise" Madame de la Rue from a distance by concentrating upon her when he was travelling by coach, and he began to do so while Catherine sat beside him in the open air. Suddenly his wife let her muff fall and when he turned to her he found that she was "in the Mesmeric trance, with her eyelids quivering in a convulsive manner . . ." His magnetic concentration had somehow eddied across to her, and it was with some difficulty that he revived her and put her back inside the carriage. For Dickens it was proof of the "strange mysteries that are hidden within this power" but it also suggests, perhaps, how firmly and easily Catherine fell under the will of her husband. How sensitive she was, and always remained, to his various and bewildering moods.

Madame de la Rue's condition seemed to deteriorate in the absence of Dickens, however, and he became worried about the reappearance of the dark phantom; "I *cannot* beat it down, or keep it down, at a distance," he told her husband. "Pursuing that Magnetic power, and being near to her and with her, I believe that I can shiver it like Glass." Curiously enough, he had said nothing about his arrangement with the de la Rues to Catherine, but it was certainly at his instigation that the Swiss banker and his wife travelled to Rome in order to join the Dickens family. Now he magnetised her every day, "sometimes under olive trees, sometimes in vineyards, sometimes in the travelling carriage, sometimes at wayside inns during the midday halt". At one time during this visit Madame de la Rue displayed very alarming symptoms indeed; "she was rolled into an apparently impossible ball, by tic in the brain, and I only knew where her head was by following her long hair to its source." What is perhaps most remarkable about this whole episode is the extent to which Dickens trusted his powers; here was a woman in an extremity of mental anguish, but he possessed such self-confidence that he believed he could cure her. By himself. Dickens fighting the invisible world. And indeed his confidence may not have been misplaced; by the time the Dickens family left Italy her phantom had departed, although in later years her symptoms gradually returned. But something else happened; at some point, on their return to Genoa after their travels, Catherine must have complained to Dickens about his close relationship to his "patient". He in turn felt compelled to speak to the de la Rues, transmitting, if nothing else, his wife's concerns. Catherine was already pregnant once more and it may be that her condition renewed that old nervous depression and anxiety from which she always seemed to suffer at these times, but the fact that she found the courage to speak to her husband suggests how upset she was by his intimate association with Augusta de la Rue – the phrase to describe the process, "animal magnetism", perhaps sufficiently suggests the emotional element which must surely have entered into the transaction. Not sexual in overt ways but physical nonetheless. Yet it is also quite clear that Dickens was indignant about any such suggestion; he remembered the whole incident well enough to refer to it some eight years later when he returned to Genoa, and even at such a late date he manages to convey his annoyance at his wife's intervention. There is always a kind of innocence about Dickens on such occasions; his self-righteousness and denial of harm were no doubt quite genuine, but always there is a striking inability to see his conduct on anything other than his own terms. Suspicion normally aroused him into a fury, and there is no doubt that Catherine's doubts (perhaps they went as far as accusations) provoked in him his usual intense response. It may have been one of defiance, however, since he stayed with the de la Rues when the preparations for departure from Italy made life in the Palazzo too chaotic for his tidy temperament. But at least Catherine had spoken out and, perhaps for the first time, had temporarily checked or diverted his wishes.

There were other reasons why the de la Rue episode proved to be a memorable one since, for the first time, Dickens had entered and in some ways controlled the consciousness of another human being. So was it perhaps now that he began even more completely to understand the complexity of human consciousness and human behaviour? All his life he had moved forward instinctively, never questioning his impulses or pausing long to consider those of other people. The mysteries of the dreams of Madame de la Rue may have come as something of a revelation, therefore, leading to an enlargement and a deepening of his humane understanding. Certainly it coincided with a period in which he became more forthcoming about his own past and more open about the reasons for his own behaviour – in a letter to Forster at this time, for example, he began to talk about his earlier years, when he applied for a job as a stage comedian and when he went to work as a shorthand writer in Doctors' Commons. This may have been because Forster had just lost his brother and Dickens, eager to take that familial place, was ready to talk about his own buried past; or it may be that the psychic intercourse with Madame de la Rue broke open something of his own hard reserve and self-sufficiency. Perhaps that is why he intimates in this period that he might want to write some kind of autobiography. The strange circumstances of his Italian sojourn could have led him towards some desire to test and to understand his own life, the relationship with the de la Rues in that sense becoming part of his continuing moral education.

In addition he was having another kind of education altogether. He was seeing more of Italy. The Dickens family spent New Year in the Palazzo Peschiere where, with other English residents, they played charades and performed country-dances in the old style. And it was in Genoa, too, that the children were given their first dancing lessons. "Our progress in the graceful art delighted him," Mamie remembered many years later, "and his admiration of our success was evident when we exhibited to him, as we were perfected in them, all the steps, exercises and dances which formed our lessons". They were all still very young. Charles Culliford Boz Dickens was seven, Mary Dickens was six, Kate Macready Dickens was five, Walter Landor Dickens was now three and Francis Jeffrey Dickens was only a few months old. He gave each of them nicknames; Mary or Mamie was known as "Mild Glo'ster", Charles or Charley as "Flaster Floby", Katey as "Lucifer Box", Walter as "Young Skull", and the baby as Chickenstalker – the fact that Francis was named after a character in *The Chimes* suggests how easily Dickens moved from his fictional family to his real family, and how in giving them all nicknames he was in a sense turning them into fiction, too. But with them he was, as one of them put it,

". . . always considerate, always gentle to them about their small troubles and childish terrors". And how could he not be, the writer who in *Oliver Twist* practically reinvented childhood from the child's point of view? He loved to give them "treats", as he called them, and, when they were in England, on every Christmas Eve he would take them to a toy shop in Holborn where he "would show as much interest and pleasure in watching the salesmen demonstrate the working of the toys, and in operating them himself, as his children did". He addressed each child, too, "in a peculiar tone of voice, which they recognised perfectly". At night he liked to sing to them before they went to bed, mainly comic songs which at their insistence he would repeat again and again, and he was expert at assuaging their childish apprehensions. The children too developed a habit of writing letters or making pen-and-ink drawings, which they would leave by his plate at breakfast time. "He must have had hundreds of these," one of his daughters said, "but he always expressed much surprise on finding them, and always had something kind or funny to say . . ." A friend remembered one evening when one of his small sons took his father aside and began talking eagerly to him; Dickens was bent over his son, watching the child's face with amusement, and when he came back to the company he remarked, "The little fellow gave me so many excellent reasons why he should not go to bed so soon, that I yielded the point, and let him sit up half an hour later." As one of his daughters once said, "It is small wonder that children 'took' to him at once, and the shyest baby would hold out its tiny arms to him with perfect faith and confidence."

It might even be said that, with his children, Dickens could retrieve his own early and happy childhood. In fact he became increasingly distant with them when they grew older, and more than one of them commented upon the puzzling reserve he displayed as they grew into adolescence. But small children are still quite aware of the atmosphere which attaches itself to either parent – perhaps more aware in infancy than in later life – and there seems no doubt that even at their relatively young ages these children sensed what Henry Dickens was later to call his ". . . heavy moods of deep depression, of intense nervous irritability, when he was silent and oppressed". Touching, too, how the children realised their father hated saying goodbye – ". . . we children, knowing this dislike, used only to wave our hands or give him a silent kiss when parting." It was not until later that Dickens began privately to express his fears and doubts about his sons in particular; but even so, even in this Italian year, it must sometimes have been hard to be the child of a genius.

And what of Georgina Hogarth now, "Aunt Georgie" to the children and already an indispensable part of the household? She helped to look after the children and, when Catherine was ill or burdened with one of her many pregnancies, she managed some of her brother-in-law's affairs like the writing of letters from his dictation. Accounts of her differ but from the evidence of her letters she was direct, forceful and not much given to self-doubt. Dickens's youngest son, Henry, was to say of her that "she was charming and affectionate, and must have made a delightful hostess, but otherwise she was but an ordinary mid-Victorian lady and rather helpless and inefficient . . ." But Henry knew her in much later years, and there came a time in the intervening period when she was resented by Katey in particular; there were also occasions when she alienated, or spoke sharply to, the other children. There is no evidence for the claims that she disliked or was jealous of her sister, however, and it is also exceedingly unlikely that she ever consciously manipulated the situation in order to become, as she did, the main manager of the household. Of course the presence of a younger sister-in-law in the Dickens ménage inevitably gave cause for rumours and surmise, especially at a date later than the events we are chronicling here. But the truth is that Dickens liked her and that she admired him in return; he called her "Georgie" or, in more playful moments, "the Virgin" (in which state she remained, turning down at least two offers of marriage in order to stay in the Dickens household). She was also a very good mimic, a gift which Dickens tremendously enjoyed, and she was one of the few women who could keep up with him in his marathon walks. He was to say later, "No man on earth ever had such a friend as I have had – and have – in her . . . the most unselfish, zealous, and devoted creature." There is in addition the fact that in his own work he often celebrates the relationship between two sisters, especially when their mutual love surrounds the same man, which is no doubt why he liked to call Georgina and his wife "My ladies" and other joint endearments. But that is all. Nothing divided the Dickens household against itself. Not yet.

Nevertheless that household, or at least its leader, was constitutionally restless and, in the middle of the first month of 1845, the whole family left Genoa and began their Italian travels. Or perhaps better to say that Dickens began *his* travels, dragging alongside him Catherine, Georgina and all five small children. To Carrara, where the large pieces of earth being thrown over the side of the marble workings reminded him of the scene in the tale of Sinbad the Sailor where merchants "flung down great pieces of meat for the diamonds to stick to". To Pisa where the leaning tower reminded him of all the pictures of it he had seen so many years ago in his school-books. Both Pisa and Carrara, then, seen as images of his childhood reading. On by rail to Leghorn. And then to Rome which, from a distance, "looked like . . . like LONDON!!!" It was not "*my* Rome", the Rome of his imagination, just as America had not been the republic of his imagination; always the reality let him down, seeming smaller and greyer and more attenuated than his own visions of it. The family were in the city only for seven days but as always Dickens, with his "clutching eye", saw everything; "I believe we made acquaintance with every post and pillar in the city, and the country round . . ." The Appian Way; St Peter's; the Spanish Steps; the cemeteries; the catacombs; the churches; the prisons; the art-galleries; the theatres. Dickens saw them all. In particular he noticed the absurd expressions on the faces of artists' models who lounged around the Spanish Steps; he was always interested in the cheaper forms of artistic illusion, and he took as much interest in these models as he did in the amateur actors of London. But he was haunted, too, by the vision of etherealised, virginal beauty; in particular by the supposed portrait of Beatrice Cenci in the Palazzo Barberini and the "transcendent sweetness and beauty" of the young girl who was about to die. This recalls his immediate response to Christiana Weller; her particular beauty had suggested to him that she, too, was soon to die. It is as if his experience of the death of Mary Hogarth meant that in his response to feminine beauty there was now always some instinctive association with fatality. Murder was also on his mind; not only was he avidly reading the reports of the latest killings in the *Examiner* but, while in Rome, he also took the opportunity of attending the beheading of a murderer. Dickens's keen observation noticed how the neck of the dead man seemed to have disappeared in the process: "The head was taken off so close, that it seemed as if the knife had narrowly escaped crushing the jaw, or shaving off the ear; and the body looked as if there were nothing left above the ear."

In Rome he was, of course, surrounded by the ceremonies of the Catholic Church, but they provoked in him merely an amused contempt. The Pope in his chair reminded him of a Guy Fawkes being carried towards the bonfire, and the veneration of relics seemed to him to be nothing more than another kind of theatre; and that not of the best. His account of ecclesiastical ritual, for example, is couched in very much the same tone that he adopted for the thespian airs of the Crummles family in *Nicholas Nickleby*, and it is not at all clear that he saw any real difference between the Vatican and the Portsmouth theatre. Not for him any understanding of the terrible consolations of the faith, nor of the history that supported its elaborate framework of worship. He was so out of sympathy with the Catholic Church that he saw only its surface. He saw its comedy. In this regard, at least, he had no real cultural or theoretical sensibility; he saw only the illusions and idiocies of the present, not the presence of the past. He joined a group of Englishmen watching the ceremony of the Pope washing the feet of those impersonating the Apostles, and reported their conversation with ill-disguised sympathy. "'By Jupiter there's vinegar!' I heard him say to his friend . . . 'And there's oil! I saw them distinctly, in cruets! Can any gentleman, in front there, see mustard on the table? Sir, will you oblige me! *Do* you see a Mustard-Pot?'" Clearly the words of the woman who had appeared in his dream, to the effect that the Catholic Church was "best" for him, had already been forgotten.

Even in Rome he could not resist the humour of English life, and he delighted in the new breed of Cockney tourists; there was a Mrs Davis, for example, who was perpetually losing her husband and perpetually looking for something in her straw hand-basket "among an immense quantity of English half-pence, which lay, like sands upon the sea-shore, at the bottom of it". There was a professional guide, or cicerone, to lead this party of English people but Mrs Davis seems to have taken objection to him: if he so much as looked in her direction, she would begin, "There, God bless the man, don't worrit me! I don't understand a word you say, and shouldn't if you was to talk till you was black in the face!" This is Dickens the novelist, the inventor of crowds as large as those in Rome, of people as absurd as any prostrating themselves before statues; the creator of his own world, who was delighted when he saw traces of it in the "real" one. That is why he loved to be among the crowds of the Carnival, among the fireworks and the flares and the streets, and the noise and the light. And yet finally he returns to the ruins, which in their solitude and desolation strike the observer with a "softened sorrow". This is precisely the mood that he had evoked at the end of *The Old Curiosity Shop*, when Little Nell reaches her place of death near the ancient church; it is the same mood he recreated in *Barnaby Rudge*, among the older and darker streets of London. It is the same mood he senses here in Rome. He loves the smell of decay and desolation. He sniffs it up. He inhales it with satisfaction. Here is a vivacious temperament that slides quickly into melancholy, a man who likes the tumult but loves the silence that succeeds it; a man who in crowds sees theatricality and artifice, but who in solitude possesses an instinctive sense of time and of time's changes.

A sense which could only be heightened when, from Rome, the Dickens party travelled via Capua and Naples to Herculaneum and Pompeii where amid the ruins of Time stray objects and moments of the distant past are preserved for ever in the stone. Thus, from the great market-place of Pompeii, Dickens stood and looked at the smoking cone of Mount Vesuvius in the near distance, with "the strange and melancholy sensation of seeing the Destroyed and the Destroyer making this quiet picture in the sun". The destroyer and the destroyed in the same even light – is this an image which Dickens came to remember many years later when, in *Great Expectations*, thirty-two men and women are condemned to death by a judge? "The sun was striking in at the great windows of the court, through the glittering drops of rain upon the glass, and it made a broad shaft of light between the two-and-thirty and the Judge, linking both together . . ." Destroyed and destroyer united in a shaft of light; it is a fine image, and it may well have filtered down from the bright day of Italy to the gloomy interior of London.

In this region, though, it is the volcano which haunts Dickens, "its dark smoke hanging in the clear sky". Of course he wants to "ascend at once", despite the fact that it is in a state of eruption and that thick ice and snow encumber the summit of the mountain. He must see it. He must see it this very night. By moonlight. So a party is formed, including Catherine and Georgina, with a number of guides to help them ascend towards the fire. He described the picture thus: ". . . sunset; then darkness; then the rising of the moon; then the dark night of the black smoke; then the raging of the red fire; then the coming out again into the shining of the moon upon the waste of Snow . . ." In fact it was a hazardous expedition in these conditions, but Dickens seems literally possessed with the idea of looking into the smoking crater of the volcano. They had six saddle horses, an armed guard, and twenty-two guides; as soon as they reached the ice-covered part of the ascent, Catherine and Georgina were placed in litters (another Englishman who joined the party was similarly helped) while Dickens took a thick stick and began to clamber over the ice as, above him, "the fire was pouring out". When they had managed to cross the ice they had to walk among a mass of ashes and of cinders, Catherine and Georgina now also on foot since the path was so treacherous. Still they climbed, until they came to the foot of the cone itself. Here the guides and guided stopped, but Dickens insisted on ascending still higher so that he might stare into the very heart of the volcano itself. "There is something in the fire and roar, that generates an irresistible desire to get nearer to it." With only one guide he climbed the last few hundred feet as burning cinders and ash rained down upon him. Then they reached it. "We looked down into the flaming bowels of the mountain and came back again, alight in half-a-dozen places, and burnt from head to foot." But, as he stood upon the summit, he swigged a bottle of wine before descending to the others. Here is another real picture of Dickens: his own extraordinary and impulsive energy sending him up to the brink of Vesuvius, his hair singed, his clothes burning. As if he were Quilp drinking scalding liquor before executing one of his mad dances. As if his own wild nature could find its match only in the wildest of natural phenomena. And, when he said of the volcano that it was "blazing away prodigiously", he used the very words with which at other times he chose to describe himself.

The descent was treacherous: easy enough to clamber down over the ash and rock, but when they reached the ice-covered side of the mountain they had to descend in a single line, in a human chain. But the chain broke: the Englishman plunged down the side of the mountain, some five hundred feet, and a guide fell down after him. The English traveller was found bruised but alive; the guide had not been discovered by the time Dickens and his party had left the scene. An extraordinary journey and somehow so much "like" Dickens as to present an inescapable and unforgettable image of the novelist in his most excited and excitable state, his clothes singed, fighting his way down the treacherous ice of a volcanic mountain.

They travelled on to Florence before returning to the Palazzo Peschiere in Genoa; the whole journey had taken some three months, and it was already spring when they came to spend their last few weeks in Italy. There followed a succession of clear bright days, and the family lived quietly here until the first week of June – quietly, that is, except for the extraordinary news that their cook had decided to stay in Genoa and marry an Italian. "As my father would observe," Dickens wrote to Forster, "she has sown and must reap." They rarely attended dinners or parties, preferring to stay among the terraces and the roses of their own home, idly exchanging the latest news of Genoa; the death of an Englishwoman for whom Angus Fletcher had arranged a ghastly "English" funeral with "a very bright yellow hackney-coach-and-pair driven by a coachman in yet brighter scarlet knee-breeches and waistcoat"; two men hanged for murder, which encouraged what Dickens called a "morbid sympathy for criminals" among the rich ladies of Genoa who insisted on praying for their souls. And so the days went by, as empty as the sky. He had agreed to read *A Christmas Carol* to a group of English friends, but suddenly and peremptorily cancelled his visit when he heard that strangers were to be present; matters were resolved and he did read, although somewhat nervously. One of the guests on that occasion remembered that Dickens refused to let anyone sit behind him in the course of the reading; he did not wish anyone to be beyond the reach of his magnetic eyes.

And by now he was eager to go back to England. He had heard from Bradbury and Evans about the success of *The Chimes*, from which he had already earned some fifteen hundred pounds, and he was arranging for the house in Devonshire Terrace to be repainted and redecorated. His first choice for colour was *bright green*; this was no doubt because the colour of most of the shutters in Genoa was (and still is) just such a green, and Dickens wanted to recreate in part the atmosphere of the city in London. He wanted his house to look *Italian* – "I should wish it to be cheerful and gay . . ." he said, and it seems more than possible that Dickens himself became somewhat Italianate while remaining in the city. When in America, he had discovered some of the virtues and vices of that country within his own nature; now that he was in Italy he recognised some of the great theatrical strengths of the Italians, their vivacity and their humour, also within himself. Catherine objected to the Genoese green, however, and Dickens acquiesced. In any case it was time to go back to his real life in the whirling, active world; time once more, as he used to put it, to "earn my bread". Various projects, which he might undertake on his return to England, were already in his mind. So great had been the success of *The Chimes* that he knew he ought to write another Christmas Book, for example, and he must already have been contemplating the prospect of a new novel opening out in front of him. It was now over a year since he had finished *Martin Chuzzlewit*. Of course he could get to work at once upon a book of his Italian travels, but he was a little uncertain how to use the letters he had already written. And there was also the prospect of a new periodical which he had discussed with Bradbury and Evans before his departure for Italy.

They left Genoa in the second week of June, returning to England by way of the St Gothard Pass; yet another wild and treacherous journey of the kind Dickens loved but which the rest of his family must have viewed with less than total enthusiasm, their carriage on this occasion slipping and sliding on the brink of abysses. Charley Dickens, then eight years old, remembered making part of this journey with his father across ". . . an extremely rocky and icy walk, from one part of the steep winding road to another by way of a short cut. Indeed I can see the pair of us now, he stalking away in the distance, I struggling in vain to keep up, very tired but extremely proud of being with him . . . finally very nearly collapsing when the phantom path we had been following was found to disappear over a half-frozen little torrent, which had to be crossed by the insecurest possible arrangement of stepping stones before the road and carriage could be regained." Then on to Zurich, Frankfurt and Brussels, where they were met by Forster and Maclise. And all the while Dickens was thinking of the scenes he had left; thinking of Madame de la Rue; thinking of what he might write; thinking of Italy. In fact one such description of his retrospective vision comes close to a description of the creative process itself – "The rapid and unbroken succession of novelties that had passed before me, came back like half-formed dreams: and a crowd of objects wandered in the greatest confusion through my mind . . . At intervals, some one among them would stop, as it were, in its restless flitting to and fro, and enable me to look at it, quite steadily, and behold it in full distinctness. After a few moments, it would dissolve, like a view in a magic lantern . . ." And so we must imagine Dickens's consciousness and imagination, as restless and energetic as he, but sometimes stopping so that he might behold a scene with absolute clarity.

What effect did Italy have upon him in all this time? It is hard to believe that it in any way changed his social or religious perspective, since from the evidence of his correspondence it would seem only to have confirmed his already-stated prejudices and beliefs. Within a very few years revolutions would break out all over Europe; but Dickens had anticipated nothing of this during his travels. He saw only the surface of things, which is what gives the prose of *Pictures from Italy* its curious combination of vivacity and flatness. Perhaps his visions and phantoms meant more to him since his own vision of Mary Hogarth, and his pursuit of the phantom haunting Madame de la Rue, stand out as the most fully experienced episodes of his journey. And it can hardly be said that Italy changed his aesthetic attitudes or artistic taste; it merely confirmed them, in the way a mirror confirms identity. Just as he saw his own opinions corroborated in the world around him, so did he everywhere see the importance of his own work reflected back at him. Thus when in his little book of travels he congratulates Italian opera "for astonishing truth and spirit in seizing and embodying the real life about it . . ." there can be no doubt that Dickens also believed himself to be capable of just such depiction of the true world. But what, then, of his own aesthetic attitudes?

He did not go to Italy in order to look at paintings or sculptures; instead of taking the more aesthetic *Northern Italy*, for example, he chose the more general *Handbook for Travellers in Central Italy* published just the year before. Once more he brought his own particular preoccupations to bear upon Titian and Raphael, Botticelli and Tintoretto, and through his response to Italian art it is possible to arrive at some understanding of his attitude to his own work. In one sense he possessed merely the taste of his time; he admired Titian and Tintoretto, but had no interest or understanding of the "primitives" who preceded Raphael. (In the same way he liked the music of Mendelssohn and Chopin, although his real taste was for the sentimental songs of his childhood and adolescence.) In other words, his was a standard repertoire of Victorian values. But, if his taste was somewhat conventional, it was expressed in a way that indirectly throws light upon his own unique vision of the world. When in *Pictures from Italy*, for example, he describes, in the context of sculpture, ". . . certain expressions of face, natural to certain passions, and as unchangeable in their nature as the gait of a lion, or the flight of an eagle" we can be more or less sure that Dickens himself believed that he was able to depict just such "natural" passions in words. In general he preferred painting that was suffused with recognisable human emotion and was concerned with "telling a story" or interpreting a narrative. He liked work which dwelt in the region of the picturesque, although after his walks through the stinking streets of Genoa as well as London he knew at what human cost the picturesque was often produced. In other words, he instinctively preferred painting and sculpture which came closest to the spirit of his own fiction.

There are other resemblances between his aesthetic and his practice. From the memories of his friends and his own family, and from the records of his own collection of paintings, it is clear that in particular he liked the depiction of young people in ruined or ancient settings, that combination of youth and death which is so obvious in his own work. He also admired pictures and watercolours of idyllic rural scenes. But he was most affected by narrative or genre painting, and one contemporary remarked, "I have heard him say to a group of young painters that 'a picture which did not tell a story was no picture at all'." That is why he approved of French "academic" or "classical" painting which used historical and mythological motifs in a striking or rhetorical manner, which is precisely what he had done in *Barnaby Rudge* and would do again in *A Tale of Two Cities*. He admired the work of Hogarth, from whom his greatest visual debt comes, and for similar reasons was greatly taken by Holbein's "Dance of Death" engravings; this is part of that affection for the "grotesque" which was so powerfully emphasised by his experiences in Italy. And of course he was much affected by, and interested in, portraits; he was an excellent judge of them, as one might have supposed in a writer who so closely studied and used physiognomy, and his daughter, Katie, declared that he could "remember with distinctness any face he may have seen for however short a time . . ." She goes on to say of Dickens's general taste, "He admired more than any other quality great breadth and force in the conception and treatment of a subject, but looked for a certain delicacy and refinement of finish." Once more Dickens's own artistic methods are here transposed as a set of aesthetic principles. Perhaps this consonance also explains the fact that he liked paintings of scenes from his own novels, and collected a large number of them in the course of his writing life.

But it is interesting, also, to determine what he did *not* like; nudes in particular, especially male nudes, seem to have irritated him. For the "primitives" before Raphael, as we have seen, he shared the standard dislike or ignorance of his time, which is perhaps why he once bitterly attacked the Pre-Raphaelite movement in the shape of Millais's "Christ in the House of His Parents"; here the partial nudity of the male figures, and the accuracy of the physical details of the human body, seemed literally to revolt Dickens and to instigate one of his most powerful if inaccurate polemics. He seems to have confused the Pre-Raphaelite movement with the anachronistic idiocies of the "Young England" group, and this largely on the grounds of its name: it is characteristic of Dickens who, when he grasps the wrong end of the stick, never fails to belabour everyone in sight with it.

But Dickens also admitted to a more general dissatisfaction with English painting, and it was not long after his Italian journey that he began to perceive English painting as somehow less dramatic, less spirited and less courageous than its continental counterparts. In a sense he saw this as a further aspect of what we might call the "English disease", a combination of respectability and timidity that was ingrained in the political and social habits of the nation. Of English painting itself he was to say that "it is no use disguising the fact that what we know to be wanting in the men is wanting in their works – character, fire, purpose . . . There is a horrid respectability about most of the best of them – a little, finite, systematic routine in them . . . mere form and conventionalities usurp, in English art . . . the place of living force and truth." To be sure Dickens is describing only English painting here, but clearly he is at least suggesting indirectly that his own work has no such disadvantages – that he does possess character, fire and purpose (the last being especially important) and, to use antonyms instead of analysis, that his work is large, infinite, unsystematic, filled with all the living force and truth so signally and dismally absent elsewhere. He was not alone in his criticism; Daniel Maclise had expressed similar sentiments a few years before to Forster: "My belief is that we in London are the smallest and most wretched set of snivellers that ever took pencil in hand . . ." Dickens never paid much attention to the fashionable art criticism of friends like Wilkie Collins and Augustus Egg, but no doubt Maclise's attitude was one that he was all too willing to adopt. And, in terms of mid-nineteenth-century English painting, it also has the merit of being broadly true. It was truly an age in which the written or spoken word dominated public consciousness.

Yet, when it came to the word, Dickens was an equally robust critic of work which seemed to him to be unsatisfactory or too tame; "by far too much mention of nerves and heartstrings," he replied to one writer who had asked for his criticism, and of Nathaniel Hawthorne's *The Scarlet Letter*, for example, he merely said that the psychological aspects of the story were "not truly done". He called Wilkie Collins's *The Moonstone* "wearisome beyond endurance" and was, perhaps surprisingly, equally sharp in questions of grammar and of usage. It used to be thought that Dickens had only the most approximate understanding of the rigours of English syntax but in truth, through the many comments among his letters – ". . . you cannot make a participle in English out of a substantive," he said to one writer – it is clear that he had a detailed and working knowledge of the minutiae of the language. And why should it not be so, in a man who was its nineteenth-century master?

In fact most of his actual literary criticism tends to be technical or formal in its scope, yet there is no doubt that behind his technical expertise there were continually present certain imaginative and moral imperatives. "Pray do not, therefore," he told one correspondent, "be induced to suppose that I ever write merely to amuse, or without an object." Whether he speaks in terms of probability, of unity, of discrimination of character (and these were three themes which continually exercised him, perhaps because these were also the areas in which the more solemn critics found him deficient), he sought, or said he sought, always to achieve what he once praised in the art of Daniel Maclise, a "grand harmony" of realistic details arranged with a "plain purpose".

It is hard now to think of Dickens as in any sense a "realistic" writer, however, and even some of his contemporaries had difficulties with the melodrama and grotesquerie which he imported from the stage into his fiction. Yet he was a child of his time and, if there is any one enduring aesthetic concept of the period, it is the belief in the social purpose or the social dimensions of art – particularly in the art of fiction which was described by one critic as "by far the most perfect representation of real life to be found in literature . . ." There had to be some connection with the life of the time, therefore, some way of proving the novel's authenticity by dealing with, or reflecting, or understanding, the prevailing issues and mores of that time; this is why, for example, there was such a fashion for "social novels" in the Forties. The old interest of the "silver fork" school of novelists, in aristocratic life, had come to an end. People wanted to see the world around them, and genuine interest was aroused by the detail and by the verisimilitude which a writer provided. A novel was thought more important if it faced the reality of its period full on. As Charles Reade, one of the great minor novelists of the age, put it: "I write for the public, and the public doesn't care about the dead. They are more interested in the living, and in the great tragi-comedy of humanity that is around and about them and environs them in every street, at every crossing, in every hole and corner . . ." But "realism" in itself (however it is defined, and the definition of it changes with each generation) was not enough, since it had to be associated with the kind of moral earnestness which made sense of a world in bewildering transition. There was still a sense of "moral design" which led ultimately to the "truth" and nothing so marks the Victorians as the intensity with which they pursued – and which they believed their writers and artists should pursue – such ideals. No need for "ambiguity" or "complexity" or any of the other twentieth-century shibboleths; plainness, earnestness, and moral force were the qualities required in the endless struggle to understand the moving world and the Force or forces which maintained it.

But of course the reality in which they were interested was one of a specific and especial kind. As Thackeray put it in 1840, "The world does not tolerate such satire as that of Hogarth and Fielding; and the world no doubt is right in a great part of its squeamishness . . . The same vice exists, only we don't speak about it; the same things are done, but we don't call them by their names . . ." In other words propriety and reticence – particularly of course in physical and sexual matters – were at least as important as earnestness and intensity. Responsibility. Respectability. These were the imperatives. Later in the century this moral aesthetic, in its broadest sense, was steadily displaced by what Henry James called "the Art of Fiction"; Dickens himself lived through that transition, but in some ways it is peculiarly difficult to estimate his own opinions on these matters. He was clearly a conventional man of his age in his reluctance to introduce the wrong topics or in any way to offend his audience, but no one saw more clearly than he the fatuities and hypocrisies of mid-Victorian civilisation: in a very real sense he was always, and remained, an "outsider". That is one paradox. In addition he was always insistent upon the fact that what he wrote was "true", that he observed what was "real", and yet at the same time no novelist had a more instinctive sense of his craft. It used to be fashionable to decry his sensibility – in comparison, for example with that of George Eliot or of Henry James – but throughout his career he illustrates an interest in formal concerns which is matched only by his self-consciousness in maintaining them within his fiction. He never was the jovial improviser and story-teller of the Pickwickian tradition; he was a clever and artful writer who always knew exactly what he was doing.

Of course Dickens provides clues to his intent in his prefaces, or in his more moralistic letters, but it would be hard immediately to elicit any particular set of moral or social judgments from a fiction which is as contradictory and paradoxical as the man himself. It becomes clear in a reading of Dickens, however, that his "purpose", as he put it, might be seen in a broader and more efficacious light; that, in his fiction, he is trying at least to delineate the ways of Fate or Providence and that he sees the novelist's role as something like that of the nineteenth-century scientist – to make clear, by general laws of force and energy, the ways of God to men. Or, more accurately, he posits the role of the novelist as reflecting that of God; when he discusses the manner in which the writer ought carefully to lay the ground of his plot, or to bathe the whole narrative in the light of its fully prepared ending, he suggests that "these are the ways of Providence, of which ways all art is but a little imitation . . ." In the distribution of rewards and punishments in his fiction, also, Dickens admits to borrowing from the religious sphere: "Where the accident is inseparable from the passion and emotion of the character," he wrote, ". . . and arises out of some culminating proceeding on the part of the character which the whole story has led up to, it seems to me to become, as it were, an act of divine justice." In the same way the novelist takes on the role of the unseen and unmoved Mover: "The true romance of poetry, of human life or actual nature" is to be found "in unaffectedly presenting it, with the art of seeming to leave it to present itself". In a similar spirit, he makes it clear on more than one occasion that the characters must "act for themselves when the occasion arises". It is to this idea of an invisible creator that he most frequently and obviously attaches himself, not in any blasphemous sense but rather as an indication of his own instinctive practice and preference. Surely it is one of the most intriguing aspects of his fiction that Dickens, of all Victorians perhaps the most colourful and individual, should absent himself so remarkably from his own creations; where Thackeray, for example, interrupts his narratives with his own point of view and with his own reflections, Dickens never actively enters his own plots. He remains aloof from them, allowing them, as it seems, to unroll themselves. For all the personality and eccentricity of his art, his is in the end a remarkably impersonal vision of the world.

And yet of course he was not the kind of novelist who disdains the idea of his "audience"; he would not have understood the modernist assumption that great art can only really be appreciated by a few, and those few generally to be discovered in posterity. The fact that he was *always* aware of his audience is a large component of his genius, since it was the resonance which he set up with the English public and the English national identity which gave him his pre-eminent place among the writers of his time. He was always very careful to calculate the effect which his work had upon its readers, no less in his fiction than in his journalism; as he explained once, "Beware of writing things for the eyes of everybody, which you would feel the smallest delicacy in *saying* anywhere . . ." This is not simply an obeisance to propriety and respectability; the emphasis on *saying* conveys his growing interest in the public reading of his works. And those readings in turn suggest the kind of activity upon which he was engaged. He was writing for what might be called the community, for the widest possible audience with the widest possible set of values. This does not represent the kind of timidity and narrowness for which he castigated English painters, but rather a due recognition of the fact that part of the strength of his writing comes from its moral centrality, that broad agreement about certain essential matters which is to be found in the fairy tales and pantomimes of his youth. But with him it was a more conscious matter. Nothing too *strong*. Nothing you can't *say*. Nothing too *extravagant*. Nothing too *severe*. Be *humorous*. *Tempt* readers forward, and do not bludgeon them with morals or with ideas. *Elevate* low matter. Always strive for what is *noble* and what is *true*. Good. Plain. Healthy. These were some of his favourite mottoes when he came to consider the purpose and significance of his art. But of course one must trust the tale and not necessarily the teller. There are many writers whose actual practice is quite different from any of the principles they cared to espouse, although in Dickens's case the distinction is not so easy to find. He was, on occasions, all of the things he recommended; certainly he elevated "low" material and abjured what he called "a code of morals, taken from modern French novels". But when he disclaims extravagance – he, the creator of Miss Havisham and Ebenezer Scrooge – it is hard to take him absolutely seriously. It seems clear that he did not himself always properly understand the nature of his own writing, just as the absence of introspection suggests that he never really understood the forces of his own personality. He never realised how strange a writer he was, just as he never saw what others saw: how strange a man he was. Of course there were times when he chafed against the conventional restrictions in English writing. In an angry letter, some years after this first Italian journey, he complained about those readers who find the virtues and conduct of the standard English heroes of fiction to be "unnatural": it was precisely the "morality" of the English public which meant that he could not present "I will not say any of the indecencies you like, but not even any of the experiences, trials, perplexities, and confusions inseparable from the making or unmaking of all men!" Implicit here is Dickens's acceptance that his art is necessarily one of selection and necessarily one which must confirm the prejudices of his national audience; but in fact the very power and, yes, strangeness of his writing lift it beyond the reach of any such easy compromise or accommodation.

Once again, we must trust the tale and not the teller. And in this spirit we return once more to the Italian journey which first initiated these reflections on Dickens's aesthetic; for the real measure of his interest in Italy is to be found not in his travel book, nor in his letters, but in the novel *Little Dorrit*, which was composed some twelve years after the events here related. Even the surface incidents of his travels recur: the quarantine, the foreign jails, Venice, the journey across the Alps, the English people speaking to Italians, the attack on amateur artistic appreciation, all of these themes emerge in a novel which sees the world as prison just as he had once seen Naples as the jail of its poor inhabitants. "They look: when we stand aside, observing them, in their passage through the courtyard down below: as miserable as the prisoners in the gaol . . ." A novel in which the true horror is to be found in the fact that human identity cannot change, that travel itself only confirms the prison of the self in which each one of us is trapped perpetually. So ended Dickens's Italian journey.

Chapter 16

A ND this was his own sensation of travel – nothing changes. The identity remains. All that surrounds it remains. Nothing had changed in his absence; ". . . nothing new in London," he complained four weeks after his return and, in addition, he caught a bad cold almost as soon as he arrived home. The day after that return he visited his parents who were now living in Blackheath, and he of course did the usual round of dinners and meetings with his friends; a dinner with Lady Holland, an outing to Greenwich with Christiana Weller and T. J. Thompson, even a courtesy call upon Maria Beadnell, the young woman who in his youth had captivated him and who had now married. In the carriage back, according to Georgina Hogarth, Dickens laughed at the thought of his previous attachment – Maria Winter, as she now was, being, again according to Georgina, a "good natured woman but *fearfully silly*". Forster has described how it was also in this period that he revisited his childhood home in Bayham Street, Camden Town; a common enough phenomenon, this urge to revisit the haunts of childhood, so shrunken and debilitated in comparison with the memory of those places, but it may well have been connected with his half-formed idea to write his life. (If he was planning anything at all, it would have been along the lines of Thomas Holcroft's *Memoirs*, a book he admired and one which described the poverty and misery, as well as the excitement, of childhood in a graphic if somewhat breathless manner.) Often this return to the haunts of childhood coincides with some change in life, however, some turning point; and so it was to prove with Dickens.

He was "continually weeping" with his cold. After the decaying splendours and theatrical miseries of Genoa, London seemed "as flat as it can be". Camden Town, Greenwich, Devonshire Terrace, everything just as it was and as it would always be. Bayham Street. Maria

Beadnell a laughable Maria Winter. Even the old memories of child-hood become staler. No one can evoke that mood of sad and embittered weariness better than Dickens – Arthur Clennam's arrival in London on a Sunday morning in *Little Dorrit* is a perfect picture of urban melancholy – and few people can have experienced it so intensely. But if there is one constant and admirable quality in Dickens it is his tendency to fight against such moods with the same unwearying endurance with which he fought against circumstances that hampered him; "Never *say* die" was one of his mottoes. In any case he had work to do; he had another Christmas Book to write and he had agreed with Bradbury and Evans to consider the prospect of a new periodical to be edited by him. Almost as soon as he returned, in fact, he thought of a name for it, *The Cricket*, perhaps inspired by the constant chirruping of the cicadas in his Genoese garden but filled too with folk-tale associations of the hearth. It would be, he told Forster, a journal which would continue the "*Carol* philosophy" and which would allow him to enter people's homes in "a winning and immediate way".

Yet something for the near future engaged his attention much more easily. When he had returned briefly to London the previous winter, in order to read *The Chimes* to his friends, he had discussed, as we have seen, the idea of putting on a play; a private performance, to be paid for by the cast and to which each member of the cast would invite especial friends. In other words, an amateur night. If *Little Dorrit* is in part about the permanence and solidity of human identity, so firmly rooted that no mere change of scene or air can affect it, and if his return to London filled him with weariness and ennui, here was a way of fighting back against those sensations. His eagerness to play a theatrical role was at least in part a way of combating that stale and weary sense of familiarity, of adopting a new identity if only for an hour or so, of exorcising the London gloom by promoting all the colour and brightness of a play. Dickens himself wanted to be dressed in "a very gay, fierce, bright colour" as if in echo of his Italian experience: he was to play Captain Bobadil in a performance of Ben Jonson's *Every Man in His Humour*. Forster was to be in it, too. Clarkson Stanfield, as well. And T. J. Thompson. But it is most important to note that the rest of the cast – Mark Lemon, John Leech, Henry Mayhew, Douglas Jerrold, Gilbert a'Beckett – came from a specific group, a little band of journalists who were known as the "*Punch* brotherhood" to themselves and as "those *Punch* people" to outsiders, *Punch* being the name of a magazine founded only four years before and now under the editorship of Lemon himself. Dickens's connections with the new magazine were already evident; his new publishers, Bradbury and Evans, printed it and many of its contributors came from that world of radical journalism which Dickens had known in his days as editor of *Bentley's Miscellany*. Some of them of course were already his friends. John Leech had provided the illustrations for both of Dickens's Christmas Books; he was a quiet man, nervous and somewhat melancholy (as many cartoonists of the period seem to have been). He had attended the same school as Thackeray, but he was to a large extent self-taught in his own art; he also had a notoriously penurious and spendthrift father, and this no doubt endeared him to the novelist who always seems to have preferred the company of men who were in some way like himself. Certainly this was true of Mark Lemon, a large and even portly man who had all the geniality and boisterousness conventionally associated with fat men, but whose conviviality concealed an extremely sensitive nature; Dickens, again, always warmed to such people. The shy, the nervous, and the melancholy were to be found among his closest friends. Both Leech and Lemon were also very fond of children, a trait which further endeared them to him; Lemon was known to Dickens's own children as "Uncle Mark" or "Uncle Porpoise" (his wife was "Aunty Nelly").

But there were other reasons why Dickens would have been attached to the journalists of *Punch*; for one thing he shared many of their values and attitudes, most of them being self-made men who had struggled through difficult early circumstances and almost without exception had been drawn to what was then the familiar combination of journalism and play-writing. Mark Lemon and Gilbert A'Beckett had in fact been involved with the dramatisation of Dickens's *The Chimes* only a few months before but, more significantly, this dramatic and journalistic background generated a certain kind of radicalism. All of these *Punch* contributors were part of the general movement of opinion in England which opposed such measures as the New Poor Law, and the Corn Laws, and which supported such schemes as assisted emigration or education for the children of the labouring poor. In other words a loose-knit collection of standards and attitudes formulated by men who were united in their hatred of those who traded upon nostalgia for the past or who too rigorously defined social questions as items of profit and loss. It is a difficult amalgam clearly to describe, but it is instantly recognisable as a particularly English variant of conservative radicalism; conservative at least in the sense that the *Punch* writers, like Dickens himself, took a notoriously unsentimental attitude towards prisoners and other "liberal" causes. Of course they became even more conservative as they grew older – although none perhaps went so far as Dickens himself in that direction – but in this period, at a time of great social and political transition, they were all set upon the broad middle way of radical politics in arguing for reform rather than revolution or restoration.

Yet why should these men be so eager to take part in an amateur theatrical event and, in later years, even to form something along the lines of an amateur company under Dickens's management? Of course it was an aspect of their convivial association, and what we may now call a typically "Victorian" liking for clubs and brotherhoods is to be seen in their dramatic endeavours. As Dickens said with unconscious double reference, they were ". . . so well accustomed to act in concert good humouredly". (The prosaic truth is that they met every Wednesday evening, at the office of Bradbury and Evans in Bouverie Street, for a dinner in which ideas for the magazine were discussed, the latest gossip retailed and, again another "Victorian" addition, songs recited.) But this conviviality does not in itself explain what is on the face of it a most peculiar pursuit, this acting together in plays performed for friends. Were they simply so fascinated and dominated by Charles Dickens that they effortlessly fell in with his own wishes or preoccupations? There is a certain truth to this, at least to the extent in which Dickens was clearly one of their own number but somehow infinitely more expressive and more talented than they. Some of them – the best of them – recognised this. But not even Dickens could have single-handedly persuaded them to take part in the theatrical activities which were regularly to reoccur over the next seven years. Instead we must look for a cause in their own radicalism. The point is that their politics (and this is true in general of the radicals of the period) cannot be dissociated from their interest in the theatre, and the early experience of some of them as "hack" dramatists. It is the merest cliché to note that the whole point and excitement of the theatre lie in its wilful blending of the real and the imaginary; in its ability, therefore, to change reality. It has been well said by Arthur Symons, writing at the end of the nineteenth century, that men drawn to the theatre tend to be "dreamers of illimitable dreams" and "persist in demanding illusion of what is real, and reality in what is illusion". Cannot the same sentiments be applied to these mid-century radicals who were as eager to change the conditions of their time as they were forthright in their optimism and belief in progress? Such temperaments were fatally attracted to the theatre, so that in Douglas Jerrold, Mark Lemon, Gilbert a'Beckett, and many others, a preoccupation with social concerns and fascination for the heightened reality of drama consort together.

But what of Dickens himself? For he, too, was fascinated by actors and acting. We have already traced the effect of the nineteenth-century stage upon his own fiction but, in a more immediate sense, he was a man who preferred the theatre to practically any other form of activity. Hardly a week of his life passed when he did not go to a play, and his especial fondness was for theatrical or "green room" gossip; one friend noted ". . . his keen interest in the obscurest histrionic elements". He sometimes used theatrical slang, and stage expressions occur frequently in both his fiction and correspondence. It was an instinctive, and therefore "uneducated", taste: he loved bad plays and "ham" acting; he liked farces and melodramas; when in Paris he preferred the operatic burlesques at the Bouffes-Parisiens to the classical tragedies at the Odéon. His closest friends were often actors, and he once said that ". . . the more real the man the more genuine the actor . . .", which, if nothing else, emphasises the moral and idealistic aspects of the drama which in his more serious moments he was eager to present. But in any case for Dickens, even at the very end of his life, the theatre was an enchanted place. He often used the play as a symbol of mortality itself, the theatre a metaphor for ordinary human life when all the glitter and brightness fade and we are thrust back into a world which is "wet, and dark, and cold". The theatre was for him a kind of dream, in which all the restrictions and difficulties of conventional reality fell away, a world in which there was no susceptibility to hurt, no experience of pain. A world in which no one needed to change or to die.

Dickens was himself, according to his eldest son, "a born actor" and he is remembered by one friend as "saying he believed he had more talent for the drama than for literature, as he certainly had more delight in acting than in any other work whatever". Macready called him "unskilled" as an actor, which in a technical sense was true; one common remark seems to have been that Dickens was too "hard" in performance, by which was meant too careful, too contrived, too rigid. He was better at the detail than the broad effect, it seems, which sounds like the fault of a man who was thoroughly self-trained in the art, who had, in a sense, studied its effects too carefully and was too assiduous in applying them. Yet he had the genuine instincts of an actor; first and most importantly, as he admitted, he loved ". . . feigning to be somebody else". Those of an analytical turn of mind might suggest at this point that the drama was for him a form of therapy, helping him not only to "blow off my superfluous fierceness", as he put it, but also to discover and recreate himself by adopting a new identity or series of identities. At a time when he was not engaged in writing his fiction, as in this period, it is almost as if all that imaginative appetite for the creation of character was transferred to his own self; so that he became, as it were, a series of characters in search of an author.

He was a "born actor" in another sense, too. Carlyle said of him that ". . . his chief faculty was that of a comic actor", and Douglas Jerrold remarked with appropriate sarcasm that "if you only give him three square yards of carpet he would tumble on that" like a street acrobat. In other words, even in life he could not resist acting a part when the occasion presented itself. He was once seen by a contemporary helping a policeman arrest a vagabond in St James's Park: "His voice, his air, his walk made one think of some artist called upon to represent all this upon the stage." Indeed his sometimes excessive self-consciousness did give the impression that he was constantly trying to dramatise himself; as one friend astutely put it, "he had consciously an ideal in his mind, up to which he may be said to have acted". There was always something theatrical, at times almost over-bearing, about him; and of course he dressed accordingly. He once said that "he had the fondness of a savage for finery". Brightness was the key: bright clothes, bright houses, bright conversation. "He always was theatrically dressed . . ." one contemporary remembered, and there is a fragment of his conversation saved for posterity when he went to a party with an excessive cravat fastened with a bejewelled pin – "I hope you all like my pin," he declared. "It is uncommon, I think." But, if he was on occasions a dandy, he was perhaps one in the tradition of Baudelaire who dressed so well in order to conceal or protect a threatened identity. Of course Dickens himself found another explanation for it. "I constantly notice a love of colour and brightness, to be a portion of a generous and fine nature," he once said, no doubt with some oblique reference to himself. So it is that he walks through the more sombre colours of the nineteenth century in his own instantly recognisable and illuminated way. There is no doubt that he took great joy in playing the part of the famous author and the public man but it has to be remembered, too, that his identity was fluid enough to ebb and flow. He could end the performance as quickly as he initiated it.

Fluid enough, too, that his skills as an actor were matched by his authority as a stage manager and director. ". . . I was born to be the Manager of a Theatre," he once said, not least because he had always to be "in charge" of any activity in which he took a part. As his colleagues now discovered when he took them through their parts in *Every Man in His Humour*, and expected from them what he always demanded of himself: ". . . whatever the right hand finds to do must be done with the heart in it, and in a desperate earnest." The rehearsals were being conducted at the little theatre in Dean Street owned by a Miss Kelly, herself an actress of distinction but of uncertain administrative talent; she could be difficult, in a theatrical way, and in one letter Dickens described his own amusement at her behaviour, "especially when she choked, and had the glass of water brought". As always his stage management was impeccably precise. Patience. Perseverance. Punctuality. Order. Neatness. These were his watchwords so that, for example, in his list of orders to the actors he made it plain that ". . . every mistake of exit, entrance or situation to be corrected *three times* successfully . . ." There is a vignette of him at a slightly later date, with "a small table placed rather to one side of the stage, at which he generally sat . . . On this table rested a moderate-sized box; its interior divided into conventional compartments for holding papers, letters etc. and this interior was always the very pink of neatness and orderly arrangement." He attended everything; he supervised everything, but with "the utter absence of dictatorialness or arrogation of superiority . . ." The rehearsals were not entirely free of incident, however; on at least one occasion he lost his temper and accused Forster of "hectoring and self-sufficiency", and one of the players, T. J. Thompson, became less than enthusiastic about the whole project. In fact he came to detest it and said that he was "sacrificing myself to the vanity of others"; no doubt he had Dickens most prominently in mind. Thompson himself, a wealthy young man who considered himself something of a connoisseur, was at the time struggling to marry Christiana Weller, whose father was withholding consent; he had good reason to thank Dickens later when the author, with his usual tact and perseverance in affairs other than his own, managed to resolve all outstanding disputes. Dickens was also tactful with his younger brother, Fred, who now wanted to marry Christiana

Weller's sister. If Dickens had not himself been attached to Christiana, the Wellers would probably have remained in Liverpool unknown to name and fame. So could Dickens's presence change beyond recognition the lives of those around him.

He had been going down to Broadstairs to rest during the rehearsals, since the entire family had once again encamped there. Catherine, now heavily pregnant, did not of course accompany him on his forays into London. But no doubt she was among the small group of friends (including Tennyson and the Duke of Devonshire) who attended the first performance of *Every Man in His Humour* on 20 September; Dickens as Bobadil in his "fiery" colours, Forster playing Kitely in what everyone considered to be a pseudo-Macready manner (in other words, heavily emphasising the melodramatic possibilities of his part), and the others performing as well as can be expected. It was, according to the *Athenaeum*, a "memorable and pleasant evening" but Jane Carlyle was less flattering: ". . . not one performer among them could be called good, and none that could be called absolutely bad . . . poor little Dickens, all painted in black and red, and affecting the voice of a man of six feet, would have been unrecognisable for the mother who bore him." Dickens, however, was proud of his appearance and believed that he ". . . looked like an old Spanish Portrait, I assure you". He was also wearing a fake moustache which suggests, if it does not prove, that he had shaved off his own when he returned from Italy.

And so his "superfluous" energy was blown away in the craven and boastful character of Captain Bobadil. But by now it was mid-autumn and he needed to prepare a Christmas Book for the end of the year; already for him it seems to have become a seasonal custom in which he and his "audience", as he liked to call it, reaffirmed their close and enduring ties. It was less of a story now, more of a communal fairy tale in which all malevolence is lifted and all disputes resolved. Certainly this was the moral of a theme he had in mind which, largely revolving around the plot of a husband's mistaken jealousy, might have been inspired by Catherine Dickens's complaints about his magnetic relationship with Madame de la Rue. But he had no time to begin work on it: almost as soon as he tried to do so, he became involved in a different project altogether.

It had really all begun the year before when Bradbury and Evans had, in the course of their negotiations with Dickens, proposed the idea of establishing some kind of newspaper which Dickens would edit. On his return from Genoa, as we have seen, he contemplated a cheerful weekly periodical chirping away as *The Cricket*, but now a much more important enterprise was suggested to him. Bradbury and Evans, with the financial backing of Joseph Paxton, had decided to set up a radical liberal paper to rival such established prints as *The Times* and the *Morning Herald*. The moment was propitious; Dickens had returned to England at a time when "railroad mania", the issuing of shares in various railway companies amid the rapid extension of that transport, was at its height. The railway itself was to enter Dickens's next novel as both saviour and destroyer – he took the popular image of the moment and in the alembic of his imagination turned it into something both profound and strange – but, more immediately, it was precisely the ready availability of capital that persuaded Bradbury and Evans to launch a paper which would promote and publicise the interests which the railways served. The interests, in particular, of industrialists, of free traders, of manufacturers, all of whose radicalism in this period was directed against the people whom Dickens himself despised.

And who better than Charles Dickens to edit a newspaper which would appeal to such an audience? It was already clear from the effect of *The Chimes* (not to mention *Nicholas Nickleby*) that Dickens could directly intervene in social matters of the day, and he had been a more than capable journalist in his youth. It seemed like a good idea to Dickens, too, and, after being approached by Bradbury and Evans, he went down to Chatsworth to meet the other principal backer, Joseph Paxton. Paxton himself was an unusually gifted man who, in almost quintessential Victorian fashion, had risen in the world by perseverance, ingenuity and energy; he had begun as a gardener's boy and now, in his early forties, he was a railway promoter, architect, and manager of the Duke of Devonshire's estates. Self-help was not in the nineteenth century a mere idle slogan, but a genuine and specific course of action; it has often been said that Victorian society was authoritarian and hierarchical, but there were really no barriers to the advancement of those with ambition and the appetite for power or wealth. So it was that Paxton and Dickens, both self-made men, sat down together in order to discuss the founding of a national radical newspaper. George Hudson, another self-made man and the "railway King", was also backing the project. And Paxton himself, according to an excited letter from Dickens to his friend and financial adviser, Mitton, "has command of every railway and railway influence in England and abroad except the Great Western . . ." Thus, by the curious affiliations of technological development, a mode of transport was the single most important factor in the founding of a newspaper. With a novelist as its editor.

Once more he was in active, whirring life. Catherine was pregnant, he was planning another performance of the Jonson play to raise funds for Southwood Smith's Sanatorium, he was having more difficulties with his father over money, he was arranging for the education of his son Charley (Miss Burdett-Coutts had decided that she wished to pay for this, a favour which Dickens quickly accepted), and he still had not written the Christmas Book which was to appear in two months' time. In addition, he had his Italian travels to chronicle. Now he had agreed to take on the editorship of a daily newspaper and, even though his annual salary of two thousand pounds was to be twice that normally offered to editors, it might have seemed rash of Dickens to take on more duties than one man could ever reasonably perform. Yet, although he did not make a formal acceptance for a few days, he seems privately to have accepted the post almost at once. Almost, you might say, without thinking. With the benefit of hindsight it seems odd that a writer of genius should even wish to become the editor of a newspaper, consuming most of his time and his energy as it inevitably must do, but it has to be recalled that *Martin Chuzzlewit* had not been as great a success as the preceding novels, that the Christmas Books were considered by some to be sentimental fancies merely, and that there were critics who were already writing off Dickens as a man who had exhausted his talents before his time. He always professed great faith in himself, but there were occasions when he was deeply anxious about his prospects; indeed he admitted as much in a letter to Forster when he stated that ". . . the possibility of failing health or fading popularity" had largely influenced his decision to take what was essentially an office job. But clearly he was worried about the decision he had made. Just a day before he formally accepted the post of editor of the *Daily News*, as it was to be called, he suffered from "headache" and "giddiness"; reminiscent of the time, many years before, when a "swollen face" had prevented him from auditioning as a comic actor. But perhaps this is also an example of Dickens's actual physical frailty, his body suffering under the stress both of his energy and of his will; Forster was to write in his biography that, ". . . it may be doubted if ever any man's mental effort cost him more. His habits were robust, but not his health . . ." And already he was whipping himself up into a state of intense excitement. He had been hiring staff for the new newspaper. He had even written a prospectus. And then, the day after his formal acceptance, one of the important brokers behind the project was declared bankrupt. Dickens was so anxious and upset about the news, which materially affected the fortunes of the projected paper, that on the following day he wrote a letter of resignation to Bradbury and Evans; his originally sudden decision was equally suddenly reversed. Forster and his old journalistic colleague, Thomas Beard, advised him to do so but nothing more clearly shows Dickens's mercurial, quixotic nature than the fact that two weeks later he once more agreed to take on the post of editor – this after the project and company had been financially reorganised with a capital investment of one hundred thousand pounds.

From this time forward he went down every day to his new offices in Fleet Street, writing letters to the reporters he wished to hire, organising the administration of the business; in fact he was behaving on the *Daily News* with exactly the same firmness and decision he displayed as a stage manager. But the obvious truth that this was not a play, and that he was the editor of a project for which there were already managers in the shape of Mr Bradbury and Mr Evans, was soon to cause difficulties. Some of his friends had reservations, too; when Forster showed Macready the prospectus which Dickens had written, the actor wrote in his diary that Dickens ". . . was rushing headlong into an enterprise that demands the utmost foresight, skilful and secret preparation and qualities of a conductor which Dickens has not. Forster agreed in many if not all of my objections, but he did not seem to entertain much hope of moving Dickens." Macready, in other words, considered Dickens to be the wrong man in the wrong job. There was a celebration dinner for many of those connected with the project, at which Dickens spoke extravagantly of the potential of the *Daily News*; afterwards someone said to Charles Wentworth Dilke, then editor of the *Athenaeum*, "It is your knowledge that will be called upon to remedy the mischief done by Dickens's genius to the new paper." Which, in fact, turned out to be close to the truth.

It has been said by the chroniclers of the history of the *Daily News* that Dickens "flung himself into the work with a thoroughly characteristic energy. His energy was in its way quite as remarkable as his genius – it was, indeed, a part of his genius . . . no man could have worked harder for any conception of his own than Dickens did for the bringing out and the perfection of the new paper . . ." Yet of course it was, at least in part, his own conception; the prospectus which he had written was based upon what he had already described as his "*Carol* philosophy", since he declared that the paper "would be devoted to the advocacy of all rational and honest means by which wrong might be redressed, just right maintained, and the happiness and welfare of society promoted". This, at least, is the version which he showed to Forster – *happiness* is an important word here, suggesting how much of Dickens's role as a popular novelist he was now willing to impart to the more sober business of editing a newspaper.

Very quickly he had his staff in place and readiness, and nothing is more characteristic of Dickens's wish to stamp his own personality upon the paper than the fact that he hired several members of his own family; George Hogarth, his father-in-law, became the music and dramatic critic; John Henry Barrow, his maternal uncle, became its Indian reporter; and, most surprisingly of all, perhaps, Dickens hired his father to be the manager of the parliamentary reporting staff. Bradbury and Evans had taken offices at 90 Fleet Street next to their own printing presses – the buildings had been gutted and then rearranged as the headquarters of the new paper, and consisted essentially of two tumbledown houses with access to one another. To reach them you passed beneath an archway, out of Fleet Street, and down a narrow lane. In one house was Dickens's "sanctum" and an office for the leader-writer; the editor's office, despite absurd rumours at the time of such luxuries as a silver salver for his letters, was in fact very plain with an office table, an armchair, a reading desk, six leather-bottomed chairs, a sofa and a small bookcase in which there were such necessary works as the *Annual Register* and *Hansard*. Above Dickens were two rooms for the sub-editors and for general journalistic use; above them, and up a flight of wooden stairs, were the compositors' rooms. A staircase gave access to the house next door where the printing presses were kept. The whole works were "ill-lighted" and "ill-ventilated", and one of the journalists there recalled ". . . the worn steps, the soiled cocoa-matting, the walls that ever seemed to require painting and polishing, the windows grimed with smoke, the gas, the glare and the smell of oil and paper. The ceaseless noise of presses, moved by hand or by steam, produced a busy hum, whilst in the foggy atmosphere one could see flitting, like ghosts, the forms of men in paper caps and dusty shirt-sleeves . . ." An evocative memory of a printing era before our own, but one that lasted into the eighth decade of the twentieth century.

Amid this confusion, of all people, sat John Dickens. He was now in his sixtieth year, short, portly and "fond of a glass of grog"; he had a particular liking for gin punch which he used to mix in a Fleet Street public house called the Rainbow. He was, according to a colleague, "full of fun, never given to much locomotion . . . he was always hot whatever the weather might be". In other words he perspired a lot, which always suggests some sort of constant but low-level anxiety; the kind of fearfulness which seems to have been present in the man who squandered his family's money and managed to land them in debtors' prison, but which is often forgotten in reports of his undoubted good nature and "fun". No doubt he took a world of trouble over his new duties as manager of the parliamentary staff; no doubt he was very dignified and very precise in all his portly dealings. But opinions do differ as to his general effectiveness. One contemporary remarked that in John Dickens's department there existed "a notable deficiency of . . . care" and another has said that ". . . if his father was not really a Micawber, he was at all events destitute of the energy and experience of Delane, senior" – a reference here to the father of the editor of *The Times* who was financial manager of that paper. Another comment: ". . . it was something that 'turned up' in conjunction with his illustrious son's prosperity, and he took it with an airy grace which, however, did not hide his inefficiency from the eyes of his young staff." The references here to Micawber, who had not even been created at the time the *Daily News* was established, emphasise how potent Dickens's later mythologising of his father would be. Nevertheless it is clear enough that John Dickens was not well suited for an arduous and complicated managerial task; this was perhaps one of the reasons why Bradbury and Evans had less than complete confidence in the editorial judgment of Dickens himself. But there were times, it seems, when John Dickens could bestir himself. One of the major speeches of the day was to be Sir Robert Peel's attack upon the Corn Laws, and John Dickens went to some trouble to receive a copy of the speech as soon as it had been delivered (he wrote to Peel specifically to request it) before making sure that it was quickly printed in the columns of the *Daily News*. He even accompanied that issue of the newspaper down to western England in order to ensure its prompt distribution. It seems too, that his youngest son, Augustus, may have travelled with him. Certainly he was also employed in some capacity by the *Daily News*. Perhaps it is odd to pack a printing house with relatives – especially those of the man who satirised the propensity of the aristocratic Barnacles to arrange public employment for the various members of *their* family. So why did he employ his own father? It has been suggested that Dickens wanted to achieve some kind of psychological domination over him, and therefore over his own past. This is possible but it seems more likely that, confident as he was of his own powers to animate and control the entire enterprise, he simply wanted to provide his father with an income which would stop him being a considerable burden on his own purse and, more especially, give him something to do. There is at any rate some comedy to be found in John Dickens's evident desire to be as frugal in the service of his son as he was spendthrift in all other circumstances; "we must not through ignorance," he wrote of the newspaper's procedures, "if we can help it, throw money away . . ." But what else had he been doing all his life?

For Dickens himself, the preparations for the new paper marked a period of intense excitement: apart from anything else, they revived for him those days as a reporter on the *Morning Chronicle*, just as his recent amateur theatricals had brought back memories of the play-acting of his youth. Time was returning. There is nothing more exhilarating, at least for a period, than old time being restored. It is like the restoration of youth itself. Old time revived. "I can't sleep," he said. But this excitement also increased his propensity to manipulate and to dominate people; "Pray order your Carpet Bag, and get into the train INSTANTLY," he ordered Paxton on one more than usually fraught occasion. The fact that he had shares in the new project suggests, also, that he hoped his initial success would allow him to reap benefit in later years.

It was in any case a time of high political excitement; the riots and confrontations of the early Forties were still very much part of the political atmosphere, and there is no doubt that the middle-classes were anxious and apprehensive about what was known as "the condition of England" question – a question without an answer, perhaps, but now coming to a head, in this and the succeeding year, in the agitation over the Corn Laws which effectively prevented the price of bread from falling. Nothing could be more conducive to angering the "labouring classes" than the aristocratic network of financial and political considerations which had for so long prevented the repeal of that legislation. But now the time for change had come. There were potentialities for civil riot in Wales, in Ireland where the Potato Famine was beginning its grim work, in the south-western counties, and among the Chartists of the northern manufacturing towns: a study of poverty published in 1846 predicted "unavoidable ruin, or the most radical, and perhaps the most terrible of revolutions". It should not be forgotten that it was precisely in this period that Engels was considering the causes of working-class revolution, and that Marx joined him in England in 1849, their *Manifesto of the Communist Party* having been published the year before. There was also a more general sense of uncertainty and confusion in the face of revolutionary technological change, "railroad mania" itself being one cause of this. And there was the impact of what has been aptly called "dissolvent literature", principally those scientific works of geology or biology which called into question the religious certainties of a previous generation. As J. A. Froude said, ". . .the intellectual lightships had broken from their moorings . . . the lights all drifting, the compasses all awry, and nothing left to steer by except the stars . . ." This is the climate in which Dickens's social criticism is most clearly to be seen but, more specifically, it dominates the period when he took on the editorship of a national daily attached to the radical cause. He was caught up in the very storm of his time.

And what, meanwhile, of his Christmas Book? He called it *The Cricket on the Hearth*, as if he wanted to redeploy the material he had been ready to pour into his once projected periodical, *The Cricket*. He had arranged for the illustrations to be executed by Leech, Doyle and Maclise, but had himself been able to work on the text only sporadically, beginning and continuing it with interruptions over the late months of 1845, at a time when "insuperable obstacles crowded into the way of my pursuits". It is possible that his work upon the *Daily News*, in particular, meant that his social and political passions were deflected into the newspaper rather than into his fiction. Certainly *The Cricket on the Hearth* lacks the social dimension of its predecessors and the *Edinburgh Journal* noted that here Dickens had "turned his attention to a subject of purely moral interest", that subject being the unfounded suspicions of an elderly husband about the fidelity of his much younger wife. It is a pretty enough tale, and perhaps most affecting still for its portrait of a blind girl whose father has over the years created for her a wonderfully bright and luxurious world in which she believes she lives; no one was better at such effects than Dickens. Once again, as in all of the Christmas Books, he employs the tones of his own voice as if he were reading aloud to his audience, as if he wanted to come close to them, to take them by the arm and show them such sights as the spirits had once shown Ebenezer Scrooge. And once again, as in the other Christmas stories, the theme is concerned with a dreadful prospect which is at the last minute snatched away, a ghastly fear which is raised only to be dispelled on the last page. The effect of all of these books, quite unlike the effect of his novels, might be described as one of cheerful catharsis.

But he had been writing *The Cricket on the Hearth* in a much more discontinuous way than he had ever worked on *A Christmas Carol* or *The Chimes*, each of which seemed to have poured from him in a prolonged fit of imaginative reverie. And, to a certain extent, the difference shows. Not necessarily in its construction, which is intricate, or in its prose, which has moments of great beauty and pathos; but rather in the fact that this most recent story seems to contain certain components of Dickens's experience which he has not bothered to sharpen or suppress. It is in some ways a much more personal book than its predecessors, therefore. Is it not his mother, for example, who is satirised in the shape of a somewhat elderly woman with "a waist like a bedpost" and the distinct impression of having once been very genteel indeed? Certainly his wife enters the narrative in a direct way; first as Tilly Slowboy, the maid who is constantly grazing her legs and falling over stray objects. These were the characteristics by which Dickens had once described his wife's own clumsiness. But Catherine appears, too, in the unwarranted suspicions of infidelity which poison relations between husband and wife. And is Dickens describing his own wife, when he has the elderly and suspicious husband declare: "Did I consider how little suited I was to her sprightly humour, and how wearisome a plodding man like me must be, to one of her quick spirit; did I consider it was no merit in me, or claim in me, that I loved her, when everybody must, who knew her?" The quick spirit belonged to Dickens, and the plodding nature to Catherine; and, by the same act of fictional transference, must everybody have loved Dickens when they knew him? Was this his way of reworking the de la Rue episode in his own mind so that no blame could possibly be attached to him? For if there is one constant and pervasive presence in this book it is really that of Dickens himself; he is like the father of the blind daughter, the loving father who spreads fancies around us to beguile us and to keep us from pain. The loving friend, the loving father, the loving narrator – Dickens places himself on every level of the narrative, as if when he is working quickly and almost unconsciously his own preoccupation with himself comes most clearly forward. Even at the end we return to the narrator himself. ". . . I am left alone. A Cricket sings upon the Hearth; a broken child's-toy lies upon the ground; and nothing else remains."

It was a popular but not a critical success; it sold something like twice as many copies as *The Chimes* but those who were seeking to find evidence for Dickens's fading powers pounced upon it as an example of what one critic called "sentimental twaddle". *The Times* called it "the babblings of genius in its premature dotage", although its reviewer's critical asperity might in part have been connected with the fact that Dickens was just about to set up a rival newspaper. But he, too, seems to have been more concerned with public success than critical approval; his own popular social role was becoming of much more importance to him, and one of the reasons he accepted the editorship of the *Daily News* was to confirm his position as an arbiter of public affairs and to establish an intimate relationship with a large audience who had not necessarily read his fiction. It was in this spirit that Dickens made sure that *The Cricket on the Hearth* would be effectively dramatised as soon as it was published; he allowed Albert Smith to produce a theatrical version, to be performed by the Keeleys at the Lyceum (the Keeleys being a well respected husband-and-wife team who specialised in domestic melodramas of this kind), and he went so far as to send proofs of the story before publication so that the play could be ready at the same time. He even assisted at some of the rehearsals.

While, all the time, the excitement over the *Daily News* grew. Among the staff were now Forster and Albany Fonblanque, Douglas Jerrold and Mark Lemon. It had been agreed some time in advance that the first edition should actually be published on the day that Parliament began its crucial next session, a session which would be dominated by the battle over the Corn Laws. An advertisement had appeared in the *Morning Chronicle* and the *Morning Herald* (*The Times* refused to take it) in which a "NEW MORNING PAPER" was announced, one of "Liberal Politics and thorough Independence". And, once more testifying to the importance of railway development at this precise period in English history, "in Scientific and Business Information on every topic connected with Railways, whether in actual operation, in progress, or projected, will be found to be complete". Forster still had misgivings about his friend's hectic involvement and told Macready that Dickens was "intensely fixed on his own opinions and in his admiration of his works"; but in part this may have been because his own advice was being ignored. The chief leader writer of the paper, W. J. Fox (himself an important member of the Free Trade movement), told a friend that "Dickens and I are regularly against him [Forster] in almost everything, involving difference of opinion".

By the middle of January everything was ready, and a "dummy" edition was prepared on 17 January, 1846, the real first issue of the new paper being finally produced four days later. "On the eve of the birth of the *Daily News*," one journalist recalled, ". . . the bustle and excitement in the office rose to a high pitch." All the interested parties kept on calling in that first night of publication to see how matters were progressing – Bradbury, Evans, Paxton, Lemon, *et al*. In the event, Evans and Lemon were somehow delegated the duties of proof-reading as a result of the protracted parliamentary debate even then taking place. There had been reports of a "Saturnalia" among the printers and Joseph Paxton wrote to his wife that "all our efforts was nearly . . . floored at 4 Oclock this morning and it was only by exertion almost superhuman that it was got out at all". There is also a report that Dickens himself was drunk, and unable to write the first leader as planned; but this seems, on the face of it, highly unlikely. The whole night was a combination of efficiency and disorder, with Dickens typically trying to manage everything and everyone at once: trying to *do* everything at once, too, since he even set up some of the type himself. The first issue was finally complete. As it was being printed Dickens and his editorial staff gathered around the stone (or printer's block) and celebrated the event with speeches and of course alcohol, perhaps the gin punch which John Dickens was so expert in brewing. The editor himself did not arrive home until six o'clock the following morning, carrying with him a copy of the first edition.

It was not a complete success, however; it had been printed on poor-quality paper, and had in places been very badly "made up". In other words, the design and lay-out of the pages, perhaps superintended by Dickens himself, were ungainly. And there were also some misprints, the most egregious being in the account of stock prices, an area where accuracy above all else is necessary. One colleague at this time remembered how on the first day ". . . there was a wild rush for the first number. At the sight of the outer sheet, hope at once lighted up the gloom of Printing House Square, the Strand and Shoe Lane [the offices of rival newspapers] . . . I am not sure there were not social rejoicings that night in the editorial chambers, which had been so long beset by dread." Clearly there had to be improvements in the *Daily News* at once, although on the following day Dickens told Beard that "I am delighted to say we have a Capital paper today. I sat at the Stone, and made it up with my own hands." But, if the appearance of the new paper did not constitute a serious threat to its rivals, what of its contents? The first of its eight pages was filled with advertisements and legal notices, and the second devoted itself to precisely the causes it wished to champion: the case for Free Trade and the total repeal of the Corn Laws. Then more news and editorials and, as expected, a whole page was absorbed by railway news (many of the advertisements on the front had in fact been placed by various railway interests). There was a page devoted to the advertisement of books and magazines, as well as the usual number of auction and theatre notices. In other words, it was very much a newspaper of its time – serious, sober, closely printed, emblem of a culture which relied wholly upon the written word for its more important communications. If there was a difference at all, it lay in Dickens's own contribution; he published here the first of his accounts of his Italian travels, "Travelling Letters. Written on the Road". And, as was his custom in practically all of his publications, whether fictional or journalistic, he also wrote his own Address to the Public which epitomises his approach to public affairs: ". . . it will be no part of our function to widen any breach that may unhappily subsist, or may arise, between Employer and Employed; but it will rather be our effort to show their true relations, their mutual dependence, and their mutual power of adding to the sum of general happiness and prosperity." In other words he was not against indus-trialism or industrialists as such. His enemies, if they were anywhere, lay in parliamentary cabals and among the great landowning families who were impeding what he described here as "the Principles of Progress and Improvement".

There is no doubt, therefore, that Dickens was an energetic and hard-working editor and that, as in all the affairs of his life, he paid a great deal of attention to those details of the project which ensure its efficient operation but which are sometimes scorned by greater minds as trivial or merely technical. He knew well enough that in attention to detail, efficiency, and sheer technical competence the secret of success is to be found. In fact there are occasions when he seems more concerned with the speed with which news is transmitted than the content of the news itself, an interest which might profitably be linked to his own fiction where images of free flow as opposed to barriers and hindrances, of unimpeded circulation compared to stagnation and blockage, occur. Perhaps it is not surprising that certain metaphors in his next novel should arise from the theme of movement and release, just after the time when his major aim was to ensure the rapid and successful circulation of the *Daily News*. In fact the paper itself did improve after the near-fiasco of the first number, and that improvement was at least partly the result of the editor's own contributions; in the next few weeks he was to concentrate upon the discussion of the social questions which had always beset him, and in quick succession produced articles or "letters" on capital punishment and on ragged schools.

All of this is perfectly laudable; there is some evidence to suggest, however, that Dickens may have been a very energetic editor without necessarily being a very good one. In later years, when he was managing and editing his own periodicals, his authoritarian self-sufficiency would be a great advantage; but he was too much a man of his own opinions and prejudices, too dominant a figure, too self-assertive and in some ways too *peculiar*, to be a good editor of such a large and complex undertaking. What is needed in such a post is a man of flexible and catholic temper, who at least professes to believe (as Mark Lemon certainly did on *Punch*) that his contributors are likely to be more intelligent, and better writers, than himself. This of course was quite beyond Dickens's power to manage. One contemporary put it simply: ". . . Dickens was not a good editor. He was the best reporter in London and as a journalist, he was nothing more." Another colleague suggests that editorship was not an appropriate position for him: "Mr Dickens went on as he began, doing his best but with no experience, and no clear conception, of the duties of the post he held . . ." Dickens was as energetic and as practical as ever, and there seems no doubt that he wished to keep a controlling hand on all aspects of *Daily News* business; but in the essential role – the role of editor rather than manager or journalist – there seems to have been something lacking. One of Dickens's own leader-writers completes the story: "Had he been fit for, and had he done, his duty fully, I should have seen more of him. But my department was the economic and financial; and of political economy, or of political finance, he knew nothing . . . He thought with the 'humane public'; and with the tax-hating public; and with the 'good government and anti-corruption' public; but of how he was to serve them, except by giving way to their chief popular tendencies, as touching such matters he was really ignorant, and felt himself so . . . he could not act upon his convictions with any sort of satisfaction, because he could not see clearly, what he was about. This was a source, to him, occasionally of much uneasiness; and my presence always roused and intensified this uneasiness . . . he was absent-minded and indisposed to say anything definite; and never would *discuss* any topic properly within the lines of my department." This critical passage has been quoted at some length, partly because of the apparent justice of its complaints, Dickens's pronouncements on political and social affairs tending to be of the most generalised kind, but also because it reflects another aspect of Dickens, that "uneasiness" and "absent-mindedness" in difficult circumstances.

For it was precisely the onset of these characteristics, no doubt daily magnified by the work around him, that led him within a few days of the first publication of the *Daily News* to become restless and dissatisfied with his role. There seems little doubt that he had by now realised that he had made a mistake, that he was essentially a novelist and that any long disruption of his real work would be injurious to him. In fact he already had vague schemes of a new novel and it seems highly likely that, as soon as he had been granted shares in the company (on the first day of publication, he formally signed an agreement in which he was given shares without any need to bring in capital), he started planning to leave. But his general dissatisfaction was exacerbated by specific factors. He soon came to believe that the paper was too closely connected with the railway interests to be entirely independent. More importantly, he came to resent the "interference" of Bradbury and Evans in his running of the paper; this was precisely the complaint he had made against Bentley and *Bentley's Miscellany* some eight years before and, once again, he seems to have had very little real justification for his complaints. The point was that, in the contract to which Dickens had agreed, Bradbury and Evans were declared to be the "managers" and had the power "to engage appoint and remove the Editor Sub-editors Contributors Agents Clerks Servants and all other persons . . ." In other words, they had the perfect right to be consulted and in their own turn to act. But Dickens could not see this. In every project which he entered he had always to be both chief actor and stage manager, and he could never acquiesce in any situation where he was not *primus inter pares* and where his own choices and judgments were not of paramount concern. By the end of January – within ten days of first publication – he had decided that he could no longer stay, and was already taking that demanding and peremptory tone with Bradbury and Evans which he had assumed with Chapman and Hall only a short time before. He went down to Rochester with his family and Forster, for a weekend away from the bother and bewilderment of the *Daily News* office, and there is no doubt that it was during this visit that he fully discussed the matter with them. Here, among the scenes of his childhood, he might once again tap the sources of his true genius and reinstate it as his primary activity. In fact there was really very little for him and the others to discuss, and even Forster told Macready at this time that "no one could be a worse editor than Dickens". As on other occasions, he just needed a suitable excuse to leave in order to alleviate any sense of guilt or responsibility he might have felt; and, with the behaviour of Bradbury and Evans (which had in fact been exemplary on all other occasions), he thought he had found it. On 9 February he formally resigned; since he could now blame the managers rather than himself for his abrupt departure, at once he became much more cheerful. His must have been one of the shortest editorships of a national daily, just eighteen days, and the manner of his departure does suggest a degree of wilfulness or even ruthlessness in any matters pertaining to himself and to his own concerns. He often dropped such causes as copyright legislation very soon after he had taken them up with enthusiasm, and there seems little doubt that he "dropped" the newspaper as soon as he felt it to be interfering with his own real pursuits. Now that he had a book in mind, all the high hopes and high declarations about the *Daily News* weighed less than nothing against his own resolve. But his was not, as it turned out, a calamitous decision. Forster took over as editor and Dilke was appointed as manager; between them the *Daily News* stayed in business and eventually began to flourish as a truly radical newspaper.

Dickens was not wholly free of his connection with the paper, despite the fact that he liked to pretend that his decision was swift and final. Of course he retained his shares in it, and it seems that he continued drawing a salary from Bradbury and Evans until the end of April. But at least he was free of editorial responsibilities, and in these months he went back to his writing while planning another long sojourn on the continent; he wanted to live with his family in a country where expenses were less heavy than in England, and the writing of *The Chimes* in Genoa seems to have persuaded him that he could compose as easily abroad as at home. Nevertheless he did not want wholly to lose that position as public reformer which the editorship had provided for him, and over these next few months he contributed a series of articles on social matters which were published in the *Daily News*. In his articles on capital punishment, for example, he made it clear that he opposed all forms of judicial murder (a position he was later to modify), but once again he does so by a keen and sympathetic entry into both the mind of the murderer and the mind of the judge who condemns him. That is really where Dickens's genius lay. Not in editing. Not in the analytical survey of social affairs for which, as his newspaper colleagues explained, he was quite unfitted. But rather for the fictional representation of social matters in which his polemic is striated with the memories and experiences of his own life. That is why his essay or "letter" in the *Daily News* on the importance of the ragged schools contains such a powerful account of lost childhood: "I know the prisons of London, well . . . I have visited the largest of them, more times than I could count; and that the Children in them are enough to break the heart and hope of any man . . ." It is as if he could see his own face among the faces of the blighted and, although at a later date the problems of Dickens's true religion must be considered, it is appropriate to repeat here the prayer which he taught his children: "Hear our supplications in behalf of the poor, the sick, the destitute and the guilty, and grant Thy blessing on the diffusion of increased happiness and knowledge among the great mass of mankind, that they may not be tempted to the commission of crimes which in want and man's neglect it is hard to resist." Hard to resist. There, but for the grace of God . . . his fictive imagination and social observation work together.

At the same time as he was composing these short social essays he was busily preparing for the volume edition of *Pictures from Italy*; he was asking friends for his letters to them during that period and he was consulting his own diary, primarily to introduce new sections and not to rely totally on the "Travelling Notes" currently appearing in the *Daily News* (in fact that newspaper carried only about half of the subsequent travel book). There was one problem. Clarkson Stanfield had agreed to illustrate the text for Dickens but, when he read those passages of the narrative in which Dickens satirises the excesses of Catholic devotion, he resigned from the project. Stanfield was himself a prominent English Catholic, after all, as Dickens knew, and he could scarcely be connected with a publication which treats his Church's ritual as little more than a parade of mummers; it is difficult, too, to see how Dickens could have been so cavalier or thoughtless in choosing Stanfield for such a project. Until we remember one important fact already illustrated in his departure from the newspaper. Nothing he ever did was wrong. Nothing he ever wrote was wrong. If other people saw things differently, well, that was entirely their problem; and a problem with which he had little sympathy. In his letter to Stanfield, for example, he offers no apology. "You are the best judge whether your Creed recognises and includes, with men of sense, such things as I have shocked you by my mention of. I am sorry to learn that it does – and think far worse of it than I did." It was the Church's fault, in other words, and not Dickens's. As usual, he went at once into action in order to find a substitute; fortunately and curiously, he chose a young artist who then had no real reputation, Samuel Palmer, whose wonderful illustrations are not the least of the merits of *Pictures from Italy* in its final state.

But, perhaps most importantly in the months after his resignation, he was considering once more the possibility of a new novel. He knew that his public expected and wanted another, despite the sneers of the more intellectual of the critics, and it was in his usual uneasy, vexing, open state of mind that he began his search for a theme and a story. Certain minor incidents seem to have entered his consciousness even as he was making his preparations. He managed somehow to run over and kill a dog in Regents Park "and gave his little mistress – a girl of thirteen or fourteen – such exquisite distress as I never saw the like of". Clearly the incident shook Dickens, for he restores the little dog to life in the novel he was contemplating, *Dombey and Son*, where Diogenes is given by Mr Toots to its own "little mistress", Florence Dombey, of much the same age as the distressed girl in Regents Park. That is one of the secrets of Dickens's art in miniature: to compensate for life, to restore the dead, to revive the past, to make amends in fantasy and like the fairy to grant his own wishes. Other aspects of Dickens's life in this period enter *Dombey and Son* as well. He had met, through Joseph Paxton, the "railway King" George Hudson, and in this next novel the theme of business or at least the men of business takes a central place. A famous broker had failed just before the publication of the newspaper; in *Dombey and Son* there is a similar business failure. The "railway mania" had suffused the entire period, and in this novel the railways of course play a central part; in the narrative he names one area of Camden Town soon to be engulfed by the railways as Staggs's Gardens, and a "stag" was the slang of this period for a speculator in railway stocks. In *Dombey and Son*, too, there are echoes and reflections of Dickens's Italian trip, particularly in his meditations on the need for progress amid the decaying stillness of those who try to forestall or ignore such advance. It would not necessarily be true to say that all of these themes and meanings were consciously deployed by Dickens, only that they are the circumambient life in which he moved and in which he planned his novel. All the while restoring lost time and reviving lost contours; connecting the world and making it lucid; brightening the colours and bringing forth the meaning.

Yet still he could not start; he had too many other matters "on his mind". For one thing, although he had resigned the editorship, he was still materially caught up in the future welfare of the *Daily News*. The various other shareholders in the paper could not decide how best to move forward, however, and so Dickens waited. He said that he was "at Sixes and sevens". He contracted some kind of nervous pain in his face. In addition, despite his failure to stamp the *Daily News* in his own image, he was still eager to take an active role in that world of effort and discipline which the Victorians had created in their own tireless and enthusiastic image. Work on the newspaper, as well as his wish to find another well-paid post independent of his literary fortunes, seems to have fired his determination to take up public employment: once again he contemplated the idea of becoming a magistrate or assuming "some Commissionership, or Inspectorship . . .". As he had said when he first considered the idea three years before, ". . . I would never rest from practically shewing how important it has become to educate, on bold and comprehensive principles, the Dangerous Members of Society". Not an arrogant and authoritarian magistrate, therefore, of which there were all too many in the courts of London; instead he subscribed to the definition by another magistrate of his task as "an adviser, an arbitrator and a mediator". It was in this spirit that he arranged a dinner at Devonshire Terrace for three men who were actively involved in prison management – specifically so that Chesterton, the Governor of the Middlesex House of Correction, and Tracey, Governor of the Westminster House of Correction, could meet Alexander Maconochie, a penal reformer who shared Dickens's distaste for the "separate system" of prison management and had during his time as Governor of Norfolk Island (the penal colony in Australia) perfected a system of "marks" as a way of rehabilitating prisoners. It is not difficult to imagine the kind of conversation held at that table in Devonshire Terrace. The animated and speculative conversation of the governors, combined with the more obsessive and private interest of Dickens who nonetheless could talk just as persuasively and knowledgeably about prison conditions as any of his companions.

It is in precisely this spirit of social improvement that one should consider Dickens's most interesting activity in this period between the *Daily News* and his eventual removal to the continent, an activity that was in fact to engage his animated attention for many years and to become his most significant social project. It was Miss Burdett-Coutts who first conceived the idea of a "Home" or "Asylum" for "fallen women", but at once Dickens took it up and elaborated upon it with all the ferocious enthusiasm of his fervent nature. His scheme to set up a ragged school with Kay-Shuttleworth had come to nothing, and so all his thwarted energy was directed towards Miss Burdett-Coutts's much more promising project. Almost as soon as the plan for it was broached he sent a long letter to her in which he outlined the nature and the regimen of the Home to be founded. The system of discipline. The practical training. The daily routine. The very lay-out of the building itself. It is curious how the plans are so detailed that they appear to be ready made; as if Dickens had in his imagination been constructing such a place for some time. The conversations with prison governors, the outline for a ragged school, all played their part – for him, as for the more enlightened of his contemporaries, social reform, educational reform and prison management were seen as aspects of the same effort. He would continue to plan and discuss and agitate about them even while he lived abroad.

Before this second departure for Europe, there were of course the usual excursions and celebrations. He went to Richmond with Forster, Macready, Maclise and Stanfield; "we had," Macready noted in his diary in his usual rather lugubrious way, "a very merry – I suppose I must say *jolly* day – rather more tumultuous than I quite like . . ." The fact that Clarkson Stanfield joined the party, despite his refusal to illustrate *Pictures from Italy*, suggests that his anger at Dickens's attitude to his faith had already subsided. It was difficult to stay angry for long with Dickens, when he himself was so mercurial. There was also some kind of celebration when the latest member of his family was christened – by the name of Alfred D'Orsay Tennyson Dickens, in honour both of the poet and of the French count whose wit and judgment Dickens readily admired. But the name was enough to delight those who secretly, or not so secretly, considered Dickens to be rather vulgar. "Ah Charlie, if this don't prove to posterity that you might have been a Tennyson and were a D'Orsay . . ." So Robert Browning wrote to Elizabeth Barrett, and he went on, ". . . when you remember what the form of sponsorship is, to what it pledges you in the Church of England – and *then* remember that Mr D is an enlightened Unitarian – you will get a curious notion of the man, I fancy . . ." (Dickens, in other words, was a little on the vainglorious rather than the literary side, and his professed religious beliefs were indecisive if not hypocritical.) There were other engagements, too: he gave a speech to the General Theatrical Fund, in which once more he extolled the virtues of the actor. He attended a Royal Academy Dinner and from there went on to see a performance of General Tom Thumb, the celebrated midget, in Albert Smith's *Hop o' My Thumb*; in these two quite varied outings we may see, if nothing else, that the starched rectitude, so beloved of the denigrators of the nineteenth century, really never existed.

And he was still waiting for some decision about the *Daily News*. Waiting to find out what might happen to his shares. Waiting to see if his resignation had inflicted a fatal blow on its prospects. Waiting until he could wait no longer, and finally, in April, he decided to leave for Switzerland at the end of the following month. His preferred choice had been Genoa but Catherine, still no doubt concerned about his magnetic relationship with Madame de la Rue, seems to have vetoed that idea; so it was Switzerland, and Lausanne. Two weeks before his departure *Pictures from Italy* was published, in the preface to which Dickens confessed to "a brief mistake I made, not long ago, in disturbing the old relations between myself and my readers . . ." He meant his editorship of the *Daily News*, of course, although the proprietors of that paper might have been excused for believing that the mistake was theirs in hiring him in the first place. *The Times* commented tartly on Dickens's statement about his old "relations" with his public: "Let him not, we entreat him, be too eager to resume them. He has not only to sustain his past reputation, but to repair the mischief which we assure him has been done by his latest publications . . ." Dickens may not have seen this complaint, since it was published the day after he had left for the continent, but no doubt its reproaches and its sentiments were very well known to him by now. He had invited Tennyson to join him in Switzerland but the poet had said to a friend, ". . . if I went, I should be entreating him to dismiss his sentimentality, and so we should quarrel and part, and never see one another any more . . ." So even among his admirers there were some who had disliked the tone of the Christmas Books. It was indeed time to resume his old pursuits. It was time to embark upon his novel. There was another reason for his departure; he wanted to put as much distance as he could between himself and the *Daily News*. It is quite likely that, despite his best efforts, he still felt some residual guilt about his role in its affairs; more than any single person he had come close to ruining it. But he never could have admitted such guilt. And what did he wish to do instead? To leave the scene of the crime. To take flight. To Switzerland.

Chapter 17

H E planned to be away for a year, enough time to complete a great deal of the novel he now had in mind. So once more the whole large family set forth on its travels, accompanied again by their courier in Italy, Louis Roche. Set forth for Lausanne. Many years later, Dickens remembered the mountains. The wooden cottages. The little wooden bridges. The streams. The hillside pastures. Of course Switzerland was not at all like Italy, and Lausanne was not at all like Genoa – except for the fact that they were both built beside water which was such a potent imaginative force for Dickens (in his next novel the doomed little Dombey gazes out at the waves), and that both were surrounded by mountains. Mountains which haunted certain aspects of Dickens's fiction, too, with a vision of cold and brightness which D. H. Lawrence was to explore in another century in *Women in Love*.

They arrived in Lausanne eleven days after their departure from England, in three separate coaches, and took rooms at once in the Hotel Gibbon. For the next two days Dickens roamed around the town, looking for a suitable house for what was now a family of nine, with servants. It was not a large town but, unlike Genoa, it was neat and clean and orderly – all the things which appealed to Dickens, and it was quite in character that just after writing a Christmas story about a maker of dolls he should now find something which he described as a "doll's house" for his family. It was a villa called Rosemont, lying upon a hill which overlooked the lake and the mountains beyond; only a few minutes' walk to the water's edge among green fields and vineyards. Altogether a different atmosphere from Genoa, then; quiet, industrious, and almost studious in its retirement; Dickens noticed the number of bookshops he passed on the daily walks which soon became his speciality here. There was an English church in the town, but only a few English residents. In Genoa he had tried to meet as few of his countrymen as possible but those who lived in Lausanne were of a different sort – literate, wealthy, but with radical and philanthropic sympathies quite other than those of the more blasé expatriates in Italy. Neither were they the privileged and impervious holders of inherited wealth who for Dickens so stultified the air of England. They were just people who preferred the cleaner air of Switzerland. Among them, William Haldimand, a former MP and Director of the Bank of England, now a philanthropist who had helped to establish an asylum for the blind in Lausanne itself; he had also written a number of books, such as *Conversations on Chemistry*, although it is not clear how much this impressed Dickens. Since Haldimand owned a large estate just below Rosemont, Dickens soon became acquainted with him, and it was not long before the expatriate introduced his famous neighbour to his friends, the de Cerjats, a rich but artistic and philanthropic couple. And, most importantly, Richard and Lavinia Watson, who, like the Dickens family, had come to Lausanne only for the summer. Richard Watson had been an MP, too, a liberal who had supported the Reform Bill despite the fact that he owned a very large estate in Northamptonshire (his house there later became the model for Chesney Wold in *Bleak House*). But Dickens seems to have been most impressed and delighted by his wife; there are many occasions, in fact, when he is much more at ease with women than with men.

All lived within walking distance of one another, although carriages were generally still used for social purposes, and in later years Dickens was to remember the times when he strolled at dusk outside Rosemont, smoking with the men, while the women played and sang within. It was in fact generally these dusky and bosky scenes that he associated with Lausanne, and in *David Copperfield* they were to be transmuted into his own particular poetry: ". . . I heard the voices die away, and saw the quiet evening cloud grow dim, and all the colours in the valley fade, and the golden snow upon the mountain-tops become a remote part of the pale night sky . . ." The diaries which Mrs Watson kept of this period in Lausanne suggest a more animated life; they describe dinners, parties, and various excursions, of which Dickens was always the centre. And yet, in a later memoir, she said that she wished to emphasise ". . . the unusual absence of all affection or conceit in him . . . no one could resist the wonderful (so to call it) tyranny he exerted, not for himself, but for the carrying out of the

object in hand! His face expressed all this in a most amusing way . . ."
Most of the first-hand accounts of Dickens in this period do indeed
stress how natural and spontaneous he was, by which is meant how
little he carried with him the air of a "great writer". In company he
was singularly unaffected in manner and conversation, and if such
accounts do not seem to correspond with those which emphasise
Dickens's theatricality, it ought to be remembered that in society he
was quite different from the person who was glimpsed in the thoroughfares of London or on the platforms of public assemblies. When
he was being watched, or thought that he was being watched, he put
on a performance; when involved in the normal courtesies of life he
could forget himself to a degree that rendered him the perfect companion. It was part of his nervous self-consciousness, however, that he
found it difficult to make the first move in social relations. "To
strangers he was somewhat reserved," a friend of this period recalled,
"but a warm reception ever met those who made the slightest
advance . . ." And how else did Charles Dickens now appear to
others, this famous novelist, quondam editor of the *Daily News*, and
still a man of only thirty-four? T. A. Trollope, the brother of the
novelist, had met Dickens the year before in Italy and had remarked at
the time upon the "lustrous brilliancy" of his eyes. But Trollope also
recorded a more unfamiliar fact; Dickens was in fact near-sighted but
". . . continually exercised his vision by looking at distant objects, and
making them out as well as he could without any artificial assistance".
Dickens did sometimes wear spectacles, at least in the later part of his
life, but the idea of his training or *forcing* his eyesight is yet another
example of his remarkable will. Mrs Watson also remembered another
extraordinary characteristic which he demonstrated in Lausanne; it
was ". . . his marvellous quickness of vision, taking in everything at a
passing glance. Thus, driving through a town with tall houses [no
doubt this was Geneva], he described with all the details of a weird
portrait, the appearance of an old woman looking out of a top-storey
window. Though he had seen her but for a moment, the impression
was complete and indelible." Mrs Watson naturally associates this gift
with the "power of detail" in his novels, but it can also be linked with
his similarly extraordinary power of memory. A female friend of his
was once complaining of the dullness of her neighbourhood and
remarked that she had only one acquaintance in the area; it was a man
called Maddison. Dickens did not see this woman for three or four
years later, until he spotted her at an evening party. He made his way

through the crowd towards her and eventually reached her side. "Well," he asked, "and *how's Maddison?*"

Dickens's eldest son, Charles, had his own memories of his father in Lausanne; of ". . . walks along the lake-side or among the beautiful hills behind the town, or visits to open air fetes in the heart of the green woods where he was always anxious that I should join and distinguish myself in the boyish sports that were going on . . ." There is perhaps a criticism of his father implied in the suggestion that Dickens always wanted his son to "distinguish" himself, and it ought to be remembered that Dickens as a child did not partake of any boyish sports. Among his activities "my father found time for many pleasant mountain excursions; to Chamounix, to the Great Saint Bernard, which always had a weird fascination for him . . ." and elsewhere. Charles also remembered one occasion, of "my sister Mamie sitting at the piano and singing the Queen of the May, and Alfred Tennyson unexpectedly strolling in among us through the window that opened on to the lawn, as if the odd coincidence were quite a matter of course".

It took only a little while for Dickens to "settle" in this new environment, and almost at once his attention turned to the two projects which were absolutely necessary for him to complete: the new novel, which he had now already promised to Bradbury and Evans, and the Christmas Book which had become almost a seasonal necessity both for him and for his readers. His study was on the first floor of the villa, with a long balcony and a window which looked out upon the lake and mountains: beside him was the town of Lausanne, its steep streets seeming to him like the streets in a dream, and the green hills beyond. It was his custom to walk nine or ten miles every evening, all the time thinking of the books he was about to write; he already had a notion for the Christmas Book, one which concerned the peace that suffuses an ancient battlefield. And in this vision of calm succeeding battle, was he perhaps trying to create a mood in which his own recent struggles on the *Daily News* could be co-opted into a saner and more comprehensive vision of the world? Certainly there is something of this eventually to be discovered in the novel he was also contemplating, *Dealings with the Firm of Dombey and Son. Wholesale, Retail, and for Exportation.* A novel which ends, too, on a note of peace and hope after the struggles of the day. And as he walked through Lausanne, planning *Dombey and Son*, he was looking towards just such an ending, constructing much of the plot in advance so that, by the time he began, he had a clear view of the narrative he wished to complete. This is the first novel for which Dickens's number plans survive and, although it cannot be assumed that there were not similar number plans for his previous fiction, it can at least be tentatively suggested that this was the first novel in which Dickens paid as much attention to construction as he did to composition. The number plans themselves are simply sheets of blue paper, one for each instalment of the novel, folded in half; on the left side he would write down general themes or topics which he wished to introduce, and on the right side the contents of each chapter were summarised. The plans acted, then, both as a structural key and as an aide-mémoire, a way of organising his material in easily accessible form and of maintaining a close scrutiny upon the dynamics of each number. There are often occasions in the novels of Dickens where he introduces a chapter or scene simply to alter the mood or tempo of the narrative, and there is no doubt that it was only by constant reference to his abbreviated notes that he was able to achieve what might be called the symphonic effects in his writing.

So it is that, in the first of the number plans for *Dombey and Son*, on the left hand side of the sheet, Dickens jots down among other references "Wet nurse – Polly Toodlie" and "Wooden Midshipman"; the name is eventually changed to Toodle but the contrast here, implicit and not necessarily conscious, "Wet" and "Wooden", is one that recurs throughout a novel in which various types of solidity and hardness (male) are placed against free movement and liquidity (female). His central female character, Florence Dombey, breaks down in tears some eighty-eight times and this sub-text of tears, of flowing water, of the sea at which Paul Dombey gazes, lends the novel much of its power. It has already been noticed how many of the events of this year take their place somewhere within Dickens's wonderfully capacious consciousness, to be transformed into fiction, and it can also be said that the world of commerce and offices which Dickens describes in *Dombey and Son* bears at least oblique relationship to the world of newspapers and railways which he had just quitted. There is a sense in which Dickens seems to wish to separate himself from the world of men, the solid world, and in *Dombey and Son* to reach out to the water and the sea, to describe and to celebrate those specifically female virtues which he longed for – the absence of which had so disheartened him in his own struggles with the commercial men who owned the *Daily News*.

That this is not simply a fantasy of the biographer is perhaps confirmed by the fact that there are many references to what might be called the "feminine" side of Charles Dickens, by which is meant those qualities which were considered "feminine" in his own period. One friend declared that "there was something feminine in the quality that led him to the right verdict, the appropriate word . . ." Even at the end of his life an American friend and confidante, Mrs Fields, noticed that "exquisite delicacy and quickness of his perception, something as fine as the finest woman possesses". A contemporary extends the perception with a characteristically mid-Victorian note that ". . . his imagination, like a woman's, conquers his more reasoning faculties . . ." while in a review of his work reference was made to his ". . . feminine, irritable, noisy mind . . ." And there was, too, that neat domestic interest in furniture and decoration; as his daughter, Mamie, once recorded, "he was full of the kind of interest in a house which is commonly confined to women . . ." It was also said by more than one contemporaneous critic that Dickens did indeed possess a "feminine" sense of dirtiness or ugliness in men and, although of course his sensitivity to mood and atmosphere, marked as being "feminine" by his contemporaries, would not be so treated today, it is still worth noting that passive component of his vocabulary which, especially in his correspondence, describes the way in which things "master" or "take possession of" him. It is worth recognising, too, how in his fiction characters must relinquish oppressively male qualities in order to attain some state of grace or quietus. Certainly this "feminine" quality within his writing partly explains why he is always so ambivalent about money, about power, about the nature of "progress" and, in the novel he was now about to write, the dominance of the railway. Again and again he asserts the importance of gentleness, kindness, sympathy, generosity; at the time these were seen as specifically feminine characteristics, at least in their purest state, although Dickens understood better than many of his mid-Victorian contemporaries that they were the proper attributes of all human beings. Understood imaginatively, at least. It is clear enough that, while Dickens's creative instincts were fully engaged with his whole experience of the world, his stated motives and methods were very much of his period. Perhaps that is why there are so many monstrous females in Dickens's work – although it is a folk-tale characteristic, it is even now specifically associated with that vision called "Dickensian" and may be seen as his attempt to ridicule or suppress the "feminine" element within himself.

That is precisely the point; he lived in an age which increasingly was creating a divide between the sexes. We might note the fact that the ready emotionalism of men, so prevalent an aspect of life in the first decades of the century when men would weep in public, was now being replaced by something much more suitable to an age in which commerce and power were the twin deities of the male world; we might note that beards and moustaches became fashionable in the mid-Fifties; we might note that the conventional male costume was being reduced to the sober tones of the morning suit and the black dye of the stove-pipe hat. All these were characteristic of a society in which the worship of commercial force was matched only by the continuing scientific enquiry into the principles of energy, where the constant refrain concerning "the battle of life" was complemented by the exploitation of the poor and by the often violent acquisition of overseas territories. This is the context in which Dickens was seen by many of his contemporaries to have an essentially "feminine" genius; the context in which he was often said to lack wisdom or reason or sagacity, all characteristically seen as male qualities of dominance and control. And it is clear enough that Dickens resented such implied denigration, of himself in particular and of fiction in general; that is why he constantly emphasised what he considered to be the moral force of his writing, why he always insisted that he described what was "true". True, however, in a much larger sense than he often consciously intended. He thought he was part of his age, and yet he was creating a large, echoic, mythic structure out of it. He saw beyond the conventional stereotypes of "male" and "female"; he saw more permanent and enduring characteristics.

He walked among the hills behind Lausanne; he walked beside the lake; he looked across at the mountains; all the time thinking of the work in hand. But he could not begin, not yet, not until the "big box" which contained all the appurtenances of his desk arrived at Rosemont; these were not just his writing materials, his goose-quill pens and his blue ink, but also the bronze images of two toads duelling, of a dog-fancier with the puppies and dogs swarming all over him, a paper-knife, a gilt leaf with a rabbit upon it. He grouped all these images around him on his desk; as his son-in-law explained after Dickens's death, these were the images "for his eye to rest on in the intervals of actual writing", and so great was his love of habit and order that he could not write without their silent presence in front of him. As soon as they were placed in his study at Rosemont, he began.

First, while he was still contemplating *Dombey and Son*, he got on with the necessary tasks: "I had a good deal to write for Lord John [Russell] about the Ragged schools. I set to work and did that. A good deal for Miss Coutts, in reference to her charitable projects. I set to work and did *that*. Half of the children's New Testament to write, or pretty nearly. I set to work and did *that* . . ."

It is necessary to interrupt his almost obsessive list of works performed, of obligations fulfilled, to consider this children's New Testament – not least because the novel and Christmas story which Dickens was about to write have often been said to incorporate a religious tone or sensibility which had previously been noticeable only by its absence from his writing. He called it *The Life Of Our Lord*, a handwritten manuscript begun while at Lausanne but not completed for three years, in which he recounts the story of the New Testament (largely drawing upon the gospel according to Luke) in the simple language of a children's tale or fairy story, the latter influence perhaps suggesting the extent to which Dickens turned all of the most significant aspects of his life into just such a story. A story to be read aloud since, in a later letter, Dickens recounts how his children "have had a little version of the New Testament that I wrote for them, read to them long before they could read, and no young people can have had an earlier knowledge of, or interest in, that book. It is an inseparable part of their earliest remembrances." A slight exaggeration here, since the eldest children were already well beyond the stage of their earliest remembrances (Charley was now nine years old), but the sentiment is clear enough; as Dickens said of his own work, ". . .one of my most constant and most earnest endeavours has been to exhibit in all my good people some faint reflections of the teachings of our great Master . . . All my strongest illustrations are derived from the New Testament; all my social abuses are shown as departures from its spirit." He goes on explicitly to link his Christmas Books with that Testament: "In every one of those books there is an express text preached on, and that text is always taken from the lips of Christ." Dickens's religious sensibility is of the broadest kind, in other words, and *The Life Of Our Lord* reflects the sentiment which he had inscribed upon a silver cup presented to the Unitarian minister, Mr Tagart, "For his labours in the cause of that religion which has sympathy for men of every creed and ventures to pass judgment on none". The little biography itself is artlessly and apparently spontaneously written. "I think you have seen a camel?" he asks at one point. "At all events they are brought over here, sometimes; and if you would like to see one, I will show you one." The text throughout is suffused with sentiments which are precisely of the kind Dickens introduced into his secular writing. "Never be proud or unkind, my dears, to any poor man, woman or child. If they are bad, think that they would have been better, if they had had kind friends and good homes, and had been better taught. So, always try to make them better by kind persuading words; and always try to teach them and relieve them if you can . . . And always pity them yourselves, and think as well of them as you can."

It can fairly be said, then, that the New Testament was at the core of Dickens's own religion. "I hold our Saviour," he once wrote, "to be the model of all goodness, and I assume that, in a Christian country where the New Testament is accessible to all men, all goodness must be referred back to its influence." He told his youngest son, on the eve of the latter's departure for Australia, that the New Testament was ". . . the best book that ever was or will be known in the world . . . I now most solemnly impress upon you the truth and beauty of the Christian religion, as it came from Christ Himself . . ." It is convenient to disparage Dickens's religious sense, of course, just as it is easy to forget how central religious debate was to the orthodox culture of the age. But, just as sermons, tracts and religious texts were the literary staple of the period, so Dickens's own religious beliefs are of crucial significance when we come to consider his relationship to his own time. Nevertheless it is a vexed question, this religious sense in Dickens, largely because most of his critics and biographers have been content to ignore it or to characterise it as some vague Pickwickian attitude of universal benevolence. There is a certain truth to that, since on many occasions Dickens seems to possess a religious sensibility without any specific religious beliefs; but it does not go far enough. It is clear what he did *not* like, for example. Catholicism remained a pet hate, as did the revival of Anglo-Catholicism in his own century; from his accounts, the adherents of the latter seem to be no more than amateur actors of the kind who haunted the penny gaffs of London. In his fiction he castigates Dissenters and especially Dissenting ministers; he was never very fond of Henry Burnett, his sister's Nonconformist husband, and no doubt Burnett's freeze-dried religion had something to do with that dislike. His childhood memory of being dragged to a chapel in order to hear a more than usually pompous sermon has often been used to suggest that Dickens's hatred of Dissenters was part of some childhood trauma; but this seems unlikely. There are a great many more interesting adult reasons why he should despise Nonconformity, chief among them being its dislike of both fiction and theatre. His anger was in any case often directed at those who placed themselves in a position somehow "superior" to his own; as he said of one Anglican clergyman in later life, "I cannot sit under a clergyman who addresses his congregation as though he had taken a return ticket to heaven and back . . ." But he also came in the end to be "disgusted" by the Established Church, and this primarily because of the internecine arguments which dominated religious debate in the middle decades of the century, a debate where authority was ranged against authority, text against text. He came to hold "in unspeakable dread and horror, those unseemly squabbles about the letter" while the same men of faith were doing nothing to alleviate the plight of the poor and the wretched who surrounded them and their churches. These controversies were largely concerned with the literal truth of the Bible, especially when such truth was being questioned by recent developments in geological science; Dickens himself took the sensible view that "nothing is discovered without God's intention and assistance", and he remained appalled by the concentration upon what he considered to be the minutiae of faith when God's own creatures were dying of disease and malnutrition in the slums of England.

That he had a more constructive religious sense is not really in doubt, however, and on many occasions he proclaimed his Christianity; ". . . in this world," he told one friend, ". . . there is no stay but the hope of a better, and no reliance but on the mercy and goodness of God . . ." His image of Jesus was of an orthodox New Testament variety, if touched by the somewhat sugary benevolence which Dickens sometimes lavished upon his "good" characters, a figure who ". . . never raised his benignant hand, save to bless and heal . . ." But he was in no sense pietistic and was for example very amused when a charity boy, taught to learn the Scriptures by rote (a practice Dickens also detested), came out with "Our Saviour was the only forgotten son of his father . . ." In practical terms it seems that Dickens said his own private prayers each morning and each night; and that he taught his children to do the same, giving them as their text, among other sentiments, "Make me kind to my nurses and servants and to all beggars and poor people and let me never be cruel to any dumb creature, for if I am cruel to anything, even to a poor little fly, you, who are so good, will never love me . . ."

The religion of hate or vengeance was not one in which he particularly believed, therefore, and his championship of the spirit over the letter of the faith is one indication of the rather relaxed attitude he took in doctrinal matters. Of course he believed what most of his contemporaries believed – his attachment to Unitarianism lasted only for three or four years, and was in fact related to his admiration for the Unitarian minister, Mr Tagart – and on the whole his religion could be said to encompass that of the broad Anglican Church. Certainly the Redemption and the Resurrection were articles of his faith (both themes, in secular guise, were also to appear in his fiction). He believed the New Testament to be of infinitely more importance and significance than the Old, and he discarded the concept of a wrathful and avenging God as firmly as he rejected the doctrine of original sin and the concept of eternal damnation. In fact he seems to have had very little concept of "sin" at all, his own interests being more obsessively centred around the secular concept of "crime" instead. His was a religion of natural love and moral feeling, therefore, and was in spirit not remarkably different from the rational "cult of sensibility" which was part of his eighteenth-century inheritance.

One could put the same point differently by saying that his was essentially a faith established upon practical philanthropy and conventional morality, the kind of generalised belief which was in tune with his temporary attachment to Unitarianism and which a later generation would suspect of being no more than wishful piety. It is perhaps interesting in this context that the grandson of a Unitarian minister, T. S. Eliot, would reject such laxity as little better than heresy and would in turn espouse a hard and dogmatic Christianity of his own. But Dickens was part of an earlier and in some way much freer period, the important fact really being that he remained a Christian all his life at a time when many of his contemporaries rejected that religion on intellectual grounds and became either sceptics or atheists. But not Charles Dickens. He remained faithful to the broad beliefs of the typical mid-nineteenth-century gentleman; in this, as in other matters, he was not afflicted by the doubts which exercised many of his contemporaries. In any case his attachment to his audience, and his belief in its reality as one extended family, would have effectively prohibited him from espousing non-Christian or anti-Christian precepts.

Of course his life and opinions are one thing, his art quite another. It is interesting to note that in his actual novels no character seems ever to be primarily impelled by Christian motives, and churches themselves tend to be portrayed as dusty places of empty forms and rituals. He usually mentions ministers only to parody or to attack them. And in fact this disparity, between his vigorous public expression of Christian sentiment and his almost total lack of interest in Christian institutions or Christian representatives, is close to the essence of the matter: he was a man of religious sensibility, but his beliefs were determined by his own vision of the world rather than by any inherited or specific creed. That is why the Christian faith becomes, for him, a larger and brighter version of the sentiments he promulgated in his Christmas Books; at no point does it seem that Dickens relied upon any religious "authority" other than his own will or temperament. In the last resort, he believed no one other than himself. His religion was in that sense part of his extraordinarily self-willed and self-created personality, and cannot be separated from it.

If this is the religious spirit which permeates *Dombey and Son*, as has often been suggested, it is not something deliberately introduced by Dickens but is rather part of the very act of creation. So much part of the writer that he did not choose to reveal it. It is simply revealed. That he was contriving the plot of the novel well in advance is not of course in doubt: he was at work upon his number plans, as we have seen, and the cover design which Hablot Browne completed on his instructions shows the main design of the novel. So, on the long evening walks at Lausanne, Dickens meditated on what he called the "general idea" or the "leading idea"; he was planning so far ahead that he already knew that his proposed removal to Paris in November would, with its "life and crowd", materially help him with a much later number. From his own notes it becomes clear, however, that he is looking forward in terms of story and character rather than of theme; despite the extraordinary amount of attention which has in the past been lavished upon Dickens's symbolic intent, from his own correspondence and working plans it is clear that he did not pay attention – at least any conscious attention – to matters which are conveniently paraphrased as "symbols" or "images" or "emblems". He was concerned with the story and with his characters, and with the complicated relationships which can spring up as both move forward. As he moved forward with them. Seeing nothing but them all around him in the evening air of Lausanne.

It was time to begin. Being a superstitious man he used his own variant of the *sortes Vergilianae*, and took a copy of Laurence Sterne's

Tristram Shandy from his shelf, opened it at random and, with his eyes closed, placed his finger somewhere upon the printed page; then he read, "What a work it is likely to turn out! Let us begin it!" And so he began, looking out over the lake, with a birth and death; the birth of Paul Dombey and the death of his mother, both caught up in the stern presence of Dombey Senior and the timorous gestures of little Florence Dombey. Here in miniature is the whole family saga in which lineage and commerce go together, a fatal union expressed in the title, *Dealings with the Firm of Dombey and Son. Wholesale, Retail, and for Exportation.* He was proud of the title, and wanted it to remain a secret until the last possible moment; he was nervous about the illustrations, too, and kept sending Browne a variety of often imperious instructions. But this was really only part of his general nervousness at the prospect of once more resuming his old relations with the public. The first number seems to have come relatively easily to him. He had planned well ahead, he knew where he was going, and his prose has a new measure of deliberation and restraint; despite the relatively clean state of his manuscript, with far fewer emendations than usual, it is almost as if he were actively working against his fluency, working to create more prolonged effects and to unite the narrative from its very opening. The novel is in part about the loss of natural affections within one family, and how without them nothing else can grow, and Dickens builds upon the achievement of his previous novel, *Martin Chuzzlewit*, by attempting something close to moral analysis. In these opening pages Dickens sets himself the task of creating a more elaborate interior life for his protagonists; a life which of course will be revealed in speech and in action but which is less theatrical, more measured and more powerful than anything in his previous fiction.

Two years had passed since the completion of his last novel. Now at last he was beginning again, and this new start released the full flood of Dickens's previously hampered creativity. His head was filled with ideas; ideas for other novels and for other stories, even as he worked upon this one. He conceived the plot of a man imprisoned for many years and then released (a notion which was eventually to emerge in *A Tale of Two Cities* more than ten years later). He soon thought of another "very ghostly and wild idea" which eventually turned into a Christmas Book. He had plans for a character who was slowly emerging in *Dombey and Son* as Walter Gay. He was also meditating upon the eventual demise of little Paul Dombey, as if he were trying to repeat the national success of Little Nell's death. This plethora of ideas seems also to have induced a general restlessness; even as he was writing the first number of the novel he was concerned about the approaching deadline for this year's Christmas Book. But, as soon as he had finished that first number, he went on an expedition with his family to Chamounix; amidst the glaciers of which he hoped to glimpse the outlines of the Christmas story which still perplexed and eluded him. On this journey he saw "waterfalls, avalanches, pyramids and towers of ice, torrents, bridges; mountain upon mountain until the very sky is blocked away . . ." He tumbled about the Mer de Glace, and was both fascinated and appalled by Mont Blanc, its cold white summit seeming to lure him forward. Always in landscape he sees the same vistas – the grand, the awful, the sublime as if his imagination, catching fire upon the narrative he was even then writing, could not bear to rest upon more homely things.

Then, at the beginning of August, he returned to his novel; to the second number of *Dombey and Son* in which there is an "Icy christening", according to his own number plans (how much the ice surrounding him entered his imagination!), as well as "Paul's Second deprivation" of his wet nurse. And the effect of the novel itself stayed with him. He describes meeting a rich man with a "monomania", in some ways like the Dombey he was creating, and even his remarks to Forster about English politics are now tinged with Dombey associations; he remembered the "fishy coldness" of Lord Grey, and his description of the failure of the government to help with the assisted emigration of the poor touches upon a theme he was even now exploring in his novel. "Not all the figures that Babbage's calculating machine could turn up in twenty generations," he said, "would stand in the long run against the general heart." Yet he could not keep his mind entirely on the novel when the shadows of his next Christmas Book were gathering around him so fast; the weather was oppressive; he was finding it difficult to work, and there were complications in the design of his narrative which forced him to transpose chapters. Everything meant that he was writing very slowly, although he ascribed that slowness to other causes as well, not least the number of social engagements to which he was bound within the English community of Lausanne.

But his main difficulty was this small Swiss town itself and the "absence of streets". He missed the thoroughfares of London; he missed the crowds which hurried through them. "I can't express how much I want these," he told Forster. "It seems as if they supplied something to my brain, which it cannot bear, when busy, to lose . . . a day in London sets me up again and starts me. But the toil and labour of writing, day after day, without that magic lantern, is IMMENSE!!" The crowds of London, in which he could lose himself and then find himself again. Gaslight. Mist. Mud. The pace of urban life. This world of change and dislocation through which Dickens could walk with the sudden sense of reprieve which liberates a man so in thrall to his work. The idea of purposiveness without purpose. The solitude in which, at one remove, he could re-enact his old childish feelings of homelessness and isolation. Seeing the poor and the mad and the unhappy. Restoring his vision of the world. Looking into the brightly-lit windows of the shops and the darker interiors of the houses. One of his daughters reported how he was "sometimes obliged to seek the noise and hurry of a town to enable him to struggle through some difficult part of a long story . . . a long walk in the noisy streets would act upon him as a tonic . . ." Of course like many of his contemporaries he was fascinated by crowds; the crowds who appear so memorably in Carlyle's *History of the French Revolution* and in Frith's naturalistic paintings, the crowds who attended choral societies or went on railway excursions, the crowds who emerge in Dickens's fiction as if by right, as if this were indeed the right time to celebrate urban energy at a moment when its possibilities were becoming evident. And, as he walked among these crowds, did Dickens feel for himself what he had once written in *The Old Curiosity Shop*: "In busy places, where each man has an object of his own, and feels assured that every other man has his, his character and purpose are written broadly in his face." Did Dickens look upon the faces of the crowds as he made his way through London, through all the streets and alleys, the rookeries and courts, which he missed now in this small and quiet town in Switzerland? For in London Dickens was ubiquitous; as one contemporary put it, ". . . the omnibus conductors knew him, the street boys knew him . . . he would turn up in the oddest places, and in the most inclement of weather". He was to be seen at "lodging houses, station-houses, cottages, hovels, Cheap Jacks' caravans, workhouses, prisons, barbers' shops, schoolrooms, chandlers' shops, back attics, areas, backyards, dark entries, public houses, rag-shops, police courts, markets . . ." This topographical list itself suggests the endless diversity of London, this city of small enclosed spaces, of darkness and light, of wealth and squalor. This was what Dickens missed in Lausanne.

He had not been able to finish the second number of *Dombey and Son* when once again he was forced to break off; he had rashly agreed to join an expedition to the Great St Bernard with his "ladies" and with a small group of expatriate English friends. It was a cold journey, and a rough one, but they climbed the mountain and made their way to the famous convent where travellers are welcomed. "Nothing of life or living interest in the picture, but the grey dull walls of the convent," Dickens wrote. "No vegetation of any sort or kind. Nothing growing, nothing stirring." The scene was later to be transposed by Dickens to *Little Dorrit*, where it is viewed as yet another kind of prison, but the ice, the absence of life, the deadness, also find their way into the portrait of Mr Dombey. The English party stayed one night in the place and then made their cold and cumbersome journey back to Lausanne. Where once again Dickens took up his novel, and where once again he worried about the Christmas Book which he had to start almost at once in order to meet the deadline for publication by the end of the year. Within a few days he had in fact been able to finish the second number of *Dombey and Son*, and, two days later, he began on the Christmas tale which he had already entitled *The Battle of Life*. He had hoped to finish it by the end of September; but he could not manage any such rapid composition. He found it extremely difficult to work on two books at once; any creative effort expended on *The Battle of Life* should have been reserved for *Dombey and Son*, or so he thought, and in any case *The Battle of Life* now seemed to him to contain too good a story to be thrown away as a seasonal offering. In his earlier years he had been quite confident of his powers to work on two novels at once – *The Pickwick Papers* and *Oliver Twist* were of course written contemporaneously – but now that particular elasticity of imagination appears to have deserted Dickens. In addition he had never *begun* two books at the same time, and the difficulty of keeping both in his head (as it were) seemed to disconcert and even to paralyse him. Towards the end of September he told Forster that "I fear there may be NO CHRISTMAS BOOK!" Never before had he abandoned a project already begun and he felt "sick, giddy, and capriciously despondent. I have bad nights; am full of disquietude and anxiety; and am constantly haunted by the idea that I am wasting the marrow of the larger book, and ought to be at rest." So he was worried about *Dombey and Son*, an anxiety redoubled in view of the fact that it was his first full-length novel for so long; he was worried about *The Battle of Life*, and the fact that he might have to sever the relationship he had established with his Christmas audience; he was worried about worrying; he needed rest and ease, but he could not get it. He had neuralgic pains across his brow, and thought that he might have to be "cupped" – that is, to have blood drawn from him. He was to say later that at this point he felt himself to be "in serious danger", by which he must have meant some kind of nervous collapse, but he rallied. He found streets, after all, streets in which he could grow more self-forgetful, for in pursuit of that urban "magic lantern" he had made the short journey to Geneva and restlessly walked the narrow and winding thoroughfares of that city.

Within three days he felt well enough to begin the second part of *The Battle of Life*. "If I don't do it," he had told Forster, "it will be the first time I ever abandoned anything I had once taken in hand; and I shall not have abandoned it until after a most desperate fight." So he carried on, working against the grain, using all his massive powers of will to urge himself forward, until by the time he left Geneva for Lausanne, two days later, he knew that he would be able to complete it after all. Six days on, and he had finished the second part; his eye, he said, was now "pretty bright!" Then, as a relaxation from his labours, he used that bright eye to transfix a small audience when he read to them the second number of *Dombey and Son* and provoked "the most prodigious and uproarious delight", the success of which venture led him to think aloud to Forster about the possibility of undertaking public readings in England. Once again we sense the need for crowds in what was a new (and, for Forster, bizarre) notion. Dickens was heartened, too, by the initial success of *Dombey and Son*; the first number had sold approximately 25,000 copies and he wanted to complete *The Battle of Life* as soon as possible in order to return to a novel for which he had great plans – plans enough to retain the interest and excitement of his readers. So he worked at the Christmas Book in a fury, finishing its third and final part within five days; as he did so, he dreamed that the book was "a series of chambers impossible to be got to rights or got out of . . ." Even the short (and remarkably well conducted) radical revolution in Geneva seemed to be aligned to it in his dreams, as if the battle of his title was being mocked or copied by the sparse and scattered battles near Lausanne.

On 17 September *The Battle of Life* was completed; he sent the manuscript to London and, through the agency of Forster, arranged for his usual friends to illustrate it for him. Not all of them shared his own enthusiasm, however, and Daniel Maclise in particular seems to have resented receiving Dickens's instructions through an intermediary. Maclise had not been happy with his treatment over his illustrations for *The Cricket on the Hearth* a year before – ". . . I would give anything that I had kept my original resolve and had nothing to do with the thing," he had told Forster – and now with *The Battle of Life* he informed Forster that "it is clear to me that Dickens does not care one damn whether I make a little sketch for the book or not . . . but I do that at your bidding, and not at all for Dickens, and on the whole would much prefer not engaging in the matter at all . . ." From the short but breezy letters which Dickens addressed to Maclise in the following year it would seem that no impediment existed between them; but this is clearly not the case. There are fewer letters, certainly, but Dickens was quite able to go on as if nothing had happened; even while close friends considered his behaviour cavalier, or selfish, or both. The Christmas Book itself was published in the middle of December, to less than glowing reviews. But nevertheless it sold well, and there were to be some seventeen dramatic adaptations of the little story; Dickens himself now always had the stage in mind when he wrote such books (it was after all an extension of his public persona) and he had agreed that the management of the Lyceum should have an early copy of the proof-sheets for one hundred pounds.

His Christmas story was done. Finished. And what of it now? Written with difficulty and in despondency, almost abandoned and then completed in a rush, it is not the most successful of Dickens's stories. And, with its theme of two sisters loving the same man, it has been considered too close to Dickens's own domestic situation to have that objectivity which his best work commands. Of course the theme of two loving sisters, their love devoted to the same male, is one that seems always to have attracted Dickens; but the real importance of the story is to be found in its title. *The Battle of Life* was a phrase which meant a great deal to mid-Victorian Englishmen: it was even something of a truism in a world for which struggle and domination were the twin commandments, where the worship of energy and the pursuit of power were the two single most important activities, where there was a constant belief in will, in collision, in progress. Darwin and Malthus both described "the great battle of life" and "the great battle for life", the significant confusion between the two phrases materially assisting the evolutionist's case; Gladstone was to talk of life as one "perpetual conflict"; Browning wrote, "I was ever a fighter, so – one fight more . . ."; and Samuel Smiles, that wonderful exponent of what we have now come to call Victorian values, noted that "all life is a struggle".

So the title of Dickens's Christmas Book was immediately recognisable to those who read it, and yet what does Dickens do with the narrative itself? He reverses the significance of the title. He turns it into a moral fable of cheerfulness, goodness and self-abnegation, a story in which a young woman willingly renounces love for the sake of her sister. He turns conventional mid-nineteenth-century values on their head, an apt harbinger of what he would achieve in later fictions. The only battles here are echoes from an ancient battlefield upon which much of the action takes place, a scene of ruin which brings back memories of Dickens's account of Italy. It is an odd book, no longer widely read, and one which even at the time drew mainly unfavourable comment. Dickens himself was not altogether pleased with it. "I was thoroughly wretched at having to use the idea for so short a story. I did not see its full capacity until it was too late to think of another Subject . . ." Instead he poured some of the sentiments which might have been reserved for this tale into subsequent passages of *Dombey and Son*; it is clear that its mood, of patience and resignation, was one that entered the larger work upon which he was engaged. It has often been remarked that from this time forward, in Dickens's novels, some of his wonderful improvisatory abilities are held in check; there is indeed a new and slower movement within his work now, but can it not also be seen as related to that other gentler, more resigned, sense of life which his work is beginning to evoke? And he was changing, too. His books were changing him. Dickens had projected various images of himself – in the elderly and rapacious Chuzzlewit, in the proud and cold Dombey, both of whom are almost miraculously restored to grace – and in that very act of transference his own being seems subtly to be rearranged. It is not that he becomes "like" his books or that his novels "reflect" his personality; rather that, in the symbiotic relationship between himself and his writing, he creates a new order, a new harmony, of which he is also a part. When he recreates the world, he recreates his own self.

Two days after he had completed the Christmas story he went back once again to Geneva; he had to start work on *Dombey and Son*, simply in order to maintain the monthly publication which had already begun, but he needed to rest first and for a week he managed to subdue his nature to a regimen of complete idleness. Nevertheless he knew where he wanted to go, and what he wanted to do, with the novel; immediately on his return to Lausanne, he began the third number and wrote of Paul Dombey, of Mrs Pipchin, of Captain Cuttle and of Major Bagstock who, when he meets the proud and cold Mr Dombey, begins his course of rubicund flattery: "'By G—, Sir,' said the Major, 'it's a great name. It's a name, Sir,' said the Major firmly, as if he defied Mr Dombey to contradict him, and would feel it his painful duty to bully him if he did, 'that is known and honoured in the British possessions abroad. It is a name, Sir, that a man is proud to recognise. There is nothing adulatory in Joseph Bagstock, Sir. His Royal Highness the Duke of York observed on more than one occasion, "there is no adulation in Joey. He is a plain old soldier is Joe. He is tough to a fault is Joseph:" but it's a great name, Sir. By the Lord, it's a great name!' said the Major, solemnly." One of the marvels of Dickens is the way that he can create a kind of speech which effortlessly evokes a character, a speech both unique and identifiable, a speech which he hears among all the others lodged in his imagination and which he can draw out at will. He had begun the number at the very end of October and completed it on 9 November; a rapid movement forward, but the manuscript contains so many heavy corrections that he was clearly telling the truth when he described himself in "agonies" over the last chapter. Then almost as soon as he had finished, according to prearranged plans, the Dickens family left for Paris. "I have no doubt," he wrote to Forster, "that constant change, too, is indispensable to me when I am at work . . ." This had not always been the case but, from this time, Dickens's general restlessness becomes a marked feature of his life. He had to move on. To take flight. To match his external surroundings against the great restlessness that he harboured within his own self.

Chapter 18

IT took three carriages to get the whole family to Paris, on a journey
which took them five days. It was impractical as well as expensive
for them all to stay in an hotel so, on the first day of their arrival,
Dickens looked for a suitable residence. And he quickly found one; a
small house in the Rue de Courcelles, an extravagantly shaped and
oddly furnished place which appealed to the more whimsical aspects
of his imagination. On the night of his arrival he also took a long walk
through the city "of which the brilliancy and brightness almost
frightened him", according to Forster; and yet he was really quite used
to brilliancy and brightness. They were in fact the two qualities most
often associated with his own presence in the world, and there is
no doubt that he took amazingly to the city on this second visit; he
was soon to think more highly of the French than of the English as
". . . the first people in the universe", and in later years Paris became
for him a place of refuge, a bolt-hole, when he grew tired of England
and of that less bright or brilliant London life. On this second visit
it was very cold. It snowed. And yet Dickens did not seem to
mind. According to his son Charley, he and his father visited a
"good many theatres to 'consolidate my French' as my grandfather
once expressed it", and in Paris Dickens by his own account
went ". . . wandering into Hospitals, Prisons, Dead-houses, Operas,
Theatres, Concert Rooms, Burial-grounds, Palaces, and Wine shops."
This was a whole "Panorama" of "gaudy and ghastly" sights, the
metaphor itself suggesting just how theatrical Dickens's vision of the
world could sometimes become, the painted or scenic representations of the Panorama being one of the chief entertainments of the
day.

In particular he enjoyed going alone to the Morgue, a typically
French institution where the unidentified bodies of those recently

found dead were put on display for the Parisian public at certain times of the day. In later years Dickens was to describe this spectacle in horrified terms – ". . . the ghastly beds, and the swollen saturated clothes hanging up, and the water dripping, dripping all day long, upon that other swollen saturated something in the corner, like a heap of crushed over-ripe figs . . ." Yet he kept on visiting it. He came back all the time, since the Morgue had infected him with a state which he liked to call "the attraction of repulsion". On later visits to Paris he confessed that "I am dragged by invisible force into the Morgue", and he recounted how on one occasion he became obsessed for some days with the image of a man found drowned (a man who was to resurface in *Our Mutual Friend*), an obsession which he himself connected with the fears of childhood. For is there not something of childhood terror and childhood curiosity in his morbid inspection of the dead? In his general fascination with the idea of death and of extinction? He loved fires, as we have seen, and he loved all accounts of murders or of murderers. Of course in this he was truly a man of his age, since the mid-Victorians seem always to relish the theme of death, to revel in public executions and even to turn such ceremonies into festivals. It was a way of dealing with the horror all around them and a way, too, of finding scapegoats or victims for a life which was getting progressively more difficult and darker but for which there seemed to be no responsible parties. But Dickens had an obsession which went beyond the conventional morbidity of his time. He once wrote that "in seasons of pestilence, some of us will have a secret attraction to the disease", and it is in this same sense that he seems always implicitly to sympathise with the act of killing. He liked to visit the scenes of murder and to dwell upon the events of the crime itself; he even had a pamphlet of murder, one of the "last confessions" which were commonly hawked about the streets at the time of an execution, which he had carefully marked and annotated. It has often been said, of course, that his "evil" characters – Murdstone, Carker, Heep – reflect elements of himself which he has felt it necessary to externalise. Certainly it is true that they exercise more fascination for him than the "good" characters who similarly abound in his fiction; as David Copperfield says of Uriah Heep who is sleeping in the room next to his own, ". . . I was attracted to him in very repulsion, and could not help wandering in and out every half-hour or so, and taking another look at him". It is this fascination, this "invisible force", that links Dickens so closely to the murders in his fiction. Of Tulkinghorn. Of Drood. In a very real sense the act of killing evokes for him a kind of poetry, a poetry of suffering, a poetry of violence. Bill Sikes's murder of Nancy which he repeated endlessly in his public readings, Jonas Chuzzlewit's murder of Montague Tigg, all the butcheries in *A Tale of Two Cities* and *Barnaby Rudge*, are part of this terrible threnody. Dickens was fascinated by death, too. Death. Decay. Tombstones. Graveyards. Whether they are the graveyards of London with their ruined iron gates and railings, untended, decaying with the already decayed, or whether they are the graveyards out on the marshes near Rochester, surrounded by low flat land. There were emblems of death everywhere for him; as he wrote in one of his later Christmas stories, ". . . the stopped life, the broken threads of yesterday, the deserted seat, the closed book, the unfinished but abandoned occupation, all are images of Death . . ." He hated to make farewells even to his closest friends; he detested ostentatious funerals precisely because they were in a sense merely triumphal chariots for Death; when he grew older he refused to believe that he had in any sense aged and forbade his grandchildren to call him "Grandfather". These also suggest the fear of death and, when they are associated with his nervous haste and his constant preoccupation with clock time, perhaps we see a man who deeply feared any sense of his own ending.

And so, in the year of Our Lord 1847, Charles Dickens visited and revisited the Paris Morgue, lingering there over the faces of the drowned. There were other intimations of death, too, in this period. He had an imaginary death to arrange with all due ceremony: "Paul, I shall slaughter at the end of number five," he wrote to Forster. And he had just heard that his sister, Fanny, "was in a consumption", then a generally fatal illness and one which showed all of its distressing symptoms in advance. There was even a connection between the imagined death and the real disease; Fanny's son, Henry Burnett, was a weak crippled child upon whom Dickens had actually based the character of the ailing Paul Dombey. At least this was how Fanny's pastor, a Reverend James Griffin of Manchester, told the story: "Harry was a singular child – meditative and quaint in a remarkable degree. He was the original, as Mr Dickens told his sister, of little 'Paul Dombey'. Harry had been taken to Brighton, as 'little Paul' is represented to have been and had there, for hours lying on the beach with his books, given utterance to thoughts quite as remarkable for a child . . ." Perhaps Harry, who had been born in 1839, had also suggested to his famous uncle the character of Tiny Tim in *A Christmas*

Carol; Tiny Tim did *not* die while Paul Dombey did, of course, and it seems surprising that Dickens should decide to "slaughter" a child based upon his own ailing nephew. Yet it was fiction. Only fiction. And in the coldest days of the year Dickens was planning the death of little Paul.

There was one interruption when, in the middle of December, he went back to London for a few days. As effective if not titular head of the Dickens family he came over to discover more about Fanny's mortal illness, but there were also pressing matters of his own; he wanted to supervise the dramatic version of *The Battle of Life*, correct the proofs for the number of *Dombey and Son* about to be published, and also to go over the details of the cheap edition of his novels which Bradbury and Evans were soon to issue. The image of the visit which Dickens gives in his correspondence is characteristically of one constant hurricane of activity, excitement, arduous labour and success; twenty-three thousand copies of *The Battle of Life* sold on the day of publication, terrific crying when he reads the book to the actors, huge success at the first night. "There was immense enthusiasm at its close, and great uproar and shouting for me." And then swiftly back to Paris where he began once more to contemplate the coming death of Paul Dombey. *Presently he told her that the motion of the boat upon the stream was lulling him to rest. How green the banks were now, how bright the flowers growing on them, and how tall the rushes!* New Year's Day was bitterly cold, and in a later description of this occasion Dickens emphasises only his own visit to the Théâtre des Gaîtés that cold evening; but really his mind is elsewhere. Paul Dombey must die. *Now the boat was out at sea, but gliding smoothly on. And now there was a shore before him. Who stood on the bank?* "Everything that is capable of being frozen," he writes of his house in the Rue de Courcelles, "freezes". He is working very slowly upon the novel. "I am slaughtering a young and innocent victim," he says with barely suppressed satisfaction. *He put his hands together, as he had been used to do at his prayers. He did not remove his arms to do it; but they saw him fold them so, behind her neck.* The story now had such a hold upon him that he was working upon it both night and day. *"Mamma is like you, Floy. I know her by the face! But tell them that the print upon the stairs at school is not divine enough. The light about the head is shining on me as I go!"* He killed Paul Dombey on Friday night. *The golden ripple on the wall came back again, and nothing else stirred in the room. The old, old fashion! The fashion that came in with our first garments, and will last unchanged until our race has run its course, and the wide firmament is rolled up like a scroll. The old, old fashion – Death!* Then he walked through the streets of Paris until dawn.

Thus did his story exert its mastery over him, sending him out into the bitter night to recover from the excitement and sorrow generated by his own hand. So it was, at this time, that he began to believe that "a book called Dombey . . . the only reality in life, and to mistake all the realities for short-lived shadows". Here the world is viewed as if it were a dream, but his own fiction partakes of a similar condition; it was at this time, too, that he first began to talk about his own novel-writing as "my month's dream" and "a dream of work". And how was the death of Paul Dombey received? It "flung a nation into mourning", according to one account. (And this is the question which Dickens is struggling to ask – what is real and what is feigned, and how is it we can weep at imagined events more piteously than at real ones?) Thackeray is supposed to have thrown that number upon the desk of Mark Lemon at *Punch* and to have cried, "There's no writing against such power as this . . . it is stupendous!"; and this at a time when *Vanity Fair* was beginning to appear in monthly numbers, a novel in which death is treated both more obliquely and more abruptly. With the death of Paul Dombey Dickens created the same sensation as he had with the death of Little Nell in *The Old Curiosity Shop*. He was to do it again, with the death of Dora in *David Copperfield* and with the death of the crossing sweeper, Jo, in *Bleak House*. There were some critics who felt that Dickens had, once again, gone too far in pathos. Others who believed that he killed off any interesting child within reach simply in order to maintain the allure of his narrative. There is some truth in this. Truth enough to provoke a parody of Paul Dombey's death in a satirical magazine, *The Man in the Moon*, where, during a fake inquest into the death of the Late Master Paul Dombey, Dickens himself is called as a witness – "Had once thought of making 'Son' the agent of retribution on 'Dombey'. Abandoned the notion. Did not see his way in working it out. Considered that he had a right to do what he liked with his own. Took things as they came. Did not know what a chapter or a page might bring forth. When he had no more use for a personage, or did not know what to do with it, killed him off at once. It was very pathetic and very convenient . . . If he was asked to name the disease of which Paul had expired, thought it was an attack of acute 'don't-know-what-to-do-with-him-phobia'. Had it not supervened, he would have suffered under, and probably succumbed, at last to a chronic affection, technically called 'being-in-the-way-ism'. These complaints were very prevalent in the literary world, and very fatal . . ." And yet the public loved it, loved the pathos, loved the deaths, and some years later there was still a popular song based upon Paul's demise and entitled "What are the Wild Waves Saying?"

Forster arrived in Paris for a long-anticipated visit the day after Dickens had walked the streets in mourning for his dead child, and at once the novelist recovered from his melancholy. We will see just how often in *Dombey and Son* he introduces the notion of the fairy-story and now, himself transformed like a character in just such a story, he was "borne again like an enchanted Rider" in his expeditions around Paris with his friend. Once more he was back in "prisons, palaces, theatres, the Morgue and the Lazare, as well as the Louvre, Versailles, St Cloud . . ." Forster later characterised this regimen of sight-seeing as one of "dreadful insatiability", and he sounds very much like Wilkie Collins who commented on Dickens's companionship at a later date: "A man who can do nothing by halves appears to me to be a fearful man." Then there were the theatres, a myriad theatres: the Français, the Conservatoire, the Odéon, the Variétés, the Gymnase, the Porte Saint-Martin, the Palais Royal, the Historique as well as the Cirque and the Opéra Comiqûe. Then they met all the lions of the city: Dumas, Sue, Gautier, Lamartine, Chateaubriand, Scribe and, most importantly, Victor Hugo. Dickens hardly mentions these men and says little enough about Hugo himself, confining himself to the remark that he "looks a Genius" and then goes on to describe the furnishings of his house "which looked like a chapter out of one of his own books". Thus did the great English novelist meet the great French writer whose work his own most closely resembles: Hugo, the great poet of the poor and the dispossessed, the great chronicler of the urban darkness. And what do we learn of him from Dickens? Nothing at all. There was a sense in which he *did not care* about other writers, except on those occasions when they were involved with his life or with his activities.

Two weeks with Forster, and then back again to *Dombey and Son* with his aim now of throwing all the interest after the death of Paul onto his sister, Florence. The story needed this shift of emphasis, for the death of the boy was only a prelude to a story in which the intrigue must grow and in which the collapse of Dombey has to be all the more powerfully conveyed. But again, after all the excitement of little Dombey's death, he was working slowly; he was feeling ill, it was snowing, and he could not seem to find his way forward. He turned down social invitations in order to remain at his desk – no book had caused him so much endless concentration and trouble – and at a late stage reversed the order of two chapters so that the pain of Paul's death in the previous number might be more pleasantly dissipated. But to his horror he found that this new first chapter was two pages too short, so on the following day he travelled to London in order to work near the printer. His son was already back at King's School in Wimbledon, and on this visit he remembers his father taking him for "a long tramp" around Hampstead Heath before they dined with Lady Blessington at Gore House; a dinner, incidentally, at which Charley sat next to Louis Napoleon. Dickens spent only three or four days in London and, on the day he left for Paris, Charley contracted scarlet fever. His father learnt of this the day after he had returned to the French capital and so, with that energy and address so customary to him, he returned at once to London with Catherine. They could not stay at Devonshire Terrace, which was still let to tenants, and instead they moved to Chester Place. This was just a street away from the Hogarths, where Charley was now lying during the worst stages of his illness; Catherine, being pregnant once more, was not allowed to go near her son and Dickens was also forced to remain at a distance until the contagious period had passed.

So he was altogether unsettled and troubled. Did he in some way blame himself for the illness of his son, so soon after he had killed his imaginary child in *Dombey and Son*? The curious fact is that, once again, even when he is anxiously uncertain about his son's health and pressed for time by an always exhausting monthly schedule, he is also at his funniest and most inventive; it was while staying at Chester Place that he takes Dombey on the shrieking, whirling train journey in which the passage of the locomotive is epitomised as "Death!" and then a few pages later introduces the grotesque Mrs Skewton. "I assure you, Mr Dombey, Nature intended me for an Arcadian. I am thrown away in society. Cows are my passion. What I have ever sighed for, has been to retreat to a Swiss farm, and live entirely surrounded by cows – and china . . . I want Nature everywhere. It would be so extremely charming." She is a wonderful creation, and Dickens enjoyed her company so much that he even begins to imitate her speech. During one of her prolonged ecstasies on Nature she declares that music has "so much heart in it – undeveloped recollections of a previous state of existence – and all that – which is so truly charming". Of course Dickens is here parodying Wordsworth and by implication the Romantic movement (of which he himself was the most important legatee) but, more interestingly, he repeats the same sentiments in a letter only a few days later in a slightly ironical manner: "All the Savage (I am sure in some former state of existence I was a slap-up Chief: a little Buffalo or a Great Bear or something of that sort) stirs within me, and impels me to go and look out for cottages on banks of Thameses." His characters were very real to their author, often appearing within his own sight, as it were, and there is reason to believe that, as he wrote, he took on something of the manner and the vocabulary of the individuals whom he was creating; that in ordinary life he might become Skewtonish after Mrs Skewton has arrived, and Dombeyish with Dombey.

And what of *Dombey and Son* itself? There were some who believed that the death of the child was its high point, and that all the passion and intrigue which followed were of a lower order of invention. Yet this is to underestimate the clear sense of construction which unites the otherwise disparate parts of the novel. No doubt fuelled by previous criticism of his inability to create a plausible and coherent narrative, animated by the clear need for a different kind of achievement after *Martin Chuzzlewit*, and inspired by the popular success of the Christmas Books which had taken up much of his power during the last three years, Dickens commands techniques of contrast and repetition in *Dombey and Son* which mark a development – as he had hoped and expected – away from his previous novels. He is almost too much with us in this novel; he seems to be doing all the work, determining the readers' reactions to events, suggesting the nature of the characters; he is very much the performer and stage manager here, aware of every possible trick to capture and maintain the attention of the audience. Those of a more puritan sensibility (and they exist even among the readers of novels) may even be embarrassed by the plenitude of the writing – as if, somehow, there were some innate virtue in the more obvious marks of pain or of labour. But one thing ought to be noticed in any account of Dickens's "progress" as a writer. It has become customary to talk of the development of thematic or symbolic coherence in his novels, as if there were some steady grade of ascent up which he climbed throughout his career. But this would to misinterpret the nature of his work; it could in fact be said that *Oliver Twist* or *The Old Curiosity Shop* have more symbolic or emblematic coherence than this novel. It is true that Forster in the *Examiner* was to describe and celebrate the "poetical expression" of *Dombey and Son*. "The recurrence of particular thoughts and phrases is an instance of the kind," he wrote, "running like the leading colour through a picture" – but this concept of repetition has very little to do with the mid-twentieth-century interest in symbolism as rampant and as ostentatiously visible as heraldic emblems. Those who look for symbolic wholeness or fullness will have to be content with the knowledge that these were not matters to which Dickens attended but rather the unlooked-for and often unnoticed residue of his conscious intentions.

Of course the work changes as much as Dickens changes over these years, just as it remains the same in precisely the way that Dickens remains the same; he said once that he was always aware of a basic identity within him which never altered, despite all the vicissitudes of fortune, and there is a similar basic identity which persists through all his novels. That is why certain theatrical elements survive in *Dombey and Son*. But what kind of theatricality is it that still enters Dickens's fiction? Or, rather, what is his attitude now to the devices and the mannerisms of the theatre which he knew so well and which he had in the past incorporated almost without revision into his own work? That there *is* a change is not in doubt – and it is best represented by the words of the bartered bride, Edith Dombey née Skewton, to her ghastly mother. "It is surely not worth while, Mama . . . to observe these forms of speech. We are quite alone. We know each other." When we *know* each other, we need only speak simply. In other words, exaggerated and theatrical speech, to which Mrs Skewton is addicted, is directly associated with the fact that most characters remain *unknown* to each other, and are continually forced to assert their identity through their speech. Just as in their appearance and gesture they signal their uniqueness all the more frantically within a culture where urban cohesion and the growth of "public opinion" was creating a much greater degree of conformity in both public and private spheres.

But these are the larger matters sailing like clouds over the pages of Dickens, their presence recognisable really only by the shadows they cast upon Dombey and Carker, Mrs Skewton and Major Bagstock. Dickens told Forster that *Dombey and Son* would concern itself with Pride, just as *Martin Chuzzlewit* had been concerned with Selfishness. Certainly it describes the ways in which pride and greed supplant natural affections, but it is a much more intensely conceived novel than its predecessor. It might even be called the first of Dickens's "moral novels", and this at least in part because it followed his work on the Christmas Books which had shown him the way to outline a moral narrative with no loss of power. To suggest the virtues of forgiveness and the possibility of redemption. To invoke the presence of grace. There are universal stirrings in *Dombey and Son* which had only been implicit in his previous novels but which have now been elicited, as it were, by his seasonal fables. Of course, he is quite ready still to parody the things which most closely touch him – as Mrs Skewton is allowed to say, ". . . there are so many provoking mysteries, really, that are hidden from us. Major, you to play!" Yet, even so, there *are* mysteries within the book. The sea. The waves. "All is going on as it was wont. The waves are hoarse with repetition of their mystery; the dust lies piled upon the shore; the sea-birds soar and hover; the winds and clouds go forth upon their trackless flight; the white arms beckon, in the moonlight, to the invisible country far away." Dust. Water. Birds in flight. Birds caged. The wind. Light. A country far away. These are some of the entries into Dickens's secret world, a larger world beyond each novel but one to which all of the later novels return. On the sea shore the absurd and somehow pathetic Mr Toots follows Florence at a distance, Mr Toots aware from the sound of the waves "of a time when he was sensible of being brighter and not addle-brained"; and the small dog, the dog which Charles Dickens had killed in the park now miraculously restored, wanders with Florence along the strand. This novel has a sense of the numinous, is more profoundly touched by the sense of last things, than any of Dickens's previous novels. It is larger in conception, so that human life is seen in terms of its beginning and its end, so that grief and forgiveness become more powerful forces within it. It is a much more satisfactory work of art than its predecessors, not because of its "symbols" or its "complexity", but rather because Dickens is aware of its status as art and provides here a simulacrum of human life touched by majesty and purpose.

In no way demeaning or anticlimactic, then, to note the presence of the fairy-tale within it. The folk art of a century yearning towards transcendence. The harbour of lost wishes and dreams. The home of the illimitable. Coincidentally it was precisely in this period that Dickens first met Hans Christian Andersen; as a distinguished foreigner he was to be found in Lady Blessington's drawing room and at their first encounter, according to Andersen, "We pressed one another by the hand, gazed in one another's eyes, spoke together, and understood one another . . . My eyes filled with tears . . ." This gives an indication of Andersen's somewhat lachrymose temperament; whether they "understood one another" is debatable, however, unless it were on matters about which Dickens, at least, would not have been readily able to speak. Was he in any case wholly aware of the fairy-story in the novel he was even then writing? From the horrible old woman who captures little Florence Dombey, so much like the ancient crone whose image in the *Tales of the Genii* he had once feared, to the Dombey house where Florence is far more solitary than in any "magic dwelling-place in magic story, shut up in the heart of a thick wood", but where she blooms "like the king's fair daughter in the story"; to the scene where Florence and Captain Cuttle are said to represent "a wandering princess and a good monster in a story-book . . ." In fact the presence of the young girl seems to elicit most of the fairy-story elements in the novel, as if the plight of the neglected child recalled to Dickens all the associations of his own childhood. It was in this novel, too, that Dickens decided to take on the infant consciousness of Paul Dombey or, as he put in his memorandum to himself, "His illness only expressed in the child's own feelings – Not otherwise described". In unlocking the consciousness of the child, he also unlocked in his own consciousness the stories and fables of childhood.

He was to say in one of his essays that "in an utilitarian age, of all other times, it is a matter of grave importance that Fairy tales should be respected . . ." For it is in their "simplicity, and purity, and innocent extravagance . . ." (what a marvellous description of Dickens's own fiction at its best) that they teach, "Forbearance, courtesy, consideration for the poor and aged, kind treatment of animals . . ." Fairy-tales contain for him religious associations, then, and it is not at all clear where Dickens's adult religion begins and his childhood love of the marvellous ends. They seem to be part of that same condition of awareness, first glimpsed in infancy but which can be retrieved by the adult; for in the fairy-story we enter the realm of the mysterious and the wonderful, the magical and the fantastic, where the world becomes a place for those "old romantic stories" of which all people have some recollection. Sometimes this association is used as part of a deliberate strategy on Dickens's part. In some of his speeches, particularly, he invokes the elements of fairy-stories in order to forge a common link with his audience that no contemporary event or allusion could have achieved. But it is also an instinctive part of his being, this entry into a magical world, this departure from the real one. There were to be times of sadness and anxiety in his life when it was ". . . as if I had walked (I wish to God I had) out of a fairy tale!" and when "I wish I had been born in the days of Ogres and Dragon-guarded castles . . ." In such a world he might become the bold bright champion, in which guise he often pictured himself; he wanted to stay inside the fairy-story just as he wanted to stay inside the play, to forsake the dreary shades of the real world for the fierce colours of the stage or story. It was in this secondary world that his feelings had all the power and the unity which they possessed in his imagination, where the complicated recesses of the heart were brought out in solid colour and with solid outline. But Dickens understood the need to enter that world only temporarily, and in his necessary departure from it we may see some of the sources of his own melancholy – and see, too, the springs of his quick, voracious, energy. The energy of his attempts to redeem the diurnal world. To make it brighter; to keep on moving; to keep on writing.

To keep on being busily employed. His concern over his son's scarlet fever made it imperative to stay in London with Catherine, who was now heavily pregnant, and so he rented the temporary accommodation in Chester Place until the end of June. It was here, in the small street off Regent's Park and only a short distance from the Polygon as well as other haunts of Dickens's childhood, that Sydney Smith Haldimand Dickens was born. The seventh child. But, if even by nineteenth-century standards this was now a large household, there are clear signs that Dickens's financial anxieties, at least, were coming to an end. *Dombey and Son* itself was selling very well, and from the first four numbers alone he received something like fifteen hundred pounds from Bradbury and Evans; in fact, from the sales of all his books during the last six months of the previous year, he earned altogether more than three thousand pounds. He was also banking on (almost literally) the imminent publication of a new and inexpensive edition of his novels; this was known as "working the copyrights", and the plan was to issue all of Dickens's previous novels in cheap weekly and monthly formats. In order to emphasise the novelty of the venture new illustrations were to be used, and Dickens himself decided to write original prefaces for each of his works. He dedicated this new series somewhat grandiosely to "the English people", and in a preliminary advertisement he touched upon all those issues which remained most important to him; he wished his work to become "easily accessible as a possession by all classes of society . . .", and in addition he was happy to become "a permanent inmate of many English homes where, in his old shape, he was only known as a guest . . ." Of course there was also his belief that ". . . the living Author may enjoy the pride and honour of their widest diffusion, and may couple it with increased personal emolument . . ." This last phrase, so redolent of his father in more loquacious moments, represented something of great importance to Dickens; he expected to make a great deal of money out of this venture and, although the receipts for the first year were not altogether satisfactory, within a short time he was earning a relatively large income from what was known as the Cheap Edition. In a sense he was merely keeping up with his time, since the ever-cheaper methods of printing and the ever-widening audience of literate readers meant that novels of his kind could be diffused far more widely than had been the case even ten years before. Certainly he was now one of the highest-paid authors of his day, and it was in these summer months of 1847 that he bought six hundred pounds worth of Consols, the first of many investments he made from this time forward.

And then he was attacked by a horse. A silly accident, perhaps, but one that seemed severely to shake Dickens. He had been working very hard on the eighth instalment of *Dombey and Son* and, in pursuit of physical activity at a time of mental exhaustion, he had gone down to Chertsey for some riding. It was here that a horse in the stable attacked Dickens's arm and shoulder; his coat sleeve and shirt sleeve were torn off and the horse had come close to actually ripping the great muscle of his arm; luckily, as it turned out, it was merely heavily bruised. But something about this incident unnerved Dickens, for he became very ill; not only with the bad bruising upon his arm but also with something which he described as "a nervous seizure in the throat". He felt much more unwell than he told anyone at the time – the remedy seems to have been the sniffing of pungent salts and the taking of wormwood – and admitted only to "a low dull nervousness of a most distressing kind". It is impossible to know precisely what he meant. The nervous prostration may have had entirely physical origins but it is also possible that he had an underlying fear of being attacked, and that even the sudden violence of an animal provoked those fears. In addition he told his sister, dying of consumption, that at times of great anxiety or exhaustion he was sometimes gripped by "dreadful" ideas and oppressive mental "sufferings". The "nervous seizure in the throat" may be another clue to his suffering; a few years later, when he was again affected by nervous exhaustion, he would sometimes wake up in the night with the sensation of choking. A man of immense nervous and imaginative susceptibility could become just such a prey to various horrors. Hence the distress which he experienced now; and, when Landor saw him in the month of the accident, he wrote that he seemed "thin and poorly". Certainly he felt "poorly" enough to travel down to Brighton for peace and sea air; he found lodgings there and worked on the next number of *Dombey and Son*, the novel in which he made imaginative use of his accident some time later when Mr Dombey himself is thrown from his horse and is kicked insensible.

For nothing in his life was so strong as his desire to keep on working, to keep on with business and busy-ness. Even while in Lausanne and Paris he had been contemplating the scheme which he had concocted with Miss Burdett-Coutts, for the building of a "Home" for "fallen women", and within a month of his return to England he was consulting with prison governors about possible candidates for benevolence while looking in the suburbs of London for a suitable house. By May he had found one, in Shepherds Bush, and at once made an offer for the lease. Yet while he was doing that, and while he was writing the central sections of *Dombey and Son*, he plunged himself ("plunged" being one of his own favourite words) into yet more amateur theatricals. The first occasion two years before had been for strictly private reasons, a kind of outburst of high spirits and conviviality, but now Dickens was intent upon adopting the same course for more public ends: Leigh Hunt, as always, was in financial difficulties and the man whom Dickens was later cruelly to parody in *Bleak House* was now the object of Dickens's charitable endeavours. It was decided, or rather Dickens decided, that amateur theatricals would raise enough money to give Hunt a considerable lump sum. A meeting at John Forster's chambers in Lincoln's Inn Fields set the seal upon the idea, and much the same cast of amateur players who had performed in the autumn of 1845 was now dragooned into perform- ances at London, Manchester and Liverpool. The members of his family were asked once more to enter the maelstrom, and Catherine (perhaps in order to help dispel her usual depression after giving birth) was writing out circular letters on various theatrical matters. All of this activity meant that Dickens was leaving his novel to the last minute, not beginning work until the middle of the month and finishing some ten days later, thus leaving just a few days for the setting and correcting of type. Clearly he felt confident enough of the narrative to work on it in this fashion; he was quite sure both of what he wanted to do and the speed with which he could do it. Nevertheless there are signs in these sections of undue haste: in point of invention, and even seriousness, the chapters are some of the weakest in the novel.

After a cold winter, the summer. The Dickens family moved down to Broadstairs, as had now become the custom when they were in England. Dickens came up to London during this period, and stayed at the Victoria Hotel while attending rehearsals of his amateur cast; they had been going to play *The Merry Wives of Windsor*, but the extra work involved was too great and it was agreed that they should perform once more Ben Jonson's *Every Man in His Humour*. So Dickens worked on *Dombey and Son* during the day at Broadstairs, then travelled up to London and rehearsed once more at Miss Kelly's theatre in the evening – rehearsals which were not pre-empted by the sudden news that Leigh Hunt was about to receive a state pension. Dickens cancelled the London performance but so enthusiastic was he about the general idea of his "Amateurs" that he simply changed the object of his benevolence to John Poole, a poor broken-down writer of quondam dramatic "hits" such as *Paul Pry* and one of that large number of nineteenth-century writers who remained almost at the level of destitution while being compelled to engage in "hack work" for the small theatres or for minor periodicals. So the cast went up to Manchester at the end of July, for two nights, and then moved on for one night's performance to Liverpool. At Manchester the farce went very well and, according to Dickens, "the people laughed so, at it . . . that it was impossible to keep a grave face, and all but impossible to go on . . . The people were dropping over the fronts of the boxes like fruit." Another wonderful Dickensian simile there, and no doubt his account is true enough; at least it is corroborated by the accounts of the local press. Of the performance in Liverpool, the *Liverpool Mercury* declared that "never was greater enthusiasm evinced by any audience". But Dickens was by now exhausted; he had been dancing at an evening party for much of the night, had been busy in the Manchester theatre for most of the next day and by the time he arrived in Liverpool was so worried about his voice that he used an old stage recipe. He put a mustard poultice on his throat and swallowed a bushel of anchovies. In fact Dickens was very much the "star" of the occasion and when he appeared in person to address the audience at one of the two nights in

Manchester he was granted ". . . enthusiastic applause . . . which lasted, not seconds, but minutes". But they were all there with him: Mark Lemon, Dudley Costello, John Forster, George Cruikshank, Frank Stone, Douglas Jerrold, John Leech, and two of Dickens's younger brothers. It is characteristic of him, however, that in his letters he often addresses these friends by their stage names, rather than their real ones, just as he calls himself by the names of the variety of characters he assumed. This instinctive wish to dramatise, and thus to control, is also evident in a short narrative which he now wrote about his cast, under the assumed character of Mrs Gamp – a little effusion which, being in somewhat poor taste on the subject of child birth (Leech's wife experienced labour pains on the train coming back from Liverpool and had had a baby almost immediately on their arrival in London), was never published in Dickens's lifetime. That he did make jokes in sometimes questionable taste is not in doubt – it was part of his almost overbearing gaiety that he should do so – but it should not be forgotten that even on occasions such as this he could also muster a proper sense of tact and occasion.

That is why he is reluctant to discuss his theatrical affairs in his long and frequent letters to Miss Burdett-Coutts in this period, no doubt because he wished to appear in her eyes the serious custodian of her philanthropic interests. Certainly his relations with her had been growing in strength, although there is some evidence to suggest that there was a slight cooling of that friendship in the early months of the year, at the time when she was actively pursuing the hand of the Duke of Wellington; it was not perhaps an entirely unsuitable match, since she was the richest woman in the kingdom, but it was one that the elderly Duke felt bound gently to reject. Miss Burdett-Coutts herself remains something of an enigma; her wealth rendered her to a certain extent isolated from her contemporaries, but she seems also to have been a reserved and somewhat hesitant person. Her wish to marry the Duke of Wellington, and her implicit reliance upon Dickens's judgment, suggests that she needed the guidance and support of a stronger or older person. From the evidence of her later activities without the assistance of Dickens, in fact, it is clear that by herself she was not a particularly good manager of her money.

In this period, however, Dickens was willing to organise practically everything on her behalf, and it is noteworthy that throughout their dealings with each other he treated her on terms of absolute equality. Noteworthy, because unusual, in his relations with women; he generally tended to idealise them or to exaggerate their frailties so that they turned into characters from one of his unwritten novels. But he saw Miss Burdett-Coutts clearly, never condescended to her, and always told her the direct truth. Certainly he was working extremely hard on the scheme for the "Home" located in Shepherds Bush and, once Urania Cottage had been leased, Dickens busied himself about its general arrangements. Nothing was too small to deflect his attention, and in a series of letters to Miss Burdett-Coutts he displays his immense zeal and energy in such things as the appointment of matrons and of a chaplain, in the furnishing of the house itself, in the colour and cut of the girls' clothes (he even shopped for them himself), in the daily routine and administration of the Home, in the contents of the girls' reading, in their playing of music, in the disciplinary code, in the arrangements for washing, in domestic duties, in the drainage of the land around Urania Cottage, and in the writing of an appeal to them in which he declared that ". . . do not think that I write to you as if I felt myself very much above you, or wished to hurt your feelings by reminding you of the situation in which you are placed. GOD forbid! I mean nothing but kindness to you, and I write as if you were my sister."

There is no reason at all to doubt this, since Dickens's philanthropy was as comprehensive as his charity was instinctive. If there is philosophy here, it is of the most practical kind; this is clear in his exhortation to a contemporary to ". . . action, usefulness – and the determination to be of service . . . The world is not a dream, but a reality, of which we are the chief part . . ." There could be no better description of the nineteenth-century spirit of charity than this, and Dickens's own practice copiously exemplifies it. It has been calculated, from his bank statements, that he gave grants to thirteen separate hospitals and made forty-three donations to benevolent funds. His charity to individuals seems also to have been extensive. Indeed he was well known among begging-letter writers for being a "soft touch", and there are occasions in his correspondence when that benevolence becomes apparent. "I have thought a great deal about that woman, the Wardswoman in the Itch Ward, who was crying about the dead child. If anything useful can be done for her, I should like to do it." He had read an article in the *Daily Post*, entitled "Poverty at Home", and privately sent five guineas to its writer – to be distributed among the poor families he had described. And then again: "I should like to brighten Somebody's Christmas with a couple of Guineas or so." All the indications are that his response to pathetic descriptions was immediate and sorrowful, and that spontaneously he would give away his money to those whose lives made him weep. But even his replies to begging-letters were valuable, and the more enterprising of that trade knew that they could always get one shilling for Charles Dickens's signature from Mr Waller, the autograph dealer in Fleet Street.

There are other stories, too, of Dickens's charity. There was the case of the crippled boy who attended a costermongers' school in Saffron Hill; Dickens asked to see him but the boy, too frightened of the grand house in Devonshire Terrace, simply sat down in front of the door until a servant found him. Dickens gave him half-a-crown and also found him employment at his publisher's. "Oh sir," the boy said to his master later, "he did put me through a catechism – he asked me everything . . ." And here we see, too, the curiosity of the novelist as well as the charity of the private man. He wanted to know everything; to see, to hear, to understand. He took a small impoverished girl into service. He paid for a shoe-black boy to be taken into a ragged school and then assisted to a new life in Australia. There is the story of his calling to a poor woman and baby while he sat in an inn, and offering her brandy – "drink that up," he said – before giving her a shilling to help her on her way. Apart from giving money spontaneously to the distressed, in later years he was well known for helping the parish charities of Higham in Kent. Of course this was the message of the prayer which he had taught his children, always to be kind to the afflicted, even though he also expressed the more rigorous precept that help should most readily be given to those who help themselves.

Yet it was an essential benevolence which was evinced, for example, in his personal relations with his servants. He seems to have been in some ways more tolerant of them than he was of his own family, which is perhaps not surprising in a man whose paternal grandparents were "in service" and who understood only too well the humiliation of being in a lowly position. Had he not, too, once been in a similar condition? Thus, when a servant mismanaged a "dumb waiter", he rushed over and exclaimed, "Never mind the breakage. Is your arm hurt?" But these are necessarily stray incidents and stray records; it is evident from his letters that he did not care to talk about, or publicise, his charitable exploits. In fact the reminiscences of friends and colleagues are of more help in demonstrating the trouble to which he went in order to cheer up – or "brighten", to use one of his favourite verbs – the unhappy or the depressed. With the sick in particular he seems to have been singularly kind and tactful. He possessed, according to one who saw it, a "curious life-giving power" so that his surplus energy, radiating through his brightness and optimism, seemed actually to help the curative process of those whom he visited; a curious phenomenon but one that was also widely perceived of a later Victorian figure, Oscar Wilde. At its most practical it represents the kind of self-confidence and cheerful optimism which actually act as a tonic upon those blessed with less of those attributes. At its most mysterious it represents . . . what? The transference of human energy by touch or look? And there is a description, too, of his behaviour when a friend badly injured his hand. "Before the arrival of the medical man, Dickens took charge of the patient himself, doing everything that was necessary – bathing the injured part with vinegar, binding it up and performing to perfection . . . He even appeared on the scene at midnight, provided with medicines and liniments ordered by the doctor . . ." This all the more remarkable in a man who always tried by an effort of will to dispel any sickness from which he suffered, to *work* through it, and who in his fiction is often alarmingly sharp about permanent invalids whose condition he generally castigates as self-inflicted.

And so it was that he planned with Miss Burdett-Coutts the Home For Fallen Women with all the fervour of his philanthropy. Now that he had found the right house on the Acton Road in Shepherds Bush, he visited the prisons in order to find likely candidates for its shelter; he was on terms of close friendship with the governors of Cold Bath Fields prison and the Westminster House of Correction, as we have seen, and it was primarily to these institutions that Dickens went in search of what might be called the right material. "I have taken some pains," he told Miss Burdett-Coutts, "to find out the dispositions and natures of every individual we take; and I think I know them pretty well . . . A most extraordinary and mysterious study it is, but interesting and touching in the extreme." That last remark suggests again how much of the novelist went into the philanthropist, how closely he observed and studied the mysteries of these young women whose lives he described as "hazardous and forbidden". To Miss Burdett-Coutts he described the circumstances of their "fall" and would volunteer physical descriptions which might have come from the pages of his fiction; ". . . she had a singularly bad head, and looked discouragingly secret and moody." As soon as Urania Cottage was formally opened (in the November of this year) he began to attend meetings there regularly and to oversee the major part of its routine. Even here he was in a sense still the novelist, still keeping in touch with the poor, still attending to their habits and their ways of speech, still keen to penetrate their mystery. "My anxiety to know that secret reason of Sarah's," he wrote about one of the girls, "is so intense that I will call on Monday between one and two . . ." When he was not able to discover all that he wanted, he readily used his powers as a novelist imaginatively to reconstruct events and details. Perhaps his own sense of "power" here is the most appropriate. It is in fact also the word that Dickens used when, in the course of an argument that the girls should always emigrate together, he added that "it would be a beautiful thing, and would give us a wonderful power over them, if they would form strong attachments among themselves . . ." This sounds very much like one of the situations he idealised in his fiction; the idea of young women forming strong attachments with each other was at the centre of his last Christmas Book and plays some role in the development of *Dombey and Son.* In this context it might be noted how Dickens believed that these girls with "wretched histories" might be improved by a course of "education and example" and thus be led to a happier fate; there should be "variety in their daily lives" but "rigid order" introduced into their habits so that they might all become an "innocently cheerful Family". They were, also, to be implicitly guided by rules but would never be informed of them. But is this not precisely what happens to the characters in his fiction, characters who are guided by forces which they do not understand and who proceed through tribulation to a generally happier fate, and does it not give extra point to his suggestion that each inmate should have a "book" of her life at Urania Cottage with a final page entitled "Subsequent History"?

But of course art and life were not necessarily confused in the process. All we can say is that Dickens adopted the same set of attitudes in life as he did in fiction, and that these attitudes were literally his way of structuring and interpreting the world. His need for order, for system, remained constant. How he dealt with that world in language, however, is quite different from the way in which he mastered it through daily activity. In his fiction he presented highly sentimentalised and conventional stereotypes of women who were "fallen" or were in some other sense connected with crime – the most famous example being the fate of Nancy in *Oliver Twist* – whereas in his actual life he was severely practical in all aspects of the administration of Urania Cottage. "Rise at 6 : Morning prayers and scripture reading 7.45 : Breakfast : Dinner at 1 : Tea at 6 : Evening prayers 8.30 : Bed at 9. School at 10.30 for 2 hours. Bath once a week . . ." This bears the imprint of Dickens's personality, with its extraordinary capacity for organisation and administration, in just the same manner as the mark system which he arranged under the heads of "Truthfulness, Industry, Temper, Propriety of Conduct and Conversation, Temperance, Order, Punctuality, Economy, Cleanliness". The motto of the place, according to Dickens, was "Don't talk about it – do it!" Yet of all offenders (apart of course from juveniles) Dickens sympathised most readily with prostitutes. He is reported to have said that "he was sure God looked leniently on all vice that proceeded from human tenderness and natural passion" and, during an after-dinner conversation with Emerson, he remarked that "if his own son were particularly chaste, he should be alarmed on his account, as if he could not be in good health". Sympathy combined with discipline; pity with control. Thus did the great novelist define the moral order of the world.

And after the exertions of Urania Cottage, after the exhaustion of the short dramatic tours to Manchester and Liverpool, Dickens went back to Broadstairs and to his family. Hans Christian Andersen, so recently met, came to visit him here and described the ". . . narrow little house, but pretty and neat . . . The windows facing the Channel, the open sea rolling in almost underneath them; while we were eating the tide went down, the water ebbed at amazing speed, the great sandbanks . . . rose mightily up, the lighthouse was illuminated." And so the little town of Broadstairs was in turn illuminated by the imagination of the world's greatest writer of fairy-stories. Unfortunately his English was not as good as his imagination, and during this and subsequent meetings there seems to have been a large degree of misunderstanding and general social difficulty. But there were differences of other kinds, too; as so often with authors, their conversation turned to the question of payment and Dickens seemed quite unable to believe the low royalties which Andersen received. "Oh," he said, in that echo of his speech which so vividly brings him to life, "oh, but we must be misunderstanding one another." The morning after Andersen's arrival Dickens walked with him the two and a half miles to Ramsgate in order that his guest might catch the steam-boat to Copenhagen; Andersen's last sight of England was of Dickens, "in a green Scotch dress and gaily coloured shirt", standing on the quay as the boat slipped over the water.

Two and a half miles was of course no distance at all to Dickens (the "Scotch dress", by the way, is less likely to be a kilt than a pair of fashionable plaid trousers) for, in this first full year he was spending in England for some time, he was filled with restlessness and energy; what he described as his "superfluous steam". And there were many ways of distributing it. He had a sudden idea of editing a standard series of great British novelists, but dropped the plan almost as quickly as he had picked it up. Then, while he was writing *Dombey and Son*, he began to make preparations for the next Christmas Book, even though his experience in the previous year had shown him how difficult it now was for him to work on two fictions concurrently. But again he changed his mind and postponed his next Christmas Book for a year, despite the fact that he was "loath to lose the money" and more importantly to leave "any gap at Christmas firesides". So there was "superfluous steam" left, and he promptly expelled it in a new scheme he had conceived; a scheme for a mutual insurance fund for writers and artists. It was to be called The Provident Union of Literature, Science and Art, and the funds for it were to be raised by a series of amateur theatricals every year. Thus did Dickens hope to combine business with pleasure, and to turn his always much-anticipated and much-longed for theatricals into a *system*; just as he turned the routine of Urania Cottage into a *system*; just as he organised his responses to begging-letter writers into a *system*.

Even as he planned the Provident Union, he was coming to the climax of *Dombey and Son*. Edith Dombey flies from the Dombey household and elopes with Carker. (At the urging of Forster and ever mindful of public taste, he decided that she would not commit adultery; but, in any case, sex rarely enters his novels except in the shape of grotesque lust. For the simple reason that sex renders people all alike, while the whole momentum of Dickens's fiction is towards uniqueness and peculiarity.) Dombey in his furious anger strikes his daughter, Florence, who runs from the house. Dombey pursues his wife and Carker. The chapter concerned with Edith Dombey's elopement was written by Dickens in a furious passion, but even as he wrote so rapidly he included passages which touched upon his other concerns of the moment. For here also was a plea for the outcast – ". . . some ghastly child, with stunted form and wicked face . . ." – in the very week when Urania Cottage was opened. And he was writing here too about "the polluted air, foul with every impurity that is poisonous to health and life" just a few days after he had read a report in *The Times* about the possibility of yet another cholera epidemic in the poorer parts of London. This fear of epidemic disease was also to be evoked in *Bleak House*, a later novel but one which even now was beginning to enter the capacious imagination of Charles Dickens. For he read this most vivid number of *Dombey and Son* to the Watsons in Rockingham Castle, the very place which became the model for the dank Chesney Wold in that same *Bleak House*. So does the reading aloud of one novel seem to plant the seeds for another; so does time return and revolve so that we see the beginning of one novel in the end of another; so do the permanent imaginative concerns of Dickens become imbued with the topics and alarms of the day. He was already looking forward to the climax of *Dombey and Son* as he left Rockingham Castle. As he travelled up by train to Scotland with Catherine, he was thinking of the train which would destroy Carker; the train which plunges upon him and turns him into blood and "mutilated fragments"; Dickens thinking of all this, not knowing that in eighteen years time he would experience a greater railway disaster; all of us thinking of Dickens as we read this, and realising how great a distance separates his world from our own when we learn that the speed of an express train was then twenty-six miles per hour.

He had gone with Catherine to Scotland, the scene of his first public triumph, in order to attend a soirée for the Glasgow Athenaeum. They travelled to Edinburgh, and then from Edinburgh to Glasgow; but on this later ride Catherine was suddenly taken ill and suffered a miscarriage on the train. She was put to bed and was compelled to remain there as her husband experienced "unbounded hospitality and enthoozymoozy". He goes on, ". . . I have never been more heartily received anywhere, or enjoyed myself more completely." Even though his wife was forced to remain in bed after her miscarriage. Is there not in the contrast between these two scenes of domestic life some warning for the future? They returned to London on the third day of the new year, 1848, a date which began the succession of what in his biography Forster called Dickens's "happiest years". And why should he not be happy? He was now wealthy enough no longer to need to worry about money, he was very famous and very well loved. The enthusiasm at Glasgow had been enormous and, just a month before, when he had walked onto the platform of a meeting for the Leeds Mechanics' Institute, "the whole audience rose, and the applause became almost deafening . . ."; it was several minutes before silence could be restored. He was on the same platform as George Stephenson, the great founder of the railways, but it was he, Charles Dickens, who was singled out for that "prolonged and deafening" applause. 1848. A year of revolutions, too, which inspired and animated Dickens; the revolt of the Italians against their Austrian rulers; the revolt of the Hungarians; the abdication of Louis-Philippe and the inauguration of the Second French Republic. No matter that he had not detected any signs of these rebellions when he had travelled through France and Italy. He was on the side of revolt. He might have been reliving the crowd scenes in *Barnaby Rudge*, and now he declared himself to be "CITOYEN CHARLES DICKENS".

But if this year marked a certain happiness and excitement in Dickens's life, now more than ever firmly planted in public affection and respect, it also inaugurated a period during which his actual pre-eminence as a novelist was first seriously called into question. It has to be remembered that in 1847 had appeared *Jane Eyre*, *Wuthering Heights* and of course *Vanity Fair*, all of which novels were recognised as great or at least as significant works. It had been in this year, too, that Dickens entered a more private relationship with William Makepeace Thackeray. His position among his friends of *primus inter pares* meant that he was sometimes called upon to resolve disputes or give assistance in various domestic or financial crises, so it is not surprising that he should have been asked to intervene in a quarrel between Thackeray and John Forster. The details are no longer particularly interesting. Forster told a mutual acquaintance that Thackeray was as "false as hell", the remark was repeated to Thackeray who then "cut" Forster in public. In fact through the agency of Dickens the dispute was quickly resolved, and it is significant now only for the ambiguous position of Thackeray with regard to Dickens and Dickens's intimate friends. He was never very close to Dickens and, although they were for many years on perfectly friendly terms, no two writers could in fact have been more different. Thackeray was the scion of Charterhouse and Cambridge, Dickens of Chatham dockyard and Warren's blacking factory. Thackeray was a gentleman who never quite shook off his amateur status – indeed at times seemed to revel in it – while Dickens was the entire professional whose own class status was insecure enough to make him grandiloquent in his support for "the dignity of literature". There was another difference, too, which was well put by Mrs Lynn Linton, a woman who had had the opportunity of observing both men closely: ". . . Both these men illustrated the truth which so few see, or acknowledge when even they do see it, of that divorcement of intellect and character which leads to what men are pleased to call inconsistencies. Thackeray, who saw the faults and frailties of human nature so clearly, was the gentlest-hearted, most generous, most loving of men. Dickens, whose whole mind went to almost morbid tenderness and sympathy, was infinitely less plastic, less self-giving, less personally sympathetic. Energetic to restlessness . . . he was a keen man of business and a hard bargainer, and his will was as resolute as his pride was indomitable." No truer comparison between the two men could be made: Thackeray, benign, somewhat mournful, aware of human folly; Dickens, sharp, eager, blind to his own faults, somehow much more *driven* than Thackeray by whatever angel or demon was perched upon his shoulder. They were always generous about each other in public, although Dickens's compliments tended to be more general than Thackeray's, and it is not at all clear that he had read any of his contemporary's novels very closely or with any great enthusiasm. But their private relations were quite another story, and as one contemporary remarks, ". . . it was observed at the Garrick that if one of them entered a room where the other was talking or reading, the newcomer would look around as if searching for something he had mislaid or someone he wanted to see, and then go out". Any such coldness is likely to have been of a later date than this history has yet reached; nevertheless even in these earlier years their private comments about each other were not necessarily always favourable, Thackeray in particular feeling himself to live under the shadow of Dickens in ways which must surely have threatened even his own gentle and ironic self-esteem.

Some of his comments have survived and, apocryphal or not, they are worth mentioning in this place: ". . . He can't forgive me for my success with *Vanity Fair*, as if there were not room in the world for both of us." This seems less than fair to Dickens; he was never envious of other writers' success, and in any case the cultured praise of *Vanity Fair* would not particularly have concerned him, since his own work was infinitely more popular and (as important to him) very much better paid. On this occasion it seems likely that Thackeray was projecting his own feelings onto Dickens, for he wrote to his mother after the serialisation of *Vanity Fair*, "There is no use denying the matter or blinking it now. I am become a sort of great man in my way – all but at the top of the tree: indeed there if the truth were known and having a great fight up there with Dickens." Thackeray again: "He doesn't like me. He knows that my books are a protest against his – that if the one set are true, the other must be false." Again most unlikely; Dickens never took part in any internecine rivalry of that sort. Thackeray: "It took Mr Dickens a great while to discover that I had written a book;" the implication here, of self-absorption or neglect of other contemporary writers, is probably true. "There is nobody to tell him when anything goes wrong . . ." This was emphatically true. And so remarks were made; reports spread; gossip interchanged. Only the broad context need really be of concern at this late date – the point being that, after the publication of *Vanity Fair*, the two writers were always being compared and contrasted, by friends or enemies or critics, and even such indirect antagonism was bound to affect the principal parties. The subject can best be left now to Macaulay's rancid verse:

> Touching Thackeray and Dickens, my dear,
> Two lines sum up critical drivel,
> One lives on a countess's sneer,
> And one on a milliner's snivel.

No awards for guessing which "one" is which. But the point is that by 1848, in his thirty-sixth year, Dickens entered a new age in which writers of more recent celebrity than himself entered the field. The éclat of his sudden rise to eminence had faded, and he was no longer the unique and almost inexplicable phenomenon which in his youth he had been. He was now one novelist among others. There were those who applauded the new "naturalism". There were those who admired the classical or at least neo-classical serenity of Thackeray's writing. There were those who praised the moral passion of *Jane Eyre*. It was natural that all these changes in the literary world around him pro-voked changes in Dickens's sense of his own art. In his sense of his own self. He always rose to any challenge and, if Thackeray or Charlotte Brontë had achieved effects outside his own range – well, then, he would extend that range. He would go further. There was much still to be done.

And what is the nature of this change? It has often been suggested that, from this time forward, Charles Dickens's imagination became imbued with subtler colours. That the transition from *Martin Chuzzlewit* to *Bleak House*, for example, represents a significant strengthening of his social vision. That he no longer attacks merely rich or proud individuals in the old theatrical fashion but rather explores a whole society in order to discover the forces latent within it. There is no more than a certain truth to this since, from the time of *The Chimes* four years earlier, Dickens had a pretty shrewd idea of the nature of the society in which he lived. There is an unmistakable change in his art during this period, of course, but it would have been astonishing if it had *not* changed in so rich and self-conscious an artist. Something else was happening, something connected with his own sense of literary challenge but also working under the surface of Dickens's own life and opinions, a change which is best exemplified by the extraordinary amount of conscious and unconscious self-revelation that was about to issue from him. All the evidence suggests, as we shall see, that he was turning back to face his own past and to understand the forces that had shaped him; he was beginning to observe himself in the context of time and history, in other words, and this new sense of himself spread outward, changing everything that it touched, creating new perspectives, encouraging Charles Dickens to recognise the broader and less easily identifiable aspects of the world around him.

Certainly he had every opportunity to do so, for this new year also marked a transition of another kind. John Forster had just taken over from Albany Fonblanque the editorship of the *Examiner* and, no doubt in deference to his close friend's new role, Dickens agreed to write occasional articles and reviews for the newspaper. He had once been a successful reporter, he had once been an unsuccessful editor, but now he took on a task which seemed to combine the best of these roles; he could be both observer and pundit, combining his interest in the local and specific detail with the broadest of moral brush strokes. That is why these occasional pieces, no longer read except as extensions of his fiction, are still entertaining. They are lively, opinionated, ironic, animated by sarcasm or by pity and adopting an expressive style which uses italics, dashes, brackets, short sentences, pithy phrases to encapsulate a point or to offer an opinion. His first article was an unsigned review of a book about ghosts, but over the next twenty-three months he wrote essays upon crime, urban sanitation, poverty, capital punishment – in fact upon all the issues that touched him most deeply. That is perhaps why his position does not really change, from an article he wrote in April 1848 which contained the remark that "side by side with Crime, Disease, and Misery in England, Ignorance is always brooding . . ." to one which he wrote in October 1849 with the sentiment that ". . . drunkenness is the inseparable companion of ignorance. Drunkenness, dirt, and ignorance, are the three Fates of the wretched." In addition he confirms a lifelong opinion and anticipates his later attacks with a scathing commentary upon various Christian missionary societies which seemed wilfully to neglect conditions at home in order to preach the gospel abroad. "It might be laid down as a very good general rule of social and political guidance," he wrote, "that whatever Exeter Hall champions, is the thing by no means to be done . . ." In fact missionaries were always one of Dickens's pet hates, principally because he had no very high opinion of the "savages" of Africa or the West Indies whom they were trying to convert. In modern terminology Dickens was a "racist" of the most egregious kind, a fact that ought to give pause to those who persist in believing that he was necessarily the epitome of all that was decent and benevolent in the previous century. He came close to supporting the Confederate side in the American Civil War, and on one occasion observed in a letter that ". . . the old, untidy, incapable, lounging, shambling black serves you as a free man. Free of course he ought to be; but the stupendous absurdity of making him a voter glares out of every roll of his eye, stretch of his mouth, and bump of his head. I have a strong impression that the race must fade out of the States very fast." So, when in the *Examiner* he talks about the "march of civilisation", we must know precisely what is meant and not meant by that standard nineteenth-century phrase. The essential point, however, is that in these essays for the *Examiner* Dickens was choosing to use a public forum for those matters which he had already implicitly raised in his fiction. He was addressing his own fantasies or preoccupations, in other words, and it is quite characteristic that in his private correspondence he rarely mentions general topical affairs at all; the great Chartist National Convention of April 1848, for example, is material only for a short parody addressed to Tracey, the prison governor who was soon to be responsible for the custody of Ernest Jones, one of the Chartist leaders, and for a brief remark addressed to his brother, Fred. "I take it for granted you were not killed today." It is noteworthy, perhaps, that his close friend, John Leech, enrolled himself as a special constable for the authorities on the day of the National Convention and that troops were stationed in the house of Miss Burdett-Coutts. His friends were on the side of the government, and there is no reason to believe that Charles Dickens saw the matter any differently.

So the public affairs of the year progress with Dickens as no more than a casual observer, all the time in his own journalism providing further evidence for his confession that ". . . the ideal world in which my lot is cast, has an odd effect on the real one . . ." Thus everything became an echo chamber for Dickens's secret voice, the voice of his imagination. This was the voice he must at all costs listen to; and, at the end of February 1848, he went down to Brighton in order to finish *Dombey and Son* in the relative tranquillity of that resort. Yet, restless once more, he came back again to London a fortnight later in order to be "near the printer" as the final pages of his novel emerged. He actually completed it in the last week of March, bringing this extraordinary study of one man's broken pride to an end with his usual feeling of desolation at being parted from the characters of his imagination. Finished. Finished at last. Until he suddenly remembered that he had left out Florence's little dog from the happy tableau at the end of the novel. So he instructed Forster to add a sentence on that theme and, four days later, tried to work up his spirits once more in an expedition to Salisbury and Stonehenge. Forster, Lemon and Leech went with him and all these men formed part of a *Dombey* celebration dinner which took place two weeks later, a dinner at which Henry Burnett sang. Dickens was still describing his "forlorn" condition some days after this event, so bereft did he feel after despatching his novel into the world, but at the dinner itself he was, according to Macready, "happy". He had every reason to be; the sales of *Dombey and Son* had risen to something like thirty-five thousand, at least ten thousand more than those for *Martin Chuzzlewit*, and Dickens declared that ". . . I have great faith in Dombey, and a strong belief that it will be remembered and read years hence". So he had recovered all of his old hearty self-confidence; the fact that he did not feel it necessary to begin another novel *at once* suggests also that his new financial security removed that anxiety about the future which had dogged him through all the years before.

Of course he could still be "difficult"; there is ample evidence that even his friends treated him warily, or fell in with his ways, simply because his moods could change suddenly and unpredictably. One example may suffice. As soon as he was within sight of finishing *Dombey and Son* his attention had turned once more to that other outlet for his imagination, amateur theatricals. The old team was assembled, and rehearsals had begun, when Dickens peremptorily withdrew from the enterprise on the grounds of "lack of steadfastness" and "common consideration" among some of the cast. It is almost as if he felt that in some way he had been personally slighted. But then, no less peremptorily and unexpectedly, he reassembled the group. Partly this was a result of his continuing enthusiasm for the Provident Union which his "Amateurs" were supposed to finance but, more significantly, he was asked to raise money for the curatorship of the Shakespeare House in Stratford; the beneficiary was to be Sheridan Knowles, and the prospect of dispensing immediate literary aid seems to have decided the matter. The cast were "steadfast" once more, and he began arranging fresh rehearsals with his energy apparently undiminished. In fact his enthusiasm was such that he took away all the business from the Shakespeare House Committee and placed it in his own hands, even to the smallest matters such as the colour of the tickets. There had originally been arrangements only for two London performances, but Dickens hatched plans for a provincial tour also; he took care not to tell the company, however, until after the London engagements.

So, having completed *Dombey and Son*, he was ready once more to rush up and down the country; and this at a time of mass unemployment, riots, and the threat of general insurrection. His enthusiasm was certainly greater than any other member of the company, but this may partly have been because he was at the same time performing as himself as well as his various stage characters. As he declared, "Go where I will . . . I always find something of personal affection in people whom I have never seen, mixed up with my public reputation . . ." There were two different productions; the first included *The Merry Wives of Windsor* together with a farce, *Animal Magnetism* (this latter being a not entirely negligible or unamusing piece in which a doctor, played by Dickens, is fooled into thinking that he can "magnetise" the people around him); the second comprised *Every Man in His Humour* once more as well as another farce, *Love, Law and Physic*, to round off the evening. The Amateurs played in London; then Birmingham; then Manchester; then Liverpool; then Birmingham again; all this through the month of June. And then, in July, they performed in Edinburgh and Glasgow – still with enough spirit and energy to include another farce, *Used Up*, in which Dickens played the part of an aristocrat whose ennui is eventually cured by the realities of simple farm life. It would be invidious and unnecessary to go through all the details of rehearsing and performing once more, and the lengthy tour is perhaps best seen through the eyes of one of its principal players, Mary Cowden Clarke, author of *The Complete Concordance to*

Shakespeare and willing amateur actress who met Dickens in this year. She was eager to play the role of Mistress Quickly in *The Merry Wives of Windsor* and Dickens, no doubt aware of the happy coincidence of the author of a Shakespearean concordance actually playing in one of Shakespeare's plays, willingly added her to his little band of actors.

For her the experience was an "enchanting episode" and her account of the Amateurs' travels across England is most notable perhaps for its picture of Dickens as a man of extraordinary spirit and gaiety. "There was a positive sparkle and atmosphere of holiday sunshine about him," she wrote in a later memoir, "he seemed to radiate brightness and enjoyment . . ." But there are small vignettes, too, which show Dickens in more diffident mood. When the party were about to leave their Glasgow hotel for an expedition to Ben Lomond (which of course Dickens had organised), a crowd began to form in the street outside in order to see the famous author. Dickens noticed the people from the window and, muttering "I don't think I can face this", told the party to go on ahead without him and draw off the crowd so that he might escape from the hotel unobserved. He left with Charles Knight, to which gentleman a lady came up and said, "Could you tell me, sir, which is Charles Dickens?" At which point Dickens surreptitiously gave Knight's arm a pinch and his friend duly replied, "No, ma'am; unfortunately I couldn't." It was typical of Dickens, however, to mock Knight afterwards. "I don't know how you could have the heart to answer her so, Knight, I don't think *I* could have done it!" These were the days before Dickens's face became famous through a thousand reproduced photographs, and there is in the incident a pleasant glimpse of the author in a moment of instinctive shyness. There is another moment that Mrs Cowden Clarke remembered, also, a moment when Dickens was so exhausted that he stretched out upon five or six chairs and, using his wife's knee as a pillow, fell quietly asleep. The "glorious eyes closed, the active spirit in perfect repose . . ." Charles Dickens dreaming. And there are also echoes of his voice in Mrs Cowden Clarke's pages . . . "Oh, I'm well wrapped up" . . . "Well, I think I was never more astonished in my life than at your saying you would have some of this cold roast beef!" . . . the exaggeration and the humour reaching down the years and with it, too, the portrait of "Dickens's alert form and beaming look . . . the endless stories he told us; the games he mentioned and explained how they were played; the bright amenity of his manner at various [railway] stations, where he showed to persons in authority the free-pass ticket . . . the courteous alacrity with which he jumped out at one refreshment room to procure food for somebody who had complained of hunger towards the end of the journey, and reappeared bearing a plate of buns which no one seemed inclined to eat but which he held out, saying, 'For Heaven's sake, somebody eat some of these buns . . .'" For a moment he is back with us. We can see him and hear him. And then again he is gone.

It is clear enough from this account, however, that Dickens was at the centre of everything, so much radiance spilling out from him that the faces of all his companions were suffused with light. Parties. Dinners. Games like "Twenty Questions" at which he excelled. Magic tricks. Jokes. So it seemed, at least, to one admirer. But there are also occasions when Dickens seems too relentlessly jolly, when his efforts to make sure that everyone is lively all the time have an element of hysteria or panic attached to them. As if he could not bear the world to be ordinary or dull even for a second. There was one occasion when he literally forced a sick Mark Lemon out of bed to join the festivities; Lemon was a benevolent and funny man who could normally be expected to keep up the spirits of the party, too, and in this gesture of heaving him out of bed there seems to be a kind of desperation in Dickens as the fun began to fade. That is of course one further reason why he loved these amateur theatricals into which he could "plunge" himself, but there is always the same anxiety and disquietude as the bright lights are dimmed, ". . . especially when, as now, those great piled up semi-circles of bright faces at which I have lately been looking – all laughing, earnest, and intent – have faded away like dead people. They seem a ghostly moral of everything in life to me." Dead people. The people who came to the surface of his mind whenever the laughter and the cheering stopped. Amid all this liveliness there is always, deep within him, a brooding preoccupation. Dead people. And his sister, Fanny, was dying.

He had visited her in Manchester when he had played in his amateur theatricals, he had frequently written to her with his characteristic messages of hope and encouragement, but it was clear by the end of June that she had little time left; with her husband she came down from Manchester to Hornsey, both to be near her family and close to the doctors who might best be able to treat her. But there was no hope; she was thin to the point of emaciation and worn down by the constant cough of the consumptive. Dickens visited her often, almost daily. "She shed tears very often as she talked to her brother," Mamie

Dickens recalled many years later. ". . . He was deeply moved, and greatly impressed by her calmness and courage." Dickens has left his own account of one such painful interview. "I asked her whether she had any care or anxiety in the world. She said No, none. It was hard to die at such a time of life – " for she was only thirty-seven years old – "but she had no alarm whatever in the prospect of the change; felt sure we should meet again in a better world . . ." This was the sister with whom he had grown up and first gone to school, the sister who seemed to have deserted him when she attended the Royal Academy of Music while he was consigned to the blacking factory, the sister who sang and acted with him in their early years. She had seen him grow into a famous man, and now she was dying. "She showed me how thin and worn she was; spoke about an invention she had heard of that she would like to have tried, for the deformed child's back; called to my remembrance all our sister Letitia's patience and steadiness; and, though she shed tears sometimes, clearly impressed upon me that her mind was made up, and at rest." He came back from this meeting and, before going to bed, wrote out a detailed account and sent it to Forster; in moments of great emotion he could only understand his feelings when he wrote them down. That is the time when they became real for him, and when he could begin to understand himself. And it was at this time, too, that he began to contemplate the next Christmas Book, a book concerned with "the revolving years", with "the memory of sorrow"and the significance of time past.

So it was in no very sanguine frame of mind that he went down to Broadstairs for the annual summer holiday. Georgina and the children were already there; and so was Catherine, who was once again pregnant and once again in poor health as a result. Dickens now cancelled most of his own social engagements; after the efforts of the spring and summer, he needed time to rest. And to think. The next Christmas Book was very much on his mind, and the shadow of a coming novel, itself concerned with time past, might also have brushed across him. He went up to London on at least one occasion, mainly on business concerning the Home for Fallen Women, and it was on his return from this visit that he was greeted by the sight of Catherine ensconced in a carriage-and-pair and surrounded by a large crowd. It seemed that the pony which drew her phaeton had panicked for some reason and started bolting down a steep hill; Dickens's servant, John Thompson, had thrown himself out of the phaeton while Catherine, screaming in fright, was borne down the hill. The pony plunged down a bank, the shafts of the phaeton broke, the carriage came to rest, and Catherine emerged shaken but unhurt. In the past he had always been annoyed by her propensity for accidents, and had often directed against her that momentary irritation and annoyance which were very much part of his attitude towards her. But not now. Not when she was pregnant again. Not when his sister was dying.

They left Broadstairs at the end of August, and returned to Devonshire Terrace. Fanny was sinking, and she knew now that she had only a little time. As soon as he had returned, Dickens went once more to see her and she told him that "in the night, the smell of the fallen leaves in the woods where we had habitually walked as very young children, had come upon her with such strength of reality that she had moved her weak head to look for strewn leaves on the floor at her bedside". It was a remark which Dickens did not forget and he revives it in his next novel, *David Copperfield*, ". . . I remember how the leaves smelt like our garden at Blunderstone as we trod them underfoot, and how the old, unhappy feeling, seemed to go by, on the sighing wind." The death of his sister is associated here with the death of David Copperfield's young mother, and in that strange concatenation we see the presence of time past. Time returning. On the second of September, Fanny died, in the presence of her father. The funeral was conducted at Highgate cemetery where her Dissenting pastor noted that "Mr Dickens appeared to feel it very deeply . . ." On his return to Devonshire Terrace he wrote a letter to Miss Burdett-Coutts about Urania Cottage business, as if he were forcing himself back into the active world, but his hand was unsteady and the letter is filled with blots.

The next day he went back to Broadstairs where he stayed for three weeks before returning to London via Rochester, making his way back through the town where he and Fanny had once walked. He had not written his next Christmas Book, but was still considering it even as he was being visited by "dim visions of divers things"; this might be the first mention of the semi-autobiographical novel he was about to write, *David Copperfield*, but it is also possible that he had something else in mind. Had he decided, while consumed with remembrance of things past, to write down his own life story? Certainly the past was much with him now. Only a few months before, he had attended the funeral of William Hall, the publisher who had printed his first story, and now with the death of Fanny it was as if the whole period of his childhood had re-emerged within him – all the sensations and emotions of which could only be understood by him when he wrote them down. And so he began. It is not clear precisely when he composed the autobiographical fragment which he sent to Forster, and which Forster was later to publish; Dickens himself was to say that he had written it "just before Copperfield" which strongly suggests this period just after Fanny's death. But he had been considering the possibility of writing his life for some time. "Shall I leave you my life in MS when I die?" he had written two years before to Forster, although this sounds very much as if he were simply leaving material for a putative biographer: "Remember that for my Biography!" he once counselled Forster after he had told him how he had got out of bed one winter's night to practise the polka for his son's birthday party the next day. But events of this period hastened his approach to the more private aspects of his past and of his character. The hero of *Great Expectations* was to say of a passage in his own life that ". . . the secret was such an old one now, had so grown into me and become a part of myself, that I could not tear it away". But Dickens did now tear it away. He had reached a point where the episode of his childhood humiliation could remain his own "secret" no longer. For it was now that Forster told Dickens a story. He told him that Charles Dilke, a friend and colleague of John Dickens, had once seen Dickens working in a warehouse near the Strand, "at which place Mr Dilke, being with the elder Dickens one day, had noticed him, and received, in return for the gift of a half-crown, a very low bow". When Forster told his anecdote, Dickens was silent for a few minutes. Clearly he had touched upon a theme too close to Dickens for comfort. The secret of his past, which had played so large a part in his later self-development, was one that he had been able to keep to himself. No longer.

There were other reasons, too, which impelled Dickens towards this first act of self-revelation; he had entered the consciousness of little Paul Dombey in order to re-enact the child's death, and it is at least possible that this return to childhood had unlocked memories of his own past. In addition his son, Charley, was now of much the same age as he had been when he had entered the blacking factory. So the buried past was forced back to the surface once more, and at some point Dickens began to write the fragment of autobiography which survives; a fragment in which for the first time he recounted the details of his time at Warren's, his boyhood wanderings through London, the incarceration of his father for debt in the Marshalsea Prison, and his own eventual release from the torment of the blacking factory. The whole exercise is of approximately seven thousand words, long enough in itself to make a sizeable contribution to any short life which he might have contemplated, but it breaks off at the time he leaves Warren's. He did not show this fragment to Forster until January of the following year, when Forster noted in his diary that it had "no blotting, as when writing fiction; but straight on, as when writing ordinary letter". The absence of emendation suggests that it emerged fully formed from Dickens's goose-quill pen – that out of his anger and anxiety he had shaped this piece of autobiography slowly in his mind and imagination over a period of years, that it was the fully formed view of his past upon which he often reflected and in which he must surely have found comfort as well as pain. For was it not precisely through his transcendence of these experiences that he had become the man and writer that he was? It might even be said that he wrote this autobiographical fragment at this stage in his life precisely in order to assert his own sense of self-worth, and indeed to justify the extent of his adult ambition. For on one level it conforms to the very pattern of Victorian autobiography, in its concentration upon the privations and miseries of a child who will overcome them by his own energetic determination to fight and win in the "battle of life". The fact that his autobiographical reminiscences remained unfinished suggests that it was only this passage of his childhood that he needed to remember; although indirectly it does also suggest that Dickens broke off when he realised how difficult it would be for him to express himself in factual guise. His narrative is both revealing and unrevealing, for example, turning Dickens into a passive sufferer without giving any clue as to the necessarily tough or self-willed nature of the child who struggled through such early setbacks to become a rich and famous man. In other words it is overbalanced on the side of pathos, and it seems likely that Dickens realised that a book couched in such a tone would not convey half the truth of his own life. That it might even, in a sense, be incredible. So the fragment was eventually incorporated into his next novel, a novel which was provisionally to be entitled *Mag's Diversions* – a humorous title which suggests muddle and folly, and one in which a predominantly comic tone might have been expected to place the suffering of the young Dickens into more than one perspective. A novel which contains the hero's "Personal History . . . Which He never meant to be Published on any Account". So did Dickens project his own concerns. He eventually sent what he had finished of his autobiography to Forster who was no doubt pledged to secrecy as to its contents; which may be why in *Bleak House* Tulkinghorn, the lawyer who knows the secrets of the great, is placed by Dickens in Forster's own chambers in Lincoln's Inn Fields. It has been stated by one of Dickens's sons that his father also showed what he had written to Catherine, who persuaded him not to publish his childhood memories on the grounds that they defamed his own mother and father. This may or may not be true. It seems more likely that he had already decided not to publish anything in this form.

Yet the urge to write about his past was still very great and, as soon as he returned from Broadstairs to London, he started work on the Christmas Book he had for so long been contemplating, a book about lost time. *The Haunted Man and the Ghost's Bargain* is concerned with the power of memory, with family life which is destroyed and replaced only by the wretched anxieties of a distinguished but solitary man; it is a story in which the central character's mournfulness is linked closely with the death of a beloved sister. It is a strange and powerful book in which memories "come back to me in music, in the wind, in the dead stillness of the night, in the revolving years". The theme itself revolves around Dickens's belief that memory is a softening and chastening power, that the recollection of old sufferings and old wrongs can be used to touch the heart and elicit sympathy with the sufferings of others. In his autobiographical fragment he had written of his parents' apparent neglect only to add that "I do not write resentfully or angrily: for I know how all these things have worked together to make me what I am . . ." Now, in the last words of this Christmas Book he was writing, he put it another way; "Lord, keep my memory green . . ." For it was his suffering and the memory of his sufferings which had given him the powerful sympathy of the great writer, just as his recollection of those harder days inspired him with that pity for the poor and the dispossessed which was a mark of his social writings. It has been said that in this autobiographical fragment Dickens is only suppressing his feelings of hurt and jealous rage, but it seems more likely that he was actively involved, after Fanny's death, in the process of transcending them.

The Haunted Man and the Ghost's Bargain, the first Christmas Book for two years, was carefully planned; the manuscript shows evidence of forethought and afterthought, as Dickens crosses out, amends, and adds to such an extent that in its original form it is actually very hard to read. He was working on it slowly through November, while Mark

Lemon was preparing a dramatic version of the same story, and by the third week of that month he had finished the first two chapters. Then he went to Brighton, to finish the third and last chapter in the winter's quiet of that seaside town which always seemed to him to be a place of "gay little toys", a small and bright resort where somehow he could master his material with more ease. By the end of the month he had completed it. On the first day of December he told his publisher, William Bradbury (no doubt eager for "copy"), that "I finished last night, having been crying my eyes out over it"; and indeed the manuscript does look in part as if the ink has been blotted by tears. He read it to Mark Lemon, so that Lemon could finish the dramatic version, and then he sent it off to Bradbury and Evans. Twelve days later he was reading it "with his usual energy and spirit" to a group of friends which included Miss Burdett-Coutts, Forster and Clarkson Stanfield. In the larger world it was received with rather more enthusiasm than the less approachable *Battle of Life* but it was not a particular commercial success, not at least when compared to the sales of *A Christmas Carol* and *The Chimes*. Indeed this was to be Dickens's last Christmas Book, as if in this tale of memory restored he had come to the end of that series which had combined private memory, religious feeling and social satire in equal measure. In *The Haunted Man and the Ghost's Bargain* particularly, intense personal feeling had been closely allied with a religious message of hope and redemption; thus it was that the death of Fanny and the abandoned autobiographical fragment worked together to form a purer and larger statement. This was indeed Dickens's genius: to remove his private concerns into a larger symbolic world so that they became the very image of his own time.

But, even as he infused the power of grace through these pages, his forgiveness of his own real family was only partial. In the last month of the year he attended the marriage of his younger brother, Augustus, but firmly refused to have anything to do with that of Frederick to Anna Weller. For a while he set his face against a brother who, he believed, had all the worst attributes of their father. And once more he was restless. There were vague plans of Italy, which came to nothing. For he had something else to do, something for which travelling would have been a poor substitute; he was restless because another novel, closely related to everything he had just written, was stirring within him. He had been contemplating a new book in the last months of 1848, and at some point in this period Forster suggested to him that he use a first-person narrative – a suggestion which Dickens took very seriously. It has often been said that Dickens was thinking of *Jane Eyre*, and the success of that novel in creating a narrator who tells her own story, but it is also likely that he was aware of his own success in dealing with Paul Dombey's illness from the child's point of view and wished to achieve such an effect on a much larger scale. He always possessed the ability to build upon his achievements. He had written in *Dombey and Son* about the loss of natural affection, he had written in *The Haunted Man and the Ghost's Bargain* about the importance of memory, and from both of these there now emerged another story.

And, as he considered it, everything began to come together once more; one of the oddest aspects of Dickens's writing of fiction, in fact, is the extent to which it seems to magnetise the surrounding area of his life, turning everything into an aspect of the novel he is contemplating. He had decided, for example, to take a brief holiday with John Leech and Mark Lemon. Originally they or, rather, Dickens had planned a visit to the Isle of Wight but the weather in that area was so bad that he switched his attention to East Anglia and, in particular, to Norwich and Stanfield Hall – the latter house being chosen because it was the site of the notorious Rush murders. Dickens had a fascination with places where blood had been shed, and only two months before James Rush, disguised in a woman's dress and bonnet, had killed the owner of Stanfield Hall together with his son. (Of course Dickens was not alone in his interest; ballads and posters of Rush were enormously popular, and railway excursions were even arranged to the site of the crime by this latest "monster in human form".) So on the first Sunday on the new year, 1849, the three men travelled to Norwich and, having explored the city, visited Stanfield Hall itself. That afternoon they went on to Yarmouth, spent the night there, and on the following day walked from Yarmouth to Lowestoft and back again; a total distance of some twenty-three miles. The next morning they left for London. A brief visit but, as it turned out, a fruitful one.

Yarmouth, Dickens told Forster, ". . . is the strangest place in the wide world"; he had been looking at the flat shore and the even sea and the marshes all around, a landscape so much like that of the Medway he had known as a child. Or, rather, like a dream or hallucination of the area he knew so well. It is possible that he also saw the Yarmouth boathouse, an odd structure with its roof made from the bottom of a boat. Like an object from a dream. The "strangest place", then, with its flatness and silence and miles of marshes reaching towards the sea.

And there were fishermen here, too, fishermen who might have reminded him of the men he had once known at Chatham and at Portsmouth. A scene both like and unlike the scenes of his childhood, just as *David Copperfield*, the novel upon which even now he was meditating, would be both like and unlike his own memories of infancy. Other things caught his attention. On the walk back from Lowestoft to Yarmouth, he had passed a signpost pointing to the village of Blundeston – he seems to have read it as "Blunderstone" – and the name stayed in his mind. He had, after all, an attraction to names which included stone; Bradley Headstone, Edward Murdstone, the Sliverstones, Thomas Balderstone, "Stony" Durdles. So he read Blunder*stone* and, if he had indeed already the idea of chaotic *Mag's Diversions* in mind as the title for his new book, then *Blunder*stone would also have seemed appropriate. So it was that the novelist found or, rather, invented the name for the birthplace of David Copperfield. Who was himself originally to be called Copperstone. Stone. Heaviness. Weight. Age. Churches. Ruins. Gravestones. All that aspect of Dickens's imagination may surface in a word.

There are other events which cast their shadow over the approaching novel. On 15 January, 1849, Catherine was delivered of another son; Dickens christened him Henry Fielding Dickens in "a kind of homage to the style of work he was now so bent on beginning", according to Forster – which, if so, must be the first occasion when an infant has been baptised in honour of an unwritten book. Two weeks later Fanny's crippled child, Henry, died: the boy who had acted as model for Paul Dombey and perhaps even for Tiny Tim, so strange a presence to bequeath to posterity. He had survived his mother by only four months, and without doubt died of a broken heart. While on the subject of children it might also be recalled that Dickens's eldest son was now at exactly the age when Dickens himself first entered the blacking factory. A birth; a death; an echo of himself.

In this same period Dickens was also writing a series of articles for the *Examiner* on the plight of mistreated and wretched children. They were the victims of what was known as "baby-farming", by which the parish and local authorities gave the orphaned or the abandoned into the care of minders who were paid a certain amount each week per head of child; "a trade," as Dickens wrote, "which derived its profits from the deliberate torture and neglect of a class the most innocent on earth, as well as the most wretched and defenceless . . ." He was writing about the deaths of no less than one hundred and eighty children at the Juvenile Pauper Asylum in Tooting run by a certain Benjamin Drouet, deaths which had mostly occurred during the cholera epidemic of that winter but which were materially assisted by under-nourishment as well as lack of basic care and hygiene. The Board of Health (whose secretary was Dickens's brother-in-law, Henry Austin) had recommended that the uninfected children should be moved to some other place, but the Poor Law Commissioners rejected the suggestion; so more children died. Drouet was indicted for manslaughter; but then he was acquitted on the grounds that the children, even when they first entered Drouet's "care", would probably have been too weak to resist the disease. This incident called forth from Dickens four separate articles, an apt measure of his disgust at the systematic starvation and mistreatment of children who were emaciated, covered in boils, unable to eat, and who ran the risk of being horse-whipped if they complained of their treatment. The episode helped to focus and to systematise Dickens's feelings about the need for proper urban sanitation and rigorous administrative control of institutions such as the pauper asylum, but it is significant, too, that he was writing about child neglect at precisely the time he was fashioning *David Copperfield* in his mind. Everything was coming together.

In February he went down to Brighton once again, with his own family and with the Leeches; he wanted to be near what he called now the "great hoarse ocean" which seemed in its roar to be asking, "won't anybody listen?" But Dickens did. He listened to everything. He saw everything. And was sometimes granted the strangest recompense: he believed that extraordinary things were always likely to happen to him and, true to form, the landlord of his lodgings as well as the landlord's daughter went "mad" before being taken away in strait-waistcoats, raving, to the local asylum; ". . . quite worthy of me," Dickens said with less than charitable concern for the poor couple, "and quite in keeping with my usual proceedings." And as he looked out at the hoarse ocean his own mind was "running, like a high sea" on the possible names for his new novel. He knew by now that it was going to be a narrative couched in the first person, and he knew that it was to become the saga of a young man's life; that is no doubt why he was thinking of Henry Fielding's *Tom Jones* and why Hablot Browne in his cover drawing gave only the most general incidents of a life from cradle to grave. But the names were now the important things. Without the names, he had no characters and no real story. Without the names, he could not begin. His working notes provide evidence of the care with which he was proceeding. *Mag's Diversions and experiences, observation Being the personal history, of Mr Thomas Mag the Younger of Copperfield Blunderstone House* went through a variety of changes, some seventeen in all, until Dickens emerged at the end triumphant with *The Copperfield Survey of the World as it rolled. Being the personal history, adventures, experience, and observation, of Mr David Copperfield the Younger of Blunderstone Rookery.* All this in a firm hand, with his characteristic two underlinings of each word; and then, in a fainter and slightly narrower hand, he added: "which he never meant to be published, On any account." The name Copperfield had itself emerged through a rehearsal of such names as Wellbury, Magbury, Topflower, Copperboy and Copperstone. Just as Murdstone was to emerge through Harden, Murdle (later revived as Merdle in *Little Dorrit*) and Murden. Announcements of a new novel were made at the end of February; at which time, too, Charles Dickens began.

Chapter 19

A ND how did he begin? He began by considering what he called
the "central idea" or the "leading idea" which he then, according
to his publisher, "revolved in his mind until he had thought the
matter thoroughly through". Finally, again according to his publisher, he "made what I might call a programme of his story with the
characters" and on that rough base he would begin his work. Dickens
himself said that at this early stage he also needed to be sure of the
"purport of each character" as well as the "plain idea" each might come
to embody. Of course he might still be struck by, or imagine, scenes
and characters (even incidents) which had an independent existence of
their own; there were occasions when he chose a particular London
street or district, for example, before detailing the plot which would
eventually lead into it. But all the time he was looking for that one
chain of being, that one clear line to which everything else could be
attached – the important point being that he invariably saw this in the
form of a *story*. The story which would bring ideas or characters to
light and life.

It was not an instant or an easy process, and throughout Dickens's
writing life the symptoms at the beginning of a new novel are the
same. "Violent restlessness, and vague ideas of going I don't know
where . . ." And then again, ". . . it is like being *driven away*." Here is
the idea of a new story actively repelling him, thrusting him outside its
own field of force. Dickens became irritable, solitary, preoccupied,
". . . going round and round the idea . . .", not being able to settle on
any one thing and therefore not able to rest; ". . . walking about the
country by day – prowling about into the strangest places in London
by night – sitting down to do an immensity – getting up after doing
nothing . . ." This was for him the agony of birth, ". . . wandering
about at night into the strangest places . . . seeking rest, and finding

none". That last phrase is strikingly reminiscent of the fate of the unclean spirit in the Bible, as Dickens stalks the streets of London, both by day and by night, the amorphous shape of the narrative within him like some burden from which he needs to be relieved. Then, as the time came close for the strange story to be born, he would shut himself away in his study, contemplating, looking out of the window, not writing a word.

Thus did he "lay the ground". And it is not surprising that a man who went to so much trouble to arrange and to learn his speeches in an orderly fashion should wish to take infinitely more trouble over his novels; never was a writer so exact, so thorough, so careful in his plans. He told one contemporary that ". . . the plot, the motive of the book, is always perfected in my brain for a long time before I take up my pen". And he told another that ". . . he never began to write before having settled the work in its minutest detail, in his head". But this is not to say that he knew every aspect of his novel in advance; far from it. He had the architectural plans drawn up, as it were, but he needed to build freely and instinctively. He began with the story and with the ideas which that story suggested; but then, as he writes, he lets that story take on its own most appropriate shape. Then the characters come and settle within the narrative, bringing with them their own lines of force which complicate the essential plot. And so a double focus is at work; the characters seem for a while to career off at a tangent, but then the "leading idea" draws them back again and reasserts itself until the characters once again break free and roam before being once again retrieved.

And he would *see* it – ". . . *see it*, and write it down". In his letters he often says, if only you could have seen it, or, if only I could show it to you. But the whole process is immeasurably more important in his fiction. "In the excited and exalted state of my brain," one of his central characters is heard to say, "I could not think of a place without seeing it, or of persons without seeing them . . ." And what is said by Pip can also be said of his author; "I can as distinctly see with my own eyes any scene which I am describing as I see you now . . ." he told one acquaintance. For him the important thing are the *pictures*; they are more significant to him than ideas or themes or even, sometimes, words. He talks of his fiction on occasions as a "picture-frame" but his pictures within the frame are not like the still lives of an artist; Dickens sees objects and images as if they had suddenly been illuminated by lightning. A character "came flashing up . . . and I had only to look on and leisurely describe it . . ." Thus the advice he gave to an aspiring writer: "Whatever she writes about must be going on before her . . ." and must affect her more than anyone else. So everything happens before Dickens. We may recall how in childhood the heroes of his reading seemed to be literally bodied forth in front of him; and so it was in his own fiction, as he summons forth visions which he must describe. It was in itself a restless and irritable process, this form of second sight, and one friend has remembered his ". . . muttering to himself, walking about the room, pulling his beard, and making dreadful faces . . ." There was one occasion when his daughter, Mamie, was convalescing from a long illness and he allowed her to remain in his study as he worked. "On one of these mornings, I was lying on the sofa endeavouring to keep perfectly quiet, while my father wrote busily and rapidly at his desk, when he suddenly jumped from his chair and rushed to a mirror which hung near, and in which I could see the reflection of some extraordinary facial contortions which he was making. He returned rapidly to his desk, wrote furiously for a few moments, and then went again to the mirror. The facial panto-mime was resumed, and then turning toward, but evidently not seeing, me, he began talking rapidly in a low voice . . ." An extra-ordinary scene – the father looking at his daughter but not seeing her, muttering to himself, acting out scenes in the mirror, alert and alive only to the world of his imagination, peopling his study with other men and women and children, hearing other voices.

But how did he shape his working day? Georgina Hogarth said after his death that "everything with him went as by clockwork . . ." And his eldest son said that "no city clerk was ever more methodical or orderly than he; no humdrum, monotonous, conventional task could ever have been discharged with more punctuality or with more business-like regularity, than he gave to the work of his imagination and fancy". He arose from his bed at seven, breakfasted at eight, and shortly after nine o'clock he was ensconced in his study where he remained until two. Then he walked until five through the country-side or through the streets of London; he dined at six (sometimes staying with friends at the table until ten); afterwards he spent the evening with family or friends and retired at midnight. He had, in other words, to be systematic in order to endure his life. When he returned to his study in the morning, everything was neatly and precisely arranged; a vase of fresh flowers on his desk, together with the usual objects which have already been described, the desk itself always placed in front of the window so that he might look, unseeing, out at the world. And he needed quiet, dead quiet; in Devonshire Terrace an extra door was added to keep out the noise. He was surrounded by books also, and those who have suggested that Dickens was in some ways an ignorant or uneducated man should look at the list of the volumes in his library at Devonshire Terrace. "There are books all round," Mrs Gaskell wrote to a friend about Dickens's study, "up to the ceiling, and down to the ground . . ."

Of course there were the intervals for meals, as his daughter, Mamie, recorded; ". . . he would come in, take something to eat in a mechanical way – he never ate but a small luncheon – and would return to his study to finish the work he had left, scarcely having spoken a word in all this time. Again, he would come in, having finished his work, but looking very tired and worn. Our talking at these times did not seem to disturb him, though any sudden sound, as the dropping of a spoon, or the clinking of a glass, would send a spasm of pain across his face." We can see them at their table – Dickens and his family, the children talking in low voices, the father seemingly in a trance. Eating mechanically, and then hastening back to his quiet and neat study. He used a goose-quill pen with blue (or occasionally black) ink. He wrote on blue-grey slips of paper, eight and three quarter inches by seven and one quarter inches. On an ordinary day he would complete approximately two thousand words (some two to two and a half "slips") but when he was writing in a furious vein he might cover four "slips" and complete almost four thousand words. Sometimes, of course, nothing came at all; and yet he stayed in his study, keeping to his hours. On these occasions he might draw figures or dots, or doodle. Or he would simply stare out of the window. "But I always sit here," he said, "for that certain time." His son adds, "Whether he could get on satisfactorily with the work in hand mattered nothing. He had no faith in the waiting-for-inspiration theory . . . It was just his business to sit at his desk during just those particular hours in the day, my father used to say, and, whether the day turned out well or ill, there he sat accordingly." He would occasionally come into lunch and complain of having had a "bad morning" – "but I have known from the expressive working of his face and from a certain intent look that I learnt to know well, that he had been, almost unconsciously, diligently thinking all round his subject . . ." So the novelist sat at his desk, from nine until two, and, when the time came for his three-hour walk, "I go at once, hardly waiting to complete a sentence".

Yet even as he walked he continued to think of his story, "his eyes looking straight before him, his lips slightly working, as they generally did when he sat thinking and writing . . ." This is part of the process which he once described as ". . . searching for some pictures I wanted to build upon". Looking steadily at them. Following them through. Dickens once compared the imagination to a "powerful Locomotive", and there is in his descriptions of the actual composition of his novels a strong sense of continual forward momentum; he would talk about a "move" coming up in his story and in his working notes he would often employ the phrase "*carry through*". He invariably placed number and title before each chapter in his manuscript, but would always paginate according to the whole monthly part rather than each separate chapter; thus by small things he kept up the momentum. The movement which would carry him forward to "the great turning idea"; the idea which would keep the images steady as he contemplated them. Harmony. Consistency. The maintenance of the appropriate tone. These were the matters which most concerned him as he carried on with each novel.

So the process of composition goes on, the quill pen moving across the sheet of grey-blue paper. "I never copy," Dickens said, "correct but very little, and that invariably as I write." Of a particular effect in *Oliver Twist* he once wrote, "I thought that passage a good one *when* I wrote it, certainly, and I felt it strongly (as I do almost every word I put on paper) *while* I wrote it, but how it came I can't tell. It came like all my other ideas, such as they are, ready made to the point of the pen – and down it went." In later years he would become more careful or more costive in terms of invention, and there is a marked increase in the additions and emendations in each manuscript. But the principle remains the same; Dickens found it difficult to write "cold", as it were, and it was in the extraordinary if fitful heat of the imagination that he was able to fashion his sentences. He made the same point in a slightly different context – "I never commit thoughts to paper, until I am obliged to write, being better able to keep them in regular order, on different shelves of my brain, ready ticketed and labelled to be brought out when I want them". This is an excessively mechanical way of describing it, although Dickens often took a certain amount of crude pleasure in comparing his invention to a mechanical or scientific process. The truth is that he wrote instinctively, swiftly, adding or amending as he went along. All the time weighing up the tone and the effect of what he was about to write and instinctively, too, engaged in what he called the "incessant process of *rejection* . . ."; by which he meant "rejecting things, day after day, as they come into my thoughts, and whipping the cream of them". The formula on which he proceeded through this movement of rejection or acceptance went something like this. "How much of this will tell for what I mean? How much of it is my own wild emotion and superfluous energy – how much remains that is truly belonging to this ideal character and these ideal circumstances?" His own wild emotion might send him straying forth in one direction, seeing the comic possibilities or the pathetic elements in a scene to such an extent that he goes chasing after them; but then he comes back to himself, comes back to the strict organisation and discipline which must always be part of his narrative. So he was ". . . eschewing all sorts of things that present themselves to my fancy – coming in such crowds! . . ." Coming in such crowds; and in that phrase one has a glimpse of the novelist at work, surrounded by the possibilities and potentialities of his own imagination, in a cloud of characters and phrases and words. There must have been times when it seemed to him that he might populate an entire universe, when his imagination was as strong and as fertile as life itself, laughing at the comic scenes which presented themselves to his imagination – "Some of it, made me laugh so, that I couldn't see the paper as I was writing" – and weeping as the more pathetic scenes took their place. No one was more affected by his writing than he was himself. Laughing and crying alternately.

"Streaky, well-cured bacon" – that was what he had called it in *Oliver Twist*, ". . . the tragic and the comic scenes . . . sudden shiftings of the scene, and rapid changes of time and place . . ." There is nothing artless about it. Indeed in his private diary he had once made an undertaking to himself not to "paint" his entries; in other words, not to write them as a novelist. When he wanted to, he could write as plain and as sober English as any other author; but when his feelings are truly engaged, as in the act of composition, then his language sometimes dips and soars. Those interested in the overall shape of his narrative might note how even the most demotic prose seems to fit into the elaborate rhythmic structure of his narratives, of which his instinctive use of blank verse is only the most obvious example. In fact he reaches for the cadence of blank verse whenever his feelings are deeply engaged, and indeed he admitted that at such times he even started talking in rhythmic patterns. This probably has more to do with the many nights he spent watching Macready play Shakespeare than with the actual reading of Shakespeare; but it is curious nonetheless, and suggests just how much poetry Dickens brought into the novel at a time when the great "romantic" poets had finished their own work. It is not simply that his more serious characters speak in blank verse at times of sorrowful feeling, but rather that all of his most powerful and successful characters speak in metrical patterns or with a cadence close to that of blank verse; not just Little Nell but also Mrs Gamp, Dick Swiveller as well as Florence Dombey. There are similar effects in Sterne and Richardson but to nothing like the same degree as in Dickens; in fact it might be said that this heightening of his characters' speech is one of his most distinctive contributions to the novel. But what of the more technical matters? Dickens's spelling is erratic; and words like labour or honour are just as likely to be written as *labor* or *honor*. He can sometimes be simply a bad speller, and it was left to the printer to correct such errors as *stationery* for *stationary*, *suspence* for *suspense*, and *chimnie* for *chimney* – although the last two might well have been simply a residue of the eighteenth-century English which he had read as a child and which had so powerfully affected his imagination. His punctuation is as erratic and as inconsistent as his spelling, but his main effects were superintended by the comma and the colon.

And then the final moments. He signs off each manuscript with "The End", both words underlined twice. The end of each novel which for him was always a parting from "companions", the companions he always needed, even if they were those of his imagination. So at the close of each book he was almost as agitated as he was at its beginning, and he would go wandering once more in "sorrowful" mood. This was the time when ". . . wildnesses come over me, and I go off unexpectedly into strange places . . ."; when he seemed to be left in a ". . . condition of temporary and partial consciousness . . ." But he was not just leaving his imaginary companions behind, he was also surrendering a part of himself; at the end of *David Copperfield* he told Forster that "I seem to be sending some part of myself into the Shadowy World". But then of course the order and the discipline returned, for never has a writer's life been so divided between wild feeling and strict control, between helpless sensations of loss or abandonment and the stern will for power and domination. There was, after all, the obligation to read and correct the final printers' proofs, as he had done for each number printed a few days before publication; as might be expected, he made much heavier changes in galley proof than he did in the final set of page proofs. He was generally and reasonably careful in his reading, and paid particular attention to the importance of proper paragraph breaks. He would often change words, and delete whole sentences or paragraphs if the need arose; if he was over the necessary limit for each monthly number he would usually excise passages of improvised humour or external description, but at a later stage his changes tend to maintain the even tone of the narrative and avoid the more sententious passages of pathos or of violence. He cut very well, although he did not always ensure that newly-connected passages were in complete harmony with each other; he worked instinctively and quickly on the proofs, and some-times he failed to notice errors which the printer had made as well as errors of his own. In fact there were occasions when he corrected a printer's error without reference back to the original manuscript, and thus compounded the mistake. This can be a nightmare for textual editors and it has been recorded of *Hard Times*, one of Dickens's shortest novels, that there are over 1,500 textual variants. And yet, as far as Charles Dickens was concerned, this was the end of the process. The printers would return the sheets of manuscript to him, together with the proofs; he collected these and bound them together with his working notes. These were his memorials for posterity, and there is no doubt that he now had such a sense of his historical importance that he considered the retention of these items to be no more than his literary duty. They were the relics of his art.

And what of *David Copperfield*, now that Dickens had walked and contemplated, had found a title and a theme? Now that he was ready to begin? Since he had decided to set part of the narrative in Yarmouth, he purchased a copy of *Suffolk Words and Phrases* in order to find expressions he might use to lend authenticity to his local characters' speech. In fact the intensity of his care over, and work upon, the new novel is a mark of its importance to him; there were no theatricals and no foreign excursions in this first year of its writing, nothing but hard and constant effort upon a novel which he was always to consider his best. It was in this early stage of preparation that he concocted the name of Murdstone and the first entry on the right-hand side of his working plan says simply, "Father dead – Gravestone outside the house". Murdstone. Gravestone. So did name and theme intertwine in an immediate and almost instinctive pattern of association. He began the actual novel slowly and with some difficulty in the last week of February and worked on it steadily for much of the next month; the first page is filled with emendations as Dickens made his way through the thicket of memories and inventions in a chapter simply entitled "I Am Born". Dickens wrote, "Here is our pew in the church" in the second chapter, entitled "I Observe", and in his own copy of the novel Forster has written "actual" in the margin beside it – no doubt Dickens told him of the truth of this. And in the same chapter, beside the account of David reading to Peggotty from a book about crocodiles and alligators, Forster has written "true". He makes no such mark a little earlier, where the young David is terrified by the story of Lazarus rising from the dead, and associates it with his own dead father; but that was for Dickens "true" and "actual" in quite another sense. He was making slow progress – so slow, in fact, that in the end he was forced to write quickly in order to finish the number in time for publication. But still he had written too little, and at a late stage added passages on the characters both of Mrs Gummidge and of Little Em'ly, whose fate is for an instant unveiled. So the scene was gradually being established: in these first three chapters Dickens had introduced David, Mr Murdstone, Little Em'ly, Peggotty and Betsy Trotwood. Their story is set in the 1820s and 1830s, and Dickens makes sure that David Copperfield is of an appropriate age so that, when he is eventually sent to work in a factory, he is the same age as Dickens was at the time of his arrival in London. Thus did autobiography merge wonderfully with fiction. Each chapter was sent to the printer as soon as it was completed, and then at least two sets of proofs were despatched back to Dickens who, in turn, sent one set to Hablot Browne for the purposes of illustration. This was a much more sensible arrangement than the conveyance of messages from Lausanne and Paris while Dickens was deep in *Dombey and Son*, and in fact the relationship between author and illustrator now returned to its previous cordial and professional shape. So the first number was completed and ready at last, everything prepared for Dickens's long sojourn in the Shadowy World.

And yet which for him was the world of shadows and which the world of reality? There are occasions when he does not seem to know and, even as he wrote the first number, Dickens was also completing his articles on the deaths of the children at the Tooting juvenile pauper asylum. He was dealing with two kinds of child abuse one after another; the private abuse of David Copperfield at the hands of the Murdstones, and the public abuse of the abandoned children in the baby farm, the emotion induced by both spilling over into each other.

And it was at this time, too, that the real world assumed the shape of Dickens's own fiction. Just at the end of his labours on the first number of *David Copperfield*, he was walking along the Edgware Road with Mark Lemon when a young man picked Lemon's pocket. In Dickens's own words as recorded in the police court, "I was with Mr Lemon, and saw him turn suddenly round upon the prisoner, who speedily ran away: we pursued him, and when he was taken he was most violent; he is a very desperate fellow, and he kicked about in all directions. There was a mob of low fellows close by when he tried Mr Lemon's pocket, and we were determined that he should not effect his escape, if we could prevent it." "A mob of low fellows" – here is the authentic voice of Dickens. And then, too, the authentic voice of London as the prisoner, one Cornelius Hearne, aged nineteen, makes his defence against Dickens's charges:

Mr Dickens: "When at the station I said I thought I knew the prisoner, and that I had seen him at the House of Correction."

Prisoner: "Now, your worship, he must have been in 'quod' there himself, or he couldn't have seen me. I know these two gentlemen well; they're no better than swell-mob men, and get their living by buying stolen goods. (Laughter.) That one (pointing to Mr Dickens) keeps a 'fence' and I recollect him at the prison, where he was put in for six months, while I was there for only two."

It is as if the Artful Dodger had risen up from the pages of *Oliver Twist* to accuse the author of his being. Thus the voices of the past come back, echoing through the police court, illuminating a vanished world, memories of Dickens's own fiction colouring our interpretation of words and people. The real world. The shadowy world. Although Cornelius Hearne had in fact been able to steal nothing from Mark Lemon, he was sentenced to three months' hard labour at the House of Correction. But who is more real? Cornelius Hearne or the Artful Dodger? Dickens returned from the court to Devonshire Terrace, and to the next stage of David Copperfield's fortunes.

But he was finding it very difficult: "I am lumbering on like a stage-waggon." In the chapter he was now trying to write, in the course of which little David falls under the control of the Murdstones, he made a great many alterations and corrections, changing his mind as he wrote, trying to find the right tone, the right word. While his daily life, the real Shadowy World, went on as before. He gave a dinner party at which one guest became sick while another fell prostrate on the carpet, and Albany Fonblanque laughingly described

Dickens as another Benjamin Drouet for failing to take care of his charges. He went to the opera with "Mary Barton", his assumed name for Mrs Gaskell. He gave a speech at the General Theatrical Fund. He attended the Derby. And what of his family in this period? One of his daughters, Kate, was in later life to give a portrait of Victorian domestic life which is undoubtedly based upon her own experience of the Dickens household; she reports that, in the mid-century, women of the upper-middle class, to which class Catherine Dickens and Georgina Hogarth by right of Dickens's position were now attached, "lived a pleasant if uneventful life of peace and plenty; plenty of rather monotonous amusement such as garden parties, croquet, long walks, drives and rides and in the evening occasional rather dull dinner parties, dances and the always popular opera and theatre parties. Their mornings were occupied with the usual small domestic worries . . . Business disposed of, they managed to get through a large amount of letter-writing, embroidery and reading . . . many of them were thoughtful in those days, and greatly given to introspection . . . Their manners were gentle and unobtrusive . . . low voices . . ."

And as they talked in low voices Dickens was sitting in his study, behind the green baize door, working steadily forward. "I hope David Copperfield will 'do'," he said. "The world would not take another Pickwick from me, now; but we can be cheerful and merry I hope, notwithstanding, and with a little more purpose in us." Cheerful he still was, as he introduces the character of Barkis who is forever "willin'", and he was also slowly moving towards his "purpose"; he had managed to finish the fifth chapter by the first of May and then four days later completed the last chapter of the number. In June he went down to Cobham, just beyond Chatham, in order to engage in a little local research for the pilgrimage he had in mind for his hero to make, a pilgrimage away from London to the peace of the country-side, and by the third week of that month he had killed off David's mother and left him an orphan in the care of the Murdstones: "Get a clean pocket-handkerchief ready for the close of 'Copperfield' No 3 . . ." he told Mark Lemon. By now he knew in which direction he was moving, and had planned well ahead. So he found time to attend Hampton Races. To visit the Vauxhall Theatre. To give a speech at the annual dinner of the United Law Clerks' Society. And all the time he was getting ready to introduce the account of his own past into *David Copperfield*, taking it directly from the autobiographical fragment he had already written. He was restless again as he came close to this revelation, and one day he walked fourteen miles into the country to consider what he had to do. Just before he began this fifth number, he had written a memorandum to himself, "what I know so well"; and so it was.

These were the chapters in which David Copperfield becomes a "little labouring hind" in a crumbling warehouse along the Thames, in which the Micawbers are incarcerated within the King's Bench Prison in the Borough, in which young Copperfield leads his own lonely life in the streets of London. Dickens wrote these chapters very quickly and without the least sign of difficulty; there are far fewer manuscript emendations here than anywhere else in the novel, and this no doubt because he was working directly from his own autobiographical paragraphs. But even as he was writing the chapter in which David Copperfield is placed in the crumbling warehouse Dickens fell and somehow managed to injure his left side, the very "weak" side which had disturbed him when he had been a real "labouring hind". He had inflamed his old injury, had to be cupped and blistered, writhing in agony once more in just the way he had writhed in agony on the floor of the rotting warehouse by the Thames. His childhood condition returned, as in his imagination he relived the terrors of the old days; "what I know so well." But who could have believed that even the physical pain could be revived? He went down to Broadstairs to recover, and a few days later was in good enough spirits to write a parody of "Sloppy", a waterman at the Charing Cross cab-stand whose peculiar habits of speech rendered him memorable to Dickens. He was also well enough once more to work quickly on the novel, and by the middle of July he had managed to finish the entire "autobiographical" number. It is a measure of his brilliance that he was able to bring in all the private material on the blacking factory and the debtors' prison without once losing his objective sureness of tone; he was able to connect fully with his childhood while at the same time turning it into fully realised fiction, so that it becomes both solid and haunting, both memorably real and at the same time fantastic, magical, bizarre.

As soon as he had finished the number he went down to the Isle of Wight with John Leech, his purpose being to find a suitable spot for the summer months. They stayed at a lodging house in Shanklin while they reconnoitred the area, and within a couple of days Dickens had found "Winterbourne" in Bonchurch, a converted barn some hundred and fifty feet above sea-level with an estate which extended down to the seashore and included a stream as well as a waterfall. It was owned by the Reverend James White, an aspiring playwright whom Dickens had met through Macready some time before (he described White as "comically various in his moods", which suggests that he was not entirely in sympathy with him – in fact, as so often with Dickens, he preferred the company of White's wife, Rosa), and it was here that he decided to retreat while he carried on with his writing through the summer months. He returned to Devonshire Terrace in order to pick up family and servants, and a week later came back to Bonchurch with all of them in tow; Thackeray by chance encountered them on the pier at Ryde and, as he put it, saw them "all looking abominably coarse vulgar and happy".

There are many reminiscences of their time at Winterbourne, not the least among them being that of Dickens's eldest son who remembered ". . . continual excursions and picnics during the day; constant impromptu dances, and games, and forfeits, and such like diversions; performances of conjuring tricks, with my father as the magician and John Leech as his attendant, in the evenings". At first Dickens was delighted by the place; ". . . the variety of walks is extraordinary; the things are cheap, and everybody is civil." Also the gardener was able to turn the waterfall on the grounds into a shower bath; a large tub, with holes cut into the sides and bottom, was placed beneath the water and it was into this which Dickens dipped. He "believed in" cold water as a sovereign remedy for all sorts of conditions, and had what was then the relatively unusual habit of bathing every morning. (In London, at a later date, he was to have a shower bath of such strength that it was known as "The Demon"). His delight at the shower materially affected his powers of measurement, however, and his descriptions of the waterfall's height vary in his correspondence from one hundred and fifty to five hundred feet. He was soon well known to the islanders – the population of Bonchurch being something under five hundred – and according to one report his "blunt and forthright manner offended many locally". This seems unlikely; it is much more probable that his occasionally silent and remote manner surprised the natives as much as it had once disappointed those who sailed with him across the Atlantic. But there are also stories of his high spirits, of the picnics and dances and garden parties and amateur theatricals and games and expeditions which he organised. One local described him as having "a very rapid decided way of talking" and of being "excessively full of fun and spirits". Among those who came to join the two

families, at Dickens's always insistent invitation, were Jerrold and
Beard, Egg and Stone, Browne and Austin.

The fun only began, of course, when he had finished his day's
portion of *David Copperfield*; he wrote in a first-floor room overlooking the sea, and throughout the first month of his residence in the Isle
of Wight he found the composition very difficult. So it is that the
thirteenth chapter, in which David makes his long pilgrimage to Aunt
Betsy, is filled with emendations; all the evidence suggests that the
succeeding chapters were also written with far more labour than the
long sequence which he had taken from his autobiographical reminiscences. This is not to suggest that Charles Dickens disappears once
more from the narrative. Quite the contrary. He was pleasantly
surprised when Forster now pointed out to him that the initials of
David Copperfield were his own initials reversed; in addition the
mad old second-hand-clothes dealer who screams at David is called
"Charley", as is the kind but ineffectual schoolmaster who plays the
flute. More importantly, still, it was in the first number he wrote at
Bonchurch that "Mr Dick" appears, the companion of Betsy
Trotwood who cannot help but put "King Charles the First's head"
into the "Memorial" he is forever trying to complete. Charley.
Dick. King Charles. Dickens is both schoolmaster and madman,
idiot and king; are these images of all his potential selves, as David
Copperfield is seen to search desperately for his own identity and
destiny?

He was working slowly, then, and almost as soon as he arrived he
began to be troubled by a persistent cough. As so often he tried to
subdue his infection by harsh exercise, and started taking long walks
across the downs. Where he was sometimes encountered.

Charles Dickens to Edmund Peel, the local poet: *You* must like these
downs as I do.

Edmund Peel: Yes, but I cannot climb them as you do. *Charles
Dickens smiles and passes on.*

By the end of August he had finished the fifth number and almost at
once set to work on the next. It was at this time too that, in proof, he
hit upon the idea of Mr Dick being haunted by King Charles the First's
head; just as, now, his own head was filled with ague and fever. His
symptoms were alarming; ". . . an almost continual feeling of sickness, accompanied with great prostration of strength, so that his legs
tremble under him, and his arms quiver when he wants to take hold of
any object." He was writing this account to Forster in the impersonal

third-person, as if he wanted to distance himself from his own sickness, and it is typical of him that despite his loss of strength and concentration "I make no sign, and pretend not to know what is going on". He blamed the climate of Bonchurch for his condition, but the symptoms he describes sound like some sort of generalised nervous debility: "Extreme depression of mind, and a disposition to shed tears from morning to night . . ." Mental exhaustion must have induced at least part of this condition, and it seems likely that Dickens's own efforts to write were proving as wearying as the weather. He had just revealed to the world his own past in fictional guise, and even now he was writing the chapters which would take David Copperfield to the age of seventeen, the very years about which he said he often dreamed. It is often forgotten what a nervous and anxious man Dickens was, even at the height of his fame, and Forster describes how in this particular period he had "a nervous tendency to misgivings and apprehensions". There can be little doubt that these apprehensions were at least indirectly related to that great effort of self-revelation which he had recently undergone, a revelation which Dickens may neurotically have believed to entail some form of retribution or punishment. So he fell sick, and became severely depressed. Yet still he blamed the climate, and professed to believe that the other members of his family were secretly as weakened as he was; he began to make plans to leave the island, and finished the number of *David Copperfield* later than usual.

But then there occurred an incident which put his plans in jeopardy. John Leech, while bathing, was knocked over by a giant wave and suffered some kind of concussion – "congestion of the brain" it was called, and leeches were placed upon his temples to draw off the blood. But he remained ill, restless, and in pain; until, that is, Dickens offered to mesmerise him into a magnetic sleep. Which he did, successfully. Leech slept and, as he slept, recovered. As soon as he felt able to leave him, Dickens abandoned the Isle of Wight and at the very end of September travelled down with the family to Broadstairs. It was here, ensconced once more in the house next to Ballard's Hotel by the sea-front, that he set to work on *David Copperfield*. By the time he left, almost three weeks later, he had in fact completed an entire number. But he was also the recipient of bad news: the sales of the novel were markedly down on those of its predecessor, and were to average something like twenty thousand copies a month as contrasted with approximately thirty-five thousand for *Dombey and Son*. Dickens did not yet have the exact figures but their drift was clear enough; he was not going to earn as much on this novel as he had anticipated. But he was not wholly cast down. Not now. He had other plans. After the relative failure of *Martin Chuzzlewit* he had turned eagerly to the *Daily News* as a form of recompense, of release, of refuge. Now once again he was maturing the idea for another periodical, albeit of a more personal kind. He had in fact been considering it throughout the summer, even while at Bonchurch, but the bad news about *Copperfield* made it of more pressing and even paramount concern. He was already discussing specific details with Forster: a weekly periodical at a price of three-halfpence or twopence, and featuring a character to be called "THE SHADOW" who would be a kind of correspondent at large and who might be assumed to have some secret intelligence on the latest subjects of the day. This journalistic spectre would also provide the kind of framing device for various pieces which Dickens always seemed to prefer; it is yet another example of that unity in diversity which is the mark of his fiction as well as of his journalism, and might without portentousness be described as an aspect of his aesthetic sense. As soon as he returned to London he informed Bradbury and Evans of his plans, in which they broadly concurred. Dickens was, you might say, back in business.

But as he set to work on the chapters of *David Copperfield* which would lead ineluctably to Steerforth's ravishment of Little Em'ly, he was also back in a London which he characterised as "a city of Devils". One more he was faced with the horror of life, in the life he saw around him as well as in the fiction he was about to conceive, for once more he attended a public execution – of the Mannings, a couple who had conspired to kill Mrs Manning's young lover. They were hanged outside Horsemonger Lane Gaol, and Dickens had gone to this place the night before expressly in order to watch the behaviour of the crowd. In two subsequent letters to *The Times*, he described "wickedness and levity", "cries and howls", "screeching, and laughing", "brutal mirth or callousness"; in a typically nineteenth-century sense he conceived it to be his "duty" to bring such matters to the attention of the public, and suggested that in future hanging ought to be conducted in a secret place within the prison walls. But he was affected by less public sentiments, too, and after the execution of the Mannings he was haunted by two figures: ". . . the man's, a limp, loose suit of clothes as if the man had gone out of them; the woman's a fine shape, so elaborately corseted and artfully dressed, that it was quite unchanged in its trim appearance as it slowly swung from side to side . . ." Here was true horror, too, in the absence of life; and in the crowd itself Dickens shrank from his fellow creatures and even from himself "as fashioned in the image of the Devil". His letters to *The Times* were printed as handbills and distributed in the streets, but the feeling of horror is genuine and private. Private anxiety fuelling public denunciation. The horror of life. The pity of life.

And at Urania Cottage, too, he was brought face to face with the sorrowful mysteries. He and Miss Burdett-Coutts had already suffered disappointment; the first young women who had been sent out to Australia in order to start new lives had apparently taken up prostitution on the ship itself which, as Dickens put it, came as "heavy disappointment and great vexation" to those engaged in running the Home. And now there was dissension within Urania Cottage itself when one Isabella Gordon, in league with two others, began to stir up resentment against the Matron and her assistant. Dickens arrived to investigate the complaints, and at once it becomes clear that it was he whom the girls most feared. He was the famous novelist, although it is to be doubted that this impressed them very much; but, more importantly, he was shrewd, sharp and strict sometimes to the point of severity. It was Dickens who heard the complaints of Isabella Gordon and then, in his redolent phrase, ". . . she danced upstairs before Mrs Morson, holding her skirts like a lady at a ball". But her story was found to be untrue and maliciously intended; in order to uphold the authority of the Home, her two friends were severely warned (one of them Dickens evocatively described as being "a draggled piece of fringe upon the skirts of all that is bad") and Isabella Gordon was dismissed. "As she had no clothes she departed, of necessity, in those she had on, and in one of the rough shawls. We gave her half a crown to get a night's lodging . . . The girl herself, now that it had really come to this, cried, and hung down her head, and when she got out at the door, stopped and leaned against the house for a minute or two before she went to the gate – in a most miserable and wretched state . . . We passed her in the lane, afterwards, going slowly away, and wiping her face with her shawl." No more is ever heard of Isabella Gordon; the last recorded sight is of her wiping the tears from her face with the rough shawl which Charles Dickens had given her. Certainly the novelist was moved by the sight – "the sad picture", as he put it, remained in his mind all that evening – and no doubt it was with some intention to exorcise his own guilt or sorrow that only a few days later he described, in that month's episode of *David Copperfield*, the departure of Martha to a life of prostitution in London. "Then Martha arose, and gathering her shawl about her, covering her face with it, and weeping aloud, went slowly to the door. She stopped a moment before going out, as if she would have uttered something or turned back; but no word passed her lips. Making the same low, dreary, wretched moaning in her shawl, she went away." So did the real world enter Dickens's fiction, helping to shape the novel even as it emerged under his hand. A smaller example may add to the sense of this process. At the beginning of November he wrote a letter in defence of Street Punches, the Punch and Judy acts which were performed at street corners and at fairs, and a few days later, in *David Copperfield*, he characterises Mr Spenlow as "like Punch". Thus do the daily matters attracting his attention play their own part in a novel which has transcended its day, its own century, and even the century after. With words he was actually writing very quickly, through the weeks of November 1849.

In fact he wrote two chapters in just four days before travelling, with the rest of the family, to Rockingham Castle in Northampton-shire in order to stay once again with the Watsons. They remained for four days and Mrs Watson wrote in her diary, on the day of their departure: "Nov. 30. Dickens and Family left. Last night he and Miss Boyle acted a scene out of *Nicholas Nickleby* and from the *School for Scandal* in the Hall most admirably. He afterwards performed some conjuring tricks." One might be forgiven for thinking that Dickens had known "Miss Boyle" for some time, since he felt able to enact with her a scene out of one of his own novels. In fact he had just met her; she was Mrs Watson's cousin, and had been specifically invited to Northamptonshire in order to meet the great novelist. The scene from *Nicholas Nickleby* which they played together was the one in which a madman, fallen deeply and hopelessly in love with Mrs Nickleby, throws an assortment of vegetables over the garden wall to display his affection. Dickens himself seems to have been infected with the part because only a few days later, after his return to Devonshire Terrace, he sent Mrs Watson an extravagant missive of love about her cousin, complete with a heart and the initials C.D. being pierced by an arrow. To Mary Boyle herself he sent a parody of Gray's *Elegy in a Country Churchyard*:

The small dog Spitz has given a shrill bark,
And gone off with her tail uprais'd in air;
I don't know where she's gone, it is so dark,
And (what is more) I don't think that I care . . .

Over the next few years he was to write equally extravagant and affectionate letters to her; of course it was all a "joke" with no adulterous intent, but there was a reality beneath it, too, a reality which in a later letter he described to Miss Boyle as the feeling that "I seem to be always looking at such times for something I have not found in life . . ." Which was precisely the sentiment he was expressing in *David Copperfield* at the time he met her: ". . . I felt a vague unhappy loss or want of something overshadow me like a cloud." Clearly Catherine could not provide what it was that Dickens so longed for. She was much stouter, her size in part owing to the number of pregnancies she had undergone; she was now in her late thirties, but already looked middle-aged; according to a contemporary she was also "heavy in her manners and conversation"; she was slower in action and reaction; she was sometimes unaccountably ill and nervous. And her husband, the most famous and most adored writer of his age, wanted something else, something more . . . the fact that he should instantly if facetiously fall in love with another woman is some indication of what it was that he thought he was missing.

Altogether it was, for him, a difficult period. In December, particularly, he was being harassed on two sides. The first instance was certainly the most disagreeable, and the most invidious. One Thomas Powell, an employee of Thomas Chapman and colleague of Dickens's younger brother, Augustus, had three years before been detected embezzling money from the firm; he tried to commit suicide by taking laudanum and, out of pity for his situation, Chapman never pressed charges. On a later occasion he was detected in forgery but feigned madness and was for a while detained at a lunatic asylum in Hoxton. Then he had decamped for America where he earned his living as journalist and writer of cheap books. Powell had known Dickens reasonably well and, through the agency of Augustus, had even dined with him; it was not a connection he was likely to forget and, in this year, he had written a distinctly unflattering life of Dickens which was even now appearing in the American newspapers. In this account Dickens is branded as a snob and parvenu; perhaps more importantly, he is also accused of having based the character of Mr Dombey upon

Thomas Chapman himself. Dickens had already learnt of all this in October, and immediately took steps to denounce Powell as a liar and forger (which undoubtedly he was). Now, in December, he had dispatched to America a series of documents convicting Powell of the offences charged, plus a pamphlet of his own in which he went through the same charges. It was at this point that Powell threatened to sue him for libel, to the amount of ten thousand dollars.

Of course he had no real chance of launching let alone winning any such case, and Dickens was more angry than anxious about the matter. But unfortunately it coincided with another threatened action, and this time from a more unlikely source. A certain Mrs Hill, a chiropodist and manicurist, a neighbour of Dickens, and a dwarf, felt that she was being portrayed as the untrustworthy and tiny Miss Mowcher in *David Copperfield*. She was right; Dickens had obviously seen her on many occasions, and had caricatured at least her appearance in the novel without any thought of the consequences to Mrs Hill herself. So she sent a pained letter about his use of her "personal deformities"; "Should your book be dramatised and I not protected madness will be the result." Dickens sent her a conciliatory reply, in which he admitted the justice of her rebuke in part but went on to say (quite untruthfully) that the main element of the characterisation was based upon someone else. But immediately he wrote a more honest letter to Forster in which he concluded, ". . . there is no doubt one is wrong in being tempted to such a use of power." Again that word with which he characterises his fiction. Power. A few days later he received a letter from Mrs Hill's solicitor, in which an action for libel was vaguely threatened. Dickens tried to mollify the man, and promised to repair the damage by changing the character of Miss Mowcher in order to throw a creditable light upon Mrs Hill herself. He was as good as his word, eventually, but there can be little doubt that he was perturbed by all that had taken place. Perturbed in other ways, too. A few days later he resigned from the Garrick, for reasons which remain unknown, and in the same period he was offended by Daniel Maclise apparently because he had been unable to attend the usual Christmas celebrations at Devonshire Terrace. In other words, there was anger and resentment in Dickens during this period, particularly against Thomas Powell. Certainly it is possible that the memory of the experience of these feelings was one he used to direct David Copperfield's hatred against Uriah Heep in the chapter he was then writing. Just as his "mock" passion for Mary Boyle is likely to have been fictionally transformed into David Copperfield's "real" passion for Dora Spenlow; just as his experience with Isabella Gordon had been incorporated within his portrait of poor Martha. And so it goes on, this shuttling between literature and life, this cross-fertilisation; no doubt the closest examination of each day in Dickens's life, if such a process were at all possible, would reveal other associations and resemblances. But they are not to be unearthed now, not at this late date, and in any case *David Copperfield* must temporarily give way to what had become for him more pressing matters. For, at the end of December 1849, Dickens announced in handbills that he was about to begin editing a "WEEKLY MISCELLANY OF General Literature". It was a role he would maintain until the end of his life.

Chapter 20

THE old year ended and the new decade began with his work on the new periodical, and he was attending quickly to the next instalment of *David Copperfield* in order to give himself more time to concentrate on its preparation. He was receiving manuscripts from friends, and even soliciting useful material, as early as January 1850; he was preparing "dummy numbers" (he had learnt something from his brief editorship of the *Daily News*) and even before he had thought of an appropriate name for the journal he was already announcing its aim as the ". . . raising up of those that are down, and the general improvement of our social condition". He had in mind some clear aspects of that social condition; in particular sanitation, education and housing. These were the three issues that lay beneath the "condition of England question", as it was still being called, and it was genuinely part of Dickens's determination to fight for those causes even as he tried to beguile and to entertain. But after his experience on the *Daily News*, as well as on *Bentley's Miscellany*, he was determined that this time he should be in sole charge of the editorial content of the periodical; he knew himself well enough to realise that he could brook no interference in the pursuit of his own designs. But he needed assistance; he could not edit a weekly periodical on his own and, on Forster's advice, Dickens decided to employ W. H. Wills, once his secretary on the *Daily News*, as sub-editor of the magazine. He could not have made a better choice. Wills was already experienced in what might be described as the administrative side of publishing, having been assistant editor of *Chambers's Journal* as well as Dickens's quondam secretary. He was two years older than Dickens, a small, thin man with a quick, nervous eye; one colleague described him as a ". . . very intelligent and industrious man . . . but rather too gentle and compliant always to enforce his own intentions effectually upon others . . .", while another contemporary called him ". . . friendly and good-natured but with a certain *literal* or pedantic air . . ." In other words, he was precisely the man Dickens needed to take charge of all the minutiae of the daily administration of the magazine – the negotiations with printers, the dealings with contributors, the "make-up" of the periodical, and all the myriad business matters which surround any consistent undertaking. He had a reputation also for being more cautious and frugal than Dickens, a reputation which no doubt derived from the fact that, within certain broad limits, it was he who decided upon the payments to contributors. Dickens's own opinion of him was just if somewhat severe – "Wills has no genius, and is, in literary matters, sufficiently commonplace to represent a very large proportion of our readers"; a decidedly backhanded compliment but in fact over the years of their association Dickens grew very fond of his assistant until in the end, according to Forster, he "had no more intimate friend". He may not have had "the ghost of an idea in the imaginative way", as Dickens also said, but the novelist himself had more than enough imagination for the enterprise; what Wills provided was painstaking work, loyalty, and discretion. And compliance: he was exactly the kind of man who deferred to Dickens's often arbitrary and authoritarian manner.

So the ground was being laid for the new periodical and, on the second day of February, Dickens, after several attempts at finding a title (among those considered were *Charles Dickens* and *Everything*), hit upon *Household Words*. It was taken from one of the many Shakespearian tags he seemed to carry in his head. "Familiar in their mouths as Household Words" was placed upon the masthead of the periodical, although the actual line from *Henry V* is slightly different and reads "Familiar in his mouth as household words". Now that he had found a name he also needed a local habitation, and a few days later he took a lease upon 16 Wellington Street North, a small and narrow thoroughfare just off the Strand, the headquarters of the new periodical itself being "exceedingly pretty with the bowed front, the bow reaching up for two stories, each giving a flood of light". Like much of London it stood upon a haunted spot, the site of an old tenement where, according to legend, Hogarth had seen the final tableau of "The Harlot's Progress". In the first-floor front of the older house the artist had seen the woman in her coffin, the ancient drunken crones in various postures around her, and it was this scene which Dickens often "conjured up", he said, as he sat beside the bow window on the first floor. He soon became as familiar in this area as in many other parts of London, and local tradesmen told one of his earlier chroniclers that "they noted regularly his lithe figure briskly flitting past as the clock struck, his little bag in hand".

So it was that Dickens busied himself about the preparations for a new weekly periodical even at the time he was still heavily engaged with the working out of *David Copperfield*. And with the working out of other, more intractable, destinies. His children were to say in later years that he seemed to love his fictional children as much as his real ones, but in this period especially he was very concerned with those flesh-and-blood creatures whose father he happened to be. His eldest son, Charles, was just about to go to Eton (his education there being paid by Miss Burdett-Coutts), and there is no doubt that Dickens was preparing his son for precisely the kind of straightforward middle-class life which he had never himself experienced. At the same time, again at the instigation and indeed at the expense of Miss Burdett-Coutts, he was actively planning to have his second son, Walter, enrolled in an East India Company cadetship which would eventually take him out to business in India; again, a straightforward, middle-class option. There is no sense in which Dickens brought up his children to be "rebels" against the system which he himself so consistently attacked, and there is also no sense in which he thinks of their education as anything other than preliminary to "making their way" in the active, adult world. It is clear enough that he wanted to ensure that his own children acquired none of his own father's characteristics, that they remained both reliable and self-reliant (although, alas, the burden of inheritance was such that the sons eventually displayed temperaments closer to that of John Dickens than that of Charles Dickens). His daughters were to be educated at home, and there is little independent testimony about their lives in this period – except for a revealing remark by one of Thackeray's daughters, Anny, who remembers a children's party given by Dickens at Devonshire Terrace. Of Katey and Mamie she says, "I remember watching the white satin shoes and long flowing white sashes of the little Dickens girls, who were just about our own age but how much more graceful and beautifully dressed." Mrs Gaskell said of the children that they were ". . . so polite, and well-trained". In other words, they were being brought up as "model" children, impeccable, good-mannered and very well-dressed.

Nothing like Dickens's own childhood, of course, which is perhaps one of the reasons why he lavished such attention on his children in their younger days; it was not just a means of protecting them from a similar fate, but also a way of asserting his own transcendence of it. In any case the disparity between his own childhood and theirs was mirrored for him in his constant visits to the ragged schools and on his journeys through the poorer quarters of the city. He saw there how different the children of the poor and destitute were; how experienced, how precocious, how lost. It is precisely in this period, for example, that he read in the *Examiner* an account of the cross-examination of a fourteen-year-old boy, George Ruby, who earned his living by sweeping the mud and manure from the streets of London. Here is the exact account, which Dickens later republished in his own periodical:

Alderman Humphrey: Do you ever say your prayers?

Boy: No; never.

Alderman: Do you know what prayers are?

Boy: No.

Alderman: Do you know what God is?

Boy: No.

Alderman: Do you know what the Devil is?

Boy: No. I've heard of the Devil, but I don't know him.

Alderman: What do you know my poor fellow?

Boy: I knows how to sweep the crossing.

Alderman: And that's all?

Boy: That's all. I sweeps the crossing.

Here is the germ of Jo in *Bleak House*, here in these plain and corroborated words of a fourteen-year-old boy. And there are still those who accuse Dickens of melodramatic exaggeration.

Appropriate, here, to mention the small book which Dickens began at this time and which he was eventually to finish some three years later. In his spare time, while resting from his labours on his fiction or on the new periodical, he was in the habit of dictating to Georgina Hogarth a narrative which he entitled *A Child's History of England*. It was meant primarily for his own children, but it was also in part serialised in *Household Words* so that it can fairly be said to have some general or public import. The actual contents are not in themselves particularly original; Dickens seems to have derived most of his information from Keightley's *History of England* and from Charles Knight's *Pictorial History of England*. Certainly the latter book was in his library, and was heavily annotated by him. It is often said that historical writing, like biography, says more about the period in which it is written than about the period which is its ostensible subject; in a sense, Dickens's own attempt proves the truth of this. It has very much the timbre of the mid-nineteenth century, and its character might best be summed up in the slightly later words of Froude in *Short Studies in Great Subjects*: "One lesson, and only one, history may be said to repeat with distinctness; that the world is built somehow on moral foundations; that, in the long run, it is well with the good; in the long run it is ill with the wicked." A very "Victorian" sentiment, and one which is confirmed by Froude's statement that what is wanted is "a positive, manly and intellectually credible explanation of the world".

That is precisely what Dickens was trying to impart to his children some twenty or so years before Froude's own comments. *A Child's History of England* is in many ways a melodramatic and theatrical account – in parts it is very close to the caricature tradition of Rowlandson and Hogarth – since Dickens had deliberately decided that his historical narrative must have a "romantic and attractive air" in order to inveigle the children into reading it. But it is also very sharp and very opinionated; "true", as Dickens said in a letter, and not "genteel". He was not interested in dictating the kind of book he satirised later in *Little Dorrit*: "Even the said great personages dying in bed, making exemplary ends and sounding speeches; and polite history, more servile than their instruments, embalming them!" There is nothing polite about Dickens's own account of England's past and, from a reading of the volume, you would think the history of that country to be no more than a continuing "battle of life"; a frenzied, active, heaving controversy which ends in the death of a monarch, only to begin all over again. In fact the book bears a strong resemblance to his two historical novels, *Barnaby Rudge* and *A Tale of Two Cities*; it is essentially history as theatre, with crowds, confrontations, clashes, battles, death scenes and sundry noises off. But it is also energetically written; Dickens's imagination simply pours into everything he writes or speaks, and so there are moments of great power. When, for example, an old man is being burned at the stake: "And then he was seen to make motions with his hands as if he were washing them in the flames, and to stroke his aged face with them . . ." Dickens is fascinated by punishments or executions, and throughout the narrative he goes to no great pains to hide his own opinions; he calls James I "his Sowship", and Henry VIII ". . . a blot of blood and grease . . ." Those who seek for the meaning of his historical novels might find some evidence in a narrative where monarchs in general are reviled and where the people in rebellion are cheered; he takes the side of Wat Tyler and, on the French Revolution, he comments that ". . . I know of nothing worse, done by the maddened people of France in that awful time, than was done by the highest judge in England, with the express approval of the King of England, in The Bloody Assize". So it is a narrative of action, movement, conflict and one in which key adjectives are "turbulent", "relentless" and "dreadful"; a narrative, too, in which the permanent and unassuageable English character is extolled. Dickens says of the "English-Saxon" that "it has been the greatest character among the nations of the earth". And, a little later, "Wheresoever that race goes, there, law and industry, and safety for life and property, and all the great results of steady perseverance, are certain to arise." No clearer statement of his belief exists, and it ought always to be kept in mind when Dickens himself in later years attacks the English government for its folly and the English people for their complaisance.

Which leads back to one of the more salient facts in this year of transition – after so long a period working almost exclusively on *David Copperfield*, Dickens was once again preparing to take up a public role as editor of a weekly periodical and to resume the public duties attendant upon that role. Even the cheap edition of his *Sketches by Boz*, which was printed in this year, some fourteen years after its first publication, suggests what a change had come upon him since those days as an ironist and sketch-writer. Dickens was now at pains to remove anything which smacked of bad taste or flippancy; the typically ebullient and sometimes callow language of the young man is chastened for this reprint, just as the more exaggerated aspects of his humour are mollified. It has sometimes been said that great art must of its necessity shock, offend or perplex any putative audience; Dickens, perhaps the greatest artist of his century, convincingly disproves such assertions.

This of course does not mean that he was uncontroversial, and his public pronouncements in this year suggest how firmly he had reached conclusions about the major issues of the period. At the beginning of February, for example, he delivered a speech to mark the establishment of the Metropolitan Sanitary Association, an Association which was instituted as a direct result of the cholera epidemic of the previous winter, and which united various interests in the cause of sanitary reform, public health, housing, and the closing of the City churchyards. All these were "causes" which Dickens would also directly champion in *Household Words* and, during his speech at the Freemasons' Tavern on that February day, he proclaimed that the members of the new Association "found infancy was made stunted, ugly, and full of pain; maturity made old, and old age imbecile; and pauperism made hopeless every day. They claimed for the metropolis of a Christian country that this should be remedied, and that the capital should set an example of humanity and justice to the whole empire." His speech, according to newspaper reports, was greeted with "loud and prolonged cheers". And it might be noted in passing that this was one of the first occasions when Dickens mentioned the "empire", a concept which in his later fiction can be glimpsed as part of that large mysterious world beyond the individual self.

Even as he was preparing his speech for the Metropolitan Association he was working quickly on the next number of *David Copperfield*, wanting, as it were, to get it out of the way at this busy time. He managed to complete it on 21 February, and only three days later he was back on his round of *Household Words* business with a visit to Mrs Elizabeth Herbert in order to discuss the arrangements of the Family Colonisation Loan Society, a body which, as its name suggests, assisted the passage of needy and worthy families to Australia. Mrs Herbert was clearly impressed by his devotion to this "cause" (indeed it was one of the main planks of the liberal or radical platform), and wrote to the founder of the society, Mrs Chisholm, that "he is so singularly clever and agreeable that I hope you will forgive me for having made this appointment without your direct sanction . . ." The appointment was for two days later when indeed he did call upon Mrs Chisholm to discuss her scheme; Dickens, however, seems to have been most impressed by the somewhat neglected state of her children. "I dream of Mrs Chisholm, and her houskeeping," he wrote to Miss Burdett-Coutts. "The dirty faces of her children are my continual companions." Familiar companions, too, since this image of them was one which fully embodied his own disgust at the way certain philanthropists attended to distant causes while ignoring those closer to home, and of course it was one which would be resuscitated in the house of Mrs Jellyby in *Bleak House*; one of a number of episodes and scenes from this period, which, blocked from access into *David Copperfield*, found their way into Dickens's next novel. The day after he had seen Mrs Chisholm, for example, he was sent by his brother-in-law, Henry Austin, a *Report on a General Scheme for Extra-Mural*

Sepulture which contained harrowing detail on the state of city graveyards. "I began to read it last night, in bed," he told Austin, " – and dreamed of putrefaction generally." This was also a theme which was to enter *Bleak House*, particularly in the description of the small urban graveyard in which Nemo is buried and against the bars of which, within sight of walls where ". . . a thick humidity broke out like a disease", Lady Dedlock dies. There is always a sense in which he is preparing the ground for the next novel even while working upon the present one – an activity which gives some justification to G. K. Chesterton's view that there are not really distinct fictions but rather a continuing production of Dickensian *stuff* which is cut off into separate pieces and given separate names. That is also why his activities and reading at this time are able to nourish both *Household Words* and his own fiction. If *Household Words* becomes the secular companion of Dickens's imaginative work, a novel such as *Bleak House* can in turn be seen as a fantastic and mysterious counterpart to Dickens's journalism.

Emigration and transportation were in any case close to his real interests at this point, particularly with regard to the possibility of sending the young women from Urania Cottage to Australia in order to make a "new start". This is of course the destiny of Little Em'ly in an episode of *David Copperfield* yet to be written, but his continuing interest in real "fallen women" was one which he took to extraordinary lengths. He rented a room near the Magdalen Hospital in order to interview girls whom the Hospital did not take in and, in one letter to Miss Burdett-Coutts, he describes how "in the course of my nightly wanderings into strange places, I have spoken to several women and girls . . ."; in a letter to Daniel Maclise in the same month he said of an unknown person, "The young lady was *not* interesting, and I was after you in three or four minutes." He had, in other words, stopped to talk to a girl or young woman while his friend wandered away. It ought to be remembered that in a much earlier letter to Maclise he had let him know of a brothel in Margate; of course that was nine years before, but it suggests, at least, how much philanthropy was intermixed with a certain kind of sexual voyeurism. This is not to suggest that Dickens consorted with prostitutes (the evidence for which does not exist and, given Dickens's almost puritanical abstemiousness and rectitude in other matters, it must in any case rate as a very remote possibility), only to emphasise how much female prostitution was on the minds, and indeed in front of the very eyes, of the middle-classes in this period. The number of prostitutes in London at this time has been estimated at anything from ten thousand to one hundred and twenty thousand; certainly they were an accepted sight on most of the major thoroughfares, in the theatres and the pleasure gardens. Nineteenth-century London was in many ways a much less restrained city than its late twentieth-century counterpart – the possibilities of chaos, the prevalence of disorder, always lurking just beneath its surface.

Philanthropy was of course one way of keeping disorder in check and, even as Dickens was engaged on Urania Cottage business, he accepted an appointment on the Central Committee of the Working Classes for the Great Exhibition. That particular jamboree was now in active preparation, and Dickens was a member of the Committee which was to look into the role of, and arrangements for, the "working classes" in what was supposed to be a national celebration: it was already realised what a danger those classes could pose if they were actively excluded from participation. In fact, on a motion of Dickens himself, the Committee dissolved itself some four months later, after meeting obstruction on the part of the Commissioners. But the episode confirms the evidence of Urania Cottage on the extent to which Dickens himself was seen as a possible representative, or guardian, of the less affluent members of the community.

But all of this frantic activity meant that in London Dickens was too pressed and too bothered to work properly on *David Copperfield*, for which project he needed at least two weeks in every month. So at the beginning of March he took lodgings in King Street, Brighton, in order to work in peace. Here he began those chapters which deal with Copperfield's burgeoning romance with Dora Spenlow, a romance in which there are shades of Dickens's love for his mother and his sister, as if the novelist himself were looking helplessly back at the time of his own infancy. Back towards his dream of a girl or young woman; young, beautiful and good. A dream which descended on him again as he travelled on the railroad, which he described as ". . . a wonderfully suggestive place to me when I am alone . . ." He was coming from London back to Brighton, and was concerned with the want of "something tender" in the second issue of *Household Words* which he was even then preparing. As the train made its way towards the coast Dickens looked up at the stars through the window of his carriage, and something in that sight of immensity reminded him of the night-sky of his own childhood – of the time when he and his now dead sister had looked out the window of their little room in Chatham, had seen the adjacent graveyard, and had looked up at the heavens together. Even as he is writing about Dora Spenlow, therefore, his mind is roving back towards his young sister; out of his nocturnal meditation came "A Child's Dream of a Star", a short but in many ways attractive piece which certainly contributed to the tenderness of *Household Words*. "'My age is falling from me like a garment, and I move towards the star as a child.'" It was not the only time in this year when he went back to his infancy; in the seasonal story he eventually wrote, "A Christmas Tree", he returned to the scenes of his childhood and described them in vivid and exact detail. In both of these shorter pieces there is both nostalgia and true memory; it is almost as if his work on *David Copperfield* had unlocked the mysteries of his own childhood, so that at last he is able to go much further back than the period he described in his explicitly autobiographical fragment; to go back to the beginnings of his life, to the Eden time.

He was only in Brighton for thirteen days, and a week after his return to London he finally signed the articles of agreement for the new periodical with Bradbury and Evans. He was to have a half share in all profits, Bradbury and Evans to have one quarter, Forster and Wills one eighth each. Bradbury and Evans were to manage all the commercial details, while Dickens was to be in sole charge of editorial policy and content. In the first year, he earned an extra seventeen hundred pounds and, in the second year of trading, two thousand pounds. A good agreement for Dickens, therefore, especially since he was also to be paid five hundred pounds a year as editor and recompensed separately for each of his contributions. From this time forward he never needed to rely solely upon his fiction in order to maintain himself and his large family.

The first issue of *Household Words* bears the date 30 March, 1850; this was a Saturday, and the periodical actually appeared on the Wednesday before. Underneath this title, on the front page, were the words "Conducted by Charles Dickens", which also appeared as a running head throughout its twenty-four pages of double-columned and unillustrated type. Contributions were anonymous but, when Douglas Jerrold saw this constantly reiterated phrase, he said that it was really "*mono*nymous throughout". It was published weekly and priced at twopence – although it was also released in monthly form and, eventually, as a bound volume. This first number contained an "Address" to its readers written by Dickens, in which he once more staked his place beside the hearths of English families and pledged that nothing in his journal would render his readers "less ardently persevering in ourselves, less tolerant of one another, less faithful in the progress of mankind, less thankful for the privilege of living in the summer-dawn of time". He promised not to be in thrall to the "mere utilitarian spirit" with its "iron binding of the mind to grim realities" but instead to illuminate the Fancy and demonstrate that "in all familiar things, even in those which are repellent on the surface, there is Romance enough, if we will find it out . . ." Here is the prospectus for *Bleak House* and *Hard Times*, too, and indeed both of these novels – written as Dickens edited *Household Words* – can be seen in conjunction with the periodical. In this first issue there also appeared the first instalment of Mrs Gaskell's story "Lizzie Leigh", an article partly written by Dickens and entitled "Valentine's Day at the Post-Office", a specimen of dramatic blank verse called "Abraham and the Fire Worshipper", another article by Dickens entitled "The Amusements of the People", a piece about a French tragedienne entitled "An Incident In the Life of Mademoiselle Clairon", a poem called "The Wayside Well" and the fruit of his meeting with Mrs Chisholm, "A Bundle of Emigrants' Letters". Dickens was responsible for almost a third of the copy in this first issue, thereby hoping no doubt to entice prospective readers, and although he wrote less in subsequent issues the basic "mix" of the periodical remained much the same. There tended to be some four or five articles on subjects of topical interest, or travel, or history, or literature; a story; a poem; and an essay; most if not all of them couched in a deliberately "bright" tone in which entertainment was combined with instruction. It says something about the nature of the publication that books were not reviewed in its pages, and were described only when they had some "direct present bearing on social advancement and convenience". As for poetry, Dickens seems to have possessed ordinary middle-class taste *in excelsis* and one contemporary remarked that "I don't believe he cares a rush for Poetry in the stricter sense".

Dickens was pleased with this first issue, however, and sanguine about the prospects of the periodical in general: "The Household Words I hope (and have every reason to hope) will become a *good property* . . . The labor, in conjunction with Copperfield, is something rather ponderous; but to establish it firmly would be to gain such an immense point for the future (I mean *my* future) that I think nothing of that." Some of his contemporaries were not as impressed, and Mrs Browning said that it "won't succeed, I predict, especially as they have adopted the fashion of not printing the names of contributors". She was wrong: the circulation settled down to approximately thirty-nine thousand and, although this figure is not nearly as high as for other periodicals of the period, it was enough to generate a reasonable profit. Nevertheless it did not satisfy a large number of Dickens's contemporaries, and this largely because it was unashamedly popular or middle-class in tone and inspiration. It was nothing like such serious journals as *The Edinburgh Review* – it was not in any sense "intellectual" – but rather took its place among the magazines which heralded or exploited the growth of the reading public throughout this period. In 1832 Chambers's *Edinburgh Journal* and Knight's *Penny Magazine* had both been established, and over the next two decades the growth of Sunday papers and weekly family periodicals was matched only by the rise of the popular penny papers which relied upon sensationalised fiction for the labouring classes. In this context *Household Words* was not unlike the *London Journal* or the *Family Herald* (although the former had a circulation of some four hundred and fifty thousand), since it catered for a respectable middle-brow domestic audience. Since this was not the cleverest, the most scholarly or even the most imaginative audience in Britain, *Household Words* had to be cheerful, bright, informative and, above all, readable.

It says something about the nature of Dickens's genius that he felt able to edit such a weekly periodical for the next twenty years; for the rest of his life he was to engage in laboured and often difficult editorial work, day by day, week by week, correcting the articles of others, cutting and reshaping, entitling, collaborating with other writers, corresponding, dealing with printers and distributors. He was doing a job that any number of nineteenth-century journalists could have accomplished but here we have the greatest author of his age working continually without complaint or apology. In 1852, for example, on his own estimate he read nine hundred manuscripts (of which only eleven were suitable for publication, and that after substantial rewriting by himself), as well as receiving and answering over two thousand letters. The month after the inauguration of the periodical he also began a *Household Narrative of Current Events*, a monthly supplement of the news compiled by his father-in-law, George Hogarth, and including a leading article which was usually written by John Forster (Forster was also to remain editor of the *Examiner* until 1855 and, with some judicious praise, materially assisted the reputation of *Household Words*).

And so Dickens began to *conduct* his journal; that sense of the conductor is close to his continual interest in stage-management, as if the nation were a vast theatre for each week's performance of *Household Words*. It was an audience for which Dickens took every possible pain; each week for twenty years he bent over ". . . that great humming-top *Household Words* which is always going round with the weeks, and murmuring, 'Attend to me.'" Of course it was not to be expected that a man who turned all of his duties into a "system" would not soon adopt a routine in his weekly journalism. So it is that, according to one of his secretaries, on certain days of the week he arrived at the offices in Wellington Street North at eight in the morning and then left at eleven. Each week's issue was printed on the Wednesday, and on the following day he and Wills and others met at five for the weekly editorial conference which might go through dinner and into the evening. It was at this meeting that most of the articles were chosen (characteristically Dickens managed to work three weeks ahead of publication), but it was Dickens himself who decided upon the order in which they would appear; this was a very important point with him, and it was with the instinctive skill of the novelist that he knew how to balance and to lighten an issue. He was always very business-like, too, in the administration and organisation of editorial matters; his own manuscripts, for example, were always returned to him by the printer in a sealed envelope. And, as was to be expected, he had a perfect memory of contributors and of their pieces.

For it was always *his* journal, and every article published had to bear the stamp of Charles Dickens; he once described it as the diffusion of himself through its pages. That is why he was such a perfectionist in the revision or rewriting of articles; sometimes he might add a phrase or a paragraph, and on other occasions he might append a footnote which he signed "CD" or "The Conductor of this Journal". He had a horror of being wrong about anything and, as one contemporary remembered, "When an inaccuracy, however slight, was brought home to him, it made him miserable . . ." It was precisely this which prompted him to write to Wills, "Nothing can be so damaging to Household Words as carelessness about facts. It is as hideous as dullness." Accuracy was also to be matched by coherence of opinion; Dickens wrote, again to Wills, that ". . . the journal itself is blowing hot and cold and playing fast and loose, in a ridiculous way". That is why he also tried to keep to certain fixed rules in matters of syntax and punctuation, and nothing more clearly shows the energy and persistence of the man than in the care he took over even the shortest piece which was to appear in his pages. He added, amended, revised, shortened, condensed and rewrote (it has been estimated that *Household Words* incurred some two thousand printers' corrections each week). It has been reported that "when one of the long slips had been corrected it looked like a blue network covering the print – so profuse and lavish were his alterations". And Percy Fitzgerald, one of his chief contributors, has remembered "the way he used to scatter his bright touches over the whole, the sparkling word of his own that he would insert here and there, gave a surprising point and light". This did of course mean that some articles written by other hands were in fact attributed to Dickens, although one such contributor declares that he had "no remotest notion that he was putting a bushel over the lights of his staff". Yet of course there were writers who cavilled at such treatment. It seems that Wilkie Collins, for example, was worried that an article by him might by these methods be mistaken for an article by the "Conductor". Dickens replied rather tartly to Wills, ". . . such a confusion of authorship . . . would be a far greater service than dis-service to him. This I clearly see." He cut, too, with a trained eye and when Percy Fitzgerald, on seeing Dickens remove a large passage, commented, "There's fifteen shillings lost to him for ever," Dickens "laughed immensely". Thus did *Household Words* become a true vehicle for HIMSELF.

That is why there were also occasions when he "tabooed" an article because its sentiments or sympathies were so different from his own. There were even times when he accepted an article only to reject it later, generally on the grounds that it "won't do". The important point was that Dickens wanted nothing in his periodical which would upset, anger or depress his putative audience; his best advice to his contributors was to imagine a reader who was pleasant, intelligent but "rather afraid of being bored". Throughout his career as an editor there are warning notes to those whom he considered to be going too far in one direction or another. Of an article by Mrs Lynn Linton, Dickens told Wills "I don't know how it is that she gets so near the sexual side of things as to be a little dangerous to us at times". And of an essay by Wilkie Collins he told Wills "not to leave anything in it that may be sweeping, and unnecessarily offensive to the middle class". He had an instinctive sense of what was right and proper within his periodical, then, but this does not mean that he failed to explain patiently and constructively why a certain piece did not meet his requirements. In fact his letters are generally concerned with the effectiveness of presentation, since this was the quality he recognised immediately. Percy Fitzgerald again: "As I read over his many letters on those points, I am amazed at the good-natured allowance, the untiring good humour, the wish to please and make pleasant, the almost deference, the modesty . . ." Another contemporary editor has recorded that "many a time have young would-be contributors called upon me, and produced from their breast-pockets as passport to my attention a letter of rejection, torn and frayed, and bearing tokens of having been read a hundred times, from the Master. 'He wrote me this letter himself,' they would say, as though there were but one 'He' in the world. It was generally a pretty long one, though written at a time when minutes were guineas to him, full of the soundest advice and tenderest sympathy."

So it was by trial and error that Dickens was able to assemble a team of writers around him. Among the first of his regular contributors were Henry Morley, R. H. Horne, Dudley Costello and Blanchard Jerrold; some of them had worked with him on the *Daily News* and some of them were young aspiring writers who naturally tended to copy him and were for a while branded as "slavish imitators" of his style. In later years others joined this inner circle of regular writers, among them Percy Fitzgerald, G. A. H. Sala, and Wilkie Collins. They made regular contributions and were sometimes paid a fixed salary rather than a sum for each article. They were in that sense the "backbone" of the journal and were often given certain specialities; Henry Morley tended to write on educational matters, for example, while Sala made his reputation with his descriptions of London life. There were also less regular writers, such as Mrs Gaskell, whom Dickens would call upon from time to time. He was known to be a quick and generous payer, also, which helped to endear him to his contributors. It was his practice, too, to send newspaper cuttings or articles to various interested parties in the hope that they would provoke some sort of piece for *Household Words*. In all this he did not differ from any other editor of the period, however – except perhaps in the sense that, as one contemporary noted, he "was a born trader, with a considerable power of organisation, and his plans were laid down with financial prudence".

Sala has left an account of his first meeting with Dickens in the office of the periodical. ". . . I was overcome with astonishment at the sight of the spare, wiry gentleman who, standing on the hearthrug, shook me cordially by the hand – both hands, if I remember aright . . . He was then, I should say, barely forty; yet to my eyes he seemed to be rapidly approaching fifty." Sala goes on to discuss Dickens's editorial persona in the years they knew each other; he "seldom talked at length on literature, either of the present or the past . . . What he liked to talk about was the latest new piece at the theatres, the latest exciting trial or police case, the latest social craze or social swindle, and especially the latest murder and the newest thing in ghosts. He delighted in telling short, droll stories, and occasionally indulging in comic similes and drawing waggish parallels. He frequently touched on political subjects – always from that which was then a strong Radical point of view, but which at present [1894] I imagine would be thought more Conservative than Democratic; but his conversation, I am bound to say, did not rise above the amusing commonplaces of a very shrewd, clever man of the world . . ." This description has been quoted at some length because it gives a fair and accurate portrait of one aspect of Dickens, but it has to be remembered that he was so sensitive a man that he would adapt his conversation to the standard of his interlocutor. Sala himself was a "very shrewd, clever man of the world", and there is no doubt that Dickens reacted accordingly. It ought to be remembered, too, that his silence on matters of literature (and on his own work) is perfectly understandable; he took it too seriously to be able to talk about it freely or easily, and preferred instead to steer his conversation onto less pressing journalistic subjects.

But there was one other large area in which he did differ from most other editors, and that lay in his attention to style. "Brighten it, brighten it, brighten it!" was his message once to W. H. Wills, and all of his editorial practices were designed towards that end. He liked to put smart or punning titles on the articles, and he always emphasised the need for liveliness and brightness in even the most humble pieces; it was the quality which Mrs Gaskell, in a not particularly complimentary spirit, defined as "Dickensy". One contributor, John Hollingshead, said that "the driest subjects" were to be imbued with "some degree of fancy and imagination"; and Percy Fitzgerald has also described that principle of lively exaggeration which Dickens always favoured. "Everything, even trivia, had to be made more comic than it really was. This was the law of the paper . . ." So *Household Words* remained "Dickensy" until the end.

There is no doubt that Dickens was indeed a great popular journalist, although it has to be said that the particular tone and quality of the journalism he espoused have not remained popular. The style of Addison and Steele, embodied in the *Spectator*, is one that has had some continuing attraction; but the same cannot be said of the bright domestic tones of *Household Words*. At the time, however, Dickens wielded great power with the periodical. His own most important articles were always printed on the first page, and on many occasions *The Times* or the *Examiner* would reprint them. John Henry Newman said in a sermon in the year of the first publication of *Household Words* that confusion and doubt had led to a great rise in the power of the press. "Hence the extreme influence of periodical publications at this day," he said, "quarterly, monthly, or daily; these teach the multitude of men what to think and what to say." Clearly this was part of the role Dickens designed for himself; *Household Words* dealt with the topics of the day, and with the great social issues, in a style which was designed to reach the largest possible number of people in the most palatable and entertaining way. It could not be said that *Household Words* ever really advanced a subject which was not already before the nation, but its purpose was to *publicise* the causes of the day.

The example of another nineteenth-century writer can be employed here to illuminate an important aspect of Dickens's editorial personality. Justin McCarthy wrote of the sociologist, H. T. Buckle, that "he brought to his task . . . an ardent spirit full of faith in his own theory, and a power of self-will and self-complacency which enabled him to accept as certain and settled every dogma on which he had personally made up his mind". Precisely true of Dickens, too, which is why *Household Words* bore so recognisably the stamp of its editor's public personality. Again he might be said to share another Victorian characteristic with Thomas Arnold, as described in the *Edinburgh Review* of 1845: "Arnold could do nothing by halves . . . Whatever it was on which he was engaged he threw himself headlong into it, almost bodily, as into a volcano . . ." – one remembers here not only Dickens's painstaking editing of *Household Words*, but also his own journey up to the very summit of Mount Vesuvius – ". . . from whose depths forth he came again – argument and sentiment, emotion and burning words – rolling and thundering." As might be said of Dickens's own words, in his contributions to *Household Words*; perhaps not boiling, but certainly in the upper reaches of the Victorian thermometer. He wrote a great deal in the first two or three years but, as the magazine grew more stable both in spirit and in circulation, he began slowly to intervene less actively himself. Carlyle described

Dickens's pieces here as "Word-Spinnings", that in no complimentary sense, and in fact his journalism was not without its critics.
Yet he knew what he was doing. He knew his journalism to be a thing
quite different from his fiction, and with that instinctive rapport with
his audience which never left him he was able effortlessly to write in a
quite different style. It has been suggested that the predominantly
middle-class readers of *Household Words* would have been precisely the
people who had read and admired his earlier novels, so it is perhaps not
surprising that the sprightly benevolence of *The Pickwick Papers* and
Oliver Twist infuses the pages of the journal. An instructive contrast
might here be made with Douglas Jerrold, a radical journalist whose
style was less restrained by Fancy or by Delicacy than that of Dickens.
In the *Weekly Dispatch*, for example, it was declared that "Dickens
likes to dwell upon and magnify the better qualities of human
nature . . . though he sketches bad men and base passions, he never
leaves off without reforming the former and annihilating the latter.
His means of effecting good is the opposite of Douglas Jerrold's for
that writer always attacks the follies of the age, and by severely lashing
with cutting satire the baseness of the world, seeks to affect an
amelioration in the condition of his fellow men." The ingrate Thomas
Powell added to the contrast in his *Pictures of the Living Authors of
Britain*: "Jerrold flies at his enemy like a tiger, and never lets go while
there is life in him; while Dickens contents himself by giving him a
sound drubbing. Jerrold is most in earnest, but Dickens is more
effective." A salutary comparison, therefore, but the two men were
not so far apart that they could not come together in a different sense.
In this period, for example, they had quarrelled over the matter of
capital punishment (Dickens being in favour of private hanging
behind the walls of the prison, as we have seen, while Jerrold was in
favour of total abolition), only to be cordially reunited. They had not
met for several months, so serious had been their disagreement, until
they both found themselves dining in the Garrick Club. Dickens did
not make the first move; he was too nervous of a rebuff ever to do
so. But Jerrold turned his chair around and, according to Dickens,
". . . said aloud, with a bright and loving face that I can see as I
write . . . 'For God's sake, let us be friends again! Life's not long
enough for this!'" Another writer, David Masson, was introduced to
Dickens by Jerrold just after this moment of reconciliation and he
reports that Dickens "in his satisfaction at the happy termination of the
estrangement, took me by the arm and walked around the room with

me, pointing out this and that one of the dramatic portraits which hung on its walls, and for which it was famous".

Dickens's actual writing within the pages of *Household Words* took many different forms, and he certainly no longer needed to write letters to *The Times* about public executions. It has already been demonstrated how closely and carefully he revised articles for the periodical which, as it were, diffused his spirit through the nation. But there were also many occasions when with Wills, Morley or others he would collaborate in "composite" articles, Dickens characteristically providing the opening and ending to set the tone of the piece, while his collaborator filled in the rest. Sometimes these articles were the result of a joint expedition by Dickens and his companion to a post office, or to a factory, or to a market, or to a school, or to a race-meeting; they would visit the site of their investigation together, and then write separately the portions of the article to which each had been assigned. Dickens would then knit the pieces together. In particular he relished what were called "process articles" in which the secrets and techniques of a modern industrial process or system were disclosed to the reader; paper mills, plate-glass manufactories, and dockyards were all covered in this manner. Dickens's imagination seems to quicken upon these subjects and, in his introduction to an article on the factory which manufactured plate glass, he writes thus: ". . . we stood on the edge of a foul creek of the Thames, so horribly slimy that a crocodile, or an alligator, or any scaly monster of the Saurian period, seemed much more likely to be encountered in such a neighbourhood than the beautiful substance that makes our modern rooms so glittering and bright . . ." Crocodiles and alligators bring back memories of Peggotty and David Copperfield. But, in this sudden vision of primeval shapes lumbering through contemporary London, there is also an inkling of the imagination which created the opening pages of *Bleak House* in which a "Megalosaurus" is envisaged roaming along Holborn Hill.

Some of his articles were also written in collaboration with their subjects, and in these first months of the new journal Dickens was arranging to meet various members of the Detective Department at Scotland Yard in order to obtain material or anecdotes for *Household Words*; one of these men, Inspector Fields, was later assumed to be the original of Inspector Bucket in *Bleak House*, and there is no doubt that Dickens was sufficiently impressed by him to turn him into yet another token of his always-admiring interest in the efficiency and doggedness of the London police. Inspector Fields's recollections of his cases were not always reliable, however, and there is some evidence that Dickens's own tendency to exaggerate the facts was amply assisted by the officer himself; the famous detective had once been an amateur actor at the Catherine Street Theatre, and once more in that typically nineteenth-century association with the theatre there is a clue not only to the somewhat melodramatic nature of the New Police but also to the Victorian temperament. Even its representatives of authority and of the law had theatrical as well as investigative instincts. Is that not what Dickens was trying to reveal in his accounts of Parliament or of Chancery? Society as theatre?

But Dickens also collaborated on articles of a more prosaic nature; on money-orders, on church registries, even on the office of *Household Words* itself. Of course he remained permanently interested in the great social crusades of the period and on many occasions added his own observations to articles on charity schools, ragged dormitories, asylums, prisons, cheap lodging houses and workhouses. In fact it is in articles such as these that some of his most effective writing is to be found, whether it be in his account of "the doomed childhood that encircles you out of doors, from the rising up of the sun unto the going down of the stars . . .", or in his description of an emaciated weaver of Spitalfields. "Again his loom clashes and jars, and he leans forward over his toil. In the window by him, is a singing-bird in a little cage, which trills its song, and seems to think the loom an instrument of music. The window, tightly closed, commands a maze of chimney-pots, and tiles, and gables. Among them, the ineffectual sun, faintly contending with the rain and mist, is going down." There are passages here which, even if they do not contain the true genius of Dickens, do at least demonstrate how the sparks of that genius fly off him in the course of his ordinary journalistic observations. And perhaps the most notable example of these collaborative writings occurs in the Christmas Supplements which he instituted in 1852 and which replaced his Christmas Books of previous years; once again his favourite "framing device" was used to incorporate a sequence of linked stories, written by several hands but with Dickens composing the transitional passages as well as some of the stories themselves.

Of course there are many articles in the pages of *Household Words* which he wrote entirely himself; it was his desire to add "something tender" to the second issue which prompted him to write "A Child's Dream of a Star", the small lament inspired by the train-ride from

London to Brighton. There were other occasions on which he wrote an essay or article specifically to alter the tone and substance of a particular issue, just as there are times when his lifelong concerns prompt him into accounts of the prisons or of the poor. In the first six months of *Household Words*, for example, he wrote nineteen separate pieces, ranging from an attack on the pre-Raphaelite movement to an anatomy of the begging-letter writer to the state of Smithfield meat market. It is even possible to link some of these items with the novels of later years. So it is that in "A Walk in a Workhouse" he comes across a young domestic servant who has been removed to this place "on account of being subject to epileptic fits" and then later revives her as Guster in *Bleak House*; in "A Poor Man's Tale of a Patent" his attack on the twin evils of bureaucracy and the suppression of patented inventions heralds the much larger disquisition on the same themes in *Little Dorrit*. Dickens's fiction is not some separable entity, to be extracted from his life and other works, but rather part of the fabric of his existence as he makes his way through the world.

That is why, even as he plotted and planned over *Household Words*, his work on *David Copperfield* was continuing at the same high level of intensity. By the beginning of May he had come to a crucial point in the narrative. "Still undecided about Dora," he wrote to Forster, "but MUST decide to-day." The decision was whether Dora, David Copperfield's child-wife, was to live or to die. As was his custom on such mortal occasions he took long walks to contemplate the matter and spent some of his evening simply thinking; keeping his mind steadily on the object of his thought and trying to trace its path forward. Tracing its path through the avenues of his own life also. He was reading Carlyle's *Latter-day Pamphlets*, even then being issued, and he was about to read Tennyson's newly published *In Memoriam*; both of these books would have an influence upon *David Copperfield* itself. But he was now suffering from tiredness as a result of his ceaseless attention both to the novel and to *Household Words*. His letters in May are short and infrequent, testifying to the amount of time taken up by these twin pursuits, and he was planning to take a short "break" in Paris with Daniel Maclise – Maclise being a less stuffy friend than Forster and one with whom he could still go wildly out into the night. Clearly he was longing to get away but throughout most of June he remained in London "as busy as a bee". (He misspelt it "be" as if his mistaken use of the "Verb unprincipiant", to use James Joyce's phrase, resounds with his sense of his own being.) It was very hot but he kept going; "that remarkable man", that "amazing man!", to use just two of the expressions about himself with which Dickens was now supplementing "the Inimitable". No doubt the full flood of his creativity in *David Copperfield* led to this surplus of self-worth.

Then, the day after he finished *David Copperfield* for the month, he was off to Paris. It was very hot in that city, too, and the general round of theatre-going and dinners and excursions was larded over with a thick coating of perspiration and fatigue; "I can do nothing but drink, and go to sleep in the daytime," he told his wife. After a few days they left Paris for Rouen and travelled home on the first day of July by way of Dieppe. It had been a short trip but for Dickens a necessary one; it had given him a respite, and almost as soon he was back in Devonshire Terrace he had planned *David Copperfield* to its end. The last four numbers were sketched out in his working notes, and the main stages of the narrative signalled well in advance. He set to work upon the next number, the one in which Little Em'ly is finally discovered (a chapter over the melodrama of which he expended great pains), but clearly he was finding it very difficult to write during the London summer, quite apart from the fact that he was constantly being waylaid by office business and by reportorial excursions. So he negotiated the summer lease of Fort House in Broadstairs; this relatively large house, a little away from the main town and sea-front, had always attracted his attention, and for him and his family it must have seemed the perfect seaside retreat – the house itself separated from the harbour by a cornfield, overlooking the sea and the lighthouse.

On the fifteenth of August, before he left London, he made up another issue of *Household Words* with the assistance of Wills; on the next day Catherine was confined and gave birth to a daughter, Dora Annie Dickens; that same afternoon Dickens and the rest of the family travelled down to Broadstairs as had been originally planned to take up their newly rented summer quarters. Georgina went with him in order to look after the children, while Catherine remained in London with the new baby; not necessarily an unusual or unsympathetic arrangement. What *is* odd, however, is that, just five days after Dora was born, he wrote to his wife – ". . . I have still Dora to kill – I mean the Copperfield Dora . . ." As if he could mean anything else. But how strange it is for him to call his infant child after a character whom he intended to "kill". He had written in his memoranda: "Dora to die in THIS No.? Yes. AT THE END." And that fatal end came in his first week at Broadstairs just after he had written exceptionally affectionate letters to his wife, as if in some way he was trying to negate the implication in the death of his heroine. Nevertheless Dora was indeed to become what Dickens later described as an "ill omened name", and it was at Broadstairs, too, that he further confused what he called "my various children – real and imaginary . . ." For in "A Poor Man's Tale of a Patent", written this summer, the central character declares that he has two sons in Australia and one son dead in India; which was precisely what was to happen to Dickens's offspring in future years. A strange precognition, then, as strange as the fact that the death of "my Dora" was a year later to be terribly reflected in reality. Yet how odd of Dickens to create this fictional image of a son dead in India just months after he has agreed with Miss Burdett-Coutts that his own son, Walter, should join the cadets of the East India Company. And what must Catherine have thought of the death of the imagined Dora so soon after the birth of the real one? Surely it cannot be that her husband was obliquely wishing death upon his children? More likely that he did not know *what* he was doing, and one is tempted to use Betsy Trotwood's words on David Copperfield, that character himself so strange a simulacrum of Dickens – ". . . blind, blind, blind!"

Dickens and family were to stay at Broadstairs from the middle of August until the end of October; by now a town, according to George Eliot, "which David Copperfield has made classic". She is talking here of the location of "Betsy Trotwood's cottage" in the vicinity; thus did Dickens's work descend like a tongue of fire upon a locality, its scorch marks lasting for ever. Fort House was the ideal location for Dickens himself and his study, reached by a small staircase, had large windows letting in the brightness of the day, as well as affording a fine view of the open sea. But in some respects Broadstairs was becoming less attractive than before. In particular Dickens was bothered by the sounds of street-sellers and street musicians as well as by noise in the vicinity of Fort House itself. There was a coastguard station not far from the house, and the wife of the coastguard gave her recollections of the famous novelist to one of his first biographers. "Mr Dickens," she said, "was a very nice sort of gentleman, but he didn't like a noise." Whenever the children were too raucous, Dickens would gently ask the coastguard "to take the children away" or "to keep the people quiet". There were other kinds of disturbance, too. When Forster came to stay he snored so loudly at night that Dickens could not sleep; he wandered around the house and even woke up Georgina to keep him company. The scene was suitably transformed by Dickens in the chapter of *David Copperfield* he was just about to write, the chapter in which the fatal storm at sea keeps David up. "For hours I lay there, listening to the wind and water . . ." Is it too fanciful to imagine Dickens lying in his own room, listening to the wind and water of Broadstairs and revolving so many matters in his head?

For he had to work on more than just the novel. Even though he was out of London he kept in constant touch with W. H. Wills on *Household Words* business; discussing ideas with him, proposing contributors, sending articles of his own, correcting proofs. He even developed a particular style of correspondence with his assistant, and had a habit of writing in short paragraphs underneath capitalised headings like a tally sheet. There were in fact many occasions when he criticised his assistant severely for want of editorial taste or judgment, and one exchange of letters brought forth a rather hurt reply from Wills to Dickens's complaint that *Household Words* lacked "fancy" and brightness. "No one, not even yourself (as you said the other day) can sparkle to order, especially writers who have only an occasional sparkle in them . . . If you could regularly see and go over each sheet before it is put to press there would be a very thick sprinkling of the excellence in which you say *Household Words* is deficient . . . I cannot (less perhaps than many other men) be *always* right . . ." There is a suggestion here that Dickens was not taking as much care as he should over certain of the essays prepared for publication. Nevertheless he always tried to get to London at least on one day each week, when he generally arranged the "make-up" with Wills in Wellington Street before embarking on reportorial excursions or attending the meetings of the committee at Urania Cottage. And there were times when the pressures of work affected even his seaside repose. Many years later he recalled an occasion this summer when he visited the stationer's shop in Broadstairs to buy writing paper. He had not yet begun that month's number of *David Copperfield* and as he entered the shop he "overheard this strange lady asking the person behind the counter for the new green number. When it was handed to her, 'Oh this,' said she. 'I have read. I want the next one.' The next one she was thereupon told would be out by the end of the month. 'Listening to this, unrecognised,' he added, in conclusion, 'knowing the purpose for which I was there, and remembering that not one word of the number she was asking for was yet written, for the first and only time in my life, I felt – frightened!'" A small story, but evidence enough of the strain under which Dickens continually placed himself – to produce each month a certain number of chapters, despite sickness or fatigue or any unforeseen eventuality. And it says something about the order and discipline of his life that he maintained such a regimen until the end.

Of course he managed to rest after each morning's labours in Broadstairs; there was an expedition to the North Foreland lighthouse, various picnics and excursions and, when Sir Frederick Pollock met him here, he wrote that "he never talked about himself or his books, and was thus in great contrast with Thackeray . . ." One episode concerning Dickens and his children gives some indication of their holiday mood. He, Georgina and the children were playing in the garden of Fort House when Dickens asked Sydney, his son now aged three, if he would go and meet Forster at the railway station. Sydney boldly answered "Yes" and set off through the garden gate and down the street, until finally he was overtaken and brought back by one of the children. Then they all began a game: of Sydney flying out of the gate and into the street, always to be hauled back a few moments later. Then on a whim, after Sydney had disappeared with Alfred (two years older), Dickens closed the garden gate and all the family crouched in hiding until the two children decided to return. Dickens takes up the story in a letter to his wife: "Presently, we heard them come back and say to each other with some alarm, 'Why, the gate's shut, and they are all gone!' Ally began in a dismayed way to cry out, but the Phenomonon, shouting 'Open the gate!' sent an enormous stone flying into the garden (among our heads) by way of alarming the establishment." A pleasant little story of domestic life but illuminating, too, about the nature of Dickens's own temperament when he becomes a child playing with his children. (It is interesting to note, too, how Dickens spells "phenomenon" as "phenomonon", perhaps misled by some faint echo of the Greek *monos* meaning unique and individual. Inimitable.) Time. Another time. Sydney died at sea two years after the death of his father, one of the many foreshortened lives of the children. And Dickens called him, while he was still an infant, "The Ocean Spectre".

In his study, looking out to sea, Dickens completed the next number of *David Copperfield* by the middle of September; this instalment is perhaps the most notable of all, since it contains the chapters which describe the emigration of Little Em'ly and the Micawbers as well as the death of Steerforth in the terrible storm. Images of the sea here as he gazed out of his window – the sea which propels new life or the sea which destroys; and, in his notes about the storm, Dickens wrote in his memoranda, "at Broadstairs here, last night" although in fact no storm has been recorded during this period. These are some of the most memorable passages in the novel and, although the storm scene has been justifiably described as a fine piece of marine description, the departure of Little Em'ly with Mr Peggotty has a tone and resonance that bring it close to the poetry of Dickens's being, the slow, sad music which is often to be heard within his fiction and indeed which may be its most enduring presence. "Surrounded by the rosy light, and standing high upon the deck, apart together, she clinging to him, and he holding her, they solemnly passed away. The night had fallen on the Kentish hills when we were rowed ashore – and fallen darkly upon me." As he wrote he had "been believing such things with all my heart and soul . . .", and, afterwards, he was so disturbed by his own powerful narrative that ". . . I can't write plainly to the eye . . . I can't write sensibly to the mind". Yet almost as soon as he had finished this number he began the next and last, the double number in which David Copperfield travels abroad, as Dickens had done, and in which all his travails are finally resolved with his marriage to Agnes Wickfield. He was still in Broadstairs on the twenty-third of October when, finally, he completed the novel. Two days before he had written to Forster while in that uneasy state of mind with which he finished all his works. "Oh, my dear Forster, if I were to say half of what *Copperfield* makes me feel to-night, how strangely, even to you, I should be turned inside-out! I seem to be sending some part of myself into the Shadowy World." He liked that last phrase so much that he used it again in the preface he wrote two days later. And now he was so agitated, so restless, so sorrowful, that he wanted to go back to Rochester for a few days; as if in the scenes of his infancy he might restore his sense of himself.

Towards the end of his life Dickens had the following conversation: *Charles Kent* (a friend): Which of all your books do you think I regard as incomparably your best?
Dickens: Which?
Kent: *David Copperfield*.
Dickens: You are quite right.

This remained his constant belief. Another acquaintance tells a similar story: "I asked Charles Dickens, about a year before his death, which of his books he considered the best. 'Unquestionably David Copperfield,' he replied."

Immediately after it was published, in fact, the general critical reaction was almost as favourable as his own; it soon became clear that this was his "masterpiece" although, even so, Dickens himself retained a peculiarly private relationship with the novel. ". . . I never can approach the book with perfect composure," he once wrote, "(it had such perfect possession of me when I wrote it) . . ." And in his preface to the novel he declared that ". . . no one can ever believe this Narrative in the reading more than I have believed it in the writing". For, yes, he was sending part of himself into a shadowy world where the novel becomes a narrative among other narratives, part of a larger history than that of his own self, revolving slowly with the borrowed motion of its creator and of its time until it takes its place in the permanent literature of its country. Compared with Dickens's previous novels *David Copperfield* has much less movement, much less speed and glitter; it is stiller, retrospective, the sentiment chastened, the comedy deepened. This tone had been implicit in *The Battle of Life*, apparent even in the miniature, "A Child's Dream of a Star", but this is the first occasion when it can be detected on a sufficiently large scale to represent a change of direction. It is a change towards a certain kind of plangent lyricism, and it is not unrelated to the fact that this is the first novel in which Dickens consistently uses the first-person singular, the first novel in which he *sees* himself as he breathes and moves.

Of course we might say in the modern idiom that this is a fiction which is really "about" itself. It is both a novel of memories and a novel about memory. Memory brightens: ". . . I have never seen such sunlight as on those bright April afternoons . . ."; memory creates in the mind fresh associations: ". . . the Martyrs and Peggotty's house have been inseparable in my mind ever since, and are now;" memory revives the clearest and most detailed impressions: "the scent of a geranium leaf, at this day, strikes me with a half comical, half serious wonder as to what change has come over me in a moment . . . ;" memory retains the sharpest of all impressions: "the face he turned up to the troubled sky, the quivering of his clasped hands, the agony of his figure, remain associated with that lonely waste, in my remembrance, to this hour. It is always night there, and he is the only object in the scene." And memory brings back the earliest and most permanent impressions of childhood, like the occasion when David sees his mother for the last time: "I was in the carrier's cart when I heard her calling to me. I looked out, and she stood at the garden-gate alone, holding her baby up in her arms for me to see. It was cold still weather; and not a hair of her head, or a fold of her dress, was stirred, as she looked intently at me, holding up her child. So I lost her. So I saw her afterwards, in my sleep at school – a silent presence near my bed – looking at me with the same intent face – holding up her baby in her arms." But there is also the mystery of other memories, preconscious memories: ". . . a feeling, that comes over us occasionally, of what we are saying and doing having been said and done before, in a remote time . . ." Memory, then, as a form of resurrection and thus of human triumph; as David Copperfield looks out of the window he had known so many years before and sees the old sorrowful image of himself as a child. "Long miles of road then opened out before my mind; and, toiling on, I saw a ragged wayworn boy forsaken and neglected, who should come to call even the heart now beating against mine, his own." Thus does memory recreate the self out of adversity, linking past and present, bringing continuity and coherence, engendering peace and stillness in the very centre of the active world. It is the purest and best part of Dickens's self, the source of his being, the fountain of his tears. All of his writing and experience over the last two years had brought him to this point, this resurrection.

Yet memory here is also such a troubling force. It is associated with "the old unhappy loss or want of something . . ." as if in the act of remembrance the narrator must confront and once again experience some central bereavement; it is linked, too, with the fear and sense of "change in everything"; and somehow memory is associated in Dickens's imagination with the pain which men cause women. It is related to David Copperfield's own fear of death and of discontinuity, and it also bears some strange relation to the city which is seen as an emblem of forgetfulness. And so there is contrapuntal movement within the book, a narrative which goes both backwards and forwards. Memory as triumph and restoration; memory as loss and grief. The novel's thematic centre lies in the success of young David Copperfield; it is on this level a *Bildungsroman* which bears more relation to "In Memoriam" and "The Prelude" than it does to *Tom Jones* or *The Adventures of Peregrine Pickle*. But it is also a novel which laments the loss of that innocence which precedes success, a novel which celebrates the frustrated and the disheartened, the mad and the innocent, the retired and the retiring. All those who fail – whether it be

Uncle Dick or Dora Spenlow, Wilkins Micawber or Dr Strong – are surrounded by a shining and irrepressible light; it is the successful man and writer, David, who bears the shadows with him everywhere he goes. One can place in this context Chesterton's remark about Lord Macaulay: "But above all he typifies the two things that really make the Victorian Age itself, the cheapness and narrowness of its conscious formulae: the richness and humanity of its unconscious tradition." It was an era that seemed to worship power and success, but how strange the yearnings within it; how filled with a sense of loss, and the longing to be free of all its relentless activity. David Copperfield's own remark might even act as a commentary upon it: "I sit down by the fire, thinking with a blind remorse of all those secret feelings I have nourished since my marriage. I think of every little trifle between me and Dora, and feel the truth, that trifles make the sum of life. Ever rising from the sea of my remembrance . . ." Ever rising are the small unconsidered moments, the strange words of those who have failed, the kindness of those who have retired from the fight, the eccentricities of those who have had to defend themselves against the world. What is David Copperfield's success to all that?

Of course there is some confluence of feeling between Charles Dickens and David Copperfield; how could it not be so when he introduced all of his autobiographical passages within the career of Copperfield himself? He is like the young David himself who, after the death of his mother, watches himself in the mirror to examine the sorrow on his own face. But the identity runs deeper than that, for Dickens sees his own face everywhere. In a letter of this period he signs himself "Wilkins Micawber", and in the novel David himself also writes a letter in the style of Micawber; and yet the novelist is also Micawber's son, who sings in public houses just as the young Dickens once had done. He is David being comforted by surrogate mothers, but he is also the motherless and fatherless Little Em'ly: yes, he is the prostitute Martha, too, for the rules of the school in which David Copperfield is enrolled are the same rules which Dickens applied to the "fallen women" of Urania Cottage. Everything becomes thus entangled, the further we stare down into the novel; yet everything has to remain entangled, because nothing can be worked through or worked out. It would be death itself to do so, and the fate of Dickens would be that of the gorgon who on seeing its own reflection was turned to stone. This is a novel in which all his ". . .contradictions and inconsistencies", all those ". . . erratic and perverted feelings constantly at war within his breast . . .", as Copperfield says of himself, are projected outward, sent spinning into the shadowy world, and are thus for the moment quietened but not resolved. As Dickens puts down his pen in the study which looks out to sea and observes ". . . the phantoms of those days go by me, accompanying the shadow of myself, in dim procession".

He came back to London almost as soon as he had finished the novel, not only to be close to the printer but also, in late October, to begin that round of frantic social engagements and social activities into which he always plunged at the end of a long novel. Expeditions. Theatres. And dinners. Always dinners. It was in fact in October of this year that Bradbury and Evans published *What Shall We Have for Dinner?*, a volume comprising a number of recipes taken from the table of Devonshire Terrace and compiled by Catherine Dickens under the theatrical pseudonym of Lady Maria Clutterbuck. Long meals. Heavy meals. Course following course. Rich soups. Legs of mutton stuffed with oysters, eggs and minced onions. Elaborate desserts. Dressed crab. And toasted cheese, endless toasted cheese – "no man," one reviewer wrote, "could possibly survive the consumption of such frequent toasted cheese." But this was another aspect of the Victorian age and its concern with *force* and *energy*. For such things a plentiful supply of fuel is needed. And for Dickens himself, too, who finished *David Copperfield* only to plunge at once into more amateur theatricals. He had been arranging matters while he was at Broadstairs, and it had been agreed that Sir Edward Bulwer-Lytton should put Knebworth Castle at his disposal for a small number of performances.

Dickens had met Bulwer-Lytton on many occasions in the Thirties and Forties, but they had never forged the same kind of intimate bond as existed between Dickens and the "self-made" men of his generation; Bulwer-Lytton had a much more difficult and in some ways more complex character than that of Lemon or Jerrold. He was the son of a general and landowner who became a Radical MP, the author of "silver-fork" novels of the aristocratic school who turned his attention to "social problem" novels as well as historical melodrama. R. H. Horne, in *A New Spirit of the Age*, described him as "very frank, easy, careless (sometimes perhaps studiously so), good natured, pleasant, conversible . . ." But later and perhaps more astute biographers have noted how much of this apparent ease was on the surface only; in truth Bulwer-Lytton was a deeply troubled man who was unsure of his standing as a writer and who tried to mask his anxieties with a strange amalgam of defiance and *politesse*, diffidence amounting to shyness combined with a prickliness which sometimes turned into open contempt. The long face, the wary and watchful eyes, the extravagant dress, were the weapons of his terrifying self-consciousness and lack of confidence. Nevertheless Dickens had a high opinion of him, for in a sense he was drawn to Bulwer-Lytton as he was drawn to William Macready – both of them difficult, defensive, uneasy, and sometimes overbearing men whose true qualities of sympathy and generosity Dickens was able to detect beneath the surface persiflage. In addition Bulwer-Lytton had demonstrated his radical credentials in a now unread novel, *Paul Clifford*, and Dickens had never forgotten certain lines in one of Bulwer-Lytton's plays which might be seen as one of the seminal statements of the age:

> Then did I seek to rise
> Out of the prison of my mean estate;
> And with such jewels as the exploring mind
> Brings from the caves of knowledge, buy my ransom
> From those twin gaolers of the daring heart –
> Low birth and iron fortune.

The last two lines particularly appealed to Dickens, perhaps as a reminder of how successfully he had triumphed over just such gaolers.

It had been at some point in July that Bulwer-Lytton, inspired by reports of Dickens's amateur theatricals on behalf of John Poole, had suggested that the stage manager and his cast should perform at Knebworth, his country house and estate close to Stevenage. At once Dickens, with his customary animation, replied that the idea of a play "stirs my blood like a trumpet" and over the next few months, while he worked on *David Copperfield* in Broadstairs, he eagerly discussed the details of the production. The rehearsals were postponed until Dickens had completed all the necessary work on the last stages of his novel, but they had begun in earnest by early November; the play was once again *Every Man in His Humour* (with a farce attached at the end), and the cast was much the same as before. Catherine Dickens was herself going to play a role but, during the London rehearsals, she fell through a trap-door and sprained her ankle. There were to be three separate performances at Knebworth and, as usual, Dickens drilled his cast relentlessly; in addition he had all the trouble of turning the banqueting hall of that house into a temporary theatre, attending to all the details of gas lighting, negotiating with Nathan the costumier and Wilson the wig-maker, and arranging for a Choremusicon to be delivered by railway to Stevenage – the instrument itself being one of those cumbersome nineteenth-century ingenuities, which imitated piano as well as string music. The performances were given in the middle of November but, since the stage manager's enthusiasm and energy always needed fresh outlets, he also agreed to a performance of *Used Up* at Rockingham Castle two months later; the evening was arranged for the principal families of the county and, once again, it seems to have been a huge success. It is only necessary to note, in this roll-call of theatrical outings, the comment of one of his amateur actresses, Mrs Compton: ". . . he was both sensitive and irritable, and a restless disposition (another personal characteristic) made him desirous of continually *doing* something."

That need to be continually *doing* received fresh impetus, however, at Knebworth itself; Bulwer-Lytton was impressed by the performance of Ben Jonson's play, and said to Dickens: ". . . this is a great power that has grown up about you, out of a winter-night's amusement, and do let us try to use it for the lasting service of our order." The "order" in question was the literary one, Bulwer-Lytton sharing Dickens's belief that the vocation of writers was one of great seriousness and merited the highest degree of independence. For some years, in fact, he had been interested in the idea of establishing some kind of pension fund or provident institution for authors; his efforts with Forster and Ainsworth in 1845 to set up a benefit fund for the children of Laman Blanchard, after that writer had committed suicide, only served to increase his belief in the need for such an arrangement. Two years later, in 1847, Dickens had drawn up a prospectus for a "Provident Union of Literature, Science and Art", but the proposal had come to nothing. Now Bulwer-Lytton and Dickens, inspired by the success of the Knebworth theatricals, came together with one mind and in the weeks following those performances established a scheme which became known as the "Guild of Literature and Art" – an ambitious project designed to help writers "in difficulties" with a system of annuities and pensions as well as the provision of a number of special houses on Bulwer-Lytton's estate. Both men seem to have been disillusioned by that organ of charity, the Royal Literary Fund, precisely because the money dispensed by it was indeed "charity"; in the Guild they wished to emphasise the fact that money was given as an "award" to writers and artists of distinction. So their plans were laid. Bulwer-Lytton agreed to write a play, and Dickens's company were to perform it both in London and in the provinces in order to raise money to support the Guild's schemes. Once proposed to Dickens, of course, he plunged into the preparations as if his life depended on them. "Once in a thing like this," he had said to Bulwer-Lytton about the Knebworth theatricals themselves, "– once in anything, to my thinking – it must be carried out like a mighty enterprise, heart and soul." And so it proved.

On his return from Knebworth to London, however, he also had other mighty enterprises to superintend. In particular he had to write a seasonal piece for the first Christmas number of *Household Words*. No longer would he have the time or the inclination to write a Christmas Book; the last of them, *The Haunted Man and the Ghost's Bargain*, had appeared two years before. So now he wrote a short essay, "A Christmas Tree", in which he evokes in extraordinary and wonderful detail the toys of his childhood; it is perhaps not a coincidence that, only a few weeks later, he was explaining to a correspondent how he dreamed characteristically of his youth and early manhood. Of those enchanted days before his marriage, before his success, before his fame. When he turned his attention away from those lost years and looked at the present life surrounding him, he was nothing if not gloomy. He wrote two other pieces for *Household Words* in the same period; one entitled "A December Vision" and the other "The Last Words of the Old Year". In the first he depicts England as a place of ruin and disease, a place where children are neglected or whipped for small crimes, ". . . hunted, flogged, imprisoned but not taught . . .", where illiteracy and brutishness and death triumph, where "not one miserable wretch breathed out his poisoned life in the deepest cellar of the most neglected town, but, from the surrounding atmosphere, some particles of his infection were borne away, charged with heavy retribution on the general guilt". In the second essay he portrays a country in which degradation and neglect are rampant, and where the Court of Chancery shockingly mismanages justice. Both essays are powerfully written, and it is of some interest to note that they foreshadow the themes which he was to explore only a few months later in *Bleak House*. He was slowly approaching a deeper understanding of the world, but it would take some private miseries of the next year to act as the lightning rod of the vision even now taking shape.

He had been sitting to the portrait-painter, William Boxall, but he broke off the sessions when he found that on the canvas he first resembled a famous boxer, Ben Caunt, and then a murderer, Greenacre. He was inordinately restless, the work on the amateur theatricals seeming only to increase that restlessness, and he was also feeling extremely unwell; what he called a "bilious attack", but one which has all the marks of nervous prostration. Then, on the last night of the old year, he held a country dance for the members of his amateur company at Devonshire Terrace. A party that heralded a year in which Dickens would be forced to endure much distress and many changes, the year in which all the bleakness of *Bleak House* seems to descend upon him.

IV

IT WAS ON a bright April morning that they all made their way to Greenwich Fair, some in spring-vans, some in hackney-coaches, and many on foot – the short and the tall, the old and the young, the whole procession led by Dick Swiveller and Barnaby Rudge, who were walking arm in arm and singing loudly into the mild air:

> What were the wild waves saying
> When they came against the strand,
> Oh what sweet truth conveying
> As they whisper to the land?

"An old song," Dick Swiveller says, with some satisfaction, "Which is why we have the water lapping against the Strand, which was previously not in London but in Brighton." Barnaby nods solemnly, and promises to remember the information; then with a wild "Halloo" he tosses his scarlet slouch-hat into the air.

A vendor of gingerbread struggled to keep up with them as they strode at the head of the throng. It was Pecksniff. "All so sweet and so light," he said. "And all so freshly made it is a charity to sell them." His assistant, Uriah Heep, was weaving in and out of the crowd, with a supply of spice-nuts, calling by rote "Do me the honour, sirs and gentle ladies, do come and buy." Among the crowd making their way to the Fair were Mr and Mrs Micawber who, together with their children, had been joined for this occasion by the Crummles family. The infants were playing "Ring in the Air" and "Threading my Grandmother's Needle"; the Jellyby family, vainly endeavouring to hide their dirty faces and their patched clothes, looked on sadly until they were led away by the always sympathetic Oliver Twist. (He had been hired by Mrs Jellyby on the understanding that he was "good with children".) Wilkins Micawber watched them depart. "Can it be," he observed to Vincent Crummles, who was even then examining with professional interest an actor impersonating an eighteenth-century lawyer with a tie-wig, "can it really be that there are children who do *not* know how to play?"

Crummles adopted one of his more famous mournful expressions. "It is too true, sir. Too, too true. It is a skill as rare as acting, sir, although of course not so noble. And while we talk of acting –". He pointed to a large booth, outside which John Jasper was playing a jew's harp. Beside the unfortunate musician was a large notice upon which was inscribed in straggling black capitals "OBSERVE THE FAMOUS POSTURE MASTERS IN THEIR MOST CELEBRATED SCENES, AS LAST PERFORMED TO ALL THE CROWNED HEADS OF AFRICA". The two companions did not enter the exhibition but instead were swept along to the main site of the Fair by the concourse around them; but one ragged boy, Jo, slouched close to the entrance of the booth. He had no penny for admission but he lingered outside and, by sundry cranings and bendings, managed to glimpse two of the exhibits closest to him. One was of Little Nell, lying upon her bier with her hands crossed upon her innocent breast; the other was of Miss Havisham, her arms held up straight in the air and with an expression of agony upon her face. Jo watched and watched, and he could have sworn that he saw Little Nell wink at Miss Havisham (in truth they were daughter and mother) until Sam Weller, posted as a guard, moved him on.

And at the Fair itself what junketings of strangers and what secret pledgings of lovers, what dancing and clanging and screaming and bellowing; and all so neatly intertwined that it might have been the handiwork of some secret fair-master. Quilp and Mrs Skewton were enjoying each other's company with the help of several glasses of gin-and-water, until Mrs Skewton's wig tumbled into the grass and was promptly mounted upon his own head by the dwarf. Krook and Magwitch were devouring vast quantities of whelks and pickled salmon, while Pip and David Copperfield indulged in a bout of arm-wrestling for which there seemed to be no certain winner. Their contest seemed so real, in fact, that Florence Dombey burst into tears once more and had to be led away by Mrs Gamp; the old nurse was now so unsteady on what she called her "appendages", however, that she fell upon poor Florence and both females had to be helped to their feet by Edwin Drood.

But now it was time for the pantomime. The celebrated Gradgrind family were to play the flutes and violas, and a silence gathered over the company as they made their way to the spot on the hill where the performance was to be held. And as they struck up their famous air, "The Hippodrome Prelude", Columbine (Miss Mowcher) drifted gracefully into the centre of the area, closely followed by Pantaloon (Thomas Traddles) and Harlequin (Harold Skimpole). It was always the same drama, but it always elicited the same tender sentiments in the audience who responded to the adventures as if they were truly real. The tears ran down the face of Mrs Harris, and Fagin buried his nose in his pocket handkerchief. But then, as so often happens, everything changed. The acrobats, the Mantalinis, appeared; and then among them stepped the Squeers family, the jugglers whose most famous trick was to keep several boys up in the air at once.

But, as they continued with their performance, the sky darkened and a cold mist rolled in from the Thames across the fields of Greenwich. "What can this be?" cried out Paul Dombey.

"It is nothing," Little Nell replied. She had left her post in the posture-masters' booth in order to watch the pantomime, for secretly she wanted to be a dancer. "It is nothing at all, dear little Paul."

"No." Ebenezer Scrooge was standing behind them. "I have seen something like this before. It is a prelude to some change in the narrative." Little Nell and Paul Dombey clung tightly to each other when they heard this. Martin Chuzzlewit merely laughed. "Nothing can happen to us," he called across to them. "We are immortal." But, like the others, he fell silent when he heard the sound of laboured, heavy breathing which filled the firmament like thunder. And then he heard a sigh, which rolled across the fields like a wind.

"Something is happening," Lady Dedlock whispered to her companion, Mr Barkis. "Something is dying."

"No!" Mr Pickwick stepped out from behind a stall selling toys and put his beaming, rubicund face against the dark sky. "We can go on. We can outface the storm of dying. We cannot die." They murmured among themselves for a little and then, with one common shout of joy, they continued with their dancing and singing upon the hill.

Chapter 21

CHARLES DICKENS was now approaching middle-age. His "bilious attack" was succeeded by a very bad cold. His tenancy of Devonshire Terrace was coming to an end, and so he was planning to move house. A restless and disagreeable start to the new year in every way, and one which was compounded by the behaviour of his brother, Frederick, who was using his name to obtain credit from various sources; ". . . rasping my very heart," Dickens said. But, more importantly, his father's health was failing. Both his parents had moved to Keppel Street, near Russell Square, in order to live with a certain Mr and Mrs Davey; Davey was a surgeon acting as a medical attendant to John Dickens, who was now severely afflicted by the urological complaint (probably bladder stones) which had beset him for the last thirty years. Mrs Davey recalled later that Dickens would often visit his parents here. "He was not a very talkative man," she said, "but he could be extremely pleasant when he chose." An implication here, perhaps, that with his parents Dickens relapsed into silence or monosyllables.

He told Mary Boyle, half-jokingly and under one of the assumed theatrical names he used with her, that he was "confoundedly miserable". Indeed his misery now seems to have been on a large scale. "London is a vile place, I sincerely believe," he wrote to Bulwer-Lytton. "I have never taken kindly to it since I lived abroad. Whenever I come back from the Country, now, and see that great heavy canopy lowering over the housetops, I wonder what on earth I do there, except on obligation." The canopy of fog, soon to be evoked on the first page of *Bleak House*. And what were the obligations? To join a deputation to the Chancellor of the Exchequer to seek the repeal of paper duty; to take the chair at the Royal Society of Arts; to arrange the details of the theatricals at Rockingham Castle; to discuss the Guild play with Bulwer-Lytton, and arrange for its performance later in the year; to arrange the details of a farewell banquet in honour of William Macready, about to give his last performance (as Macbeth) at Drury Lane Theatre; to keep the wheels of *Household Words* turning, and to continue writing articles in order to keep it "bright". And, just ten days after he had described to Bulwer-Lytton that canopy of fog obscuring London, he perceived ". . . the first shadows of a new story hovering in a ghostly way about me (as they usually begin to do, when I have finished an old one) . . ." He was planning to go to Italy but abandoned the idea when it conflicted with the projected rehearsals of Bulwer-Lytton's play. Instead, with John Leech and Spencer Lyttelton, he took off for a five-day trip to Paris; ostensibly on *Household Words* business, since he wanted to make a distinction between the horrors of Smithfield and the efficiency of French meat-markets, but really he just wanted to get away for a while. Away from the pressures and responsibilities which were building up. Plunging back into them as soon as he returned.

On the first evening of March he stood up in the London Tavern and made a speech in praise of Macready, whose final performance on the stage he had witnessed two nights before. John Coleman, an actor present on that occasion, remembered that Dickens "was at his best . . . indeed his speech was as florid as his costume . . . He wore a blue dress-coat, faced with silk and aflame with gorgeous brass buttons, a vest of black satin, with a white satin collar, and a wonderfully embroidered shirt. When he got up to speak, his long curly hair, his bright eyes, and his general aspect of geniality and *bonhomie* presented a delightful picture. I made some ingenuous remark upon the subject to Thackeray, who blandly rejoined, 'Yes, the beggar is as beautiful as a butterfly, especially about the shirtfront.'" A blue coat. Brass buttons. An embroidered shirt. He concealed himself well. You would not guess that Dickens was at this moment in a mood of restlessness and depression. And yet he was there, resplendent among his peers and his contemporaries, like them no doubt reduced to tears by Macready's own speech on the occasion. As Coleman put it, ". . . As far as I could see through my own tears, there was not a single dry eye in the vicinity." And, after the cheering and the laughter, Macready moved away "through an avenue of overwrought men, excited and hysterical . . . Many, who could not get near him, cried 'God bless you, sir!' or 'God bless you, Mac!'" Overwrought men. Tears. This is the Victorian period, as it truly was.

At the same time as Dickens was organising the banquet for Macready, he was looking for a suitable site in which to present Bulwer-Lytton's play, *Not So Bad As We Seem*, especially important now that both writers had decided that the Guild would get off to the best possible start if they could perform it in front of the Queen. As a result Dickens wrote a long letter to the Duke of Devonshire, in which he asked if the Guild players might make use of Devonshire House for the play; the Duke agreed at once and confided to his diary, "I have made a friendship with Charles Dickens. I worship him." The Duke worshipped the son of a debtor. This is the Victorian period, as it truly was.

But, amid these public signs of friendship and even honour, Dickens's private life was growing yet more troubled. Catherine had become "exceedingly unwell", as he put it, although her illness was really only the culmination of a prolonged period of anxiety and distress. Not that this was always visible to Dickens's acquaintances; it was in this year that Henry Morley, one of the contributors to *Household Words*, declared that "Dickens has evidently made a comfortable choice. Mrs Dickens is stout, with a round, very round, rather pretty, very pleasant face, and ringlets on each side of it. One sees in five minutes that she loves her husband and her children, and has a warm heart for anybody who won't be satirical, but meet her on her own good natured footing. We were capital friends at once, and had abundant talk together. She meant to know me, and once, after a little talk when she went to receive a new guest, she came back to find me when I had moved off . . ." The reference to her stoutness and her "very round" face, clearly the appearance of a woman approaching middle-age, testifies to her ten years of child-bearing. But there were other consequences of her pregnancies; all the evidence suggests that she suffered from a peculiarly intense form of post-natal depression and illness, as we have seen, culminating in bad attacks of migraine as well as a general "giddiness" or "sickness". It seems evident, too, that in more recent years she had suffered from other forms of nervous or hysterical prostration; intermittent but severe nonetheless, and it was something of this kind that was now beginning to affect her. Catherine herself wrote to a friend with an account of her symptoms: "I have been suffering for some time from a fullness in the head, which has lately increased so much, & caused me such violent headaches &c, that I have been ordered to go at once to Malvern and try what change of air and cold water will do for me." Dickens himself described the symptoms as including "a tendency of blood to the head", "giddiness and dimness of sight" as well as "alarming confusion and nervousness at times" – all of which manifestations he had observed at periods over the last three or four years. He also explained to a Dr James Watson, a "hydropathic practitioner" at Malvern under whose care he wished to place her, that she grew uneasy if she stayed in other people's houses. Depression leading, in other words, to anxiety and even perhaps paranoia. One of his characters in a sketch for *Household Words*, "Smuggled Relations", written by him some four years after this, has a wife called Susannah who "is not distinguished by closeness of reasoning or presence of mind" and who on occasions "would have gone into hysterics but that I make a rule of never permitting that disorder under my roof". Of course this is not a portrait of Catherine or of Dickens himself but his rather hostile attitude towards female "hysterics" is one that reappears very often in his fiction, generally with the belief that such behaviour by women is a sign of amateur theatrics rather than serious disability. Was it something of this latent disapproval which Catherine herself provoked?

At any rate her condition was now serious enough to persuade Dickens that she ought to travel at once to the more bracing air and water of Malvern; together they went down and took Knutsworth Lodge, where Dickens stayed with her for two or three days before returning to London. Over the next few weeks he was to commute between Malvern and London, spending two or three days each time with Catherine at the health resort; in other words, at a time of great personal business and vexation, he was behaving as a considerate and careful husband. Even at Malvern in these conditions, however, his sense of humour did not desert him and his descriptions in a comic account of the "Cold Waterers" to Forster might be applied to "fitness fanatics" of any period; especially an old man who was engaged in the Victorian equivalent of "jogging" and "who ran over a milk-child, rather than stop! – with no neckcloth, on principle; and with his mouth wide open, to catch the morning air".

From the scene of these monstrosities he came up to London to continue with his always-pressing business and, in addition, he was still actively looking for a family dwelling to succeed Devonshire Terrace. His offer for a certain Balmoral House in North London was rejected but this was fortunate since a few years later a barge filled with gunpowder, travelling along the Regent's Park Canal, exploded opposite the house and all but destroyed it. And of course he was coming to London to manage the rehearsals for Bulwer-Lytton's comedy, *Not So Bad As We Seem*, which were being held at Covent Garden Theatre until a temporary theatre had been erected in the Duke of Devonshire's house. When one of the actresses from the amateur theatricals of 1848 appeared to take part in this new play, Dickens said that he "nearly fainted" with the rush of memory – "The gush of recollection," he wrote, "was so overpowering that I couldn't bear it."

But then the world rushed in upon him, too. The day after the first rehearsals he was told that his father was seriously ill and about to undergo an operation from which it was doubtful he would recover. The bladder stones had now grown so large that John Dickens could no longer urinate and the operation, "the most terrible . . . known in surgery" according to Dickens, would entail an incision being made between the anus and the scrotum so that the stones could be physically removed. And this John Dickens would be forced to endure without anaesthetic. His son arrived soon afterwards and found his father's room awash with the consequences of what must have been a terrifying and almost unbearable surgical procedure; "a slaughter house of blood," as Dickens described it to his wife. And yet the native optimism of the father, which may have played some part in his son's description of Mr Micawber, helped him to rally; he was according to Dickens "wonderfully cheerful and strong-hearted". But.Dickens felt the blow himself almost as if he were a part of his father. "All this goes to my side directly," he said, experiencing once more the terrible agonies of his childhood (when, it has been said, his own kidneys became inflamed in response to his father's urinary troubles of that period), "and I feel as if I had been struck there by a leaden bludgeon." He returned to Devonshire Terrace, and, while his father slept, awaited more news. The next morning he went to the *Household Words* office. It was a miserably wet day in late March, and he looked down from his first-floor study onto the scene in Wellington Street North. "It is raining here incessantly . . . A van containing the goods of some unfortunate family, moving, has broken down outside – and the whole scene is a picture of dreariness." A family moving, just as his family had moved when he was a child, just as he was attempting to move now. Dreariness. The past and present coming together through a prospect of rain as he waited for news of his father. He attempted to carry on with his normal work, and on 28 March he went down to Malvern once again to see Catherine. But by now it was clear that his father was dying; Dickens was sent for and returned to London. He arrived at Keppel Street at a quarter past eleven on the night of 29 March, and with his mother stayed at the bedside of the dying man. ". . . he did not know me, nor any one. He began to sink at about noon . . . and never rallied afterwards. I remained there until he died – O so quietly . . ."

Charles and his mother were reunited in the hour of suffering. "In the hour of her sad bereavement," Mrs Davey recalled, "his conduct was noble. I remember he took her in her arms, and they both wept bitterly together . . . He told her that she must rely upon him for the future. He immediately paid whatever his father owed, and relieved his mother's mind on that score." So even at this hour Dickens was involved in the world of money and of debt, so closely connected with all his experience of his family. He was aware of it, too, and complained some days later that his father's death had caused "more expence". It was no doubt his generosity which prompted his younger brother, Alfred, to write to their mother, "It is something to know how nobly Charles has behaved in this trial . . . we are all not in a position to show such substantial proof of affection for the memory of our dear father . . ." Dickens was in fact severely shaken by this death. "I hardly know what to do," he told Forster, "I am going up to Highgate to get the ground." Yet he continued with all of his familiar duties and two days before the funeral, ". . . so worn by the sad arrangements in which I am engaged, and by what led to them, that I cannot take my natural rest . . .", he came to the somewhat surprising decision that he wanted to spend the night at a police station-house in order to write an article on the subject for *Household Words*. It has been suggested that beneath this extraordinary wish there was a buried sense of guilt about his father's death, prompting the desire to be somehow near the police and near the cells. But is there perhaps not something equally extraordinary here? Is he not going back in sad reprise to the days of the Marshalsea Prison, when he and his father had been so intimately connected? When he and his family had been so closely bound together by prison doors?

John Dickens was buried at Highgate Cemetery on 5 April, and upon his gravestone Dickens had composed a tribute to his "zealous, useful, cheerful spirit". After the funeral Elizabeth Dickens stayed for a while at the home of her daughter, Laetitia, in Notting Hill and planned later to travel up to Yorkshire in order to stay with Alfred. And what of Dickens, after the first shock of the death had passed?

From now on, when he referred to John Dickens, characteristically he used the phrase "my poor father"; all his resentment and anger seemed to have been dissipated, leaving only the pity of circumstances behind. Circumstances to which John Dickens had been as much a victim as his son. (It is not inapposite to note that it is precisely the power of circumstance which envelops his next novel.) Dickens still could not sleep and, from one letter, it is clear that he began once more to worry about his finances, as if the death of John Dickens had revived in him all the old fears of debt and imprisonment. For three nights he walked the streets of London until dawn – just such a night as he recreated in *Bleak House*, his next novel, when ". . . every noise is merged, this moonlight night, into a distant ringing hum, as if the city were a vast glass, vibrating". Some years later he could still recall these nocturnal walks so clearly that he commemorated them in an essay, "Night Walks", where he also evokes this month of March with "the weather damp, cloudy, and cold. The sun not rising before half-past five, the night perspective looked sufficiently long at half-past twelve: which was my time for confronting it." And, as he walked the streets after his father's death, "the wild moon and clouds were as restless as an evil conscience in a tumbled bed, and the very shadow of the immensity of London seemed to lie oppressively upon the river". Dickens walked on. Past deserted theatres. Past the stone walls of Newgate. Past the King's Bench Prison where he had once imprisoned Mr Micawber, so sad a simulacrum of his father. Past Bedlam hospital for the mad. Past churches. Past graveyards where it occurs to him that, if those buried there rose from their resting places, ". . . the vast armies of dead would overflow the hills and valleys beyond the city, and would stretch away all round it, God knows how far". A strange image. In *David Copperfield* he had associated the death of David's father with the boy's fear that the dead man might rise from his grave like Lazarus. Did that same fear haunt him now, a grown man? Certainly he was walking endlessly, as obsessively as those characters of his who labour under some great affliction. Still he walks on and, as the chimes of the City churches ring out over the sleeping city, their sounds ". . . go opening out, for ever and ever afterwards widening perhaps . . . in eternal space . . ." He passes the homeless and the poor, the mad and the wretched, and one night there is a strange meeting. "The creature was like a beetle-browed hair-lipped youth of twenty, and it had a loose bundle of rags on, which it held together with one of its hands. It shivered from head to foot, and its teeth chattered, and as it stared at me – persecutor, devil, ghost, whatever it thought me – it made with its whining mouth as if it were snapping at me, like a worried dog. Intending to give this ugly object, money, I put out my hand to stay it – for it recoiled as it whined and snapped – and laid my hand upon its shoulder. Instantly, it twisted out of its garment, like the young man in the New Testament, and left me standing alone with its rags in my hand." What kind of being is this, this young man like some demented image of the city itself? A creature such as *he* might have become? Dickens walked on and on until dawn broke.

He did, on just such a night, visit the police station-house which at the time of his father's death seemed so important to him. He must have spent a night there soon after the funeral, and he composed an article on his experience for *Household Words*; it is a wonderfully descriptive essay in which once more he warns his readers of that circle of "doomed childhood" growing up in their midst, but in which he also includes dialogue which might have come straight out of one of his own novels. This is the speech of London as it existed, whether it be in the slurred speech of the drunk who calls himself a "Solirrer" (solicitor) and who seems to have been robbed of a watch – "I doro how much. I'm not par-TICK-ler . . . abow the war. It's not my war. It's a frez of my." It's not my watch. It belongs to a friend of mine. And as he speaks we can see Dickens close to him, listening so intently that he can almost miraculously repeat the sounds of drunken speech. Or whether it be in the speech of a "very indignant matron with a very livid face" who keeps a coffee-house – "'. . . I had just been hissuing directions to two of my servants, when here come between us a couple of female persons which I know to be the commonest dirt, and pushed against me.'

'Both of them pushed against you?'

'No sir,' with scorn and triumph, 'they did *not!* One of 'em pushed against me' – A dead stoppage, expressive of implacable gentility.

'Well, ma'am – did you say anything then?'

'I ask your parding. Did I which, sir?' As compelling herself to fortitude under great provocation . . ."

Dickens's comic sense does not fail him; even now when he, too, was under great strain. The death of his father had coincided with Catherine's own sickness, and at a time when he had been expressing his gloom about the life of London. In a letter to Catherine from that city, he declared that after this death "I have sometimes felt, myself, as if I could have given up, and let the whole battle ride on over me". He was now approaching middle-age, and it seems likely that the death of his father affected him as it seems to affect all bereaved sons or daughters: he had a sudden awareness of his own mortality. He was fatherless now, like so many of the characters he had created, and all the perceptions which had shaped his novels were being deepened.

As it will appear in the novel he began to write seven months later, *Bleak House*, in which the Court of Chancery is seen as the wearying and inescapable condition of life itself. If it is true that the Law is often seen as the image of the Father, then in the novel's portrayal of the Court as a vast plain, upon which the weary traveller never finds rest or safety, is there not some sense of Dickens himself lost within some huge image of his father, caught in his toils, struggling to break free but unable to do so except in death? Can we see the head of John Dickens, monstrous as if in a Dali painting, looming over the streets of the metropolis as Dickens walks them? What else surfaces in *Bleak House*? Decrepitude. Weariness. *Anger* against the world. None of the nostalgia of *David Copperfield* but rather an intense, fierce drama. Strangeness. Wildness. And a constant refrain – "a terror of myself", used in *David Copperfield* but marshalled here upon a large scale. And how often that phrase rings through Dickens; ". . . dread of myself" in *David Copperfield*; ". . . in mortal terror of myself" in *Great Expectations*; ". . . afraid of myself" in *David Copperfield* again; ". . . afraid of himself" in *Little Dorrit*; ". . . afraid of myself" in *Our Mutual Friend*; ". . . frightened at myself" in a later story, and in *Bleak House*, once more, that ". . . terror of myself". A true litany of anxiety combined with something like self-disgust and the fear of private darkness. Is this what Dickens felt, too, as he made his night walks through London?

After the funeral of his father, Dickens again took up his routine of going between London and Malvern; and, as he did so, he was making his plans for the year ahead. He had already decided to spend the summer once more at Fort House in Broadstairs, and was hoping to begin a new novel during the late autumn or winter in London; at least as soon as he had found a suitable new house, and had settled there. On 14 April he came up to London in order to take the chair at a meeting of the General Theatrical Fund, one of those theatrical charities which appealed both to his sense of justice and to his delight at the professional actor's skills. Of course, with Catherine recuperating in the country, Dickens was also trying to spend as much time as possible in the company of his children; so on this day he went straight from the station to Devonshire Terrace and, according to one of his daughters, spent much of his time "playing with the children and carrying little Dora about the house and garden". Little Dora, named after the heroine of *David Copperfield* who dies. The "ill-omened" name. Then the time came for him to change and to go on to the London Tavern for the annual dinner. The affair was conducted as usual but, half an hour before Dickens was to speak, Forster was called out of the room. When Dickens rose he was greeted with "prolonged cheering", and after a few words on the general subject of the Fund he went on to express his gratitude to the theatrical profession: "Not because the actor sometimes comes from scenes of affliction and misfortune – even from death itself – to play his part before us; all men must do that violence to their feelings, in passing on to the fulfilment of their duties in the great strife and fight of life."

Forster himself was soon to speak but he knew now that he had a much harder task to face; he had left the room at the urgent bidding of one of Dickens's servants, who came with the news that the infant Dora had died quite suddenly. Forster decided to keep the news from Dickens until all his part in the proceedings had been completed, and in his biography Forster recalls how with anguish he listened to Dickens's remarks about the need to leave even the scene of death in order to carry on with the battle of life. No doubt Dickens had been thinking of his father's death then, steeling himself to go forward into the world once more, but how apposite his words were in another sense. Forster rose to speak; when, in the course of his speech, he referred to Dickens's "practical philanthropy" someone at the back of the hall called out, "Humbug!". But Forster carried on unperturbed. It was only at the end of the proceedings, and with the help of Mark Lemon whom he had called to assist him, that he told Dickens about the sudden death of his infant daughter. She had been seized with "convulsions" and expired within a few minutes. Dickens did not then break down but came back home. "I remember what a change seemed to have come over my dear father's face when we saw him again," Mamie recalled, ". . . how pale and sad it looked." All that night he sat beside the death-bed, keeping watch over the little girl's corpse with Mark Lemon. The next morning he wrote a tender and careful note to Catherine, clearly anxious that this latest news might augment her own suffering and even lead to some kind of break-down. "I think her *very* ill," he told her, although he knew his daughter to be dead. Forster went down to Malvern with the letter and, when the news was eventually broken to her, Catherine fell into a state of "morbid" grief and suffering. Then, after some twelve hours or so, she seemed to recover something of her self-control. Dickens himself remained "in control" for a while, but his daughter remembered the time when he could no longer restrain his grief: "He did not break down until, an evening or two after her death, some beautiful flowers were sent." He "was about to take them upstairs and place them on the little dead baby, when he suddenly gave way completely". There are only one or two other recorded occasions when Dickens "gave way", but those who saw it never easily forgot.

But he maintained his duties. On the same morning that he wrote to Catherine, he also composed a letter to the Duke of Devonshire in order to explain that his loss made it necessary to postpone the first night of the Guild play and thus the Queen's attendance at it; interesting, this, too, for the way in which he writes with perfect self-assurance about his decision to change Victoria's plans. And yet so great was Dickens's need for some expression of his grief that he felt compelled to *write down* a prayer after his daughter's death; only in words could he find true relief. He found a grave for her in Highgate Cemetery, on a spot from which it was possible to see the great city spread out beneath. At a place, too, which Dickens noted to be filled with bird-song. The strife and the song. Life continuing. Just as now his energy had to be directed towards Catherine's recovery. She had returned to London and, as part of his campaign to keep her going out "under a variety of pretences", he began seriously to negotiate for the purchase of a new home – Tavistock House, in Tavistock Square. It was to be the last in which Catherine and Charles Dickens would live together.

So the shocks of this year had been great indeed: the sickness of Catherine, the death of his father and the death of his child. Yet pre-eminent in Dickens's mind was the need for self-sacrifice and for continuing ardent labour; in this he was so much like his contemporaries that we might even on this occasion describe him as "Victorian". The preparations for Bulwer-Lytton's play went ahead and, as soon as Joseph Paxton had designed a portable stage for Devonshire House, the rehearsals began to take place there. Bulwer-Lytton's deranged wife made a comment on Dickens's activity in this period that suggests how close the mad are to sanity, even if it is sanity of the strangest kind – "Oh," she said, "Mr Dickens makes a habit of acting with a dead father in one pocket and a dead baby in the other." The

Duke of Devonshire's reaction to the rehearsals now taking place in his house was perhaps more predictable; as he had said, he "worshipped" Dickens and took nothing from the author in bad part, but he had reservations about some of Dickens's acting companions, especially those who came from the sphere of journalism in general and *Punch* in particular. ". . . The young heroes," he said, "are acted by very common hard-favoured vulgar-looking men . . ." These of course were the men with whom Dickens generally chose to surround himself. At the same time a prospectus on the Guild of Literature and Art was issued in which Dickens praised these "very common" players and, of his own services, records: "He would be false to the trust placed in him by the friends with whom he is associated and . . . of the calling to which he belongs, if he had any dainty reserve in such a matter. He is one of an order beyond which he affects to be nothing, and aspires to be nothing." He was saying, in other words, that he wished only to be a novelist and that his role as an actor was simply instrumental to that end. Certainly he was bringing together as many disparate influences as he could to shape the Guild – his literary colleagues, his journalistic colleagues, his amateur actors – and, as usual, he ruled them with that mixture of cheerfulness and firmness which was his speciality in the marshalling of men and affairs. One contemporary recorded Dickens's manner at a meeting of the Guild itself: "His smile was enough . . . As a chairman he was as precise and accurate in carrying out the traditions of the post. Before business began, his happy laugh rang through the room; he had a word for every friend, and generally they were his associates as well as friends. Voices were high in merriment, and it looked as though business would never begin; but when Mr Dickens did take his seat, 'Now gentlemen, Wills will read us the minutes of the last meeting. Attention, please. Order!' It might have been the most experienced chairman of the Guildhall . . ."

Yet not every writer agreed either with the aims or with the methods of Dickens in establishing such an association for the relief of writers and artists; Thackeray, in particular, took exception to this form of charity. On the very night of the first performance of *Not So Bad As We Seem*, he spoke at a dinner of the Royal Literary Fund to this effect; "Literary men are not by any means, at this present time, that most unfortunate and most degraded set of people whom they are sometimes represented to be . . ." To Mrs Carlyle he wrote, "And dont you understand that there are a set of men who will be martyrs, who are painting their faces and asking for your money, who want to make literature a chronic beggary under the name of the Guild . . ." There is something of the disdain of the intellectual here combined with the self-consciousness of the artist, and in a letter to Forster he added, ". . . I don't believe in the Guild of Literature I don't believe in the Theatrical scheme; I think *that* is against the dignity of our profession . . ." In other words he did not believe that writers should cavort as actors upon a stage, or expressly raise money for the more unfortunate of their brethren. Of course he had a point – there *was* something slightly absurd or pathetic about it – even if that point can be subsumed under the larger heading of his self-imposed rivalry with Dickens for the supreme position in contemporary English literature. In addition he was no friend to Bulwer-Lytton, whom for some reason he despised; perhaps for the reason that people tend to dislike the thing they themselves most resemble. Even so, he asked Forster "to tell Dickens and you his familiar friend, that I'm not his enemy: and I think the world is large enough for fifty such coaches as he and I drive, but we're on different sides of the house . . ." Truly they were now, and relations between the two novelists were to grow a great deal cooler as a result.

Dickens was driving his own coach fast enough, at any rate; the dress rehearsal of *Not So Bad As We Seem* was held on 14 April and then, two days later, the play was performed at Devonshire House "in the Presence of Her Majesty and His Royal Highness The Prince Albert". It was a success. The audience sat in the picture gallery while the adjoining library had been transformed by Joseph Paxton into a stage; a special box had been erected for the Queen and her consort, of course, but among the other guests were the Duke of Wellington as well as various dukes and peers and members of what in our century has been called "the Establishment". The Queen herself was amused. "All acted on the whole well," she confided to her journal. "Dickens (the celebrated author) admirably, and Dr Jerrold, a funny little man, who writes in 'Punch', extremely well . . . The dresses and scenery were beautiful. After all was over, we had a *select* supper with the Duke, only getting home after 1." But not everyone enjoyed the proceedings and, although the press reports of the play were generally favourable, the Duke of Wellington confessed that he "sat out two Acts" only. Yet the play itself, set in the early eighteenth century, was both sufficiently conventional and sufficiently intriguing to capture the attention of a contemporary audience. It is a complicated drama of political and emotional intrigue, of feigned and true love, in which Dickens played Wilmot, a dandy and man-about-town, while Forster took the role of the difficult, stern and self-made Hardman. Thus Dickens was able to assume an alien identity; and did he see in this character of the dandy "with-the-heart-of-gold", ranged against a selfish self-made man, any possible criticism of his own self-made and arduous ethic? *Not So Bad As We Seem* ended with a rhyming epilogue on the establishment of the Guild –

Wilmot: Yes! Other vocations, from Thames to the Border,
　　　Have some esprit de corps, and some pride in their order . . .
　　　Why should authors be spitting and scratching like tabbies,
　　　To leave but dry bones –
　　　　　Softhead: – For those grateful cold Abbies!

At the second performance in Devonshire House a new farce, written by Mark Lemon and Dickens himself, was given an airing. It was entitled *Mr Nightingale's Diary* and concerns a hypochondriac who goes down to take the cold-water cure at Malvern (a trip perhaps inspired by Catherine Dickens's own journey). It is amusing enough, but was at the time chiefly notable for the number and variety of quick character-changes that Dickens was able to make – in manner, if not in method, so similar to the impersonations of Charles Mathews so many years before. In rapid succession and with equally rapid "patter" Dickens took the shape of a deaf sexton and an invalid, as well as characters not a million miles removed from his own Sam Weller and Mrs Gamp. As Sam Weller on this occasion, he also utters a line which bears a remarkable similarity to those pathetic tones soon to be heard in Jo of *Bleak House*, "Ah, those wos the days, Sir – them wos!", and his trick of singing snatches of popular song during his dialogue bears affinities to the earlier behaviour of Mr Dick Swiveller in *The Old Curiosity Shop* and the later habits of Mr Silas Wegg in *Our Mutual Friend*. (It has to be remembered, however, that the printed text bears very little relation to the performance, since both Lemon and Dickens were well known for their impromptu repartee and for their "gagging" on stage.) The Duke of Devonshire arranged a supper and ball for all the performers after this second night on 27 May; again much "merriment", to use the word so often employed by Dickens and his friends, but for Dickens himself the entry into the glare and light and heat of the stage only produced a more profound melancholy after the play had finished. He found in the fall of the curtain after the performance ". . . something of the shadow of the great curtain which falls on everything . . ." – although of course such considerations did nothing to deter him from launching into his plans for yet another "provincial tour" with his company.

First, however, he had to make his arrangements for the summer. He managed, as planned, to rent Fort House once more; Catherine, Georgina and the children went on ahead of him while he completed his business in London. But he did not stay in Devonshire Terrace; he was so dismayed at the prospect of so many people arriving for the Great Exhibition, some of them no doubt bearing with them letters of introduction to the famous novelist, that he rented out his house and himself took refuge in the office of *Household Words*. He also went down to Epsom for two days, in order to work up some material for the periodical, but he did not linger over the Great Exhibition itself. It had formally been opened at the beginning of May and Dickens's reaction was notably reserved about an event which, for most of his countrymen, marked the plain supremacy of England in the world of commerce and invention. This is not to say that he did not hold shares in what he once described as "the spirit of the Time"; he, too, believed in what he called "the march of civilisation" and "the great progress of the country". In a speech at a dinner in honour of Joseph Paxton he declared, for example, that "this was a great age, with all its faults . . ." Even at the very end of his life he was praising the major discoveries and inventions of his period – electricity, railways, all those aspects of the nineteenth century which less complete men like Ruskin or Morris disparaged or neglected. In that sense he was very much a modern man, very much a man of his period, and he never ceased to attack those who endorsed the myth of "the good old days". In the fake bookshelves which he was to have constructed later, he even had seven "volumes" entitled *The Wisdom of Our Ancestors* – the first volume on Ignorance, the second on Superstition, and so forth down to the last on Disease.

And yet Dickens would have strongly disagreed with Macaulay's description of this year, 1851, as ". . . a singularly happy year of peace, plenty, good feeling, innocent pleasure and national glory". As far as Dickens was concerned, it was nothing of the kind but rather a year of Crime, Disease, Poverty and Ignorance; and as a result he detested that self-congratulatory tone which was so marked a part of the Great Exhibition itself. Why not, he had said at the beginning of the year in *Household Words*, have an alternative exhibition of "England's sins and negligences"? It was not just that he was profoundly out of sympathy with the pomposity and narrowness of the "new" England – a dislike which occurs even in a random remark of his on ". . . the hideous coats and waistcoats of the present day" – but also he feared that the emphasis on England's commercial glories would blind governors and governed alike to the real needs and demands of the country. Of course he did have a real animus against the Exhibition itself; it has already been reported how he was instrumental in the dissolving of the Working-Class Committee of that extravaganza, when it became clear that no special attention was to be paid to the needs of the labouring classes. And of the Exhibition itself he wrote that "so many things bewildered me. I have a natural horror of sights, and the fusion of so many sights in one has not decreased it." He had visited it twice but had clearly wandered around to no marked effect; as in his own fiction, he could not bear profusion without order, variety without coherence. And yet, even still, he was so much a man of his period. His vigour. His earnestness. His energy. His will. His probity. His compulsive need to work. So many people compared the body to a machine that it becomes one of the dominant metaphors of the age – "We must make the machine of the brain go. It does not do to let it stop. Whatever happens, energise." This is Symonds but it might also be Dickens. And here is Charles Kingsley: "Do not be afraid of my overworking myself. If I stop, I go down. I must work." And this might be Dickens, too. He was also a man of his age in his optimism and in his benevolence. Mary Mitford wrote of his friend, Talfourd, words that could just as easily be applied to the novelist himself: Talfourd being a man "who takes people at their best, and sets forth their beauties instead of their defects . . . He has a talent for admiration and enjoyment." And yet Charles Dickens was perhaps most like his age in his own inconsistencies. He was both vigorous and sentimental; filled with a self-certainty matched only by self-doubt; a man of great sincerity whose greatest pleasure lay in play-acting; a pragmatist as well as a romantic; both coherent and uncertain. And so when we consider the Great Exhibition of 1851, laid out beneath Paxton's glass domes in Hyde Park, we must think less of the objects and the statues and the inventions – and rather more of the people who flocked to see them, people as uncertain as Dickens himself, people as bewildered and contradictory, people who did not know that they were part of an "age" at all. There is something which exists beyond the ordinary reaches of chronology; and it is to be found in Dickens's novels.

The family were once more ensconced in Broadstairs, and Dickens found the repose there exhilarating after the exhaustion of that year. "Corn growing, larks singing, garden full of flowers, fresh air on the sea." But it was still necessary for him to travel regularly to London, and this partly because at last he had managed to buy the house he and Catherine had inspected: Tavistock House, a plain brick house just off Tavistock Square and screened from the public thoroughfare by iron railings, a garden and trees. It was of some eighteen rooms, larger than Devonshire Terrace and in a grander district; it had been owned by a friend of Dickens, Frank Stone, but the Stones were to move to the next house but one. And so Tavistock House was prepared for its new family. In fact it was to have something of a chequered history; a later owner, Georgina Weldon, suffered a nervous collapse within its walls and subsequently issued a pamphlet entitled "The Ghastly Consequences of Living in Charles Dickens's House", in which, among other things, she claims that her fate was "that of a sane person shut up in a lunatic asylum, put there for the purpose of being slowly or 'accidentally' murdered". She might be said intuitively to have picked up something of the atmosphere which was to be engendered here. Dickens himself always believed in the personality of houses, too, in that constant slow life which accrues to them, but at this early stage there seemed no reason to believe that Tavistock House would not be for him and his family a perfectly happy place.

And even now, even as he managed and performed in the Guild play at the Hanover Square Rooms in London, even as he conducted an extensive correspondence on the subject of the forthcoming provincial tour, even as he remained deeply engaged on *Household Words* business, shades of a new book were beginning to thicken around him; as usual he became afflicted by that "violent restlessness . . ." which presaged a new novel. But he could start nothing until Tavistock House, described by Frank Stone's son as a "dirty, dismal, dilapidated mansion", had been redecorated and thoroughly repaired. For throughout the summer Dickens had also been directing busy letters to his brother-in-law, Henry Austin, asking for advice and assistance on various domestic and sanitary arrangements. Turning painting rooms into drawing rooms; preparing curtains and carpets; lengthening the entrance passage; attending to the drains; turning a recess into a cupboard or perhaps, on second thoughts, a bookcase; arranging a shower bath, ". . . *a Cold Shower of the best quality, always charged to an unlimited extent . . .*"; shielding the water closet from that shower, since "I have not sufficient confidence in my strength of mind, to think that I could begin the business of every day, with the enforced contemplation of the outside of that box. I believe it would affect my bowels." And, as usual, he wanted everything done *at once*. "I have to request that no time may be lost in executing this work"; "VITALITY OF EXPEDITION"; "*punctuality and dispatch*"; speed, always. What Henry Austin thought of his brother-in-law's state of permanent hyper-activity is not recorded. Nor are the impressions of the workmen who were constantly being stared at, questioned, and generally chivvied by Mr Dickens. "Inimitable hovering gloomily through the premises all day, with an idea that a little more work is done when he flits, bat-like, through the rooms . . ." And who better than Dickens to appreciate the comedy of his own behaviour, as he sits disconsolately upon a ladder and "Irish Labourers stare in through the very slates". Nevertheless any delay caused him agonies. And he was also worried about money; as the refurbishment of Tavistock House went ahead, he was anxiously scanning the half-yearly accounts from Bradbury and Evans. He had not earned as much as he would have liked, and it was clear to him that he would have to begin a new serial fiction as soon as possible. Yet he could not commence anything until he was settled into his new house and at the moment, ". . . having all my notions of order turned completely topsy-turvy", there was nothing to be done except to wait for the workmen to finish. There was no chance of another holiday, either, and by October he was once again having to plan the next Christmas issue of *Household Words*. In addition he had a bad cold – always a sure sign that things were not going forward as he had hoped and planned. That his "system of Order" had been disrupted.

He was hoping to move into Tavistock House by the middle of November but, before so doing, he embarked with his cast upon their first provincial tour of *Not So Bad As We Seem* and *Mr Nightingale's Diary*; it was a "first" in other ways, too, since it has been suggested that the travels of Dickens's amateur company marked the first occasion when actors toured the country with a complete play. But it was a modest beginning, compared with some of Dickens's later peregrinations, and the players stopped only at the Assembly Rooms in Bath and the Victoria Rooms in Bristol. The cast comprised most of the same players, although now the female parts were taken by professional actresses; the theatre itself was transported with them, since as a result of Paxton's ingenious construction it could be unpacked and erected within a matter of hours. The timetable was of course meticulously arranged and observed by Dickens – and since, according to one of the players, ". . . he always liked to do things on a handsome scale" on this and subsequent tours he would generally book the largest rooms in any hotel for the Guild players. They would dine at two in the afternoon before the play, and then take supper together afterwards. Sometimes they were joined by the local worthies but there were also evenings in the ensuing months when they would be left to themselves, on which occasions a series of after-supper entertainments were arranged; ". . . the favourite game on these particular occasions," according to the same member of the cast, "was leap-frog, which we played all round the supper-table . . . Dickens was fond of giving a 'high-back' which, though practicable enough for the more active, was not easily surmounted by others, especially after a substantial supper; while the immense breadth and bulk of Mark Lemon's back presented a sort of bulwark to the progress of the majority." On one occasion Dickens was sent flying under the table by an inexpert leaper, but "Mr Dickens rose with perfect enjoyment at the disaster, admirably imitating the action in pantomimes under similar circumstances . . ." The fact that it is impossible to imagine senior editors, journalists and novelists of the present day engaged in leap-frog with each other perhaps offers some clue as to the difference between the late twentieth century and the middle of the nineteenth. There was only one unfortunate incident during the performances themselves, when a lamp was knocked over and the scenery caught alight. Showing his usual presence of mind, despite or perhaps because of his own great fear of fire, Dickens rushed upon the stage with Mark Lemon and summarily put out the blaze with a thick overcoat.

John Forster was absent for at least one of these performances, and there is some evidence that Dickens became somewhat disenchanted with him. If so, it was only one of the many occasions when a fundamental incompatibility of temperament between the two men reasserted itself; Forster loud, domineering and getting somewhat more "stuffy" as the years passed in a manner that did not endear itself to Dickens. And in fact one unintentional consequence of this first provincial tour was the friendship established between Dickens and one of his Guild actors, Wilkie Collins, a friendship that in some respects at least was to supplant that between Dickens and Forster. Indeed Collins was quite a different person, this slight, short, bulbous-headed young man (some twelve years younger than Dickens) who was notable for his geniality, his good temper and his cheerfulness. He already knew such friends of Dickens as the artists Augustus Egg and Daniel Maclise – and this because his father had been a famous painter while his brother, Charles, was already a modestly talented one. In addition, Collins was a keen admirer of amateur theatricals and had in fact arranged some of his own before joining Dickens's Guild troupe; at the time he met Dickens, he also had plans of becoming a novelist. There was a great deal, in other words, to bring them together. Of course there were also many and great contrasts between them, but these personal differences seemed only to endear Collins to Dickens; the younger man was untidy, unpunctual, indolent and alarmingly vague on occasions but for once Dickens did not seem to mind. It is almost as if he saw in Collins some alternative image of himself. This was what he meant when he described himself as the "Genius of Order" and Collins the "Genius of Disorder". There were also some ways in which Collins was more unconventional than Dickens. He was still a bachelor living with his mother when he first became acquainted with the famous novelist, but within a few years his private life was to take a bizarre turn.

It was not long before Collins was writing for *Household Words* itself, and eventually he became a member of its small permanent staff. Certainly he began to take his writing seriously after he formed a friendship with Dickens, and there is no doubt that Dickens encouraged and advised the younger man; his first proper novel *Basil*, was published the year after they met and it seems probable that Collins not only listened to but also took Dickens's advice on the craft of fiction. There were many occasions when they discussed such matters (it also surfaces in their extant correspondence) and as a result Collins came to share the older man's own high claims about the "order" of novelists. He also came to understand the need for care and labour in the preparation of fiction, and it was not long before Dickens was prophesying success for him in the high art which they both espoused. In fact it would not be going too far to say that Wilkie Collins became Dickens's protégé and, with the exception of Harrison Ainsworth, it could also fairly be said that he was the only novelist with whom Dickens ever formed a close relationship. Of course their friendship was not founded on literary matters alone – even if Dickens did not subscribe to Collins's "code of morals", as he put it, he realised that he was an easy-going companion with whom he could explore the darker recesses of urban life. In that sense Collins took over the place which Daniel Maclise had once held in his life; as Maclise became more reclusive and wayward, Dickens turned to the young man for companionship in what he would describe as voluptuous or sybaritic jaunts. By which he seems to have meant nothing more than a kind of high-spirited lounging through the more louche areas of London and Paris, as well as visits to the "low" theatres of both capitals. Wilkie Collins was part of a younger generation, in other words, and there is a sense in which he embodied for Dickens all the easy-going and open-hearted bravura of youth which he himself had never experienced. The older man had always been too ambitious, too concerned to win money and fame, to allow himself to taste the real pleasures of the young. Was this now something he was trying to recapture in his new friendship? Could he forget himself with Collins; forget his fame, forget his responsibilities, and for a passing time become young again?

But this is to move ahead too far. Their friendship had only begun at the end of this first provincial tour of the Guild, and in any case Dickens had other matters on his mind. Most importantly, after his return, in the middle of November, he and the family were at last able to take possession of Tavistock House. It had been transformed; now it was indeed a grand house, fully refurbished and redecorated, and one of Dickens's first concerns was to keep the iron gates in front of the driveway locked. In this way he hoped to avoid the depredations of the street traders and the street musicians, whose noise was one of the principal discomforts of his London life. He had already promised his daughters that their old attic room in Devonshire Terrace would be replaced by what he called a "gorgeous" room in Tavistock House; but "they were not allowed to see the room at all until it was quite finished, and then he took them up to it himself. Everything that was pretty, dainty and comfortable was in that room . . ." Hans Christian Andersen was later to visit the house and recalled how "in the passage from street to garden hung pictures and engravings. Here stood a marble bust of Dickens . . . over a bedroom door and a dining room door were inserted the bas-reliefs of Night and Day after Thorwaldsen. On the first floor was a rich library with a fireplace and a writing-table, looking out on the garden . . . The kitchen was underground, and at the top of the house were the bedrooms." Andersen's room itself looked out over the towers and spires of London which "appear and disappear as the weather cleared or thickened". But no weather, no fog or rain, could affect the neatness and orderliness inside the house. Marcus Stone, his neighbour's son, recalled that in the newly refurbished house Dickens's influence was everywhere visible, with ". . . his love of order and fitness, his aversion to any neglect of attention, even in details which are frequently not considered at all. There was the place for everything and everything in its place, deterioration was not permitted . . . There was no litter or ˀccumulation of rubbish, no lumber room or glory hole. The Pneumatic cleaner of today [1911] would not have gathered a rich harvest of dust in any house of his. If he was something of a martinet he certainly spared himself less than anybody. A Napoleonic commander in chief, he found able and active allies in his sister in law and elder daughter who were geniuses in carrying out his ideas." It may be interesting to note that Marcus Stone does not include Catherine Dickens among his "allies" in this war against disorder. And then Marcus Stone goes on to say that, in Tavistock House, "all the order and completeness of Devonshire Terrace was established on a more important scale . . . In the drawing room his pictures were arranged exactly as they had been in the Devonshire Terrace dining room but as this room was twice the size they had more space between them". Among these pictures were portraits of his own characters – Dolly Varden in the wood, Kate Nickleby in Madame Mantalini's show-room, Mrs Squeers administering brimstone and treacle to the pupils of Dotheboys Hall, Little Nell among the tombstones. Thus did Dickens surround himself with his own imagined world. And indeed with his own imaginative preoccupations as well; one of the volumes which he wished to have as a "dummy book-back" was *History of a Short Chancery Suit*, precisely the theme he was about to explore in his next novel.

His study at Tavistock House was a large room with sliding doors which led into the drawing room; Dickens liked to open these doors and thus, during the mornings given over to composition, walk up and down the whole length of the house. Pacing around as he contemplated the next sentence, the next word. And it was here, in his new study, that he began work on *Bleak House*. This title was only given to the novel after much experimentation, perhaps while at Fort House in Broadstairs; the first title was almost as simple as the last, and on off-white paper he had written in black ink "Tom-All-Alone's" and, beneath it, "The Ruined House". There had been a place known as Tom-All-Alone's near Chatham, a patch of ruined houses cleared to make way for a new prison, and it seems likely that at this point Dickens was imagining the setting of his story in some similar ruined house in the country. His second attempt at a title included: "That got into chancery/And never got out." So already he saw this ruin as part of the interminable processes of the law, the Court of Chancery being notorious for its inefficiency and dilatoriness. There is a pun here too, the phrase "in chancery" being used for a hold in boxing. Then he added "Building/Factory/Mill", as if he wished to incorporate the state of industrialised Britain. After a few more attempts he tried out "Bleak House Academy", as if some part of the national education were to be included in his plan. Then "The East Wind" was introduced as a title, a wind which to Londoners was often a harbinger of disease, spreading as it did from the East End of London to the more salubrious areas of the West. Until eventually the title emerged plainly as *Bleak House*. But how important the process had been to him, how many half-formed ideas and images had attached themselves to Dickens's search for a name.

But, if these ideas and images seemed to spring from his "playing", as it were, with words and phrases, they were also provoked into life by the very issues of the day. Thus in the spring and summer of 1851 there had been reports in *The Times* concerning the extraordinary delays which regularly occurred in Chancery suits, and in a legal history of the period it is reported that ". . . never had the public mind been more inflamed; a competent observer declared that the most popular measure which could be introduced into the House of Commons would be one for the abolition *sans phrase* of the Court of Chancery". It was a theme which Dickens himself often addressed, linking it characteristically with the general state of the poor and the deprived, since the legal system had become "a by-word for delay, slow agony of mind, despair, impoverishment, trickery, confusion, insupportable injustice" – this litany from the pages of *Household Words* sounding like Miss Flite's caged birds, "Hope, Joy, Youth, Peace, Rest, Life, Dust, Ashes, Waste, Want, Ruin, Despair. . ." And in that transition, from the accumulation of complaints to the very image of living creatures in their cages, do we see the curve of Dickens's imagination.

So although it has often been said that a contemporary read Dickens as he would a newspaper, picking up all the topics and allusions of the day, this is true only in a special sense. The world is transformed once it is shut up in *Bleak House*. Of course there had already been many pieces in *Household Words* both on the neglect of the poor and on the horrors of London, and just a few months before he began *Bleak House* he had in fact made a speech at the first anniversary banquet of the Metropolitan Sanitary Association in which he said that ". . . certain as it is that the air from Gin Lane will be carried, when the wind is Easterly, into May Fair, and that if you once have a vigorous pestilence raging furiously in Saint Giles's, no mortal list of Lady Patronesses can keep it out of Almack's . . ." There in abbreviated form is one of the central perceptions of the novel he was soon to write; how rich and poor are bound to one another, how contagion spreads so quickly that it becomes an image of chaos itself. *Jo struck with mortal illness, moving on, infecting others in the course of his "strange existence upon earth". Esther Summerson in all the fever of disease.* Then, in the same speech, Dickens declared, "What avails it to send a Missionary to me, a miserable man or woman living in a foetid Court where every sense bestowed upon me for my delight becomes a torment, and every minute of my life is new mire added to the heap under which I lie degraded . . . Would he address himself to my hopes of immortality? I am so surrounded by material filth that my Soul can not rise to the contemplation of an immaterial existence!" *The Reverend Chadband tries to preach to the unreformed Jo.* So out of public statements the fictional images are formed. Neglect. Irresponsibility. Poverty. Disease. Ruin. Decay. One of the central emblems of *Bleak House* concerns the possibility of explosion and conflagration, of various combustible materials given a brief fiery life, of a system that has putrefaction at its heart and which must one day dissolve in noxious vapours. What "picture", to use Dickens's word, may illustrate this? Could it not be the burial ground which had been described in the *Narrative* for *Household Words* only a few months before: "The *Cholera Nursery* is a name which has been given to the churchyard of St Clements Dane. It is crammed with human remains, yet augmentation of corpses and of noxious vapours are daily made . . ." *Lady Dedlock lies dead before the iron gates of the burial ground.* The dead bodies of the poor. The dead bodies of the rich. Interconnectedness. The East wind. In the *Narrative* of *Household Words* there had also been a plea for the education of the poor because of the "startling depths of mental ignorance and neglect concealed beneath our hollow shows of civilisation". *Krook writing words in chalk upon the wall, writing the words backwards, writing words which he does not understand.* The poor. The outcast. The excluded. The possibility of fire welling up from within. Revolution. Spontaneous combustion. *And the glutinous ashes of Krook cling to the very walls and ceiling.* Everything is combined, journalism and fiction, fact and romance, truth and image. Everything is touching else, so that it becomes impossible to know where the reality ends and the vision begins.

And no more so than in the crossing sweeper Jo. Jo, the illiterate boy who seems to owe so much to the cross-examination of George Ruby reported in the *Narrative* of *Household Words* with the facts ". . . that he did not know what a New Testament was; that he could not read; that he had never said his prayers; that he did not know what prayers were; that he did not know what God was; that, though he had heard of the devil, he did not know him; that, in fact, all he knew was how to sweep the crossing . . ." Facts only partly transformed in Jo's cross-examination in *Bleak House*: "Name, Jo. Nothing else that he knows on . . . No father, no mother, no friends . . . Knows a broom's a broom, and knows it's wicked to tell a lie . . ." There was another child, too, who may be said to act as a model for Jo, if that is not too loose a word for so strange and instinctive a process of combination. It is a boy whom Dickens encountered in one of his many visits to the ragged schools and one whom he described in "A Sleep To Startle Us", an essay for *Household Words* written as he was composing the early chapters of *Bleak House*: ". . . an orphan boy with burning cheeks and great gaunt eager eyes, who was in pressing peril of death, too, and who had no possession under the broad sky but a bottle of physic and a scrap of writing . . . He held the bottle of physic in his claw of a hand, and stood, apparently unconscious of it, staggering, and staring with his bright glazed eyes; a creature, surely, as forlorn and desolate as Mother Earth can have supported on her breast that night. He was gently taken away, along with the dying man, to the workhouse; and he passed into the darkness with his physic-bottle as if he were going into his grave." The child goes into the darkness, and then there emerges Jo. The real boy touches hands for a moment with his imaginary counterpart who will live for ever. George Ruby. The dying orphan. Jo.

There were many others, too, from whom Dickens could have taken his story. It is clear enough that Dickens had seen Henry Mayhew's *London Labour and the London Poor*, published in this same year, 1851, when Dickens began *Bleak House*. He may have read some of the observations closely related to his own interests, such as the fact that "taken as a class, crossing sweepers are among the most honest of the London poor . . ." But there were terrible stories in Mayhew's account, stories of the poor and the desperate, more terrible than anything depicted by Doré or by Hogarth, more terrible than anything described by Dickens himself. There was the thirteen-year-old boy wearing only a ragged cloth jacket, fastened with bits of tape, and a pair of ragged trousers. "He wore two old shoes; one tied to his foot with an old ribbon, the other a woman's old boot. He had an old cloth cap. His features were distorted somewhat, through being swollen with the cold". This is what he told Mayhew on the death of his mother: ". . . when I went back to the lodging house they told me she was dead. I had sixpence in my pocket, but I couldn't help crying to think I'd lost my mother. I cry about it still. I didn't wait to see her buried, but I started on my own account . . . I have been begging about all the time till now. I am very weak – starving to death . . . I would do anything to be out of this misery." And an interview with another boy: "Had heer'd on another world; wouldn't mind it if he was there hisself, if he could do better, for things was often queer here. Had heered on it from a tailor – such a clever cove, a stunner . . . was an ignorant chap, for he'd never been to school, but he was up to many a move, and didn't do bad; had heer'd of Shakespeare, but didn't know whether he was alive or dead, and didn't care. A man with something like that name kept a dolly and did stunning; but he was sich a hard cove that if *he* was dead it wouldn't matter. Had seen the Queen, but didn't recollec' her name just at the minute; oh yes, Wictoria and Albert." Mayhew adds to this account that the boy "answered very freely, and sometimes, when I could not help laughing at his replies, laughed loudly himself, as if he entered into the joke".

There is no sense, then, in which Dickens needed to exaggerate the already original and idiosyncratic speech of the poor, or to magnify their miseries. It was all there before him, on every corner of every street; and perhaps what is more remarkable still is the extent to which the poor represented not so much an under-class as a state within a state, a community of persons who had no real connection with the external world of events and characters which is chronicled by history. These are people who had no religion of any kind, no sense of their country, no knowledge of their rulers, and indeed no real sense of their own selves. Thus Mayhew's report of a conversation with a crippled bird-seller who never read the newspaper: "It don't come in my way, and if it did, I shouldn't look at it, for I can't read over well and it's nothing to me who's king or who's queen. It can never have anything to do with me. It don't take my attention. There'll be no change for me in this world." These are our forgotten ancestors, the unknown people who lived and died in a world which offered them little but misery and disease, who went down into the darkness; that toiling mass which we may briefly glimpse in the pages of Dickens but which he could not present in all its enormity, for then it would have been too terrible to bear, too appalling to witness. In his life of course he knew the worst; he had seen it over and over again, and one contemporary witnessed his journeys into this inner world: "I watched Dickens intently as he went among these outcasts of London, and saw with what deep sympathy he encountered the sad and suffering in their horrid abodes. At the door of one of the penny lodging-houses (it was growing towards morning, and the raw air almost cut one to the bone), I saw him snatch a little child out of its poor drunken mother's arms, and bear it in, filthy as it was, that it might be warmed and cared for . . ." So he knew and had seen the worst; he was even trying to mitigate the worst. But he could not write about it as it was. He had no desire gratuitously to alienate his largely middle-class public, and took care to retain the social and sexual proprieties of the period. One could put the point another way by noting that he was as reticent about his own past as a "labouring hind" in the blacking factory as he was about the conditions of the working poor. There were some things that could not be said. In any case nineteenth-century fiction is too much implicated with the theatre, with melodrama itself, with the demands and expectations of the literate, with the concept of power and order, with the notion of historical reality – it was in a literal sense unable to reproduce (perhaps unable even to *see*) the real lives of the urban poor. In *Bleak House* Dickens intervenes directly with political and social comment, but he sees the world itself as infused with melodrama, changed by images and "pictures". So he created Jo, the street-crossing sweeper, and upon his frail shape he heaps the mud and the filth, the poverty and the illiteracy and the disease. Everything is touching everything else. The city is the fog-covered sphere which Dickens revolves in his hand, trying to peer into the centre where past and future are gathered.

And so he begins. In his new study in Tavistock House he takes out his blue paper, dips his quill pen in black ink, and begins. "London. Michaelmas Term lately over, and the Lord Chancellor sitting in Lincoln's Inn Hall. Implacable November weather. As much mud in the streets, as if the waters had but newly retired from the face of the earth, and it would not be wonderful to meet a Megalosaurus, forty feet long or so, waddling like an elephantine lizard up Holborn Hill." A Megalosaurus in Holborn Hill – he had invented a similar image just a few months before when in *Household Words*, as we have seen, he had imagined a "scaly monster of the Saurian period" in a creek of the Thames. The image had appealed to him, and so he had retained it; it is precisely what he was to call, in the preface to this novel, ". . . the romantic side of familiar things". A fact balanced against an unfamiliar impression, reality suffused with wild fancy so that it both is and is not the same – the kind of magic Dickens had imbibed from his childhood reading and now somehow recreated in this present world of mud and November weather. The balance between fact and marvel, reality and grotesquerie, sense and romance – a balance which for some reason seems quintessentially of the mid-nineteenth century when all forms of scientific and historical enquiry were discovering the marvellous within the domain of the familiar. It had been precisely this sense which Dickens wished to capture in the early stages of preparing *Bleak House*. He had a notion of setting his ruined country house in a valley in Gloucestershire because it reminded him of a valley in Switzerland; thus, in conflating them, he would be able to introduce the foreign into the familiar.

But it was of London which he now wrote. The city where the Megalosaurus might stalk and which on this November day is suffused with fog. "Fog everywhere . . . Chance people on the bridges peeping over the parapets into a nether sky of fog, with fog all round them, as if they were up in a balloon, and hanging in the misty clouds." So the fog brings mystery, too, diffusing "the romantic side of familiar things" as the people hurry through the pearly darkness. And yet such a fog was real enough. It was no wraith of Dickens's invention. One contemporary wrote about "the vast city wrapt in a kind of darkness which seems neither to belong to the day nor the night . . ." The fogs of London were famous then. White, green, yellow fogs, the exhalation of coal fires and steamboats, factories and breweries; one afternoon, only a few years before, ". . . the mingled vapour and smoke grew thicker and thicker until it was literally pitch-dark. Torches appeared on all the streets . . ." The city as the mystery. That is at the heart of *Bleak House*. The city where the familiar becomes foreign, just as the words of the law are "foreign" to those who cannot read.

There was a sense in which Dickens loved this alien city; he loved that unearthly darkness which made it a place of fantasy and a harbinger of night. This was the city that harboured all the grotesques and the monsters which he created in *Bleak House*, fashioning them out of the mud and dirt which fill its pages. Dickens loved the city of mist, the city of night, the city lit by scattered lights – perhaps it might be described as a form of urban Gothic, like the architecture which was even then appearing in the grander thoroughfares of London. "There is nothing in London that is *not* curious," Dickens once wrote. But that which was the most curious was also "the most sad and the most shocking". This was "the great wilderness of London" in which we are able even at this late date to fix the precise places which Dickens chose to depict. The graveyard outside which Lady Dedlock dies was located at the corner of Drury Lane and Russell Street, with its entrance through Crown Court. It is now a playground for children. Krook's Rag and Bottle Warehouse was to be found in Star Yard, near Chichester Rents; at the time of writing, this whole area has been demolished to make way for new building. But, even if by a feat of the historical imagination we stand upon the same pavements and see the old buildings and gates rising up once more, they would still not be the same places which Dickens saw. For him they were emblems of a new order and thus charged with unfamiliar mystery, the whole great city becoming as extraordinary as the Thames of his vision, the Thames which in *Bleak House* "had a fearful look, so overcast and secret, creeping away so fast between the low flat lines of shore: so heavy with indistinct and awful shapes, both of substances and shadow: so deathlike and mysterious". One other thing ought to be remembered, too: London was as interesting to its own inhabitants as it was to Dickens himself, and there is no doubt that they were eager to see, to read, and to learn all they could about their novel circumstances in a city which was growing and changing at an unparalleled speed. It was their sensibility, for example, that encouraged the growth of a more strident melodrama in the "low" theatres, in its dramatic contrasts mimicking the change and uncertainty of metropolitan life; there were new forms of comedy, too, particularly the comedy of shiftless street life; and a harsher kind of romanticism emerges, the romanticism which springs from the urban dark. The urban dark which Dickens was even now creating as he worked upon *Bleak House*.

By the first week of December he had finished all but the second chapter of its opening instalment, but then he had to break off in order to start work on his Christmas essay for *Household Words*. Never was he able to free himself from the trammels of his weekly periodical and in this short piece, "What Christmas Is, As We Grow Older", he establishes a melancholy note in his memories of the dead, and in his memories of past Christmases. "Lost friend, lost child, lost parent, sister, brother, husband, wife, we will not so discard you!" But in this little seasonal vignette there is also a plea for forbearance, for acceptance and understanding of the past; this Christmas, the Christmas after the death of his father and the death of his daughter, this Christmas becomes for Dickens a time of reconciliation. A time to sit and pause. A time to cease to complain and to strive. A time to incorporate the past. This, at the end of 1851, when he was beginning *Bleak House*.

Chapter 22

A TIME, too, for festivity. *Laus Deo!* was his general response to the birth of a new year and, for the first party in Tavistock House, Dickens organised a New Year's Eve celebration. He had also built a stage in the back room of the first floor of Tavistock House for the usual Twelfth Night entertainments, which rivalled those of Christmas and the New Year, and he called it "The Smallest Theatre In The World". This year he and the children put on a burlesque by Alfred Smith, *Guy Fawkes*, but such festival productions became an annual event in the Dickens household. Charley has described his father's omnipotent role in these proceedings: "He revised and adapted the plays, selected and arranged the music, chose and altered the costumes, wrote the new incidental songs, invented all the stage business, taught everybody his or her part . . ." No wonder the male children of Dickens were in later life to feel inadequate (the daughters had more of Dickens's own spirit) – how could it be otherwise with such a father? A few days later he took the children to see a panto-mime, *Harlequin Hogarth; or The Two London 'Prentices*, at Drury Lane. But what a life of contrasts his was: the night before the pantomime he had toured some of the poorest quarters of London in the company of Inspector Field, with the intention of finding an area in which Miss Burdett-Coutts might carry out her plan of erecting modern dwelling houses for the working classes (just such an area was eventually found in Bethnal Green). And what contrasts in his own life, too, at least for those who cared to look for them. George Eliot described Tavistock House to a friend and mentioned "splendid library, of course, with soft carpet, couches etc. such as became a sympathiser with the suffering classes. How can we sufficiently pity the needy unless we know fully the blessings of plenty?" Not the first or the last sarcastic remark about Dickens by Eliot and an indication, perhaps, of the envy which his success and popularity could inspire in even the most high-minded contemporaries. The sort of remark which, if he heard of it, he brushed aside or affected to ignore.

Nothing now was so important to him as the writing of *Bleak House*. By the end of January he had come close to completing the first two numbers; he had interpolated a new chapter, "In Fashion", which he paginated from A to E and then inserted between the original first two chapters. Now "In Fashion" could be seen as a parallel to the first chapter, "In Chancery", and the structural principle on which Dickens was working becomes quite evident. His notes on this new second chapter – "*Lady Dedlock. Law Writer.* work up from this moment" – make it clear also that the elaborate parallels he was setting up in the narrative were accompanied by a very clear sense of the direction of the plot. As he writes he sees the comprehensiveness of what he is about to achieve like a half-glimpsed vision in front of him. It is this vision towards which he proceeds. And now he wanted to move ahead as quickly as possible. Yet another appeal had come for him to stand for Parliament (it was the third), and once more he rejected it; in the past he had done so on financial grounds, but on this particular occasion he cited his work on *Bleak House* as the main reason for his refusal. He told Wills that ". . . it is impossible that I could go into it with the new book in hand. If I had only H. W. I might possibly make the dash, but I should be worried to death if I did it now." It was in a similar spirit that he cut down upon all his social engagements while he was working on the novel; it became his practice now to accept only two public dinners a month, and he resolutely refused to go to any others. His attitude towards "society" had in any case suffered a sea-change; in *Bleak House* for the first time it is seen as an absurdity, an irrelevance, almost a madness. A dark force from which the real people must escape in order to create another society of their own.

So his early routine for *Bleak House* was now settled. He generally worked on the novel from ten until two and, under normal circumstances, he hoped to finish his work by the twentieth of each month. At the end of this period he generally found himself in a state of what he once called "blackguard restless idleness", and would be constantly asking friends to join him on nocturnal tours, walking expeditions and various country jaunts. The paucity of references to *Bleak House* in his correspondence during the time of composition strongly suggests that he was quite in command of his material and felt no need privately to agonise over its composition; in a way it could be said that he had been preparing for this novel all his life and, despite the calamities and general weariness which had helped to provoke it in the first place, there can be little doubt that while he was actually working he remained relatively content. Despite the generally oppressed and oppressive tone of the book, in fact, there is ample evidence to suggest that Dickens was even happy while he was writing it – certainly happier than he had been in the previous year, when no proper creative work had been accomplished. Any amount of misery can afflict a writer, but in the actual process of writing that misery is dissolved. It might even be said that *Bleak House* cured the very malaise which was responsible for its composition.

Evidence for this rather more cheerful state of mind emerges in the reminiscences of the son of George Cattermole, the illustrator whom Dickens had befriended and whose house was often visited by the novelist in search of relief and release from the labours of his study. Cattermole lived in Clapham Rise, then a country retreat some way out of town, and on many occasions Dickens, Forster and others would take the omnibus there from the Ship tavern at Charing Cross – an omnibus stop, incidentally, served by a "tout" known to Dickens as "Sloppy". Cattermole's son describes this man as "one of those melancholy, faded, red-nosed, gin-and-watery, whelk-and-periwinkly men, always 'half-muddled' yet never drunk, never noisy, never jolly . . . nodding to Bill, drinking with Jack, asking Tom 'how is that party with the wooden leg?' . . ." In fact exactly the kind of person Dickens swooped upon in sheer delight, and in letters to Cattermole he expertly parodies Sloppy's hesitant and awkward conversation. He and his friends retold various "Sloppy-isms" and the ancient omnibus tout's verbal mannerisms became the object of a long-standing joke between the men; as in one letter from Dickens to Cattermole where he talks about "Claphim" and "Tucker'seseseseseseseseseseseses in the Strand". These Clapham Rise dinners – celebrated by "The Portwiners", as they called themselves – were apparently very jolly, and Leonard Cattermole remembers Dickens brewing gin punch, admiring a water-colour drawing "with his legs rather wide apart", and even on one occasion hiding in a cabinet – ". . . running up playfully before dinner when no one was in the room, and hearing himself enquired for when company entered". At this point he burst forth, just as many years before he had burst into the drawing room of the Hogarths and executed a sailor's dance on the spot.

Thus did the novelist still release his naturally high spirits. By 7 February he had finished the second number of *Bleak House*, and only now did he discover that he had overwritten and had to delete some seventy-six lines. At least it looks as if they were excised for reasons of space, although it is interesting to note that the majority of these cancelled lines concern the manner and conversation of Leonard, later hurriedly changed to Harold, Skimpole. The point was that, for the "model" of this irresponsible and fickle creature, Charles Dickens had taken Leigh Hunt, a friend of long standing, and the very man whom he had originally tried to assist with his amateur theatricals. That it was meant to be a close study of the original is evident in Dickens's admission later that "I suppose that he is the most exact portrait that ever was painted in words! I have very seldom, if ever, done such a thing. But the likeness is astonishing . . . It is an absolute reproduction of a real man." He had even lifted some of the material of Skimpole's conversation from a book which Leigh Hunt had written eight years before, *A Jar of Honey from Mount Hybla*. So astonishing a likeness, in fact, that he asked Forster and another friend to look over these passages in early proof stage; both men told him that the resemblance was too close, and that changes or excisions ought to be made. So Dickens altered the name from Leonard to Harold, cut out some of the more egregious parallels, and hoped for the best. But in truth nothing could alter the obvious identification with Hunt, and it soon became common knowledge that Dickens had pilloried his friend in the latest number of *Bleak House*. It was soon well known in London, at least, and, according to one contemporary, ". . . the general opinion was strongly in favour of Hunt". Another contemporary recalled that when the portrait of Skimpole was published the reaction among friends of Leigh Hunt was "intensely painful" and had "the effect of estranging one from the friends of Dickens who were most like flatterers and partisans".

Of course, as is the way with such things, Hunt himself did not recognise the likeness at first and had to be prompted by several friends before he understood the gravity of Dickens's attack. He had no idea why it had been launched in the first place and wrote, "Did my not joining the Guild of Literature and Art offend him? But I had never refused to do so. I underwent real distress in not knowing what step I ought to take." It seems that he protested about the matter to Dickens himself when he attended a dinner at Tavistock House; according to Wilkie Collins, ". . . Hunt directly charged Dickens with taking the character of Harold Skimpole from the character of Leigh Hunt, and protested severely. I was not present, but Dickens told me what had happened." Dickens's precise words in reply are not known, but his response no doubt went on the usual lines: he had taken only a few traits from Leigh Hunt, the character was based upon many different men, and so forth. It was also reported that in subsequent years, according to a friend of Hunt's son, "Dickens has been wonderfully attentive to Leigh Hunt". But in fact, despite his protests, Dickens did not change the portrait of Skimpole as he changed that of Miss Mowcher; if anything, the description becomes harsher and more unforgiving. Dickens no doubt assumed that Hunt had accepted his protestations of innocence, and may not have fully realised that it remained a matter of some distress both to him and to his family.

It was in fact a savage attack and it is doubtful if anything more wounding could possibly be said about the man, Dickens himself compounding the problem when in later numbers he seemed to be describing Hunt's own family in vivid and sarcastic terms. So why had Dickens done it? It is true that Leigh Hunt had irritated him four years before with an appeal for another theatrical benefit to be arranged on his behalf. It is also true that in his *Autobiography*, published in 1850, Leigh Hunt paid scant tribute to the help he had received from contemporaries like Dickens and Forster. But the fact that he had not joined the Guild would perhaps have only confirmed to Dickens the central irresponsibility or even fecklessness of Leigh Hunt. But none of this really matters. The point is that Dickens could not help doing it. The picture of Harold Skimpole was so exactly right for *Bleak House* that Dickens could no more have changed it than he could have abandoned the novel itself. He was always notoriously sure of the accuracy of his own perceptions, but he was equally sure of the rightness of his literary judgment. The twin themes of irresponsibility and neglect run everywhere through *Bleak House*, and Skimpole is an intrinsic part of a much larger design. He *had* to go in, and the force of this creative compulsion should never be underestimated: the fact that Dickens made no attempt to mitigate the severity of the portrait is only one indication of the extent to which he felt driven to write in this manner. He simply could not stop himself from doing it.

But the origins of characters are deeper and more disturbed than that. Of course there are the easy identifications to be made in the pages of *Bleak House*, from the grand (Lawrence Boythorn was meant to be a sketch of Walter Savage Landor) to the trivial (Inspector Bucket bears some idealised resemblance to Inspector Field and Mooney the beadle is apparently taken from a real beadle, Looney, who superintended Salisbury Square). But the point is that all of these characters, in the very act and art of composition, become, as we have had occasion to note elsewhere, part of Dickens himself. The point might even be made with that character who in *Bleak House* seems furthest from Dickens himself – Esther Summerson, the artless humble little body who is always rattling her keys and whose narrative acts as a kind of counterpoint to Dickens's own. Now it is possible that at least part of Esther Summerson may have been derived from Dickens's observations of a certain Esther Elton who, after the death of her father, exhibited what at the time Dickens called ". . . patient womanly devotion; a little piece of quiet, unpretending, domestic heroism . . ." This may well be transmuted into Esther Summerson's own selfless devotion, ". . . half ashamed of not entirely believing in him myself . . . hoped I might always be so blest and happy as to be useful to some one in my small way . . ." But this was precisely the artless little tone that Dickens on occasions could himself adopt quite seriously, as for example when he wrote to Miss Burdett-Coutts in the following year that "my old Lausanne friends were all so cordially happy to see me that I felt half ashamed of myself for being liked so much beyond my deserts". Half ashamed – the very same phrase and, since the letter was written just after the completion of *Bleak House*, it is possible that Dickens had actively co-opted the character of Esther Summerson as part of his own response to the world. But we have already seen how often passivity and gentleness emerge as the great virtues of Dickens's characters, as if there were some part of himself that yearned to be reinvested with that innocent infantile state; Dickens could only create Esther Summerson because she was a part of his own self. Just as Harold Skimpole was also part of his own self; that is why he went almost blindly forward with the characterisation, for in the heat of composition (and we have seen how sometimes he mouthed words in the mirror before he wrote them down), he *was* Skimpole and had to exorcise him.

So he worked on through February, and at the end of that month the first number of *Bleak House* appeared – on this occasion in bluish-green wrappers (Dickens did not return to the bright green wrappers of his earlier novels until the commencement of *Our Mutual Friend*, his last completed work). Such was the pressure of time that some of the narrative was set very hurriedly, and in fact over forty different compositors worked upon it over the months that followed, but the advertising space included in each number was at a higher premium than ever. On the inside cover of the first number there was an advertisement for Edmiston's Pocket Siphonia, or waterproof overcoat, which was followed by a section called "Bleak House Advertiser"; advertisements here included one for Rowland's Macassar Oil, for Life Pills, for Chrystal Spectacles, for Cough Lozenges, Pulmonic Wafers, Hair Lubricant, Shawls, Self-Acting Pipe Tubes, and Parasols. Some twenty-four pages of advertising in all, and on the inside back-cover an "Anti-Bleak House" advertisement for overcoats and trousers. The back cover itself was devoted to Heal and Son's Bedsteads. So did the life of nineteenth-century England surround, and even compete for attention with, Dickens's own evocation of it. Of course there were also advertisements *for* Bleak House in the periodicals of the period, and in fact it could be said that Bradbury and Evans's promotional campaigns were at least a modest element in the success of Dickens's work. Posters were placed on walls, bills fixed around lamp-posts, wrappers and plates displayed in bookshop windows. Not the least of the selling points for the new serial, however, emerged in Phiz's "dark plates" for such scenes as the London slums; this was a new technique by which Hablot Browne machine-ruled the whole plate with very fine parallel lines, thus spreading a darker tone throughout. So did Browne maintain a visual commentary upon Dickens's style, the artist developing alongside the novelist in a symbiotic relationship which was extremely important to the first reception of Dickens's work. Browne's actual relationship with Dickens was still cordial but no longer really close, however, and they maintained between each other a strict business arrangement. They both needed each other (Dickens of course always remaining the dominant partner), but Browne's own growing shyness as well as Dickens's burgeoning responsibilities meant that their association was in large part now only a professional one.

So, as Dickens finished each chapter or each number of *Bleak House*, proofs would be sent on to Hablot Browne with Dickens's specific recommendations for subjects to be illustrated. Then, customarily, Dickens would see a proof of Browne's plate for final approval. He was writing quickly now, in any case; he wanted to get ahead on the novel so that he could find time for those journeys of the Amateur Players to Manchester and Liverpool which he had arranged on the Guild's behalf for February. In Manchester they played at the Free

Trade Hall, and then went on for two performances at the Philharmonic Hall in Liverpool. And, as far as Dickens was concerned, there was always the same "triumph", the same "rapturous auditors", the same prodigious scenes in which he and the cast were ". . . blinded by excitement, gas, and waving hats and handkerchiefs". There never can have been a man whose enthusiasm expressed itself in such hyperbole, and throughout his life everything is either the *best* or the *worst*; there was no middle way. "I have been so happy in all this," he told Bulwer-Lytton, "that I could have cried on the shortest notice any time since Tuesday." And to his wife he added a more personal note; ". . . indeed the earnest admiration and love of the people towards one, is something quite bewildering – or would be, if one were not steady in such matters." When he returned from this short tour he suffered the usual symptoms of withdrawal from the gas and the excitement; he was, as always, exhausted, stiff, and with weakened voice. As he used to tell his correspondents, he made fourteen costume changes each night. Nevertheless the festivities could not be allowed to end so abruptly, and a few days later he gave a dinner for the whole cast at Tavistock House.

It was at Tavistock House, too, that in the middle of March Catherine Dickens gave birth to her tenth child – named, in honour of the baronet, Edward Bulwer Lytton Dickens (Bulwer-Lytton himself was godfather). It was to be her last child, the conclusion of her long and unhappy history of pregnancy. The tour or perhaps the birth seemed to have unsettled Dickens; although he had to finish as much of *Bleak House* as possible in order to make room for yet more provincial theatricals in May, he was working on the novel only fitfully, felt "anxious", and was taking eighteen- to twenty-mile walks in order to quieten or exhaust his restless spirit. He remained relatively content as long as he could work systematically and consistently on the novel; but to work on it discontinuously, abruptly, quickly – this he disliked. He was also concerned about Leigh Hunt's reaction to the portrayal of Harold Skimpole (he still found himself automatically writing Leonard, and then crossing it out). Once more he was thinking of going abroad; to Paris, to Geneva, anywhere. In fact, in the end, he only went as far as Dover; but he did visit Rockingham Castle for one night, no doubt in part to refresh his memory concerning the model for his own Chesney Wold in the novel. But this was his normal reaction at times of self-imposed or external stress; to escape, to get away, to flee. And this despite the fact that all the news concerning *Bleak House* ought to have cheered him. Bradbury and Evans reported that sales were very high, and indeed they remained at over thirty thousand for the whole run of the novel.

It is not hard to see why, despite his mood, he needed to work quickly on *Bleak House*; not only was he in charge of all the administrative arrangements concerning the second provincial tour but a glance at his engagements for the first week of May, even before he departed with the Amateurs, reveals just how occupied he was. On the first day of May, a Saturday, he was trying to finish the next number of the novel (chapters eleven to thirteen), before attending a dinner for the Royal Academy that evening. On Sunday he had to prepare another large section of his *A Child's History of England*, ready to dictate it to an amanuensis at Wellington Street North. On the mornings of Monday, Tuesday and Wednesday he had to be present at the office, in order to "make up" the next two numbers of *Household Words*. On Wednesday he took the chair at a meeting for the removal of trade restrictions on literature; George Eliot was also present on that occasion and remarked how Dickens was ". . . preserving a courteous neutrality of eyebrows, and speaking with clearness and decision", but she did add that he was "not distinguished-looking". Two days later there was a dinner at Tavistock House to celebrate his son's christening, and on the following afternoon his time was taken up by a number of welcome and unwelcome callers. Then, two days later, he was off with his Guild players for performances in Shrewsbury and Birmingham.

There were only a certain number of days, therefore, when he was able to concentrate upon *Bleak House* and, almost as soon as he returned from the short provincial tour, he was once more "hard at work" on the fourteenth chapter, trying to keep free of interruptions and making sure that all his attention was concentrated on the working out of the story. Presumably that is why he went down to St Albans as soon as he had corrected the proofs of that number; he was thinking ahead, thinking of poor Jo's vagrant route, Jo, who, in his mortal illness, talks of travelling along "the Stolbuns Road". Certainly he was in his mind now, since the number he had just finished had concentrated upon the sufferings of the poor street-crossing sweeper; to such an extent, in fact, that the narrator *becomes* Jo as he shuffles through the streets of London. "To be hustled, and jostled, and moved on; and really to feel that it would appear to be perfectly true that I have no business, here, or there, or anywhere . . ." And it is in this spirit, and with this access to Jo's consciousness, that Dickens reflects upon a world controlled by what Jarndyce calls "this monstrous system". As the poor Chancery litigant, Gridley, puts it, "The system! I am told, on all hands, it's the system. I mustn't look to individuals. It's the system."

That *system* now seems to us a quite ordinary concept but at the time of *Bleak House* it was of new and pressing relevance. It becomes, in fact, one of the organising principles of the novel itself. Disraeli, four years before, in 1847, had heralded its emergence: "No one has confidence in himself; on the contrary, everyone has a mean idea of his own strength and has no reliance on his own judgement. Men obey a general impulse, they bow before an external necessity . . . Individuality is dead . . ." It is the presence of this "external necessity" which make *Bleak House* such a different novel from its predecessors, and we must see in that change a whole grouping of impersonal forces which were just now coming into public consciousness. Thus in a review this year of Herbert Spencer's *Social Statics*, he was criticised largely because his own version of "individualism" was considered to be out of date. And at the end of the decade John Stuart Mill, in *On Liberty*, was proclaiming that ". . . there is also in the world at large an increasing inclination to stretch unduly the powers of society over the individual, both by the force of opinion and even by that of legislation; and as the tendency of all changes taking place is to strengthen society and diminish the power of the individual, this encroachment is not one of the evils which tend spontaneously to disappear but, on the contrary, to grow more and more formidable." ". . . the powers of society" – are these not the mysterious forces which do their work within *Bleak House*, condemning not only the poor to further hardship but also implicitly cutting down, destroying, the individuality of those like Mr Gridley and Miss Flite who find refuge from these "powers" only in death? Just as Dickens and the sanitation reformers had repeatedly made the point that the sickness of the poor very quickly becomes the sickness of the rich, that cholera can move rapidly from Whitechapel to Whitehall, so now political philosophers were also discovering the same process of social assimilation on other levels. In a world where everything is touching everything else, in the world of *Bleak House* and of encroaching "public opinion", individuality was now no more than a past or passing deity, lost in the fog and darkness of the novel, the fog and darkness of the law which, like disease, spreads its errors everywhere.

Dickens was preoccupied with the novel throughout the summer and, when an American woman congratulated him on the narrative of Esther Summerson, he asked anxiously "Is it quite natural, quite girlish?" He went down to Folkestone in order to write among more peaceful surroundings; in Tavistock House he was being "persecuted" by callers with various letters of introduction and his own writing had suffered as a consequence. "I feel," he said, "as if I had been thinking my brain into a sort of cabbage net." He stayed at Folkestone for a few days, returned to London briefly, and then took lodgings for his family and himself at 10 Camden Crescent in Dover. He intended to stay here for three months, from the end of July to the beginning of October, with a regular weekly visit to London on *Household Words* business as well as the always-pressing work for Miss Burdett-Coutts and Urania Cottage (work now amplified because of her new scheme for model homes in East London). In his usual manner, however, he was imploring his friends to come and stay with the family; and one who took up the invitation was Wilkie Collins who, in his letters home, vividly described the Dickens regimen in Dover. Breakfast at ten minutes past eight *sharp*, after which Dickens would vanish into his study and remain there until two. The afternoon, however, was given over to walks, expeditions, swimming. His fame could sometimes prove an impediment, however, and Collins described how people "used to waylay him . . . and have a good long stare at the 'great man'. . ." Dinner at half-past five. Then card-games (a pastime which Dickens did not particularly care for – his daughter remembered how, during such sessions, his attention would wander and he would get up to straighten a picture). Bed between ten and eleven. In fact Collins liked the atmosphere so much that he readily agreed to stay an extra week, but some of the guests found the Dickens family (and especially Dickens himself) rather overwhelming; Kate Horne visited Camden Crescent and wrote that "I think with the Dickens's almost more than anyone else you require to have some room to breathe alone".

Much of the merriment left this little gathering, however, when Dickens was informed of the sudden death of Richard Watson. Dickens, who had dined with him only three weeks before, was clearly distressed at the news. "When I think of that bright house, and his fine simple honest heart, both so open to me, the blank and loss are like a dream." A little later he visited the bright house, Rockingham Castle, in order to comfort Mrs Watson in her affliction; they went up together to the gallery and walked into "the very part which he had made and was so fond of, and she looked out of one window and I looked out of another . . ." and they said nothing. But that was satisfactory, that was as it should be; already Dickens had written her a powerful letter of condolence and Mrs Watson knew, as did others, that he could write the things which he could never bring himself to say. But it was a "blank" to him, death upon death in these months. D'Orsay was soon to die; and Mrs Macready; and he visited the dying Lady Lovelace who had asked to see him. Death upon death, a sequence of them which casts its shadows over *Bleak House* even as he wrote it. "What a field of battle it is!" Dickens told Forster, and it was at this time that he sensed "some odd electrical disturbance in the air" which rendered everyone nervous. Certainly he seemed to be in an anxious and even aggressive mood. He described one of his female contributors as "an impudent bitch" and wrote an incandescently angry letter to Evans about one of the publisher's employees who had, apparently, interfered with some business at *Household Words*.

Nevertheless he had said some months before that actors are to be valued precisely because of their ability to rise from scenes of death and suffering in order to entertain their audience of that evening and all evenings to follow; and this is precisely what Dickens now had to do. The Amateur players were about to start on another provincial tour; Dickens was not only responsible for all the administrative arrangements (in which task he was helped by Catherine, who sometimes wrote his more impersonal letters for him), but he had to superintend the rehearsals. Almost as soon as he had finished the next number of *Bleak House* at Dover, he went to London and rehearsed in a city which now, during the heat of the summer, was sending up intolerable stenches from the alleys, from the polluted river, from the tenements. And then on to Nottingham, to Derby, to Newcastle-upon-Tyne, to Sunderland, to Sheffield, to Manchester, and finally to Liverpool. Everywhere a triumph. Everything going "wonderfully well". But there were minor anxieties. In Sunderland Dickens was so concerned with the roof of a new hall that at any minute he expected it to collapse, and as a result suffered agonies during the rounds of applause and cheering. He was so worried about the possibility of a stampede that he placed Catherine and Georgina at the front of the hall and, as he acted, he looked with apprehension at this precarious roof; "I am sure I never acted better, but the anxiety of my mind was so intense, and the relief at last so great, that I am half-dead to-day, and have not yet been able to eat or drink anything or to stir out of my room." An apt indication, this, of the susceptibility of Dickens to nervous shock.

A banquet had been arranged at Manchester in order to honour the Guild, and naturally Dickens spoke; during the course of his remarks he paid tribute to the Manchester Athenaeum itself and remarked that it ought to become a "pattern to the rising enterprise and energy of England . . .", which was hardly the image of the country then being created in *Bleak House*. He made another speech two days later, at the opening of the Free Library in Manchester, in which he made clear his belief that "capital and labour are not opposed, but are mutually dependent and mutually supporting . . ." So it is that Dickens's explicit political utterances tend to be of a suitably orthodox if vaguely radical sort; what he poured into his books, when he was alone, is something far more difficult and secretive. For as soon as the tour was finished he rushed back to Dover in order to work upon chapters twenty-three and twenty-four of the novel, chapters in which he takes on Esther Summerson's voice, and in which Miss Flite cries out at the death of Gridley – "Oh no, Gridley! . . . not without my blessing. After so many years!" These were the chapters which Dickens read to Wilkie Collins and to his own family, Dickens taking on the voice of Esther Summerson, mimicking the accents of Mrs Jellyby and becoming Miss Flite, screaming beside the death-bed of a man worn down by the Law.

He had rented Camden Crescent until the beginning of October, at which time the children returned to London (Mamie and Katie being superintended by a French governess) while Dickens, Catherine and Georgina travelled across to Boulogne. He wanted to finish the next number of *Bleak House* there and, as soon as he had done so, to return to London and his ordinary professional life. It is remarkable, incidentally, for a man of such fixed habits, how easily he could accommodate his writing to any surroundings; London, Folkestone, Dover and now Boulogne seemed to provide no distraction or difficulty in the constant daily process of writing. Only a man who was so fully in his imagined world that the real one no longer obtruded could manage such changes of scenery with Dickens's equanimity. They stayed in Boulogne for two weeks, at the Hotel des Bains, and clearly appreciated the area; it was in fact to take the place of Broadstairs as their summer retreat, although on this first visit Dickens brought back with him only one souvenir – a little figure of a Turk seated, smoking, as the sign for a tobacconist's shop, which he considered to be unmatched for its "grotesque absurdity". As soon as he had returned to London, he went straight to the office in order to discuss with Wills the shape of the coming Christmas issue. He also brought back the next two chapters for *Bleak House* and, since he did not in fact return until 18 October, less than two weeks before publication, he was cutting his "deadline" rather fine.

And then straight on to the next number, leading up to what he called "the great turning idea", by which he clearly meant the revelation to Esther Summerson that her mother is indeed Lady Dedlock. Gustave Flaubert used to say that he suffered with his characters even as he created them, that he became invaded by nervous anxiety at the same time as his characters, and even shared in the agony induced by the arsenic poisoning of Emma Bovary. Dickens's symptoms were not so severe but he did manage to contract a very bad cold at the time he was consigning Esther Summerson to a bout of smallpox; although, curiously enough, W. H. Wills became, like Esther, temporarily blind at the time that particular episode was published. And then there was rain. Rain in London for three months; heavy rain through which Dickens insisted on walking; hallucinatory rain, since with his bad cold "my whole room looks swollen and giddy, and it seems to be incessantly *raining* between me and the books"; fictional rain in *Bleak House*, the rain which further weakens Jo in his short passage to death.

He was indeed "shut up" in *Bleak House*, as he put it, and everything in his exterior life seems in some sense to reflect that condition. So it was that at this time, when he is chronicling the progress of poor houseless Jo, he is working intently upon Miss Burdett-Coutts's schemes to provide model houses for the poor; looking over surveys and plans, taking part in negotiations with recalcitrant landlords, superintending the estimates and costs. Even the controversies upon which he was engaged are concerned with the novel. The December number had culminated in the death of Krook by the mysterious process of spontaneous combustion, for example, leaving behind only a "thick, yellow liquor" and some white ashes. This form of internal combustion has been recorded over many centuries, sensationally or otherwise, and is even now the subject of scientific debate; but, in a period when the energetic forces of nature were being celebrated and in a book where the potential for violent explosion lies just beneath the rags and patches of its characters, the phenomenon serves a double purpose. It is indeed integral to the plot, but that did not stop G. H.

Lewes, in his "Literature" column for the *Leader* that same month, ridiculing the event; Dickens, he said, ". . . has doubtless picked up the idea among the curiosities of his reading . . ." and, perhaps more woundingly, went on to say that ". . . Captain Marryat, it may be remembered, employed the same equivocal incident in *Jacob Faithful*". Nothing stung Dickens more than the accusation of unreality, unless it was the accusation of plagiarism, and in the next number of *Bleak House* he tried to launch a counter-attack by listing (through the medium of a coroner's inquest on the strange death of Krook) all the "authorities" which supported the existence of the phenomenon. But posterity has been as unconvinced as the more sceptical of his contemporaries, and it has been demonstrated that Dickens took the original account of Krook's unnatural death from a published report in either the *Gentleman's Magazine* or the *Annual Register*; in other words, he had read about the incident, recalled it when it became necessary for his own purposes, and then gone back to the periodical in order to copy out the appropriate details. In his attempt to defend himself he borrowed a lecture on the subject from John Elliotson, and in a private letter to George Henry Lewes three weeks later claimed that ". . . I looked into a number of books with great care, expressly to learn what the truth was". But this was a lie; despite all his show of learning, which suggests assiduous personal research, all he had done was to open a copy of Robert Macnish's *The Anatomy of Drunkenness* and transcribe all the "authorities" from this second-hand source. And this at a time when he was counselling Wilkie Collins about "taking great pains" upon his work! In other words, he was trying to dissimulate his own lack of knowledge; nevertheless he maintained his confident position, and refused on any account even to hint that he might in any small way be mistaken. He was right, as far as he was concerned, and not even a battery of scientific authorities would ever have persuaded him otherwise. The man who could forget nothing might also have drawn some comfort from the notes of Michael Faraday which, the year before, had been employed in a series of articles for *Household Words*; the salient sentence reads, "It is said that spontaneous combustion does happen sometimes; particularly in great spirit drinkers. I don't see why it should not, if the system were to become too inflammable." And again that word – *system*, used in political discussion and in scientific discourse, in social surveys and in geological investigation.

It was in terms of the movement of *Bleak House*, then, that Dickens believed in the phenomenon; everything in the book leads up to this point and, if spontaneous combustion had not existed, Dickens might well have wanted to invent it. But this sudden explosion of heat at Krook's Rag and Bottle Warehouse is in turn related to the whole climate of scientific enquiry in which Dickens worked. It does not in the least matter that he himself was not acquainted with all the discussions and discoveries of his period, although at the time of his death he did have in his library copies of Darwin's *On The Origin of Species by means of Natural Selection* and Lyell's *Principles of Geology*. It is enough that he was part of his period, and that much of its *energy* (to use a key word of that time) ran through him and his language. In fact it has been suggested that Darwin's own scientific narratives owe much to his reading of Dickens's novels; in similar fashion, Dickens's own understanding of the symbolic forces of the world is charged with the same group of perceptions defined by contemporary scientists and geologists. Even the very form, the expansiveness, the detail, the momentum of Dickens's novels seem to be intimately associated with the discovery of *fields of force*, the understanding of the dynamics of *systems*, the enquiries into *magnetic centres*, the research into *thermodynamics*, the hypothesis of *evolution*. Is it inappropriate to note that the specifically English contribution to the science of the period lay primarily in physics and in the analysis of energy – that this particular concern should emerge in the country that had inaugurated the industrial revolution of the late eighteenth and early nineteenth centuries? In Dickens's own narratives all the fecundity of detail is absorbed within the drive of the narrative itself, all its abundance chastened by the need for symbolic transformation and the will to power; in their very form, Dickens's novels reflect the leading scientific preoccupations of his time. For the world was no longer seen in terms of discrete particles uniting and dividing within empty space on some set of mechanistic principles; the world was seen as an organism, not a machine, and the characteristic momentum of this organism was seen in terms of *waves* and *systems*. Light. Electricity. Magnetism. Electro-magnetism. Thermodynamics. These are the forces which exist within the very shape of *Bleak House* itself and, in the year before Dickens began to write that narrative, the second law of thermodynamics was proposed – how energy is converted into heat rather than useful work and so moves ineluctably towards its quietus, how the entropy of closed systems leads ultimately to disorder. How the forces of poverty and disease build up and spontaneously combust in the form of Krook. How the world of *Bleak House* is wearing down.

So perhaps science might even provide a moral framework for the perceptions of the period. In *Household Words* itself, in 1850, a contributor had discussed the manner in which science proved that ". . . we live in a world of paradoxes; and that existence itself, is a whirl of contradictions. Light and darkness, truth and falsehood, virtue and vice, the negative and positive poles of galvanic or magnetic mysteries, are evidences of all pervading antitheses, which acting like the good and evil genii of Persian Mythology, neutralise each other's powers when they come into collision." It is significant that the forces of the scientific universe are here associated with the fairy-tales of childhood, confirming once more how mythopoeic the Victorian imagination was; how much fact and discovery were seen in terms of mystery and even magic. And there was that other direction in which Victorian enquiry progressed – the direction of the past, the distant, the inconceivable past. The discovery of what was then called "Neanderthal Man" was to be made in 1856, and already excavations in Egypt, in Sumeria and in Greece had taken back the development of the human race into remote antiquity. It has already been suggested how the concept of the individual was even then being displaced by the idea and by the reality of "the system"; now in related fashion the individuals of the nineteenth century were seeing themselves as part of some extrinsic historical movement which could neither be reversed nor denied. Progressive evolution. Biological evolution. Antiquity itself. All the forces of the period seemed to be suggesting that the individual is imprisoned within a deterministic process. Faraday himself, the contributor to *Household Words*, believed in the presence of some universal force to which all the local forces of magnetism and electricity were related. The awareness of the interconnectedness of all things, the resistless momentum of the "system": these are also some of the most notable characteristics of *Bleak House* as well as of *Little Dorrit* and *Our Mutual Friend*. These novels belong solely to Dickens's genius, but his genius in turn is a component of the period in which he lived and wrote. And behind him, behind Faraday, behind Darwin, was the belief that there were fixed laws of the universe which could be discovered and explained – there was no uncertainty, no *relativity* in their accounts – and it is this certainty, this belief in the knowability of the material world and the continuity of all living things, which lends Dickens's own imagined world the same coherence and sustenance.

We understand now that the interpretations of nineteenth-century scientists and geologists were in a sense fictions, fictions as much part of their period as *Little Dorrit* or *David Copperfield*; Darwin and Faraday were telling stories, or fables, which created a world where the vigorous and the happy survive and multiply, where social hierarchy was confirmed by all the appearances of nature, where purpose and drive could be measured and maintained. Yet, in Dickens, that very sense of system, of interconnectedness, also led to gloom, anxiety, a sense of closeness and suffocation. It was at this point that science and literature might be said to part.

By the middle of December Dickens had come close to "the great turning idea" and at the last minute he added, on a separate piece of paper, the passage in which he used various authorities to confirm his own use of spontaneous combustion. Already he could see to the end of the story. He was planning to complete it by the following August, and then to travel once more to Switzerland. In the interim, between numbers in this bleak December, he rushed out once more into the world in order to refresh himself. With Wilkie Collins he went on a prowl around Whitechapel, and with Frank Stone he went back to Chatham, revisiting this site of childhood memories just after completing a short essay, "Where We Stopped Growing", in which he evokes some of the sharpest memories of his own childhood. He was also dictating sections of *A Child's History of England* concerned with the reign of Henry VIII, and in the number of *Bleak House* he had just finished he had written of ". . . the lamplighter going his rounds, like an executioner to a despotic king, strikes off the little heads of fire that have aspired to lessen the darkness. Thus, the day cometh, whether or no." We have just observed how great matters may come together in the language of the age, but there is room also for these small connections and affiliations, leading to the overwhelming truth that all parts of Dickens's life are related one to another. And is it true, then, as he said, that trifles make up the sum of life? He attended a dinner for the Poor, given by Miss Burdett-Coutts, and then three evenings later celebrated the coming of the New Year. A year in which the direction of Dickens's public activities was radically to change.

It all started in Birmingham. He had travelled there in the first week of January 1853, to receive the present of a diamond ring and a silver-gilt salver from a citizens' association formed to award prizes in the field of Fine Arts; in fact Dickens already wore a diamond ring, but he removed it and placed the Birmingham gift on his finger instead.

While at the banquet in his honour he had heard from his hosts about their plan to open a new Industrial and Literary Institute in the city – this would be a slightly grander version of a Mechanics' Institute, in which the working people of Birmingham would receive instruction and (so the theory ran) at the same time engage in various forms of profitable or useful entertainment. It was precisely the kind of plan which Dickens endorsed, encouraging as it did the labouring classes to be reunited with the rest of the community in that always perilous journey towards enlightenment. And, on the way to the railway station after the banquet, it suddenly occurred to him that he could help raise money for the venture by giving a public reading in Birmingham. As soon as he returned to London he wrote to one of the founders of the Institute and offered to read *A Christmas Carol* the following December; ". . . there would be some novelty in the thing, as I have never done it in public, though I have in private and (if I may say so) with a great effect on the hearers." He asked, in return, that the "working people" should be admitted free – free, therefore, to experience Dickens's own vision of the nation as one happy extended family which his first Christmas Books had incorporated. They would sit along with the "middling classes", and their common interests would be revealed by Dickens himself in his role as chief fireside entertainer. The Birmingham committee enthusiastically accepted the novelist's proposal, and a date was set for the Christmas of that same year. So it was that the public readings of Charles Dickens, which were to play so large and in some respects so fatal a part in his life, were from the start specifically associated with his philanthropic activities.

But he could really only maintain such a stance by emphasising one other aspect of his belief – specifically his faith that "Literature" was a serious enterprise with serious ends. This was in fact the theme of the speech he had given at Birmingham that evening. ". . . Literature cannot be too faithful to the people . . . cannot too ardently advocate the cause of their advancement, happiness, and prosperity." There had been a time when Dickens had wished for a less exalted role; the role of a writer, as he said in the preface to *Nicholas Nickleby* almost fifteen years before, ". . . who wished their happiness, and contributed to their amusement". But he lived in different times; the new age demanded some obeisance to its proprieties, and in any case Dickens clearly considered himself to be more than an entertainer. Even the attacks upon *Bleak House* as it was being composed, attacks in which its "unreality" was emphasised, only served to increase his belief that what he wrote was *true*; and, if true, also *important*. There is nothing unusual about a writer slowly acquiring more gravitas, at least in his public pronouncements, but Dickens's own sense of mission was materially affected by his work on the Guild of Art and Literature; his was a profession, even a vocation, but not a trade. And it was the responsibility of all artists to stand up for their "order". It is also likely that his experience of deaths over the past few months, particularly that of his father, had prompted him to see his own work in the perspective of mortality and therefore of true "significance". Thus all the forces of his life encouraged him to make such a pronouncement.

And it was one to which he added in the same Birmingham speech. He made it clear, for example, that literature was not some cloistered pursuit but one that should be available and accessible to all. ". . . I believe no true man, with anything to tell, need have the least misgiving, either for himself or for his message, before a large number of hearers . . ." Dickens was no modernist, in other words, and in fact it was precisely the broader or more apparently "populist" elements of Dickens's art which prompted the negative reaction first of Oscar Wilde, then of the fin-de-siècle poets, then of such writers born at the end of the century as Eliot and Pound. And there was something else in Dickens's Birmingham speech, arguably the most important speech he had yet made, which deserves consideration, since it touches upon the very essence of his conception of his art. He spoke of painting but he could have been speaking of his own medium; ". . . it cannot hope to rest on a single foundation for its great temple – or the mere classic pose of a figure, or the folds of a drapery – but that it must be imbued with human passions and action, informed with human right and wrong . . ." A statement which, according to the newspaper reports, was greeted with "*Cheers*".

So what of *Bleak House*, being written in the same month and indeed the same week as this speech? Imbued with Dickens's passions, certainly. On the day after his appearance at Birmingham, and on his return to London, he visited the stagnant reaches of Hickman's Folly, a slum area off the Thames just east of Southwark Bridge, in order to make enquiries for Miss Burdett-Coutts and her slum clearance scheme. What he found here were the usual sheds and decaying wooden houses; and then in ". . . a broken down gallery at the back of a row of these, there was a wan child looking over at a starved old white horse who was making a meal of oyster shells. The sun was going down and flaring out like an angry fire at the child – and the child, and I, and the pale horse, stared at one another in silence for some five minutes as if we were so many figures in a dismal allegory . . . Lord knows when anybody will go in to the child, but I suppose it's looking over still – with a little wiry head of hair, as pale as the horse, all sticking up on its head – and an old weazen face – and two bony hands holding on the rail of the gallery, with little fingers like convulsed skewers." It is a remarkable description. The abandoned child and the decaying wooden house had for a long time been essential elements of Dickens's imaginative repertoire – and, to see them here in front of him, it must have been as startling as if one of the scenes in his novels had come to life. As if the imagined aspects of his own neglected childhood were being re-enacted in dumb show in front of him. These were the human passions and human scenes which Dickens innately understood and with which he "imbued" his fiction; if they seem a world away from his confident social pronouncements at the Birmingham dinner, it is because they come from a source much deeper and darker than Dickens's moral conscience. He did not forget the scene, and that "pale horse" reappeared in the number of *Bleak House* he was even then writing as "the gaunt pale horse" which carries Richard Carstone back to London and to his eventual death.

Dickens was working hard on *Bleak House*, but his time was also being taken up by *Household Words*: Wills was ill, and for the last few weeks Dickens had to conduct all the usual business of the journal. He went down to Brighton for a fortnight specifically in order to work in peace, Catherine and Georgina having gone ahead of him in order to make sure that their lodgings in Junction Parade were in perfect order for him. Then, as soon as he was back in London, he was rising at five o'clock even on a Sunday morning in order to carry on with the novel. He was writing, and then reading episodes to family and friends; constant toil over the book which had taken so strong a hold upon him, constant toil leading up to the climax of the story. It seems likely, also, that he rented rooms in this period where he might work undisturbed. Certainly at a later time he took an apartment for just such a purpose at the corner of Hatcham Park Road and New Cross Road, and there is some evidence to suggest that he had taken up the accommodation while he was composing *Bleak House*. The other location mentioned as Dickens's temporary habitation is (or was) Cobley's Farm in North Finchley; the site of the rented rooms is less significant, however, than the fact that Dickens was beginning what would become a lifelong habit of providing himself with a "bolt-hole" for the purposes of work and anonymity. New Cross, or Finchley, was a long way from his normal centre of operations; and a long way, too, from Tavistock House. For there had been interruptions even there. He had wanted to hire a gun, with small shot, in order to get rid of some dogs which barked in Tavistock Square and then, a little later, he had been horrified to see the local baker's man relieving himself outside the gates of Tavistock House itself. Dickens, who was always aware of his personal dignity on such occasions, remonstrated with him; the man was "*very impertinent*" in return, and Dickens threatened to have him taken into custody under the Police Act. This was not the only occasion when Dickens threatened less distinguished members of the community with the law – another thing he detested was swearing in public places – but nevertheless he saw the humorous side even of his own actions. The baker's man, he said, ". . . was rather urgent to know what I should do 'if I was him' – which involved a flight of imagination into which I didn't follow him".

But was there a further reason for his wanting to absent himself from Tavistock House? Did he by any chance want to get away from his large family? Catherine was described at this time as ". . . a good specimen of a truly English woman; tall, large and well developed . . ." This was the account given by Harriet Beecher Stowe, an author whom Dickens did not very much admire but whose remarks about Catherine "greatly amused" him when they were published, presumably because "large" and "well-developed" were euphemisms for Catherine's gathering stoutness. She seemed to be putting on fat as Dickens grew leaner and more raddled with the years – as physical proof, perhaps, of the growing disparity between them. His children had been causing him concern in recent months, too. His eldest son, Charley, had decided to become a businessman and had gone to Germany to learn the language. In a letter to his German publisher, who had agreed to look after the boy, Dickens made it clear that he wished his son to be treated as a "gentleman" but in no way to be "*pampered*" – which sounds like his own especial recipe for bringing up a family. But he was more concerned about another son, Frank, whom he only now discovered to have a stammer; somehow or other the news had been kept from him by Georgina and Catherine, which suggests, if nothing else, a less than close relationship between father and son. Catherine had told a friend that Dickens was very fond of babies and that he liked them to be as "new" as possible; another and somewhat rueful indication of the fact that his interest in his children decreased in direct proportion to their age. As for Frank's stammer, that was to be rectified in Dickens's usual thorough and methodical way. He gave him elocution lessons in his study each morning.

So the dominant note of his life at this time is still one of overwork: ". . . the journey is ever onward and we must pursue it or we are worthy of no place here." That was one way of putting it. And there was another way, too. Only a few weeks later he was concerned once more about prisons in *Household Words*, and in the course of his revisions to an article by Henry Morley he twice underlines punishment as the goal of all good prisons; "some degraded kind of hard and irksome work" is what he recommends. Is there not in this emphasis something of Dickens's own attitude towards himself? His son once declared him ". . . angrily unwilling as he always was to admit that he could possibly be doing too much", and throughout his life there is this need for *work. Hard work.* Hard labour. Certainly in this period, with his constant concern over both *Household Words* and *Bleak House*, he was definitely over-exerting himself. He said that he felt "rather limp" and in a letter to Forster he admitted that ". . . hypochondriacal whisperings tell me that I am rather overworked. The spring does not seem to fly back again directly, as it always did when I put my own work aside, and had nothing else to do . . . What with Bleak House and Household Words and Child's History and Miss Coutts's Home, and the invitations to feasts and festivals, I really feel as if my head would split like a fired shell if I remained here." If he remained in London, that is, and even now he began actively to make preparations for a summer in Boulogne. It was in this period, too, that his appearance began to show signs of his stress and exhaustion. There were people who now commented that they "would not recognise him" as the young man they had once known, and Mrs Yates, a quondam actress who had not seen him for fifteen years, told her son that ". . . save his eyes, there was no trace of the original Dickens about him". The young man with the flowing locks had gone; only the bright eyes remained the same.

He had said the whisperings of sickness were "hypochondriacal" but he became truly sick; once more it was the inflamed kidney of his childhood, now causing him such discomfort that he took to his bed for six days; his pain rendered his face gaunt, his eyes wide, and, as he told Wilkie Collins a few years later, "I was stricken ill when I was doing Bleak House, and I shall not easily forget what I suffered under the fear of not being able to come up to time". On doctor's advice, from this time forward, he always wore a broad flannel belt around his waist to protect his weak kidney. And he had to get away. He went down to Folkestone en route to Boulogne, where all the arrangements for his summer residence had now been made.

Boulogne was to become his principal summer home for the next three years. He had said the year before that "it is as quaint, picturesque, good a place as I know . . . everything cheap, everything good . . ." and in "Our French Watering Place", an essay which he wrote for *Household Words* in 1854, he described it as ". . . a bright, airy, pleasant, cheerful town . . ." And he liked the people; he liked their brightness and their animation, what one might almost call their theatricality in the business of life (of course there were times when he himself was described as "French" because of his own vivacious manner). In the essay he refers to his "landlord", a certain M. Loyal Devasseur; in fact his real name was M. Beaucourt and in the middle of June Dickens and family took up residence in a house which he owned near the Calais road, the Château des Moulineaux. It was on the side of a rather steep hill, facing the old walled city of Boulogne and surrounded by gardens and terraces which climbed steadily up the hill towards woods beyond. In his semi-fictional essay Dickens described how ingeniously his French landlord had united English comfort with native elegance, and the general atmosphere of the house – tiny rooms furnished with great neatness and arranged with dexterity – was one that Dickens came to appreciate and even to love. His idea of perfect comfort was in any case always that of a small room, like a ship's cabin, carefully arranged. In his letters from Boulogne in the summer of this year he described the château as a "doll's house" (always for him a term of praise) and M. Beaucourt himself might have walked out of one of Dickens's own novels, so spritely and characteristic he seems.

M. Beaucourt: "In the moonlight last night, the flowers on the property appeared, O Heaven, to be *bathing themselves in the sky*. You like the property?"

Mr Dickens: "M. Beaucourt, I am enchanted with it; I am more than satisfied with everything."

M. Beaucourt (laying his cap upon his breast, and kissing his hand): "And I sir, I equally!"

On an occasion some five years later, Dickens records an act of signal generosity by M. Beaucourt, only the conclusion of which need detain us now.

M. Beaucourt: "Ah, that family, unfortunate!"

Mr Dickens: "And you, Monsieur Beaucourt, you are unfortunate too, God knows!"

M. Beaucourt: "Ah, Monsieur Dickens, thank you, don't speak of it!"

And this is the point of the anecdote: in one of the most wonderful descriptions in all of Dickens's letters the Frenchman "backed himself down the avenue with his cap in his hand, as if he were going to back himself straight into the evening star, without the ceremony of dying first. I never did see such a gentle, kind heart."

On this first visit to Boulogne, Dickens visited the local theatre, attended the various Sunday fêtes, inspected the pig-market (for some reason, the antics of pigs always amused him), and of course walked. Walked for miles after his work, and a friend has recalled that ". . . it was amusing to find that the friends who on the first days after their arrival gladly agreed to accompany him, mostly slackened by degrees in their readiness to do so". It is perhaps worth noting, too, that Georgina often accompanied her brother-in-law on such expeditions while Catherine did not do so. He did not make "calls" upon his walks. He did not care for the English abroad, certainly not the English residing in France, and he took pains not to "know" anybody for the duration of their stay; thus, at one stroke, cutting through the complex and insidious bonds of Victorian etiquette. In addition he had grown a moustache and beard after his illness; he had done the same in Genoa a few years before, which suggests that he enjoyed even the physical act of changing his English identity when he was staying on the continent.

Immediately after his arrival he rested for a week, and began to recover his strength. As soon as he had done so he set to work once more upon *Bleak House*, even now reaching its climax as Lady Dedlock is tracked down by Inspector Bucket and Esther Summerson. By the end of the third week of June – less than two weeks after his arrival – he had managed to complete the number; and, by the end of the month, he had fully sketched out all the steps which would lead him to the end of the book. As soon as he had done so he was once more asking friends to join him in the château; clearly his intention to finish the novel in the course of August meant that he could have companions with him by the time he was ready to celebrate its completion. He even planned a banquet at the château formally to signal that event. Before he began this final entry into *Bleak House* he rested again for a few days, if rest it can be called, with his daily and energetic expeditions to fêtes and fairs, theatres and markets. He even took a two-day trip to Amiens. Then on the first day of August he began the final double-number, his aim being to finish it by the eighteenth or nineteenth and then to take the final chapters personally to London. Dickens set timetables for himself with an iron determination, as if he could work best within punishing and self-imposed constraints, and on this as on many other occasions he fulfilled his own demands to the letter. So it was that in the first seventeen days of August he completed *Bleak House*. Lady Dedlock had been killed at the end of the previous number, and now in this last instalment the narrative unfolds; the death of Lady Dedlock is balanced by the marriage of her illegitimate daughter, the Chancery case tumbles down, Richard Carstone dies of weariness. Dickens was so preoccupied with his composition that he forgot things, his actual penmanship deteriorated, he composed only very short letters. Characters meet, glimpse each other in the street, are reunited, all of them part of the "system", that dark network which has its centre at the cemetery for the poor where Nemo is buried and outside which Lady Dedlock dies. Everything comes together, the art and the life in communion; after a time in which Dickens experienced the death of his father and daughter, as well as the deaths of friends like d'Orsay and Richard Watson, he is writing a novel about the power of last things. It is in this perspective that the whole of human life can be seen. "'It was all a troubled dream?' said Richard, clasping both my Guardian's hands eagerly." And the panorama of this whole sad world is to be found in that short scene when ". . . poor crazed Miss Flite came weeping to me, and told me that she had given her birds their liberty".

He had finished on time, and at once set off on the short trip to London in order to complete all necessary preparations in person. In the preface which he now wrote, he declared that, "In 'Bleak House' I have purposely dwelt upon the romantic side of familiar things. I believe I have never had so many readers as in this book. May we meet again!" He stayed in the capital only for two or three days, and then returned to Boulogne where in the Château des Moulineaux, he read the final number to his family. "May we meet again!" This was how he now saw his intimate relationship with his readers, as if he were about to shake hands with them, fix them with his bright eyes, and hold them in leisurely converse. The interest was to a certain extent reciprocated; as the *Illustrated London News* now said, ". . . 'What do you think of *Bleak House*?' is a question which everybody had heard propounded within the last few weeks." Clearly there was something different in it, something odd, something unexpected to prompt the question. In later years it was seen by nineteenth-century commentators as the beginning of Dickens's unfunny and ponderous "decline", and even the criticism at the time was not as laudatory as the actual sales of the novel might suggest; once more the power of his characterisation was acknowledged, and the word favoured to describe it was "daguerreotype" with all its contemporaneous associations of sharpness and clearness of focus. But the *Spectator* was not alone in ". . . having found it dull and wearisome". Even Forster believed that it lacked the "freedom" and "freshness" of Dickens's previous novels, and thus inaugurated works of quite a different and more cumbersome kind. Apparently there were few readers able to detect the pattern which Dickens had laid down within his story. Chancery? The ruined slums? The churchyard? These were not seen as emblems of some larger design, but rather Dickens's specific response to specific abuses. And how could it be otherwise? The book was seen as part of its time, part of the ceaseless forgetful flow which was the experience of life. It was a book to be set alongside the other books published in this year – Matthew Arnold's *Poems*, Ruskin's second and third volumes of *The Stones of Venice*, Charlotte Yonge's *The Heir of Redclyffe*. *Bleak House* appeared in a year when the eighth edition of the *Encyclopaedia Britannica* was first published, in which Verdi's *Rigoletto* was produced in London, in which Browning's *Colombe's Birthday* was staged, and in which Holman Hunt unveiled *The Light of the World*. It was the year in which Turkey and Russia went to War. *Bleak House* was part of that year, that world, and could not then be separated from it.

But what of it now, this narrative which now stands in a sense outside of time? It has often been suggested that *Bleak House* does indeed mark a change in Dickens's style but one that is to be welcomed; the novel, according to many recent critics, inaugurated the novelist's "dark period". It is agreeable thus to mark off the stages of Dickens's progress, but it is hard to find any real evidence with which to do so. The development of a novelist can really best be understood, not in terms of his "moods" or even of his "themes", but rather in that slow process of experimentation and self-education which changes the techniques of his prose. In that sense, the "darker" aspects of Dickens's novels are merely an aspect of their more assiduously unified structure. There are scenes in *The Pickwick Papers* and in *Oliver Twist* as dark as anything in *Bleak House*; what has changed is the way in which he closely packs together all the aspects of his vision, thus excluding that free play and improvisation which we consider to be the "light" pitted against the "darkness" of his structural control. There is another change as well; as Dickens wrote each novel he came to a much more intimate understanding of his own vision of the world, and this closer acquaintance with his own genius inevitably precluded a certain kind of improvisation or elaboration which in a lesser novelist can be seen as "charming" or "ingenious". Forster had noticed it, too, this loss of "freedom"; but it was a necessary part of the restraining and refining force of Dickens's imagination. He was seeing things more clearly, he was seeing them as a whole.

So *Bleak House* seems more deliberate and more closely written than its predecessors, the very device of creating an alternative narrative in the voice of Esther Summerson only serving to emphasise the coherence of that other, impersonal narrative voice. Thus, like nineteenth-century ideas of God, Dickens has his centre everywhere and his circumference nowhere. And, just as his narrative shows a greater depth of coherence, so everything in the book is attracted towards that centre. As Dickens had said in the novel, "What connection can there have been between many people in the innumerable histories of this world, who, from opposite sides of great gulfs, have, nevertheless, been very curiously brought together!" Jo, Lady Dedlock, Nemo, Tulkinghorn, Inspector Bucket, Esther Summerson, Guppy, Boythorn, Skimpole, Chadband, Flite, Guster, Snagsby, Krook, Smallweed. A world in which people are tightly bound together – in ties of duty, ties of love, ties of charity, ties of relationship, ties of debt so that the novel itself grows dark with the mass of lives fluttering together within it. And yet at the same time this world is so perilous, so cruel, so close to death and disaster. All of them coming together, the rich and the poor, the sick and the well; while "in such a light both aspire alike, both rise alike, both children of the dust shine equally". Children of the dust dissolving into fog and mud.

What kind of vision is this? There are mysteries here; mysteries of parentage as well as mysteries of the law. Mysteries of the past. Mysteries of origin. And, for a man who believed that the dreamer always awoke with a head filled with *words*, the final mystery is the mystery of language itself. The mystery of writing in particular; writing which is the mark of the rich and the mark of the law, to be set against those like Jo and Krook who cannot read. After his stroke Sir Leicester Dedlock, too, can no longer read. So this sense of writing goes with some deeper understanding of power and of powerlessness, and it was also at this time that Dickens retold one of his own frequent dreams ". . . when I am in a strange country and want to read important notices on the walls and buildings, but they are all in an unknown character". Dickens's own writing in *Bleak House* is filled with power, containing the language of sentiment as well as the rhetoric of political satire, the cadence of polemic and the expression of wonder. His language can contain these things because it has not become as *specialised* as the English of the later half of the nineteenth century; it is neither "abstract" nor "concrete"; it has not been separated out into its component parts. That is why those readers who have looked for social "solutions" to social "problems" in this novel have not been successful, since at this early stage in the Victorian comprehension of "system" there is no special language to analyse it; there is no clear distinction between the powers of society and the nature of free individual and moral choice. It was a period of transition, and the marks of that transition are to be glimpsed through the fog which obscures the ancient streets of London. Thus the solitary voice of Esther Summerson, the illegitimate child, "can't be kept out" of the narrative, as she puts it, any more than the narrator's direct assault upon the iniquities of mid-nineteenth-century justice. And can one not hear in Esther Summerson's voice also something of the strangeness and wildness and pain which is audible in the first-person narrative of *David Copperfield*? At that moment, for example, when on a cold and wild night Esther sees towards London "a lurid glare overhung the whole dark waste" and she ". . . had for a moment an undefinable impression of myself as being something different from what I then was". Like David, Esther is given many names; and like David, too, she experiences a "terror of myself". And is Dickens present here, also, amid all the wildness and pain and strangeness? Can we hear the still, almost suppressed, voice of Charles Dickens? The shifting identity. The terror of himself. And all the pain of the world.

At the beginning of September he returned once more to London in the company of Wilkie Collins, who had been staying with the Dickens family in Boulogne; it was a stormy crossing and Dickens suffered from sea-sickness. Collins, however, passed the time in profitable observation, and he noticed in particular how all the ladies lying on the deck with white bowls beside them resembled a damp and enormous picnic party. Dickens had come back upon *Household Words* business but fashionable London itself, "out of season" since July, was deserted. Dickens wandered through the barren tracks of the West End, peeping into his tailors' shop and visiting a hosier's, seeing nothing around him except solitariness and dreariness. But one thing cheered him: he had been trying to purchase a portmanteau and ". . . near the corner of St James's Street saw a solitary being sitting in a trunk-shop, absorbed in a book which, on a close inspection, I found to be Bleak House. I thought this looked well, and went in. And he really was more interested in seeing me, when he knew who I was, than any face I had seen in any house . . . including my own." A charming story, the shop assistant reading *Bleak House* just as the great novelist himself enters, the recognition and the interest. But he was just as easily discomfited as he was cheered; he discovered that he had earned from Bradbury and Evans two hundred pounds less than he expected, so at once he wrote to Catherine to inform her that there would be no Christmas Party that year. (It ought to be remembered that one of the things that had attracted him to Boulogne was the cheapness of living expenses, and he mentioned on more than one occasion the fact that a good wine was only tenpence a bottle.)

Then he travelled back to Boulogne. In fact a general feeling of restlessness after the completion of *Bleak House* seems to have affected him since he went back and forth between France and England, completing all necessary business before he set off upon a long excursion to Switzerland and Italy in the company of Wilkie Collins and Augustus Egg. The journey had in fact been discussed with Collins as early as January of that year because Dickens had realised even then that, after the completion of his novel, he would need a holiday in order "to clear my mind and freshen it up again". And so, in the second week of October, the three travellers – together with a courier Dickens had recently employed for the purpose – set off from Boulogne on a journey of nine weeks that would take them to Lausanne, Geneva, Chamounix, Martigny, Milan, Genoa, Naples, Bologna, Rome, Florence, Padua, Venice and Turin. It was a standard route for the English traveller, but such a consideration did not disturb Dickens; he seems to have preferred the familiar trail, since he knew that he would never be far from proper accommodation and splendid "sights". He was also travelling in his own old footsteps, having visited precisely the same Swiss and Italian cities some years before; he was revisiting the haunts of his glorious early adulthood.

They were a well-matched trio, Dickens and Collins and Egg, and, although there were times when their misadventures seem to come very close to those of Jerome K. Jerome's later trinity of imagined travellers, they got on well enough. As Dickens told Georgina in one of his many and long letters home, "I lose no opportunity of inculcating the lesson that it is of no use to be out of temper in travelling . . ."; and Wilkie Collins, in a letter to his mother, describes how "we travel in a state of mad good spirits, and never flag in our jollity all through the day . . . Egg is constantly exercised in Italian dialogue by Dickens." This continual jollity sounds in itself something of a strain, and there is little doubt that it was Dickens himself who liked to keep the days at fever pitch. In fact Collins knew Italy well – he had travelled there extensively with his family – but Dickens was the definite leader of the party, the one who made all the arrangements with the courier, the one who kept a record of all expenses in his pocket-book. Collins and Egg seem even to have copied him by attempting to grow moustaches, an exercise which Dickens considered with a certain ironic disfavour. As a result, he cut off the beard he had grown and sported only a luxuriant moustache, no doubt on the principle he had enunciated some years before when he decided to wear the brightest waistcoat at T. J. Thompson's wedding in order to ". . . ha ha ha ha! *Eclipse* the Bridegroom!" And it was Dickens, too, who hurried his travelling companions along from place to place; as he confessed to Miss Burdett-Coutts, ". . . I am so restless to be doing – and always shall be, I think, so long as I have any portion in Time – that if I were to stay more than a week in any one city here, I believe I should be half desperate to begin some new story!!!"

And what is to be said of the journey itself? Paris to Strasbourg on the new railroad, and then on to Lausanne where Dickens almost at once went to see Rosemont, the old house where he had written the first chapters of *Dombey and Son*, before revisiting his old friends of the area, Cerjat and Haldimand, still the same, still argumentative, and very pleased to see him. But he had another reason to visit the old scenes. Already he had some "vague Swiss notions" for another novel and, no doubt, he wanted to experience once more the effects of the Alpine ranges upon his imagination, an experience he was not in fact to describe until he began to write *Little Dorrit*. Then from Lausanne to Geneva, and then on to Chamounix. It was here that the party ascended to the Mer de Glace and, by his own account at least, Dickens was so agile and nimble in his climbing that the Swiss guides nicknamed him "the Intrepid"; he always prided himself upon his athleticism but it was now an integral part of his belief that, at the age of forty-one, he was not about to grow old. And this was the scenery he loved – the precipices, the abysses beneath his feet, the narrow ledges, the rocks, all making up a picture of "general desolation". It was one of the permanent landscapes of his imagination. It is perhaps significant to note that in a letter to Forster he described how close he and his party came to disaster when a large rock almost fell upon them, but in a letter to Catherine the same day he made no reference to it at all; surely this is evidence of the fact that he knew of his wife's nervous disposition, and had no intention of unduly alarming her. He was in fact concerned about her health in general, and wrote privately to Georgina: "Pray tell me how Kate is. I rather fancy from her letter, though I scarcely know why, that she is not quite as well as she was at Boulogne." Clearly the nervous illness of the previous year had not entirely vanished and it is significant, in the light of later events, to see at what length and how often he writes to his wife; how, in all manner of ways, he managed to suggest what he later wrote from Rome: "I miss you *very much.*" They travelled on from Chamounix to Martigny, Dickens making the whole journey by foot, and then crossed the Simplon Pass on a clear bright day on their way to Milan. Nothing to report here except an image Dickens himself conjured up; they had been advised to keep a hold of their possessions for fear of thieves, so cords were attached to each trunk by which they held on to them throughout the journey. "You will imagine the absurdity of our jolting along some twenty miles in this way, exactly as if we were in three shower-baths and were afraid to pull the string." In Milan Egg and Collins went to visit the "Lions", as Dickens termed the local notables, while he stayed in the hotel room and caught up with his letters, in the course of which he described his companions in generally cheerful terms. Collins ate and drank everything. He was, besides, rather too careful with money. And so was Egg – although Dickens might have stopped to consider the fact that they were poor men compared with Dickens himself, and were not used to the little comforts and luxuries with which he liked to surround himself in the grander hotels en route. And of course, as Dickens explained to his wife, "We observe the Managerial punctuality in all our arrangements, and have not had any difference whatever." There is no doubt that Catherine had learnt all too much about that "Managerial punctuality" for herself.

They all had their own routines. Egg put everything down in a diary, and was perpetually asking Collins the names of the places they had visited. Collins himself was contemplating a series of travel articles for *Bentley's Miscellany*, and so he sent home letters in which characteristically he described the scenery and the art of the various places they had visited, clearly with an eye to later publication. So, where Collins's letters were filled with mountains and paintings, Dickens's letters were stocked with characters and stories. They had in any case quite different ways of seeing the world, and during these weeks Dickens travelled through a landscape of gloom and grandeur which was inhabited only by grotesque, absurd or comic people.

From Milan to Genoa, where Dickens took Egg and Collins to see the Palazzo Peschiere, in which he had written *The Chimes* so many years before. Then he called upon such old friends as the de la Rues and such relatively new residents as the Thompsons – T. J. Thompson and Christiana Weller, whose somewhat unorthodox domestic arrangements were immediately apprehended by Dickens. "We had disturbed her at her painting in Oils; and I rather received an impression that what with that, and what with music, the household affairs went a little to the wall." All his old romantic enthusiasm for Christiana had disappeared, leaving only his sharp observations in its wake. And in Genoa, too, he met an old friend, the wife of the British Consul, who had heard of his recent illness. Dickens rang the bell of the villa in which the couple resided. Mrs Brown came out "and stared at me".

Dickens: "What! You don't know me!"

Mrs Brown: "I expected to find a ruin, we heard you had been so ill. And I find you younger and better looking than ever. But it's so strange to see you without a bright waistcoat. Why haven't you got a bright waistcoat on?"

She had said all this in her "old quiet way", one of Dickens's friends who was not particularly impressed by his enormous fame but who liked and respected him. And who would talk to him quite frankly and normally about her "minutest affairs".

They had had a slow journey by road from Milan to Genoa, some thirty-one hours of travelling without any real break upon the road. It is easy to forget just how exhausting continental travel could still be, despite the advent of the railway, and when for example the three travellers sailed from Genoa to Naples they found themselves on a severely overcrowded boat which had no room even for first class passengers; both male and female passengers were lying on the decks and on the stairways, ". . . arrayed like spoons on a sideboard". Dickens, Collins and Egg lay down on bare planks with only over-coats for covering during the night, and then of course "a perfectly tropical rain fell". But Dickens was nothing if not resourceful in such situations, and he managed to bully or charm the captain into giving him the steward's cabin while Egg and Collins were consigned to the store-room in the hold, from which they eventually emerged smelling of cheese and spices. There was of course no question of Dickens being forced into such an ignominious position. Yet it is no wonder that, in a letter to Georgina, he looked forward to ". . . coming home again, to my old room, and the old walks, and all the old pleasant things". And he kissed every child he came across in remembrance of his own.

In Naples they stayed in an hotel apartment facing the sea; agreeable enough, but Dickens seems to have been annoyed that Vesuvius was not in the fiery condition which had so exhilarated him eight years before. Fortunately human absurdity never changed, as Dickens knew very well, and he pounced with glee upon an Englishwoman, a ". . . noble specimen – single, forty, in a clinging flowered black silk dress . . . and with a leghorn hat on her head, at least (I am serious) *six feet round*. The consequence of its immense size was, that whereas it had an insinuating blue decoration in the form of a bow in front, it was so out of her knowledge behind, that it was all battered and bent in that direction – and viewed from that quarter, she looked dead drunk." All this was written to his wife who, despite everything that had happened, retained a sense of humour very similar to her husband's. And, since Dickens went on to describe how the lady in question had "designs" upon an "ancient Lieutenant", Catherine, unlike many women of her period, was clearly not to be shocked by the details of sexual frailty. Living with Dickens must have been, in some sense, an education in good-humoured tolerance.

From Naples to Rome and, while his two companions went out to see the local sights, Dickens began work on "The Schoolboy's Story" which he sent on to Wills to be included in the forthcoming Christmas issue of *Household Words*; even on holiday, his prompt sense of duty never deserted him. In fact the actual circumstances of travelling had to be *subdued* by him; he never wished to be mastered by force of circumstance. ". . . I am particularly anxious to overcome the dif-ficulties of so unsettled a life," he told Catherine, "and do something on the Xmas No." So what did he see of Rome on this trip? A performance in the Coliseum, that great monument to intolerance and cruelty which perpetually fascinated him. A marionette theatre in the stable of a decayed palace, where ". . . so delicate are the hands of the people who move them, that every puppet was an Italian, and did exactly what an Italian does". And he was fascinated, too, by the areas outside Rome which were laid waste by malaria; the mouldering houses from which all life has fled, the stagnant waters, the mist, the ruined arches and the heaps of dung. Yet "here is a world of travelling arrangements for me to settle, and here are Collins and Egg looking sideways at me with an occasional imploring glance as beseeching me to settle it. So I leave off. Good-night."

They moved on from Rome to Florence, where Dickens's less than reverential attitude towards art and art appreciation was signally different from the more knowledgeable attitudes both of Egg and of Collins. Dickens was someone who knew what he liked (with the corollary that what he liked *must* be good) and never seemed to realise that he might learn something from his two companions. He was always ready, too, to note the absurdities of other English travellers without ever realising that he too in his own hurried, restless way, might be rather distinctive. But, if he lacked that kind of self-knowledge, it meant also that he lacked false pride; of one party of English travellers he told Georgina ". . . I was extremely intimate with them, invited them to Tavistock House when they come home in the spring, and have not the faintest idea of their name". From Rome to Padua by coach. From Padua to Venice by railroad. And once more the old dream of beauty laps around him; he stayed in the same hotel as before, the Danieli, and once more his descriptions float upon the water. But this did not mean that he forgot the self-imposed duties of his life; he was already fretting because W. H. Wills had not kept him "up to date" on *Household Words* matters, and in the Danieli he managed to finish another short story for the Christmas issue of the periodical, "Nobody's Story", a tale of the poor, the forgotten, the "rank and file of the earth". They were in their way home now; from Venice the three companions travelled to Turin and then on to Paris, where Dickens picked up his son, Charley. From Paris back to London. By way of the Channel, of course, and Charley recalled that ". . . my father considerably astonished me at Calais – it was perfectly calm and smooth – by lying down on the deck enveloped in all the rugs and overcoats he could get hold of; becoming of the complexion of a damaged orange, and delivering himself, an absolutely unresisting prey, to sea sickness. From this unpleasant malady he suffered on the smallest provocation for many years". For many years, in fact, until he literally trained himself not to be sick. His will, as always, triumphed in the end. And there were in any case advantages in being such a famous man; when it was learnt that the Channel boat was carrying Charles Dickens, a message was telegraphed ahead to Dover to hold up the train until he came ashore.

He was back in London in the second week of December and, although he was once more deep in *Household Words* business as well as the management of Tavistock House theatricals for Twelfth Night, his main concern was with the Readings he had promised to give in Birmingham for the Industrial and Literary Institute. There were to be three of them – *A Christmas Carol* on 27 December, *The Cricket on the Hearth* on the following day and then, on the thirtieth, *A Christmas Carol* once more. This last performance was the one in which he was most interested, since the audience would be comprised entirely of the "working people" who would be sold tickets at the low price of sixpence. Catherine, Georgina and the older children accompanied him to Birmingham, while Wills seemed to be acting in the capacity of manager for the occasion.

For the first Reading, in the Town Hall, he rose a little nervously before the seventeen hundred people who had endured a snowstorm in order to hear him. But he soon got into his stride and, as he told a friend a few days later, ". . . we were all going on together, in the first page, as easily, to all appearance, as if we had been sitting round the fire". This was the first large public reading he had ever given, and all his skills as an actor could not have prepared him for such an occasion; yet he took to it very easily, he took to it *naturally* simply because it was natural for him to become intimate – as if "round the fire" – with seventeen hundred people. One of the secrets of his genius was his ability to project himself in just such a fashion so that, although his own domestic life might not always have been a model of sympathetic union, he could represent and instil the idea of domesticity and comfort in those who watched and listened to him. A reporter from the *Birmingham Journal* noted "how Mr Dickens twirled his moustache, or played with his paper knife, or laid down his book, and leant forward confidentially . . ." He misjudged only one particular; it took him three hours to read *A Christmas Carol*, where he had predicted two, but judicious cutting in later years substantially shortened this tale of comfort and joy. It always remained his favourite among his readings, at least until his last years, since of its very essence it conveyed precisely the mood of familial and national harmony which he was even then attempting to instil with his presence in Birmingham. Although the second night's reading of *The Cricket on the Hearth* seemed to have been equally successful, Dickens never enjoyed it so much.

So the great triumph of his Birmingham visit was his reading of *A Christmas Carol* on the third night to the "working people". Two thousand of them packed the Town Hall – it had been at Dickens's own instigation that the tickets were priced so cheaply – and as soon as he appeared on the platform the *Birmingham Journal* recorded how they all "rose up and cheered most enthusiastically, and then became quiet again, and then went at it afresh". Before he began to read, he stepped forward to address them. "My Good Friends . . ." he started to say, and at once there was "a perfect hurricane of applause". They were his good friends indeed, and as he made his preliminary speech he was interrupted by cheers and laughter and applause, as if he were the very first man who had understood them and who represented them. For had he not in his Christmas Books stood up for the rights of the poor? And here he was, telling them that he had always wished "to have the great pleasure of meeting you face to face at this Christmas time" – more applause and cheering – and going on to instil the central lesson of his own political philosophy. "If there ever was a time when any one class could of itself do much for its own good, and for the welfare of society – which I greatly doubt – that time is unquestionably past. It is in the fusion of different classes, without confusion; in the bringing together of employers and employed; in the creating of a better common understanding among those whose interests are identical, who depend upon each other, and who can never be in unnatural antagonism without deplorable results, that one of the chief principles of a Mechanics' Institution should consist." He went on in this vein, again with much cheering and applause, until he ended with "I now proceed to the pleasant task to which I assure you I have looked forward for a long time".

He began, "Marley was dead . . .", and carried on through that great lament for the poor and that insistent wish for pity and for sympathy. "They lost nothing," Dickens reported afterwards, "misinterpreted nothing, followed everything closely, laughed and cried with the most delightful earnestness." Here he had full proof of what he called his "Power", evidence of his ability to sway large masses of men and women, and to "imbue" them, too, with something of his own beliefs. And at the end, to renewed cheers and applause, he came forward to say ". . . I am as truly and sincerely interested in you . . . any little service to you I have freely rendered from my heart . . ." It had been a triumph, and there is no doubt that the reception he received from this working-class audience materially affected his description of the same men and women in the novel he was just about to begin, *Hard Times*. But now he also knew more about his own gifts and capacities, and Wills wrote to his wife, "If Dickens does turn Reader he will make another fortune. He will never offer to do so, of course. But if they *will* have him he will do it, he told me today." He was ready to enter one of the most extraordinary periods of his own life.

Chapter 23

*C*HARLES DICKENS: "Mrs Morson, this is the girl who wants to go, I believe."

Mrs Morson: "Yes."

Charles Dickens: "Take her at her word. It is getting dark now, but, immediately after breakfast tomorrow morning, shut the gate upon her for ever."

Thus Dickens with some of his first words of the New Year, at Urania Cottage. And, as always, he listened eagerly to the words of these young women in reply, noting them down to Miss Burdett-Coutts as precisely as if they had stepped out of one of his own novels: ". . . she didn't suppose, Mr Dickerson, as she were a goin to set with her ands erfore her . . ." And then again: ". . . which blessed will be the day when justice is a-done in this ouse." The banished girl was left in a state of miserable consternation for the night but then, as Dickens had planned all along, the order was revoked for the sake of "the great forgiving Christmas time". Thus authoritarianism is mixed with pity, and may be seen as a picture in miniature of Dickens's attitude towards the poor and the dispossessed.

Similarly it was in the spirit of the great Christmas time that once more he organised the Twelfth Night theatricals; in fact the children had already settled upon some form of play but Dickens saw them rehearse it, decided that it was not good enough, at once began to marshal them in *Tom Thumb*, and observed that "they have derived considerable notions of punctuality and attention from the parental drilling". No doubt they did. Dickens himself played the ghost of Gaffer Thumb (under the stage name of "The Modern Garrick"), and in fact was dressed for the part in so "hideous and frightening" a manner that his young son remembered being taken up to the dressing room to see his father in advance, so that he might not break down in terror on the stage of the "Theatre Royal, Tavistock House". This same son, Henry, then five, also sang a nineteenth-century comic song for this occasion:

"SPOKEN: Now comes the conflabbergastation of the lovier:
As Vilikins was valiking the garden around
He spied his dear Dinah laying dead upon the ground,
And a cup of cold pison it lay by her side,
With a billet-dux a-stating 'twas by pison she died.
Too ral lal, loo ral lal, too ral la."

Thackeray, who had brought his young daughters to see the performance, actually fell off his seat laughing as the infant Henry sang this; and, after the play, there were various country dances and games.

It was also the birthday of Dickens's eldest son, Charley, but for him it was not a particularly happy time. He had come home from Germany and had already disappointed his father, who told Miss Burdett-Coutts that ". . . he has less fixed purpose and energy than I could have supposed possible in my son". But how hard it must have been, to live up to the demands of such a father. "He is not aspiring, or imaginative in his own behalf. With all the tenderer and better qualities which he inherits from his mother, he inherits an indescribable lassitude of character . . ." Here it is at last; here is his central dissatisfaction with his wife. Lassitude. In other words, want of ardour. Want of enthusiasm and quickness. Want of all the qualities on which Dickens prided himself. It is clear enough that he was discussing matters with Miss Burdett-Coutts which he would not have discussed with his wife herself and, worst of all, he is actually blaming Catherine for the defects in his son. Odd that he did not wander further abroad genealogically, and remember the behaviour of his own father and his brothers. Did he not want to believe that any defects could be transmitted through *him*? Yet he really knew better than that and Forster remembered how "the question of hereditary transmission had a curious attraction for him . . ."; Dickens himself had written that "it suggests the strangest consideration as to which of our own failings we are really responsible for . . ." In the event his son returned to Germany in order to consolidate his hold upon the language but, in the meantime, Dickens set him to work at the office of *Household Words*. He had already been struck by the eagerness of the working people of Birmingham, and it is possible that he saw in his eldest son a distinct and unflattering contrast to those who, like himself, had been compelled to force their way through an uncongenial world. Yet what he did so quickly and peremptorily in his life, what he felt and believed, soon sent down echoes into the darker and stranger regions of his imagination. What kind of education should a parent give a son? How much was the ambition of the self-made man really worth? These were the questions which he began to explore in his next novel.

He had not wanted to write it; he had not wanted to write anything of that kind so soon after the completion of *Bleak House*. He had been looking forward to at least a spring and summer of relative idleness. But the sales of *Household Words* had fallen alarmingly, and in the last set of returns its profits had been cut by more than half. Of course he knew his own drawing power but, on this occasion, it was Bradbury and Evans who asked him whether he might consider writing a serial expressly for the periodical in order to improve its sales. There is no evidence that he even questioned his ability to do so; despite the fact that he had been exhausted to the point of collapse during the latter stages of *Bleak House*, he was ready to begin again. He knew that the new work had to be fiction; his own serialisation of *A Child's History of England* had not been a great success (certainly it had not prevented the decline in sales), and he must have recalled the occasion so many years before when *The Old Curiosity Shop* had boosted the flagging sales of *Master Humphrey's Clock*. And, in a sense, he had a subject already to hand. It had been the cheers and applause of the working people of Birmingham which had brought him into the new year and they would bring him, too, to his next novel.

He set to work in the third week of January 1854. He took out a sheet of his characteristic light blue writing paper, and calculated the amount he would need to fill five pages of *Household Words* each week. He was no longer used to writing in the weekly format and so, to expedite matters, he actually decided to arrange the new novel in monthly parts which he would then subdivide into the necessary weekly portions. On the same day he took out another sheet of paper and began to consider titles. On the left hand side he wrote simply, "Mr Gradgrind/Mrs Gradgrind". Then on the other side he began with his title, "Stubborn Things". Then he wrote "Fact". Which was followed by "Thomas Gradgrind's Facts". It is clear in which direction his imagination is running. Only a few months before he had written in Boulogne an article entitled "Frauds on the Fairies" in which he took exception to his old friend, George Cruikshank, and his attempts to introduce temperance propaganda into the fairy-stories of childhood. As a child he had detested books which had discounted the wonderful and the bizarre in favour of precept or homily, and now his old faith in the stories of his youth was crystallised in this little essay with his declaration that "In an utilitarian age, of all other times, it is a matter of grave importance that Fairy tales should be respected". This of course had wider ramifications. Mr Gradgrind, whose name he had found at once, was a teacher, and clearly was always meant to be; thus we have such alternative titles as "Two and Two are Four" and "Prove it!". A theme continued in the first words of the novel, echoing around a schoolroom, "Now, what I want is, Facts." And is there not also an echo here of Dickens's irritation when his account of spontaneous combustion was derided by Lewes as fanciful, perhaps even some continuation of his attack upon those critics who refused to see "the romantic side of familiar things"?

The opening of the novel was proving difficult, however. In the manuscript of *Hard Times*, the first page is covered with deletions and emendations; and two days later Dickens was asking W. H. Wills to obtain for him ". . . the Educational Board's series of questions for the examination of *teachers* in schools". He needed material evidence, in other words, on which to base his attack upon false education. But at some point over these first few days Dickens, in one of those acts of imaginative combination which set him apart from his contemporaries, saw through the matter of the schools to the larger question. "Facts" in an utilitarian age also meant the vogue for statistics and figures which was even then being used to abstract and anatomise the suffering of the urban poor. So everything once more was coming together; the horrors of a childhood unalleviated by Fancy could be aligned to the horrors experienced by the urban poor and by the working people of the great industrial cities. Now the real subject was in place. *Hard Times*. He had actually written it out three times in his list of possible titles, and its recurrence suggests the direction in which his imagination had been moving all along. This was the theme that had been waiting for him, and it took the question of education to act as a catalyst for it.

Hard times. He had been in Birmingham, after all, where, among the workers of that great industrial city (that "machine" as Dickens once described it), his support for the new Educational Institute had been cheered and applauded. In an essay he wrote for *Household Words* directly inspired by travelling on the Birmingham railway he created a landscape which was to reappear in *Hard Times* itself; with the "glare in the sky, flickering now and then over the greater furnaces . . . Tongues of flame shoot up from them, and pillars of fire turn and twist upon them." And of course his reception had encouraged him in his belief that the labouring classes needed the sustenance of Fancy as embodied in *A Christmas Carol*; the connection between childhood, fairy-tales and the labouring poor was made again. Just as importantly, his enthusiastic welcome confirmed him in his belief that they were on the whole generous and true people.

But why sometimes did they behave in a manner quite inconsistent with Dickens's belief in them? He had been reading about a strike of weavers in Preston, and in a letter to Miss Burdett-Coutts he explicitly linked the matter with his own experiences in Birmingham. "I have never seen them collected in any number in that place," he said, "without extraordinary pleasure . . . ." So why did they go on strike? Dickens's own feelings on the more and more troubled question of industrial relations are clear enough. Three years before he had criticised a threatened strike by engine-drivers and firemen of the North Western railway line, and had stated that ". . . we must deny the moral right or justification . . . to exert the immense power they accidentally possess, to the public detriment and danger". But he was by no means unsympathetic to the workers' case; as he said, ". . . We firmly believe that these are honest men – as honest men as the world can produce . . ." His essential complaint was that the organisers of the strike ". . . are, sometimes, not workmen at all, but designing persons who have, for their own base purposes, immeshed the workmen in a system of tyranny and oppression". In the following year he made a similar comment about a strike being organised by the Amalgamated Society of Engineers: "Honourable, generous, and spirited themselves, they have fallen into an unlucky way of trusting their affairs to contentious men, who work them up in a state of conglomeration and irritation . . ." His position, then, was clear and it can only have been confirmed when he contrasted the enthusiasm of the Birmingham workers with the realities of the Preston strikers. Who had misled the latter? All these reflections now came together and on a sudden decision, five days after he had begun the novel, he set off for Preston in order to see for himself the conditions and attitudes of the workers there.

The strike of the Preston weavers had actually begun in October of the previous year, and it quickly became a crucial test of the relative powers of Capital and Labour; the mill-owners closed their factories in order to prevent the workers from picking them off one by one, and the dispute over whether it was a straightforward strike or a management "lock out" was only one issue during a protracted struggle in which each side waited for the other to surrender. The strike was in its fourth month when Dickens arrived in Preston and attended one of the workers' meetings, a visit which was picked up by the Chartist journal, *Reynolds's Weekly Newspaper*. "Mr Charles Dickens, the author, was a spectator of the proceedings on Monday for about ten minutes. That gentleman now rejoices in a luxuriant pair of moustaches, and not being recognised, was taken by many for some 'distinguished foreigner'." Ten minutes: not a long time but quite long enough for Dickens's preconceptions to be confirmed. As he explained in an article which he wrote for *Household Words* two weeks later, he was impressed by the workers themselves and their "astonishing fortitude and perseverance; their high sense of honour among themselves . . ." but, if blame were to be found, it should be directed against "some designing and turbulent spirits". This was precisely the line he had taken before, and ". . . I left the place with a profound conviction that their mistake is an honest one . . ." The strike was an honest mistake – rather cool comfort for those engaged upon it but his sentiment emphasises the central message which he had been repeating in articles and speeches and correspondence; there must be some mutual trust and regard between employers and employees because they needed each other, and in harmony between them lay all the hopes for the prosperity of the country. In the same article he also declared that ". . . into the relations between employers and employed, as into all the relations of this life, there must enter something of feeling and sentiment; something of mutual explanation, forbearance, and consideration . . ." Now these are precisely the virtues encouraged by Fancy, as Dickens had also often repeated, so in condemning the aggression between workers and masters at Preston he was also implicitly condemning the loss of Fancy in their lives. That is why he was so concerned to support educational institutes in the large industrial cities; the delight in Fancy, the delight in literature, would encourage just those virtues of harmony and sympathy which were necessary in the maintenance of good industrial relations.

There was a specific reason, also, why Dickens decided to widen his attack from educational matters alone. When he had first begun to

write *Hard Times* he had immediately assaulted certain pronouncements from an educational body known as the Department of Practical Art, which concerned itself with the teaching of drawing and
design. Its art superintendent, Richard Redgrave, had recently published a lecture in which he insisted that taste depended upon "acknowledged principles" and "rules" rather than "innate feeling or
perception"; he also declared, in the light of such principles, that
"colours must be arranged together in specific and absolute quantities
to be agreeable to the eye . . ." This is precisely the kind of statement
which Dickens rejected and despised, and the fruit of Mr Redgrave's
remarks is to be found in the opening pages of the novel itself. "You
must use . . . combinations and modifications (in primary colours)
of mathematical figures which are susceptible of proof and demonstration. This is the new discovery. This is fact. This is taste."

But the immediate and topical object of Dickens's scorn soon
widened. Just a few days before he visited Preston he read a speech
delivered by his acquaintance, James Kay-Shuttleworth, in which the
Department of Practical Art was praised for its work in schools. But
in the same speech Kay-Shuttleworth condemned the weavers of
Preston and asserted that the relations of capital and labour were only
to be understood by a study of "abstract truths, easily obscured or
perverted to an uneducated people". So had "abstract truths" become
one of the most egregious platitudes of the day, reaching downwards
from the sphere of social philosophy even to that of practical art and
design. Everything in Dickens's experience would have led him to
reject such a "philosophy", and so it is not at all surprising that his
immediate assault upon the "Fact" school of hard-grind education
should have developed into a larger polemic on the very future of the
country. No doubt he would have had more than a little sympathy,
therefore, with the speech which a leader of the Preston strikers,
George Cowell, made just six days before Dickens himself arrived in
Preston, a speech in which he explicitly attacked the remarks of James
Kay-Shuttleworth. "The sooner we can rout political economy from
the world," he said, "the better it will be for the working classes of this
country."

And what of Preston itself, this city without the beneficent presence
of Fancy in its internecine struggles? Dickens found it bleak, "a nasty
place". And was he reminded by it of some of the forbidding realities
of his own childhood? Here once again he might see the connection:
his own childhood would have been just as bleak and "nasty" without

the nourishing power of his Fancy. In fact there is for him some deep horror, no doubt springing from his childhood reading, in *not* seeing the world as fancy; some fear that, without the mediating power of the imagination, its nastiness and dreariness would be overwhelming. This is expressed in Louisa Gradgrind's declaration that for her Fancy could have become ". . . my refuge from what is sordid and bad in the real things around me . . ." The loss of imagination is connected, too, with the loss of natural affection, and with the creation of unnatural families, all the conditions of Dickens's own childhood being re-instated in this alien landscape of factories and furnaces beneath the glaring sky.

This is how it appears in *Hard Times*, in Coketown, where the whole sad saga of Stephen Blackpool is seen in terms of the individual experience of suffering and isolation; he is a man apart, rejected by his fellow-workers, condemned by union agitators. Yet in his article on the strike itself in *Household Words* Dickens had been notably more restrained in his criticisms of the mill-workers; and, when the *Illustrated London News* reported that the novel was based upon the Preston action, he immediately wrote an angry letter denying the claim and stating that the story had ". . . a direct purpose in reference to the working people all over England". In other words, his novel was not the same thing as his journalism; it served larger purposes and existed in a different sphere. Which, in turn, raises the question of Dickens's fiction as a simulacrum of what under certain circumstances is called "real life". Of course he claimed that everything he wrote was "*true*", and of all charges against him the one he most detested was that of purveying unreality – hence his angry response to Lewes's attack on the subject of spontaneous combustion. This was partly because his conception of literature was now so high that in a sense he saw himself as a teacher, as an important writer whose pronouncements were to be taken seriously. But his was not just a private belief, since the whole tone and movement of the period encouraged the supposition that writers were the guardians of, or spokesmen for, the "Truth". The tendency towards dogmatism in certain Victorian writers, and the no less fervent belief in the existence of certain absolute and fundamental principles, meant that a serious novelist was more likely than not to take up Dickens's position. What he said was true, what he described was real.

Of course it is not as easy as that, and the tendency in late twentieth-century criticism of Dickens has been to emphasise the unreality of his novels; to see them as magical, obsessive, haunted fables. Clearly there are ways in which Dickens's novels are at odds with the "real" world of the nineteenth century and the evidence of *Hard Times* itself suggests that his fiction bears little relation even to his own descriptions of that world in his journalism and in his letters. We have already described how his melodramatic depiction of the prostitute, Martha, in *David Copperfield* is quite at odds with his pragmatic and indeed somewhat severe treatment of the "fallen women" at Urania Cottage. Similarly his descriptions of London in his novels owe much more to his childhood experience than to adult observation. Anyone who reads of the haunted city in *Our Mutual Friend* would never guess that in the same period London possessed the first underground railway in the world (the "Inner Circle" line which is still in use at the end of our own century). But of course there is a larger point here. Dickens's powers of assimilation were equalled only by his powers of imaginative combination, particularly in his gift of seizing upon the essential elements of a scene or character and turning them into the constituents of his overwhelming vision. He changed the "reality" of a scene or character in the light of an imagination which characteristically fused fancy and reality, raised problems in order to resolve them, incorporated the idea of order within the most disordered events, and all the time worked quietly through to a harmonious resolution which was as much a demand of Dickens's own nature as it was an obeisance to the expectations of his audience.

Yet, when we talk about Dickens's own nature, how much can his fictions be said to represent the "real" man who wrote them? The man who went to Preston, the journalist who described the strikers, the novelist who composed *Hard Times* from all the disparate elements of his experience as man and his skills as a reporter? It might be said that in his life, as well as in his art, he simplified people and events in order imaginatively to dominate them. This is not to say that he did not see them clearly enough; his son, Charley, has revealed how, in his father's relations with his school-friends, ". . . it was always a source of wonder and delight to me to see how quickly my father got at the keynote of a young man's character and seemed to know by instinct exactly what to say to him and exactly how to say it". This instantaneous perception was clearly part of Dickens's awareness of the world but, equally clearly, his perceptions were augmented or altered to fit the patterns of his imagination; an imagination which, like the electromagnetic fields discovered in his lifetime, charged the visible world with an invisible order. That is why, in his correspondence, he tends to recreate the world of his fiction so that we cannot look in his letters for any reality extending beyond his novels but rather a continuation of those novels themselves. In these letters he treats the real world rather as people treat the past in memory, smoothing it, idealising it, heightening the episodes of comedy and pathos. For him, writing itself seems to become a form of ritualised memory. There is another connection, also, between his life and his art. In his discussions about his fiction, he is always concerned to point out what he calls the pattern of "divine justice" which he is intent on following in his own narratives. Surely that fictional pattern is related to his attempts to become a magistrate and, as it were, to dispense justice outside the pages of his books? It is often held up as a matter of ridicule that in Dickens's fiction the good end happily and the bad unhappily (Miss Prism, in *The Importance of Being Earnest*, declared that "that is what Fiction means"). But for him it was not simply a literary convention to be deployed for the sake of his audience. He believed in the truth and efficacy of that ethical dispensation; witness the mark system he deployed at Urania Cottage and the fact that, some years later, he dispensed prize tickets to his household staff on the basis of their behaviour. As in his fiction the good are to be rewarded – and, if possible, materially. This "aesthetic" concept was in fact a real part of his life.

Which in turn leads to the larger issue, and the one most difficult to unravel. How did Dickens's fiction reflect the temperament of the man himself? There are some preliminary clues. The man who was well known to his children for his changes of mood is the writer of novels which interleave comedy and pathos like "streaky, well-cured bacon". The man known to his friends for his gaiety and his cheerfulness was the comic novelist who often extolled the virtues of brotherhood. But we must also remark the characteristic Dickensian hero or heroine; the reserved, lonely, isolated figure, making its way through a world which presses down inexorably. Oliver Twist no less than Arthur Clennam, Smike no less than Little Dorrit. And can we not see in the lineaments of these characters something of Dickens himself – a man who, despite his cheerfulness and good humour, remained characteristically reserved and taciturn? Ranging from the long descriptions by his children to the specific observations of a fellow passenger on the ship taking him to America, there is a general and genuine sense of his *apartness* in the world. Is this what Carlyle meant when he looked down into Dickens, and saw beneath the dazzling radiances "the elements of death itself"? Certainly this is the quality which many of his major characters carry with them everywhere, in their guilt as well as in their isolation, in their self-willed effort to create an identity no less than in their death-like passivity at moments of crisis. And can we not see in them the outline of Dickens himself, bending over the images he has created and glimpsing there something of the mystery of his own being? But, if he is "like" his novels, it is also in another and more bewildering way. His gestures in the world are appropriated by his fictional works; the way he walked, the way he conversed, the way he changed from subject to subject, are themselves to be found in the formal movement of each novel and in the underlying shape which all of his novels in sequence reveal. Yes, even the way he walked, that quick, steady, purposeful walk of his. The extraordinary distances he covered as he walked. The observations he made as he did so. All of these living attributes can be found in the very shape and momentum of his fictional narratives. And of course the novels impart to the careful reader precisely that sense of emptiness which Dickens carried around with him everywhere, and to which he adverted at times of crisis; not in the emptiness of the novels but rather in their attempt to fill that emptiness with speech and characters, to create order out of disorder, to raise anxieties in order to experience the pleasure of resolving them, to purify the self in words of fire.

And so he set to work on *Hard Times* after his return from Preston. The narrative had been conceived for *Household Words* and everything about it reflected that condition, even to its appearance on the front page of the periodical as if it were a cross between a journalistic report and an editorial. He began writing it in a deliberately sparse style and the fact that, as he told Miss Burdett-Coutts, he still had "motes of new stories" floating in front of him as he did so suggests what is evident enough from a reading of this small book: Dickens did not in any sense think of it as a novel in his usual vein. In fact it reads like a fable, in a style which is very close to Victorian translations of fairy-stories in the same period. Its intentional simplicity also brings it much closer to the tone of his Christmas stories and it is possible that, in the absence of his old Christmas Books, Dickens was trying to write something on a similar scale and with a similar purpose – to bring his listeners together around the fireside of his imagination, just as he had managed to do at the Birmingham meeting, and to impress upon them the virtues of comradeship and sympathy. Of course it is "topical", too, in the same way that *The Chimes* had been topical. It was even associated with a series of articles which Dickens was about to publish in *Household Words* on industrial accidents: in fact he added a passage about such accidents, and a footnote drawing attention to the series in the periodical, but both references were excised at proof stage. His satire on the facts of Mr Gradgrind's classroom was aimed at a number of specific targets as well; primarily the Department of Practical Art, as we have seen, but it was also directed against the contents of Charles Knight's *Store of Knowledge* (which in fact introduced the ludicrously literal definition of a horse); against the "tabular reports" of library reading compiled by the Manchester Free Library and discussed in *Household Words* one month before; against the new regimen of pupil-teachers who were even now issuing from the training colleges only recently established; and of course against those people in general "who see figures and averages" only. In a later letter he attacked what was generally known as the "Manchester School" of political economics for what he called ". . . its reduction to the grossest absurdity of the supply-and-demand dogmatism" and its belief that self-interest was the major factor in human decisions. "As if the vices and passions of men had not been running counter to their interests since the Creation of the World!" The vices and passions of men; these are what Dickens wanted to chasten and reveal as he moved steadily forward upon his story.

He had planned for it to commence serialisation in *Household Words* at the beginning of April, so by the time he returned from Preston he had two months still in hand. He was busy turning down as many public engagements as he could (in particular, every sanitation organisation in the country now seemed to want him as a guest speaker), but there were private festivities which went ahead as usual. There was his birthday dinner at Gravesend, which was to become something of a ritual, and a few days later he went over to Paris for a short visit; principally because of those "motes of new stories" which were hovering beside him even as he prepared *Hard Times*. He was still eager to write a novel with a continental setting, and it was as a result of his French trip that he seems deliberately to have ignored a special jury summons. The judge got his own back, as it were, since it was reported in the *Illustrated London News* that "having finished his Chancery suit, his Lordship observed, Mr Dickens, by attending, might have added to his knowledge of a suit at common law. The Lord Chief Justice seemed unwilling to fine the distinguished novelist for his non-attendance."

When Dickens did come back to London in the middle of February he set to work properly upon *Hard Times*, and it was at this stage in his early writing that he decided to enlarge upon Mr Sleary's circus troupe who are the sole representatives of "Fancy" in the fact-hard town of Coketown. It was said by one of his friends that "he arranged with the master of Astley's circus to spend many hours behind the scenes with the riders and among the horses . . ." This is unlikely but, on his return from Paris, he did write to Mark Lemon and ask him to ". . . note down and send me any slang terms among the tumblers and circus people . . ." Yet some of that circus seems to have derived from his own memories; there is in *Hard Times* a performing dog known as Merrylegs, and in an essay a few months before he revealed that in his childhood he had christened a dog with the name of Merrychance. And that is precisely the point. Dickens's vision of the circus is primarily derived from childhood memories of its entertainment and with it, too, all those other associations of his boyhood and of early nineteenth-century culture – the puppet shows, the pantomimes, the circuses, the fairs, the boxing matches, the Punch and Judy. So what would be more apt, in a novel which is concerned with the blighting of the imagination in childhood, than to identify the springs of Fancy with the circus and its performers? To go back to an earlier time, before the encroachment of Facts and Statistics. There is another reason also. Coketown is in thrall to the factory and to the machine; in a later letter Dickens suggested that those whose lives are dominated by machinery would also want for their amusement "*something in motion*", the motion in this novel provided by the very acrobats and the performing animals themselves. And, now that he was writing *Hard Times* in earnest, certain other perceptions re-emerged. In a letter written in March he declared that "the English are, so far as I know, the hardest-worked people on whom the sun shines". A sentence which he liked so much that he promptly inserted it, with minor variations, into the novel. In an essay written for *Household Words* some time before he had said that ". . . these people have a right to be amused", a demand reiterated by Sleary, the circus manager in *Hard Times* who through his lisp declares, "People mutht be amuthed . . ." So again and again Dickens emphasised the need for entertainment, for recreation, for "rational amusement" in "these cast-iron and mechanical days . . ." His voice rang out in the assembly rooms and town halls and institutes, reaffirming what is arguably the most important position of his life. For in it, too, he is reaffirming the value of his own work.

"I say really, gentlemen, in these times, when we have torn so many leaves out of our dear old nursery books, I hold it to be more than ever essential to the character of a great people, that the imagination, with all its innumerable graces and charities, should be tenderly nourished . . ." *Loud cheers.*

". . . do not let us, in the laudable pursuit of the facts that surround us, neglect the fancy and the imagination which equally surround us as part of the great scheme." *Hear, hear.*

". . . there can be no efficient and satisfactory work without play; that there can be no sound and wholesome thought without play." *Hear, hear.*

And through the early months of 1854 he worked on. He said later of *Hard Times* that ". . . the idea laid hold of me by the throat in a very violent manner", but at the time all he could see was the labour and difficulty of a narrative which was being serialised in weekly parts almost as he wrote it. The requirements of "compression and close condensation" gave him "perpetual trouble", and in a letter to Forster he complained that ". . . the difficulty of the space is CRUSHING. Nobody can have an idea of it who has not had an experience of patient fiction-writing with some elbow-room always, and open places in perspective. In this form, with any kind of regard to the current number, there is absolutely no such thing . . ." In fact the form he had chosen was less strict than that of the familiar monthly numbers, at least in the sense that he was writing for his own periodical and could increase at will the space given to the story in each issue; which he did, for example, in the last instalment. But his constant meticulous effort, week after week, was in itself exhausting; his doctor ordered him to have a "regimen of fresh air" for a week, and it is likely that his need for a respite became obvious just after he had finished, at the beginning of March, an instalment of some eleven thousand words.

At the beginning of April the first number was published; it was displayed on the front page as "HARD TIMES by Charles Dickens", the only time that a signed article had appeared in its pages. No illustrations. Just two columns of print going from page to page, and presented in such a way that it might just as well be a leading article as a story – a confusion which undoubtedly proved fruitful to a novelist who was as keen to catch the atmosphere of the time as to create a fable of the machine age. It was, in a sense, an inauspicious time, for this was the month that Britain declared war against Russia, ostensibly over the defence of Turkey but in reality as a check against the growing power of that nation under Czar Nicholas. This war, described by one historian as initiated by a potent combination of British liberalism and jingoism, was not one which would necessarily be criticised by Dickens; but his early comments on the issue are concerned only with its effect upon the sale of books. (There would come a time when the conduct of that war, however, provoked some of Dickens's most bitter condemnations of the "system" by which Britain was governed.) But the publication of *Hard Times* was inauspicious in a much smaller way as well: Mrs Gaskell had already started writing a novel, eventually entitled *North and South*, which anticipated Dickens's location and broad theme. In January Forster had written to tell her to ". . . go on with the story whether it be for Dickens or not". In fact it was for Dickens, and appeared in *Household Words* almost immediately after the conclusion of *Hard Times*. By April, however, it was clear that there was more than a passing resemblance between the two tales, but Forster wrote to encourage her. "As to the current which Dickens's story is likely to take I have regretted to see that the manufacturing discontents are likely to clash with part of your plan but . . . I *know* with what a different purpose and subsidiary to what quite opposite manifestations of character and passion *your* strike will be introduced, and I am your witness, if necessary, that your notion in this matter existed before and quite independently of his." It has been suggested that Dickens was guilty of plagiarising Mrs Gaskell's novel but there is no evidence or justification for this. Dickens really did not begin editorial work upon her manuscript until he was well into his own and, if anything, he went to some pains not to clash with *North and South*. That is why, in *Hard Times*, the theme of union and management is quickly raised and just as quickly forgotten. In any case the two novels are barely alike in any respect, Dickens's mythical and fabulist imagination working on quite different principles from Mrs Gaskell's more naturalistic and domestic preoccupations.

Yet, even after he had begun actual publication in April, Dickens was still "planning and planning the story", apparently not sure how to use the material he had collected. All the time he was desperate to keep ahead, as he maintained the regular momentum of his day's work at the office (Wills still away) and his evening's entertainments. Some scenes of that period can even be revived.

Forster and Dickens at the theatre together, watching a more than usually ridiculous drama.

Forster: "My dear Dickens, Good God, what does this mean?"

Dickens (embarrassed by Forster's loud voice): "Hold your tongue and be damned." Work on *Hard Times* continues.

Catherine is excited by the imminent marriage of their neighbour at Tavistock House, Mr Cardale, and makes preparations to attend the wedding. But then her husband sees her. "Caught putting bonnet on for that purpose, and sternly commanded to renounce idiotic intentions." Work on *Hard Times* continues.

Dickens, having just rejoined the Garrick Club, is asked to take the chair at a dinner to commemorate the birthday of William Shakespeare. His speech, in which he celebrated the birth of Shakespeare's characters as well as Shakespeare himself, was "one of the most remarkable" one listener had ever heard and had a "startling effect" upon the members of the Garrick. Work on *Hard Times* continues.

Mark Lemon has agreed to accompany Dickens on a "jaunt". "I have been awaiting travelling orders from Mr Sparkler . . ." he writes. This is not Lemon's pseudonym for his famous friend, but rather one of Dickens's own. Lemon and he eventually go down to Rochester for the day, where they visit Watts's charitable hostel for poor travellers in the High Street. Dickens signs the visitors' book but, unlike everybody else, leaves no comment. Work on *Hard Times* continues.

Still working, through April and May, despite the fact that "Mrs Dickens is in the meantime picking up all manner of conditional engagements, and firing me off like a sort of revolver". So he wanted his holiday and he was already looking forward to another summer in Boulogne, for which purpose he had rented a slightly larger house from M. Beaucourt at the top of the hill above the town. (Georgina had already gone over to inspect the property, a sure sign of the importance which she now enjoyed in the Dickens household.) He had agreed to take it from June until October and, as the time for leaving approached, beset by social engagements, by friends, by dinners, he was desperate to keep up the pace of *Hard Times*. But he was looking ahead, too, looking much further ahead; with Forster he was discussing the idea of giving a series of paid public lectures but, at this juncture, he decided against the idea. It was only to be considered if and when the "higher calling" of the writer, as Forster put it, should have "failed of the old success".

By the end of May he was writing only two weeks ahead of publication in *Household Words*; which meant that, just before setting off for Folkestone en route to Boulogne, he was still in the process of killing Mrs Gradgrind as well as giving her one of the most famous lines in the history of death-bed scenes. "I think there's a pain somewhere in the room . . . but I couldn't positively say that I have got it." Then off to Boulogne. In fact Dickens left earlier than he had previously intended, simply because he was anxious to continue *Hard Times* in the relative privacy of his French retreat; he wanted to finish it and then properly relax, to enjoy, as Catherine said, "a complete country holiday". He arrived in France in the middle of June, and he was aiming to complete the story by the end of July. Leaving him at least two full months of idleness. The new house, Villa du Camp de Droite, was at the top of the hill above the château where they had spent the previous summer; the rooms were larger than those in the former place, and it had a pleasant garden as well as a field to itself. It was so high that Dickens said that it was like being in a balloon, a pleasant sensation for a man who on his visits abroad liked to feel himself cut off from all English bonds. Except the inevitable ones: the children came over a few days later, accompanied by Mark Lemon's children, but their father rapidly arranged the details of their French life. Mamie and Katey had a French governess, and the boys were to be enrolled in a local school run by an Englishman.

Everything was as it should be, the only problem consisting in the very tangible shape of an army camp nearby. Dickens was afraid that the sound of drums would disturb his concentration, and in any case he found it hard to get on with the novel. It was not until the end of June that he began in earnest, and he worked steadily through into July; his aim now was to finish by the nineteenth of that month, and then to take the manuscript to London. So he was what he called ". . . stunned with work . . ." He was coming close to the discovery of Stephen Blackpool in the deserted mine-shaft, leading ineluctably to the mill-hand's death. Dickens's head was feeling "hot"; he was for some reason nervous; and it was at this moment that he has Rachael, the hapless friend of Stephen, declare, ". . . I fall into such a wild, hot hurry, that, however tired I am, I want to walk fast, miles and miles." A wild, hot hurry: that was Dickens's state now as he came to the concluding chapters. Stephen dead. Gradgrind's son fleeing from the scene of his crime. And in Dickens's notes: "Wind up – The ashes of our fires grown grey and cold." He had, in the interim, sent a letter to Carlyle asking if he might dedicate the book to him; which was duly done, although Carlyle's reply was not as enthusiastic as perhaps it might have been. To lend his name to a *fiction*?

Dickens finished two days sooner than he had anticipated, in his own wild, hot hurry; completed on the Monday, and then on Tuesday he took the manuscript back with him across the Channel. But by now he was feeling very tired and "used up". In fact he was more exhausted than he realised and, when he arrived in London, he suffered severely from the ". . . very hot, close, suffocating, and oppressive" weather. The climate, as always, seemed to reflect his moods. As soon as he had a complete set of proofs he sent them over to France, for Catherine to read; and, now that he was preparing an edition in volume form, he gave titles to all of the chapters and divided the novel into three "Books". This may or may not have been partly in imitation of Thackeray who had divided *The History of Henry Esmond* in such a manner; whatever the cause, Dickens liked the arrangement, and he was to employ it for all subsequent completed books. He commuted in the hot weather between Tavistock House and the office of *Household Words*. He was sitting for yet another portrait. He was annoyed by Catherine's mother, who for some unaccountable reason wished to take out life insurance at her advanced age. And then something strange occurred, something which might be put down to Dickens's own state of nervous exhaustion. He was walking along the street one morning when "I suddenly (the temperature being then most violent) found an icy coolness come upon me, accompanied with a general stagnation of the blood, a numbness of the extremities, great bewilderment of mind, and a vague sensation of wonder. I was walking at the time, and, on looking about me, found that I was in the frigid shadow of the Burlington Hotel. Then I recollected to have experienced the same sensations once before precisely in that spot. A curious case this, don't you think?" The hotel itself was at 19 Cork Street (the building now contains an art gallery), on the corner of Burlington Gardens, and assiduous research has yielded no earthly clue to the source of his sensation. Yet it is a case "curious" enough, especially for a man who had only recently been condemning the contemporary craze for "spirit rapping" and who was in the habit of poking mild fun at Bulwer-Lytton's own fascination with the occult.

But he did attend seances, with whatever misgivings, and he did have a real sense of the numinous. What could be more natural, then, that his own nervous debility should render him susceptible to all those influences which linger in the avenues and alleys of the great, wild city? Of course he could feel his tiredness; but it was not his way to yield to such things and in his own hot way he tried to conquer that feeling of being exhausted, frayed, empty, "used up". He met a friend at the theatre, the playwright Buckstone, and proceeded to drink gin-slings with him until dawn. Not a usual practice of Dickens's, but he was on his own and, most importantly, he was intent upon ". . . knocking the remembrance of my work out".

And what a work it had proved to be. Written quickly and almost feverishly, begun in order to boost the sales of his periodical, laying hold of its author "by the throat" as it proceeded, it is in some ways the most puzzling and revealing of Dickens's novels. There are the usual "inconsistencies", although the term should really be applied to a theorem and not to a novel, where the very paradoxes are part of the theme. The more unpleasant characters, for example, are also the most substantially imagined and the most entertaining; the social and political dimension of the narrative is quickly supplanted by an emphasis on individual goodness and individual charity; the claims of Fancy and entertainment are embodied in an old-fashioned circus whose lisping manager barely makes himself understood. Everything is united by the one constant element in the novel, however, the one that has always had so strong a hold upon its author's imagination that it twists everything into its own shape – "an unnatural family", as Dickens terms the Coketown operatives, is at the root of all the suffering and uncertainty. The cold and unfeeling husband; the proud and self-willed wife; the feckless young son. These are here again, as they have been in *Dombey and Son*, *Bleak House*, everywhere. And of course the pattern of the narrative is laid down by these primal figures of Dickens's art. Mr Gradgrind's treatment of his wife is precisely like the mill-owners' treatment of their workers; Mr Bounderby's disparagement of his mother like the mill-workers' disparagement of the employers. We do not need Dickens's speeches to confirm that he saw industrial relations primarily in terms of familial duty and mutual respect. But *Hard Times* is the work of his imagination, not his social conscience, and the theme of the family cannot help but be affected by all the obsessions and strangenesses he brings to it – the peculiar virginal women, the shrewish spinster, the helpless father, the prattling mother, all the same figures emerging from and then retreating into the shadows of Dickens's imagination. The cold man is always humbled, the thoughtless young man is either killed or in some less tangible way injured beyond repair. In all respects *Hard Times* is more like the work of William Blake than of Friedrich Engels, fuelled as it is by the components of a private vision which is given public significance. And when Stephen Blackpool, the abandoned mill-worker, dies, the presence of the "God of the poor" and the "Redeemer" emerges in the text itself. Dickens really did now have a sense of the numinous, that "infinite world", as he calls it here, which is seen by him in stars, in shafts of light, in bodies of still water.

Yet how are we then to take the savage comedy of the novel, the wonderful cruelty with which Dickens raises up figures like Mrs Sparsit and Mr Bounderby? How strange, in that sense, that Mr Bounderby himself, the most ludicrous and despicable character in the novel, should sound like a caricature of Dickens himself, this self-made man who unjustly accuses his mother of neglecting him and who says of his own career, "How I fought through it, *I* don't know . . . I was determined, I suppose." But once we start looking for images of Dickens and of those closest to him, in the biographical equivalent of spirit-rapping, we see their shapes everywhere. Is it Dickens recreating himself in Stephen Blackpool's loveless marriage, for example, and in his sense ". . . that he was never, in this world or the next, through all the unimaginable ages of eternity, to look on Rachael's face or hear her voice. Wandering to and fro, unceasingly, without hope, and in search of he knew not what (he only knew that he was doomed to seek it) . . ." Do we see John Dickens in the absconding father of little Sissy Jupe? And Dickens's own son in the feckless wastrel son of Mr Gradgrind, a character who takes the reader towards a concluding scene that could only have been written by this novelist? Mr Gradgrind, the philosophic radical, the utilitarian, the stern schoolmaster, sits in the "Clown's performing chair in the middle of the ring" of the circus while his feckless son, Tom, parades in black-face in front of him. "The father buried his face in his hands, and the son stood in his disgraceful grotesqueness, biting straw: his hands, with the black partly worn away inside, looking like the hands of a monkey. The evening was fast closing in; and from time to time, he turned the whites of his eyes restlessly and impatiently towards his father. They were the only parts of his face that showed any life or expression, the pigment upon it was so thick." A miraculous scene, written quickly by Dickens in the early days of July, hurrying to finish the story before publication, desperate for rest; out of the hurry comes this spare and vivid language, this directness of presentation, this sparseness and determination. But it shows signs of his tiredness, too, and there are times when it becomes mechanical and forced, the quickness amounting almost to haste, a deep dissatisfaction with the world seeping through everything like a stain.

". . . A mere dull melodrama," *The Rambler* said, "in which character is caricature, sentiment tinsel, and moral (if any) unsound." The *Westminster Review* commented upon its topical nature, and suggested that Dickens's language was one which "speaks especially to the present generation" and may not be intelligible to the next. And, later, there was a sharp parody of Dickens's style in *Our Miscellany*: "The crowd gathering. Like a snowball. Much dirtier, though. Rather." Dickens professed untruthfully never to read reviews of his own work but, even if the majority of them did remain unread by him, they created the critical atmosphere which he sensed and through which he had to move. It is hard now to imagine Dickens as he was then: a writer whose great reputation was secure but whose progress into a "serious" novelist was uncertain; who would suffer throughout these years the imputation that he was "declining" as a creative force; but who fought back on his own terms, even to the extent of readily embracing once more his role as an "entertainer" and using that as a weapon against his many detractors.

The book was finished. Dickens travelled back from London to Boulogne, and at last began that "country holiday" of which he was so sorely in need. He lay on the grass and read, he lay against the haystacks and slept; ". . . reading books and going to sleep" was his phrase, the luxury of retreating to his childhood experience of reading and resting. But with it too there was now the intimation of adult exhaustion – the dropping of the book, the page unturned. He visited the fêtes and fairs, as he had last year, and went for his usual fifteen- or sixteen-mile walks; since he was walking in the rain for some of the time, however, he suffered an inflamed ear for several days and placed compresses of poppies against his head to relieve the swelling and the pain. Thackeray was in Boulogne, too; his daughters were now on very friendly terms with Dickens's daughters, and it seems likely that it was the children who brought the two novelists together here. They dined on at least one occasion, and then played "forfeits" with the boys. There were also house-guests of course and Wilkie Collins, suffering agonies of rheumatic gout, stayed for some weeks. In his letters to his brother, Charles, he describes their expeditions on windy days with a kite which he and Dickens had manufactured. And, when the Prince Consort visited the Emperor of France in the neighbourhood, Dickens and Collins arranged for a candle to be placed at every window of the Villa du Camp de Droite; at a signal from Dickens with a small dinner-bell, all the candles were lit at once. There were one hundred and fourteen in all and, according to Collins, "the effect from a distance was as if the whole house was one steady blaze of light. It was seen for miles and miles around. The landlord went into hysterical French ecstacies [Dickens said in his own account that he literally *screamed* with delight] – the populace left their illuminations in the town, and crowded to the ramparts opposite our hill, to stand in amazement. We let off fireworks besides, and to crown all we had not the slightest alarm or accident." How characteristic, too, that in his taste for spectacle and incandescent display Dickens should actually out-French the French with what he called his "palace of light".

There were other house-guests beside Collins; among them Chauncy Townshend, Augustus Egg, Thomas Beard and W. H. Wills bearing, on Dickens's express instructions, some red shirts from Dickens's wardrobe, some essence of ginger, and Burnett's Disinfecting Fluid. The last no doubt, one of Dickens's favourite household items. To disinfect. To clean. To *purify*. He had in fact been in constant correspondence with Wills, effectively editing and running *Household Words* from a distance; in these ostensibly lazy weeks, almost all his letters were concerned with that subject. In particular he was worried about Mrs Gaskell's *North and South*, which was proving too long and too unwieldy for serial publication. Mrs Gaskell herself was also somewhat difficult, particularly in her inability or slowness to cut her text as Dickens desired; nothing irritated him more than unprofessional behaviour, especially in novelists whom he knew to be inferior to himself, and although he kept his own communications with Mrs Gaskell relatively courteous he was far from flattering about her to his deputy. And so his life went on. He could never remain indolent for very long and, just after he had been listing the pleasures of idleness to his friends, he was in fact starting to write articles for *Household Words* and preparing for that year's Christmas issue.

Boulogne itself was untypically animated. The outbreak of the Crimean War explained the large army camp which had been established in the vicinity, and what with Napoleon III, and what with the

Prince Consort, the whole place came alive (in Dickens's descriptions at least) with flags and bugles and guns. And fires. If there was one thing that Dickens enjoyed, both in art and in life, it was a good fire; so he was positively enthusiastic when a theatre in Boulogne was burnt to the ground. He went to the scene of the accident as quickly as he could, and found that ". . . the spectacle of the whole interior, burning like a red-hot cavern, was really very fine, even in the day-light". There was not much other news for him to report otherwise; except, perhaps, one thing. He and his family went to the performance of a conjuror, and in a detailed letter to Forster he describes some most extraordinary feats of clairvoyance. In one trick the conjuror gave Catherine a half-sheet of paper and then asked her to think of two things; she did so, a lion and a rose, and when she opened the sheet of paper she found that these were the precise items which he had written down in advance. In another trick he guessed which names two army-officers had written on slates, and then proceeded to alter one of these names without being in the slightest contact with the slate itself. And, in a third trick, blindfolded and with a cloth thrown over his head, he was able to "see" what particular dates had been written down by members of the audience. Remarkable in itself and, in an age which was beginning to understand such unseen powers as electromagnetism, this exhibition of clairvoyance had a significance which those of later generations may not be able readily to appreciate. But then some other Boulogne news displaced all other gossip. An epidemic of cholera was suspected, although the terrible nature of the disease did not seem to affect Dickens's always alert presence of mind. His coolness in face of present danger was remarkable; his friend and family doctor, John Elliotson, was also spending the summer in Boulogne and they discussed the situation together, but Dickens does not seem to have been particularly worried. He was still asking his old friend, Thomas Beard, to join the family; and in fact they all eventually left Boulogne at the time they had originally intended. When the disease broke out in England, however, especially when it began once more its depredations upon the London poor, he went on the offensive.

For the last three years he had been campaigning on the vital necessity of proper sanitation for the city and its environs, yet still nothing had been agreed or attempted. (The fact that over twenty thousand people died from this year's epidemic only serves to emphasise how appalling such a visitation of illness remained.) So Dickens struck back at the various authorities who had delayed or actively impeded the scheme for a centralised plan of sanitation. None of the anger and dissatisfaction which he had discharged into *Hard Times* had gone, and in a number of articles in September and October (written in Boulogne and then posted to Wills) he attacked Parliament and the Law with a ferocity which was altogether new. Of Parliament in particular he told Forster that his hope was ". . . to have made every man in England feel something of the contempt for the House of Commons that I have. We shall never begin to do anything until the sentiment is universal . . ." In other words he wished somehow (and the method is never very clear) to effect a wholesale revolution of attitudes among the English people, and it was this polemical aim which was behind the most ferocious political statement he had yet made. It came in an address, "To Working Men", which he wrote quickly and spontaneously for *Household Words* in the latter half of September. Of the authorities who had allowed cholera to spread unchecked, Dickens said that ". . . they are guilty, before GOD, of wholesale murder" and then went on to address the "working men" directly. It was this latter part of his article which caused the most consternation among his more respectable friends; he advised the workers to unite and, with their strength, to turn out from office those who had misled and mistreated them. It is the closest he had come to suggesting some kind of social revolution and, when Miss Burdett-Coutts wrote to him in her alarm, he condemned ". . . a worthless Government" and said of cholera itself, "Let it come twice again, severely, – the people advancing all the while in the knowledge that, humanly speaking, it is, like Typhus Fever in the mass, a preventible disease – and you will see such a shake in this country as never was seen on Earth since Samson pulled the Temple down upon his head."

Hard words for a hard time. A time of disease and a time of war. And yet, perhaps most importantly for Dickens, a time in which he himself was restless, anxious and miserable. He could never rest for very long, and the weeks of relative idling in Boulogne seem really only to have increased his sense of unease as he contemplated the return to England. He was ready to begin yet another novel in *Household Words*, since the publication of Mrs Gaskell's *North and South* had depressed the sales of that publication. This is proof, if nothing else, of his stamina. And yet, unusually, it was not simply his preparation for another novel which was provoking his unrest. His misery seemed to have a deeper cause, and in a letter to Forster he explained something of what it was: "*Restlessness*, you will say.

Whatever it is, it is always driving me, and I cannot help it. I have rested nine or ten weeks, and sometimes feel as if it had been a year – though I had the strangest nervous miseries before I stopped. If I couldn't walk fast and far, I should just explode and perish."

He had reached middle-age, and he had attained unprecedented success, and yet he was still not content. Not happy. This must have seemed the strangest thing of all to him, to have achieved so much and still to be looking for contentment. And what could he see ahead of him except further disquiet? If he had not found that one thing he was always looking for by middle-age, how could he be expected to find it later? That need for love and admiration, born in childhood, was still not satisfied; that wound which had opened in his earliest years was still not healed. And perhaps this is the most terrible thing of all, so disconcerting as to provoke all his intense restlessness and his desire for escape – it had been the dislocation and privation of his childhood in the blacking warehouse which had helped propel him towards success. But, now that he had achieved that success, and its novelty had waned, all the miseries of his childhood were returning with redoubled strength. The fame and fortune of his years as a novelist had effectively repressed all the symptoms of his old panic and disorder but now, as he entered middle-age, they were reasserting themselves once more. He had never escaped his past – he knew that as well as anyone – he had merely prevented it from swallowing him up. There is a curious passage in Forster's biography, when discussing the problems of this time, which takes us to the heart of one of Dickens's fears; ". . . there were moments (really and truly only moments) . . ." but a moment can last a lifetime! – ". . . when the fancy would arise that if the conditions of his life had been reversed, something of a vagabond existence (using the word in Goldsmith's meaning) might have super-vened. It would have been an unspeakable misery to him, but it might have come nevertheless." If the conditions of his life had been reversed . . . and he had returned to the precarious existence of his childhood. This is what Dickens feared; he had feared it as a child, when he saw how easily he might have taken up the street-life of the other children around him; and now, even at the pinnacle of his success, that childhood terror of vagabondage had revived. He could not escape his past, or the anxieties of his past which sometimes had more reality than the real world all around him. There is that image at the end of *Hard Times* – Gradgrind sitting in the Clown's chair in the middle of the circus-ring, his son capering around him with blackened face and hands. The scene has the quality of a vision or what Dickens would have called a "picture"; and could not the son, covered in blacking, be a "picture" of the young Dickens? A young Dickens, in a nightmare of degradation, capering before his father? Or is it the young Dickens capering and gibbering before the older version of himself? Swallowed up, at last, by his past.

Chapter 24

W HEN he returned to England, he retained his moustache and in addition had grown very brown in the sun (an indication of the fact that Dickens had a slightly dark or what was once termed a "muddy" complexion). But he said that he was feeling "too old"; clearly the recuperation in France had not materially affected his anxious state. He plunged himself into work as if it were some shower bath of the spirit and at once began composing the Christmas issue of *Household Words*, using the idea of the Watts's charitable hostel in Rochester as a venue for certain moving or entertaining stories written by several hands. Of course some of these stories were Dickens's own, and in his account of Watts's Charity itself he managed to arouse the anger of the Rochester worthies; the *Maidstone and Kentish Journal* berated him for inaccuracy and bad taste, since ". . . the matron of the Charity has been vulgarised and the provisions of the founder's will misunderstood". A reminder that Dickens was not often concerned with the reaction of those real people about whom he chose to write; in a sense, he did not see them when he was writing, he saw only his *idea* of them. In addition he was preparing another round of public readings; this was only the second year in which he had agreed to give them, but already he had come to think of them as a settled and satisfactory activity into which he could pour all his ferocious energy. So satisfactory in fact that, despite Forster's protestations and his own occasional misgivings, he was happy to increase their number when the opportunity arose. He was also writing for *Household Words*, of course, trying to "brighten" each number in his own "inimitable" style, although it cannot be said that he did so in one of his stranger essays of this period when, in outraged terms, he attacked the idea that the recently-lost expedition of Sir John Franklin to the Arctic had indulged in cannibalistic practices. It is so strange an article, in fact, that it throws more light on his own excitable and anxious state of mind than upon the ostensible subject of his concern. Besides launching an attack upon the "savage", by which he meant non-white, races (". . . we believe every savage to be in his heart covetous, treacherous, and cruel"), he persistently and cavalierly denied that ". . . any of the members [of the Franklin expedition] prolonged their existence by the dreadful expedient of eating the bodies of their dead companions . . ." And, by some curious associational link, he returns to his childhood reading rather than any contemporary evidence to corroborate this statement: "In the whole wide circle of the *Arabian Nights*, it is reserved for ghoules, gigantic blacks with one eye, monsters like towers, of enormous bulk and dreadful aspect, and unclean animals lurking on the sea-shore . . ." The idea of cannibalism was one which horrified him, but his response to what had been a serious and well-argued case became in the end no more than a litany to the virtue and hardihood of the white explorer. Of course he was no tyro in such matters; one of his favourite pastimes was the reading of travellers' memoirs. And, if he had an especial fondness for the Arctic waste and its white landscapes, perhaps it was because he saw himself in some sense as an ice-bound traveller, driven towards the extremities. This story can be completed with the news that, in 1986, the corpses of some members of that same Franklin expedition were found preserved in permafrost. And Dickens was right, after all: they appear to have died of tuberculosis and starvation. In the newspaper photographs they are to be seen preserved in their icy beds, their faces and clothes clearly visible; the contemporaries of Dickens returned to our own time. The past does not wholly fade.

Here is another Victorian story which can be revived in a different sense, released into the present just for a moment before it crumbles. It is a true story which, on Dickens's return from Boulogne, touched his heart. A letter had been sent to him in Boulogne: "I have heard much of your goodness to unfortunate people – and your writings have emboldened me to pray for your advice . . ." The letter came from a certain Frederick Maynard, who explained the unhappy situation of his two sisters and himself. His eldest sister "became acquainted with a gentleman and lived with him 9 years but I regret to say not as his wife –". But she became "a Mother" both to him and her young sister, feeding and clothing them, and going so far as to have him articled to an architect, with a "handsome premium", when he reached the age of seventeen. But then "her protector left her and she was plunged in great distress with the chances of a frightful life before her –". His articles of course were cancelled, since she could no longer afford to maintain him, and she herself had little prospect of obtaining honest employment. So she was now earning her living as a prostitute, in the very house where she lived with her brother. "She must not be judged by her unhappy condition, for I affirm in spite of it – a more virtuous minded woman never lived." And so what were they to do? Charles Dickens read this extraordinary letter, and made an appointment to meet the young Frederick Maynard at Tavistock House after he had returned to London. Dickens found him "suitably dressed, in black", as he told Miss Burdett-Coutts, and his manner perfectly accorded with the quiet and civilised tone of the letter. "He cried, at several parts in our conversation: but he sat in my room with his back to the light, and always made an effort to hide it, and was evidently relieved when I appeared not to notice it." This is Dickens at his best, calmly but sympathetically learning of misfortune and hoping to resolve it. He discovered that the sister had a two-year-old daughter – "Although she is what she is," Dickens went on to tell Miss Burdett-Coutts, "in the very house to which the brother goes home every night of his life, he has an unbounded respect and love for her, which presents one of the strangest and most bewildering spectacles I ever saw within my remembrance." She had educated her younger sister to be a nursery-governess; they had a mother, who had a "situation" in a Kensington workhouse, but they had no love for her. Dickens would have noticed this with interest, this dislike of a mother who had clearly abandoned them to their unhappy fate. Frederick Maynard was now an architectural draughtsman on a salary of thirty-five shillings a week, but he was trying to get some kind of menial evening employment in a theatre in order to increase his income. "If he could make enough to keep his sister and her child he would be heartily thankful, and they would joyfully maintain a home together, and he would ask no help."

How strange and how touching a story, so much a part of its period that it might almost serve as a lesson in the uses of history; to see how the true affections have neither grown nor diminished in the last one hundred and fifty years, how familial love can find an echo in our own hearts just as it did in that of Charles Dickens. Yet a lesson, too, in the constraints which in any period mortally affect the lives of those who live within them – the constraint here being that of the quondam mistress and her illegitimate daughter, quite banned from respectable society and from any "honest" position, her sudden fall into prostitution bringing down with her the sister and brother whom she so much cared for. Was there anything to be done? At this painful interview Dickens at once seems to take command of her situation; he suggested to the brother that she might emigrate and start a new life, a prospect which had never occurred to him or to the young woman herself.

"Ask her," Dickens said to Frederick as he was about to leave.

The young man came back into the room: "Mr Dickens, I know it would be utterly in vain to ask her to leave her child behind her –"

"No one would propose that. Let us suppose that she was to take it with her."

Immediately he wrote to Miss Burdett-Coutts, outlining the case, and, while he waited for her answer, did nothing. Then the young lady herself wrote to the novelist. "Altho' as you may imagine I should prefer remaining in this Country, still for my Child's sake I should gratefully accept any honorable opportunity of redeeming my position, even to the breaking of all ties that hold me here . . . I have no words to thank you for your goodness . . ." Dickens visited her and found her exactly as her brother had described – "I cannot get the picture of her, out of my head. I particularly wish that you could see her and speak to her." This to Miss Burdett-Coutts again, the aim being to persuade her to pay for the young woman's emigration to the "Cape" (South Africa) where she might start a new life. It is no wonder that the situation had affected him so powerfully; with the neglectful mother, with the remorseful prostitute, with the affection between brother and sister, it was as if the elements of one of his own novels had sprung into life. Just as it had done, months before, when he had seen the boy and the pale horse of Hickman's Folly. But even he could hardly have written a story in which this delicate and intelligent young woman acted as a prostitute within the house of her child and brother; it is, Dickens said, ". . . a romance so astonishing and yet so intelligible as I never had the boldness to think of". And it is noteworthy, too, that at no point does Dickens make any moral judgment about prostitution in general or this prostitute in particular; surely once again evidence for the unspoken acceptance and understanding of that phenomenon in the middle of the nineteenth century. Some weeks passed, while Miss Burdett-Coutts and Charles Dickens pondered the young woman's situation, until she felt constrained to write to the novelist again. "I cannot express the deep gratitude I feel for the kind sympathy and interest you have shewn in my affairs – Will you tell me if there is a possibility of my being able to leave England soon, as indeed I am very anxious to do so." Miss Burdett-Coutts then saw her, liked her or pitied her (it does not matter which), and agreed to help. But complications of an unknown kind obtruded, and eventually it was agreed that Miss Burdett-Coutts should rent and furnish for the young woman a house in a neighbourhood where she was not known, and there earn her living by taking in lodgers. Again, how much a part of its period this solution is. But the lodging house was not a success, and a year later it was agreed that Mrs Thompson (as she was always called, despite the fact that she was not married) should sell the furniture of the house and, with the proceeds, emigrate with her child to Canada. At this point she passes out of Dickens's life and out of our history, one of those constrained and difficult nineteenth-century lives which has been recorded here simply because for a moment it came to the attention of Charles Dickens. What became of Mrs Thompson in Canada, whether she married again, what life her daughter led as a new Canadian, all of this is lost to us.

Dickens had been arranging these matters in what he had once called that "great forgiving" Christmas time, and it was to be in this season too that he read for various charitable or civic institutions. In fact his success at Birmingham the year before had been so "prodigious", to employ one of his own favourite words, that he had been obliged to refuse most of the many requests which were now made to him. It was this enthusiasm for his new role as reader that persuaded him to make more commercial arrangements in future years, but, for the moment, he was the charitable speaker; on 19 December he went to the Literary, Scientific and Mechanics' Institution in Reading, and then two days later read at Sherborne for the Literary Institution; immediately after Christmas he went to Bradford and read on behalf of the Temperance Educational Institution. What a time it was for Institutes and Charitable Groups of all kinds; one of the glories of the period lies in the fact that, at a time when the idea of state funding was still in its infancy, it was considered a duty of the average Victorian to support and to encourage the various foundations which were established over the whole country. On all three occasions Dickens had decided to read *A Christmas Carol*, so obviously appropriate for the season, but now a new element was introduced into its delivery. Before he began to read, he announced that he would be treating his audience as if it were grouped around a Christmas fire; then he went on to say, ". . . if you feel disposed as we go along to give expression to any emotion, whether grave or gay, you will do so with perfect freedom from restraint, and without the apprehension of disturbing me." This recommendation to laugh and to cry vociferously was greeted with "Loud applause". He was indulging in what might anachronistically be described as a form of group therapy or, to put it in another context, he was creating the conditions for a nineteenth-century version of that *catharsis* which was supposed to be the experience of watching Greek tragedy. Here the *catharsis*, which was readily associated with Dickens's plea for sympathy between the various classes of the country, was more like that of a child who is asked to believe that the fairy-stories, after all, are true.

His largest audience was at Bradford, where some 3,700 people were packed into St George's Hall; as was now becoming his habit, he and Wills went up the night before in order to inspect the reading arrangements, and on this occasion Dickens found to his consternation that two rows of seats had been set up behind his lectern. "These (on which the committee immensely prided themselves) I instantly over-threw: to the great terror and amazement of the bystanders . . ." Dickens *never* allowed anyone to sit behind him; partly no doubt from some half-superstitious, half-obsessive, fear that he might be attacked, and partly because much of the power of his reading lay in his eyes and in his gestures. He was asked where the Mayor was supposed to sit and, characteristically, he replied that ". . . the Mayor might go – anywhere – but must not come near me". The reading was another success, with all the laughter and the tears and the cheering he hoped for, expected, demanded. And there was a little private drama as well; he seems to have been greatly taken by the landlady of the hotel in which he was staying. He confessed this, not to Catherine, but to Mary Boyle. Restlessness again. The restlessness of the heart revealed in half-joking asides, as if the subject were never very far from his thoughts.

Two days after the Bradford reading he gave an address for the Commercial Travellers' Schools at the London Tavern. The fact that Dickens was to speak meant that ". . . as dinner hour approached the ticket bureau of the tavern was literally besieged by applicants . . .", an anticipation here of the extraordinary scenes which were to accompany Dickens on his later reading tours. When he spoke he was greeted with "loud and protracted cheering"; whatever the critics might say, it was Dickens the popular author who was still triumphant. It was on this occasion, too, that for the first time he alluded publicly to the Crimean War which had been all but monopolising public attention for the last six months. He had already touched upon the matter in one of his Christmas stories, where the union of France and England is greeted with some satisfaction; a satisfaction all the more real, of course, since Dickens had learnt at first-hand the pleasures of France and of the French. But now he extended that affection into a public pledge of support for the war: ". . . if ever there were a time when noble hearts were deserving well of mankind by exposing themselves to the obedient bayonets of a rash and barbarian tyrant, it is now, when the faithful children of England and France are fighting so bravely in the Crimea." Close to jingoism, perhaps, but also close to Dickens's real mood; the Russian empire was for him, as it was for most Englishmen of the period, a cruel autocracy bent upon subduing the smaller states of Europe. In that sense it was a force literally against civilisation, a civilisation of which England and France were the two major examples. But he had many private reservations; for one thing the conduct of the war was being seriously mismanaged by that fatal combination of incompetence and vested interest which he observed in the ordinary conduct of affairs. Indeed the phenomenon was being repeated on a massive and perhaps fatal scale; supplies gone astray, equipment useless, medical treatment appalling. Out of an army of 54,000 men so many dead and most of the others unfit for duty. His contempt for Parliament had been evident long before the start of the War itself, his address to working men at the time of the cholera epidemic being sufficient evidence of that. But the growing reports of sloth and stupidity in the actual business of warfare only confirmed his belief that the rulers of England were close to destroying the country which they had "inherited", or being destroyed in turn. He was not content with standard denunciations, however, and as a practical step for helping the British troops he had persuaded Miss Burdett-Coutts to pay for the manufacture and transportation of an ingenious "drying machine" for the linen of the soldiers who were even then suffering the mortal effects of the bitter climate. But there were wider ramifications than the conduct of the war itself, since for Dickens it seemed that the declaration of warfare meant that all efforts at domestic reform would be postponed or frustrated. Sanitation, education, and public health in general could all be left to one side while the administration concentrated upon its war "effort". "I feel," he said to Mrs Watson, "as if the world had been pushed back five hundred years." But he said nothing of this in his speech to the Commercial Travellers, and went on from his patriotic remarks about the war to discuss the changes in modern travelling. After he had made his toast, "The Orphan's Prayer" was sung by the children of dead travellers, who then proceeded to walk through the rooms. Then, at the close of the proceedings, the celebrated entertainer, Albert Smith, sang "Galignani's Messenger". Forgotten songs. A forgotten culture in which orphans paraded in front of their benefactors and men sang to one another after a dinner.

It was in this same spirit of communal entertainment that Dickens was rigorously marshalling his own children for the next Twelfth Night play at Tavistock House – on this occasion, *Fortunio and His Seven Gifted Servants* – in which Dickens played the part of the angry "Baron Dunover (A Nobleman in Difficulties)". Georgina Hogarth presided at the pianoforte, and Mr "Wilkini Collini" played Gormand. A comic song against the Czar was performed, and there was dancing afterwards. Another year had gone by, a year for Charles Dickens of arduous labour followed by low spirits, exhaustion swiftly succeeded by intolerable restlessness.

And how did his public reputation stand now? There is Nathaniel Hawthorne's comment, confided to his notebook after a visit to England in this new year, 1855: "Dickens is evidently not liked nor thought well of by his literary brethren – at least, the most eminent of them, whose reputation might interfere with his. Thackeray is much more to their tastes." A true enough assessment, for there is no doubt that the intellectual and literary leaders of opinion were considerably less impressed by Dickens than the middle-class or working-class audiences whom he addressed. Of course he had his loyal allies – Forster, Collins and the regular contributors to *Household Words*; but even they were somewhat suspect and Ruskin wrote in this same year that "he is in a bad set . . . Yet he is I believe a good man (in the common parlance) and means well –". In the same month that Ruskin made this comment, *Blackwood's Magazine* observed that Dickens was "a *class* writer, the historian and representative of one circle in the many ranks of our social scale . . . it is the air and breath of middle-class respectability which fills the books of Mr Dickens". There is a certain truth here, too, and it is that particular kind of middle-class appeal which was responsible for some of the more highbrow disdain of the man Trollope was to dub "Mr Popular Sentiment". But there was more to it than that. *Hard Times*, and his subsequent address to working men in the pages of his periodical, had also laid him open to the charge of what Macaulay termed "sullen socialism". This was what Marx had in mind when he told Engels that Dickens had "issued to the world more political and social truths than have been uttered by all the professional politicians, publicists and moralists put together". Harriet Martineau saw Dickens's position as one of "pseudo-philanthropy", however; Mary Russell Mitford described it as "liberal cant" while Bagehot defined it as "sentimental radicalism" which was a "pernicious example" to those who imitated or followed the novelist. In other words Dickens was increasingly being seen as a dangerously misguided iconoclast whose political opinions were at best based upon romance rather than reason and at worst were products of class-bound resentment. Forster obliquely makes a similar point when he reports that ". . . the inequalities of rank which he secretly resented took more galling as well as glaring prominence from the contrast of the necessities he had gone through with the fame that had come to him . . ." All of the forces which had propelled him forward to success were, now that that success was assured, being seen clearly for the first time: we have already noted how in his own life the old conditions of childhood misery seemed to be re-emerging and it is part of the circle of his fate that it was in the same period that the weaknesses and failures of his genius were being emphasised by his contemporaries. He had reached a difficult transitional phase of his fame which could only exacerbate the discontents which, sometimes "secretly" and sometimes not, he suffered.

His resentlessness was, if anything, aggravated still further now, and, within a week or two of the New Year, he was planning a few days in Paris with Wilkie Collins, Dickens turning more and more often to Collins for relief from all his familiar responsibilities. (It was at Collins's dinner table that he first met Millais and, apparently not the least embarrassed by his vicious attack upon Millais's "Christ in the House of his Parents" five years before, he wrote a short note to the painter the following day in which he expressed admiration for his genius.) Certainly these responsibilities were getting no lighter, and from this time forward there emerges in Dickens's correspondence a line of pained and anxious rumination over the fate of his children; none of whom, daughters excepted, were "turning out" as he had once hoped and expected. Charley had come back from Germany and was trying to find work with a London firm; Walter was about to enter a school in Wimbledon where he would be spetifically trained for his duties in India. And their father, meanwhile, was taking long daily walks through the snow. Thinking of their future. Thinking of his future. Thinking of the further series of readings he had planned; already he was moving on from the success of *A Christmas Carol* and wanted to take extracts from one of his novels. Thinking of a new novel, the "motes" of which had been hovering around for some months. In fact certain elements of it had entered his consciousness, and, in an essay entitled "Gaslight Fairies" which he wrote for *Household Words* in February, many of the characteristics of the Dorrit family – as yet unborn – are to be found. Thinking of these things as he trudged through the snow, walking from Tavistock Square to Highgate and beyond during one of the coldest of winters.

And it was now than he did an unusual thing. He bought a notebook, of coarse paper and with green covers, and started making "Memoranda". Lists, names, plots, stories, characters, observations, reflections, anything which would help him in the construction or composition of the next novel. He used black ink at first, and half of the contents were inscribed in the first five months of 1855, although he continued to refer to it (some twenty-five pages in all) right up to the time of his death. Thus:

> The man who is incapable of his own happiness. One who is always in pursuit of happiness. Result. Where is happiness to be found then. Surely not everywhere? Can that be so, after all? Is *this* my experience?

These notes were never meant to survive, and it is only by accident that they have been recovered from the darkness into which Dickens tried to consign all of his most private reflections.

> A misplaced and mismarried man. Always, as it were, playing hide and seek with the world and never finding what Fortune seems to have hidden when he was born.

Dickens himself? Perhaps. But then again perhaps not. But how significant that even these most intimate asides are transmitted in the form of story, of anecdote, of character.

> The man whose vista is always stopped up by the image of Himself. Looks down a Long walk, and can't see round himself, or over himself, or beyond himself. – Is always blocking up his own way. – Would be such a good thing for him, if he could knock himself down.

Some of the memoranda written in the early months of 1855 are directly related to the novel which Dickens was soon to begin, but there are passages here which demonstrated the author in the act of observing the people among whom he walked.

> Bright-eyed creature selling jewels. The stones and the eyes.

This is Dickens in that preliminary act of creation, noting down significant details before they have been transformed into the material of his art. Watching.

> Found Drowned. The descriptive bill upon the wall, by the waterside.

Dickens also cut out an extract from *The Times*. And, on this occasion, was he thinking: and so, despite what I have written, it still goes on?

> Education for Little Children. Terms 14 to 18 guineas per annum; no extras or vacations.

Here are the materials of the nineteenth century, found objects resurfacing once more without the mediating power of Dickens's imagination. In their raw state. And his ideas, too, in their raw state, the stray reflections which occur to him as he walks through the snow of a London winter.

> Thinking of altered streets as the old streets – changed things as the unchanged things – the youth or girl quarrelled with all those years ago, as the same youth or girl now. Brought out of doors by an unexpected exercise of my latent strength of character, and then how strange!

This last passage was soon to be transposed into a larger context, but the important point is that Dickens was now writing down what he had seen or what he had imagined. Of course it is always possible that he had kept such memoranda from his earliest days as a novelist, and that it is merely by chance that one notebook has survived; but this is unlikely. He filled only half of the surviving notebook, but continued to use it for fifteen years: this does not suggest that he was a regular or habitual recorder of such episodes and perceptions. Forster has another explanation, and suggests that this little green-covered notebook is ". . . proof that he had been secretly bringing before himself, at least, the possibility that what had ever been his great support might some day desert him . . . He could no longer fill a wide-spread canvas with the same facility and certainty as of old; and he had frequently a quite unfounded apprehension of some possible breakdown, of which the end might be at any moment beginning." And how terrible a fear for a novelist who had written habitually and permanently, whose whole force of life and reality depended upon his writings. To fear a sudden "breakdown" when everything might end. And it was this, again according to Forster, which accounts for his "impatience and restlessness" in this period. Boulogne back to London. Now London to Paris which, in a sense, was a mission of despair. ". . . You will hear of me in Paris, probably next Sunday, and I *may* go on to Bordeaux. Have general ideas of emigrating in the summer to the mountain-ground between France and Spain. Am altogether in a dishevelled state of mind – motes of new books in the dirty air, miseries of older growth threatening to close upon me." It has been suggested that these old "miseries" have a direct connection with Dickens's increasingly unstable marriage, but they are older even than that. They go back to the beginning of his life, to the roots of his whole being, to that sense of being deprived and unfortunate, of being unloved and rejected by those whom he most needs. Or by someone in particular. Someone. "Why is it, that as with poor David, a sense always comes crushing upon me now, when I fall into low spirits, as of one happiness I have missed in life, and one friend and companion I have never made?" Certainly memories converge upon him so that at times it might seem as if he were literally being imprisoned by his past; just as, in the novel he was contemplating, images of prison radiate through the narrative. And what was the first memory of his past to return?

Gad's Hill Place; the house just outside Rochester, hallowed by its association with Falstaff, and hallowed, too, because of its association with his father. This was the house which John Dickens had shown his small son, and which he had held out to him as the possible reward for a successful man. This was the house he suddenly saw for sale at the beginning of February, on one of his many trips back to the landscape of his childhood. At once he made enquiries about it; "The spot and the very house are literally 'a dream of my childhood'," he told Wills. And how strange, that this dream should have persisted through all the years of his fame. Particularly since Gad's Hill Place is not in itself an altogether prepossessing house – certainly not as grand as Tavistock House itself – and yet so strong was the hold of Dickens's infancy upon him that it remained an enchanted spot. Perhaps he also wanted to placate his father's shade by purchasing it, just as his father had once wished. He had decided to visit it again three days later, but then suddenly he changed his mind. Something more significant had just occurred. Quite by chance, another aspect of his past had returned. The night before he was to leave for Rochester, he received a letter.

He had been reading by the fire, when some letters were given to him; he looked at them in a desultory fashion (he received and sent so many that he used to refer to himself as a sort of Home Office), and then found his mind to be "curiously disturbed" and "wandering away through so many years to such early times of my life"; he could find no reason for the change of mood, but he picked up the pile of letters once again and looked through them. It was then he saw certain handwriting, for the first time in over twenty years, and he recognised it at once: it was that of Maria Beadnell, the girl for whom he had conceived such a strident passion in the days when he was working as a shorthand reporter in the House of Commons. The days before any of his novels had been conceived. The days before his fame. So it was exactly to that time of his life that her letter sent him spinning. At least this was how Dickens described his reaction to Maria Beadnell herself, since he needed something of a theatrical overture for the recommencement of a friendship which had once been so important to him.

He wrote to her the next day, and it was no doubt in order to do so that he cancelled his arrangement with Wills to visit Gad's Hill Place; he explained to Wills that it was because of the heavy snow, but in fact only a few days before he had walked from Gravesend to Rochester through banks several feet high. He really needed time and quietness to reply to this letter from an emblem of his past. What Maria Beadnell (now in fact Mrs Maria Winter) wrote is not recorded, although to judge from Dickens's reply it was simply a letter to a famous friend in which she recounted news of her marriage, of her daughters, and of her family. It was later reported that she was fond of a little drink in the afternoon, and she may have decided to write to Dickens at a time of more than usual sentimentality or nostalgia. Dickens himself replied in a full flood of the same commodity. "I forget nothing of those times," he told her. This was almost the literal truth; he could still recall the details of conversations and clothes as if the events of his youth had happened just the day before. When we talk of Dickens's "nostalgia", then, it is wise to remember that it was of a special kind; he still *saw* and *heard* everything very clearly. "They are just as still and plain and clear as if I had never been in a crowd since, and had never seen or heard my own name out of my own house. What should I be worth, or what would labour and success be worth, if it were otherwise!" He ended with something of a peroration, indicating not for the first time that he was stylistically most conscious when his deepest emotions came into play. "In the strife and struggle of this great world where most of us lose each other so strangely, it is impossible to be spoken to out of the old times without a softened emotion." Incidentally in this same letter he had no "softened emotion" for Elizabeth Dickens: "My mother has a strong objection to being considered in the least old, and usually appears here on Christmas Day in a juvenile cap which takes an immense time in the putting on." Leaving aside the fact that Dickens himself had borrowed from his mother this reluctance to admit to ageing, his reference to her is remarkable here precisely because of its rarity – allusions, when they do occur, are usually of a dismissive or derisory kind. If it were not for the evidence of those who recalled how he cared for her after the death of John Dickens, one might be forgiven for thinking that he had altogether written her out of his life. But, if it is true that he found it difficult to talk about her, this was not from neglect but rather from a complex of emotions and associations upon which, perhaps, he did not want to dwell. In many ways he was still too close to her, and had once been too much hurt by her, to be anything but dismissive and abrupt about her now. The case of Maria Beadnell was quite different however; he had a "softened emotion" for her because she reminded him of the best part of his youth, and because she could no longer wound him as once she had. And so the peroration goes on. "You so belong to the days when the qualities that have done me most good since, were growing in my boyish heart that I cannot end my answer to you lightly. The associations my memory has with you made your letter more – I want a word – invest it with a more immediate address to me than such a letter could have from anybody else. Mr Winter will not mind that. We are all sailing away to the sea, and have a pleasure in thinking of the river we are upon, when it was very narrow and little."

Dickens travelled to Paris with Wilkie Collins the next day, clearly still in the thrall of his old passion or the old image of himself. Maria Winter had herself been so entranced by his reply – and how could she not be so, receiving what was practically a love letter from the greatest writer of the day? – that she sent another communication which Dickens received while in the French capital. It was a letter requesting him to make certain small purchases in Paris, but at once he sent back another long and even more affectionate reply. Among the contents of which: ". . . never was such a faithful and devoted poor fellow as I was . . . one perpetual idea of you . . . one creature who represented the whole world to me . . . you made me wretchedly happy . . . the most innocent, the most ardent, and the most disinterested days of my life had you for their Sun . . . the Dream were all of you . . ." This was a love letter in all but name; and how strange that Dickens should have surrendered so helplessly to his own remembrance that he seems almost to have believed that Mrs Winter, now in her forties, was still the same young girl he had once known. What is more remarkable still, it is not as if she had just emerged in his life after twenty years of silence; he had kept in intermittent contact with her family over the years and Dickens had in fact visited her soon after her marriage. After which occasion, according to Georgina Hogarth, he "had laughed about his former love for her in the carriage coming home". So his sudden passion (for want of a better word – affection is too light, and love too strong) is all the more extraordinary. But not so extraordinary, perhaps, if the real object of his devotion was not so much Maria as his own younger self. Of course he felt something for her; some regret, perhaps, that he had not married her. A regret sharpened by the increasingly burdensome presence of Catherine. A regret deepened still further by the middle-aged man's lament for the weakening of his own sexual attractiveness and sexual potency. And how much more poignant such memories must have seemed to him now that he was in Paris, "free", away from his family; the letter he composed in the French capital is notably more ardent than the one which he had written in London five days before.

He had written it from the Hôtel Meurice where he had taken an apartment with Wilkie Collins; he had decided to stay here rather than at the Hôtel Brighton, his normal quarters, because it allowed the two men more freedom in dining out – a necessary freedom for Dickens at a time when he needed what he called the "festive *diableries de Paris*". Collins described their rooms in the hotel as a ". . . delightful apartment, looking out on the Tuileries, gorgeously-furnished drawing-room, bedrooms with Turkey carpets, reception-room, halls, cupboards, passages – all to ourselves". In preparation for these days of pleasure Dickens had described Collins as his "vicious associate", by which hyperbolic phrase he meant no more than that he was what was then known as a "man of the world" and infinitely more amenable to the pleasures of the *boulevardier* than someone like John Forster. Unfortunately Collins suffered a sudden attack of rheumatic gout, and was for most of the day "laid up" in the gorgeous apartment while Dickens walked and walked through the city. But together, in the evening, they did manage to visit the restaurants and the theatres; although it cannot be said that Dickens was a particularly good audience on such occasions. Collins remembered many years later how in Paris "the second act generally exhausted his powers of endurance. I implored him to respect the *development of art*. He generally answered . . . 'I'm off, for a walk in the streets' . . . I firmly believe he never read one of Balzac's novels." No doubt there were occasions when Wilkie Collins walked the streets with him, although the younger man's capacity for exercise was severely limited and in any case he preferred the pleasure gardens or the dance halls to the alleys and by-ways of Parisian life. It has sometimes been suggested that Dickens took such excursions with Collins for the purpose of "picking up" prostitutes; Collins's reputation for venery was well deserved, perhaps, but it is unlikely that Dickens himself ever took part in anything more than close observation. His were often *mental* and *verbal* passions, not physical ones; his extravagant expressions about Parisian "diableries" were followed only by his usual reserved, watchful, and restrained behaviour.

He was back in London by the twenty-first of the month, having spent only nine days in France. There was another letter for him from Maria Beadnell, arrived the very morning after his return, and at once he sent another long reply addressed now to "My Dear Maria". Clearly it was sent to a secret address, or sent privately to her by some other means, because only two days later he was addressing a perfectly discreet letter to "My dear Mrs Winter"; in other words, he was writing her a letter which could be shown to her husband without embarrassment. It all sounds very much like a reprise of the sub-terfuges of youthful lovers. The first and more private letter was in response to an obviously impassioned communication from Maria, in which she tried to explain her coquettish behaviour so many years before. The game of "might have been" was one that Dickens on occasions liked to play, and in his response he dealt in tremulous tones with his own thwarted passion; ". . . nobody can ever know with what a sad heart I resigned you . . . My entire devotion to you, and the wasted tenderness of those hard years . . . whether any reputation the world can bestow is repayment to a man for the loss of such a vision of his youth as mine . . ." That was what he lamented, the vision of his youth. In all these letters to Maria there is revealed an almost hysterical willingness to love or to be loved, an eagerness to return to his youthful state matched only by the sorrow which he experiences when he realises that such a retreat is not possible. Yet none of these letters would have been written, none of this terrible thwarted feeling could have existed, if it were not for the deep unhappiness of Dickens's present life. He had returned to London, so dreary a city after the brightness of Paris, and a thaw had followed the snow. "Everything is weeping," he said. He had come back to a city damp and dirty and wet, and on the Sunday morning after his return the intolerable jangling of church bells disturbed him. In *Little Dorrit* this is also the vision vouchsafed to Arthur Clennam on his return to London, himself exasperated by the bells, in a city where there was "nothing for the spent toiler to do, but to compare the monotony of his seventh day with the monotony of his six days, think what a weary life he led, and make the best of it – or the worst, according to the probabilities". City of streets, of ". . . close wells and pits of houses . . ." The doleful, dark city; the city of the wrathful and the sad; the great prison of life. The lines from *Little Dorrit* had of course yet to be written, but even now the book was running through Dickens's head; and how significant, too, that the novel should emphasise the futility of travelling when you return to the place from which you started. Should emphasise a world where every road is darkened by the shadow of the prison house. These are the sentiments, lying too deep to be expressed in anything other than his fiction, which can be perceived between the lines of his correspondence with Maria Beadnell. They decided to meet; they agreed to do so secretly or, rather, Dickens concocted a plan whereby Maria would call upon Mrs Dickens and find her "not at home". What could be more natural than that she should then be received by Mr Dickens?

As soon as he saw her, all his longing and his passion fled. Georgina described her later; she "had become *very* fat! and quite commonplace . . ." The youthful Maria, conjured up so delicately and tenderly by Dickens, turned out no longer to exist. As he put it only a few months later in *Little Dorrit*, and in a passage which Maria herself was sure to read, "Clennam's eyes no sooner fell upon the subject of his old passion, than it shivered and broke to pieces". It is difficult to envisage Maria's feelings when Dickens goes on to write, ". . . Flora, who had seemed enchanting in all she said and thought, was diffuse and silly . . . Flora, who had been spoiled and artless long ago, was determined to be spoiled and artless now." But there was something crueller still.

In one of her letters to Dickens Maria had pointed out that she was now "toothless, fat, old and ugly" but Dickens had brushed aside this as the merest playful nonsense. But now he remembered it, all too well: "'I am sure,' giggled Flora, tossing her head with a caricature of her girlish manner, such as a mummer might have presented at her own funeral, if she had lived and died in classical antiquity, 'I am ashamed to see Mr Clennam, I am a mere fright, I know he'll find me fearfully changed, I am actually an old woman, it's shocking to be so found out, it's really shocking!'"

Two things call for notice here. How was it possible for Dickens not to realise that Maria *must* have changed over twenty years? He had evidence enough for that in his wife, as well as in himself. But this is where the extraordinary nature of Dickens's imagination has to be understood; the fact was that he *saw* Maria just as she had been in her youth, down to the smallest items of her clothing, and so vivid a picture literally bore down any existing or hypothetical reality. We have already seen how fictional characters were as real to him as the people among whom he lived and moved; Dickens had recreated Maria in his imagination, and nothing on earth could shake him from his vision. Until, that is, he actually saw her. And in that revulsion from her, that cruelty only too apparent in his portrait of Flora Finching, it is as if he were revenging himself upon the real Maria for shattering what he had called his "Dream". One of his constant laments concerns the sad and mournful manner in which reality falls short of the imagination – the central image here is the return to the dark streets after a night in the theatre – and in the case of the now stout and unprepossessing Maria all of his resentments found an easy target. And there was something else, too. According to Georgina Hogarth (who in this as well as in other matters reveals a sharp tongue), Maria ". . .was always romantic, and used to talk a great deal about her early love". Her early love, of course, being Dickens himself. Is this the origin of one of the observations in Dickens's green note-book of memoranda: "The sentimental woman feels that the comic, undesigning, unconscious man is 'Her Fate'. – I her fate? God bless my soul, it puts me into a cold perspiration to think of it. *I* her fate? How can *I* be her fate? I don't mean to be. I don't want to have anything to do with her. Sentimental woman perceives nevertheless that Destiny must be accomplished"? If this is a pen-portrait of Maria Beadnell and Charles Dickens, it is of course one well advanced towards fiction; and that is precisely the point. In his passionate letters to her and in his subsequent revulsion, the only important and real thing to Dickens is his own vision. His own image of Maria is the one thing that matters and, when it is destroyed, he does not scruple to parody the real woman in his next novel. Of course in his actual treatment of Maria after their meeting, he is as tactful as it was possible to be: the passionate epistles are followed by letters of excuse or delay, in which he invokes the sacred name of his art in order to explain his inability to meet her. But the real feeling is expressed in the novel itself, where he redirects his anger and where also he finds solace in the imaginative reconstruction of a situation for which he bears no personal blame. Whereas in fact the opposite was the case; *he* had pursued Maria, *he* had over-ridden her objections and raised her hopes. The most pleasant letter he now wrote was in fact to Maria's daughter, Ella, where some of his old playfulness and tenderness re-emerge. Is it any wonder that so many of his contemporaries found him "strange"? And what of Maria in her later life? A nursemaid in the Winter household recalled that she was "sweet and kindly" in the early part of the day, but that then she would begin to drink. "All her refinement and restraint seemed then to break down, and it would be during these times . . . that she would refer to Dickens. She had a tremendous collection of his books by that time. They were to be found all about the house. When excited she would take them from the shelves and run through their pages, commenting on their contents, interspersing them with references to the author." Did she take down *Little Dorrit*, too, and read over the descriptions of the woman modelled so unflatteringly upon her? "At other times she would lie on the couch and say, 'Nurse, it was here that he used to sit', and I have seen her, in one of these moods, actually kiss the place on the couch, and recall something that Charles Dickens had said to her . . ." A sad story, this sentimental, lost, bibulous woman – blasted, as it were, by Dickens's fame.

And what of Dickens, too, his fame meaning nothing to him? All his old restlessness had returned, the brief episode with Maria Beadnell only emphasising the miseries with which he felt himself to be surrounded. In "Gone to the Dogs", an ironic essay on private and public misfortune, which he now wrote for *Household Words*, he once more laments the loss of his first innocent love and chronicles the growth of seedy worldliness in men and women; themes which he has deployed before but here they are explicitly linked first to financial chicanery and disgrace, then to national ruin itself. The last two subjects were also to be explored in *Little Dorrit*, the novel which he was now contemplating. So, in his short essay, the loss of innocent love, the prevalence of financial malpractice and the conduct of the Crimean War are linked together as expressions in miniature of the same anger and bitterness which were soon to break out elsewhere. That there was anger in him now is not in doubt. He let slip in one letter that he was ". . . dead sick of the Scottish tongue in all its moods and tenses", which can only be a reference to his wife and to her family. There was also, as Forster himself suggested, a direct link between this anger and his interventions both in literary matters and in public polity.

The literary matters may have been the less serious, but they were certainly the more protracted. Dickens's scheme with Bulwer-Lytton for the Guild of Literature and Art was for the moment in abeyance, for complex legal reasons, and all of his energy was directed instead towards the reform of the Royal Literary Fund. The controversy is now of relatively marginal interest, significant perhaps only for Dickens's behaviour during the course of an immensely protracted dispute between those members of the Royal Literary Fund who wanted to change its charter and make it genuinely a professional organisation dedicated to the rights of authors and those who wished it to remain what it had been for some years, a charitable body on the model of many such nineteenth-century institutions which spent a great deal of money in administration and rather less on its charitable deeds. In other words, Dickens, temporarily baulked by the slow progress of the Guild, wished to incorporate some of the Guild's principles into the much older Fund.

He and his supporters (among them Forster) met secretly two days before the next annual meeting in order to plan their strategy; their tactic was one of surprise, and it was only on the morning of the meeting itself that Dickens sent a letter to the secretary of the Fund, Octavian Blewitt, announcing that he would move a motion demanding the re-organisation of the Fund's charter. His speech was in fact at the time greeted with applause and with laughter; there was no one so good as Dickens at the kind of irony which needed to be directed against the antiquated structure of the Fund, and by the time the meeting was over Dickens was so pleased with his success that he told Collins, "Virtually, I consider the thing done." But he over estimated his powers of persuasion. The thing was not "done" at all, and over the next three years there were a series of proposals, counter-proposals, pamphlets, speeches and special meetings which left matters more or less as they had always been. On this first occasion of dispute, however, there was a conversation between Blewitt and Dickens which gives some sense of Dickens's demeanour as the "clubbable", responsible public man. It is recorded by Dickens himself but there is no reason to doubt the general accuracy of his report. Blewitt, a defender of the status quo, was obliquely suggesting that Dickens had been able to set up a special committee by fraudulent voting procedures.

Blewitt: "O, I'm very glad to see you, because here's a curious point has arisen, and I want your opinion on it very much. Supposing three of four partners in a firm, and the firm to have given ten guineas, one of the partners has got a right to vote, has he?"

Dickens (in tones of gentlest suavity): "Oh dear me! that seems to me to be perfectly clear. If you doubted whether that partner represented the firm in voting, you would write to the firm to ask the question, and on their replying 'yes', there would be an end of it."

Blewitt: "You feel quite certain about that?"

Dickens: "Perfectly."

Blewitt: "Well then, here's another curious thing. We think there were people here yesterday holding up their hands who were not members. Did you see P—— here?"

Dickens: "No."

Blewitt: "Well, Sir Henry Ellis says *he* saw him, and he is not a member. I myself saw a gentleman, with his back to the door, who, when I offered him a ballot paper, told me he was not a member."

Dickens (with the utmost gravity): "Aye-aye! On which side do you suppose these people voted?"

Blewitt (colouring): "Oh, I say nothing about that. We have all an equal interest in keeping them out, that's all I mean."

Dickens: "But whose business is it to see that none but members are in the room on such an occasion?"

Blewitt (colouring again): "Why, if I had proposed to challenge them, Mr Dilke might have charged me with some sinister object."

Dickens: "But how about ascertaining all that before they got into the room at all?"

Blewitt made a proposal on this, to which Dickens assented, and "we parted with infinite affection". A long dialogue, but one that neatly epitomises Dickens's presence of mind, his mental agility, and his desire always to come out "on top" in any situation. In fact his own attitudes to the controversy are an interesting index of his temperament. He had said that he wanted to do what was "generous and right" only a few days after he had been exploring the possibility that the Queen herself might be persuaded to withhold her subscription to the Fund; and then, when at a later stage it was clear that the argument was going against him, he told Macready that "I am resolved to reform it or ruin it – one or the other". Clearly nothing was meant to survive the force of Dickens's irate will, even to the point where he would destroy that which he could not control. Yet just as he had over-estimated the effect of his original speech, he vastly over-stated his own capacity either for "reform" or "ruin"; he failed in his bid, and the Royal Literary Fund carried on much as before without the benefit of Dickens's membership. The important thing, for Dickens, had been his own *rightness* and not the survival of the Fund itself. It is reminiscent of his treatment of Maria Beadnell, where it had been his own needs and attitudes rather than the woman herself which claimed his attention.

Nevertheless there had been a certain justice in Dickens's attempt to reform the Fund, based as it was upon aristocratic patronage and the distribution of charity to deserving members of the literary tribe; it was precisely his dislike of amateurish organisation and of conventional patronage which informed most of his political and social judgments in this period, and so it was for exactly the same reasons that, even as he was conducting the battle against the Royal Literary Fund, he agreed to join the Administrative Reform Association. His interest in it had been aroused by Austen Layard, an M.P. who became the chief spokesman for the Association in Parliament. Dickens had met Layard at the house of Miss Burdett-Coutts in March and, although they had in fact encountered one another before, it was only now that Dickens formed a closer association with him. Layard himself was, like Dickens, quintessentially a man from the early years of the century, liberal, enthusiastic, energetically at home in any number of activities; he was already famous for his excavations at Nineveh but he had entered Parliament in 1852 and by the following year was Under-Secretary for Foreign Affairs. His membership of the Administrative Reform Association was largely the result of his disgust at the maladministration which had taken such a terrible toll upon the British troops in the Crimea, Sebastopol and Balaklava having become bywords for military incompetence and administrative bungling on a massive scale. And Layard was by no means alone –

it was precisely Dickens's own horror in the face of what was happening in the Crimea which had led to his friendship with him and to his joining the Association. As soon as they had met, in fact, Dickens was pledging support to his cause; and, such was the novelist's influence, he was also able to ensure that similar support was expressed in *Punch*, in the *Illustrated London News* and the *Weekly Chronicle* as well as his own *Household Words*. There was much to be said. Reports (especially those by William Russell in *The Times*) had already begun to convey the full effect of the mismanagement both of troops and of supplies. Disease; malnutrition; the failure of the War Office (or, rather, the Commissariat department) to dovetail men and supplies, leading to the deaths of thousands of soldiers; the lack of medical facilities; the lack of proper clothing to withstand the extreme cold. These were the issues which Layard and his associates tried to raise again and again, with only limited success. But, although the débâcle in the Crimea was the single most important reason for the formation of the Administrative Reform Association, it also embraced larger aims which were very much those of Dickens himself. And how could it not have done so since its membership was made up of professional men, businessmen, self-made men – in fact the whole range of practical, energetic mid-Victorians who disliked what was still the aristocratic and "'tuft-hunting" bias of government, of toadying and patronage, of the sons of sons who packed the various offices of the Civil Service? They were very much like the Benthamite radicals of the earlier part of the century, but shorn of the ideology or cant and concerned only to campaign for the proper conduct of public affairs and the wise use of public money. To attack what Dickens called, in an open letter to the Association, ". . . the present system of mismanaging the public affairs, and mis-spending the public money . . ."

Dickens did not in fact speak publicly until the third meeting of the Association in June, when in some of his most powerful language he derided the conduct of the war and denounced a government which seemed to stand against the real interests of the country it purported to serve. "With shame and indignation lowering among all classes of society, and this new element of discord piled on the heaving basis of ignorance, poverty and crime, which is always below us . . ." In the course of the speech he used a phrase, ". . . what is everybody's business is nobody's business . . ." which was to prove a signal towards the novel he was now actively contemplating; the original title of *Little Dorrit* was to be *Nobody's Fault*. Thus do Dickens's political, social and imaginative concerns congregate together at a time when he, the greatest novelist of his age, mounted a platform with politicians and businessmen in order to express that "true politics" which Layard, in a subsequent speech, associated with him. He was as always perfectly dressed, in white waistcoat and evening dress, and one of the reporters observing the occasion noticed how clearly and cleverly he spoke; telling a joke ". . . with a jump in the voice and an archness of expression which showed Dickens to be a consummate actor". It was in fact the theatricality of the speech and the setting which impressed this reporter, the setting itself being Drury Lane Theatre and Dickens himself having ". . . acquired the habit, peculiar to all good speakers, of opening wide his mouth to give full effect to the charm of oral delivery". But Dickens was also very angry, and very determined. He launched a savage attack upon Lord Palmerston in *Household Words* and, at a private dinner given by Lord John Russell, where other politicians were present, ". . . I gave them a little bit of truth . . . that was like bringing a Sebastopol battery among the polite company". And one can picture him on that occasion; talking down any opposition, talking quickly in his own fierce and determined way.

We may in fact take the Crimean War as an index of Dickens's "true" politics for it was in this year, 1855, that his convictions were sharpened and strengthened. Of course his instincts had always been the same, and his attack upon the maladministration of the war was only a further extension of those attacks which he had made in earlier life – against parishes, against vestries, against a national government which refused to co-ordinate proper sanitation even in the face of constant misery and epidemic disease. From his early manhood, also, Dickens had acquired a distrust of, and even distaste for, the public manners and public service of the "aristocracy". And, although in public he was generally concerned to suggest that all classes should work together, in private he was much more scathing about a "political aristocracy" which would ruin the country and which had already implicitly set itself against the claims and demands of the other classes. That was his basic position then, and it was one which the conduct of the Crimean War only confirmed. There was another central stance from which he never moved, his hatred of Parliament, and his disgust at a "rotten" system of representative government. At this time Aberdeen had replaced Russell as Prime Minister, only to be replaced in turn by Palmerston; the administration of the country was being arranged through varying alliances, deals and coalitions which owed less to a concern for national welfare than the need to satisfy various political interests. An unstable time; a difficult time; but in its way only an exaggeration of those characteristics of hypocrisy, self-interest and even bribery which Dickens always associated with the House of Commons. In that sense he was and remained a "Radical" (sometimes, at the end of his life, he would substitute "Liberal"), one who four months before his death declared that ". . . our system fails" and who had earlier confessed that "I have come to the conclusion that representative Government is a miserable failure among us". He hated Parliament always, therefore, but in the period under review he particularly hated Palmerston; "the emptiest impostor," he called him, ". . . ever known". So it is interesting that a friend of Dickens, Sir Arthur Helps, should after the novelist's death see many points of comparison between Palmerston and Dickens himself. "There was . . . a considerable resemblance between these two remarkable men in several points. They both had a certain hearty bluffness of manner. There was a sea-going way about them, as of a captain on his quarter-deck. They were both tremendous walkers, and took interest in every form of labour, rustic, urban, or commercial. Then, too, they made the most and the best of everything that came before them: stood up sturdily for their own way of thinking; and valued greatly their own peculiar experiences." Dickens only lacked the politician's "supreme serenity of temper", an attribute which in any case Dickens did not particularly admire (principally because he never possessed it himself). But in this consonance between the two men are we not reminded of the fact that some people despise most heartily those whom they most closely resemble? And, when Dickens called Palmerston "the emptiest impostor", was he not divining in Palmerston's character a particular vice which he himself might on occasions possess?

So in this period Dickens would have swept away the current form of representative government without compunction (without being very clear, perhaps, about what to put in its place), and in a letter to Layard he suggested that if the people were to "array themselves peacefully, but in vast numbers against a system, that they know to be rotten altogether – make themselves heard like the Sea all round this Island – I for one should be in such a movement, heart and soul, and should think it a duty of the plainest kind to go along with it (and try to guide it), by all possible means". Strong words although, perhaps, one should remember from his threats against the Royal Literary Fund that he sometimes allowed his words, or his pen, to run away with him. In any case there was clearly no possibility of any such mass movement arising in England, and one of the salient aspects of Dickens's political rhetoric lies in his awareness that the "people", however they were to be defined, were so alienated from the administration of the country that they did nothing now but look gloomily on. They were lethargic and "you can no more help a people who do not help themselves, than you can help a man who does not help himself". So their rage and dissatisfaction were simply "smouldering", but it would take only a chance event or grievance to set off the "devil of a conflagration as never has been beheld since". He even compared the state of England to that of France before the Revolution and, although it has seemed odd to many commentators that Dickens should so misread the mood of the nation that he seriously believed it to be at least close to some kind of general revolution, it ought to be remembered that the images of smouldering and burning owe as much to his recent work on *Bleak House* as to any more general political understanding.

Indeed this leads to the heart of the matter, and sometimes the rather puzzling matter, of Dickens's political beliefs. He took the world personally; he often adopted in his imagination the role of victim, and was thus able to deal in powerful and poignant manner with the sufferings of the poor and the afflicted. It often seems, in fact, that his reforming zeal sprang from a sense of personal injury or personal fear; he so disliked any kind of authority wielded over him that, as we have observed, it was precisely against those two areas where he had once been in a subordinate position, the House of Commons (as reporter) and the Law (as shorthand copier), that he directed his most strident attacks. But just as he was quick to forget issues which he had once raised with all his usual fervour, so he seems always to have been relatively uninterested in those matters which did not touch upon that secret self at the heart of all his formulations. Indeed, in those social issues with which he did not feel himself to be directly engaged, he tended to become conservative and moralistic. But this is not to diminish the full scope of his reforming vigour; just as he could never settle in a room until he had arranged all the furniture to his own specifications so he found it difficult *not* to suggest changes or clamour for improvements with a manner which one contemporary described as ". . . . full of ardour for the public good" but also "somewhat despotic". It could be said, therefore, that his political principles sprang from emotional needs and not from argument; as a result they are not really susceptible to rationalisation, and cannot be said to form a coherent whole. This in turn explains a number of paradoxes which can be found throughout Dickens's life and career. He disliked magistrates in general but on more than one occasion wished to become one. He detested and pilloried the Law but it was only in this year that he formally withdrew his application to join the Bar. He was an opponent of insularity and that species of jingoism which trusted only in this "right little, tight little, island" but on more than one occasion was excessively jingoistic, particularly in regard to those "savages" who disliked British colonial rule. We shall see how his urgent belief in social peace and stability came to be expressed in a philosophy (if that is the word) of social paternalism; but even here there are doubts and ambiguities, his own experience of fathers leaving him less than fully convinced about the nature of paternalism itself. That is why, in *Barnaby Rudge*, in a novel dominated by fathers, Dickens seems most intently to sympathise with the rioters and incendiaries bent upon destroying the prison of the state. Again, his firmest belief is in the family, and in society itself assuming the structure of a family, and yet of course in his fiction families tend to represent disunited, difficult and even dangerous areas of human conflict. There are inconsistencies here, inconsistencies springing from the constant battles between his emotional needs and perceptions, which cannot really be reconciled. That is partly the explanation for that commonly advanced description of Dickens's social and political creeds: he knew what he was *against* but found it far more difficult to give a convincing or even half-substantial idea of what precisely he was *for*. The closest we can get to it, in general terms, is in his attitude to the game of cricket.

Two years before his death, while he was in America, he sent a letter to his son, Harry, concerning the organisation of the Gad's Hill Cricket Club, which was to be composed both of "gentlemen" and "working men". "The first thing to be avoided," he told his son, "is, the slightest appearance of patronage . . . The second thing to be avoided is, the deprival of the men of their just right to manage their own affairs . . ." He then goes on to suggest that Harry should nominate himself as captain on the grounds that he would be better able to deal with the "gentlemen" whom they wished to join the club, that he should then propose that the "gentlemen" should pay twice the subscription of "working men" but that all members, regardless of class, should have an equal vote. Then . . . "draw up the club's rules and regulations, amending them where they want amendment". And he concludes thus: "Whatever you do, let the men ratify; and let them feel their little importance, and at once perceive how much better the business begins to be done." Here we have Dickens's dream of society in miniature, an harmonious arrangement of all classes in which the paternalism of the gentleman captain is linked with the due recognition of the "little importance" of the workers, in which the doctrine of self-help is balanced by the notion of financial subvention. But it is the need for co-operation between the classes that lies at the heart of his design, and indeed is the one theme to which he reverts again and again in his public speeches, amounting to a demand for ". . . a fusion of several classes on a good, common, mutual ground". That is why, despite his private distaste for the "aristocratic" class, in public at least he continually urged the connection of class with class for the purposes of mutual benefit. "I wish to avoid placing in opposition here," he had said during his speech to the Administrative Reform Association, "the two words Aristocracy and People. I am one of those who can believe in the virtues and uses of both, and, I would elevate or depress neither, at the cost of a single just right belonging to either."

There is plenty of evidence to suggest, also, that he was instinctively and often expressly conservative in his real social attitudes. There is no need to rehearse here once again his penal policies, which amounted to a general call for harsh discipline, real punishment, and, for some offenders, literal life imprisonment. In that area he was closer to Carlyle than to any of the liberal reformers, to such a degree that he might well be called "reactionary". But, if he was an authoritarian in such matters, how could he be otherwise – this man who ran his own house as if it were a little machine of domesticity, and whose central impulse in any social activity was to dominate and to organise? He was also a strict disciplinarian when it came to matters of public morals, an amusing instance of which is cited by Dickens himself when, quite unconscious of any irony, he declared in *Household Words* that he had felt compelled to take action against those who used bad language in public places. "The writer has himself obtained a conviction by a police magistrate . . . for this shameful and demoralising offence – which is as common and as public as the mud in the streets. He obtained it with difficulty, the charge not being within the experience of anyone concerned; but, he insisted on the law, and it was clear (wonderful to relate!); and was enforced." We can see Dickens hauling in an offender; insistent, peremptory, in the face of what was no doubt the incredulity of the authorities. This sort of authoritarianism or paternalism is connected, too, with the evident fact that he never really sympathised with the working class as such; he pitied and helped individual members of that class, but he had scant sympathy for any kind of collective or organised groupings within it. Here was a man who had, after all, successfully suppressed any public knowledge of his own working-class experience in the blacking factory and who had, at the time, shrunk from contact with his "low" companions. He was, as we have seen, hostile to those Chartist and trades union leaders who took advantage of their position to incite demonstrations or strikes. But he was not opposed to public demonstrations as such; in fact it was in June of this year that he expressed sympathy for disturbances by a crowd in Hyde Park demonstrating against a "Sunday Bill", currently before Parliament, which would severely curtail any right of Sunday trading. For Dickens this was yet another instance of the fatal miscomprehension of what he once called the "People governed" by the "People governing". Yet at the same time he abhorred the violence among the demonstrators themselves and on many occasions stressed the need for peacefulness, order, and stability even in the actions of the dispossessed. His main objective was for a "great peaceful constitutional change" and even if he was, as he explained, "a Reformer heart and soul . . ." his greatest fear was of the anarchy which can succeed riot and demonstration, precisely the anarchy which he evokes so masterfully in *Barnaby Rudge* and in *A Tale of Two Cities* but which he detested when it came closer to home. Towards the end of his life, for example, he opposed any demonstrations on behalf of a Fenian amnesty; ". . . the time must come," he wrote, "when this kind of threat and defiance will have to be forcibly stopped." There was such a thing as "unreasonable toleration", he added, and went on to say that such demonstrations would attract ". . . all the ruffian part of the population of London, and that is a serious evil which any one of a thousand accidents might render mischievous". These are not the remarks of a reactionary middle-aged man. He had been saying the same kind of thing all his life. It is the belief of a man who would give money to tramps but then follow the gift with what he called "moral admonitions". It is the expression of a man who believed in the virtues of self-help; as he had said at a meeting of the Newsvendors' Benevolent Association, ". . . it is only by your thoroughly helping yourselves that the public can ever be got to help you".

It is also the sentiment of a man who, in political and social reforms, was thoroughly practical both in his aims and in his methods; who believed in the importance of provident societies, mutual insurance companies and savings banks. Yet although he asserted the need for state intervention in the areas of housing and education, he never really attacked the nature or structure of the industrial society growing up around him; nor did he have much to say against specific commercial institutions. There is no doubt, either, that he believed in an "élite", an élite made up not of blood relations but of professional men, practical men, self-made men. That is why he had great faith in the possibility of progress but, if we return once more to that speech at the Administrative Reform Association with which we began, he knew ". . . that our public progress is far behind our private progress . . . we are not more remarkable for our private wisdom and success in matters of business than we are for our public folly and failure . . ." A thriving industrial and commercial society; an essentially paternalistic state, one in which the class system would not be abolished but in which class worked harmoniously with class; a political system based on some other principle of representative democracy, and preferably excluding conventional parliamentary government; state intervention in certain key areas of education and sanitation, but nothing beyond that. A curious amalgam of stated beliefs, perhaps, but political attitudes cannot really be transposed from one century to the next; this was a politics for the nineteenth century, and one peculiarly bound up with the conditions of that time. To look at it now is like looking at those wonderful specimens of nineteenth-century factory machinery – large, cumbersome, heavy but powerful and efficient nonetheless. It ought also to be remembered that these were Dickens's *stated* beliefs; his imaginative concerns and preoccupations often work against them, undermining them, deflecting them, even destroying them. Just as Dickens in evening dress at the Administrative Reform Association is not the same figure as that haunted, driven man who made faces in his mirror as he fashioned his characters out of his own voice.

He was driven still. He was thinking of travelling to Spain, and had dinner with Richard Ford, author of a *Handbook for Travellers in Spain*; an American guest on the same occasion "did not think him agreeable or quite at his ease". Of course, at this juncture, he may well have been neither. ". . . I am in a state of restlessness impossible to be described –

impossible to be imagined – wearing and tearing to be experienced. I sit down of a morning, with all kinds of notes for my new book (for which by the bye, I think I have a capital name) – resolve to begin – get up, and go out, and walk a dozen miles – sit down again next morning – get up and go down a railroad . . . make engagements and am too distraught to keep them . . .'' So at least he had embarked upon his new novel, despite all his restlessness, the "capital name" being *Nobody's Fault*. He began the first chapter and by the end of May had reached the middle of the first number, but, as he had intimated, he could not work on it continuously or successfully. In fact he broke off altogether for three weeks in order to dash into another round of private theatricals. On this occasion he decided upon *The Lighthouse*, a melodrama of a sufficiently sentimental kind which Wilkie Collins had just written and which Dickens thought could be performed to advantage in the schoolroom of Tavistock House. He consulted with Collins, who could hardly have disagreed, and rehearsals began at the beginning of June; among the cast Collins himself, Mark Lemon and Augustus Egg. Dickens also asked Clarkson Stanfield to paint the backdrop for the little play, and in fact the artist produced two scenes – one of the interior of the lighthouse in question, and the other a seascape (which was Stanfield's speciality). How odd, incidentally, that he should wish to put words in Stanfield's mouth; on Tuesday afternoon Dickens wrote to him with a lament that "O, what a pity it is not the outside of the Light'us, with the sea a-rowling agin it!" and then the following day wrote to Mark Lemon with the news that "Stanny says he is only sorry it is not the outside of the lighthouse with a raging sea . . ." Dickens spread his own sentiments liberally across all of his friends, on these occasions of "communal" effort, and in the rehearsals he was once again the source of all wisdom and authority. The members of the cast nicknamed him Mr Crummles, after the grandiloquent actor-manager in *Nicholas Nickleby*, although there were times when he seems to have behaved more like Mrs Squeers.

Rehearsals were at seven each evening in the two weeks before the first performance, and Dickens's oldest son remembers how carefully his father arranged all of the scenic and atmospheric effects. "Marcus Stone . . . turned the wind if I remember rightly – the long box of rain, the flash for the lightning, the sheet of iron for the rattle of the thunder, besides half-a-dozen cannon balls to roll about on the floor to simulate the shaking of the Lighthouse as it was struck by the waves – and we dropped, I recollect, various heavy articles to represent the thud and crash of the billows.'' How carefully Dickens prepared, even for a theatre which could hold no more than twenty-five people at a time. Charles Dickens junior goes on: "It was nervous work, this riding on the whirlwind and directing the storm. It had to be done all through the first act, exactly at the word, of course, and only on each occasion, for a rigidly defined time, and I could always tell by the very look of my father's shoulders at rehearsal as he sat on the stage with his back to me that he was ready for the smallest mistake, and that if I didn't wave that flag at exactly the right moment, or if the component parts of my storm were at all backward in attending to their business, there would promptly come that fatal cry of 'stop!' which pulled everything up short, and heralded a wigging for somebody.'' It all sounds rather terrifying for everyone involved as Dickens, balked at his work on his new novel, threw himself into the play with an intensity which his son here describes very well. Dickens even wrote a song for the play which, curiously enough, was derived from his childhood reading, more than thirty years before, of the story of a shipwreck. The East Indiaman, *Grosvenor*, had been wrecked off the coast of Africa and the remains of her crew carried with them a seven-year-old boy in a fruitless journey overland to the Cape, a painful story of suffering and childhood death, and one which must have powerfully impressed the young Dickens. Impressed him enough, at any rate, to write a series of verses on the subject so many years later –

> The winds blew high, the waters raved,
>   A ship drove on the land,
> A hundred human creatures saved
>   Kneel'd down upon the sand.
> Three-score were drown'd, three-score were thrown
>   Upon the black rocks wild,
> And thus among them, left alone,
>   They found one helpless child.

The song was performed by Mamie in the production, and these verses on the sad fate of a "helpless child" were set to the music of "Little Nell" by George Linley. A helpless child, fruitless travel, the return of Little Nell; these were some of the matters concerning Dickens at a time just before *Nobody's Fault* was changed to *Little Dorrit*, and another child made her appearance on the stage of Dickens's imagination.

The Lighthouse itself was performed on four separate occasion; the first in front of servants and tradespeople, and the other three before a "select" audience, the handbill for the occasion promising a "Domestic Melo-drama, In Two Acts" at "The Smallest Theatre in The World". Dickens in the role of Aaron Gurnock, the head Lightkeeper, was deemed to be a great success of the tragic style; his son remembered that he had an "extraordinary melodramatic intensity and force", and Dickens himself noticed with satisfaction afterwards that the audience "were crying vigorously". One member of the audience observed in particular how Dickens had ". . . a sad, sacred, lost gaze, as of one whose spirit was away from present objects, and wholly occupied with absent and long-past images". Elizabeth Yates, quondam actress, came up to him after the performance and declared, "O Mr Dickens what a pity it is you can do anything else!" The last performance was followed by a supper and dance which lasted until five the next morning; among those not invited to the occasion, however, was poor Maria Winter. Her baby died just a few days before the first performance, and Dickens wrote to tell her that "it is better that I should not come to see you. I feel quite sure of that, and will think of you instead." Enough said. She had been effectively written out of his life before he wrote her back into his fiction, and not even the death of her baby would mitigate his early portrait of the garrulous Flora Finching.

Now it was to the new novel that he turned again. There was one more performance of *The Lighthouse* at the Kensington house of a certain Colonel Waugh (it was a presentation for charity) and then Dickens took part in a rowing expedition from Oxford to London before going down for the summer to Folkestone. He had chosen the resort because of its reputation for quietness (Broadstairs had now become far too noisy) and it was here, at 3 Albion Villas, in a small house, ". . . always to be known by having all the windows open, and soap and water flying out of all the bedrooms", that he was intent upon the narrative he had been contemplating so long. He was in daily communication with W. H. Wills and once a week went up to the office of *Household Words*, but his real work, as he sat and looked out to sea, was now here.

He was clearly in a highly receptive and excitable mood. He was profoundly affected by a story submitted to him, in which a man is wronged by the woman whom he loves – ". . . I have never been so much surprised and struck by any manuscript . . ." – and just a few days later he was moved by Holme Lee's novel, *Gilbert Massenger*, in which the most important theme is that of inherited madness. He told Wills that "it was more painfully pathetic than anything I have read for I don't know how long". Clearly he was willing to be touched by almost anything (except Maria's grief at the death of her child). A man affected equally, then, by private restlessness and the spectacle of public decay. The "vision" of his youth shattered. The country close to ruin. Images of desuetude. Images of dreary London. *Nobody's Fault* has begun.

Never since *Barnaby Rudge* had any novel so long a period of gestation; he had finished half of the first number by the middle of May but had, as we have seen, then broken off to perform *The Lighthouse*. (The first number would not in fact be published until December.) But this interval was only the symptom of a larger confusion and difficulty. His son, Charley, was to say of *Little Dorrit* that ". . . my father started [it] in a panic lest his powers of imagination should fail him", a domestic comment which lends weight to Forster's description of his friend's "sluggish fancy" in the preliminary stages of composition and Forster's belief that ". . . the old, unstinted, irrepressible flow of fancy had received temporary check". All these factors are meant to explain what Forster called ". . . a droop in his invention". Posterity has not shared that judgment, however, and the signs of delay and confusion in the early stages of writing have less to do with any diminution of inventive skill than with what was for Dickens almost a unique problem; he had no "guiding idea", or leading theme, which would propel him through the narrative, and all the preliminary memoranda suggest that he was casting around for some time in an effort to make all of his "pictures" and preoccupations cohere. We have already seen how the original title, *Nobody's Fault*, sprang directly from his disgust with the maladministration of the country and the Crimean War – even though in his typical manner he was about to embody those concerns in the figure of a man who was to say at every calamity, "Well it's a mercy, however, nobody was to blame you know!" The epitome of bureaucracy and Red Tapeism located in a phrase. But this in itself was clearly not enough to fructify Dickens's imagination, and when he went down to Folkestone in the middle of July he was still uncertain about his general direction. It was only after he had completed a version of the first number and had already started the second that the "leading idea" occurred to him; he wrote it down in his working notes as: "People to meet and part as travellers do, and the future connexion between them in the story, not to be now shewn to the reader but to be worked out as in life." No longer just the theme of bungling and mismanagement, but a deeper note; a note which had sounded through his own travels on the continent, and one which emerged in the new second chapter he now wrote, "Fellow Travellers", which ends: "And thus ever, by day and night, under the sun and under the stars, climbing the dusty hills and toiling along the weary plains, journeying by land and journeying by sea, coming and going so strangely, to meet and to act and react on one another, move all we restless travellers through the pilgrimage of life." It is clear from the manuscript of the novel that Dickens now began what was to become chapter three, and after that threnody on the pilgrimage of life he brings Arthur Clennam home to a London which is ". . . gloomy, close and stale", a London of melancholy streets and soot-blackened houses. Now that the mood of the novel had been set and some of its central themes settled, he went on in better spirits. From this time forward he maintained the routine of composition which was so important to him: he wrote from nine until two, and then walked until five. It is as if the energy expended on the new story only increased the restless physical energy which he had to expel in violent exercise, on some occasions ". . . swarming up the face of a gigantic and precipitous cliff in a lonely spot overhanging the wild sea-beach".

He worked straight on from the first to the second number, taking up the threads he had so lately introduced. He was still more tentative than usual, casting about in his notes to himself for the proper continuation, until it was clear that a girl named "Dorrit" was to be given a larger context and a home; the home being the Marshalsea Prison where Dickens's own father had once been imprisoned and where now "Little Dorrit", as he had decided to call her, returns to her father and her ungrateful siblings. The novel was growing, and changing, all the time. Wilkie Collins came down to spend some time with the Dickens family in Folkestone, and some relatives also arrived, but he was now confident enough of the drift of his story to inform his German publisher, Tauchnitz, about the publishing arrangements for the new novel. And, as he moved on to its third instalment, all those elements which had been lying quietly unworked beneath the surface of his imagination could now be used. He wrote a satirical chapter on the Circumlocution Office, that epitome of "tuft-hunting" amateur bureaucracy; ". . . I have been blowing off a little of indignant steam," he told Macready, "which would otherwise blow me up . . ." But this was no longer just to be the satirical novel which Dickens had at first intended; he was now extending his theme, so that Circumlocution becomes the whole vast babble of the world, the world of travellers, the world of hypocrisy, the world of imprisonment. He now decided, too, that he would raise up the Dorrit family from poverty and make them rich, and in that transition show the emptiness of wealth. Now the story was "everywhere – heaving in the sea, flying with the clouds, blowing in the wind . . ." The sea is beneath his window, and he looked out upon the sky and ocean as he worked; ". . . such movement in it, such changes of light upon the sails of ships and wake of steam-boats, such dazzling gleams of silver far out at sea, such fresh touches on the crisp wave-tops as they break and roll towards me . . ." And the novel everywhere. Working upon it from nine until two, and then dashing out of the house. ". . . I can still in reason walk any distance, jump over anything, and climb up anywhere," he said in an essay he was writing for *Household Words*. He had almost finished the third number of *Little Dorrit*; this was the title which even now he decided to give to the work upon which he was so eagerly embarked. But it is an indication of his uncertainty, his need to take great pains even in the full flood of his inspiration, that the next number was not to be completed for another three months.

In early October, just after he had finished the third number, he recited *A Christmas Carol* in aid of the Mechanics' Institution of Folkestone; he read in a carpenter's shop and was, according to Mark Lemon's daughter, "very nervous". At any event, the next day he reported himself to be climbing, swimming and generally leading the life of a "fighting-man" in training. Five days later he went up to London in order to preside at a dinner for Thackeray, who was about to cross the Atlantic in search of American gold, and then returned to Folkestone. But he was still travelling. Travelling now back to France, where he was spending more and more of his time – partly, at least, in order to keep away from London while he was writing. With Georgina he went across to Paris and, after some difficulty in finding the right apartment, rented strange lodgings in the Avenue des Champs-Elysées for the next few weeks. They had in fact taken two apartments, on two floors above a carriage shop, but the rooms were small and there was a general air of dirtiness which Dickens managed to dispel only after numerous imprecations to the porter and proprietor, ". . . explaining that Dirt is not in his way, and that he is driven to madness, and that he devotes himself to no coat and a dirty face until the apartment is thoroughly purified". And so it was, leaving clean apartments which looked down upon the Champs-Elysées and what Dickens described as ". . . the wonderful life perpetually flowing up and down" and "a moving panorama". When Dickens describes London as seen from a window, it is generally through a prospect of mud and drizzle. In Paris Dickens was not so thoroughly at home and everything appeared different, brighter, more garish, more spectacular – just like a "moving panorama", in fact, where scenes were painted on canvas and then with the help of machinery slowly rolled past the spectators. There was in that sense for him an unreality about the French capital but, as he watched the moving show from the window of his apartment, it was an unreality that confirmed his own sense of life. ". . . as we French say . . .", he added as a comic afterthought in one letter back to England, and indeed there had already been observers who had noticed that, with his facial expressions, his gestures, there was something "floridly Parisian" about his manner. But in truth it was not Parisian at all. It was just a different kind of Englishness, an early nineteenth-century Englishness, which was out of fashion and out of favour in the mid-Victorian dispensation.

But of course the differences went deeper than that; many Englishmen had come to Paris in the course of this winter in order to visit the grand Art Exposition, but Dickens was not impressed by the standard of English art. "There is a horrid respectability about most of the best of them – a little, finite, systematic routine in them, strangely expressive to me of the state of England itself." This is the mood which was to envelop *Little Dorrit* and it is one also which shapes an essay he was now writing for *Household Words*, "A Slight Depreciation of the Currency", in which he objects to the palliative uses of "Money" at a time when national duty and national honour should be the principal agents of social change. It was at this time, too, that he decided to divide *Little Dorrit* into two books, "Poverty" and "Riches", with the clear understanding that the latter may bring no benefit. And, as he examined English painting, as he considered the state of England itself, he expressed once more ". . . my despondency about public affairs, and my fear that our national glory is on the decline . . . mere form and conventionality usurp, in English art, as in English government and social relations, the place of living force and truth." From Paris he could see the situation of his country clearly (at least so he thought), but it is hard not to believe that his own inchoate feelings of loss and restlessness did not materially affect his judgment of all these other matters. Never was a man so heavily dependent upon private circumstances in all his more generalised prescriptions, and there never was a man who was less willing to admit to such a fact.

It is clear also that he liked Paris because he was now very famous there; in shops any presentation of his card was met with, "Ah! C'est l'écrivain célèbre!" He was invited to grand dinners, some of which he described in tones worthy of the *Arabian Nights*, and he knew or was introduced to most of the literary "lions", among them George Sand, Lamartine and Scribe. He struck up a particular friendship with the actor, Régnier, and the demands of amity were such that he congratulated Régnier on a drama, *La Joconde*, which in a private letter to Forster he condemned. He was sitting to the painter, Ary Scheffer; the *Moniteur* was serialising *Martin Chuzzlewit*; the eminent French critic, Hippolyte Taine, was about to write at length about him in *La Revue des Deux Mondes*; the French publishing firm of Hachette were negotiating with him on the terms for a complete edition of his novels. In other words, Paris had taken to him as once London had done, and part of his pleasure in living in the capital has to do with the fact that the early stages of his English fame were here being revived. Yet it would be wrong to consider Dickens in Paris as some wholly new or different creature; his restlessness and frustration were apparent even here and, if he criticised England for its narrowness and its mercenary values, he was in turn criticising the French drama for its absurd and frozen classicality at the same time as he was noting that the Parisians in particular seemed mesmerised by the Bourse. False-seeming; the worship of money; stale theatricality; narrowness. These were conditions which he seemed to confront wherever he turned.

In the beginning of November he returned to London for a week; he had at last decided to buy Gad's Hill Place, that dream of his childhood which he had seen a few months before and which had quite fortuitously come up for sale. At this stage he thought of it only as an investment, and had no definite plans of inhabiting it, but he had come back to the city to supervise negotiations for its purchase. Equally importantly, he had taken upon himself the responsibility of arranging the funeral of a Dr Brown, the husband of Miss Burdett-Coutts's chief confidante and friend. So he returned to take care of the dead, the capital as unwelcoming as if it had taken on the murky colours of his description in the opening chapters of *Little Dorrit*. "Perpetual rain,"

Dickens wrote to his wife from the office of *Household Words*. "Storms of wind." There were charity children in the street outside, braving the gusty showers in order to attend a morning performance by Anderson the Wizard in the Gaiety Theatre just opposite in the Strand. He had a bad cold, and his eye was infected. London. A few nights after his arrival he went wandering with Albert Smith through the streets of the East End, and quite by chance came upon a forlorn group who had been refused entry to the Whitechapel Workhouse on a "very dark, very muddy" night; ". . . five bundles of rags," he called them. Dickens at once rang for the Master of the Workhouse in order to speak to him, but the man was not at fault; the casual ward of his institution was already full, and nothing could be done for these five souls. Dickens then went up to question them; they were all women, and when one of them told him that she had not eaten for a day and a night he seemed not to believe her. *"Why, look at me!"* she said. Then: "She bared her neck, and I covered it up again." He gave her a shilling for supper and a lodging (in that part of London, such a lodging would have been of the meanest sort). "She never thanked me, never looked at me – melted away into the miserable night, in the strangest manner I ever saw." In this silent flight she resembles the young man who had, chattering at Dickens, twisted himself out of his rags on an earlier London night; and it is as if in these worn and silent creatures he was beginning to see the soul of London itself.

Four days later he returned to Paris – ". . . must go to work diligently," he wrote, on the next and much delayed instalment of *Little Dorrit*. But it was difficult still. He had to organise that year's medley of Christmas stories for *Household Words*, a task which was more than usually onerous since he thought very little of the ones he had commissioned. He had completed two of his own and was just about to start work again on the novel when he found it necessary to write a third – this latter, "The Boots", in fact proved to be one of his most popular, concerning as it did the run-away match of two small children. Work on the novel was also delayed because of his interminable sittings to Ary Scheffer, a duty which became more and more wearisome. When the portrait was eventually finished, in the following year, Dickens did not believe that it resembled him but, then, ". . . it is always possible that I may know other people's faces pretty well, without knowing my own . . .", a comment which might be applied to other aspects of Dickens as well. Then he had to read *The Cricket on the Hearth* to sixty people in Ary Scheffer's studio. *Then* he had to correct the proofs of the Christmas stories. *Then* he had to supervise the printing of a *Household Words* almanac for the coming year; this had originally been Henry Morley's idea, but of course it was soon suffused with Dickens's spirit as a "Chronicle of Progress" which ". . . in the contemplation of the beautiful harmonies by which Man is surrounded, and of the adorable beneficence by which all things are made to tend to his advantage, and conduce to his happiness, we hope we may have necessarily infused into our work, a humble spirit of veneration for the great Creator of the wonderful Universe, and of peace and good-will among mankind". It was to be "Sold by all Booksellers, and at all Railway Stations", proving just how the beneficient Creator had changed the modes of distribution in the years since Dickens had begun to write. In fact it did not sell as well as had been predicted and Dickens explained to Wills that "it is a pity (I observe now) that my name is nowhere upon it". A panegyric, then, to the nature of Creation, but it was not a joy which Dickens seemed really to share as he contemplated *Little Dorrit*. His vision of the world was closer to his experience outside Whitechapel Workhouse a few weeks before, a vision of a wild and weary London in which there is no rest, no peace, no hope. This was what was closest to him now, this city of unrest which corresponded so well to his own restlessness.

At the beginning of December the first number of *Little Dorrit* was published. Bradbury and Evans had in advance conducted a large publicity campaign, with some four thousand posters and no less than three hundred thousand handbills. The first instalment was itself, in Dickens's phrase, a ". . . brilliant triumph" and the printing order for the second number was increased to thirty-five thousand. In the middle of that month he returned to London to savour his triumph, and then went on to Peterborough to give a reading of *A Christmas Carol* at the Mechanics' Institute there; a member of the audience on that occasion remembered how ". . . a broad high forehead and a perfectly Micawber-like expanse of shirt collar and front appeared above the red baize box . . ." Then back to London where ". . . the people I met, on their way to offices, were actually sobbing and crying with cold". Then off to Sheffield where once more he read *A Christmas Carol*; when he came to the line, ". . . and to Tiny Tim, who did NOT die", there was a tremendous shout from the audience who in that act of revival perhaps saw something of themselves. One contemporary report explains how ". . . a universal feeling of joy seemed to pervade the whole assembly who, rising spontaneously, greeted the renowned and popular author with a tremendous burst of cheering". And what of the author himself who had managed to create that universal joy, who seemed somehow to have the force of the world flowing through him? He could not sleep that night. He felt like "an enormous top in full spin". He purchased his usual almanac from a shop in Oxford Street, and then returned to Paris.

Now at last he could work on *Little Dorrit*, and in these final days of the old year Dickens depicted the passage of his heroine through the waste of London. The narrative seemed to enlarge and expand as he wrote it; originally it was to be only part of a chapter, but now he renumbered the chapters so that the whole instalment ended with that sad nocturnal expedition. The footsteps and the street-lamps. The rushing tide and the shadows. The sounding of the clocks. The homeless. The drunken. The vision of Whitechapel Workhouse is here enlarged and deepened, bringing with it all of the weariness and sadness which Dickens now associated with the city: ". . . the flaring lights . . . the ghastly dying of the night". The strange scene of the woman bending over Little Dorrit: "I never should have touched you, but I thought that you were a child". And her "strange, wild cry" as she turns away. And Dickens himself at the closing of the year? He said that he was overworked. That he was depressed. Here we may see in part the origins of that image of imprisonment which critics have detected running through the novel. For even in Paris Dickens was weary, and there was nowhere else to turn.

V

"A STRANGE meeting, this."
       "Have we met before?"
"We met at the beginning, in Kingsland Road, when
you were a young man."
       "Ah yes. So long ago. Pickwick."
       "And Nickleby. And Oliver Twist."
       "And now?"
       "And now everything. You have created everything."
       "Is that why I seem to myself to be so diminished?
Have my characters taken away my life?"
       "Not diminished but enriched. Changed."
       "Yes, certainly that. Certainly I have changed."
       "No, I mean that you have enriched the world."
       "And yet the curious thing is that I seem to have had no
part in it. It has taken place beyond myself. Or, rather,
the books seem to have been written by someone else. Do
you understand that?"
       "I think so. I'm not sure."
       "Or else how could it be that I feel so bereft, so tired, so
ill at ease?"
       "Could it be that the author is not so important, so
central, as we tend to believe? That he is in some sense not
responsible for his creations?"
       "Come now. I am not so tired as all that." Dickens
laughed. "But there is another remarkable thing. You
talked of the beginning, but did you know that there are
times when I feel as young now as I did then? There are
even times when I experience the same sensations as I

753

once did as a child. And then the novels matter not at all. Is *that* why I feel bereft? Bereft of my own work?" He shifted uneasily in his seat. "But this mood will never last. In a few moments I will be myself again."

We were sitting in the Mid-Victorian Room of the Geffrye Museum. It was late at night, and the staff had all departed. Dickens got up from his chair, and started touching or rearranging the small domestic objects which had been placed within the interior for the purposes of authenticity. He was humming the old song, "Long time I courted you, Miss . . ." He sat down after a few moments, and adjusted the crease in his blue serge trousers: I noticed the stripe of dark satin running down both sides. "You just said now that you understood me," he went on as if we had not stopped talking. "But I don't think that you do. How could you understand me when I do not even understand myself?"

"The biographer –"

"– Oh, biographers. Biographers are simply novelists without imagination!" He looked across at me with that full, direct glance which I had come to know so well; and then he smiled. "Forgive me. As I said, I am tired. And some of my best friends are biographers."

"When you say that you do not understand yourself, do you mean that you don't care to?"

He snatched at the word. "And there's another thing. I never really know what I *mean*. That is the question I can never bring myself to ask anyone when they talk about my writing. But what does it mean? What does it mean?"

"What does a novel mean? It *means* only that you have managed to complete it."

He laughed. "Yes. Very good. And that, after all, is the principal matter. Tell me more about myself."

"You are nervous, although you try not to show it. You are proud, although you pretend not to be –"

"But I am the least arrogant of men. And as for nerves –". He was turning his signet ring around and around upon his finger.

"You see people so clearly, and yet really you never see them at all."

"Are you saying that I live in a world of my own devising?" He gave me a quick, funny glance.

"Actually, I don't know. I'm making all this up."

Now he laughed out loud. "Precisely. You know as little about me as I do. But the important thing, upon which we are agreed, is that you should finish your work. And it is in the very act of completion that some new truth will be revealed."

"And, when your own career upon earth is over, will the truth of your life also be revealed?"

"Let us not talk of that. Let us not discuss dying. I am not concerned with myself, you understand, but with the books that will remain unwritten and the characters who will stay unborn. I have so many of them in my head, you know, I *see* so many of them in front of me – what will happen to them if they cannot come into the world? Will they migrate to the imaginations of other writers? Yes, that is it. Like transported criminals they will find a new world. Perhaps in centuries to come . . ." He got up from his chair in order to wander along the narrow corridor which connected the rooms of various periods in this museum; he turned to his right and walked past the interiors of the eighteenth and seventeenth centuries; then he retraced his steps, passed me, and stopped to consider the bakelite wireless and the linoleum flooring of the Thirties Room. He walked up to the edge of this exhibit and seemed about to enter the room itself, but then he checked himself; he did not want to cross the threshold. Instead he came back to the mid-Victorian interior, where I was waiting for him. He picked up a small jar containing lavender. Then he laughed, and put it down again. "The mystery is too deep to fathom."

"The mystery of time?"

"No, no." Charles Dickens laughed again. "The mystery of my own self." Dawn was breaking when I left him.

Chapter 25

1856. A year before his life was irrevocably to change. Fourteen years before his death. A year of restlessness. A year of continual movement from place to place. Dickens's plan was to stay in Paris until May, and then move on for the summer to Boulogne where, once again, he would stay on "the Property" of M. Beaucourt. Not that the routine of his life had changed; it had just found another, and perhaps more garish, setting. He liked to walk still. Walk endlessly. He walked the old walls of Paris, and at night he used to wander into "strange places". He invited friends as old as Beard and as new as Sala (the young man who had impressed him so much with his articles on London for *Household Words*) to stay in Paris with him and his family. But there was something wrong, something troubling him . . . in one letter in this first month of the new year, he addresses himself in the character of Boots, the servant with whom he had just attained a signal success in his Christmas story. Dickens was always good at imitating servants, and perhaps it has something to do with the fact that his paternal grandparents themselves were both "in service" that in such a voice he comes close to revealing his true feelings. "When you come to think what a game you've been up to ever since you was in your own cradle, and what a poor sort of chap you are, and how it's always yesterday with you, or else to-morrow, and never today, that's where it is." Three months later he was expanding upon the same mood in a more intimate and less facetious letter to Forster: "However strange it is to be never at rest, and never satisfied, and ever trying after something that is never reached, and to be always laden with plot and plan and care and worry, how clear it is that it must be, and that one is driven by an irresistible might until the journey is worked out! It is much better to go on and fret, than to stop and fret. As to repose – for some men there's no such thing in this life." There is a coda to this letter which we will examine shortly, since within it lies the source of Dickens's restlessness. It is enough to note now that at the beginning of the year he also had visions of the Pass of the Great Saint Bernard, visions of travel, visions of escape, visions of solitude; he did manage to bring them into *Little Dorrit* as he had planned but in that novel, where all his diurnal aspirations are seen for what they really are, the solitary and ice-bound place becomes a symbol only of the impossibility of escape. Of the permanence of the past. Of the continuing presence of the Marshalsea Prison in lives that should be quite at liberty. It has often been suggested that the novel is itself filled with images of imprisonment – and now even the writing of each number ". . . will hold me prisoner".

He went back to England at the beginning of February, specifically in order to bring with him the number of *Little Dorrit* he had just completed but also to continue the protracted negotiations over his purchase of Gad's Hill Place. London was no longer his chosen city, however, and he told Catherine that "the streets are hideous to behold, and the ugliness of London is quite astonishing". He had a tooth extracted almost as soon as he arrived, and of course plunged into his usual maelstrom of self-imposed activity. "I began the morning in the City, for the Theatrical Fund; went on to Shepherd's Bush; came back to leave cards for Mr Baring and Mr Bates; ran across Piccadilly to Stratton Street, stayed there an hour, and shot off here. I have been in four cabs today at a cost of thirteen shillings. Am going to dine with Mark and Webster at half-past four, and finish the evening at the Adelphi." He ran across streets; he "shot off"; he took cabs in his haste.

While he remained in London there was a spectacular bankruptcy, and only a few days after his return Sadleir, a prominent financier, took poison and killed himself on Hampstead Heath; this was another aspect of England which he detested, its burgeoning and often corrupt financial empire, and he was to introduce it at once into *Little Dorrit* in the character of Merdle, the financier whose power is proportionate to his chicanery. Of course commercial speculation was not confined to England alone; at the same time there was a fever of speculation in Paris, and the strong smell of what Dickens called a "pecuniary crisis", but it was of England which he wrote. So it is that within a week of his return to the French capital he started work on a new instalment of the novel, and began his portraits of Merdle and of that fashionable "Society" which is no less a prison or forcing-house than the

Marshalsea gaol itself; as he told Forster, "Society, the Circumlocution Office, and Mr Gowan, are of course three parts of one idea and design." The Circumlocution Office was his attack upon that lethal combination of ineptitude, bureaucracy and snobbery which constituted the administration of England; Gowan is an idle dilettante and "painter" to whom nothing is serious, and as such embodies for Dickens all of his earlier comments on what was wrong with English art and the English imagination. But there were so many aspects of England now which horrified and infuriated Dickens. His feelings about Palmerston were only one degree removed from disgust, as we have seen, and the end of the Crimean War negotiated at the Congress of Paris in the first months of 1856 did nothing to alleviate them; "the twirling Weathercock" he was and he remained. Dickens was also infuriated with a number of other prominent national figures, chief among them Harriet Martineau, the ardent "reformer" and propagandising atheist ("There is no God, and Harriet Martineau is His prophet," was Jerrold's characteristically caustic comment), who had recently been questioning the attacks in *Household Words* on those industrialists who refused to attend to the safety of their factory employees; Dickens referred to her "vomit of conceit" and systematically blasted her in "Our Wicked Mis-statements", an essay in the periodical. Even Elizabeth Gaskell was beginning to anger him, and he commented to Wills that, if he were her husband, he would feel compelled to "beat her!". So much for Dickens's stand upon the rights of women.

So it is that in *Little Dorrit* Dickens mounts his single most ferocious onslaught against England and English society; against its government, against its financiers, against its artists, and even against its ordinary citizens who, at least in Bleeding Heart Yard, believed that ". . . foreigners were always immoral . . . that foreigners had no independent spirit, as never being escorted to the poll in droves by Lord Decimus Tite Barnacle, with colours flying and the tune of Rule Britannia playing". He had of course made attacks of such a kind before but they had always been directed against specific abuses and, in *Oliver Twist* for example, the powers of money and benevolence together could at least rescue the doomed orphan child. In *Little Dorrit*, money itself is seen to be a faithless and corrupt delusion. Even when the Dorrits become rich, they cannot escape their past. The only hope is to be found in *endurance*, which was precisely the message he was giving to some of his correspondents in the same period.

He worked on through the next instalment, correcting the proofs in Paris as soon as they were returned to him by the London printers. Then once more back to London with the final sections of the number, arriving at eight o'clock in the morning on 10 March and returning to Tavistock House only briefly before going to his office in Wellington Street. Then straight on to inspect the ruins of Covent Garden Theatre, which had burnt down only four days before; he loved fires, as we have seen, and, next to fires, the blackened relics of the conflagration. ". . . the theatre," he said, "still looked so wonderfully like its old self grown gigantic that I never saw so strange a sight." And he noticed everything; the iron pass-doors, the chandeliers, and even pieces of material from the men's wardrobe from which ". . . I could make out the clothes in the Trovatore". He had already pledged himself to make one or two speeches on public occasions during this fortnight's visit, and he contracted a cold so fierce that he felt obliged to stay in bed for most of each morning in order to cope with the rigours of the rest of the day. "I weep continually," he told Mary Boyle (it had become one of his favourite phrases), in a letter which only half-facetiously announces his usual undying devotion to her. But then he was given news that "flattened" him more than any cold. John Forster, his old bachelor companion, the occasional invalid, the gregarious but always essentially solitary inhabitant of an apartment in Lincoln's Inn Fields, was about to marry. And to marry an heiress. Dickens described it to Georgina as ". . . the most prodigious, overwhelming, crushing, astounding, blinding, deafening, pulverizing, scarifying secret . . ." Usually he congratulated his friends on their marriages and spoke of them in a blind mist of what Mrs Gaskell would probably have called "Dickensy" sentiment, but his attitude to Forster's marriage was from the beginning one of astonishment not unmixed with a sort of jocosity. The Lincolnian mammoth had at last found a mate and, for Dickens, it was another stage in the gradual separation between the two men. Forster had become much more conservative, much more sure of himself ("my dear boy" was one of his ways of addressing Dickens), much more bourgeois – to use a perhaps anachronistic term – and, as a result, Dickens no longer had the same intimate relationship with him. He seemed increasingly to mock him in his letters and, although Forster remained his literary confidant and editor-in-chief, it was to younger friends that the novelist increasingly turned. Friends who were admirers as much as companions, funnier, sharper, more quixotic, somehow looser and freer in the ways of the world.

There had been one especial reason for his return to London, however; he had finally, after delays and negotiations that seemed to him to be stretching on as long as an amateur Chancery suit, purchased Gad's Hill Place. The house he had seen with his father, so many years before, was at last his own. There are certain people who seem doomed to buy certain houses. The house expects them. It waits for them. Gad's Hill Place and Dickens had just such a fatal affinity. It was the house which had once been pointed out to him as the very summit of achievement, and it was the house in which he was to die. He paid £1,790 pounds for it. "After drawing the cheque I turned round to give it to Wills . . . and said: 'Now isn't it an extraordinary thing – look at the day – Friday! I have been nearly drawing it half-a-dozen times, when the lawyers have not been ready, and here it comes round upon a Friday, as a matter of course.'" The point was that Friday had become a sort of superstition with him, being the day on which he considered that the most important things in his life always happened to him. It was his "lucky" day. Unfortunately he could not move into the house he had purchased in so timely a fashion; it still had its tenants, a rector with his daughter, and Dickens's plan was eventually to refurbish it before letting it out by the month. If there were no tenants, it could then become a retreat for himself and for his family. A few days after he had signed the agreement he travelled down with his son, Charley, together with Mark Lemon and Wilkie Collins. "We inspected the premises as well as we could from the outside –" his son later recalled, "my father, full of pride at his new position as a Kentish freeholder, and making all manner of jokes at his own expense, would not take us into the house for fear of disturbing the rector and his daughter who were then inhabiting it – and we lunched at the Falstaff Inn opposite, and walked to Gravesend to dinner, full of delightful anticipation of the country life to come."

Now that matters were settled, Dickens felt able to return to Paris. Wilkie Collins joined him there and, although on a previous visit he had stayed in bachelor apartments a few doors away from their own lodgings, now he stayed with the Dickens family and dined with them every day. The fact that Collins himself was often ill from gout or rheumatic fever did not in any sense strain their relationship, as illness was wont to do in other cases with Dickens, ". . . my old Patient" he called him once, as if his position were that of doctor as well as friend. In fact he also had another role to play, perhaps the most important of all, since it is clear that in this period Dickens was in a sense training

Collins to be a writer. Of course there were their usual walks, nocturnal or otherwise, on one of which, incidentally, Collins found some of the material for his finest fiction. "I was in Paris wandering about the streets with Charles Dickens," he said, "amusing ourselves by looking into the shops. We came to an old book-stall – half shop and half store – and I found some dilapidated volumes and records of French crime – a sort of French Newgate Calendar. I said to Dickens, 'Here's a prize!' So it turned out to be. In them I found some of my best plots." But Dickens played much more than this passive role in Collins's development as a novelist; he counselled him on publication arrangements, he discussed "Fiction" on many occasions (one of the few recorded examples of Dickens taking anyone into his confidence on that subject so close to him, so close to his most secret impulses), he listened to Collins's stories and then endeavoured to correct or advise the younger man. "Keep all this a secret," Collins wrote to his mother in this year, ". . . for if my good-natured friends knew that I had been reading my idea to Dickens – they would be sure to say when the book was published, that I got all the good things in it from him . . . He found out, as I had hoped, all the weak points in the story, and gave me the most inestimable hints for strengthening them . . ." In other words Collins became something of an apprentice and those critics who have suggested that it was Dickens who learnt from Collins (*The Mystery of Edwin Drood* is always cited for an example, as a work to a certain extent modelled upon *The Moonstone*) should look again at the available evidence. Dickens may have learnt some things from Collins, but they were not of a literary nature.

It was in this period, too, that his assistance to Collins bore what might be described as its strangest and certainly, as far as Dickens himself was concerned, its most powerful fruit. For it was from Paris that Dickens wrote to Wills, "Collins and I have a mighty original notion (mine in the beginning) for another Play at Tavistock House . . ." This "original notion" was a drama to be performed at Tavistock House on the next Twelfth Night, a drama to be set in the Arctic regions and eventually entitled *The Frozen Deep*. Dickens had already celebrated the denials and rigours of Arctic life in his articles on the Franklin expedition; in addition the idea of the solitary traveller, the explorer, was one that he found deeply sympathetic at a time when all the normal conditions of his life provoked in him nothing better than unrest and gloomy despair. Certainly in his letters and articles during this period he reverts to the theme of solitariness, of monkish devotions, of the grandness and mystery of ice-bound regions – a region he was soon to explore in *Little Dorrit*, also. In other words he was seeking some idealised and almost inhuman retreat. A world specifically, perhaps, without women. Without his wife. Without his family. These are the very ideas which now found an outlet in the first preparations for the play, but so advanced was Dickens's own conception of the drama that even in these early months he seems to have had a good idea of its eventual shape. That Collins wrote the play is not in doubt, but it is clear that he was doing so almost entirely at his friend's direction; as Dickens had said in an early letter to Wills, he was quite able to "infuse a good deal of myself" into Collins's own essays for *Household Words*. He also told Wills that the younger writer ". . . is very suggestive, and exceedingly quick to take my notions".

But why did Dickens not work upon the play himself? It ought not to be forgotten that his own experience of writing "drayma", as he once called it, had not altogether been a success but, more importantly, all his creative energies were perforce directed towards the writing of *Little Dorrit*. Even with Wilkie Collins present with him in Paris, for example, it is clear that he was keeping the last two weeks of March and the first week of April free of all engagements so that he could work at peace upon the novel. In fact it was now that he was writing the seventh number, clearing the ground for the sudden wealth of the Dorrit family and at the same time composing some of the funniest scenes in the novel. Flora Finching was again in full flight – ". . . ere we had yet fully detected the housemaid in selling the feathers out of the spare bed Gout flying upwards soared with Mr F. to another sphere." Dickens laughed out loud as he wrote this, as surprised by his own extraordinary invention as any of his readers. And what of the "real" Flora, Maria Beadnell? He had written a shamefaced letter to her, thanking her rather belatedly for one of her own letters; significantly he superscribed the letter as from 49 Champs-Elysées when in truth he was at the time writing to her from the *Household Words* office in Wellington Street. It may even be that he suffered from conscience of a sort; as Flora Finching progressed through the narrative, she becomes much more sympathetic until by the end she has the makings of a comic heroine. Thus in his art Dickens could be reconciled to those whom, in life, he never wished to see.

By the first week of April he had written the first two chapters of the instalment; then Macready came to Paris for a short visit, and after he had gone Dickens fell to work and finished the number at once. He took a long walk through Paris in preparation for the next, but in fact did not begin. Not yet. There were dinners. There were other visitors. And his internal restlessness always came back to the surface, leading him into those "strange places". One night, in a cheap venue where there was wrestling as well as other more familiar nocturnal pursuits, he was attracted by the face of a young woman, "handsome, regardless, brooding . . ." He did not speak to her, but the next night he returned to the same place in order to look for her – ". . . I have a fancy," he told Wilkie Collins, his old companion on such pilgrimages who had now returned to London, "that I should like to know more about her. Never shall, I suppose." Here is the yearning of the famous man, ready to return to a tatty Parisian "night-spot" in order to seek out an anonymous woman.

He went back once more to England at the beginning of May; he was supposed to be staying in London at Tavistock House but his wife's family, the Hogarths, were there and his dislike for them was now so intense that he preferred to stay at the Ship Inn, Dover, for four days until they had left the premises. He had told Wills from Paris that "the Hogarth family don't leave Tavistock House till next Saturday, and I cannot in the meantime bear the contemplation of their imbecility any more. (I think my constitution is already undermined by the sight of Hogarth at breakfast.)" On the same day he wrote to Mark Lemon that ". . . I cannot bear the contemplation of that family at breakfast any more . . ." And this about a family he had once admired and about a man, George Hogarth, of whom he had been especially fond. What had gone wrong? It was in part the result of the sometimes extraordinary behaviour of Mrs Hogarth, a woman of apparently volatile temperament, but his rage against "that family" had much more to do with his growing estrangement from Catherine herself. It is not easy to chart the course of this. In the letter to Forster already quoted, in which Dickens had discussed his restlessness in vivid terms, he had gone on to say, as if in extenuation, "I find that the skeleton in my domestic closet is becoming a pretty big one . . ." So here was the root of his dislike of the Hogarths, his growing dislike of a wife who seemed to him to have inherited, in what might be described as a typically Dickensian manner, all of the less amiable characteristics of her parents.

Over the years he had complained about her clumsiness, her slowness and her occasional absent-mindedness; characteristics especially irritating to a man as quick, neat and decisive as Dickens.

There were times, as we have observed, when he had also been rather callous about her child-bearing propensities, especially since she suffered from post-natal depression amounting almost to mental disorder; it was as if Dickens had no responsibility at all for the emergence of his children into the world. Reports about his actual behaviour to his wife differ and, as is usual in such cases, rely more upon rumour and conjecture than evidence. One young contributor to *Household Word* noted that "it had been obvious to those visiting at Tavistock House that, for some time, the relations between host and hostess had been somewhat strained; but this state of affairs was generally ascribed to the irritability of the literary temperament on Dickens's part, and on Mrs Dickens's side to a little love of indolence and ease, such as, however provoking to their husbands, is not uncommon among middle-aged matrons with large families." This seems accurate enough, confirmed as it is by Dickens's own occasional remarks about his wife's "indolence". But it is by no means the whole story – there had been times when Catherine, far from being lazy or relaxed, suffered from severe nervous depression and obvious insecurity. In the days of their engagement this had sometimes manifested itself in bouts of petulance or complaint; then, as now, she lacked confidence in herself, and therefore lacked confidence in the affection of those closest to her. But, as so often happens, the passage of the years had only exacerbated her condition; it is possible, even probable, that her apparent lethargy was a symptom of anxious defensiveness or a means of withstanding acute distress. A grandchild later remembered her nervous habit of "winding the first fingers of both hands round and round a chain" and her own daughter, Katie, told a later biographer that her mother ". . . could not be herself – she was (as it were) in prison, not allowed to say what she felt". Was this why she was also what one relative called a "complaining woman" and what Macready's grand-daughter called "a whiney woman"?

Her daughter is also supposed to have said that her mother was "jealous" of Dickens, a remark which Dickens himself corroborated when later he described how she had fallen into the "most miserable weaknesses and jealousies". And Harriet Martineau said (for what it is worth) that "*fretfulness and jealousy*" were charged against Catherine. Georgina Hogarth, after Dickens's death, declared that Catherine ". . . is a very curious person – unlike anyone else in the world". And she more or less accused her of being unfeeling. Her daughter is also supposed to have told a friend that her mother "was heavy and unregardful of her children", although this is contradicted by the evident affection she both gave and received. But clearly there was something "odd" about her in later years: a strange stillness, an unwillingness to be moved, perhaps even a heaviness of spirit.

There are other reports. Evans, Dickens's publisher, is supposed to have said in later years that he could not bear Dickens's "cruelty" to his wife – "swearing at her in the presence of guests, children and servants . . ." This is most unlikely, not least because Dickens had a sense of social obligation matched only by his reserve. It is inconceivable that he would have sworn at her in front of guests, equally inconceivable that he would have done so in front of the children. Given his dislike of public swearing, already recorded, it is unlikely, to say the least, that he swore at all. More probable is the kind of icy anger reported in another story when, at a dinner party given by Talfourd a few years before, Dickens had been explaining how his "thoughts" came to him at odd hours of the night and how he needed to jot them down at once. Apparently Catherine said, "That is true. I have reason to know it, jumping out of bed and getting in again, with his feet as cold as stone." But then "Dickens left the table, and was afterwards found sitting alone in a small room off the hall – cold and angry". At least this is a possible scene; Dickens's behaviour was often odd and unpredictable, and the idea of his being "cold and angry" with his wife seems to fit all the known facts of his relationship with her. But matters are never that simple in any marriage, let alone that of Dickens. For in this year it was also reported "how careful he was of his wife, taking on himself all possible trouble as regards his domestic affairs, making bargains at butchers and bakers, and doing, as far as he could, whatever duty pertains to an English wife". In other words, he was *protecting* Catherine as well.

It is best to look instead at internal evidence, which although not conclusive provides less ambiguous clues. In his letters to his wife Dickens continually addresses her as "My dearest Catherine" and repeats expressions of affection which are not unfelt. But something else is clear as well; his letters to Georgina ("My dear Georgy . . .") are far longer and far more intimate in a "chatty" kind of way; he wrote to both women from London on the same day at the beginning of May, for example, and the differences in tone are instructive. The letter to Catherine is relatively short and clearly restrained, opens with "My Dear Catherine" and ends abruptly with "This is all the theatrical news I know". The letter to Georgina is three times the length, more intimate and has the message "Kiss the Plorn for me"; this instruction to kiss his youngest child is significantly not made to Catherine herself, thus suggesting that Georgina had in a sense supplanted much of her sister's role in the Dickens household. Certainly she was now attending to most of the domestic details: for she was efficient, intelligent, and devoted to her brother-in-law. She had had at least one offer of marriage, from Augustus Egg, but had refused it. It is clear that she had made a definite decision to attach herself permanently to the Dickens family and to Dickens himself; and although there were occasions when he was concerned for her future, and in a sense troubled by a loyalty so great that it might foreclose on other possibilities in her life, at this stage he was implicitly relying upon her for all those duties which Catherine did not or could not perform. Georgina taught the smallest children, for example, and acted occasionally as an amanuensis to Dickens himself. But she seems to have been of a less placid temper than her sister. She was intelligent rather than clever, sharp, observant (she was, to Dickens's delight, a wonderful mimic); and it seems that on occasions she could be severe with the children. Yet she was also described as ". . . a really delightful person, plain, unassuming . . ." Henry Charles Dickens, Dickens's grandson who was born many years after these events, said that she was quite "an ordinary mid-Victorian lady" and ". . . no great figure in history at all".

Conflicting and even contradictory accounts of both women exist, therefore, and on this occasion a biographical narrative must settle for something like a compound portrait; of a nervous, uneasy and depressed wife whose essentially loving nature had been undermined both by her continual pregnancies and by the peculiarities of her husband's temperament; of a sister-in-law who was more practical and more efficient, even in a sense more *devoted* to Charles Dickens largely because she had never suffered the strain of being his wife. And ". . . no great figure in history at all". There is the real truth of it, as true of Catherine as it is of Georgina, two "ordinary" women placed in an extraordinary situation precisely because of their relationship to the great novelist, and whose understandable human frailties seem much larger in the glare of the light which has as a result been thrown upon them. And Charles Dickens himself, restless, perplexing, peculiar, impetuous, of sudden moods. A man whose childhood haunted him, whose memory of his closest female relatives was one of neglect and betrayal – what did he demand from other women, therefore? Did he even know or recognise what it was? Is it not possible that he felt the need to enact the old infantile story of abandonment again and again? A man whose childhood had left him with a permanent although sometimes camouflaged feeling of hurt, of imprisonment, of yearning; where is the wife who could satisfy such a man? His feelings about sexuality were in any case complicated, and it is possible that his physical relationship with Catherine turned him against her in ways that of course would not apply to his sister-in-law. Two sisters united only in their love for Charles Dickens. Two sisters whose characters were in a very real sense formed and manipulated by Dickens, although he himself, in his usual fashion, could not see that he was in any way responsible for Catherine's unhappiness or Georgina's increasingly false position. He was never to be blamed for anything; this was his constant if unacknowledged rule. Here, then, we have the makings of a domestic tragedy.

So Dickens stayed at the Ship Hotel, Dover, unwilling to see the parents of the two women. He had hoped to work upon *Little Dorrit*, but he could do nothing. Instead he went for what were now becoming his customary twenty-mile walks; the more restless he was, the more imprisoned he felt himself to be, the longer his walks became. Dover itself was "out of season" and in an essay he wrote for *Household Words*, on the very subject of not being able to write, he described the closed shops, the empty theatres and the deserted bathing-machines. He looked in at a window of a shop selling literature, and saw *Dr Faustus*, *The Golden Dreamer* and *The Norwood Fortune Teller* at sixpence each. He walked on the Downs and there encountered a "tramping family in black" to whom he gave ". . . eighteen-pence which produced a great effect, with moral admonitions which produced none at all". And there again is the essential Dickens, an unhappy man standing on the Downs and giving "moral admonitions" to a family of vagrants. As soon as the Hogarths had left Tavistock House he moved back to London; one of the things that irritated him most about his wife's family was their general untidiness, and on his return to the house he swept the floors, washed the study and drawing room, ". . . opened the windows, aired the carpets, and purified every room from the roof to the hall". The carpet was in the corner "like an immense roly-poly pudding, and all the chairs upside down as if they had turned over like birds and died with their legs in the air . . .", this last image one which can truly be given the much-abused term "Dickensian". And then he returned to his London life – a party at the *Household Words* office, a visit to Drury Lane Theatre, an evening with Macready, a visit to the Egyptian Hall in Piccadilly. He was given permission to mount the dome of St Paul's in order to see the fireworks and illuminations in celebration of the end of the Crimean War, and there had a vision of "blazing London" so much like his own description of it in *Barnaby Rudge*. He made short trips to Kent on Gad's Hill Place business. He gave an address at the Royal Hospital for Incurables, and it is a measure of his own unsentimentality about illness, as well as the sometimes hard temper of the age on such matters, that even on such a mournful theme he managed a number of jokes; he did not want to hint, for example, that ". . . there was any connection between a Hospital for Incurables and the Houses of Lords and Commons ⟨*Laughter*⟩". He wrote an essay for *Household Words* at this time on the demeanour of a certain murderer, William Palmer, and noted the fact of his ". . . complete self-possession, of his constant coolness, of his profound composure, of his perfect equanimity". Curiously, this is also a description which Dickens liked to give of himself. In this same month he had in an argument somehow managed to reduce Miss Burdett-Coutts's recently-widowed companion, Hannah Brown, to "showers upon showers of tears". And Dickens in the face of this emotion? "I remained, of course, quite composed . . ." It is in this same essay on the murderer that Dickens imagines himself in the place of a man who has poisoned his wife . . . During this visit to London George Meredith left for him at Tavistock House an inscribed copy of *The Shaving of Shagpat: An Arabian Entertainment*. And Dickens very much admired a painting being newly exhibited, "Chatterton" by Henry Wallis, who had used Meredith as his model for the dead poet. He saw a man sobbing in front of the picture; it was Frank Stone, crying because the image of Chatterton was so much like that of his own dead son.

While he spent May in London, he continued with his work on *Little Dorrit*, now so much in command of his narrative that he made for himself only the briefest of notes and memoranda. Even as he was hastening around the city this spring at his usual feverish pace, therefore, he was at the same time writing about a melancholy, deserted London of summer, on ". . . a grey, hot, dusty evening". A city that contained "Wildernesses . . ." In these chapters of the novel he infuses the narrative once more with images of travellers, of the strange roads down which they all drive, of uncertain futures. There is also a wonderful image here of the Thames as a symbol of change, of forgetfulness, of destiny; ". . . and thus do greater things that once were in our breasts, and near our hearts, flow from us to the eternal seas." And is he here also mourning the loss of his love for Catherine?

He stayed in London for the whole month, and then in the second week of June he travelled to Boulogne where the rest of his family had already established themselves for the summer in the Château des Moulineaux. Dickens once more grew a beard, to complement his moustache, and dressed in what John Forster called a "French farmer garb" of blue blouse, leather belt and military cap. M. Beaucourt had planted new flowers in the gardens and now, again according to Forster, "at work it became his habit to sit late, and then, putting off his usual walk until night, to lie down among the roses reading until after tea . . . when he went down to the pier". The boys had their own little cottage in the garden, and Dickens devised a "code of laws" for their holiday home; everything was to be kept in its place, and each boy in turn was appointed "Keeper" for the week. The washing arrangements were to be conducted like those on "a man of War" and Dickens solemnly inspected the cottage three times a day. There are anecdotes of Dickens on this last trip to Boulogne with the whole of his family, in some way a sacred time because never again were the Dickens family to be so united. Memories of Dickens with his youngest son, Plorn, or "the Baby"; his eldest daughter had "the remembrance of these two, hand in hand, the boy in his white frock and blue sash, walking down the avenue, always in deep conversation . . ." And of Dickens going to a fair at Boulogne and carrying "his baby-boy on his shoulders or on his head all the way". Perhaps the last time we shall have a vision of the relaxed Dickens. The contented Dickens. Even if contented for only a day, a moment.

Yet he had his work still to do. ". . . Now to work again – to work! The story lies before me, I hope, strong and clear. Not to be easily told; but nothing of that sort IS to be easily done that *I* know of . . ." He was writing the final chapter of the instalment he had started in London, and the whole of the next number; difficulties did exist even so, as he confessed, but these were primarily the result of the fact that he had now to prepare for the ending of Book One, for that moment when the Dorrit family walk free from the Marshalsea and Little Dorrit herself collapses at the prospect of liberty. It has been said, fairly enough, that scenes such as these emphasise how Dickens's satire on the Circumlocution Office and the Barnacles is gradually displaced by more private concerns. But that is not to suggest that his distaste for, and assault upon, the failures of English "civilisation" had weakened in any sense. In an essay published in *Household Words* a little later in the year he referred once more to John Sadleir, the financier who had killed himself upon Hampstead Heath and who had become the unwitting model for Merdle in *Little Dorrit*; and, in the same context, Dickens denounced ". . . ignorance enough and incompetency enough to bring any country that the world has ever seen to defeat and shame, and to lay any head that ever was in it low . . ."

Dickens was inviting guests to stay with the family at Boulogne even as he resolved his difficulties with *Little Dorrit* – Mary Boyle, Mark Lemon, Thomas Beard and Clarkson Stanfield among them – but he realised that these were people who knew him too well to dream of interrupting him at his work. Most other social invitations he declined, even one from Lord John Russell for dinner, since he knew that such excursions unsettled and delayed him. He entertained "at home", as it were, and the only variation from this self-imposed quietness lay in his frequent trips across the Channel to London, bearing with him some more pages of manuscript or proofs. Gradually he was reaching the end of the first "Book", only to discover from the proofs that he had underwritten the last chapter of all. So at this point he added a scene in which the other debtors in the Marshalsea watch the Dorrits depart: "It was rather to be remarked of the caged birds, that they were a little shy of the bird about to be so grandly free, and that they had a tendency to withdraw themselves towards the bars, and seem a little fluttered as he passed." How apposite, perhaps, that while staying in Boulogne Dickens had his own caged bird, a canary which he called *Dick*. And that when finally he left Boulogne he described the grounds as resembling a ". . . dreary bird-cage with all manner of grasses and chickweeds sticking through the bars". Images of cages emerged everywhere around him as he wrote the novel and, in this same period, he wrote a brief résumé of his biography to Wilkie Collins only to add that ". . . I feel like a wild beast in a caravan describing himself in the keeper's absence". He felt himself to be imprisoned, perhaps, but was there not a part of him that believed that he *deserved* to be imprisoned?

He took the remaining pages of the last chapter to London with him and then, three days later, travelled back to Boulogne on the Folkestone boat; on which he discovered his old friend, Chauncy Hare Townshend. There may have been no car ferries in 1856 but the mid-nineteenth-century version certainly existed, and Townshend was sitting in his private carriage which had been hauled onto the deck. "I could not but mount the Royal Car," Dickens wrote, "and I found it to be perforated in every direction with cupboards, containing every description of physic, old brandy, East India sherry, sandwiches, oranges, cordial waters, newspapers, pocket handkerchiefs, shawls, flannels, telescopes, compasses, repeaters (for ascertaining the hour in the dark), and finger-rings of great value." And here is an example of Dickens's instinctive irony: "He was on his way to Lausanne, and he asked me the extraordinary question 'how Mrs Williams, the American actress, kept her wig on?' I then perceived that mankind was to be in a conspiracy to believe that he wears his own hair."

He suffered from stomach pains when he got back to the Château des Moulineaux, but Dr Elliotson, who was again staying for the summer nearby, managed effectively to cure him. And then, a few days later, Wilkie Collins joined the household. Not before time; both men were eager to work together upon *The Frozen Deep*, having planned and discussed it at length, although Collins's habits did not entirely conform with those of his host. Dickens's rule was that breakfast should be served at nine o'clock and no later. Collins, who on more than one occasion preferred the pleasures of the Casino to early nights, often did not rise until eleven o'clock and was to be seen eating pâté de foie gras by himself. Their play was far enough advanced, however, at least in its conception, for Dickens to be giving instructions to Clarkson Stanfield and another painter, William Telbin, about the sets for each Act. Certain aspects of the play were very much on his mind, in fact, although it is hard to say precisely where *Little Dorrit* ends and *The Frozen Deep* begins in a comment about "unnatural" heroes which he made at this precise juncture. In a letter to Forster he was lamenting the absence in fiction ". . . of the experiences, trials, perplexities, and confusions inseparable from the making or unmaking of all men! . . ." But is he speaking here of Arthur Clennam, so confused a hero in *Little Dorrit*? Or of Richard Wardour, the complex figure of love and anger at the centre of *The Frozen Deep* whom he was about to portray upon the stage (part of his enthusiasm for the play being written sprang from his anticipation of enacting it *himself*)? And is he also thinking of himself underlying both of these men, informing them with something of his own passion and his own fear? Dickens and Collins had been expecting to spend at least two months together at the Château des Moulineaux, time enough to complete the play even to Dickens's satisfaction, but a sudden out-break of cholera in Boulogne meant that the entire household had to return hurriedly only two weeks later at the end of August. The children returned first with their mother, then Dickens, and then finally Georgina; the staggered departure necessary because of all the truncated arrangements involved with the disconsolate M. Beaucourt. The Channel crossing was not a success, for Dickens at least, and a fellow-traveller observed that he carried with him "a box of homeopathic globules"; in fact it was Dickens's habit to take a dose of laudanum on such occasions, to steady his stomach and no doubt his nerves, and it seems in later years that laudanum (or tincture of opium) became for him something of a necessary palliative.

As soon as he had returned to Tavistock House at the beginning of September he threw himself once more upon *Little Dorrit* and, although he had begun the second "Book" and was "hard at it", he was now in arrears and beginning to lose his reserve of two months' work before publication. He even added one chapter at a late stage, which suggests that, even though he could now see clearly to the end of the whole novel, he was experiencing certain local difficulties. At the same time he was sending out instructions for the next round of stories in the Christmas issue of *Household Words*, while his own contribution to that seasonal fixture was being directly affected by his work upon *The Frozen Deep*. Of course it was in essence Collins's play but Dickens was sending letters to him through these weeks of early composition, suggesting changes or additions; then the first two acts which Collins had completed by the beginning of October were revised by Dickens, fair copies of his revisions being made by himself, his eldest son and by Mark Lemon. He described these changes to Collins as "some cuts" but in fact they are much more extensive than that, since his purpose was to emphasise the role and the character of the man he himself was to play, Richard Wardour, the "hero" who helplessly loves a woman but who in the end sacrifices himself to save the life of a rival. Dickens's revisions of Collins's script were intended fully to dramatise both his dilemma and the revelation of his self-sacrifice, and Collins seems to have accepted his extensive changes with good grace; it may have been clear to him by now that this was an exercise for Dickens in self-revelation of a suitable theatrical kind. By the tenth of October a list of invitations for the Twelfth Night drama was being drawn up, and a reading of the complete play was held at Tavistock House. Plans had been agreed with Clarkson Stanfield for the staging of the play in the schoolroom; the windows of the room were taken out and a wooden stage erected just beyond them, so that the whole house now resounded with the noise of carpenters and gas-fitters and joiners and painters. The care which Dickens took over details was as usual extraordinary; he wished the scenery to be as realistic as possible (substituting a hammock for a bed at one point) and he even asked William Cooke, the manager of Astley's, to give his advice.

Dickens himself was already deep into his part, and on one of his twenty-mile walks through the country fields of Finchley and Neasden he rehearsed it out loud. "*Young, with a fair sad face, with kind tender eyes, with a soft clear voice. Young and loving and merciful. I keep her face in my mind, though I can keep nothing else. I must wander, wander, wander – restless, sleepless, homeless – till I find her!*" These were some of the words which he shouted out into the air. In the first week of November full-scale rehearsals actually began; twice, and sometimes even three times, each week. But not everything was being rehearsed. Dickens, in the early days, omitted one of his own long soliloquies as Richard Wardour, a scene in which, as another participant noted, ". . . he had all the stage to himself". He did not want to over-prepare it, or perhaps he did not want the others to see in advance precisely how much of the play now *was* him. In fact he was making adjustments and revisions through the whole period of these rehearsals, all the time concerned to make his role that of a good man, a virtuous man, a dignified man, whose soul has become "ice-bound" through the loss of love. Wilkie Collins had at first delineated him as a conventional villain or even maniac, but Dickens saw something quite different in the role of a man perpetually seeking and never finding true affection. It was a part into which he could pour himself, and even at rehearsals his identification with it was seen to be something quite extraordinary. His son, Charley, remembered his "realism"; "in his demented condition in the last act he had to rush off the stage, and I and three or four others had to try and stop him. He gave us fair notice, early in the rehearsals, that he meant fighting in earnest in that particular scene, and we very soon found out that the warning was not an idle one. He went at it after a while with such a will that we really did have to fight, like prize-fighters, and as for me, being the leader of the attacking party and bearing the first brunt of the fray, I was tossed in all directions and had been black and blue two or three times before the first night of the performance arrived." This was the "frenzy" that others also noticed in his performance, a frenzy which suggests some external passion precipitating him upon the stage.

Even as he was rehearsing the part he was writing his own contribution for the Christmas issue of *Household Words*. "The Wreck", in which the theme of the beleaguered explorer is taken up once more in an account of the horrors inflicted upon shipwrecked travellers. Once again he was delineating the extremities of suffering and he told Wills that "I never wrote anything more easily, or I think with greater interest and stronger belief". Images of ships appear in the chapters of *Little Dorrit* he was also writing in November, but the concept of "The Wreck" goes beyond his customary interest in the sea and the things of the sea; in this story the death of a little golden-haired child, Lucy, becomes the central theme; both in spirit and in content it is closely related to the death of the boy taken across the Cape by shipwrecked travellers, about which Dickens had read many years before and which he had recently commemorated in verse. It has also been surmised that the "Golden Lucy" of the Christmas story is related to Lucy Stroughill, the small girl who was one of his neighbours during his childhood days at Ordnance Terrace. So the memories of childhood return in a story of suffering and desperation, just as Dickens is reviving the "frenzy" of lost love and abandonment in *The Frozen Deep*. Then in the last month of the year he included this passage about marriage in *Little Dorrit*: ". . . and after rolling for a few minutes smoothly over a fair pavement, had begun to jolt through a Slough of Despond, and through a long, long avenue of wrack and ruin. Other nuptial carriages are said to have gone the same road, before and since . . ." *The Frozen Deep*. "The Wreck of The Golden Mary". *Little Dorrit*. Travellers in all of them. The journey suddenly stopped. Wreckage. A broken marriage. Lost love. Dead children. The struggle to endure. The quietus found only in death. Dickens was feeling strangely unwell; ". . . a digestion, or a head, or nerves, or some odd encumbrance of that kind . . ." He was living amid the "usual uproar", which are the last two words of his novel, and yet, as he put it in a letter before he reached that ending, "Calm amidst the wreck, your aged friends glides away on the Dorrit stream, forgetting the uproar for a stretch of hours . . ." Once more the image of shipwreck. Yet he worked on amidst "the wreck", into the year that was to signal the end of his marriage and the start of a very different life.

Chapter 26

THERE was a dress rehearsal of *The Frozen Deep* on Monday, 5 January, 1857, this in typically Victorian fashion for servants, tradespeople and their friends. The main performance was on the following evening in the schoolroom at Tavistock House, and there were two performances after that. Curiously, although these were private gatherings in a very small space, Dickens had decided that the newspaper reviewers should still be allowed to attend; it suggests, above all else, some overwhelming need to display himself in his new guise as tragic hero. He wanted his new identity to be recognised and confirmed; in part, perhaps, to contradict those critics who found the heroes of his fiction to be "un-natural". How could an author who displayed such intense feeling create anything un-natural? So he could not have been anything but pleased when *The Leader* described the "savage energy" of his performance. The play itself reads now as a melodrama marked by the formality of its passion, but there are lines in it which seem to have come straight from the pen of Charles Dickens as he revised and extended Wilkie Collins's original script. "Never you give in to your stomach, and your stomach will end in giving in to *you*." Pure Dickens. And again: "I would have accepted anything that set work and hardship and danger, like Ramparts, between my misery and me . . . Hard work, Crayford, that is the true Elixir of *our* life!" Then there are lines which seem to come from some deeper source within him; his character, Richard Wardour, appreciates the Arctic "because there are no women here" and in the same Act he exclaims that "the only hopeless wretchedness in this world, is the wretchedness that women cause". Here speaks the boy, the adolescent and also the man, each stage in his life marked by the supposed enmity or failure of women. His mother. His sister. Maria Beadnell. Catherine Dickens. And, in the last words of the play, the audience and other actors wept with Dickens. "Nearer, Clara – I want to look my last at *you*. My sister, Clara – Kiss me, sister, kiss me before I die!" Dickens's acting in this scene had an extraordinary effect upon those who watched it, and how could it not be so? All the emotion of his life was being poured into these broken lines, and, according to Dickens, Wilkie Collins muttered, "This is an awful thing!" Sometimes he was so drained by this last scene, in fact, that he was "floored" for ten minutes and could do nothing; but then he was up again and ready to take part in the "screaming" farce, *Uncle John*, which ended the evening; although at least one participant recalled that Dickens had the "constrained expression" of Richard Wardour on his face for some time afterwards.

John Oxenford, one of the critics invited to the private theatricals, said of his performance that "his appeal to the imagination of the audience, which conveyed the sense of Wardour's complex and powerful inner life, suggests the support of some strong irrational force". He was also the first to notice that it was the performance of a novelist rather than of an actor, and in that potent combination of fiction and the irrational we can see the twin origins of Dickens's dramatic power. Thackeray attended one of the performances and remarked of Dickens that "if that man would now go upon the stage, he would make his £20,000 per year", a prediction which was closer to the truth that he could then have realised. Dickens himself was pleased with the performances; he said to at least four correspondents that it was "the most complete thing", by which he meant that there was a sustained emotion throughout the play. The audiences, he said, were "excellent" and he had never seen any so ". . . strongly affected by theatrical means". They wept buckets, in other words, which of all the responses Dickens was the most eager to elicit. He, too, was strongly affected, even though in his customary manner he stated that he was "calm" after the excitement of his performance. At the dance after the first night, however, he asked a certain Mrs Lankester to waltz with him and she recorded that "I was whirled around almost to giddiness . . . a wild tulle flounce which adorned my new pink silk skirt as it caught in one of the wires of the footlights, becoming entangled and torn, so that it had to be cut asunder with a pen-knife from the pocket of my distinguished companion, who handed the yards and yards of diaphanous material to me with a bow". She kept the material as a relic of her mad dance with the famous man.

The theatre in the schoolroom was now dismantled and Dickens returned to his postponed work on *Little Dorrit*, composing the extraordinary scene in which William Dorrit breaks down at a grand dinner-party and reverts to his former life as a prisoner. The past, revived, had surfaced once again; the wealthy and distinguished gentleman had become once more "the Father of the Marshalsea", the sad old man with the shades of the prison house upon his face; and were there times, now, when Dickens felt himself returning helplessly to his own past? He had called William Dorrit's dilapidated brother Frederick, which was of course the name of his own brother, his own family again reappearing in his imagined families. But what of the reality itself? In this period Frederick had in fact been sponging off Dickens's friends, and trying once more to obtain money from his own brother. Dickens refused, and on the day of his birthday received the following letter from Frederick: "I cannot help saying that the tone of your letter is as *cold & unfeeling* as one Man could pen to another – much less one Brother to another . . . the World fancy from your writings that you are the most Tolerant of Men – let them individually come under your lash . . . & God help them . . ." A man is never a hero to his own relations. But there were more sympathetic companions than the members of his own family, and his birthday dinner that evening was attended by men such as Wilkie Collins and Thomas Beard.

He was very tired after his extraordinary efforts in *The Frozen Deep*. He went down to Brighton for a few days with Collins, and while he was there Benjamin Webster, the theatrical manager and actor, read to him a play, *The Dead Heart*, a tale of self-sacrifice at the time of the French Revolution which leads to a substitution at the foot of the guillotine, strangely corresponding with the self-sacrifices of Richard Wardour. In fact the story made such an impression upon Dickens that it emerged two years later in *A Tale of Two Cities*. All his life Dickens used such external influences or coincidences to reinforce his imaginative impulses. Just before going down to Brighton he had visited the Zoological Gardens, for example, and seen the snakes there being fed with live guinea pigs and rabbits – ". . . I have ever since been turning the legs of all the tables and chairs into serpents and seeing them feed upon all possible and impossible small creatures . . ." And that is why, while working on *Little Dorrit* in Brighton, he described the hands of Rigaud ". . . with the fingers lithely twisting about and twining one over another like serpents. Clennam could not prevent himself from shuddering inwardly, as if he had been looking on at a nest of those creatures." Exactly as Dickens had done in the Zoological Gardens.

He was embarked upon the twenty-eighth chapter of the second Book, and now he had to prepare for the final double number and the conclusion of his story. He organised his notes carefully and, in order to remind himself of precisely what he had already done, he summed up the action for himself in a series of memoranda. He came back to London after a few days but then went down to Gravesend, partly to work on the conclusion of the book in peace, but also partly to superintend the repairs which were being made to Gad's Hill Place. But he was back in London at the beginning of May, and it was in his study at Tavistock House that he finished *Little Dorrit*. He had at this time been writing to a novelist, Emily Jolly, and in his letters he had besought her to "strive for what is noblest and true" in her work; it was in this spirit that he approached the closing pages of *Little Dorrit* itself. Certainly there is a religious sense at work in the book. "Set the darkness and vengeance against the New Testament," he wrote in his working notes, and in his description of a sunset over London he introduced this new sense of life. "From a radiant centre, over the whole length and breadth of the tranquil firmament, great shoots of light streamed among the early stars, like signs of the blessed later covenant of peace and hope that changed the crown of thorns into a glory." But is there not in this vision of redemption something of the weariness and sorrow which had been expressed in Dickens's first vision of London in the same book, the London of "melancholy streets in a penitential garb of soot . . ."? A vision of faith and of despair, then, subsumed in Dickens's vision of the world itself as a place of imprisonment. "Far aslant across the city, over its jumbled roofs, and through the open tracery of its church towers, struck the long bright rays, bars of the prison of this lower world." He needed to finish "at a heat"; the manuscripts of these last pages show many revisions and additions; he cancelled a visit to Joseph Paxton; he could do nothing else until the novel was finished. On the first Sunday in May it was completed, and three days later he went back to the Marshalsea Prison, the site of his father's imprisonment and his own childhood suffering, the scene of the last pages of his novel. The yard had gone. So had the gates and the spikes. The buildings had been converted and the walls lowered. Dickens did recognise the outer courtyard and the inner wall but, more importantly, he discovered the "great block of the former prison" where once had been ". . . the rooms that have been in my

mind's eye in the story", the rooms to which so many years before his
father had been consigned. He had not visited the prison as he was
writing the story; his own vision of it was too elaborate and too
substantial to admit of any comparison. But, now that he had fixed the
Marshalsea for ever in his prose, he could face the ruined reality. And
so, as he said in his preface to the now completed novel, ". . . whoso-
ever goes into Marshalsea Place, turning out of Angel Court, leading
to Bermondsey . . . will stand among the crowding ghosts of many
miserable years". Angel Court has become Angel Place but parts of
the Marshalsea still survive; now there is a small park where once the
front yard had been and, until recent years, there was a plaque upon part
of the old wall which read: "This site was originally the MARSHAL-
SEA PRISON made famous by the late Charles Dickens in his well
known work 'Little Dorrit'." And Charles Dickens himself passed this
way on Wednesday, 6 May, 1857. He stopped to talk to a small boy
who, taking pity on this stranger, ". . . told me how it all used to be.
God knows how he learned it . . . but he was right enough . . ."

Sales of *Little Dorrit* had been good; they had held up until the end,
and the final double number had a circulation of approximately
twenty-nine thousand copies. Dickens, in his preface, remarked
upon the number of his readers and repeated the phrase he had used at
the end of *Bleak House* – ". . . May we meet again!" The critical
reaction, if he had cared to read it, was less encouraging. In fact it was
largely treated as a failure, a bad novel, a sign of Dickens's sad decline;
this reaction was partly political, partly the "intellectual" response to a
popular author, partly the need to pull down an idol. *Blackwood's
Magazine* called it simply "Twaddle" (a reference which Dickens saw
by accident and which upset him for at least a moment). And one of his
first biographers, writing a sixpenny pamphlet which was published
in the following year, said of *Little Dorrit* and of *Bleak House* that they
"have not been greatly relished by the public any more than they have
been praised by the critics". It was in this period that a handsome
Library Edition of Dickens's novels first started to be published (it was
yet another way for him to "work" his copyrights), and one of the
reviewers of that edition suggested that "it does not appear certain to
us that his books will live . . ." But what did Dickens make of such
criticism? A few weeks later he was walking with Hans Christian
Andersen, who had been hurt by the reviews of his latest book (in fact
he had been found lying face down, in tears, on the lawn of Gad's Hill
Place). "Never allow yourself to be upset by the papers," he told

Andersen, "they are forgotten in a week, and your book stands and lives." They were walking in the road, and Dickens wrote with his foot in the dirt. "That is criticism," he said. Then he wiped out his marks with his foot. "Thus it is gone."

The completion of *Little Dorrit* meant that he could turn his attention properly to Gad's Hill Place. He had frequently made trips into Kent in order to superintend the repairs he had ordered, but it was only now that he began seriously to move into his new house; as usual, he was hurrying along the various workmen still on the premises, who were only to "be squeezed out by bodily pressure". He was demanding speed because he wanted Catherine to come down on 19 May, which was her birthday, and on this occasion the family party was joined by his extended family of Wills, Collins and Beard. But this was only a preparatory "house-warming", and on the first day of June the family travelled down for the entire summer; Tavistock House meanwhile was left in the charge of Anne Brown, Catherine's old maid, so that it was ready for Dickens to use on his frequent business trips to London. He wanted the quiet of the countryside, however; he had somehow managed to catch influenza, and he felt that the Kentish air might act as a restorative for him. But what of Gad's Hill Place itself? Dickens called it "old-fashioned, plain, and comfortable". It is a house of Queen Anne's period, a three-storey red brick affair with a bell turret on the roof and wooden porch complete with seats and pillars. It is not a grand or even a large house; it might be considered, in fact, somewhat solid and unprepossessing. But for Dickens it had the spell of his childhood upon it. From the roof it is possible to glimpse the river Thames and the dark shape of London, to see Rochester and the valley of the Medway and, to the north, to view the flat and desolate marshes. So many compass points of Dickens's imagination. The rooms are relatively small – on the ground floor a drawing room and a dining room, a study and a billiard room. Dickens's bedroom, on the first floor, looked over the fields towards Strood; this may once have been Dickens's study but in fact Dickens changed what Auden once called "the cave of making" on at least three occasions until eventually it was sited on the right-hand side of the entrance hall, overlooking the garden. Here he was surrounded by his books, as well as by more of his famous counterfeit book-backs. He looked out upon a lawn and drive and then, on the opposite side of the Gravesend to Rochester Road, beyond the lawn, there was a shrubbery with two large cedars of Lebanon.

Dickens often remarked upon the fact that this was the spot where Falstaff had committed his robbery and then run away; in other words it was a place already hallowed by the exploits of fictional characters which Dickens almost deemed to be true. He loved the area in any case, this spot of his childhood, although, as his son remarked, it could not be said that Dickens was in any sense a "countryman". He liked the "effect" of bright flowers (he had scarlet geraniums planted neatly in the gardens) and the general pastoral scene; but he had no intimate or extensive knowledge of the natural world. In fact he had severe problems with it at first; the water supply was not extensive enough for his needs and, after a great deal of trial and error, it was decided that a large pump would have to be built upon the grounds. And at first the quiet of the area seems to have disturbed him; his daughter, Mamie, recalled that "when he first went to Gad's Hill, he used constantly to get up in the middle of the night, arm himself with a loaded gun, unchain the dogs, and walk about the garden, thinking he had heard footsteps and determined to protect his property". Here is a stray indication of what a nervous, highly-strung man he was. But gradually these midnight sorties abated as he grew accustomed to the solitude, and his inspections took place just after breakfast instead; before he began his writing for the day, he would walk around the house and grounds, looking at everything and making sure that everything was in its place. His son, Charley, remembered how he checked even the books and the pictures. He could not set to work until he had satisfied himself about the neatness and order of the world around him. There were one or two other problems connected with rural life; almost as soon as they arrived Catherine, in the approved urban fashion, left her husband's calling cards with their more prosperous neighbours. But this was a solecism in a rural area, implying that Dickens did not wish to be visited; she should have waited until the neighbours had visited Gad's Hill Place and left *their* cards for the new arrivals. Such were the demands of social life even in this Kentish backwater.

But it became a famous backwater, with any number of prominent guests making the pilgrimage by railway from London Bridge Station to Higham or Gravesend. One of the first was Hans Christian Andersen. Dickens expected the famous Danish writer to remain for about two weeks, but in fact he managed to stay for five and, in the process, severely to test the patience of the Dickens family. Dickens himself, of course, was the one who was most able to dissimulate his feelings in the sacred name of hospitality; Andersen said of him that he

". . . seemed to be perpetually jolly, and entered into the interests of games with all the ardour of a boy . . ." Of Gad's Hill Place itself, he stated that "in every room I found a table covered with writing materials, headed notepaper, envelopes, cut quill-pens, wax, matches, sealing-wax and all scrupulously neat and orderly". In his own room Andersen found *The Fairy Family*, *The Arabian Nights*, *Spectator* essays and the works of Washington Irving – a highly appropriate selection, and one no doubt made by Dickens himself. Andersen's diary at the time also throws a certain oblique light upon the arrangements of the Dickens household. He arrived at Higham station to be met by the novelist; "I was much moved; he embraced me, I kissed him on the forehead." But Dickens's family were not quite so welcoming. Of Mamie, Andersen said that she resembled her mother, while Katie was "very like her father's portrait in the early editions". Charley seemed to "suffer from moods" while Walter was sometimes "silly!" and showed no interest in helping him with his luggage when he arrived back at Higham station from a London excursion. Catherine, it seems, was much more agreeable, and some eighteen days after his first arrival Andersen noted in his diary, "Miss Hogarth is not at all attentive, nor are the sons; there is altogether a great difference between the whole family and Dickens and his wife." Yet he added, four days later, "When Dickens is present they are all extremely kind to me." The master of the house clearly also mastered the behaviour of its occupants. In fact Andersen seems to have got on extremely well with Catherine; they even went to the theatre together, which perhaps suggests that she looked with some sympathy and even fellow-feeling upon this rather gawky, clumsy, sentimental "outsider". There is also a strange report at second-hand, and some time later, that Andersen had occasionally met Catherine "crying, and he had also seen her come out of a room together with her mother with her eyes full of tears". This report adds that Georgina was "piquant, lively and gifted, but not kind". For a short time, perhaps, one veil is lifted. Eventually Andersen left, and Dickens kissed him at parting. No doubt the kiss was also one of relief, since above a dressing room mirror he put a card which read, "Hans Andersen slept in this room for five weeks – which seemed to the family AGES!" Katie called the Danish writer a "bony bore" and Dickens himself, according to one of his sons, once described him as a cross between Pecksniff and the Ugly Duckling. Perhaps it was only by considering him as a fictional character (a joint creation by him and Andersen, it seems) that he could properly discard him; discard him without guilt, at least. Certainly his subsequent relationship with him was rather more subdued, and there is clear evidence that in later times he ignored the Danish writer's letters to him. Andersen sent him books and photographs as well, but Dickens responded to none of them.

There were other matters on Dickens's mind during this period of enforced hospitality, none more serious or more powerful than *The Frozen Deep*. The drama seemed literally to haunt him. At the beginning of February he had begun to hear rumours that the Queen wished to see a performance of the play at Windsor Castle but, more pressingly, the death of Douglas Jerrold at once suggested to Dickens that performances should be given for the benefit of the man's family.

Jerrold had died very suddenly. Dickens had been travelling on the train from Higham with Catherine and Georgina, when a man in the same carriage looked over a newspaper and said to his companion, "Douglas Jerrold is dead." The night before, Dickens had had a dream in which Jerrold came up to him with a piece of writing which Dickens could not decipher. An old dream of powerlessness and helplessness, this, connected with his reliance upon language and now obviously to be seen in prophetic or admonitory terms. But there was never a man who so quickly cast away the irrationalities of his dream life and at once, in the full glare of day, he began actively to make plans for Jerrold's immediate family. Within a few days he had arranged that various friends and colleagues should lecture, that he himself should give readings of *A Christmas Carol*, and that there should be performances of *The Frozen Deep*; all of which activity was designed to raise some two thousand pounds. The importance of the play was enhanced when the Queen let it be known that she would like to attend one of its charity performances. Although it had already been agreed that these performances should be held at the Gallery of Illustration, in Regent Street, Victoria asked if the actors might play somewhere in Buckingham Palace. Dickens, very politely, refused; his daughters had not been presented at Court and he did not want their first visit to the Palace to be in the guise of actresses. And, as usual, Dickens got his way. Not even Queen Victoria could match the subtle powers of his will, and she agreed to attend a private "evening" a week before the subscription performances began.

In the meantime Dickens was arranging his readings of *A Christmas Carol*, and at the end of June he read his story at St Martin's Hall, near Leicester Square. The hall itself was crowded hours before he walked on stage and, as *The Times* reported, "so large was the number sent away from the doors through want of room that long before the assembly had dispersed placards were affixed in various parts of the building . . . announcing a repetition of the 'reading' at the same place on Friday, the 24th instant". *Town Talk* suggested that many had come simply "for the purpose of looking at the man who has, for so many years, been an unknown though most familiar friend . . ." – a salutary reminder that, in these early days of photography (M. Daguerre's new process had not been perfected until 1839), Dickens's face was not necessarily familiar to those who knew his works (although in February of this same year, 1857, he had declared himself in danger of being "mobbed" if he went to India House). For those who had not seen him, *Town Talk* provided a brief portrait; of a man now in his forty-sixth year, slight, with long brown hair, moustache and pointed beard. The journalist also noted, as had others, that he had a slight lisp or hiss when he tried to pronounce 's'. As soon as Dickens appeared there was such prolonged applause that "it threatened to postpone the reading indefinitely"; although when Dickens did commence reading, in a "serio-comic" tone, the first words, "Marley was dead: to begin with . . ." there was a slight *frisson* when it was recalled that he was reading in remembrance of Jerrold's own death. But the occasion was a success; particularly noted were Dickens's expressive eyes, his hand movements, his well-controlled voice and his ability dramatically to render the speech of his characters. At the end there was ". . . a long outburst of cheers, mingled with the waving of hats and handkerchiefs".

In the period he was preparing for these readings Dickens was also rehearsing his amateurs once more in *The Frozen Deep*; since the venue had changed from Tavistock House to the Gallery of Illustration, Dickens had once more to attend to all the details of lighting and setting (the fact that he seems to have been a master at lighting *The Frozen Deep* may itself provide an interesting light upon similar effects in his novels). One participant in these proceedings remembered how he was to be found in the Gallery, ". . . resting one arm in the hand of the other, looking at the drops and cogitating upon their effect for the coming night, or working like any scene-shifter at the properties". His participation did not end there, however, and on at least one occasion he acted as ticket-seller. A certain Mr Hipkins recalled how Dickens ". . . related to me how a Yorkshireman had applied for a ticket and told him (of course not knowing him) that the purpose of his long journey was to see him". Dickens did not reveal himself to this admirer, and Hipkins suggests that the Yorkshireman might in fact have been disappointed since Dickens had lost his "jauntiness of appearance" and ". . . looked furrowed and careworn".

The performance in front of the Queen was held on 4 July and, according to Georgina Hogarth, ". . . the Queen and her party made a most excellent audience – far from being cold, as was expected, they cried, and laughed and applauded and made as much demonstration as so small a party (they were not more than fifty) could do". Yet on this occasion, too, was evinced another example of Dickens's will; Victoria asked for him to be presented to her but, when the message was relayed "behind the scenes", Dickens refused. An almost unprecedented thing to turn down such a regal request, but he said later that "I could not appear before Her Majesty tired and hot, with the paint still upon my face . . ." He was wearing his costume for the farce – dressing gown, absurd wig and red nose – and it is clear enough that both his own dignity and his sense of pride as a writer deterred him from being presented to her under such circumstances. Charles Dickens, in red nose and make-up? It could not be. The Queen politely gave way.

The cycle of his readings and performances was only momentarily interrupted when he travelled down to Southampton in order to witness the departure of his son, Walter, for India. Partly as a result of Miss Burdett-Coutts's influence, he had joined the East India Company as a cadet and, after suitable training in England, was now at the age of sixteen about to set sail. He was in fact sailing to the place of his death. He died six years later, and Dickens was never to see him again, one of the many tragedies and disappointments that were to mark Dickens's children; as if his own great success had left some kind of stain upon his offspring. As if, in some form of natural compensation, they *had* to fail. Dickens had always found Walter "a little slow", with a good sense of "duty" and "responsibility" but with no "uncommon abilities"; no doubt he saw in him something of his wife, and there is in the extant photographs of the boy a hint of Catherine's "sleepy" expression. But now, at this time of separation, Dickens wrote that ". . . I don't at all know this day how he comes to be mine, or I his . . ." And yet, watching Charley and Walter mount ahead of him onto the gangplank which led to the ship, Dickens saw himself as a young man in their shapes. He had always found partings difficult but now he had come to believe, in his own uneasy and restless state, that ". . . the best definition of man may not be, after all, that he is (for his sins) a parting and farewell-taking animal . . ." There is no evidence to suggest, however, that Dickens was particularly upset about Walter's departure for Walter's own sake; his lament is generalised, and his own response to seeing his son leave was to think of himself at a similar age. With him, the pity here seems to be a form of self-pity, as if in parting with his son he was parting with some aspect of his own self.

Two further performances of *The Frozen Deep* followed at the Gallery of Illustration and, at the end of one of them, John Deane, the manager of the Great Manchester Art Exhibition, suggested to Dickens that he might like to perform in that city's New Free Trade Hall. At first Dickens did not consider the idea to be feasible and refused but, when he discovered that the London performances alone would not guarantee the two thousand pounds he was attempting to raise for the Jerrold family, he promptly changed his mind. He went up to Manchester in order to read *A Christmas Carol* there, and took the opportunity of inspecting the Hall itself. It was certainly adequate for the play itself, but clearly it was too big for Georgina or for his daughters to act in; they were not trained in the arts of the stage, and would be neither seen nor heard to best effect in a building which could hold upwards of two thousand people. They had managed extraordinarily well during the public performances at the Gallery of Illustration, but the time had come to find professional actresses and, the day after his return from Manchester, he began to search for them.

He was assisted in this by Alfred Wigan, the manager of the Olympic; he had already engaged two young actresses, Fanny and Maria Ternan, at his theatre and now at Dickens's suggestion he approached them to see if they would take part in *The Frozen Deep*. Wigan in turn recommended to Dickens their younger sister, Ellen Lawless Ternan, and their mother, Frances Eleanor Ternan. And so the Ternans enter this history. A family which would otherwise have remained unknown to posterity, a family of struggling actresses who have been caught in the brilliant light which has fallen around Charles Dickens. When at least one member of that family would have preferred to remain in subdued shadow. It would be easy to compare them to that other dramatic family, Vincent Crummles and Company of *Nicholas Nickleby*, but the Ternans were at once more intelligent and more refined than their fictional counterparts. The Ternan parents had themselves acted from their earliest years and, by the time Frances Eleanor Ternan married Thomas Ternan in 1834, they had a solid record of performances behind them. Together they travelled to America in search of that fabled "gold" available to English performers but they were only relatively successful and, on their return to England, took a succession of engagements in various parts of the country; at one time Thomas Ternan simultaneously managed both the Newcastle Theatre and the Doncaster Theatre, but this northern eminence was not to endure and seven years later he died in Bethnal Green Lunatic Asylum of "General Paralysis" (by the nomenclature of the age, this suggests that he died in the tertiary stage of syphilis).

Mrs Ternan was now alone with three daughters, Fanny, Maria and Ellen. All of them had been brought up in the ways of the theatre, and all of them had already started their stage careers; Ellen herself, the youngest, having first appeared on the boards at the age of three. This was still a time when actresses were not always considered to be "respectable", of course, but Mrs Ternan was a matron of the new "Victorian" school; she was eminently respectable, and ensured that her daughters remained so. Certainly they had led a nomadic life, going from one theatre to another, but they could not be dismissed as mere "strolling players". Theirs was a mid-century thespianism. They were *serious*. They were exponents of a high art. Frances Ternan had even acted with Macready on several occasions, in *Hamlet*, *Lear*, *Macbeth* and other Shakespearian productions (in fact Macready helped the finances of the family immediately after Thomas Ternan's death). Mrs Ternan and her daughters had continued their careers in various London theatres – Drury Lane, Sadler's Wells, the Princess's Theatre – but by this period Mrs Ternan herself had all but retired from the stage. She came forward only on occasions such as this, in the performances of *The Frozen Deep*, although she could also sometimes be persuaded to appear in parts which she had formerly played with some success.

There exists a certain amount of information about the Ternan girls in the year of *The Frozen Deep*. The eldest, Fanny, said of her family that "we are a nervous crew, but we have our compensations . . ." Fanny herself was always considered to be the cleverest of the three and, in fact, she was to have some sort of career as a novelist and general writer in her later life; Maria was the liveliest and the most entertaining; Ellen, the youngest, was described by an intimate of the family as "outwardly placid but firm underneath". She was also the least gifted actress in the family and, despite her early experience of the theatre, she never seems to have created much of an impression in her theatrical roles. She was an actress by inheritance, in other words, and not by vocation. Yet since there was something about her which powerfully affected Charles Dickens, perhaps in the exploration of her personality we may learn something of the novelist himself. She was just eighteen when she played in *The Frozen Deep*; the same age as Dickens's daughter, Kate. She had in fact been born in Rochester, and her uncle, a barge-owner, still lived there. One might call this a coincidence, to have been born in the very place which was at the centre of Dickens's imagination, if it were not for the fact that, as the novelist himself knew, there is really no such thing as coincidence. "And thus ever, by day and night . . . coming and going so strangely, to meet and to act and react on one another, move all we restless travellers through the pilgrimage of life." It is clear enough that Dickens knew of the Ternan family before he met them in the course of the Manchester production; the father had appeared at the Theatre Royal, Rochester, when Dickens was a boy in that place, and he might have seen Mrs Ternan on the stage at Covent Garden in the late Twenties. He would no doubt have heard of the Ternans in any case through Macready who, as we have seen, knew them well and had acted with both parents. So when Dickens encountered them he was in effect encountering a known quantity, a branch of that theatrical life which he understood so well and which he never ceased to appreciate. He might even have already seen Ellen Ternan upon the stage since, four months before, she had appeared at the Haymarket as Hippomenes in Frank Talfourd's *Atalanta*. There is a story that he comforted her "behind the scenes" when she feared that, in her male part, she was too scantily clad; but this is undoubtedly one of those apocryphal stories which spring up unaided about the lives of great authors. Certainly he comforted Maria Ternan during *The Frozen Deep* but that is, as they say, quite another story.

And what of Ellen herself at this time? Dickens's daughter, Kate, described her as ". . . small, fair-haired, rather pretty . . ." She went on to say that she was not a particularly good actress but that "she had brains". The *Era* described her in *Atalanta* as ". . . a debutante with a pretty face and well-developed figure . . ." but noticed her apparent lack of confidence on the stage. Ellen emphasised that lack of confidence when she described herself as having ". . . a figure like an oak tree and a complexion like a copper saucepan". But the fact that she did not consider herself to be pretty, despite the opinions of others, may have something to do with her growing up in the company of two older and more vivacious sisters. It seems that she also suffered from occasional migraines and from "nettlerash", a skin condition now more commonly linked with psychosomatic tension; so we are entitled to think of her as a somewhat nervous young woman. In later life she showed herself to be practical and clever; the daughter of her closest friend, a certain Helen Wickham, has remarked that, in later life, she was witty, warm, sympathetic, charming, cultured and charitable. If this litany of praise sounds perhaps too fulsome, the same observer adds that she also occasionally "victimised" her household, that she let her husband "make a perfect doormat of himself for her", that she read all of her daughter's letters until she was twenty-five and that sometimes "when she didn't get her own way" she made extraordinary scenes. She could also be "rather a cruel tease" and "quite a little spitfire". So she was self-willed, and could on occasions be rather domineering. Her commonplace book also suggests that she was highly intelligent and, for a woman who had been educated only in the course of a peripatetic theatrical childhood, remarkably well read; among her favourite authors were Huxley, Arnold, Schiller, Hume and George Sand. In addition, she was not particularly "domesticated", which, given the nature of her life as a young girl, is not altogether surprising. So by indirection a composite portrait of Ellen Ternan emerges – self-willed, intelligent, her shyness or reserve concealing a young woman of remarkable natural gifts. Nevertheless it ought to be remembered that most of these descriptions of her date from many years after Dickens's death, and it is possible that her very contact with the famous novelist gave her a certain self-confidence as well as that delight in her intellectual prowess which she might otherwise have not so convincingly displayed. Of course she must also have possessed these capacities when she was younger, but it seems likely that they were effectively suppressed or only occasionally evident in a family of older and more experienced women. The only token of her difference from her mother and sisters at this stage lay in the fact that she was not a particularly proficient actress; nor, as far as the evidence indicates, a particularly enthusiastic one.

But this was the young woman who brought to the surface Dickens's most dangerous and powerful emotions. He first encountered her at rehearsals of *The Frozen Deep* with her mother and sister, rehearsals which took place intensively for three days just before they all travelled up to Manchester on the railroad. At first, from Dickens's own descriptions, it would seem that he was most struck by Ellen's slightly older sister, Maria – struck, at least, by the ready emotionalism of her response to his performance as Richard Wardour. She had already seen one of the performances of the play at the Gallery of Illustration and, when she arrived for the rehearsals, she said, according to Dickens himself, "I am afraid, Mr Dickens, I shall never be able to bear it; it affected me so much when I saw it, that I hope you will excuse my trembling this morning, for I am afraid of myself." She might have said something like this, but the actual speech bears all the marks of having been half-invented by Dickens himself; "I am afraid of myself" being, as we have seen, one of his own favourite expressions. In another account of the same conversation Dickens has her saying, "I cried so much when I saw it, that I have a dread of it, and I don't know what to do." Which sounds more likely to be correct.

In this period of preparation, as if he had an anticipatory sense of some extraordinary change in his life, Dickens was altogether restless and was taking a little opium to help him sleep. Catherine in turn was very ill; ill enough, certainly, to have a doctor despatched from London to Gad's Hill Place in order to attend her. The exact nature of her complaint is not clear, although it may well have been a repetition of that nervous prostration which had afflicted her in the past; perhaps she, too, had some uneasy anticipation of what was to occur in her own life. She was recovered sufficiently, however, to travel with her husband to Manchester together with the rest of the cast. The train was delayed and, while they all waited, Dickens (known facetiously as 'The Manager') passed conundrums from his carriage to that of the actors.

Question: "Why is Dickens's stomach at this moment like a butler's pantry?"

Answer: "Because there is a sink in ⟨sinking⟩ there."

The first night was held in the New Free Trade Hall on 21 August, and the night belonged to Dickens. Wilkie Collins recalled that "he literally electrified the audience". As Dickens put it himself, "It was a good thing to have a couple of thousand people all rigid and frozen together, in the palm of one's hand . . . and to see the hardened Carpenters at the sides crying and trembling at it night after night." The carpenters were not the only ones to cry. At the end of the play Maria Ternan had to cradle the dying Dickens in her lap, and "when we came to that point at night, her tears fell down my face, down my beard . . . down my ragged dress – poured all over me like Rain, so that it was as much as I could do to speak for them".

Dickens (whispering): "My dear child, it will be over in two minutes. Pray compose yourself."

Maria Ternan: "It's no comfort to me that it will be soon over. Oh it is so sad, it is so dreadfully sad. Oh don't die. Give me time, give me a little time! Don't take leave of me in this terrible way – pray, pray pray!!"

Dickens went on, "And if you had seen the poor little thing, when the Curtain fell, put in a chair behind it – with her mother and sister taking care of her – and your humble servant drying her eyes and administering Sherry (in Rags so horrible that they would scarcely hold together), and the people in front all blowing their noses, and our own people behind standing about in corners and getting themselves right again, you would have remembered it for a long, long time."

Another witness of the last night at Manchester (a third was arranged, even as they were there, because of the crowds flocking to both of the scheduled performances) remarked that it was ". . . too real, too painful, the men were sobbing, and Mark Lemon on the stage was crying every night, although he had seen and played in it so often . . ." In other words, something extraordinary was happening in the New Free Trade Hall. There was some power coming out of Dickens which, in Collins's word, "electrified" those watching him – the power of what? Of thwarted emotion? Of all the loss and helplessness embodied in Richard Wardour's self-sacrifice and death? And what did he feel as Ellen Ternan, already with some extraordinary hold over him, spoke her own lines with her sister:

Ellen: "My dear, I shall always remain what I am now, because the man I loved with all my heart is . . ."

Maria: "Dead?"

Ellen: "Dead to me. Married . . . I don't think he ever suspected how dearly I loved him."

Here was the young and pretty actress who somehow provoked in Dickens all the longings he had once attached to others like Christiana Weller. She acted as a catalyst for the idealised love he seemed to harbour within himself, that aspiration towards, and passion for, *the one thing missing in his life*; and it would not be going too far to suggest that, when she spoke those lines in *The Frozen Deep*, Dickens himself was caught in the momentum of the drama to such an extent that he saw himself as Ellen's actual love. This was why the play was so real for him, and why in his desperate last moments as Wardour his pain transmitted itself to actors and audience alike. Yet there was a part of him that remained detached and watchful even now; as he lay dying with the audience weeping in front of him, ". . . new ideas for a story have come into my head as I lay on the ground, with surprising force and brilliancy". (He is likely to have glimpsed the sacrificial death for love of Sydney Carton in *A Tale of Two Cities*.) And then, as quickly as he could, he dressed himself for the farce.

There was of course a party after the last night, but Dickens retired to bed early. And the cause was Ellen Ternan. "I have never known," he wrote to Wilkie Collins some while later, "a moment's peace or content, since the last night of *The Frozen Deep*. I do suppose that there never was a man so seized and rended by one spirit." He had returned to London but was embroiled in a state of intense restlessness, dreariness, misery. It had broken out at last, that feeling which he had kept under control with hard work and long walks and vivid theatricals and constant activity. That feeling which he had always sensed in himself as part of himself. ". . . I feel," he told Miss Burdett-Coutts, "as if the scaling of all the Mountains in Switzerland, or the doing of any wild thing until I dropped, would be but a slight relief;" it is as if he literally had to tear his feelings out of his own breast. ". . . I want to escape from myself," he wrote to Collins the day after his outburst to Miss Burdett-Coutts. "For when I *do* start up and stare myself seedily in the face, as happens to be my case at present, my blankness is inconceivable – indescribable – my misery amazing." And then again, four days later to Henry Austin, "Low spirits, low pulse, low voice, intense reaction. If I were not like Mr Micawber, 'falling back for a spring' on Monday, I think I should slink into a corner and cry." But the spring was almost broken; on the same day he wrote to Hans Christian Andersen from Gad's Hill Place, and the whole sad pitch of his feelings infects the outer world. "The cornfields that were golden when you were here are ploughed up brown. The hops are being picked, the leaves on the trees are just beginning to turn, and the rain is falling as I write – very sadly – very steadily." Of his family he says hardly anything, except that "when I come back I shall find them dining here by lamplight", and even in this picture of the family meal (once so beloved in his fiction) there is nothing but the intimations of sadness. When he is discussing his plans for the future, in another letter, the same weariness creeps in. "I shall have to give myself up for a week or two to some friends who are coming, and then the dreary leaves will

begin to fall and my wintry plans will gather about me." At Gad's Hill
Place he was jotting down notes for the story which he had conceived
as he lay upon the stage, but nothing was to come of them for many
months. There was no escape from the feeling which had always been
latent within him – this weariness, misery and blankness so much like
the sensations of his childhood. The feeling of being "neglected and
hopeless"; the "miserable blank" of his life; the time when "I felt as if
my heart were rent". All these are words from his own memories of
his childhood, but they could equally well be applied to this period of
his life also, all the old feelings triggered off by the sight of a young,
attractive and unattainable girl. And compounded now by the sense of
his own ageing, of life closing down. Forster was to say of this period
in his friend's life that "there was for him no 'city of the mind' against
outward ills, for inner consolation and shelter". But this is to do
Dickens less than justice; he had a "city of the mind" in his fiction
itself. But he had to suffer the disadvantages of his gifts; his quick
imaginative excitement and his loss of self-possession in the characters
of his imagination were now the very qualities which unnerved him,
saddened him, rendered him desperate. He saw too much; he *experienced* too much; he conjured up too readily images of decay and
suffering. Perhaps, at such moments, he turned too easily to tragedy
or melodrama. All the characteristics that made him a great novelist
were now directed against his own self. Yet, in Dickens's life, there
was always somebody else to blame and even as his own misery
increased so did his disaffection from his wife; ". . . the years have not
made it easier to bear for either of us," he told Forster, "and, for her
sake as well as mine, the wish will force itself upon me that something
might be done. I know too well it is impossible. There is the fact, and
that is all one can say." Some months before he had written in
Household Words that "the Law of Divorce is in such condition that
from the tie of marriage there is no escape to be had, no absolution to
be got . . ."

But his was not a character to succumb to mere resignation. He
followed Ellen Ternan, and some words in *Our Mutual Friend*, a novel
in part concerned with helpless passion, may be significant here. "You
draw me to you. If I were shut up in a strong prison, you would draw
me out. I should break through the wall to come to you. If I were lying
on a sick bed, you would draw me up – to stagger to your feet and fall
there." These are sufficiently alarming sentiments and Dickens immediately observes, "The wild energy of the man, now quite let loose,

was absolutely terrible." Lines which in themselves evoke Wilkie Collins's comment on Charles Dickens at this time, as conveyed in a narrative they were soon jointly to write: "To me you are an absolutely terrible fellow. You do nothing like another man. Where another fellow would fall into a footbath of action or emotion, you fall into a mine." Collins wrote these lines of a man who was in the thrall of a complete passion. Dickens had heard that the Ternans were about to travel to the North, to appear in a special season at Doncaster, and, within a week of his return from Manchester, he started preparing for a journey in precisely the same direction. He was arranging an expedition of some two weeks with Collins, ostensibly to write some articles on the North of England for *Household Words*. But he was drawn towards Ellen Ternan as towards a lodestone; at the beginning of September he was booking rooms for a week at the Angel Hotel, Doncaster, since he already knew that the Ternans were to be performing at the Princess's Theatre there. On the same day he sent a solution of a riddle to a friend; unexceptionable in itself but, as we shall see, the notion of a "riddle" stayed in his mind. Four days later he and Collins took the train from Euston Square terminus to Carlisle, and from there on the following day they rode on to the little village of Heske. Dickens had an end in view; he had read about ". . . a certain black old Cumberland hill or mountain, called Carrock, or Carrock Fell". And almost as soon as they had arrived Dickens wanted to exhaust himself, wear himself out, *climb a mountain* as lovers do in fairy-stories. As Dickens said in the narrative he and Collins were to weave out of their adventures, *The Lazy Tour of Two Idle Apprentices*, "If I fell into that state of mind about a girl, do you think I'd lay me doon and dee? No, sir . . . I'd get me oop and peetch into somebody." Through the parodic Scottish brogue can be heard the true voice of Dickens. So with a reluctant Collins, and the landlord of the inn where they had decided to stay, he made his way resolutely towards Carrock Fell; a gloomy and lonely eminence indeed into which he could "peetch" all his wildness and despair.

As on Mount Vesuvius so many years before, Dickens began doggedly and earnestly to ascend, followed with varying degrees of enthusiasm by his two companions. Then mist descended. It began to rain very heavily. Dickens still had to "go on". A keen wind started to blow, the mist became impenetrable. Still he had to ascend further, to move forward. But they were lost; even the landlord had no idea of their location. Then Wilkie Collins slipped upon a wet stone, fell heavily to the ground, and badly sprained his ankle. Again it was like the trek upon the side of Vesuvius: Dickens wanted to go on to the top, regardless of the fears and mishaps of the others. It is almost like one of Dickens's primal scenes, this remorseless ascent while others are injured or fall behind. But he carried Collins on their descent; just like the self-sacrificing Richard Wardour "in private life", he said. (So he was still, after all, in the play!) Eventually the three mountaineers found their way to safety and to the inn, but the injury to Wilkie Collins meant that one of the aims of this Northern expedition – to see as much of the country as possible – had to be in part curtailed. Yet nothing could stop Dickens's resolution to go on with the trip; they travelled to Wigton,˙ from there to Allonby, and then on to Lancaster, Leeds and eventually to Doncaster. Collins could still move a pen despite his inflamed ankle, of course, and even as they travelled they established a routine for the writing of their journal; breakfast at half-past eight and then work, Dickens all the time tidying up the room after Collins. After work, for Dickens, long walks while his companion remained in the relative comfort of the inns and hotels. From Allonby he had written to Georgina and, for the first time, sent his love to his children but not to his wife. He did not write to Catherine at all but at the end of one letter he addressed Georgina as "My dearest Georgy", and from his tone it seems clear that he had already entered into some kind of compact with her; a compact not about Ellen Ternan, but rather about his feelings for Catherine.

By the middle of the month, a week after setting out upon their journey, he and Collins arrived at Doncaster. To the real object of his journey. It was the famous race week here and, although one of their ostensible purposes had been to describe that jamboree, Dickens was far more interested in the Ternans who were now billed to appear as part of Charles Kean's company. Certainly he visited their theatre; there is a newspaper report of Dickens and Collins being sighted in the boxes and becoming "objects of the most marked attention and conversation". Dickens recorded the same incident rather differently, and seemed annoyed when actors and audience alike gave "Three cheers for Charles Dickens, esquire!" He had all at once to become the smiling public man even while he was on a private mission, even while his real self was wounded and desperate. It is not clear that he actually watched the Ternans perform at that theatre, but it is almost inconceivable that he did not in fact see Ellen, on Tuesday, 15 September, in her minor roles in *The Ladies Club* (written by Mark Lemon) and *The*

Pet of the Petticoats. It seems likely also that she was subject to some ribaldry from the largely louche and drunken race-course "set" who frequented the theatre in this week, since in *The Lazy Tour of Two Idle Apprentices* he launches a vicious diatribe against odious gentlemen who "put vile constructions on sufficiently innocent phrases in the play . . ." So was this the occasion when Dickens comforted Ellen in the dressing-room? Had she wept after some more than usually disgusting remarks from the pit? Certainly it is possible. It is also possible – indeed likely – that Dickens asked the Ternan ladies to allow him to escort them to the races on the following day, and there are indications that he went on excursions with Ellen and her mother. In two rather cryptic letters to W. H. Wills he explains that he has come to Doncaster ". . . along of his Richard Wardour! Guess *that* riddle, Mr Wills!" And then two days later, "I am going to take the little – riddle – into the country this morning . . . So let the riddle and the riddler go their own wild way, and no harm come of it." The activities of Dickens in Doncaster, then, are camouflaged by his own penchant for mystery and dramatic irony as well as by his pressing need for secrecy. It seems, however, that, accompanied or unaccompanied, he attended the Corn Market, visited some local ruins and then left rather precipitately on the following Monday. The cause of his unexpected departure is not known, but in a letter a short while later he wrote that "the Doncaster unhappiness remains so strong upon me that I can't write, and (waking) can't rest, one minute". Something had happened. Some kind of rebuff, perhaps, or some kind of misunderstanding. It is not at all obvious what it might be, however, just as the actual relationship between Dickens and Ellen Ternan at this time is also unclear. There is no reason why he should not have felt himself able to attract a much younger woman – he at the age of forty-five, and she eighteen. It ought not to be forgotten that Ellen's own father had died when she was seven years old, and she might therefore have been impressed by the idea of a "father figure". It seems also that Dickens still conceived of himself as a young man, or even younger; in one of his letters to Wills he declared that he meant to be "as good a boy" as he had ever been. Similarly, in *The Lazy Tour of Two Idle Apprentices* he calls himself Francis *Goodchild.* Yet there is something odd here. A good boy. A good child. These are his images of himself at the time when he was following Ellen Ternan to Doncaster; this does not suggest the hope or prospect of any sexual relationship but something more pervasive and more infantilist. Something very peculiar was happening to Dickens at this period in his life, and one might recall here what he had written at an earlier date. "I think I'd rather *not* love, unless I could do it in an original manner. I seem to have been always doing it in the regular way, ever since I ran alone."

As soon as he returned to London he began work upon those portions of *The Lazy Tour* . . . which he had not written in the North, since the short narrative was to begin publication in *Household Words* at the start of the following month. It is not in itself a particularly interesting piece of travel-writing; not surprising, perhaps, since the whole venture was merely a device to visit Ellen in Doncaster. But there are moments when it becomes unwittingly revealing about Mr Goodchild *aka* Dickens ". . . who is always in love with somebody . . ."; who is ". . . a bold, gay, active man in the prime of life"; who repeats rhapsodically "O little lilac gloves! And O winning little bonnet, making in conjunction with her golden hair quite a Glory in the sunlight round the pretty head, why anything in the world but you and me!"; who laments "the desert of my heart". How odd that Dickens should, even in such an oblique fashion, declare his love for the little person with the lilac gloves and the golden hair (Ellen Ternan had golden hair); but the fact is that he could no more have stopped himself writing this than he could have stopped breathing. He only really felt it when he had composed it; to have left these sentiments unstated would have meant that, for him, they did not really exist. Dickens was not "idle" at all. He was desperate, or at least close to desperation, and throughout the short narrative there are images of thwarted or misshapen love. In one story included within the fabric of these travels, a man literally *wills* his wife to death; but the wife's name is *Ellen*. Strange reaches of consciousness here; and in the story's sequel, too, where a young man ("Dick") falls asleep while an older man tried to prise him awake. Can we see here the restless torment within Dickens's own self, the older man trying to keep awake the younger man, trying to warn him – "Get up and walk, Dick! . . . Try!" – but being unable to do so. "I can't . . . I don't know what strange influence is stealing over me." Who issued the warning, and who needed it? Thus did he entangle himself, fight with himself, in the same week that he wrote to Forster, "Poor Catherine and I are not made for each other, and there is no help for it." And then, a few days later, ". . . Too late to say, put the curb on, and don't rush at hills . . . I have now no relief but in action. I am become incapable of rest. I am quite confident I should rust, break, and die, if I spared myself. Much better to die, doing."

By the beginning of October Ellen Ternan had returned from the Doncaster theatricals and Mrs Ternan found rooms for herself and two of her daughters (Fanny had taken up an engagement in Dublin) in Canonbury. Within a matter of days Ellen herself was engaged at the Theatre Royal, Haymarket, where she remained for much of the next two years; this seems like a natural move, but in fact Dickens had more than a small role in negotiating it. For in the middle of the month, after Ellen had joined the company, he was thanking the manager, Buckstone, for his help in arranging matters so well; "I need hardly tell you that my interest in the young lady does not cease with the effecting of this arrangement . . ." And, in the meantime, something had happened further to estrange Dickens from his wife. It is not clear what it might have been; there were any number of misunderstandings between them and, according to Dickens's own report to Emile de la Rue, Catherine was often jealous of his relations with other women and was inclined to suspect the worst. It is possible – even likely – that Catherine had discovered that the Ternans were appearing at the Doncaster Theatre just when her husband visited the town. Likely, too, that she had read her husband's encomium on the golden-haired, lilac-gloved sweetheart in *A Lazy Tour* . . . It is even possible that she had found out about Dickens's successful efforts to enrol Ellen Ternan at the Theatre Royal. Did she say something? Something which enraged him? It has already been suggested how he detested those who placed a ribald construction on Ellen's innocent lines in the Princess's Theatre, and his savagery was often elicited when he believed that something innocent and sacred to himself was being misinterpreted or abused; he had, for example, reacted angrily, almost hysterically, to the less than awestruck comments in the visitors' book at Niagara Falls. So if Dickens was at this time suffused by an innocent and almost infantile love for Ellen Ternan, if she had for him become something of a sacred and untouchable object, it is not difficult to understand his fury if anyone, even his wife, should place what he considered to be a false construction upon his behaviour. But all this is mere surmise; the facts are clear enough. Finally, irrevocably, he turned away from Catherine. On 11 October he asked her maid, Anne Brown, radically to alter the sleeping quarters for his wife and himself; what had been a shared room was to be cut in two and henceforth Dickens would sleep alone, a partition between his wife and himself. He was withdrawing from her, literally sealing himself off from her. Three or four days later he left Tavistock House after a quarrel with Catherine; he left his bed at two o'clock in the morning, unable to sleep, and walked all the way to Gad's Hill Place. A distance of some thirty miles. "The road was so lonely in the night," he wrote later, "that I fell asleep to the monotonous sound of my own feet, doing their regular four miles an hour. Mile after mile I walked, without the slightest sense of exertion, dozing heavily and dreaming constantly." More than seven hours' walking. In his broken pedestrian sleep he made up verses, spoke in a foreign language, believed that he was about to breakfast in an "Alpine Convent". Seven hours, never once stopping. And of what else did he dream in this extraordinary nocturnal expedition? Only a few weeks later he was telling Mrs Watson about the Princess of the fairy-stories, ". . . you have no idea how intensely I love her!" In fact on more than one occasion he obliquely describes Ellen as a "princess" out of the story-books. Yet how strange it is that she seems already to have become less a living human being than a creature from his imaginary world and a figment of his heart's desires. Even in the heat of Dickens's passion we may look for explanations to Dickens the fabulist.

But there was also and always Dickens the public man, who even in these days must work on; work on with *Household Words*, work on with his speeches and engagements, work on with the next Christmas issue of the periodical. For the latter, at least, he found his theme readily enough; the Indian Mutiny had erupted earlier in the year, and the carnage inflicted upon the British community in India by the native inhabitants seems to have provoked in Dickens a rage which blended easily with his private discontents. It is hard otherwise to understand what was a mood of rabid violence; he told Miss Burdett-Coutts that he wished he was Commander-in-Chief in India and ". . . that I should do my utmost to exterminate the Race upon whom the stain of the late cruelties rested . . . with all convenient dispatch and merciful swiftness of execution, to blot it out of mankind and raze it off the face of the Earth . . ." It is not often that a great novelist recommends genocide . . . Something of this mood and theme was now also reconstructed in his story for the Christmas issue of *Household Words*. It was entitled "The Perils of Certain English Prisoners" and, unlike previous Christmas supplements in *Household Words*, it was composed by him and Collins alone (Dickens himself writing the major part of it). It is a curious story about an uprising on a tropical island, where a combined force of natives and pirates attacks a garrison of English settlers; the settlers are captured, taken into the jungle but eventually, after a series of heroic deeds and painful setbacks, manage to escape. It was clearly based in part upon the Indian Mutiny, although Dickens emphasised that he did not want to make any "vulgar association" with current events; it is appropriate, then, that his genocidal rage is at least partly kept in check and no stridently jingoistic or patriotic note is introduced. Instead it become once more a tale of heroism, hopeless love, and self-sacrifice – just as Richard Wardour's had been – and, interestingly enough, it features a certain Captain Carton who would later be resuscitated as Sydney Carton in *A Tale of Two Cities*. In other words, Dickens's imagination clustered around the same theme or set of themes throughout this period – struggle, heroism, endurance, self-sacrifice and, running beneath all of these, a thin strain of unrequited and unfulfilled love for an object too far out of reach, too sacred to be touched. And he was very restless. "I weary of rest, and have no satisfaction but in fatigue." He gave two readings of *A Christmas Carol*, one for the Mechanics' Institute at Coventry and one for a similar organisation in Rochester. He invited Miss Burdett-Coutts to dine "with us" at the end of November, so there was at least some pretence of, or approximation to, ordinary domestic life in the Dickens household. But there was no Christmas party this year at Tavistock House.

Uncertainties pursued him into the following year. He was not sure whether or not to begin a new novel; he had written down the notes which had occurred to him during *The Frozen Deep*, but he could not yet settle to such a long task. He wanted something to divert and preoccupy his "worried mind" but he found that, for the first time in his life, he could not properly discipline himself. He still planned to work on the novel through the summer in order that he might begin publishing in the late autumn; he even had a title in mind, of a sufficiently foreboding kind, *One Of These Days*; and yet, and yet . . .

He was reading, but not in a desultory way; he realised at once that *Scenes of Clerical Life*, by the unknown author George Eliot, had in fact been written by a woman. He considered it a fine novel as well, and Mary Ann Evans "treasured" the enthusiastic letter which Dickens sent to her. But there was no doubt that he remained in a fevered and overwrought state. He had a powerful sense of "change impending over us", in itself debilitating for a man of fixed habits, and a mild letter from Catherine to Miss Burdett-Coutts, asking for her help in placing Catherine's brother in a "situation", provoked a rage in Dickens quite disproportionate to its cause; he wrote at once, apologising for his wife's perfectly reasonable request and added, ". . . I hope you will forgive her more freely and more readily than I do." His birthday dinner, a few days later, was a somewhat bleak affair, the only guests being Collins and Forster, and Dickens no doubt took advantage of the occasion to give vent to his feelings. He was angry, unsettled, and yet two days later he gave what is arguably his finest and most powerful address. It was on behalf of the Hospital for Sick Children in Great Ormond Street which, after six years, still had only thirty-one beds at its disposal in a city where over twenty thousand children died each year. It was a theme close to Dickens, for did he still not think of himself at times as a *child*, and a sick child at that? But it was also one which could elicit all that was noblest and most humane in his nature. In the course of a long speech, he recalled a visit he had made to the slums of Edinburgh; ". . . there lay, in an old egg-box which the mother had begged from a shop, a feeble, wasted, wan, sick child. With his little wasted face, and his little hot worn hands folded over his breast, and his little bright attentive eyes, I can see him now, as I have seen him for several years, looking steadily at us. There he lay in his little frail box, which was not at all a bad emblem of the little body from which he was slowly parting – there he lay, quite quiet, quite patient, saying never a word. He seldom cried, the mother said; he seldom complained; 'he lay there, seeming to wonder what it was a' aboot'. God knows I thought, as I stood looking at him, he had his reasons for wondering . . . and why, in the name of a gracious God, such things should be!" The whole speech needs to be read before its full impact can be understood but it had a "quite startling" effect upon its auditors, according to Forster, and Dickens ". . . probably never moved any audience so much . . ." Three thousand pounds was raised that night, and Dickens promised to read *A Christmas Carol* a few weeks later for the same fund; as a direct result of his efforts, in fact, the Hospital for Sick Children was properly endowed for the first time. So here is another measure of the man and of his influence; no doubt his pathetic picture of the sick infant was fuelled in part by his own feelings of misery and weariness but, at the time of greatest personal crisis in his life, he was able to make such a speech for such a cause.

It was a speech which had more than a public effect, however. It helped to alter the direction of Dickens's life. For the extraordinary responsiveness of the audience to this address, all the tears and the laughter and the cheers, served to confirm something which he had always known – he had a great power at his command. He had known it during *The Frozen Deep*. He had known it during his charitable readings. Was there any way he could now make use of it? So it was that in his restless and dissatisfied state, unable to start a new book, he turned his mind once more to the possibility of giving a series of paid public readings from his works; if he could not resume contact with his audience by writing another novel, he could nevertheless remain in close touch with it. He was even thinking, somewhat vaguely, of returning to America and reading there. He needed something in which he could lose himself and forget his misery. He needed *activity*. He needed to *exhaust* himself. He also needed the money; in February, for reason or reasons unknown, he had borrowed from his solicitors on the security of his copyrights. Everything conspired to turn him towards this new direction, therefore, and to take commercial advantage of a skill he knew he possessed.

It was in March that he began seriously to plan an extended season of readings, beginning in London and then extending to the provinces, although even still he was keenly aware of the possible dangers involved in turning himself into what was essentially a public entertainer. Ever since the early Forties he had emphasised the dignity and the value of the novelist's calling, of course, and now he began a series of conversations with his friends and his publishers to test whether that calling would be in any way diminished by his new role. He asked Bradbury and Evans about the possible effect upon his next book; and of course he talked to Forster, who seems to have been alone among his friends in objecting to the idea as an abrogation of his powers and his responsibilities. Since Dickens's mind seems to have been firmly made up even before he began to take advice from his friends, he quickly dismissed Forster's objections as "irrational" and presumed that his new wife's money had in some way gone to his head (typical of him to make such a judgment about even an old friend who opposed his wishes). By the end of the month, in fact, his plans were set; he would read *A Christmas Carol* both in London and in the provinces, by the end of which tour he hoped to have netted ". . . *a very large sum of money*". Arthur Smith was to be his manager; they had worked together on the administration of *The Frozen Deep*, and Smith had the added advantage of being the brother of Albert Smith whose own performances, albeit of a very different kind from those which

Dickens envisaged, might yield profitable clues about the best way of proceeding. The fact was that Dickens was following in a long tradition, and Albert Smith was only one of many entertainers who performed in one-man shows. As a young man Dickens had been powerfully affected by Charles Mathews's "monopolylogues", for example, and actors often recited Shakespearian verse at various provincial and metropolitan theatres; more particularly, there was a tradition of writers giving series of lectures, Coleridge, perhaps, being the most notable exponent of that public art. Dickens himself knew instinctively what skills were involved. On one occasion, for example, he and Forster had attended a recitation by Westland Marston of one of his own plays; at the conclusion Dickens went up to Marston and said "You don't know the way to read", and then recited to him the second act. "The change was surprising," according to one observer. "As Dickens read the characters seemed to stand out and almost walk about the room. 'There, Marston,' he said, 'that is the way to do it.'" But there was a difference. It was not usual for novelists to recite from their own books in the same way, and it is significant that Dickens had decided to read only from his Christmas Books on this first tour, to be succeeded in the following year by another Christmas story written especially for the occasion. These seasonal books seemed to him to be the best way of connecting himself to any audience, therefore, relying as they did upon the kind of directness and intimacy of address which were not always evident in his novels. But they were also his most conventionally "serious" work. If he saw himself as a public entertainer, it was one who would stir the conscience as well as excite the laughter of his audiences.

First there came a test; some time before he had agreed to read for the Philosophical Institution of Edinburgh, and he decided now to rehearse with them *A Christmas Carol* before beginning the series of paid readings. The event was held towards the end of March, just after Dickens had been solemnly if single-mindedly conferring with friends and colleagues, and it confirmed all of his instincts. He had been very careful about the arrangements in advance. He travelled to Edinburgh with Wills and inspected the Music Hall before the reading itself. "There must be no one behind me," he told one of the organisers, ". . . I must see everyone's face and they must see mine . . . everyone must see my face." The organiser whom he addressed, David Douglas, also recalled that "I was surprised to meet a somewhat carelessly dressed little man, wearing a short coat, figured or tartan waistcoat, apparently travel stained . . . His complexion was a dull brick red, his jowls strongly marked and the face clean shaven. He might easily have been mistaken for a sailor just returned from a voyage."

The reading was, according to Dickens, a "tremendous success". As he arrived on the platform he was greeted with great applause, and at once, in the coolest possible manner, he explained to his audience that they should allow their emotions to be expressed "in the most natural way" and that he hoped they would resemble "a small group of friends assembled to hear a tale told". This was, again, greeted with applause. And then he read once more the story of Ebenezer Scrooge. Wills noted "wonderful unanimity. Wonderful happiness. Cheers and guffaws and pocket-handkerchiefs all in their right places." Dickens was encouraged and gratified by the success. "It is an unspeakable satisfaction to me," he told Wills, "to have left such an impression in Edinburgh." He knew, now, that he could perform the same feat elsewhere, although he was rendered somewhat nervous by the news that the Queen would very much like to hear a reading of *A Christmas Carol* at some favourable opportunity. Dickens was disturbed at the thought of reading it to her alone; he needed an audience with whom he could conspire, and suggested very gently that the Queen might care to listen to him under those circumstances. Of course there were still dissenting voices and a certain John Tulloch, who had been present at the Edinburgh reading, noted ". . . that it was too *histrionic*"; he said of Dickens's appearance that "it is a sort of mixture of the *waiter* and the actor, Frenchified in his dress to a degree quite disagreeable. He has not a pleasant face, singular lines – I don't know whether of care – running under his eyes and from his mouth – in short, not very gentlemanly." The lines of care were certainly there by now, but the idea of his not being "gentlemanly" might have more concerned the novelist on the verge of taking up what was in all practical senses a new and ambiguous career. He read *A Christmas Carol* once more for charity, on behalf of the Hospital for Sick Children, and then at the end of April he gave his first paid public reading in St Martin's Hall. It was of *The Cricket on the Hearth*, and over the next three months he read at least twice a week in London; after which, he set out upon his provincial tour. So he embarked upon a course of readings that he was to follow for the next twelve years. In fact, for the rest of his life.

A large audience had assembled for this first one in St Martin's Hall. Dickens stepped onto the platform, flower in his buttonhole and gloves in hand. He showed no outward signs of nervousness but, according to Edmund Yates, he was "walking rather stiffly, right shoulder well forward"; but at once he was greeted by a "roar of cheering which might have been heard at Charing Cross". Dickens remained composed. Before he began, he made an announcement. He had decided, he said, to take up "reading on my own account, as one of my recognised occupations" and he went on to say that "firstly, I have satisfied myself that it can involve no possible compromise of the credit and independence of literature. Secondly I have long held the opinion, and have long acted on the opinion, that in these times whatever brings a public man and his public face to face, on terms of mutual confidence and respect, is a good thing". Then he went on to speak of the ties almost "of personal friendship" between himself and his readers. "Thus it is that I come, quite naturally, to be here among you at this time; and thus it is that I proceed to read this little book, quite as composedly as I might proceed to write it, or to publish it in any other way." One of the audience remembers Dickens's "clearness of articulation, as though he were particularly desirous that every word should be thoroughly weighed by his hearers . . ." Dickens was in fact trying to suggest that it was a natural and even almost inevitable development of his art, that there was nothing unusual about reading in public, and that it could only confirm the relationship he had already established with his audience. That he believed this there is no doubt; but of course he had left out of account the two most pressing reasons for his decision to read. He did not mention the feverish restlessness which had destroyed his domestic happiness and which had almost driven him to this fresh activity, and he did not mention (as he had done to his friends) his hopes of earning a great deal of money in a relatively short space of time.

He still recognised problems, of course, and was particularly nervous about reading *The Chimes*. "To tell you the truth," he told Thomas Beard, ". . . I *can not* yet (and I have been at it all the morning) command sufficient composure at some of the more affecting parts, to project them with the necessary force, the requisite distance. I must harden my heart, like Lady Macbeth." He had struck upon the real secret of any such undertaking: in order to move his auditors he must not himself be moved. He was determined to acquire whatever skills he needed for such work; all his life, he had taken on challenges only to wrest victory from them. And this was now something that he knew he had to do. "I must do *something*," he told Forster, "or I shall wear my heart away." Here the single most important reason for the readings emerges once more in his own words; his misery at home, his unsatisfied longings for Ellen Ternan, were pushing him forward and ". . . the mere physical effort and change of the Readings would be good, as another means of bearing it". It is even possible that he rehearsed his readings in front of Mrs Ternan (and perhaps Ellen, too), since she knew a great deal about the art of elocution. And so he had begun, his unsatisfied love for a young woman turning his life around.

Chapter 27

DICKENS had once told an actress, "in his rapid, earnest way, and with a slight lisp which he had, 'Ah! When you're young you want to be old; when you're getting old you want to be young . . .'". It was in this spirit that Dickens was about to set in train a series of events which would forever change his life. "Who then could have conceived or prophesied," Percy Fitzgerald wrote later, "that in the year of grace 1858, the whole fabric should have begun to totter, and that a strange, sudden change should have come about. This literally – I remember it well – took away all our breaths . . .". And if Dickens could have foreseen precisely what would happen, would he have changed his course? No. No will could ever be set up against his own and, at a time when he seems to re-experience something of his old childhood misery and sense of abandonment, he exhibits once more that firmness of purpose, that ardour against the barriers of the world, that belief in self-transformation, which had animated his earliest years. This was his second battle, even if it were essentially a battle against himself, and he was not about to shirk it. So much of his life and struggle seemed to him at such times to be a dream, and yet what of his own dreams now? "Only last night," he told Macready in the middle of March, "in my sleep, I was bent upon getting over a perspective of barriers, with my hands and feet bound. Pretty much what we are all about, waking, I think?"

In the early months of 1858 he was just as disaffected from Catherine, but the tone of his remarks is one of solemn weariness and endurance. "A dismal failure has to be borne," he said to Forster, "and there an end." But he had burst into tears, had cried and sobbed, when he watched a play by Westland Marston in which a man falls in love with a young woman. As soon as he returned from Edinburgh he had felt himself to be beset by "a crowd of cares" and, in a strange letter to a certain Mrs Hogge, he seems to be comparing himself to an abandoned orphan. "He is crying somewhere, by himself, at this moment. I can't dry his eyes. He is being neglected by some ogress of a nurse. I can't rescue him." Once more the conditions of his life sent Dickens hurtling back to his infancy, or at least to a myth of his infancy in which he is once more the poor, sick child in need of female comfort. He is Goodchild again, without his nurse. As for his public, adult life, "All the rest of my world turns as it did, and that's not saying much for it." But it was an endurance and weariness shot through with flashes of desperation, with a kind of helpless longing for some other life; in a short article for *Household Words*, published at the beginning of May, "Please To Leave Your Umbrella", he explains how he is haunted by a "little reason" (shades of the "little riddle" in Doncaster) and how "my little reason" took him visiting Hampton Court Palace. Any interested party would have been quite able to read between the lines of this somewhat coy essay and to recognise Dickens's infatuation with someone unnamed; ". . . I and my little reason, Yorick, would keep house here, all our lives, in perfect contentment . . ." Once again, he simply could not help but proclaim his own passion. Just as he could not help parodying Leigh Hunt or ridiculing his own mother, so he could not help but put down in writing that which preoccupied him. He never really paused to consider its effect upon others, and was therefore always surprised by disgruntled or bitter reactions. It was hardly likely, however, that he would care about Catherine's reaction to this particular piece of imaginary infidelity.

For it was at this time, at the beginning of May, that something happened to provoke from him rather more than weariness at an unhappy marriage. There were one or two specific episodes which affected the events of the next few months, even though the incidents themselves have since been obscured in a cloud of gossip and speculation. One had to do with a small piece of jewellery. It was not unusual for Dickens to reward members of his amateur cast with "keepsakes" at the end of a season; Francisco Berger, who organised the musical aspects of Dickens's theatre, was for example given a pair of cuff-links. So it was that he had given a piece of jewellery to Ellen Ternan. In some accounts Dickens presented her with a brooch which contained his portrait or his initials; in other accounts he gave her a bracelet. Whatever the item, such a gift would have been given to the young actress in the autumn of 1857. Reports differ again about the revelation to Catherine of this gift; in one, the brooch needed to be mended and the jeweller to whom it was sent, seeing the initial or the portrait of Charles Dickens, had returned it to Tavistock House. Georgina told Catherine, who then "mounted her husband with comb and brush". But in another account the jeweller informed Mrs Dickens that "her" bracelet was ready for collection and it was at this point that she discovered her husband's gift to the young actress. Both reports are further muddled by the fact that, in the story of the brooch, Georgina Hogarth is said to have told Catherine because she was jealous of *Mrs* Ternan. Ellen Ternan is also described as Dickens's "god-daughter". In other words all the confusions which can be expected from hearsay and rumour abound in these accounts; if there is any truth in them at all, it can only be the reflection of the fact that, at some point, Catherine Dickens was rendered jealous by Dickens's gift or gifts to Ellen Ternan.

There are further ramifications. According to Dickens's daughter, Kate, she found her mother sobbing – ". . . seated at the dressing table in the act of putting on her bonnet, with tears rolling down her cheeks. Inquiring the cause of her distress, Mrs Dickens – between her sobs – replied: 'Your father has asked me to go and see Ellen Ternan.' 'You shall not go!' exclaimed Mrs Perugini [Kate], angrily stamping her foot. But she went . . ." Unfortunately, Kate seems to have given at least two other versions of the same story. In one of them she is supposed to have said that "her father asked her mother to go and see his 'woman' [Ellen Ternan] but my mother, rightly refused . . ." And, in another account, Dickens ordered his wife to see Mrs Ternan and not Ellen at all. The truth therefore is hidden somewhere at the bottom of the well – if anything can be made out of it all, it is perhaps as a reflection of Dickens's previous quarrels with his wife. It is undoubtedly true, for example, that he asked Catherine to apologise to the de la Rues over her unfounded suspicions about her husband's relationship with Madame de la Rue; perhaps we can reconstruct a scene in which Catherine, piqued by jealousy which Dickens believed to be unfounded, was asked to apologise to Ellen Ternan or to Mrs Ternan for her misconstructions. This seems the most probable course of events, but there is no doubt whatever about the sequel. Dickens had dinner with Forster on 4 May, and on the following day he saw Mark Lemon. He had decided that he must separate from his wife.

He wanted the actual process of separation to be handled as informally and as discreetly as possible; a man in his prominent public position could hardly act otherwise, and he proposed to his wife that they should lead separate lives while remaining to all outward appearances the same married couple as before. At first he suggested that she should have her own apartment in Tavistock House, and should appear at parties in her old role; a neat and agreeable solution for him, but not one that was likely to recommend itself to Catherine who would be forced to live a kind of charade. Then Dickens suggested that they should take it in turns to occupy the town house and the country house – she remaining at Tavistock House while he lived at Gad's Hill Place, and vice versa. There even seems to have been an idea that Catherine should live abroad, without her children, while Dickens remained in England. Of course Catherine rejected all such suggestions; or, rather, she and her family rejected them. Faced with her husband's sudden and no doubt bewildering desire to break all marital and domestic ties, she went for advice and for comfort to her parents. Her sister, Georgina, it seems, tacitly supported Dickens in his desire for new arrangements in which she inevitably would play a much larger role although her own somewhat anomalous position in any new household would have been (and was) a distinctly uncomfortable one.

Within days of his proposals for an informal separation being rejected, Dickens suggested that Catherine should set up house elsewhere and that he would then give her four hundred pounds a year, plus brougham – the latter article, the carriage, suggesting just how precisely Dickens thought he could "tie up" matters in this way. Certainly he seemed intent upon something as carefully arranged as one of his own fictions. Later he would declare that Catherine had first broached the idea of leaving home, but that is clearly not the case: whatever shortcomings she possessed as a mother (and these were only suggested by Georgina and Dickens) she had no desire whatever to abandon her children. It was he who wanted her to leave but, as soon as the Hogarths themselves began to take an active part in the negotiations, his hope for a quick, clean resolution evaporated. He was slowly but inevitably drawn into a protracted dispute, and part of the reason for his subsequent extraordinary, in some ways inexplicable, behaviour can be laid to the fact that he had lost control of events – a situation almost unique in his life, and one with which he really did not know how to deal. Mrs Hogarth came to stay with Catherine at Tavistock House, and on the following day Dickens left the house and moved into his offices at Wellington Street North. Forster was deputed to act for Dickens (he was to negotiate directly with Mrs Hogarth, whom Dickens detested), while it was agreed that Mark Lemon, a friend of both parties, should act as Catherine's representative.

It was from his office that Dickens now wrote to Miss Burdett-Coutts, no doubt an emblem of Victorian respectability he wished to placate. "We have been virtually separated for a long time," he wrote. "We must put a wider space between us now, than can be found in one house." But even at this early stage he found it necessary to defend himself from any reproach – it was he, after all, who had determined upon a separation – by attacking his wife. (He had of course used the same tactic in his often unfair diatribes against his publishers.) "If the children loved her, or ever had loved her," he told Miss Burdett-Coutts, "this severance would have been a far easier thing than it is." His logic here seems to have vanished. "But she has never attached one of them to herself, never played with them in their infancy, never attracted their confidence as they have grown older, never presented herself before them in the aspect of a mother." He went on to say that ". . . Mary and Katey (whose dispositions are of the gentlest and most affectionate conceivable) harden into stone figures of girls when they can be got to go near her . . ." On the evidence of the children themselves, all this was quite untrue. As Alfred Dickens was to say, "When the separation took place it made no difference in our feelings towards them: we their children always loved them both equally . . ." And how extraordinary for Dickens so to malign the woman with whom he had lived for the last twenty-two years. Whom he had once loved and praised. Tempting though it is, it would be too easy to say that he was simply lying in order to protect himself. This would be to misunderstand the very particular nature of the man. For him nothing was real until it was written down; he actually believed what he wrote as he wrote it, just as he "believed" in his novels; in the act of composing them they were more real to him than anything surrounding him in the actual world. So, too, with his strictures against Catherine; the imagery of the unnatural mother and of children turning into "stone", borrowed from his fiction, again took on vivid life before him. It was all now true for him, and in a sense he was reliving his childhood nightmares even as he was in the act of breaking up his own home. He said of stage management that it was like writing a book in company; during this marital separation, with his desire to control the participants, to determine negotiations and even to manipulate the reactions of onlookers, he was, in a sense, attempting to write a book out of real people and real events.

On the following day he summoned his eldest son and told him what was happening. Dickens was later to state that he persuaded his son to live with his mother (while the rest of the children were to remain with him) but again this looks as if the wish or fantasy were determining his recall of circumstances. All the available evidence suggests that the decision to stay with his mother was wholly or partly Charley's. The young man was so shocked by his father's news that it was only after he had left him, and gone to his bank in the City, that he was able to collect his thoughts sufficiently to write his father a short note – in the course of which he stated that: "Don't suppose that in making my choice, I was actuated by any feeling of preference for my mother to you. God knows I love you dearly, and it will be a hard day for me when I have to part from you and the girls. But in doing as I have done, I hope I am doing my duty, and that you will understand it so." His filial responsibility, in other words, determined that he should remain with, and look after, his abandoned mother.

And so, through the first two and half weeks of May, Forster and Lemon, with Catherine and Mrs Hogarth, tried to draw up a suitable deed of separation which would satisfy all parties without the need to enter a court of law. But Dickens's hopes of keeping the business secret were necessarily misplaced; rumours about the impending separation began to spread and, as is usually the case, rumour begat rumour. That he was having an affair with an actress. An actress at the Haymarket. Ellen Ternan. Maria Ternan. Mrs Ternan. No one seems to have been sure about the exact identity. That Mrs Dickens had written to the Haymarket, exonerating the said actress. That he had eloped with the very same actress to Boulogne. And then there were rumours, infinitely more damaging, that he was having an affair with his own sister-in-law. With Georgina Hogarth. That she had given birth to his children. More astonishing still, it seems likely that these rumours about Georgina were in fact started or at least not repudiated by the Hogarths themselves. The point was that Georgina had elected to stay with Dickens and his children even as Catherine was being forced to leave them and, in addition, it seems likely that she knew in advance of Dickens's plans to separate from his wife; his letters to her in the months before these events suggest that she was altogether in his confidence. As a result her mother and her younger sister, Helen, turned upon her; *she* was still in the confidence of the great novelist, while *they* were repudiated and despised. Could it be from these feelings of jealousy that so much malice spread? It can happen even in the best of families. "The question was not myself; but others," Dickens later wrote to Macready. "Foremost among them – of all people in the world – Georgina! Mrs Dickens's weakness, and her mother's and her younger sister's wickedness drifted to that, without seeing what they would strike against – though I had warned them in the strongest manner."

Events were now slipping even further out of Dickens's control, and it was at some point in these crucial days that Mrs Hogarth seems to have threatened Dickens with action in the Divorce Court – a very serious step indeed since the Divorce Act of the previous year had decreed that wives could divorce their husbands only on the grounds of incest, bigamy or cruelty. The clear implication here was that Dickens had committed "incest" with Georgina, which was the legal term for sexual relations with a sister-in-law. At Dickens's instigation Forster wrote an urgent letter to Dickens's solicitor, asking for clarification of the new Act; and at the same time, too, Georgina was examined by a doctor and found to be *virgo intacta*. At this point, it seems, the Hogarths implicitly dropped the threat of court action. Yet the bare facts of the matter can hardly suggest the maelstrom of fury and bitterness into which the family, now divided against itself, had descended. And what of Dickens himself? From the beginning he had tried to keep everything as neat and as ordered as everything else in his life, but it had spiralled out of control. The case for an informal separation had degenerated into a series of formal negotiations which in turn threatened to lead to public exposure of his domestic life; he, the apostle of family harmony, had even been accused of incest with his own wife's sister. He reacted badly to stress and now, during the most anxious days of his life, he ceased to behave in a wholly rational manner. "My father was like a madman . . ." his daughter was later to say. "This affair brought out all that was worst – all that was weakest in him. He did not care a damn what happened to any of us. Nothing could surpass the misery and unhappiness of our home . . ." It was at this unhappy point that Catherine and her mother visited Miss Burdett-Coutts in order to ask her to act as a mediator; but Dickens reply to her subsequent letter was one of complete and absolute rejection. "If you have seen Mrs Dickens in company with her wicked mother, I can not enter – no, not even with you – upon any question that was discussed in that woman's presence." On the same day

Catherine wrote thanking Miss Burdett-Coutts for her efforts; "I have now – God help me – only one course to pursue."

The following day she sent a letter to Mark Lemon, which she asked him to pass on to her husband; the contents are not known but Lemon now made it clear that he wanted to extricate himself from what was becoming a more and more unpleasant and difficult business. And then, the day after, perhaps in defiance of her mother's wishes, Catherine agreed to accept the deed of settlement; to accept, in other words, her husband's terms. Trustees were now appointed to look after her interests – Lemon, despite his reservations, being one and Frederick Evans, Dickens's publisher, being the other. In fact Catherine also employed Evans's solicitor, and eventually set up house only half a mile from Evans himself; he clearly felt the need to protect her, even at the cost of incurring the enmity of his most profit-able author. But, at this stage, Dickens was eager only that the whole affair should be settled. On the Saturday, the day after Catherine had accepted the terms, her solicitors conferred with her father and then, three days later, they met Dickens's solicitor, Ouvry, and began the formal preparation of the deed of settlement. As far as Dickens was concerned the matter was over now, and he asked Wilkie Collins to visit him so that he might tell him the whole long story.

But his sense of bitterness remained, and at this juncture he wrote what became known (by him, at least) as the "violated letter", a long statement in which once again he exculpated himself and implicitly blamed his wife for all the woes of their marriage; at the end of the affair, it seems, he could not resist reshaping it to fit his own preconceptions as if he were writing the conclusion to a novel. In this extraordinary letter he even accuses his wife of a certain "peculiarity of character" which led her to relinquish all care for her children, and then goes on to refer to her "mental disorder". And this in a letter which, as we shall see, he allowed anyone and everyone to read. There was one additional note which betrays the very depth of his anger against the Hogarths: "Two wicked persons who should have spoken very differently of me, in consideration of earned respect and grati-tude, have (as I am told, and indeed to my personal knowledge) coupled with this separation the name of a young lady for whom I have a great attachment and regard." It was previously thought that Dickens was referring here to Ellen Ternan, but clearly he means Georgina Hogarth. "I will not repeat her name – I honour it too much. Upon my soul and honour, there is not on this earth a more virtuous and spotless creature than this young lady. I know her to be innocent and pure, and as good as my own dear daughters." Dickens then gave this letter to Arthur Smith, the manager of his readings, and told him to show it to whomever might be interested; in other words, he wished his own account of the separation to be in circulation before that of any rival. Thackeray saw it a few days later and wrote to his mother, "To think of the poor matron after 22 years of marriage going away out of her house! O dear me its a fatal story for our trade." In fact Thackeray had himself played some part in the affair, albeit by accident; as he said to his mother in the same letter, "Last week going into the Garrick I heard that Dickens is separated from his wife on account of an intrigue with his sister in law. No says I no such thing – its with an actress – and the other story has not got to Dickens's ears but this has – and he fancies that I am going about abusing him!"

Dickens was hearing the abuse on all sides and, in a number of letters, he refers to the "lies" which were being spread about him everywhere. Then on the very day after he had written the "violated letter" he heard that Mrs Hogarth and Helen Hogarth were, even as the negotiations about the settlement were being concluded, still spreading rumours about Georgina. If Catherine had agreed to the settlement against the advice of her mother, as seems likely, then Mrs Hogarth's own bitterness was leading her into a fresh assault upon the integrity of the daughter who had taken Dickens's side against her own sister; it ought to be noted, however, that Catherine herself seems to have borne no grudge against her younger sister, and in fact seems to have been relieved that the children remained under her care. But as soon as Dickens heard of this fresh outbreak of rumour he wrote to his solicitors and demanded that they obtain an undertaking from the Hogarths that all such gossip would stop; otherwise, he would proceed no further with the negotiations. Catherine's solicitors then wrote back and declared their ". . . conviction that the Hogarth family could not have originated them". But this was not enough for Dickens; he was still hearing a variety of lies and slanders directed against him and Georgina, and he wanted Ouvry to be "relentless" with Mrs Hogarth. In the event, on the same evening, George Hogarth, the mild-mannered, gentle man who must have been im-mensely distressed by all this familial rivalry and hatred, wrote a letter to his solicitor in which he assured him ". . . that the report that I or my wife or Daughter have at any time stated or insinuated that any impropriety of conduct had taken place between my daughter

Georgiana [sic] and her Brother in Law Mr Charles Dickens is totally and entirely unfounded". Of course Hogarth himself was not being accused of anything and, in any case, the slanders against Dickens went wider than the charge of incest with Georgina. So Dickens's solicitor wrote back to say that ". . . Mr Dickens will not sign any deed with these charges hanging over him, and supposed to be sanctioned by some members of his wife's family". He enclosed a statement which he wished only Mrs Hogarth and Helen Hogarth to sign. In the meantime, Dickens was reading *A Christmas Carol* at St Martin's Hall, followed on the next evening by *The Chimes*. Stories of familial harmony after discord. Peace. Good will upon earth. No record remains of his appearance or demeanour on these occasions.

The choice for Mrs Hogarth was obvious; either she signed the statement prepared for her by Dickens's solicitor, or Dickens would refuse to proceed with the deed of settlement, a settlement which now raised Catherine's annual income to six hundred, rather than the first proposed four hundred, pounds. Catherine's misery would only be lengthened by any delay, and Mrs Hogarth must have known well enough by now that her son-in-law was not the man to yield to any entreaty. But still she held out against signing the piece of paper which would be tantamount to confessing she had spread rumours about her own daughter, Georgina – until, that is, Mark Lemon and Dickens's eldest son pleaded with her to do so and thus to end the uncertainty under which they were all now living. Clearly, for Catherine's sake as much as for anyone else, the matter should finally be resolved. So, on 29 May, Mrs Hogarth and Helen Hogarth reluctantly put their names to a document which said in part, ". . . certain statements have been circulated that such differences are occasioned by circumstances deeply affecting the moral character of Mr Dickens and compromising the reputation and good name of others, we solemnly declare that we now disbelieve such statements. We know that they are not believed by Mrs Dickens, and we pledge ourselves on all occasions to contradict them, as entirely destitute of foundation." Catherine's solicitor then proposed to present this document in return for the deed of settlement itself, but Dickens believed that such a transaction would be an outrageous attempt at something close to a "bargain" where only simple justice was involved. Catherine's solicitor immediately gave way, and the statement was handed to Dickens. On the same day Catherine left Tavistock House for the last time, and travelled to Brighton with her mother.

William Charles Macready

Daniel Maclise

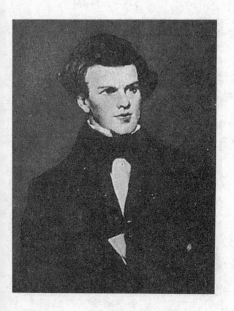

John Forster

Hablot Knight Browne

George Cruikshank

William Harrison Ainsworth

Angela Burdett-Coutts

William Makepeace Thackeray

W. H. Wills

Wilkie Collins

Mark Lemon

· John Forster

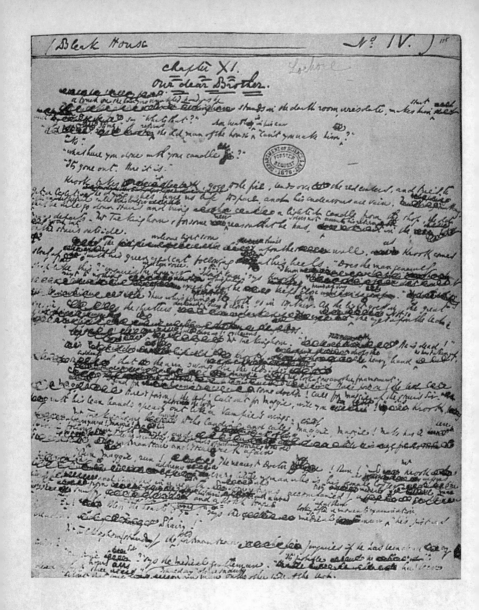

The opening of chapter 11 from the manuscript of *Bleak House*

CHAPTER XI.

Our dear brother.

A TOUCH on the lawyer's wrinkled hand, as he stands in the ~~death~~ *dark*
room, irresolute, makes him start and say " What's that ?"

" It's me," returns the old man of the house, whose breath is in his
ear. " Can't you wake him ?"

" No."

" What have you done with your candle ? "

" It's gone out. Here it is."

Krook takes it, goes to the fire, ~~bends~~ *stoops* over the red embers, and ~~tries~~
to get a light. The dying ashes have no light to spare, and his endeavours
are vain. Muttering, after an ineffectual call to his lodger, that he will
go down stairs and bring a lighted candle from the shop, the old man
departs. Mr. Tulkinghorn, for some new reason that he has, does not
await his return in the room, but on the stairs outside.

The welcome light soon shines upon the wall, as Krook comes slowly
up, with his green-eyed cat following at his heels. " Does the man
generally sleep like this ? " inquires the lawyer, in a low voice.

" Hi ! I don't know," says Krook. " I know next to nothing of his
habits, except that he keeps himself very close."

Thus whispering, they both go in together. As the light goes in, the *is shaking his*
great eyes in the shutters, darkening, seem to close. Not so the eyes *head and lifting*
upon the bed. *his eyebrows*

" God save us ! " exclaims Mr. Tulkinghorn. " He is dead !"

Krook drops the heavy hand he has taken up so suddenly that the arm
swings over the bedside.

They look at one another for a moment.

" Send for some doctor ! Call for ~~Maggie~~ up the stairs, sir. Here's
poison by the bed ! Call out for ~~Maggie~~, will you ? " says Krook, with
his lean hands spread out above the body like a vampire's wings.

Mr. Tulkinghorn hurries to the landing, and calls " ~~Maggie, Maggie~~ !
Make haste, here, whoever you are ! ~~Maggie~~ !" Krook follows him
with his eyes, and, while he is calling, finds opportunity to steal to the
old portmanteau, and steal back again.

" Run, ~~Maggie~~, run ! The nearest doctor ! Run !" So Mr. Krook
addresses a crazy little woman, who ~~is~~ his female lodger, who appears and
vanishes in a breath, ~~and~~ who soon returns, accompanied by a testy
medical man, brought from his dinner, ~~and~~ with a broad snuffy upper lip,
and a broad Scotch tongue.

" Ey ! Bless the hearts o' ye," says the medical man, looking up at
them after a moment's examination. " He's just as dead as Phairy."

Mr. Tulkinghorn (standing by the old portmanteau) inquires if he has
been dead any time?

H

The opening of chapter 11 from the proof of *Bleak House* with Dickens's
own corrections

FROM WHOM WE HAVE
GREAT EXPECTATIONS

Caricature of Dickens, 1861

Dickens giving a reading, c. 1859

Gad's Hill Place

'The Empty Chair', Gad's Hill, June 7, 1870. Painting by Luke Fildes on the day of Dickens's death.

The Swiss Chalet

Dickens reading to
Mamey and Katey
on the lawn of
Gad's Hill

Dickens with
friends on the porch
at Gad's Hill, 1865

Dickens reading in
his garden at Gad's
Hill, c. 1866

DOLBY.—"Well, Mr. Dickens, on the eve of our departure, I present you with $300,000, the result of your Lectures in America."
DICKENS.—"What! only $300,000? Is that all I have made out of these penurious Yankees, after all my abuse of them? Pshaw! Let us go, Dolby!"

Caricature of Dickens
and Dolby, c. 1868

Dickens, 1861. From a caricature
by Andre Gill

Dickens at the Staplehurst accident, June 1865

Ellen Ternan c. 1870

Ellen Ternan.

Dickens, 1867

Dickens dreaming about his characters, c. 1870. From a painting, *Dickens's Dream* by Robert William Buss.

Dickens after death, by J. E. Millais

Two days later Dickens was back at the house. Georgina and the children were with him, and in a letter to a friend Dickens spelled out the nature of the separation; Charley was to live with his mother while his eldest daughter, Mary, was to be "mistress of the house". She was, in other words, to be in titular command of the servants and household management while in fact Georgina herself was really in charge of such matters. It was Georgina who now wrote to Maria Beadnell about the whole affair, although the tenor and vocabulary of the letter strongly suggest that Dickens simply dictated it to her. Once again it was written ostensibly "more in sorrow than in anger" and, once again, the real responsibility for what had happened was heaped upon Catherine; a strange letter for her sister to write, even at Dickens's dictation, but an indication of how far the ordinary loyalties of family life had broken down under the pressure of Dickens's anxiety and uncertainty. But such private letters were not enough for him, and on the following day he consulted his solicitor about the possibility of issuing some kind of public statement exonerating himself from all the false charges that had been levelled against him. Ouvry's private advice is not recorded, but it is doubtful in any case if anything would have stopped Dickens from taking the extraordinary step of issuing to the newspapers a personal statement on his "domestic trouble". Yet, even as he began to draft it, he was clearly ill at ease and, when he took a walk that day to prepare for a speech he was about to give for The Playground and General Recreation Society (how strangely his private and public lives conflicted now), "the first thing I saw, when I went out of my own door, was a policeman hiding among the lilac trees apparently lying in wait for some burglar or murderer. After observing him with great dread and anxiety for a minute or two . . ." he realised that the policeman was on a harmless errand. But why had he been filled with such "great dread and anxiety" at the mere sight of a policeman? Was it already some guilt which was haunting him, not letting him rest? Some irrational fear of imprisonment?

By the beginning of June the two sets of solicitors had agreed upon a draft of the terms of the separation. Catherine was to be given an income of six hundred pounds; at Dickens's instigation, she was granted unlimited access to the children; and both parties agreed not to "disturb" each other or take legal action against each other. In other words Dickens was to give his wife exactly what she would have been granted if there had been an act of judicial separation, while in turn Catherine (and of course by implication her mother) would no longer hint or threaten any proceedings under the new Divorce Act. Catherine's solicitor sent a copy of the document to her in Brighton. At the same time Wills travelled down to see her, with a copy of Dickens's personal statement; he found her on the pier, reading a novel (the title of which remains unknown). Dickens intended to issue his statement to the newspapers and also to publish it in *Household Words*; he had already shown it to several friends, such as John Forster and Edmund Yates, who advised him not to issue such a private account of domestic conflicts. But Dickens also consulted the editor of *The Times*, John Delane, who believed that it should so be published. It was his advice Dickens decided to take, although it is of course unlikely that he ever had any other plan in mind. With a copy of this statement he sent to Catherine a letter, asking her to read the "article" since it contained a reference to herself (although at no point requesting her permission to divulge the details of their married life), and adding, "Whoever there may be among the living, whom I will never forgive alive or dead, I earnestly hope that all unkindness is over between you and me." Catherine (perhaps somewhat weakly) said that she did not object to the allusion to her, but then sent a copy of it to her solicitors. They promptly asked Dickens to postpone its publication, but events were already in motion. On the following day it appeared in *The Times* and then in the succeeding issue of *Household Words*. In part it read as follows: "By some means arising out of wickedness, or out of folly, or out of inconceivable wild chance, this trouble has been made the occasion of misrepresentations, most grossly false, most monstrous, and most cruel—involving, not only me, but innocent persons dear to my heart . . . and so widely spread, that I doubt if one reader in a thousand will peruse these lines, by whom some touch of the breath of these slanders will not have passed, like an unwholesome air."

But in this respect, if in no other, he misjudged the extent of his fame. A pamphlet about Dickens's life, printed later in this year, suggests that very few people outside the London literary "world" knew anything about the matter. Nevertheless, "called upon by the first novelist of the day thus to ventilate a vague denial of nothing that anybody seemed to know about, the press generally printed the manifesto". One of his first biographers was a boy at the time this statement was issued, and he said that ". . . I well remember the feeling of surprise and regret which that article created among us of the general public . . . So far as one could learn at the time, no great dissimilarity existed between the author and the man . . ." But the statement, simply entitled "Personal", altered that equilibrium; a gap opened between Dickens the novelist and Dickens the husband and father. Percy Fitzgerald recalled that "people were all but bewildered and almost stunned . . . Everyone was for the most part in supreme ignorance of what the document could possibly refer to . . . the delusion that all of his readers had heard of some particular slander that had grown out of the domestic trouble, the fact being that nearly everyone who had read the dark allusion was in the completest ignorance". Of course it is easy to see, at least in hindsight, that elevating gossip to the level of public rebuttal meant that the press could now proceed to anatomise the gossip itself; five days after the statement appeared in *The Times*, the *Court Circular* suggested that Dickens preferred ". . . his wife's sister to herself, a preference which has assumed a very definite and tangible shape". Wills asked Ouvry if such a statement was actionable, but Ouvry wisely advised silence. At the same time an editorial in *Reynolds's Weekly Newspaper* went so far as to say that "the names of a female relative and of a professional young lady, have both been, of late, so intimately associated with that of Mr Dickens, as to excite suspicion and surprise in the minds of those who had hitherto looked upon the popular novelist as a very Joseph in all that regards morality, chastity and decorum . . . Let Mr Dickens remember that the odious – and we might almost add unnatural – profligacy of which he has been accused, would brand him with lifelong infamy . . ." Matters became ever worse when, three months later, Dickens's "violated letter", with its reference to Catherine's incapacity as a mother, found its way into the English press. The *Liverpool Mercury* was to say that ". . . we consider this practice outrageously impertinent as regards the public, and so wantonly cruel as regards the private persons whose names are thus forced into a gratuitous and painful notoriety, that we feel called upon to mark it with indignant reprobation". It is hard not in part to accept the newspaper condemnation of Dickens in this instance. So why was it necessary for him to go into print at all? Why did he issue his first "personal" statement to a generally bewildered and uncomprehending public?

Of course he genuinely thought that everyone was talking about him. There is what might be considered an anticipatory passage in *Dombey and Son*, anatomising Dombey's feelings after the flight of his wife from the Dombey home. "The world. What the world thinks of him, how it looks at him, what it sees in him, and what it says – this is the haunting demon of his mind. It is everywhere where he is; and, worse than that, it is everywhere where he is not." Dickens literally could not bear it; he, the celebrant of the domestic hearth, was even now being whispered against, accused of hypocrisy, condemned for putting away his wife, disparaged even for "preferring" his wife's sister. His anger and bitterness could simply not be held in check; he believed himself to be a good man who had been wronged, and this was the truth which he had to convey to his public. If he kept his silence, it might appear that he was indeed admitting his guilt. All his life he had depended upon an audience for applause and praise – ever since the days when his father had put him on the table of the Rochester tavern – and now, in this grave crisis, he had to maintain contact with that audience; he had to speak to it; he had to persuade it. For, if he were to lose his hold upon it, he would lose hold of everything. It was not just that he was about to embark upon a series of provincial readings (although the prospect of a disastrous tour must have occurred to him) but, more importantly, he was afraid of isolation. Of public failure. And perhaps there was another fear too, a fear which he described a few years later in *Great Expectations*. "The death close before me was terrible, but far more terrible than death was the dread of being misremembered after death. And so quick were my thoughts, that I saw myself despised by unborn generations . . ." In the context of the novel this statement seems a little far-fetched, but its presence is explicable if it is seen as Dickens's compulsive memory of the time when he, too, faced something far worse than death – shame, obloquy, derision. It is easy to see, therefore, why he felt he had to speak out even at the risk of alienating certain friends. He had to clear himself. He had to be *clean* so that he might appear before his public, that of the present and that of the future, as he always had before. He may have cared more about his audience than about his own family, but what was left for him otherwise? And so the statement appeared. Within a few days he was afflicted once more by kidney pain, the old suffering of his childhood resurfacing now just as his childhood vision of the world had re-emerged in his attacks upon Catherine herself.

And what were the reactions of those closer to him than the public itself? It has to be remembered that a separation of this kind, on the grounds of incompatibility, was a relatively rare occurrence. And that adultery itself (which comprised part of the rumours about him) was considered a very serious offence; in the staple fiction of the period, for example, marriage is a sacred institution, the destruction of which leaves the man a wretch or miscreant for the rest of his life. Of course there were those who took his part – Wills, Forster and Mrs Macready among them – but it is hard not to suspect that there was a general uneasiness about his behaviour even amongst his closest friends. Miss Burdett-Coutts had tried to mediate, and Forster himself admitted to Landseer that "both are in the wrong . . . But yet I wish you could know *everything* – because, upon the whole, Dickens bears this test better than you would be prepared to think . . . ." But others were not so charitable or, perhaps, so partisan. Harriet Martineau, who knew Catherine's trustee, Evans, declared that Dickens was really "wild" with "conflict of passion". Mrs Gaskell thought that it had made him "extremely unpopular" and James Payn described it as "a public outrage, a blazoned defiance of all ordinary rules of conduct". Elizabeth Barrett Browning said of Catherine, "Poor woman! She must suffer bitterly – that is sure." Some of the comment was more satirical, and Shirley Brooks said of Mrs Dickens that she had been "discharged with a good character". Of course Brooks was a member of the *Punch* group, and there is no doubt that, as a whole, the writers of that periodical turned against the man who had for a while been one of their favourites. Their dinner-table gossip has been recorded for posterity in the diaries of Henry Silver, and a flavour of the general reaction against Dickens can be revived. ". . . Thackeray recalled how Dickens, questioned at the Athenaeum about the quarrel, had broken down and wept. But this, the Table declared, merely proved that Dickens was always acting. It was probably the applause at the amateur theatricals that had first turned his head, Mark [Lemon] thought, and brought on his unforgivable conduct to Catherine . . . So arrogant, said Percival Leigh, that it would not surprise him if Dickens should proclaim himself to be God Almighty. Commented Shirley Brooks with his usual pungency, 'Thinks himself God now. If he is we are atheists, for I don't believe him . . .'." And so it went on.

And what of the other principal players in this drama? Of the reactions of Ellen Ternan or Mrs Ternan nothing is known; their silence at the time can be taken for granted. Catherine herself removed to 70 Gloucester Crescent; she made little outward comment upon her misfortune, although in a letter to her aunt she declared that ". . . you will understand and feel for me when I tell you that I still love and think of their father too much for my peace of mind . . . I trust by God's assistance to be able to resign myself to His will, and to lead a contented if not a happy life, but my position is a sad one, and time only may blunt the keen pain that will throb at my heart, but I will indeed try to struggle hard against it." About two months after the separation her eldest son came to live with her, as she had wanted, and there were occasions when she was visited by her other children. But her position was indeed a "sad" one, a wife only in name, publicly alienated from her famous husband's affections, and a woman who became increasingly lonely through the passage of years. Her husband's remaining letters to her are short and infrequent, beginning formally with "Dear Catherine" and ending with his usual signature and flourish; the letters are addressed to "Mrs Charles Dickens". But not the least touching aspect of her long privation is to be found in the efforts which she made to keep up with her husband's career; she avidly read the novels that were to follow, and often went to the theatre to see dramatic adaptations of his fictions. And, in a sense, he and his work were so close to her that he could never really be separated from her. "She was always kind," it was reported later. "She delighted to give children's parties at her house, although on these occasions her own loved children were never among her little guests."

And what of the children? Walter was in India; Francis was in Germany; Alfred, Harry and Sydney were at Mr Gibson's boarding school in Boulogne; and Charley was at Baring's Bank (he left for Hong Kong a year later). Edward, still only six years old, remained at home under Georgina's care. Dickens said of his eldest children that, "between them and myself, there is a confidence as absolute and perfect as if we were of one age". A curious remark, echoed in the "violated letter" where he said of his children that "all is open and plain among us, as though we were brothers and sisters"; interesting, perhaps, as much for his own implicit reduction of his age as for the manner in which he instinctively idealises the relationship between brother and sister. It is not at all clear, however, that his children would have agreed with him about the amicable relationship he had formed with them; most of them were in any case out of England, and played no part in the separation proceedings. And Edward (or Plorn) was too young to understand what was taking place. It has been suggested that Charley went unwillingly to his mother's house, and there may be truth in that – although, of course, it does not minimise the affection he felt for her. He loved his mother and yet must have realised that to live with her in Gloucester Crescent was a kind of exile from his father's brighter presence. Yet it may be significant that, as we shall see, despite his father's enmity, he remained on good terms with Evans and with Thackeray. The position of Mary and Katie is more complicated. In retrospect Katie was very harsh about her father: "My father was a wicked man – a very wicked man . . . My father was not a gentleman – he was too mixed to be a gentleman . . . My father did not understand women . . . he was not a good man, but he was not a fast man, but he was wonderful!" These are the mixed comments attributed to Katie in her later life and, despite the occasional contradiction, it is clear enough that she blamed her father for what had happened to the household. She is reported to have said of her mother, "We were *all* very wicked not to take her part; Harry does not take this view, but he was only a boy at the time, and does not realise the grief it was to our mother, after having all her children, to go away and leave us. My mother never rebuked me. I never saw her in a temper. We like to think of our geniuses as great characters – but we can't." And yet the evidence about her relationship to her mother is far from unambiguous; that she did sometimes visit her is not in doubt, and it is recorded that Dickens could sometimes scarcely bear to speak to her after such visits. But she did not see her very often and in later life seems to have suffered a fair measure of guilt about this. Her older sister, Mary, visited her mother even less often and seems instinctively to have sided with a father whom she admired and loved. There was no conflict of interest here. And of course Georgina never saw her. Quite clearly Katie and Mary preferred the excitement and glamour of their father's company and their father's household to the respectability and boredom of their mother's more straitened circumstances. They were growing up, going into "society", and there were obvious advantages in being connected to the greatest novelist of the day. But it seems that, as a result, they somewhat neglected their mother; which in turn led to all the ambiguities and self-recriminations which surface in Katie's later memories of her parents.

"My father was a wicked man – a very wicked man . . ." So what are we to make of him at this juncture? It could be said that Catherine stood in the way of his desires or his aspirations, and that he got rid of her with less compunction than that with which he despatched his fictional characters. He had never really needed her. He had never really needed anyone. Yet, from his own account, he is the victim. He is the wronged party. In his letters after the formal separation, he draws attention continually to his own sufferings. To Edmund Yates he wrote, "If you could know how much I have felt within this last month, and what a sense of wrong has been upon me, and what a strain and struggle I have lived under, you would see that my heart is so jagged and rent and out of shape, that it does not this day leave me hand enough to shape these words." A letter almost Shakespearian in its cadence, a literary effect often elicited from Dickens under the stress of great passion; but not a word about Catherine or her more obvious sufferings. But did he nevertheless realise that in some sense he had committed a wrong against her and against their children? Did he perhaps feel, or instinctively feel afraid, that his very writing might be affected by this? All his beliefs and attitudes would have encouraged him to suppose that a flawed man could not write great prose. In the novel he wrote next, *A Tale of Two Cities*, there is a stray comment which seems to speak of this period on his life. "He knew very well, that in his love for Lucie, his renunciation of his social place, though by no means new to his own mind, had been hurried and incomplete. He knew that he ought to have systematically worked it out and supervised it, and that he had meant to do it, and that it had never been done." Is there some sense of self-recrimination here, in this apology for a botched-up job, a hasty series of mistakes? He was about to undertake a tour of readings, and he now flung himself into them with something like ferocity; it might be true, after all, that only his public could save him from his own sense of unworthiness. He nerved himself to go on, to go forward. All his life calamities had only spurred him on to fresh effort, and this was truly the case now. But there is also a subtler sense, a softer subject, a deeper music; in his novels from this time forward, the twin themes of forgiveness and death find a more prominent place in the arena of his imagination. As if, even as he continued his life as a public man, there were deeper regrets and sadnesses which lay just beneath the surface.

"If my father had lived," Katie once said, "he would have gone out of his mind." And, at the time of the separation itself, she said that he had acted like a "madman". Certainly there is something very curious, almost incredible, about aspects of his behaviour during this period. For, in a sense, the separation from his wife was only the first act of a drama which was permanently to estrange Dickens from a number of his closest friends and colleagues. He was never to forgive or to forget, as he had said, the conduct of Mrs Hogarth or of Catherine's sister, Helen: he laid a solemn injunction upon his children that they were never again to see their grandmother or their maternal aunt, and told his eldest son to make sure that his brothers and sisters never called upon their mother when the two offending relatives were there. "I positively forbid the children ever to utter one word if they are ever brought into the presence of either of the two, I charge them immediately to leave your mother's house and come back to me." His anger is perhaps understandable, since these two women had (as far as he was concerned) maligned Georgina and himself in the most vicious way. But much more odd was his similar injunction to the children never to see, or to speak to, Mark Lemon or Frederick Evans. Lemon was one of his oldest friends, and Evans was one of his most trusted colleagues; yet such was his mental turmoil at the time that they were transformed almost overnight into his bitterest enemies. The point was that *Punch* had not printed Dickens's "Personal" statement on the woes of his marriage; since Lemon was the editor, and Evans one of the proprietors, of that journal, Dickens took it as a personal affront and an implicit rejection by them of his honesty. At the same time, since both Lemon and Evans had been acting for Catherine Dickens in the negotiations over the deed of settlement, Dickens seems to have seen behind their refusal some malign conspiracy against him. To Evans he wrote, "I have had stern occasion to impress upon my children that their father's name is their best possession, and that it would be trifled with and wasted by him if either through himself or through them he held any terms with those who had been false to it in the greatest need and under the greatest wrong it has ever known. You know very well why (with hard distress of mind and bitter disappointment) I have been forced to include you in this class. I have no more to say." He also decided that he would somehow sever his partnership with Bradbury and Evans in *Household Words* although, with his reading tour imminent, he realised that any such action would have to wait until he had time and opportunity to arrange matters. The *Punch* table of course fluttered over, and fed upon, these sensations. "There were stories of how Dickens had publicly cut Bradbury and Evans, how he had passed Mark [Lemon] without recognising him. Evans insisted that he had never been able to find out how he had offended Dickens . . ." Dickens was in fact so estranged from Lemon that he paid his wife's allowance to Ouvry, who then passed it on to Lemon as Catherine's trustee; for many years he spoke to neither man, and it can be said that he died without fully being reconciled to them. Yet his eldest son took a different course; despite his father's prohibition he still visited Evans's house and in fact married Evans's daughter (Dickens refused to attend the wedding). So Dickens struck out even against his own son; when Charley wrote an article mocking Edmund Yates in *Punch* (Yates had been a staunch defender of Dickens during the separation), Dickens withdrew his son's name from a list of proposed members for the Garrick.

It was Yates, too, who prompted Dickens's most serious quarrel with Thackeray. He was a young journalist, in a sense one of Dickens's "squad" (as Carlyle called the young men who clustered around him and around *Household Words*), one of those young men of plausible manner and ready talent who ingratiate themselves with famous but somewhat insecure men like Dickens. As one contemporary of Yates put it, he ". . . was very fascinating too. Superficially, mind you." Such young men can be dangerous, and Edmund Yates had written an unflattering profile of Thackeray in *Town Talk*. Thackeray objected and, since Yates was a fellow member of the Garrick, he asked the committee of that club to expel him on the grounds that his conduct was "intolerable in a society of gentlemen". Thackeray was behaving in a sufficiently ridiculous manner, therefore, and it is perhaps no surprise that Dickens – now a great hater of "society" in every sense – should take the young man's part. He drafted Yates's reply to Thackeray, spoke up for him at the committee meeting of the Garrick, and resigned from the club when that committee took Thackeray's part in the dispute. Thackeray wrote to a friend, "I'm not even angry with Dickens now for being the mover in the whole affair. He can't help hating me; and he can't help not being a – you know what, I dare say." The word Thackeray omits here is "gentleman". "His quarrel with his wife has driven him almost frantic. He is now quarrelling with his son . . . the poor boy is very much cast down at his father's proceedings." Thackeray indulged in another bout of sarcasm when Dickens, faced with the prospect of a court hearing over the Garrick affair and of himself being summoned into the witness box to explain his assistance to Edmund Yates, wrote to Thackeray in order to suggest some private mediation. Clearly enough, Dickens did not wish to be questioned in public about *anything*. As Henry Silver, the diarist of the *Punch* dinners, said of his general behaviour, "Wheels within wheels."

But of course the wheels were powered by one great source of energy, Dickens's hurt and anger during the separation from his wife. And it is even fair to say that he quarrelled with Thackeray precisely because he believed him to have been positively hostile in his attitude towards his domestic affairs. It is clear enough that Thackeray, as a "clubbable" gentleman, helped to spread the gossip about Dickens's problems. It was he who had mentioned the young actress at the Garrick, however innocently, and his daughter, Anne, reported to a close friend later in the year, "Papa says the story is that Charley met his Father and Miss whatever the actress's name out walking on Hampstead Heath." But there was also a warmer and more charitable aspect of Thackeray's behaviour; he kept up his friendship with Catherine and, in fact, in the very heat of the controversy in June, he invited her and her son to dine with him. But of course this is also all the evidence we need to account for Dickens's dislike – as Thackeray himself realised and, in an essay which he wrote for the *Cornhill* magazine two years later, he seems implicitly to be describing Dickens in an account of ". . . the man qui croit toujours avec raison. His anger is not a brief madness, but a permanent mania. His rage is not a fever-fit, but a black poison inflaming him, distorting his judgment, disturbing his rest, embittering his cup, gnawing at his pleasures, causing him more cruel suffering than ever he can inflict on his enemy." A year later they met at Drury Lane; Thackeray recalled that "Dickens and I shook hands and didn't say one single word to each other . . . he knows now that I have found him out . . ."

Thackeray was right about one thing; Dickens was indeed suffering from the consequences of his behaviour. And, when his "violated letter" attacking Catherine appeared in the English press (as he must have known it would, sooner or later), he became even more fiercely and justifiably criticised. There were times when his depression became so great that he was utterly cast down. "Sometimes I *cannot* bear it," he told Mary Boyle. Desolation. A feeling of loss. Bewilderment. Rage. Misery. Is this also the feeling he pours into Rogue Riderhood of *Our Mutual Friend* – ". . . like us all, every day of our lives when we wake – he is instinctively unwilling to be restored to the consciousness of this existence, and would be left dormant, if he could". Years of overwork and of pressing anxiety had finally taken their hold upon him; there was no doubt that he was suffering from nervous exhaustion, and his sometimes extraordinary behaviour, seeing plots against himself in every quarter, suggests strongly that he was now experiencing something very close to a nervous breakdown. There had been reports in earlier days of Dickens's "madness" – that is often how people respond to such extraordinary energy and productivity – and even after his death there were critics who described his "monomania" or his "hallucinations". But there was nothing "mad" about Dickens at all. In this period of nervous exhaustion it would seem that all of his usual characteristics simply became exaggerated to the point of unreality. If we are to understand his behaviour at this time, we need to understand his behaviour at all times.

There is no doubt that he was a man of highly-strung and mercurial temperament. His children have recalled how he was ". . . full of confidence at one time, depressed at another". How he experienced ". . . heavy moods of deep depression, of intense nervous irritability, when he was silent and oppressed. These, however, were never of long duration . . ." And Percy Fitzgerald has remarked that "no one was ever so highly strung as Charles Dickens. He suffered in the most acute way from any mental strain . . ." And of what did this strain consist? The fear of failure. The fear of breaking down. The fear of being ridiculed. The fear of being laughed at. The fear even of feeling itself; we have discussed before that curious reserve which he exhibited towards those closest to him. And then there was also his extraordinary restlessness. One of his earliest biographers quotes an acquaintance who said that "with all his sagacity, Dickens is eternally afraid of being *slighted*. He never seems to be at ease – not even in his own house. His restless eye wanders . . . He has always seemed to me as if he had something *on* his mind as well as *in* it . . ." And this seems to be a true description. It is not hard to understand, therefore, his sense of panic and of urgency, as well as his inability to think about what he was doing to other people, which mark his behaviour during this period. And there is, too, his immense susceptibility to slights which, at the time of the separation, seemed to turn for him the most innocuous act into one of hostility and vengeance. There is always to be found within Dickens that inner person – hurt, watchful, afraid – who looked out through the eyes of the successful writer and the famous man. It is often said that his novels suggest the intense sensitivity of the child's vision of the adult world, but Dickens possessed in equal measure the susceptibility of the anxious child. The dread. The fear of being abandoned. The fear of being unloved. That is why he was quick to anger and resentment, but just as quickly mollified by praise and by admiration. As a friend said, ". . . his buoyancy was readily chilled by lack of appreciation or indifference". And it is this same nervous susceptibility which led him to idealise others just as he used to idealise himself. He lived in a world of his own creation, a brighter or darker world as the case might be. There were times when the darkness predominated, of course, and it is significant that throughout his work – from the portrait of Newgate in his earliest *Sketches by Boz* to the depiction of John Jasper in *The Mystery of Edwin Drood* – Dickens seems most readily and most easily to sympathise with condemned men, guilty men, trapped men.

Guilty. Is there also some sense of guilt in Dickens? It is not necessary to wield the theatrical vocabulary of psychodrama to note certain aspects of his character which lead towards that conclusion; his excessive punctuality, his obsessive love of order, his neatness and precision of dress, even the habit of constantly combing his hair in case a strand of it had fallen out of place. And was it the obscure working of guilt, or of the consciousness of guilt, which prevailed even when he was so ostentatiously declaring his righteousness? ". . . nobody in the world is readier to acknowledge himself in the wrong than I," he once declared only half-jokingly to Frith; "only – I am never wrong." There is never any indication that he believed himself to be mistaken in any of his public pronouncements, or in fact that he ever confessed to being wrong about anything. He had always to be right. He was the good man. He was the moral man. He was the man who never fell prey to self-criticism. And, with this fixed belief in himself, came also the pressure of that will with which he controlled the responses of others towards himself. That is why, in a sense, he never bothered to understand himself or paused to reflect upon himself. His inner life was a kind of fruitful chaos, taking on the shape of the characters he created, its very amorphousness an indication of Dickens's genius no less than his latent fearfulness. If he understood himself at all, it was in a half-exaggerated and half-whimsical manner, as if he, too, were a character from one of his own books. He would often refer to himself in the third person and the manager of his last readings, George Dolby, recalled that "he had a singular habit . . . of regarding his own books as the production of someone else, and would almost refer to them as such". It is the same disregard of himself, the same refusal to look at himself, which led to his apparent composure when he was being wildly applauded or cheered at public gatherings. Dolby noticed, too, his ". . . inattention and apparent deafness to the applause with which his name was greeted" in theatres or assembly halls. He would look around at the decorations, or up at the ceiling, as if nothing at all was being said about him. But sometimes, too, he fled from himself; sometimes, in the phrase we have had cause to notice before, he was truly "afraid of himself". Perhaps that is why he never really enjoyed solitude but always surrounded himself with friends; he was not even solitary when he was alone with his work, since at these times he invoked his characters who plucked at him and spoke to him. Does not everything suggest some inner dread, some guilt of an inexplicable kind which he preferred not to notice but the promptings of which so surely mark his outward behaviour?

The roots of that guilt, if such it is, can never adequately be fathomed. There are those who have seen in it the reaction against his infantile desire for the mother, and the rejection or killing of the father. There are others who view it as the result of his infantile wish to kill those other siblings who needed his mother's love. And yet it is more interesting to see these somewhat banal and possibly over-rated childhood responses working at higher pitch within his own adult life. Not just in his life as a man – for had he not effectively replaced his father as "head" of the family, even becoming for a while his employer? But also in his life as a writer – on the most obvious level, he had attacked and "written off" his parents in a variety of partial character portrayals. But there was also a more important kind of filial betrayal; in a sense he had rejected both of his parents when he recreated himself in language. In that self-engendering which takes place in the act of composition he was in a sense divesting himself of origins and claiming a kind of imaginative orphanhood. Partly out of ambition, partly out of egotism. That is why the constant note in his correspondence is his feeling of his own uniqueness – the "Inimitable"! – and why he is always so sure that all those who knew him would be preoccupied with *his* concerns and feelings. But the reverse side of the self-concern is paranoia: everyone is watching me, everyone is talking about me. Precisely the paranoia which led him to make his "Personal" statement about his marriage, and precisely the paranoia which caused him to destroy his friendship with Mark Lemon and Frederick Evans on the flimsiest of grounds. Of course it is easy to wield such terms as paranoia, and there are times when psychoanalytic description becomes simply a way of avoiding any real understanding of the subject; but it is hard not to see in Dickens's behaviour during the separation all the fears and anxieties of his childhood revived, all the latent and necessary confusions of his own personality brought to the surface.

Chapter 28

IT was a hot summer, the summer of 1858. The Thames stank, and the sewage of three million people boiled under the sun in what was now no more than an open sewer. In the public buildings along the banks of the river, blinds were soaked with chloride and tons of lime were shovelled into the water itself. Boiled bones. Horse meat. Cat gut. Burial grounds. All of them putrefying and fermenting in the heat. This was the climate in which Charles Dickens began his London readings in the second week of June, to be succeeded in August by a provincial tour. He had changed his programme from the original series of Christmas Books, and began the London season in St Martin's Hall with the story of *Paul Dombey*. A week later he added two of his Christmas stories, the *Poor Traveller* and *Boots at the Holly Tree Inn*, as well as including a monologue entitled *Mrs Gamp*. *Paul Dombey* itself was "a prodigious success", Dickens reported, and the audience wept so much that his manager, Arthur Smith, was not sure about using it again. But Dickens knew better; he repeated the reading twice in the next month.

How did he look now? His hair was much shorter, thinning on the forehead and growing more grizzled; it was darker but in places there were now hints of grey. He had a moustache and beard in the American fashion – the sides of his face and jaw clean-shaven – and the effect of this was to cover up part of his mouth. As a result, according to Katie, he looked "grave". Dickens had his own account of it, later reported by Frith: "The beard saved him the trouble of shaving [Dickens said], and much as he admired his own appearance before he allowed his beard to grow, he admired it much more now, and never neglected; when an opportunity offered, to gaze his fill at himself . . . besides, he had been told by some of his friends that they highly approved of the change, because they now saw less of him . . ."

Eleanor Christian, the lady with whom he had been so sportive at Broadstairs so many years before, met him again in this period and noticed how much older he seemed, ". . . his face lined by deep furrows, hair grizzled and thinned, his expression care-worn and clouded". Other people noticed the care upon his face, too; ". . . the deep lines on his face – almost furrows . . ."; ". . . his face looked furrowed and care-worn". Those who saw him for the first time, however, noticed a relatively small, well-knit, neat, rather dressy man. "His face was ruddy," Mrs Ward remembered, ". . . his eyes were remarkably brilliant, and he held his head very uprightly, thus adding to the general vivacity of his bearing. His dress was, perhaps, rather 'loud' . . ." So some things had not changed; he still "carried himself very erect, walking with almost military precision", and his eyes still had that wonderfully lustrous and expressive quality which had always been noticed. And he was still something of the dandy; even as he came through the mid-part of the century, he refused altogether to subscribe to the sombre stateliness of orthodox male dress. He liked wearing velvet dinner-jackets or velvet waistcoats, and now he sported a large gold watch-chain which hung across his breast. For his readings he wore a white waistcoat and white geranium in his buttonhole; he walked precisely on stage at the precise time, looked at his audience and then began to read.

And he knew now that he needed his audience more than ever. Ellen Ternan was about to go up to Manchester for two months, since the whole company at the Haymarket was due to open in the Theatre Royal there. It has sometimes been suggested that by now Dickens was having some kind of "affair" with her, but all the evidence suggests otherwise. He seems still to have been in that dazed and infatuated state with which he had first seen her; certainly all the protestations of innocence which mark his public statements in this period have the ring of genuine and literal truth. It was almost a childish innocence, in fact. As he said to Mary Boyle in an affectionate letter, one of the many he wrote to her, his heart itself was "like a child," in the sense that it was both tremulous and uncertain even in the company of those he knew well. But his relationship with the whole Ternan family was clearly growing stronger. In the summer, even as he was continuing with his reading tour, he was trying to find a proper singing master for Ellen's sister, Fanny; she wanted to study in Italy, and he went to some trouble to assist her. In fact he was even forced to defend Fanny Ternan's innocence against rumours which connected her name with his own, and on one occasion he was obliged to thank her cousin, Richard Spofford, for believing in his honesty and in her blameless integrity. He even compares her to his own daughters, which suggests that Dickens found in the Ternans something of an extended family without the discord which had overpowered his own household.

It had been a terrible year and in July, only a few days after the deed of separation had been formally signed, Dickens started to go down to Gad's Hill Place as often as possible between his London readings; joined there by such loyal friends as Forster and Beard, reassured by the tranquil countryside which he had known since childhood, "I am quite myself again". He was comforted, too, by the realisation that his public had not, after all, deserted him (even though he still had to face the potentially sterner test of the provinces); his readings were crammed and, when he made a speech at the foundation of a Dramatic College, he was "received with acclamation". As soon as he had finished the last of the readings in St Martin's Hall he went back to Gad's Hill Place and there began the final preparations for his provincial tour. He was always concerned with finance of course; he hoped to make something like one thousand pounds per month, which in fact was an under-estimate, and before embarking on the tour he wrote to the stationmaster at Euston to see if he, as a "public man", could expect any concessions from the railway company during his forthcoming travels. No doubt he had in mind some kind of discount on the price of the five tickets (two first class for Smith and himself, and three second or third class for his ancillary staff – he was not an egalitarian). The stationmaster wrote across the letter, "I am quite unable to see what special privileges can be granted except not being too particular with the luggage". So, at normal prices, Dickens started on his travels with his four assistants. Arthur Smith was to act as his manager; John Thompson, his personal servant, was to be his dresser; a man named Boycett looked after the gas-lighting of Dickens's performance; a man named Berry acted as Smith's assistant and general factotum. Part of the pleasure to be derived from Dickens's account of the tour in fact lies in his relationship with these men, the three servants, in particular, playing in his eyes the role of comic turns to his "straight" act. Thompson was fond of doing imitations and had "the absurdest little gingerbeery giggle", Berry was perpetually "unfortunate" and from time to time broke out in boils, Smith was always being waylaid and buffeted by the multitudes who wanted tickets. Boycett was the most sober or most nondescript member of the group, but seems occasionally to have delivered himself of oracular utterances which always favourably impressed Dickens with their vacuity.

The five of them set off on the first day of August, their first stop Clifton. The reading programme was planned well in advance, and Dickens would ring the changes on the *Carol*, the *Chimes*, the *Trial in Pickwick*, *Paul Dombey*, *Boots at the Holly Tree Inn*, the *Poor Traveller* and *Mrs Gamp*; Gamp, Pickwick, Dombey and Carol proved (as one might expect) to be the most popular, although the sentimental comedy of Boots had its admirers. It was to be a lengthy tour, beginning at Clifton and finishing at Brighton; there were more than eighty readings altogether, and visits to more than forty towns in England, Scotland and Ireland where Dickens read in warehouses, assembly rooms, booksellers, offices, halls, hotels and pump rooms. There would come a time, as we shall see, when his performances themselves became miniature works of art, creating a wholly new form of entertainment, but on this first provincial tour he was primarily watching and learning. Of course he repeated his now customary appeal for the audience to create the atmosphere of "a small group of friends assembled to hear a tale told", and slowly he was beginning to create the right conditions for such an intimate gathering. At first he had used a high desk, like a lectern, but quickly changed this for a lower one so that his audience could see more of him and of his gestures. For a while he employed a paper knife for emphasis, but soon dropped this prop; perhaps it was too reminiscent of the pointer which Albert Smith used in his one-man entertainments and thus slightly vulgar. He was learning how to use his voice for dramatic purposes, too; of course he had had practice on the amateur stage, but it was necessary for him now to carry much of the weight of the readings on his varied enunciation and pronunciation. As one observer noted during a reading of the *Poor Traveller*, "He dwelled on the separate syllables, and tolled out the 'r's . . ." He took such pains, in fact, that on this first provincial tour he frequently lost his voice. But he was acting too; when he adopted the role of Boots the servant, for example, *The Critic* noted "the swaying to and fro of the body, the half-closing of the eyes, and the action of the head, when any point in the narrative is supposed to require particular emphasis to make it clear, and the voice sounding as if affected by the chewing of a straw . . ." All the time he was observing himself as well as the audience and, unlikely though it might seem, he was also willing to take advice from interested parties. Of course he did so in his usual blithe manner. Frith, who was about to paint his portrait (especially commissioned by Forster), ventured to criticise Dickens's performance as Sam Weller in the *Trial in Pickwick*; Dickens promptly changed it but coolly declared that "I only made Sam a little smarter". These readings were still an unusual experience for him – "this strange life" he called it on more than one occasion – and he was compelled to learn and to adjust as he went along.

His own correspondence with Georgina, Mamie and Katie (he wrote to each one in turn on a sort of rotary system) reveals just how strange that life still seemed to him; the endless railway journeys, the boat trips, the nights in hotels, the dinners at three or four in the afternoon, the visits to the hall, the endless crowds, the money taken in, the misadventures, the applause, the brightness of the gas, the heat. And there were the visits to the industrial towns of the North and the seaside resorts of the South, the slums of Edinburgh and the streets of Dublin, all passing before him like some diorama of British life in the middle of the century. His accounts of the readings themselves tend to be broadly repetitive – never seen such audiences, deafening applause, never read better, money pouring in, hundreds turned away, universal crying. There is no doubt that it was indeed a success; there had been nothing quite like it before, and the novelty of the enterprise was combined with the extraordinary popularity of Charles Dickens to create the kind of crowds and the kind of applause which were generally reserved for the more famous singers of the period. Certainly no novelist, no writer, had ever achieved such national acclaim. So it was that in the scenes of pathos the audience wept; at the death of Paul Dombey one man cried openly for a while and then "covered his face with both hands, and laid it down on the back of the seat before him, and really shook with emotion". And then of course there was the comedy. Here is Dickens's description of another member of the audiences: ". . . whenever he felt Toots coming again he began to laugh and wipe his eyes afresh, and when he came he gave a kind of cry, as if it were too much for him." Dickens could not help but laugh, too, and one of the most charming aspects of these first readings was the extent to which he was infected by the audiences so that "I *could not* compose my face" and began to laugh with them at the remarks of his own creations. And he was cheered, too, by what he considered to be the intimation of his own "Fame" when a woman stopped him in the street and said, "Mr Dickens will you let me touch the hand that has filled my house with many friends?" – although he rather spoils the effect of this anecdote by putting the same words in the mouths of other "common people and gentlefolks". There were at least two occasions, however, when the stress of travelling and performing gave Dickens violently bad colds; the danger was of his voice disappearing, of course, so he dosed himself liberally with barley water and mustard poultices. ". . . I think I sang half the Irish Melodies to myself, as I walked about to test it." This is a reminder that Dickens could still sing from memory the melodies he had first learned as a child – Tom Moore's songs being one of the staples of his childhood performances at the Mitre Inn in Rochester – which in turn indirectly suggests how the performances of his childhood are linked to those of his middle-age. There were times when he felt too tired and too "oppressed" to face the audiences but, whenever he nerved himself to do so and stood in front of them, all his old spirit and energy returned.

It was while he was on tour in Ireland that he met an admirer, Percy Fitzgerald, on the platform of a railway station; and in Fitzgerald's account of this meeting it is possible to catch something of Dickens's manner in the world. When he first approached him Fitzgerald noticed ". . . the uneasy twinkle in Boz's eye . . . he had been waylaid – caught by some enthusiast". But in fact Fitzgerald was already a contributor to *Household Words* and, when he caught his name, he responded warmly:

Dickens: How *do* you do? I am very glad to see you.

Fitzgerald says that this was spoken in a strong "burr" or accent; which may be roughly what was meant when others talked about the strange "metallic burr" in his conversation, a thickness or heaviness of speech that was sometimes mistaken for a lisp. He went on to tell Fitzgerald that he had just been to Belfast.

Dickens: Tremendous houses, curious people, they seem all Scotch, but quite in a state of transition. I walked a long way by sea to Carrickfergus. Had a letter from Forster yesterday. He's worried to death with old Landor's business (Laughs). What a pity.

Fitzgerald: Yes. And he is so wrong-headed.

Dickens: Yes. (Snatching at the word). That's it, so very wrong-headed, and yet there's a great deal behind that . . . Lord bless you, yes! Known him for years. (Then abruptly) Well, Forster is deep in the Swift. I tell him he'll never get through it. But he does go at a thing with all his soul . . . Oh Lord, no. *He'll* never have done it, never.

Fitzgerald catches here the quickness and abrupt pace of Dickens's conversation, and he adds that "all the while his words were spoken in a sharp, jerky way, off-hand to a degree, but very engaging". Fitzgerald also records that his manager, Arthur Smith, was with him and that he had a "calm, quiet assurance . . . invaluable to Dickens". This impression of a nervous, abrupt, excitable man is confirmed in another report of Dickens conversing on a railway platform. "During the whole of the time we were pacing up and down the long platform – for he seemed to be one who could not stand still, but must be moving . . . The dramatic action that accompanied his earnest words, drew upon him the notice of all the bystanders."

So we begin to see him, the short man not quite at ease in the world. The greatest and most popular novelist of his period, walking quickly up and down, gesticulating, talking abruptly. There are other snatched records of his conversation; here, for example, was his discussion with Augustus Egg about a pencil drawing. "What is the history of this? Can you tell us? Who is this good-looking young fellow? And what is the meaning of this discoloured stuff, which looks as if it had been white at one time?" Some of his favourite phrases included "Oh lor no"; "God bless my soul"; "It has amazed me for life!" He always said "Good day" rather than "Goodbye" and used to address household servants in the morning with a "How are we today?" (to which they sometimes did not know how to reply). When he was listening to people, he would nod his head and often repeat "surely" or "certainly"; and he had a habit of interjecting with "capital, capital".

And of what did he speak? By fortunate chance a memoir of his conversations at Gad's Hill Place has survived and, from the apparently bald transcript (someone working from memory soon after the event), it is possible to gain some idea of the suddenness and abruptness of his talk. "Dickens had not read *Jane Eyre* and said he never would as he disapproved of the whole school. [This apropos of Miss Hogarth saying that it was an unhealthy book.] He had not read *Wuthering Heights* . . . They met she shrieked and married him. His wife is always sending contributions to *All The Year Round*. Lever was a very good whist player and was an army surgeon . . . Albert Smith's last productions very poor stuff. Had himself a very queer notion of the plot of *Oliver Twist* Praised Wingrove Cooke's book – thought it superior to Russell's. Saw Peter Cunningham on the top of a coach in a very wretched condition Remarked on the price of Frith's picture. Was reserved while walking and complained of his side and sleepless nights. Read the *Arabian Nights* all one evening and made references. Preferred Smollett to Fielding. Spoke of the evident demoralisation of London since the early closing movement." And then in a second transcript: "Dickens spoke with great vehemence against the Chinese and their Exeter Hall sympathisers. Believed that if we struck off the heads of 500 mandarins we should achieve more than by the greatest of victories. Webster who passed through the Court the other day was he believed a nephew of the comedian and had eloped with his wife . . ."

There is more to similar effect but in this sudden, rapid and changeable speech we catch something of the manner of Dickens. It is not necessary at this late date to elucidate all of the references, but perhaps it is significant to note that he admitted to having a "very queer notion" of the plot of *Oliver Twist* (it was rather tortuous, in other words), that he was suffering from the pains of his childhood, and that he spoke so fiercely against the Chinese with whom the English were then at war. But how did others react to this conversation? G. H. Sala said that it never really rose above "amusing commonplaces", but George Eliot noted its "real seriousness along with his keenness and humour"; in other words, like other men of genius, Dickens varied his conversation in order to suit the taste and the mood of his interlocutor. There were of course times when his reserve was the single most noticeable aspect of his behaviour; there were occasions, especially when he was being "lionised", when he simply retreated into himself. But those who have recorded their memories of his talk have most often noted the ease and freedom with which he spoke to everyone. He had no pomposity and no affectation; instead he had "plenty of light easy talk and touch-and-go fun without any effort or humbug of any kind". He was always genial. He never dominated conversation but rather let it take its way and spoke freely on whatever topic arose; and he was very good, too, at "drawing out" shyer or more reserved people. He was also a very good listener, and there were many times when he seemed genuinely to prefer that role. In fact, as Forster reports, to his friends he was ". . . the pleasantest of companions, with whom they forgot that he had ever written anything". And that in a way is the most important point; his conversation was so agreeable, so little self-concerned, so genuinely pleasant, that those who encountered him could hardly believe that he was the most popular novelist of his age. He could not be the man who had created Bill Sikes and Oliver Twist and Little Dorrit, this easy and agreeable conversationalist. Of course there were those who were, as a result, disappointed; Longfellow said that "Dickens saved himself for his books, there was nothing to be learned in private . . ." and Forster said of his conversation that ". . . with every possible thing to give relish to it, there were not many things to bring away". Forster adds, significantly, that this aspect of his personality fitted in with so many other of Dickens's qualities and ". . . he seemed to be always the more himself for being somebody else, for continually putting off his personality". But this is not to suggest that he was always an actor in conversation; he did not "put off" his personality so much as subdue it, allow it to take on the light and the shade of the person with whom he talked. In other words he was not a memorable talker; he had neither the cadence of Samuel Johnson nor the wit of Oscar Wilde. In that sense Longfellow was right. He did save himself for his books for it was in *writing*, with all its richness and complexity, that he dwelt; in *talk* he showed only the more superficial aspects of himself, and that is because conversation was, for him, of small import beside his compositions.

Yet he was never boring or flippant. He could speak on any number of subjects, as the transcripts of his conversation at Gad's Hill Place suggest, and there is no doubt that there were times when his conversational humour reminded his interlocutors that he was, after all, the greatest comic novelist ever to write in English. His daughter recalled how the servants waiting at table "were often convulsed with laughter at his droll remarks and stories". And, in a section of this biography which has necessarily dwelt upon the darker and more sorrowful aspects of his character, it is important also to record how to most people he seemed to be "the *cheerfullest* man of his age"; both Forster and an American friend, J. T. Fields, use this quotation of Johnson about Garrick to suggest Dickens's conversational manner. Trollope described him as "a *hearty* man"; he laughed a lot (he had an infectious laugh) and he said himself that "if *I* were soured, I should still try to sweeten the lives and fancies of others"; however coy it sounds, this seems to have been no less than the truth. And although such a comment suggests that Dickens was adept at concealing all those aspects of his character which we have taken care to describe here – we must always remember his reserve about all those matters which touched most closely upon his own self – it cannot be doubted that to the world he was no more and no less than what he seemed; ". . . so bright, so merry, and – like his books – so human . . ."

This was how he appeared to his audiences, too, who clustered around him, shook hands with him, as if he were the very model of the cheerfulness which his earlier books had spread into their homes. From Ireland he came back to London, and then on to Gad's Hill Place; he needed rest now, and yet he could not altogether rest. He was still editing a weekly periodical, and it is often forgotten that Dickens managed what to most others would seem a "full-time job" even as he set out upon his reading tours. It was often said by his children that he disliked the thought of growing old, and that he refused to believe that any of his vigour had diminished with the years; in truth it had not, but the source of that energy was now not so much youthfulness and enthusiasm as perseverance and willed determination. Then he set off again – Huddersfield, Wakefield, York, Harrogate, Scarborough, Hull, Leeds, Halifax, Sheffield and Manchester in a period of eleven days. Two days' rest in London, then on to Darlington, Durham, Sutherland and Newcastle in a four-day tour. He *walked* from Durham to Sunderland, and then *walked* from Sunderland to Newcastle. Then on to Scotland; to Edinburgh, Dundee, Aberdeen, Perth and Glasgow. He described this visit to Edinburgh as a "brilliant victory" as if his reading tours were some sort of military campaign, as if he were trying to fight against some kind of enemy – which, in a sense, he was. Even as he carried on with the tour there were reports in the press about the "violated letter" which had only recently been made public, and he was in a sense trying to face down his critics by demonstrating the love and enthusiasm which the public still had for him. That is why in his accounts of his triumphs some of his hyperbole seems self-defensive. "The welcome they gave me was astounding in its affectionate recognition of the late trouble, and fairly for once unmanned me. I never saw such a sight or heard such a sound." The reading tour finally came to an end at Brighton, in the middle of November, and there was a celebration dinner. For he had much to celebrate. He now felt assured that recent events had in no way damaged his reputation, or the affection which he inspired, and as an added bonus – in more ways than one – he realised that he had found a welcome means of guaranteeing his income in the years ahead. As *Saunders's News-Letter* explained in the following month, "A photography likeness sells a book; how much more likely that it would sell when the living author stands before you." The little green "reading books", which contained a printed version of the material he used on stage, were certainly selling very rapidly; but in addition he was surprised to discover that the novels from which the readings were adapted also increased their sales. This would seem the obvious result and his amazement at the fact suggests just how unfamiliar in the mid-nineteenth century was the phenomenon of what we have come to call "publicity". It might even be suggested that Dickens, of all nineteenth-century authors (with the possible exception of Oscar Wilde), was the one who did most to encourage and extend that concept. But of course these were not the sole reasons for , or the only rewards of, the lengthy tour. He himself knew that it had become for him almost a rite of exorcism after the agonies of the previous months; ". . . perhaps it is best for me," he told Wilkie Collins, ". . . to wear and toss my storm away – or as much of it as will ever calm down while the water rolls – in this restless manner." When he stood upon the stage, behind his reading desk, he forgot everything except the book and the audience. And that was part of the charm of the readings for him, the charm of forgetfulness. When that winter he gave a series of readings in London he noted to Miss Burdett-Coutts the contrast between the "bright crowd" at St Martin's Hall and the "dark" of the great city itself. He needed that brightness; sometimes he said that it "cooked" him, but he needed the glare and the applause in order to rescue himself from the dark.

For there were still rumours and whispers following him, precisely the kind of slanders which sometimes truly weighed him down with anxiety and depression. He threatened to sue a man in Scotland who had said that Georgina had had three children by him; in an election for the rectorship of Glasgow University he scored the lowest number of votes and was described as ". . . a cowardly calumniator, the cuckoo of his own merits . . ."; he was also receiving unpleasant letters, like the following from a certain Newton Crosland, ". . . my general knowledge of your character induced me to believe that certain obnoxious rumours against you were true when I heard them about ten days ago, at the corner of every street and in every social circle . . ." In December Thackeray told his daughters that "he is 1/2 mad about his domestic affairs, and tother 1/2 mad with arrogance and vanity". Dickens himself may also have been indiscreet; as Georgina said, "I often used to tell Charles that he was too open with many people . . . that he did not remember how small things and sayings of his were noted down by those about him . . ." There were rumours, too, about his daughters; he said in a letter at this time that ". . . my girls are very pretty, and keep house here [Gad's Hill Place] in great state" but so sensitive an observer could hardly have been unaware of the fact that Mary and Katie were experiencing a certain amount of social coldness because of their decision to stay with their father and, more particularly, with Georgina rather than their mother. As one of Catherine's relatives put it, ". . . they, poor girls, have also been flattered as being taken notice of as the daughters of a popular author. He, too, is a caressing father and indulgent in trifles, and they in their ignorance of the world, look no further nor are aware of the injury he does them." But in fact they must have been aware, at least in part, of precisely that "injury". An unfriendly letter, from a certain Eneas Sweetland Dallas to John Blackwood, reported how Dickens's daughters ". . . are not received into society. You would be excessively amused if you heard all the gigantic efforts the family make to keep their foot in the world – how they call upon people that they never called on before and that they have treated with the most dire contempt." Eneas Dallas goes on to record how Dickens and his family called upon the Samuel Carter Halls and invited them to Tavistock House, only to be told ". . . that it was with Mrs Dickens they were acquainted – that if Mrs Dickens were at Tavistock House they should be happy to call, but otherwise – afraid – very sorry – but etc. etc." This sounds very much like malicous gossip, but the fact that it could be spread in these terms does suggest something of the animus against Dickens and his household in the more "respectable" families; it should not be forgotten that Samuel Carter Hall was supposed at the time to have been Dickens's model for the hypocrite Pecksniff in *Martin Chuzzlewit*.

No doubt there was also gossip about the Ternans, and perhaps about Ellen in particular. It should be remembered that, in this period, a woman who was thought to have sexual relations with a man outside marriage was considered to be little more than a prostitute and that, in addition, the term "actress" still carried a certain amount of moral opprobrium. Ellen could have been, and no doubt was, as virginal as Dickens always insisted; but this would not have stopped the malice and the rumour. It is for this reason, no doubt, that Dickens became incensed about what has become known as the Berners Street affair. Dickens's efforts to find a singing master for Fanny Ternan in Italy had been successful, and it seems likely that he helped to pay for her trip to that country together with her mother who was to act as chaperone; the two other daughters, Maria and Ellen, were still working in London but they had moved on Dickens's advice from Canonbury to rooms at 31 Berners Street (just off Oxford Street and closer to the theatres). It was during their residence here that the policeman on that particular "beat" questioned the two women. Ellen told Dickens what had happened, and at once he flew into one of those indignant passions during the course of which he lost all sense of reality; if the incident was reported in *The Times*, he told Wills, there would be "public uproar". In his vociferous letter he went on to tell Wills to see the two women, and then to make a complaint at Scotland Yard against the officer. Dickens seemed to think that the policeman had been bribed to find out more about the Ternan girls from some "Swell"; this seems likely, but his reaction to the incident suggests the extent to which he felt himself threatened from all sides. And, to complicate matters still further, his own family were behaving in a less than "respectable" manner. His brother, Frederick, had left his wife, and Anna Weller had now applied to the recently-established Divorce Court for a legal separation on the grounds of adultery. Yet another brother, Augustus, had deserted his wife, too, and gone to America with another woman. Who in the period, knowing of these matrimonial entanglements as well as that of Charles Dickens himself, would have failed to consider the whole family to have, in one of the phrases of the time, "bad blood"? And who even now can doubt that the legacy of John Dickens's fecklessness had not in some sense imprinted itself upon his children – even if, in Dickens's case, it was to be all the more sternly repudiated?

Yet there is a sense in which Dickens, despite all of these familial and amatory anxieties, seems to have confronted the worst and to have overcome it. He had of course removed one source of discomfort. He had separated from Catherine and, in so doing, he had sloughed off the life he once thought that he wanted. Instead he had now got the life he *really* wanted all along; all the available evidence suggests (though of course it does not prove) that he had entered a strange mythical relationship with the idealised virgin of his fiction, and that his affection for Ellen Ternan was quite outside the familiar Victorian pattern of clandestine mistresses. Of course the readings had helped, as we have seen, to bolster his self-esteem at a time when it was most severely under threat. "I consider it a remarkable instance of good fortune," he told Miss Burdett-Coutts, "that it should have fallen out that I should, in this autumn of all others, have come face to face with so many multitudes." He was happy to have *faced down* the world, too, and the idea for a Christmas story which occurred to him in the course of the reading tour suggests precisely his attitude at the time; it was to be a story that ". . . shows beyond mistake that you can't shut out the world; that you are in it, to be of it; that you get into a false position the moment you try to sever yourself from it; and that you must mingle with it, and make the best of it, and make the best of yourself into the bargain." It was the same force of life which made him always watch the world; while on a railway trip, he told Georgina, "it was a most lovely morning, and, tired as I was, I couldn't sleep for looking out of window".

In fact the actual Christmas story he wrote was of a quite different complexion and, furthermore, it was the last to be published in *Household Words*. The grievance which Dickens had held against Frederick Evans since the time of the separation had not perceptibly abated and, now that the readings were completed, he set to work at once to sever all connection with the publishing firm which had served him so well and for so many years. In particular he wanted to take *Household Words* away from them; so in November he appointed Forster as his representative and, through him, asked his publishers to agree to the dissolution of the periodical. In the meantime Dickens went down to Gad's Hill Place and prepared to start work upon the next, and last, Christmas issue of *Household Words* with Wilkie Collins. For a while he had thought of using his Christmas contribution as the opening of a new novel – he had been jotting down notes for one at the beginning of the year – but in fact it was eventually combined with some stories of Collins and others to produce *A House To Let*. Dickens's own piece, "Going Into Society", was a moral fable on the dangers of "Society"; a subject, you might say, which he now knew by heart. So perhaps something of Dickens is to be found in the "Showman" who tells this story, a man who ". . . had led a wandering life, and settled people had lost sight of him, and people who plumed themselves on being respectable were shy of admitting that they had ever known anything of him".

Negotiations with Bradbury and Evans were proceeding even as he wrote and published this cautionary tale. The publishers refused to discontinue *Household Words* and in fact they denied the legality of Dickens's proceedings; he then asked them, instead, to sell their interest in the periodical to him. They replied that they might be interested in selling their share, but only as part of an arrangement in which he would purchase their interest in all of his works. Dickens then offered one thousand pounds for *Household Words* alone. Again, they refused. It was a complex and acrimonious dispute as Wills and Forster, directed by Dickens, refused to do anything other than purchase the periodical or dissolve it. (It is not recorded how difficult it was for Wills to take a stand against men whom he had previously liked and admired, yet another instance of the havoc which Dickens could wreak in private relationships when he was set upon some end of his own.) Matters were further complicated by the fact that Dickens was already thinking ahead to a new periodical, to be conducted wholly by himself. He had also decided to return to Chapman and Hall for the publication of his novels, despite the fact that this was the firm which he had left in a similar outburst of anger and indignation so many years before. But that was now long in the past; Hall was dead and Chapman was about to retire, leaving the running of the company in the hands of his cousin, Frederick. Once more Dickens was fighting against his "enemies" real or imagined, changing his old allegiances, abandoning those who stood opposed to his will, forcing his way through the world.

It was with something like fellow-feeling, therefore, that towards the end of the year he delivered a speech at a prize-giving of the Institutional Association of Lancashire and Cheshire; it was an occasion when he gave prizes to working men who had completed courses of study under difficulties, men who represented the individual triumph of skill and assiduity over poverty and disadvantage, men whose will to succeed had overcome all obstacles. And how close such men were to Dickens at this time of his life! Two poor brothers who worked in coalmines during the day and then, three nights a week, walked eight miles to a college. A moulder in an iron foundry who got up at four o'clock in the morning to learn industrial drawing. A piecer who at the age of eighteen had been illiterate, but who then taught himself how to read and write, how to work in algebra, and who wrote of himself ". . . that he made the resolution never to take up a subject without keeping to it . . ." It is often suggested that the 1850s were in England a time of social and political stability, of national pride and wealth. But such individual histories demonstrate that it was also an era of transition, of marked but uneven change. The progress in science did not necessarily mean progress in urban sanitation or practical medicine; developments in industrial technology did not necessarily lead to factory reform. So in some ways this was a decade of anxiety; John Stuart Mill wrote in his diary in 1854 that "scarcely anyone, in the more educated classes, seems to have any opinions, or to place any real faith in those which he professes to have". There were new kinds of finance. New forms of labour. But there was also the decline of belief in organised religion. The decline of faith in the family itself, when, as Walter Bagehot put it, "a man's household are the special foes of his favourite and self-adopted creed". So it was that Bagehot described this as a time of "confusion and tumult", and Matthew Arnold, in 1853, spoke of "the bewildering confusion of our times". We have the paradox of a more prosperous age undermined by doubt, a politically more stable era marked by intellectual and moral confusion, a much more powerful society but also a more anxious one; this is precisely the paradox which Dickens explores in his later fiction, and it is in this context that we can properly and most fruitfully see Dickens in his own time of change, of anxiety, of private doubt underlying prosperity. It is in this context, too, that we must see those young men to whom he was awarding prizes – men fighting out of poverty, aspiring towards a better life, just as Dickens himself had once done, with all the vitality and ambition which Dickens still possessed.

On the day after the prize-giving he left Manchester for Coventry, where he was to be presented with a seventy-five guinea watch (purchased by subscription after Dickens had read for the Coventry Institute in the previous year). He made an agreeable speech, as everyone expected, and then at the end he made an impromptu toast to the women. "We know that the Graces were all women (*renewed laughter*); we know that the Muses were women, and we know every day of our lives that the Fates are women (*Roars of laughter*). I think that as we receive so much from them, both in happiness and pain, we ought at least to drink their healths. (*Cheers.*)". No one who knew anything of Dickens's domestic trials could doubt the significance of what were, for him, remarkably frank words; ". . . both in happiness and pain . . ." The last days of the year, at Gad's Hill Place, were wet and dreary. Dickens, Frith and Collins played bagatelle and talked.

He had no desire to celebrate his forty-seventh birthday two months later. "I have not had the heart to make any preparation for it," he wrote to Wilkie Collins, "– you know why." But he did not want his gloom to infect his children, and he planned to take them down to Brighton for a few days. He also had a bad cold, always a sure sign with Dickens that he was either depressed or overworked. "– you know why . . .", he had said, and it is likely that the reason was that "little reason", that "riddle", Ellen Ternan. Fanny Ternan and her mother were about to return from Italy, and Dickens seriously thought of letting Tavistock House to the entire family; until, that is,

Forster argued him out of the idea. It would no doubt have been a provocation to those who already suspected "the worst". Even so, when the Ternan family were reunited, they took steps to move from the unfurnished lodgings in Berners Street; somehow the two older sisters were able to afford to take a lease on 2 Houghton Place, Ampthill Square, in Camden Town. It has been suggested that Dickens himself provided the money with which they purchased the lease, but the evidence for this remains circumstantial – consisting mainly of the fact that, a month before, Dickens sold at least fifteen hundred pounds' worth of government stock and, a few weeks later, agreed to write a short story for the *New York Ledger* at the then astonishing price of one thousand pounds. Clearly he needed money for something, but it may just have been for "improvements" at Gad's Hill Place. Whatever the truth of the matter, the Ternans (without Fanny, who had decided to remain at her studies in Italy) moved into the new house in March. Five months later Ellen appeared for the last time on the stage and, from that time forward, seems to have earned her living in Houghton Place as a teacher of elocution. The house itself was a four-storied, terraced affair in a suitably residential and middle-class area of London. Francisco Berger, who had met the Ternans when he was arranging the music for *The Frozen Deep*, often visited the new family residence; he remembered the occasions when he met Dickens there, too, playing cards and singing duets with Ellen at the piano. Perhaps they sang together two popular songs of that time, Mendelssohn's "Fast, ah, too fast fade the Roses of Pleasure" and John Barnett's "I will gather the Rose".

In the first months of this new year, 1859, Dickens was sitting to Frith; Forster had commissioned a painting of his friend, and Frith had willingly accepted it. Dickens was, he said later, "a delightful sitter, always punctual to the moment, and always remaining the full two hours . . ." He even went to the trouble of having himself photographed by a celebrated exponent of the new art, Watkins, and to the photographer's studio were brought Dickens's table, chair and velvet jacket – the point being that Frith could work from the artificial image when the great original was absent. The photograph itself shows a grave, rather tired man, his hair pushed back from his forehead, sitting back in his chair in an indefinably wary or uneasy posture. He seems to be holding a paper knife, or quill pen, in his right hand. Frith thought nothing of the photograph itself, although he used the basic position. In his portrait the tiredness has been replaced by something very much like exaltation, and the gravity has been combined with intense watchfulness.

Frith's diary:

> *Jan 21*: Arranged Dickens's portrait till he came at 1.30. He sat delight-
> fully . . . talking all the while.
> *Jan 22*: Dickens again . . . most pleasant. No wonder people like him.

Frith said of the novelist that he had "the expression settled into that of one who had reached the topmost rung of a very high ladder, and was perfectly aware of his position". Dickens himself said of the completed picture that "it is a little too much (to my thinking) as if my next-door neighbour were my deadly foe, uninsured, and I had just received tidings of his house being afire . . ." And, when Dickens was not talking during each of the two-hour sessions, he had time to think.

Thinking of more readings. Thinking of a reading tour of America, although there was what he called a "private reason" for his regretting a long absence from England. Thinking of the successor to *Household Words*, which he was still determined to dissolve. Thinking of titles for a new periodical. Astonishingly enough, considering his present position, he first came up with *Household Harmony*, and became rather annoyed when Forster gently hinted at the incongruity. "I am afraid we must not be too particular about the possibility of personal refer-ences and applications: otherwise it is manifest that I never can write another book." But he assented, and considered *Charles Dickens's Own* and *Time and Tide* among other titles. Until triumphantly he arrived at,

"'The story of our lives, from year to year.' – *Shakespeare*.

ALL THE YEAR ROUND.

A weekly journal conducted by Charles Dickens."

He had even found an office for the new periodical, only a few doors down Wellington Street North from his old headquarters; but a much plainer set of rooms than those for *Household Words*, described by Percy Fitzgerald as ". . . a shop rather than an office". One visitor noticed the plainness of the new offices, too, and remarked that there was not ". . . a square yard of carpet of any kind, but daily scrubbings had made the floors and stairs scrupulously clean. Nowhere in the building did I see a single article of furniture excepting an oblong table and a pair of large rush bottomed armchairs in the editorial room''. Nevertheless Dickens did fit up for himself an apartment on the top storey of the house; he was planning to let Tavistock House and needed somewhere to stay in London on his frequent trips from Gad's Hill Place. Finance was now a very important consideration in a venture to be organised entirely by himself, and within a matter of weeks he concluded an agreement with an American entrepreneur whereby Dickens would ship across the Atlantic stereotype plates of each issue so that it could be published simultaneously in the United States. He also made an arrangement with Harper and Brothers to send over proof sheets of the magazine before publication. But there was one much more important matter which he had to resolve. He realised that, in order to send *All The Year Round* successfully into the world, it would be necessary to begin a story of his own in the first issue; nothing else was so likely to attract or to keep readers as a new novel from an author who had published nothing now for eighteen months. He had his rough jottings, conceived at the time he was lying on the floor of the stage as Richard Wardour, which had no doubt been amended or enlarged in the course of the last few months; but, as always, he needed a title before he could begin. *Buried Alive. The Thread of Gold. The Doctor of Beauvais.* Then it came to him. *A Tale of Two Cities.* Even as the title emerged he was considering the publication arrangements; it would be printed each week in *All The Year Round* and then bound up at the end of each month in the old green-covered Numbers. It was, in fact, a narrative which emerged powerfully and naturally. Just eight days after he had invented its title, he was hard at work upon it; almost at once the story had taken "complete possession" of him and, in its spare dramatic style, there are echoes of his role as Richard Wardour in *The Frozen Deep* as well as of his more recent experiences as a public reader. The differences between *A Tale of Two Cities* and Dickens's previous novels have often been described, but they are most clearly to be seen in the circumstances of its prolonged genesis.

There was of course still the pressing necessity to wind up *Household Words*, before his attention could be fully engaged upon the new journal, and he went about that business with his usual speed and steely determination. He had three hundred thousand handbills and posters printed, in order to advertise the new journal, at which point

Bradbury and Evans issued an injunction to stop the distribution of leaflets announcing his departure from *Household Words* and the imminent publication of *All The Year Round*. For once Chancery acted speedily; the case came up the next day, and judgment was largely given in Dickens's favour. The Master of the Rolls also ordered that *Household Words* be put up for auction, and the proceeds distributed fairly between all the parties concerned. Dickens's determination to buy the periodical, now that the opportunity presented itself, could only have been strengthened by a rumour that Bradbury and Evans wished themselves to purchase *Household Words* and make Thackeray its new editor. So at the auction Dickens, represented through the bidding of Arthur Smith and the diversionary tactics of Frederick Chapman, bought out his old journal for £3,550, a sum which he later recouped by selling the stock of stereotype plates to Chapman and Hall. He had won, as he had always insisted he would, and in the last number of *Household Words* he could not resist proclaiming the fact of his own rightness. "He knew perfectly well, knowing his own rights, and his means of attaining them, that it *could not be* but this Work must stop, if he chose to stop it. He therefore announced many weeks ago, that it would be discontinued on the day on which this final Number bears date. The Public have read a great deal to the contrary, and will observe that it has not in the least affected the result." In a private letter Dickens said of his old publishers, "What fools they are!"

Household Words and *All The Year Round* finally merged in the issue of Saturday, 4 June, 1859, after *All The Year Round* had been issued by itself for the previous five weeks. In some respects the two periodicals were identical – the same size, the same sober appearance, the same double-columned page, approximately the same mixture of articles, and the same price of twopence. The contributors were also much the same; "my brothers", as Dickens sometimes called them although he himself was known as "the Chief" and many of the journalists were less flatteringly known as "Mr Dickens's young men". And yet, as Dickens announced in his prospectus, "in some important respects I am now free greatly to advance on past arrangements". The principal "advance" for him lay in the fact that, for the first time in his life, he had sole control of his own periodical; the legend at the top of every issue, "Conducted by Charles Dickens", was now literally true. He owned it, he edited it, and only he could take the major decisions concerning it. One such decision became obvious at once; the first issue of the new journal began, on the front page, with the opening episode of *A Tale of Two Cities*. It was a beginning, too, in another sense. He had been thinking about the nature of the new periodical, and the defects of its predecessor, and had come to the conclusion that *All The Year Round* would always carry the serialisation of a novel (sometimes, in fact, two novels were published concurrently); he remembered how *The Old Curiosity Shop* had once saved *Master Humphrey's Clock*, and *Hard Times* had materially assisted *Household Words*. In fact novels were now to be the main feature of the new periodical, among them *The Moonstone* and *The Woman In White*, as if in obeisance to a culture which demanded more comfortable and leisurely reading. There were of course the more familiar ingredients; there was generally a short story, for example, and some relatively topical matter which in the first few numbers was of a sharply satirical kind. (One innovation was the inclusion of comic paragraphs under the heading "Lost" or "Wanted" – which was exactly the device he had used as a schoolboy on the small "newspapers" he compiled at Wellington House Academy.) Dickens had not lost his belief in the necessity of drawing attention both to the privations of the poor and the abuses of the government, but there is no doubt that there was actually less social and political matter in *All The Year Round* than there had been in its predecessor. There were several reasons for this, one of them being of a technical nature; since he had agreed to ship stereotype plates of each number for simultaneous publication in the United States, it was necessary for each issue to be prepared two and half weeks in advance of publication. Such a delay inevitably meant that the more topical items could not be introduced. But, perhaps more importantly, Dickens's own interest in the political and social affairs of the day seems from this time to have been waning. In his correspondence, too, he seems to be losing heart or losing interest (it is difficult to decide which); he saw only public indifference everywhere, but no doubt his own private unrest and anxiety meant that he was also less active, less eager, and less engaged. He was, in addition, now so familiar with the techniques and business of periodical publication – *Household Words* had appeared every week for over nine years – that he must inevitably have lost some of the interest which had once spurred him forward. Certainly some contributors noted a diminution of spirit in the new periodical. Percy Fitzgerald considered it to be less personal, more conventional and ". . . seemed to lack the tranquil unaffected simplicity of the old journal". And yet something of this change can be attributed to the nature of the age itself; the blander forms of impersonality, the larger element of "entertainment", as opposed to the analysis of political or social issues, bear all the marks of their period.

Of course this is not to suggest that Dickens neglected his property; far from it. Even when he was engaged on his arduous and lengthy reading tours, he carefully went over manuscripts and proofs and "make-up"; his letters to Wills are shorter than in the early years, but this was primarily because they had reached such an understanding that Wills almost instinctively knew what it was that Dickens appreciated or detested. There were occasional arguments between them, but nothing like the blunt and often peremptory messages which Dickens used once to direct at his employee. Dickens was also very concerned with its success; he was now fully convinced of the virtues of advertising (another aspect in which the nature of the period seems directly to be reflected by him) and he spent a great deal of money on billboards, placards and newspaper advertisements. The placards were six feet in length with black and red letters on a golden orange ground, in themselves sufficiently striking and certainly effective; there were occasions when the offices of *All The Year Round* were almost besieged by those who wanted the next episode of a successful serial. And, as a result, *All The Year Round* was much more successful than *Household Words* had ever been. The earlier journal had sales of something between thirty-six thousand and forty thousand, while *All The Year Round* never dipped below one hundred thousand copies. Although this was still not in excess of the more popular middle-class journals, it was certainly enough to afford Dickens (and Wills) a large and sustained income. It confirmed Dickens, too, in his favourite belief; that he was, after all, right all the time.

So what was the nature of his reputation and his popularity at this point in his life; what did ". . . this great audience . . .", as he described the readership of *All The Year Round*, think of him now? That he was very popular there can be no reasonable doubt. Justin MacCarthy said that "no one born in the younger generation can easily understand . . . the immensity of the popular homage which Dickens then enjoyed . . . He was almost worshipped by the lower-middle-classes in our provincial towns . . . the only author they knew." And Percy Fitzgerald noted that "no one indeed can even conceive the singular veneration, admiration and love that was felt for him . . ." As photographs of his visage became more and more widely disseminated, in the late Fifties and early Sixties, he was also instantly recognised in any town or city in the country. There were times when he thought of himself merely as "public property", however, and was not wholly pleased by the reproduction of his image in booksellers' windows; he said at one time that he had promised enough photographic sessions ". . . to haunt mankind with my countenance". There is in fact one disadvantage with all of these photographs; because of the necessity for the image to "take", Dickens had to remain still for some time, which is why all of the images show him in rather dour or unsmiling mood. None of them catch that gaiety of spirit and animation of countenance which were his single most obvious characteristics. He knew as much himself, and generally damned all photographs of himself as either grim or ferocious.

But they were all, as it were, designed to add further to the idea of the literary man as hero. This was a period in which the cult of the "great man" was widespread and there was a sense in which Dickens was for most of those who read him truly "larger than life". There is a pleasant story of a boy looking at a picture of Dickens in the window of a bookshop near St Paul's Churchyard, and then looking up to see the novelist himself scrutinising the same image; the boy's expression immediately became one of "wonder and worship". Dickens laughed at this and then gave an affirmative nod – as if to say "It is so, young man. It is Charles Dickens" – before walking briskly away down Cheapside. To see Dickens in the street was an event worthy of comment and his son, Henry, recalls that "to walk with him in the streets of London was a revelation . . . people of all degrees and classes taking off their hats and greeting him as he passed". (Dickens said knowingly of one acquaintance, "He was immensely pleased to be with me," by which he meant, to be *seen* with me.) His son also remembered that, when he and his father were touring a factory in Birmingham, the working people continually stopped Henry and asked, "Is that Charles Dickens?" His reading manager of later days, George Dolby, records how one day he was walking in the countryside with "the Chief" when two young men came upon them on the road – one young man fell back into a wood on the side of the road, pulling his companion with him. "Make way!" he said. "Blow me if that ain't Charles Dickens." He said this in such a Cockneyfied and theatrical way that Dickens laughed out loud; then he asked the young man if he might have "the honour of shaking him by the hand". And, again, there was the incident of the young girl at the zoo which Dickens was visiting with Henry – "Oh mummy! mummy!" she shouted. "It is Charles Dickens!" And Henry adds, "My father, who had heard and seen it all, was strangely embarrassed; but oh, so pleased, so truly delighted." In fact he did have an apparently ambivalent attitude towards his fame, and Percy Fitzgerald noted that "he was always quite unconcerned at the staring and whispering. He was so unaffected; he behaved just as though he were alone." This is like the story of Dickens feigning indifference when his name was mentioned at the circus or in the theatre. But this was the apparent indifference of someone who was in fact mightily moved by all such signs of admiration and praise, just as he used to feign coolness at the "enthoosemoosy" which greeted him as a young man while nevertheless excitedly writing back to Forster and Catherine about it later. Of course there were occasions when it became too much; sometimes he went to the theatre in cap and muffler precisely in order to avoid being recognised. But Fitzgerald noticed, for example, how ". . . he liked little deferential attentions from railway guards and such persons . . ." In great things as in small he was of a piece; it can be taken for granted that he really enjoyed the admiration and the instant recognition.

But, if in a certain sense he now required it to bolster his own sense of self-worth, what of his general reputation as a writer in the same period? Perhaps it is enough at this point to recall that in the last half of his life and writing career there were constant criticisms of his exaggeration, his sentimentality, his grotesquerie, his inability to create character and his propensity for caricature, his melodrama, his theatricality, his pathos, his reliance upon the role of the "entertainer" (thus a man of too little culture). In fact he was severely criticised for precisely the faults which are now considered to be some of his greatest virtues. But there was even then no doubt that, despite these "blemishes", he was perhaps the most significant writer of his age. Mechanics' Institutes and Literary Societies would debate his merits – "What is the influence upon society of the writings of Charles Dickens? Do they elevate or degrade our literature?" – and he was recognised as a man of genius, a writer who had changed the shape of the English novel. But there was something more, for in an obscure sense it was already being recognised that he was a representative figure. "Charles Dickens is preeminently a man of the middle nineteenth century . . ."; ". . . a child of his age"; ". . . the novelist of his age"; Sir Arthur Helps once told Queen Victoria that Dickens's ". . . name will hereafter be closely associated with the Victorian era". Just *how* closely he would be identified with the nineteenth century would probably have come as a shock to his contemporaries, however; no one of that period could have guessed that "Dickensian" would become a term of opprobrium for any disagreeable aspect of the century, and no one would have believed that his fame as a popular novelist would be undiminished more than one hundred years after his death. Of course he also exerted a tremendous influence in his own time; he knew as much, and even counted upon it. He said of his own fiction that it was composed "to interest and affect the general mind in behalf of anything that is clearly wrong . . .", and at one reading of *A Christmas Carol* he spoke of the need to keep imaginative literature in close touch with "private homes and public rights". The effect of the portrait of Dotheboys Hall in *Nicholas Nickleby* is only one of the examples which might be adduced to reveal the extent of Dickens's influence upon the consciousness of his time. When he was told how popular and revered he was even in Russia, he is reported to have said, "Yes, there is so much suffering there that what I have tried to say would almost certainly find many hearts open to receive it." So on one level he was conscious of the didactic, or at least exhortatory, purposes of his fiction. But he exercised just as much influence through *Household Words* and *All The Year Round*. It is not just that many of their more controversial articles were instantly reprinted by the national press, but rather that the middle decades of the century marked a period in which middle-class England took its opinions from the periodical press. Of course many of them preferred to trust the longer essays of such intellectual journals as the *Edinburgh Review*, but there was a large public (as the circulation of *All The Year Round* proved) ready to take its attitudes from articles in a journal "Conducted by Charles Dickens". As Lecky declared, in his *Religious Tendencies of the Age*, "It is our lay writers who are moulding the character and forming the opinions of the age", thus superseding ". . . the clergy in the direction of the thought of England".

And what was Dickens's attitude towards this "multitude", this "audience" which he addressed throughout his life? For him the relationship was personal and almost loving. "Wherever I go," he said in this period, "I find myself affectionately cherished in the homes of honest men and women, and associated, as their friend, with their domestic joys and troubles." For him the "public" was not some amorphous entity but at times a group of friends and at other times an extension of his family. If he conceived of it abstractly at all, it was as a real force and an equally real consolation; a force that he could move and, in making it laugh or weep, come to feel the power within himself. In a very real sense he identified himself with his audience, and, as the events around his separation demonstrated all too clearly, the reactions of the people "out there" were more important to him than those of his family or of his closest acquaintances. The point was that he had achieved enormous popularity so early in his career and with such ease that he never thought of his audience as in any way estranged from, or alien to, himself. To keep faith with it, then – that was the important thing. But equally important, in retrospect at least, was his understanding of it; there never was a writer more adept at judging his readership than Charles Dickens. He knew precisely what effect to achieve, and precisely the means with which to do it. That is why he was always so skilful at creating the right "mix" of articles within each issue of his periodical; he knew how to vary the emphases and change the moods so that the publication had an effect larger than the sum of its parts. But it is not often understood that he used a variant of the same technique within his fiction; he gauged the extent to which pathos and comedy could be employed, and was very careful never to weary or to bore the reader. This sounds like a matter of infinite calculation, but it was not so. It was a matter of instinct; the instinct to see his own work, as it were, from the outside; to understand it as his public understood it. If he could see his characters in dumb-show in front of him, then he ensured that his readers would also see them: it is, after all, one of the things which comprise Dickens's greatness. It has often been said that in the process he merely picked up the prevailing opinions of his middle-class audience and reflected them, just as it is often said that his work suffers from too great a surrender to "popular entertainment" in the matter of melodrama or pathos. But the reality of the matter is actually much more interesting. Dickens impressed his fiction upon his readers with almost mesmeric intensity precisely because of his very closeness to them; he conveyed his themes and predilections with such force and openness that by some alchemical process they adopted them as if they had been theirs all the time. Yet in this midst of this strange but fruitful confusion there were occasions when Dickens himself was not able to distinguish between his private and public lives – when it is not at all clear that he knew himself where Dickens "the public man" ended and where Dickens the individual began. He often described himself half-regretfully as a "public personage" or "public property", but this was a condition he in fact positively encouraged. There were times when he seemed to live only to display himself and his feelings, when his emotions and reactions only became real after they had been presented to the public for approbation. But what of that great audience he could not yet see? The audience to come?

When Dickens planted some lime-trees at the front of Gad's Hill Place, he told Forster that "he had no idea . . . of planting only for the benefit of posterity, but would put into the ground what he might himself enjoy the sight and shade of". Which is a fairly accurate description of his attitude towards his own work. There is no doubt that he enjoyed both the acclaim which he received and the influence which he possessed, but there can also be no doubt that at least part of his attention was directed towards posterity. What he said of the fictional instalments in *All The Year Round* might equally be said of his own novels – that he hoped they would ". . . become a part of English Literature". He once admitted in *Household Words* that the idea of posterity was ". . . a topic of much speculation with me"; that is why he was at great pains to collect together the working notes for his novels and bind them in with his manuscripts, and why most of his original material was given to Forster and became part of what Dickens only half-jokingly described as the "collection". Certainly he attached enormous importance to his public reputation; in his earlier career, for example, he tried to manipulate his public persona by arranging discreet "puffs" of his own work, writing letters to prominent people, and befriending critics. He was also adept at issuing short and censored biographical details, thus ensuring that nothing would be transmitted to his contemporary audience or to posterity without his official approval. This was why he came so close to hysteria at the time of the separation when, for the first time in his life, his public reputation began slipping out of his own control. Of a small article he wrote in the year before his death, in fact, he explained that "I have thought it best to make it a piece of personal testimony which can be quoted a hundred years hence"; and it seems likely that this gradually became one of his major preoccupations. And yet, as of all the things closest to him, he spoke of this to no one. "No man in his inner mind felt so sure of Westminster Abbey and immortality," one colleague has said, "and no man kept that inner mind more carefully concealed." Instead he tended to display his usual air of impenetrable modesty; "utterly uspoilt by his long sustained and immense popularity", as one friend put it. Dickens was always unassuming about his fame, easy and amenable in conversation (as we have seen), but all the time he retained deep within himself his real sense of his own achievement. As Forster said of his apparent indifference to criticism, ". . . the secret was that he believed himself to be entitled to higher tribute than he was always in the habit of receiving".

And, as always, he worked on. By the time the first issue of *All The Year Round* appeared, Dickens had already written at least the first three weekly episodes of *A Tale of Two Cities*; he had in fact been working quickly upon it, after so long a period of gestation, and would continue to do so. But it did not spring fully-armed, as it were, from his imagination. He had always admired Carlyle's *History of the French Revolution*, and asked him to recommend suitable books from which he could research the period; in reply Carlyle sent him a "cartload" of volumes from the London Library. Apparently Dickens read, or at least looked through, them all; it was his aim during the period of composition only to read books of the period itself, and so great was his enthusiasm for the story that it had indeed "taken possession" of him. He was a "slave" to it by the middle of May and managed to complete it by the beginning of October. Dickens's knowledge of the French Revolution was strengthened by Carlyle's wonderful history, which had appeared twenty-two years before, but it was a subject which seems always to have fascinated him. In truth his opinion on the matter never really changed, since it was his primary belief that the French *ancien régime* had itself created the conditions which provoked the revolution. ". . . It was a struggle on the part of the people for social recognition and existence," Dickens had written in the *Examiner*, in the heady period of the Forties when Chartism itself seemed to bear witness to the threat of an English revolution of a similar kind. ". . . It was a struggle for the overthrow of a system of oppression, which in its contempt of all humanity, decency, and natural rights, and in the systematic degradation of the people, had trained them to be the demons that they showed themselves when they rose up and cast it down for ever." It was a social philosophy, or, rather, a social obsession, which he had emphasised in all his writings.

A Tale of Two Cities was unusual for Dickens, however, in the sense that he explicitly conceived it as a novel of story and incident rather than of character or dialogue. He was reading the first four of Tennyson's *Idylls of the King* through the summer months while he was working on the book, and that is perhaps why he also described it as ". . . a *picturesque* story". He was often susceptible to stray influences of this kind, although this in turn raises the troubled question of the sources which affected his composition of the novel. Troubled in the sense that he was now being directly charged with plagiarism – not plagiarism of Carlyle but of *The Dead Heart*, a play by Watts Phillips which opened three weeks before the conclusion of *A Tale of Two Cities* in *All The Year Round* and which had the same historical setting, much the same story and approximately the same climax. In fact, as we have already discovered, Dickens had been given a reading of the play some two years before at Brighton; and, at a time when the twin themes of self-sacrifice and amatory renunciation were pressing closely upon him in, *The Frozen Deep*, it is not at all surprising that Phillips's play should set up a series of echoes and resemblances which have less to do with conspicuous plagiarism than with the need to write *this* story and no other.

Nevertheless many other sources have also been suggested for it; among them Bulwer-Lytton's *Zanoni*, Matthew Lewis's *The Castle Spectre*, Arthur Young's *Travels in France*, Louis-Sébastien Mercier's *Tableau de Paris* and Beaumarchais's account of his imprisonment during the Terror (the last three were no doubt recommended by Carlyle, who also employed them). There is also an account of the trial of a French spy, very much like Dickens's account of the trial of Charles Darnay, in *The Annual Register* of 1781, but in this case, as in so many others, the reason and context of the borrowing are more interesting than the fact of the borrowing itself. For the account of the trial of the French spy was sandwiched between two long narratives concerning Lord George Gordon – in other words, while Dickens was undertaking research for *Barnaby Rudge*, he had come across an interesting trial, and the vague outline of it re-emerged for him when he came to write *A Tale of Two Cities* some twenty years later. It is quite possible that he reproduced the details of that trial without even knowing that he was doing so, and an understanding of this phenomenon suggests the extent to which "plagiarism" is the wrong word for the wrong activity; certainly the emphasis upon likely sources of the novel tends to discount the evident fact that, as with all of his novels, Dickens had been preparing to write it all of his life. There is a clue to his intention when, in any essay written in 1853, he recalls his childhood interest in ". . . the wicked old Bastile" where ". . . was shut up, in black silence through so many years, that old man of the affecting anecdote, who was at last set free" but who ". . . prayed to be shut up in his old dungeon till he died". Here, in embryo, is the central theme of the novel. Similarly, as early as 1855, Dickens was jotting down in his notebook stray suggestions – "How as to a story in two periods – with a lapse of time between, like a French Drama?" – which were to culminate in *A Tale of Two Cities* itself. And, in 1846, he had outlined in a letter ". . . the idea of a man imprisoned for ten or fifteen years . . .", the time of imprisonment itself representing the gap between the two parts of the story. In other words all the forces which propel *A Tale of Two Cities* forward had been present in Dickens's imagination for many years. Certainly the image of the prison, and the even more unsettling idea of the prisoners who love their confinement, had been with him from his earliest days; from his childhood, by his own account, but certainly from the days of *Sketches by Boz* and *The Pickwick Papers*. It is striking only that it should at this time have been so powerfully revived. And that it should be associated now with the idea of secrets; with the horrors of the condemned man; with the concept of self-sacrifice, apparently so important to him at this point in his life; with the idea of the renunciation of love for some higher good. And connected, too, with the uncertainties or obscurities of love itself – "'. . . mysteries arise out of close love, as well as out of wide division; in the former case, they are subtle and delicate, and difficult to penetrate. My daughter Lucie is, in this one respect, such a mystery to me; I can make no guess at the state of her heart.'" It has often been suggested that Lucie Manette is a partial portrait of Ellen Ternan but the evidence for any such identification is not needed to demonstrate how much *A Tale of Two Cities* was a part of all his preoccupations and long-standing themes. Part, too, of his own immediate unrest: "Throughout its execution," Dickens said of the novel, ". . . it has had complete possession of me; I have so far verified what is done and suffered in these pages as that I have certainly done and suffered it all myself." He told Mary Boyle that he would like to have acted the part of Sydney Carton, the man who willingly goes to his death on the guillotine in order to save his "rival" for the love of Lucie Manette, and in his anguished letters of this time, letters in which he describes his "suffering" at the unmerited abuse which he is forced to endure, is there some image of himself as a similar hero who must love without hope? Who must be patient even unto death? All these themes came together in *A Tale of Two Cities*. He had to write it not merely because of the pressing demands of *All The Year Round* but because these elements, so long meditated and now so powerfully stirred within him, emerged in just this form. He had no need for characters or dialogue in his usual manner, since the material he now possessed needed no elaboration. It emerged as it was, and Dickens "suffered" within it.

Yet there is the influence of Carlyle still to be understood, and the way in which his notions of Providence and Divine Justice consorted so easily with Dickens's sense of his own fate at this time. There are of course linguistic echoes of Carlyle in the novel itself – "Indeed they were at sea, and the ship and crew were in peril of tempest" is a notably Carlylean image of the state of France – but they would have been purely instinctive on Dickens's part. Just as his most powerful feelings were comprehended by him in terms of *words*, so the words of others most powerfully affected him. According to Carlyle's biographer, Froude, Dickens carried with him everywhere a copy of *A History of the French Revolution* at the time of its publication in 1837; that he referred to it often is exemplified by a photograph of him later in life, reading upon the lawn of Gad's Hill Place, with an edition of that same volume in his hands. Dickens, in his preface to this novel, called it a "wonderful book". Certainly some episodes from *A Tale of Two Cities* are established upon Carlyle's own narrative, particularly the accounts of the revolutionary crowds and the events of the September massacres. Carlyle's history may also have prompted Dickens's use of hidden documents which play so large a part in the working out of his plot. But it would be hard to establish, from these borrowings, that Dickens derived anything like a "philosophy of history" from Carlyle; he took from him what he needed for his immediate purposes, that is all, and it seems likely that whatever general inspiration Dickens received from him in earlier days was now largely dissipated.

There is an interesting anecdote from this period, which perhaps expresses the nature of their relationship better than any disquisition. Carlyle went to hear Dickens read the trial scene from *The Pickwick Papers* and, when Dickens arrived on the platform, the two men nodded at each other. They were on the best of terms and, in fact, shared a similar sense of humour; one contemporary observed of this occasion that "I thought Carlyle would split, and Dickens was not much better. Carlyle sat on the front bench, and he haw-hawed right out, over and over again till he fairly exhausted himself. Dickens would read and then he would stop in order to give Carlyle a chance to stop . . ." During the interval Carlyle went backstage, and had a brandy-and-water. "Carlyle took his glass and nodding to Dickens

said, 'Charley, you carry a whole company of actors under your hat.' "
A compliment, of course, but there is little doubt that, even at this
relatively late stage in Dickens's career, Carlyle could really only think
of him as an entertainer, his constant bias against fiction leading him to
disregard the more serious aspects of that pursuit. Dickens was too
keen an observer not to realise this and, in turn, he treated Carlyle with
an admiration and friendliness not unmixed with reserve. It would in
any case have been quite alien to his own self-sufficiency and self-
regard ever to take wholesale from Carlyle any of Carlyle's broader
themes; in particular Dickens distrusted his love of the past and his
worship of power, and it is noteworthy that both these aspects of
Carlyle's history are missing from the novel.

But what of Dickens's general borrowings? Goldsmith, Smollett,
Sterne, Marryat, Addison, Scott, Fielding, and Hogarth are only a few
of the artists from whom Dickens is supposed to have taken effects,
characters or scenes. Of course it is true that Hogarth, for example,
provides Dickens with something very much like a mythology upon
which he could draw when necessary; but, in general terms, the
materials which Dickens stole or borrowed are never as important as
the principles upon which they are transformed by him into the
constituents of his own especial art. There are in fact two types of
borrowing in his work. One is purely instinctive and unconscious,
and it is fair to say that he would have been astonished by the number
and variety of passages or characters he is alleged to have taken from
previous novelists. The work of Smollett or Sterne, of Defoe or
Addison, was simply part of the world in which he moved; one might
as well say that he stole the image of Newgate from the actual
Newgate Prison as to suggest that somehow he consciously plagiarised material from the favourite authors of his early years. The second
type of borrowing is more deliberate. As in the case of Carlyle's
History of The French Revolution, he took certain passages or incidents
which struck him as being significant and then redeployed them.
These passages were for him a source of inspiration; he abbreviated
them, elaborated upon them, adapted them, but in all cases the
original material is only of significance by reason of its place in the
fresh combinations of Dickens's fiction. To suggest that they are
"stolen" or "borrowed" or "plagiarised" is little different from stating
that the words Dickens used are "stolen" or "borrowed" from the
English language itself. So it is that in *A Tale of Two Cities* Dickens
took from Carlyle what he needed and then refashioned it in the light

of his own highly idiosyncratic or immediate preoccupations with imprisonment, with rebirth – and, more particularly, with self-sacrifice and the renunciation of love.

Chapter 29

HE was planning to stay at Gad's Hill Place for the whole of this summer of 1859, while he carried on with the weekly instalments of *A Tale of Two Cities*. And how different his life was now. This was the first full year in which he was separated from his wife and, perhaps just as importantly, the first full year in which he maintained his isolation from such old companions as Mark Lemon. Even friends like Miss Burdett-Coutts saw and heard much less of him now, as if he had decided to deliver some kind of reproof to all those who had even a partial sympathy for Catherine. He had also contracted a heavy and prolonged cold, complete with sore throat and congested chest, which left him tired and enervated for weeks at a time.

These spring and summer months of 1859 marked the period after the first series of public readings, too, and as always the applause and brightness of his travelling life were succeeded by a period of increased gloom and disappointment. Somehow he needed to find a fresh source of excitement, some new stimulus – all the more reason, then, for his being taken into "complete possession" by the novel he had now started to write. For him it was the next best thing to *acting*, the excitement which he poured into his presentation of Sydney Carton and of this world of terror. He planned to stay in the country until October, time enough to complete *A Tale of Two Cities*, at which point he would be ready to set off on a second provincial reading tour. As always the most orderly and methodical of men, he quickly developed a routine; going to London on Monday afternoon and spending Tuesday at the office in Wellington Street, returning to Gad's Hill Place on Wednesday and working there on the novel until the next Monday. For a short time he was diverted from his main work by the story he had agreed to write for the *New York Ledger* for a thousand pounds – "Hunted Down" it was called, and it is not in itself a particularly memorable piece of fiction, except perhaps for its demonstration of Dickens's general fascination with the idea of the murderer and his particular interest in the case of Thomas Wainewright, the poisoner whom Oscar Wilde was later to immortalise in his much more interesting composition, "Pen, Pencil and Poison". There will soon be occasion to describe daily life at Gad's Hill Place, but it is enough at this point to suggest that, for Dickens, it was a sufficiently quiet and retired place to allow him to work undisturbed upon his novel. Of course there were visitors – Thomas Beard, W. H. Wills and Edmund Yates among them – but Georgina now organised the household very competently. The only incidents seem to have been those of ordinary rural life at this period in the nineteenth century; the celebration of various rustic occasions at the Falstaff Inn just across the road; the long country walks accompanied by Turk, a bloodhound, and Linda, a St Bernard. It was a very hot summer, and the nights were for Dickens particularly disagreeable; but he worked on, buoyed up by the success both of his serial and of *All The Year Round* itself.

In a letter in this period he asked Wills to send proofs of the current number of *A Tale of Two Cities* to Ellen Ternan (it is conceivable that he wanted her to see how he had portrayed Lucie Manette) but he was not inseparable from his new companion. There was, after all, his notion of travelling to America. A country which promised him *money*. It had been a New York journal which had paid him a thousand pounds for one short story, but there was the prospect of yet larger sums if he would agree to an extended reading tour of the major cities. His interest in what was already a much-discussed project had been revived by the arrival in England of James Fields, a young publisher and partner in the Boston firm of Ticknor, Reed and Fields; he was very enthusiastic about Dickens's work in any case, and came down to Gad's Hill Place specifically to persuade him that the time had come for him once more to take the United States by storm. Fields has left a description of this first visit to Kent. "He drove me about the leafy lanes in his basket wagon, pointing out the lovely spots . . . and ending with a visit to the ruins of Rochester Castle. We climbed up the time-worn walls and leaned out of the ivied windows, looking into the various apartments below. I remember how vividly he reproduced a probable scene in the great old banqueting-room, and how graphically he imagined the life of ennui and every-day tediousness that went on in those lazy old times . . . That day he seemed to revel in the past." And why not, since he was even then writing his own account of eighteenth-century France? The guest with Fields at dinner that same night was Wilkie Collins, and afterwards they lay down on the grass while Dickens told them anecdotes about his new pet raven. And so life went on. He was still anticipating a journey to America (although, as he said, no doubt in relation to Ellen Ternan, "I should be one of the most unhappy of men if I were to go . . .") and opened negotiations with an American agent who had also visited him. The agent proved to be no more than an entrepreneur who would sell him to the highest bidder, however, and when negotiations broke down Dickens considered the possibility of travelling during the following year instead. It was something of a personal misfortune, then, that the Civil War should break out only a few months later. Dickens was not to visit the United States for another five years, at a time when his own health was much less able to withstand the rigours of the journey.

Even now he could not shake off the persistent low illness which so enervated him, and he decided to travel down to Broadstairs to see if the sea air and sea-water might help him to recover. He was with Wilkie Collins's brother, Charles, and seems to have diverted himself as much as he could under the circumstances; spending one evening, for example, enjoying the performance of a particularly bad mesmerist in the Assembly Rooms. But he was too ill to bathe in the sea, and his head felt "addled". Throughout these months, in fact, there is a general feeling of dilapidation and weariness about him; just before he left for Broadstairs he wrote a letter to Forster which ended with a prospect of death. "I am a wretched sort of creature in my way, but it is a way that gets on somehow. And all ways have the same fingerpost at the head of them, and at every turning in them." This is very much the mood that suffuses the passages of *A Tale of Two Cities* which he was now writing, the mood emerging, too, in one of his characters who reveals that, ". . . as I draw closer and closer to the end, I travel in the circle, nearer and nearer to the beginning". And how close this is to his own life, reading now in public as he had once performed in public as a child, once more haunted by the theme of imprisonment as he had been when his father was incarcerated in the Marshalsea. Could it be that Dickens himself felt that he was also close to the end of his own full circle, returning to the anxieties and loss of childhood? So it is that, in the closing pages of the novel, he invokes the image of the small stream being absorbed into the sea; but with it, too, there is hopefulness in the refrain repeated throughout the narrative, "I am the resurrection and the life . . ." In his letters during this period he describes his working out of the story as equivalent, in little, to the ways of "Providence" and of "divine justice"; so, if there is resignation here, it is compounded with hope.

He was taking great pains over this weekly serial, then, particularly since he had to work simultaneously on the formal composition of both weekly and monthly parts; the difficulties of condensation were, however, always his most immediate and pressing problem. "The small portions thereof, drive me frantic . . ." he said, since it was necessary for him to unify, to abbreviate, to anticipate, within this double framework. Of course there is a sense in which he relished the formal challenge of such a task, but an examination of the manuscript shows how often his writing gets smaller and smaller as he nears the end of a chapter; clearly he was trying to press as much as possible within the smallest space, and the number of additions and deletions which litter the written pages show how carefully he was now working. His problems were to a certain extent aggravated by the fact that he was no longer on satisfactory terms with Hablot Browne, the faithful "Phiz" who had been the illustrator of his books for so long; he was now relaying his instructions to Browne through his publisher, and the cooling of their relationship is probably the consequence of Browne's agreement to work on *Once a Week*, the periodical which Bradbury and Evans had established as a rival to Dickens's own. In fact *A Tale of Two Cities* is the last book that Browne was ever to illustrate for Dickens: in the matter of his separation from Catherine and his estrangement from Bradbury and Evans, he was not a man to forgive even the most unintentional of slights. And he worked on, through the hot days, through his lingering illness. ". . . I am at work, and see the story in a wonderful glass."

Soon after Broadstairs he went to London for a few days, and then returned to Gad's Hill Place where, at the very beginning of October – just in time to prepare for the public readings a week later – he finished the novel. It was published in volume form by Chapman and Hall in the following month, although it seems less to require a book than a theatre. For in some sense it is the most dramatic of his novels; almost literally so, since its theatricality and rhetoric spring from his stated wish to act out the life and death of Sydney Carton. Clearly Dickens has learnt something from his public readings as well as from his amateur theatricals; the style is insistent, repetitive, and almost gestural. It is significant, too, that almost as soon as he had completed it he was making plans to have the story dramatised both in Paris and in London. The French scheme was abandoned because of the possibility of government censorship, but Tom Taylor adapted the novel for the Lyceum under the management of Madame Celeste. Dickens was in fact so eager to provide a proper dramatic version that he played a large role in the rehearsals – there is evidence that he practically directed the play – and even changed the famous ending specifically for theatrical purposes. The last lines of the novel, "'It is a far, far better thing that I do, than I have ever done; it is a far, far better rest that I go to than I have ever known", were now supplemented in the stage version with a final "Farewell Lucie, Farewell Life!". *Curtain*. The fact that the Lyceum was only a hundred yards away from his office made his participation in the play all the easier; we must imagine him walking briskly down Wellington Street, recognised by those he passed, and crossing to the other side of the street just before he reached the Strand. The theatre is still there, a dark, grimy adjunct to a now undistinguished thoroughfare.

And of the story itself? In some ways a dark one, filled with images of horror and of destruction, of dirt and disease, of imprisonment and violent death. The central image is one of resurrection, but this encompasses the stealing of dead bodies from their graves as well as the more spiritual resuscitation which Sydney Carton so much longs for. This is a world of enormous shadows, of the setting sun, of night; the only illumination occurs in the glare of the French Revolution itself, as if the only alternative to the darkness of despair lies in the rage and destructiveness of that event. And yet in his fiction (as opposed to his journalism) Dickens never really adopts an attitude without at the same time embracing its reverse and it cannot be expected, particularly at this time of his life, that he would be able to resolve all of those contradictory impulses and ambiguous attitudes that comprise so large a part of his genius. The force of the novel springs from its exploration of darkness and death but its beauty derives from Dickens's real sense of transcendence, from his ability to see the sweep of destiny. "Eye to eye, voice to voice, hand to hand, heart to heart, these two children of the Universal Mother, else so wide apart and differing, have come together on the dark highway, to repair home together, and to rest in her bosom." Forster was wrong to say that Dickens had no "city of the mind", no inner resource to combat the changes of the world; he had a sense of the numinous, and he had a sense, too, of that common fate which transcends all social divisions and diurnal battles. This, in the year after the start of his new life, is what emerges most clearly from one of his shortest and most powerful novels.

The brief provincial tour began on 10 October with a reading in Ipswich and ended on the 27th with one at Cheltenham; fourteen performances in all, punctuated by visits to Gad's Hill Place or Tavistock House, and of which nothing need be reported except the usual prodigious enthusiasm and Dickens's own restless energy. He went back to Gad's Hill Place at the conclusion of the readings in order to celebrate Katie's twentieth birthday (Forster and Wilkie Collins joined him there) and then at the beginning of November he returned to London and to Tavistock House; he had decided to remain here at least until Easter, and to lease Gad's Hill Place in the interim. Now that he had returned for the duration, he at once set to work; not only to clear up the vast arrears of correspondence but also to settle down to his regular periodical business. In particular he wanted to decide well in advance the length and nature of the serial stories which would follow *A Tale of Two Cities*, to be completed at the end of the month; he had already arranged for Wilkie Collins's *The Woman In White* to begin in *All The Year Round* immediately after the conclusion of his own story, but now he was looking even further ahead. That is why he went to dinner with Mr and "Mrs" Lewes, the latter now becoming better known as "George Eliot". He had admired *Scenes of Clerical Life*, and was equally laudatory about *Adam Bede* which had appeared this year – in fact he was so enthusiastic that he wrote what can only be described as "fan letters" to the female novelist. "Adam Bede," he wrote, "has taken its place among the actual experiences and endurances of my life . . . The conception of Hetty's character is so extraordinarily subtle and true, that I laid the book down fifty times, to shut my eyes and think about it." And what a persuasive picture this is: Dickens putting aside the book and closing his eyes in order fully to understand the character of pretty Hetty Sorrel (did he see in her some echo of Ellen Ternan?). Just four days after dining with them, Dickens wrote to George Henry Lewes, suggesting that Mrs Lewes (he used the term quite blandly, although he must have known that theirs was not a legal union) might care to contribute a tale to *All The Year Round* after *The Woman In White* had run its course. Mrs Lewes was undecided and indecisive, but eventually demurred on the grounds of "*Time*". Dickens had already been in touch with Mrs Gaskell, however, in case of just such a refusal; and a little later he was also coming to an agreement with Charles Lever for the serialisation of his next novel. He was nothing if not a "professional". At the same time he was preparing himself for the first Christmas issue of *All The Year Round*; in the past, on *Household Words*, it had often been difficult to find a "peg" upon which to hang the seasonal stories from various contributors, but this year an idea was handed to him ready-made.

It all began with a series of arguments which he had been conducting with well-known "spiritualists" of the period. The Fifties and Sixties were, after all, the decades which saw an enormous increase of interest in what we would now describe as psychic phenomena; ghosts, table-rapping, seances and the whole panoply of effects from what was known by devotees as the "spirit world". This interest may partly be attributed to the decline of faith in orthodox Christianity, now being demythologised by the twin forces of scientific enquiry and biblical scholarship, but it was also a perfectly natural extension of the interest in those invisible energies and forces which the physical sciences of the day had been disclosing. Few writers were more interested in the subject that Dickens, as we have already seen, but his fascination with ghosts and spirits was matched only by his dislike of "humbug" and fraudulent religiosity. That is why he indulged in animated controversy with such devotees of the pyschic world as William Howitt, and why in the course of one argument he proposed that Howitt's account of a "haunted house" should be investigated by one of his writers. It was then the idea occurred to him; he decided to call the Christmas story sequence "The Haunted House", and under his direction it became a systematic satire against the proponents of psychical phenomena. He himself did visit one of the haunted houses which Howitt had proposed; or, at least, he went to the area. The house was located at Cheshunt, just outside London, and Dickens decided to make an expedition of it in the second week of December. Wilkie Collins and W. H. Wills went on ahead in a brougham, taking with them some fresh fish "as Dickens did not care to trust altogether to the local hotel or inn", while Dickens and one of his contributors, John Hollingshead, walked the sixteen miles. They seemed to have had some trouble in locating the house itself, but eventually they found a semi-detached villa which stood upon the haunted ground; Dickens wrote afterwards to Howitt, "I can hear of no one at Cheshunt who ever heard of anything worse in it . . . than rats, and a servant (one Frank by name), said to have a skilful way of poaching for rabbits at untimely hours." In fact ghosts of various sorts plagued

Dickens at this time, and only a few months later the household at Gad's Hill Place was alarmed by news that there was a spirit haunting a local monument. "Plorn was frightened to death," Dickens reported and, in order to quell any lurking consternation among his family or staff, he decided to take prompt action. He gave his son, Frank, and a schoolboy friend, two short sticks while he equipped himself with a double-barrelled gun (he also had a pistol in his bedroom, no doubt kept there because of his continuing fear of being robbed).

Charles Dickens (to his domestics): "Now observe, if anybody is playing tricks and has got a head, I'll blow it off."

He and the two boys then walked to the monument.

Charles Dickens (out loud): "Now look out! If the ghost is here and I see him, so help me God I'll fire at him!"

It is hard not to resist the impression that, for all his bluster, Dickens is almost as frightened as the children; especially so when he now hears what he called a "terrific noise – human noise – and yet superhuman noise".

Frank: "Did you hear that, pa?"

Charles Dickens: "I did."

They advance cautiously, towards the superhuman sound, towards the ghost. And then they discover that it is the noise of an asthmatic sheep. As Dickens concludes the story, ". . . triumphant return to rum-and-water".

No, Dickens was preoccupied with ghosts of quite another sort and, in one of his own stories for "The Haunted House", he wrote of ". . . the ghost of my own childhood, the ghost of my own innocence, the ghost of my own airy belief". Dickens was now a haunted man, but his spirits were not those which bell, book and candle could exorcise.

The general impression of Dickens at this juncture, in fact, is of a melancholy and in many ways dissatisfied man who was trying at all costs to keep *busy*, to fill his days, to cultivate forgetfulness. Of course there were also the unanticipated and unhappy chances of life which required his attention. His friend and neighbour, Frank Stone, had died suddenly, for example, and Dickens went to enormous trouble in order to find employment for his sons; he started by finding work for Marcus, who was then a budding painter and illustrator, but he also took in hand the task of trying to teach Arthur Stone shorthand. By strange chance some of the notes he compiled for Arthur's benefit have been discovered, with exercises in shorthand complemented by what seem like stray phrases dictated out of Dickens's consciousness; "the bill is due today . . . the sea is deep . . . *Thr* ws ons a boy *and he said* to his master, shall *I have* a *good character* from you . . . *The world* is *subject* to *Providence, and* wt*ever* Prov*idence* dsns is for the best . . . My pr*ivileges* are *the* privileg*es of a Plaintiff* not *the privileges of a defend-ant* . . ." Strange sentences and phrases, perhaps, to spring unbidden from the mind. But how much more extraordinary is this painstaking effort on behalf of the boy, from a man already half-dazed with work, from the greatest writer of his day.

He was busy in another sense, too, since, between reading tours and between novels, he went back to a largely public role. He visited a commercial travellers' school in Pinner the day before making a speech to the Commercial Travellers' Association, for example, but even on this occasion he made a reference to the dominant note in his life at this time. "Gentlemen, we should remember tonight that we are all Travellers, and that every round we take converges nearer and nearer to our home; that all our little journeyings bring us together to one certain end . . ." Death. After his speech the orphan children of dead commercial travellers were paraded around the dining hall and "excited the deepest interest"; they sang several songs and then a toast was given to Dickens himself ". . . who appeared overcome by the manner in which his health was received". Now it was time for his annual series of Christmas readings in St Martin's Hall (his last performances here, since the hall burned down eight months later), and then four days after Christmas he travelled to Wales to see, and to report on, a terrible shipwreck of the *Royal Charter* off the coast near Llanallgo. The local clergyman had played the major part in retrieving the bodies of the dead and in a little Welsh church Dickens ". . . remarked again and again . . . on the awful nature of the scene of death he had been required so closely to familiarise himself with . . ." Death. He stayed in Wales for four days.

When he returned to London, the long illness from the earlier part of that year manifested itself once more and, on doctor's orders, he was forced to remain in the city. So it was in this first month of the New Year, closeted in London, that he took advantage of an idea which seems to have occurred to him when he addressed the Commercial Travellers three weeks before – for it was now that he took on the persona of an "Uncommercial Traveller" in order to write a series of essays for *All The Year Round*. They are wonderful pieces which, if they had to be characterised, might take as their motto the words which Dickens had just used in his Christmas story when he deemed himself to be haunted by the ghosts of his childhood innocence. Over the next few months he wrote essays in which he raised once more the spectre of a lost past. The spectre of lost childhood. In a letter to Miss Burdett-Coutts in this period he told her that ". . . the old time never grows older or younger with me". It remains as it was, always present and always being invoked. As it is in these essays themselves, sixteen of them written between January and October of 1860 – essays concerning the Paris Morgue and the bodies of the dead; concerning broken sleep; concerning his lonely walks through the streets of London at night; concerning sad and dismal metropolitan neighbourhoods; concerning suicides and paupers in Wapping; concerning the figure of "the very queer small boy" who is the spirit of his own infancy; concerning the lonely chambers in the Inns of Court; concerning the deserted churches in the City of London, St James Garlickhithe, St Michael Paternoster Row, St Martin Vintry, St Michael Queenhithe; concerning his visit to his childhood haunts from which he returns with his early imaginations ". . . so worn and torn, so much the wiser and so much the worse!"; concerning the grim and frightening stories of his childhood nurse. These are chronicles of sometimes desolate and unhappy wandering, filled with nostalgia, solitude, weariness and melancholia (even his letters in this period are much quieter and much plainer, less buoyant with the vivacity of Dickens's inventiveness). The wanderings of a man haunted by his past and by images of death – and we recall once more the words in *A Tale of Two Cities*, "For, as I draw closer and closer to the end, I travel in the circle, nearer and nearer to the beginning." And yet how much Dickens still sees and notices of the world around him, how much he is still part of his world even if the London which he resurrects in his "Uncommercial" essays is a faded or faint city with nothing of that crowded and almost "modern" life which burgeoned during the Sixties. These are the essays of a man who remembers an earlier time with infinite longing and infinite regret, a writer who could not help but pour out these thoughts between the writing of *A Tale of Two Cities* and the writing of *Great Expectations*.

In a speech to the Royal Society of Musicians which he gave soon after beginning the series of essays, the old refrain is heard again when he says of music, "You know it can give back the dead . . ." This was a time when, as he said in a letter to Edmund Yates, ". . . the dream that we are all dreaming seems to darken . . ." This was a time when his mother was slipping into senile decay, although even now he could not help laughing at her with his same mercilessness – ". . . got up in sables like a female Hamlet," he said; ". . . the instant she saw me," he added at a slightly later date, "she plucked up a spirit and asked me for 'a pound'." This was a time when his wife seemed to him to be "that figure [who] is out of my life for evermore (except to darken it) and my desire is, Never to see it again". This was the time of what Nina Lehmann described as "a queer dinner" at Tavistock House: "no games – nothing but a Chopin and Mendelssohn from me with Dickens and Wilkie as attentive auditors, and a piece alarmingly played by Mamie herself".

He went down to Gad's Hill Place in April but then was back at Tavistock House where he wanted to remain until June. But he no longer liked this house, this harbour of so many memories. He wanted to get rid of it. He wanted to sell it. A few weeks later he began to suffer from rheumatism which attacked his left side, yet another involuntary memory of childhood, and so he decided to leave London a little earlier than he had planned in order to recuperate in the country air. The month before he had also been attacked by neuralgia of the face; all these were in fact harbingers of serious ill-health, but they were signs which he chose to disparage or to ignore. And now another part of his past was about to leave him. His daughter, Kate, was going away from home – and this the daughter who in manner and in temperament was most like her father, who had the same slow pulse and the same occasionally fiery temper, the same nervous habits and the same ready wit. She had always been her father's favourite, the one who was pushed forward by the others to ask for special dispensations, but now she was leaving him. She had decided to marry Charles Collins, the younger brother of Wilkie; not because she was in love with him, she explained later, but simply because she wanted to get away from "an unhappy home". Which gives at least a modicum of substance to Harriet Martineau's gossip about Dickens at this time: "He is *awful* at home now, – restless, despotic & miserable." In later life Kate admitted that, before this engagement to Charles Collins, she had fallen in love with Edmund Yates but that he had not noticed, or had pretended not to notice, the nature of her feelings. Collins was quite another matter. Wilkie, a few months before the decision, said that his brother ". . . is still trying hard to talk himself into believing that he ought to be married". Dickens was very much opposed to the match, not least because he was unsure of Collins himself; he had already employed him to write for *Household Words* and *All The Year*

Round, and thought enough of him to take him to Broadstairs with him ten months before, but for one reason or another he objected to Kate's marriage to him. It has been suggested that he was homosexual. Kate herself seems to have told her father that her husband was impotent. Certainly they had no children, and in addition he suffered from a mysterious, wasting illness throughout most of their married life. He was also a timid and rather melancholy man, who in later years seems to have wilted under Dickens's fierce glare.

From Dickens's description of the marriage ceremony itself, held at Higham parish church on 17 July and followed by a lavish wedding breakfast at Gad's Hill Place, the casual reader might be forgiven for thinking that it was a cheerful and even glorious occasion; the village blacksmith firing off guns the previous night (although no one at Gad's Hill Place knew why at the time), the triumphal arches of flowers constructed by the villagers, and, as Dickens reported, albeit in tones that suggest how little he thought of the match itself, ". . . the whole was a great success – SO FAR". Dickens, as witness, signed himself "literary gentleman"; but of course the other most important member of the family was not allowed to be present. Catherine Dickens sat at home in Gloucester Crescent and, with her eyes on the clock, followed the ceremony in her imagination. According to Kate herself, Dickens was delighted by the response of the villagers, and Frederick Lehmann, a friend of the family, wrote to his wife of the occasion that "the breakfast was a gorgeous affair. Everything on the table in the way of decoration was white, flowers and all. After breakfast (without a single speech, and only one toast) we had games on the lawn, and Aunt Sally was the great attraction. About three o'clock we all drove to Rochester, and had a good time in that delicious old ruin, Rochester Castle . . . Thence to Chatham, where we listened to a military band performing in the park . . . About 6.30 we were back at Gad's Hill, had time for a game of croquet, saw the children of the neighbouring people get tea and cake, and went into dinner at seven . . . Dinner over at nine; a cigar in the garden . . . a country dance; and we all fly at eleven to our special waiting our return at Higham." Clearly Lehmann was swept up by the almost frantic merriment which Dickens seemed able to induce in a group of his friends (in its general drift, in fact, this might be taken as an accurate account of the kind of day usually spent by guests at Gad's Hill Place), but other reports indicate that the occasion was not as agreeable as it might on the surface have seemed.

For one thing, many of the guests, aware of Dickens's disapproval of the marriage, did not quite know how to behave; as Dickens told Mrs Dickinson, a lady with whom he had struck up an especially relaxed friendship, "They didn't know whether they were to look melancholy, beaming or maudlin; and their uncertainty struck me as so uncommonly droll, that I was obliged to hide my reverend parental countenance in my hand on the altar railing". How strange that he should be laughing – and almost congratulate himself for laughing – for this reason at his daughter's wedding. Odd, too, that he should laugh even in the midst of his distress, for his real displeasure, and even grief, at the marriage were clearly visible to others. Holman Hunt, for example, noticed that "Dickens was overstrained and inclined to be argumentative", and the two men entered a pointless argument about David Roberts's painting, "A Recollection of the Desert: on the Approach of the Simoom", which Dickens owned. Hunt pointed out to him that Roberts had painted the sun setting in the south, but Dickens, in Leonee Ormond's account, "irritably countered by saying that he particularly liked the setting sun". When Hunt then suggested that the Sphinx was meant to face it, Dickens just as irritably declared that he still liked the painting as a "poetical conception". So did the merriment continue. At the end of the day ". . . Mamie went up to her sister's bedroom. Opening the door, she beheld her father upon his knees with his head buried in Katie's wedding gown, sobbing. She stood for some moments before he became aware of her presence; when at last he got up and saw her, he said in a broken voice: 'But for me, Katie would not have left home', and walked out of the room . . ." This account comes from Kate herself, relayed by her amanuensis and confidante, Gladys Storey; given the circumstances of the occasion, and the detail of Dickens sobbing into the wedding dress (we have already seen how much importance he attached to the clothes of the women he loved), it seems likely to be a faithful report of Dickens's real distress at this time. The newly-created Mr and Mrs Collins travelled for their honeymoon to France and to Belgium and, since it was cheaper to live on the Continent than in England, both of them seemed willingly to prolong their stay. "I have not even told any of them at home about the odd life we are leading," Kate wrote to her new mother-in-law, Harriet Collins, "for fear that they should fancy we were really frightfully badly off." They did their own shopping, their own cooking and their own bed-making (which, for two middle-class English people in Europe, was something of a novelty), and in one letter Kate told Harriet that "we have lived for four weeks today on food of our own cooking".

And what of the other children? From his correspondence in these years after the separation from Catherine, it is clear that much time and anxious attention were being devoted to his sons and daughters. It is likely that, after the removal of their mother, Dickens felt an especial responsibility towards them. Much of what we know of them in fact stems from his accounts, and it can hardly be said that he was indulgent to their faults; but it is possible also, from their own memories and from reports of them by contemporaries, to create an at least partly authentic family picture. Kate is reported to have said that, with one exception, she did not believe her siblings to be entirely sane; hardly a fair description (although, like her father, she was not readily known for her objective judgment) and yet there was something in the children of Charles Dickens that appeared to make them peculiarly unsuited to the world and to each other. But it is possible that we exaggerate their characteristics, just as everything pertaining to Dickens becomes exaggerated; perhaps they were in a sense almost too "normal", too little like their father, and have as a result suffered at the hands of disappointed commentators.

There was Charles Dickens junior, or Charley, twenty-three in the year of his sister's marriage. He had just left his mother's house and set out for China on behalf of the firm for which he worked; but he seems to have been generally a somewhat uncertain, unfixed person who allowed his life to be in large part guided by his father's wishes. He had inherited his father's love of order and neatness, but in no other respect did he resemble him. He was dutiful but suffered from a certain lassitude of spirit which was, in the end, to lead him into precisely the kind of financial calamities which his own father dreaded. There was Mamie – now twenty-two – amiable, somewhat sentimental, but high-spirited and with a love for what might be called the life of London society. She seems to have attached herself to her father with an almost blind affection; certainly she never married and, of all the children, she was the one who stayed closest to him for the rest of his life. Walter Landor Dickens was of course in India in the year of his sister's marriage; not much of his life there is known, except that he was now nineteen and already piling up debts. Next, in order of seniority, comes Francis Jeffrey Dickens; the one most like his father "in face, gesture and manner", but a most unsettled and anxious boy whom Dickens professed not to understand. It seems that he could decide upon nothing, wanting at first to be a doctor and then changing his mind, taking up languages in order to enter business, but eventually going to work for his father on *All The Year Round*. He was the least self-reliant of his brothers, and in some ways the saddest of them; he had given up all hope of being a doctor because he was afflicted with a very bad stammer. In addition, he suffered from sleep-walking. He was sixteen now – could it be that the departure of his mother two years before had brought on this anxious sleep-walking? And was he now further aware that in some way he had failed his father? Alfred Tennyson Dickens, now fifteen, was "a good, steady fellow", according to his father, who had decided upon an engineering course in order that he might join the Army. He failed to qualify, however, and eventually migrated to Australia; but, of all the male children, he seems the most straightforward, the most reliable and the most independent. Sydney Smith Haldimand Dickens was thirteen, at this time attending the naval college in Southsea in order to be trained as a naval officer. As a boy he showed great energy and character – a "born little sailor", his father said – and eventually he was to join the Royal Navy as a midshipman. But something happened to him; perhaps as the result of a terrible fever (the explanation put forward at the time) and then again perhaps not, he became reckless and improvident. There came a time when Dickens refused to allow him into the house, and in later life Mamie said that she thought of him with "contempt" and even "horror". Henry Fielding Dickens, "bright and clever", again according to his father; he was now only eleven but he was already quick-witted and energetic, and was to turn out to be the most successful of the Dickens children. Edward Bulwer Lytton Dickens – a child of eight, amiable, shy, affectionate, but a boy of no real ability and, as it turned out, of no real application or energy. He, too, eventually emigrated to Australia where his life as a putative sheep-farmer was not a success. It is he who provides perhaps the most poignant memorial for all of the children. "Sons of great men," he said, "are not usually as great as their fathers. You cannot get two Charles Dickens in one generation."

His father would no doubt have agreed with him. In a speech he once declared that "hereditary talent . . . is always an exceptional case"; and, in his accounts of his own children, there are constant intimations of his disappointment and even on occasions hostility. Of course he had loved them as babies and as small children; but he described, in one of his periodical essays, ". . . the sorrowful feeling sometimes awakened in the mind by the idea of a favourite child's 'growing up'", and it certainly seems to be the case that he lost affection for them as they grew older. An American friend in whom he confided some years later reported that "he appears often troubled by the lack of energy his children show . . .", and he said himself that he had ". . . brought up the largest family ever known with the smallest disposition to do anything for themselves". But this does not mean that he was a stern father, at least not stern by the standards and practices of the time. There is only one extant account of any real strictness; it comes from a local preacher at Shorne, a village near Gad's Hill, who recalled the occasion when he saw Dickens chastising one of his boys in the open air. The preacher apparently "pleaded" with Dickens to spare the boy; " 'What!' exclaimed the enraged father, his breath coming in palpitating gasps, 'he has told *his own father a lie!* . . . I cannot spare him!'" The reverend gentleman added, "When I looked at the poor boy I pitied him; but when I gazed at the sorrowful face of the outraged father, my heart fairly broke down, and I turned aside to weep. The father suffered more than the child. It was a strange sight to witness, and I hope I shall never see the like again." An overwrought account, and local preachers are not necessarily always to be believed. But, as it stands, it is the only record of Dickens punishing his children in the conventional "Victorian" manner. Yet it seems likely that his strictness sprang, where it existed at all, from his own obsessions rather than from the orthodox pieties of the period; that is why so much attention was paid to the need for absolute neatness in his children, with his daily inspections and his habit of leaving little notes of reproof in their rooms. Noise and untidiness were the two things he could *not* bear, and so his children were brought up in a hard school of almost military order. If he wanted to teach them anything other than that, it was self-reliance; this had been the one virtue which his own parents and his own brothers had so notably lacked, and it was with something like desperation that he saw his own children falling into exactly the same traps of recklessness and improvidence which he had observed in his family. He was different from other fathers, also, in that strange remoteness and that reluctance to display his feelings which all of his children seemed to notice; and of course different, too, by reason of the attention which he paid to his fictional "children". Charley and Katie, as well as the others, knew that there were many occasions in which the creatures of his imagination took precedence over anything of flesh and blood; perhaps it was a partial absence of self-worth which made them so curiously estranged from each other after their father's death. Certainly at the time, with the exception of Henry, the boys realised that they were all "failures" in their father's eyes; but perhaps they felt doomed to failure, in any case, when they realised that they could never match their father's own high standards. In many ways a sad family, therefore, marked by early deaths, business failure, sorrow, always living in the shadow of the extraordinary Charles Dickens, perpetually aware of the fact that all they had inherited from him was the name. It is not coincidental that at the time of his daughter's marriage, a time when he was also most concerned with the future careers of his other children, he should begin the novel which shows the folly of spendthrift youth. It was called *Great Expectations*.

There were family problems of other kinds, too, and only a few days after Kate's marriage Dickens's brother, Alfred, died of pleurisy. He had been an engineer working in Manchester, and the only one of Dickens's brothers to have made anything of his life – Dickens had already given up on Frederick and totally rejected Augustus, both of whom had been almost criminally careless with money and both of whose lives seemed like some broken reflection of their father's. Now Alfred was dead, leaving behind a widow, Helen, and five children. Dickens went up to Manchester at once, and brought his brother's family back with him to London. The funeral was held at Highgate, where John Dickens was buried, and then Dickens returned to Gad's Hill Place with the bereaved family. He found a farmhouse nearby where Helen and the children could stay while he looked around for a London house, all of which activity meant that he was preoccupied with their affairs for some weeks. It is even possible that the five children reappeared in *Great Expectations*, the novel he was soon to begin, as the five lozenge-shaped tombs in Cooling Churchyard (there is in fact a row of six stone lozenges there). Not an indication that he wished them dead, not that, but rather a sign of how powerfully the events of his life intruded into his fiction, even the most stern and obvious realities being transformed into the shape of his own fears and preoccupations.

Another part of his past was about to be abandoned, too; after having lived there for some nine years, he was now in the process of selling Tavistock House. He was planning to spend the summer and autumn months in Gad's Hill Place and then renting a furnished house in London from February to March. When he was at his "Kentish freehold", as he sometimes called it, he would use his set of rooms in the *All The Year Round* office as a temporary base. In fact, like most of the other activities in his life, he managed to sell the house very quickly, and by August it had gone for two thousand guineas; the bargain, he said, had been made with the prospective purchaser in five minutes. He moved out in the following month; some of the furniture was taken to his rooms at Wellington Street North, and he gave the rest to his sister-in-law, Helen, for whom he had found a house in Highgate. Helen, perhaps in way of recompense, had agreed to take on the care of Mrs Elizabeth Dickens whose senile decline made her unsuitable for orthodox nursing. All the mouldings and pictures, of course, were taken down to Gad's Hill Place which, now that it had become Dickens's sole permanent residence, was to be continually "improved" by him over the next ten years.

So this is what it had come to by the late summer of 1860. His favourite daughter married and living away from home, his brother dead, his mother decaying, his old house sold. All these were marks of loss or separation, and in August he had exclaimed to Mrs Dickinson, his unofficial confidante, "Well! Life is a fight and must be fought out." Nevertheless he was suffering from low spirits and found that he could not sleep; and it was at this low point, at the beginning of August, that he began "meditating a new book", as if the only cure for this depression of spirits was a return to his imaginary world. "But we must not think of old times as sad times," he explained to Mrs Watson in September, "or regard them as anything but the fathers and mothers of the present. We must all climb steadily up the mountain after the talking bird, the singing tree, and the yellow water, and must all bear in mind that the previous climbers who were scared into looking back got turned into black stone." DON'T LOOK BACK. That is the sentiment here, and it can be seen to act as some kind of anticipation of the novel he was to begin three weeks later, *Great Expectations*; a novel in which he is engaged in exorcising the influence of his past by rewriting it. The talking bird and the singing tree sound like the very emblems of his fiction, but he can only reach them by climbing steadily forward and ignoring the path which has brought him to this point. DON'T LOOK BACK.

And, in the month when he handed out this injunction, he burnt all of his past correspondence. It was part of the general "clear up" necessitated by the selling of Tavistock House, but it has wider ramifications as yet another example of his desire to resist his past, to efface it, to rewrite it, to turn his separation from his wife and the start of his new life into something much more real, more tangible. He burnt the letters in the field behind Gad's Hill Place; Mamie and two of her brothers brought out basketful after basketful of them, from Carlyle, Thackeray, Tennyson, Collins, George Eliot . . . the letters of twenty years. Mamie asked him to keep some of them, but he refused. No. They all had to be burnt. And as he completed this sacrificial pyre it began to rain very heavily; " . . . I suspect my correspondence of having overcast the face of the Heavens." Jean Cocteau never burnt any of the letters he received from his contemporaries ". . . out of a sort of respect for the pains taken by the people who sent them . . ." Clearly Dickens did not have the same respect. In his new life there is almost some kind of hatred of the past. But what was the shape of this new dispensation? In an otherwise anodyne letter to a friend, Marguerite Power, he makes a remark which is omitted from the published text; someone is to visit him at the office in Wellington Street, but the name of that person was at a later date cancelled out. It looks as though the words inked over might have been "the Charmer", however, in which case it may safely be assumed that he is referring to Ellen Ternan: but to speak of her in such an open way to another female friend suggests very strongly that his relationship with her was similarly open, and that Ellen was not at this stage his clandestine mistress. In the following month he made the first of a number of payments to a certain Miss Jeffries (they varied between five pounds and forty pounds), and in the census of 1861 no doubt the same Miss Jeffries was listed as a "visitor" at the Ternans' house in Houghton Place. Was he paying her for some service to the Ternans? Certainly the whole family was now living at Houghton Place, and in an aside within a slightly later letter to Bulwer-Lytton Dickens mentions ". . . a woman whom I could implicitly trust, and in whom I have frequently observed (in the case of my own proofs) an intuitive sense and discretion that I have set great store by". This may of course be one of those female friends, like Marguerite Power or Frances Dickinson, with whom he had a close and confiding relationship (they were high-spirited, clever women who shared his own sense of humour and in whose company he could relax); but the strongest possibility must be that he was once more obliquely alluding to Ellen Ternan who, in the course of these years, emerges only occasionally to remind us of her presence and of the importance which she continued to possess for Charles Dickens. But she remains as discreetly concealed as so many other aspects of Dickens's private life in these years. All we have are stray hints and indirections, brief references and brief omissions, and yet even these have their place in this history; for they tell us that much must remain hidden from view, and that even our most comprehensive efforts must necessarily remain incomplete. Perhaps it is better that some things should remain concealed, in order to remind us of that which is ultimately unknowable.

At the end of September he began work on *Great Expectations*; or, rather, he began writing another essay in the guise of the "Uncommercial Traveller". Forster had suggested to him that he might try his hand once more at the humour which had been so much a part of the sketches of his early years (it was Forster, too, who had deplored the relative absence of humour in *A Tale of Two Cities*), but as he started writing in the old manner there occurred to him what he called "a very fine, new, and grotesque idea". ". . . I begin to doubt," he went on, "whether I had not better cancel the little paper, and reserve the notion for a new book . . . I can see the whole of a serial revolving on it, in a most singular and comic manner . . ." Forster states that this "grotesque" idea contained the germ of the relationship between Pip and Magwitch which was to be at the centre of *Great Expectations*. This is certainly possible, but it is also true that the actual form of *Great Expectations* had much more to do with the troubled state of *All The Year Round* than with Dickens's own creative imperatives. He had begun the story almost as soon as the "idea" occurred to him, apparently believing that he was starting work on the basis of the usual twenty numbers, but then certain commercial considerations altered his plans. The problem lay with Charles Lever's novel, *A Day's Ride: A Life's Romance*, which was then being serialised in the periodical but was proving to be a heavy liability in terms of falling sales. Something had to be done quickly before *All The Year Round* suffered what might have been irretrievable damage to its circulation. So, on 2 October, only a few days after he had begun the new novel, Dickens decided that it would have to be written as a weekly serial for the periodical and that it should be of approximately the same length as *A Tale of Two Cities* – this despite his previous complaints about the shortness and difficulty of weekly instalments. So was *Great Expectations* born. By 4 October he had determined upon a name and started work upon it in its new format – the first episode was to be published at the beginning of December, and he wanted to have at least two months of the book in hand before that date. At least he had his broad theme already prepared; it was to concern the adventures of a "boy-child, like David" but, in order to avoid any kind of unconscious repetition, ". . . I read *David Copperfield* again the other day, and was affected by it to a degree you would hardly believe . . ." So did his past, inserted within the narrative of the earlier novel, still haunt him; even now as he was beginning the life of Pip, an anxious and guilt-ridden child, sensitive to the point of hysteria and altogether a very queer, small boy.

By the middle of the month he had completed the first four chapters, so spontaneously and so instinctively that he dispensed with working notes and barely used anything from the notebook which he still kept (all he took from his memoranda are a few names). Then he went down to Gad's Hill Place in order to work undisturbed, and by the end of October he had completed seven chapters; he was back in his old routine, of fierce work followed by equally fierce exercise, and at least for a while he seemed more cheerful. He also had a brief holiday in view; he had already agreed with Wilkie Collins that they should make a tour of Devon and Cornwall in order to gather material for the next Christmas issue of *All The Year Round*. So, as soon as he had finished the seventh chapter – had finished, in other words, a month's amount of material – he returned to London and prepared for his Western expedition. They were in fact away for only four days. "We had stinking fish for dinner," Dickens reported to Georgina on their arrival at Bideford in North Devon, "and have been able to drink nothing . . . There is nothing in the house but two tarts and a pair of snuffers. The landlady is playing cribbage with the landlord in the next room (behind a thin partition), and they seem quite comfortable." But out of this brief visit came that year's seasonal tale, "A Message from The Sea", a somewhat convoluted story concerning a message in a bottle which causes consternation in a Devon fishing village. It is of no real interest now except to the extent it emphasises Dickens's extravagant admiration for sailors. Thus was Dickens occupied throughout November, and he wrote "A Message from The Sea", at the same time as he maintained his progress on *Great Expectations*; he was spending much of his time in London during this bout of writing, principally because he liked his new bachelor quarters in Wellington Street North. Perhaps he was reminded of his old days of self-sufficiency, when he was first beginning to write in chambers at Furnival's Inn . . . and, within a few weeks, he was to place Pip in quarters at Barnard's Inn.

Yet he was no longer so resilient, no longer able to maintain the same rate of composition. He felt himself to be overworking; he was suffering once more from pains in his left side, which seem to have been an extension of his summer rheumatism; and he could not sleep. The longevity of these pains in his left side suggests that even now he was suffering the preliminary symptoms of the stroke which would finally kill him. And yet, he said at the beginning of December, ". . . I MUST write". He was now in his fiftieth year, growing a little bald, unwell, driven by no stern economic necessity but nevertheless driven by something. ". . . I MUST write." He was feeling so ill that he went back to Gad's Hill Place, and here he continued with his self-imposed routine of work. ". . . I MUST write" were words he had used in a letter from his country "retreat", and the chapters he wrote during this period of ill-health, effort and exhaustion are invested with a strange, hallucinatory, murderous tone. Orlick's irrational attack upon Mrs Joe Gargery, as if he were a surrogate for Pip's own suppressed feelings of rage and hurt; allusions to George Barnwell, the murdering apprentice made famous in song and story; Pip's confession to Biddy of "the madness of my heart"; the appearance of the strange Mr Jaggers; Pip's last visit to Miss Havisham before his departure and his entering into his great expectations. The humour is here as much as in any of Dickens's earlier books, but it is darker now and somehow more vicious. It was bitterly cold at Gad's Hill Place, and he was still feeling very unwell; the thermometer was well below freezing, the pipes stopped, the water in the bedroom jugs froze and broke the crockery.

He spent Christmas Day with the household (because of the low temperature they could barely sit at the dinner table), and then on the following day he went back to London; primarily this was in order to be close to his doctor, Frank Beard (who was Thomas Beard's brother). It was warmer in London and, in addition, Beard advised him not to continue his "commuting" between Gad's Hill Place and Wellington Street. So he stayed in his quarters at the office, writing on, pleased by the early success of his serial which was hailed at once as a return to his old "humorous" manner. In fact he stayed in London until the middle of January, while the rest of the household were still ensconced at Gad's Hill Place – doing nothing but work, swallow his medicine, and take a stall at the theatre every night. No doubt he was seeing Ellen Ternan (although no word of her escapes into his correspondence) but his principal male companion in these wintry

London days was Wilkie Collins, whose irregular love life Dickens now viewed with equanimity. In fact he often visited Collins's lodgings in Harley Street where the young writer lived with Caroline Graves and her daughter, Harriet; Dickens even invented affectionate nicknames for them.

Caroline Graves herself, because of her "rescue" by Wilkie Collins some years before, has often been considered to be the original inspiration for *The Woman In White*. In reality matters were more complicated than that. Matters always are. It would be wrong to assume with some critics, for example, that *The Woman In White* was in turn the primary source for the character Dickens was even now creating, his own woman in white, Miss Havisham of *Great Expectations*. The origins of that lady are more complex, and certainly more interesting, than any specific source; and, if we turn for a moment from the history of the author to the history of one of his characters, we may see Dickens himself "in a wonderful glass". For from what depths of his being does Miss Havisham emerge? There is Dickens's memory from childhood of what he called, in one essay, "The White Woman" of Berners Street, a simpering madwoman ". . . dressed entirely in white, with a ghastly white plating round her head and face, inside her white bonnet". Berners Street was also the thoroughfare in which Ellen Ternan was exposed to the attentions of the inquisitive policeman, so we may be able to see in this congruence of place Dickens's association of "The White Woman" with something close to sexual guilt. Then, in the *Household Narrative of Current Events* for January 1850, there is an account of a certain Martha Joachim, a recluse who dressed entirely in white after her suitor blew out his brains in front of her. In the same issue of that *Narrative*, there is also a description of the transportation of convicts to Australia as well as the story of a woman whose gown is set on fire – both of which subjects emerge in *Great Expectations* itself, as if the very germ of the novel had been planted by Dickens's casual reading of some journalism eleven years before. Yet in these two examples it is possible to understand how heterogeneous themes and ideas seem to attach themselves one to another, acquiring fresh power and resonance as they do so; it is in this very act of combining, perhaps, that the story itself begins to emerge. As if storytelling itself were part of the process of consciousness rather than some neatly defined and independent activity. As if it were a way of creating a pattern out of these random and fortuitous items which somehow lodged in Dickens's consciousness.

There were other images, too. There was the murder of a duchess who lived on the Champs-Elysées, close to Dickens, in 1856; a duchess who, according to the novelist in a letter to Forster at the time, "lived alone in a great house which was always shut up, and passed her time entirely in the dark". Then there was the part of Miss Mildew, dressed in white, which was played by Charles Mathews during his "At Home" of 18 April, 1831. There is the blighted bride in white who appears in *The Lazy Tour of Two Idle Apprentices*, ". . . a white wreck of hair, and dress, and wild eyes . . ." And of course there is also Wilkie Collins's famous woman in white, ". . . a solitary Woman, dressed from head to foot in white garments". All of these images, from the remote past of his childhood to the most recent fictional creation, come together in Miss Havisham – a figure made up of folk-tale, journalism, theatrical review and fiction. And behind it, too, some horror in the idea of rancid virginity, of sexuality stopped up and therefore become threatening, of some monstrous creature living outside of time and thus the very image of infantile fears. All of it coming together as Charles Dickens and Wilkie Collins sit together in Harley Street, talking to Caroline Graves, the woman who according to contemporary report had fled from a villa off the Finchley Road and presented ". . . the figure of a young and very beautiful woman dressed in flowing white robes that shone in the moonlight".

In the early weeks of the new year, 1861, Collins and Dickens would call a brougham and visit the theatres together or, on one occasion, listen to Buckley's Serenaders at St James's Hall. Not all of the theatrical experiences were quite so agreeable, however. When he and Collins realised that Mr Lane, proprietor of the Britannia Theatre, was to stage a dramatised version of their composite story, "A Message from The Sea" on 7 January, they threatened to issue an injunction preventing any such unauthorised performance. This was a rare occurrence – it was the merest custom for theatres to make adaptations of the latest novel or story – and Dickens felt obliged to write a letter to *The Times* on the following day in which he stated his belief that ". . . it is in the power of any English writer of fiction legally to prevent any work of his from being dramatised or adapted for the stage without his consent . . ." In fact he was not as sure of his "power" as he suggested and was not at all convinced that, if it came to it, the Court of Chancery would uphold any such legal right; but a compromise was reached with Lane, and it was announced that ". . . arrangements have been made for the representation of the piece". What Dickens and Collins really wanted was a share of the profit in the stage version, but they also took the precaution of issuing an eight-page booklet, entitled "*A Message from The Sea*, a Drama in Three Acts", which was clearly designed to assert their copyright.

While he stayed in London Dickens's progress on *Great Expectations* was rapid. "As to the planning out from week to week," he told Forster later, "nobody can imagine what the difficulty is, without trying. But, as in all such cases, when it is overcome the pleasure is proportionate." He had decided to divide the novel, like its predecessor, *A Tale of Two Cities*, into three books; he had issued the previous novel in monthly numbers as well as in the weekly instalments of the periodical, but the experiment had not been a success and Dickens did not repeat it; *Great Expectations* accordingly appeared only in thirty-six consecutive numbers of *All The Year Round*. His innate and instinctive orderliness was such, however, that the three books (or "Stages", as he called them) were almost exactly the same length even though the weekly portions sometimes varied in quantity. And he had not entirely forgotten his original plan to write his usual twenty monthly numbers; he still calculated the series on a monthly basis, and paginated afresh at the beginning of each month's manuscript.

By the middle of January his health had improved sufficiently for him to return to Gad's Hill Place, and for the next few weeks he travelled back and forth in his usual manner; although at first much of his time in London was taken up with house-hunting rather than with writing. It was his plan to spend the next five months in rented accommodation in the capital – primarily for Mamie's benefit, since she enjoyed the delights of the "season" – and it did not take him long to find a "really delightful house" at 3 Hanover Terrace, facing Regent's Park. Here he wrote, went to the office, gave dinners, met his friends; and from here too he emerged to take his long walks through London, that ambulatory routine he had begun in his childhood and of which he had never grown tired. Four days before he moved into Hanover Terrace, in fact, he took just such a walk from his offices in Wellington Street – along the Strand which passed Wellington Street, then down Whitehall to Westminster, then through Westminster along the Thames to Millbank; ". . . the day was so beautifully bright and warm," he told de Cerjat in a letter the following day, "that I thought I would walk on by Millbank, to see the river. I walked straight on *for three miles* on a splendid broad esplanade overhanging the Thames, with immense factories, railway works, and whatnot erected on it, and with the strangest beginnings and ends of wealthy streets pushing themselves into the very Thames. When I was a rower on that river, it was all broken ground and ditch, with here and there a public-house or two, an old mill, and a tall chimney. I had never seen it in any state of transition, though I suppose myself to know this rather large city as well as anyone in it . . ." This was the very area where, in *David Copperfield*, the prostitute Martha is tracked – Dickens now, on the last day of January 1861, following her route in a neighbourhood which he had then described as ". . . oppressive, sad, and solitary by night, as any about London. There were neither wharves nor houses on the melancholy waste of road near the great blank prison. A sluggish ditch deposited its mud at the prison walls. Coarse grass and rank weeds straggled over all the marshy land in the vicinity. In one part, carcases of houses, inauspiciously begun and never finished, rotted away. In another, the ground was cumbered with rusty iron monsters of steam-boilers, wheels, cranks, pipes, furnaces, paddles, anchors, diving-bells, windmill-sails and I know not what strange objects . . ." But now this area of wooden piles, and rotten buildings, and discarded machinery, had been transformed into the broad esplanade along which Dickens walked.

How much London had changed in just ten years of his life. Where once this place had been no more than the outer reaches of a tumble-down eighteenth-century city, it was now the harbinger of the modern capital of the late nineteenth century – cleaner, more stately, more organised. The great arterial sewers north and south of the river were now in place, and the Thames itself was no longer the open cesspool which it had been in the earlier decades of the century. Seventeenth- and eighteenth-century London was now being altered beyond recognition by street improvements; cut up and excavated by the encroachment of the railways; razed in the commercial redevelopment of the City. Even the early nineteenth-century London of Nash was itself being destroyed in the course of the enormous transition through which the capital now was passing. Queen Victoria Street cut through from Blackfriars to the Bank of England. Cannon Street extended. Farringdon Street. Garrick Street. New Oxford Street. Clerkenwell Road. Southwark Street. All now being built on the "open cut" or "cut and cover" methods, which turned parts of London into vast building sites of dust and wooden scaffolding. Westminster Bridge and Blackfriars Bridge rebuilt. The Hungerford Suspension Bridge torn down. Hungerford Market torn up. Cannon

Street terminus. Victoria Station. St Pancras. Broad Street. The line from Shoreditch to Liverpool Street. And, most spectacular of all, the underground railway from Paddington to Farringdon Street was opened in 1863 – the vast building programme which this particular development entailed meant that much of the old Clerkenwell, described in *Oliver Twist*, was gone for ever. For inhabitants like Dickens, who had known London since the Thirties or Forties, it might well have seemed as if the old city were being extirpated and a new one erected in its place. It is only in the earliest photographs of London, those taken in the Thirties and Forties, that it is still possible to see the lineaments of the city in which Smollett lived and Defoe worked; the stillness and quiet of these first photographs truly give the impression of a place rescued from the oblivion of lost time. But later photographs, of the Sixties and Seventies, show a different capital; the advertising hoardings, the omnibuses carrying men in stove-pipe hats, the cabs, all the rush and blur of the traffic, evoke a city much closer to modern times. Much closer to ourselves. The old and the new lived precariously together just for a moment – this moment, with Dickens striding between the two.

And so, even as Charles Dickens strolled along the new esplanade of the embankment, London was being transformed. It was no longer the city which he had known as a child and young man. This was now becoming the London of wide streets and underground railways, the orderliness and symmetry of the old Georgian capital quite displaced by the imperialist neo-Gothic of mid-Victorian public buildings. Something of the old compactness had gone for ever and with it, too, the particular gracefulness and colour of the previous century. In its place rose a city which was more massive, more closely controlled, more organised. The metropolis was much larger but it was becoming emptier, as the suburbs around London took up some of the displaced population, and it was also much more anonymous; it was a more public city, the seat of empire and of commerce, but it was also a less human one. It is not possible to see Ebenezer Scrooge or Miss Havisham, Fagin or the Artful Dodger, in the new thoroughfares and squares of the 1860s; this was no longer the wild and barren place of Dickens's imagination, nor was it the extravagant and eccentric locale where all his characters had met and moved together. And yet Dickens never ceased to live in that old city. Even as he walked along the Thames Embankment, he was still walking with Pip through the city of forty years before. Dickens was observing the new city at a time when his own imagination was dwelling in the older London of *Great Expectations*, when his own vision was of a lost past. For the old city was the one in which he always lived. It was the city that had made him. It was the city which had almost destroyed him but which had then raised him up. It was the city of his dreams and the city of his imagination. In his work it is the city that will live for ever. But, with all the change around him, did he think now that he, too, was part of a vanished dispensation – that he, in this new city, was himself growing old?

VI

Are there any particular virtues to this biography?

Well, the first thing to say is that it is very thoroughly
researched. I have a kind of complex about discovering
everything there is to know, but this is probably because I
realise just how much cannot be known. Cannot now be
recovered. I even made a point of reading all the books
about Dickens and, in most cases, reading them all the
way through.

Doesn't that make the book too academic?

That is always a problem. Not just with the more
obvious "critical" material, which I always feel obliged
to include even though it is precisely the kind of passage
most readers will skip. I also have a nasty habit of taking scholars, or perhaps I should say academics, too
seriously. Take the example of the footnotes. I was
determined not to have any at all but then, in the last
stages of composition, my nerve failed. I certainly did not
intend to sit down and list every source for every quotation but I did compromise: I wrote little essays on my
sources for each chapter. In a way this is a sort of
confidence trick, but it was a trick I felt compelled to
perform because instinctively I believed that a book
without footnotes would not be taken seriously. Now I
know scholarly footnotes themselves have always been a
sort of trick, an academic habit established upon the
nineteenth-century illusion that scholarship can fulfil the

demands of a science and based, too, upon the nineteenth century preoccupation with *origins*. Theoretically I knew all that, but practically I was still under the influence of that derelict and now often farcical practice. So I did it. I put them in.

What other faults do you recognise now?

I thought we were discussing the book's virtues.

They are often the same thing.

Is it a fault, or a virtue, that I often imply more certainty and assume more authority than in fact I possess? Take the relationship of Charles Dickens with his wife. Certain incidents are recorded and certain matters became the object of gossip and speculation, but the real nature of their marriage cannot be recovered; but of course that did not stop me from interpreting it in a very direct way. I might be quite wrong. I might be half-wrong and half-right. I suppose you might call it the uncertainty principle, but it is a principle quite impossible to build into biography; of all forms, the biographical one seems to demand certainty and clarity. Once you introduce ambiguities and doubts, the whole enterprise starts to collapse.

On the subject of certainty, I notice that you spend a good deal of space trying to relate specific passages of his fiction to events of his own life. And sometimes this really doesn't work.

Sometimes it works and sometimes it doesn't. I was just so tired of conventional literary criticism, and so tired of the orthodox "life and work" divide in most biographies, that I wanted to find a new way to interanimate the two at the same time as I wanted to discover a different way of describing the novels themselves. Now I know from my own experience that a great deal in a novel happens by chance: you see something, you hear something, you think of something, and then you put it in. I wanted to trace a similar process in Dickens – like the time he ran over a dog belonging to a small girl, and then gave Diogenes to Florence Dombey a few weeks later. A small incident, perhaps, but significant. And then there was the occasion, after he was attacked by a horse, when he had Dombey injured by a fall from his own horse. Of course there are connections which are not quite so obvious, and it is quite likely that I have sometimes imposed a pattern where no pattern really exists. And there is another fault related to that. At all costs I wanted to keep up the momentum and the smooth texture of the prose – I suppose that comes from my work on novels – so, whenever there might have been a gap or a discontinuity in the narrative, I made a point of hustling together events and images in order to effect a smooth transition. In other words, I cheated.

What other aspects of the book worry you?

I was always concerned about the length of the chapters – sometimes they seemed too long, sometimes they seemed too short, and I was forever altering or abbreviating or expanding. And I'm worried about the opening chapters – family ties and early childhood are the two most boring elements in anyone's life, but they simply cannot be wished away. I'm also worried about certain passages of difficult writing which, significantly enough, tend to occur in my descriptions of the novels. I'm worried about relating Dickens to his period – in the sense that there may not be an analysable relation at all. I suppose, in the end, I'm worried about everything.

Do you admire other biographies of Dickens, then?

Yes and no. Of course you have to make ritual obeisances to biographers like John Forster and Edgar Johnson – otherwise everyone thinks that you're being too arrogant – but in actual fact I don't even really care for Forster's Life. Some of it is really very dull. And Edgar Johnson himself can be awfully wrong-headed.

But no doubt you will seem wrong-headed in thirty or forty years' time.

Every biography is a prisoner of its time, yes, and I'm sure that anyone who may happen to open the book in the twenty-first century will recognise at once that it was written in the fin-de-siecle of the twentieth century. I have probably made too much of the fact, for example, that Dickens *saw* reality as a reflection of his own fiction. That his novels dominated his understanding of people and even of himself. It sounds perfectly reasonable now, but no doubt in two or three decades it will seem no more than the bias of a particular writer in a particular era.

So why did you decide to write the book in the first place?

I don't know. It just seemed like a good idea at the time. I had some vague attraction to the *idea* of Dickens, but I didn't really know a great deal about his work or his life. In fact it came as a shock to realise just how much I would need to read, and to assimilate. But it was a challenge and, after writing the biography of T. S. Eliot, I wanted another challenge. In any case much of the difficulty resolved itself into matters of organisation –

So how did you organise it?

I used files and card boxes and indexes. Into the card boxes went all my notes on every book I read about Dickens. Into the files went all my own reflections, all my general reading, all my biographical and bibliographical research. I started actually writing the book in September 1988, but for months before that I was collating a vast amount of information into a day-by-day account of Dickens's life. I forgot to mention that I had determined to read at least three times everything that he ever wrote – which meant letters and journalism as well as fiction. To read all his fiction just once takes three or four months, so you can see how extensive and involved the work actually was. Eliot was a breeze in contrast – you can get through his collected works in the course of a long weekend.

And did you like Dickens at the end of it?

I'm always being asked that question, and I never have an answer. I never did like or dislike him – such matters just don't come into it. All I wanted to do was understand him, which is quite a different thing. In that sense he was like a character in a novel I might write – I never like or dislike any of the characters I have created. I simply try to understand them and, in understanding them, to bring them to life.

So in that sense biographies are like novels?

I always used to say that, but I never really believed it. It just sounded good at the time. The only real connection between the two, as far as I am concerned, is in the need to make the narrative coherent. To impose a pattern upon the world. That is all. You also need similar skills, of course, the most important being to cover up your own inadequacies.

You said that you were really only concerned to understand Dickens. Do you?

At the time of the actual writing, I certainly did. Immediately after the book was finished, I thought I did. Now I'm not so sure. Only the reader has the answer.

Chapter 30

HE was now forty-nine years old. On his birthday, perhaps as a present to himself, Dickens bought Mary Green's *Lives of the Princesses of England* and Agnes Strickland's *Lives of the Queens of England*. On the same day he held a dinner for himself at 3 Hanover Terrace; his old friend, Beard, was among the guests and most of his family were also present. His son, Charley, had now returned from China and was working in the City – he had in fact already had an effect upon his father's *Great Expectations*, in which the young Herbert Pocket was originally a "merchant" who was to trade ". . . to China for teas". But Dickens struck out these references at proof stage. He did not strike out a description of Herbert, however, which might almost be that of Dickens about his son, "There was something wonderfully hopeful about his general air, and something that at the same time whispered to me that he would never be very successful or rich". It is worth noting in this place that Dickens was angered and distressed by the fact that his son was still intent upon marrying Bessie Evans, the daughter of the publisher whom Dickens had utterly rejected and abjured ever since the time of the separation. Was fiction one way for Dickens, then, to express all those aggressive impulses which could not emerge in ordinary waking life? Frank was at home, too; Dickens, despairing of his competence in business matters, had taken him on as a general factotum in the *All The Year Round* offices. Mamie of course was present, as was Georgina who, in the 1861 Census, was described somewhat unflatteringly as "servant-housekeeper". Kate and Charles Collins were now back from the continent, and were living in the apartment of Kate's mother-in-law at Clarence Terrace. Dickens still did not think much of that marriage, either, and at the same time he was being compelled to subsidise his other children from a distance; Walter had already been accruing large

897

debts in India, and in the previous months Dickens had sent him £115. 14s. Then there was his brother Alfred's widow, Helen, and her five children; and then there was his mother in her senility. It is no wonder that in a letter the following month he was describing how ". . . I am quite weighed down and loaded and chained in life" – and this just after he had written in *Great Expectations* of the convicts who were ". . . handcuffed together, and had irons on their legs . . ." In the narrative at this point Pip tries imaginatively to understand the plight of these chained criminals, but surely we can see behind the text itself the shadow of Dickens identifying himself with the prisoner if not with the outcast.

He was being pressed in by his own engagements also. He wanted to complete *Great Expectations* as quickly as possible – he had a date early in June in mind – but his work upon it was disrupted by a series of six readings which he had undertaken to give in St James's Hall in March and April. When the time came to give them, some people in the front row ". . . plainly saw the tears provoked by the wonderful reception given to Dickens directly he stepped upon the platform". One member of the audience at St James's Hall was Thomas Beard himself, but he always sat at the end of the row and was too shy to go "backstage" in order to drink brandy and water with Dickens. He did not wish to impose upon his old friend. He was both too stalwart and too bashful to do so, and perhaps a better companion for Dickens than some of his more effusive contemporaries. As Thackeray said at this time, "There is nobody to tell him when anything goes wrong. Dickens is the Sultan, and Wills is his Grand Vizier". At the end of the readings Dickens was delighted to have made five hundred pounds, after all expenses had been paid, but nevertheless he was relieved to be able to concentrate on the continuing story of Pip and Magwitch. At some point it seems that, for quietness, he took rooms near the Five Bells public house in New Cross (he had stayed in lodgings here once before), and by the end of April he was well into the third "stage" of Pip's expectations and his knowledge that all of his wealth and his status as a "gentleman" had come from the pocket of the convict Magwitch.

After the political and social concerns of *Little Dorrit*, then, Dickens returns to a highly personal vision. Once more, as in *A Tale of Two Cities*, the theme includes that of sexual and emotional renunciation; but here it is shorn of its heroic context and is imbued instead with elements of guilt and aggression. So why is it that Dickens projects himself into so essentially flawed a figure as Pip – might it have been a sudden access of self-knowledge, held away, warded off during these recent difficult years, which could only really be explored in fiction? It is in any event a book of great psychological accuracy and observation, as if Dickens were secretly examining himself as he writes, analysing the nature of passion, of hypocrisy, of psychological meanness, all those things "low and small" of which Pip eventually realises himself to be guilty. The idea of false expectations, the notion of being a true gentleman, the violence just below the surface of conventional life; these are the themes which seem to touch Dickens most deeply. And by what other tokens can we measure him now? Everything in this novel is grey, rainy, melancholy – "So cold, so lonely, so dreary all!" The shadowy darkness which crowds the narrative in *A Tale of Two Cities* had been dispelled by the garish light of the Revolution itself. But here a dying light, and a pale flare across the marshes, make up the only illumination. *Great Expectations* is filled with small rooms: Wemmick's miniature castle; Jaggers's office; the little room where Orlick sits; the garret of Pip's childhood. Perhaps we can see the true vision of Dickens's own childhood in this wilderness of small rooms, just as it seems likely that he is going back to the sensations of his own earliest years when he connects childhood here with feelings of guilt and of terror. For never has any novel been so imbued with the horrors of infancy. It has already been made clear how Miss Havisham is in part derived from the woman in white whom Dickens had seen as a child, but is not the convict straying upon the marshes near Cooling another emblem of early fear? There are other intimations of his childhood, too. Jaggers is said to live in Gerrard Street, where the young Dickens used to visit his uncle, Thomas Barrow; Miss Havisham dwells in Satis House, closely modelled upon an old Rochester mansion; Pip's sense of being "common" while engaged in manual work bears obvious relation to Dickens's own early life; similarly, Joe Gargery's visit to the "Blacking Ware'us"; the fact that Pip's benefactor has been shaped by prison has its own connection with the problems of the early Dickens household, too (". . . if the ghost of a man's own father cannot be allowed to claim his attention, what can, Sir?"); and there is a "secret" kept for ever.

Everything from his childhood is coming together for Dickens now; it is almost as if his old miseries had been stirred into life by the story of Pip's love for Estella, the story of a man devoted to a woman who cannot and does not love. Old anxiety and sadness returning when love is denied – is that the truth of it? In many ways, therefore, it is a much more frankly autobiographical work than *David Copperfield*; and if this book does indeed reflect a fresh access of self-knowledge on Dickens's part (who could have gone through the events of the last two years without being in some sense invaded by it?) it is as if that self-knowledge had also opened up the doors of self-perception. That is why all the previously inchoate and shadowy fears of his childhood are allowed to emerge without impediment. Combining into strange shapes so that Dickens himself seems to be part Pip and part Magwitch, the convict representing all that is guilty and all that is beneficent, all that is "common" and all that is powerful. Creating strange currents of thwarted love and sexuality in Miss Havisham and Estella. Lamenting the hopeless search for love. Fashioning a self-made "gentleman" in Pip who has no real place in the world and whose own values, created out of self-love, are impossibly frail – what aspect of the author might we see in *that*? It is as if Dickens were in a fever which allows him to speak freely for the first time, just as Pip, in his own sickness, reverts helplessly to the state of a child – ". . . I fancied I was little Pip again". And Dickens, writing in Wellington Street North, was only a few steps away from Chandos Street where little Charles had tied up pots of blacking as he sat in the window. Towards the end of *Great Expectations* Pip waits beside the deathbed of Magwitch, and it is almost as if the young Charles Dickens were sitting at the deathbed of the old Charles Dickens. ". . . I knew there were no better words that I could say beside his bed, than 'Oh Lord, be merciful to him a sinner!'"

He was almost constantly in pain as he wrote. He was suffering from what he called "facial neuralgia", and was too ill on 20 May to take the chair at the annual dinner of the Newsvendors' Benevolent Association (Wilkie Collins, rather reluctantly, took his place). But he was able, two days later, to hire a Thames steamer so that he might more accurately convey the chase and recapture of Magwitch on the river. Forster and other friends joined him on this excursion and Forster noticed that ". . . he seemed to have no care . . . except to enjoy their enjoyment and entertain them with his own in shape of a thousand whims and fancies; but his sleepless observation was at work all the time, and nothing had escaped his keen vision on either side of the river." When he returned, Dickens made out a list of the tides and their times. On the following day he went down to Dover for a week, principally so that he could work undisturbed on the last chapters of the novel but also because he hoped the sea air might cure his neuralgia. He went for his customary walks (on one day he actually walked from Dover to Folkestone and then back again, a distance of some fourteen miles) but he was concentrating upon the book so that he might finish it by the middle of the following month. "I work here, like a Steam Engine, and walk like Captain Barclay", the "Captain" being a famous pedestrian who once walked one thousand miles in one thousand hours. And, by the time he returned to London, he was indeed coming to the end of his story; in order to help himself with the construction of its last scenes, he drew up memoranda on dates and characters which had already occurred. He had been expecting to finish the book on 12 June and so orderly were his calculations that he in fact completed his narrative just the day before. More remarkable still is the fact that his neuralgic pains vanished as soon as he had finished his work. As the book ends with Pip walking along Piccadilly seeing there Estella and understanding, then, that "suffering . . . had given her a heart to understand what my heart used to be". A lonely, poignant ending which is perfectly in accordance with the whole tone and theme of the novel.

But it was to be changed – not at Dickens's own instigation but rather at the urging of Bulwer-Lytton. Dickens had for a long time planned to visit him at Knebworth, and only a few days after completing the book he made the journey; not only did he want to show him the last sequences of his own novel but he wanted to go through the proofs of Bulwer-Lytton's *A Strange Story*, which was to be serialised in *All The Year Round* immediately after the conclusion of *Great Expectations*. In some ways they were still an ill-assorted pair, Dickens and Bulwer-Lytton, both of them famous and popular novelists, but how great a gulf between them in their lives and in their art, Bulwer-Lytton, always essentially the aristocrat, the eccentric, the dabbler in the occult. A brief but accurate specimen of their conversation can be gathered from a report of it by George Eliot. Bulwer-Lytton had been describing a Frenchwoman who could raise the dead, but only at great expense.

Dickens: "What is the cause of this expense in raising the dead?"

Bulwer-Lytton (seriously): "The Perfumes!"

While at Knebworth Dickens, with some others, visited the tumble-down mansion of a local eccentric and hermit, one James Lucas, who after the death of his mother lived in an unwashed and unkempt condition; he wore an old blanket fastened with a skewer, slept on cinders, and conversed with passers-by through a barred window. Investigation has since revealed that he was suffering from an acute mental disorder and feared that he was about to be murdered by his own brother; but Dickens, on his visit, gave him scant sympathy and was merely confirmed in his hatred of those who cut themselves off from human society and seem to parade themselves as somehow noteworthy specimens of individualism. He hated anything which smacked of hypocrisy just as much as he scorned the cloistered virtues of the nun or monk. He never understood Lucas's madness, therefore, and saw only the horrors of dirt and exhibitionism. He remained quite cool and collected during his visit (although he admitted later that, if he had known how many rats lived with Lucas, he would have been less composed), but in fact he was so incensed by what he witnessed that Lucas became the subject of his next series of Christmas stories. Dickens violently attacked him as "Mr Mopes the Hermit" – an attack which did little other than increase the poor man's notoriety, and the Great Northern Railway even put on special cheap weekend excursions to see "the Hermit".

But something of greater significance occurred during his visit to Hertfordshire. Bulwer-Lytton read the proofs of the last chapters of *Great Expectations*, and persuaded Dickens that he ought to change the ending in order to render the fates of both Pip and Estella less harsh; in this way, he could avoid alienating the reader who might have expected something more compassionate than Dickens's somewhat bleak coda. Dickens saw the force of Bulwer-Lytton's objection at once – a few years before he had suggested to one of his own contributors, after all, that the close of her story was "unnecessarily painful" and urged her to soften its effect for the sake of her readers. He went back to Gad's Hill Place, and within four days had revised the conclusion so that it is indeed softened like the evening mist with which the book ends.

If Dickens had thus been revising for the sake of a favourable reaction, he still could not have hoped for a warmer reception than the book actually received. It was issued in three volumes soon after its conclusion in his periodical (this strange format, unique in Dickens's writing career, was actually designed to cater for the growing library trade; Mudie's, the great exponent of the circulating library, took most of the first edition), and the general reaction was one that celebrated his return to the humour and pathos of his earlier fiction. This is what Forster had wanted and, since it really meant that Dickens had abandoned the social and political satire of *Little Dorrit* or *Bleak*

House, it was also clearly what many of his other readers wanted as well. Just as he employed only his earlier fiction in his public readings, so Dickens now seemed to have reverted to his old role as "entertainer" in his most recent work. *The Rambler* said that ". . . we may rejoice that even in Mr Dickens's ashes still live his wonted fires", and a university magazine noted that most people had approached *Great Expectations* with no more than curiosity "to see what further ravages time might have yet in store for the mental frame of a novelist already past his prime . . ." (one understands perfectly why Dickens made it a rule never to read reviews); but this particular reviewer, like most others, experienced "a rather agreeable surprise".

The house in Hanover Terrace had now been given up, and Dickens returned to spend the summer at Gad's Hill Place; it was his custom to come up to London on Wednesday, in order to arrange the "make-up" of the next issue of *All The Year Round*, but most of the week was spent in Kent. The younger boys were also back from school for the summer, and now there were opportunities for cricket, for country expeditions, for walks, for hours on the lawn. But of course for Dickens there also had to be time for work; there never was a period in which he could be truly said to relax, and even during these quiet summer months he began assiduously and earnestly to prepare for the series of readings which were to begin in the autumn. For a long time he had been wanting to devise a reading out of *David Copperfield* and, now, with almost four months before the start of his tour, he had found the perfect opportunity to do so. In the same period he prepared reading scripts which were provisionally entitled "Nicholas Nickleby at the Yorkshire Schools", "Mr Chops, the Dwarf", "Mr Bob Sawyer's Party", "The Bastille Prisoner" and "Great Expectations". The last two were never performed but all of the others were, the reading version of *David Copperfield* being some two hours in length while the extract from *Nicholas Nickleby* ran for one and a quarter hours. We will come to see later how Dickens poured all the resources of his art and personality into these readings (his favourite always remained the adaptation from *David Copperfield*) but, even at this preliminary stage, his perfectionism and punctiliousness were as marked as ever. He would choose what portions of the novel he wished to read, then he would cut out the passages he needed and paste them into a book; these would then be run off by his printer at Chapman and Hall, so that he had something like a fair copy on which to work. This became his "prompt copy", on which he would then go to work in order to elicit the greatest possible range of effects for the benefit of his audience. He distilled the material into a few powerful or comic scenes; he made the jokes funnier or the humour more exaggerated; he dispensed with elaborate descriptions, because he knew that his own acting would more than compensate for any loss of focus; he excised sub-plots and incidental characters; he cut out all social or political references, on the grounds that they were not suitable in an "entertainment"; and, as he practised reading the texts out loud, he would underline certain passages in a variety of inks, or add stage directions to himself in the margins. Alongside the text of "The Bastille Prisoner", for example, Dickens wrote such directions as "Sigh", "Moan" and "Low". In other words, he turned his novels or stories into a quite different form of art. They became short dramatic entertainments, designed for the peculiar gifts of this solitary actor behind his reading desk. Each day at Gad's Hill Place he practised for two or three hours, talking out loud, groaning, making faces in the mirror, turning himself into a veritable medium for characters as diverse as Bob Sawyer and Mrs Squeers, Smike and Dora Copperfield, the dismal whine of one and the high feminine note of the other. Then, at the end of the three hours' rehearsal, he "collapsed" and did nothing for the rest of the day. His characters had exhausted him.

Yet even as he planned for the reading tour he was disturbed by news that threatened to ruin it before it had begun: Arthur Smith, his manager, had grown dangerously ill; Dickens was greatly worried and did not know what to do. He could make no definite plans while Smith lay sick but, on the other hand, he did not want to employ anyone in his place; it was only when Dickens perceived that Smith would not recover that he decided to employ a certain Arthur Headland. And then Smith died – the friend who Dickens said was his "right arm". The day after Dickens returned from the funeral, his brother-in-law, Henry Austin, the man to whom he had often turned for support and advice, died also. More deaths crowding in. And yet he declared that the coming readings ". . . must be fought out, like all the rest of life". This was always Dickens's reaction in the face of death – to fight. The world was one in which we are ". . . all to suffer, and strive, and die"; but for Dickens the emphasis is upon the *striving*. In fact he felt the death of Arthur Smith much more keenly than that of Henry Austin. Nothing now could be the same, and, without him, he felt quite lost and helpless. Smith had arranged everything, had dealt with tickets and audiences, with transport and with hotels. What he also missed, in his absence, was the sense "of compactness and comfort about me" which was so important to him in the long and arduous travels around the United Kingdom. In that invocation of comfort and compactness, there is also an oblique sense of being cosseted, of being protected, even of being loved – so it is perhaps not surprising that he should react to his manager's death in such a powerful and explicit manner. He also attended the funeral of Henry Austin, a ceremony which he observed with his usual grisly comicality (he was always adept at noticing the hypocrisies of mourners of such occasions), and for the next few months he spent a great deal of time exhorting and comforting his widowed sister, Laetitia. He suggested that she go away to a seaside town to recover some of her spirit; he advised her to recommence all the ordinary activities of life as a cure for sorrow; he warned her against taking boarders, and so on. No one could be more practical than Dickens at such times. But he tired of his duties and, by the following year, had handed over the problems of all his widowed relatives to Georgina; in particular he was pleased to divest himself of Helen, his sister-in-law, whose importunate behaviour came to "disgust" him. Of course when it came to public matters he himself stepped forward in the guise of public man – it was he who had to write to Palmerston, a politician he despised, to request a civil list pension for his sister.

So it was that in the autumn of the year, while he was assisting Laetitia, he set out upon the second series of readings which, he feared, would be dull and wearisome without the presence of Arthur Smith. The ancillary team – Boycett, Thompson and Berry, now with the addition of Headland – accompanied him, and they stopped first at Norwich on 28 October. The tour was to last until the end of January and was to encompass places as far apart as Brighton and Edinburgh, Hastings and Preston. But it did not begin well. The audience at Norwich "were not magnetic", he reported, by which he meant that there was no current of energy between himself and his listeners; sometimes he described this in moral terms as a "common bond", but as often as not it seems to have been almost a more tangible link. It is significant, too, how on this second major tour he was able subtly to discriminate between the responses of the various audiences whom he addressed, which suggests in turn how much his own performance depended upon his "peculiar personal relation" with each audience. It was for him almost a physical charge, a surge of energy that lent him the power to impersonate the scores of characters whom he "read" each night. Even now it was beginning to take its physical toll, however; one child was allowed into his dressing room after a reading in Colchester at the beginning of November, and even many years later remembered the way Dickens ". . . in his shirt-sleeves, was walking rapidly up and down, as a means of getting through with the cooling and calming process . . ." Later he ate a large supper but ". . . was absolutely never still, mentally or physically . . ." *Never still.* And, as so often in his life, Dickens was now describing the world in words that might have been applicable to his own condition. In his own accounts of his travels in his correspondence there are now storms everywhere, as if he were a giant altering the climate as he storms across the country. Storms and raging seas at Dover; gales and fierce rain in Edinburgh; snow storms at Colchester; fierce storms at Berwick-upon-Tweed. In fact the imagery of storm and sea comes so naturally to him at this period that the most important aspects of his life are described in its terms. The audience is ". . . taken by storm" by his reading from *David Copperfield*; there is ". . . a terrible wave in the crowd . . ."; the people "roar" around him; the audience is taken to ". . . the top of a wave". Then, when he returns to Gad's Hill Place he is confronted by ". . . a raging sea of correspondence"; an employee mishandles matters but "I cannot be very stormy with him . . ."; and, when he comes to the end of his tour, he begins ". . . to see Land now". So this was how he saw himself: caught in a storm upon the face of the deep, like so many of the travellers he had read and written about. And how close did he feel now, to shipwreck and drowning?

In the middle of November he returned to Kent; he had arranged for a break of ten days in the intense schedule of readings in order that he might work on that year's Christmas issue of *All The Year Round*, but then once more he was back on his travels. It was from this time forward, however, that all the problems he foresaw in the absence of Arthur Smith began to plague him. It was in the third week of November that the readings started to go wrong, with an accident at Newcastle-upon-Tyne. The audience "were all very still over Smike" when the gas apparatus which illuminated Dickens fell over; one woman screamed and ran towards him, and there was "a terrible wave" in the crowd. But these were times when Dickens was effortlessly able to keep his composure. He spoke out loudly to the woman, "There's nothing the matter, I assure you; don't be alarmed; pray sit down." The panic subsided, the equipment was reassembled, and the reading continued. But it had been a difficult moment; the packed halls, the excitement of the crowd (often seeming to amount to hysteria), the difficulties of exit, the fragility of the gas equipment, meant that such occasions carried a constant risk of fire or fatal crushing. And it was at this time, of all times, that Dickens had cause to regret Arthur Smith's absence even more; for it was clear that Headland, an agreeable but apparently incompetent man, could not cope with the management of so complex a thing as a reading tour. Previously he had worked at St Martin's Hall in London, but Dickens's enterprise was quite a new thing in the world of public entertainment. Now handbills advertising the readings were going astray; the wrong readings were advertised; printed cards contained the wrong details. Dickens, who of all people demanded the utmost precision and rigour in business arrangements, was as concerned as he was enraged. He sent Berry, the general factotum, ahead of him to clear up as many of the difficulties as possible; and Headland was not employed by him again. An indication of what might happen, when affairs were mismanaged, is given by the last reading at Edinburgh in the Queen Street Hall: Dickens was dressing when he heard more than the usual commotion and, when he had finished his preparations, he went outside to find the street, the passages of the hall and the hall itself rapidly filling up with crowds upon crowds of people. The local agents or (more probably) Headland had so badly organised matters that too many tickets had been sold and too many people let into the body of the hall. Dickens, again almost frigid in his composure in the face of alarming excitement, walked onto the platform and waited until the noise of the crowd subsided – he waited and waited until there was what he called "dead silence". Then he told the people assembled there that he would adjourn the reading to the larger Music Hall nearby or, alternatively, could read another night.

Voice from the crowd (amid cheering): "Go on, Mr Dickens. Everybody will be quiet now."

Another voice: "We *won't* be quiet. We won't let the reading be heard. We're ill-treated."

Charles Dickens: "There's plenty of time, and you may rely upon it that the reading is in no danger of being heard until we are agreed."

Another voice: "Mr Dickens!"

Charles Dickens: "Sir."

Same voice: "Couldn't some people, at all events ladies, be accommodated on your platform?"

Charles Dickens: "Most certainly."

Same voice: "Which way can they come to the platform, Mr Dickens?"

Charles Dickens: "Round here to my left."

So the ladies of Edinburgh congregated on the platform around, and in front of, Dickens; he said that it looked like a "gigantic picnic". He went on to read from *Nicholas Nickleby* and *The Pickwick Papers*; again, as always, huge success; roaring crowd; cheers; laughter; tears; and applause. And so he went on around the country, on to Carlisle, Lancaster, Preston. In the latter place he knew, from his last visit, the young woman who sold newspapers at the local station – she told him that she had tickets for that evening's performance and was coming "with a person".

"*The* person?" Dickens asked.

"Never *you* mind."

And on again. It was while he was in Manchester that the news of Prince Albert's death arrived and stopped all public proceedings of that sort; Dickens was not at all pleased, since it meant that he had to postpone the six readings he was to give in Liverpool and instead return to London. He had in any case no particular interest in Albert, a man whom he considered to be of no more than ordinary mind and spirit; ". . . the Jackasses that people are at present making of themselves on that subject!" was his kindest comment. After his unexpected return to London he went down to Gad's Hill Place, where he stayed until the end of Christmas week with the family – Mamie remembered that, during the Christmas festivities of these years, the house "was always filled with guests" and she recalled the long walks, the games of "Proverbs" and "Dumb Crambo" in the evening. After this week of rest he went straight on to Birmingham where, for the first time, he read "Mr Bob Sawyer's Party" and scored an indubitable success with it. ". . . he laughed till the tears ran down his cheeks over Bob Sawyer's party," a friend said of this particular entertainment, "and the remembrance of the laughter he had seen depicted on the faces of the people the night before."

By the end of the reading tour, in January 1862, he could not sleep and was ". . . dazed and worn by gas and heat . . ." He came back again for rest to Gad's Hill Place, but in February he decamped with his family to another London residence which he had taken for the season (not rented on this occasion, but exchanged for Gad's Hill Place), 16 Hyde Park Gate South, just a few yards from Kensington Gardens. But he did not like it at all all – ". . . this odious little house," he called it, this "London box". And his work was not over yet. He had agreed to give further readings in London in the Hanover Square Rooms, and these were to continue until the end of June; in other words, he had characteristically determined to keep himself occupied the whole time he remained in the capital. Clearly he had no thought of rest or recreation – perhaps for the sake of the money, perhaps for the sake of the applause and glare to which he had now become accustomed, more likely for the potent combination of all of these. He also had plans to begin work on a new novel, for which characters and subjects had already occurred to him – a strange father and son he had seen in Chatham, "Found Drowned" posters by the London wharves – but it proved impossible to work in the little house in Kensington. So after breakfast he left each morning for the office, no doubt making a habit of walking the four miles to Wellington Street, and spent many evenings in the company of friends like Yates, and Wills, and Collins. He was now also well acquainted with two other men who were to become almost "fixtures" in his life from this time forward, men for whom he had the strangest affection, and whose friendship casts another light upon Dickens's own character.

The most interesting of these two companions was Charles Fechter, an actor of French parentage whose strong accent had not inhibited his success upon the London stage. He had first achieved that success with his portrayal of Hamlet at the Princess's Theatre in 1861, and the remark of a theatre employee on that occasion is still worth recording one hundred and twenty-nine years later – "Sir, it's wonderful. We all know Mr Kean. Mr Kean was great. But with 'im '*Amlet* was a tragedy, with Mr Fechter it's quite another thing. He has raised it to a mellerdrama." In fact melodrama was not quite Fechter's forte; he was a remarkable actor on the stage of the period precisely because of his ability to subdue the rant and gestural theatrics which were so common amongst his contemporaries and to replace them with something which seemed at the time much more "naturalistic", more "romantic", more "picturesque". These were precisely the qualities to which Dickens aspired in his own amateur dramatics, and it is perhaps not surprising – given Dickens's own sensitive condition during this period – that he first recognised Fechter's genius when he saw him playing a lover. He had seen him in Paris. "He was making love to a woman," Dickens told a friend, "and he so elevated her as well as himself by the sentiment in which he enveloped her, that they trod in a purer ether, and in another sphere, quite lifted out of the present. 'By heavens!' I said to myself, 'a man who can do this can do anything.' I never saw two people more purely and instantly elevated by the power of love." It is hard not to think of Dickens's own situation at this time in his extraordinary attachment to a man who could play the elevated and romantic lover, the man who took love into a purer sphere than that of earthly pleasure.

Many of Dickens's acquaintances, however, were puzzled about his interest in Fechter. The actor had, according to one observer, ". . . a very dark sallow face and close black hair". Marcus Stone remembered how "none of his friends could understand Dickens's obsession for the man. He was a waster . . . He was not worth the trouble Dickens went to in his behalf." But acquaintances like Stone, aside from the fact that they may have been jealous, did not realise how in Dickens's sensibility drama and life were so compounded that he could not separate the man from the actor. And in truth those who knew Dickens better also shared an affection for Fechter. He was sometimes moody and quarrelsome, and it is true that he had absolutely no conception of financial management, but he seems to have had a wonderful vein of geniality not unmixed with an impetuous and impulsive temperament. Wilkie Collins was a frequent guest at his house in St John's Wood and remembered how at dinner guests chose their own wine (there were no servants) and, on occasions, wandered into the kitchen to help the French cook. At this time in Dickens's life, when all the platitudes and conventions of society seemed only to be the weight he was forced to bear, there is no doubt that Fechter's playful and "bohemian" society gave him more pleasure than that of his more respectable contemporaries. In addition Fechter was a wonderful mimic, and no gift pleased Dickens more than that. He lent him money, he conceived the idea of directing a play with him, and, when the actor took over the management of the Lyceum in 1863, Dickens seems for the next four years to have acted as unpaid adviser and even "play-doctor"; he partly rewrote a melodrama, *Belphegor*, for one of his productions. Fechter was also a regular visitor to Dickens at Gad's Hill Place on Sundays, when the horrors of the metropolitan Sabbath became quite insupportable.

Another constant visitor to Gad's Hill Place was Henry Chorley, a music critic and occasional novelist; he was on such good terms with Dickens, in fact, that he was one of the few men who was able to invite himself down to Kent for weekends. Yet he was a stranger partner for Dickens than Fechter – Chorley was a mild, broken-down, sad bachelor in late middle-age (he was five years older than Dickens). He had a thin voice, a shuffling gait, and a depressive temperament which he never could quite quench with drink. Yet Dickens understood him, liked him and tried on all occasions to cheer him. By all accounts Chorley was a disappointed man who thought he had failed in life, and no aspect of a man's character was more likely to win Dickens's instinctive care and sympathy; we need go no further than his fiction to recognise to what extent Dickens could "identify" with those who had been vanquished in the "battle of life". Of course he himself had never failed, but the fact that he had spent half a lifetime terrified of any such eventuality meant that he could be wonderfully generous with those who had not been able to avert it. But there was another tie between men otherwise so dissimilar in their destinies. Chorley, too, was almost entirely self-educated, thwarted from his early vocation by a mother who put him to work in a mercantile office when he was still a boy. Here, in this congruence of early life, we see also one of the roots of Dickens's sympathy – no story could stir him as much as that of maternal mistreatment (we might recall how moved he was, in early life, by Samuel Johnson's description of the fate of Richard Savage in *Lives of the Poets*), and there were times indeed when he seemed to treat Chorley almost as some sad alter ego, some version of Charles Dickens if Charles Dickens had failed. So it was that, during these spring months in London, he and Chorley would make long expeditions together – on one occasion, for example, after listening to Arthur Sullivan's music for *The Tempest*, walking from Crystal Palace back to Chorley's house in Knightsbridge.

Yet as soon as the period of house exchange was over, and he could remove himself from the disagreeable "box" in Kensington, he returned to Gad's Hill Place for the summer; another summer of sports in the afternoon (cricket in the field behind the house or croquet on the front lawn), and evening games of whist, of riddles, or of conundrums. But these idle pleasures were not to be enjoyed for long since, in June, Georgina Hogarth became ill. Dickens described her condition as "degeneration of the heart", or "aneurism of the aorta", and in fact she grew so seriously ill that he began to doubt whether she would be able to recover. She was low-spirited, confused, and suffered great pain in her chest. Dickens himself, seeing the rapid decline of the woman who had stood by him during the time of the separation, went around in an "altogether dazed" condition. She had recovered a little by the end of June, but was still very ill indeed and suffered something of a relapse towards the end of July. But was his own anxiety at Georgina's condition in part amplified by guilt? Why was it that Georgina's "heart" had been so suddenly afflicted? It has been suggested that she had heard, or knew, of something about her brother-in-law's life which deeply disturbed her. This would be merely fanciful speculation, were it not for the fact that in this very period of Georgina's illness Dickens's own movements become strangely and even mysteriously uncertain.

In the third week of June, even while Georgina remained very ill, he went to France for a week, returned for his last London reading on 27 June, and then almost at once set off for France again – these two journeys being only the beginning of a number of short but regular visits to France he made over the next three months. Certainly his wandering back and forth between the two countries, combined with his anxiety about Georgina's illness, meant that he could settle down to nothing in any continuous way; it is clear that he wanted to begin the novel which he had already been contemplating for some months, but he did not find sufficient time or peace of mind to do so for another two and a half years. His correspondence during the period is remarkably uninformative, however, compared at least with the wealth of detail which he usually lavished on his travels. "I have been in France . . . I am away to France forthwith . . . going back there immediately . . . a visit at a distance . . . My absence is entre nous . . . On the Sunday I vanish into space for a day or two . . ."

Significant, and probably unintentional, is his employment of the word "visit" – whom was he visiting? And where, at a "distance", did he go? The second question can, at least, be answered with some certainty; Dickens was crossing the Channel to Boulogne, and then travelling a few miles south to the village of Condette. The Mayor of the Commune of Condette at that time has recorded how "Charles Dickens, le célèbre écrivain, a habité la maison de M. Beaucourt-Mutuel – il y faisait en 1864 son séjour favori et y restait, de temps en temps, une période de 8 jours; il a laissé quelques souvenirs parmi quelques habitants . . ." The house which M. Beaucourt-Mutuel owned in Condette was a modest chalet, certainly modest by the standards of the previous dwellings he had owned in Boulogne and in which Dickens had stayed. But there lies the story itself: M. Beaucourt-Mutuel's expenditure on the "Property" of Boulogne was so large that he went bankrupt, and in 1860 he was forced to sell up and to purchase instead the modest bungalow some ten miles outside

Boulogne. This is the "chalet" where Dickens stayed. The plaque affixed to its wall states that he resided here from 1860 to 1864, while the Mayor of Condette gives 1864 as the time of the first visit; in fact all the evidence from the hints and indirections in Dickens's correspondence suggests that he visited Condette regularly from this time, 1862, until the summer of 1865. So what was the attraction of such a place for Dickens? It was a quiet, even secluded, village; and the chalet itself, with its courtyard and gardens, had nothing close to it except for the scattered dwellings of the small farmers of the locality. It can be inferred, in other words, that Dickens liked the privacy of this area and of this particular house.

And so to whom did he pay these "visits"? It is unlikely, to say the least, that he would be constantly crossing the Channel in order to pay his respects to the Beaucourt-Mutuels. The answer lies closer to home, but it would probably never have been revealed had it not been for a railway crash which occurred in June 1865 – at the time of the terrible accident at Staplehurst, as we shall see, Charles Dickens was travelling in a first-class carriage with Ellen Ternan and Mrs Ternan. They had all come over from Boulogne. There can be no certainty in this matter but the balance of probabilities tilts one way: that, from 1862 onward, Ellen Ternan and Mrs Ternan were paying guests at the chalet of the Beaucourt-Mutuels (who now needed any additional income rather badly) and that Dickens's frequent and continuous journeys to France were for the sole purpose of visiting them in their seclusion. Perhaps just as significantly, the constant travelling of 1862 (one might almost say that Dickens was "commuting" between France and England) coincided with a period in which, as he told his closest friends, he was consumed by "misery". In September he told Wilkie Collins that "I have some rather miserable anxieties which I must impart one of these days . . ." Three months earlier he had written to Forster about ". . . the never to be forgotten misery of this later time . . ." which he compared to the miseries of his childhood (the miseries of the time when he felt himself to be abandoned). In December he also told Laetitia that he had ". . . quite enough of my own cares".

And what provoked this anxiety and pain? It is hard to avoid the conclusion that it had something to do with his continual visits to Ellen Ternan and her mother in Condette. There have as a result been many speculations about the exact nature of the relationship between Dickens and Ellen in this period – that they were unhappy lovers, that

Ellen had had a child and was bringing it up secretly in Condette, that she had had a miscarriage or abortion, that the child had died. It has to be said at once that no evidence has been found for any of these more dramatic possibilities, and we may perhaps approach a little closer to the truth of Dickens's unhappiness in a letter which he wrote in October to his sister, Laetitia, who was still in deep distress after the death of her husband. "But in this world," he said to her, "there is no stay but the hope of a better, and no reliance but on the mercy and goodness of God. Through these two harbours of a shipwrecked heart . . ." A shipwrecked heart – a strange although not entirely inapposite phrase to use to a widow, but how easily it springs from Dickens's pen. How much it seems to reflect his own concerns, too, is evident when he adds that "the disturbed mind and affections, like the tossed sea, seldom calm without an intervening time of confusion and trouble". Again Dickens seems in part to be addressing himself here; it has already been conveyed how often he employed the imagery of storm and sea to describe this period in his own life. Just as instinctive as his reference to the "shipwrecked heart", and to that underlying faith in God which bolsters it.

But these do not sound like the remarks of an adulterer, or of a man who has fathered a child upon a young woman living in banishment in France. It is unlikely, too, that Madame Beaucourt-Mutuel or Mrs Ternan would have permitted anything other than the greatest respectability of manner and conduct under what might be considered to be their joint roof. But we are left, then, with the enduring and perhaps unanswerable question: what precisely was the nature of the relationship between Ellen Ternan and Charles Dickens? That he was obsessed with her, there can be little doubt. That he maintained his relationship with her until the end of his life, there can be no doubt. That he maintained his affection for her, also, is undeniable. Perhaps an "ordinary" man might in such circumstances have become her sexual partner, but one needs only to look back over these pages to realise at once that Dickens was not "ordinary" in any sense. In many ways he was decidedly odd. His hysterical reaction to the death of Mary Hogarth – his keeping her clothes so that he might on occasions take them out and look at them, his longing to be buried with her – indicates as much. And since his behaviour was always quite exceptional, we should not fall into the trap of expecting him to behave in a conventional way with Ellen Ternan. Perhaps one might recall the remark which he had made to Mrs Watson eleven years before: "I think I'd rather *not* love, unless I could do it in an original manner. I seem to have been always doing it in the regular way, ever since I ran alone." In this context it is important, too, to remember the idealism in which all his most fervent expressions about love are couched; certainly, if there is to be found one paradigm for his continuing obsession with Ellen Ternan, it is indeed in his enduring and idealised love for Mary Hogarth whose image he had seen again and again in the young women (like Christiana Weller) to whom he was attracted. It may also be significant that Mary Hogarth died in her eighteenth year, which was the age of Ellen Ternan when he first met her, so that his love for her might be seen as some kind of idealised continuation of that first love for Mary. As late as 1867 he was still calling her "my dear girl", and is it too fanciful or extravagant to suppose that his love for her was all along as pure as it was obsessive? If we are to learn any lessons of the heart from his fiction, it may be from the central matter of Arthur Clennam's love for Little Dorrit that we can most fruitfully do so: ". . . there were ties of innocent reliance on one hand, and affectionate protection on the other; ties of compassion, respect, unselfish interest, gratitude, and pity." Just as Dickens called Ellen Ternan "my dear girl", so did Clennam call Little Dorrit his "poor child".

This in its turn leads to the other aspect of the matter which has to be explored. Throughout Dickens's fiction, and particularly in the Christmas stories of these later years, there is a continuing fascination with infant sexuality; in the Christmas adventure of three years before, for example, Dickens had fantasised about a harem of infants, a "Seraglio" or "Hareem" of quite innocent children at play. This infant sexuality is complemented, too, by what one might call the sexless passion conveyed in Dickens's constant references to the love between brother and sister, or between adult and child; ". . . as if he were a very little boy, and she his grown-up nurse" is one variant, as is ". . . the old bachelor brother and his maiden sister". Arthur Clennam refers to Little Dorrit at one point as his "adopted daughter" and, in Dickens's last completed novel, the central vehicle of safe passion is to be found in the playful relationship of father and daughter. Could it not be precisely this form of love which Dickens had for Ellen Ternan? The whole parade of his heroines might come to this, then – this sexless marriage between brother and sister, or father and daughter, a union like that which he had established with Mary Hogarth and which seemed to him to be the very pattern of idealised love. Is it any wonder that he treated most ordinary marriages as absurd or comic, and most forms of sexual passion as illicit and inducing guilt? Purity and innocence are the two single most important qualities for him – when a woman loses those, as the inmates of Miss Burdett-Coutt's Home undoubtedly had, they are immediately treated by Dickens in a much more objective manner; not exactly coldly, but dispassionately. That is why, when Christiana Weller married, she ceased to be for Dickens the idealised young virgin doomed to an early death and became instead a rather ordinary young woman somewhat remiss in her domestic duties. All the engagement of his nature, all the idealism and veneration, were elicited only by the innocent young girl or young woman; and, since this is the tone that Dickens always adopted towards Ellen Ternan, it seems almost inconceivable that theirs was in any sense a "consummated" affair. We might consider this at least as a hypothesis, therefore – all the evidence about Dickens's character, and all the evidence we possess about Ellen Ternan herself, suggest that the relationship between them acted for Dickens as the realisation of one of his most enduring fictional fantasies. That of sexless marriage with a young, idealised virgin.

It has generally been assumed, however, that their relationship was indeed consummated, and that Ellen Ternan became his mistress. The rumours were only given wide currency in the 1930s when a certain Thomas Wright passed on the remarks of a Canon Benham – to whom, it seems, Ellen "disburdened her mind" in later life in an apparently very generalised way. Where there is a mistress, however, there may be also a child; and in recent years there has as a result been a constant game of "hunt the baby", complete with its panoply of scholarly misunderstandings, family secrets, biographical gossip, asides in letters marked "confidential", elaborate investigations into rate books and parish registers and railway timetables – all of it, in the end, amounting to nothing. This pursuit is only to be expected, however; legitimate children are rarely a subject of any great interest since their relationship to their famous parent tends to be quite transparent. But the idea of Dickens siring an illegitimate child who grew up in the late nineteenth century, and even survived into the twentieth, has more resonance; an illegitimate offspring seems somehow to acquire more power, as if its status as an outcast brings it closer to the genius who was its father. At least two people have been nominated for this role but, again, the suggestions have proved to be quite without foundation. It is true that a servant who had worked for

Ellen Ternan claimed that "there were children", but for every statement suggesting a sexual liaison there is an equally authoritative one asserting quite the opposite. Ellen Ternan's maid, Jane Wheeler, who was in her employment from 1866, left a message for Ellen's daughter – ". . . if you had asked she would have told you the truth, your dear mother never was the mistress of Charles Dickens".

So from where do the rumours about the illegitimate child or children spring? Curiously enough, they primarily come from Dickens's own daughter, Kate. In much later life she told a confidante, Gladys Storey, that her father and Ellen had set up an establishment together and that there had been a "resultant son (who died in infancy)". Miss Storey duly published this information in her book, *Dickens and Daughter*, while in her unpublished papers there are references to conversations she had also held with Dickens's son, Henry: "Sir Henry and I . . . talked about Ellen Ternan – there was a boy but it died . . ." It all sounds highly plausible, for what could be more authentic than the remarks of Dickens's own children? Nevertheless there are significant problems with any such testimony. For one thing Henry could only have heard the story from his sister since, at the time of these events, he knew nothing whatever about Ellen Ternan except that she was an occasional visitor to Gad's Hill Place. And from where did Kate learn of the dead infant? She offered no proof – no letters, no diaries, no papers – and, indeed, all that really survives are her own unsubstantiated remarks relayed at second hand. We *do* know, however, that both Mamie Dickens and Georgina Hogarth maintained a close and steady friendship with Ellen Ternan after Dickens's own death. Would they have done so if she had indeed been the partner in an adulterous liaison with the man they both venerated? It is as unlikely as the possibility that Mrs Ternan would have accepted – and indeed, on the evidence available, supervised – a relationship which would have turned her daughter, in the eyes of the mid-Victorian world, into little more than a harlot.

There can be no certainties here. But it is appropriate, at least, to recall the words of Ellen Ternan's daughter: "My mother very often talked about Dickens. She always spoke of him with affection and said what a good man he was. Never was there a suggestion of sadness or sorrow or trouble in her references to him. She just spoke of him as a great man, and a great and well-liked friend . . ." Perhaps this is too anodyne a description, but it seems likely that there is a truth somewhere within it. Nevertheless we are not talking of any ordinary friendship between a "great man" and a young woman; it was something very extraordinary indeed, more extraordinary than an adulterous liaison and almost bewilderingly odd. We must imagine Dickens, in middle-age, haunted by a young woman who became for him a surrogate sister, daughter, virgin mother, child; a man obsessed, and unhappy with that obsession to the end of his life; a writer who had formed in life precisely the kind of relationship he had so helplessly created again and again in his fiction; a genius who held on to his ideal against all the odds and who, it might be said, was eventually destroyed by it. His was the "shipwrecked heart" after all, and could it not have been Ellen's reluctance to take on so strange a role that accounted for all the misery piling up against him in this year? The year when he first started travelling to Condette?

For this had become the shape of this life, this constant travelling between England and France, with his refrain on miseries which had "gathered and gathered". But he knew that there was at least a temporary cure for distress; he had even recommended it to his widowed sister, and, yes, it was *activity*, *busyness*, *work*. "In a determined effort to settle the thoughts," he told her, "to parcel out the day, to find occupation regularly or to make it, to be up and doing something . . ." And what activity did Dickens find at this time of his own distress? Of course he continued his constant and punctilious work upon *All The Year Round*. He was contemplating, too, a long novel – it would be his first since *Little Dorrit* five years before, and the very fact of this lengthy interval suggests how much the shape of his life had changed since the separation from Catherine. He had ideas but he did not yet have any plot, and he told Forster that ". . . all this unsettled fluctuating distress in my mind" made it almost impossible for him to work upon it. But he could still perform on the stage, and he was thinking of a series of readings in Paris; there he could earn money while remaining within easy reach of Condette. He did not care to abandon his family for so long a period, however, and it was agreed that Georgina, Mamie and he should spend the last months of the year together in the French capital. Forcing himself, as he said, back to his reading desk.

Georgina had slowly begun to recover her health in the late summer and autumn, and in early October Dickens took her down to Dover to try his favourite remedy of sea-air and sea-water. Then he was mysteriously absent again for a few days but, on his return, decided to remain with her at Gad's Hill Place because, since his departure, she had stayed there alone; Kate and Charles Collins had been in Scotland, while Mamie had been with friends. In the middle of October he travelled back to France, on the understanding that Georgina and Mamie were to follow him four days later. It was probable that he spent those four days at Condette, since he planned to meet his two relatives at Boulogne; but the sea was too high, the wind too strong, and eventually the channel boat found its harbour in Calais. Dickens went to meet them there and they travelled on by train to Paris – to an apartment at 27 rue du Faubourg Saint-Honoré which was very expensive but ". . . pretty, airy, and light". Of course he now knew Paris very well, and his general sense of being "at home" in France (indeed it had become almost literally his second home) was increased by the fact that "I see my books in French at every railway station great and small". Wills came over for a few days to decide the contents of the next Christmas issue, his journey indicating that this was no longer a mere routine part of the periodical – each Christmas number sold in the region of two hundred thousand copies, and represented an important part of Dickens's income. Wills reported back to his wife that "Dick" was "very cheery", and indeed his sense of humour was not impaired despite his miseries. Bulwer-Lytton, who was growing somewhat deaf, had dinner with Dickens one evening here and was talking about someone of his acquaintance.

"Was he wealthy?" Dickens asked.

"Healthy! One of the healthiest men I ever knew; never had a day's illness in his life."

At which answer Dickens glanced at their dinner companion, Marcus Stone, with one of those comical looks which no photograph was ever able to capture. "Dickens turned one eye on me," Stone said, "and I had to get up and look out of the window, to avoid bursting out into laughter." Dickens loved those moments of comical embarrassment, of suppressed laughter which one of his glances was enough to set off; as Stone went on to say, "He had an extraordinary power of making you laugh, under trying conditions when it was not wise to laugh." That is why he was such a menace at funerals, where even his genuine grief could not impair this mischievous, boyish, and sometimes almost hysterical gaiety. And yet, even amidst the dinners and the theatrical outings and the spirited laughter, there is no doubt that he was also miserable and highly overwrought. Anything to do with lost love or doomed love, for example, seemed to reduce him to tears; after a performance of Gluck's *Orphée* "I was disfigured with crying", and during a scene showing Marguerite yielding to her fatal love in *Faust* "I couldn't bear it, and gave in completely". To Georgina he said of the latter opera that ". . . it affected me so, and sounded in my ears so like a mournful echo of things that lie in my own heart". So Georgina, at least, knew something of the unhappy state of his affections.

A state that drove him to extreme restlessness. To thoughts of reading in Australia. To plans for the new novel. All the time commuting between Paris and London. But there was no escape, not for a man of his age, of his fame, of his responsibilities. For he had his children's lives to manage as well as his own, in the absence of any hint that they could cope for themselves. He tried to get Francis into the Foreign Office and, when he failed the competition, was eager to have him installed in the Bengal Mounted Police; Alfred, too, was set to fail his examinations at Woolwich and Dickens decided that he ought to pursue a mercantile career – preferably in tea, and preferably in India or China; he was worried about Edward's general shyness and so took him away from Wimbledon School; in addition, Charley's business affairs were not prospering. There was no sense, then, in which Dickens neglected his sons during this period of private distress; he was in fact almost over-active on their behalf, although his interventions were what might be called of a managerial rather than paternal kind. It is hard to resist the suspicion, also, that he was happy to send them overseas; whether this was to encourage self-reliance or to minimise the strain upon his own pocket is not clear. It may perhaps be surmised that he also wanted them as far away as possible from the circles of gossip and rumour concerning his attachment to Ellen Ternan. More restlessness. More travelling. Christmas week at Gad's Hill, where finally he was reconciled to the fact of his son's marriage to Bessie Evans; they had had a child and the man who had cried at *Orphée* and *Faust* could hardly withhold his blessing from the fruit of a much happier union. From Gad's Hill to London. From London to Paris in the second week of the new year, 1863.

He had arranged to read from *David Copperfield* at the British Embassy there but this was not to take place for another week and, in the meantime, he said that he had to visit "a sick friend concerning whom I am anxious". So he vanished into space, as he put it to Wilkie Collins – which really meant that he vanished in the general direction of Condette. He did not arrive in Paris until four days later, and then read at the Embassy to a French audience which seemed to him to be more acute in matters of gesture and expression than any of his English ones: ". . . when I was impersonating Steerforth in *David Copper-field*," he told an American friend some years later, "and gave that peculiar grip of the hand to Emily's lover, the French audience burst into cheers and rounds of applause." How odd that he should play the part of the wicked lover to perfection. He was once more suffering from facial neuralgia, and he could not sleep; principally because, as he told the physician at the British Embassy, he suffered from "an anxiety not to be mentioned here . . ." It seems in these hints and obliquities that Dickens almost *wants* to divulge his secret anxieties, to confess everything and thus be healed or reassured. But of course he could not do so for, with his appetite for self-revelation, there was an equally strong attraction to concealment and to "fiction". That is why he had told one friend that he might travel to Genoa after the reading, while informing another that he might go on to Lausanne; in other words he was covering his tracks, because he left Paris to spend another four days at Condette. Secret days, days stolen out of time, not to be measured by chronology or biography. When he returned he gave two more readings in the French capital, one of them being from *Dombey and Son*, which he had not performed for a year and which as a consequence he had to rehearse all morning. But, as usual, these readings created what he described as a "sensation", ". . . a two-hours' storm of excitement and pleasure. They actually recommenced and applauded right away into their carriages and down the street." The Parisian response so exhilarated him, in fact, that he immediately made plans to begin reading again in London as soon as he returned there.

And before that return? He went once more from Paris to Condette, "touching the sea at Boulogne" as he put it rather vaguely to his daughter, Mamie, in a letter which makes it quite clear that she, at least, did not know about Ellen Ternan or about the chalet. He was away for ten days, on a kind of "tour" which took him to Amiens and Arras, and then just after the middle of February he returned to London. To work. To activity. He proceeded with the London readings which he had already planned, beginning with two a week but eventually cutting them down to a reading each Friday. Then once more he travelled back to France on "anxious business" and he remained as a result "in dull spirits". Back to London where in a speech at the beginning of April he declared, "Depend upon it, the very best among us are often bad company for ourselves (I know I am very often) . . ." Then he was again summoned back to France by "a sick friend". Those biographers who have suggested that the sickness in question was either Ellen Ternan's miscarriage or her pregnancy must explain why it had been continuing now for almost a year. And there is something more to be said on this matter. We have seen how the young women whom he idealised in the past seemed always to be destined, in his eyes, for an early death – as if the image of Mary Hogarth imprinted itself upon their outlines. Ellen's protracted sickness, if such it was (and it should be remembered that in later life she did suffer from prolonged ill-health) would only have had the effect of endearing her more to him, of persuading him to idealise her all the more hopelessly. Then, after this visit to a sick friend, he returned to hear news of Augustus Egg's death. "We must close up the ranks and march on . . ." he told Wilkie Collins, and two weeks later repeated the phrase during a speech on behalf of the Royal Free Hospital. Death and mortality all around him. The first four months of 1863 have in this bare biographical account comprised nothing more than work and sickness, constant travelling and constant anxiety. But anxiety can twist time out of shape. A moment may last a lifetime. Four months in this account, therefore, but of how long a duration to Dickens?

He was still too unsettled to begin work on any novel, anything which would require continuous and regular energy, so instead he began another series of his "Uncommercial Traveller" papers. The first one deals, appropriately enough, with the Channel crossing to France, but it is a journey which seems to induce in him sensations of tremulous anxiety. "The distant dogs of Dover," he writes, "bark at me in my misshapen wrappers, as if I were Richard the Third." And, in this new series of occasional essays, how sombre is the general mood: the Paris Morgue; the memory of an inquest into the death of a child; the churchyards of the City of London churches, among which he wanders on Sunday like "the Last Man"; the memories of lost or unhappy love affairs; the demise of stage-coach days; the shabbiness of London and of its inhabitants; memories of funerals; the dilapidation of alms-houses. On these occasions his language is contemplative, melancholy, resigned. Yet in the company of others he still seemed as gay and cheerful as ever. For the purpose of one "Uncommercial" essay he had visited a ship filled with Mormons about to emigrate, and an acquaintance with him at the time recalled how Dickens ". . . talked and laughed the whole way, and was in great form as we passed through Ratcliffe Highway". This account also reveals another, equally jovial, aspect of his personality. "There was a small boy, who had nothing to do with the Mormons, who was attracted by Dickens in a curious way, and hung about our party on board the ship . . . Dickens was very pleased with him, and he with Dickens." But this same acquaintance goes on to describe how, some time later, ". . . it was almost painful to see his worn looks". There is no discrepancy here. Dickens was a man who was characterised by his laughter and by his high spirits in the company of others, but these do not preclude or pre-empt that anxious and melancholy tone which he had acquired in his childhood and which re-emerged when he was alone; that character which, he had told Forster, he had lost "under happier circumstances" but which had now reappeared. It may not be coincidental, then, that it was in this very period that, for the purpose of a new reading, he began to rehearse from *Oliver Twist* the murder of Nancy by Bill Sikes: a brutal murder in which the woman is bludgeoned to death, and one in which Dickens assumed the roars of Sikes and the shrieks of Nancy, one, in fact, that he considered to be too "horrible" to put before an audience. Indeed he did not do so for another five years, but the seed was there already. Amongst the gloom and the misery, therefore, the acting out of violence *in extremis*. The fire which must burst out, even among the shadows.

There are happier things to record, however, since it was while he remained in London now that he finally healed his breach with Thackeray. Dickens claimed that it was he who made the first move, while he was hanging up his hat in the Athenaeum. He looked up and saw Thackeray's haggard face. "Thackeray," he said, "have you been ill?" And thus, according to Dickens, were they reconciled. A rather more convincing account is given by Sir Theodore Martin who was speaking to Thackeray at the time when Dickens came into the club. He passed close to Thackeray "without making any sign of recognition". Suddenly Thackeray broke away from his conversation, and reached Dickens just as the latter had his foot on the staircase. "Dickens turned to him, and I saw Thackeray speak and presently hold out his hand to Dickens. They shook hands, a few words were exchanged, and immediately Thackeray returned to me saying 'I'm glad I have done this.'" This sounds much more likely to be true than Dickens's self-serving version, particularly in light of the fact that he was notoriously bad at being the first to "make up" in such circumstances. He said once that ". . . quarrelling is very well, but the making up is dreadful", and this was largely the result of his own shrinking sensitivity in emotional matters of this kind. He could not bear even the prospect of being rebuffed, and so he held his peace. In fact Thackeray himself seems to have been prompted in his action by Kate Dickens; he was visiting her and her new husband when in the course of one conversation he said to her, by his own account, "It is ridiculous that your father and I should be placed in a position of enmity towards one another." Kate urged Thackeray "to say a few words . . ." – her father was, she said, "more shy of speaking than you are". And so they were reconciled in a conversation on the staircase of the Athenaeum during the course of which, according to Thackeray, Dickens cried. This is unlikely in such surroundings but, if true, it is only another sign of that generally overwrought condition in which he was now living.

He divided his time between Kent and his London office (since he had been forced to spend so much time in France, he had not rented a London house) but even here, in the midst of his familiar life, he was dreaming of Ellen Ternan; dreaming of her in a red shawl with her back turned towards him. And again he was unwell. For a man who had always prided himself upon the vigour and elasticity of his physical spirit, he had become surprisingly susceptible to all the ills of the flesh. He was also growing tired of London; it was in this period, as the "Uncommercial Traveller", that he was describing the hopeless shabbiness of the city, and he now spent as much time as possible at Gad's Hill Place. There had been occasions in the past when he had discussed with Forster the possibility of renting or even selling that house, but now it had truly become his domain.

So what of this "estate" now, this "little country house", to use two of Dickens's own descriptions? Everyone agreed that it was a very well-appointed and comfortable house, the perfect setting for a writer who had all his life celebrated the virtues of the household hearth. Many visitors (as well as relatives) have described some of its more notable characteristics; the scarlet geraniums, Dickens's favourite flower, in the beds in the front garden; the library with its false bookcases and with Dickens's desk in front of three large windows which overlooked the lawns; the neatness of that desk with its usual carefully arranged quill, ink bottle, pencil, india-rubber, pin cushion, and date-calendar; the billiard room and its green-and-white tiles; the conservatory built on to the dining room; the modest drawing room; the guest bedrooms with everything laid out for neatness and comfort; the walled croquet garden and children's schoolroom he had constructed; and everywhere the mirrors which Dickens loved, and which were so much part of his character that after his death the looking-glass panels in the dining room gave to his infant granddaughter ". . . quite an eerie sense of realisation of the life that had been . . ." As if she might have seen, if she had looked closely into those bright surrounding mirrors, the faces and clothes of an age that had gone, the ordinary conversation and laughter of the man who had recreated that age in his fiction, the man who died in that very room. Died surrounded by mirrors.

It is only to be expected that there was a routine to life at Gad's Hill Place. Breakfast at eight, when Dickens had his usual rasher of broiled ham; then a walk around the house and grounds to make sure that everything was in perfect order – Mamie recalled how he ". . . invented all sorts of neat and clever contrivances, and was never happier than when going about the house with a hammer and nails doing some wonderful piece of carpentering . . ."; then the answering of correspondence immediately after his "rounds"; work until one, or sometimes even three if he decided to forgo lunch; lunch (bread and cheese and perhaps a glass of ale); then his long walk or "tramp" or "blow" accompanied by the two dogs, Linda and Turk, who padded behind him; dinner at six or six-thirty, beginning with a glass of Chichester milk-punch and ending with a dish of toasted cheese; and then an evening of reading or music when Mamie might play Mendelssohn or the music of popular ballads on the pianoforte. Dickens smoked a cigar after dinner, strolled around the gardens in the early evening or sometimes, as one of his children remembered, "paced up and down the room". At midnight he always retired.

Of course he was well-known in the neighbourhood for his afternoon walks – sometimes into Rochester to pick up his mail, sometimes to Chalk or to Cooling marshes, sometimes to Shorn and Cobham, sometimes past his boyhood home of Chatham to the Lines. It was inevitable, then, that local legends came to associate him with a variety of places and houses; the room he slept in, the garden gate against which he leaned, the inns he visited, all in due course becoming objects of pilgrimage for the curious. It is in fact something of a pleasure to read topographical accounts of "Dickensland", principally the areas of Rochester and Chatham, the items of its landscape neatly fitting into place and creating a half-real, half-fictional world which seems to be perpetually the same and perpetually welcoming.

Sometimes his children accompanied him on his walks, although he was generally silent for the twelve miles which remained his daily average. Henry Dickens recalled that "I have accompanied him through the *Great Expectations* country; I have stood by his side in the churchyard where Pip was turned upside down by the convict; I have looked down with him upon the tombstone of 'Pirrip', also 'Georgiana, wife of the Above'; we have wandered together over the marsh country down by the river – that dark, flat wilderness, as he described it – without a word being exchanged between us". He was a familiar sight. One local remembered that he was ". . . quick in all his movements, walked fast, and had a sharp glancing eye noting everything around . . .", although in later life the same observer noticed that Dickens ". . . appeared greatly to have lost his old vivacity, and his face was lined, rugged and careworn, and apparently he took little notice of his surroundings". But this is to anticipate the end of this history. The postmaster at Rochester recalled him ". . . when walking by himself and unobserved, apparently acting some character, as you could see his face in constant motion. He always was theatrically dressed . . ." He was so famous that some people dogged his footsteps or hastened around another corner to get a better look at him (this was always happening in London, too, where people would actually run ahead, turn around and then walk past him very slowly and casually). It was observed that he walked quickly, that he tended to walk in the middle of the road, that he carried a small dog-whip (which he never used), that ". . . he held his head high up when he walked and went at a great pace", that he "always passed the time of day" but that sometimes he would simply nod cheerfully rather than say "good day", that he liked to speak to children, that he dressed ". . . more like a jockey than a *littérateur*". He sometime stopped for "refreshment" at the Crispin and Crispianus, an inn just outside Strood, and the landlady remembered him to be ". . . habited in low shoes not over-well mended, loose large check-patterned trousers that sometimes got entangled in the shoes when walking, a brown coat thrown open, sometimes without waistcoat, a belt instead of braces, a necktie which now and then got round towards his ear and a large-brimmed felt hat, similar to an American's, set well at the back of his head. In his hand he carried by the middle an umbrella, which he was in the habit of constantly swinging, and if he had dogs (a not unfrequent occurrence), he had a small whip as well". When he entered the public house for a glass of ale or a little cold brandy-and-water, ". . . he walked straight in, and sat down at the corner of the settle on the right hand side . . . he rarely spoke to any one but looked around as though taking in everything at a glance . . ." He did not precisely fit in with country life, therefore, and, as his son made clear, ". . . he never took at all to what most people understand by a country life . . . he never acquired, or cared, I think, to acquire the accurate knowledge of country sights and sounds . . ." which belongs to the countryman. It was recalled, too, that he did not often mix with his country neighbours, and no doubt this was principally because he did not want to get inveigled into the round of dinner-party engagements and other various social occasions which the richer and more respectable of them would have expected of him. But he did take a particular interest in the tramps who haunted the dusty roads of Kent, and would often stop to speak to them; they sometimes returned the compliment by being interested in him, and Dickens himself recalled one occasion when he was sitting in the garden and a tramp looked over the wall at him, muttering, "Ugly lazy devil, *he* never did a day's work in his life!"

Of course he had some connection with the people around him, even if it was generally in a managerial capacity. He acted as scorer, for example, during the annual cricket match between Gad's Hill Place and the local villagers. One contemporary remembered ". . . him in his white jean coat, and his grey hat set a little on one side, his double glasses on, going conscientiously through his work: scoring down 'byes', and 'overs', and 'runs'; at times cheering an indifferent 'hit' with an encouraging 'Well run! Well run!' " There were also foot-races and various other games but at the end it was always Dickens who made a speech and gave out the prizes to the winning contestants. Not the squire of the village, of course, but certainly the next best thing. One incident is worth recalling: at one of these cricket matches a Sergeant of the Guards walked up to Dickens and asked, "May I look at you, Sir?"

"Oh yes!" – just what Dickens would say, quickly and without thought. But he was "blushing up to the eyes".

One of his early chroniclers can finish the story. "The Sergeant gazed intensely at him for a minute or so, then stood at attention, gave the military salute, and said 'God bless you, sir!' He then walked off, and was seen no more."

The cricket matches, and other items of local interest, were recorded in the *Gad's Hill Gazette*, a small newspaper written and published by Dickens's sons, and therefore available only in the summer and Christmas holidays. It was at first handwritten and then "run off" but the last of the editors, Henry, was given a proper printing set by Wills and from then on produced the little newspaper in methodical fashion. Henry even wrote a poem or two for its pages but it was characteristic of his father that, when the boy sent one to *All The Year Round*, Dickens ". . . made it quite clear to me in suitable language that I was not destined to become a great poet and had better stick to things mundane, like the study of the law". Which, of course, is what he did. But he was a respectable amateur journalist in the days of the *Gad's Hill Gazette*. "Miss Dickens and Mrs Collins went to London, this morning (Friday) and are to return this evening, accompanied by M Stone Esqre. Ch Dickens Esqre left on Wednesday . . . We are glad to inform our readers that Linda is much better . . . We are very sorry to have to inform our readers that Mr C Dickens has been suffering from neuralgia, during the past week; he is better now, though still not quite well."

There were his own children around him at Gad's Hill Place, but soon there were also grandchildren – no less than six of them before his death, the offspring of his son, Charley, and Bessie Dickens, née Evans. Dickens, who had an aversion to the process of ageing, did not care to be addressed by them as "Grandfather", however; so he was always called "Venerables" instead. Kate Dickens remembered her father escorting two of them on a tour of the house – and how they talked merrily to each other as Dickens pointed out the various attractions of the place, how Dickens took his grandson into his arms when the child grew tired and how the three of them then sat on a seat beneath the great mulberry tree while ". . . the little boy dreamed his dreams – and my father, no doubt, dreamed his . . ." One of these children was Mary Angela, the first of his grandchildren, and even in later life Dickens seems to have haunted her imagination. "If I were to reproduce pictorially the old Gad's Hill scenes," she wrote, ". . . I think I should inevitably surround the figure of 'Venerables' with a coloured light, or a peculiar line of isolation." When playing in the garden, at a time when her grandfather was writing, she felt a ". . . vague sense of dread, only to be described as 'creepy' . . ." There were other memories of hers which seem pervaded by a similar mood; of a time, for example, in the drawing room where there is ". . . a tall stand of flowers, too, in the corner beyond the window and the door, and close to it a group of men in evening dress. Somebody is late for dinner and, I think, even the small observer in the muslim pinafore has a notion that 'Venerables' does not like people to be late. But

'Venerables' himself seems to be wholly unconcerned. He is laughing and talking at a great rate, there, by the stand of flowers." What a strange picture, this, the little girl perceiving the unease or anger beneath Dickens's convivial laughter. There was a time, too, in the dining room. Or, rather, a moment out of time – a roaring fire, a view from the windows of the garden covered in snow, and "my grand-father, handsome, alert, but for the moment a little at a loss, looks down at me. I, a very small girl in a pinafore look up at him. And I am afraid . . ." And her memory, too, of Dickens reading *A Christmas Carol* in St James's Hall. ". . . I count among the most dreadful moment of my childish existence the moment when 'Venerables' cried." But there are happier memories of Dickens and of Gad's Hill Place – "I can see the figure at the head of the table standing with his glass in his hand, alert, laughing, full of the zest of the moment . . ."

The servants and tradesmen at Gad's Hill Place provide information of a more specific but no less intriguing kind; how Dickens liked to bathe in cold water in the mornings; how he read *The Times* every day; how he never wore a nightcap; how he carried a Gladstone bag with him on his travels; how he autographed his bottles of wine; how he was a good carpenter and "handyman"; how he hated to be called "Sir"; how his favourite colour was light orange; how he preferred cold, bright weather; how he had a mania for opening windows to the fresh air; how he kept his own books neatly in a row, in the order of their publication; how he wrote out instructions to the servants about their various duties; how he loved candle-light; how the flag was hoisted above the house when he was in residence. Those who worked for him also recalled how kind and considerate he was (perhaps not surprising in a man whose paternal grandparents had also been servants); when they left his service, he would give them a photograph of himself with his name signed on the back. No servant was allowed into his study, however, which was "sacred", with the door locked when he was not occupying it; nevertheless it was always "the perfection of neatness". At times, then, he might have seemed rather forbidding. On one occasion a new parlour-maid noticed a man looking intently at her and, when she reported this downstairs, she was told that it was the "master" and that "he was reading your character . . . he now knows you thoroughly". The tradesmen re-membered him as being very precise and methodical; in particular, he insisted always upon absolute punctuality. He was not very talkative, either, and some thought him "rather masterful". One of his earlier biographers has narrated the story of his believing the water from his well to be polluted and how, when the well-sinkers told him that the water was pure, he refused to believe them. He even called in the Rochester road-foreman, who then hit upon the idea of picking up a dead cat from somewhere else, deluging it in water, and then presenting it to Dickens as the offending object. Dickens was highly satisfied by the discovery, and never complained again about his supply. A neat little story, but not for that reason necessarily to be disbelieved. Another local, a Mr Acworth of Rochester, left his own memorial: Dickens's "appearance was always very neat and prim, as if he had just come out of a band box," he said. And he related Dickens's odd system of giving tickets to tradesmen who then exchanged them for drink at the Falstaff Inn opposite the house, ". . . the tickets being graded in value according to the age and standing of the individual". This, in its way, is a typical piece of Dickensian "business".

The guests of Dickens have left their own accounts, too, of life at Gad's Hill Place. The routine of the house was much the same, with the difference that he was rather more visible to his guests than he was to his family. He took his meals with them, and was unfailingly courteous and cheerful even when (as sometimes happened at breakfast) he was clearly anxious to get on with his own work; many guests commented, too, upon the strange paradox of complete domestic comfort with the relative invisibility of servants. Their rooms had comfortable beds, generally with a sofa and the cane-bottom chairs which Dickens preferred (this preference no doubt the result of the operation to remove his fistula in 1841), as well as a writing-table, paper, quill pen and small library of books. He also installed a kettle with cup, saucer, milk and tea so that the guests could make their own beverages. In the afternoons, after he had completed his work for the day, he might take them out to participate in various games. He was not himself particularly "sporty", possessing more nervous energy than physical energy (although he did enjoy rowing on the Thames and had a certain fascination for the then rather bloody art of boxing), but on the lawns of Gad's Hill Place he played battledore or shuttlecock and occasionally, even though he detested the game, croquet. But, more often than not, he would take his guests on various walks and excursions in the immediate neighbourhood. The walks of course were rather an ordeal for those who were not used to the kind of exercise which Dickens habitually took – twelve miles in two and a half hours, with only a five-minute break. But these were not the silent marches upon which he was sometimes accompanied by his children; as Edmund Yates recalled, Dickens could be tempted into speaking about his own work, ". . . to tell how and why certain ideas occurred to him, and how he got such a scene or character. Generally his excellent memory accurately retained his own phrases and actual words, so that he would at once correct a misquotation . . ." There were the walks to Cooling and Shorne and Cobham; in particular Dickens liked to point out the stile in Cobham Park near which the painter, Richard Dadd, had killed his father in 1843. "Dickens," one guest remembered, "acted the whole scene with his usual dramatic force . . ." Sometimes he would take out the basket-carriage (it had jingling bells on it, brought to him from Norway by a friend) which was drawn by the horse known as Newman Noggs through the hop-gardens and the cornfields of the region; sometimes, too, he took out his Irish jaunting car and, on at least one occasion, in the last year of his life, he hired two post-carriages with postillions in old-fashioned red jackets and breeches: a scene that might have come out of *The Pickwick Papers* or *Nicholas Nickleby*, and one that suggests that Dickens knew precisely how to be "Dickensian" when he chose. And of course there were the excursions to Rochester Castle; to Maidstone; to Canterbury and its cathedral where, one American guest recalled, "Dickens, with tireless observation, noted how sleepy and inane were the faces of many of the singers . . ."; to Cooling churchyard with its lozenge-shaped graves immortalised in the opening scene of *Great Expectations*.

It was in this last place that something of Dickens's vivacity can be evoked in an incident one summer's day. As James Fields, the American publisher, recalled, Dickens "had chosen a good flat gravestone in one corner . . . had spread a wide napkin thereon after the fashion of a domestic dinner-table, and was rapidly transferring the contents of the hamper to that point. The horrible whimsicality of trying to eat and make merry under these deplorable circumstances, the tragic-comic character of the scene, appeared to take him by surprise. He at once threw himself into it . . . with fantastic eagerness. Having spread the table after the most approved style, he suddenly disappeared behind the wall for a moment, transformed himself by the aid of a towel and napkin into a first-class head-waiter, reappeared, laid down a row of plates along the top of the wall, as at a bar-room or eating house, again retreated to the other side with some provisions, and, making the gentlemen stand up to the wall, went through the whole play with the most entire gravity." It conjures up what Dickens would have called a "picture" – the church on the edge of the wild marshes, a few cottages and a decayed rectory beside it, the distant sea-line, the tall grasses of the marshes with the wind going through them. And here is Dickens, who had so often mimicked the tones of the waiter in his fiction, going through this "routine" by the very graves of the children of Cooling. If it is reminiscent of anything, it is of the scene in *The Old Curiosity Shop* where Little Nell and her grandfather come across the image of Punch perched cross-legged upon a tombstone. It is quintessential Dickens, in fact, this wild humour in a melancholy landscape. Which is then followed by his benevolence. He saw two tramps watching them eat, and at once offered them wine and food, but saying first to the ladies, "*You* shall carry it to them, it will be less like a charity and more like a kindness if one of you should speak to the poor souls!" At the end of this feast he would have done what he did on all such picnics – on another occasion, for example, "Dickens would not let us start again until every vestige of our visit to the wood in the shape of lobster shells and other *débris* had been removed". And then, after the party had returned from Cooling churchyard, "Dickens played longer and harder than any one of the company."

Of course there were some guests who found Dickens's particular form of relaxation very exhausting, and one visitor some years later recalled life at Gad's Hill Place for Dickens's journalistic colleagues. "Everybody must work at something from 10 to 2 like the host – Sala used to take down an old bundle of proofs and make believe correct them . . . Poor Wilkie Collins who needs rest used to sneak off to the library and go to sleep with a cigar. Dickens pried him out and said, 'None of this. No smoking in the library in the daytime – you must work at something.'" There follows a description of the usual afternoon walk "and woe to the laggards"; then dinner, billiards, charades, and at ten o'clock the visit to the smoking room "where you must drink more gin punch than was good for you". (Dickens, like his father, prided himself on his ability to mix that concoction.)

But these were his junior colleagues, his "young men", with whom he did not necessarily have to observe all the social niceties. With those he knew less well, or with whom he was on quite different terms, the effect was different. One guest noticed how at dinner ". . . his vivacity never flagged, nor was it for one person alone. He appeared to hear what every one at the table said and turned from one end of it to the other with the utmost rapidity . . . without seeming to make any effort or ever talking in loud boisterous tones." After dinner it was the same, and "very soon Dickens moved off to talk to the little lady who was too shy to play, but whom he evidently managed to set at her ease . . ." He was also a very generous host. One menu for dinner at Gad's Hill Place has survived, in the handwriting of Georgina Hogarth, and it provides one more indication of the dining habits of the period in general and of Dickens in particular – with its clear soup and Palestine soup, soles with herbs and cod-oyster sauce, chicken with spinach, sweetbreads with peas and truffles, beef gravy, saddle of mutton, pheasants with oysters, ginger pudding, mince pies, pudding of orange jelly, fondu, apricot cream ice and orange water ice. In the evening, after dinner, there were games like whist or vingt-et-un, guessing games like "Yes and No" by which the name of an object was discovered by interrogating one person; Dickens was adept at such things and on one occasion managed somehow to guess, by questioning Charles Collins, that the object Collins had in mind was "the top boot of the left leg of the head post-boy at Newman's Yard, London . . ." Charades were sometimes played; an American guest remembered Dickens appearing with a black handkerchief on his head and a fire shovel, as an axe, in order to mimic the beheading of Charles I. Wilkie Collins was the victim. There were also memory games which, his son said, Dickens ". . . played as if his life depended on his success"; Percy Fitzgerald remembered how, in such games, Dickens "forced" his way to a solution. There was often music in the drawing room after dinner – Dickens had a particular affection for George Linley's ballad, "Little Nell", as we have seen, but he also enjoyed the Lieder of Mendelssohn as well as the music of Chopin and Mozart. And on occasions, too, there was dancing. Dickens himself was not a particularly good dancer but when others did the Sir Roger de Coverley his daughter, Mamie, recalled how "he would insist upon the sides keeping up a kind of jig step, and clapping his hands to add to the fun, and dancing at the backs of those whose enthusiasm he thought needed rousing, was himself never still for a moment until the dance was over". Sometimes he did an impromptu dance of his own, however, and during one game of charades executed a sailor's horn-pipe (which has some claim to being his favourite step). After dancing and games, there might be billiards; Dickens liked contests of this kind for, he used to say, "it brings out the mettle". Percy Fitzgerald had a memory of him ". . . stooping over the table, his coat off, his large double glasses on – which gave him rather an antique, 'old-mannish' look". He always retired at twelve and, at the end of the day, he would tell one of his sons (or his most intimate male guest) "to see the gas out all right" and take care of the keys of the sideboard until morning.

There are many anecdotes of him in this period of his life at Gad's Hill Place. How, for example, he had a detestation of bats which sometimes used to fly into the house and how on one occasion, as Henry recalled, Dickens put a hip-bath on his head as protection before climbing a ladder to get at a bat nestling in a corner. But the hip-bath began to wobble as he mounted the ladder and, while standing on the steps, "he burst into a fit of uncontrollable laughter" at his ridiculous appearance; how he would speak to each of his pets in a different voice, how one kitten would follow him everywhere and sit with him while he was writing; how he had a "double" in Chatham, a Mr John Baird, who was often mistaken for the novelist and how on one occasion Dickens "walked up to him and shook hands, cordially, without the usual ceremony of introduction"; how he was seen in a railway carriage, going up to town from Higham station, ". . . sitting quietly in a corner. It was at the time that one of his serial novels was appearing, and most of the passengers were reading the current monthly number. No one noticed Dickens . . ." In these anecdotes and scenes the man comes before us again as once he was, the real Charles Dickens rising up to greet us as we follow his story to the end.

Chapter 31

THE summer of 1863 was as unsettled as the spring. He went back once more to France in August, but had returned to Gad's Hill Place by the end of the month, with two projects now firmly on his mind; one was the Christmas issue of *All The Year Round*, the writing of which had become part of his settled routine, and the other was the novel which he had been contemplating for at least the previous two years. Now, at last, he thought he was ready to begin; he wrote to Chapman and Hall in order to fix the appropriate terms for what would be his first long novel for seven years; he wanted six thousand pounds for half the copyright, and he got it. He was so eager to begin now that nothing really could stop him, not even the deaths of those around him. He had once said that to live through middle-age was to walk through a kind of cemetery, and so it was to prove in this last half of the year. His hated mother-in-law, Mrs Hogarth, died in August but this was of no real interest to Dickens; he sent a very curt note to Catherine about her rights to the grave where Mary Hogarth was buried. And then in September his own mother died – not a moment too soon, Dickens seems to have felt, since for some time she had been in a state of bodily and mental decay. She had been living with her daughter-in-law, Helen, in a house at Grafton Terrace (for which Dickens paid), and it was here that he had occasionally visited her, in her "fearful state". But there are no real signs of loss or grief in Dickens's response to her death; certainly nothing remotely comparable to the bleakness which had descended upon him after the death of his father. But, if there was no explicit or even conscious grief on Dickens's part, something close to sorrow emerges in the work upon which he was now engaged. Mrs Dickens was buried on a Thursday at Highgate Cemetery, next to her husband, and only three days before Dickens had begun that year's Christmas story with the portrait of a garrulous female, Mrs Lirriper, who seems not unlike the mother whom he was about to bury. But there is a difference now; Mrs Lirriper, far from being one of the silly women so characteristic in his fiction, is, despite her tendency to talk, a kindly and sensible old party. Surely it is possible to see in this contemporaneous portrait some kind of oblique, posthumous tribute to Mrs Dickens which her son could not give her in her lifetime? He had been too close to her, and she had wounded him too much, for any such emotional openness in his life; but, in his art, and after her death, she lives again as a good and decent woman. In the story, too, she has a male lodger, Major Jemmy Jackman, who is not unlike John Dickens in speech: "I esteem it a proud privilege to go down to posterity through the instrumentality of the most remarkable boy that ever lived . . ." This might have been John Dickens talking about his son, Charles, but this "remarkable boy" is a young orphan whom Mrs Lirriper and Major Jackman bring up. Just the three of them – a mother not a mother and a father not a father, with one male orphan; almost a holy family, one might say, but a holy family of Dickens's imagination. This is how it might have been, no siblings, no distractions, no real parents, with the extraordinary power of Dickens's fantasy lending this fable its strength. And, although there were other stories and contributions to this Christmas issue, it was his presentation of Mrs Lirriper – the entire story is entitled "Mrs Lirriper's Lodgings" – which characterised the number and which accounted for its extraordinary success. It sold more than two hundred thousand copies and was, in every sense, the most popular thing he had written since *A Christmas Carol*. Everywhere he turned, he said, he found the same enormous enthusiasm for his creation of the benevolent lodging-housekeeper; one of his earliest biographers has also recorded the "immense *furore*" which the story created. Dickens's office boy at this time, William Edrupt, recalled the sensation, and added that "the street in front of the office was crowded with folks . . . I loved all his successes, though I don't think he cared anything about them so long as his work was done." This is not altogether true, of course, and there are times when Edrupt's memory fails him altogether. But he does provide incidental details which are valuable for any view of Dickens's less august behaviour as an editor in this period; how he used to ask Edrupt to purchase for him ices "of which he ate considerable"; how he ". . . lived a lot by his nose. He seemed to be always smelling things . . ."; how he would sometimes dip his head into a bucket of cold water and then dry himself with a towel; how Edrupt was never allowed to sharpen the quill with which Dickens wrote; how his memory was so good that after he had heard an address only once "he could name the street and number" more than a week later; how he was always prompt and how he would scold Edrupt for being late; and how sometimes they would talk. When Dickens asked him if he had read anything of his, Edrupt always replied, " 'No, Sir' . . . he would slap me on the back and laugh every time". In fact it is mainly the laughter that Edrupt remembers – "Mr Dickens threw back his head and laughed and laughed . . ." – and at this time of anxious misery for Dickens it is remarkable how funny "Mrs Lirriper's Lodgings" is, and how close to the comedy of his earliest novels. It has often been said that Dickens was now well into his "dark period" or his "bleak period" as a novelist; but all the evidence suggests that he had lost not one jot of his former humour, and that indeed in some ways he had improved upon it.

Yet we have seen how, at Cooling, Dickens could laugh in a graveyard and in the same period as he was writing "Mrs Lirriper's Lodgings" he was preoccupied with his own miseries. ". . . my heart faints sometimes under such troubles as I do know," he told Charles Lever in the November of this year, "and if it were not for a certain stand-up determination, I should be down. 'Who is hit?' Nelson said, without looking round, when they shot his Secretary. 'I am hit,' ten thousand of us may cry at once instead, 'in a mortal place, but our rest is before us, and we will work our way to it.' " There is an intimation here of the desire for death on Dickens's part, and it is significant that he was writing this even as he was working upon the early chapters of the new novel, a novel in which he could already see his "opening perfectly"; an opening on the banks of the Thames, a river which had once seemed to him to be a very "image of death". He was already "closely occupied" upon his narrative when there were more deaths. Thackeray died suddenly on the Christmas Eve of that year. One might invoke here Dickens's words to William Edrupt on the ending of one of his stories, ". . . *they all die sooner or later.*" Augustus Egg dead. His mother dead. Now Thackeray. They all die in the end. Dickens attended Thackeray's funeral and as he stood at the graveside he ". . . had a look of bereavement in his face which was indescribable. When all others had turned aside from the grave he still stood there, as if rooted to the spot, watching with almost haggard eyes every spadeful of dust that was thrown upon it. Walking away with some friends, he began to talk, but presently in some sentence his voice quivered a little, and shaking hands all round rapidly he went off alone." Was he thinking also of his own death as he watched the dirt being thrown upon the novelist's coffin? And how strange that, at this funeral, he wore not the customary clothes of mourning but "trousers of a check pattern, a waistcoat of some coloured plaid and an open frock-coat". It is reminiscent of the scene at Cooling churchyard.

On the last night of what had been for him an anguished year he played charades at Gad's Hill Place with his guests; they had to guess, among others, his rendition of The Pathetic History of the Poor Little Sweep, Mussulman Barbarity to Christians, and Merry England. One of his props for this game was placed against the wall of his bedroom and, when he noticed that it looked like one of "the dismal things that are carried at Funerals", he quickly cut off the black calico draped around it. On retiring to bed that night he saw that the prop was still in his room, and that its shadow still kept its resemblance to a funereal pike. That same evening, at a quarter past five, his son Walter fell dead in Calcutta with a gush of blood from his mouth. More death. Walter left nothing behind, only a little trunk which contained some changes of linen, some prayer books, and the photograph of "a woman believed to be a member of the family". Could that have been a photograph of his mother, Catherine, living alone in Gloucester Crescent? A friend later recalled that she was "in great grief" at the death of her son. Her estranged husband sent out to India an inscription for the boy's tomb, but he sent not one word of condolence to Catherine herself. Death and gloom and estrangement everywhere around him.

And what of the novel being written all through this time? He had decided to call it *Our Mutual Friend*. He had begun it in November, as we have seen, and he already had the "main line" of the story in front of him; now, after more than two years of attempting to write, he was desperately eager to carry on with it in case he lost the impetus or became in any other way unsettled and distracted. Certain characters and themes had stayed with him for a long time; he had jotted down notes for the character known as Podsnap as early as 1855, and the title itself was one of those stray phrases which seemed to lodge in his memory like a talisman. It occurs in truncated form on at least three occasions in *Little Dorrit* – ". . . very proper expression mutual friend", as Flora Finching says. But, more importantly, the themes and emblems of the book can be traced much further back; for, in *Our Mutual Friend*, the songs of his childhood re-occur in almost hallucinatory state as the wooden-legged Silas Wegg recites the words of a sentimental ballad, "The Light Guitar", which Dickens learned as a child and which he had quoted almost thirty years before in his first published volume.

> "And if my tale (which I hope Mr Boffin might excuse) should make you sigh.
> I'll strike the light guitar."

Wegg also misquotes, among others, Tom Moore's famous "Eveleen's Bower" – "Oh! weep for the hour . . ." – and Alexander Lee's "The Soldier's Tear". The music and words of Dickens's infancy thus ascend into the air of Sixties London, in a novel which itself aspires towards a kind of timelessness. There is another principal source, too, although it is one which Dickens may well have scanned just once some fourteen years before; an article by R. H. Horne in *Household Words* of 13 July, 1850, "Dust; or Ugliness Redeemed", contains in inchoate form many of the principal elements which emerge in *Our Mutual Friend* itself. Here, too, there is a dust heap which contains marvels; a one-legged man who sifts through it with two companions (one of whom is named Gaffer, like Gaffer Hexam of Dickens's novel, and the other with "poor withered legs" like Jenny Wren); a drowned man restored to life. All these elements combine together in *Our Mutual Friend* but, perhaps more importantly, even the short journalistic essay contains the seeds of Dickens's vision; for in Horne's account the dust heap can act as a place of resurrection, the cinders used as some kind of restorative, and in that place of filth and decay each of the three dust-contractors sees visions of redemption and eternity.

So this essay may properly be seen at the catalyst which brought together for Dickens all the wealth of his reading and of his observation. It attracted all those strange dreams of antiquity and modernity which he had chronicled in "Down With The Tide", an essay about London with its vision of "mummy-dust" and "dry atoms from the Temple at Jerusalem" being blown across the Thames which itself is ". . . such an image of death in the midst of the great city's life . . ." It catalysed, too, the sights he had depicted in another essay, "Wapping Workhouse"; the posters proclaiming the discovery of drowned men, and the sight of a young man, alive, but "all dirty and shiny and slimy, who may have been the youngest son of his filthy old father, Thames . . ." Images of death by drowning. Of ancient dust. Of the old river god. Ancient myth and modern urban life co-exist and interpenetrate. Dust. The river. Mud. Out of which springs life. Ash. From which life rises like the fabulous bird. These images are particularly potent in *Our Mutual Friend*, since the ash and dirt of London are thus placed within a perennial myth of death and rebirth. It is one of the strangest components of Dickens's imagination, always present as a consistent low note in his accounts of the "Great Oven" but only in his later years coming to the surface as a persistent, almost obsessive, preoccupation with death and its aftermath. And how appropriate, too, that it is now he hears once again the songs of his childhood.

The permanence of his childhood vision of London, overlaying the modern metropolis, is one that has already been explored in these pages; but it is not the whole truth. If this was a man who could glance once at a row of shops and remember the details of every one, how could he do otherwise than instantaneously recognise and understand the contemporary life around him? Not just the filth and wretchedness which persisted in London through the years of reconstruction – Hippolyte Taine said of Shadwell in this decade, "I have seen the lower quarters of Marseilles, Antwerp and Paris: they come nowhere near this." But Dickens sensed and recognised something else as well; he sensed in the change of London a change in the nature of civilisation itself. A civilisation that he anatomised in *Our Mutual Friend* with the Veneerings and the Podsnaps. Speculation. Peculation. Overseas investment. Short-term money markets. Brokering. Joint stock banking. Discount companies. Limited liability. Credit. A world in which human identity was seen in terms of monetary value. A world of barter and exchange. And thus, in the houses of the middle-class and upper middle-class, the fake "marbling". Veneer. Imitation wood. Chinoiserie. Exaggerated ornamentation. Blankets of fabric. Stifled silent rooms. Death. Gold. Filth. This is the world of his last completed novel.

As soon as he had the "main line" of the story he worked upon it closely and continuously. He knew from the beginning how the story was slowly to be divulged, his suggestions for each instalment in his working notes closely following the writing of the one before, his memoranda emphasising how sustained and unified a design he had in mind – "lay the ground carefully . . . *This to go through the book* . . . clear the ground, behind and before . . . Lead on carefully . . ." Sometimes his notes to himself in the course of the composition mention just a name, or a place, as if the whole vast panorama were ready to unfurl in his mind at the smallest hint. Yet he was writing much more slowly than before, the style of the narrative so much more elaborate, the conversations reading in part like ritualised drama; his handwriting is small now, sloping downwards to the right, with many additions and emendations. He even told Wilkie Collins that the effort of going back to the large scale of twenty monthly numbers, after the serials in *All The Year Round*, left him "quite dazed".

It is almost as if he were starting again, starting something in quite a new vein, and this sensation of novelty was emphasised by the fact that he was now working with Marcus Stone rather than Hablot Browne as illustrator. He had dropped Browne abruptly and the illustrator, an innocent, shy and unworldly man, never really understood the reasons for Dickens's decision: ". . . lately (Authors and Artists will sometimes squabble) I have not been on very good terms with him . . ." he had said before their separation and, after the event, he told his partner, "I don't know what's up any more than you do . . . Dickens probably thinks a new hand would give his old puppets a fresh look . . . Confound all authors and publishers, say I; there is no pleasing or satisfying one or t'other. I wish I had never had anything to do with the lot." It seems likely, as we have seen, that Dickens decided to dispense with Browne's services after the illustrator had started working for *Once A Week*, the periodical published by Dickens's rivals and enemies, Bradbury and Evans; but this is only speculation. The effect, however, was to end a partnership which had lasted almost thirty years and which had encompassed novels as different as *The Pickwick Papers* and *Little Dorrit*. Despite Browne's relatively mild words it seems that he was mortally wounded by the publication of *Our Mutual Friend* with the illustrations of another artist, and his work sadly deteriorated after this time. It would be unfair, however, to blame Dickens's decision entirely upon spite or even pique. Browne's surmise that the novelist wanted a "fresh look" for his "puppets" is also probably true; certainly his own work for Dickens had been falling off, and his illustrations for *A Tale of Two Cities* were woefully sketchy and undramatic. He had also been appearing in many different places, which cannot have helped him concentrate upon his Dickensian contributions. The really important fact remains, however, that the particular symbiotic relationship between writer and artist had now disappeared; Dickens no longer needed Browne to give visual strength to his imaginative conceptions, and Browne had ceased to develop and enlarge his range in response to Dickens's own progress as an artist. A separation was, in that sense at least, understandable.

Marcus Stone was younger and fresher than Hablot Browne, but by no means so good an artist. After the death of his father, Frank Stone, Dickens had taken the young man "in hand" and had already been responsible for several large commissions for so young (and, it has to be admitted, relatively untalented) an artist. He suggested his name to friendly publishers as an "admirable draughtsman" and commissioned him to provide woodcuts for the Library Edition of *Great Expectations* and *Pictures from Italy*. He also designed the frontispiece for the Cheap Edition of *A Tale of Two Cities* in the same year that he started work on *Our Mutual Friend*. Dickens wanted a new "look" for his first serial novel in seven years and, indeed, Stone's illustrations lent a quite different aspect to the text. His work was much more contemporary and much more fashionable – more "modern", in a word. He was a member of a younger generation who no longer paid their obeisances to Hogarth; he was "correct", naturalistic and sentimental where Browne had been vivid, emblematic and grotesque. Stone worked in wood where Browne had worked in steel, and this not only in a technical sense. There are no Squeerses or Scrooges in the work of the younger artist, only men in Sixties dress and ladies in the bonnets and skirts of the same period. But Dickens had moved on, too, and Stone was in some ways a more appropriate artist for a story which, in Dickens's own words, provided a "combination of drollery with romance". If there are times when Stone's drawings anticipate the illustrations in the *Strand* magazine at the end of the century, there are also occasions in *Our Mutual Friend* when the conversation of Eugene Wrayburn might have come from a drama by Oscar Wilde.

Stone designed the cover of the monthly parts after seeing only the first two numbers and, although Dickens had specific corrections to make to it, he seemed altogether pleased by the result. "Give a vague idea, the more vague the better," he told the young man, and Dickens was for once himself quite vague. When Stone asked him which of Silas Wegg's legs was wooden, for example, he did not know, "I do not think I had identified the leg." Stone also quotes him as saying, on the subject, "It's all right – please yourself." This in turn suggests that Dickens himself was less interested in the illustrations to his work, perhaps because he realised that they were no longer as necessary to his design as once they had been. In fact the story of his collaboration with

Stone over these months indicates a certain decline of enthusiasm and concern. At first he gave him specific instructions, but soon he permitted him his own choice of good "moments". Then, towards the end of the serialisation, Dickens allowed Stone to choose and illustrate whatever subjects he liked best, scarcely bothering to raise any objection. But this is to anticipate the entire composition of *Our Mutual Friend*. By the third week of January 1864, he had just written the first two instalments, and at once he started work upon the third, his assiduity largely a result of the fact that he wanted to have five numbers in hand before he began publication. A large amount, perhaps, but he realised that he was now working much more slowly than before, and that he could not automatically rely upon that old exuberant inventiveness which had always brought him up to the deadline with enough material. In addition he was about to rent another London house for the "season", which in its turn would cause further interruptions.

It was while he was looking for a house, at the beginning of February, that the news arrived of Walter's death in India; he did not tell Georgina of the proximate cause of his son's sudden collapse, because it turned out that he had been suffering from precisely the same "aneurism of the aorta" which afflicted Georgina herself. He was distressed, but not exactly prostrated with grief, and in any event went ahead with the renting of 57 Gloucester Place just north of Hyde Park. It was here that he was to settle until June, and it was here in February that he worked on the third number of *Our Mutual Friend*. The last chapter of the previous instalment had turned out to be too long to be used, and it was while Dickens was contemplating a fresh subject to fill the gap that Marcus Stone arrived with news which was to change the entire narrative. Stone had been looking for a stuffed dog to act as a model and had in the course of his enquiries come across a certain Willis, a taxidermist whose shop was in St Andrew's Street near Seven Dials. Stone had already heard Dickens say that he needed to find a peculiar avocation for *Our Mutual Friend* – "it must be something very striking and unusual," he said to him one night in a theatre they were visiting – and, as soon as he had found the taxidermist, Stone went around to Gloucester Place in order to tell him that he had come across something very striking indeed. At once Dickens accompanied him back to the shop and, although Willis himself was not there, he took note of everything; in a novel which came to anatomise society and the confusion of human identity, this articulator of skeletons and stuffer of dead animals proved to be precisely the man he needed for the purposes of his design. And so Mr Venus was born.

In March Dickens was back in his old routine of commuting between Gad's Hill Place and London, working on *All The Year Round* as well as *Our Mutual Friend* but for once not spending much time in the office itself. He seems to have taken to the house in Gloucester Place, and found himself able to work on the fourth number there without undue strain. It had the additional advantage of being large enough to accommodate the various dinners and engagements which were now an inevitable part of his metropolitan life. One frequent guest, of course, was John Forster – even though, at this precise time and in this precise number, Dickens was satirising him in the guise of Mr John Podsnap, the first chapter of the fourth number being itself entitled "Podsnappery". That Forster was the original of Podsnap admits of very little doubt, and the accumulated irritations and anger of a lifetime's friendship can be seen to emerge in what is a crude if effective portrait; his peremptoriness, his self-righteousness, his dismissal of inconvenient truths, even his correction of his guests' pronunciation were all aspects of Forster in his more domineering moods. In the novel, too, Podsnap represents the disdain of "Society" for the relationship between the respectable Eugene Wrayburn and the low-born Lizzie Hexam, which may in its turn suggest that Dickens was disturbed and irritated by Forster's attitude towards his friendship with Ellen Ternan. For increasingly, as Dickens moved away from the demands and standards of conventional mid-Victorian society, Forster came to embody them; the very distance between the two men can be marked out with this novel. Perhaps that is why, as Dickens reported to Georgina a little later, "Forster fluttered about in the Athenaeum, as I conversed in the hall with all sorts and conditions of men – and pretended not to see me – but I saw in every hair of his whisker (left hand one) that he saw Nothing Else".

But it was not just Forster who now provoked Dickens's anger and even, sometimes, contempt. Or, rather, in his worst moments Forster became one aspect of a system which Dickens now altogether despised. Not so much the false emphasis on what he calls here "bargain and sale", nor the language of speculation and commerce which threatened to destroy his quintessentially early nineteenth-century belief in human perfectibility: it is rather that, in *Our Mutual Friend*, all social life is seen in terms of a game, a preposterous game in which the counters are false values and in which the players are merely actors. An unreal game, its unreality confirming Dickens's intermittent sense of waking life as a kind of dream which must be "dreamed out" before we dead awaken. So now, after the attempt at self-analysis and self-knowledge which marked *Great Expectations*, Dickens returns to a full-frontal assault upon English life. The personal pain of renunciation and the general shadow of unhappiness are not as strong in *Our Mutual Friend* as they had been in the previous novel; they have been placed instead within the context of general national decay which is sufficiently symbolised by Silas Wegg's unskilful reading of the ". . . declining and falling off the Rooshan Empire". "*This to go through the book*", as Dickens adds in his working notes. In fact this is the first novel in which he directly confronts and attacks contemporary English social behaviour (*Little Dorrit* had been much more concerned with its institutions and its bureaucracy), all the marriages, arranged or otherwise, all the dinner parties and Commons business now seeming *quite* false and unreal, in a world of morbid vacancy, stale routines and universal hypocrisy. Social events are depicted as occasions of torment and even the act of eating and drinking in company, so joyful a social ritual in Dickens's earlier novels, is now seen as no more than another twist of the knife. And the gossip, the dreadful gossip, the gossip of which Dickens was so often the subject and which he truly feared and hated, is also anatomised. There is here, then, a general hatred for society; a hatred which he had as a child and young man but which now returns in a savage attack upon the world in which he lived and moved and of which he was, indeed, a principal ornament. That is why his sympathies in *Our Mutual Friend* lie with the odd and the outcast; those who, as it were, are forced to clean up and live off the waste and detritus of the rich (such large dust heaps, in reality dominating the landscape of Battle Bridge and Liverpool Street!). And perhaps that is also why, in the figure of the distressed Betty Higden running from the spectre of the workhouse, he returns to the attack he had made upon the New Poor Laws twenty-seven years before in *Oliver Twist*. All the radicalism of his youth is returning again, in his last finished novel.

London itself, too, has become again a "heap of vapour" and "circling eddies of fog", a hopeless, rainy, leaden place with an "air of death" and general melancholy. The citizens of London are seen departing from the City in the evening like ". . . a set of prisoners departing from gaol"; just as Dickens's constant journeys between France and England, and his wild exhilaration as he travelled during his public readings, suggest the nature of a man who felt himself, too, to be sometimes locked within a prison. All the bustle and vivacity of London, exemplified in his earlier novels, have now departed; it is a dark prison, a grim and gloomy place, a city made up of solitaries. A city in which its inhabitants deal with dust and detritus. In which the "low" characters are also those who trade in skeletons, the anatomical form without soul, or who prey upon and dissect the dead – indeed that is a clear theme of the novel, since one of the reasons why Betty Higden is fleeing from the workhouse must surely reside in the contemporary rumours that the bodies of the poor who died there were dissected by surgeons and used in medical research.

And yet it is these "low" characters who are sometimes vouchsafed a glimpse of another world. "Come up and be dead!" the crippled Jenny Wren calls out. "Come up and be dead!" There is a world beyond ordinary reality. Just as dead objects and even dead people can be revived in the dust heap, can be restored to the light, so here there is a vision of another world which fitfully illuminates this sublunary sphere. And that is why there is, in Dickens's narrative, such a longing to escape from the prison of the earth. So it is that he returns to an image he had employed for the first time in *A Tale of Two Cities* – of life as an imprisoning circle, the end returning to the beginning, just as he had now returned to his old childhood miseries. "And, like most people so puzzled, he again and again described a circle, and found himself at the point from which he had begun. 'This is like what I have read in narratives of escape from prison,' said he, 'where the little track of the fugitives in the night always seems to take the shape of the great round world, on which they wander; as if it were a secret law.'" And how can they escape from the imprisoning circle? "Come up and be dead!" In one letter of this period Dickens remarks upon ". . . the Great Mystery of Death", and it is almost as if he were dealing with his own fear of that final condition (remember how he had laughed and joked in Cooling graveyard) by treating it as a form of rebirth. What is buried must eventually come to light, just as surely as the bodies come up from the Thames in the first chapter of this story. Death is everywhere but it cannot be directly felt or understood, and it is this paradox which lends so strange and almost hallucinatory a tone to the book. Serenity combined with anxiety. For ". . . it seemed as if the streets were absorbed by the sky, and the night were all in the air". There is a poetry here, the poetry of absence. Sublimity and comedy mixed. Contradictions. Dust. Ashes. Rebirth. And at the end of

March, even as he contemplated these things, Dickens was walking through the streets of London: ". . . I walked long against the dust . . . Utterly abominable and unwholesome." By the end of April he had completed the fifth instalment, as he had planned, and by the time he left London on 23 April, to celebrate the third centenary of Shakespeare's birth with Wilkie Collins and Robert Browning, he saw everywhere around him the advertisements and hand-bills announcing his new serial novel. Did this give additional emphasis to his remark, when asked to subscribe to a national memorial for Shakespeare, that that poet's ". . . last monument is in his works . . ."? Posters advertising *Our Mutual Friend*, Dickens's own last complete work, were now on omnibuses and even steamboats; posters on the major outlets of W. H. Smith; posters at railway stations and bills wrapped around gas-lamps. And when the first number of *Our Mutual Friend* appeared in May it, too, bore all the signs of the new age which it was about to survey; with advertisements within its green covers for Mudie's select library, crinolines, Slack's electro-plate, Cash's cambric frilling, metallic pen-makers, and the Passport Agency.

His constant refrain from Gloucester Place in May is that he is "closely occupied". In fact he was involved in rather fewer public engagements than usual: just two speeches in April and one meeting in May, the latter being for the Royal Dramatic College, at which he disappointed one admirer by delivering only "a thoroughly business-like address". He seems to have been beset instead by private engagements; dinners, parties, gatherings, which filled the London "season" from March or April through to July. Dickens now had an aversion to formal social occasions, as his account of them in *Our Mutual Friend* might imply; he hated parties of almost any kind and was inclined to "bolt" or to "slip away", to use two of his own expressions, as soon as he decently could. This sometimes meant that he disappointed those who had come to see him; as Lord John Russell's daughter recalled, one constant enquiry was "But where is Mr Charles Dickens?" He was desperate to get away from London, from hot rooms where he always had to be "Mr Charles Dickens", the famous public man – his hatred of that role perhaps all the more intense now that he had acquired a "secret" or at least concealed private life of quite another kind.

And how did he appear now to those who met him? He was looking much older, in this decade of his life ageing very rapidly, with grizzled beard and moustache, even scantier hair and a face which showed all the furrows and lines of his internal conflicts and anxieties. Holman Hunt said of him in this decade that ". . . all the bones of his face showed . . . and every line of his brow and face was a record of past struggle . . ." It was a face which showed also his resolution, his will, but there were those who thought they saw in it a self-confidence which verged upon aggression. A young London solicitor, Arthur Munby, encountered Dickens in the street during this period, and left a perceptive account of that encounter in his diary.

"*Tuesday, 10 May, 1864.* Near Covent Garden this afternoon I met Charles Dickens, walking along alone and unnoticed. A man of middle height, of somewhat slight frame, of light step and jaunty air; clad in spruce frockcoat, buttoned to show his good and still youthful figure; and with brand new hat airily cocked on one side, and stick poised in his hand. A man of sanguine complexion, deeply lined and scantly bearded face, and countenance alert and observant, scornful somewhat and sour; with a look of fretfulness, vanity; which might however be due to the gait and the costume. Thus he passed before me, and thus, in superficial casual view, I judged of him. Anyhow, how unlike the tall massive frame, the slow gentle ways, the grave sad self-absorbed look, of Thackeray!"

And how did those who met him in social life now react to him, in his late middle-age? He himself realised, and laughed about, the fact that many people were disappointed and even dismayed when they first saw him; he seemed to them too short and altogether too slight to be the great novelist of their imagination. But everyone noticed how neat, how quick, how "dapper", he was – his characteristic stance with his hat cocked to one side, his head thrown back, one hand in his pocket, ready with what Percy Fitzgerald called his gentle "raillery on some little presumed weakness". In contemplative mood he would often place his face in the hollow of his right hand, with his forefinger extended over his cheek, the second finger over his upper lip and his thumb under his chin. When he was relaxed, he would sit with his hands clasped behind his head and his legs crossed in front of him. Sometimes, when talking, he would bend forward in his chair and put his hand on his interlocutor's knee and sometimes, in his enthusiasm, he would seize somebody's hand with both of his own. For he was rarely seen at rest. He was always active, nervous, quick of move-ment, with rapid glance and quickly-changing expression. He was eager to go, and eager to leave; if he was inviting someone down to Gad's Hill Place he would pull out a little notebook straight away, and begin jotting down the times of trains.

So many memories of him, then, even if some of them are almost contradictory. As one of his earliest chroniclers, Edwin Pugh, noted in 1912, ". . . there are already almost as many versions of the man Dickens as there are people who remember him in the flesh. I have talked with some of his contemporaries, and have been amazed at the diversity of their varying impressions of his personality. In a few more decades I predict that he will be as much a mystery as Edgar Allen Poe." Pugh went on perceptively to note that ". . . Dickens was essentially a self-contained and self-sufficient man. Underneath all that bubbling effervescence of his perennial youth, his high spirits and his gay insouciance, there was all the time the grave, sad, moody man who peers forth at us from those later portraits . . . these innate powers of stern reserve and self-restraint which were never broken down in his moments of freest expansion, were fostered in him in his childhood." It might also be said, of so contradictory a figure, that beneath the grave, stern and self-restrained man there was always a genial and high-spirited child waiting to jump out. But it does mean that there are, as Pugh suggested, almost as many judgments of him as there are observers. At a dinner party given by Lady Waldegrave in this period, for example, he was taciturn and even rather boring, managing to utter "a few commonplace remarks and no more". But at Lady Molesworth's dinner party in the same period he "bubbled over with fun and conversation, laughed and chaffed". Of course it is no surprise that he seemed different to different people – that is simply the condition of being human – and it would be absurd to expect any consistent or steady "personality" to be exhibited on all occasions. Perhaps all that one can say of Dickens is that, in his highly attuned and highly developed state, he displayed more paradoxes than most. Of course to most people he seemed to be simply a cheerful and genial man filled with bonhomie. "However animated a roomful of people might be," one friend observed, "his appearance upon the threshold gave them an instant sense of exhilaration. It was like turning the Bude light upon a half-lit chamber . . . The contagion of his high spirits infected everybody . . ." But then again, to others, he seemed taciturn and reserved. For some he was the most delightful of companions, to others he appeared too masterful and domineering. He could not have been a more kind and gentle man, according to some, but others recalled his sudden bursts of anger or his sharp temper whenever he felt himself slighted. There are other paradoxes as well, which this biography has attempted both to demonstrate and to explain; he was impulsive and yet disciplined, restless and yet systematic, modest in manner but driven always by the need for pre-eminence. He was of genial disposition, but he also possessed an inflexible and paramount will. He often maintained a cool or grave demeanour, even while hiding the "savage" or "wild animal" which he sometimes sensed within himself. He spoke many times of life as a "dream", and yet one of his constant characteristics was his restless and relentless activity in the world. He mocked theatrical conventions while at the same time always remaining instinctively theatrical himself. He worried a great deal, and yet maintained a determination to triumph over all difficulties. He had an unshakeable belief in his own rightness, and yet he was extraordinarily sensitive to criticism. But above all there was his tremulous susceptibility and imaginative sympathy combined with his persistence, his hardiness, his need to do the impossible, his constant temptation to stand back and look on, amazed, at himself.

Many contemporaries saw these paradoxes, or disparities, and concluded that he was extremely "odd". It is one of the most common remarks passed about him by acquaintances and even friends. This related not only to his behaviour but also to his dress: "His appearance in walking dress in the streets during his later years," Sala explained, "was decidedly 'odd', and almost eccentric, being marked by strongly-pronounced colours, and a fashioning of the garments which had somewhat of a sporting and somewhat of a theatrical guise." And this led the more "respectable" of commentators to regard him also as somewhat vulgar, an attitude summed up by *The Times* in the year after his death. "That he was often vulgar in manners and dress, and often overbearing; that he was ill at ease in his intercourse with gentlemen; that he preferred being a King in very low company; that even in his early days he lived rather in a clique than in society; that he was something of a Bohemian in his best moments – all these are truths . . ." It is not hard to understand why Dickens so bitterly attacked that very "society", which *The Times* represented, in *Our Mutual Friend*.

Of course the more perceptive of his contemporaries saw something quite different, something which even frightened some of them. It is the merest cliché to observe that he was very good at divining character, but he also had a habit of trying to guess what people were actually thinking even before they started talking to him. On one occasion he heard and recognised a friend's footfall and, as soon as he entered Dickens's study, the novelist said, "I know what you've called about!" The friend, Charles Kent, went on to explain: "As it happened I had not seen him before this for about a week. Observing a look of surprise on my face upon hearing the words he had just uttered, he added laconically three more by way of explanation. He was quite right! Yet the matter he was referring to, and which was in truth the main reason for my having then looked in upon him, we had never once, upon any previous occasion, spoken of, or I believe, ever thought of before. 'I was certain of it!' he said, laughing." There was also his strange certainty about his understanding of human behaviour. A friend, James Payn, once told him of an incident he had witnessed, in which a woman at a ball tossed from a window her bouquet of flowers to a man dressed in rags. Payn thought that the tramp was in fact the woman's lover in disguise, but Dickens disagreed. "'No,' he said, as though the facts were all before him, 'he was not her lover; he was merely a messenger waiting for the bouquet to be thrown to him, a signal that had been agreed upon beforehand.'" And he was probably right.

He was always scrutinising, always examining, and this alone was enough to make certain people feel nervous in his presence. "As you talked to him he was still observing," Percy Fitzgerald recalled, "and you felt a sort of uneasiness when telling him something, as his keen, brilliant eyes roved up and down and finally settled on you, while his expressive mouth broke into a smile. Could he be 'reckoning you up' all the time?" There were others who professed to be positively frightened of him. Justin McCarthy, who was a young newspaperman at the time, remembered that ". . . Dickens rather frightened me; I felt uneasy when he spoke to me, and did not quite see what business I had to be speaking to such a man. His manner was full of energy; there was something physically overpowering about it, as it then seemed to me; the very vehemence of his cheery good-humour rather bore one down . . . Dickens somehow or other always made me feel rather afraid." Henry James, seeing Dickens in America on his second reading tour, observed another aspect of this in "the offered inscrutable mask . . . which met my dumb homage with a straight inscrutability, a merciless *military* eye, I might have pronounced it, an automatic hardness, in fine, which at once indicated to me, and in the most interesting way in the world, a kind of economy of apprehension . . ." But perhaps Emerson, who met him on this same visit to the United States, had the most interesting observations. When he was told by the Fields, Dickens's hosts, about the great man's cheerfulness and high spirits, Emerson replied, "You see him quite wrong, evidently, and would persuade me that he is a genial creature, full of sweetness and amenities and superior to his talents, but I fear he is harnessed to them. He is too consummate an artist to have a thread of nature left. He daunts me! I have not the key."

That consummate artist had, in this June of 1864, at last managed to get away from London and all the ". . . public speechifying, private eating and drinking, and perpetual simmering in hot rooms . . ."; he went down to Gad's Hill Place and there continued work on the seventh number of *Our Mutual Friend*. Since he was planning another journey across the Channel he was working very hard and very steadily on the narrative, so that he would be sure to finish that instalment before he went away. He was about to reach the moment when Jenny Wren, from the roof of the counting house in St Mary Axe, calls down, "Come up and be dead! Come up and be dead!"; he knew the strength of his story now and, perhaps for the first time in his life, was not unduly concerned by falling sales. (There had been a drop of something like five thousand between the first and second numbers, and by the final double number sales were down to nineteen thousand after beginning at thirty-five thousand.) Of course he no longer needed to be concerned with any disastrous financial loss; for one thing, he could rely for his livelihood upon his readings and his ownership of *All The Year Round* as well as the steady "working" of his copyrights in the various editions of his previous novels. Indeed his annual income climbed steadily year by year in this period, and it seems likely that increased financial security materially assisted his artistic self-confidence; or, rather, he was no longer so troubled by extraneous factors. He just kept on with his steady hard work, and managed to complete the seventh number on time, just before leaving the country in the last week of June. He might have been going to France, as he told one acquaintance, or he might have been travelling to Belgium, as he informed a second correspondent; he was either unclear himself, and planned to take a touring holiday with Ellen Ternan and her mother, or he was deliberately if vaguely trying to cover his tracks. Certainly, in a letter to Wills, he joked about another "Mysterious Disappearance". He was back at Gad's Hill Place in the first week of July, however, and immediately started work on correcting proofs: his brief holiday meant that he had already almost "lost" one number of the five he wished to hold in advance. Matters were not helped, either, by a sudden illness of Wills which meant that Dickens had to take on more editorial work than was customary.

But his main complaint seems to have been quite a new one with him; he told Forster that he was now "wanting in invention, and have fallen back with the book". This had always been one of his greatest fears, to lose his creativity, to break down, so it is no wonder that he was also feeling "very unwell". He had been suffering from a sore throat, and now he was visited by some more serious but non-specific physical affliction which left him weak and depressed. It was very hot at the beginning of August, too, and as a result he still could not work properly. But by the middle of the month his health and spirits had sufficiently improved; he was "working hard" again, and was turning down invitations so that he might write undisturbed and catch up on the amount by which he had fallen behind. By the beginning of October he had in fact managed to finish the ninth instalment, and was thus, at last, almost half-way through the novel. But he still had to write his Christmas story for the year. It had now become of serious financial moment to him, and time was pressing. So he stayed at the office in Wellington Street and there worked steadily upon "Mrs Lirriper's Legacy", the successor to "Mrs Lirriper's Lodgings" with which he hoped to achieve a similar success. He went to see *The Streets of London* at the Princess's Theatre one evening in order to "cool" his "boiling head" after his work, and then a few days later he finished the seasonal story. He was so concerned about its success, in fact, and so worried about the possibility of piracy or imitation, that he told his printer to lock up the type once it had been set and to pull no proofs without Dickens's written instructions. It is a pleasant enough tale, with its kindly and garrulous heroine at the centre, and even in this comic format Dickens was able once more to spread a moral for his audience – in this case not his old Christmas message of comradeship and conviviality but rather the more sombre theme which was also at the heart of the novel upon which he was now engaged, that "Unchanging Love and Truth will carry us through all!".

But his boiling head had not cooled, not at all, and as he finished the story he confessed that he felt "something the worse for work" and was thinking of decamping to the seaside in order to recuperate. He chose Dover, and took rooms with a sea view at the Lord Warden Hotel where he had stayed before. He rested here for a few days but, as soon as he had returned to the office a week later, he wanted to get back to work. He wanted to; but could not. His old companion, John Leech, died suddenly. Of all recent deaths it was the one that most affected Dickens, and Forster described it as one of the many "unwonted troubles" through which the novelist now had to force his way. Life was no longer that easy ascent, no longer even that plateau of fame and fortune, but rather a slow descent with obstacles and abysses continually marking its course. Leech's death meant that he could not write; he ". . . seemed for the time to have quite lost the power; and am only by slow degrees getting back into the track . . ." *Our Mutual Friend*, which had begun with deaths and dereliction, was continuing within that same unhappy atmosphere. His letters during this period are also marked by the sombre presence of mortality, whether it be in his decision that his biography should only be pursued "when my life is over" or in his remark to Wills that their friendship ". . . never can have any break now (after all these years) but one".

In November he travelled again to France – no doubt once more to see Ellen Ternan, whose presence (it can be surmised) was also casting a shadow over his writings. The danger is of seeing her everywhere, in fact. Can it be Ellen Ternan who stands behind Lizzie Hexam, for example, the "low born" but gentle heroine of *Our Mutual Friend*? Is it she who informs Dickens's description of Bradley Headstone's passionate and violent attachment to Lizzie: "'Yes! you are the ruin – the ruin – the ruin – of me. I have no resources in myself, I have no confidence in myself, I have no government of myself when you are near me or in my thoughts. And you are always in my thoughts now. I have never been quit of you since I first saw you. Oh, that was a wretched day for me! That was a wretched, miserable day!'" Then, again, there is Charley Hexam's rejection of her: "'But you shall not disgrace me . . . I am determined that after I have climbed up out of the mire, you shall not pull me down'." Can we sense in this ambivalence, projected into the contrasting responses of two characters, something of the complexity of Dickens's own feelings? Or perhaps we may see the shadow of Ellen Ternan behind the portrait of Bella Wilfer in the same novel, the girl who says that "'. . . I am convinced I have no heart as people call it; and that I think that sort of thing is nonsense'". Which is uncannily reminiscent of Estella's declaration in *Great Expectations*: "'You must know,' said Estella, condescending to me as a brilliant and beautiful woman might, 'that I have no heart . . . I have no softness there, no – sympathy – sentiment – nonsense.'" Are these, too, echoes of a real woman?

Perhaps. Perhaps not. A writer whose life had been marked by astonishing and abundant invention cannot be presumed to rely upon Ellen Ternan for his portraits of young women. What is certainly true is that in these last two novels, *Great Expectations* and *Our Mutual Friend*, Dickens has for the first time given serious consideration to the theme of unrequited love. In earlier books it may have been secret or ill-timed, but there was always an equilibrium in which both parties seem to accept that they loved or can be loved; and that, when eventually they declare their love, it is not rejected. But in these last two novels – and in his uncompleted final fiction also – there is torture in love, and despair, and madness. There is some necessary connection between courtship and death in them, too, so that in these last works it is possible to trace the strange curve of Dickens's temperament exploring extremity in art if not necessarily in his life.

The Christmas gathering that year comprised Charles and Kate Collins, the Fechters, Marcus Stone and Henry Chorley; as the *Gad's Hill Gazette* stated, "The guests remained on and off from Dec. 24th 1864 until Jany 5th 1865." It was not necessarily a very merry gathering. In particular Dickens seems to have been uneasy about the protracted ill-health of his son-in-law, Charles Collins, which in fact proved in the end to be cancer of the stomach. "I have strong apprehensions," he said, "that he will never recover, and that she will be left a young widow." The complexity of his feelings towards his favourite daughter suggests that the wish here was very much the parent of the thought itself. As for the others at this happy time? "All the rest are as they were. Mary neither married nor going to be; Georgina holding them all together . . ." But there was some relief. Some excitement. As his Christmas present Fechter had brought to Dickens a Swiss chalet – a real one, disassembled into pieces. It was too cold to participate in any outdoor games, and so Dickens suggested that the "bachelor guests" (by which he presumably meant the strong Stone rather than the weak Collins) should unpack the pieces – ninety-four altogether, in fifty-eight boxes – and help to put them together. But it was too complex and difficult an undertaking for the men to manage and Fechter's French carpenter at the Lyceum, M. Godin, was summoned from London to help. It was in fact larger than anyone (except, perhaps, Fechter) had anticipated – a real chalet on two floors, with a ground floor room and a first floor room, the latter having six windows. So Dickens arranged for it to be erected on that piece of ground belonging to him on the opposite side of the Rochester

High Road; there the chalet was shaded by the cedars and stood in a place from which Dickens could see the fields of corn beneath him and, in the distance, the Thames with its yachts and steamboats. Eventually he also had a tunnel excavated beneath the road itself, so that he might pass from his house to his chalet undisturbed; the building of this, like the building and furnishing of the chalet itself, filled him almost with boyish delight. One of his children remembered how expectantly he watched as the workmen approached each other from the opposite ends of the tunnel, and how he ordered an impromptu celebration when they broke through and completed the work. And the chalet itself was like a fantasy of boyhood, this secret place among the trees. It became his place of work in the spring and summer, an alternative to his study in the house, one which was even brighter and lighter. He had a telescope placed there so that he might observe the world around and above him but, more importantly, he had mirrors fastened along the walls so that the whole interior sparkled and shone with the sunlight even as he wrote at his desk.

His routine in the early months of 1865, as he continued his work on the last half of *Our Mutual Friend*, was one in which he "commuted" between Gad's Hill Place and the office of *All The Year Round*. In January he was asking for a copy of *Merryweather's Lives of Misers* in order that he might detail the reading matter of the Golden Dustman, Mr Boffin: "'Now, look well all round, my dear, for a Life of a Miser, or any book of that sort . . .'" Working on Mr Boffin's decline and fall; watching from his office window at the crowds streaming over Waterloo Bridge; Silas Wegg singing "auld lang syne"; a fire at the Surrey Theatre. So did his life, interior and exterior, continue. At the beginning of February he was again in France "for a week's run"; apart from anything else he seems to have been crossing the Channel "perpetually" because his visits to Condette helped to soothe the neuralgia from which he was now constantly suffering. But it was never entirely alleviated, and in the third week of February he became troubled by a swollen left foot. Yet it was only the harbinger of greater pain and distress; as Forster justifiably said, it represented "a broad mark between his past life and what remained to him of the future". So did the signs multiply, the bars of the prison house closing round. Dickens, who believed always in triumphing over illness by determination and hardihood, declared that he had simply contracted frost-bite from too much walking in the snow around Gad's Hill Place. This was where the first fierce attack came upon him, after all —

he was walking with his two dogs, Linda and Turk, when he suddenly fell lamed to the ground. He managed to rise only with much difficulty and then had to limp home for three miles, the dogs creeping beside him and never turning from him as he slowly made his way. He was greatly moved by his pets' reaction, in fact, which provided him with further proof that they had distinctive intelligence and temperament (a belief that was not necessarily widely shared at the time). "Turk's look upward to his face was one of sympathy as well as fear", according to Forster, "but Linda was wholly struck down".

"Never *say* die," was, as we have seen, one of his mottoes; by which he meant that the acquiescence in a disease can aggravate or even induce it. That is why he was eager to carry on as if nothing whatever had happened; he was "laid up" on the sofa at Gad's Hill Place but then, a few days later, travelled to London. He had, among other business, to find a rented house for the season. But he was still suffering so severely from the pain that there were days when he could not leave the office after he had finished his day's work on *Our Mutual Friend*. In March he took possession of a house at 16 Somers Place, once more beside Hyde Park, but here he was again "laid up" and suffering from sleepless and agonising nights. He did not have frostbite at all – or, rather, some temporary condition of that kind only exacerbated what was essentially the slow process of vascular degeneration. There can be no certainty in any medical diagnosis so long after the event, but it seems likely that the afflicted kidney which had affected him since childhood was now causing high blood pressure, which in turn had resulted in arterio-sclerosis and the possibility, at any time, of small or transient clots within the blood stream. If a clot had fixed in the leg it would indeed lead to all the swelling and agony of the foot which Dickens now experienced. The fact that his condition seemed to be exacerbated by his nervous exhaustion, as we shall see, would itself fit the case; tiredness and anxiety would raise his adrenalin level, which would in turn put pressure on his vascular system. The combination of anxiety, high blood pressure and kidney weakness might truly be a fatal one under such circumstances, the possibility always existing that a clot or haemorrhage could result in paralysis or death. Yet, in the months and years ahead, it never seemed to occur to Dickens that the agonies he suffered descended upon him when he was in a condition of nervous prostration. He saw only local and immediate causes, which could be alleviated by local remedies and the power of will. A man who had achieved so much, and who had

come so far, by the exercise of that very faculty was not likely to lose
faith in it now. And of course his attempt to work through illness
was part of his hatred of growing old; "he could not bear the idea of
losing any of his activity," one of his sons said, "either of mind or
body."

He remained in pain and ill-health until the spring, only finally
recovering in the last week of April. He went out to dinner for the first
time on the twenty-seventh of that month and then, almost immediately, took himself off to France where he spent the first week of
May. But his general nervous exhaustion, of which the swollen foot
may have been one manifestation and of which his previous "want of
invention" was certainly another, was not to be so easily cured. He
gave a speech for the Newsvendors' Benevolent Association, on which
occasion he "covered" for Edmund Yates who lost the thread of his
own speech ("I saved you that time, I think, sir!" he told him. "Serves
you well right for being over-confident"). He was away again for
some three days, and then on the twentieth of the month delivered an
address to the Newspaper Press Fund in which he recounted his
memories of his own days as a newspaper reporter. So many years ago
now. A time when he could stand for hours in pelting rain in order to
transcribe political speeches, could gallop through the dead of night in
post-chaises, could sit huddled in the House of Commons; the audience, according to one reporter present, were ". . . carried away by
the extraordinary charm of that speech". But, for Dickens, what were
the feelings as he recounted those bright and dashing days? So long
ago. Clearly there was something wrong with him even as he made
the speech. For some reason he wrote two identical letters to Austen
Layard on succeeding days, having forgotten that he had written the
first. And he needed to get away. ". . . Work and worry," he told
Forster before he left once more for France, ". . . would soon make an
end of me. If I were not going away now, I should break down. No
one knows as I know to-day how near to it I have been . . ." He told
Mamie that ". . . I had certainly worked myself into a damaged state".
He left for France at the end of May, therefore, and at once began to
feel better; perhaps the company of Ellen Ternan itself was enough to
assuage much of the nervous tension under which he seems to have
laboured. But then something happened, something which was to
affect the rest of his life.

While in France he had managed to work on the second chapter of
the sixteenth number – he was drawing towards the close of *Our*

Mutual Friend – and he brought the manuscript back with him in the pocket of his overcoat (he had a Gladstone bag, which he took everywhere with him on his travels, but for some reason he never trusted his own work to it). With Mrs Ternan and Ellen Ternan he boarded the ferry which took them from Boulogne to Folkestone, and it may well have been on this occasion that a fellow-passenger noticed him: "Travelling with him was a lady not his wife, nor his sister-in-law, yet he strutted about the deck with the air of a man bristling with self-importance, every line of his face and every gesture of his limbs seemed haughtily to say – 'Look at me; make the most of your chance. I am the great, the *only* Charles Dickens; whatever I may choose to do is justified by that fact.'" The three of them were booked into a first-class carriage and they took the 2.38 tidal train from Folkestone to London. They passed the town of Headcorn thirty-three minutes later and were approaching the viaduct over the river Beult just before Staplehurst at a speed of fifty miles an hour on a downward gradient. At that moment repair work was being conducted on the viaduct itself (in fact it was little more than a bridge) and two of the rails had been lifted off and placed at the side of the track. Even as the train was speeding down towards them. The foreman in charge of these works had consulted the wrong time-table; he did not expect the tidal train for another two hours and, against regulations, the flagman who was supposed to give warning to oncoming trains of any obstruction was only 550 yards from the site of the work. So everything happened too late. The driver of the train saw the red flag and applied his brakes, but he had no time. He whistled for the guards to apply their brakes (there was no consistent braking system then) but it was not enough. The train approached the broken line at a speed of between twenty and thirty miles per hour, jumped the gap of forty-two feet, and swerved off the track as the central and rear carriages fell down from the bridge onto the bed of the river below. All of the seven first-class carriages plummeted downwards – except one and that one, held by its couplings onto the second-class carriage in front, was occupied by Charles Dickens and the Ternans. It had come off the rail and was now hanging over the bridge at an angle, so that all three of them were tilted down into a corner. Dickens himself composed a graphic if slightly inaccurate account of what ensued (without, of course, mentioning the names of his companions).

Ellen screamed, and Mrs Ternan cried out, "My God!"

Charles Dickens (catching hold of them both): "We can't help ourselves, but we can be quiet and composed. Pray don't cry out."

Mrs Ternan: "Thank you. Rely upon me. Upon my soul I will be quiet."

Charles Dickens: "You may be sure nothing worse can happen. Our danger *must* be over. Will you remain here, without stirring, while I get out of the window?"

He managed to climb out and, when he stood upon the step of the carriage, he saw that the bridge had gone (in fact it had only been broken). Then he saw two of the guards running up and down.

Charles Dickens: "Look at me. Do stop an instant and look at me, and tell me whether you don't know me."

Guard: "We know you very well, Mr Dickens."

Charles Dickens: "Then, my good fellow, for God's sake give me your key, and send one of those labourers here, and I'll empty this carriage."

With a makeshift arrangement of planks he managed to extricate the Ternans from the upturned carriage, and it was at this point that he saw the other first-class carriages lying at the bottom of the river bed. With his familiar cool self-possession he went back into the carriage, and took out a travelling flask of brandy as well as his top hat. He filled the hat with water, clambered down the bank, and then started his work among the dying and the dead. He found a man with his skull cut open; he gave him a little brandy, poured some water on his face, and laid him on the grass beside the stream. He said only "I am gone", and then died. A woman was propped against a tree, her face covered in blood; he gave her a little brandy from his flask, but the next time he passed her she was dead. The dead and dying lay everywhere. "No imagination can conceive the ruin . . ." he said in a letter, and this was one of his constant remarks – unimaginable, I could not have imagined it – the reality of the scene too great even for him. One young passenger, Mr Dickenson, recalled later how it was the urging and assistance of Dickens which ensured that he was rescued from beneath a pile of twisted wreckage. Another passenger recalled how Dickens, with his hat full of water, was "running about with it and doing his best to revive and comfort every poor creature he met who had sustained serious injury". One other instance will suffice. A man was looking for the woman he had just married, so "Dickens led him to another carriage and gradually prepared him for the sight. No sooner did he see her corpse than he rushed round a field at the top of his speed, his hands above his head, and then dropped fainting." And then, as he prepared to quit the scene of death, Dickens did a remarkable thing. He remembered that his manuscript was still in the pocket of his overcoat and, ". . . not in the least flustered at the time", he clambered back into the swaying carriage and retrieved it. He said that it was soiled only, although any such marks of the accident have now faded from the pages themselves. Then he travelled back to London with the other survivors on an emergency train, and was met by Wills at Charing Cross station. It was only now that his self-possession and calmness vanished; now that he was safe in London once more, he felt "quite shattered and broken up". He spent the night at his quarters in his office, with Wills sleeping next door in case Dickens should need him.

He returned to Gad's Hill Place the next day, and told the landlord of the Falstaff Inn that "I never thought I should be here again". His eldest son immediately travelled down to see him and found his father "greatly shaken, though making as light of it as possible – how greatly shaken I was able to perceive from his continually repeated injunctions to me by and bye, as I was driving him in the basket-carriage, to 'go slower, Charley' until we came to foot-pace, and it was still 'go slower, Charley'." Charles Collins was also at Gad's Hill Place, and reported to his mother that Dickens ". . . does look something the worse for wear". He had also lost his voice – "I most unaccountably brought someone else's out of that terrible scene . . ." he said, in strange parallel to that theme of lost or double identity which informs *Our Mutual Friend* – and did not properly recover it for more than two weeks. Of course he had to write many letters, some of them dictated to Georgina, in which he dwelt briefly upon the horrors of the accident but in which he constantly ascribes his own shakiness not to the crash itself but to his work among "the dying and dead". All his life he had been haunted by the sight and memory of corpses (as at the Paris Morgue), and even now he was writing a novel in which death and the effects of death play a paramount part; suddenly he had been plunged into all of its frightful reality. Some of the letters were quite long, and not without that hint of unconscious exaggeration without which Dickens's letters would not be complete (his was not the only carriage to be saved, for example); others were very short, however, and, in response to one from his wife, he sent only the briefest of notes. In the longest letter, to his old but now partly estranged friend, Thomas Mitton, he made it clear that he did not on any account wish to be examined at the inquest into the disaster. The reason for this is clear enough; he did not want the fact that he was travelling with Ellen Ternan to become public knowledge. The matter could not be altogether avoided, however, and in a letter to the stationmaster at Charing Cross he asked if a gold watch-chain, a bundle of charms, a gold watch-key and a seal engraved "Ellen" had been retrieved from the carriage. It may or may not be significant that he wrote this letter in his own hand, and did not leave it to Georgina. He was also anxious about Ellen's welfare in other respects and, while he was staying at Gad's Hill Place, he wrote a note to his manservant, John Thompson, asking him to deliver a basketful of various delicacies to "Miss Ellen". In fact there is at least the possibility that she was injured or in some way deeply disturbed by the train crash; from this time forward he tends to call her in his letters "the Patient" and in later life she suffered from intermittent bad health which her friends believed to have been caused in an "accident"; in particular her upper left arm seems to have been a constant source of pain and uneasiness. (When she developed cancer in 1907, it was the left breast and left armpit which proved susceptible.) There is also a stray reference in Forster, when he remarks that Dickens "was beset by nervous apprehensions which the accident had caused to himself, not lessened by his generous anxiety to assuage the severer sufferings inflicted by it on others . . ." He may be referring here to Ellen Ternan but, then again, he may not. Even at this most anxious period of her life with Dickens, she remains very much in his shadow. Certainly Dickens did assist others, too, and in particular he took a great interest in the young man named Dickenson whom he had, perhaps literally, saved from death. Could it have been his surname – Dickenson, suggesting "son of Dickens" – which helped to arouse his interest? We have seen in the past how much importance he attached to names. He had taken him to the Charing Cross Hotel immediately on their arrival from the scene of the crash, and visited him several times as he lay ill there; he also invited him down to Gad's Hill Place for the next New Year celebrations and, even two years later, he was still taking a friendly interest in his future. In fact Dickens's general conduct at the time of the disaster was so exemplary that the directors of the railway company sent him a piece of plate in gratitude (it was no doubt by pulling these particular strings that he was indeed able to avoid appearing at the public inquest which followed).

But what of Dickens himself? Some days later he was still overwhelmed by "the shake". He felt weak, but he experienced a "faint and sick" sensation in his head rather than in his body; his pulse was low, he felt generally nervous and when travelling by train he suffered from the illusion that the carriage was "down" on the left side. In fact this was not the side which went down in the actual crash, but we may recall that it was his left foot which had been attacked earlier in the year and that he suffered from renal colic on the left side of his body – in other words it is possible that the accident had materially affected Dickens's weak side, and that the vascular damage already recorded had been increased by his general nervous strain after the Staplehurst disaster. In fact travelling became for him the single most distressing activity, although he tried to get over his fear of trains by going back in them almost at once. He returned to London in one, for example, in order to see his doctor and no doubt to call upon Ellen Ternan. But it was not easy for him; he had to travel on a slow train rather than the express, and even the noise of his London hansom distressed him. He withdrew from all public engagements, and "the shake" certainly affected his writing in more than a physical sense; the rest of that number of *Our Mutual Friend*, snatched from the crash, is curiously dull. In addition it was far too short – ". . . a thing I have not done since Pickwick! . . ." – and he had to lengthen it at proof stage.

But the permanent results were equally serious. The effect of the Staplehurst accident "tells more and more", he noted in 1867, and then a year later he confessed that ". . . I have sudden vague rushes of terror, even when riding in a hansom cab, which are perfectly unreasonable but quite insurmountable". This sudden sensation of horror remained the most obvious consequence. How could it not be so in a man with a visual memory as powerful as his imaginative capacity, forever reliving the old crash and forever *seeing* the crash into which he might again be plunged? His son, Henry, recalled that "I have seen him sometimes in a railway carriage when there was a slight jolt. When this happened he was almost in a state of panic and gripped the seat with both hands." And Mamie remembered that ". . . my father's nerves never really were the same again . . . we have often seen him, when travelling home from London, suddenly fall into a paroxysm of fear, tremble all over, clutch the arms of the railway carriage, large beads of perspiration standing on his face, and suffer agonies of terror. We never spoke to him, but would touch his hand gently now and then. He had, however, apparently no idea of our presence; he saw nothing for a time but that most awful scene." The great conceiving power of Charles Dickens was thus turned into a medium for recurrent and conscious nightmare; once he had seen the characters of Smollett and Fielding around him, now he saw only the dead and the dying. There were even times when he had to leave the train at the next station, and walk the rest of the way home. But surely there must have been some further reason for this scene to be etched upon his consciousness in characters of fire? In much of his fiction the railway is seen as a terrifying and destructive force, no more so than when it tears up the landscape of London and runs down the guilt-ridden Carker in *Dombey and Son*. Was it as if some terror from his own imagination had now come alive, just as the dead had surrounded him at Staplehurst even as he was writing a book about death itself? Not only had he been involved in a crash but that accident may have injured Ellen Ternan and certainly threatened to expose his "other life" with her. His own worst fears must then have loomed in front of him, and was there not also some sense of guilt and punishment following him as relentlessly as the train once pursued Carker? We know only that, as his son said, Dickens "may be said never to have altogether recovered" and that he actually died on the fifth anniversary of the Staplehurst disaster.

He was back in the office by early July, but he now had no intention of being away from Gad's Hill Place for more than a day or two at a time. It was the usual summer, with his children back from school and his friends visiting for long weekends. The *Gad's Hill Gazette* has news of a cricket match, too, but one son was noticeable for his absence; at the end of May, Alfred had finally departed for Australia. He wanted to become a sheep farmer and there is no doubt that Dickens, always feeling himself beset by the number and demands of his dependants, was pleased to see him start out in life on his own account. And Dickens himself still had much to do. He had by now the whole plan of *Our Mutual Friend* sketched out, and was hoping to finish the novel by the end of August. To that end he was working very hard, and his notes demonstrate the care with which he was now completing the pattern of his narrative: "*Back to the opening chapter of the story* . . . *Back to the opening chapter of the book, strongly.*" On the reverse side of his notes for the last double number, he explains the intricacies of the plot to himself in preparation for the denouement of the story. And in fact the relative dullness of the instalment written after the Staplehurst accident seems to have lifted; by the time he begins the next his customary inventiveness and humour have returned with his cutting portrayal of the stately but gloomy Mrs Wilfer who could assume, ". . . with a shiver of resignation, a deadly cheerfulness". It is in this first chapter of the next number that Bella Wilfer addresses her new husband in words that seem so much part of the essential Dickens. "Dear John, your wishes are as real to me as the wishes in the Fairy story, that were all fulfilled as soon as spoken." For *Our Mutual Friend* is itself in part a fairy-story, that is how it acquires its power. Part fairy-story, part social realism; it has that double aspect which ensures that the fairy-story seems true while the realism is touched by enchantment. The book is filled with dolls and toys; the happy house of the married couple at the end is filled ". . . with gold and silver fish, and mosses, and water-lilies, and a fountain, and all manner of wonders" just as Dickens's letters were often filled with images of the magic mountains and the singing trees and the yellow water which were so much part of the landscape of his romantic aspirations. Certainly it is this atmosphere of fairy-story which accommodates perhaps the most startling aspect of the novel, for it is only in an enchanted landscape that characters can be dismembered and then come together again, that identity can be lost and then refound, that death can be followed by resurrection, that the broken or maimed can be restored with the glory of the other world upon them. The central character, John Harmon, assumes many identities and remarks at one point, "But it was not I. There was no such thing as I, within my knowledge." Eugene Wrayburn suffers from a similar confusion when he speaks his own name and taps his forehead and breast; ". . . perhaps you can't tell me what this may be? – No, upon my life I can't. I give it up!" And Silas Wegg talks to Mr Venus of bringing "me" to the Bower – meaning by "me" his leg. "Where am I?" he asks as he sits in the shop of the taxidermist and looks for his missing limb. Many other examples might be adduced here but they all point in the same direction; in this novel, buffeted as it is by the language of barter and the new ethos of commercialism, human identity is diffused and disrupted. Only those who have gone through the experience of the loss of identity can be restored to anything like integrity. Just as the dead re-emerge from the depths of the river.

At least this is one way of putting it, and there is no doubt that the careful reader will notice this theme – along with many others – working its way through the narrative. Yet of course this search for themes, or symbols, or meanings, is the late twentieth-century equivalent of those earlier attempts to attach localities, or inns, or real people, to Dickens's narratives; it is part of the attempt to domesticate, to explain, and therefore to control. Whether Dickens was conscious or not of such matters is quite another question; it seems unlikely, in any case, that he would have formulated them in the terms employed here. The theme of *disjecta membra* and eventual wholeness, of death and resurrection, is so powerful and permanent an aspect of story-telling that it may well have emerged without any conscious direction or purpose on the novelist's part. There is only one certain and determining feature of Dickens's work, and that is its humour – this is the merest cliché, of course, but it does have an important bearing on the subject to hand. For it is not just ordinary comedy. It is a humour that dissolves ordinary categories, that explodes or defuses the most serious attempts at meaning; so it is that, when we talk of Dickens's themes and purposes, we must always be aware that they are likely to be diverted or ignored or overturned at any time. Which is another way of saying his "meanings" and "values" change from book to book, and even within the same book. In *Our Mutual Friend*, for example, the self-help of Betty Higden is lavishly praised while that of Bradley Headstone is scornfully condemned. His "symbols" some-times remain undeveloped or are simply discarded; it is well known that fog opens *Bleak House*, but it is often forgotten that it never appears again in the same capacity but is replaced by rain. Sometimes Dickens will develop a character only to discard it; sometimes he will create an effective dramatic scene which only at the end of the book can be seen to have led nowhere at all. In the same way his language is filled with *seems* and *perhaps* and *as if* and *a kind of* and *a sort of*, as meanings and even values are improvised as he goes along with his story. Of course this is in part the result of serial publication, which meant that he never had the luxury of second or third drafts in order to resolve contradictions or clear up inconsistencies; but, more importantly, it is also part of the man himself. Realism and fantasy. Comedy and pathos. Irony and sympathy. There was never anyone more likely to see the comic side of a sombre scene, or to mock and undercut his own seriousness; when his fiction is surveyed in all its paradoxes, its inconsistencies and its complexities, it ought also to be emphasised that such ambivalences are not resolved because, given the nature of the man and of the writer, they could never be resolved. His books are in that sense as incomplete and as contradictory as his own self. As any human being.

As incomplete and contradictory, at least, as the man who could be plunged into the severest mental disorder by a railway accident and at the same time seem to an observer to be "in the highest spirits". This was Percy Fitzgerald's description of him on the day in July when Dickens, with a party of friends and family, visited Knebworth; he had come to the house of Bulwer-Lytton in order to help celebrate the opening of the first homes for indigent artists and writers which had been established in the name of the Guild of Literature and Art. Fitzgerald has in fact left an amusing memoir of the occasion, amusing principally because of the presence of Forster who seems to have behaved in a more than usually self-important way on the occasion. He was in charge of the celebrations and was seen to be pacing up and down "in great state and dignity". "'Lord bless you,' cried Boz, in a tumult of enjoyment, 'why he *didn't see me*! He wouldn't, I should say. He was in the clouds, like Malvolio'." Dickens himself was ". . . gay as a bridegroom, with his flower, bright costume, hat set a *little* on one side". He inspected the Guild houses, called in upon a local tavern which had been named "Our Mutual Friend" and made an agreeable speech. There was open-air dancing afterwards, until eventually the Dickens party took a train home. But now the gaiety suddenly disappeared. They were delayed in a tunnel because of some "wandering" luggage carriages, and Fitzgerald noticed how Dickens "grew much disturbed". Could he feel "the shake" again, and see the dying in front of him?

He continued at Gad's Hill Place with *Our Mutual Friend* and was, by August, working on the final double number. He had finished it by the very beginning of September and then, for the first time in his life, wrote a "Postscript" (rather than his usual preface) in which he justified his method of narration and described briefly his experience in the Staplehurst crash. "I remember with devout thankfulness that I can never be much nearer parting company with my readers for ever, than I was then, until there shall be written against my life, the two words with which I have this day closed this book: – THE END." It would be the last time he would be able to use those words. In this postscript he was also concerned to explain the difficulties of monthly serialisation in the exposition of his "pattern", which indicates that he was to a certain extent concerned about the critical reception of the book. It was, to use the common term, "mixed", and perhaps the most severe commentary came from the young Henry James – ". . . the poorest of Mr Dickens's works. And it is poor with the poverty not of momentary embarrassment, but of permanent exhaustion . . ."

E. S. Dallas in *The Times*, however, claimed that *Our Mutual Friend* was ". . . infinitely better than *Pickwick* in all the higher qualities of a novel . . ." It is not known whether Dickens read James's review in *The Nation* but certainly he read the notice in *The Times*. And it says something about his need for praise, especially the kind of praise that preferred his later novels to his early ones, that he in fact presented Dallas with the manuscript of *Our Mutual Friend* itself. Of all things this was what he most wanted to hear: that he had never deteriorated, that he was still at the height of his powers, that his early popularity had not been succeeded by what Henry James had called "permanent exhaustion". That he did not feel himself to be exhausted, despite the effects of the Staplehurst crash, is clear enough from the fact that even as he was completing *Our Mutual Friend* he was thinking ahead to his next novel, at least to the extent of soliciting an offer from an American publisher.

As soon as he had finished he wanted again to get away, this in part to cure the neuralgia which had been so badly affecting him. He met Wills at the office in London to expedite urgent business, and then made the journey to France. It can be assumed that he was returning over the same route as the train in the Staplehurst disaster, so this desire to leave as soon as the novel was finished must in part have been related to his need to fight out, and triumph over, his fears of travelling after the crash. He was in Boulogne for a few days; since it is clear that from this time Ellen Ternan and her mother resided in England, he may have been involved in winding up their affairs in Condette. Nevertheless he reported to Forster that ". . . I am burnt brown and have walked by the sea perpetually". He also reported that his foot was swelling again but it appears not to have prevented this perpetual walking – another example of Dickens's refusal to "surrender", as he might have put it, to physical debilities. From the Boulogne area he went on to Paris, where he stayed a few days, before crossing the Channel once more. On his return he shuttled back and forth between Gad's Hill Place and the offices in Wellington Street, and it may well have been about this time – certainly it was in this year – that the young Thomas Hardy encountered the great English novelist. It ought to rank as one of the most significant meetings in nineteenth-century literary history but, as on most such occasions, it was nothing of the sort. Hardy was then studying architecture in London and on this auspicious day he entered a coffee-shop near Charing Cross when he saw Dickens. "I went up and stood at the vacant place beside the stool on which Dickens was sitting. I had eaten my lunch, but I was quite prepared to eat another if the occasion would make Dickens speak to me. I hoped he would look up, glance at this strange young man beside him and make a remark – if it was only about the weather. But he did nothing of the kind. He was fussing about his bill. So I never spoke to him."

It was while he was in London now that the idea for the next Christmas story occurred to him – a sentimental piece, as it turned out, but remarkable for its depiction of the central character. Dickens described how it occurred to him. ". . . I sat down to cast about for an idea, with a depressing notion that I was, for the moment, overworked. Suddenly, the little character that you will see, and all belonging to it, came flashing up in the most cheerful manner and I had only to look on and leisurely describe it . . ." The character was that of a "Cheap Jack", a travelling salesman who moved around in his wagon from village to village, and precisely the sort of person whom Dickens would have seen in the lanes of Kent. The curious thing is that into the character of this itinerant salesman Dickens should pour so much of his own feeling – as if such a traveller were, at this point in his life, closer to him than anyone else. The Cheap Jack's wife has gone, his child is dead, and he takes a strictly paternal interest in a young girl with "a pretty face" and "bright dark hair" who also happens (no doubt for the purposes of Christmas sentiment) to be both deaf and dumb; together they travel around the country. He is "King of the Cheap Jacks" whose own sense of professional responsibility means that he has to hide his true feelings from the public. "Being naturally of a tender turn, I had dreadfully lonely feelings on me after this. I conquered 'em at selling times, having a reputation to keep (not to mention keeping myself), but they got me down in private, and rolled upon me. See us on the footboard, and you'd give pretty well anything you possess to be us. See us off the footboard, and you'd add a trifle to be off your bargain." This is so close to Dickens's own private lamentations in the same period, and so close to his own role as a public performer during his readings, that it is hard to resist the belief that he was in a sense writing out his own misery; or, rather, *seeing* his misery in this guise. It is perhaps only to be expected, then, that when he came to adapt this story for his real public readings, it was an enormous success, and *The Times* reported that ". . . perhaps there is no character in which the great novelist appears to greater advantage". There may well be implied sarcasm here – to suggest that Charles

Dickens himself is most at home in the guise of showman and salesman (in a sense rather like Thomas Carlyle's own definition of novelists in general) – but why Dickens should leave himself open to such an identification, and why indeed he seems actively or unconsciously to have sought it, remains an open question. Certainly this particular story, written so quickly and with such clarity during one week in London, was another popular Christmas offering. There were some reviewers, of course, who considered it to be a waste of his talents – ". . . a witty and pleasing chapter," one magazine argued, "in which Mr Dickens attempts to carry off the absurdity and dead weight of the chapters which his joint-stock company have added to his." There had been a time, as the same reviewer noticed, when Charles Dickens's Christmas Book – whether it be *A Christmas Carol* or *The Chimes* – was one of the events of the year, a definite and sustained piece of work from a man acknowledged to be one of the leading influences of the day. But now, for the same season, he wrote no more than one or two entertaining stories as part of a large Christmas "package" in *All The Year Round*. But this has as much to do with the conditions of the age as with the condition of the writer; it was becoming, after all, the period of the magazine story and leisurely or "civilised" journalism. It was not a time when the radical politics of the Thirties could be mingled with fantasy and fable.

He had finished the story by the third week of September, just days after returning from France, but it cannot be said that he had in any sense recovered his health. The journey may have done something to restore his confidence in train travel, but there is evidence that it was precisely in this period that he suffered a mild or transient stroke. He himself told a friend only that he had suffered from "sunstroke" and had been ordered to bed for a day. In fact one of his earliest biographers, writing in 1871, has indicated that Dickens suffered a stroke in the previous summer – ". . . whilst on a trip to Paris," he wrote, "Mr Dickens met with a sunstroke which greatly alarmed his friends. For many hours he was in a state of complete insensibility, but at length recovered and in due course returned home." This sounds very much like the same event, which the biographer has misdated by a year, and the evidence itself is clear; he was receiving advance warning of what might one day be a massive stroke or haemorrhage. Nevertheless he preferred to pass off the symptoms as local and specific, and continued with his usual heavy round of activity: in the latter half of September he was once more embroiled in Guild business and *All*

The Year Round affairs, for example, as well as assisting Fechter at the Lyceum with an adaptation of *The Master of Ravenswood*. Mrs Ternan herself had been recruited into the cast (one more indication that she and her daughter had left Condette), so Dickens's efforts as an unofficial and unannounced "play doctor" were no doubt redoubled.

His general equanimity was not helped, either, by the sudden eruption of what became known as the "Eyre controversy". On 11 October a few hundred blacks attacked the Court House in Morant Bay, Jamaica, and Governor Eyre declared martial law, in the course of which 439 were shot or hanged while 600 were flogged. Eyre had feared a rebellion and had acted accordingly, but liberal opinion in England was incensed by his behaviour; as a result, he was suspended while a commission of inquiry visited Jamaica. Those who attacked Eyre were essentially the orthodox liberals of the period, among them Huxley and Mill. Those in vociferous support of Eyre included Tennyson, Ruskin, Carlyle and, of course, Dickens. His view on such matters has already been described, and he was violently opposed to what he now called "that platform-sympathy with the black – or the Native, or the Devil . . ." and believed that it was wrong to deal with ". . . Hottentots, as if they were identical with men in clean shirts at Camberwell . . ." It was the same spirit which led him implicitly to support the South in the Civil War even then being fought, principally on the grounds that the Northern onslaught upon slavery was no more than a piece of specious humbug designed to conceal its desire for economic control of the Southern states. Dickens was notoriously unsentimental about such matters and it ought to be remembered, too, that in his support of Eyre, and in his attacks upon the liberals of the period, he was merely ringing the variations on attitudes which he had held as a young man. His early *Sketches*, for example, are often directed against blinkered missionaries who are more concerned with the plight of natives abroad than the poor at home. It is one of the most significant features of Dickens's life that his real opinions and real values never changed. The young and ambitious man was in essentials no different from the middle-aged and famous author; that is another reason why he was so effortlessly able to reach back and experience his own past. In some sense, as he knew well enough, he was always the same. Thirty years before, while courting Catherine Hogarth, he had been "busy all day", "completely worn out", often dizzy and unwell. Now, in 1865, he was still "perpetually occupied", and sometimes dizzy or unwell. As a young man he had almost feverishly taken on extra burdens – "The work will be no joke, but the emolument is too tempting to resist." And now, at the beginning of a new year, 1866, he decided, against the advice of friends, to embark upon another reading tour of England and Scotland in order to earn money. The same urgent need to *work*. The same fever. The same restlessness.

He had learned from his mistakes with Arthur Headland four years before, however, and had decided that he would leave all the administrative and managerial business to a firm of professionals; in the middle of January he went up to London in order to negotiate with Chappell and Company of New Bond Street, using Wills as his principal agent in the transactions (Forster, quite opposed to Dickens's readings in any case, would not have been suitable for the role), and eventually a satisfactory agreement was reached. But the point was that Dickens should not really have been working hard at all, let alone contemplating a long and arduous tour of the whole country. It was, Forster said in his biography, a "startling circumstance". In fact Dickens himself was feeling unwell through much of January and February, and there is no doubt that the effects of the train crash, as well as more general arterio-sclerotic weakness, were operating within him. His doctor, Frank Beard, diagnosed "want of muscular power in the heart" and Dickens himself recognised some diminution in his usual "buoyancy" and "tone". His pulse was abnormal, too, and he was advised to rest. But of course he could not rest: he had reasoned himself into believing that the readings might actually be of some benefit to him, and he said that the doctors themselves (he sought a second opinion, which was very much the same as Beard's) encouraged him to read occasionally. Which sounds very much like an anxious patient putting words in the mouths of others. Forster explained Dickens's eagerness to tour at this time as part of his self-imposed task ". . . to make the most money in the shortest time without any regard to the physical labour to be undergone". This is true, but there is another truth. He could no more stop himself than he could stop breathing. He had to go on. He had to face his audience in the brilliance of the gaslight. He had to confirm his own sense of being loved. He had to recreate a family around him. He had, even, to confirm to himself the efficacy and strength of his own fictions.

Once more he found a place in London for the season, primarily so that Mamie could come to "town" for the manifold pleasures to be found there; he rented 6 Southwick Place, near Hyde Park and just round the corner from the house which he had taken two years before. The coincidence of place was in fact no coincidence – Dickens employed a house agent who specialised in this area (which was then commonly known as "Tyburnia" because of its proximity to the site of the old Tyburn gallows at the top of Oxford Street), largely because it was considered to be one of the healthiest parts of London. It was conveniently near the breezy heights of Notting Hill and, of course, to the park itself. This was what might be called his official residence, then, but in the same period he also rented what can only be described as an unofficial residence. In January or February of this year he took a small house in Slough, Elizabeth Cottage in the High Street, under the name of Charles or John Tringham. It was not unusual for him to rent rooms or lodgings outside London – on several occasions he stayed in or near the Five Bells pub near New Cross – but to use an assumed name in the rate books suggests a deliberate effort to mislead. The mystery deepens (or, perhaps, resolves itself) with the fact that he also rented a cottage for Mrs Ternan and Ellen Ternan approximately a quarter of a mile away, in Church Street. Of course at this time Mrs Ternan was appearing in Fechter's play at the Lyceum and was renting a house in Harrington Square, Camden Town; in addition it seems that, for at least part of the period during which her mother was working, Ellen went down to St Leonards-on-Sea to stay with Maria, her sister. This is no doubt why the early rates for the second cottage were paid by "Tringham" and only subsequently by "Turnan". Nevertheless Ellen could not have spent all of her time at St Leonards, since Dickens made a point of being with her in London on her birthday in February – an "annual engagement," he told one correspondent, "which I cannot possibly forego". Soon, however, Ellen and her mother came to reside in Slough. It seems almost as if Dickens were trying to recreate the conditions of Condette; in a place away from London where he could work in peace, and where he could see Ellen Ternan as often as he wished. Not that it could be as close a secret; many friends and relatives knew that the Ternans were living in Slough, and Dickens was himself much too famous and public a man to go completely unrecognised. But why the name Tringham? Mrs Mary Tringham kept a tobacconist's shop close to the offices of *All The Year Round* and, as Katharine Longley has pointed out in her pioneering study of the Ternans, the name may have remained in his mind as some faint echo of a poem by Thomas Hood:

". . . learning whatever there was to learn
In the prattling, tattling village of Tringham . . ."

So the word would have suggested gossip, rumour and spying; precisely the things he spent his time fearing and avoiding. He may not have consciously been aware of these associations but, as in his fiction, the whole panoply of remembered and misremembered reading, fears and displacement of fears, encouraged him to light upon that particular surname. But it seems likely that he also derived a certain amount of pleasure from the use of aliases (and, as we shall see, of codes). It was a way of introducing the imperatives and intrigues of his fiction into his own life – had not John Harmon, in the novel he had just completed, lived under the assumed names of Julius Handford and John Rokesmith? In his last novels and stories the theme of the "double life" becomes more and more prominent, although the idea that a new identity comes as a form of liberation or renewal is balanced by the notion that the secret life, or the buried self, might be dangerous and even fatal. But, if all this effort was a way of avoiding the attentions of his contemporaries, it was also a way of fooling posterity. Dickens was quite aware of his stature, and of the use that would be made of such things as private documents after his death; what could be more natural, for a man of his temperament, than that he should try to conceal from the eyes of the future the most secret and important part of his life? (Of course he could not have anticipated the extraordinarily minute professionalism of modern scholars, nor the use of infra-red and other devices to unlock the secrets of the past.) For the time being he must have felt a certain relief, and even enjoyment, at the thought of *having got away with it*. Whether Ellen Ternan shared his amusement is another matter, however. She must have known that she would survive him.

Other members of his family were suffering from the depredations of gossip, too, in this same period. It seems likely, for example, that there were occasions when Mamie would accompany her father and Ellen Ternan on various excursions; her presence on such occasions, in the company of a woman who might be thought by some to have compromised herself, would have been enough to cast some doubt upon the moral character of Mamie herself. Certainly something seems to have been disturbing both her and her sister, Kate Collins. As Frederick Lehmann recorded in a letter to his wife, concerning a dinner which Chorley gave this year: ". . . Mamie kept darting distressed and furious glances and shaping her mouth all the time for the word 'beast' whenever Chorley looked away from her . . . Kitty looked a spectacle of woe and between Prinsep and me was quite distracted. She told me that Mamie, who looked round and matron-like [just like her mother], was to be pitied and she could not lead such a life, but added mysteriously, 'she takes her happiness when she can, and a few visits to town lately have given her all she cares for'. She added, 'Of course, it will come out. Sure to.' My dear, these two girls are going to the devil as fast as can be. From what I hear from third parties who don't know how intimate we are with them, Society is beginning to fight very shy of them, especially of Kitty C . . . Mamie may blaze up like a firework any day. Kittie is burning away both character and I fear health slowly but steadily. When she smiled something of her former pretty self reappeared, only to make the pained and woebegone expression that would follow more distressing . . . the Dickens and Collins faction was at one end of the drawing-room and Society at the other and when I came up Mamie said the Society women were beasts . . ." And, in the following year, Lehmann was calling Kate a "little hussy". It is worth quoting his letter at some length, precisely because it does provide a sharp insight "behind the scenes", as it were, of Dickens's greatness. It is not a happy picture of his daughters, certainly, and very far from his constant claims that the family were all well and flourishing. Clearly they were not – Georgina had recently been seriously ill from a condition that seems in part to have been induced by nervous anxiety, and now the two daughters were "woebegone" and on the point of being shunned by "Society". It must have something to do with their own behaviour (no doubt Katie, faced with the illness and incapacity of her own husband, found ready admirers elsewhere), but that behaviour must be seen in the context of a too-famous father who was himself implicitly breaking all the codes that "Society" enjoined. Perhaps they felt they had the *right* to be different; perhaps the unhappiness of their home life encouraged unconventional behaviour elsewhere; perhaps they, like their father, just did not care.

For, when Lehmann noticed that the "Dickens and Collins faction" were at a different end of Chorley's drawing room from "Society", he is clearly referring to the rumours about the personal lives of both men: Collins known to have a mistress living with him in his own house, and Dickens . . . what really was known about Dickens? What was suspected? The persistent rumours about his relationship with

Ellen Ternan must have continued long after the separation from Catherine, and they were certainly seen together from time to time – in the street, in restaurants, on the cross-Channel ferry. But the little cottage in Slough harbouring "Mr Tringham" must surely have remained concealed; even as they gossiped about him, he was fooling them. It may not be wise to quote from other fiction in order to elucidate Charles Dickens, but a passage from Chekhov's short story, "The Lady With the Dog", seems peculiarly relevant to his life at this point: "He had two lives: one open, seen and known by all who cared to know, full of relative truth and relative falsehood, exactly like the lives of his friends and acquaintances; and another life running its course in secret. And through some strange, perhaps accidental, conjunction of circumstances, everything that was essential, of interest and of value to him, everything in which he was sincere and did not deceive himself, everything that made the kernel of his life, was hidden from other people; and all that was false in him, the sheath in which he hid himself to conceal the truth . . . all that was open. And he judged of others by himself, not believing in what he saw, and always believing that every man had his real most interesting life under the cover of secrecy and under the cover of night. All personal life rested on secrecy . . ." There is much of Dickens in this – for this belief, that every man conducted his real life under the cover of night, was to become the plot of his last and uncompleted novel, *The Mystery Of Edwin Drood*. And did he, in his ordinary life, too, judge others in the same way? Was the conventional world merely one of deception and folly? It is close to his sensibility, at least, and it does elucidate his behaviour at a banquet of aldermen given at the Mansion House in the first month of this year. ". . . I sat pining under the imbecility of constitutional and corporational idiots . . . O! No man will ever know under what provocation to contradiction and a savage yell of repudiation I suffered . . . Mary and Georgina, sitting on either side of me, urged me to 'look pleasant'. I replied in expressions not to be repeated . . ." That "savage yell of repudiation" had already been heard in *Our Mutual Friend*, and it is one that echoes through his life now – a life divided into its public and private compartments, with all the energy and passion of his nature devoted to a "romance" which the world would hardly understand; ". . . my romance . . .", he had said mysteriously to Frances Dickinson which "belongs to my life" and would only die with it. In the latter belief, at least, he was mistaken.

By March he had reached agreement with Chappell and Company

on the nature and extent of the proposed reading tour. He would give thirty readings for which they would pay him fifteen hundred pounds. Originally he had been thinking of something in the region of two thousand guineas, but he accepted the lower offer with no misgivings. Indeed he seems to have been making some sort of point; he said later that he had informed the firm that "I offer these thirty readings to you at fifty pounds a night, because I know perfectly well beforehand that no one in your business has the least idea of their real worth, and I wish to prove it". And as always (as he might have said) he was right. Chappell themselves agreed to take care of all business and administrative arrangements, as well as paying for his personal and travelling expenses. They also appointed, with his agreement, a certain George Dolby to take care of all the business management; Dickens had met him on occasions before, but it was only now that they really came to know each other. Dolby was a tall, bald, thick-set man with a loud laugh, and a supply of humorous stories matched only by theatrical gossip. Precisely the kind of man, in other words, that Dickens liked. He was to "manage" Mark Twain at a later date, and Twain described him as ". . . large and ruddy, full of life and strength and spirits, a tireless and energetic talker, and always overflowing with good nature and bursting with jollity". He could be a little noisy and was "not over-refined" as one acquaintance put it; but there was also a quieter and sadder side to him, an aspect manifested in his stammer which, as Dickens noticed, always disappeared when he was imitating other people. The forced proximity of Dolby and Dickens, over a number of years, did nothing to destroy the true friendship which grew up between them – both of them "professional" men, both of them funny and observant. In addition, and most important of all to Dickens, Dolby remained punctilious and trustworthy. He has left his own account of his relationship with the novelist, which reveals a more humorous and light-hearted man than most biographers of his later years have cared to suggest. There is no doubt, however, that Dolby brought out the best in him; he used to make him laugh, for one thing, and was always prepared with new anecdotes and stories for "the Chief", as he came to call him. Dolby also had a fund of animal spirits – he had a trick of standing on his head upon a chair, which Dickens made a point of attempting – and a wide vocabulary. Once he was talking of a competitor and described how he had been "bested" by him.

Dickens: "Where on earth did you get that word?"

So it was in his company that Dickens began his new series of readings. It was his first extended tour for four years, and of course he prepared himself with his usual thoroughness. He also took pains to adapt a reading from the Christmas success of the previous year, the story of the Cheap Jack, and rehearsed it to himself some two hundred times. But still he was not altogether sure of it, and so he arranged for a private reading in front of friends at Southwick Place – a reading which Dickens, true to his methodical disposition, timed to the second. Among the audience were Forster, Browning, Collins, Fechter and, according to Dolby, ". . . the verdict was unanimously favourable". Even his closest friends were now surprised by Dickens's skills as a reader; again according to Dolby, they (as well as the general public) ". . . were convinced that up to that time they had had but a very faint conception of Mr Dickens's powers either as an adapter or an elocutionist . . ." So, with Dickens thus heartened, the readings began. With Dolby as business manager and Wills as travelling companion, he opened his tour on 23 March, 1866, at the Assembly Rooms in Cheltenham. He saw Macready here after his performance and noted to a mutual friend later that he seemed "on the whole much older", a condition which he ascribed to the fact that Macready had retired from the theatre. It is as if Dickens were in a sense cheering up himself – proving to himself that he should go on with his remorseless activity, the decay of a retired Macready reinforcing his determination to do so. From Cheltenham the Dickens party travelled back to London (Dickens had to give a speech at the Royal General Theatrical Fund) but then on again to Liverpool, to Manchester, to Glasgow, to Edinburgh, to Bristol, to Birmingham, to Aberdeen, to Portsmouth . . . until coming to the end of the tour in London in June. The great novelist was now the great entertainer.

Chapter 32

PUBLIC readings had once more taken their place at the centre of his life, and perhaps through them we may see something of the true nature of his genius. He had acquired his skills only with great effort and determination, precisely as he had once mastered shorthand when he was a young man. The most important first step was preparation – not just the idle rehearsal of an hour or so but a consistent, methodical and laborious process of dramatisation and memorisation. He rehearsed the story of the Cheap Jack more than two hundred times before he felt able to put it on stage, as we have just observed, and in fact most of his readings were the product of at least two months' work; on expressions, gestures, intonations, everything. In the margins of the "reading books" which he created out of his stories and novels he would add small notes as keys to his own delivery; "cheerful", "stern pathos", "mystery" and "quick on" appear in *A Christmas Carol* while in *The Cricket on the Hearth* are to be found instructions such as "very strong to the end". It is not at all clear whether he worked entirely on his own; many observers noticed how his delivery improved as he went on, and in his own advice to other speakers there is a clear professional understanding of matters to do with elocution. All of which suggests – or at least raises the possibility – that he was coached by Ellen Ternan or by Mrs Ternan. Certainly it has been suggested as a reason for his close friendship with the family, and it is not one that can entirely be discounted. And as he rehearsed his words, shouting out loud in the lanes around Gad's Hill Place, declaiming in his study, cutting and altering his stories as he went along, it was his own fiction that was being revivified. With it, too, his own identity. In a speech he gave in 1869, he refers to the fact that "it was suggested by Mr Babbage, in his *Ninth Bridgewater Treatise*, that a mere spoken word – a mere syllable thrown into the air – may go on

979

reverberating through illimitable space for ever and for ever, seeing that there is no rim against which it can strike: no boundary at which it can possibly arrive". Perhaps Dickens had this imaginative sense of his own voice, as the words of Sam Weller or Mrs Gamp ascend into the air and travel through the infinite universe.

In the process, too, these had become new creations. It was often remarked that Dickens did not like members of the audience to consult copies of his books as he was reading from them, and this was for a very good and very specific reason; they were rarely the same narratives, and certain people even complained about the fact that he departed from the text. In preparation for the readings he had already condensed and changed various passages, removed references to gesture and appearance, altered the jokes, and so forth. He also revised passages in the light of the audience reaction itself, and on more than one occasion was known to "gag" or improvise on the spot. He felt able to do so because he had his stories by heart after hundreds of previous rehearsals. Sometimes he would announce the title of his reading and then ostentatiously close his prompt book and recite from memory, but there were also occasions when he would hold the book only for effect or turn the pages mechanically without ever seeing them.

These were all stage effects, in other words, but they were only part of the complex and elaborate ritual which Dickens had devised for his entire performance. When he arrived in a new town for the next reading he would make a point of visiting the hall as soon as possible – "taking the bearings", he used to call it, when he checked the acoustics and the seating arrangements. He never let anyone sit behind him, and if he believed the place was unsuitable for his performance (although this rarely happened) he never scrupled to demand another hall. Then he supervised his staff's assembly of the props. A large maroon screen, seven feet high and fifteen feet wide, was placed behind him while a carpet of the same dark colour was laid on the floor of the stage. In front of Dickens the pipes for his gas lighting were set up in a most ingenious arrangement – two upright pipes, about twelve feet in height, supported a maroon-coloured board which shielded a horizontal row of gas-lights and their tin reflectors. At the height of Dickens's head there was a further gas-light on each pipe, protected by a green shade. In other words, the gas was designed principally to throw the sharpest possible light upon Dickens while the rest of the stage or platform retreated into shadow. But perhaps the most important stage prop of all was the reading desk which Dickens himself had designed, a flat-topped desk which reached about the height of his navel, supported on four slender legs, the top of which was always covered in a crimson or maroon cloth. There were small projecting ledges on either side of the table; on the right a space for his carafe of water and glass and, on the left, a shelf for his gloves and pocket handkerchief. On the left-hand side of the desk, too, was an oblong block of wood upon which he could rest his elbow (which had the effect, of course, of allowing him to rest his whole body); just above ground level there was also a rail upon which he could rest his foot.

When the props were assembled to Dickens's satisfaction he went back to his hotel for a rest before the evening's performance; it was his invariable rule never to stay in private houses during his tour. He hated morning readings, although sometimes he was compelled to give them, and the usual time for the start of his performance was eight o'clock. Eight o'clock *precisely*. His custom was to give a long reading of some ninety minutes, followed by a short interval, and then a shorter (and generally comic) reading with which to close. The whole entertainment lasted approximately two hours. As the audience filed into the hall, last-minute preparations were supervised by Dickens's staff. One American reporter caught the scene very well: "A little before 8 the Dickens gas man appears, takes a view, at the side of platform and contents. Returns to ante-room. In one minute and a half comes out again. Look no 2. Retires. Comes out again and goes upon the platform. Lets on gas. Blandly surveys the gorgeous spectacle. Returns quite satisfied. Audience all eyes and expectation. Enter Dolby and views the scene so charming with a tremendous air of importance – in fact several airs. Retires, reports progress, reappears, takes a concentratedly tremendous look, says to himself 'All right – perfect' and retires." And what of Dickens himself? In his dressing room he had put on his evening clothes, placed a flower (generally a rose or geranium) in his buttonhole, adjusted his gold watch-chain which hung across his waistcoat, checked his appearance. He would then stand by in the wings as the audience grew impatient with expectation, and would make a point of looking at them before he went on. As one chronicler of his tours noticed of his relationship to his audiences, "He was hardly less keenly observant of them than they of him. Through a hole in the curtain at the side, or through a chink in the screen upon the platform, he would eagerly direct your attention to what never palled upon his own, namely, the effect of the suddenly brightened sea of faces on the turning up of the gas, immediately before the moment of his own appearance at the reading desk.'' Then he walked forward briskly to the desk, book in hand.

Always he was greeted by a storm of applause but he never acknowledged it and went straight to the desk, poured himself a tumbler of water from the carafe, and waited for the clapping to subside. He stood in silence for a few moments, looking around at the audience. ''His wonderful eyes seemed to have the power of meeting those of every separate individual in the audience,'' it was reported. An American observer recalled ''. . . his intelligent glance around and through the audience, as if he were rapidly taking stock of them, and his own apparent cool and decided manner, as if confident that in a few minutes that eager crowd would be under his spell . . .'' He always waited here, in perfect silence, until the last straggler had found a seat. And then, without any introduction, he took up his book. ''Nicholas Nickleby at Mr Squeers's School,'' he would say in his clear voice. ''Chapter the First.'' And then he began. He said that he always came ''with a feeling of perfect freshness'' to each of these readings, quite as if he had never done it before; there were many times when he had been ill with cold or fever or some unexplained depression, but on every occasion his spirits returned as he stood and waited for the audience to settle. He always managed to find his energy and his voice, even at times when he was most in danger of losing them. And this had something to do with that immediate relationship he created when he looked at his audience, a relationship which one observer described as ''. . . the magnetic current between reader and listener . . .'' It might be usefully described as a mesmeric effect, as the audience in turn became what one American called ''one eye-ball'' watching him. And yet Dickens needed the audience, too; when he read unsatisfactorily he said that the audience ''was not magnetic'', as we have seen, since he depended for his performance upon their response.

And what did the audience notice as the reading began? There was first of all Dickens's voice which he had trained for just such times, or, rather, a distinctive voice for each character; the high sombre delivery of Paul Dombey; the husky and unctuous tones of Mrs Gamp; the snappish voice of Mrs Pipchin; the orotund accents of Sergeant Buzfuz saying ''respon-see-bee-lee-ty''. When he became Fagin he found within himself a ''hoarse, rasping voice'' with what one auditor remembered as combining an ''Israelitish lisp, and East-end Cockney

of the Thirties". "*Thuppothe* that lad – *thuppothe* he was to do all this –
what then?" He snarled as he spoke and, according to the same
observer, "again and again he made his audience shudder". In the
reading from *Nicholas Nickleby* itself, one observer noted "the harsh
dissonant voice of Squeers, the well-modulated tones of Nickleby, the
grating treble of Mrs Squeers, the mincing language and hysterical
passion of Miss Squeers . . . and, above all, the dispirited heart-
broken utterance of poor Smike . . ." All of them emerging from the
mouth of Charles Dickens. His own characters inhabiting his body.
And there were other effects, too – his exact use of the Cockney "w" in
place of "v" (wery rather than very) which is in fact half "w" and half
"v", as well as the Cockney pronunciation of opposite as oppo-sight,
joints as jints, owner as howner, rather as rayther. But, most importantly, it became characteristic of Dickens that he chose a rising
inflection in passages of comedy. "Child being fond of toys, *cribbed*
nec*lace*, *hid* nec*lace*, cut string *of* nec*lace*, *and* swallowed a *bead*!"
And then there were his gestures, the movements of his hands as he
read. Hands which according to one newspaper report provided ". . .
an unlimited power of illustration". As another observer noticed, "He
rubs and pats his hands, he flourishes all his fingers, he shakes them, he
points them, he makes them equal to the whole stage company in the
performance of the parts." During the scene of the Fezziwigs' party in
A Christmas Carol, his hands "actually perform upon the table, as if it
were the floor of Fezziwig's room, and every finger were a leg
belonging to one of the Fezziwig family". Then there was also "the
roll or twinkle of the eyes, and above all the wonderful lift of the
eyebrows . . ." He turns up the corners of his mouth, a comic twist to
the right, a savage curl to the left; he elongates his face; he rubs his eye
and stares; he bites his fingers nervously; he points. It is as if he were
watching himself as once he watched the old ghost in *The Lazy Tour of
Two Idle Apprentices*: ". . . the right forefinger . . . seemed to dip itself
in one of the threads of fire, light itself, and make a fiery start in the air,
as it pointed somewhere . . ."

It was a complete performance, but it was more than a performance.
It was a kind of spectacle. And it was a kind of haunting. When Bob
Cratchit sniffs and smells the pudding in his little house, Dickens bent
over and did the same; when Peggotty slaps Ham's shoulder it "makes
us wonder how Mr Dickens can poke the air so naturally as to make
believe it to be 'Ham'". Then he becomes Steerforth, and his face
"darkens". Similarly, in the death of Paul Dombey, "Paul's little

wistful face looked out every now and then . . . from among the fantastic forms and features grouped around him . . ." And in that sensation of a face peeping out as Dickens reads there is an intimation, too, of all the characters who hovered around Dickens during these performances – grouped around him as they are in many portraits of him, where characteristically the artist depicts him surrounded by the people of his imagination. And, as he read the death scene of Paul Dombey, Dickens's voice grew lower and lower except once when "HE CRIED OUT" and then dropped again *sotto voce*. In the same way, in the trial of Mr Pickwick, he literally *became* Justice Stareleigh. "His little round eyes, wide open and blinking; his elevated eyebrows that are in a constant state of interrogation; his mouth, drawn down by the weight of the law . . . the stern iron-clad voice, apparently measuring out justice in as small quantities as possible and never going faster than a dead march". (It was said that Dickens based this upon the manner of Samuel Rogers, so that mimicry is for once aligned with impersonation.) There was a little boy of six in the audience on one occasion when Dickens became Stareleigh, and many years later he still remembered his childhood impression that instead of Dickens there appeared ". . . a fat, pompous, prosy little man, with a plump imbecile face . . . The upper lip had become long, the corners of the mouth drooped, the nose was short and podgy, all the angles of the chin had gone, the chin itself had receded into the throat, and the eyes, lately so humorous and human, had become as malicious and obstinate as those of a pig." And then he became the young female servant who interrupts Bob Sawyer's party. "Please, Mister Sawyer, Missis Raddle wants to speak to *you*" in a "dull dead-level voice". And of course there was Fagin in ". . . his rounded shoulders, in his sunken chin, in his pinched cheeks and hanging brow, in his gleaming eyes and quivering, clutching hands, in the lithe shiftiness of his movements, and the intense earnestness of his attitude". Dickens could do all this simply by standing at a desk in front of an audience. In *A Christmas Carol* alone he impersonated some twenty-three characters, and now we may understand plainly the force of Forster's remark that he ". . . seemed to be always the more himself for being somebody else, for continually putting off his personality". Yet it was as real for Dickens as it was for his audience; "so real are my fictions to myself," he had said in a letter, his whole bearing exemplifying what had once been explained by the narrator of *David Copperfield*. "I do not recall it, but see it done; for it happens again before me." There is, too, the description of Peggotty's narration. "He saw everything he related. It passed before him, as he spoke, so vividly, that, in the intensity of his earnestness, he presented what he described to me, with greater distinctness that I can express. I can hardly believe, writing now long afterwards, but that I was actually present in these scenes; they are impressed upon me with such an astonishing air of fidelity." That was how it also seemed to Dickens's auditors; when Dickens read from the "storm scene" of *David Copperfield*, "It was not acting, it was not music, nor harmony of sound and colour, and yet I still have an impression of all these things as I think of that occasion. The lights shone from the fisherman's home; then after laughter terror fell, the storm rose; finally we were all breathless watching from the shore, and (this I remember most vividly of all) a great wave seemed to fall splashing on to the platform from overhead . . . Someone called out; was it Mr Dickens himself who threw up his arm?" The audience were in a kind of trance, a state deepened by the absence of ventilation and the consumption of oxygen by the gas flames, which in turn provoked a mild form of hysteria. All of it being conducted by Dickens with "his head thrown back, his large eyes bright with a sense of enjoyment of what he was doing, confident, unfaltering . . ." with all "the intense mental activity blazing in his face . . ." A hint of aggression here, too, in that hypnotic power which Dickens was able to exercise.

There was an interval of ten minutes after the long reading. Dickens would leave the platform, again apparently oblivious to the applause, and go back to the dressing room where he took a glass of brandy and water or sometimes iced champagne, put a new flower in his button-hole, and rested a little. When he returned he generally read a short comic item and the mood of the hall changed. "Call Sam Weller!" and there was a roar of applause and cheers among the audience. Mrs Gamp. Miss Squeers. Boots. When the audience laughed Dickens could not help himself: he would begin to laugh, too. "Dickens, the author," as one observer remembered, "comes in at intervals to enjoy his own fun; you see him in the twinkle of the eye and the curve of the mouth." Sometimes he would interpolate a new joke which was "received with peals of laughter"; for of course the audience would know the books thoroughly, know them almost as well as Dickens himself. It is as if he were a child again, standing on the table in the Rochester inn, entertaining his father's friends grouped around him. So, when one New York newspaper said of his readings that ". . .

what he is doing now is only the natural outgrowth of what he has been doing all the days of his life . . .", the reporter was expressing a greater truth than he could have known. Dickens was once more the entertainer he had always been, applauded by his family and by his family's friends; but he was also the entertainer he had been as a young man, in the springtime of *The Pickwick Papers* and *Nicholas Nickleby*. That is why he never read from his later novels, and why even from his earlier books he cut out anything which was not directly and immediately entertaining or pathetic. No social polemic. No apostrophes. Only sadness and humour and drama. He was once more creating a family who loved him. He was reverting to his early days in another sense, also. What he was doing on stage was close in spirit and in manner to the one-man performances of Charles Mathews which he had watched as a young man. It was Mathews whom he had copied when he, too, wished to join a theatrical company; and it is to the example of Mathews he returns in these last years of his life. In some sense Dickens had managed to regain his youth.

Of course his act was necessarily close to the theatre of his own day, and the *Spectator* said that his reading of the death of Paul Dombey "was precisely the pathos of the Adelphi theatre". Nevertheless there were signal differences. The very starkness of the lighting and setting of Dickens's stage performance suggests something of this; it was quite a different experience from any previous one-man shows, for it created drama out of Dickens's presence. And he was never, in the colloquial sense, a "ham". It has been noticed before how powerfully restrained his acting was, how he was less interested in the grand gesture than in the careful intermingling of small details to create a combined whole. The same is true of his readings. There was something sober, almost severe, about the general effect. In his performances he was careful to control every rehearsed look, gesture and accent in order to create the desired result; that is why one of his audience believed that "he resorted to no tricks and few arts, in voice or manner". He did not act out the scenes but suggest them, evoke them, intimate them. He remained a reader, in other words, and not an actor. No mannerisms. No artifice. No affectation. Somehow he created his startling effects by an economy of means which was unique to himself, so it is truly as if the novels themselves spoke through him.

He never acknowledged the applause at the end, and he never took "curtain calls". He merely bowed and left the stage, going straight to his dressing room and taking off his clothes which were by now wet through with sweat. The audience eventually dispersed, Dickens's staff dismantled the stage apparatus and packed it into boxes, Dolby started to count up that night's "takings". And Dickens himself? He was always utterly exhausted and drained of life. After reading the death of Paul Dombey, for example, the "most acute suffering" still showed on his face later. And his daughter, Mamie, said that after the readings in London Dickens would come home ". . . voiceless and unable to eat any supper . . . still over-done and restless, and unable to sleep". She said that he always remained "cheerful", however, but Dolby, who was in a position to know better, recognised instead a "great depression of spirits" which did not last very long. It did not last long because Dickens had in a sense triumphed again; he needed that contact with his public in order to reinforce his own sense of himself, for never has any man needed an audience to validate his emotions more than Dickens. He no doubt justified and explained the readings as part of his life-long campaign for "elevated" popular entertainment, but they also confirmed and strengthened his own belief in himself. There is no doubt, either, that the readings had an effect upon the fiction he was even then writing; one of the salient characteristics of his later novels is the manner in which the author withdraws from the narrative, and it seems plausible to suppose that the direct contact which Dickens now had with his audience obviated the need for any such directness in his writing. That is why his last novels are more impersonal, more formally cohesive, and therefore apparently "darker".

But were there other effects, too? Effects upon himself? It has often been said that all the work and worry and travel involved in the reading tours materially hastened his death, a view first put forward by Forster and then taken up by others, although generally by those (like Forster) who believed that the readings were in any case detrimental to his art and injurious to his status. Ruskin probably voiced the majority opinion when he said that it was ". . . his effort to make more money by readings, which killed him" – almost as if he *deserved* to die for abandoning the higher claims of his calling. But the medical evidence is less certain. Of course worry and excitement, let alone the nervous strain of travelling everywhere by train even after the Staplehurst crash, must materially have affected his nervous regimen and therefore his physical sturdiness. High blood pressure, and the resulting vascular problems, could very well have been exacerbated in such circumstances. But it has also to be remembered that Dickens enjoyed his readings; he looked forward to them when he was inactive and in the course of them, as we have seen, he regained his strength even as vicariously he relived his youth. Who can say what beneficial effects such activity, well ordered and well regulated as it was, might not also possess in turn? George Dolby said that in his forced retirement towards the very end of his life ". . . he did not cease to long for a return to the Reading life" and that the doctors' permission for him to do so ". . . did more, I think, to promote his recovery to health than anything else could have done". The minor strokes and the swollen limbs suggest that he was in any case a marked man, for whom the medical practice of the time could not afford a cure, but a man's life is all of a piece. The public readings might have injured his health but, on the other hand, they might have for a time revivified him.

So the tour continued. From Cheltenham to London in the spring of 1866. From London to Liverpool, and then onwards again. Dolby was taking care of all business matters and spent very little time with Dickens. Wills was the reader's principal companion and, much to Dickens's discomfort, he cross-examined Dolby on the preliminary journey to Liverpool in order to decide upon his suitability. In fact Dickens, too, had worried that Dolby might not be "a man of resources". But he passed all the tests and soon he was not only sharing the first-class carriage with Dickens but also using the sitting room which he invariably booked at each hotel. It was Dolby, too, who, on this first trip together, has left a record of Dickens's own excitement and enthusiasm. How he visited the circus whenever he could; how he danced a hornpipe in the train carriage as Wills and Dolby whistled an accompaniment; how he always provided the sandwiches of egg and anchovy, and made the iced gin punch; how he was once told off by the manageress of a station refreshment room for helping himself to milk and sugar; how he lay down like a pantomime clown along the steps of the houses in his home town. It is a striking portrait of Dickens with, as Dolby said, "the iron will of a demon and the tender pity of an angel"; with his pea-jacket, his d'Orsay cloak and soft felt hat "broad in the brim" and "worn jauntily on one side"; with his "wiry moustache", "grizzled beard", and deeply lined, bronzed face like the face of "a Viking". In Liverpool three thousand people were turned away from his reading; in Glasgow two files of policemen kept the crowds from the doors of the City Hall; in Manchester there was so wild a demonstration of cheering and applause that Dickens, for once, was overcome. But there was no doubt that the whole tour, in the long intervals between those demonstrations of joy and gratitude which revived him so easily, was wearying in the extreme. Railway travelling now disturbed and exhausted him; Dolby has recorded how he used to nerve himself with a pull of brandy from his travelling flask. (On one occasion, compounding his terror of travelling by express, a fire broke out in one of the carriages.) It was a hard life: getting up at six-thirty, travelling on to the next place, lying in a hotel bed unable to sleep, eating very little, the whole process repeated day after day. Forster said that "it was labour that must in time have broken down the strongest man . . ." but Dickens, now in his fifty-fifth year, was not so strong as that. Even during the tour he was still suffering from what he called "irritability of the heart", and his general restlessness and insomnia made the condition worse. Only the performances themselves seemed to help him and, during the short interval, he always took a dozen oysters with a little champagne in order to refresh himself. He ate but little apart from this. He was hoarse with cold at Manchester, and was compelled to read with a husky voice; and one observer at a Birmingham reading noticed "how fatigued" he seemed in comparison with his visit in 1859. In May Wills informed his wife that Dickens was suffering from headache and what he called "brow neuralgia"; Dickens himself said that he was feeling very gloomy and "dull" but, as was his habit, he tried never to show this to his travelling companions. To them he remained cheerful – what Wills called "plucky" – and it would be hard from Dolby's own account of Dickens's animated behaviour to realise that he was a man who had just suffered from a terrible nervous shock and the effects of a transient stroke. But the effects were nevertheless there; towards the end of the reading tour he began to suffer severe pain in his left eye, and his left hand, too, was in the grip of "neuralgic" spasms. He went on, in low spirits each day, only to spring up again at the expected time. He went on but, by the time he had finished the tour in June, he said that he felt "very tired and depressed". But there is the extraordinary thing – even before this tour was over he had already opened negotiations with Chappell and Company to undertake another in the following winter. Nothing could stop him now.

He had been away for some three months; when he went down to Gad's Hill Place in order ". . . to rest and hear the birds sing", it was his first visit since March. No doubt he was comforted, too, by the fact that the gross receipts of the tour amounted to some five thousand pounds; he had kept his bargain with Chappell, and they had been rewarded. Then he went back to London, partly in order to be "disposed of" at various dinners and social engagements (although he seems to have been able to limit himself now to three or four days each week) and partly to catch up with all the arrears of office business and correspondence. He also had to set to work upon a projected new edition of his works, the "Charles Dickens Edition", each of his novels appearing once a month in a single volume for 3/6, freshly set, with new prefaces by Dickens himself and, as the prospectus explained, "a descriptive headline will be attached by the author to every right-hand page". In fact this became the most popular of all Dickens's editions in his lifetime; with the gilt lettering on the back, and a facsimile signature on the red cover, it might be seen as encompassing and defining a lifetime's work. It was truly his memorial. His last edition.

In July he was spending much of his time at Gad's Hill Place, and this because he had a great deal of entertaining to arrange there, what with guests he and his family had invited, or guests who had invited themselves. He travelled up to the office for at least two days a week, however, and future work was very much on his mind. It was not long before he had come to an arrangement with Chappell for the next series of readings, although the success of the first tour was such that Dickens could now more or less dictate his own terms; he was to receive sixty pounds a night (an increase of twenty per cent on the last series) and would perform for forty-two nights, with Chappell as usual paying all of his travelling and business expenses. He would begin in the new year and he calculated that, in the six months remaining of the old, he could write the next Christmas story for *All The Year Round* and make some progress upon a novel which he wished to serialise in that periodical during the following spring. Again he had ideas and conceptions floating somewhere within the recesses of his consciousness, but as yet no firm thread upon which to bind them.

So much of the future, but what of the past? A letter from his wife had come at the beginning of August, in which she had asked for his advice and intimated that he might care to visit her at Gloucester Crescent. Dickens refused to go anywhere near her, and told Georgina to reply to her on his behalf, the latest in a series of rebuffs and rejections which suggest Dickens's unrelenting determination in all matters that affected him personally. Catherine herself was still seeing her children, except for those abroad and except, of course, for

Mamie. One of the reasons for Mamie's apparently wayward behaviour in this period might have been her sense of guilt or shame at the way in which she had severed all relations with her mother in order to stay close to her famous father. Catherine also maintained her friendships with some of the people whom she had met during her life with Dickens, George Cruikshank among them. She seems to have maintained a reasonably "social" life (she lived very close to her sister, Helen), and often went to the theatre, but there is no doubt that beneath the surface of her existence there was a low tone of privation or sorrow which broke out at intervals. She and Kate had agreed never to talk about Dickens, since it caused only pain to both of them to do so, but on one of her daughter's visits Catherine looked at a photograph of her husband and asked, "Do you think he is sorry for me?" On another occasion, at the theatre with friends, she suddenly burst into tears when she saw her estranged husband enter a box opposite her own. She was taken home by a friend, who commented later to her husband, "I thought I should never be able to leave her; that man is a brute." Clearly Dickens remained at the centre of her life – she always went to see the dramatisations of his novels and, on the publication of *Our Mutual Friend*, she wrote to Chapman and Hall asking, "Will you with your usual kindness to me send me my husband's new periodical as it comes out each month?" She also had a photograph album with the images and autographs of most of the famous men and women whom she had known through Dickens, among them Andersen, Leech, Cruikshank, Tennyson, Jerrold, Macready, Longfellow, Ainsworth, Frith and Collins. And she kept all of his letters to her; at one time she sent them to Miss Burdett-Coutts in order to prove how happy she and Dickens had been, and to demonstrate that "he had loved her". She even kept the envelopes which he addressed to her, and with these mementoes she also kept a prayer in Dickens's handwriting. It is entitled "Prayer at Night" and the paper is so badly creased that it may well be that Catherine carried it around with her. It contains the lines ". . . be held together in a bond of affection and mutual love which no change or lapse of time can weaken". Catherine will hardly enter this history again.

Throughout the summer Dickens was never completely well. He was bothered by flatulence and stomach pains and was on two occasions seized "apparently in the heart". More warning signs, but again Dickens chose to ignore their seriousness by suggesting that they had to do with something "in the atmosphere". And of course he carried on with his duties regardless, including the time-consuming but not necessarily unwelcome work with Fechter at the Lyceum; the actor-manager was about to put on Dion Boucicault's sensation drama, *A Long Strike*, and Dickens was a constant and regular adviser in all the theatrical preparations. But he was also getting on with his own necessary business. He had begun the Christmas story for that year, and used as his starting point his embarrassment at being reprimanded during his last reading tour by the manageress of the station refreshment room; he took his belated literary revenge by parodying and mimicking the harridans behind the counter in "The Boy at Mugby". But this was only one of his contributions to that Christmas issue of *All The Year Round*; he also appended a number of other stories, among them the famous ghost tale, "The Signal-Man", which serves as an apt reminder of Forster's remark that Dickens liked nothing so much as to tell or to be told ghost stories. In fact he wrote almost half of that year's Christmas issue, and was at work on it throughout September and the first half of October. Certainly there was no diminution of inventiveness in this last period of his life; the comic impersonation of the boy in the refreshment room was followed by the ghost story, both of them preceded by the sentimental narrative of a disappointed man. The last is perhaps the most interesting for in two stories, "Barbox Brothers" and "Barbox Brothers and Co", Dickens reverts to what had become his most enduring fantasies and images. Here once more is a weary and anguished man – disappointed in love, disappointed in life, disappointed in the absence of any real childhood and youth. And here again, as in two of his previous Christmas stories, a melancholy middle-aged man takes up with a small girl and protects her; there is no suggestion of a sexual tie here, of course, but rather the kind of plaintive infantilism (Dickens was adept at creating "baby talk") which seems now to spread over any story of his which is at all concerned with human love. Is this what it had come to? The murderous lust in *Our Mutual Friend* or *The Mystery of Edwin Drood*, counterpoised by a sexless but powerful infantilism? It was in any case a successful formula; the new Christmas edition sold more than two hundred and fifty thousand copies, and Dickens was so pleased with his work upon it that in more than one letter he signed himself "The Boy".

It sounds like a quiet summer and autumn, then, after the excitement of the readings, but it was not without its moments of local drama; he was forced to shoot the dog which Percy Fitzgerald had given him, Sultan, because of its propensity to lunge at any human shape apart from that of Dickens himself (he was led ceremoniously out to the field, and there shot through the heart); he was in the process of suing a Mr Cave, the proprietor of the Marylebone Theatre, who had accused Dickens of turning up drunk at a production of *The Black Doctor* (untrue); his renegade brother, Augustus, died in Chicago. And then something far more shocking occurred – eight sovereigns had been stolen from the office in Wellington Street North, only to be just as mysteriously replaced when the theft was discovered. A police detective was called in and, as a result of his investigations, the culprit was found. It was John Thompson, the man who had been Dickens's manservant and valet for twenty-four years. He has not been prominent in this history precisely for the reason that he was a man-servant – he was discreet. Dickens relied upon him, liked him, and was always considerate to him (it was he who looked after Thompson's welfare during a bout of severe illness), but he rarely mentions him; in this life of Charles Dickens he remains a shadow slipping away from us, from time to time caught in his employer's mimicry of him, but that is all. What he thought of his "master" is as a result unknown; but the fact that, as it turned out, he had been stealing for a number of years suggests that he had no very high respect for him. Dickens had come to trust him, however, and the news of these thefts came as a terrible shock. In one moment the relationship of twenty-four years was severed, and Dickens said that ". . . I have had to walk more than usual before I could walk myself into composure again". He sent John Thompson away, but could not bear to discharge him with a "bad character", knowing full well that it would be almost impossible for him to find any other decent employment. So the matter was hushed up. And then his daughter, Kate, became seriously ill with something known then as "nervous fever", which sounds as though it might have been related to Lehmann's observation earlier in the year that she was ". . . burning away both character and I fear health . . ." And so the year came to an end: a houseful of guests at Christmas and Dickens reading his adaptation of "The Boy At Mugby" to the assembled company, a sports competition on Boxing Day with Dickens as judge and referee ("The All Comers' Race. Distance – Once round the field. First Prize, 10s . . ."), and Ellen Ternan close by in Rochester where she was staying with her uncle.

On 29 December of the following year, Dickens lost his pocket diary while he was staying in New York. It is a small book, immediately notable only for the fact that Dickens very carefully writes out the day of the week before each date. He lost it in New York, and now it is to be found once again in the same city, in the Berg Collection of the Public Library there. It opens with a "*Laus Deo!*", in recognition of the fact that he has survived another year, and there follow brief entries in Dickens's smallest and neatest hand. Some of the entries for this new year, 1867, are in truth so brief and elliptical that they have had to be decoded, sometimes with surprising results, but the main lines of his life in this period are clear enough. We learn, for example, that he was in the habit of arranging to meet friends in the Burlington Arcade, that he liked to dine at Verey's restaurant, and so forth. Those who want a daily account of Dickens's movements will certainly find it here. On Monday, 7 January for example, we read "at G.H. All go. To Sl at 2" – which, roughly translated, means that he was at Gad's Hill Place, that the Christmas Party finally disassembled, and that he went on to Slough, no doubt to his own "secret" cottage there before visiting the Ternans just a short walk away. (It might be mentioned at this point that he was now placing money for Ellen in something he called the "N Trust", "Nelly" being the familiar name by which he knew her.) For the next few days he slept at the office or commuted back and forth from Slough (he usually caught the train at Windsor Station, perhaps to expose himself less to public comment on the platform), but on Saturday, 12 January he returned to Gad's Hill Place in order to rehearse his new readings scripts, taken from the "Mugby Junction" stories, in front of Dolby, Chappell and a few others.

For, two days later, the second reading tour began. It opened at St James's Hall, in Piccadilly, where the "Mugby Junction" readings were not altogether a success (after a few more performances, Dickens in fact dropped them from his repertoire). Then he went on to Liverpool with Dolby. But it was after only the second night's reading there that he became so faint that he had to be laid down on a sofa, not a particularly auspicious beginning for another arduous season. Once again, however, Dickens ignored the possibility of serious symptoms and put down his faintness merely to his insomnia. It was freezing weather all over the country, and he found that he and his usual party (in the absence now of the dismissed Thompson) had to battle their way through gales and snow-storms in the provincial towns which they visited. Dickens's spirits were not helped by an incident at Wolverhampton, a few nights after Liverpool, when one of his gas appliances was misplaced and began to burn through the copper wires which held up the reflector. But as usual his constitutional presence of mind in emergencies saved the situation; he calculated how long it would take for the wire to burn through and, without any appearance of haste, shortened his reading to finish just before it did so. Dolby and the gas man, Barton, watched anxiously from the wings and, as soon as he had come to an end, quickly turned off the flame.

Already, a week after beginning the tour, he was exhausted. He was obliged to get off the Leicester–London express at Bedford, because he could not bear the rocking of the carriages. A short while later he began to experience "soreness all round the body" which, for some reason, he ascribed to the excessive use of his voice. Then he began to experience discharge of blood from his old complaint, piles, and was obliged to seek a medical remedy at once – the discharge of blood providing one more sign of vascular degeneration. He was sleepless and "not quite right within" before travelling on to Ireland for the next stage of the tour. What it all pointed to was severe debilitation of some kind. Yet he could not see that this was true. He could not believe it. It was becoming another difficult test for him, in other words, begun with enthusiasm but quickly followed by all the privation and monotony of living "on the road". He was pursued by galley proofs of *All The Year Round*, and such of his correspondence which had arrived at the office marked "Private". They were moving from Birmingham to Leicester to Manchester to Glasgow to Leeds to Dublin to Preston. Always the same arrangements in each town and city. Always the same routine. As Dolby said in his memoir of the "Chief", "Day after day we were doing the same things at the same time – packing our portmanteaus, travelling to a fresh town, unpacking the portmanteaus . . ." On an average of once a week Dickens returned to London in order to give one reading at St James's Hall before being dispatched again to another destination; in the short intervals of rest between readings (generally at weekends) he would customarily stay in Slough or, on occasions, at the office in London where a certain Ellen Hedderly, servant, was now engaged to look after him and his apartment. On one occasion when she was ill, he stayed instead at the Great Western Hotel. And then forward again. In the labour and trials of this life, however, Dolby remarked that Dickens remained always patient and, in bad hotels, ". . . invariably put the best construction on the discomforts . . . in the most trying situations [he] was always more cheerful and good-humoured than any public man with whom I have ever been associated".

Of course there were occasions when travel was positively useful to him. It was while on tour, for example, that a theme or motif he had been carrying around in his head at last emerged in coherent shape. He had been walking with Dolby the twelve miles from Preston to Blackburn, amongst the factories and mills of that region, when quite by chance the two men came across the ruins of Hoghton Towers. He had been implicitly preparing for a new novel, but had found no way of making his ideas come together; now, in the spectacle of the ruined house, and in the sensations it provoked in him, Dickens found the key to unlock his main design. They wandered over the old mansion, and something about these ruins – so redolent to Dickens of his own childhood, of the ruined warehouse where once he had worked – crystallised for him everything that had remained incoherent. "It seemed to have been frozen before, and now to be thawed," he wrote in the story that eventually emerged from this visit. "The old ruin and all the lovely things that haunted it were not sorrowful for me only, but sorrowful for mother and father as well." Thus does the past, locked in time and then released, cause the onset of private misery. And so emerged this strange story, "George Silverman's Explanation". He had expected to use its main theme for the novel he planned to serialise in *All The Year Round*, as we have seen, but an offer of a thousand pounds from an American publisher diverted his creativity into another channel. The novel was forgotten and a story emerged instead. He wrote it in a relatively short time, and to him it seemed to have ". . . the strangest impression of reality and originality . . . I feel as if I had read something (by somebody else) which I should never get out of my head!!"

It is indeed a most peculiar narrative, related by a timid and apparently unworldly man whose motives are continually misunderstood by those around him. To himself he is gullible, gentle, almost saintly; to others he is a self-serving and sanctimonious hypocrite. It sounds like an exaggerated version of Dickens's own situation – suspected of the worst, and yet aspiring to the best, in his relationship with Ellen Ternan – and in his account of the neglected childhood of George Silverman ("I hid in a corner of one of the smallest chambers, frightened at myself. . .") he returns once again to his old preoccupation with the mistreatment of passive characters. Indeed in its catalogue of woes – George Silverman is rejected by his mother, misunderstood by a putative lover – there is an echo of Dickens's life as it might have been if it had gone altogether wrong. And the narrator himself, whose tone of humility and self-neglect is so ambiguous and so easily misconstructed, is in fact the first of a number of Dickens's narrators and characters whose own vision of themselves is not shared by the outside world. There may be some secret confession here but it is impossible to puzzle out; there is a preoccupation with motives misconstrued and actions misinterpreted, but there is also hovering over the plight of this apparently innocent man an inexpressible taint of horror and guiltiness. And did the name Hoghton Towers remind him of Houghton Place, where Ellen Ternan and her mother had once lived? In the last years of his life Dickens goes so deep into the most unfathomable areas of narrative that any "truth" is difficult to uncover.

As he considered this story he went on with the reading tour. There were on occasions incidents which broke the monotony; like the time Dickens was improvising a song-and-dance routine in a railway carriage when his sealskin cap was blown out of the window, or the excitement of the journey to Ireland during a period when the Fenian crisis was at one of its intermittent heights. As always, of course, he was at least momentarily cheered and revived by the reactions of the audiences who came to see him; his letters speak continually once more of huge crowds, incredible applause, tears, laughter. But by the time it had come to an end he was sick to death of it all – of the hot rooms, and the glare, and the exhaustion. In his diary entry for 13 May, 1867, beside his brief notation that he read "Dombey & Bob" at St James's Hall, he underlined the word *Last*. It was all over. Yet even before reaching this happy quietus he was contemplating yet another tour; and, this time, the most arduous and exacting yet. He had for a long time been receiving letters and invitations to read in the United States and these offers of engagement had now become "the chief topic" of his discussions with Dolby. Should he travel to America, to the "Loadstone Rock", as he called it? He believed that he could make a "fortune" there, but he could not bring himself to contemplate the absence from Ellen Ternan. He wanted to triumph in the United States as he had already triumphed in England, to stamp his image upon the moving spirit of the age, but he could only do so at the risk of his mental and physical health. He was so distraught and distracted – of all things, he hated uncertain or unresolved business – that he could hardly bring himself to think about the sudden but not entirely unexpected death of his old friend, Clarkson Stanfield. Nevertheless his grief was genuine. Just a few weeks before he had sent Stanfield a letter in which he had described to him a seascape at Tynemouth, when behind a fleet of merchantmen there appeared a "most glorious rainbow . . . arching one large ship, as if she were sailing direct for heaven". This concatenation of light and another world is one of Dickens's constant "pictures" and, after Stanfield's death, the letter was found beneath his pillow. There was some comfort to be derived, perhaps, from the intimation of "heaven" and, in his obituary for *All The Year Round*, Dickens recalled how the painter ". . . had laid that once so skilful hand upon the writer's breast and told him they would meet again, 'but not here'". Yet, even as Dickens's mournful attention was being directed towards another world, he could not suspend his immediate preoccupation with the more mundane problem of America. It had become for him ". . . this spectre of doubt and indecision that sits at the board with me and stands at the bedside". And yet, and yet ". . . the prize looks so large! . . ."

He decided that he could come to no real conclusion without the benefit of a first-hand report about his prospects and so, one July morning as he and Dolby walked across Hyde Park to the office from Paddington Station, it was agreed between them that Dolby should travel to the United States at the beginning of August in order both to judge the financial prospects of an extended reading tour and to inspect halls for likely venues (he would in addition take with him the manuscript of "George Silverman's Explanation", and another story, which Dickens had written for the American journals). At the same time Dickens was intent upon changing his life in a more immediate way. Since the end of March he had been sporadically searching for a house in the London suburb of Peckham, which he might lease for Ellen Ternan and her mother. Clearly there was some inconvenience in their inhabiting the cottage in Slough, not least because it was a relatively small place and Dickens himself had a proportionately higher degree of visibility there. Peckham was a little more anonymous and, although it had the advantage of being closer to London than Slough, it still preserved an air of remoteness from metropolitan concerns; more importantly still, it was only about twenty minutes' walk from the apartment which Dickens seems intermittently to have kept near the Five Bells Inn in New Cross. It took some time, however, to find an appropriate house. Dickens was still at Slough during the first three weeks of June; on the sixth of that month he had sent a letter to Wills on stationery embossed with the legend "ET", in which he admitted that the "Patient" (Ellen) was the "gigantic difficulty" in the way of his travelling to America. And, later in the month, Ellen's sister, Fanny, certainly stayed there during a visit from Italy (where she now lived with her husband, T. A. Trollope). The evidence of Dickens's diary strongly suggests, however, that he or Ellen had found a suitable house by the twenty-first of the month, and that on the following day he waited there some time for her in order to examine the property. It was at 16 Linden Grove, a comfortable two-storeyed house surrounded by a large garden and settled among fields. A more prosperous house than the previous one; a more *genteel* house. But first it had to be redecorated and the Ternans remained in temporary accommodation until it was ready for occupancy. They moved in on 18 July, at which point it seems that Dickens returned to Gad's Hill Place. It has generally been assumed that he shared both the temporary and permanent houses with the Ternans, although there is no direct evidence to that effect; the notations in his diary are too elliptical to afford any real clues. In fact it seems just as likely that Dickens maintained his lodgings near the Five Bells during this whole period – what better reason could there have been for choosing a house in this vicinity in the first place? He paid the rates for Linden Grove (again under the assumed name of Charles Tringham), but it is at least possible that he simply visited the Ternans regularly rather than lived there. The fact that he sometimes travelled back to Gad's Hill Place from New Cross Station (which is just a short stroll from the Five Bells) certainly suggests that he still maintained his old quarters even at the time when the Ternans were close by.

Of course it would be absurd to suggest that everything was open and, to adopt the English expression, "above board". He employed assumed names; he kept up "secret" apartments; and in a letter to Wilkie Collins in this period he was actively concealing his absence from Gad's Hill Place. At the beginning of July he also wrote an odd letter to his friend, Frances Dickinson, in which he alludes to "the story" and "the history" – ". . . it would be inexpressibly painful to N to think that you knew the history . . . She would not believe that you could see her with my eyes, or know her with my mind. Such a presentation is impossible. It would distress her for the rest of her life . . . If she could bear that, she could not have the pride and self-reliance which (mingled with the gentlest nature) has borne her, alone, through so much." We can conclude from this only that Ellen had suffered anguish of no ordinary kind, and that what most heavily weighed upon her was "the history". This can hardly refer to her early life as an actress – almost anyone could have known about that – so it must apply to some more recent chain of events. It seems likely to be connected with the relationship between Ellen and Dickens, although Dickens can hardly have believed that this relationship in itself would cause her such bitter anguish; no, there is something else, something not known, some other sequence of events, which caused her and Dickens distress over a long period. Some illness? Something to do with her family? But in the same letter Dickens expresses his dislike of Ellen's sister, Fanny, in terms that allow no ambiguity. Her "share in the story" is "a remembrance impossible to swallow" and she herself ". . . is infinitely sharper than the serpent's Tooth". These again are puzzling references. He had sent all possible good wishes to her and T. A. Trollope after their marriage (in fact, it had been he who was responsible for her introduction to Trollope), and by this time he had already begun to serialise her novel, *Mabel's Progress*, in *All The Year Round*. Some explanation, however, may be found in the fact that two months before Fanny had arrived back in England, and had been staying with Ellen and her mother in Slough; the point is that Fanny was much tougher, and more conventionally ambitious, than her younger sister. It seems plausible – to say no more – that she objected even to the possibility of a domestic scandal which might materially affect her relationship with the expatriate community in Florence. Did she feel so protective towards Ellen, or towards the reputation of her family, that she cast what Dickens would have considered to be unjustified suspicions upon his relationship with her younger sister? Certainly such suspicions always provoked in him a resentment close to fury, and it might explain his angry tone in this strange letter. Had she also heard rumours of Dickens's trip to America, and the possibility of Ellen accompanying him? Was her visit to England something to do with the renting of the new house in Peckham rather than the two cottages in Slough? All these are merely speculations, suggesting, if nothing else, the complexity of familial and domestic arrangements; and intimating, too, the weight of cares which Dickens now seemed to carry with him everywhere.

On the second day of August he accompanied Dolby to Liverpool in order to "see him off" on his Atlantic crossing. He made the journey even though he was once again suffering from a swollen and painful left foot which made it necessary for him to walk everywhere with a stick – when the two men boarded the ship he was recognised everywhere, and both men and women offered him their seats.

Nothing seemed to minimise his own curiosity, however, and Dolby records how "he examined everything, even to the little bunk in the state-room, as if it had been a bed at Gad's Hill, to see that it was comfortable". Dickens returned to London the next day, dined that evening at the Athenaeum and, because he was too lame to go the railway station, took a hansom cab out to Peckham. The following day was a Sunday, but he came to London expressly in order to receive the advice of an eminent surgeon, Sir Henry Thompson. Thompson diagnosed "erysipelas" – a fevered inflammation of the skin – consequent upon walking, which might be classed as yet another example of a doctor telling the patient precisely what the patient most wants to hear. Erysipelas itself was a serious disorder, however, and was sometimes known as "St Anthony's Fire" because of its connection with severe nervous affliction. Dickens returned to Peckham at once, but on the following day came back again to London in order to consult the doctor once more; the condition of his foot was now so bad that he was "laid up" at the Wellington Street offices for the next four days. While in this unhappy condition he was visited by a somewhat sanctimonious clergyman from Philadelphia. "I am quite a cripple as you will perceive," Dickens said as he greeted the man at the top of the office stairs, and the clergyman at once noticed ". . . his exceedingly poor taste in the matter of dress. He wore a blue cloth dress coat trimmed with black velvet collar and gilt buttons, a flowered purple velvet vest and checkered cashmere pantaloons, while around his neck was the usual high shirt collar turned down in front, and the black silk tie loosely fastened with a gold ring." Certainly very striking attire, especially for an invalid, and the clergyman's account of the interview unintentionally suggests that Dickens had not lost his sense of humour.

American: ". . . I hold that a man must have really loved a woman if he would fully interpret the secrets of a woman's heart."

Dickens (smiling): "You are correct again, sir."

If only the clergyman had known how "correct" he was.

By the end of this week of being "laid up", Dickens felt strong enough to undertake a ride in the open air and a visit to the Olympic Theatre; and, from that time forward, he commuted between Wellington Street and Peckham while also of course making sure that he made regular visits to Gad's Hill Place. All the time he was waiting anxiously for Dolby to telegraph his news from America but, in this interval, he could not of course be expected to *stop working*. So he began that year's story for the Christmas issue – so much a matter of routine now, but Dickens was too great an artist not to distil something of himself in even the most minor or improvised piece. The new story, or rather serial, was entitled "No Thoroughfare" and it was once again a collaborative effort by Dickens and Wilkie Collins. It is, in general terms, a mystery story in which murder and flight and embezzlement are played out against that setting of the Alps which so haunted Dickens's imagination. It was characteristic, too, that Dickens should once more direct his imagination into the mind and consciousness of a murderer, the same smooth, hypocritical murderer who had appeared in "Hunted Down" and would reappear in *The Mystery of Edwin Drood*. He was working on the story at Peckham and, at the end of August, he read the first portion of it to Wilkie Collins at the office. He wanted to finish it as quickly as he could, and this primarily because America was so much on his mind that nothing else seemed to be of much consequence; this may in part explain the somewhat conventional nature of the narrative. Certainly he was so preoccupied with his reading affairs that, despite his best intentions, he was only able to make slow progress on the story – to repeat his telling image, he was working ". . . at the pace of a wheelbarrow propelled by a Greenwich Pensioner". It was primarily because of America, too, that he was anxiously and comprehensively denying rumours about his health in the same period. Whether this was out of fear of insurance problems with the Eagle Star Office, or from concern that the Americans would think him unfit to maintain the stress of a long tour, is not clear. But in a number of angry letters he denied newspaper reports that he was very ill, that his doctors had told him to rest, that he was travelling to America simply in order to take a break from "literary labours". Of course he went too far in his denials, and claimed that he had ". . . NOT consulted *eminent surgeons* . . ." when in fact he had seen Sir Henry Thompson only a few weeks before; he even said that he had "not had so much as a head ache for twenty years" which, as we have seen in this history of his perennial illness, was rather far from the truth. But the truth was always a very fluid concept for Dickens; he did not so much lie as believe in whatever he said at the time. Nevertheless there was also a part of Dickens that truly believed he was not, *could not*, be sick – a man who had triumphed over the agonies of childhood must also be able to triumph over the ailments of the flesh. All sorts of conscious arguments and unconscious presumptions were brought into play in order to convince himself of this, some indication of which is imparted in a letter he had written to Wills a few weeks before in which he claimed that ". . . my habit of easy self-abstraction and withdrawal into fancies, has always refreshed and strengthened me in short intervals wonder-fully . . . I do really believe that I have some exceptional faculty of accumulating young feeling in short pauses, which obliterates a quan-tity of wear and tear". Reading his stories in public, in other words, revitalised him. But beneath this is a sterner and older sense that he must *keep on working* – "I shall never rest much while my faculties last, and (if I know myself) have a certain something in me that would still be active in rusting and corroding me, if I flattered myself that it was in repose." He is making the astonishing suggestion here that, if he indulged in rest, it would start to destroy him. But who knows if there was not a truth even in that?

Dolby returned to England in late September, having fulfilled the commands of his "Chief" to the letter. He had inspected various halls in Washington, New York and Boston; he had carefully calculated the likely profits of the enterprise, down to the most recent rate of dollar conversion; he had spoken to the most eminent and influential men of the country, including the famous P. T. Barnum. Dolby immediately travelled down from London to Gad's Hill Place – he was greeted on his arrival at the house by the sound of a dinner gong which Dickens described as "real show business" – and it was here that he announced to "the Chief" his overwhelming conclusion. Dickens should go to the United States. It was then agreed that Dolby should make out an official written report on the subject, which Dickens could show to his advisers (foremost among them Wills, Forster and his solicitor, Ouvry). But these three gentlemen were scattered all over the country and could not conveniently be brought together so, instead, Dickens wrote out his own account which he entitled "The case in a nutshell". Dolby's advice is tendered, but the main thrust of this "nutshell" report is directed towards the probable financial gains from the American tour.

By strange chance Forster himself was staying in Ross, which happened to be Dolby's own home town, and it was there that the two men came together at an acrimonious and peremptory interview in which Forster once more announced his settled dislike of the readings in general, as detrimental to Dickens's art and injurious to Dickens's health. The novelist himself came up to Ross to join in this unhappy conference, but the combined efforts of the two men were not enough to sway or to placate Forster. In the end they agreed only to disagree – Dickens had to all intents and purposes already made up his mind to travel to America and, when Dolby parted from Forster at Ross railway station, ". . . he gave me . . . a parting injunction to take care of Mr Dickens, which would have been really comic, but for the earnestness with which it was delivered". Of course it was largely on financial grounds that Dickens was drawn to a positive decision. He was supporting three establishments now, that of his family, that of his estranged wife, and that of the Ternans. His son's firm was about to be declared bankrupt, his other male children were as unsettled and unreliable as ever (with the sole exception of Henry, who had gone up to Cambridge), and now he was being forced to support his son-in-law, Charles Collins, whose ill-health and general debility made it almost impossible for him to earn his own living (Dickens paid him some three hundred and fifty pounds in the September of this year). So it was that, on the last day of September, he cabled "Yes" to his American publishers. He was off to the Loadstone Rock.

There were a great many arrangements to be made, but none more sensitive and more important than the question of Ellen. She had been "the gigantic difficulty" of his going at all, principally because he could not bear the contemplation of such a long absence from her. And so, throughout these months of planning and negotiation, he had been scheming to bring her with him to the United States. Of course she could not travel with such a public man in any compromising capacity, and it seems that at first he thought of taking her with him ostensibly as a companion to his daughter, Mamie. Mamie herself has said that her father had asked her to accompany him to America, and only reluctantly abandoned the idea when it was clear that his would be only a "business trip". Certainly there is a note in his pocket diary about a ladies' state room for the Atlantic crossing, "2 berths for'ard in front of machinery". The importance here lies in the note about *two* berths; Ellen, if she should come, was not to come alone. Mamie did not go, however, although the excuse of a "business trip" does not sound entirely plausible. It seems that she had in any case a fear of travelling by sea, and it is possible that she rebelled at the prospect of travelling simply in order to legitimise Ellen's position. Whatever the reason, that particular plan had to be dropped. But Dickens had not given up. Not yet. Dolby was to travel to the United States ahead of his employer, in order to make sure that preparations for the readings were well advanced, and three days before his departure he dined with

Dickens and Ellen Ternan. Some new plan had already been concocted, and it is clear from the extant correspondence that Dolby was
to consult with James Fields, Dickens's publisher in Boston, and his
wife whom the novelist had already met and liked – to see if it was at all
possible for Ellen to come over without causing undue scandal or
offence. Since Ellen had a cousin, Richard Smith Spofford, who lived
just north of Boston (it had been he who had written a letter of support
to Dickens at the worst moments of his separation crisis) it was at least
possible that Ellen might travel separately to the United States on the
excuse that she was visiting her relative. In any case, Dolby was
to send back a transatlantic cable with the message either "Yes" or
"No"; but Dickens was not so sanguine about the prospects that he
did not readily envisage a negative response to Dolby's discreet
enquiries.

While he waited, however, he worked with Wilkie Collins in order
to finish "No Thoroughfare" before he crossed the Atlantic. He had in
fact just started to delineate the mind and character of the murderer in
the story, Obenreizer, when it occurred to him that it would be an
ideal dramatic role for Fechter; so it was quickly agreed between the
two authors that Collins should also write a dramatic version of the
serial which might then be put on by Fechter during the Christmas
season while Dickens was in America. He carried on working against
time, then, finishing his own part of the serial and even helping Collins
with its dramatic adaptation. On 26 October, finally, the telegram
from Dolby arrived. "No." That same evening, Dickens dined at
Verey's with Ellen. It was something in the nature of a farewell dinner,
since Ellen and her mother were in any case about to travel to Florence
in order to stay with Fanny and her new husband. Had Fanny, or her
mother, decided to get Ellen out of the way? Had they feared that she
might be persuaded to go to America, after all? Dickens, as we shall
discover, was only vaguely aware of their plans and did not realise at
the time that Ellen was to stay in Italy for an undefined period; she did
not actually return to England until April of the following year. After
that dinner at Verey's he returned to Gad's Hill Place to prepare for his
own departure, and did not go down again to Peckham.

He had much to prepare, much to arrange. He set out in advance to
Forster a memorandum concerning all payments which were due to
him from Chapman and Hall. With his son, Charley, he left detailed
instructions about the dramatic adaptation of "No Thoroughfare". In
effect he left him in charge of the play should disputes arise between

Fechter, Collins and Webster, the manager of the Adelphi where the Christmas drama was to be performed; as it turned out, Charley was more than eager on his father's behalf, and on his own initiative engineered large cuts in the length of the play. But his most important instructions were left with W. H. Wills. He arranged all the details concerning not only *All The Year Round* but also his letters, his private bank accounts and various necessary payments. Most significant of all, he left Wills instructions concerning Ellen Ternan; he gave Wills her address in Italy, Villa Trollope, but also wrote, "If she needs any help will come to you . . ." Dickens added that Forster "knows Nelly as you do, and will do anything for her if you want anything done". He also told him to write out the exact words of a telegram which he would send to Wills the day after his arrival at Boston, and he asked him to send them on, precisely as written, to Ellen herself in Italy. He was, in fact, passing on a coded message, the solution to which is to be found on one of the back pages of Dickens's pocket diary for 1867 – "Tel: all well means *you come* Tel: safe and well, means *you don't come* . . ." There can be no real doubt that he was still, even at this late moment, attempting to arrange for Ellen's passage to the United States – *you come* or *you don't come* clearly being the signal to her. The telegram, as it turned out, had the latter message. Ellen did not go to America; although quite how she was supposed to extricate herself from her family in Italy, and then travel alone across the Atlantic, is not at all clear. It seems possible that Dickens was merely refusing to give up hope entirely while there was still hope to be found, and this principally for his own reasons; he could not face the American expedition without at least the faint prospect of Ellen joining him at some stage but, when he arrived in America, he was able to look forward to the pressure of business with a steadier heart. Thus *you don't come*, after months of uncertainty, was finally dispatched. No thoroughfare.

Meanwhile, in the first days of October, he prepared himself for his journey. Amidst the press of business one occasion stood out, however, and this was the farewell banquet given to him by his friends and contemporaries at the Freemasons' Hall seven days before his departure. It was a lavish affair, even by mid-Victorian standards; there were some four hundred and fifty guests at the banquet itself while, according to custom, some one hundred women were sitting in the gallery above. The lobbies and the corridors had already been decorated with statuary and exotic plants, there were English and American flags entwined together, and the walls of the hall itself had been decorated with twenty panels, representing the works of the novelist, each one announced in gold lettering. It seemed to one observer that "the noble room had all the semblance of a temple especially erected to the honour and for the glorification of England's favourite author". The doors were thrown open and, when Dickens appeared on the arm of Bulwer-Lytton, "a cry rang through the room, handkerchiefs were waved on the floor and in the galleries . . . and the band struck up a full march". During the dinner the band of the Grenadier Guards played music by Mozart, Meyerbeer, Verdi, Strauss and Offenbach. Grace was sung, various speeches were made (by, among others, Landseer, Trollope and Bulwer-Lytton) until eventually Charles Dickens himself rose from his seat. But he could not make himself heard, since the assembled company rose and cheered continually; some people crowded the aisles around him while others leaped upon chairs. Dickens now almost lost control of himself. He tried to speak but could not do so and, according to one observer present, "the tears streamed down his face". He told Wills the next day that he was forced to take "a desperate hold of myself", before he could begin. "Your resounding cheers just now would have been but so many cruel reproaches to me if I could not here declare that, from the earliest days of my career down to this proud night, I have always tried to be true to my calling. [*Great cheering*] . . . I trust that I may take this general representation of the public here, through so many orders, pursuits, and degrees, as a token that the public believe, that with a host of imperfections and shortcomings upon my head, I have as writer, in my soul and conscience, tried to be as true to them as they have ever been to me [*Loud cheers*] . . ." This was truly Dickens's testament. Here in front of the cheering crowd was again the young man who had written *The Pickwick Papers* and *The Old Curiosity Shop*, the author who more than any other embodied the moving spirit of the age. (Yet how odd it is that this great and famous man should even then be conducting a "secret" life in the purlieus of New Cross and Peckham!) He went on to talk of America, and he took this occasion to make peace with the men and women among whom he was soon to move by repeating some words from one of his Christmas essays. "I know full well, whatever little motes my beamy eyes may have descried in theirs, that they are a kind, large-hearted, generous and great people. [*Cheers*]." And this was how he ended a speech which had been interrupted so many times by cheering and applause: "'And so,' as

Tiny Tim observed. 'God bless us every one!'" He sat down to the sound of continual cheering.

At the beginning of the following week, just four days before his departure, he was back in the office, making his final preparations for departure. Percy Fitzgerald came to see him there and observed ". . . the worn, well frayed man, now looking at a letter brought in hastily, now engaged with some businessman". It was from there, also, that he wrote a short and somewhat curt note to Catherine, who had clearly written to him with her own message of *bon voyage*. It read only, "I am glad to receive your letter, and to accept and reciprocate your good wishes. Severely hard work lies before me; but that is not a new thing in my life, and I am content to go my way and do it." On 8 November he travelled in a special railway carriage – a "royal saloon carriage", someone called it – from London to Liverpool. Wills travelled up with him and noticed curiously how, after lunch, Dickens "actually took out a clothes brush and flicked away all the crumbs from seats and floor". Then, on the ninth of the month, Dickens sailed on the *Cuba* for the United States.

Chapter 33

H E had been given the second officer's cabin – on deck, which meant that with his window and door open he received all the fresh air he needed. But he was still not entirely sanguine about the pitching and rolling of these cross-Atlantic ships, and so he carried with him a medicine chest filled with laudanum, ether, and sal volatile. In the event, however, he found that baked apples were the best precaution against sea-sickness. With him, but in less commodious quarters, were Scott, his new valet; Lowndes, the new gas-man; and a general factotum called Kelly whose ill-health seems to have infuriated his employer. He also took a large number of books with him, among them the proof sheets of a new life of Garrick; he was, as he said to his daughter, a "great reader" on board ship. From his own account it was a voyage punctuated by the intense merriment which Dickens's joviality produced and interrupted by gales of the most frightful nature; par for the course, one might say, on any journey involving the author. He took particular pleasure in describing the Sunday service during a heavy sea, when clergyman and congregation rolled around together and provided what Dickens called an "exceedingly funny" spectacle. As usual in these circumstances, he could not restrain his laughter: ". . . I was obliged to leave before the service began." But no doubt he had time amidst all this comicality to reflect once more upon the country he was about to visit again after an absence of some twenty-five years, years in which, it must be said, Dickens had not materially changed his opinion about it at all. Despite his friendship with various Americans, it is clear that he still distrusted the country as a place where "smartness" vied with financial malpractice as the chief household god. Despite his attacks upon the institution of slavery in *American Notes* he managed implicitly to support the Southern states in the Civil War only lately ended; and this principally, as we have seen, because he believed the Federal cause to be based on dollars and cents with the anti-slavery cry as no more than mere camouflage for the grosser economic motives. But he had caused for more private antagonism also. He had never really mastered his anger at the wholesale pirating of his novels in the United States, and so sensitive a man could hardly have been expected to forget the bitter attacks which had over the years been launched upon him by the more "yellow" sections of the American press. Yet both of these complaints provided reason enough for him to travel back – to triumph over the press and his enemies and, at the same time, to make a "fortune" as some recompense for the fortune of which he had been unjustly deprived.

Dolby's advance arrival in Boston had alerted that city to Dickens's coming and just before he docked, according to a report in one newspaper, ". . . everything was immediately put into apple-pie order. The streets were all swept from one end of the city to the other for the second time in twenty-four hours. The State House and the Old South Church were painted, offhand, a delicate rose pink." The booksellers' windows were filled with his novels, and once more there appeared the "Little Nell Cigar" and the "Pickwick Snuff" and the "Mantalini Plug". It had already been arranged that Dickens, true to his custom on his reading tours, would stay in an hotel for the duration of his stay; and, for this "first stop" in Boston, rooms had been prepared for him at the Parker House. Dolby had already decided that Dickens should not be exhibited free of charge, as it were, and had demanded strict privacy for his employer; so the manager of the hotel assigned a private waiter to serve Dickens's meals in Dickens's own sitting room, and placed a servant outside the door at all times to prevent access to the apartment. And already, days before his arrival, the queues for tickets for his "readings" were enormous; the attraction consisted not only in his own fame and genius but also in the novelty of the enterprise, since no one in America had ever seen public readings of the kind which he proposed. On the first morning the tickets were on sale the queue was over half a mile long, and many people had arrived the night before with straw mattresses, food and tobacco.

Dickens eventually arrived at Boston on Tuesday, 19 November at 8.30 in the evening; somehow the *Cuba* became "grounded" on a mud bank, but he left the ship an hour later to be greeted by Dolby, Fields and a crowd of newspapermen and well-wishers. He was taken straight to the Parker House, and was forced to make his way through a crowd which had gathered to greet him there. He had supper (he noticed at once that the "cost of living is enormous"), and said to his assembled friends that he would have been quite prepared to give the first reading that same night. It was not mere bravado on his part – he did want to start on his work as soon as possible, and this largely because he wanted to expedite what already seemed to be him no more than a long ordeal. Only two days after his arrival he wrote that ". . . I yearn to begin to check the Readings off, and feel myself tending towards Home". But this was in a private letter to Wills. To American reporters he was more circumspect and said merely that "I came here for hard work, and I must try to fulfil the expectations of the American public". But from the start he seemed to Dolby to be "very depressed in spirits" and somewhat unsettled in his behaviour; during their first conversation on the night of his arrival, after the others had left, he noticed Americans trying to look at him through a crack in the door, and he became peevish and irritable as a result. He regretted his decision to come and added, "These people have not in the least changed during the last five and twenty years – they are doing now exactly what they were doing then."

Two days after his arrival he had dinner with his publisher, James Fields, and his wife Annie Adams Fields; the two became his closest friends during this visit, Annie herself being then thirty-three while her husband was fifty, and from Annie's diaries it is possible to elicit a sympathetic if occasionally too romantic portrait of Dickens himself. The first dinner went well enough – "he bubbled over with fun," Mrs Fields wrote. But his real thoughts were elsewhere and on the same day he wrote to Wills, explaining that he would send letters to Ellen Ternan ("my Dear Girl . . .") through him. On the following day he had breakfast in his sitting room, before commencing what would become a daily rehearsal of the readings; in this room there was a large mirror surrounded by decorated black walnut, and it is likely that he paraded his facial impersonations in front of it. Then, after a light lunch, he took the first of his long walks which varied somewhere between seven and ten miles. A reporter noticed what he was wearing for this first excursion: "Light trousers with a broad stripe down the side, a brown coat bound with wide braid of a darker shade and faced with velvet, a flowered fancy vest . . . necktie secured with a jewelled ring and a loose kimono-like topcoat with wide sleeves and the lapels heavily embroidered, a silk hat, and very light yellow gloves . . ." A gorgeous specimen among the conventionally dark-suited and dark-coated inhabitants of Boston and one small boy, a certain John Morse junior, "remembers distinctly that Dickens was the most magnificent-ly attired pedestrian that he had ever seen". Whenever he stopped a crowd gathered but, on the whole, the Bostonians left him to himself. He was compelled to go to the local theatre incognito, however, to avoid any inconvenient demonstrations.

He was not actually to begin his readings until 2 December and the delay of almost two weeks, originally arranged in order to allow him time to recover from the voyage, became a source of intense irritation to him. He kept himself as secluded as possible, worked in his hotel apartment, walked, and hardly "socialised" at all; as he told one journalist, "I am come here to read. The people expect me to do my best, and how can I do it if I am all the time on the go? My time is not my own, when I am preparing to read, any more than it is when I am writing a novel; and I can as well do one as the other without concentrating all my power on it till it is done." Grand public dinners, which had been such a feature of his last visit, were to be avoided. But he saw Putnam again – George Putnam who, twenty-five years before, had been the young man who had acted as secretary for him and Catherine. He was now looking old, his teeth gone, and when he saw Dickens ". . . he laughed and cried together". He also visited a school ship and made an impromptu speech to the boys there: ". . . if you have ever cause to remember me, think of me as a visitor who had sincere interest in your welfare and who told you above all to tell the truth as being the best way and the only way to earn God's blessing." How different from the kind of speech he was giving in America twenty-five years before. How much wearier he sounded now, how much less he had to say. He was dining only with those whom he knew best. Among them Longfellow, although dinner at the poet's house was marred for Dickens by the fact that Longfellow's wife had burnt to death there. She had run, aflame, screaming into his arms and Dickens, as he sat there, could not get the picture out of his head. Like the insistent memory of the Staplehurst disaster, he saw only the burning wife and heard the screams. Perhaps that is why other guests noticed how much more quiet he was than usual, and Longfellow himself recognised a change in him. He said that he was "as elastic and quick in his movements as ever"; but saw also that "he seemed very restless, as if driven by fate; *fato profugus*." *Fato profugus*: Vergil's description of Aeneas who was driven from his native shore, driven from his love for Dido, in search of a higher destiny. So Longfellow saw in this small, quick, brightly-dressed man, this restless, weary novelist, the makings of a tragic fate. Yet Dickens himself did not perhaps see it quite that way. At another dinner with Longfellow he noticed the row of his own novels in a bookcase and remarked, "Ah, I see you read the good authors!" And there was still sometimes that gaiety; at a dinner with Fields and Dolby, he ". . . had been giving imitations and acting pantomimes all the evening until they were convulsed with laughter". Nevertheless the intermittent good spirits of the first days were, as usual, striated with something very much like gloom; by the end of November he was feeling depressed. He was meant to attend a small gathering at the house of James and Annie Fields but wrote saying that "he was overtaken by a sudden access of melancholy wh. must prevent him from leaving the fireside and solitude of his own room". Yet by the following day he seemed fully recovered, and spent the next evening performing another series of comic impersonations for the Fields.

His first reading was held on 2 December at the Tremont Temple. There had been a snow-storm that morning, but the evening was bright and clear; according to the *New York Tribune*, "The line of carriages ran down all manner of streets and lost itself in the suburbs . . . the gay, struggling, swarming multitude that was trying to get inside the doors, watched by the long-faced silent multitude that crowded round the doorways without tickets . . ." Among the audience were Longfellow, James Russell Lowell, Oliver Wendell Holmes, R. H. Dana and Charles Eliot Norton. It took time for the audience to settle but then Dickens, to an accompaniment of loud cheers and applause and waving of handkerchiefs, walked briskly onto the platform in his evening tail-coat with its lapels faced in satin, and with two small red and white flowers in his buttonhole. The "set" was unchanged – the same maroon back-cloth, the same maroon carpet, the desk and the array of gas pipes. Without acknowledging the applause in any way, he began to read from *A Christmas Carol*. The reception was by all accounts (and not only that of Dickens) remarkable for its length and vociferousness; the applause between the first two chapters, or "Staves", even gave Dickens time to speak in an "aside" to Dolby who had gone behind the screen.

Mr Dickens: Is it all right?
Dolby: All right.
Dickens: Hall good?
Dolby: Excellent; go a-head, sir.

Dickens: I will, when they'll let me.

Dolby: First-rate audience.

Dickens: I know it.

After the interval, when he *could not* get off for the applause and against all his custom had to reappear in order to acknowledge the enthusiasm, he came back to read the trial scene from *The Pickwick Papers*. Again he elicited a wonderful response and afterwards, in the dressing room, he laughed and embraced Fields in his happy excitement.

He read three more times in Boston and then travelled down to New York, where he stayed at the Westminster Hotel in Irving Place. The hotel manager had thoughtfully arranged for his sole use of a private staircase which led to his door and, as in Boston, a servant was posted outside Dickens's apartment to prevent any unwanted intruders. The next morning he and Dolby visited the Steinway Hall, where the readings were to be given, and then spent the rest of the day walking about the city. And how much it had changed. He did not even recognise the area in which the hotel was situated; Union Square and Fourteenth Street had scarcely existed in 1842, and Dickens found that the city seemed to have outfaced nature by growing younger rather than older. He was indeed in a new civilisation. *Fato profugus*. The boy who had writhed in pain on the floor of the blacking warehouse was now the most famous writer in the world. His portrait everywhere in New York. His novels dramatised in a score of theatres there. The queues for tickets to his readings stretching down the streets, with all "the shouting, shrieking and singing . . ." suggesting, Dolby said, ". . . the night before an execution at the Old Bailey . . ." But he was tired and miserable. Unable to sleep. He had a cold which seemed, in the freezing weather, to be turning into influenza. Dolby found him standing at the window of the hotel, looking out at the falling snow and "literally streaming at the eyes and nose from the effects of his influenza". And yet, forlorn, sick, he carried on. He spent a day at the studio of Jeremiah Gurney, having his photograph taken; photographs which show him alert and dominating but with a penumbra of weariness which is to be seen in the deep lines around the eyes. He went once to the theatre, to see a sensation-drama. He visited a police station-house at three in the morning, and was so fascinated by its photographic book of criminals that he could not close it. He rode around the city in a carriage and pair. He drove in a sleigh through Central Park. But nothing could shake his sickness and weariness. Dolby was doing everything for him now; the days when Dickens was intent upon stage-managing the entire perform-ance were now over, and he was happy merely to turn up at the right time with the right readings. His two most often repeated remarks to Dolby were, "Do as you like" and "What are you going to do about it?" He read six times in the Steinway Hall and, once again, he received tremendous ovations. As the janitor of the hotel said to him, in words beautifully transcribed by Dickens, "Mr Digguns, you are gread, mein-herr. Ther is no ent to you! Bedder and bedder. Wot negst!" One senses, in his evident delight in reproducing the sound of these words, his old sharpness and observation. It could not be said, however, that he was seeing much of the country on this visit – in these first weeks, he was travelling only between Boston and New York – but, then, he had no interest in seeing it. He was no longer the young man of 1842, wide awake and desperate to know everything. Now he was interested only in his performances, and in the amount of money which he was able to earn from them; he sent his "takings" back to England almost as soon as Dolby had collected them, and his corre-spondence in this period is rendered almost wearisome by his constant emphasis on the sums acquired and the sums expected. But what did the Americans themselves see, and think, of him now? The descrip-tions are of course various, as Dickens realised (to his evident amuse-ment). Hawthorne's son thought him ". . . erect, virile and animated; the eyes under his dark brows were brilliant and strong, as one used to command." But those who had known him during his previous tour of the United States found him, of course, much changed: ". . . hair thinned and whitened, marks of age and the trials of life. Wrinkles, deeper setting of the eyes. The whole face, once so round and beaming, has become furrowed and shrunken." Of the description of the author at his readings, however, the comments all tend in the same direction – ". . . slight brisk man . . . he might pass for a shrewd Massachusetts manufacturer, or an active New York merchant . . . a dapper air . . . a genial expression . . . Quick, curious and beautiful, that smile is the secret of the man's whole nature . . . might have been taken for an American, or perhaps more likely a Frenchman . . ."

By the time he was back in Boston at the end of December he was feeling more unwell and depressed than ever. On Christmas Day, a day on which he and his party were compelled to travel by railroad back to New York, Dolby has recorded that he was "suffering from the most acute depression . . ." His friends had come to present him with their Christmas greetings but "these were a signal failure, and the kindly wishes ended in a perfect break-down in heart and speech . . ." He stayed silent on the journey; it ought not to be forgotten that he was still very alarmed by railway travel, and the American trains were constantly being "banged up hill or banged down hill", to use his own evocative phrase. And when on this journey to New York his fellow passengers cheered him, the writer who had done so much to infuse the Christmas day with benevolence, he became yet more depressed. His thoughts were elsewhere, as they must have been for the greater part of his time; during December alone he had written some six letters to Ellen Ternan and, although their contents are unknown (it must be presumed that Ellen burnt all the letters she ever received from him), his own comments in the covering letters to Wills are indication enough of their tone. ". . . my spirits flutter woefully towards a certain place at which you dined one day not long before I left, with the present writer and a third (most drearily missed) person . . . I would give £3000 down (and think it cheap) if you could forward *me*, for four and twenty hours only, instead of the letter . . . Another letter for my Darling, enclosed." His influenza made him weep continually. And, when he read the following night in New York, he had a card especially printed, "Mr Charles Dickens Begs indulgence for a Severe Cold, but hopes its effects may not be very perceptible after a few minutes Reading." And indeed, as usual, they were not. He was unwell throughout the last days of the year; he was so demoralised in fact, that against all the habits of a lifetime he was not rising from his bed until the afternoon and not eating anything until three o'clock. But it was not simply a cold, or influenza; there were times when he felt so faint that he had to lie down and rest. A doctor was called, but Dickens himself had already sensed what he called the "low action of the heart . . ." Perhaps it was for this reason that, contrary to all his usual practice, he decided that he wished to stay with the Fields in Boston rather than entrust himself to the Parker House.

In the first month of 1868 he read in New York, Boston, Philadelphia, Baltimore and Brooklyn; hard work for him, but hard work also for his staff which had to be augmented with some American recruits. Numbering and stamping six thousand tickets for Philadelphia, eight thousand tickets for Brooklyn; answering business correspondence; arranging advertising; preparing accounts; organising all travel arrangements. And, in response, the excitement of the American public. "People will turn back, turn again and face me, and have a look at me . . . or will say to one another, 'Look here! Dickens coming!'" When he sat in his carriage people would gather around it and "in the railway cars, if I see anybody who clearly wants to speak to me, I usually anticipate the wish by speaking myself". But he was in poor health still and would remain so for the rest of his visit, the "influenza" having settled down into a cold and catarrh which stayed with Dickens while he remained on American soil. This often made him very depressed; he was sleeping only for about three or four hours each night, and he told Georgina that he was losing his hair "with great rapidity". He was indeed almost visibly growing older, day by day and week by week. But the most extraordinary aspect of this extra-ordinary tour was the extent to which he was able to recover when he stood on the public platform for his readings; he had a strange power of "coming up to time", no matter how drained and debilitated he seemed beforehand, and indeed it was often the case that the more prostrated he was in advance the more powerful his performance. All his nervous energy seemed at once to expel the signs of ill-health, like an organism through which an electric current is passed. Then after-wards the faintness, the sickness and the depression: they had not been expelled but simply suppressed, and Dickens himself fully realised that ". . . one's being able to do the two hours with spirit when the time comes round, may be co-existent with the consciousness of great depression and fatigue".

A depression which co-existed, too, even with hilarity. Many of the most noteworthy incidents of this visit confirm Dickens's high spirits in periods of the greatest distress; the time when he began playing the pantomime clown on the edge of a bath for the amusement of Dolby, and promptly slipped fully clothed into the water; the time he sang comic songs from the "low" theatre. All these are manifestations of Dickens's wonderful, almost childish, good spirits which emerged as suddenly as lightning – and it is perhaps no coincidence, therefore, that the most touching stories of his travels are connected with his con-versations with children. There was the young boy who had come to see Dickens in his hotel, was detained by the clerk, and arrived long after the time he was supposed to have met the great author. At first Dickens was very stern. "You were late," he said after carrying on with his work for several minutes. "I do not like people who do not keep their appointments with me." But, when the reason for the delay was explained, the "atmosphere was instantly cleared" and he took the boy's hand, asked him questions about school, told him jokes and did a variety of impersonations for his benefit. Then there was the little girl who brought a young friend to see him "to my infinite confusion", "A friend all stockings, and much too tall, who sat on the sofa very far back, with her stockings sticking stiffly out in front of her, and glared at me and never spake word. Dolby found us confronted in a sort of fascination, like serpent and bird . . ." There was also the small girl who suddenly sat next to him on a train. "God bless my soul," he said, "where did you come from?" She told him how much she liked his books. "Of course," she added, "I do skip some of the very dull parts once in a while; not the short dull parts, but the long ones." Dickens laughed very much. "Now," he said, ". . . I distinctly want to learn more about those very dull parts." Then he took out a notebook and pencil in order to question her about what he called his "long thick books".

On the first day of February, he travelled down to Washington for his readings there; he visited President Johnson ("Each of us looked at the other very hard . . ."), and attended one dinner at which a guest noticed how he was ". . . extremely nervous, quick in his motions and changing his expression like a flash". On this occasion he heard many stories about the last days of Abraham Lincoln, and in particular his strange dream before his assassination. "Mr Dickens sat back in his chair and listened, I thought with tears in his eyes, at times, and remarked once in a while, 'God bless my soul.'" He remembered the story well and, in the months ahead, retold it many times: it is almost as if he diverted his fears about his own death into his constant dwelling on Lincoln's. But this is to move too far ahead; now, on his fifty-sixth birthday, he was at a low ebb. He had hardly any voice left, and was applying a series of mustard poultices to draw off his catarrh; he still slept only fitfully, stayed in bed until twelve and could take very little solid food. Every night, he said, he was dreaming of Mamie's pet dog, Mrs Bouncer – a strange picture to carry with him everywhere, unless in the dream image of the small dog he saw something of himself, unattached, forlorn, lost. In fact most of the images which struck him during this tour were of nightmare or horror. During one great thaw in the ice-bound landscape some sheep had been compelled to eat each other in order to stay alive, and he noticed ". . . the haggard human misery of their faces". He also retold a story imparted to him by Longfellow of a murderer, Webster, who put a bowl of some burning mineral in front of his friends and then placed his face over the weird light which issued from it – ". . . *with a rope round his neck*, holding it up, over the bowl, with his head jerked on one side, and his tongue lolled out representing a man being hanged!" These were some of the images that Dickens kept in his head.

And then, after Washington, off to Baltimore, Philadelphia, Hartford, and Providence where, when he marched up the steps of his hotel accompanied by two policemen and surrounded by a crowd, he remarked to Dolby, "This is very like going into the police van in Bow Street, isn't it?" But everywhere the cold, the snow-storms, the gales. He was now so exhausted that he had decided to cancel some of the readings already planned; he cut out Chicago, the West and Canada, so that he might be able to return home a month earlier than he had originally envisaged. And all the time he was writing letters to Ellen Ternan – four in February alone. For a few days at the beginning of March he was able to rest, since his projected readings had to be cancelled in the week of the President's impeachment. But then he was off again. Syracuse ("We . . . supped on a tough old nightmare called buffalo . . ."), Rochester, Buffalo, Albany, New Haven, Hartford, even though the brief respite had done nothing to ease his depression or fatigue. His only relief seemed to lie either in the constant calculation of the profit he was making – he estimated, rightly to within a thousand, that he would make for himself some twenty thousand pounds – or in his excitement at witnessing the enthusiasm of his audiences. "They have taken to applauding too whenever they laugh or cry," he said of the Bostonians, "and the result is very inspiriting." Particularly he noticed, one night, that "one poor young girl in mourning burst into a passion of grief about Tiny Tim, and was taken out". He was dosing himself with laudanum by now simply in order to sleep (although the soporific had an enervating effect upon him the next day) and his foot had once more broken out in all the agonies of swelling. He was so badly lamed, in truth, that he hobbled everywhere, through the snow and the slush of the American streets, on a stick. Dolby now never left him and, even during the readings, sat by the side of the platform and carefully watched his progress.

But the worst was over. April was the final month, and on its first day he read again in Boston. One member of the audience on that occasion remembered how he came in ". . . leaning heavily on the arm of his manager, who assisted him up the steps of the platform and behind the screen; from which he entered to commence his reading alert, quick, and apparently in the best of health, and went through it with all the fire and vigour imaginable, only to fall into the waiting arms of his manager at the close". Annie Fields noticed, the next day, that he was coughing all the time and was in very low spirits; she observed, also, that he was extremely rude to Dolby and behaved generally, as her husband said, "like a spoiled child". (Mrs Fields believed that his temper was the direct result of low takings the night before.) He was so ill on the third of the month that an American doctor told him not to perform that evening. Of course he paid no attention and went ahead, but nevertheless he felt it necessary to cancel all social engagements afterwards in order to preserve his rapidly waning strength. Three days later he read again, once more leaning upon Dolby as he made his way slowly onto the platform; ". . . he appeared to be very lame and entirely unable to walk alone," one witness commented, but as soon as he was on the stage he was "erect and brisk". But something had gone from him. He no longer seemed able to regain his vitality afterwards. He did not change his clothes after the readings, as was his custom, but lay on the sofa for twenty or thirty minutes "in a state of the greatest exhaustion". He would take only soup or beef-tea back in the hotel, and would then retire to what were fast becoming relentlessly sleepless nights. In fact there were times now when even he thought that he might altogether break down, and be unable to go on with his tour. He was continually "nervous and shaken", he admitted, and on 7 April Longfellow and Fields urged him to give up that night's reading. He took a biscuit and sherry at twelve and then drank a pint of champagne at three (for someone with vascular degeneration, this alcoholic diet was one of the worst imaginable) but that night, as he told his daughter, he ". . . read as I never did before, and astonished the audience quite as much as myself. You never saw or heard such a scene of excitement." He had been on the point of taking his friends' advice and stopping altogether, but after the "excitement" of that night he seems to have sensed something like a return of his powers. In any case he was sustained by the knowledge that he was coming to an end and the following day, Wednesday, 8 April, he gave his last reading in Boston. He read the story of the "Cheap Jack" and "Mrs Gamp", once more putting on the features and assuming the voice of that redoubtable old party, until at the end the prolonged applause brought him back to his reading desk. "In this brief life of ours," he said, "it is sad to do almost anything for the last time . . . Ladies and gentlemen, I beg most earnestly, most gratefully, and most affectionately, to bid you, each and all, farewell."

The hall erupted in applause and cheering, while Dickens stood there with the tears in his eyes.

Only the last readings in New York were left now. He was clearly exhilarated by the prospect of his imminent departure, and after the first reading there his spirits once more rose in an improvised routine of comic songs and "patter" in the company of his friends. He read again the next night and Mrs Fields noticed that one of the signs of his fatigue was ". . . the rush of blood into his face and hands". Four days later, on 18 April, a farewell banquet was held for him in New York; so serious was his lameness, however, that he arrived very late. He had been in such pain all day that he could not fit a boot on his foot, and in the end Dolby had to drive all over the city looking for such a thing as a gout-stocking. But eventually he arrived, an hour after the appointed time, hobbling in on the arm of Horace Greeley, the editor of the *New York Tribune*, with his foot swathed in something resembling a carpet-bag. Dinner was conducted to the sound of national airs being played by a band and, at the end, he rose to speak. "When the storm of enthusiasm had quieted," one guest remembered, "Dickens tried to speak but could not; the tears streamed down his face. As he stood there looking on us in silence, colour and pallor alternating on his face, sympathetic emotion passed through the hall. When he presently began to say something, though still faltering, we gave our cheers . . ." When he returned to his hotel (where, incidentally, he repeated his long speech word for word to Annie Fields), it was observed that the main source of his anxiety lay in the prospect of the news of his illness being telegraphed to London. But whom did he most fear upsetting, Ellen or Georgina? The next day he could hardly rise from his bed, and was constantly attended by friends and by his doctor. But there was only one reading left now, the farewell reading for New York. A card was sent out in advance, signed by his doctor, Fordyce Barker: "I certify that Mr Dickens is suffering from a neuralgic affection of the right foot, probably occasioned by great fatigue in a severe winter. But I believe that he can read tonight without much pain or inconvenience (his mind being set on not disappointing his audience) with the aid of a slight mechanical addition to his usual arrangements." That evening he limped slowly to his table and sat down, with his leg supported by the "mechanical addition". Then he read *A Christmas Carol* and the trial scene from *The Pickwick Papers*. He left the stage to "tumultuous applause", but returned on the arm of Dolby. "Ladies and gentlemen, The shadow of one word has impended over me all this evening, and the time has come at last when the shadow must fall. It is but a very short one, but the weight of such things is not measurable by their length, and two much shorter words express the whole round of our human existence . . . Ladies and gentlemen, I beg to bid you farewell – and I pray God bless you, and God bless the land in which I leave you." Now, as one member of the audience recalled, "the vast audience stood cheering and tearful as, gravely bowing, and refusing all assistance, as if in that final moment he wished to confront us alone, the master lingered and lingered, and slowly retired". It was his last appearance in the United States. His last public occasion in a country with which he had fought an unending contest but in which he had an unending interest – a country in some ways so like himself, so eager and impetuous, that there are times when his battles with it seem like battles with his own shadow.

The day after the reading he was unable to rise from his bed, so tired he had become. That night Fields told him that a statue ought to be raised in honour of him and of his heroism. "No, don't," he replied characteristically, "take down one of the old ones instead!" Then, on the following day, he sailed for England. He was surrounded by a large crowd as he left his hotel for the last time, and bouquets were thrown to him from the windows nearby. It was a fine day as he went down to the harbour by Spring Street, to step onto the private tug which would take him to the *Russia* which was lying off Staten Island. As soon as Dickens saw the water, he said, "That's *home*!" Fields and other friends had accompanied him to this final point of departure. "As the tugboat hooted, all left save Fields . . . The lame foot came down from the rail, and the friends were locked in each other's arms. Fields then hastened down the side, and the lines were cast off. A cheer was given for Dolby, when Dickens patted him approvingly upon the shoulder, saying 'Good boy'. Another cheer for Dickens, then the tug steamed away." The group left on the shore shouted, "Goodbye!" Dickens ". . . put his hat upon his cane, and waved it, and the answer came 'Goodbye' and 'God bless you every one'". Anthony Trollope, who had arrived in New York that same day, visited Dickens in his cabin just before the *Russia* sailed; he found him with his foot bound up, but remarkably cheerful. Dickens had finished his tour at last.

The journey back to England was uneventful but speedy; and this much to Dickens's liking, since he found the other passengers on board to be "Jackasses". Within three days his catarrh disappeared and the swelling of his foot eased; he was able to sleep (he had taken the steward's cabin on deck for its air) and his appetite had returned. Eight days at sea, and then they were back in England. But what of those whom he had left behind? When the Fields returned to Boston they embraced each other and sobbed. Annie Fields, now free at last to consider the man with whom she had spent so much time, noted some of the reflections in her diary which have been ably chronicled in George Curry's *Charles Dickens and Annie Fields*. "He is swift, restless, impatient, with moods of fire . . ." She thought of his return to England and to Gad's Hill Place. "But even now he might be lonely such is his nature. When I recall his lonely couch and lonely hours I feel he has had a strange lot. May his mistakes be expiated." And then, on the day of his arrival in England, she wrote, "I cannot help rehearsing in my mind the intense joy of his beloved – It is too much to face, even in one's imagination, and too sacred. Yet I know today to be *the day* and these hours, *his hours* – Surely among the most painfully and joyfully intense of his whole life . . . Tomorrow Gad's Hill!!" It is clear from this that she knew, through Dickens himself or through her husband, of some "beloved" who was not at Gad's Hill Place and whom Dickens had been longing to see. It can only have been Ellen Ternan, but the curious fact remains that Mrs Fields was not the sort of woman who would have spoken in such rapture about a mistress. She was a respectable and respected Bostonian from a distinguished family, an American Victorian of the old school, one might say. This is made quite clear in a later entry in her diary of that year when she condemns a man from her husband's firm "found in adultery – the cause of ruin to two women besides the wreck of his wife's happiness . . ." On the matter of this sexual chicanery she adds that ". . . he had been dealing with the life and death of his own soul . . ." It is inconceivable that a woman who spoke in such terms about marital unfaithfulness would also have described in so glowing and rapturous a way Dickens's relationship with his "beloved" – unless it were something quite different from a normal sexual affair. She would not have written in this way if she had not considered Dickens's relationship with Ellen Ternan to be above reproach. This must also be connected with the constant expression of her feeling that he was in many ways a sorrowful and lonely man; certainly such remarks should be seen in the light of her knowledge of his relationship with Ellen, and they lead towards a conclusion quite different from that which suggests that he was living "in sin" with her and even, as some have believed, with their illegitimate child or children. Of course it would be unwise to place too much emphasis upon stray thoughts in a diary, but they do help to suggest a much stranger relationship between Dickens and Ellen Ternan than has in the past been supposed.

And what of Dickens himself now? What had been the effect of his American tour? Both his sons believed that it injured him. Henry said that it actually shortened his life, and Charley has written that ". . . the American work had told him upon him severely. The trouble in the foot was greatly intensified, and he was gravely out of health." But there is something more to be discovered in the record of these five months, something which Carlyle discerned when he read Forster's account of them in his biography: "Those two American Journies especially transcend in tragic interest to a thinking reader most things one has seen in writing." It is reasonable to assume, for example, that Dickens almost killed himself in order to make more money; he risked everything in order to become more "secure". And yet this had always been the case. Certainly it had been true at the time of his earliest childhood, when the search for security was the one constant aspect of a life so bedevilled by pain and anxiety. And it may be precisely here that the proper significance of his American journey can be understood – that, somehow, in the vision of the mature Dickens making his way through an alien country, we catch sight, from time to time, of the young Dickens making his way through the streets of London.

There was that same desperate need for security, and that same sense of the "dreariness" of life which he had experienced as a child; his Christmas journey on the train from Boston to New York, when he sat in silence and looked out of the window, evokes the journey he made in the coach which brought him from Rochester to London as a child. A journey in which ". . . I thought life sloppier than I expected to find it". In adult life as in childhood, also, he was racked by pains of a predominantly nervous origin; what he called his "ailing little life" as a child, when, as Forster said, he was "subject to continual attacks of illness", had surely now returned. But now, as then, he preferred to keep his agony to himself and once more "suffered in secret". There was a similar attempt to conceal his life in other ways, too. Where once he had hidden from Bob Fagin and his warehouse companions the fact that his father was in the Marshalsea, so now he hid from most people his liaison with Ellen Ternan. There was the same need to perform as well; in the blacking warehouse he had entertained his little companions "with the results of some of the old readings" just as now, in

America and England, he entertained audiences with readings from his own books. As a child he had been considered a "prodigy" by the adults, and he was considered a prodigy still. As a child he had also felt the need to work skilfully and hard, saving as much money as he could in the process; and nothing of that had changed. The continual fevered sicknesses, the sense of dreariness and desolation, the secret life, the need to entertain, the urgent desire to work, the interest in money – all these echoes of his childhood resound through these last years. Of course many things had changed. He no longer took his breakfast in prison, he no longer hated his mother and his older sister, he no longer felt himself to be "beyond the reach of all such honourable emulation and success", he no longer felt himself to be neglected and humiliated, and the crowd no longer watched him tying up the labels of blacking pots in the window of Chandos Street. But do we not feel the pressure of these things still propelling him forward through all the days of his life? It is not so tragic as Carlyle would have it, but, rather, part of the ineluctable process of life – Charles Dickens returning, despite his genius and all his fame, to the state of his childhood. As if nothing that had ever happened to him could exorcise the presence of that child. As if nothing, in the end, were of any account beside that sense of the world which first visited him as a child.

Chapter 34

THE *Russia* arrived at Queenstown Harbour on the last day of April, 1868, but Dolby and Dickens did not hurry home. They dined in Liverpool on the following day and then took the morning train the day after that, arriving back in London in the middle of the afternoon. But Dickens did not go down to Gad's Hill Place. He went instead to Peckham in order to be with the Ternans, Ellen and her mother having returned from Italy only two days before. He stayed here for a week, making occasional visits to London, principally to catch up with the dramatic version of *No Thoroughfare* at the Adelphi and to consult with Fechter about its chances in Paris. (He also lent money – something like two thousand pounds – to the actor who was then, as ever, hard up.) On 9 May he finally returned to Kent, although Georgina and Mamie must have known that he was staying in Peckham in the interim because they warned him in advance that the local inhabitants wanted to signal his arrival by dragging his carriage from Higham station to the house. He forestalled this rumbustious greeting by travelling instead to Gravesend station; nevertheless, his route home was marked by flags on the neighbouring houses and by the cheers of the villagers. But life soon settled down into its familiar routine. "I feel the peace of the country beyond all expression," he said and, in fact, both his spirits and his health seemed quickly to revive. They had reasserted themselves even while he was crossing the Atlantic and now, when his doctor saw him, he exclaimed (according to Dickens), "Good Lord! Seven years younger!" But he did not rest for long. He "returned to the ordinary routine of his London life, as if he had never left it", according to Dolby, but in reality it was more than simply "routine". He had arrears of some six months' correspondence and in addition the pressure of work was materially increased later in the month when Wills, while hunting, fell from his horse and suffered severe concussion. He said that it was like having doors slamming in his head all the time and, as a result, he could not resume office work for several months. But this meant that Dickens had to superintend all the financial and business arrangements of the magazine, which were Wills's especial province, as well as the customary weekly editorial work. In other words, the exhaustion of America was quickly followed by severe work at home. Henry Morley acted as a substitute for Wills (Wilkie Collins was not at all eager to return to office life at Wellington Street) but the additional labour meant that Dickens was granted very little rest. He began once more his relentless round between Wellington Street and Peckham (and no doubt his "secret" apartment near the Five Bells), between Peckham and Gad's Hill Place.

He was also much occupied over the play which Collins and he had adapted from their Christmas story. It had opened at the Adelphi at Christmas and had been an enormous success, the pursuit and capture of the murderer, Obenreizer, fitting appropriately within the climate of a perfervid "sensation drama" as popular in this period as "sensation fiction" itself. *No Thoroughfare* ran for more than one hundred and fifty performances, and a critic in *The Mask* noted that "Charles Dickens and Wilkie Collins have made their dramatic hit at last! . . . in *No Thoroughfare* they are both at liberty to enjoy their triumph to the utmost. It is a hit in every sense of the word, more particularly in the sense which is the pleasantest of all in managerial consideration. Its 'money' draw has never been equalled in the annals of the theatre." In truth this is something of an exaggeration but the purport is clear enough; Collins and Dickens, grouped together very much as if they were some new playwriting team of the Sixties, had achieved what in the new language of the era was called a "hit". One is reminded of Dickens's phrase to Dolby, "real show business"; this had not been the vocabulary of the Thirties, when Dickens first began to write for the stage, but his triumph in this new atmosphere suggests how malleable in one sense his genius was.

The play was also to be performed in Paris, and Fechter left the "run" at the Adelphi towards the end of May in order to superintend rehearsals at the Vaudeville there, Dickens in the meantime sending out somewhat peremptory instructions to him. The novelist himself went over at the end of May, and stayed at the Hôtel du Helder; he was specifically there to attend the first night three evenings later, but in fact he was too apprehensive about the reactions of the Parisian audience to do so. He took a ride with Fechter in an open cab on that first night and then they sat together in a café near the theatre as the translator, Didier, came out to them with news of each act. Dickens *was* about to enter the theatre but then, getting "nerves" at the last minute, changed his mind and ordered a cab to take him to the station so that he might catch the Boulogne train. He was back at Gad's Hill Place the next day, having heard that the play had been a complete and signal success.

He was still preoccupied for most of the time, however, with business at *All The Year Round*, and had managed to organise for himself a summer routine from which he rarely, if ever, departed; from Monday to Thursday he worked and lived in London, while at the weekends he returned to Gad's Hill Place where he entertained the various guests who arrived throughout the summer months (among them Longfellow and Frith). In fact his work on the periodical was at last providentially lightened, although for a reason with which Dickens could possibly have dispensed. His son, Charley, was involved in bankruptcy proceedings, having lost all of his money in his paper-mill business (for which he had already received a great deal of help from Miss Burdett-Coutts) and owing something like one thousand pounds. This was for him a very serious matter, since he had a wife and five children – Dickens was at a loss to know what to do for him, but eventually arrived at the conclusion that he was best placed to work with him at Wellington Street. So Charley reported on the daily "mailbag" and answered most correspondence. There were family problems of another kind also; his daughter's husband, Charles Collins, was now in very bad health and, Dickens reported, "*I* say emphatically – dying". In fact Collins had stomach cancer and would die in 1873 but, as far as Dickens was concerned, his demise could not come a moment too soon. This was partly because of his resentment at Collins marrying his daughter in the first place (after Dickens's death Georgina told Annie Fields that he had for a long time been exercised by the "dreary unfortunate fate" of Kate), but partly because of his deep dislike of constitutional weakness of any kind. Collins was now vomiting a great deal, remained very feeble, and could not leave his room at Gad's Hill Place – "totally unfit for any function of this life," Dickens told Wills in a description not notable for its sympathy with the invalid. And Mrs Fields, in her diary, remarked, taking her cue from comments by Fechter, that Dickens "could not understand the prolonged endurance of such an existence and in his passionate nature which must snap when it yielded at all, it produced disgust". Again according to the Boston lady, Dickens used to regard his son-in-law with a look which seemed to say ". . . astonishing you should be here to-day, but to-morrow you will be in your chamber never to come out again". This attitude must have caused dissension within his own family but, in addition, it also provoked an estrangement from Charles's brother. For Wilkie Collins could not be led to believe that his brother was seriously ill, and was naturally hurt and annoyed by Dickens's attitude towards him; Dickens seems to have repaid in kind and made a point of telling Wills that *The Moonstone*, then being serialised in *All The Year Round*, was "wearisome beyond endurance". Relations between the two novelists, previously so close, never recovered.

But it was also in this period that Dickens's problems wore a more private aspect. It seems that the Ternans left Linden Grove in Peckham – by October Mrs Ternan was staying at 32 Harrington Square (very close to the house the family had occupied before they moved to the Slough cottage in 1866), and from December to June she and, most likely, Ellen were staying at 10 Bath Place in Worthing. After that they moved into an apartment house at 305 Vauxhall Bridge Road. The evidence is circumstantial and incomplete but it does suggest that, from this time forward, Charles Dickens and Ellen Ternan no longer lived with or near each other; Dickens himself seems to have kept on the Peckham house for a while, and perhaps paid someone to maintain it for him. Nevertheless there is no evidence of any estrangement between them – it seems clear, as we shall see, that Ellen accompanied him on all or part of his next reading tour – and it is even possible that she sometimes remained *sub rosa* at Peckham after her mother had moved away. In what capacity, if such is the case, is of course not known. But perhaps one might pick out some stray sentences from the novel which Dickens soon began to write, and repeat the words of Rosa Bud to her "lover", Edwin Drood. "'That's a dear good boy! Eddy, let us be courageous. Let us change to brother and sister from this day forth.'

'Never be husband and wife?'

'Never!'"

And, when Longfellow came to visit Dickens at Gad's Hill Place, he noticed his "terrible sadness".

What else was there for Dickens to do, now, except to work on and to work hard? By the end of July he was trying to begin that year's story for the Christmas issue of *All The Year Round*, but he was starting drafts only to abandon them; he could see nothing beyond what had now become for him a dreary routine of stories around a theme. One such draft, written partly in Peckham, may be what has since become known as the "Sapsea Fragment"; it is a short episode narrated by a pompous auctioneer which bears the seeds for some parts of *The Mystery of Edwin Drood*. It may actually be this piece of narration which Dickens described to Wills as tending towards a new book rather than a Christmas tale but, even so, it remained only a fragment. Eventually he abandoned altogether the idea of writing a Christmas number for that year, despite the evident financial advantages of the old scheme. He simply seemed unable to work at his old pace or with his old instinctive energy, and it is significant that Forster should notice this summer ". . . manifest abatement of his natural force, the elasticity of bearing was impaired, and the wonderful brightness of eye was dimmed at times". He added, more ominously, that on one occasion ". . . he could read only the halves of the letters over the shop doors that were on his right as he looked". Dickens ascribed this to the effects of the medicine he was taking for his injured foot and, according to Forster, no one really understood ". . . the fact that absolute and pressing danger did positively exist".

For it was at this very time that Dickens, unable to manage any continuous writing, plunged once more into the fevered hard work of his readings. Even before he had left America he had been negotiating with Chappell and Company for a further, "farewell", series of readings; Chappell had suggested seventy-five in all, but it is some measure of Dickens's wild over-estimate of his own strength that he insisted upon giving one hundred readings for the sum of eight thousand pounds. It is strange, perhaps, that, according to Dolby the prospect of such hard labour came to Dickens positively as ". . . a relief to his mind". But it is stranger still that at this time, when the old vigour of his spirit seemed to be ebbing, he returned to something which he had been putting off for the last five years: he began to arrange a reading from *Oliver Twist* of the murder of Nancy by Bill Sikes. Five years before he had considered it but had been afraid that it was too "horrible" to launch upon the public. But now its horror no longer concerned him; or, rather, he embraced it and heightened it in what was to become the nearest approach to "acting" which he ever managed in the readings. The appropriate scenes from the novel – beginning with Fagin's decision to have Nancy followed, and ending with her death – were of course abbreviated in his usual style. There are two extant versions of the reading script which emerged from these cuts and changes, but the second of them has the most explicit instructions concerning Dickens's performance. All the way through there are stage directions in the margins: "Beckon down . . . Point . . . Shudder . . . Look Round with Terror . . . Murder coming . . . Mystery . . . *Terror To The End.*" And then there was the text itself. ". . . he beat it *twice* upon the upturned face *that almost touched his own . . . seized a heavy club,* and *struck her* down!! . . . *the pool of gore that quivered and danced in the sunlight on the ceiling* . . . but *such* flesh, *and so much blood*!!! . . . *The very feet of his dog were bloody*!!!! . . . *dashed out his brains*!!" So much blood and death. So much horror. One summer's afternoon Dickens's son, Charley, was working in the library when he heard the sound of two people involved in a serious and violent quarrel. He stepped outside, and then saw his father at the end of the meadow behind the house, ". . . striding up and down, gesticulating wildly, and, in the character of *Mr Sikes*, murdering *Nancy*, with every circumstance of the most aggravated brutality". Killing her. Seizing the heavy club and striking her down to the ground. Bellowing. This was Dickens now. At the climactic end of his career as a public reader. Less than two years before his own death. *Terror to the end.*

So why did he do it now? Of course he wanted a new "sensation" for his final tour, and he said that he wished to leave behind him the memory of ". . . something very passionate and dramatic, done with simple means . . ." And of course, as we have seen, sensation drama and sensation fiction were now very popular with a public which, in any case, had always possessed a taste for murder and for death. But were there reasons other than these purely external ones? In going back to *Oliver Twist*, and in going back to Fagin, Dickens was in some sense also reliving again the period of his own childhood from which he had so largely drawn his inspiration for that early novel. We have seen how his travels in America suggest some return to the condition of his childhood, and can we not see it also revived here? But, on this occasion, only the horror and hatred which he had once felt. Killing his mother. Killing his sister. Mocking the boy who had pitied him in the warehouse, mocking the boy whose name he had given to Fagin. And yet also becoming him, identifying with him; he played the part of Fagin, just as he played the part of Sikes. There may be some other private disturbance here, too, some echo of his own more recent feelings in this bloody account of a man killing "his" woman. Yet on the stage Dickens played the part of Nancy, too, as well as those of Sikes and Fagin – he said at one point in the new year that he was ". . . at present nightly murdered by Mr W. Sikes . . ." To be both murderer and victim. To be the man and yet to be the woman. All the strange pathways of the novelist's imagination come to a central point. It is as if he stands lost and bewildered here, shouting out the words, terrifying his audiences. It is impossible to say exactly what he meant, or what he thought he was doing. We are simply eavesdropping on his secret dialogue with his own self, a self which had always been the same, always watchful, always waiting. Love, despair and hate are all too strangely intermingled to be considered apart.

Perhaps it says something about his frayed state of mind in this period that, when his son Edward ("Plorn") emigrated to Australia, he was plunged into a quite uncharacteristic paroxysm of grief; and this despite the fact that Dickens himself had been largely instrumental in sending Plorn, not yet seventeen, to seek his fortune in the outback. He had seen in him what he had observed in other of his children, a lack of determination and application which he blamed upon their mother but which might equally have been ascribed to his own family. In preparation for Plorn's emigration he had sent him to Cirencester Agricultural College for eight months – he considered this quite long enough under the circumstances – and then dispatched him to join his brother, Alfred, in New South Wales. But he had always been an impressionable and rather vulnerable boy, and it seems somewhat rash of Dickens to send him to a life in the outback which he himself knew only from "books and verbal description". (How typical of him, though, to trust in "books" for a true depiction of the reality.) But, when the time came to take his leave of Plorn on the platform of Paddington station, "the scene that followed was tragic in its emotional intensity". These are the words of Dickens's son, Henry, who went on to describe how "my father openly gave way to his intense grief quite regardless of his surroundings". On another occasion he added that "I never saw a man so completely overcome", which suggests that Dickens's passionate outpouring of sorrow must have been of an extraordinary kind. Certainly Plorn himself was not accustomed to seeing his father so moved, except perhaps when he gave public readings, and he looked the other way until the train was ready to depart. He took with him, however, a complete set of his father's books; how touching that this young man should be seeing his father for the last time, while carrying with him the novels by which Charles

Dickens would be remembered for ever. Dickens also handed to his son a letter in which he impressed upon him the lessons of the New Testament as well as the "truth and beauty of the Christian religion". And so his young son left him – Plorn, the child whom Dickens had carried on his shoulders around the countryside of Boulogne, who used to accompany his father on cab rides, whose comments on life in general Dickens found "wonderful", his favourite son. In letters after the event Dickens talks again and again of the "sad parting" and the "hard parting". Was there in the sadness perhaps some measure of guilt that it was he who had pushed him away? But there was more to it than that. It is likely that Dickens realised well enough that he would never see his son again and, in this parting on Paddington station, there was some token of death's final separation. Is that what provoked that passionate and unprecedented burst of sorrow from Dickens, the father who had never been able to express his true feelings to his children? Days later he admitted that "I find myself constantly thinking of Plorn". But he was not alone in this. Catherine Dickens wrote from Gloucester Crescent that "I miss you most sadly, my own darling Plorn". Georgina is almost equally moved in her own letter, although hers is clouded somewhat by her apology for any harshness or "hasty words" that she might once have uttered. Which suggests that Plorn was not altogether at ease in Gad's Hill Place after the departure of his mother. Which suggests in turn that, despite Dickens's protestations to all of his friends, Georgina was no real substitute for Catherine.

Certainly Henry Dickens was now spending a great deal of time with his mother – she tells Plorn as much in her letter to him. While he remained at home he was a burden about which Dickens still often complained; he had expressed a wish to go to Cambridge rather than immediately to embark upon a professional career, but it was only with misgivings that Dickens allowed him to attend university. In fact Henry had gone up to Trinity Hall just a week before Plorn sailed, and Dickens was very careful about ensuring that his son received just enough money *and no more*. His refrain is always the need to keep out of debt, and to depend upon his own resources; his injunctions are always the same, too. Do not waste your father's hard-earned money. Remember what your father's life was like at the same age. Nevertheless he was genuinely proud of his son, and was delighted when in the following year Henry won a scholarship at Trinity Hall which promised him an annual stipend of fifty pounds. Henry told him the news when he arrived from Cambridge at Higham station and was met by his father in the pony carriage. At first Dickens only murmured "Capital! Capital!" but, half way home, he ". . . broke down completely. Turning towards me with tears in his eyes and giving me a warm grip of the hand, he said, 'God bless you, my boy; God bless you!'" Henry was the only one of his children to have achieved any success in life, and it must have sometimes seemed to Dickens that he had attained his great distinction at the price of everybody else's happiness. But now, in Henry, he had some proof that at least a particle of his extraordinary talents might survive his passing.

In other respects the world was, as he had said, very much a cemetery. Just a few weeks after Plorn had left him for ever, his younger brother, Frederick, died of asphyxia induced by the bursting of an abscess on his lung – Frederick, the boy whom Dickens had taken into chambers with him when he was a young reporter, whose education and prospects had always been a source of concern to him, the brother to whom he always felt closest. He had become something of a lounger, something of a wastrel (although he had always retained that sharp humour and sense of the comic which his older brother also possessed) and, in recent years, his improvidence and irresponsibility had been yet another burden on Dickens. But the news of his death erased all traces of their previous arguments and Dickens remembered only the bright, active boy for whom he had taken all the "parental" responsibility. He had been, as it happened, his last surviving brother. "It was a wasted life," Dickens wrote to Forster, "but God forbid that one should be hard upon it, or upon anything in this world that is not deliberately and coldly wrong . . ." There is a tone of resignation and forgiveness in this that consorts easily with Dickens's more fragile state, a new tone that also found relief in a friendly letter which he now wrote to Mark Lemon after twelve years of cold hostility and suspicion. Towards the end of his life he was beginning to see matters in a longer perspective, even those affairs which had once so closely moved him and enraged him.

It was Dolby who told him about his brother. He had received the news of Frederick's death from a friend who lived in the same town and, when he broke it to Dickens, it had a "serious effect" upon him – to such an extent that his "distress of mind" seemed to make it impossible for him to read that same night in London. And yet the sight of the hall and the little reading desk acted as a kind of drug; they "banished all this depression, and he forgot himself and his own sufferings in the excitement of his duty". This of course was, for him, one of the inestimable benefits of his public readings; even now, ill, prematurely old, depressed (as he so often announced himself to be), he was revived by the momentum of his reading scripts and literally forgot himself in the excitement of taking on the very characters he himself had created. He could forget his own mortality. That is why, even at the very height of his exhaustion and overwork, he knew that he would greatly miss these public performances once the "farewell" season was over.

It had begun on 6 October. Hard work, as always, and his letters during this period are much shorter and much less exhilarated than those he had written at similar times in the past; Forster said that it was a "fatal mistake" for Dickens to embark upon this hectic schedule of one hundred nights, shaken by loss of sleep, deeply fearful of railway travel which still induced in him "rushes of terror", dependent upon a quite unsuitable diet. In Dolby's own account, which tends to stress Dickens's high spirits, there nonetheless emerges the portrait of a man who was mentally agonised, sleepless, depressed, who broke down in paroxysms of grief at the death of friends, and who was terrified for his life during train journeys. There exists at least the possibility that he knew that he was dying (and dying so young!) but could not cope with that knowledge. Liverpool. Manchester. Brighton. He was sick. Unable to sleep. Having to spend half the day lying upon a sofa. His foot was swelling again, and this time the vascular degeneration was affecting the right as well as the left leg. There were still times when he could make out only the right halves of words and one evening, when Charley heard his father reading in St James's Hall, he noticed that ". . . he found it impossible to say Pickwick, and called him Picksnick, and Picnic, and Peckwicks and all sorts of names except the right with a comical glance of surprise at the occupants of the front seats which were always reserved for his family and friends". On two occasions Dickens compared himself to Mariana in Tennyson's poem. He did not state in what exact particular but her final refrain is eloquent enough:

> "I am aweary, aweary,
> Oh God, that I were dead!"

And yet this is the man whom Dolby found "laughing immoderately" in his hotel room. He was laughing at *The Old Curiosity Shop*, a copy of which Dolby had purchased for him and which he was now reading "as if he had never seen it before". He told Dolby that he was not laughing at his own words but, rather, at the recollection of the circumstances and incidents which had accompanied their writing. The period when he was with Catherine, in the fullness of his fame and youth. It might be thought that, at this time in his life, this was truly laughter in the dark. But it was not necessarily so. It has already been observed how the highest spirits could in his life accompany the truest grief; it was in part an accident of temper but also practically a philosophy for, as he said at this time, there was always ". . . something comic rising up in the midst of the direst misery . . ."

There was at least one brief respite from his readings now, since the general election of November meant that Dickens could safely leave aside any performances for the duration of the campaign (he supported Gladstone and the Liberal party, particularly since he maintained a lifelong aversion to Disraeli, but it cannot be said that he had any great faith or hope in representative government even on the newly re-formed model). Of course he did not rest. There was no longer time to rest. He had already decided to begin a new series of "Uncommercial" essays (in the event he wrote only seven) and, in preparation for one of them, he visited the purlieus of Limehouse; his main object was to visit the recently-established East London Children's Hospital at Ratcliff Cross but he also went to Gin Alley, Three Foxes Court, Butcher Row, and the other sad streets clustered around Commercial Road and Nicholas Hawksmoor's church of St Anne's Limehouse. He saw here the children suffering from poison ingested as they worked at the lead-mills in Waterloo Place close by but, perhaps more significantly, he was visiting once more an area which would become central to his next and last novel. A book smelling of graves and of old dust. A story of violent passion. Of death. And it can hardly be coincidence that now, just before resuming his reading tour, Dickens declaimed for the first time to a private audience that bloody murder which he had been rehearsing, "Sikes and Nancy". He had performed it for his son, Charley, who had advised him not to undertake it in public; knowing that his father would react violently to any suggestion that he was too frail or too ill to bear the strain, Charley preferred to keep his reasons to himself. Dolby also tried to dissuade him from taking on the additional excitement of this particular reading. But he was unwilling to listen to such advice and, finally, it was agreed that the decision should be left to Chappell and Company. In turn they proposed that

Dickens should read it to a group of friends, and that their reaction should act as final judge and arbiter of the matter. And so it was arranged. On 14 November, in St James's Hall, Dickens killed Nancy in public. Fagin was in front of the audience. And then Sikes. And then the woman herself, beaten down, gasping and shrieking, to the ground. ". . . *such* flesh, *and so much blood!!!*" Dickens becoming all of them in turn. The audience were, according to Dickens, "unmistakeably pale, and had horror-stricken faces". He himself had had doubts about it immediately before he began but afterwards, when the famous maroon screen was thrown back to reveal a table of oysters and champagne (how "Dickensian" this is – this feast after the horror), the reaction of his audience only served to increase his determination to perform it. One friend, William Harness, explained to Dickens later that it was "a most amazing and terrific thing" but that he had had ". . . an almost irresistible impulse upon me to *scream*", and a famous doctor told Dickens that ". . . if only one woman cries out when you murder the girl, there will be a contagion of hysteria all over this place". Precisely what Dickens wanted to hear. And Mrs Keeley, the celebrated actress, replied to Dickens's enquiry, "Why, of course, do it. Having got at such an effect as that, it must be done. But the public have been looking out for a sensation these last fifty years or so, and by Heaven they have got it!"

Those closest to Dickens were still unhappy about the prospect. His son and Dolby himself were as resolutely opposed as ever; so, of course, was Forster. Edmund Yates was opposed to it. Percy Fitzgerald was opposed to it. They had watched Dickens in the agonies of possession upon the stage in front of them, and they knew how it was affecting him. There may even have been something too dangerous, too alarming, almost *too* odd, in the sight of this man tearing himself to pieces in front of an audience. But nothing could stop Dickens now. At least two of those present, Charles Kent and Wilkie Collins, had more technical objections. They were unhappy at the sudden termination of the reading at that point where Sikes drags the dog from the room of the murder and locks the door. Perhaps the flight of Sikes should be shown, and then his death as he falls from the rooftop on Jacob's Island? At first Dickens was much opposed to this – ". . . no audience on earth could be held for ten minutes after the girl's death," he told Kent. ". . . Trust me to be right. I stand there, and I know." But this was just his usual tone of certainty, and in fact he did append a short narrative to the murder itself. In three pages of manuscript he condensed all that part of *Oliver Twist* which deals with the flight and death of Sikes, and the whole reading was as we have it now. Dickens also arranged an addition to his familiar set in order to take account of the unusual nature of this particular reading. Two large maroon screens were placed on either side of the regular back screen, like wings, and curtains of the same colour were placed to enclose any other opening upon the stage. Dickens, in other words, was creating a confined space in which the figure of the actor and reader was entirely isolated – each gesture distinct, each movement lit by gas against the dark cloth. It had become a Theatre of Terror.

But he did not begin it, not yet, for at the end of 1868 he travelled up to Scotland for a conventional series of readings which were (as usual) met with great acclaim. The general press of business around him, too, was even greater than before. He had still to maintain all his work on *All The Year Round* since, although Wills was now back at work, he was according to Dickens really "no better". And this at the time when the "New Series" of the magazine was about to appear, a series marked by distinctive changes in typography and size. The Christmas issue was, however, finally abolished; Dickens explained his decision by the number of other journals which now imitated it and rendered it almost "tiresome". But he could not admit to staleness or fatigue in any other sense, and actually had to deny in public a rumour that he had given up the editorship. He said at the end of the twentieth volume, just before the beginning of the "New Series", that ". . . my fellow labourers and I will be at our old posts, in company with those younger comrades whom I have had the pleasure of enrolling from time to time and whose number it is always one of my pleasantest editorial duties to enlarge . . ." At the same time, too, in compliance with a request in the will of Chauncey Hare Townshend, he felt obliged to collect the scattered writings of his dead friend on the subject of religion; a thankless task at the best of times but one rendered more dreary by the amount of material through which Dickens had to sift. "Are they worth anything as religious views?" Fitzgerald asked him while he was still engaged on this laborious task.

"Nothing whatever, I should say."

Yet of course Dickens finished the job as an act of friendship. As a duty. It was once remarked by Annie Fields how difficult it must have been for him always to respond to the affection or admiration which he inspired in others; there are in fact many occasions on which those who seemed almost to idolise him were upset or depressed by his conduct, although in any other man it would be considered perfectly normal. Percy Fitzgerald, in a postscript to Dickens's remark on Townshend, adds that Dickens ". . . had to put up with a vast deal of this admiring worship, generally from retiring creatures whom his delicate good-nature would not let him offend". It is yet another light on the man, coming now as he entered the last year which he would see to its close.

He gave his first public performance of "Sikes and Nancy" on 5 January, 1869, in St James's Hall. He had been rehearsing it for some days and, when it was completed, according to Dolby, he was "utterly prostrate"; it was only after he had quickly left the platform that the audience was able to recover its composure, too, and realise what had taken place upon the stage – ". . . that all the horrors to which they had been listening were but a story and not a reality". The accounts in the press were generally very favourable and nothing further was needed to steel Dickens's determination to make it an essential, and indeed the central, part of his repertoire. He read it approximately four times a week and nothing on earth seemed able to prevent him from doing so, even at the cost of life and health. It took on, for him, an hallucinatory reality. It became almost a monomania. It was, Dolby said, ". . . one of the greatest dangers we had to contend against", and still Dickens went on. His letters were filled with it. "I am murdering Nancy . . . I have a vague sensation of being 'wanted' as I walk about the streets . . . My preparations for a certain murder . . . The crime being completely off my mind and the blood spilled . . . my fellow-criminals . . . I commit the murder again . . . imbue my hands in innocent blood . . . I have a great deal of murdering before me . . ." Edmund Yates watched his performance: "Gradually warming with excitement he flung aside his book and acted the scene of the murder, shrieked the terrified pleadings of the girl, growled the brutal savagery of the murder . . . The raised hands, the bent-back head, are good; but shut your eyes and the illusion is more complete. Then the cries for mercy, the Bill! dear Bill! for dear God's sake! uttered in tones in which the agony of fear prevails even over the earnestness of the prayers, the dead dull voice as hope departs, are intensely real. When the pleading ceases, you open your eyes in relief, in time to see the impersonation of the murderer seizing a heavy club and striking his victim to the ground." It is chilling even now to contemplate this, but how chilling then. Dickens believed that the audience had a "horror of me after seeing the murder". And there were times when he had a horror of himself – Dickens, too, feeling guilty and "wanted" as he walks the streets, so strange an image of this famous public man. As if it all counted for nothing and he were no more than the vagrant or outcast which, in his childhood, he had feared that he might become. It is what killed him – according to his son – this endlessly repeated murder. And Dolby has agreed.

On the night after the first London reading he went on to Ireland. Percy Fitzgerald saw him when he was about to catch the train and noticed how his face was "worn and drawn, and delved with wrinkles, and scored with anxiety, bronzed and burnished, and also wearing a very sad expression . . ." Had Ellen Ternan come to see him depart, too? Or even to travel with him? There is an oblique aside in Percy Fitzgerald's account which suggests as much for, when he took this opportunity of telling Dickens that he was to be married, "I recall his saying that I must let him tell it to one who was with him." One who was with him . . . Fitzgerald does not amplify upon the unnamed companion, but it is hardly likely to have been Dolby, Georgina or any of the other frequently mentioned members of Dickens's staff or family. It is clear, too, from Dickens's own unusual confession later, that Ellen Ternan had been with him for at least one of the later readings in the North of England; so she was his companion still and, again according to his own unexpected reference, was the only person who could tell him those "home truths" about his health which others like Dolby tended to avoid.

And then, after Ireland, on again – London, Bristol, Torquay, Bath . . . ". . . the older I get, the more I do and the harder I work," Dickens admitted almost exultingly in one letter, and it is hard not to notice at least a tendency towards self-punishment in such a diagnosis and such a life. A self-punishment that may be reflected by the fact that all the time he was delivering himself up to be "murdered" by Bill Sikes, just as he in turn became the foul murderer of a woman. His foot was again beginning to swell and to provoke the usual agonies, but he had *to go on*. In his ceaseless journeying and neglecting of all the symptoms of ill-health, it is permissible to quote back at Dickens something he himself had written three years before of another writer: "To have saved her life, then, by taking action on the warning that shone in her eyes and sounded in her voice, would have been impossible, without changing her nature. As long as the power of moving about in the old way was left to her, she must exercise it, or be killed by the restraint." There is a truth here, in this introduction to Adelaide

Anne Proctor's *Legends and Lyrics*, which Dickens did not need to go very far to divine; to those of active and impatient disposition rest can be as great a killer as activity, and it could be said that Dickens would have died just as surely and just as quickly if he had been prevented from public reading.

But there were times when even he could not ignore his symptoms; by the middle of February his foot was so bad that his doctors insisted the next London reading be cancelled, and that a forthcoming tour of Scotland be postponed. For a few days Dickens remained in London – to judge by his correspondence, clearly impatient and fretful but determined to rise triumphant from his pain. Eventually the swelling abated, and Frank Beard allowed Dickens to travel only five days after the original diagnosis, despite the fact that this was against what Forster called the "urgent entreaties" of his family and close friends. Dolby noticed, when his "Chief" did arrive in Scotland, that he was "very lame" but that he tried to "disguise the fact" of his ill-health with his usual "vivacity of manner". On that visit he read "Sikes and Nancy" in Edinburgh, and afterwards he was again so "prostrate" that he had to lie on the sofa in order to regain something of his strength and composure. After a glass of champagne he returned to the stage for the second reading "as blithe and gay as if he were just commencing his evening's work". Nevertheless Dolby noticed with some alarm that "these shocks to the nerves were not as easily repelled as for the moment they appeared to be, but invariably recurred later on in the evening, either in the form of great hilarity or a desire to be once more on the platform, or in a craving to do the work over again". That is the strangest aspect of all, this craving to go on and do it all again. A craving allied with unnatural high spirits. Dickens's strange manner seemed even to have affected his friends and, after the Edinburgh reading, Dolby noticed how people were reluctant to join him after the performance; Dolby believed that they might in part be alarmed by the demonstration of what Dickens himself called (apparently jokingly) his "murderous instincts". But he was himself being murdered, too, by his own determination to go on. Indeed it was at this point in Scotland that Dolby suggested to him that the "Sikes and Nancy" reading might be used less often or reserved for the larger towns.

Dickens (angrily): "Have you finished?"

Dolby: "I have said all I feel on that matter."

Dickens (leaping up from his chair and smashing his plate with his knife and fork): "Dolby! your infernal caution will be your ruin one of these days!"

Dolby: "Perhaps so, sir. In this case, though, I hope you will do me the justice to say it is exercised in your interest."

There was silence for a few minutes and Dolby, turning round, found Dickens in tears. He embraced Dolby, and asked his pardon – the small episode yet another token of the extraordinary nervous strain which was now apparent in Dickens's behaviour.

His foot had recovered but the constant slow wearing down of his health and vitality proceeded apace; the sudden death of his old friend, Emerson Tennent, and the necessity of attending his funeral, for example, meant that one reading at York had to be almost desperately quickened. In order to reach the train to London on time that night, he went through his readings without a normal interval, stepping behind the screen only to moisten his lips with champagne before continuing from "Boots" to "Sikes and Nancy" to "Mrs Gamp". On the train back to London Dickens recalled the time when he and Tennent had climbed Mount Vesuvius together – so many years ago, now – and at the funeral Forster found his friend looking "'dazed' and worn". There is something almost maniacal about this constant effort, this constant travel and this no less constant fatigue – and how like him, at this juncture, to spend a whole morning in clearing up Wills's office, throwing away everything, straightening out shelves and corners, getting himself covered in dust, relentlessly determined to reduce everything to "good order".

His reading life was, from this time forward, a sheer catalogue of woes. In Liverpool at the beginning of April he tripped over a wire and badly cut his shin. But he was well enough to attend a dinner given in his honour in that same city, and once again with almost obsessive interest concentrated upon the need for ceaseless labour. "All that I claim for myself, in establishing the relations which exist between us, is constantly fidelity to hard work . . . what seems the easiest done is oftentimes the most difficult to do, and that the smallest truth may come of the greatest pains . . ." That these "relations" did exist between himself and the English public was of course now beyond a doubt. He walked to the railway station at Liverpool the next morning and was "repeatedly stopped by people of all classes, eager to take him by the hand and to thank him for the pleasure his books had afforded them". It would be impossible to gauge the extent of his popularity from newspaper accounts or reviews – even as his popularity increased, the critics were writing him off – and the best evidence lies in sales. For it is a remarkable fact that, during the last years of his life, each successive edition of his work sold better than the one before and that the sales of all his novels managed to increase year by year.

Then, more agony. A discharge of blood from his old complaint of piles. His foot swelling painfully again (for which complaint Scott, his valet, was now provided with emergency medicines). Sleeplessness and weariness which he called "unendurable". Dolby said of Dickens's condition at this point that "his mind was more disturbed by it than his manner would lead any one (not knowing him well) to suppose". Edmund Yates, who dined with him one evening in Leeds, noted that he ". . . looked jaded and worn, and had to a certain extent lost that marvellous elasticity of spirits which was his great characteristic". He was depressed and, again according to Dolby, "the old geniality had disappeared"; even now he realised that his chances of finishing the tour were greatly weakened and, in conversation with Dolby, he regretted the likely financial loss to Chappell and Company. At Chester, two days later, he was suffering from giddiness and mild paralysis; his doctor questioned him later and Dickens told him that, at the time, he was "giddy, with a tendency to go backwards, and to turn round. Afterwards, desiring to put something on a small table, he pushed it and the table forwards, undesignedly. He had some odd feeling of insecurity about his left leg, as if there was something unnatural about his heel . . . Also he spoke of some strangeness of his left hand and arm; missed the spot on which he wished to lay that hand, unless he carefully looked at it; felt an unreadiness to lift his hand towards his head, especially his left hand . . ." In an article he wrote for *All The Year Round* not long after he spoke of his being, for the first time in his life, ". . . giddy, jarred, shaken, faint, uncertain of voice and sight and tread and touch, and dull of spirit". In fact he was close to a paralytic stroke. Nevertheless, after Chester, he went on to read in Blackburn and then at Bolton – although at his last reading he felt so giddy that he almost fell before the audience. Later in the year Dickens told his American publisher, James Fields, that ". . . when he was ill in his reading only Nelly observed that he staggered and his eye failed, only she dared to tell him". It is not clear to which particular reading he is referring here, but it seems most likely to have been the one in Bolton; Ellen Ternan, therefore, was with him for at least part of his Northern tour.

It was only now in the extremity of these circumstances that Dickens felt it necessary to write two successive letters to his doctor, Frank Beard, with an outline of his symptoms. The first letter was itself alarming enough to bring Beard up to Preston for an immediate examination and, while he waited for Beard's arrival, Dickens admitted in another letter that he was "half dead" with overwork. In fact his letters, to such friends as Norton, were now very short, the writing clumsy and the characters badly formed. Then Beard arrived from London, immediately examined his patient and forbade any more readings. The only possible cure was "instant rest", Beard turning to Dolby and saying, ". . . if you insist on Dickens taking the platform tonight, I will not guarantee but that he goes through life dragging a foot after him." There was no help for it; as Dickens later remarked, "being accustomed to observe myself as if I were another man, and knowing the advice to meet my only need, I instantly halted . . . and rested." Of course that night's reading had to be cancelled. The landlord of the Bull, where the Dickens party was staying, took it upon himself to telegraph as many localities as possible with the news of the cancellation, and the Chief Constable ordered that mounted police be despatched to stop "every carriage or cab coming in that direction". Dickens and Beard had gone at once to London, and on the following day Dickens was examined by Sir Thomas Watson. "When I saw him," Watson wrote later, "he *appeared* to be well. His mind was unclouded, his pulse quiet. His heart was beating with some slight excess of the natural impulse. He told me he had of late sometimes, but rarely, lost or misused a word; that he forgot names, and numbers, but had always done that." Watson's recommendation was the same as that of Beard; Dickens must at once stop his public performances, and rest. They issued a certificate which ended: "In our judgment Mr Dickens will not be able with safety to himself to resume his readings for several months to come."

Dickens then returned to Gad's Hill Place, feeling now "greatly shaken". In the joint communiqué by Beard and Watson, part of his condition was ascribed to his "long and frequent railway journeys", and this was a diagnosis with which Dickens agreed; he said that his ailment was in large part due to railway "shaking" and he found suddenly that he could not bear to travel on express trains. The Staplehurst disaster, in other words, continued to haunt him. He was sleeping and eating normally, but he admitted that he felt dazed and very tired. He was avoiding stimulants of any kind and, instead of his usual tea or coffee, was now drinking homoeopathic cocoa. He had to stay very quiet for at least a month, and was of course severely disappointed by the necessary cancelling of the readings and by the subsequent loss of revenue. Yet it says something about his remarkable will, as well as his powers of apparent recovery, that a few days later he announced himself to be in a "brilliant condition" and was even ready to resume his London life. But did he also now have some sense that his death was coming; or had he, even, in that incipient paralysis, had some intimation of what death was *like*? Two days after his return to London he wrote to his solicitor, Ouvry, asking him to draw up his will. Which was speedily done – it was made out by 12 May and then executed at the office of *All The Year Round*. He had rented no house in London this season but instead, when he did not wish to be confined to the office, he took rooms at the St James's Hotel in Piccadilly. While "in town" he would go to the theatre, dine at Verey's or at the Blue Posts tavern in Cork Street; other favourite inns, where dinners were served, were the Cock and the Cheshire Cheese in Fleet Street as well as the Albion opposite Drury Lane Theatre. One of his most constant companions now was Dolby and, during this period in London just after the enforced retreat from Preston, he noticed ". . . the change that was coming over him. I missed the old vivacity and elasticity of spirit . . ."

But he put a brave face upon his condition, not least because his American friends, the Fields, had come to England and Dickens had decided that they were to be entertained and diverted on a very large scale. One of the reasons he took rooms at the St James's Hotel was to be close to their own hotel in Hanover Square. Certainly he was concerned to put them at their ease about the condition of his general health and, in a letter before he saw them, he explained that he had been disturbed by railway travel but was now "myself again". On the first day he met them, almost as if to prove his fitness, he took James Fields on a long walk beside the Thames. Both Fields and his wife have left records of their time with Dickens. How he took them to the rooms in Furnival's Inn where he had begun *The Pickwick Papers*. How he guided them through the Temple, and showed them the room where Pip had lived in *Great Expectations*, the dark staircase on which Magwitch had stumbled and the narrow street where Pip had found lodgings for his unwanted benefactor; yet how strange a picture this is, Dickens pointing out these dwellings as if his characters had been real. As if his novels were now part of the bricks and stone of London. As if he had filled the city with his own creations. Dickens walking through the streets of London on a spring evening, evoking the very contours of his fiction, as ". . . a belated figure would hurry past us and disappear, or perhaps in turning the corner would linger to 'take a good look' at Charles Dickens".

Then on at least two occasions he took Fields with him on expeditions to see what he called "the darker side of London life"; they went to the station house at Leman Street and were then guided by police inspectors through the poor quarters of the city. In particular through Whitechapel, Shadwell, Wapping – those areas of the East End where poverty, misery and vice were the only fates visited upon those who lived there. They visited an opium den in New Court off Bluegate Fields which, it is popularly supposed, was the original of the opium den with which Dickens opened *The Mystery of Edwin Drood* only five months later. "In a miserable court," Fields wrote, "we found the haggard old woman blowing at a kind of pipe made of an old penny ink-bottle." They walked among the poor and the outcast and the criminals and the dying. In a casual ward they stepped among the men and women, lying upon the floor, "worn out with fatigue and hunger". Outside a penny lodging house Fields saw Dickens "snatch a little child out of its poor drunken mother's arms, and bear it in, filthy as it was, that it might be warmed and cared for". In a lock-up Dickens entered into an animated conversation with a lost child, a girl of four or five years old wearing her mother's huge bonnet which looked like "a sort of straw coal-scuttle". This was the world which had not changed since his own childhood, the dark world of London, the shadowy areas of the city he sometimes called "Babylon" or the "Great Oven" and where, as Annie Fields noted, ". . . he seemed altogether at home". For in a sense it was his home. It was that which he had always most feared and by which he had always been most fascinated. It was the unchanging part of this city, and of his own self.

In the following month, James and Annie Fields went down to stay with Dickens at Gad's Hill Place; again there were more expeditions, more long walks, more parties, more dinners. They all went to Canterbury in large four-horse carriages, complete with postillions in red coats and top-boots, and it was here that Dickens found another clue to the novel he was about to write. In the cathedral there, he was depressed by a service which seemed no more than a token of worship and which would find its place in the pages of *The Mystery of Edwin Drood*. It was in Canterbury that Dickens also gave one intimation of his fictional method when, asked which house was the original for Dr Strong's school in *David Copperfield*, Dickens laughed and replied that several "would do". It was here, too, that he was happy to lose his identity. A crowd collected around the carriages and one man, pointing to James Fields, shouted out, "That's Dickens!" Dickens then handed Fields a small parcel and said, in tones loud enough to be heard by the crowd of onlookers, "Here you are, Dickens, take charge of this for me." It was during the Fields' stay at Gad's Hill Place, that Dickens laid out lunch on the wall of Cooling churchyard, in a scene which has already been included in this history. The scene has been described but not its immediate context, however – his clowning in the presence of death, but not the fact that it was during this period when he had intimations of his own death. In the memoirs of Joseph Grimaldi which Dickens had edited more than thirty years before, there is a description of Grimaldi's father who had such a horror of death that he haunted graveyards and speculated upon the fate of their occupants. But it was he, too, who introduced the well-known "skeleton scenes" for the clown in pantomime. How like Dickens – laughing at death even when he was most fearful of it, laying out the food in Cooling churchyard like Grimaldi the mime. Of course it would be wrong to consider Dickens in any way derelict or depleted. Dolby himself had noticed how much better he seemed after a few days' rest in Kent, and how sanguine he was about his return to a "brilliant" condition. Yet, despite all the merriment and all the activity, Anne Fields noted in her diary of this period that ". . . it is wonderful the fun and flow of spirits C.D. has for he is a sad man. Sleepless nights come too often, oftener than they ever would to a free heart. But the sorrows of such a nature are many and must often seem more than he can bear." Again the reference to a heart not "free" points to his suspected or known relationship with Ellen Ternan, a relationship which seemed to bring only "sorrows" now.

It was the last full summer of Dickens's life – "a very happy summer", too, according to both Kate Collins and Georgina Hogarth. He spent the weekends, as usual, in Gad's Hill Place but made a point of being in London on Thursday for "make-up" day at the office. Wills was now almost retired from the business as a result of the injury to his head, and Dickens's son, Charley, rescued from the disgrace of bankruptcy, now seems to have taken on many of his old duties. Dickens himself wrote only a few short articles for the periodical during the period of recuperation. But he did also manage to write an essay on Fechter, destined for the *Atlantic Monthly* and designed to bolster the actor's reputation just before he began a tour of the United States, an essay which has an interest beyond that of the mere "puff" since within it Dickens reverts to his one apparently inescapable subject. For he talks about Fechter as a romantic actor and mentions in particular how the loved object is redeemed, rendered brighter and worthier, by the very interest and passion of the lover himself. "I said to myself, as a child might have said, 'A bad woman could not have been the object of that wonderful tenderness, could not have so subdued that worshipping heart, could not have drawn such tears from such a lover.'" And once again in this account of love it is remarkable how Dickens puts himself in the place of a child and, with a child-like vision, describes an earnest and almost spiritual passion. The article was not quite seen in that light in the United States, however, and one American newspaper printed a cartoon showing Dickens blowing up a gigantic india-rubber figure of Fechter – "You just keep still and I'll do hall the blowing for you. I know 'ow to 'umbug those blasted Yankees, as I've done it before." He had other small writing assignments, too; he was finishing off his abbreviated series, "New Uncommercial Samples", but his general depression of spirits is most evident in his review of Forster's *Life of Landor* in one of the July issues of *All The Year Round*. "The life of almost any man possessing great gifts," he wrote, "would be a sad book to himself . . ." There was other melancholy or troublesome business during the summer; he was busy in negotiations over the unsuccessful Guild of Literature and Art, the charitable schemes of which seemed to be getting nowhere, and in the same period he had also reluctantly agreed to mediate in the separation proceedings between his friend, Mrs Frances Elliot, and her husband. No doubt he could have been spared this reminder of his own unhappy history but, as always, he paid more attention to the calls of "duty" than of private convenience.

Yet it was now, in the summer of 1869, only a little while after the physical suffering induced by his readings, that Dickens became once more eager to begin the composition of a new novel. He had considered the possibility the summer before, and had managed to produce at least one fragment, but it was only now he felt that he could begin seriously to write. This probably had less to do with the "free time" available to him (he had had just as much to spare in the previous year) than with the fact of his illness; the shock of his debility and the first intimations of death seem to have propelled him once more towards expression, towards the writing of a novel which would be dominated by images of death and by the presence of unacknowledged passions running beneath the observable surface of life.

How did it begin? By July certain stories were occurring to him, even though they were at this stage no more than motes in the air; to Forster he disclosed the idea of a novel based upon the fortunes of a betrothed couple who do not marry until the end of the book. It sounds very much like the theme of life's wandering "travellers", so prominent in *Little Dorrit* and *Bleak House*, but one redefined in the context of passionate love. It was not, in any case, a new idea; Forster claims that it was first mentioned to him this July, but in fact it is only a reworking of a plot Dickens had jotted down in his book of memoranda at least nine years before. In addition he was to include within the novel some of the names and traits of characters which he had already explored in the "Sapsea Fragment" written a little while ago. *The Mystery of Edwin Drood*, in other words, represented not so much a radical new departure in Dickens's preoccupations but, rather, a distillation of those which had remained with him over the years. Yet no one could possibly have anticipated the use to which they would be put, in a narrative so strikingly dissimilar from anything he had written before.

As so often, other ideas swiftly followed his initial determination to write, and in August he told Forster that he had ". . . laid aside the fancy I told you of, and have a very curious and new idea for my new story". In fact he did not lay aside the first "fancy" of the betrothed couple but redeployed it within the subsequent one, part of the wonderful combining power of his imagination which did not reject, but encompassed and incorporated, material. By 20 August he was already considering titles for the new novel; he set down a list of seventeen of them on a sheet of paper, beginning with "The loss of James Wakefield" and ending with "Dead? Or alive?". On the same day he wrote to Frederick Chapman, projecting the idea of a new story in twelve shilling numbers, thus suggesting that Dickens, aware for the first time that his powers could be exhausted as rapidly as his readings had been terminated, was not eager to trust himself to a twenty-month series on the old pattern. Market conditions had also changed, and what had been acceptable in the Forties and Fifties was not, in the days of Mudie's Lending Library and the railway bookstalls, necessarily the right formula for the late Sixties and Seventies. Dickens himself was never afraid, in the cant phrase, to move with his times. It was one of the secrets of his permanent and growing success. Contracts were soon drawn up, but it is another indication of his anxieties that, at his insistence, a clause was inserted which stipulated that, in the event of the author's death or incapacity, arbitrators would estimate the amount to be repaid to Chapman and Hall. He did not want to sign any contract under false pretences, and his worries about the financial loss to Chappell and Company after the abandonment of the readings suggest how careful he now wanted to be with his publishers. Contracts were not finally completed and accepted until the winter of this year but, in the event, Dickens was paid £7,500 and a half share of the profits for the copyright in this last book.

By the middle of September Dickens began his real planning for the novel. At some point in this month, or the one before, he explained to Forster the "very curious and new" idea that had occurred to him. It was one that concerned the murder of a young man by his uncle, and how the truth of this familial slaying would not be revealed until the murderer himself reflects upon the stages of his fatal career in a condemned cell. This is an intriguing plot and, with its use of opium as an agent of revelation, bears a passing resemblance to Wilkie Collins's *The Moonstone*. But it does not consort very well with the list of titles and themes which Dickens had propounded to himself on 20 August, the drift of which indicates that the main character was to vanish only to re-emerge at the end of the book. It seems likely that the idea of murder, and thus the permanent disappearance of Edwin Drood, only occurred to Dickens once he had begun to draw up the main lines of the plot in his number plans. This in itself would explain his strange treatment of a story by Robert Lytton, "The Disappearance of John Acland", for which he had already arranged publication in *All The Year Round* – this is a short narrative in which the disappearance of a young man is only later discovered to have been, after all, murder. Dickens accepted this story when he was not sure about the main lines of his own novel but, as soon as he had decided that *his* disappearing character should also be murdered, he abruptly terminated Robert Lytton's story with only the briefest of excuses. He did not want his new thunder to be stolen, in other words, and "The Disappearance of John Acland" was sacrificed to *The Mystery of Edwin Drood*.

But Dickens was not interested simply in the machinations of crime and detection; his was to be a crime based upon the experience of violent and thwarted love, and it was to be explored through the consciousness of the murderer himself, John Jasper. This was not a new development – he had been working towards a similar effect with Bradley Headstone in *Our Mutual Friend* and with Obenreizer in "No Thoroughfare". But although there are hints of both these characters in Jasper, in the portrayal of this divided, driven man there is a greater intensity of focus on the nature of aggression and sexual obsession. Even as Dickens was able in conversation to outline the plot and the theme of his novel to Forster, his real and incommunicable interests were working their own way towards resolution. So it is that *The Mystery of Edwin Drood* becomes essentially the mystery of his murderous uncle, Jasper, and the real theme of the novel lies not in its complicated plot but rather, as Dickens's daughter, Kate, has expressed it, in Dickens's ". . . wonderful observation of character, and his strange insight into the tragic secrets of the human heart . . ." And how could it not be so, at a time when his public life was dominated by his reading of "Sikes and Nancy" and his private existence conditioned by what seems to be an increasingly sorrowful love for Ellen Ternan?

Certain key themes were evident, however, from the beginning. The first number plan opens with the line "Opium-Smoking", and at once we are in the world of Limehouse and Bluegate Fields: the area which in the months before Dickens had visited both as guide to his American publisher and as the "Uncommercial Traveller". But then, in that same first number plan, another locale emerges – "*Cathedral town running throughout*". In the novel it is called Cloisterham but every available detail suggests how strongly it is related to the city of Dickens's childhood, to Rochester and its environs. London, then, conjoined with Rochester. At the end of his life he is returning to the twin sources of his creativity. Not only returning to them, but actually seeing them as one. For, in a novel which is concerned with the nature of the divided life and the dual personality, it is not so strange that Limehouse and Rochester should meet, should in a sense be superimposed upon one another to create a composite landscape of the imagination; even down to the very details of topography when St George's-in-the-East, the wonderful and barbaric church which looms over the opium dens of Bluegate Fields, comes to resemble Rochester Cathedral itself. The visions of his childhood and his experience as a man, mingled together.

Throughout the period of planning and composition, in fact, we can find Dickens himself in the two worlds of London and Kent. He had already visited the opium dens with Fields, but he returned to them in the autumn of this year as he began writing *The Mystery of Edwin Drood*. He seems also to have recalled an essay on the same subject in his own journal three years before. In "Lazarus, Lotus Eating" there is an account of the opium dens of New Court which might serve as an introduction to the first chapter of the novel itself. "The visions this miserable little hole has seen, the sweet and solemn strains of music, the nightly feasts, the terrible dramas, the weird romances, the fierce love, the strange fantastic worship, the mad dreams, the gorgeous processions, the brilliant crowds, the mystic shadows which have occupied it would fill a volume." It has already been described how Dickens himself took laudanum, both in order to sleep and to mitigate some of the pains of sickness, but we do not need to presume that he was an "addict" (all the evidence works against such a presumption) to understand why, in this period of his life, such visions of passionate transcendence would exercise a profound attraction for him. But how appropriate, too, that they should be rooted in the poverty and filth of London which Dickens had always observed with mingled horror and fascination. Another element of his "darker" London emerges in the novel almost by indirection. He had once in an essay described the man who kept a low lodging-house in the Borough and who was known as "Deputy", and it is this name which Dickens gives to the "hideous small boy" who haunts Cloisterham and *The Mystery of Edwin Drood* like some imp of the perverse. Thus the duality again: the intimations of bliss and the awareness of destitution.

But, if the darker elements of London creep and eddy through this novel, so also do the obscurer elements of Rochester. It is appropriate, too, in a book of secrecy and passion, that one of the main sources of its plot should come from Ellen Ternan. One of her uncles, who had been staying in Rochester, had one morning set out for Fort Pitt and was, like Edwin Drood, never seen again. But the city enters also in more immediate ways; there are accounts of Dickens lingering in the vicinity of the cathedral at Rochester with pencil and notebook in hand, and several ecclesiastical dignitaries later prided themselves on being copied down by Dickens. But he knew Rochester so well that he hardly needed to observe it in the manner of a reporter; all that was important about this place already lay within him, and the city which emerges in his novel is really the one which he knew as a child. That is why, when Dickens thought of a condemned cell for the murderer, John Jasper, his imagination wandered back to the Rochester gaol he had seen as a small boy. Thus, in *The Mystery of Edwin Drood*, does he bring to the landscape of his childhood and youth the themes of camouflage, secrecy and self-division.

Certainly these were the elements which were in his mind when, at the end of September, he began seriously to work upon the new story; the extant number plans suggest that he could see his way through the first stages of the novel without undue difficulty. He had already agreed that Charles Collins should undertake the illustrations to the new monthly series. Whether this was at Collins's suggestion, or at Dickens's actual request, is not certain; but it seems likely that he was happy to grant a commission which would not only occupy his son-in-law's time but also afford him at least the basis of an income. In any case Collins himself, as Dickens knew very well, had a higher reputation than Marcus Stone who had illustrated Dickens's previous novel. In order to prepare Collins for the work ahead, Dickens asked Frederick Chapman to send down to Gad's Hill Place copies of the old green covers which Hablot Browne had designed in the past. He wanted Collins, in other words, to work on the basis of approved models. Now he, too, was ready to begin. During the autumn and winter he often went to the office in Wellington Street but he did not set up living quarters there, as he had in the past; he went there only to work. The rest of his time was spent either at Gad's Hill Place or at Peckham, in which retreat some of the planning and composition of this final work were undertaken. Of course there were interruptions. At the beginning of October, for example, the Fields came to visit him at Gad's Hill Place once more before their return to Boston. Almost as soon as the American couple had arrived, Dickens told them of the new story which he had just begun. "It had taken strong hold upon him already," Annie Fields wrote in her diary, "and he begins to be preoccupied with it." He read out what he had already written to James Fields, "acting as he went on". When eventually they came to part at the railway station, Dickens was there to "see them off". "He in his cheery way making us look at and think of other things until the signal came. A crowd had collected to see him by the time we started but he did not seem to see it and the blood rushed all over his face as the tears came to ours, and we were off. He ran forward a few steps and all was over – except eternity." Eternity. And Annie recalled, principally, Dickens's "dear suffering face".

By the third week of October he had finished the first instalment of the novel, and promptly read it out at Forster's house "with great spirit". Stone. Dust. Old churches. The presence of the past. These are some of the aspects of the vision which Dickens was now imparting to his listeners. It is the smallest and most intense world that he had ever created, beginning with the strange opium dreams of Bluegate Fields and then moving on the "old Cathedral town" of Cloisterham. Or shall we say Rochester? Transformed now, in any event, to an oppressive and echoic place; it is as if Dickens were finding within himself, and within the landscape of his childhood, a stranger aspect of human passion and a permanent reminder of human mortality. Stories of antiquity. Stories of the English past. It was not for Dickens a new theme – in an essay for *Household Words* nineteen years before he had spoken of "an old Cathedral town" characterised "by the universal gravity, mystery, decay, and silence", but one so badly embodied in "the drawling voice, without a heart, that drearily pursues the dull routine . . ." How odd and how significant, then, that he had been dismayed by just such "drawling" voices when he had visited the cathedral at Canterbury a few months before. There are times in Dickens's life when a perception suddenly returns with undiminished vigour.

In *The Mystery of Edwin Drood*, however, all the old perceptions are shadowed and deepened with Dickens's own painful reflections on the nature of time and of mortality, reflections which elicit in turn some of his finest writing. "Old Time heaved a mouldy sigh from tomb and arch and vault; and gloomy shadows began to deepen in corners; and damps began to rise from green patches of stone; and jewels, cast upon the pavement of the nave from stained glass by the declining sun, began to perish . . . In the Cathedral, all became grey, murky, and sepulchral, and the cracked monotonous mutter went on like a dying voice, until the organ and the choir burst forth, and drowned it in a sea of music. Then, the sea fell, and the dying voice made another feeble effort, and then the sea rose high, and beat its life out, and lashed the roof, and surged among the arches, and pierced the heights of the great tower; and then the sea was dry, and all was still." It is the nearest Dickens came to a Gothic novel, a novel springing out of his own childhood memories, compounded by hard experience, and mixed with the strange promptings of his own heart – "'If the dead do, under any circumstances, become visible to the living . . .'" The mingling of the living and the dead is at the centre of nineteenth-century Gothic but of course it had also been at the centre of Dickens's own imagination; the opening of *David Copperfield*, with the infant fear of the father rising from his grave, is only one indication of the extent to which it affected him. But now, at the end of his life, with how much troubled ambiguity does he approach the dead and address the question of death itself. As he looks down upon Cloisterham and sees ". . . its river winding down from the mist on the horizon, as though that were its source, and already heaving with a restless knowledge of its approach towards the sea". This wonderful passage is part of a scene in which John Jasper and the stonemason, Durdles, wander through the crypt of the Cathedral, until it is time for Durdles to be stoned homewards by the imp Deputy. The whole cycle of life and maturity and death is seen in this strange ritual of guilt and punishment and mad joy, unfolding through the pages of *The Mystery of Edwin Drood* and culminating in what is now Dickens's constant theme. ". . . so have the rustling sounds and fresh scents of their earliest impressions, revived, when the circle of their lives was very nearly traced, and the beginning and the end were drawing close together." The constant theme of his life. The constant theme of his art. Yet in a way how different all this is from Dickens's earlier fiction; the picture he creates here is of Christmas Eve in Cloisterham, but quite changed in spirit from the day which he used to celebrate in his novels and in his Christmas Books. For it is also on Christmas Eve that Edwin Drood is murdered. A day which had once acted as a prelude to all the joys of beneficence and brotherhood now marks only the onset of death and mystery. The end coming, subduing and changing the beginning.

Dolby has said that the writing of the novel came with more difficulty to Dickens; it gave him "trouble and anxiety", and Dickens told him that he "missed the pressure" of former days. But in fact the manuscript suggests that the writing of it came to him with relative ease, since there are fewer emendations than in some of his previous novels. His major alterations, indeed, are in the sphere of addition and augmentation; which in turn emphasises how in this novel Dicken's prose seems instinctively more economical and more restrained. *Our Mutual Friend* had been established in part upon periphrasis and comic grandiloquence but *The Mystery of Edwin Drood* is much more austere, all the corrections and additions adding only to the specificity and detail of the narrative. This may partly spring from Dickens's desire to harbour his powers at a time when he was not sure how long they would last or how far they could be extended; but, more importantly, it may be that the power and significance of his final vision did not encourage any of the free-wheeling exercises of the past. Of course he had in his most recent novels explored the theme of the "secret" life, of dual identity and self-division, just as he had also analysed the necessity of masks and camouflage in a world which depends upon appearances. And of course all these matters must have seemed germane to the life which, even as he was writing the novel, he felt compelled to lead. But in *The Mystery of Edwin Drood* they are enlarged and strengthened in the pursuit of a larger vision, a vision which depicts the "lanes of light" between the dark pillars of a crypt and which reflects upon ". . . that mysterious fire which lurks in everything . . .", even in the cold stone walls of an ancient church. It is the same power which informs the dialogues and soliloquies in the book. The conversations are lucid and precise but yet they command an almost Jamesian complexity; and they are suffused, too, with another sense, what Dickens in the narrative calls the ". . . curious touches of human nature working the secret springs of this dialogue". Again the idea of secrecy, but it is associated with the true nature of human power and human life. And had his poor health, opening the door to another world, also unlocked for him the springs of such a music?

He had been writing the second instalment during November, despite being affected by a heavy cold, and he managed to finish it by the end of the month. He was trying to move on quickly, not least because he knew that he now had to prepare for that short season of "farewell" readings which his doctors had permitted. But he completed these first two numbers only to discover, to his horror, that he had underwritten both of them; each one was something like six pages too short, and he had at once to set to work to make up the deficiency. He added an entirely new scene, transposed a chapter from the second instalment to the first, and then added another chapter to the second – all of which meant that he was using up his material too fast. He was also vexed by his illustrator. Charles Collins, having sketched out a cover, found that he could no longer draw without weakening his health. Some other artist had to be found at once and Dickens went up to London in order to consult with Frederick Chapman. In the event he discovered a young artist, Luke Fildes. Or, rather, it was John Everett Millais who found him for Dickens – the painter, who was staying at Gad's Hill Place, went into Dickens's study one morning and showed him the first issue of *The Graphic*. "I've got him!" he shouted and then pointed out to his host an illustration, "Houseless and Hungry", which Fildes had executed. It was exactly the kind of realistic and detailed examination of social misery which would have appealed to Dickens, and he wrote to the young artist asking to see other specimens of his work. These, too, proved satisfactory and so he gave him the commission, an extraordinary honour and indeed opportunity for so young an artist; Fildes himself, in a jubilant letter to a friend, exclaimed, "This is the tide! Am I to be on the flood? My heart fails me a little for it is the turning point in my career." Within a few days Fildes was conducted into an interview with the great man. Fildes was a rather serious young person and, on this occasion, informed Dickens that he would probably be best at illustrating the graver aspects of the author's fiction. And so it proved; Fildes's drawings lend a serious *and* contemporary tone to Dickens's otherwise "timeless" concerns. So it was settled. Three days before Christmas, too, Dickens had managed to finish all the necessary rewriting.

But once more, only a week or so away from his last season of readings, he was suffering great pain. Dolby noticed ". . . a slow but steady change working in him . . .", and on Christmas Day his foot was so swollen that he had to remain in his room. He could not walk because of the pain and discomfort but, in the evening, he managed to hobble down to the drawing room in order to join his family in the usual festivities after dinner. It was his last Christmas on earth; he, who had in his own work so often celebrated the blessings of that season, could now experience it only as an invalid. He lay on the sofa and watched the others at their games. And of what was he thinking now? There is one clue, at least, to his state of mind. His family had been playing "The Memory Game"; it was one which Dickens could hardly ever resist and, after observing the others for a while, he decided to join in. Henry recalled one of his contributions. "My father, after many turns, had successfully gone through the long string of words and finished up with his own contribution, 'Warren's Blacking, 30 Strand'. He gave this with an odd twinkle in his eye and a strange inflection in his voice which at once forcibly arrested my attention and left a vivid impression on my mind for some time afterwards." Warren's Blacking, 30 Strand. The blacking warehouse. The site of his childhood labour and humiliation. The source of all his agony. And yet the name meant nothing to his family; none of them knew of his past. Just another phrase in the course of a Christmas game; but, to Dickens, how pregnant with the whole mystery of his life. Yet it remained a mystery, even to those who knew and loved him best. Although he was here for the first time openly alluding to that terrible period, his family would not know the truth about his early life until they read of it in Forster's biography.

The following afternoon, after the usual Boxing Day sports, Dickens made a little speech to the assembled guests and contestants, at the end of which he said that ". . . please God we will do it again next year". But they did not. On New Year's Eve he attended a party at Forster's house, where he read out the second instalment of his new novel. At the stroke of midnight the company stood with their glasses in their hands to mark the turn of the time. Later one guest said that "I never saw him again".

VII

I HAVE only dreamt once of Charles Dickens. In my dream I heard an acquaintance talking in an adjacent room, and I knew that he had just returned from a dinner at which the novelist had been present. And yet this was a dream of the present: so Dickens still lived. "He could not have been more natural," my acquaintance was saying. "Laughing. Telling stories. But the important thing is, that I have actually been in the company of Charles Dickens." At once I felt the phantom of the presence of Dickens hovering about me as I stood in the empty room: a beneficent presence, certainly, but one not unmixed with fearfulness or, perhaps, a kind of holy terror.

I entered the other room. "Philip!" I shouted at my acquaintance. My voice was too loud, and everyone fell silent. "Don't you realise that if he really *was* Dickens, he would be 128 years old!" This was the age I mentioned in my dream, although of course in reality he would have been older still. Philip merely nodded, hardly bothering to conceal his boredom; it was clear that this posed no hindrance to his meeting Charles Dickens. And in truth, since this was a dream, it seemed no disqualification to me either. In any case why should he wish to talk to me when he had just talked to the great novelist? And so it was that the phantom of the presence of Dickens was joined by the phantom of my own inadequacy. I was lost in some time between the mid-nineteenth century and the late twentieth century, and I could not speak. I was adrift between two worlds which now seemed to exist simultaneously – or, rather, had become one world.

And then I was sitting next to Dickens in the carriage of an underground train which was travelling somewhere in Essex. I saw him in profile, and he did indeed seem very old with his white beard and long white hair. It was not so much an image of him, however, as an image of old age imbued with all the characteristics of Dickens. He was chuckling about something, and was talking animatedly to other people in the same carriage. He was saying something about his old age, but he did not actually address any remark to me. And, again, I think my primary sensation was one of fear – fear that he was still alive even as I was writing my biography of him. Fear that he might turn and *attack* me. But he was still laughing and joking. "This is where I get off," he said. "I have to see my children." And in my dream he was now standing on the platform as the automatic doors began to close and now, for the first time, he looked straight at me. And, when he smiled, I knew that it truly was Charles Dickens. That, in some sense, he had not died. I never saw him again.

Chapter 35

IN the New Year, the last year of his life, Dickens broke the rule he had always maintained – he was both writing a novel and doing a series of public readings at the same time. He was trying not to allow the readings to interfere with his composition but, nevertheless, he was now appearing at St James's Hall approximately twice a week and, in addition, he felt it necessary to spend some time in "getting up" his subjects once more. There is no evidence, however, that he would willingly have forgone the opportunity of this "farewell" series of twelve performances; he needed the money (or thought that he did, which is much the same thing) but he also felt a sense of responsibility to others beside himself. He had been much impressed by the considerate behaviour of Chappell and Company towards him at the time of his infirmity the year before, and according to Forster this sense of duty alone ". . . supplied him with an overpowering motive for being determinedly set on going through with them".

But there were warning signs of the risk he was courting even before he began. Five days before the first of the readings he had travelled up to Birmingham in order to distribute prizes at the Birmingham and Midland Institute, where it was noticed that "his face wore a hectic flush, his hair was greyer and thinner . . ." In fact he had been severely shaken by the railway journey to the Midlands, so shaken, indeed, that he felt it necessary to consult Frank Beard once more as soon as he returned to London. So how did he appear now to others, in this final year? Everyone agreed that he looked much older than his fifty-eight years; the man who had seemed almost preternaturally youthful at the beginning of his fame had now prematurely aged. Blanchard Jerrold saw him by chance in the street and scarcely recognised him. "It was he, however; but with a certain solemnity of expression in the face, and a deeper earnestness in the dark eyes. Those who had not seen him for some time were now struck with the sudden whiteness of his hair . . ." He dined one evening with George Eliot, and she said later that she had found him "looking dreadfully shattered", and Percy Fitzgerald had already noticed "the worn, buffeted face, the strained eyes . . ." Dolby told a mutual friend in conversation that ". . . he seems to be getting smaller – in fact, shrinking up – besides this he is getting irritable in his temper and worries himself over little things, which he never used to do". He was also now limping almost all the time and, as one friend noticed, "dragging one leg rather wearily behind him". How different even from the middle-aged man who had remained in brisk and vigorous health, who had walked twelve miles a day without the slightest sensation of fatigue. But all that had gone now and ". . . the elastic spring which had carried him forward at the rate of over four miles an hour, without pause or rest, had departed".

Yet there can be no doubt that, despite his obvious disabilities, Dickens had wanted to read again – had actively looked forward to his next engagements with his public. Dolby reveals that, when Sir Thomas Watson gave him permission to undertake these last readings, it "inspired him with new hope, and did much to promote what we all hoped would be his perfect recovery". So he began in good heart on 11 January, and Forster noticed that, after the slight roughness of delivery noticeable on his return from the United States, he now spoke with "the old delicacy" and with "a subdued tone" which had all the "quiet sadness of farewell". He also gave readings on three separate mornings, and this for the benefit of "the theatrical profession" whose other engagements meant that they could never attend his evening performances. This of course also materially affected his stamina and now, no doubt at his family's urgent request, Frank Beard stayed with him and monitored his pulse both before and after each reading. His records survive, showing clearly how Dickens's pulse leaped up as he came to the conclusion of each narrative. His ordinary pulse on the first night was 72 but soon it was never lower than 82 and, on the last nights, rose to over one hundred; during the readings themselves it rose rapidly higher and, at the close of his last reading from *David Copperfield*, it had risen to 124, which was in fact the mark it reached after all the "Sikes and Nancy" performances. So did his body respond to its work, manifesting evidence of slow but steady deterioration. Indeed his son, Charley, believed these final readings to have actually killed him and he remembered Frank Beard addressing him in words that were hardly reassuring. "I have had some steps put up against the side of the platform, Charley. You must be there every night, and if you see your father falter in the least, you must run up and catch him and bring him off with me, or, by Heaven, he'll die before them all." Forster agreed that he was being killed by his exertions: ". . . there will be no presumption in believing that life might yet have been for some time prolonged if these readings could have been stopped." And Dolby has given a graphic description of what was actually happening to Dickens now after the "Sikes and Nancy" readings; ". . . he would have to be supported to his retiring room and laid on a sofa for fully ten minutes, before he could speak a rational or consecutive sentence." So there were times when he may have been talking incoherently before returning to full consciousness, all the while augmenting what Dolby called ". . . his feverish excitement and his bodily pain . . ." There were others with him, too. Dickens himself mentioned that "the Patient" (in other words, Ellen Ternan) attended his reading on 23 January. So she remained with him still, even up to the end.

He had rented a house at 5 Hyde Park Place for the duration, principally because he wanted to remain in the capital during the readings, and thus avoid any of the railway "shaking" involved in commuting between Gad's Hill Place and London. He was once more back in "Tyburnia", and this last of his London houses directly overlooked Hyde Park, with what is now Bayswater Road beneath its windows. His bedroom and study were on the first floor, directly above the road, but Dickens seemed in no way to be affected by the constant roar and hurry of the traffic; he told Dolby that even at dawn he liked to hear the noise of the waggons bringing produce from Paddington station to the markets of the city, because it reminded him of that active and busy world which revolved even as he slept. And why should he care about London noise now? He had known it all his life. Of course he still had his "secret" retreat in Peckham, and his charwoman there remembered that at the time "Mr Tringham" was writing "a mystery story"; so it may be assumed that parts of *The Mystery of Edwin Drood* were composed in Linden Grove. It seems that in this period the Ternans themselves were living in an apartment house on the Vauxhall Bridge Road, as we have seen, but Ellen Ternan's attendance during at least one London reading admits the possibility that she was still close enough to share his house on occasions. The nature of their relationship at this late date cannot now be ascertained, but it is reasonable enough to quote some words from *The Mystery of Edwin Drood*, words which he wrote this spring, words which concern the decision of Rosa Bud and Edwin Drood to take on the relations of brother and sister rather than affianced lovers. "The relations between them did not look wilful, or capricious, or a failure, in such a light; they became elevated into something more self-denying, honorable, affectionate, and true." We cannot extrapolate from the art to the life but there is a tone here that is quite new in Dickens's work, and it is hard to see from where else it might have come.

There were occasions now when he talked of death, particularly of his desire for a sudden death. "A death by lightning most resembles the translation of Enoch," he is supposed to have said, although the words do not sound like those of Dickens. But the sentiment is clear enough. Nevertheless he still made a determined effort to remain cheerful, at least when he was in the company of others. Carlyle had dinner with him at Forster's house in January and wrote later that "Dickens was very cheery . . . a son, a d*r*, and Miss Hogarth with him . . . he has got, I doubt, some perman*t* nervous damage from that conquest of the £20,000 in Yankeeland, and is himself rather anxious now & then ab*t* it – a *foot* that goes occasionally wrong (part *powerless*, I think), and now latterly some finger of a *hand* do: – but he was now *very* nearly done with these final London 'readings', & promises to be all himself ag*n*. What a tragedy & hideous *nemesis*, were it otherwise! He talked to me ab*t* America as a *wonderer*, by no means as a *lover* . . ." So he was "very cheery" in front of Carlyle, and his daughter, Kate, said that ". . . my father's brain was more than usually clear and bright during the writing of *Edwin Drood* . . . the extraordinary interest he took in the development of this story was apparent in all that he said or did, and was often the subject of conversation between those who anxiously watched him as he wrote, and feared that he was trying his strength too far . . . the book he was now engaged in, and the concentration of his devotion and energy upon it, were a tax too great for his fast ebbing strength. Any attempt to stay him, however, in work that he had undertaken was as idle as stretching one's hands to a river and bidding it cease to flow . . ." So the river must go on, "heaving with a restless knowledge of its approach towards the sea".

His left hand was swollen, as he had told Carlyle (it seems to have been the thumb which was most badly affected), and he had to support it in a sling; as a result he cancelled dinner with Gladstone at the end of

January, but of course carried on with the third instalment of his novel in the dull and gloomy weather of the later winter. He respected Gladstone to a certain extent, but it cannot be said that at this stage he had any more real faith in him than in any other legislator or parliamentarian. Indeed his very last words on the subject of political life are as plain as they could possibly be; he told Bulwer-Lytton in February, four months before his death, that ". . . our system fails". He had been moving towards this conclusion all of his life and now, in a sense, he was returning to all his old allegiances in his hatred and contempt for Parliament; he was as proud now of what he called his "radicalism" as he had been when he was a young man. In fact five months before, while attending a meeting in Birmingham, he had tried to encapsulate his opinions in a short sentence. "My faith in the people governing, is, on the whole, infinitesimal; my faith in The People governed, is, on the whole, illimitable." In print the use of capitals, as later explained by Dickens, makes his sense reasonably clear; he had no trust in the governors, every faith in the governed. But at the time his remarks were misconstrued and even misrepresented. Did Mr Dickens mean that the people should not be allowed to govern themselves? And how could he have faith in the people who elected such governments in the first place? The latter point is hard to answer, but, then, Dickens was in no sense a coherent political theorist. Instead he remained, to use one of his favourite words in this period, a man "apart". A man apart who believed that ". . . our system fails". He had been saying as much all his life. It is almost as if he saw England once more as a huge workhouse presided over by Bumble, a vast and terrifying school administered by Squeers.

The days passed by. The last days. He gave his final reading from *David Copperfield* on the first evening of March. Two days later he attended, with Wills, a birthday party for Ellen Ternan at Blanchard's in Regent Street. On the eighth of the month he gave his last performance of "Sikes and Nancy", the reading which more than all others had weakened him. It was while he was on his way to the platform in order to play murderer and victim for the last time that he whispered to Charles Kent, "I shall tear myself to pieces." A few weeks before he had confessed to Dolby that ". . . it was madness ever to have given the 'Murder' reading, under the conditions of a travelling life, and worse than madness to have given it with such frequency". Yet even though he saw his madness he could not stop it. He went on.

The day after this reading he had an interview with the Queen in Buckingham Palace, at the sovereign's own request. Despite his lame foot he had to stand throughout the audience, according to protocol, while Victoria leaned against the arm of a sofa. He thought her "strangely shy", he told Georgina, "and like a girl in manner". In her journal the Queen described him as ". . . very agreeable, with a pleasant voice and manner". And of what did they talk? The servant problem. Lincoln's dream before his assassination (a topic of which Dickens never grew tired). Dickens's own public readings. The time when, thirteen years before, she had attended a performance of *The Frozen Deep*. The American attitude towards the Fenians. National education. The price of butcher's meat. Thus did the two greatest representatives of the Victorian era address one another, just as if they were unaware of their place in the history of their time. There were rumours afterwards that Dickens had been offered a knighthood or even a peerage, but there was nothing to them; he had in any case decided that he would remain what he had always been. Charles Dickens.

The time had now come for him to prepare himself for his final reading, his last appearance before the public. Two days before, he gave a dinner for all those connected with the business side of the reading tours and then, on 15 March, he prepared for his final reading that night. He was suffering from a bad throat, and had to have a poultice placed on it. He saw Luke Fildes about the illustrations for the fourth number of *The Mystery of Edwin Drood*. And then in the evening he went from Hyde Park Place to St James's Hall in order to read "A Christmas Carol" and "The Trial from Pickwick"; for the last time his audience would hear the voices of Ebenezer Scrooge, Bob Cratchit and Sam Weller. A huge audience had assembled, and many hours before the time of the reading crowds had gathered outside the two entrances in Regent Street and in Piccadilly. But punctually, at eight o'clock, Dickens walked onto the platform with his book in hand, "evidently much agitated", Dolby said, by the emotion of this final performance. The audience then rose to its feet, cheering and applauding, and he could not proceed for several minutes. Everyone watched him as he stood smiling behind his desk, that "spare figure . . . faultlessly attired in evening dress, the gas-light streaming down upon him, illuminating every feature of his familiar flushed face . . ." And then eventually he began. "I thought I had never heard him read . . . so well and with so little effort," Charley said. Charles Kent believed that ". . . he was keyed to a crowning effort". After he had finished the second of his readings, the trial scene from *The Pickwick Papers*, once more the audience burst into applause and cheering which lasted for several minutes. He had left the platform but had been recalled by the enthusiasm – almost the hysteria – of the audience several times. Until finally the noise and sensation abated. Dickens stood in front of them for the last time, and delivered a short speech that he had prepared for this occasion. "Ladies and Gentlemen, it would be worse than idle – for it would be hypocritical and unfeeling – if I were to disguise that I close this episode in my life with feelings of very considerable pain." Then he spoke briefly of the fifteen years in which he had been engaged in his readings, of his duty to the public and of their ready sympathy in return. He mentioned the imminent appearance of *The Mystery of Edwin Drood*, and then his voice faltered as he came to the end – ". . . but from these garish lights I vanish now for ever more, with a heartfelt, grateful, respectful, and affectionate farewell." There was a brief hush in the audience followed by something very like a common sigh and then, as his son recalled, "a storm of cheering as I have never seen equalled in my life". His head was bowed and the tears were streaming down his face as he left the platform. But the cheering and applause would not stop; after several minutes he returned, faced his audience once again, raised his hands to his lips in a kiss, and then left the platform for the last time. "He was deeply touched that night," his son said, "but infinitely sad and broken . . ." So much had come to an end now. So little left ahead of him. For a man who could never bear to say farewell, and for whom that direct relation to his public had been at the centre of his life, it was a moment of terrible sorrow.

Afterwards he wanted to destroy his reading desk – "I have no more use for it," he said – and his daughter, Kate, begged him to give it to her. But he did not wish these fifteen years to be entirely forgotten; he was delighted that Charles Kent was about to write a history of the readings, and he gave him all the material he needed for that task. He proposed, in addition, to leave his reading books to Forster, so that they might enter the "collection" of his work which was to be transmitted to posterity. But something had gone, something that could never return. To Fechter's son, Paul, he wrote in French the shortest epigraph of his public life. "Mon petit ami Paul, je t'envoie mes adieux au public. C'est fini, je tâcherai d'écrire encore, mais je ne parlerai plus." He signed it "Ton vieil ami".

In the third week of March, just a week after his final public reading, Dickens read the fourth number of *The Mystery of Edwin Drood* to Forster; the fact that Forster had once again become his confidant, and that he was still to a certain extent estranged from Wilkie Collins, suggests that Dickens at the end of his life was now returning to some of his oldest allegiances. He also told Forster on this occasion about the problems he was once again having with his sight. He could not read the right-hand half of the names above shop-doors. Then, a few days later, he experienced a massive haemorrhage of blood from his piles. All the signs were now pointing in the same direction. But there were also things to cheer him. At the beginning of April the first number of *The Mystery of Edwin Drood* was published in the familiar green cover, and it was an immediate success. Something like fifty thousand copies were sold, and the critical reaction was largely concerned to celebrate the fact that the novelist had reacquired his "old" manner. The actual peculiarities of the novel were not generally noticed, and instead the reviewers praised the humour present in characters like the stone-mason, Durdles, and the Tory "jackass", Mr Sapsea. That is why the *Spectator* believed Dickens to have returned "to the standard of his first few works", and yet of what a different world those first works had been a part. In the "Advertiser" purchased with *Nicholas Nickleby* there had been advertisements for such things as the Poor Man's Pill and Hussar suits for boys. Now, in *The Mystery of Edwin Drood*, the advertisements were for washing machines and self-raising flour.

His deteriorating sight and the disorder of his piles meant that he was seeing Frank Beard at least once a week, generally on the day before "make up" day at the office of *All The Year Round*. Nevertheless, when he gave a speech to the Newsvendors' Benevolent Association on 5 April, one spectator observed that ". . . he was full of merriment and overflowing with humour". The next day he attended a Levee at Buckingham Palace, for which notable occasion he was forced to wear court dress, including a cocked hat which, unsure of the proper direction it was meant to point, he tucked under his arm. Then on the following evening he gave a grand reception at Hyde Park Place, complete with Joachim playing Schumann and Tartini as well as the sound of the massed ranks of the London Glee and Madrigal Union. "Everyone" was there – it was, you might say, his final tryst with "Society" – but Dolby noticed that Dickens himself, although as bright and as animated as ever, was "suffering very much" and looked "jaded and worn".

It was a busy month. He went to the circus on one evening and saw an elephant standing on its head, which feat led him to wonder out loud why "they've never taught the rhinoceros to do anything . . ." He visited the theatre. He attended private dinners with friends. And, of all marks of respect and homage, he seemed most pleased by the gift from a successful Liverpool timber merchant, George Holme, of a silver table ornament. Georgina, in a letter to Annie Fields, said that Dickens could not remember anything more "gratifying" and "pleasant" during the whole of his career. One part of the gift was a silver centrepiece for the table, on the sides of which had been etched designs to represent·the seasons – spring, summer and autumn only, however, so that Dickens might be reminded simply of the more agreeable and hopeful months. But he told Forster, in words that disclose his state of mind during this last period, "I never look at it, that I don't think most of the Winter." Even if the real winter was never to surround him again.

Mamie said that in this period of busy activity he "grew quickly and easily tired", and in truth he just as rapidly became bored with dining out and general socialising. He was growing restless and even by the middle of April had made up his mind not to accept any public engagements for the rest of the year. He was also tired of London and longed for the country, a mood which he expressed in the instalment of the novel he was writing at this time – ". . . deserts of gritty streets, where many people crowded at the corners of courts and bye-ways, to get some air, and where many other people walked with a miserably monotonous noise of shuffling feet on hot paving-stones, and where all the people and all their surroundings were so gritty and so shabby." He was working slowly on the story now, transposing chapters in order to create the precise dramatic effect he desired, moving on carefully but anxious in case he was using up his material too quickly.

But his concentration upon the narrative was then profoundly disturbed by the death of Daniel Maclise, one of his oldest companions, the young man who with Forster and Ainsworth had comprised the first real circle of friends to which Dickens ever belonged, the oddity and solitude of whose final years only served to remind Dickens of how much they had all gone through, how much they had all changed. He could not really "get over" the artist's death – in a letter to Forster he said that he was "at once thinking of it and avoiding it in a strange way" – and it is almost as if in the shock of that fatality he had some intimation of his own end. He had already agreed to deliver a speech at the annual dinner of the Royal Academy three days later, and he took the occasion – he had, at least, that much command of himself – both to mourn the passing of his old friend and to lament the loss to his chosen profession. Towards the close he added this: ". . . I already begin to feel like that Spanish monk of whom Wilkie tells, who had grown to believe that the only realities around him were the pictures which he loved [*cheers*], and that all the moving life he saw, or ever had seen, was a shadow and a dream. [*Cheers*]." One of the guests said of Dickens that night, ". . . he then looked like a man who would live and work until he was four score. I was especially struck by the brilliance and vivacity of his eyes." But in fact it was the last public speech that Dickens ever made.

He had been making plans with his gardener, Brunt, to prepare plants for the newly-built conservatory at Gad's Hill Place, plants which would flower next year, but, as he said in a letter to his old friend Mrs Watson, "the dear old . . . days are always fresh in my heart". Blanchard Jerrold met him in the street this spring, and noticed how the settled gloom and sadness of his countenance lifted when they met and spoke; ". . . he spoke cheerily, in the old kind way – not in the least about him – but about my doings, about Doré, about London as a subject [Jerrold was about to write a text to accompany Doré's pictures of suffering London] . . . about all that could interest me, that occurred to him at the moment." But after they had shaken hands, ". . . the cast of serious thought settled again upon the handsome face, as he turned, wearily I thought for him, towards the Abbey". Towards the place where he would be buried in the following month. In the same period he had been discussing *The Mystery of Edwin Drood* with a friend. "Well, you, or we," he said to Dickens, "are approaching the mystery –" Dickens, "who had been, and was at the moment, all vivacity, extinguished his gaiety, and fell into a long and silent reverie, from which he never broke during the remainder of the walk".

On an evening that month he had been visited at Hyde Park Place by a young author, Constance Cross, who had been recommended to him by Bulwer-Lytton. They spoke together for about an hour and in the course of their conversation he told her that he was considering a stay of two years in Germany, and that he was hoping to travel there "accompanied by his daughter". He told her also about Gad's Hill Place – ". . . I love the dear old place; and I hope – when I come to die – it may be there." Then he described his evenings "generally in the society of a much-loved daughter, to whom he often affectionately referred". Or perhaps this was his way of talking of Ellen Ternan, these references to his "daughter"? Constance Cross eventually asked him what might happen if he died before one of his books was completed. "That has occurred to me – at times." But then he added, more cheerfully, "One can only work on, you know – work while it is day."

He had breakfast with Gladstone, early in the month of May, and seemed to those present to be looking "very ill"; after he had left, the prime minister said to the assembled guests, "Anyone can see that he is sacrificing his life to his work." But he had been doing that all his life. Other engagements followed; dinner with the American minister, dinner with Lord Stanhope and Benjamin Disraeli. On 7 May he read the fifth number of *The Mystery of Edwin Drood* to Forster but three days later the "neuralgia" in his foot returned so painfully that he had to swathe it in constant hot poultices and take laudanum simply in order to sleep. He cancelled all social engagements, begged off the Theatrical Fund dinner at which he was supposed to speak – "I could no more walk into St James's Hall than I could fly in the air," he told one of the organisers – and was forced to miss the Queen's Ball which he had promised to attend with his daughter. Mamie went without him.

Dickens was away from Hyde Park Place for three days in May; no doubt he had gone to Peckham, and Ellen Ternan may have been the "sick friend" upon whom he said that he was "in attendance". On 22 May he dined with his old friends, the Lehmanns, and began the last social round he would ever be forced to endure. He was "extremely jolly", Lehmann reported later. Also present that evening was John Forster; the two men talked of the sudden death of Mark Lemon, of which Dickens had heard that day. Dickens then spoke of their other friends who had died in the past few years. "And none beyond his sixtieth year," he said, "very few even fifty." Dickens was now fifty-eight. Forster suggested that it did no good to talk of such matters. "We shall not think of it the less," he replied. Forster was never again to see him alive.

A few days later Dickens was dining with the Houghtons, specifically to meet the Prince of Wales and the King of the Belgians; he had not wanted to go, so bad his foot had become, but eventually he managed to make his way there. He was too lame to walk upstairs to the drawing room, however, but instead was helped into the dining room where he waited for the others. Yet at a dinner with Lady Molesworth towards the end of the month he was once more bright and animated. "Dickens simply bubbled over with fun and conversation," another guest remembered, "talking in a way which resembled nothing so much as some of the best pages in his own books." He visited the theatre, too, and "Dickens was in high spirits, brim-full of the *joie de vivre* . . . he was at times still so young and almost boyish in his gaiety . . ." We must imagine a man now who, when alone, settled into a grave and melancholy state but who, in the company of others, still retained all the cheerfulness and animation of his youth; a man whose temperament remained indomitably bright but who was so susceptible to thoughts of his own mortality that he could fall very silent.

A measure of his high spirits even now is to be found in the fact that he was actively superintending rehearsals for an amateur play to be performed at the beginning of June. Both of his daughters were to take part, and in fact some of the rehearsals were conducted at Hyde Park Place; Dickens had expressed some interest in playing a part himself, but now he was too lame to be able to do so. Instead, according to one of the actors, Herman Merivale, he "superintended and managed the whole thing . . . and he threw himself into every part with each actor in turn in a way not to be forgotten . . ." Even though he was suffering from his lameness, he directed the rehearsals ". . . with a boy's spirit, and a boy's interest in his favourite art; 'coaching' us all with untiring kindness, marking his 'prompt-book' as he marked his readings, and acting all the parts *con amore* one after another, passing from the 'old man' to the 'young lover' with all his famous versatility and power". Passing from the old man to the young lover – this seems like the very simulacrum of his life now, all the boyishness and gaiety seeming to spring unimpeded from the recesses of his being. For here once again he was surrounded by the pursuit of his youth; once more he was taking on the stage management of a production, as he had done when he had put on *Clari* at the house of his parents in Bentinck Street thirty-seven years before. He left Hyde Park Place at the end of May and went down thankfully to Gad's Hill Place for two or three days' repose – "dead lame," he said. As Dolby remarked towards the close of his memoir of the "Chief", ". . . it would really seem, in looking back, that all things pointed to the great end".

On the first day of June, a Wednesday, he wrote a few lines to conclude the amateur play which was to be performed the following evening; he wrote them in his own hand and then added "Curtain" at the conclusion. He was at the office in Wellington Street the next morning. Here he wrote the last codicil of his will, leaving *All The Year Round* to his son, Charley, and for the rest of the morning he was preoccupied with office business. Percy Fitzgerald came to see him, and together they looked at the posters which Dickens had prepared for the advertisement of Fitzgerald's next serial: "I see his figure now before me, standing at the table – the small delicate formed shoulders . . ." Dolby visited him later that same morning – they lunched together regularly on Thursdays – but "on this particular occasion," Dolby wrote, "I was much struck by the alteration of his demeanour – not that he was less genial than usual, but that he appeared to me to be suffering from such great depression of spirits that even his gaiety of manner under these circumstances could not disguise." After lunch they parted and, as they shook hands across the table, Dickens said, "Next week then." But Dolby noticed "the pained look on his face". In another account he described the "great mental agony" imprinted on his features, as well as the tears which came into his eyes, but the more restrained account seems the more likely.

That night Dickens attended the first performance of the play which he had rehearsed during the last days of May; once more he was busy and active behind the scenes as stage manager, prompter, bell-ringer and lighting expert, going through these old and familiar routines, according to the actor Merivale, "with infectious enjoyment". But Fitzgerald was also present and has said that ". . . he left the impression on those he met of being oppressed with ill-health and dejection. His face became more lined with care or suffering, and a sort of sad look overcast it." So was he "oppressed", or filled with an "infectious enjoyment", on this occasion? One is tempted to reply with the words he had used to Herman Merivale that day – the actor was not sure whether his part was meant to be comic or serious, and Dickens replied, "My dear boy, God alone knows. Play it whichever way you feel at night." But there was no doubt that he was tired. His son-in-law, Charles Collins, found him sitting behind the scenes at the end of the play with a "dazed" expression. And, as he left, he is supposed to have replied, to an enquiry, "I am tired. I want rest – *rest*." That night he stayed at the office, unusually for him, and on the following morning his son, Charley, found him working there on *The Mystery of Edwin Drood*. He was about to leave for the day and went in to see his father, who was still "writing very earnestly". After a moment "I said, 'If you don't want anything more, sir, I shall be off now,' but he continued his writing with the same intensity as before, and gave no sign of being aware of my presence. Again I spoke – louder, perhaps, this time – and he raised his head and looked at me long and fixedly. But I soon found that, although his eyes were bent upon me and he seemed to be looking at me earnestly, he did not see me, and that he was, in fact, unconscious for the moment of my very existence. He was in dreamland with *Edwin Drood*, and I left him – for the last time." There is something very disturbing about this anecdote, the prematurely aged man still so immersed in his images and words that he could not even see his own son standing in front of him. And what of Charley himself? In retrospect he must have been disturbed, too. This was the last time he would ever see his father, and yet he was ignored by him in favour of the creatures of his imagination.

Dickens was now on the last chapter he would ever write, concerned that he had already used up too much of the material he had prepared and anxious lest he had inadvertently disclosed too much of his complete design. But he wrote on now, as Rosa Bud arrives in London and glides in a boat along the Thames, ". . . and, all too soon, the great black city cast its shadows on the waters, and its dark bridges spanned them as death spans life, and the everlastingly green garden seemed to be left for everlasting, unregainable and far away." He wrote only a few thousand words after this, and the fact that he left the novel unfinished has in turn led to what has generally been called "the Drood controversy". Was Drood really dead? Was Jasper really the murderer? How was Drood murdered? Who is the strange figure of Datchery? Woman, or man? But in a sense all these enquiries miss the central point; that Dickens was not really concerned with plot at all, at least not in the mechanical sense which such speculations imply. Of course it has afforded a great deal of harmless amusement to those who enjoy games and puzzles but it has left out of consideration the true nature of Dickens's art which, in this final novel, was so deeply implicated in the extraordinary and haunting portrayal of John Jasper – a murderer perhaps, an opium addict certainly, an artist, a frustrated lover. Jasper who, even when he plays his music, is "'. . . troubled with some stray sort of ambition, aspiration, restlessness, dissatisfaction, what shall we call it?'" We may call it the very conditions on which Charles Dickens himself held his life, a life of struggle and work and anxiety lit by the intense glare of fame. Again, of Jasper, Dickens writes that, although "constantly exercising an Art which brought him into mechanical harmony with others . . .", he possessed a spirit which was ". . . in moral accordance or interchange with nothing around him". It may well have been on the afternoon of this day, after writing his novel all the morning, that Dickens was seen near the Athenaeum ". . . grey-haired, careworn, and so absent and absorbed in his thoughts . . ."

Dickens returned to Gad's Hill Place that night, and was never to leave it again alive. He spent the weekend walking and writing letters. On the Sunday afternoon he became very tired after a relatively short walk and his daughter, Kate, was shocked to see him "a good deal changed". But he seemed to improve during dinner and then, afterwards, he smoked his usual cigar and took a stroll in the garden with both his daughters, the air filled with the sweet scent of syringa shrubs. Afterwards he sat in the dining room and contemplated his new conservatory, which had just been completed as an extension to that room. Mamie had gone into the drawing room to play the piano, and Dickens listened to her solitary music as he sat looking at the flowers. Kate had mentioned to her father that she wanted to talk to him about a decision she was about to make – she wanted to go on the stage, in order to earn some money for herself and her ailing husband – and at eleven o'clock, when Georgina and Mamie had retired to bed, and the lights in the conservatory had been turned down, father and daughter talked together. They discussed her plans, of which Dickens disapproved since there were people in the theatrical profession "who would make your hair stand on end". They considered the matter for a while but then, when Kate rose to leave, Dickens asked her to stay because he had more to say to her. He talked of his hopes for *The Mystery of Edwin Drood*, "if, please God, I live to finish it". Then, he added, "I say *if*, because you know, my dear child, I have not been strong lately." He went on to talk of the past but not of the future, and it seemed to his daughter that "he spoke as though his life were over and there was nothing left". Then he went on to regret that he had not been "a better father – a better man". Kate said, in a later unpublished account, that he also mentioned Ellen Ternan. Father and daughter did not leave each other until three in the morning.

But Dickens was up the next day, Monday, at 7.30 – "Sharp, mind," he had said to his parlour-maid, since he had a great deal of work to manage that week. He went over to the chalet early in order to continue with his writing of the novel, and it was here that Kate came to see him before she left for London with Mamie. She knew how much he hated partings, so she had merely left her love to be given to him by Georgina; but, as she waited on the porch for the carriage to take her to the station, she had "an uncontrollable desire to see him once again". So she hurried through the tunnel to the chalet on the other side of the road, and mounted the wooden staircase to the upper room where he always worked. "His head was bent low down over his work, and he turned an eager and rather flushed face towards me as I entered. On ordinary occasions he would just have raised his cheek for my kiss, saying a few words, perhaps, in 'the little language' that he had been accustomed to use when we were children; but on this morning, when he saw me, he pushed his chair from the writing-table, opened his arms, and took me into them . . ." It was the last time they would speak to one another. That afternoon he walked to Rochester with the dogs and, in town, he bought a copy of the *Daily Mail*. He was seen by several people leaning against the wooden railing across the street from Restoration House, and "it was remarked at the time that there would be some notice of this building in the tale then current . . ."

On the next day he wrote, as usual, and then drove to Cobham Wood with Georgina, dismissing the carriage once they had arrived there and walking round the park back to Gad's Hill Place. It is impossible not to quote an account of precisely the same walk from his first novel. "A delightful walk it was: for it was a pleasant afternoon in June, and their way lay through a deep and shady wood, cooled by the light wind which gently rustled the thick foliage, and enlivened by the songs of the birds that perched upon the boughs. The ivy and the moss crept in thick clusters over the old trees, and the soft green turf overspread the ground like a silken mat." A June day. So it was then, and so it was now. In the beginning we see his end. It was his last walk, but it had been beautifully anticipated thirty-four years before. That evening he fixed some Chinese lanterns in the conservatory, and sat in the dining room to consider their effect in the twilight.

He awoke early on the following day, Wednesday, 8 June, in excellent spirits. He talked a little with Georgina about his book and then after breakfast went straight over to the chalet in order to continue work on it. He came back to the house at one o'clock for lunch, smoked a cigar in the conservatory and then, unusually for him, returned to the chalet where he remained occupied on the novel which had taken such a hold upon him. These last pages were written with relative ease, marked by fewer emendations than usual, and

Dickens's final passage of narrative opens with an encomium to light –
"A brilliant morning shines on the old city" – which echoes the very
first sentence of his first novel, *The Pickwick Papers*. "The first ray of
light which illumines the gloom . . ." Light calling to light, the figure
of Dickens bent between them. That light even penetrates into the
cold stone of the cathedral and manages to "subdue its earthy odour",
again in echo of his first novel where Jingle had spoken of the same
place, "Old cathedral too – earthy smell . . ." The circle was almost
complete. His first novel and his last novel. One opening with the
light and with Rochester, the other closing on the same two notes. The
circle of life. "For, as I draw closer and closer to the end," it had been
said in *A Tale of Two Cities*, "I travel in the circle, nearer and nearer to
the beginning." Charles Dickens coming to his end now, in the house
he had seen as a child and which he had never forgotten. He wrote the
last words of *The Mystery of Edwin Drood*, "and then falls to with an
appetite"; after which he formed the short spiral which generally
marked the end of a chapter. The end. He came back to the house an
hour before dinner and seemed "tired, silent and abstracted". While
waiting for his meal he went into the library and wrote two letters.
One to Charles Kent, in which he arranged to see him in London at
three o'clock on the following day: "If I can't be – why, then I shan't
be." The other to a clergyman to whom, in response to some
criticism, he declared that "I have always striven in my writings to
express veneration for the life and lessons of Our Saviour . . ."

Georgina was the only member of the family with him and, just as
they sat down together for dinner, she noticed a change both in his
colour and his expression. She asked him if he were ill, and he replied,
"Yes, very ill; I have been very ill for the last hour." She wanted to
send immediately for a doctor but he forbade her to do so, saying that
he wanted to go to London that evening after dinner. But then
something happened. He experienced some kind of fit against which
he tried to struggle – he paused for a moment and then began to talk
very quickly and indistinctly, at some point mentioning Forster. She
rose from her chair, alarmed, and told him to "come and lie down".

"Yes," he said. "On the ground."

But as she helped him he slid from her arms and fell heavily to the
floor. He was now unconscious. A young servant went at once on the
pony, Newman Noggs, into Rochester in order to summon the local
doctor, Mr Steele, who arrived at 6.30. "I found Dickens lying on the
floor of the dining-room in a fit. He was unconscious, and never

moved. The servants brought a couch down, on which he was placed. I applied clysters and other remedies to the patient without effect." Rugs were wrapped around him and pillows were put beneath his head.

Telegrams had already been sent to Frank Beard, and to Dickens's daughters. When they arrived at Gad's Hill Place, Kate could hear her father's deep breathing, "We found him lying unconscious on a couch in the dining room where he and I had talked together; a sudden gloom had fallen upon the place, and everything was changed; only the still, warm weather continued the same, and the sweet scent of the flowers he had so much admired floated in through the open doors of the new conservatory." They watched him through the night, taking it in turns to place hot bricks against his feet which were now so cold. He did not move at all, and yet they could not help but still believe that, suddenly, he would revive and be himself again. They could not believe that this unconscious form was Charles Dickens. But he never stirred.

"On the ground." His last words. And is it possible that he had in some bewildered way echoed the words of Louisa Gradgrind to her errant father in *Hard Times*, "'I shall die if you hold me! Let me fall upon the ground!'"? And were his other characters around him as he lay unconscious through his last night? He had often recalled the image of Sir Walter Scott dying ". . . faint, wan, crushed both in mind and body by his honourable struggle, and hovering round him the ghosts of his own imagination . . . innumerable overflowing the chamber, and fading away in the dim distance beyond". He had spoken these words, as a young man, in America, at the height of his fame. And can we see them now, the ghosts of Dickens's imagination, hovering around him as he approaches his own death? Oliver Twist, Ebenezer Scrooge, Paul Dombey, Little Nell, Little Dorrit, the Artful Dodger, Bob Sawyer, Sam Weller, Mr Pickwick, Barkis, David Copperfield, Pip, Quilp, Fagin, Stephen Blackpool, Nicholas Nickleby, Mrs Nickleby, Bumble, Jo, Martin Chuzzlewit, Bob Cratchit, Fagin, the Crummles family, Edwin Drood, Peggotty, Mr Dick, Mr F's Aunt, Mrs Gamp, Uriah Heep, Pecksniff, Micawber, the Infant Phenomenon, the Jellybys, the Smallweeds, the Mantalinis, the Father of the Marshalsea, Barnaby Rudge, Rogue Riderhood, Miss Havisham, Bill Sikes, Nancy, Smike, all of them now hovering around their creator as his life on earth came to an end.

But there were other shadows hovering about him which he could not have seen. Shadows of the future. Shadows of the real people he was now leaving behind him. Of John Forster kissing his friend's face as he lay in his coffin and writing, "The duties of life remain while life remains, but for me the joy of it is gone for ever more." Of Ellen Ternan visiting Mamie and Georgina in the years ahead, marrying a schoolmaster, teaching French and elocution to schoolchildren. Of Mamie and Georgina sharing a house with Henry. Of his children fighting bitterly amongst themselves. Of Kate painting and looking after her invalid husband, until he died and she married again. Of Georgina and Catherine Dickens reconciled at last. Of Catherine herself, living out a true widowhood after the enforced separation of twelve years. Of Sydney buried at sea two years later. Of Plorn bankrupt. Of Alfred lecturing on his father. Of Charley giving readings from his father's books. Of a Christmas fund raised for the benefit "of the descendants of Charles Dickens". Of the sale of his effects two months later, when the stuffed body of Grip, his favourite raven, was sold for one hundred and twenty pounds. All this came to pass.

They watched him through the night – Frank Beard, Georgina, his daughters – but he never stirred from his unconsciousness. Doctor Steele returned in the morning and observed that "there was unhappily no change in the symptoms, and stertorous breathing, which had commenced before, now continued". He and Frank Beard advised that another doctor should be summoned and Charley, who himself had now arrived, sent a telegram to London: "Mr Dickens very ill. Most urgent." But there was nothing now to be done. When Russell Reynolds arrived in answer to the urgent entreaty he said at once, on seeing him. "He cannot live." Ellen Ternan, summoned by Georgina, came that afternoon to be present at the side of the dying man. He lingered all that day, his breathing becoming louder. And then at five minutes before six o'clock in the evening his breathing suddenly diminished and he began to sob. Fifteen minutes later he heaved a deep sigh, a tear rose to his right eye and trickled down his cheek. He was dead. Charles Dickens had left the world.

Postscript

NONE among those who stood around him that day really wished him back. He had suffered too much. He had become too sad. It was Kate who remarked that "if my father had lived, he would have gone out of his mind".

Lived through what? There were thirty more years of the century. Charles Dickens died at the very height of the "Victorian" age, and yet in his death one of its moving spirits had crept away. Part of its soul had gone. So, looking back at the record of this one life, can we see the traces of the larger world in which he moved? He was born at the beginning of the century and never quite reconciled himself to the developments which took place in his maturity. He was already the most famous novelist in England when Victoria ascended the throne, and throughout his life Dickens was unmistakably an early Victorian; anyone who knew him in the Fifties and Sixties would instinctively have known that his temperament and vision came from an epoch that had already disappeared, just as even in our period it is possible to recognise the salient characteristics of men and women who came to maturity in the Thirties or Forties. He was an early Victorian, or perhaps more accurately a pre-Victorian; in his capacity for excitement and exhilaration, in his radicalism, and in his earnest desire for social reform, he was one of those who came to prominence in the first three decades of the century. The joy in discovery, the belief in progress, the largeness of spirit – all these were characteristics of the men who grew old with Dickens. In his ardour, in his theatricality, even in his vulgarity, he is a man from the beginning of the century. By the time of his death most of these characteristics had left the English; or, rather, they had become less prominent and had been supplanted by a certain practicality and a certain steadiness. Just as the larger movement of the age was towards centralisation and uniform-ity, so the single-mindedness and indeed eccentricity of the early Victorians were in turn replaced.

There is no doubt that such changes occur, but perhaps it is only in the processes of an individual human life like that of Dickens that they can be mostly clearly discerned. Yet they can be recognised, too, in Dickens's own fiction, no less in its comedy and sentiment than in its brooding poetry and in its capacity to transform the world into myth. In Dickens's work – in Dickens's life itself – there is the same unmistakable urge to encompass everything, to comprehend everything, to control everything. In this he is a part of his period, the man exemplifying the spirit of his time in his energetic pursuit of some complete vision of the world. The intricacy, the complexity, the momentum, the evolution, the very length of his narratives indicate as much – narratives which contain so much humour (and there never was a period so capable of laughing at itself), so great a concern for the central human progress of the world, and yet such a longing for transcendence also. Charles Dickens was the last of the great eighteenth-century novelists and the first of the great symbolic novelists, and in the crushing equilibrium between these two forces dwells the real strength of his art. The newspaper editorials after his death noted how fully he had chronicled his period but he had done more than that; he had made it larger, brighter, more capacious than anything they could possibly have imagined for themselves. It may be true that he created or recreated his age in his own image but, as we have seen in this history, in his own person he experienced powerfully the most genuine forces of his time. The plunge from relative gentility, the manual labour in the blacking warehouse, the ambition, the endless hard work, the energy, the battle against circumstance, and then the triumph of the will. To be followed in turn by exhaustion and illness. And by the ultimate triumph of sorrow and fatality. So do all ages, and all men, go into the dark.

In some ways it can be said, therefore, that he represented the Victorian character, both in his earnestness and in his sentimentality, in his enthusiasm and in his sense of duty, in his optimism and in his doubt, in his belief in work and in his instinct for theatricality, in his violence and in his energy. For him life was conflict, it was "battle" always, but one which contained vivid colours and grandiose visions. The nature of that "battle" is clear enough. It was not just his own private battle against the world and against the demands of his own divided nature; it was also a struggle in which all the forces of his time were ranged beside him, for it was a struggle to maintain a vision of the coherence of the world, a vision of some central human continuity. In this sense it was also a battle against all the self-doubt, anxiety and division which lay beneath the surface of his own nature, just as they dwelt beneath the progressive formulations of nineteenth-century power.

But these are generalities, no longer close to the life as it was conducted or to the century as it moved forward. ". . . trifles make the sum of life": David Copperfield's words have a place in this history, for surely it is in the "trifles" of Dickens's life that we have found the source and measure of the works which comprise his greatness. Not trifles, then, but origins. For what do Dickens's own novels tell us, but that a passing gesture, an image, or mood, can form a whole network of meaning. That the coincidence, the chance remark, the unexpected meeting, can change a human being. That the significance of a whole lifetime of endeavour can be altered by the sudden confusion of events. But this is not simply a novelistic device. It is a perception into the very nature of the world, and it is one which biography itself must strive to exemplify. To see Dickens day by day, making his way, the incidents of his existence shaping his fiction just as his fiction alters his life, the same pattern of emotion and imagery rising up from letters and novels and conversations, the same momentum and the same desire for control – to see Dickens thus is to turn biography into an agent of true knowledge, even as we remember that the greatness of his fiction may lie in its absolute *difference* from anything which the life may show us. But once we have made that leap, from the man to his works, then we can also begin to carve out that unimaginable passage from the single human being to the age in which he lived. Seeing in his gestures, his conversations, his narratives, his dress, his moods, even in his moments of blindness and self-deception, the lineaments of the age itself – an age which existed in him and through him, but which also existed beyond him. An age which may also be seen as an exhalation of human lives. The spirit of the time. The breath of the time. People, known and unknown. And among them Dickens, whom we have come to understand.

A few weeks after his death, just as everything had been prepared for the auction of his effects, Georgina, Mamie and Kate walked through Gad's Hill Place, "going into every room, and saying good-bye to every dear corner". Mamie wrote that ". . . We three, who have been best friends and companions all our lives, went out of the dear old Home, together". Three years later Catherine Dickens attended the first performance of *Dombey and Son* at the Globe Theatre in London. But she could not watch it. She broke down and wept.

Notes on Text and Sources

I HAVE not given page numbers to my quotations from Dickens's work for the simple reason that, until the Clarendon edition of his fiction is completed, there is no standard uniform text for his novels. For the purposes of continuity, as well as accuracy and general accessibility, I have chosen to refer to the eighteen volumes of The Charles Dickens Library, an edition published by the Educational Book Company in 1910 as a suitably expanded version of the Soho Edition of 1903. It is reliable and, most importantly, it has been my companion (and benefactor) during all the years I have been working on this biography. I could no more abandon it now than I could abandon my own first love of Charles Dickens's writing. This edition does not, however, include *The Mystery of Edwin Drood* and for that text I have used the edition published by Oxford University Press under the aegis of "The World's Classics". Dickens's published letters fall into two distinct parts – there is, primarily, the Pilgrim Edition of his correspondence which at the time of writing has reached Volume Six. The years so far encompassed by this wonderful enterprise are 1820 to 1852. The other major source of Dickens's published correspondence is to be found within the volumes of the Nonesuch Dickens. This work, patchy and sometimes even misleading, is still the best complete edition of Dickens's correspondence for the years not covered by the Pilgrim Edition. There are also several smaller and more specific collections, among them the *Letters from Charles Dickens to Angela Burdett-Coutts, 1841–1865*, edited by Edgar Johnson, and *Mr and Mrs Charles Dickens: His Letters to Her*, edited by Walter Dexter. There also remain the piles of Dickens's unpublished correspondence, lying in the various institutions of England and America to which I have referred in my acknowledgments.

Certain other books of primary material call for especial mention: *Charles Dickens: The Public Readings*, edited by Philip Collins (London, 1975); *The Speeches of Charles Dickens*, edited by Kenneth Fielding (Oxford, 1960); *Charles Dickens: The Critical Heritage*, edited by Philip Collins (London, 1971); *The Uncollected Writings of Charles Dickens: Household Words, 1850–1859*, edited by Harry Stone (London, 1969); *Dickens's Working Notes for His Novels*, edited by Harry Stone (London, 1987). And of course the thanks of any biographer must go to the massed ranks of the editors and contributors of *The Dickensian* over many years. There is more information and pertinent material within those green-covered magazines than in a host of more apparently imposing volumes.

Of course no biographer of Dickens can refrain from mentioning John Forster's *Life of Charles Dickens*, published in three volumes between 1872 and 1874. All other biographies, together with the host of critical and scholarly studies which I have found helpful, are to be found in the bibliography which follows my notes.

Prologue

There are various descriptions of the events after Charles Dickens's death. Some of them are to be found in the recollections of his children – most notably in *Recollections* by Henry Dickens and a long contribution by Mamie Dickens in F. G. Kitton's *Charles Dickens: By Pen and Pencil*. Kitton's book is especially valuable for other first-hand accounts of this period; it is there, for example, that we can find the remarks of the man who sculpted Dickens's death-mask, Thomas Woolner. Other first-hand reports are to be found in W. R. Hughes's *A Week's Tramp in Dickensland*, which was written in 1891 and offers invaluable evidence from those who were in a position to know Dickens in his "home" surroundings. Other details can be gleaned from the remarks of Kate Dickens as broadcast to the world by Gladys Storey in *Dickens and Daughter*, and some interesting items can also be collected from early issues of *The Dickensian*. The first number of that invaluable journal, dated January 1905, in fact carries an article by Henry Dickens on the events surrounding the death and funeral of his father. Of course Forster, in the last pages of *The Life of Charles Dickens*, is also very informative; it is he who prints Dickens's will in an appendix, but for a hint of the notoriety surrounding that document it is interesting to read the remarks of one of Dickens's first biographers, J. H. Friswell, in *Modern Men of Letters*, published in the year of Dickens's death. Contemporary accounts of the death and obituary tributes are also to be found in all of the newspapers and periodicals of the period – particularly of note are those in the *Daily News*, the newspaper which Dickens edited for a very brief period, and in *The Times*, the *Spectator* and the *Illustrated London News*. Very full and interesting accounts of the funeral itself are to be found in G. A. Sala's *Charles Dickens*, also published in the year of Dickens's death, and in Percy Fitzgerald's *Memories of Charles Dickens*.

Chapter 1

No one has written more poignantly about Charles Dickens's childhood than Charles Dickens, although his aptitude for fiction was such that not all his reminiscences are free of invention. One of the hardest tasks for any biographer, in fact, lies in the attempt to separate the real truths from the penumbra of romance, nostalgia and fantasy which surrounds them. For, in a sense, Dickens's childhood can be found everywhere – in the elaborate narratives of *Great Expectations* and *David Copperfield* no less than in shorter journalistic essays such as "A Christmas Tree", "New Year's Day" and "What Christmas Is, As We Grow Older". But there are levels of truth, just as there are different levels of narrative. The fictional accounts can be taken as just that – fiction, even though there are many passages in the novels which reflect aspects of Dickens's childhood and Dickens's childhood aspirations. Then there are the essays which he wrote as himself or as the "Uncommercial Traveller"; in these there tends to be a charming if sometimes confusing mixture of fictional narrative and true memory. And then there is the famous "autobiographical fragment" which Dickens employed in *David Copperfield*, and which John Forster later published in the life of his friend. This again owes as much to the tradition of autobiographical writing as it does to Dickens's memories of his childhood, but there is no doubt that in the general drift of the narrative is to be found an essential truth about Dickens's childhood. Dickens also sometimes spoke to Forster about his earlier years and these oral reminiscences, to be found in the early pages of Forster's biography, have the ring of genuine and momentary recollection. These, at least, we can transmit without the precaution of exegesis.

There are three separate accounts of Dickens's childhood. The first is Robert Langton's *The Childhood and Youth of Charles Dickens* which, published in 1912, has the benefit of some first-hand testimony. There are also Christopher Hibbert's *The Making of Charles Dickens* and Michael Allen's *Charles Dickens's Childhood*, the latter being noticeable for its meticulous scholarship. Of great value, also, are F. G. Kitton's *Charles Dickens: His Life, Writings and Personality* and the same author's *The Dickens Country*. Both of these studies also have the benefit of first-hand testimony, as does W. R. Hughes's *A Week's Tramp in Dickensland*. One of Dickens's earliest biographies, R. Shelton Mackenzie's *Life of Charles Dickens*, published in 1870, is also surprisingly well-informed about Dickens's family and parents.

The matter of Dickens's ancestry has been thoroughly explored, most notably by William Carlton in two essays in *The Dickensian* – "The Barrows of Bristol" (Volume 46) and "More About the Dickens Ancestry" (Volume 57). A great deal of unpublished but fascinating documentary material is also to be found among Carlton's scholarly papers, which are now preserved at Dickens House. There are also two long and valuable essays in Volume 45 of

The Dickensian, "The Dickens Ancestry: Some New Discoveries", taken from the notes of A. T. Butler and Arthur Campling. More genealogical material is to be found in John Noakes's *Rambler in Worcestershire*.

Reminiscences of Dickens's paternal grandmother are to be found in *The Life, Letters and Friendships of Richard Monckton Milnes, first Lord Houghton* by T. W. Reid; more information is given by "J.E.A." in Volume 4 of *The Dickensian*, as well as in Langton, Mackenzie and other sources. Reminiscences of her are also vouchsafed in some unpublished letters to Kate Perugini, Dickens's daughter, from Lord Crewe and J. C. Parkinson; these, and much else that is fascinating on Dickens's relatives, is to be found among the Storey papers preserved at Dickens House. For Dickens's maternal grandparents, the most reliable source remains "The Huffams, the Barrows and the Admiralty", by E. Bechhofer Roberts in *The Dickensian* (Volume 24).

There is a wealth of information about Dickens's mother to be found in all of the standard biographies, although the material preserved in the earliest of these biographies tends to be the most interesting; it has to be remembered on all occasions, however, that gossip and speculation find their way into even the most anodyne descriptions. Of more particular and local relevance are reminiscences of Mrs Dickens in *Lippincott's Magazine* of June 1874 and in *The Story of a Lifetime* by Lady Priestley; curiously enough, there are some intriguing details in Charles F. Rideal's *Charles Dickens's Heroines and Women Folk*. There is also a letter from Elizabeth Dickens to Samuel Haydon, on the subject of her husband; it is undated but it is to be found among the many papers preserved in Dickens House. Material is also to be found in Gladys Storey's *Dickens and Daughter*. I shall not make it a practice to footnote every remark or quotation from Dickens's published writings, but I will document the more arcane references. So for example, the remark ". . . excuse my curiosity, which I inherit from my mother . . ." is to be found in an essay, "Bill-Sticking", which was published in *Household Words* of 22 March, 1851. There are as many accounts of Dickens's father as there are of Dickens's mother, but the most specific and detailed is undoubtedly "John Dickens and the Navy Pay Office" by Angus Easson in volume 70 of *The Dickensian*. Dickens's own parodies of his father's circumlocutory style are sprinkled throughout his correspondence, both in Pilgrim and in Nonesuch; one passage of parody, for example, is to be found in a letter to Forster in the last months of 1844 and is printed in Pilgrim Volume 4, pp. 243–244.

The songs of Dickens's childhood are transmitted in a series of articles by J. W. T. Ley in *The Dickensian* (Volume 27) and, while on the minutiae, there is some interesting additional extra information on the subject of Dickens's birth to be found in the catalogue of the Dickens Birthplace Museum in Portsmouth. In fact those who wish to experience at first-hand something of Dickens's life should visit the Portsmouth house itself; the houses in Hawk Street and Wish Street have now been torn down, but it is still possible to recapture something of the historical essence of Dickens's native town simply by walking around it. The sense of place is useful, if for no other reason than for the sense of scale which it introduces into any discussion of Dickens's childhood; the fact that Hawk Street, for example, is so close to the docks and the harbour suggests the very presence of the sea in the author's infancy. Similarly, the close-packed streets beyond Oxford Street intimate something of the echoic closeness which would have formed part of Dickens's first experience of London. Those, by the way, who search for Dickens's speech on Shakespeare's birthday, the speech which I quote in association with his own birth, will not find it in the published collection of his speeches. He made the speech, at the Garrick Club, on 22 April, 1854 and a record of that occasion is to be found in "Some Uncollected Speeches by Dickens" by Philip Collins in *The Dickensian* (Volume 73).

Other material for this chapter has been gleaned from the pages of *Dickens: Interviews and Recollections*, edited by Philip Collins. Invaluable information is also to be found in *Dickens and Women* by Michael Slater, and in *Charles Dickens and His Family* by W. H. Bowen.

Chapter 2

There are many topographical and topoliterary studies of Chatham and Rochester, often under the soubriquet of "Dickensland", that mythical place where the characters of his imagination congregate in real inns and real houses. Three studies are essential, however, both for their first-hand testimony and for their descriptions of places which have now, alas, vanished for ever: *Charles Dickens and Rochester* by Robert Langton, *The Dickens Country* by F. G. Kitton and a pamphlet, *References in the Works of Charles Dickens to Rochester, Chatham, and Neighbourhood and to Persons Resident Therein* by Leonard Miller. For the area known as "the Brook", there are at least four sources of primary information. Most importantly Hughes's *A Week's Tramp in Dickensland*, to which reference has already been made; but *The Real Dickens Land* by H. S. Ward, is also useful, as are the relevant passages in Thomas Wright's *The Life of Charles Dickens*. There are also memories of the area in Michael Harrison's *Charles Dickens*. Of course Dickens himself played some part in the mythical aggrandisement of that region, most notably in "One Man in a Dockyard" in *Household Words* of 6 September, 1851 (although this was a "composite" article with R. H. Horne, the most evocative passages are certainly by Dickens) and "At A Dockyard" in the second series of "The Uncommercial Traveller". There is also an unpublished letter, dated 4 February, 1868, in which he expresses his admiration for the navy. On a more mundane level, at least one of his neighbours in Chatham is anatomised in "'The Old Lady' in Sketches by

Boz" by William J. Carlton in *The Dickensian* (Volume 49). Of course there is no substitute for an actual visit to contemporary "Dickensland": Chatham is now almost unrecognisable, although the house in Ordnance Terrace remains and even in its present situation it is possible to see what *kind* of locality the young Dickens knew. The Brook, however, has disappeared beneath arterial roads and a shopping centre. Rochester itself remains, if not in pristine condition, at least in a state resembling the market-town of Dickens's time. The centre has been "preserved", the Cathedral and Castle are still visible, and many of the surrounding buildings are in good repair. The reader of *The Pickwick Papers* or *The Mystery of Edwin Drood* may, however, be struck by the compactness and even smallness of the central area – so different a place from the townscape of Dickens's imagination. Those who cannot revive the past for themselves, however, may find some comfort in *Rochester from Old Photographs* produced by the City of Rochester Society.

Dickens himself alluded on several occasions to the details of his education – to his dame school in a speech to the Printers' Pension Society on 6 April, 1864 (reprinted in his collected *Speeches*, edited by K. J. Fielding), as well as in "Our School", published in *Household Words* on 11 October, 1851. He also passed on many details and descriptions to John Forster, who duly makes use of them in his biography. Other accounts and relevant details are to be found in Langton's *Charles Dickens and Rochester* and in a book by his daughter Mamie, *Charles Dickens*. There is also a brief reference in the diaries of Mrs Watson, as reprinted in *The Dickensian*. But the fullest account of his time at the school of William Giles is to be found in *Charles Dickens and His First Schoolmaster* by Arthur Humphreys. There are also memories of that school in John Hallewell's *Dickens's Rochester*. Further information is to be found in the anonymous *Charles Dickens: The Story of His Life* which was published in the year after his death. There is a letter in the *Daily News* of 9 June, 1870, from William Giles's grandson, and the collector of trivial memorabilia might like to know that Dickens's name was used as a referee in William Giles's advertisement for his own school in the *Liverpool Mercury* of 17 January, 1845. The matter of Dickens's religion is in part covered by some of the above, but the most reliable account of the Dickens family's attitude to the Christian faith is to be found in *Memories of the Past* by the Reverend James Griffin; he was minister to Fanny Dickens in later life, and clearly she confided in him. Dickens's own account of "Boanerges Boiler" is to be found in his essay in the first series of the "Uncommercial Traveller", "City of London Churches".

On the subject of Dickens's early reading, specifically of "picture-books", there is a wealth of testimony from Dickens himself. He refers to them in that speech to the Printers' Pension Society already mentioned, but his longest account is to be found in "First Fruits", an article which he wrote with G. A. Sala for *Household Words* of 15 May, 1852. Two of his Christmas Stories, "The Child's Story" and "A Christmas Tree", are also interesting in this connection. "New Year's Day", in *Household Words* of 1 January, 1859, also contains significant references.

Dickens's juvenile reading in general is of course covered by Dickens's own autobiographical fragment as transferred to *David Copperfield*; Forster adds more detail, but there are numerous individual references scattered throughout Dickens's published and unpublished writings. Particular mention might be made here of "Discovery of a Treasure near Cheapside" in *Household Words* of 13 November, 1852, in which he dilates upon the wonders of *The Arabian Nights*. J. T. Fields, in his *In and Out of Doors with Charles Dickens*, bears witness to his detestation of Sandford and Merton, and his daughter, Kate, describes her father's reading habits as a child in *The Magazine of Art* (1903). There is some additional knowledge to be gained, however, from actually reading the very editions of the books which the young boy himself knew. He used volumes from Cooke's Pocket Library, for example, with small pages and very small print; to feel these pages, and to peer at the tiny words, is to gain some insight into the experience of reading as it must have been for Dickens. Coleridge's account of childhood Fancy is to be found in the *Letters of Samuel Taylor Coleridge*, edited by E. H. Coleridge.

Dickens's general sense of loneliness and weakness as a child is adequately conveyed by at least two accounts from those who heard it from him at first hand; the first by Mamie Dickens in *My Father As I Recall Him* and the second by George Dolby in *Charles Dickens As I Knew Him*. Of course Dickens himself refers to his own childhood condition on many occasions – "I am not a lonely man, though I was once a lonely boy", from "Railway Dreaming" in *Household Words* of 10 May, 1856, adequately sums up the general mood of such reminiscences. Other references are to be found in his account of himself as a "very queer small boy" in "Travelling Abroad", part of the first series of "Uncommercial Traveller" essays, and also in his preface to the first Cheap Edition of *Nicholas Nickleby*. As for his search for literal meanings, we have Mrs Davey's account of the young boy walking down the same path all of his life in *Lippincott's Magazine* of June 1874. There is a glimpse of the adult Dickens in similar mood in *The Life of Charles Dickens, As Revealed in His Writings* by Percy Fitzgerald. He himself refers to his childhood capacity for telling the literal truth in "Smuggled Relations", from *Household Words* of 23 June, 1855, and in another "Uncommercial" essay, entitled "Medicine Men". It is in the latter that he depicts the hysterical scenes at the Flanders funeral. Dickens's childhood attachment to Gad's Hill Place is mentioned on at least two occasions in his correspondence, once in an "Uncommercial" essay, and then again in some detail by Forster. The independent witness by the childhood friend is to be found in "Memories of Charley Wag" by J. H. Stocqueler, reprinted in *The Dickensian* (Volume 62). The ghoulish nurses of his childhood appear in "Nurse's Stories" by the Uncommercial Traveller and in the first chapter of one of his Christmas stories, "The Holly-Tree Inn".

The long and detailed account of his Christmas presents is to be found in "A Christmas Tree", which was part of the Christmas Number of *Household Words* in 1850. It is almost invidious to single out specific references in Dickens's work to the spell of the pantomime on his childhood years; but the most important descriptions are to be found, once more, in "A Christmas Tree" and in his introduction to the *Memoirs of Joseph Grimaldi*. Dickens's best account of his childhood love for the theatre is to be found in an essay already mentioned, "First Fruits", and in a disguised account of Rochester, "Dull-borough Town" in the Uncommercial series. I have employed several contemporary accounts of the theatre in general and the pantomime in particular – among the most important are the descriptions given by Prince Pückler-Muskau in *Prince Pückler Travels to England*, the description by Leigh Hunt in the *Examiner* of 26 January, 1817, and the account by Francis Wey reprinted in William Axton's *Circle of Fire*. There is also a very interesting discussion of Dickens and early pantomime in Harry Stone's *Dickens and The Invisible World*.

Mary Weller's account of the young and convivial little boy is to be found in Robert Langton's *The Childhood and Youth of Charles Dickens*, and there is further testimony in W. R. Hughes's *A Week's Tramp in Dickensland*. There are also first-hand recollections gathered in A. W. Ward's *Dickens*. The best account of the songs which the young Dickens knew, and sang, is to be found in a series of articles written by J. W. T. Ley in Volume 27 of *The Dickensian* – "The Sea Songs of Dickens", "The Songs Dick Swiveller Knew" and "Some Hymns and Songs of Childhood". There is a further account by J. S. P. Grove, "Dickensian Songs" in Volume 16 of the same periodical. A more extended description is to be found in James T. Lightwood's *Charles Dickens and Music*.

The turbulent subject of Dickens's fears and dreams is not one that is susceptible to precise notation; it is so much one of the springs of his art that it is hardly a "subject" at all. There are references in *Dombey and Son*, *A Christmas Carol*, *Great Expectations*, *David Copperfield*, *The Haunted Man and the Ghost's Bargain* . . . the list could be protracted. But perhaps two specific references should be noted; his account of the figure chalked upon the door is to be found in "Lying Awake", published in *Household Words* on 30 October, 1852, while his account of the town idiot is to be found in "Idiots" in *Household Words* of 4 June, 1853. It is possible, however, to be more definite about his accounts of his dreams, or nightmares. The "shapeless things" approach him in "A Christmas Tree" and the "minute filaments" horrify him in "At A Dockyard".

On the more mundane subject of John Dickens's career in these early years, I have made use of "'The Deed' in David Copperfield" by W. J. Carlton in Volume 48 of *The Dickensian* and "John Dickens, Journalist" by the same author in Volume 53. I have also employed "Some Recollections of Dickens" by Marcus Stone in Volume 6 of *The Dickensian*.

Chapter 3

Dickens's own autobiographical remarks are of crucial significance in assessing this period of his life, although they must of course be considered as part of a literary exercise and not necessarily of a factual report; similarly, there are many passages in *David Copperfield* which throw a fitful light over the events of these months. Forster's biography contains material which he acquired from Dickens himself, and there are many revealing passages to be found in these first pages.

Of Camden Town, and Bayham Street in particular, there are a variety of contemporary accounts. Some interesting detail is to be found in the three books by Kitton already mentioned, *Charles Dickens: By Pen and Pencil*, *Charles Dickens: His Life, Writings and Personality* and *The Dickens Country*; there are also accounts of the area in Hughes's *A Week's Tramp in Dickensland*. There is relevant information to be found in *London for Dickens Lovers* by W. Kent, *The Real Dickens Land* by H. S. Ward and in Mamie Dickens's *Charles Dickens*. An "Extra Number" of *The Bookman* (1914) also contains interesting material. One of the fullest accounts of Bayham Street itself (complete with photographs) is to be found in two essays written by Willoughby Matchett for *The Dickensian* (Volume 5), entitled "Dickens in Bayham Street". A resident of that street also gave an account of it in a letter to the *Daily Telegraph* of 7 December, 1871. Dickens's own longest account of the area (as distinct from his allusions to it in his fiction) is to be found in "An Unsettled Neighbourhood", published in *Household Words* of 11 December, 1854. There is also a brief mention of "Debt at home as well as Death" in the second chapter of one of his Christmas stories, "The Haunted House".

Dickens's period in the blacking factory has been thoroughly examined by all of his biographers, and to list the sources for my own account would be to list almost all writers about Dickens in general. The most factually precise account, however, is given in Michael Allen's *Charles Dickens's Childhood* while there is much scholarly detail to be found in W. J. Carlton's "In The Blacking Warehouse", printed in Volume 60 of *The Dickensian*. The incarceration of John Dickens in the Marshalsea, and the subsequent trials of his family, have also been exhaustively detailed in most major accounts of Dickens. But it is worth mentioning here an essay published in Volume 28 of *The Dickensian* by G. F. Young, "The Marshalsea Revisited"; this was written in 1932, and includes photographs of the prison which are now of some documentary importance. For nothing now remains, except for portions of the wall and a small park where once the exercise yard was located. (It was in this park, by the way, that the present writer was inspired to write his first novel, *The Great Fire of London*.) That essay was followed by an interesting letter on the prison, and further information on the whole area is to be found in *With Charles Dickens in the Borough* by William Kent. There is a very good discussion on the nature of indebtedness and bankruptcy in the period in Nigel Cross's *The Common Writer. Life in Nineteenth-Century Grub Street.*

Other information has been gathered from the followed sources: "John Dickens and The Navy Pay Office" by Angus Easson (Volume 70 of *The Dickensian*), "'The Deed" in David Copperfield" by W. J. Carlton (Volume 48 of *The Dickensian*), "The Barber of Dean Street" by W. J. Carlton (Volume 48 of *The Dickensian*), "Fanny Dickens, Pianist and Vocalist" by W. J. Carlton (Volume 53 of *The Dickensian*), "Postscripts to Forster" by W. J. Carlton (Volume 58 of *The Dickensian*). Elizabeth Dickens's will is reprinted in Volume 67 of *The Dickensian*. Dickens himself provides much information about the nature of pawnbrokers' shops in "My Uncle", published in *Household Words* of 6 December, 1851, although the short dialogue from the interior of one of those establishments is taken from his early sketch, "The Pawnbroker's Shop".

Chapter 4

On early nineteenth-century London there are books without end; books about its topography, its culture, its architecture, its street-life, its inhabitants, its sanitation (or the absence of it) and its history. Yet, despite all the vicissitudes of time, so much of the spirit of the old city remains in its contemporary incarnation that the best way to understand the capital which Dickens knew is to re-tread the streets which were so familiar to him – the streets of the Borough, of Somers Town, of the City, of small thoroughfares like Craven Street and Buckingham Street below the Strand. To mingle with the ghosts, and to hear the echoes of the past – this is possible still. Those who prefer less direct methods of approach to that past can read any number of accounts of London in that period, but one source which is often missed are those retrospective accounts written by old men in the 1880s and 1890s. These have proved invaluable in the course of my research, and it is enough here to mention some of the most substantial of them: *Through the Long Day* by Charles Mackay, *My Lifetime* by John Hollingshead, *Glances Back Through Seventy Years* by H. Vizetely and *Retrospect of a Long Life* by Samuel Carter Hall (the last gentleman, by the way, was generally thought to be the model for Pecksniff in *Martin Chuzzlewit*). A near-contemporary account is of course given by Henry Mayhew in *London Labour and the London Poor*, but in fact an equally lively account of London life is to be found in his lesser known *The Criminal Prisons of London*. The description of the Adelphi arches in my text is taken from Michael Harrison's *Charles Dickens*, and the best account of Johnson Street and Somers Town is to be found in John Brett Langstaff's *David Copperfield's Library*. Some extracts from the songs of London are to be found in "Some Songs That Dickens Knew" by J. W. T. Ley in Volume 27 of *The Dickensian*. The quotation on the craving for "excitement and display" comes from *The Age of Equipoise* by W. L. Burn.

Of course there are also many modern accounts of nineteenth-century London; and among the more interesting of those are *The Victorian City: Images and Realities*, edited by H. J. Dyos and Michael Wolff; *The Making of Victorian England* by G. Kitson Clark; *Early Victorian England*, edited by G. M. Young; *Victorian People and Ideas* by R. D. Altick; *London, 1808 – 1870, The Infernal Wen* by Francis Sheppard. There are also books specifically concerned with Dickens's connection with London, among them *The City of Dickens* by Alexander Welsh, *Dickens and the City* by F. S. Schwartzbach, and *The Days of Dickens* by A. L. Hayward. Of much interest, too, is *The Other Victorians* by Steven Marcus. And we must not of course forget Dickens himself; it would be absurd to select passages from his novels concerned with the life of the city, since it is the very breath and spirit of London which animate his fiction. Enough to mention here two less well-known essays which include Dickens's own earliest recollections of London life – "Where We Stopped Growing", published in *Household Words* of 1 January, 1853, and "Gone Astray", published in the same periodical on 13 August, 1853. Some of his finest writing on the capital is also to be found in *Sketches by Boz* – particularly "The Streets – Morning" and "The Streets – Night". His remarks about the barren field behind Montagu House are to be found in a speech he delivered for University College Hospital on 12 April, 1864. Those who wish to place Dickens's autobiographical reminiscences in a wider context may be interested to read *Poor Monkey: The Child in Literature* by Peter Coveney and *When The Grass Was Taller: Autobiography and the Experience of Childhood* by Richard N. Coe.

Chapter 5

There are several accounts by Dickens's schoolfellows, some of them memories of the author himself and some of them recollections of Wellington House Academy. Robert Langton, in *The Childhood and Youth of Charles Dickens*, gathered the largest collection of first-hand testimony, but there are also important reminiscences in Volumes 7 and 22 of *The Dickensian* (particularly the former). There are interesting letters from George Merry in *The Times* of 12 December, 1871, and from Richard Shiers in the *Camden Gazette* of 16 December, 1871. Another contemporary, C. F. Walsh, wrote to John Forster on 30 December, 1871 – the contents of which letter are to be found in the Carlton papers stored in Dickens House. There is also relevant information to be found in *Notes and Queries* of 23 May, 1891. Two interesting essays by Willoughby Matchett, "Dickens at Wellington House Academy", are to be found in Volume 7 of *The Dickensian*; and in Volume 66 of the same periodical W. J. Carlton has written an essay on one of Dickens's young contemporaries, "A Friend of Dickens's Boyhood". Of course the single most important source of information remains Forster's biography, but Dickens himself provides sidelights upon his youthful career in "Our School", published in *Household Words* of 11 October, 1851, and, briefly, in an "Uncommercial" essay, "Among the Short-Timers". He also described the school in less than flattering terms in his speech at the Warehousemen and Clerks Schools Dinner on 5 November, 1857. The letter to his school friend, Owen Peregrine Thomas, is his second extant letter, and is to be found on the first page of the first volume of The Pilgrim Edition of *The Letters of Charles Dickens*; which gives me the opportunity here to pay tribute to so elaborate and extensive a work of scholarship, without which the task of any biographer would be immeasurably more difficult. The footnotes alone supply more information than is to be found in most conventional biographies of Dickens, and the enterprise – which at the date of writing has reached its sixth volume – provides the first reliable text of Dickens's correspondence. No doubt, in the seventh or perhaps the eighth volume, Dickens's letter to Frank Stone, dated 31 May, 1855, will be printed; this is the letter in which Dickens refers to his consultation of Vergil and thus proves that he did, after all, study Latin during his schooldays.

Some details of Dickens's brief legal career are to be found in Kitton's *Charles Dickens: By Pen and Pencil*; most importantly, Kitton reprints the recollections of his colleagues and of his employer. There is an interesting essay by W. J. Carlton, in Volume 48 of *The Dickensian*, "Mr Blackmore Engages An Office Boy", and more information is to be found among the Carlton papers. Additional details are supplied in R. S. MacKenzie's *Life of Charles Dickens*, published in the year of his death. Two books on early nineteenth century drama are relevant at this point, Ernest Reynolds's *Early Victorian Drama, 1830–1870* and Paul Schlicke's *Dickens and Popular Entertainment*.

The fullest accounts of Dickens's acquisition of shorthand are to be found in *Charles Dickens: Shorthand Writer* by W. J. Carlton and in an essay in the *Manchester Quarterly* of July 1892, "Charles Dickens and Shorthand" by W. E. A. Axon. Most of the important information about Doctors' Commons is to be found in the study by Carlton just mentioned, and also, once more, in Kitton. There is also an interesting account of that now-forgotten place (together with an invaluable map of its location) in "Roundabout Doctors' Commons" by W. J. Fisher in Volume 27 of *The Dickensian*. Dickens is listed as an independent shorthand writer in the *Law List* of 1831. Of course Dickens himself describes his experiences there in *David Copperfield*, but one of his Sketches is on that very subject. It is, strangely enough, entitled "Doctors' Commons". The story about Dickens's subscription to the circulating library is taken from Thomas Wright's *The Life of Charles Dickens*;

there is no reason to doubt its authenticity. Wright's accuracy was once unjustly impugned, but recent research has shown him to be, on almost all occasions, more accurate than many apparently "reliable" biographers. The reminiscences of Thomas Mitton's sister are to be found in Edwin Pugh's *The Charles Dickens Originals*; she is included in that volume on the strength of her claim that he used to call her "Little Dorrit" – a most unlikely story. Additional information for this chapter has been found in "The Strange Story of Thomas Mitton" by W. J. Carlton in Volume 56 of *The Dickensian*; in "Fanny Dickens, Pianist and Vocalist" by W. J. Carlton in Volume 53 of *The Dickensian*; and in "John Dickens, Journalist" by W. J. Carlton in Volume 53 of *The Dickensian*. A letter from John Dickens to the Royal College of Music, on the subject of his daughter's fees, is reprinted in Volume 9 of *The Dickensian*.

Chapter 6

Information about Maria Beadnell is not easy to acquire. There is material to be found in Thomas Wright's *The Life of Charles Dickens* and, more substantially, in J. H. Stonehouse's *Green Leaves: New Chapters in the Life of Charles Dickens*. But the best general discussion is to be found in Michael Slater's *Dickens and Women*. More particular references are to be found in "Maria Beadnell's Album" by A. De Suzannet, published in Volume 31 of *The Dickensian*. There is a facsimile of other verses Dickens wrote in *another* album, that of Ellen Beard, in Volume 28 of the same periodical. Also important is "David to Dora: A New Dickens Letter" by Michael Slater in Volume 68 of *The Dickensian*.

There are many accounts of Dickens's early career as a shorthand reporter in parliament. Contemporary descriptions are to be found in *An Old Man's Diary, Forty Years Ago* by John Payne Collier and in Grant's *The Newspaper Press*. A description of the parliamentary press corps in this period is to be found in Samuel Carter Hall's *Retrospect of a Long Life*. Other material on this period in Dickens's life is to be found in a sixpenny pamphlet isused in 1858, *Charles Dickens: A Critical Biography*; it is anonymous but was probably written by J. Friswell. A short account of penny-a-line journalism is to be found by the young William Makepeace Thackeray in an essay, "Solitude in September", published in the *National Standard* of 14 September, 1833. Other important material on this period in Charles Dickens's life is to be found in the following essays: "Dickens: An Early Influence" by Talbot Penner in Volume 64 of *The Dickensian*; "Dickens and the Two Tennysons" by W. J. Carlton in Volume 4 of *The Dickensian*; "Dickens's First Experience as a Parliamentary Reporter" by Gerald R. Grubb in Volume 36 of *The Dickensian*. The best accounts of the general political situation in the same period are to be found in E. L. Woodward's *The Age of Reform*, Asa Briggs's *The Age of*

Improvement, W. L. Burn's *The Age of Equipoise* and *Early Victorian England, 1830–1865*, edited by G. M. Young. The shorthand report of the murder trial, which may or may not have been compiled by Dickens, is to be found in the British Library under the press-mark Dex 306 (1). The extract from the novel on the parlous and excitable state of London is taken from William Maginn's *Whitehall*. Of course Dickens himself, on more than one occasion, referred to his life as a shorthand reporter and to his distaste for parliamentary procedure. One of his early essays, "A Parliamentary Sketch" (originally made up of two, "The House" and "Bellamy's"), is to be found in *Sketches by Boz*. He returns to the subject in "Our Honourable Friend" in *Household Words* of 31 July, 1852, and of course described a similar phenomenon in the appropriate pages of *David Copperfield*. His account of the unhappy state of England during these years is to be found in a speech which he delivered to the Newsvendors Benevolent Institution on 9 May, 1865.

Much of Dickens's theatrical experience and ambition have already been covered in earlier chapters, but there are certain items which are relevant at this point. Information on his production of *Clari*, for example, is to be found in "Home and the song 'Home! Sweet Home!', Their Enchantment of Dickens" in Volume 9 of *The Dickensian*. Material on the rehearsals and playbills for that production is to be found in the Pierpont Morgan Library. The surviving portions of his burlesque tragedy, *O'Thello*, are printed in Volumes 26 and 73 of *The Dickensian*. And there is an interesting account of Dickens's early dramatic writing by Malcolm Morley in "Plays and Sketches by Boz" in Volume 51 of that periodical. The comparison of Dickens's acting with that of Charles Mathews is to be found in *Macmillan's Magazine* of January 1871. And there is a contemporary account of some of the actors whom Dickens admired in G. H. Lewes's *On Actors and the Art of Acting*.

Other miscellaneous material. The information about Dickens's desire to emigrate to the West Indies is to be found in a letter which his cousin, Culliford Barrow, wrote to Thomas Wright on 21 January, 1895; this letter is to be found among the Wright papers at Dickens House. More information on his early life is to be found in "A Companion of the Copperfield Days" by W. J. Carlton in Volume 50 of *The Dickensian* and in "Two Early London Houses of Charles Dickens" by The Editors in Volume 47 of *The Dickensian*. There are two sketches of Dickens in this period – one is reprinted as the frontispiece to Volume 2, no 2, of *The Dickensian*; the other is to be found in Volume 4 of that same periodical. The remarks which Dickens made to an American journalist on the poverty and heartbreak of the London poor are to be found in C. Lester's *The Glory and Shame of England*. The remark about Dickens embodying the "time-spirit" is to be found on page 534 of *Dickens: The Critical Heritage*, edited by Philip Collins.

Chapter 7

Dickens's own first contributions to the *Morning Chronicle* are to be found in two succeeding issues of that newspaper, for 17 September and 18 September, 1834. Much time and ingenuity have been expended in locating other reports and contributions which were the work of Dickens. Some, of course, are now beyond recovery: his shorthand reports of Parliament are necessarily merged with the larger whole. But, through careful perusal of his letters and careful attention to style, it is certainly possible to pick out many of his dramatic criticisms; much work in this connection has been done by the indefatigable and invaluable W. J. Carlton in "Charles Dickens, Dramatic Critic" in Volume 56 of *The Dickensian*. Another source of information is the republication of "A New Contribution to the 'Monthly Magazine' and an Early Dramatic Criticism in 'The Morning Chronicle'" in Volume 30 of *The Dickensian*. It is also worth looking at "Journalistics" by T. Kent Brumleigh in Volume 48 of the same periodical. For more general accounts of these days as a reporter, much interesting material is to be found in a very early biography, *Anecdote Biography of Dickens*, by R. H. Stoddard and published in 1874; it is he, for example, who prints the "Resurrectionist" card which Dickens gave to Vincent Dowling. More valuable information is to be found in Kitton's *Charles Dickens: By Pen and Pencil*, which contains recollections by Dickens's contemporaries on the *Morning Chronicle*, and in the anonymous *Charles Dickens: The Story of His Life* published in the year after his death. Other material is to be found in James Fields's recollections of Dickens's conversation in the *Atlantic Monthly* of August 1870. Other selective but necessary detail is to be found in four further essays by W. J. Carlton who must rank as the single most persistent and thorough scholar of Dickens's early years: "Dickens reports O'Connell: a legend examined", "'Boz' and the Beards", "An Echo of the Copperfield Days" and "The Story Without a Beginning" (respectively in Volumes 65, 58, 45 and 47 of *The Dickensian*). John Stuart Mill's account of Black and the *Morning Chronicle* is taken from his *Autobiography*. Of course there is also a great deal of information volunteered by Dickens himself, beyond the ambit of his fiction; most notably in four separate speeches, to the Commercial Travellers Schools on 30 December, 1854, to the Newspaper Press Fund on 20 May, 1865, at the Farewell Banquet in his honour in New York on 18 April, 1868 and, briefly, in a speech for the Newsvendors Benevolent Institution on 21 November, 1849. All these are to be found on the relevant pages of *The Speeches of Charles Dickens*, edited by K. J. Fielding.

Information about the *Monthly Magazine*, which had the distinction of printing Dickens's first fiction, is to be found in an essay which Percy Fitzgerald wrote for the third volume of *The Dickensian*. Dickens's account of delivering his story to the *Monthly Magazine*, and then seeing it in all the glory of print, is taken from his preface to the first Cheap Edition of *The Pickwick Papers*. "Portraits in 'A Parliamentary Sketch'" is an essay by Carlton in Volume 52 of *The Dickensian*, which emphasises how contemporary and topical Dickens's allusions frequently were. And, for the earliest reviews which Dickens provoked, it is worth looking at an essay by Walter Dexter, "Contemporary Opinion of Dickens's Earliest Work" in Volume 31 of *The Dickensian*. The excited letter which he wrote to Henry Kolle, on first seeing his name in print, is reproduced in Volume 30 of that periodical; interesting to note his large rounded hand, which was soon to be displaced by the more compressed and familiar handwriting. There are two general studies of Dickens's Sketches which are both scholarly and readable: Virgil Grillo's *Charles Dickens's "Sketches by Boz"* and Duane De Vries's *Dickens's Apprentice Years: The Making of a Novelist*.

On the subject of Dickens's early lodgings, there are at least three essays which provide not only information but also (and perhaps equally importantly) photographs. There is an account of "Where Pickwick Was Conceived: Furnivals Inn" by Percy Fitzgerald in Volume 3 of *The Dickensian* and, in Volume 31 of that same periodical, there is to be found "Dickens's Tenancy of Furnivals Inn: Some New Documents". Dickens himself adverts to this period of his life in his essay as the "Uncommercial Traveller", entitled "Chambers"; but of course such melancholy piles reappear through his fiction. The house in Selwood Place is discussed in an "An Early Home of Dickens in Kensington" by Carlton in Volume 61 of *The Dickensian*. Furnivals Inn has of course long since been demolished, but the house in Selwood Place remains. The entire Hogarth family has been discussed on many occasions, but the single most important introduction to the subject remains Arthur A. Adrian's *Georgina Hogarth and the Dickens Circle*. Other items on the same subject are "George Hogarth: A Link with Scott and Dickens" by W. J. Carlton in Volume 61 of *The Dickensian*. Catherine's earliest letter about Dickens is to be found in "New Letters of Mary Hogarth and Her Sister" by L. C. Staples in Volume 63 of *The Dickensian*. The story of the young writer executing a sailor's hornpipe in the Hogarths' house is repeated by Mamie Dickens in her *Charles Dickens*. The letter from John Dickens to Thomas Beard is reprinted in Michael Harrison's *Charles Dickens*.

Chapter 8

Much of the material on Dickens's *Sketches by Boz* has been considered in the notes for the previous chapter, but it is appropriate to mention in this place all those accounts of George Cruikshank and Charles Dickens. In particular, *Charles Dickens and George Cruikshank* by J. Hillis Miller and D. Borowitz. There is also a fascinating discussion of the two men in Jane R. Cohen's

Charles Dickens and His Original Illustrators (from which the remarks about Buss are taken), as well as in J. R. Harvey's *Victorian Novelists and Their Illustrators*. For Dickens's working methods and procedures, however, the single most important study remains *Dickens At Work* by John Butt and Kathleen Tillotson. Of more technical interest is "The Reception of Dickens's First Book" in Volume 32 of *The Dickensian*. The negotiations over *The Pickwick Papers*, and the monthly appearance of that novel, have of course been exhaustively explored, and there is space here only to mention the more significant and interesting contributions by biographers and critics alike.

As so often happens in Dickensian matters, the best accounts are also some of the first – not simply that of Forster, whose presence as guide and interpreter must be taken for granted in the pages of this book, but also that of his other early biographers. There are interesting sections on Pickwick, for example, in *Charles Dickens: The Story of His Life*, published anonymously in 1870, and in R. Shelton MacKenzie's *Life of Charles Dickens* published in the following year. Perhaps the most authoritative account, however, comes from W. Dexter and J. W. T. Ley in their *Origin of Pickwick*, while Arthur Waugh provides valuable information in his *Charles Dickens and His Illustrators*. There is also interesting material in R. H. Stoddard's *Anecdote Biography of Charles Dickens*. A modern scholarly account must also be given pride of place here: Robert L. Patten's *Charles Dickens and His Publishers* is an invaluable study of the whole of Dickens's career. My account of the political and social effect of *The Pickwick Papers* is indebted to that most interesting study, Gerald Newman's *The Rise of English Nationalism: A Cultural History, 1740–1830*, truly indispensable reading for anyone who wishes to understand this period of English history.

The early negotiations over *The Pickwick Papers* are thoroughly aired in all the preceding volumes, but more specific accounts are to be found in "The Birth of 'Pickwick'" by Arthur Waugh in Volume 32 of *The Dickensian*, and in "A Note on the Payment for 'Pickwick'" in Volume 40 of the same periodical. Kitton's *Dickens and His Illustrators* also contains much first-hand testimony. The unhappy subject of Robert Seymour is well covered in "Where Robert Seymour Died" by Leslie Staples in Volume 13 of *The Dickensian*, and by Kitton in *Dickens and His Illustrators*. There is also a letter which Dickens himself wrote on the subject of Seymour to *The Athenaeum* on 28 March, 1866; a letter from Weld Taylor to Kitton on the same subject simply dated "April 14", is to be found among the Kitton papers stored at Dickens House. An important and long letter from Robert Buss on his role in the genesis of *The Pickwick Papers*, dated 11 December, 1871, is reprinted in Volume 32 of *The Dickensian*. There is material on both Seymour and Buss in Kitton's study of the illustrators and in the volume on *Pickwick* jointly written by Dexter and Ley. There is of course much more material on Hablot Knight Browne himself, and there are three books in particular which ought to be mentioned in this place: *Phiz and Dickens* by Edgar Browne, *Dickens and Phiz* by Michael Steig, and *The Life and Labours of Hablot Knight Browne* by David Croal Thompson. Of course all the books about Dickens's illustrators, already mentioned, contain much valuable material on his life and career. But in this period two other short analyses ought to be mentioned: Robert Patten's study in Volume 66 of *The Dickensian* and an essay, "Portraits of Pott: Lord Brougham and The Pickwick Papers".

For more specific topics in connection with *The Pickwick Papers*, the following essays are invaluable. "How Dickens Wrote His Descriptions of Bath for 'The Pickwick Papers'" by T. J. Bradley in Volume 23 of *The Dickensian*; "Speculations on the source of Bardell vs Pickwick" by Percy T. Carden in Volume 32 of *The Dickensian*; "Sam Weller's Double Million Gas Microscope" by C. H. Green in Volume 12 of *The Dickensian*; "The *Pickwick* Advertisement and Other Addresses to the Public" in Volume 32 of *The Dickensian*; "Dickens and the Naming of Sam Weller" by Harry Stone in Volume 56 of *The Dickensian*. There was also an interesting correspondence on the early anticipations of "Wellerisms" in Volumes 2 and 4 of the same periodical.

For the first response to *The Pickwick Papers* it is necessary to read "Some Early Reviews of Pickwick" (in two parts) in Volume 32 of *The Dickensian*. I have also made use of reviews in *The Athenaeum* of 3 December, 1836, the *Quarterly Review* of October 1837, *The National Magazine and Monthly Critic* of December 1837. A more general survey of the effect of *The Pickwick Papers* is to be found in *The Victorians and Their Books* by Amy Cruse. Further material is to be found in R. J. Cruikshank's *Charles Dickens and Early Victorian England* and of course the fullest survey of contemporary opinion is gathered in *Charles Dickens: The Critical Heritage*, edited by Philip Collins.

The reaction to Dickens's pamphlet, *Sunday Under Three Heads*, is reviewed in "Early Propaganda" in Volume 32 of *The Dickensian*. On the subject of Dickens's plays, one of the most substantial guides remains F. W. Fawcett's *Dickens the Dramatist* but there are also specific studies of *The Village Coquettes* and *The Strange Gentleman*. These are "Charles Dickens and the St James's Theatre" by S. J. Adair Fitz-Gerald in Volume 16 of *The Dickensian*; "Dickens and His 'Ugly Duckling'" by T. W. Hill in Volume 46 of *The Dickensian*; and, finally, "Dickens and His Correspondence with John Hullah. Some New Light on His Early Dramatic Works" in Volumes 29 and 30 of *The Dickensian*. The manuscripts for these two early plays are to be found in the Manuscript Department of the British Library, with the press-marks Add Ms 42938 (346–447) for *The Village Coquettes* and Add Ms 42939 (571–644) for *The Strange Gentleman*.

It is time to move away now from purely literary matters. The chambers in Furnivals Inn have already been discussed but it is worth mentioning here the description of the second set of rooms there in John Greaves's *Dickens at*

Doughty Street. First-hand accounts of those who attended the marriage of Charles Dickens and Catherine Hogarth are to be found in Kitton's *Charles Dickens: By Pen and Pencil* and the Special Marriage Licence for that ceremony is reproduced in Volume 43 of *The Dickensian*. There are accounts of the honeymoon in Langton's *The Childhood and Youth of Charles Dickens*, in Kitton's *The Dickens Country* and in Shelton MacKenzie's *Life*. The letter from Mary Hogarth about the domestic arrangements of the young couple is to be found in "A letter from Mary Hogarth" by Kathleen Tillotson in the *Times Literary Supplement* of 23 December, 1960. For Dickens's appearance in this period I have gone both to the exhaustive accounts in Kitton's *Charles Dickens: By Pen and Pencil* and to an interesting short sketch in the *Pictorial Times* of 20 April, 1844. His speech about the dignity of literature was made at St George's Hall, in Liverpool, on 10 April, 1869.

Chapter 9

Details of Dickens's arguments with Richard Bentley will be furnished in a later chapter; at this earlier, and relatively peaceful, point it is enough to mention Percy Fitzgerald's essay in Volume 3 of *The Dickensian*. There is a letter from Dickens to W. B. Archer reprinted in Volume 75 of *The Dickensian* and Dickens's announcement about his intentions in "The Extraordinary Gazette" is reprinted and discussed in Volume 26 of that periodical. Drafts of the agreements with Richard Bentley are to be found in the Pierpont Morgan Library, and certain unflattering remarks by Bentley and his son are to be found in the Berg Collection of New York Public Library.

The early and formative stages of *Oliver Twist* are ably discussed by Kathleen Tillotson in her introduction to the Clarendon Edition of that novel, and there is also a very interesting analysis by Burton M. Wheeler, "The Text and Plan of Oliver Twist", in Volume 12 of the *Dickens Studies Annual*. The controversy over Cruikshank's claims to have initiated the idea of Oliver are fully detailed in the books concerning Dickens's illustrators, which have already been mentioned; perhaps the most lively discussion, however, is to be found in Stoddard's *Anecdote Biography of Dickens*. His use of Mr Laing, the magistrate, is discussed in "The Hatton Garden Philanthropist" in Volume 37 of *The Dickensian*. The best discussion of the relation of *Oliver Twist* to the New Poor Laws is in Dennis Walder's *Dickens and Religion*.

The stage history of *Is She His Wife?* . . . is discussed in two articles, "A Stage Aside. Dickens's Early Dramatic Productions" in Volume 33 of *The Dickensian*, and "Pickwick Makes His Stage Debut" by Malcolm Morley in Volume 42 of the same journal.

The subject of Dickens's friends and friendship has been discussed by both scholars and biographers, but the best general survey remains J. W. T. Ley's *The Dickens Circle: A Narrative of the Novelist's Friendships*. Of course many of those friends have been considered worthy of biographical treatment in their own right, and the best study of Ainsworth is S. M. Ellis's *William Harrison Ainsworth and His Friends*. Ley has written an article on the specific relationship between the two men, "Dickens and Ainsworth" in Volume 9 of *The Dickensian* (in Volume 28 of that periodical there is an article on Ainsworth's rebarbative relative, Mrs Touchet). The best study of Ainsworth's fiction, as well as its relation to Dickens's own, is to be found in K. Hollingsworth's *The Newgate Novel, 1830–1847*.

John Forster has claimed the attention of almost anyone who has written about Dickens's life, although still the best introduction to that subject must remain Forster himself in his *Life*. There are two separate studies of him, however; *John Forster: A Literary Life* by J. A. Davies and *John Forster and His Friendships* by Richard Renton. Percy Fitzgerald devotes a chapter to him in his *Memories of Charles Dickens* (and retells many of the funniest stories about him in the course of it), but more scholarly disquisitions on the Forsterian phenomenon are to be found in "Forster and Dickens: The making of Podsnap" by James A. Davies in Volume 70 of *The Dickensian*, and "Forster: Critic of Fiction" by K. J. Fielding in the same volume. There is also an interesting discussion by Jean Ferguson Carr in Volume 52 of *English Literary History*. Less than fully flattering asides on Forster by Dickens's own children are to be found in an essay by Kate Perugini in Volume 3 of the *Pall Mall Gazette*, and in the preface written for *Little Dorrit* by Charles Dickens junior. Various less than kind comments are also to be found scattered through Dickens's unpublished correspondence – correspondence, in other words, which postdates the most recent volume of the Pilgrim Edition The best life of Maclise is by James Dafforne and is entitled, simply, *Daniel Maclise R.A.* The fullest account of Dickens's house in Doughty Street is to be found in John Greaves's *Dickens at Doughty Street* while the present curator of Dickens House, David Parker, has written a fascinating article on some of the furnishings of that establishment in "The Reconstruction of Dickens's Drawing Room" in Volume 78 of *The Dickensian*. Reminiscences of domestic life in that house, before the death of Mary Hogarth, are to be found in Kitton's *Charles Dickens: By Pen and Pencil*. The Pilgrim Edition of Dickens's correspondence also contains several appendices which are of crucial importance in evaluating this period in his life – his diaries for 1838 and 1839 have been reprinted, and there are further appendices on his cheque book counterfoils and on his agreements with multifarious publishers. Further light on Dickens's domestic arrangements is to be found in "New Letters of Mary Hogarth and Her Sister Catherine" in Volume 63 of *The Dickensian* and in "The Death of Mary Hogarth" by W. J. Carlton in the same volume. John Dickens's begging letter to Chapman and Hall is reproduced both by Percy

Fitzgerald and by Kitton. An account of Dickens's election to the Garrick Club is to be found in Volume 33 of *The Dickensian* and a drawing of the author, c. 1837, is placed as a frontispiece to Volume 4, No 2, of that journal.

Chapter 10

The death of Mary Hogarth, and Dickens's intense reaction to it, are of course subjects of perennial interest to all chroniclers of his life. A scholarly approach is to be found in "The Death of Mary Hogarth: Before and After" by W. J. Carlton in Volume 63 of *The Dickensian*. In the same volume is reprinted Catherine's letter to her cousin on the subject of Mary's death. In Volume 37 of *The Dickensian* there is to be found an essay on "Collins's Farm, Hampstead" where Dickens rested after the shock of the death. Henry Burnett's recollections of New Year's Eve are to be found in Kitton, and Macready's account of dinner there is to be found in his *Diaries* under the date of 26 June, 1837.

The effect of Mary's death upon the shape and structure of *Oliver Twist* is not a matter to be easily resolved; but an interesting discussion of the context of those changes is to be found in F. S. Schwarzback's *Dickens and the City* and in an essay by Neil Forsyth, "Dickens and Coincidence", in *Modern Philology* of November 1981. For Dickens's account of Fagin not letting him rest, see James Fields's *Yesterdays With Authors*. On the history of the negotiations with Richard Bentley, the appropriate letters in Volume 1 of the Pilgrim Edition are the best and obvious source; many of Richard Bentley's own papers are to be found in the Berg collection of the New York Public Library but, for those readers unable or unwilling to make the journey, the footnotes of the Pilgrim Edition offer a perfectly satisfactory history of the affair.

The delights and sights of early nineteenth-century Broadstairs are discussed by B. W. Matz in "Dickens's Association With Broadstairs" (Volume 4 of *The Dickensian*), although the best way of understanding Dickens's pleasure in the resort is to visit it; it still retains many of the features which rendered it so attractive to him, and many memorials to his visits to the town are also to be found there. Other miscellaneous items to be mentioned at this point: the remarks about not liking *The Pickwick Papers* in later life are to be found in Richard Watson's diary entry of 31 December, 1846, reprinted in Volume 47 of *The Dickensian*, and also in Percy Fitzgerald's *The Life of Charles Dickens As Revealed in His Writings*. An account of Fanny's marriage to Henry Burnett is given in the Reverend James Griffin's *Memories of the Past*. The fact that Dickens and Ainsworth were planning to write a book together on the subject of London is revealed in Ainsworth's correspondence, printed both in Ellis's biography and in *The Dickens Circle* by J. W. T. Ley. The fight in the slums, in which Dickens may have been a participant, is disclosed in James R.

Anderson's *An Actor's Life*. The whispers about Dickens being acquainted with "low life" are repeated in J. H. Friswell's *Modern Men of Letters* published in the year of his death, and a brief account of the Pickwick dinner is given by Macready in his *Diaries*, in the entry for 18 November, 1837. For the details of Dickens's bank account, the best source is "Charles Dickens: A Customer of Coutts and Co." by M. Veronica Stokes in Volume 68 of *The Dickensian*. An account of "Dickens In The Witness Box" is given in Volume 70 of that journal and, for Carlton's general discussion of Dickens's diaries, "The Dickens Diaries", see Volume 55.

The subject of Dickens's interest in mesmerism or "animal magnetism" is best handled by Fred Kaplan in his *Dickens and Mesmerism: The Hidden Springs of Fiction*. His visits to mesmeric session are discussed in Ellis's *W.H. Ainsworth and His Friends*, and also in Weld Taylor's reminiscences as recorded by Kitton.

The visit to Yorkshire with Hablot Browne in order to see the state of the schools is recorded in T. P. Cooper's *With Dickens In Yorkshire* and in Cumberland Clark's *Charles Dickens and the Yorkshire Schools*. The subject is also fully discussed in John Manning's *Dickens On Education*. More specific information is also to be found in the wonderfully entitled "Burials of Boys in the Delightful Village of Dotheboys" by T. P. Cooper in Volume 35 of *The Dickensian* and in "Treasures at the Dickens House: Education at Shaw's Academy, Bowes" by S. J. Rust in the same volume. An earlier account, including photographs, is to be found in Volume 7 of that same periodical. A short biographical sketch of Dickens appeared in the *Durham Advertiser* of 26 January, 1838, and Dickens's rebuttal appeared in the issue of 10 February of the same year.

For the parallels of characters in *Nicholas Nickleby* with those in "real life", see Kitton's *Charles Dickens: By Pen and Pencil* – at least for Henry Burnett's somewhat coy insinuation that he was one of the models for Nicholas. See also "The Original of the Infant Phenomenon. An Interview with Otis Skinner" in Volume 11 of *The Dickensian* and "The Cheeryble Brothers" by F. R. Dean in Volume 26 of that journal. For the fact that Dickens saw the book as a "diary" of its composition, see Macready's entry in his *Diaries* for 5 October, 1839. For people in turn being influenced by Dickens's fiction, see an interesting entry in the Manuscript Collection of the British Library, with the press-mark Egerton MS 2154. Henry James's remark about Craven Street is mentioned in G. H. Ford's very useful *Dickens and His Readers*; Craven Street still exists in very much the same state although, at the time of writing (December 1989), it looks as if it is going to be pulled down at any moment.

It would be absurd to list the occasions of Dickens's humour; readers of his novels will know as much about it as the present writer. Examples are also to be found dotted through most of the books written about him, from

Fitzgerald to Kitton to Ley to Hughes to a solitary reference in the March 1961 issue of *Notes and Queries*.

Chapter 11

The history of the dramatisations of *Oliver Twist* is most fully explored, as one might expect, in "The Dramas of *Oliver Twist*" by Malcolm Morley in Volume 43 of *The Dickensian*. The same author has written "Nicholas Nickleby on The Boards" in the same volume. Further information is to be acquired in "Charles Dickens and the St James's Theatre" by S. J. Adair Fitz-Gerald in Volume 16 of the same periodical. A report (false) that Macready offered a great deal of money to secure Dickens's services was aired in the *Theatrical Observer* of 15 November, 1837. For Macready's own comments on Dickens during this period, see his *Diaries* under the entries for 27 April, 1838 (when Dickens "pained" him) and for 5 December, 1838 and 12 December, 1838.

Those wishing to see a portion of the manuscript of *Nicholas Nickleby* should make for the Manuscript Room of the British Library and ask for it under the press-mark of Add Ms 57493. In fact this portion of the manuscript, in Dickens's large clear hand, was once in the possession of Mr Hicks, the foreman of the printers at Bradbury and Evans. It is worthy of notice, too, that it is bound up with two letters – one is from a certain George Brookes, a pupil at Shaw's school at Bowes, which contains the sentiment "I feel very happy and comfortable and have been ever since I came . . ." – a letter no doubt dictated by Shaw himself, or written under his gaze. The letter is dated 14 November, 1825. The second letter is from Shaw himself, dated 2 February, 1826, in which Shaw writes to announce the fact that the same boy, Brookes, had become very seriously ill – ". . . I am afraid my next Letter will have to state his final departure . . ." Someone has written in pencil above this, "the boy George Brookes died 10.55 the same night". This may or may not be in Dickens's handwriting; it is difficult to be sure. How all this material came into the hands of the foreman of the printers is impossible to guess. Was it a gift from Dickens? Or had he been asked to "set" this material (perhaps for use in a pamphlet) and had inadvertently or deliberately kept it? Such discoveries are one of the incidental pleasures of research.

The story about Dickens falling ill and travelling across the Channel to write in peace is to be found in *James T. Fields: Biographical Notes and Personal Sketches*. The details of Dickens's wishing to join the Middle Temple are explored in Volume 17 of *The Dickensian*. For some sense of the summer retreat at Twickenham, it might be worth examining "The Balloon Club: Some Unpublished Documents" in Volume 37 of *The Dickensian*. Even the lightest and most inconsiderable of Dickens's pastimes have become the object of serious scholarship! Dickens's article on the coronation festivities is to be found in *The Examiner* of 1 July, 1838, and the extract from "Scott and His Publishers" is taken from *The Examiner* of 2 September, 1838.

Angela Burdett-Coutts's comments on Dickens are to be found in *Angela Burdett-Coutts and the Victorians* by Clara Burdett Patterson, and it is also well worth examining *Lady Unknown* by Edna Healey. The remarks by Dickens's offended neighbour in Doughty Street are reprinted in Volume 1 of *The Dickensian*.

There is much material and information on the tour to Midlands and the visits to Manchester. There is "Dickens and Manchester" by F. R. Dean in Volume 34 of *The Dickensian* and, in Volume 9 of the same periodical, J. W. T. Ley has written "Dickens and Ainsworth: Boz's First Friend". Material is also to be gathered from *Dickensian Inns and Taverns* by B. L. Matz and an account of Dickens's evening with the Grants (or Cheerybles) is given in William Glover's *Reminiscences of Half-a-Century*. There is more detail, too, in Ellis's biography of Ainsworth.

The quarrel between Bentley and Ainsworth has been detailed in the notes to previous chapters, but it is worth mentioning at this point the strangely entitled *Dickens v Barabbas* by "C. J. S. and F. J. H. D" which deals in more detail with Dickens's relationship both with Bentley and Ainsworth at the time he ceased to edit the *Miscellany*. The story about his continuing grief over Mary Hogarth is given in a letter from a certain Mary Howitt, reprinted in Volume 17 of *The Dickensian*. The best discussion and description of the Dickenses' cottage near Alphington is given by John Greaves in *Dickens at Doughty Street*. The report of Dickens's demeanour at the Farewell Dinner for Macready is given in *Recollections of Writers* by C. and M. Cowden Clarke. Mrs Cattermole's reminiscences of Dickens are to be found in Kitton's *Charles Dickens: By Pen and Pencil*. Macready's account of the Nickleby dinner is in his *Diaries* under the entry for 5 October, 1839.

There are many separate accounts of Devonshire Terrace. Mamie Dickens adverts to it in her *Charles Dickens* and Henry Burnett refers to life there in Kitton's book just mentioned. There is also an interesting article by Michael Allen and David Parker in Volume 75 of *The Dickensian*. Gissing's account comes from an essay he wrote in *Homes and Haunts of Famous Authors*. The interview Dickens granted to a American journalist is to be found in Lester's *The Glory and Shame of England*.

Dickens's notation in the antiquarian's visitors' book is detailed in Volume 20 of *The Dickensian*. Mrs Lynn Linton's comments on his trip to Bath are to be found in Kitton. A letter from the working man, John Overs, to Charles Dickens (in response to his sending him *Chartism*) is located in the Free Library of Philadelphia.

The relationship between Carlyle and Dickens has been examined on many separate occasions and in many separate articles. The best account of that relationship is to be found in Oddie's *Dickens and Carlyle: The Question of Influence* and in Macrae's *Carlyle and Dickens*, but a good general discussion of the context of that friendship is also to be found in Patrick Brantlinger's *The Spirit of Reform*. Georgina Hogarth's letter to Carlyle after Dickens's death is to be found in the Pierpont Morgan Library in New York, while his reply is located in the Berg Collection in the Public Library of that same city. Thus do related items sometimes find a related home.

The influence of the theatre on Dickens's fiction is a large subject, and one which has of course been thoroughly treated. Perhaps the best exposition, however, is Robert Garis's *The Dickens Theatre: A Reassessment of His Novels* but there are other books of considerable interest: Paul Schlicke's *Dickens and Popular Entertainment*, William Axton's *Circle of Fire* and G. J. Worth's *Dickensian Melodrama*.

Chapter 12

For the effect of *The Old Curiosity Shop* upon Dickens himself, see the memoirs of George Dolby, *Charles Dickens As I Knew Him*; the anecdote about Little Nell following him everywhere is repeated by James Fields in *Yesterdays With Authors*. For Dickens's more material hopes for the periodical, see Macready's entry in his *Diaries* for 9 April, 1840. For the effect of Little Nell upon others, the best general survey is by Amy Cruse in her *The Victorians and Their Books*. More reaction is also to be found of course in the two best sources, *Dickens: The Critical Heritage*, edited by Philip Collins and in G. H. Ford's *Dickens and His Readers*. It is also worth looking over *A Bibliography of Dickensian Criticism, 1836–1975*, edited by R. C. Churchill.

The letter which Dickens wrote about the feasibility of a Norfolk Island penal colony study is described in the *Times Literary Supplement* of 10 December, 1981 – although my attention was drawn to it by a reference in Robert Hughes's *The Fatal Shore*. Dickens's account of the Courvoisier hanging was printed in the *Daily News* of 28 February, 1846, while Henry Burnett's own description of the occasion is reprinted in Kitton's *Charles Dickens: By Pen and Pencil*.

Eleanor Christian's memories of Charles Dickens and family at Broadstairs are to be found in two separate places – the first account, published in 1871, is entitled "Reminiscences of Charles Dickens, From a Young Lady's Diary" and was printed in Volume 10 of *The Englishwoman's Domestic Magazine*. The second was published seventeen years later, as "Recollections of Charles Dickens, His Family and Friends" in Volume 82 of *Temple Bar*. There are differences between the two accounts, although not of an important kind.

The reports of Dickens's madness can be gathered from several quarters. Landseer's joke, for example, is repeated by Kitton and the story of the anonymous meeting in an inn at twilight is given in papers held in the Manuscript Room of the British Library, at press-mark Egerton 2164 (pp 16–17). For a full account of the birds which he so much admired, see "Dickens's Ravens" by O. Sack in Volume 13 of *The Dickensian*. One of those birds, now stuffed and mounted in a glass case, was last seen by the present writer in the basement of Dickens House. It may be there still; it cannot have flown away.

There are of course numerous accounts of *Barnaby Rudge* in critical, biographical and scholarly studies. One of the best essays on the subject of that novel's relation to the politics of the time is by T. J. Rice, "The Politics of 'Barnaby Rudge'" and is to be found in *The Changing World of Charles Dickens* edited by Robert Giddings. A good general survey of the political climate is also to be found in J. W. Dodds's *The Age of Paradox: A Biography of England, 1841–1851*. Dickens's success at the Edinburgh dinner is variously reported in Kitton and Mackenzie. Professor Wilson's speech on that occasion is reprinted in Volume 12 of *The Dickensian*, and an account of an eye-witness is to be found in Volume 2 of *A Review of English Literature*. Of course, as is so often the case, all the information required by the general reader is to be found in the footnotes which add so much to the pleasure of reading the Pilgrim Edition of Dickens's correspondence. Sometimes, however, odd letters turn up which have escaped the enquiries of even the most alert editors: one such is the letter to Maclise about the prostitutes of Margate, an account of which is to be found in Sotheby's sale catalogue of English Literature and History for 23 and 24 July, 1987.

Dickens's American preparations are partly revealed in the interview he gave to an American journalist, reprinted in John D. Sherwood's *Hours at Home*. The *Quarterly Review* of September 1841 describes the contemporary fashion for books of American travel, and Catherine's reluctance to make the journey is chronicled in Macready's *Diaries* under the entry for 23 September, 1841. Dickens's insurance policies are detailed (and reproduced) in "Links With the Past: Dickens's Insurance Policy" in Volume 14 of *The Dickensian*.

Chapter 13

The best, if not the most objective, accounts of Dickens's journey through America and Canada are to be found in his *American Notes for General Circulation*, and in the voluminous letters home reprinted in Volume Three of the Pilgrim Edition of his correspondence. The relevant pages of Dickens's *Speeches* also furnish interesting background information. There are of course books on the same subject, among them W. G. Wilkins's *Charles Dickens in*

America, Edward Payne's *Dickens's Days in Boston* and Michael Slater's *Dickens on America and the Americans*.

A description of him and his wife as Atlantic travellers is given in "Reminiscences of Charles Dickens. By a Fellow Passenger" in Volume 4 of *Dickens Studies*; the fellow traveller was in fact Pierre Morand, whose drawing of Dickens on deck is to be found among the Tyrell Collection preserved at Dickens House. Many accounts of him on America soil of course survive, and the handiest general compendium is to be found in *Charles Dickens: Interviews and Recollections*, edited by Philip Collins. There is also much material in Mackenzie, Kitton and Fields. For more specific and topical accounts, a wealth of information exists in the American newspapers of 1842 – among them the *Philadelphia Gazette* of March 13; the *Public Ledger* of March 9, the *Worcester Aegis* of February 9, the *Boston Post* of February 12 . . . the list could be multiplied almost indefinitely. More substantial reading, and more personal accounts, are to be found in *J. L. Motley and His Friends* edited by S. and H. St John Mildmay, *Strawberry Fair* by William Hewe, and *Personal Traits of British Authors* edited by E. T. Mason.

One of the longest and most interesting of these accounts is by Dickens's American secretary, George Putnam, in "Four Months With Charles Dickens During His First Visit to America" in Volume 26 of the *Atlantic Monthly*. It is also worth looking at "The Boz Ball" by N. Parker Willis in Volume 12 of *The Dickensian*. Volumes 60 and 74 of that periodical contain further American recollections. For a general and contemporaneous account of the American press, see an essay by P. L. Simmonds in the *Journal of the London Statistical Society* of July 1841. The letter from John Dickens to Coutts is reprinted in *The Listener* of 19 July, 1951.

Canada is similarly well covered, and such matters as arrival and departure are to be found in the columns of the *Toronto Examiner* of 11 May, 1842, the *British Colonist* of 11 May, the *Toronto Patriot* of 6 May, the *Toronto Morning Star and Toronto Transept* of 7 May, the *Quebec Gazette* of 28 May; no doubt there are many more, but these are the only ones the writer has inspected. For a modern Canadian perspective, see Tony Kilgallin's "Charles Dickens Found Toronto's Rabid Toryism Wild and Appalling . . ." in *Toronto Life* of January 1967. On the subject of the Montreal amateur theatricals, see "For One Night Only. Dickens's Appearance as an Amateur Actor" by Walter Dexter in Volume 35 of the *The Dickensian*. "The Amateur Theatricals in Montreal" in Volume 38 of *The Dickensian* and "The Montreal Theatre and Another Mystery" by Andrew Patterson in the same volume.

Chapter 14

Dickens's return to England is described in Macready's *Diaries* under the entry for 29 June, 1842, and also by his daughter, Mamie, in *Charles Dickens*.

Thomas Hood's account of the Greenwich dinner is to be found in Ley. Dickens's parodic encomium on Broadstairs is in the Pierpont Morgan Library: it is dated 7 July, 1842. For life in that resort during the succeeding year, see Catherine Dickens's letter to Mrs Felton, dated 2 September, 1843, at Dickens House.

Dickens's letter on the absence of copyright provision in the United States was published in *The Examiner* of 16 July, 1842. Mary Shelley's account of Dickens's rage against that country is to be found in Volume 1 of *The Trollopian*. For some press comment about *American Notes* itself, see *Blackwood's Magazine* of December 1842, the *Edinburgh Review* of January 1843 and the *North American Review* of January 1843. For Dickens's own later account of the controversy, see his own article in *All The Year Round* of 1 March, 1862. His article of support for Lord Ashley's Bill is to be found in the *Morning Chronicle* of 20 October, 1842. One account of Dickens's excursion to Cornwall is in Walter Dexter's *The England of Dickens*. A drawing of "Cheese Wing, Cornwall" and signed "CD" is to be found in the Gimbell Collection of the Beinecke Rare Book and Manuscript Library at Yale University. The episode at Horne's funeral is most fully and graphically evoked in W. R. Nicholl's *Dickens's Own Story*.

Much material on London during the period has already been described but, on the specific questions of sanitation and disease, the most useful and detailed account is H. Jephson's *The Sanitary Evolution of London*. The best modern account is by Andrew Sanders in his *Charles Dickens, Resurrectionist*. Also important in this connection is F. Engels's *The Condition of the Working Class in England in 1844* while two good historical surveys are J. W. Dodds's *The Age of Paradox* and J. L. and Barbara Hammond's *The Age of the Chartists, 1832–1854*. There is an interesting sidelight on Dickens's attachment to Unitarianism in a letter from Frank S. Johnson, "Dickens and the Tagarts" published in Volume 21 of *The Dickensian*. The best general account is to be found in Dennis Walder's *Dickens and Religion*. For an account of the Sanatorium, one of the first extensions of his "ethical culture", see certain contemporary documents in Volume 76 of *The Dickensian*.

On Frith's portrait of Dolly Varden, see his *My Autobiography and Reminiscences* while the story about Dickens's sarcasm on the pronunciation of model is reported by a Mr Emery in Volume 4 of *The Dickensian*. Thackeray's own sarcastic comment on Dickens's appearance at a ball is to be found in Volume Two of the *Letters and Private Papers of William Makepeace Thackeray*, edited by Gordon N. Ray. The letter from John Dickens to Chapman and Hall, dated 9 July, 1843, is to be found among the Carlton papers preserved at Dickens House. For the best account of Dickens and the Elton Committee, see George Hodder's *Memories of my Time*.

Dickens's visit to Manchester is covered of course by Fielding in his edition of the *Speeches*, but a more specific account of Dickens's demeanour and behaviour is to be found in *Alderman Cobden of Manchester: Letters and Reminiscences* by E. W. Watkin. Henry Burnett adds his own memories in Kitton, and the most detailed account of all is in "Dickens and Manchester" by F. R. Dean in Volume 34 of *The Dickensian*.

Much has been written about *A Christmas Carol*, rather less on the piracy trial which succeeded it. The best account here is in "Legal Documents Relating to the Piracy of *A Christmas Carol*" by S. J. Rust in Volume 34 of *The Dickensian*. There is a curious attack on Dickens by four publishers, listed in the Manuscript Room of the British Library under the press-mark Egerton 2154. Dickens's trip to Liverpool, and his sudden affection for Christiana Weller, are of course widely known. The best modern account is by Michael Slater in his *Dickens and Women*, while the *Liverpool Mercury* of 28 February, 1844, provides a contemporary version. A copy of the verses he inscribed in her album is to be found as the frontispiece to Volume 12 (January 1916) of *The Dickensian*, while his letter of commendation about her to an impresario is reprinted in Volume 67 of that same journal.

R. H. Horne, in his *A New Spirit of the Age*, embarks upon a discussion of Dickens in his first chapter. Evidence that Dickens was displeased by the book is to be found in a letter Elizabeth Barrett wrote to Robert Browning, dated 15 May, 1845, in *The Letters of Robert Browning and Elizabeth Barrett Browning, 1845–1846*, edited by Elvan Kintner. The story of Dickens's opening negotiations with Longman is to be found in Vizetely; there is no reason to doubt its accuracy, given Dickens's circumstances at this time. The account of his "cut and dried" manner of speaking is reprinted in Volume 63 of *The Dickensian*, while his own account of his pets is to be found in Volume 48 of the same periodical. On the move from Devonshire Terrace to Osnaburgh Street, in preparation for the departure to Italy, see Catherine Dickens's letter to Mrs Tagart, dated 1 June, 1844, in Dickens House. And, for the Dickenses' study of Italian before that departure, see *Episodes of my Second Life* by Luigi Mariotti.

On the subject of Dickens's attitude towards ragged schools, the best general account is to be found in John Manning's *Dickens on Education*; the most interesting survey of Dickens's attitude towards poor children in general is Norris Pope's *Dickens and Charity*. Of great importance, also, is Philip Collins's *Dickens and Education*. It is worth looking, more specifically, at "Dickens and the Field Lane Ragged School" by O. Sacks in Volume 4 of *The Dickensian* and at "Dickens and the Ragged Schools" by Philip Collins in Volume 55 of the same journal.

Chapter 15

The best collection of material on Dickens's Italian journey is to be found in his own *Pictures from Italy*, as well as his extensive and colourful correspondence in the fourth volume of the Pilgrim Edition. Further enlightenment is also to be found in *Little Dorrit*, if that novel is read carefully enough, and there is even a brief hint of his experiences in the Palazzo Peschiere in the first chapter of one of his Christmas stories, "The Haunted House". Of course there is also really no substitute for actually visiting Genoa itself; the Palazzo Peschiere and the Villa D'Albaro have survived the years, albeit now in very different surroundings. But the spirit and the life of Genoa remain much as they were in Dickens's own time: certainly the old quarter of that city is as labyrinthine and as ramshackle as ever it was during his residence. By walking through these streets and alleys, by looking out at the sea and the hills, the picture which Dickens presents the reader in his travel-writing and in his correspondence is immeasurably brightened and enriched.

For the armchair traveller, however, the best compact source of information is "Pictures from Genoa" by Leslie C. Staples in Volume 46 of *The Dickensian*. There are also brief memories by Mamie Dickens in her *Charles Dickens* and Charles Dickens jnr.'s comments can be found among the Storey papers preserved at Dickens House. Henry Dickens talks more generally about his father in *Memories of My Father*.

Michael Slater has written most acutely about the topical aspects of *The Chimes* in his essay, "Dickens's Tract for the Times" in *Dickens 1970: Centenary Essays*, a volume which he himself edited. Forster's invitation to the reading of that little book is reprinted in Volume 8 of *The Dickensian*, and various reviews of it are to be culled from *The Times* of 25 December, 1844, from the *Northern Star* of 28 December 1844, from the *Economist* of 18 January, 1845 and from *Parker's London Magazine* of February 1845. A slightly caustic comment by Bulwer-Lytton, in a letter to Forster dated 25 December, 1844, is to be found in *Dickens Centennial Essays* edited by A. Nisbet and B. Nevius. The account in *The Times* of the woman sentenced to death for drowning her baby is to be found in the issue of that newspaper dated 17 April, 1844. The comment about Dickens wanting to make readers cry rather than laugh is to be found among Mrs Watson's reminiscences of the author, as relayed to Kitton in *Charles Dickens: By Pen and Pencil*.

The best discussion of Dickens's revisions to the text of *Oliver Twist* is in Kathleen Tillotson's introduction to the Clarendon Edition of that novel. There is also much valuable analysis in Robert Golding's *Idiolects in Dickens*. For the most astute analysis of the mesmeric experiments with Augusta de la Rue, see Kaplan's *Dickens and Mesmerism: The Hidden Springs of Fiction*. On the subject of Dickens's appreciation of Italian art and sculpture, the most scholarly and perceptive description is to be found in an essay written by Leonee Ormond in Volume 79 of *The Dickensian*; it is from her, for example, that I gathered which particular guide-book Dickens took with him on his travels. His attack on the Pre-Raphaelites was made in an essay, "Old Lamps for New Ones", in *Household Words* of 15 June, 1850. Daniel Maclise's comments to Forster on his artistic contemporaries is quoted in the second volume of *Early Victorian England*, edited by G. M. Young. Thackeray's discussion of the need for propriety is in *The Times* of 2 September, 1840, and Charles Reade's comments on the romances of the present day is quoted in Richard Altick's *Victorian Studies in Scarlet*. On the pressing need for reality in the novel see G. L. Craik's *A Compendious History of English Literature and the English Language*, published in 1861. He makes brief mention of both Dickens and Thackeray as the pre-eminent modern authors in his last chapter, "The Victorian Era". Curiously enough, in T. B. Shaw's *Student's Manual of English Literature*, published in 1864, there is no mention of Dickens at all – although there is, for example, of Charlotte Brontë. For more general aesthetic studies of the period see J. H. Buckley's *The Victorian Temper: A Study in Literary Culture*. Peter Conrad's *The Victorian Treasure-House* provides a brilliant analysis and reconstruction of the period. It is also worth examining Ruskin's *Lectures on Art*.

Chapter 16

Comments about Dickens's love for actors and acting, and about his own propensities in that direction, abound in many published sources; the recollections of him by two men who knew him well, George Dolby and Percy Fitzgerald, describe in some detail his love for "green room" gossip and his endless discussions of plays and players. There is also a long section concerning Dickens's skills as actor and manager in Mary Cowden Clarke's *Recollections of Writers*. Dickens's remark about having more talent for drama than for literature (even as he said it he must have realised that it was not true) is recorded in "Charles Dickens: Recollections of the Great Novelist" in the *New York Daily Tribune* of 5 July, 1870. The incident in St James's Park, when he seemed so much like an actor on stage, is reprinted in J. B. van Amerongen's *The Actor in Dickens* (itself a very useful volume). Macready's comment about Dickens being unskilled is to be found in his *Diaries* in the entry for 27 December, 1845. It is also worth examining "For One Night Only. Dickens's Appearances As An Amateur Actor" in Volume 35 of *The Dickensian*. There is a wealth of material on Dickens's brief editorship of the *Daily News*, but perhaps the best sequence of articles is by Gerald R. Grubb: "Dickens and the *Daily News*: The Origin of the Idea" in *Booker Memorial Studies*, "Dickens and the *Daily News*; Preliminaries to Publication" in Volume 6 of *Nineteenth Century Fiction*, "Dickens and the *Daily News*: The Early Issues" in the same volume of *Nineteenth Century Fiction*. Two further indispensable items are "New Light on Dickens and the *Daily News*" by Kathleen Tillotson in Volume 78 of *The Dickensian* and "March 1846, 'at Sixes and sevens'; a new letter" by Kathleen Tillotson in Volume 82 of *The*

Dickensian. There are of course many recollections by contemporaries also: some of the most striking are to be found in *Reminiscences of Thirty Five Years of my Life* by Joseph Crowe, *The Life of Sir William Howard Russell* by J. B. Atkin and, most intriguingly, "Dickens as J. T. Danson Knew Him" by Kenneth Fielding in Volume 68 of *The Dickensian*. On the contents of the first issue see "Treasures of Dickens House" in Volume 34 of *The Dickensian*. Macready's misgivings are to be found in his *Diaries* under the entries for 2 November, 1845 and 27 December, 1845. The dinner at which Dickens spoke about the newspaper's prospects is described in Volume 2 of *Early Victorian England*, edited by G. M. Young. The most important of Dickens's own early articles for the journal is "Crime and Education" in the issue of 4 February, 1846. His letter on the Courvoisier hanging was printed in the issue of 28 February, 1846 and his tripartite discussion of capital punishment is to be found in the issues of 9 March, 13 March and 16 March of the same year. It is also worth examining "John Dickens, Journalist" by William Carlton in Volume 54 of *The Dickensian*. The comment on *The Cricket on the Hearth* comes from the *Edinburgh Journal* of 17 January, 1846. The copy which I have seen of that seasonal tale had the signature of his father, John Dickens, scrawled across the title page: no doubt the author's Christmas present. Browning's tart comment on the christening is from his letter to Elizabeth Barrett dated 7 May, 1846 and is to be found in *The Letters of Robert Browning and Elizabeth Barrett Browning, 1845–1846* edited by Elvan Kintner. The comment about Tennyson also comes from Browning, in a letter dated 1 May, 1846 in the same volume.

On the subject of his *Punch* friends, see *Mark Lemon: First Editor of Punch* by Arthur Adrian, "John Leech: Dickens's Friendship with the great 'Punch' Artist" by J. W. T. Ley in Volume 13 of *The Dickensian*. It is also worth looking at the relevant sections of Ley's *The Dickens Circle* and there is a very interesting chapter, "The 'Punch' Connection", in Gordon N. Ray's *Thackeray: The Uses of Adversity*. Clarkson Stanfield's life is documented in *Clarkson Stanfield* by James Dafforne, and also in the relevant sections of Jane R. Cohen's *Charles Dickens and His Original Illustrators*. The remark on the connection of radicalism and theatre comes from Arthur Symons, as quoted in Karl Beckson's *Arthur Symons: A Life*.

Chapter 17

The best descriptions and evocations of Dickens's stay in Lausanne (and Geneva) are to be found in his own correspondence, collected in the fourth volume of the Pilgrim Edition. His children have left their own memories of the same period – Mamie Dickens in *Charles Dickens* and his son Charles in "Reminiscences of my Father" in the *Windsor Magazine* of December 1934.

More of his memories are to be found among the Storey papers held at Dickens House, and also in his preface to *Dombey and Son*. Mrs Watson's diaries for the period are reprinted in "Sidelight on a Great Friendship" by Leslie C. Staples in Volume 47 of *The Dickensian*, and her reminiscences were also gathered by Kitton for *Charles Dickens: By Pen and Pencil*. T. A. Trollope's recollections, albeit of the year before, are also found in that volume. Once more, as was the case with Genoa, there is no real substitute for visiting Lausanne – even in its present state it offers something of the spirit and charm which Dickens himself experienced almost 150 years ago. Rosemont has gone, but the lake and the mountains of course survive; similarly the atmosphere of the place has survived. The old quarters of Geneva are also still redolent of that recent past through which Dickens walked. Thomas Powell has an account of Dickens in this period in *Frank Leslie's Sunday Magazine*, July 1886–April 1887, but it is not entirely to be trusted.

On his preliminary work on *Dombey and Son*, the best scholarly study is by John Butt and Kathleen Tillotson in their *Dickens at Work*. John Butt has also written an essay on the subject in his "Dickens's Notes for His Serial Parts" in Volume 45 of *The Dickensian* but the indispensable work of reference for this aspect of Dickens's genius is *Dickens's Working Notes for His Novels*, edited by Harry Stone. Interesting analysis and criticism are also to be found in Susan R. Horton's *Interpreting Interpreting. Interpreting Dickens's Dombey*. Dickens's need for the crowds of the city is aptly illuminated by his daughter, Kate, in Volume 3 of the *Pall Mall Gazette*. And, for the picture of Dickens's ubiquitous wandering through the streets of London, see G. A. Sala's *Charles Dickens*.

The subject of his religion is of course best discussed in Dennis Walder's *Dickens and Religion*, but there is also a very interesting analysis to be found in Florence Maly-Schlatter's *The Puritan Element in Victorian Fiction*. A more general account is presented in Humphry House's now classic *The Dickens World*. His children have left their own memories of his religious instruction – Mamie Dickens in *My Father As I Recall Him* and Henry Dickens in *My Father As I Knew Him*. Other contemporary descriptions of his religious practice are to be found in the recollections of Weld Taylor and Professor Ward in Kitton's *Charles Dickens: By Pen and Pencil*. There are also significant insights to be derived from Macrae's *Carlyle and Dickens*.

On the "feminine" side to his temperament, see Annie Fields's comments in *Memoirs of a Hostess: Drawn from the Diaries of Mrs J. T. Fields*, edited by M. A. De Wolfe Howe. Blanchard Jerrold adverts to the topic in *A Day With Charles Dickens*, and also brings up the subject in his reminiscences to Kitton. For contemporary reviews which mention this theme, see the *North British Review* of May 1851, the *Saturday Review* of 8 May, 1858 and the *Contemporary Review* of January 1869.

Chapter 18

Dickens himself expatiated on the joys of Paris in "A Flight", in *Household Words* of 30 August, 1851 and in "Railway Dreaming" in the same periodical of 10 May, 1856. More prosaic memories are to be found in his son's recollections in the *Windsor Magazine* of December 1934. The best discussion of the Cheap Edition of Dickens's novels is to be found in Robert L. Patten's *Charles Dickens and His Publishers*. There is an essay on the same subject, however, "The Cheap Edition" by L. A. Kennethe, in Volume 39 of *The Dickensian*. In Volume 40 of the same periodical, by the way, Walter Dexter discusses "The 'Library', the 'Peoples' and 'Charles Dickens' Editions"; this may sound an abstruse or merely technical subject, but it is of some importance in trying to gauge the nature of Dickens's sense of himself and of his own work.

The parody of *Dombey and Son* appears in *The Man in the Moon* of 1 March, 1847. John Forster describes the poetic aspects of that novel (as well as the death of Paul) in the *Examiner* of 28 October, 1846. More descriptions of the contemporary reaction are to be found in Amy Cruse's *The Victorians and Their Books*. The best account of Dickens's relationship with Hans Christian Andersen is to be found in Elias Bredsdorff's *Hans Andersen and Charles Dickens*.

There are many articles on Dickens's "Amateur" players, but perhaps the most scholarly account is the one already mentioned – "For One Night Only. Dickens's Appearances as an Amateur Actor" by Walter Dexter in Volume 35 of *The Dickensian*. The reminiscences of Mary Cowden Clarke appear in her *Recollections of Authors*, and the Gampian parody by Dickens (on the actors themselves) was published for the first time by Forster in his *Life*. It is also worth examining "The Proposed Benefit for Leigh Hunt. An Unpublished Pamphlet" in Volume 36 of *The Dickensian*.

The relationship of Dickens to his dying sister, Fanny, is best attested in the letters which he wrote to her – many of them still unpublished, but to be found at Dickens House. There are also letters here to her husband, Henry Burnett. Mamie Dickens offers some descriptive passages in her *Charles Dickens*, and for a more pious account see the Reverend James Griffin's *Memories of the Past*.

The history of Urania Cottage is dealt with by Edna Healey in her life of Miss Burdett-Coutts, *Lady Unknown*, but the primary source must remain Dickens's own letters to that lady as collected and edited by Edgar Johnson in *Letters from Charles Dickens to Angela Burdett-Coutts, 1841–1865*. The letters themselves are to be found in the Pierpont Morgan Library. Further light is shed upon his role in that venture in *Dickens and Charity* by Norris Pope, while his own account of the institution was published in *Household Words* of 23 April, 1853. The details about Dickens's autobiographical fragment are of course best studied in Forster's own account of the Dilke episode and its aftermath. (And of course Forster reprints that autobiography in the earliest sections of his own narrative.) The story about his showing it to his wife is conveyed by Charles Dickens junior in his preface to the 1892 edition of *David Copperfield* and also by Kitton in *Charles Dickens: His Life, Writings and Personality*. There are two very interesting general discussions – one, on Dickens's own awareness of his biography, by Jean Ferguson Carr in Volume 52 of *English Literary History*; and the other is a volume edited by George P. Landow and entitled *Approaches to Victorian Autobiography*.

There has been much research in recent years on the topic of Dickens's contributions to the *Examiner*, and most of the articles themselves have now been reprinted in various scholarly magazines. Suffice it to say, here, that his articles on the deaths of the children in Drouet's "baby-farm" at Tooting were published in the *Examiner* on 20 January, 1849, 27 January, 1849 and 21 April, 1849.

Writers have followed Dickens and friends to Great Yarmouth on several occasions, particularly since that visit marks the birth of *David Copperfield* in a topographical sense. The best of them are "David Copperfield and East Anglia" by Philip Collins in Volume 61 of *The Dickensian* and "The Composition of David Copperfield" by John Butt in Volume 46 of the same journal. There is also an account in Kitton's *The Dickens Country*, and Dickens describes his discovery of "Blunderstone" in an unpublished letter to Mrs Richard Watson dated 27 August, 1853. It is also worth looking at the illustration of the upturned boat on the beach of Great Yarmouth in "Peggotty's House", published in Volume 27 of *The Dickensian*.

The details of Dickens's philanthropy are scattered over all the memoirs devoted to him – among them, those of Dolby, Fitzgerald, Kitton, Mackenzie and Annie Fields. *Charles Dickens: Interviews and Recollections*, edited by Philip Collins, also contains much indispensable material on this subject – my account of the crippled boy who sat outside Devonshire Terrace, for example, is taken from the Reverend C. J. Whitmore's account in that volume. It is also worth looking at E. Wagenknecht's *The Man Charles Dickens: A Victorian Portrait*, but of course, more especially, at Norris Pope's *Dickens and Charity*.

Chapter 19

Dickens's own remarks about his working habits are scattered throughout his correspondence, both published and unpublished. What I have done in this chapter is to bring them together, and attempt to elicit some kind of system out of them. There is also a handy compendium of his relatives' observations in *Charles Dickens: Interviews and Recollections*. Georgina

Hogarth gives some indication of his working day in a letter to F. Harvey, dated 15 December, 1880, and it is to be found in the Pierpont Morgan Library. Henry Dickens discussed his father's routines both in his *Recollections* and in *My Father As I Knew Him*. Mamie Dickens performed the same service for posterity in *Charles Dickens* and in *My Father As I Recall Him*. Charles Dickens jnr's best recollections are to be found in the *Windsor Magazine* of December 1934. In Volume 3 of *The Dickensian* there is also a short and anonymous account of "How Dickens Corrected His Proofs".

For his specific work on *David Copperfield* during this period see "The Composition of *David Copperfield*" by John Butt in Volume 46 of *The Dickensian*, and "Mr Micawber and the Redefinition of Experience" by William Oddie in Volume 63 of the same periodical. Of more general import is Richard J. Dunn's *David Copperfield: An Annotated Bibliography*, while Kate Perugini's (née Dickens) account of life in a Victorian household was printed in Volume 29 of *The Dickensian*.

The account of Dickens's pursuit of the pickpocket was printed in *The Era* of 25 March, 1849, while Dickens's letters to *The Times* on the execution of the Mannings were printed in that newspaper's issues of 14 November, 1849 and 18 November, 1849. His more private and gruesome reflections are retold in "Lying Awake" in *Household Words* of 30 October, 1852. For his brief stay at Rockingham Castle, see Mrs Watson's diaries as reprinted in Volume 47 of *The Dickensian*. His fake "Elegy", after Gray, is reprinted in Volume 10 of the same journal.

For his sojourn on the Isle of Wight, the best and most substantial record is to be found in the shape of Richard J. Hutchings's *Dickens on an Island*, while his son, Charles, records his own memories of those summer months in the *Windsor Magazine* of December 1934. There are also recollections in Kitton's *Charles Dickens: By Pen and Pencil*. There is also an interesting article on that episode in Volume 61 of *The Dickensian*. For the best account of Dickens's strange illness in this period, it is best to consult David Waldron Smithers's *Dickens's Doctors*. And, finally, Thomas Powell: the best account of this controversy is to be found in two articles by Wilfred Partington, "Should A Biographer Tell? The Story of Dickens's Denunciation of Thomas Powell's Forgeries" in Volumes 43 and 44 of *The Dickensian*.

Chapter 20

The best source for material on *Household Words* is Anne Lohrli's compilation, itself entitled *Household Words*. One should also glance into a volume devoted to a later enterprise, E. A. Oppenlander's *Dickens's All The Year Round: Descriptive Index and Contributors List*. It is of course worth browsing through the actual back numbers of the periodical itself but the best anthology of Dickens's own writings from it is to be found in *The Uncollected Writings of*

Charles Dickens. Household Words, 1850–1859. The volume is edited by Harry Stone, and has an invaluable introduction. Material on the *Household Words* office itself is available in Kitton's *Charles Dickens: His Life, Writings and Personality*, and there is more detail in *The Dickens Souvenir of 1912* by Dion Calthorp and Max Pemberton. Thomas Wright, in his *The Life of Charles Dickens*, managed to obtain material from those who worked with Dickens at the time, and there is also an interesting account by G. A. Sala in Volume 4 of *Belgravia*. It is also worth looking at Percy Fitzgerald's *Memories of Charles Dickens*. A more scholarly account is given by Philip Collins in an essay in Volume 3 of *A Review of English Literature*, and he has also compiled "Dickens as Editor: Some Uncollected Fragments" in Volume 56 of *The Dickensian*. There is an interesting study of "The 'Singler Stories' of Inspector Field" by William Long in Volume 83 of the same journal. On Dickens's methods as a journalist it is worth reading an article in the *Weekly Dispatch* of 27 December, 1846, and Thomas Powell's reflections are to be found in *Pictures of the Living Authors of Great Britain*, published in 1851. Some valuable correspondence from Wills to Dickens is held in the Manuscript Room of the British Library, under the press-mark Add Ms 46469 (88–97). A discussion of the more general context of Dickens's work is to be found in R. D. Altick's *The English Common Reader*. George Ruby's cross-examination was published in the *Examiner* of 12 January, 1850; it was also published in Dickens's own *Household Narrative* for that month, although the journal itself was not issued until May of that year. It is also worth examining "Charles Dickens on 'The Exclusion of Evidence'" by K. J. Fielding and Alec W. Brice in Volume 65 of *The Dickensian*. Detail on Dickens's work for the Working Class Committee for the Great Exhibition is to be found in Volume 60 of *The Dickensian* and in Volume 10 of *Victorian Studies*. The generally favourable critical reactions to *David Copperfield* can be exemplified by the reviews in *Fraser's Magazine* of December 1850, the *North British Review* of May 1851 and the *Prospective Review* of July 1851. Dickens's own comments about his novel are to be found in Charles Kent's *Charles Dickens as a Reader* and in "George Russell's Recollections of Dickens" in Volume 78 of *The Dickensian*.

On Fort House and Broadstairs, the old sources are generally the best: in particular Hughes's *A Week's Tramp in Dickensland* and Kitton's *The Dickens Country*. And of course also "Dickens's Association with Broadstairs" by B. W. Matz in Volume 4 of *The Dickensian*. The story about Dickens's fear at the prospect of not having completed that month's number is found in Kent's *Charles Dickens as a Reader*, while George Eliot's comment about Broadstairs is in a letter she wrote to Mrs Taylor, dated 19 August, 1852, which is now to be found in *The George Eliot Letters* edited by G. S. Haight.

The theatricals at Knebworth are discussed by Mrs Compton in Kitton's *Charles Dickens: By Pen and Pencil* and it is also worth looking once more at Walter Dexter's "For One Night Only . . .", already mentioned. See also "A

Lawyer's Black Boxes: Light on the Guild of Literature and Art and the Douglas Jerrold Fund" by T. W. Hill in Volume 47 of *The Dickensian*. For the strange spectacle of Bulwer-Lytton himself, one of the best and most amusing accounts is Michael Sadleir's *Bulwer and His Wife: A Panorama*, and there is of course much information to be found in Ley's *The Dickens Circle*. R. H. Horne's description of the baronet comes from his *A New Spirit of the Age*, and there is an interesting essay by Valerie Purton, "Dickens and Bulwer Lytton: the Dandy reclaimed?", in Volume 74 of *The Dickensian*.

Chapter 21

For an account of the death of John Dickens, see Mrs Davey's article in Volume 13 of *Lippincott's Magazine*, and on the familial aftermath there are unpublished letters at Dickens House – most notably from Dickens's brother, Alfred, to his mother, dated 6 April, 1851 and to his sister Laetitia ("Tish") two days before. There is also a letter from Elizabeth Dickens herself to a friend of Dickens's childhood, Louis d'Elboux, quoted by W. J. Carlton in an essay, "A Friend of Dickens's Boyhood", in Volume 66 of *The Dickensian*. Dickens himself recalled the period immediately after his father's death in one of his "Uncommercial Traveller" essays entitled "Night Walks". It is also worth looking at "Lying Awake" in *Household Words* of 30 October, 1852.

His preliminary schemes and dreams for *Bleak House* are of course best surveyed through the medium of his correspondence, both published and unpublished; much preparatory material is discussed in Harry Stone's edition of *Dickens's Working Notes for his Novels*, and G. H. Ford has written an illuminating article on "The Titles for *Bleak House*" in Volume 65 of *The Dickensian*. The best general study of the forces working within Dickens during this period is to be found in Robert Newsom's *Dickens and the Romantic Side of Familiar Things*. His early reference to a Saurian monster in the vicinity of the Thames occurs in "Plate Glass" published in *Household Words* on 1 February, 1851.

Dickens made his speech for the General Theatrical Fund, on the evening of Dora's death, on 14 April, 1851. It is of course reprinted, and the context described, in Fielding's collection of Dickens's *Speeches*. Mamie Dickens detailed her father's reaction in the *Cornhill Magazine* of January 1885. Henry Morley's rather sanguine description of Catherine Dickens is given in *The Life of Henry Morley* by H. S. Solley, and Dickens's fictional dislike of female hysterics is included in an essay, "Smuggled Relations", in *Household Words* of 23 June, 1855.

Dickens's exemplary behaviour at a meeting of the Guild is described by Sir John Robinson, as quoted in W. T. Shore's *Charles Dickens and Friends*, while Dickens's prospectus was published in *Household Words* of 10 May, 1851. Of the Guild theatrical performances themselves there are many accounts, notably that by Godfrey Turner in Kitton's *Charles Dickens: By Pen and Pencil*, by Alfred Ainger in *Macmillan's Magazine* of January 1871, by R. H. Horne in Volume 230 of the *Gentleman's Magazine*, and by Charles Knight in *Passages of a Working Life*. Horne's recollections are also published in A. W. Ward's *Dickens*. More details are given in T. E. Pemberton's *Charles Dickens and the Stage*. Thackeray's dismal response to the theatricals is described in Ray's *Thackeray: The Age of Wisdom*.

A succinct account of Fort House, Broadstairs, is presented in an anonymous pamphlet, "Charles Dickens and His Bleak House" while the arrangements at Tavistock House are recorded in Mamie Dickens's accounts of her father, in Kitton's *The Dickens Country*, in Shelton MacKenzie's early *Life*, and in *Her Book* by Mary Boyle. Dickens's account of "doomed childhood" and of the drunken solicitor are to be found in "The Metropolitan Protectives" in *Household Words* of 26 May, 1851. The description of the doomed boy is in "A Sleep To Startle Us", published in the same periodical of 13 March, 1852. Mary Mitford's account of Talfourd is in Volume 2 of *The Life of Mary Russell Mitford* edited by A. G. L'Estrange, while Charles Kingsley's remarks are to be found in Volume 1 of *His Letters and Memories of his Life*, edited by F. E. Kingsley.

Chapter 22

The Clapham Rise Dinners, and Dickens's friendship with the Cattermoles, are described by the artist's son, the poetically named Leonardo Cattermole, in Kitton's *Charles Dickens: By Pen and Pencil*. For the Twelfth Night festivities, the best source is Dickens's eldest son's memories in the *Windsor Magazine* of December 1934. While on the subject of entertainment, it is worth mentioning in passing an essay in Volume 31 of *The Dickensian*, "Why 'Not So Bad As We Seem' was Acted in Free-Trade Hall".

Bleak House has, like all of Dickens's novels, been a separate subject of study on innumerable occasions; those who wish to examine the scholarly books on the subject need turn no further than the bibliography printed after these notes. Not mentioned in that place, but of some interest nevertheless, are "The Crossing Sweeper in *Bleak House*: Dickens and the Original Jo" by John Suddaby in Volume 8 of *The Dickensian* and "The *Bleak House* Page-Proofs. More Shavings from Dickens's Workshop" by Duane De Vries in Volume 66 of the same journal. Dickens's question about Esther's narrative being "quite girlish?" is taken from "Charles Dickens: Recollections of the Great Novelist" in the *New York Daily Tribune* of 5 July, 1870. On the inflammable subject of spontaneous combustion see the very interesting account in "Krook's Death and Dickens's Authorities" by Peter Denman in Volume 82 of *The Dickensian*; indispensable, too, are Dickens's letters to Lewes which are republished in Volume 10 of *Nineteenth Century Fiction*. Lewes's own articles on the affair appeared in the *Leader* of 11 December, 1852 and 15 January, 1853. Faraday's notes on the phenomenon appeared in the course of an article, "The Laboratory in the Chest", which was published in *Household Words* of 7 September, 1850. The encomium to science, as an almost magical practice, is to be found in "Chemical Contradictions" published in the same periodical a week later. A sample of various unfavourable reactions to the novel are to be found in the *Athenaeum* of 17 September, 1853; in the *Illustrated London News* of 24 September, 1853; in the *Spectator* of 24 September, 1853; and in *Bentley's Miscellany* of October 1853. Forster's slightly more circumspect review is in the *Examiner* of 8 October, 1853.

The Skimpole affair has been covered both by biographers and critics. For contemporary accounts, mentioned in my own narrative, it is worth examining the Journal of Benjamin Moran, under the entry for 17 January, 1858, as quoted in Volume 46 of *The Dickensian*. Wilkie Collins's remarks are quoted in W. T. Shore's *Charles Dickens and His Friends*, while there is further information in Volume 6 of the *Dickens Studies Newsletter*. Additional information is derived from a private letter from Godfrey Turner to Kitton, dated 21 September, 1886, which is held among the Kitton Papers at Dickens House. Before the most recent volume of the Pilgrim Edition reached this year, an invaluable source was to be found in "More Letters to the Watsons" by Franklin P. Rolfe in Volume 38 of *The Dickensian*. Here were printed Dickens's remarks about the original of Skimpole, all of which had been deleted from publications of his correspondence before the Nonesuch Edition of 1938 – the principal offended and offending editor being, as on other occasions, Georgina Hogarth. Of course the Nonesuch Edition is not by any means perfect – it has its fair share of mistakes and misreadings, and is woefully incomplete. The Pilgrim Edition has been filling the very large holes, volume by volume, but for those years not yet covered by that undertaking it is wise to consult other specific editions of Dickens's correspondence as well as Nonesuch. The most important of these volumes are *Letters from Charles Dickens to Angela Burdett-Coutts*, 1841–1865, selected and edited by Edgar Johnson, and *Mr and Mrs Charles Dickens. His letters to her.* This volume, with several interesting appendices, is edited by Walter Dexter. The present author has of course also read many hundreds, if not thousands, of unpublished letters.

Wilkie Collins's account of the routine of life in the Dickens household at Dover is reprinted in *Wilkie Collins* by Kenneth Robinson. For a contemporary account of the novelist's visit to Birmingham see the reminiscences of "Cuthbert Bede" in Kitton. Dickens's letter to Arthur Ryland, on the subject of reading, is to be found in Charles Kent's *Charles Dickens as a Reader*. For

Wills's description of Dickens's success, see his remarks quoted by Lady Priestley in *The Story of a Lifetime*. The account of Dickens's refuge at Cobley's Farm is given by H. Snowden Ward in Volume I of *The Dickensian* while Thomas Wright, among others, has referred to the "secret" apartment near the Five Bells public house in New Cross. The pub still stands, and across from it is a building which *might* have contained the apartment in question.

Dickens's holiday homes in Boulogne have not survived, however, and much of M. Beaucourt's estate is now covered by a school; but the situation remains the same, and aspects of the old hill and woods are visible – especially to a traveller with a certain historical imagination. The old town of Boulogne survives; along its ancient walls, and through its cobbled streets, it is still possible to relive something of the town which Dickens saw and admired. On this first trip itself, there are interesting anecdotes in *Her Book* by Mary Boyle and in letters from Wilkie Collins to his brother, Charles, now in the Pierpont Morgan Library in New York. On the Swiss tour which Dickens undertook with Egg and Collins, there is information both in Kenneth Robinson's *Wilkie Collins* and in William M. Clarke's *The Secret Life of Wilkie Collins*. There is also an account of the journey back to England, by Charles Dickens jnr, among the Storey papers held at Dickens House.

Chapter 23

The opening scene at Urania Cottage is extracted from a letter Dickens wrote to Miss Burdett-Coutts on 4 January, 1854. It is to be found in Edgar Johnson's selection of his correspondence to that lady. The *Tom Thumb* theatricals of Twelfth Night are recalled by Charles Dickens jnr in the *Windsor Magazine* of December 1934 and by Henry Dickens in his *Recollections*. There are also details by Alfred Ainger in *Macmillan's Magazine* of January 1871 and in T. E. Pemberton's *Charles Dickens and the Stage*. Dickens's absenteeism, when he was meant to be on jury service, is reported in the *Illustrated London News* of 11 February, 1854.

Dickens's brief visit to Preston was noticed in *Reynolds's Weekly Newspaper* of 15 February, 1854; there is also a significant article on the background to his visit in "The Battle for Preston" by K. J. Fielding in Volume 50 of *The Dickensian*. His own article on his journey, "On Strike", was published in *Household Words* of 11 February, 1854, and his comments on the Amalgamated Society of Engineers are quoted in *Charles Dickens: A Critical Introduction* by K. J. Fielding. On *Hard Times* itself, it is also worth reading Fielding's article in Volume 48 of the *Modern Language Review*, as well as the essay he wrote in collaboration with Anne Smith in *Dickens Centennial Essays* edited by A. Nisbet and B. Nevius. There is an important study of the novel by

Sylvere Monod, "Dickens At Work on the Text of *Hard Times*", in Volume 64 of *The Dickensian*. The belief that he sat "back-stage" at the circus during the course of his research is held by James T. Fields in his *In and Out of Doors with Charles Dickens*. Typical reactions to the novel itself are to be found in the *Rambler* of October 1854, and the *Westminster Review* of the same month. The parody of Dickensian style is to be found in *Our Miscellany* for 1857. The reference to "Mr Sparkler", sometimes known as the "Sparkler of Albion", is in a letter from Mark Lemon, dated 3 May, 1854, currently residing in the Pierpont Morgan Library.

Boulogne has already featured in these notes, but it is now worth mentioning the essay which Dickens wrote for *Household Words* on the same theme – "Our French Watering Place" is in the issue of 4 November, 1854. Some letters are also useful: Catherine Dickens to Mrs Tagart, dated 6 July, 1854, in Dickens House, and Wilkie Collins to Charles Collins, dated 31 August, 1854 and 7 September, 1854, in Pierpont Morgan. Dickens's polemic addressed "To Working Men" was published in *Household Words* of 7 October, 1854.

Chapter 24

Dickens's strange article on the Franklin Expedition, "Lost Arctic Voyagers", was published in *Household Words* of 12 February, 1855. There is one very informative article on his own contribution to this debate, "'The contents of the kettles': Charles Dickens, John Rae and Cannibalism on the 1845 Franklin Expedition" by Ian R. Stone in Volume 83 of *The Dickensian*. The story of the explorers found in permafrost was revealed in *The Times* of 26 September, 1986. That other Victorian story, of Frederick Maynard and his unhappy sister, is best retold in *The Letters of Charles Dickens to Angela Burdett-Coutts*. For his charitable readings in this period, there is "For One Night Only. Part Two. An Account of the Famous Readings" by Walter Dexter in Volume 37 of *The Dickensian*. The theatricals are, as ever, recounted in Ainger, Pemberton and in the various reminiscences of his children; see elsewhere in these notes for the references. It is a little while since we have heard from John Forster's *Life*, so it is pleasant to record a full discussion of these festive events in the second chapter of the seventh book of his *Life of Charles Dickens*. The criticism of Dickens's Christmas story about Watts' Charity is taken from the *Maidstone and Kentish Journal* of 25 December and 30 December, 1854; I am indebted to Katharine Longley for these two references.

The course of Dickens's political opinions in this period can best be traced through his own journalism; certainly he wrote often and stridently enough to leave no doubt about exactly where he stood on the affairs of the day:

the principal essays published in *Household Words* are "Prince Bull" (17 February), "Gone to the Dogs" (10 March), "Fast and Loose" (24 March), "The Thousand and One Humbugs" (21 April, 28 April and 5 May) and "The Toady Tree" (26 May). His address to the Administrative Reform Association is of course reprinted in Fielding's edition of his *Speeches*. His letters to Austin Layard are to be found in the Manuscript Room of the British Library, and a London reporter's recollections of his speech at the Drury Lane Theatre are contained in Kitton's *Charles Dickens: By Pen and Pencil*.

For notes about his literary reputation at this time, see Nathaniel Hawthorne's diary entry for 11 June, 1855, quoted in Ford's *Dickens and His Readers*, while Ruskin's comment is quoted in Volume 74 of *The Dickensian*. It is also worth examining *A Bibliography of Dickensian Criticism, 1836–1975*, edited by R. C. Churchill.

Dickens's actual Memorandum Book is now in the Berg Collection of the New York Public Library, but a faithful edition of it by Fred Kaplan, *Charles Dickens's Book of Memoranda*, is available to those who do not wish to make the journey. The best description of his motives for starting it is to be found in Forster's *Life*. The sad saga of Maria Beadnell is documented in *The Romance of Charles Dickens and Maria Beadnell Winter*, by E. F. Payne and H. H. Harper, while Georgina Hogarth's rather acid comments are to be found in a memorandum preserved in Dickens House. The maid's recollections of her were printed in the *Daily Chronicle* of 18 March, 1912. The best general discussion of the unhappy episode is found in Michael Slater's *Dickens and Women*.

Events in Paris, as seen through Wilkie Collins's eyes, are to be found in Kenneth Robinson's life of the younger novelist; but his remarks about Dickens's inability to sit through a stage performance are quoted in Volume 72 of *The Dickensian*. The details of the Royal Literary Fund affair are best summarised in a long article in the *Times Literary Supplement* of 22 October, 1954. There is also an interesting essay by K. J. Fielding in Volume 6 of *Review of English Studies*, and a further article by the same scholar in the *Times Literary Supplement* of 19 September, 1958.

Details about Dickens's frantic production of *The Lighthouse* are in his oldest son's reminiscences in the *Windsor Magazine*, already detailed, and the performance at the house of Colonel Waugh is noted in Henry Morley's *Journal* for 14 July, 1855. The sad tale of the dying child, which Dickens had remembered from his own infancy, is best discussed in "The Wrecked Dying-Child near Natal. Its Lifelong Effects on Dickens" by John Suddaby in Volume 6 of *The Dickensian*. For his reading of *A Christmas Carol* at Folkestone, see Volume 2 of *Dickens Quarterly*. And, for his "panic" when starting *Little Dorrit*, consult Henry Dickens's *Recollections*. One extra source can now be adduced for his visit to Paris, largely because it includes a photograph of the house in the Champs-Elysées where he and the family took an apartment: "Dickens in France" by Edouard Fabre Surveyer in Volume 28 of *The Dickensian*. As for his return to London, and the wretched scene outside the Whitechapel Workhouse, Dickens's own words are (as almost always) the best ones – "A Nightly Scene in London" in *Household Words* of 26 January, 1856. The *Household Words* Almanac began publication, by the way, in the issue of 22 November, 1855.

Chapter 25

Dickens's attack upon Harriet Martineau, "Our Wicked Mis-statements", appeared in *Household Words* of 19 January, 1856. For his time in Paris, it is worth looking at some hitherto unpublished letters which made their way into the *Times Literary Supplement* of 22 February, 1974; correspondence with John Leech emerges in Volume 35 of *The Dickensian* while other letters, still unpublished, are to be found in the Manuscript Room of the British Library under the press-mark MS 56081. For more information it is wise to consult Forster's *Life* for this period of his friend's career, and particularly the footnotes of these sections – which, like all good footnotes, often reveal more than their author intended.

For Dickens's purchase of Gad's Hill Place, see "Charles Dickens: A Customer of Coutts and Co" by M. Veronica Stoker in Volume 68 of *The Dickensian* for some of the financial details; his son's memories, in the *Windsor Magazine* of December 1934, are also useful. For his stay in Dover, the best source is Charles Dickens himself – in "Out of the Season" in *Household Words* of 28 June, 1856.

On the general theme of his friendship with Wilkie Collins during this period, and on the particular subject of *The Frozen Deep*, the best account is given in *Under the Management of Mr Charles Dickens: His Production of "The Frozen Deep"* by R. L. Brannan. An important letter from Dickens to Webster, dated 14 June, 1856, is reprinted in Volume Ten of the *Michigan Quarterly Review*, while the best account of the rehearsals is given by Francisco Berger in *Reminiscences, Impressions and Anecdotes*. The letter from Wilkie Collins to his mother, about Dickens's help with his composition, is dated 5 April 1856 and is reprinted in *Nineteenth Century Fiction*.

The relationship between Catherine Dickens and her husband will be more fully explored in the next chapter and its footnotes, but particular references perhaps need to be elucidated here. His letter to Mary Boyle is quoted in Nisbet's *Dickens and Ellen Ternan*, while the story of the contretemps at the Talfourd dinner is given in *From Life* by Wybert Reeve (and he says that *he* got it from Wilkie Collins who, in this and other examples, reveals himself to be something of a gossip). Dickens's care over domestic life is disclosed in Nathaniel Hawthorne's *English Notebooks*, edited by R. Stewart. It is also worth looking at Arthur Adrian's *Georgina Hogarth and the Dickens Circle*. His remarks on the demeanour of the murderer, William Palmer, are in *Household Words* of 14 June, 1856.

There is really no need to marshal independent testimony once more for the Boulogne summer – except perhaps to mention that Mamie Dickens has some references in Kitton's *Charles Dickens: His Life, Writings and Personality* and that Francisco Berger has others in the same author's *Charles Dickens: By Pen and Pencil*. The account of the Channel crossing is given by a Mr Ballentine in W. T. Shore's *Charles Dickens and His Friends*.

Chapter 26

For the rehearsals and eventual performances of *The Frozen Deep* it is natural and inevitable to look at the familiar sources: Pemberton's study of *Charles Dickens and the Stage*, the various reminiscences of Mrs Lankester, Berger and Hipkins in Kitton's *Charles Dickens: By Pen and Pencil*, Charles Dickens jnr's reminiscences in the *Windsor Magazine*, and so forth. But it is also worth reading Marcus Stone's recollections as printed in Volume 6 of *The Dickensian*, and there is an interesting unpublished letter from Georgina Hogarth to Mrs Winter, dated 21 July, 1857, which deals with the Queen's attendance at the play. This letter is in the Huntington Library.

Much has been written about Ellen Ternan and her theatrical family, and in the notes to succeeding chapters some of the minutiae will be discussed. At this early point, however, it is worth noting the major sources of information about that most mysterious young woman. By far the best discussion of the Ternan family as a theatrical phenomenon comes in the series of ten articles which Malcolm Morley wrote for *The Dickensian* under the heading "The Theatrical Ternans" (Volumes 54 to 57 inclusive). These essays comprise the single most important source of dramatic scholarship. But the palm in Ternan studies must nevertheless be awarded to Katharine M. Longley who in her *A Pardoner's Tale: Charles Dickens and the Ternan Family*, an unpublished typescript, has with patient research and scholarly investigation revealed more about the Ternan family than any previous biographer. It is impossible to write about Ellen Ternan without acknowledging an enormous debt to her work. Other scholars have of course investigated the matter, and much incidental and fruitful information is to be found among the papers which various Dickensians have bequeathed to the collection at Dickens House: among them the Storey Papers, the Wright papers, and the Aylmer papers. There are also books specifically devoted to the subject, prominent among them Ada Nisbet's *Dickens and Ellen Ternan* and Felix Aylmer's *Dickens Incognito*. Gladys Storey's *Dickens and Daughter*, purporting to be the true recollections of Kate Dickens, is necessary although not always reliable. There is also more discussion in C. G. L. Du Cann's *The Love-Lives of Charles Dickens*, but the most thorough and objective discussion is to be found in Michael Slater's *Dickens and Women*. It is also worth looking at E. Wagenknecht's *Dickens and the Scandalmongers*, and an essay by Gerald R. Grubb, "Dickens and Ellen Ternan", in Volume 49 of *The Dickensian*. Interesting later letters are revealed in "Ellen Ternan – Some Letters" by L. C. Staples in Volume 61 of the same periodical.

Gad's Hill itself is better seen than described: it survives, almost entirely intact, and is at the time of writing being used as a girls' school. Of course it has also been commemorated in any number of memoirs and biographies – among them, those of friends like Fitzgerald, Sala and Dolby as well as the recollections of the various Dickens children. Early guides, such as Hughes's *A Week's Tramp in Dickensland*, are also stocked with recollections and descriptions. The counterfeit book-backs are described (with a photograph) in Kitton's *Charles Dickens: By Pen and Pencil*, along with other details, while more information is to be found in Gladys Storey's *Dickens and Daughter*. The most concentrated account is given, naturally enough, in Edwin Harris's *Gad's Hill Place and Charles Dickens* while those who require more technical information will have to consult the auction catalogues of the house's sale, currently to be found in the Pierpont Morgan Library. For the story of Hans Andersen's protracted visit, see Elias Bredsdorff's *Hans Andersen and Charles Dickens*, while there is also "Hans Andersen: An Amusing Unpublished Dickens Letter" in Volume 31 of *The Dickensian*.

Reactions to the completed *Little Dorrit* are various and variously available, two of the most representative being in *Blackwood's Magazine* of April 1857 and in the *Edinburgh Review* of July 1857. The remark about Dickens not being read in later years is to be found in the *Saturday Review* of 8 May, 1858, while Walter Bagehot's important article on Dickens is in the *National Review* of October 1858.

There are of course any number of newspaper accounts of Dickens's early public readings for charity, and some of the comment in this biography is extracted from *Sanders's News Letter* of 26 December, 1858, the *Huddersfield Chronicle* of 11 September, 1858, the *Leader* of 4 July, 1857, the *Saturday Review* of 16 June, 1858, *Town Talk* of 5 January, 1858, and 3 July, 1858, and *The Times* of 1 July, 1857. The description of Dickens at Edinburgh is by John Tulloch and is given in Mrs Oliphant's *A Memoir of the Life of John Tulloch*.

The tours of the Amateur players have already been anticipated in various notes on Dickens's theatricals. Again, Kitton is a major source. There is also material in Lady Priestley's *The Story of a Lifetime*. Wilkie Collins's remarks come from Kenneth Robinson's biography, and there is a vignette of the theatricals by Helen Lemon (Mark Lemon's daughter) in the *Daily News* of 17 August, 1926.

Dickens's trip to the North is best viewed through the medium of his own letters, and also through the account which he produced with Wilkie Collins, *The Lazy Tour of Two Idle Apprentices*. Some of his preparatory letters, on booking hotels, are to be found in Dickens House while there is a letter to Mrs Watson in Volume 38 of *The Dickensian*. While on the subject of letters, it is appropriate to note here "Dickens to George Eliot. Unpublished Letters" in Volume 34 of *The Dickensian*. Dickens's reading of Westland Marston's play is described by Walter Wellsman in Volume 4 of that journal.

On the subject of the author's first paid public readings, the best and most authoritative source remains Charles Kent's *Charles Dickens as a Reader*, but it is also worth looking at a description in the *Illustrated London News* of 31 July, 1858.

Chapter 27

In order to understand and present the events at the time of Dickens's separation from his wife, it is necessary to bring together a variety of sources. There are of course his published letters but, just as importantly, there is the content of Dickens's unpublished correspondence – in letters, for example, to Macready and to Mary Boyle (now residing in the Pierpont Morgan Library), to Cornelius Felton (Harvard University), to Mrs Gore (Berg). There are also Mark Lemon's letters to Forster in the Pierpont Morgan; as well as some interesting if half-truthful remarks in *Harriet Martineau's Letters to Fanny Wedgewood*, edited by Elisabeth Arbuckle. More details are to be found from the mouth or at least quill-pen of Dickens himself (not necessarily the same thing) in "Letters to John Leech" in Volume 35 of *The Dickensian* and his letters to Miss Burdett-Coutts transcribed by Edgar Johnson in his edition of that correspondence but also in part available in the *Times Literary Supplement* of 2 and 9 March, 1951. There are various accounts and, more often, snatches of gossip in the memoirs of contemporaries – among them John Bigelow's *Retrospections of an Active Life*, Mrs Whiffen's *Keeping Off The Shelf*, and *The Letters and Memoirs of Sir William Hardman*. Much interesting research has been done by more recent scholars, of course, and perhaps the most active in the field has been K. J. Fielding whose essays on the separation are invaluable. Particularly one might mention "Dickens and the Hogarth Scandal" in Volume 10 of *Nineteenth Century Fiction*, "Charles Dickens and Colin Rae Brown" in Volume 7 of *Nineteenth Century Fiction*, "Bradbury versus Dickens" in Volume 50 of *The Dickensian* and "Dickens and His Wife – Fact or Forgery?" in *Etudes Anglaises* of September 1955. This last article prints the famous "Thomson-Stark Letter", sent by Catherine's aunt, Helen Thomson, to a close friend of the family. It was once thought to be a fake, but it is clear, from the amount of now-verified detail that it contains, that it is indeed a genuine account of the separation from Catherine's point of view.

Other scholars have examined this short period in great detail – most notably, of course, Katharine M. Longley whose unpublished typescript contains many useful hints and suggestions. There is also a great deal of evidence to be found among the unpublished papers of Felix Aylmer, Thomas Wright and Gladys Storey. Especially those of Miss Storey, in fact, who did not disclose everything in her published account, *Dickens and Daughter*. For a handy résumé of that material, see "The Gladys Storey Papers" by David Parker and Michael Slater in Volume 76 of *The Dickensian*. There are certain books which are essential reading – in particular Michael Slater's *Dickens and Women*, Felix Aylmer's *Dickens Incognito* and Ada Nisbet's *Dickens and Ellen Ternan*. Two books by Arthur Adrian, *Georgina Hogarth and the Dickens Circle* and *Mark Lemon: First Editor of Punch*, are also very useful. Contemporary newspaper accounts have been culled from the *Liverpool Mercury* of 9 September, 1858, the *Court Circular* of 12 June, 1858 and the *Newcastle Chronicle* of 4 June, 1858. For Dickens's demeanour during the readings of this period, see also *Town Talk* of 5 January, 1858 and 3 July, 1858.

The Dickens-Thackeray quarrel has been explored by Gordon N. Ray in "Dickens versus Thackeray: the Garrick Club Affair" in Volume 69 of *PMLA*, and also of course in that scholar's *Thackeray: The Age of Wisdom*. It is also worth looking at Adrian's *Mark Lemon*, particularly for its transcripts of Henry Silver's record of *Punch* table-talk, and at an essay by Marcus Stone in Volume 17 of *The Dickensian*. Charles Dickens jnr's attack on Edmund Yates is to be found in *Punch* of 11 December, 1858, while Thackeray's oblique account of the angry man is in the *Cornhill* of August 1860.

Chapter 28

The fullest report on the "Berners Street affair" is given by Dickens in the long and impassioned letter to Wills, dated 25 October, 1858, and currently to be seen in the Huntington Library. It is quoted, however, in Ada Nisbet's *Dickens and Ellen Ternan*. In the same volume can be found Dickens's letter to Richard Smith Spofford on the innocence of Fanny Ternan.

Dickens's letter to the stationmaster at Euston, before beginning his travels, is to be found at Dickens House. On the reading tour itself, the best brief account is to be found in Walter Dexter's "Mr Charles Dickens Will Read" in Volume 37 of *The Dickensian*. Incidental highlights are recorded by Cuthbert Bede in the *London Figaro* 15 April, 1874. His appearance in this period is described by John Hollingshead in *My Lifetime* and by Francesco Berger in *97*. His daughter Kate's description is given by Gladys Storey in *Dickens and Daughter* while Christiana Weller is quoted in Volume 1 of *Dickens Studies Annual*. Richard Stanford is quoted in Volume 21 of *The*

Dickensian. The account of the novelist gesticulating on the railway platform comes from "Cuthbert Bede" again (I use the inverted commas because it was a pseudonym), this time as he is quoted in Kitton's *Charles Dickens: By Pen and Pencil*, while the conversation with Percy Fitzgerald is quoted in that author's *Memories of Charles Dickens*. The long transcriptions of his impromptu conversations are to be found as "Some Household Words: Two New Accounts of Dickens's Conversation" by Jerome Meckier in Volume 71 of *The Dickensian*. It is also worth examining Philip Collins's "Dickens In Conversation" in Volume 59 of that periodical.

The best source of information about all aspects of *All The Year Round* is undoubtedly E. A. Oppenlander's *Dickens's All The Year Round. Descriptive Index and Contributions List*; despite its somewhat forbidding title, it is a cogent and substantial account of the journal and its contributors. It is of course always worth looking at what Robert Patten has to say in *Charles Dickens and His Publishers* while, on the tortuous controversy which led to the periodical, the best informed account is by K. J. Fielding, "Bradbury v Dickens", in Volume 50 of *The Dickensian*. It is also worth reading Philip Collins's essay in Volume 2 of *A Review of English Literature* while Volume 47 of the *Papers of the Bibliographic Society of America* contains some useful information.

The gossip about Dickens's daughters is retailed by Thackeray via Gordon Ray in *Thackeray: The Age of Wisdom*, while the most faithful account of Dickens's sitting to Frith is in that artist's own *My Autobiography and Reminiscences*. It is also worth examining "A New Portrait of Dickens. Photograph Used by W. P. Frith RA For His Painting of the Novelist" by B. W. Matz in Volume 15 of *The Dickensian*.

Chapter 29

Dickens's thoughts of America are encapsulated in Fields's account in *Yesterdays With Authors* while a more sober account is given by Gerald C. Grubb, "Personal and Business Relations of Charles Dickens with Thomas Coke Evans", in Volume 48 of *The Dickensian*.

On the subject of Dickens's plagiarism, there is an interesting discussion of Watts Phillips and *The Dead Heart* in Volume 55 of *The Dickensian*. For other accounts of his borrowings, it is only necessary to open almost any critical study of Dickens and the same litany of names – Smollett, Fielding, Sterne et al – will come tumbling out. On the theme of the dramatisations of *A Tale of Two Cities*, however, it is worth looking at Dickens's own description of James Waterson's work, "Lucie Manette", which is reprinted in Volume 7 of *The Dickensian*.

The account of Dickens's visit to the haunted house at Cheshunt is best given by Harry Stone in Volume 1 of the *Dickens Studies Annual*, while Nina Lehmann's account of the strange dinner party at Tavistock Square is reported by John Lehmann in his *Ancestors and Friends*.

The lives of the children are variously and widely discussed in Adrian's *Georgina Hogarth and the Dickens Circle*, in Bowen's *Charles Dickens and His Family*, in Storey's *Dickens and Daughter*, and so forth. A lesser-known volume, but still one of some interest, is Mary Lazarus's *A Tale of Two Brothers*, which deals with the life of Alfred and Edward in Australia – throwing much light, incidentally, on Dickens's attitude towards his sons. On Kate's marriage, the best account is given by Gladys Storey, both in her *Dickens and Daughter* and in the private papers which she left to Dickens House. Wilkie Collins's remarks are quoted by Kenneth Robinson in his life of that author, and Lehmann's enthusiastic description is to be found in *Memories of Half-a-Century* by R. C. Lehmann. Leonee Ormond details the argument with Hunt in Volume 80 of *The Dickensian*. The best account of the selling of Tavistock House is given in a letter which Dickens wrote to Frederick Chapman some years later (dated 24 August, 1860) and now at Dickens House, while there is also useful information from the author himself on the subject of burning his correspondence in a letter which he wrote to W. J. O'Driscoll on 18 May, 1870. O'Driscoll did not burn it but published it in his *Daniel Maclise*.

There is no substitute for reading the "Uncommercial Traveller" essays, although the best academic account is given in *Charles Dickens as a Familiar Essayist* by Gordon Spence. Some interesting information on *A Message from the Sea* is given in "Some Lost Writings Retrieved" in *Dickens Centennial Essays* edited by A. Nisbet and B. Nevius. It is also worth looking at "*A Message from the Sea* Dramatised" by J. B. van Amerongen in Volume 21 of *The Dickensian*.

Chapter 30

The visit to Bulwer-Lytton at Knebworth, and particularly the expedition to see the hermit Lucas, are explored in "The Truth About Mr Mopes" in Volume 26 of *The Dickensian* and in Richard Whitmore's *Mad Lucas*. It is also worth looking at a letter which George Eliot wrote to Sara Hennel, dated 6 December, 1861, in the *Letters of George Eliot*. The reaction to *David Copperfield*, with its changed ending, is best represented by *The Times* of 17 October, 1861, the *Dublin University Magazine* of December 1861, the *Rambler* of January 1862 and the *Examiner* of 20 July, 1861.

The second series of public readings is recollected in *Recollections* by David Christie Murray, and there are incidental highlights remembered by Mary Frances Morgan in Philip Collins's *Interviews and Recollections* as well as in

"An Ipswich Adventure" in Volume 36 of *The Dickensian*. Squire Bancroft recalls the St James's readings in Thomas Wright's *Life*.

On the vexed question of Ellen Ternan and Condette, the only course open to the biographer is to try and assemble the stray hints in Dickens's published and unpublished correspondence. It is an arduous business, going through all the available evidence and trying to piece together the various phrases and indirect suggestions; the effort in a sense is that of imposing form and knowability upon a subject which is formless and essentially unknowable. But the attempt has to be made. There has been one excellent study of Condette itself, W. J. Carlton's "Dickens's Forgotten Retreat in France" in Volume 62 of *The Dickensian*; and of course there is no substitute for visiting the area itself, seeing the chalet and sensing the atmosphere of the place which is so different from that of neighbouring Boulogne. The present writer was ably assisted in his researches there by Janine Watrin, who has written a splendid account of *Boulogne sur Mer. Vingt ans d'occupation anglaise 1840–1860*. Of course much help is afforded by Katharine Longley's unpublished study of Ellen Ternan; but there are also clues to be gathered in an examination of the private papers of scholars like Carlton and Aylmer who have followed the same trail. In letters from other scholars, and in their own notes, it is also possible to assemble material which can now be more easily verified or rejected. There are also occasions when material which *cannot* be used, because it remains unverifiable, seems to thrust itself forward. Such was a letter which I found at the Pierpont Morgan Library in New York: there is little enough left of it, and the name has been cut out from the salutation "My dear . . ." and it is signed "Faithfully yours always CD". Why should anyone want to remove the name of the recipient? "Faithfully yours always" is a most unusual phrase from Dickens, and there is at least the possibility that it was addressed to Ellen Ternan – a fact which someone, at a later date, wished to excise. Anyway, there it is . . . it may mean nothing. But it is an example of the kind of process of refinement and elimination which is necessary in a discussion as tentative and ambiguous as that of Dickens's relationship to Ellen Ternan. The present writer knows well enough that he might be quite mistaken in his own surmises, but he offers his interpretation of the evidence in the belief that it is the most plausible because it is the one most compatible with all he has learned about Dickens's life and character. For Dickens's time in Paris during this period there are reminiscences to be found in *Memories of Half-a-Century* by R. C. Lehmann, in *Ancestors and Friends* by John Lehmann, and in Marcus Stone's account published in Volume 6 of *The Dickensian*. For his crying at *L'Orphée*, see Madame Viardot's own description in Kitton's *Charles Dickens: By Pen and Pencil*. For his high spirits during the expedition to see the Mormons, read G. D. Leslie's account in the same volume.

On Gad's Hill and Dickens's life there, there are books and memories without end. In the accounts of George Dolby, Percy Fitzgerald, G. H. Sala, Edmund Yates, James Fields, Mary Boyle . . . in the reminiscences transcribed by Kitton and Hughes. A handy compendium of many of these is to be found in *Charles Dickens: Interviews and Recollections*, edited by Philip Collins, but the hardy traveller may wish to trudge on through the fruitful plains of scholarly journals and nineteenth-century memoirs. Here, for example, are four invaluable items from *The Dickensian*: "Charles Dickens's Study" in Volume 6, "A Sydney Man Who Knew Dickens" in Volume 9, "The Postmaster of Rochester in Dickens's Day" in Volume 19, and "Cricket Recollections of One of the Gad's Hill Team" by W. Glanvill Mason in Volume 30. The grand-daughter's memories are transcribed in *As They Saw Him . . . Charles Dickens* by Michael and Mollie Hardwick. A. B. Acworth's description of Dickens is to be found in the library of Dickens House, while the account of Dickens and his "young men" at Gad's Hill Place is given in a letter from Samuel Ward to S. Webster, dated 13 March, 1893, in the Beinecke Rare Book and Manuscript Collection of Yale University. Copies of the *Gad's Hill Gazette* are to be found in the Berg Collection of the New York Public Library.

Chapter 31

Details about his mother are given by Dickens in a frank letter to Macready, reprinted in Volume 72 of *The Dickensian*, and, for his opinion of Shakespeare's real monument, see his letter to Count Strzelecki, dated 20 April, 1860, in Dickens House.

On the subject of his reconciliation with Thackeray the two essentially antagonistic accounts are given in "George Russell's Recollections of Dickens" by Philip Collins in Volume 78 of *The Dickensian* and in Sir Theodore Martin's memory of the occasion as published by Ley in *The Dickens Circle*. Dickens's distraught behaviour at Thackeray's funeral is reported by an anonymous contributor to *Harper's Magazine* of September 1870.

The recollections of William Edrupt on Dickens as an editor and employer are to be found in "A Talk With Charles Dickens's Office Boy, William Edrupt of London" by Catherine van Dyke in the *Bookman* of March 1921 (the New York version of that magazine). More information is to be gleaned about Edrupt in "Links With Charles Dickens" by Arthur Humphreys in Volume 14 of *The Dickensian*. The description by Arthur Munby is contained in *Munby, Man of Two Worlds: The Life and Diaries of Arthur J. Munby 1828–1910*, edited by Derek Hudson. The anecdote about Thomas Hardy's strange encounter with Dickens is given in Volume 47 of *The Dickensian*, while Charles Kent's story of the novelist's prescience is included in Kitton's

Charles Dickens: By Pen and Pencil. Justin MacCarthy's feeling of being frightened by Dickens is in *Interviews and Recollections.* And Pugh's comment about the essentially fluid nature of Dickens's character is in his *The Charles Dickens Originals.* The emigration of Alfred is discussed in "The Problem of Plorn: Edward Dickens's First Days in Australia" by Mary Lazarus in Volume 68 of *The Dickensian.*

The account of seeing Dickens with a woman "not his wife", on the Channel crossing, is given by Julia Clara Byrne in the well-titled *Gossip of the Century.* There is a fascinating account of the Staplehurst disaster itself in "The Staplehurst Railway Accident" in Volume 38 of *The Dickensian* while more information is to be gathered from the *Illustrated Police News* of 17 June, 1865. Mr Dickenson's account of Dickens's assistance is given in Kitton's . . . *Pen and Pencil.* More information is to be found in Wills's letters to his wife, published by Lady Priestley in her *The Story of a Lifetime,* while Charles Collins wrote to his mother after seeing Dickens on his return to Gad's Hill Place: this letter, dated 13 June, 1865, is in the Pierpont Morgan Library. The two reactions to *Our Mutual Friend* quoted in the text come from Henry James in *The Nation* of 21 December, 1865, and from E. S. Dallas's review in *The Times* of 29 November, 1865. On the dropping of Browne, and the picking up of Stone, see *The Life and Labours of Hablot Knight Browne* by D. C. Thompson. Two other indispensable sources of reference are, Jane R. Cohen's *Charles Dickens and His Original Illustrators* and J. R. Harvey's *Victorian Novelists and Their Illustrators* – in the latter volume, some of Stone's correspondence is republished. F. G. Kitton's *Dickens and His Illustrators* contains other letters from Stone as well as angry ones from Browne. There is further material in Ley's *The Dickens Circle* as well as in "Mr Marcus Stone RA and Charles Dickens" in Volume 8 of *The Dickensian.* For the songs of Dickens's childhood in *Our Mutual Friend,* the best source is Ley's "The Songs of Silas Wegg" in Volume 26 of *The Dickensian.*

On the chalet, see Mary Boyle's *Her Book* as well as Hallewell's *Dickens's Rochester.* Charles Collins describes that edifice in the letter to his mother, dated 13 June, 1865, in the Pierpont Morgan. For a contemporary analysis of the "mirrored life" of Dickens's novels see *Blackwood's Magazine* of June 1871. The secret life in Slough has been thoroughly anatomised by both Felix Aylmer and Katharine Longley: both scholars have actually gone to the trouble of checking rate books and parish registries, although it is to the credit of Katharine Longley that she discovered the second cottage leased to the Ternans. Aylmer assumed that Dickens and Ellen Ternan (and mother) were all living beneath the same roof. Not so. It is also worth reading "Dickens Incognito" by Katharine Longley in Volume 77 of *The Dickensian.* The rumours about Dickens's daughters are reported by Frederick Lehmann to Nina Lehmann, as transcribed in John Lehmann's *Ancestors and Friends.* Michael Slater includes this and other material in *Dickens and Women.*

Chapter 32

One of the best sources of information on Dickens's career as a public reader is to be found in the reminiscences of his manager, George Dolby, in *Charles Dickens As I Knew Him*. There are also specific books on the readings themselves, all of which are valuable in their different ways. Charles Kent's near-contemporary study, *Charles Dickens as a Reader*, is especially revealing; and Kate Field's *Pen Photographs of Charles Dickens's Readings. Taken from Life* has a very good technical account of the effects which he was able to produce. A more recent account is Raymund Fitzsimons's *The Charles Dickens Show: An Account of his Public Readings, 1858–1870* while the most comprehensive survey is provided by Philip Collins in his edition of *The Public Readings*. This volume is especially valuable for Collins's prefatory notes. Of course there are also innumerable contemporary descriptions of Dickens's manners and methods as a reader: Fitzgerald, Yates, and the contributors to Kitton's *Charles Dickens: By Pen and Pencil* have left detailed accounts. His children, too, have mentioned their father's strange life on the stage. Other anecdotes and reports are to be found in Lady Ritchie's *From the Porch*, Frith's *Autobiography*, and in *The Bookman Extra Number* on Charles Dickens published in 1914. R. C. Lehmann's account is reported in Volume 59 of *The Dickensian*, and there are other appropriate articles in that periodical: "The Unique Reading Books" by L. A. Kennethe (Volume 39), "A Dickens Reading" by W. R. Kent (Volume 7), and the design of the reading desk itself is reproduced in Volume 29. An account by Herman Klein is repeated in H. C. Dent's *The Life and Character of Charles Dickens* while further information has been gleaned from the *Ipswich Journal* of 20 March, 1869, the *Belfast News Letter* of 9 January, 1869, the *Bath Chronicle* of 4 February, 1869 and the *Manchester Guardian* of 16 December, 1861 and 4 February, 1867. The actual reading texts themselves are to be found in a variety of American libraries, the Berg and Beinecke among them.

For descriptions of Catherine at this time, it is necessary to consult Jane Ellen Panton's *Leaves from a Life* and *The Letters and Memoirs of Sir William Hardman. Second Series*, edited by S. M. Ellis. Her album of photographs is described in *The Register* (Adelaide) of 3 May, 1905, and in the Storey papers held at Dickens House there are copies of her letters to Miss Burdett-Coutts. The Manuscript Room of the British Library holds Dickens's letters to her, and it is at the end of this collection that the prayer is to be discovered bound in a volume.

The house in Peckham, and Dickens's general relations with Ellen Ternan before his departure for America, are of course ably documented by Katharine Longley, Felix Aylmer and Ada Nisbet. Aylmer's papers are now at Dickens House. There is also an interesting letter on the general subject, from Edward Wagenknecht in Volume 50 of *The Dickensian*, while Mamie

Dickens discloses her father's plan to take her to America in her *Charles Dickens*. The clergyman's visit to Dickens before his departure is chronicled in "An Informal Call on Charles Dickens" in Number 27 of *University* (Princeton) while the best contemporary account of the "Farewell Banquet" is in *The Charles Dickens Dinner*, a volume published anonymously in 1867. It is also well worth examining the appropriate pages in Fielding's edition of Dickens's *Speeches*. A few stray items: Dickens's wish to sue the theatrical proprietor is detailed in "Dickens and Cave. A Theatrical Anecdote" by K. J. Fielding in Volume 50 of *The Dickensian*. The sports at Gad's Hill Place on Boxing Day are described in Robert Langton's *Charles Dickens and Rochester*, and Dickens's obituary of Clarkson Stanfield was published in *All The Year Round* of 1 June, 1867.

Chapter 33

There are no *American Notes* for this second American journey, but there are of course Dickens's own letters, both published in Nonesuch and unpublished in various university collections. There are also several books which examine the tour in some detail – chief among them George Dolby's *Charles Dickens As I Knew Him* and George Curry's excellent selection from the diaries of Annie Fields, *Charles Dickens and Annie Fields*. As an adjunct to that volume, it is still worth examining *Memories of a Hostess* by M. A. DeWolfe Howe and *Yesterdays With Authors* by James T. Fields (see also his articles in the *Atlantic Monthly* of September and October 1871). Other indispensable books are Edward Payne's *Dickens's Days In Boston* and Michael Slater's *Dickens on America and the Americans*.

His opinions on the United States, at this late date, are carefully detailed in an interesting essay, "Charles Dickens and the American Civil War", by J. O. Waller in Volume 57 of *Studies in Philology*. His letter to an American on his opinions is to be found in Volume 11 of *Nineteenth Century Fiction*, and his belief in the essential justice of *American Notes* is promulgated in some words of his in *All The Year Round* of 1 March, 1862. His attitude on copyright is expressed in a letter published in *Harper's Magazine* of December 1867. The general nature of his tour is adequately discusssed in the first books mentioned here, but there are other incidental items of interest. Noel C. Peyrouton has a very interesting piece on "The Gurney Photographs" in *The Dickensian*, while there are contemporary reminiscences of Dickens in Volumes 7, 16 and 26 of that periodical. The account of the little girl cross-questioning him about his novels is to be found in Kate Douglas Wiggin's *A Child's Journey With Charles Dickens*. Robert Tomes includes material in *Putnam's Magazine* of January 1868, and there is an article on "Dickens in Washington" by L. B. Frewer in Volume 79 of *The Dickensian*. It is also worth looking at "Dickens and James T. Fields" by W. G. Wilkins in Volume 13 of that periodical. See also Longfellow's letter to E. S. Phelps, dated 7 March, 1979, in the Boston Public Library. And, for more first-hand accounts, it is worth glancing through *Forty Years in America* by T. L. Nichols. The newspapers with eye-witness reports are legion, of course, but special use had been made here of the *Portland Transcript* of 4 February, 1868, the *New York Tribune* of 3 December, 1867 and 11 December, 1867, and *Harper's Weekly* of 25 June, 1870.

For the record of Dickens's clandestine correspondence with Ellen Ternan, the usual sources are the best; Nisbet's *Dickens and Ellen Ternan* and Aylmer's *Dickens Incognito*. See also "Dickens and Ellen Ternan" by G. C. Grubb in Volume 44 of *The Dickensian*.

For Dickens's journey home, see the account in *The Leader* of 25, April, 1868. Anthony Trollope's reminiscences are to be found in his essay, "Charles Dickens", published in Volume 6 of *The Dickensian*. Thomas Wright also has some additional information in his *The Life of Charles Dickens*. And so back to England . . .

Chapter 34

For Dickens's attitude towards Charles Collins, and his deteriorating friendship with Wilkie, see "Dickens and Wilkie Collins, A reply," by K. J. Fielding in Volume 49 of *The Dickensian*. The clearest statement of his attitude is to be found in Annie Fields's diary entry for 30 August, 1870. This is among the Fields Papers at the Huntington Library, and the entry in question is also reproduced in Volume 16 of the *Huntington Library Quarterly*. There is also relevant material in Michael Slater's *Dickens and Women*. Charles Forsyte has written interestingly on the "Sapsea Fragment" in Volume 82 of *The Dickensian*, and there is a significant correspondence between Forsyte and Katharine Longley in Volumes 82 and 83 of that periodical. On Dickens's preparations for the Nancy and Sikes reading, see his eldest son's reminiscences in the *Windsor Magazine* of December 1934. Edmund Yates is quoted to great effect in Fitzsimons's *The Charles Dickens Show* while, for a general study of the "sensation" phenomenon, see R. D. Altick's *Victorian Studies in Scarlet*.

The leavetaking with Plorn is discussed by Henry Dickens in two volumes: in his *Recollections* and in *Memories of my Father*. A full account of this, and subsequent events, is given by Mary Lazarus in *A Tale of Two Brothers* as well as in an essay, "The Problem of Plorn. Edward Dickens's First Days in Australia", in Volume 68 of *The Dickensian*.

The "Farewell" Reading Tour is of course covered by the major sources, Dolby and Kent; Dickens's pulse rate is transcribed in Volume 39 of *The*

Dickensian, while anecdotes on the Irish section of the tour are retold by F. D. Finlay in Kitton's *Charles Dickens: By Pen and Pencil*. Some interesting letters from Dickens to Finlay are printed in Volume 30 of *The Dickensian*, while Percy Fitzgerald's account of meeting him at the station is to be found in the pages of his *The Life of Charles Dickens As Revealed In His Writings*. On Dickens's illnesses, one of the best accounts is given by W. H. Bowen in *Charles Dickens and His Family*. Important, too, is David Waldron Smithers's *Dickens's Doctors*. Yates describes some of the physical effects of the illness, at least as he is quoted by Blanchard Jerrold in *A Day With Charles Dickens*. I would like to thank Dr John Gayner for discussing Dicken's medical condition with me – although of course, at this late date, the diagnosis is mine and not his. The account of Dickens with the Fields in London and Kent is most fully given by the Fields themselves in the various volumes and articles already listed, although once again George Curry's *Charles Dickens and Annie Fields* provides illuminating new information. It is also worth examining "Dickens and James T. Fields" by W. G. Wilkins in Volume 13 of *The Dickensian*. Dickens's visit to the hospital at Ratcliff Cross is described in "A Small Star in the East" by G. F. Young in Volume 30 of that periodical. It also includes a photograph of the hospital in question.

The studies of *The Mystery of Edwin Drood* are of course various and sometimes even peculiar. It is worth seeing the letter which Dickens wrote to Frederick Chapman on 20 August, 1869, which is now in Dickens House. There is also valuable information to be found in *Notes and Queries* of 25 May, 1912. Harry Johnson has memories of Dickens studying in Rochester Cathedral with more than usual intentness in Volume 20 of *The Dickensian* while in Volume 12 of that journal can be found "A Night Amongst the Drood Opium Dens" by John Suddaby. One of the most interesting books on the novel (including its preparation) is Charles Forsyte's *The Decoding of Edwin Drood*, while the best single essay on the subject is undoubtedly "*Edwin Drood* and the Mystery of Apartness" by John Beer in Volume 13 of *Dickens Studies Annual*.

Dickens's reaction to his son's scholarship is best described by the son himself in *My Father As I Knew Him*, and Henry Dickens also reveals the episode of Dickens's venturing "Warren's Blacking" in the Christmas game in the same volume. On the subject of Henry's scholarship there is also a revealing letter from Georgina Hogarth to Annie Fields, dated 15 June, 1869, in the Huntington Library.

Various of Dickens's essays and prefaces have been mentioned in this chapter, and the most important of these are: the review of Forster's *Life of Landor* in *All The Year Round* of 24 July, 1869; the introduction to *Legends and Lyrics* by Adelaide Anne Proctor, published in 1866; the article on Fechter in the *Atlantic Monthly* of August 1869; the introduction to *Religious Opinions* by Chauncey Hare Townshend, published in 1869. The New Series of *All The*

Year Round began on 5 December, 1868, and it was in that issue that Dickens denied the reports of his relinquishing the editorship.

Chapter 35

His appearance in these last months of his life is variously detailed in contemporary reminiscences, in Wright's *The Life of Charles Dickens* and in Kitton's *Charles Dickens: By Pen and Pencil*. Percy Fitzgerald, Blanchard Jerrold, John Forster, and others have given their own impressions in their own books concerning the novelist. Carlyle's record of his dinner with Dickens and Forster is transcribed in Volume 69 of *The Dickensian*.

Dickens's audience with the Queen is briefly described by Georgina Hogarth in a letter to Annie Fields, dated 4 May, 1870, in the Huntington Library. (The gift of a silver centrepiece by an admirer is described by Georgina Hogarth in the same letter.) Sir Arthur Helps's own reminiscences, "*In Memoriam*", appeared in Volume 22 of *Macmillan's Magazine* but the most substantial account appears in Volume 71 of *The Dickensian*: "Charles Dickens Meets The Queen. A New Look" by John R. DeBruyn.

The final reading is of course described by Charles Kent and George Dolby, as well as by Charles Dickens junior in the *Windsor Magazine* of December 1934. There is also a description in the *Penny Illustrated Paper* of 19 March, 1870. On Dickens's general good humour and "brightness" in the final month, see in particular Lord Redesdale's *Memories*. The breakfast with Gladstone is described in T. Sidney Cooper's *My Life*. The best source of information about the amateur theatricals of June is Herman Merivale, who described the occasion to Kitton in *Charles Dickens: By Pen and Pencil* and in a letter to *The Times* of 8 February, 1883. The account of Dickens's somewhat abstracted condition outside the Athenaeum is to be found in Volume 61 of *The Dickensian*. Dickens's last few days are chronicled by Dolby, Fitzgerald, Wright and others. Langton, Hughes and Dexter all have accounts of his last visit to Rochester. Dickens's children of course have their own memories, although the most detailed are those of Kate. Her recollections appear in Gladys Storey's *Dickens and Daughter* (as well as in the Storey papers) and she wrote her own account, "*Edwin Drood* and The Last Days of Charles Dickens" in Volume 37 of the *Pall Mall Magazine*. More details of the death are to be found in a long letter which Frederick Lehmann wrote to Dr Joachim on 13 June, 1870 and which was printed in Volume 35 of *The Dickensian*. In Volume 27 of that journal, one of the servants at Gad's Hill Place at this time, Isaac Armatage, gave his own account of these final hours.

Postscript

Kate's remark about her father going "out of his mind" is to be found in the Storey papers at Dickens House. Georgina Hogarth and Mamie Dickens wrote letters to Annie Fields in which they detailed their leavetaking of the house – letters dated respectively 15 August, 1870 and 1 September, 1870. Both are now in the Huntington Library. The recollection of Catherine Dickens weeping at a performance of *Dombey and Son* is to be found in a letter which William Farren wrote to the *Daily Mail* on 12 September, 1898. The other remarks in this postscript are, of course, entirely my own responsibility.

Bibliography

Addison William. In The Steps of Charles Dickens. London, 1955.

Adrian Arthur. Mark Lemon: First Editor of "Punch". London, 1966.

Adrian Arthur. Georgina Hogarth and the Dickens Circle. London, 1957.

Aldington Richard. Four English Portraits. London, 1948.

Allbut Robert. London Rambles with Charles Dickens. London, 1886.

Allen Michael. Charles Dickens's Childhood. London, 1988.

Altick R. D. The English Common Reader. Chicago, 1957.

Altick R. D. Victorian Studies in Scarlet. London, 1970.

Altick R. D. Victorian People and Ideas. London, 1973.

Amerongen J. B. van The Actor in Dickens. London, 1926.

Anonymous. Charles Dickens: The Story of His Life. London, 1871.

Archer Thomas. Charles Dickens. London, 1896.

Axon William. Charles Dickens And Shorthand. Manchester, 1892.

Axton Marie, and Williams Raymond. English Drama: Forms and Development. Cambridge, 1977.

Axton William. Circle of Fire. London, 1966.

Aylmer Felix. Dickens Incognito. London, 1951.

Barlow G. The Genius of Dickens. London, 1909.

Barnard R. Theme and Imagery in the Novels of Dickens. Oslo, 1974.

Barnes A. W. A Dickens Guide. London, 1929.

Becker Mary Lamberton. Introducing Charles Dickens. London 1941.

Beckwith C. E. (editor). Twentieth Century Interpretations of A Tale of Two Cities. New Jersey, 1972.

Beer Gillian. Darwin's Plots. London, 1983.

Bentley Nicolas, Slater Michael and Burgis Nina (editors). The Dickens Index. Oxford, 1988.

Best Geoffrey. Mid Victorian Britain, 1851–1875. London, 1971.

Blount Trevor. Charles Dickens: The Early Novels. London, 1968.

Boarman J. C. and Harte J. L. Boz: An Intimate Biography of Charles Dickens. Boston, 1935.

A Bookman Extra Number. Charles Dickens. London, 1914.

Bowen W. H. Charles Dickens and His Family. Cambridge, 1956.

Bowes C. C. The Association of Charles Dickens with Liverpool. Liverpool, 1905.

Boyle Sir Courtenay (editor). Mary Boyle. Her Book. London, 1901.

Brannan R. L. (editor). Under the Management of Mr Charles Dickens. His Production of The Frozen Deep. Ithaca, 1966.

Brantlinger Patrick. The Spirit of Reform. London, 1977.

Brattin Joel (editor). Our Mutual Friend: An Annotated Bibliography. New York, 1984.

Bredsdorff Elias. Hans Andersen and Charles Dickens. Copenhagen, 1956.

Briggs Asa. Victorian People. London, 1965.

Briggs Asa. The Age of Improvement. London, 1959.

Brook G. L. The Language of Dickens. London, 1970.

Brown Arthur Washburn. Sexual Analysis of Dickens's Props. New York, 1971.

Brown I. Dickens and His World. London, 1970.

Brown James M. Dickens: Novelist in the Market-Place. London, 1982.

Browne Edgar. Phiz and Dickens. London, 1914.

Buckley J. H. The Victorian Temper: A Study in Literary Culture. London, 1952.

Buckley J. H. The Triumph of Time. London, 1967.

Burn W. L. The Age of Equipoise. London, 1964.

Butt John. Pope, Dickens and Others. Edinburgh, 1969.

Butt John and Kathleen Tillotson. Dickens at Work. London, 1957.

Canning A. S. G. Philosophy of Charles Dickens. London, 1880.

Carey John. The Violent Effigy. London, 1973.

Carlton William. Charles Dickens: Shorthand Writer. London, 1947.

Cazamian Louis. The Social Novel in England, 1830–1850. London, 1973.

Chancellor E. B. Dickens and His Times. London, 1932.

Chesney Kellow. The Victorian Underworld. London, 1970.

Chesterton G. K. Charles Dickens. London, 1906.

Chesterton. G. K. Appreciations and Criticisms of the Works of Charles Dickens. London, 1911.

Christie John. The Ancestry of Catherine Thomas Hogarth. Edinburgh, 1912.

Christie O. F. Dickens and His Age. London, 1939.

Churchill R. C. (editor). A Bibliography of Dickensian Criticism, 1836–1975. London, 1975.

Clair Colin. Charles Dickens: Life and Character. London, 1963.

Clark Cumberland. Charles Dickens and the Yorkshire Schools. London, 1918.

Clark Cumberland. Dickens and Talfourd. London, 1919.

Clark G. Kitson. The Making of Victorian England. London, 1962.

Clark William Ross (editor). Discussions of Charles Dickens. Boston, 1961.

Clarke W. M. The Secret Life of Wilkie Collins. London, 1988.

Clinton-Baddeley V. C. All Right on the Night. London, 1954.

Cockshut A. O. J. The Imagination of Charles Dickens. London, 1961.

Cohen Jane R. Charles Dickens and His Original Illustrators. Ohio, 1980.

Collins Philip. Dickens and Crime, London, 1962.

Collins Philip (editor). Dickens: The Critical Heritage. London, 1971.

Collins Philip. Charles Dickens: The Public Readings. London, 1975.

Collins Philip. Dickens and Education. London, 1965.

Collins Philip. Dickens: The Critical Heritage. London, 1971.

Connor Steven. Charles Dickens. Oxford, 1985.

Conrad Peter. The Victorian Treasure-House. London, 1973.

Coolidge A. C. Charles Dickens As Serial Novelist. Iowa, 1967.

Cooper T. P. With Dickens In Yorkshire. London, 1923.

Cooper T. Sidney. My Life. London, 1890.

Coveney Peter. Poor Monkey. The Child In Literature. London, 1957.

Cross Nigel. The Common Writer. London, 1985.

Crotch W. Walter. The Secret of Dickens. London, 1919.

Crotch W. Walter. The Soul of Dickens. London, 1916.

Crotch W. Walter. Charles Dickens. The Social Reformer. London, 1913.

Cruikshank R. J. Charles Dickens and Early Victorian England. London, 1949.

Cruse Amy. The Victorians and Their Books. London, 1935.

Curry George. Charles Dickens and Annie Fields, Huntington Library, 1988.

Dabney Ross H. Love and Property in the Novels of Charles Dickens. London, 1967.

Dafforne James. Clarkson Stanfield. London, 1874.

Daldry Graham. Charles Dickens and The Form of the Novel. London, 1987.

Daleski H. M. Dickens and the Art of Analogy. London, 1970.

Dalziel Margaret. Popular Fiction One Hundred Years Ago. London, 1957.

Dark Sidney. Charles Dickens. London, 1919.

Darwin Bernard. The Dickens Advertiser. London, 1930.

David Deirdre. Fictions of Resolution in Three Victorian Novels. London, 1981.

Davies J. A. John Forster: A Literary Life. Leicester, 1983.

Davis Earle. The Flint and the Flame: The Artistry of Charles Dickens. London, 1964.

Dent H. C. The Life and Character of Charles Dickens. London, 1933.

DeVries Duane. Dickens's Apprentice Years: The Making of a Novelist. London, 1976.

Dexter W. and J. W. T. Ley. The Origin of Pickwick. London, 1936.

Dexter Walter. The England of Dickens. London, 1925.

Dickens Criticism – A Symposium. Massachusetts, 1962.

Dickens Charles the younger. Prefaces to the Novels of Charles Dickens. London, various dates.

Dickens Henry. Memories of My Father. London, 1928.

Dickens Henry. Recollections. London, 1934.

Dickens Mamie. Charles Dickens. London, 1885.

Dickens Mamie. My Father As I Recall Him. London, 1897.

Dodds J. W. The Age of Paradox: A Biography of England, 1841–1851. London, 1953.

Dolby George. Charles Dickens As I Knew Him. London, 1885.

Du Cann C. G. L. The Love-Lives of Charles Dickens. London, 1961.

Dunn Richard J. David Copperfield: An Annotated Bibliography. New York, 1981.

Dyos H. J. and Michael Wolff (editors). The Victorian City: Images and Realities. London, 1973.

Dyson A. E. (editor). Dickens: Modern Judgments. London, 1968.

Ellis S. M. William Harrison Ainsworth and His Friends. London, 1911.

Ellison Owen. Charles Dickens: Novelist. London, 1908.

Elton Oliver. Dickens and Thackeray. London, 1924.

Engel Monroe. The Maturity of Dickens. London, 1959.

Fanger Donald. Dostoyevsky and Romantic Realism. Chicago, 1965.

Fawcett F. W. Dickens the Dramatist. London, 1952.

Fawkner H. W. Animation and Reification in Dickens's Vision of the Life Denying Society. Uppsala, 1977.

Fido Martin. Charles Dickens. London, 1968.

Field Kate. Pen Photographs of Charles Dickens's Readings. Taken from Life. Boston, 1868.

Fielding K. J. (editor). The Speeches of Charles Dickens. Oxford, 1960.

Fielding K. J. Charles Dickens. London, 1960.

Fielding K. J. Charles Dickens: A Critical Introduction. London, 1965.

Fields J. T. In and Out of Doors with Charles Dickens. Boston, 1876.

Fitzgerald Percy. Memories of Charles Dickens. London, 1913.

Fitzgerald Percy. The Life of Charles Dickens As Revealed in His Writings. London, 1905.

Fitzgerald Percy. Bozland. Dickens's Places and People. London, 1895.

Fitzsimons R. The Charles Dickens Show: An Account of his Public Readings, 1858–1870. London, 1970.

Fleissner Robert. Dickens and Shakespeare. New York, 1965.

Fletcher Geoffrey. The London Dickens Knew. London, 1970.

Ford G. H. Dickens and His Readers. Princeton, 1955.

Ford G. H. and Lane Lauriat Jnr. The Dickens Critics. Ithaca, 1961.

Forster John. Life of Charles Dickens. London, 1874.

Forsyte Charles. The Decoding of Edwin Drood. London, 1980.

Friswell J. Charles Dickens: A Critical Biography. London, 1858.

Friswell J. Modern Men of Letters. London, 1870.

Frith W. P. My Autobiography and Reminiscences. London, 1887.

Frost Thomas. In Kent with Charles Dickens. London, 1880.

Fyfe T. A. Charles Dickens and the Law. Glasgow, 1910.

Garis Robert. The Dickens Theatre: A Reassessment of his Novels. Oxford, 1965.

Gerson Stanley. Soul and Symbol in the Dialogue of the Works of Charles Dickens. Stockholm, 1967.

Giddings R. (editor). The Changing World of Charles Dickens. London, 1983.

Gissing George. Charles Dickens. London, 1898.

Gissing George. The Immortal Dickens. London, 1925.

Gloag John. Victorian Comfort. London, 1961.

Gold Joseph. Charles Dickens: Radical Moralist. London, 1972.

Golding Robert. Idiolects in Dickens. London, 1985.

Gomme A. H. Dickens. London, 1971.

Gordon Elizabeth Hope. The Naming of Characters in the Work of Charles Dickens. Nebraska, 1917.

Graham Eleanor. The Story of Charles Dickens. London, 1952.

Grant Allan. A Preface to Dickens. London, 1984.

Greaves John. Dickens at Doughty Street. London, 1975.

Green Frank. As Dickens Saw Them. London, 1933.

Griffin James. Memories of the Past. London, 1883.

Grillo Virgil. Charles Dickens's Sketches by Boz. Boulder, 1974.

Gross John and Gabriel Pearson (editors). Dickens and the Twentieth Century. London, 1962.

Guerard Albert J. The Triumph of the Novel. New York, 1976.

Gummer Ellis N. Dickens's Work in Germany. Oxford, 1946.

Ham J. Panton. Parables of Fiction, 1870.

Hammond J. L. and Barbara. The Age of the Chartists, 1832–1854. London, 1930.

Harbage Alfred. A Kind of Power: The Shakespeare-Dickens Analogy. Philadelphia, 1925.

Hardwick Michael and Mollie. As They Saw Him . . . Charles Dickens. London, 1970.

Hardwick Michael and Mollie. Dickens's England. London, 1970.

Hardy Barbara. Dickens: The Later Novels. London, 1968.

Hardy Barbara. Charles Dickens: The Writer and His Work. Windsor, 1983.

Hardy Barbara. The Moral Art of Dickens. London, 1970.

Harris Edwin. Gad's Hill Place and Charles Dickens. Rochester, 1910.

Harrison J. F. The Early Victorians. London, 1971.

Harrison Michael. Charles Dickens. London, 1953.

Harvey J. R. Victorian Novelists and Their Illustrators. London, 1970.

Hassard J. R. G. A Pickwickian Pilgrimage. Boston, 1881.

Hayter Alethea. Opium and the Romantic Imagination. London, 1968.

Hayward A. L. The Days of Dickens. London, 1926.

Healey Edna. Lady Unknown. London, 1978.

Hibbert Christopher. The Making of Charles Dickens. London, 1967.

Hill Nancy K. A Reformer's Art. London, 1981.

Himmelfarb G. Victorian Minds. London, 1968.

Hobsbaum Philip. A Reader's Guide to Charles Dickens. London, 1972.

Hodder George. Memories of my Time. London, 1870.

Hollingshead John. My Lifetime. London, 1895.

Hollingsworth K. The Newgate Novel, 1830–1847. Detroit, 1963.

Hollington Michael. Dickens and the Grotesque. London, 1984.

Holman Hunt Diana. My Grandfather: His Wives and Loves. London, 1969.

Holsworth W. S. Charles Dickens as a Legal Historian. New Haven, 1928.

Hornback B. G. "Noah's Arkitecture". A Study of Dickens's Mythology. Ohio, 1972.

Horne R. H. A New Spirit of the Age. London, 1844.

Horton S. R. Interpreting Interpreting. Interpreting Dickens's Dombey. London, 1979.

Horton S. R. The Reader in the Dickens World: Style and Response. London, 1981.

Houghton W. E. The Victorian Frame of Mind, 1830–1870. London, 1957.

House Humphry. The Dickens World. London, 1942.

Hughes J. L. Dickens as an Educator. New York, 1900.

Hughes W. R. A Week's Tramp in Dickensland. London, 1891.

Humphreys Arthur. Charles Dickens and His First Schoolmaster. Manchester, 1926.

Hutchings R. J. Dickens on an Island. Bath, 1970.

Jackson T. A. Charles Dickens: the Progress of a Radical. London, 1937.

Jarmuth Sylvia L. Dickens's Use of Women In His Novels. New York, 1967.

Jephson H. The Sanitary Evolution of London. London, 1907.

Jerrold Blanchard. A Day with Charles Dickens. London, 1871.

Johnson Edgar. Charles Dickens: His Tragedy and His Triumph. New York, 1952.

Johnson W. S. (editor) Charles Dickens: New Perspectives. New Jersey, 1982.

Johnstone F. D. Dickens in our Commonwealth. Melbourne, 1909.

Jones C. H. A Short Life of Charles Dickens. New York, 1880.

Kaplan Fred (editor) Charles Dickens's Book of Memoranda. New York, 1981.

Kaplan Fred. Dickens and Mesmerism: The Hidden Springs of Fiction. Princeton, 1975.

Kaplan Fred. Dickens. A Biography. London, 1988.

Kent Charles. Charles Dickens as a Reader. London, 1872.

Kent W. With Charles Dickens in The Borough. London, 1926.

Kent W. London for Dickens Lovers. London, 1935.

Kincaid James R. Dickens and the Rhetoric of Laughter. Oxford, 1971.

Kingsmill Hugh. The Sentimental Journey: A Life of Charles Dickens. London, 1974.

Kitton F. G. Charles Dickens: By Pen and Pencil. London, 1890.

Kitton F. G. Charles Dickens: His Life, Writings and Personality. London, c. 1900.

Kitton F. G. The Dickens Country. London, 1925.

Kitton F. G. Dickens and His Illustrators. London, 1899.

Knight Charles. Passages of a Working Life. London, 1865.

Kotzin Michael. Dickens and the Fairy Tale. Ohio, 1972.

Kyle Elisabeth. The Boy Who Asked For More. London, 1966.

Lambert M. Dickens and the Suspended Quotation. New Haven, 1981.

Landow George P. (editor). Approaches to Victorian Autobiography. Ohio, 1979.

Langstaff J. B. David Copperfield's Library. London, 1924.

Langton Robert. Charles Dickens and Rochester. London, 1880.

Langton Robert. The Childhood and Youth of Charles Dickens. London, 1912.

Lary N. M. Dostoyevsky and Dickens: A Study of Literary Influence. London, 1973.

Lazarus Mary. A Tale of Two Brothers. London, 1973.

Leacock Stephen. Charles Dickens: His Life and Work. London, 1933.

Leavis F. R. and Q. D. Dickens the Novelist. London, 1970.

Levine R. A. (editor). Backgrounds to Victorian Literature. San Francisco, 1967.

Lewes G. H. On Actors and the Art of Acting. London, 1875.

Ley J. W. T. The Dickens Circle: A Narrative of the Novelist's Friendships. London, 1918.

Lightwood J. T. Charles Dickens and Music. London, 1912.

Lindsay Jack. Charles Dickens: A Biographical and Critical Study. London, 1950.

Lohrli Anne (compiler). Household Words. Toronto, 1971.

Lucas John. The Melancholy Man: A Study of Dickens's Novels. London, 1970.

Lupton E. B. Dickens the Immortal. Kansas City, 1923.

Lynn Mrs Linton. My Literary Life. London, 1899.

MacKay C. H. (editor). Dramatic Dickens. London, 1989.

MacKenzie Norman and Jeanne. Dickens. A Life. London, 1964.

MacKenzie R. S. Life of Charles Dickens. Philadelphia, 1871.

McMaster Juliet. Dickens the Designer. London, 1987.

MacPike Loralee. Dostoyevsky's Dickens. A Study of Literary Influence. London, 1981.

Maly-Schlatter Florence. The Puritan Element in Victorian Fiction. Zurich, 1940.

Manning John. Dickens on Education. Toronto, 1959.

Manning S. B. Dickens as Satirist. New Haven, 1971.

Manning S. Hard Times. An Annotated Bibliography. New York, 1984.

Marcus S. Dickens: From Pickwick to Dombey. London, 1965.

Marcus S. The Other Victorians. London, 1969.

Marshall W. H. The World of the Victorian Novel. London, 1967.

Marzials Frank. Life of Charles Dickens. London, 1887.

Mason E. T. (editor). Personal traits of British Authors. New York, 1885.

Matz B. L. Dickensian Inns and Taverns. London, 1922.

Meier Stefanie. Animation and Mechanisation in the Novels of Charles Dickens. Zurich, 1982.

Miller J. H. Charles Dickens: The World of His Novels. London, 1958.

Miller J. H. The Forms of Victorian Fiction. London, 1968.

Miller J. H. and D. Borowitz. Charles Dickens and George Cruikshank. California, 1971.

Miller Leonard. References in the Work of Charles Dickens to Rochester, Chatham, and Neighbourhood and Persons Resident Therein. Bath, 1924.

Miltoun Francis. Dickens's London. London, 1904.

Monod Sylvère. Dickens the Novelist. Oklahoma, 1968.

Moreland Arthur. Dickens's Landmarks in London. London, 1931.

Morley J. Death, Heaven and the Victorians. London, 1971.

Naeff-Hinderling Annabeth. The Search for the Culprit: Dickens's Conflicting Self- and Object-Representation. Zurich, 1983.

Nelson Harland. Charles Dickens. Boston, 1981.

Newman Gerald. The Rise of English Nationalism. A Cultural History. 1740–1830. London, 1987.

Newman S. J. Dickens At Play. London, 1981.

Newsom Robert. Dickens and the Romantic Side of Familiar Things. New York, 1977.

Nicholl W. R. Dickens's Own Story. London, 1923.

Nisbet A. and Nevius B. (editors). Dickens Centennial Essays. London, 1971.

Nisbet Ada. Dickens and Ellen Ternan. London, 1952.

Page Norman. A Dickens Companion. London, 1984.

Partlow R. B. Dickens the Craftsman. Strategies of Presentation. Carbondale, 1970.

Patten R. L. Charles Dickens and His Publishers. Oxford, 1978.

Payne Edward. Dickens's Days in Boston. Cambridge, 1927.

Payne E. F. and H. H. Harper. The Romance of Charles Dickens and Maria Beadnell Winter. Boston, 1929.

Pearce R. H. (editor). Experience in the Novel. London, 1968.

Pearson Hesketh. Dickens. His Character, Comedy and Career. London, 1949.

Pemberton T. E. Dickens's London. London, 1876.

Phillips W. C. Dickens, Reade and Collins: Sensation Novelists. New York, 1919.

Pope Norris. Dickens and Charity. London, 1978.

Pope-Hennessy Una. Charles Dickens. London, 1945.

Price Martin (editor). Dickens: A Collection of Critical Essays. New Jersey, 1976.

Priestley J. B. Charles Dickens: a pictorial biography. London, 1961.

Pugh Edwin. The Charles Dickens Originals. London, 1912.

Pugh Edwin. Charles Dickens: The Apostle of the People. London, 1908.

Quiller-Couch A. Charles Dickens and Other Victorians. Cambridge, 1925.

Quinlan M. J. Victorian Prelude. A History of English Manners, 1700–1830. New York, 1941.

Quirk Randolph. Charles Dickens and Appropriate Language. Durham, 1959.

Rantavaara Irma. Dickens In The Light of English Criticism. Helsinki, 1944.

Ray G. N. Thackeray: The Age of Wisdom. London, 1958.

Reed J. R. Victorian Conventions. Ohio, 1975.

Renton Richard. John Forster and His Friendships. London, 1912.

Reynolds Ernest. Early Victorian Drama, 1830–1870. Cambridge, 1936.

Roberts E. E. B. This Side Idolatry. London, 1928.

Robinson Kenneth. Wilkie Collins. London, 1951.

Romano John. Dickens and Reality. New York, 1978.

Rostow W. British Economy of the Nineteenth Century. Oxford, 1948.

Sadleir Michael. Bulwer and His Wife. A Panorama. London, 1933.

Saintsbury G. Dickens. Cambridge, 1916.

Sala G. A. Charles Dickens. London, 1870.

Sanders Andrew. Charles Dickens, Resurrectionist. London, 1982.

Schlicke Paul. Dickens and Popular Entertainment. London, 1985.

Schwarzbach F. S. Dickens and the City. London, 1979.

Scott P. J. H. Reality and Comic Consciousness in Charles Dickens. London, 1979.

Sheppard Francis. London 1808–1870: The Infernal Wen. London, 1971.

Shore W. T. Charles Dickens and His Friends. London. 1909.

Sitwell O. Dickens. London, 1932.

Slater M. Dickens on America and the Americans. London, 1979.

Slater M. Dickens and Women. London, 1983.

Slater M. (editor). Dickens 1970. London, 1970.

Slater M. (editor). The Catalogue of the Suzannet Charles Dickens Collection. London, 1975.

Smith Grahame. Dickens, Money and Society. London, 1968.

Smithers D. W. Dickens's Doctors. Oxford, 1979.

Spilka M. Dickens and Kafka. London, 1963.

Steig M. Dickens and Phiz. London, 1978.

Stevens J. S. Quotations and References in Charles Dickens. Boston, 1929.

Stewart Garrett. Dickens and the Trial of Imagination. Harvard, 1974.

Stoddard R. H. Anecdote Biography of Dickens. New York, 1874.

Stoehr Taylor. Dickens: The Dreamer's Stance. Ithaca, 1965.

Stone Harry (editor). The Uncollected Writings of Charles Dickens. Household Words, 1850–1859. London, 1969.

Stone Harry (editor). Dickens's Working Notes for his Novels. London, 1987.

Stone Harry. Dickens and the Invisible World. London, 1980.

Stonehouse J. H. Green Leaves: New Chapters in the Life of Charles Dickens. London, 1930.

Storey Gladys. Dickens and Daughter. London, 1939.

Straus Ralph. Dickens: A Portrait in Pencil. London, 1928.

Straus Ralph. Dickens: The Man and the Book. London, 1936.

Sucksmith Harvey. The Narrative Art of Charles Dickens. Oxford, 1970.

Swinburne A. C. Charles Dickens. London, 1913.

Symons Julian. Charles Dickens. London, 1951.

Szladits L. L. Charles Dickens, 1812–1870. An anthology. New York Public Library, 1970.

Thomas Deborah. Dickens and the Short Story. London, 1982.

Thompson D. C. The Life and Labours of Hablot Knight Browne. London, 1884.

Thurley G. The Dickens Myth: Its Genesis and Structure. London, 1976.

Tillotson K. Novels from the 1840's. London, 1945.

Tomlin E. W. F. (editor). Charles Dickens, 1812–1870. A Centenary Volume. London, 1969.

Trevelyan G. M. English Social History. London, 1944.

Trollope T. A. What I Remember. London, 1887.

Vizitely H. Glances Back Through The Years. London, 1893.

Wagenknecht E. Dickens and the Scandalmongers. Oklahoma, 1965.

Walder Dennis. Dickens and Religion. London, 1981.

Walters J. C. Phases of Dickens: The Man, His Message and His Mission. London, 1911.

Ward A. W. Dickens. London, 1882.

Ward H. S. and C. W. B. The Real Dickens Land. London, 1904.

Bibliography

Watkins William. Charles Dickens. London, 1870.

Watts A. S. Dickens at Gad's Hill. Reading, 1989.

Watts J. C. Great Novelists. Edinburgh, 1880.

Watts R. J. The Pragmalinguistic Analysis of Narrative Texts. Narrative Cooperation in Charles Dickens's Hard Times. Tübingen, 1981.

Waugh Arthur. Charles Dickens and His Illustrators. London, 1937.

Welsh Alexander. The City of Dickens. Oxford, 1971.

Welsh Alexander. From Copyright to Copperfield. The Identity of Dickens. London, 1987.

Westburg B. The Confessional Fictions of Charles Dickens. Illinois, 1977.

Whipple E. P. Charles Dickens: The Man and His Work. New York, 1912.

Wiggin K. D. A Child's Journey with Charles Dickens. London, 1912.

Willey B. Nineteenth Century Studies. London, 1949.

Willey B. More Nineteenth Century Studies. London, 1956.

Wilson A. The World of Charles Dickens. London, 1970.

Wilson E. The Wound and the Bow. London, 1941.

Woodward E. L. The Age of Reform, 1815–1870. Oxford, 1938.

Woollcott A. Mr Dickens Goes To The Play. New York, 1922.

Worth G. J. Dickensian Melodrama. Kansas, 1978.

Wright Thomas. The Life of Charles Dickens. London, 1935.

Yamamoto Tadao. Growth and System in the Language of Dickens. Kansai, 1952.

Young G. M. Victorian England: Portrait of an Age. London, 1953.

Young G. M. (editor). Early Victorian England, 1830–1865. London, 1934.

Zambrano A. L. Dickens and Film. New York, 1977.

Periodicals

The Dickensian.
Dickens Quarterly.
Dickens Studies.
Dickens Studies Newsletter.
Dickens Studies Annual.
Nineteenth Century Fiction.
Victorian Studies.

Index

1155

Index